John Curtis, OBE, FBA, is Keeper of the Middle East Collections at the British Museum. His publications include *Forgotten Empire: The World of Ancient Persia* (with N. Tallis, 2005), *Art and Empire: Treasures from Assyria in the British Museum* (with J. E. Reade, 2005) and *Ancient Persia* (2000).

St John Simpson is Assistant Keeper and Curator of Ancient Iran and Arabia, also at the British Museum. He has excavated extensively in the Middle East and Central Asia, including sites of all periods from prehistoric to recent times.

"The Persian Empire has never been out of the news, but since the great British Museum exhibition, and a spate of publications on the subject, it is more in the eyes and minds of archaeologists and historians of the ancient world than hitherto. This welcome volume offers a major guide to and an explanation of the whole phenomenon, from the acknowledged experts. It will be used and referred to more than most such compendia, and for very good reason."

Sir John Boardman, FBA, Lincoln Professor Emeritus of Classical Art and Archaeology, University of Oxford

"*The World of Achaemenid Persia* is a fine new survey of the first world empire, an empire which linked Egypt and Greece with Central Asia and India. This series of essays, undertaken by some 50 new and established scholars, discusses the whole spectrum of the Achaemenids' wealth, diversity, culture, economy and society and will become a standard work on this important area of study, a field as significant and exciting today as it has been in the past."

Georgina Herrmann, OBE, FBA, formerly Reader in Western Asiatic Archaeology, University College London

"This attractive and authoritative volume provides an unusually complete assessment of the multiple accomplishments of the Achaemenid Persians. The range of topics that is covered is quite exceptional; and the long list of contributors includes most of the principal scholars who are active in Achaemenid and ancient Persian studies at the present moment."

David Stronach, Emeritus Professor of Near Eastern Archaeology, University of California, Berkeley

"This timely book represents an outstanding contribution to the state of research on the first actual world empire in history. There can be no doubt that many of its thought-provoking articles will make a strong impact on our views of ancient Persia, and of its society and culture."

Josef Wiesehöfer, Professor of Ancient History, Kiel University

"The Achaemenid era constitutes the most brilliant period of Persia's long history, a period during which all of western Asia and part of North Africa were brought together in a vast empire under the suzerainty of the Achaemenid kings. A great deal of research has gone into the elucidation of the various aspects of the dynasty and the empire. It is wonderful now to have such an up-to-date, competent and comprehensive account of the history and culture of Achaemenid Persia between two covers."

Ehsan Yarshater, Hagop Kevorkian Professor Emeritus of Iranian Studies, Columbia University

THE WORLD OF ACHAEMENID PERSIA

HISTORY, ART AND SOCIETY IN IRAN AND THE ANCIENT NEAR EAST

Edited by
John Curtis and St John Simpson

Proceedings of a conference at the British Museum
29th September–1st October 2005

BLOOMSBURY ACADEMIC
LONDON · NEW YORK · OXFORD · NEW DELHI · SYDNEY

BLOOMSBURY ACADEMIC
Bloomsbury Publishing Plc
50 Bedford Square, London, WC1B 3DP, UK
1385 Broadway, New York, NY 10018, USA
29 Earlsfort Terrace, Dublin 2, Ireland

BLOOMSBURY, BLOOMSBURY ACADEMIC and the Diana logo
are trademarks of Bloomsbury Publishing Plc

First published in Great Britain 2010 by I.B.Tauris & Co. Ltd
Paperback edition first published 2021 by Bloomsbury Academic

Selection and editorial matter copyright © 2010 John Curtis and St John Simpson
Individual chapters © 2010 Kamyar Abdi, Bahram Adjerloo, Björn Anderson, Barbara R. Armbruster, Heather D. Baker, Oric Basirov, Pierre Briant, Maria Brosius, Annie Caubet, Alireza Askari Chaverdi, M. R. Cowell, Vesta Sarkhosh Curtis, Mehdi Daryaie, Albert de Jong, Elspeth R.M. Dusinberre, Susanne Ebbinghaus, Lisbeth S. Fried, Richard Nelson Frye, Mark B. Garrison, A. R. George, Hilary Gopnik, Thomas Harrison, Shalom E. Holtz, Despina Ignatiadou, Bruno Jacobs, Anke Joisten-Pruschke, Deniz Kaptan, Alireza Khosrowzadeh, Philip G. Kreyenbroek, Amélie Kuhrt, Judith A. Lerner, Yannick Lintz, Lloyd Llewellyn-Jones, Parvin Loloi, John MacGinnis, Peter Magee, Sabrina Maras, Bernadette McCall, S. La Niece, C. L. Nimchuk, Cameron A. Petrie, D. T. Potts, Shahrokh Razmjou, Michael Roaf, Kourosh Roustaei, N. V. Sekunda, Mojgan Seyedin, Shapur Shahbazi, St J. Simpson, Abolala Soudavar, Mohammad Hassan Talebian, Nigel Tallis, Christopher Tuplin, Melanie Wasmuth, Matt Waters, Lloyd Weeks, Wu Xin, Sima Yadollahi, Ehsan Yaghmaee, Abbas Yalvaee, Mohsen Zaidi.

John Curtis and St John Simpson have asserted their right under the Copyright,
Designs and Patents Act, 1988, to be identified as the Editors of this work.

All rights reserved. No part of this publication may be reproduced or
transmitted in any form or by any means, electronic or mechanical,
including photocopying, recording, or any information storage or retrieval
system, without prior permission in writing from the publishers.

Bloomsbury Publishing Plc does not have any control over, or responsibility for,
any third-party websites referred to or in this book. All internet addresses given
in this book were correct at the time of going to press. The author and publisher
regret any inconvenience caused if addresses have changed or sites have
ceased to exist, but can accept no responsibility for any such changes.

A catalogue record for this book is available from the British Library.

A catalog record for this book is available from the Library of Congress.

ISBN: HB: 978-1-8488-5346-1
PB: 978-1-3501-9774-9
ePDF: 978-0-8577-1801-3
eBook: 978-0-7556-3052-3

To find out more about our authors and books visit
www.bloomsbury.com and sign up for our newsletters.

The conference was organized by the British Museum and the Iran Heritage Foundation, in association with the Persian Cultural Foundation and with additional support provided by the Soudavar Memorial Foundation. This volume is dedicated to Neil MacGregor, who during his tenure as Director of the British Museum has done so much to promote interest in Iranian culture.

Contents

Editors' Introduction   xiii

Part 1: History and Historiography

1. The Theme of "Persian Decadence" in Eighteenth-Century European Historiography: Remarks on the Genesis of a Myth   3
   Pierre Briant (Collège de France)

2. Cyrus the Mede and Darius the Achaemenid?   17
   Richard Nelson Frye (Formerly Harvard University)

3. Reinventing Achaemenid Persia   21
   Thomas Harrison (University of Liverpool)

4. Portraits of the Achaemenid Kings in English Drama: Sixteenth–Eighteenth Centuries   33
   Parvin Loloi (Swansea University)

5. Light from Aramaic Documents   41
   Anke Joisten-Pruschke (University of Göttingen)

6. All the King's Men   51
   Christopher Tuplin (University of Liverpool)

7. Cyrus and the Medes   63
   Matt Waters (University of Wisconsin)

Part 2: Religion

8. The Achaemenian Practice of Primary Burial: An Argument against Their Zoroastrianism? Or a Testimony of Their Religious Tolerance?   75
   Oric Basirov (London)

9. Ahura Mazdā the Creator   85
   Albert de Jong (Leiden University)

10.	From Gabled Hut to Rock-Cut Tomb: A Religious and Cultural Break between Cyrus and Darius? *Bruno Jacobs* (University of Basel)	91
11.	Zoroastrianism under the Achaemenians: A Non-Essentialist Approach *Philip G. Kreyenbroek* (University of Göttingen)	103
12.	The Formation of Achaemenid Imperial Ideology and Its Impact on the *Avesta* *Abolala Soudavar* (Houston)	111

Part 3: Gender Studies

13.	The Royal Audience Scene Reconsidered *Maria Brosius* (University of Newcastle)	141
14.	An Achaemenid Cylinder Seal of a Woman Enthroned *Judith A. Lerner* (New York)	153
15.	The Big and Beautiful Women of Asia: Picturing Female Sexuality in Greco-Persian Seals *Lloyd Llewellyn-Jones* (University of Edinburgh)	165

Part 4: Art and Architecture

16.	The Social Dimensions of Babylonian Domestic Architecture in the Neo-Babylonian and Achaemenid Periods *Heather D. Baker* (University of Vienna)	179
17.	Why Columned Halls? *Hilary Gopnik* (Emory University, Atlanta)	195
18.	A Reassessment of Brick Motifs and Brick-Building Techniques at Achaemenid Susa *Sabrina Maras* (University of California, Berkeley)	207
19.	Empire Encapsulated: The Persepolis Apadana Foundation Deposits *C. L. Nimchuk* (University of Illinois, Springfield)	221
20.	Persepolis: A Reinterpretation of Palaces and Their Function *Shahrokh Razmjou* (The British Museum)	231
21.	The Role of the Medes in the Architecture of the Achaemenids *Michael Roaf* (University of Munich)	247
22.	Changes in Achaemenid Royal Dress *N. V. Sekunda* (Nicolaus Copernicus University, Torun)	255

Part 5: Archaeology

23. The Passing of the Throne from Xerxes to Artaxerxes I, or How an Archaeological
    Observation Can Be a Potential Contribution to Achaemenid Historiography   275
    Kamyar Abdi (Tehran)

24. Cultural Transition in Iranian Azerbaijan through the Iron Age III–Achaemenid
    Period Based on Recent Archaeological Survey and Excavations (Abstract)   285
    Bahram Adjerloo (Tehran)

25. Archaeological Evidence for Achaemenid Settlement within
    the Mamasani Valleys, Western Fars, Iran   287
    *Alireza Askari Chaverdi, Alireza Khosrowzadeh, Bernadette McCall, Cameron A. Petrie,
    D. T. Potts, Kourosh Roustaei, Mojgan Seyedin, Lloyd Weeks and Mohsen Zaidi*
    (ICHHTO, Tehran, Universities of Cambridge, Nottingham and Sydney)

26. A Review of Research and Restoration Activities at Parsa-Pasargadae:
    Analysis, Evaluation and Future Perspectives   299
    Mohammad Hassan Talebian (Tehran)

27. The Achaemenid Army in a Near Eastern Context   309
    Nigel Tallis (The British Museum)

28. The Origins of the Achaemenids (Abstract)   315
    Sima Yadollahi and Abbas Yalvaee (Tehran)

29. Excavations in Dashtestan (Borazjan, Iran) (Abstract)   317
    Ehsan Yaghmaee (Tehran)

Part 6: Seals and Coins

30. An Analytical Investigation on the Coin Hoard of the Oxus Treasure (Abstract)   321
    Mehdi Daryaie (Tehran)

31. Anatolian Crossroads: Achaemenid Seals from Sardis and Gordion   323
    Elspeth R.M. Dusinberre (University of Colorado)

32. Archers at Persepolis: The Emergence of Royal Ideology
    at the Heart of the Empire   337
    Mark B. Garrison (Trinity University, San Antonio)

33. Clay Tags from Seyitömer Höyük in Phrygia   361
    Deniz Kaptan (University of Nevada, Reno)

34. The Archer Coins: A Closer Examination of Achaemenid Art in Asia Minor   369
    Yannick Lintz (Musée du Louvre)

35. The Frataraka Coins of Persis: Bridging the Gap between
Achaemenid and Sasanian Persia ... 379
Vesta Sarkhosh Curtis (The British Museum)

Part 7: Gold, Silver, Glass, and Faience

36. Technological Aspects of Selected Gold Objects in the Oxus Treasure ... 397
Barbara R. Armbruster (University of Toulouse)

37. From Susa to Egypt: Vitreous Materials from the Achaemenid Period ... 409
Annie Caubet (Formerly Musée du Louvre)

38. Prestige Drinking: Rhyta with Animal Foreparts from Persia to Greece (Abstract) ... 417
Susanne Ebbinghaus (Harvard University)

39. Achaemenid and Greek Colourless Glass ... 419
Despina Ignatiadou (Archaeological Museum of Thessaloniki)

40. Documentary Aspects of Persepolis and the Oxus Treasure (Abstract) ... 427
Shapur Shahbazi (Formerly Eastern Oregon University)

41. Achaemenid Silver, T. L. Jacks and the Mazanderan Connection ... 429
St J. Simpson, M. R. Cowell and S. La Niece (The British Museum)

Part 8: Regional Studies

42. Achaemenid Arabia: A Landscape-Oriented Model of Cultural Interaction ... 445
Björn Anderson (University of Michigan)

43. Because of the Dread Upon Them ... 457
Lisbeth S. Fried (University of Michigan)

44. Xerxes and the Tower of Babel ... 471
A. R. George (School of Oriental and African Studies, University of London)

45. "Judges of the King" in Achaemenid Mesopotamia ... 481
Shalom E. Holtz (University of Pennsylvania)

46. Xerxes and the Babylonian Temples: A Restatement of the Case ... 491
Amélie Kuhrt (University College London)

47. The Role of Babylonian Temples in Contributing to the Army in
the Early Achaemenid Empire ... 495
John MacGinnis (McDonald Institute for Archaeological Research, Cambridge)

48. West of the Indus—East of the Empire: The Archaeology of the
Pre-Achaemenid and Achaemenid Periods in Baluchistan and
the North-West Frontier Province, Pakistan ... 503
Peter Magee and Cameron A. Petrie (Bryn Mawr College and Cambridge University)

49. Achaemenid Interests in the Persian Gulf 523
    D. T. Potts (University of Sydney)

50. Integration of Foreigners—New Insights from the Stela Found in Saqqara in 1994 535
    Melanie Wasmuth (University of Munich)

51. Enemies of Empire: A Historical Reconstruction of
    Political Conflicts between Central Asians and the Persian Empire 545
    Wu Xin (University of Pennsylvania)

Bibliography 565
Index 607

Editors' Introduction

This volume publishes the papers delivered at the conference "The World of Achaemenid Persia" that took place in the Clore Education Centre at the British Museum on 29th September–1st October 2005. From many points of view this was a landmark conference. With a few notable exceptions, it brought together from around the world all those people most active in Achaemenid studies. It has often been remarked recently that Achaemenid studies have undergone a revolution in the last 30 years, coinciding perhaps with a period when large-scale foreign excavations in Iran have not been possible and scholars have had the opportunity to undertake a radical review of the whole subject. The result has been a reappraisal of the sources that have traditionally been used to construct Persian history. It is now accepted that Greek sources such as Herodotus, Ctesias and Xenephon should be used with great caution, and that far more weight should be given to native Persian sources, particularly the Old Persian royal inscriptions and the Persepolis tablets. There is also inscribed material from surrounding areas, particularly Babylonia with its wealth of cuneiform documents dating from the Achaemenid period. All this is very much to be welcomed, but the process of reappraisal has not yet gone far enough. There is still a tendency to overlook or misinterpret the archaeological evidence from Iran and surrounding regions, and until this rich vein of evidence is properly assessed and incorporated we will still not have a rounded picture of the Achaemenid Empire. There is also a reluctance on the part of western scholars to take into account the views of Iranian archaeologists or the results of their work. It is hoped that this conference, like the exhibition which it accompanied, went a little way towards redressing the balance, although there remains far to go. In fact, nine Iranian scholars gave or shared in presentations at the conference, and two more submitted abstracts. Six of these papers are published in full, and one can only wish that it could have been more.

The conference was organized to coincide with the exhibition "Forgotten Empire: the World of Ancient Persia" that was on display at the British Museum from 9th September 2005 to 8th January 2006. This was a remarkable success and attracted more visitors—154,200—than any paying exhibition at the British Museum since "Tutankhamun" in 1972.

There was, in addition, unprecedented media interest in the exhibition, which extended its impact and influence far beyond the British Museum. There was a consequent surge of interest in Ancient Persia that is still visible today. The exhibition drew together material from four great collections, the National Museum in Tehran, the Persepolis Museum, the Musée du Louvre, and the British Museum itself. Because of the logistical difficulties in assembling such an exhibition, it was not intended that it should travel widely, and in fact it was only possible to show the exhibition in its entirety at one more venue. This was at La Caixa Forum in Barcelona, 8th March–11th June 2006, where it was seen by 127,000 visitors. The accompanying catalogue was translated into both Spanish (*El imperio olvidado: El mundo de la antigua Persia*) and Catalan (*L'imperi oblidat: El mon de l'antigua Persia*). Following this, a small number of the British Museum objects were lent to an exhibition in Speyer in Germany, where they joined objects from various museums in Germany, Belgium and Switzerland. This exhibition, entitled "Pracht und Punk der Grosskönige: Das persische Weltreich" (hersausgegeben vom Historischen Museum der Pfalz Speyer) was held 9th July–29th October 2006. The catalogue accompanying the exhibition and with the same name includes some interesting essays and makes a useful contribution to Achaemenid studies.

The conference was organized by the British Museum and the Iran Heritage Foundation in association with the Persian Cultural Foundation and with additional support provided by the Soudavar Memorial Foundation. The conference committee consisted of John Curtis, Farhad Hakimzadeh, Sam Moorhead, St John Simpson and Nigel Tallis. At the conference 49 papers on a wide

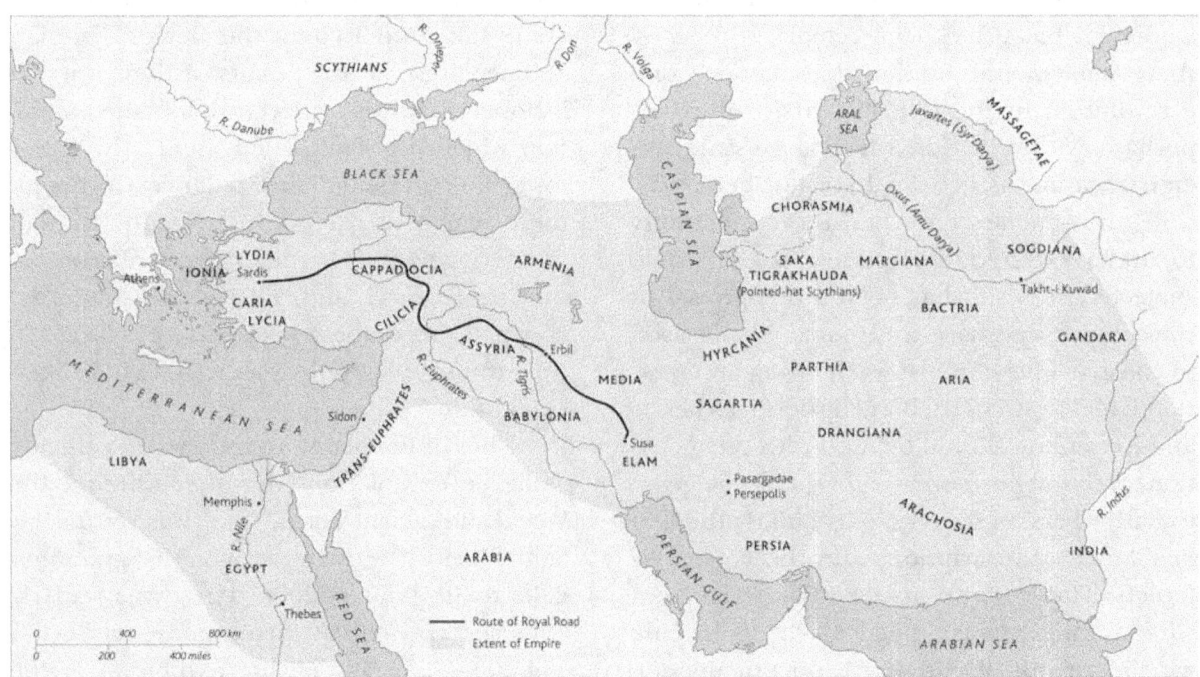

Map of the Achaemenid Empire

range of topics were delivered, and it is pleasing that 45 of those papers are published in full in the present volume. Those four papers for which, for one reason or another, we do not have the full texts, are represented by abstracts (Adjerloo, Daryaie, Ebbinghaus, Yadollahi). There are, in addition, two abstracts that were submitted by authors who were not able to attend the conference. The first of these is the abstract of a paper on the Oxus Treasure by Dr Shapur Shahbazi. He was intending to come to the conference but was unfortunately too ill to do so and passed away on 16th June 2006 before having a chance to write out his paper in full. There is no doubt this would have been a valuable contribution to Achaemenid studies, in keeping with his many other articles and books, and it is gratifying that we are at least able to include here the abstract. The death of Dr Shahbazi is indeed a great loss to Achaemenid studies, and it is a mark of the esteem in which he was held by his colleagues that a telegram expressing best wishes was sent to him on behalf of all the participants in the conference. The second of these abstracts was from Ehsan Yaghmaee, formerly of the Iranian Cultural Heritage Organization, who was unable to come for personal reasons. He was intending to deliver a paper on the important Achaemenid palaces at Bardak-i Siyah and Sang-i Siyah near Borazjan in Bushir province. There have been no further excavations at these sites since 2005.

During the conference, the film directed by Goetz Balonier, *Persepolis—A Reconstruction* was shown, and Kourosh Afhami, Wolfgang Gambke and Sheda Vasseghi of Persepolis 3D.com presented their virtual reconstruction of Persepolis. A seven-minute video from this film is now on show in the new Rahim Irvani Gallery of Ancient Iran at the British Museum.

The 45 papers and 6 abstracts have been arranged in eight parts that demonstrate the breadth and diversity of the conference. The sections are as follows: History and Historiography; Religion; Gender Studies; Art and Architecture; Archaeology; Seals and Coins; Gold, Silver, Glass and Faience; and Regional Studies. These divisions to some extent, but not entirely, are a compacted version of the 15 sessions at the conference. Those sessions were chaired by Andrew Burnett, Dominique Collon, John Curtis, Irving Finkel, Robert Knox, Andrew Meadows, Vesta Sarkhosh Curtis, St John Simpson, Nigel Tallis, Christopher Walker (all British Museum), David Bivar, Georgina Herrmann, Nicholas Simms-Williams (University of London), Sir John Boardman (University of Oxford), and Farhad Hakimzadeh (Iran Heritage Foundation). Welcome speeches were given by John Curtis and Farhad Hakimzadeh, and closing remarks were delivered by Neil MacGregor (Director of the British Museum) and John Curtis.

Since the conference was held, there have been a number of important archaeological discoveries, testifying to the dynamic nature of Achaemenid research. Foremost amongst these new findings is the discovery of a number of Achaemenid-style palaces. Thus, two Achaemenid palaces have been found in Ramhormoz in Khuzestan province (CAIS News, 30th March 2009), and the joint ICAR (Iranian Centre for Archaeological Research) and University of Sydney expedition is investigating an Achaemenid portico with column bases at Qaleh Kali in the Mamasani district of Fars province in Iran (see Potts *et al.* 2007, and Potts *et al.* 2009). There has also been work at the two major Achaemenid sites of Persepolis and Pasargadae. At Persepolis, a joint Italian–Iranian archaeological team led by Professor Pierfrancesco Callieri of the University of Bologna has carried out limited excavations and geophysical survey work in areas beyond the platform, starting in September 2008. They have established that the city of Persepolis was much larger than previously thought. The same team also conducted limited excavations on the Tall-e Takht at Pasargadae in 2006 and 2007, and found evidence of a post-Achaemenid destruction level (CAIS News, 27th November 2007). Also in connection with Pasargadae, at the 10th International Congress on Iranian Archaeology in Bandar Abbas in December 2008, Remy Boucharlat and Kourosh Mohamad Khani reported on magnetic surveys at the site. There have also been discoveries of Achaemenid significance in the Bolaghi Valley, a rescue project occasioned by the building of the Sivand Dam, particularly at sites excavated by Callieri and Boucharlat with Iranian collaborators.

In terms of publications, the most significant work to have appeared in the last five years is Amélie Kuhrt's *The Persian Empire: A Corpus of Sources from the Achaemenid Period*, two vols (London and New York, 2007), a pair of magnificent volumes that according to the fly leaf "contains the most complete collection of raw material for reconstructing the history of the Achaemenid Persian empire in existence". Students of Achaemenid religion will welcome the new book by Wouter Henkelman based on the Persepolis Fortification Texts entitled *The Other Gods Who Are?* (Achaemenid History 14, Leiden, 2008). A new and important resource for linguists is Jan Tavernier's *Iranica in the Achaemenid Period: Lexicon of Old Iranian Proper Names and Loanwords Attested in Non-Iranian Texts* (Leuven, 2007). With regard to regional studies, two works deserve special mention. The first is a comprehensive survey (in English) of the Achaemenid period in the Caucasus, with mention of the various Achaemenid palaces, by Dr Florian Knauss in *Iranica Antiqua* 41 (2006), pp. 79–118. This article is an expanded version of the Lukonin Memorial Lecture that Dr Knauss gave at the British Museum on 13th July 2004. Some of the splendid finds from one of these Caucasian sites, Vani in Georgia, were recently shown in a touring exhibition at the Fitzwilliam Museum in Cambridge entitled "From the Land of the Golden Fleece: Tomb Treasures of Ancient Georgia" (2nd October 2008–4th January 2009). Secondly, for Palestine, the collected articles of Michael Heltzer have now been published in a volume entitled *The Province Judah and the Jews in Persian Times* (Tel Aviv, 2008).

In the same period, there have been a number of important conferences or publications of conferences. They include three significant conferences held in 2006. The first was a colloquium in Paris on the Persepolis Fortification Archive. The papers have now been published in *L'archive des Fortifications de Persepolis: Etat des questions et perspectives de recherches* (Paris, 2008), edited by Pierre Briant, Wouter Henkelman and Matthew Stolper. Secondly, the controversial question of relations between Iran and Greece was revisited in a conference in Athens, which has now been published as *Ancient Greece and Ancient Iran: Cross-Cultural Encounters* (Athens, 2009), edited by Seyed Mohammad Reza Darbandi and Antigoni Zurnatzi. Thirdly, a conference in Georgia has been published as *Achaemenid Culture and Local Traditions in Anatolia, Southern Caucasus and Iran* (Leiden, 2007), edited by Askold Ivantchik and Vakhtang Licheli and appropriately dedicated to a towering figure in Caucasian archaeology, Otar Lordkipanidze. A conference that was held at Rennes in 2004, and so before our own conference, has now been published as *Persian Responses: Political and Cultural Interaction with(in) the Persian Empire* (Swansea, 2007), edited by Christopher Tuplin, and has been very favourably reviewed by Stanley Burstein in the *Bryn Mawr Classical Review* (2008.07.44).

At the time of the conference the remarkable DVD and companion book by Farzin Rezaeian entitled "Persepolis Recreated" was already available, and since then Rezaeian has produced another DVD and companion book entitled "Iran: Seven Faces of Civilization" (2007). The latter set has a long section on the Achaemenid Empire. Both these enterprises have done much to raise awareness of the Achaemenid period and to promote popular interest in this seminal period of world history. Another electronic resource that deserves special mention is more for the benefit of scholars. This is the Persepolis Fortification Archive Project, directed by Professor Matthew Stolper, which aims to digitize the large collection of cuneiform tablets from Persepolis now in the Oriental Institute of the University of Chicago. After excavation in the 1930s these tablets were loaned to Chicago for study and publication, and remain the property of the government of the Islamic Republic of Iran. They are now the subject of a legal dispute that threatens to result in the tablets being sold on the open market. This would be an unmitigated disaster on a number of counts, not least the damage that would be caused to Achaemenid studies. In order to limit the potential damage in case the worst comes to the worst and the tablets are sold, a great effort is being made to record the information in them. In this way, some good is coming out of a potentially very ugly situation.

With the exception of the incident just described, the prospects for Achaemenid studies are bright, and rapid progress is being made on a number of fronts. We are confident that the papers in the present volume will contribute to the advancement of the discipline, and the only regret is that it was not possible to make the papers available at an earlier date. Last, but by no means least, it should be pointed out that the responsibility for views expressed in this volume, including the choice of illustrations, rests of course with individual contributors and not with the editors. Efforts have been made to standardize spellings within individual chapters, but not necessarily throughout the book. Again, the editors do not take responsibility for how names are spelled, taking the view that contributors must be allowed some discretion in this matter.

For help with the preparation of this volume, the editors are indebted to Angela Smith, Nigel Tallis, Shahrokh Razmjou and Bridget Houlton. Helen Knox has undertaken the copy-editing with her usual speed and efficiency. Helen Peter compiled the index. The volume has been seen through the press by Elizabeth Stone, to whom we are most grateful. Above all, we would like to thank the Iran Heritage Foundation, who not only sponsored and helped with the organization of the conference in the first place, but also provided a generous subvention towards the cost of printing this volume and has done us the honour of making this book the first in their new series of academic monographs.

Every effort has been made to ascertain the copyright holder for images used in this book. Any missing acknowledgements will be updated for future editions.

JOHN CURTIS AND ST JOHN SIMPSON

Part 1

History and Historiography

1

The Theme of "Persian Decadence" in Eighteenth-Century European Historiography: Remarks on the Genesis of a Myth

Pierre Briant

In a recent book, I tried to show how a one-sided emphasis placed on Alexander's personality and politics in European historiography had distorted perspectives on the Achaemenid Empire, especially in the last phase of its history (Briant 2003a). The history of the Persian Empire and the history of Alexander have developed both together and in opposition to each other: to a large extent, the European vision of Persia is used to enhance the glorious enterprise of the young Macedonian king. One can extend this observation to the whole of Persian history, starting from the point when the conquests of Cyrus put the Greeks and Persians in direct contact. It is this point that I would like to come back to here, with a contribution to the historiography of ancient Persia—a question which I believe is crucial not only for assessing the stages of previous research, but also to consider more dispassionately how future research should proceed.

I have chosen to address the problem with reference to a specific theme, that of "Persian decadence". Based on well-known classical texts,[1] this historiographical subject has until now been studied above all beginning with nineteenth- and twentieth-century literature.[2] In the context of my current research on the historiography of Alexander in the Age of Enlightenment,[3] I would like to consider the modern genesis of this image, through the works of eighteenth-century scholars, philosophers and historians. This approach is all the more promising in that during this period, "Persian decadence" was contrasted with the "renovation" brought about by Alexander.[4]

1. Preliminary observations on the sources of knowledge about ancient Persia

In general, before the publication of Arnold Heeren's book[5] (at the turn of the eighteenth to nineteenth centuries), which puts the history of the empire at the centre of his thinking,[6] the internal history of Persia and the imperial institutions were never treated independently—apart from a few accounts based on interpretations of Xenophon's *Cyropaedia* (on Persia's peak) and Plato's *Laws* (on Persia's steep decline in the reign of Cambyses).[7] For eighteenth-century scholars, historians and philosophers, the only modern reference in this field was a work which was considered as an authority by Rollin,[8] namely the book by Brisson, which dates from 1590, and was regarded as authoritative until the last century (Brisson 1590; Lewis 1990). We also know that Montesquieu had read Brisson's book, without quoting it, and taken copious notes.[9] Heeren, much better informed than all his predecessors on the geography, history and even archaeology and epigraphy of ancient Persia, also often cites Brisson,[10] in order to avoid giving lists of examples that are already present in what Heeren himself describes as "a very laborious compilation" (Heeren 1840: 98).[11]

It is extremely rare on the subject of Persia that an author cites and comments on an ancient text that has not already been introduced and included by Brisson, and even more that he can give it an original historical interpretation. The best example is a passage from *The Spirit of the Laws* (XVIII.7), where Montesquieu cites Polybius X. 28, and provides his readers with a sociological and political reflection on the establishment of underground canals (*qānats*) "when the Persians were the masters of Asia". He draws important political inferences on the investments that allowed them to develop the agricultural wealth of the Persian Empire. This led him to categorize ancient Persia as one of the "industrious nations that do good things that do not end with themselves".[12]

In contrast to the classical tradition, the books of Arabic and Arabic-Persian literature, which began to be known and published, carried little weight apart from what they contributed in the field of Persian religion.[13] However, another source of information, often treated in conjunction with classical sources, is the accounts of European travellers to the East and more precisely to Persia.[14] We know, for example, how much Montesquieu relied on them,[15] and how many of his views on Persia (including ancient Persia) were taken from his reading of Chardin's *Voyages* and Hyde's book on the religion of ancient Persia.[16] When, in 1760, Bury presented a canonical work on Persian customs and mores, it was based not only on his reading of Xenophon and on the authority of Bossuet, but also on the accounts of modern travellers, especially Tavernier (p. 227).

This dialogue between past and present was also the work of travellers who established their authority with their readers by citing Greek and Roman authors[17] and interpreting them with the help of their own observations (see Briant 2006a: 35–41), based on an approach well explained by Chardin:

> Il n'y a rien qu'il nous soit plus facile de connaître dans les descriptions d'Arrian, de Quinte-Curce et de Diodore de Sicile, que la situation de Persépolis; et c'est un fort grand plaisir que de parcourir ce pays, les auteurs anciens à la main. (1711, III: 99)

Indeed, there is no doubt that the recognition of sites[18] and the observation of specific techniques[19] have enabled modern travellers and ancient historians to make sense of passages by ancient authors speaking about the Achaemenid Empire. It is sometimes a systematic approach, where the comparison, or even assimilation, between past and present seems to provide the clues to the social and political institutions of ancient Persia.[20]

At the same time, parallels between ancient authors and modern travellers can be unsafe, because they were based on the widespread assumption that, apart from conquests and invasions, the fundamental characteristics of the people had not changed profoundly. This theory, very popular in relation to ancient and modern Egypt,[21] was put forward by Bury when talking about the Persians:

> En comparant ce que les voyageurs des deux derniers siècles nous rapportent des Persans d'aujourd'hui avec ce que les Anciens ont écrit de leurs Ancêtres, on voit que leur caractère est le même à quelques nuances près qu'il était du temps de Cyrus et d'Alexandre. (Bury 1760: 226–227)

A few decades later, this was echoed in the pages that James Mill devoted to this subject: "By conversing with the Hindus of the present day, we, in some measure, converse with the Chaldeans and Babylonians of the time of Cyrus, with the Persians and Egyptians of the time of Alexander" (Mill [1817] 1975: 248–249).

The assumption tends to override historical perspectives so that, for example, for Montesquieu the Persians of the Achaemenid era were grouped together under the name of "Guèbres" (Zoroastrians), whose customs and beliefs he was familiar with, especially through the many pages that Chardin devoted to them (1711, III: 126–132). Comparisons and assimilations were also justified by the assumption of a "despotic" continuity between antiquity and modern times.[22] These comings and goings between past and present often led to the forced overlapping of two images of "decadent despotism": that of the Achaemenid Empire, on the one hand, and that of the Ottoman Empire, on the other—both resulting from an "orientalist" vision.[23]

2. Greek history and Persian history: peak and decline

Whether it be universal histories, histories of antiquity or specific works on the history of Alexander, Persian history is subordinate to Greek history. According to the method determined by Bossuet, the Persians should be judged by comparison with the Greeks:

> C'est par là que s'éleva cette Monarchie. Cyrus la rendit si puissante qu'elle ne pouvait guère manquer de s'accroître sous ses successeurs. Mais pour entendre ce qui l'a perdue, il ne faut que comparer les Perses et les successeurs de Cyrus avec les Grecs et leurs généraux, surtout avec Alexandre. (Bossuet 1681: 544)

Bossuet's inspiration is to be found in the famous manual by Charles Rollin, *Histoire ancienne des Égyptiens, des Carthaginois, des Assyriens, des Babyloniens, des Mèdes et des Perses, des Macédoniens et des Grecs*. Published in French between 1731 and 1738, it was translated in most European countries (translated into English in 1768, with the fifteenth English edition appearing in 1823).[24] The *Histoire des Perses et des Grecs* begins in Book V and continues in Books VI–IX. The account is interrupted by a description of Greek customs and mores (Book X) and of Sicily (Book XI), but continues in Books XII (*Suite de l'histoire des Perses et des Grecs*) and XIII, before focusing on the reigns of Philip II (Book XIV) and Alexander (Book XV). The books and chapters themselves are divided according to the reigns of the great kings Darius and Xerxes (Book VI), Artaxerxes "Longuemain" (Book VII), Xerxes II, Sogdian and Darius Nothus (Book VIII), the first 15 years of the reign of Artaxerxes Mnemon (Book IX), then the following years (Book XII), and finally Ochus (Book XIII). The king Darius III and his reign are evoked "in the shadow of Alexander" (Book XV §3–11).

In line with the representations transmitted by the old historiography, the model is found in all major textbooks published in the eighteenth century. It is enough to mention for example the *History of Greece* published in 1787 by the Scotsman John Gillies. He also attached great importance to the relations between Greeks and Persians:

> The Persians enslaved the Greeks of Asia Minor, and, for the first time, threatened Europe with the terrors of Asiatic despotism. This memorable revolution deserves not only to be examined in its consequence, but traced to its source, because the Grecian wars and transactions, during the space of two centuries, with the Persian empire, form an important object of attention in the present history. (Gillies [1786] 1831: 74)

On the whole, everyone was convinced of the evidence as expressed by Linguet:

> Dans ces temps reculés, il n'existe pour nous que deux peuples, les Perses et les Grecs: encore est-ce à leurs querelles que nous avons l'obligation de les connaître. L'envie de célébrer les défaites des Perses fit créer l'histoire par un Grec, et le renversement entier de cet empire sous Alexandre acheva d'en rendre toutes les parties accessibles. (Linguet 1769: 14)

For Linguet as for many other authors, the observation applied not just to political history, it was also valid for the comparative history of art. It was in the context of classical Greek art (which was then being rediscovered) that judgements on the art of Persepolis (frequently described as "coarse") were pronounced.[25]

According to a, by now, traditional model[26] based on assumptions about the relations between the Greeks and the barbarians and on a thorough reading of the ancient texts, Rollin reduced the Persian story to one of a peak (the reign of Cyrus) followed by a long and irreversible decline. The author returned to the subject three times: the death of Cyrus (IV.IV.§5: "Causes de la décadence de l'empire des Perses et du changement arrivé dans les mœurs"); at the end of the reign of Artaxerxes II (XII.1.§12): "Causes des soulèvements et des révoltes qui arrivaient si fréquemment dans l'empire des Perses"); and finally at the time of the death of Darius III (XV.§11): "Vices qui ont causé la décadence et enfin la ruine des Perses"). From one account to another, the causes remain the same with, foremost among them, "la décadence des mœurs qui entraîne toujours après elle la ruine de l'empire" (IV.IV. § 5), so that, "la mort de Darius Codoman peut bien être regardée comme l'époque, mais non comme la cause unique de la destruction de la monarchie persane…Il est aisé de reconnaître que cette décadence était préparée de loin, et qu'elle fut conduite à sa fin par des degrés marqués, qui annonçaient une ruine totale" (XV.§11). Due to a corruption of morals and minds already detectable under Cyrus, "l'on peut dire que l'empire des Perses a été presque dès sa naissance ce que les autres empires ne sont devenus que par la succession des années, et qu'il a commencé par où les autres finissent. Il portait en son sein le principe de sa destruction, et ce vice interne ne fit qu'augmenter de règne en règne" (XV.§11). In Rollin's eyes, one of the most obvious symptoms was the incredible luxury of the king and nobles when going on military campaigns: already denounced by Cyrus (IV.IV. § 5), the "madness" was described more forcefully and in greater detail during the clash with Alexander (XV.§4 and 11) thanks to Rollin's use of the famous passage by Quintus Curtius (*Hist. Alex.* III.3.22–25). The image, as is known, was as much a historiographical success as it was false.[27] Thus was born the myth of the colossus with feet of clay:

> L'éclat éblouissant de la monarchie des Perses cachait une faiblesse réelle; cette puissance énorme, accompagnée de tant de faste et de hauteur, n'avait aucune ressource dans le cœur des peuples. Au premier coup qu'on porta à ce colosse, il fut renversé. (XV.§11)

In truth, Rollin was not the first to emphasize the continuing decline of the Persians. On this as on many other things, he closely followed his master Bossuet,[28] whose authority was often alluded to in the chapters, and whose reflections on Greek and Persian history are quoted verbatim by Rollin (XV. § 20). The image even dates from before Bossuet: in 1646, during an introductory address to his translation of Arrian, intended to praise the comparative merits of Louis II de Bourbon, Prince de Condé (1621–1686), Nicolas Perrot d'Ablancourt wrote: "Alexandre a vaincu des peuples efféminés amollis par une longue paix et par les délices de l'Asie". The old model had already triumphed, just as Europe had conquered "le tyran de l'Asie" (Ablancourt 1972: 131, 135). The assumption also suited historians and philosophers who wanted to show that Alexander's plan was not a consequence of his recklessness; on the contrary, the plan was calculated, because "la terreur des Perses n'était qu'un vain appareil…On pourrait comparer l'armée de Darius à un corps gigantesque, mais mal proportionné, qui est sans force, et comme accablé sous le poids de sa masse, qui ne peut se mouvoir, et qui se soutient à peine".[29] The picture of the Persian Empire painted by Montesquieu, although highly innovative with regard to Alexander, was not fundamentally different or particularly original:

> Alexander's project succeeded only because it was sensible. The unfavourable results of the Persians' invasions of Greece, the conquests of Agesilaus and the retreat of the Ten Thousand had made known just how superior the Greek manner of doing battle and their sort of weapons were; and it was well known that the Persians were too great to correct themselves (*The Spirit of the Laws* X.13).[30]

At the end of a chapter entitled *Histoire abrégée des Perses*, Linguet (1769: 99) tried to suggest that he was the first to link Persian weakness with the Macedonian victory: "Ces observations que les historiens ne font point aident à concevoir pourquoi les progrès d'Alexandre furent si rapides". But in his statement we recognize the author's constant desire to be right, alone against everybody else. In fact, as already clearly expressed by Bossuet, the conviction that Alexander's victory was linked to "Persian decadence" was by then universally accepted.

A few decades later, the finding of John Gillies ([1786] 1831) was basically identical.[31] Questioning the failure of the Persians to prevent the invasion of Alexander, the Scottish historian responded in the following way, without surprise:

> In the space of about two hundred and thirty years, the Persians had been continually degenerating from the virtues which characterize a poor and warlike nation, without acquiring any of those arts and improvements which usually attend peace and opulence. (Gillies [1786] 1831: 424)

Gillies absolved Cyrus of any responsibility for an evolution that was considered to be catastrophic:

> The tendency towards this internal decay was not perceived during the reign of Cyrus [the vigilant shepherd of his people], whose extraordinary abilities enabled him to soften the rigours of despotism, without endangering his authority. ([1786] 1831: 85)

Basing himself on an almost unchanged model and image, he judged the critical turning point to be the capture of Babylon, which had spread the corruption of luxury to the Persian people:[32]

> The hardy and intrepid warriors, who had conquered Asia, were themselves subdued by the vices of that luxurious city. In the space of fifty-two years which intervened between the taking of Babylon, and the disgraceful defeat at Marathon, the sentiments, as well as the manners of the Persians, underwent a total change; and notwithstanding the boasted simplicity of their religious worship, we shall find them thenceforth oppressed by the double yoke of despotism and superstition, whose combined influence extinguished every generous feeling, and checked every manly impulse of the soul. ([1786] 1831: 84–85)

Taking account of traditional indicators (the luxury of the campaigning king ([1786] 1831: 99–100),[33] the adventure of the Ten Thousand presented as a glaring sign of Persian weakness and the prelude to the forthcoming defeat by Alexander [p. 402][34] etc.), Gillies also concluded that, in this state the Persian Empire in 334 "was ready to crumble into pieces at the touch of an invasion" ([1786] 1831: 402).

The idea of an empire on the verge of collapse was shared by Johann Gottfried Herder. In his *Ideen zur Philosophie des Geschichte des Menschheit* (1784–1791),[35] the German philosopher also wrote some harsh words on the Persian Empire:

> The decline began at the time of the death of Cyrus...The Persian Empire existed for a mere two centuries, and it is surprising it lasted so long...the throne, shaken even under the best princes fell of its own accord when Alexander burst into Asia, and after a few battles put an end to the old empire... Its foundations quietly undermined, the Persian Empire fell in face of the success of Alexander...Their weakness was no longer a secret, not only since the old battles of Marathon and Plataea, but especially since the retreat of Xenophon and the Ten Thousand...it [was] a tottering monarchy which for a century had just been wasting away... (Herder 1827: 360–371, 501–502)

In the face of such unanimity of ideas and inferences, dissenting voices were rare. While adopting the theory of a continuous decline from the time of Cyrus, Linguet took pleasure in contradicting his contemporaries (especially Montesquieu) about the analysis of Asian governments (1769: 96–99)[36]. Taking several of his examples from Herodotus about the Persian Empire, he declared that, "ces rois que l'on nous peint comme des despotes furieux, comme des ennemis acharnés du genre humain, n'avaient pourtant rien de plus à cœur que le maintien de l'ordre dans leurs vastes empires" (1769: 228). This may be what led the author to present an original interpretation of the excesses of the Great King on campaign, which was, however, denounced by all his contemporaries:[37] "...usage embarrassant, mais dans lequel la mollesse n'entrait pour rien, puisqu'il fut adopté par les Gaulois et par les Francs, nos ancêtres, dans un temps où ils ne connaissaient assurément ni le luxe ni la mollesse" (1769: 158).

In 1697, P. Bayle subjected another custom of the Persian kings (the 360 royal concubines) to critical analysis. Discussing Alexander's "abstinence" and "excesses", he believed that they should not be judged in the context of his adoption of the custom of the Great Kings, which he presented through Diodorus' text: "Alexander added concubines to his retinue in the manner of Darius... Each night these paraded about the couch of the king so that he might select the one with whom he would lie that night" (XVII. 77.6–7). Bayle says that in his view, this text provides no insight into the sexual life of Alexander, and therefore none into the lust of the Great Kings. Not without a certain amount of humour, he gives the following political interpretation of the custom:

> Il est certain que les princes de l'Orient, et Salomon tout le premier à leur exemple, qui se piquaient d'avoir tant de femmes, ne couchaient pas avec toutes. Ils en usaient avec elles à peu près comme aujourd'hui les sultans; ils en assemblaient un grand nombre, afin de faire un meilleur choix de quelques-unes: les autres servaient à montrer leur opulence, comme font tant de meubles inutiles des maisons riches, dont on ne se sert jamais, et que même l'on ne connaît pas. Les rois qui se piquent d'avoir les plus belles écuries ne montent qu'un très petit nombre de leurs chevaux; ils en laissent vivre et mourir la plus grande part sans jamais les essayer. Quelques-uns dressent de magnifiques bibliothèques, et ne touchent jamais à aucun livre. Ce serait donc une preuve un peu équivoque de l'impudicité d'Alexandre que d'alléguer le grand nombre de ses concubines... (Bayle [1697] 1820: 13)

Clearly, this type of anthropological analysis, far ahead of its time, was not taken up. The many comparisons made throughout the century and later, between Persian palaces and "Oriental" (Ottoman) harems, had the opposite result of further entrenching the idea of the total depravity of the Great Kings lost in luxury and lust.[38]

3. A despotic empire

Not all authors confined themselves to unilaterally insisting on the moral disintegration of Persian kings and nobles. Rather than attributing the defeat of the Persians by Alexander to their love of luxury, Gillies thought that it was due to their ignorance and their inability in the related areas of peace and war.[39] This same author repeatedly used the term "despotism", in the context of a more global analysis:

> [In 546] the Persians, for the first time, threatened Europe with the terrors of Asiatic despotism... [At Marathon] their spirits were broken under the yoke of a double servitude, imposed by the blind superstition of the Magi, and the capricious tyranny of Darius... [From Marathon onwards they were themselves] oppressed by the double yoke of despotism and superstition, whose combined influence extinguished every generous feeling, and checked every manly impulse of the soul. (Gillies 1807: 74, 84, 94)

Here speaks an eighteenth-century historian-philosopher, reader of Voltaire and Montesquieu,[40] equally opposed to despotism and to superstition. Like many of his contemporaries, his rejection of despotism was associated with a great contempt for the East, which was indirectly but clearly illustrated through his positive portrayal of Cyrus the Younger [41] or through the odious portrayal of the Cilician royal couple, Syennesis and Epyaxa.[42] This also explains his admiration for Macedonian institutions, which he contrasted with the East and with some European monarchies of his day: "We should form a very erroneous notion of the Macedonian government if we compared it with the despotism of the East, or the absolute power of many Europeans monarchs. The authority of Philip, even in his hereditary realm, was modelled on that admirable system of power and liberty, which distinguished and ennobled the policies of heroic ages. He administered the religion, decided the differences, and commanded the valour of soldiers and freemen..." (p. 396).

It is clear that here Gillies is expressing his political preferences,[43] which he showed again at length and even more explicitly in the comparison he made between Philip II of Macedonia and Frederick of Prussia.[44] This also explains the historiographical status specifically accorded to Cyrus the Elder, who of all the Great Kings, was the only one to have the capability "to soften the rigor of despotism, without endangering his authority" (p. 85).

4. An overextended and divided empire

Let us continue our analysis of the observation made by J. Gillies. In his view, eastern empires were all struck by the same evil. That is what he intended to demonstrate using the example of the "Assyrian" empire (viewed only through the lens of classical authors):

> This system of government is more favourable to the extension than to the permanence of empire. The different members of this unwieldy body were so feebly connected with each other, that to secure their common submission required almost as much genius as to achieve their conquest. When the spirit which animated the immense mass was withdrawn, the different parts fell asunder; revolutions were no less rapid than frequent; and, by one of those events familiar to the history of the east, the warlike sceptre of Ninus and Semiramis was wrestled from the effeminate hands of Sardanapalus... (p. 74)

Here Gillies assumes as his own an explanation that is essentially derived from Montesquieu and de Mably: that the vastness of an empire is also the main reason for its weakness and for its subsequent fall (Briant 2006b: esp. §3.1). Both authors continued to advocate the ideal of the "mediocre state" in the face of empires that die from over-extension. Mably wrote for example:

> Les rois de Babylone, d'Assyrie, d'Égypte et de Perse, ces monarques si puissants sembleront vous crier de dessous leurs ruines, que la vaste étendue des provinces, le nombre des esclaves, les richesses, le faste et l'orgueil du pouvoir arbitraire hâtent la décadence des empires[45]... Plus la domination de Cyrus était étendue, moins la puissance devait être formidable[46]... Plus souvent encore, la trop vaste étendue d'une monarchie fait sa faiblesse, parce qu'il ne peut régner aucune harmonie entre ses provinces, que rien ne s'y exécute qu'avec une extrême lenteur...[47].

As for Montesquieu, from 1734 on he had addressed the issue by citing the case of the Persian Empire and the Seleucid kingdom:

> Si Cyrus n'avait pas conquis le royaume de Lydie, si Séleucus était resté à Babylone et avait laissé les provinces maritimes aux successeurs d'Antigone, l'empire des Perses aurait été invincible pour les Grecs, et celui de Séleucus pour les Romains"

(*Considerations on the causes of Roman greatness and decadence*, §V).

In his major work (1748 and 1757), the philosopher took up the discussion and expressed the following opinion:

> A monarchical state should be of a medium size. If it were small, it would form itself into a republic; if it were quite extensive, the principal men of the state, being great in themselves, away from the eyes of the prince, with their court outside of his court, and, moreover, secured by the laws and by the mores from hasty executions, could cease to obey; they would not fear a punishment that was so slow and so distant… Rivers run together to the sea; monarchies are lost in despotism. (Montesquieu 1989: VIII.17)[48]

This belief was all the more readily accepted as it was matched by another fundamental idea of the Age of Enlightenment, namely the condemnation of conquerors and conquests, which caused devastation and slaughter. It is in this context that in 1731, Montesquieu had introduced the metaphor of the tree, referring specifically to the disasters caused by the Portuguese and Spanish in their colonies: "An empire can be compared to a tree with branches which, if they spread too far, take up the sap from the trunk, and do nothing but provide shade" (*Persian Letters* 121 = Montesquieu 2004: 218).

The image was later taken up by Herder: "L'empire persan eut à peine deux siècles d'existence, et il est étonnant qu'il ait duré si longtemps, car ses racines étaient peu profondes, et ses branches si étendues que chaque jour sa chute devenait inévitable…" (Herder 1827, II: 363). For Herder, the image also implied that Great Kings, considered as "insane despots and destroyers of the world" had only destroyed the civilizations of the past, without building anything else in their place:

> Insensé! des générations succèdent à des générations, mais de tels monuments ne sont pas remplacés; aujourd'hui encore ils sont en ruines, ils sont déserts. Folie de celui qui a privé l'avenir de ces merveilles des anciens â ges. Ces Perses, ravageurs du monde, ont-ils jamais fondé des royaumes, des villes, des monuments pareils à ceux qu'ils ont ébranlé et détruit? En étaient-ils capables? Les ruines de Babylone, de Thèbes, de Sidon, de la Grèce et d'Athènes sont là pour répondre…De la vient que cet empire n'a exercé une heureuse influence sur aucune nation. Il construisit sans rien édifier, il contraignit les provinces à payer d'odieux tributs, soit pour la ceinture de la reine, soit pour son diadème et son collier; mais de les réunir et de les resserrer entre elles par de meilleures lois et de meilleures institutions, c'est ce qu'il ne tenta jamais: ils sont passés, les jours d'éclat, de magnificence et d'apothéose de ces monarques; ils sont tombés comme eux, leurs favoris et leurs satrapes; et confondus sous les décombres, ils recouvrent de leurs cendres humides l'or qu'ils ont extorqué des provinces; leur histoire même n'est qu'un rêve, une fable qui, transmise jusqu'à nous, de la bouche des Grecs et des Asiatiques, ne vit que de contradictions. Jusqu'à l'ancienne langue de la Perse, tout a disparu: et les seuls monuments de sa magnificence, les ruines de Persépolis, aussi bien que les inscriptions et les figures colossales qui en faisaient l'ornement, sont des débris mystérieux dont l'explication nous est jusqu'ici interdite. Le destin s'est vengé de ces sultans; ils ont été chassés de toute la surface de la terre…"[49] (1827: 364, 367–368)[50]

For Gillies, the explanation lies not only in the almost physical considerations of the empire's vast extent. It is articulated by considering the diversity and cultural and political heterogeneity, which prevented the union of oriental empires (Gillies 1807: 74). Thus it is with the Persian Empire: "The ties of a common religion and language, or the sense of a public interest, had never united into one system this discordant mass of nations, which was ready to crumble into pieces at the touch of an invasion" (Gillies 1807: 402). The idea had already been expressed by Rollin:

> Cette multitude de provinces assujetties aux Perses ne composait pas un empire uniforme, ni un corps d'état régulier, dont tous les membres fussent unis par des liens communs d'intérêts, de mœurs, de langage et de religion;—qui fussent animés d'un même esprit de gouvernement, et conduits par des lois semblables: c'était plutôt un assemblage confus, mal assorti, tumultuaire, et même forcé, de différents peuples, autrefois libres et indépendants... Ces différentes nations, qui non seulement vivaient sans avoir de liaison ni de relation entre elles, mais qui conservaient une diversité d'usages et de culte, et souvent même une antipathie de caractères et d'inclinations, ne soupiraient qu'après la liberté et qu'après le rétablissement de leur patrie. Tous ces peuples ne s'intéressaient donc point à la conservation d'un empire qui seul mettait un obstacle à de si vifs et de si justes désirs, et ils ne pouvaient s'affectionner à un gouvernement qui les traitait toujours en étrangers et en vaincus, et qui ne leur donnait jamais part à son autorité et à ses privileges." (Book XII, §XII)

The defeat of the Persians by Alexander is not surprising, as "leur monarchie n'avait aucune ressource dans le cœur des peoples" (XV.§XI). The same opinion was expressed by Condillac,[51] Herder and many others.

It is also around these issues that the debate over the empire of Alexander compared with that of the Persians raged. If, for Montesquieu, there was a change from division to unity,[52] for others, however, Alexander did not alter the normal course of oriental empires. This is also the opinion of de Mably:

> Il semble en effet que les empires aussi considérables que celui d'Alexandre soient destinés à succomber sous leur propre poids[53]... Les Asiatiques accoutumés à ramper sous le despotisme devaient porter leurs chaînes avec docilité... La révolution qui faisait passer la couronne de Darius sur la tête d'Alexandre n'était point une révolution pour l'État, il restait dans la même situation".[54]

The same applies to Herder. The philosopher praised the one who "de cette foule de nations diverses, voulut former un peuple unique, grec par la langue, les mœurs, les arts, le commerce, et les colonies de Bactres, de Suse, d'Alexandrie, autant d'Athènes nouvelles" (p. 502). But this was in order to better emphasize the enormity of the failure:

> Les parties dont se composait l'empire étaient si mal unies entre elles, qu'à peine si elles formaient un tout dans la pensée du conquérant... Ainsi en est-il arrivé de tous les États qui, nés d'une conquête brusque, impétueuse, étendue, ne reposaient que sur le génie du conquérant. La nature individuelle de tant de nations et de contrées diverses, réclame bientôt ses droits: et ce n'est que par la supériorité de la culture grecque sur la barbarie que l'on s'explique comment des peuples unis entre eux par tant de liens ne sont pas retournés plus

tôt à leurs constitutions indigènes…Ainsi Alexandre, au milieu de ses victoires, éleva l'édifice de son empire sur un monceau d'argile. Il meurt, l'argile cède et le colosse tombe en poussière. (Herder 1827: 505–506, 520)

Although Gillies, like many others (Robertson, Vincent, Heeren, etc.), agreed with Montesquieu that Alexander's Macedonian conquest and plans enabled the creation of new channels of communication between the various countries of the empire and therefore also a "cementing" between regions that were previously cut off from one another,[55] he nevertheless considered the results of the Macedonian colonization with much scepticism: "The feeble mixture of Grecian colonization diffused through the East, was sufficient, indeed, to tinge, but too inconsiderable to alter and assimilate the vast mass of Barbarians… [Conversely], as the principle of degeneracy is often stronger than that of improvement, the sloth and servility of Asia gradually crept into Greece" (p. 437).

In other words, after the conquest of Alexander, the principles that governed the lives of eastern empires prevailed because his successors, the Seleucids and the Ptolemies, adopted the manners of the kings Alexander had ousted:

> They sunk into the softness and insignificance of hereditary despots, whose reigns are neither busy nor instructive; nor could the intrigues of women and eunuchs, or ministers equally effeminate, form a subject sufficiently interesting to succeed the memorable transactions of the Grecian Republics.

Following in the footsteps of Montesquieu and de Mably, Gillies thus opened a discussion that was not about to cease with what would be termed the "Hellenization of the East".[56] His analysis in some way validated a form of survival of the Achaemenid Empire, through its structural characteristic of "oriental despotism".

Notes

1. Briant 2003*a* (on the influence of the sources concerning the history of Alexander); also 2002*b*; Sancisi-Weerdenburg 1987*b*.
2. For the end of the nineteenth century and the first half of the twentieth century, see my study Briant 2005*a*; see also Briant 2003*a*: 85–130. On eighteenth-century England, see some remarks in Brosius 1990.
3. See the bibliography.
4. See Briant 2006*a*, 2007*a*.
5. The first edition of Heeren (1824), appeared in 1793–1796; the English translation used here was from the fourth German edition (Göttingen, 1824–1826); the whole of the first volume is devoted to the Persian Empire: *Historical Researches into the politics, intercourse, and trade of the main nations of Antiquity*, Oxford, 1833; I: *Asiatic Nations: Persia*; following a methodological introduction ("Asia", pp. 1–79), the book about the Persians is divided into two parts: 1. "A geographical and statistical survey of the Persian Empire according to satrapies" (pp. 92–320); 2. "On the constitution of the Persian Empire" (pp. 321–443).
6. In a sense, the *Researches* by Heeren (1833) are the first "History of the Achaemenid Empire", with the understanding that the author is more interested in the institutions and societies than in the political and military history. Heeren's views on ancient Persia deserve a special study; on the author, see the bibliography cited in Briant 2006*a*: n. 67.
7. See Bossuet 1681: 545–549; Rollin, Book IV, Chapter IV: *Mœurs et coutumes des Assyriens, des Babyloniens, des Lydiens et des Perses* (in fact, it is almost exclusively concerned with ancient Persia); see also Bury 1760: 223–228 (quoting Bossuet). The authors particularly hostile to the Persians deny the credibility of the *Cyropaedia* (Condillac 1775: 154–157; Linguet [1769: 88–89] describes the *Cyropaedia* as an "ouvrage chimérique", which he compares to Fénelon's *Télémaque*).
8. "Le livre de Barn. Brisson, président du parlement de Paris, sur le gouvernement des Perses, m'a été

d'un grand secours", he wrote at the end of his work on Persian institutions.
9. They figure in a manuscript from the Chateau de la Brède, to be published by C. Vopilhac-Auger, to whose friendship I owe this information.
10. Often using the following formula: "See the places cited (collected) by Brisson", e.g. *Researches* I, p. 142[h], 160[n], 161[s], 163[y], 170[q], 197[p], 415[n], 434[d].
11. The first German edition was published in 1799.
12. Montesquieu (translation by Cohler, Miller & Stone) 1989: 289; on this subject, see Briant 2007*b*.
13. See especially the very clear statement by Sainte-Croix (1804): "On [ne] trouve l'histoire véritable [d'Alexandre] que dans le récit des écrivains grecs et latins, qui va être l'objet de mes discussions" (p. 192).
14. For France, see Chaybany 1971.
15. See Dodds 1929: 41–57 ("Turkey and Persia").
16. See for example my remarks in Briant 2006*a*: 22–24; 2007*b*.
17. See, for example, Chardin 1730, ii: 247–251.
18. Travellers' accounts have provoked major debates on Persepolis: cf. the controversy in France between Sainte-Croix and Caylus (Sainte-Croix 1773, 1775: 286–287), and in Germany between Herder (1787) and Heeren (e.g. 1833, i: 401–413).
19. The example of underground channels (*qānats*) is very interesting. Described in detail in modern Persia by Chardin without reference to Polybius (1711, ii: 72–73), the system was studied by Montesquieu (1748) starting from Polybius, but without reference to Chardin or other travellers (Montesquieu 1989: XVIII.7). It was not until Morier that a careful reading of Polybius was combined with a detailed examination of a *qānat* in modern Persia (Morier 1812: 163); the collected information was first used in historical literature in Heeren's fourth edition of 1824 (1833, i: 138–139; cf. Briant 2007*b*).
20. By studying the institutions of the Persian Empire, Heeren on numerous occasions stressed their relationship with observations made in modern times; cf. e.g. Heeren (1833, i: 415, n. m), where in dealing with the assignment of villages to senior officers, and citing Chardin, he remarked: "It is astonishing how completely the same customs appear on comparison to have prevailed at the court of Xerxes, and that of the Sofis. The same thing is true also of Eastern Persia…"
21. See for example the reflections of Mallet (1735: 105–106, Letter XI): "Vous ne devez pas être surpris si ce passage fréquent d'une domination à une autre, cette inondation de peuples divers entés successivement les uns sur les autres, tous d'inclinations et de coutumes différentes, n'ont pu abolir celles qui étaient propres aux anciens Égyptiens. La nature et le climat les avaient formées et la nature reprend facilement ses droits. Aussi retrouvons-nous encore dans les Egyptiens d'aujourd'hui à peu près le même génie, presque toutes les mêmes coutumes d'hier."
22. Heeren's statement systematized this approach: "a knowledge of their [Persians] empire and its institutions, will afford a standard by which to measure those of other great monarchies established in ancient and modern times" (Heeren 1833, i: 79).
23. I am using just one word to describe an extraordinarily fruitful research theme, the results of which will shortly be published.
24. See Ampolo 1997: 26–27; for Rollin see the numerous revelations in C. Grell's comprehensive survey (1995); see also Briant 2003*b*.
25. Linguet 1769: 186–187 (describing the palace burned down by Alexander at Persepolis): "Ses débris qui subsistent encore inspirent peu de regrets…Tous les voyageurs s'accordent à dire que c'était un édifice immense et grossier" (cf. on the contrary p. 341: "Les Grecs ont mérité de devenir nos modèles"); see also de Pauw, in conflict with M. de Caylus (a keen believer in the links between Persian art and Inca architecture): "Les dessins et les plans fidèles que nous en a donnés Chardin et de Bruin, prouveront à tout jamais que ce sont des restes d'une construction désordonnée, irrégulière, élevée par la magnificence barbare des despotes asiatiques, en qui la corruption du goût est le premier fruit du pouvoir absolu" (de Pauw 1768: 325–326); on this debate, see also the position taken by Sainte-Croix, which on the whole supported Caylus against Winckelmann (1766) (Sainte-Croix 1773: 39–40, 55).
26. See Bossuet 1681: 544 (paraphrased from Plato, *Laws* III): "Mais la corruption était déjà trop universelle: l'abondance avait introduit trop de dérèglement dans les mœurs, et Darius [Ier] n'avait pas lui-même conservé assez de force pour être capable de redresser tout à fait les autres. Tout dégénéra sous ses successeurs et le luxe des Perses n'eut plus de mesure."
27. See Briant (2003*a*: 347–394; to the nineteenth-century authors cited there, one should add Rollin's contemporaries, e.g. Bossuet (1681: 550–551; 1770, iii: 555); Bury (1760: 239); Gast (1787: 22, n. 18), etc.

28. Bossuet 1681: 55–71, 542–570 (history of the Persian Empire and its decline, and its conquest by Alexander).
29. Secousse 1729: 424 (also claiming to represent Bossuet's authority).
30. Translation by Cohler, Miller & Stone 1989: 147; on Montesquieu's original analysis of Alexander, see Volpilhac-Auger 2002 and Briant 2006b, 2007b; see also Guerci 1981: 637.
31. On Gillies, see the short introductions in Clarke 1945: 106–107 and in Ampolo 1997: 58–60; on Gillies and the Persian Empire, see some brief remarks in Brosius 1990: 82–83; on Gillies, the history of Alexander and the intellectual and political context of his *History*, see my analyses in Briant 2005b and 2006b.
32. See also Rollin XV.§11, quoted in Briant (2003a: 121–122) and linked to more recent authors.
33. See above n. 31.
34. Gillies devotes no less than two chapters to Cyrus the Younger and the return of the Greek mercenaries (Chapters XXV–XXVI); see also Rollin's lengthy accounts (Book IX, Chapter II). The importance given to the expedition of the Ten Thousand is based on Polybius' reflections (III. 6–13) on the causes of war: cf. Bossuet 1681: 563–564.
35. Quoted here from the French translation by Edgar Quinet, *Idées sur la philosophie de l'histoire de l'humanité*, Paris, 1827, t. II.
36. Linguet's character and beliefs have often been studied: see Grell 1995, i: 526–538; a comparison between the two editions of *Siècle d'Alexandre* (1762, 1769) was made by Guerci (1981).
37. See above note 36.
38. See Linguet himself: "Amollis par le luxe, toujours enfermés dans leurs nombreux sérails, ils ne durent leur conservation qu'aux troubles qui désolaient la Grèce" (Linguet 1769: 97); on this theme, the book of Grosrichard (1979) is still a valuable source.
39. "Although the extravagance and vices of Susa, Babylon, and other imperial cities, corresponded to the extent and wealth of the monarchy, yet the Persians were prepared for destruction rather by their ignorance of the arts of peace and war, than by their effeminacy and luxury" (Gillies 1807: 402).
40. See e.g. Gillies [1786] 1831 (ed.): 435, n. 7.
41. "Cyrus appears to have been born for the honour of human nature, and particularly for the honour of Asia, which, though the richest and most populous quarter of the globe, has never, in any age, abounded in great characters" (p. 262): cf. Rawlinson's view (quoted in Briant 2003a: 115).
42. "A true picture of oriental manners, meanness varnished with pride!" (Gillies 1807: 264, n. 1).
43. See also the dedication *To the King* at the beginning of the book: "Sir. The History of Greece exposes the dangerous turbulence of Democracy, and arraigns the despotism of Tyrants. By describing the incurable evils inherent in every form of Republican policy, it evinces the inestimable benefits, resulting to Liberty itself, from the lawful dominion of hereditary Kings and the steady operation of well-regulated Monarchy. With singular propriety, therefore, the present Work may be respectfully offered to Your Majesty, as Sovereign of the freest nation upon earth…"
44. Gillies 1789; the comparison itself is made on pp. 1–55.
45. De Mably 1783: 16.
46. De Mably 1783: 39.
47. De Mably 1749: 203 (speaking of Alexander's empire).
48. Translation by Cohler, Miller & Stone 1989: 125.
49. Herder himself had offered his interpretation of the ruins of Persepolis (1787); on this subject he was strongly attacked by Heeren (see "Some observations on Herder's Persepolis" in Heeren 1833, ii: 401–413).
50. It is probably from Herder that Hegel borrowed his blunt judgement on the disappearance of the Persian Empire: "L'empire perse appartient au passé, et il ne reste que de tristes vestiges de sa floraison. Les villes les plus belles et les plus opulentes, telles que Babylone, Suse, Persépolis sont complètement en poussière, seules de rares ruines nous en montrent l'ancien emplacement…" (*Leçons sur la philosophie de l'histoire*, French translation by J. Gibelin, Paris: Vrin, 1963, p. 152), yet Hegel had read Ker Porter (see p. 142).
51. Condillac 1775: 208 ("un empire formé d'un débris de provinces"), 300 (hatred of peoples).
52. Montesquieu 1989: X.13–14; XXI.8 cf. Vopilhac-Auger 2002 and Briant 2006b.
53. De Mably 1749: 203.
54. De Mably 1766: 225–226; on the discussion see also my remarks in Briant 2007a.
55. See Briant 2005b: 25–35; 2006a: 41–43.
56. See Briant 2005c; also referring to another book by Gillies (1807), Momigliano (1952: 5–7) has already noted Gillies' special place in the genesis of "pre-droysénienne" Hellenistic historiography: cf. Briant 2006b.

2

Cyrus the Mede and Darius the Achaemenid?

Richard Nelson Frye

Ancient sources seem to justify Thomas Carlyle's view of history as the biographies of heroes, since they too exalt individuals as those who "make history". I would prefer to call them fanatics rather than heroes, for they would do anything to attain or hold on to power. In my opinion Alexander and Napoleon, and many others, would fit this designation, and Darius as well.

The vexed question of the rise of Darius has usually been approached by comparing the information about individuals, Cyrus, Cambyses, Gaumata or Bardiya and Darius. The motivation of each person has been investigated and surmised, with little thought about the influences of others upon our principal actors, as though each was a ruler who had companions but who acted as if all the decisions he made were only guided by personal power and authority. Is it not possible that the Iranians (Medes, Persians and others) were still in a tribal frame of mind and behaved in a manner towards their leaders different from long-settled folk? That tribal society would more likely have been similar to that of the contemporary Pushtuns with their *loya jirga*, rather than the other model, such as the blind obedience of the Baluch towards their chiefs. If we assume that Iranian leaders were not absolute dictators to their people, heeding no one, we may consider the data that we have in another light.

Based on—admittedly uncertain—remarks in various sources, I propose that at least two factions existed at court, one that may be called a pro-Mede group and the other a pro-Persian one. Of course both Medes and Persians existed in both camps but legitimacy in the first implied continuity from the old Median royal family, while the other, asserted by Darius, claimed a new legitimacy in a Persian royal descent from an eponymous ancestor called Achaemenes. What Darius did was not so much to seek his affiliation with Cyrus as attach Cyrus to his new Achaemenid legitimacy. The impetus to this proposal, after many years of uncertainty about Darius' rise to power, came to me when viewing again the cuneiform inscriptions that Darius caused to be carved on stones in Pasargadae. Other details in various sources seemed to support the existence of rival factions at court during the events leading to the triumph of Darius.

Let us begin with possibly true events in the life of Cyrus from various sources. I use the word "possibly" advisedly, since all events from that period are subject to question, and what I suggest is not new but viewed from another perspective.

Who was Cyrus? According to Herodotus (*Histories* 1.108), Astyages, the ruler of the Medes, was his maternal grandfather. Later he says that Cyrus' mother was the daughter of Astyages but his father was a Persian and inferior to his mother. He continues to say that Astyages' daughter Mandane was married to a Persian, Cambyses, and Cyrus was born from this union. Then follows the tale of how Astyages, afraid of an omen, ordered the baby Cyrus to be killed, but his minister Harpagus gave the baby to a shepherd who raised him. Later his royal birth was recognized and he was sent to his parents in Persis. Herodotus reports a fear of the magi at the Median court, who said to Astyages: "this boy is a Persian, a foreigner, and if he attains power we Medes of a different race will be despised and enslaved by the Persians". The king, however, agreed that he should be sent to his parents. The rest of the story is well known: Cyrus revolted and Harpagu and many Medes abandoned Astyages on the battlefield. Thus Cyrus became ruler of the Medes and Persians, although some Medes seem to have been resentful of the accession to power of a Persian (Herodotus, *Histories* 1.129). This has been termed the "Cyrus Saga" and much in it is probably based on contemporary folklore among the people.

If we turn to the *Cyropaedia* of Xenophon (3.10) he writes that Astyages was the father of Cyrus' mother, while Cyaxares, successor to Astyages, was the uncle of Cyrus, who was well treated at the Median court and also showed deference to Cyaxares when Cyrus attained power (5.1). The *Cyropaedia*, of course, is a paean of praise for Cyrus so it is difficult to know how much to believe, but it seems clear that Cyrus acted favourably towards the Medes and even advised his comrades to wear Median dress (7.40).

Ctesias too shows Cyrus following in the footsteps of his Mede predecessors. The Bactrians and Sagartians submitted to Cyrus because he was considered legitimate in the line of Median kings (Photius, *Bibliotheca* 72.2, Jacoby [date?] 688.PN). Thus, even though we have three unreliable sources they do converge on the proposition that Cyrus was a true successor of the kings of the Medes and may be designated as pro-Mede in his policy of conciliation between Persians and Medes. It should be remembered that Mandane, mother of Cyrus, was a Mede, as was Cyrus' wife Amytis, and so principally also their daughter Atossa. Cambyses, son of Cyrus, as well as Bardiya and Atossa were presumably three-quarters Mede and one-quarter Persian by descent.

Darius, on the other hand, was 100 per cent Persian and consequently had to have legitimacy by connection with Cyrus. In order to secure the allegiance not only of the Medes but also of other Iranians, he had to proclaim his relationship to the royal family of the Medes, and what easier way to do this than to create an eponymous ancestor for both himself and Cyrus, showing that Cyrus was in a side line of descent from Achaemenes joining the Medes, while Darius was in a direct line of kings of the Persians. In my opinion Darius ordered the carving of inscriptions on gold plates, and probably on stone, stating that his father Vishtaspa, his grandfather Arsames and his great-grandfather Ariaramnes were all kings, his grandfather and great-grandfather even having been called Kings of Kings on the inscriptions. Thus, Darius was the champion of the Persians and founder of a new dynasty, although he was linked collaterally with Cyrus and the Medes. It would be interesting to speculate on the relationship, if any, between Cambyses, father of Cyrus, and Arsames, grandfather of Darius and other members of his family.

The above explains why Darius insisted on placing the name Achaemenid in all his inscriptions, which practice was also followed on the inscriptions of his successors, for it was necessary to propagandize the name in order to convince people of his legitimacy. In Pasargadae, capital of Cyrus, Darius ordered inscriptions carved with the simple declaration "I am Cyrus the Achaemenid". Darius had to convince everyone that Cyrus was an Achaemenid like himself although Cyrus in his genealogy on the Babylonian cylinder seal does not know Achaemenes and only goes back to Teispes (Old Persian Chichpis), which is where Darius connects the two lines of descent from Achaemenes. The latter becomes the key to descent and legitimacy. So with the accession of Darius the Persian party triumphed and the Medes became subordinate partners of the Persians.

Just as the Soviets failed to force East Europeans to learn Russian, and the Ayatollahs of Tehran failed to implant Arabic among the Persians, so perhaps Darius failed to convince all his subjects that his view of the legitimacy of his family of the Achaemenids was to be believed. For the name "Achaemenid" was forgotten in Iran, which is strange given Darius' huge efforts to keep the name alive in the memories of his subjects. We will probably never know whether Darius' story of Bardiya/Gaumata and the coming to power of Darius was true or not but no one can deny that Darius was a remarkable, if not beloved, ruler.

To continue with speculation, the killing of the magi by Darius after attaining power may well reflect the defeat of the Median party of Bardiya/Gaumata and those magi at court who held on to old Aryan beliefs against the Zoroastrian convictions of Darius and many Persians, as well as some magi among the Medes. After the elimination of old beliefs the pro-Zoroastrian magi triumphed with Darius but later reconciled with those magi who favoured Mithra and Anahita. The *ayadana* destroyed by Bardiya/Gaumata and restored by Darius could have been Zoroastrian fire temples, as opposed to the general Iranian worship in high places in the open, as mentioned by Herodotus. I suggest that Darius was indeed a follower of Zoroaster but even more so his son and successor Xerxes. If we interpret his "Daiva" inscription as forbidding the worship of common Iranian deities such as Mithra and Anahita, then he was more fanatical than his father. The murder of Xerxes and his son Darius may well have had a religious as well as a political motivation. This is of course speculation but at least all the loose ends seem to tie together well.

Admittedly this paper is highly conjectural and impressionistic, but without adequate information one is forced to rely on logic and reason to paint a picture of the past that at least makes sense. The Teispes of the Cyrus cylinder and of Darius' genealogy may well have been the same person, but surely Cyrus would have mentioned his ancestor Achaemenes who would give his name to the dynasty of Darius. In this sense, however, was Cyrus really an Achaemenid? Why was the name forgotten in later Persian writings? I propose the above as a suggestion and hope others will accept it, modify it or create a better scenario for the drama of Darius' rise to power.

3

Reinventing Achaemenid Persia

Thomas Harrison

The achievement of the scholars associated with the Achaemenid History Workshop in renewing the study of Achaemenid Persian history can scarcely be exaggerated. This renewal has been the result in large part of the careful evaluation of a wealth of new evidence, and of a determination to treat Persian history in its own terms, rather than through the prism of neighbouring societies. However, it has also been driven to a significant extent by a reaction to previous Hellenocentric versions of Persian history, a desire "to break away from the dominant Hellenocentric view" as Heleen Sancisi-Weerdenburg (1987*a*) put it in her introduction to the first volume of the workshop's proceedings, "to dehellenise and decolonialise Persian history", as stated more graphically (1987*c*: 131), and somehow to launder the pejorative bias of classical Greek sources—inevitably the basis of much of any modern reconstruction of Achaemenid Persia. To summarize brutally, the new Achaemenid historiography has set itself against a narrative in which a Persian empire neutered and rendered decadent by the defeats of the Persian wars is finally put out of its misery (only 150 years later) by Alexander. In its place, and in place of the stereotypes of Achaemenid kings and queens as oriental despots, there is a new emphasis on the resilience of the Achaemenid Empire and on the tolerance and pragmatism of its rulers. The success of this academic programme[1] can be measured from the British Museum exhibition from which this volume has its origins, and which in general might be said to enshrine the main conclusions of recent work.[2]

Like any scholarly consensus, however, the new Achaemenid historiography gives rise to almost as many further questions as it settles. Questions can be asked, for example, as to whether it is legitimate to launder Greek sources—or to "distinguish the Greek interpretative coating from the Achaemenid nugget of information" (Briant 2002*a*: 256)[3]—as easily as it is sometimes done. This paper addresses another issue, however: the intellectual genealogy of the modern study of Achaemenid Persia, and whether—to put it at its most blunt—previous scholarship is as bad, or as Hellenocentric, as it is often presented as being. No one, of course, would seriously suggest that the modern historiography of Persia began from a clean slate in 1981, but it is easy sometimes to imagine so, or to suppose that the Hellenocentric version of our Greek sources was swallowed whole by previous historians. Early travellers and historians tend, at best, to be credited for adding to the sum of our knowledge, especially of monuments, not for their interpretative framework.[4] The model of Persian decadence remained frozen, according to Amélie Kuhrt and Sancisi-Weerdenburg (1987: ix–x), unmoved by decipherment or by new excavations: "The Greeks could not have been too far wrong", they comment (ironically), "they were first of all Greeks, and therefore almost infallible, and secondly, they had been contemporaries and thus had first-hand knowledge".

This paper will examine only a relatively small slice of previous historiography: mainly British writers, and mainly from the late nineteenth and early twentieth centuries, from Sir John Malcolm to A. T. Olmstead. What this slice of history-writing reveals—like the survey of eighteenth-century Greek histories of Maria Brosius (1990)—is a very much more complex and (in many instances) a more positive approach to the Achaemenid past than is commonly presented. Whether in detailed research—in the case, say, of George Curzon, later viceroy of India (1892)[5]—or in the passing impressions of less academic travellers, most commonly soldiers or missionaries,[6] these writers also in many ways pre-empt the conclusions of more recent scholarship. And, far from adhering unquestioningly to a romantic model of the Greco-Roman world, their views of the classical world—and of their classical educations—are in many cases intriguingly ambivalent.

If one looks in earlier writings for signs of the model of decadence and decline identified by the new Achaemenid historians, for stories of harem intrigues or the moral weaknesses of the Persian kings, one will—undeniably—find them. Only in rare instances, however—especially in the more detailed and scholarly histories such as George Rawlinson's *Fifth Monarchy*, or later that of A. T. Olmstead of Chicago—is it fleshed out to any great extent. Rawlinson's narrative digests all the unsavoury details of Ctesias and other fragmentary authors of the fourth century, dwelling for example on the moral weakness of Xerxes, with "scarcely a trait whereon the mind can dwell with any satisfaction" (Rawlinson 1885: 502). Similarly, A. T. Olmstead follows Herodotus in lingering on the domestic consequences for Persia of her defeat in the Persian wars, constructing the harem intrigue at the close of Herodotus' account (9.108–114) as a turning point in Persian fortunes: "failure of the European adventure opened the way to harem intrigues, with all their deadly consequences" (Olmstead 1948: 266–267).[7]

For the most part, however, decadence and decline, though present, are fairly impersonal processes without significant landmarks: the thesis of Persian decline from 479 can, after all, only really be sustained by a giant act of elision. A number of authors make the point that no one could have foretold Persian decline, that the Persian wars could only be recognized as a turning point with hindsight. "The mischief was internal", "it was situate far away in the depths of Asia, beyond the ken of the Greek of the 5th century, and it is not strange that he never appreciated the full extent of the malady" (Grundy 1901: 1–2),[8] and therefore it is somehow beyond our ken too, beyond explanation or clear identification. Signs of weakness are sometimes mentioned without being clearly identified.[9] Alternatively, a narrative of progressive decadence is presumed. So, for example, when the American traveller-historian A. V. Williams Jackson is offered water from a goatskin tankard, this leads him—meanderingly—to an observation on the Achaemenids:

> These rude vessels were made from the undressed hide of a goat, with the animal's hair left on the outside and the skin drawn tightly around a wooden rim and a circular board bottom so as to form a bucket, while three sticks were used as fastenings to give firmness to the whole and as props for the uncouth vessel to stand upon. I presume it was from tankards such as these that the hardy soldiers of Cyrus used to drink, before luxury taught them the use of silver beakers and the accompanying vices which sapped away the vigor that had conquered kingdoms. (Jackson 1906: 322)

Other writers indeed prefigure recent views. The soldier-historian Percy Sykes (1922: 18–19), for example, insists that Persia "played the leading part in the history of the known world" for the 150 years after Salamis (decadence does, like a "dry rot", creep in, in the figures of women and eunuchs, but only late on, in the court of Darius III). He also makes the argument—again familiar from recent histories—that to assume the Persian Empire decadent robs Alexander of credit for his military achievement.[10] (This is a long way, then, from the image of Persia as frozen in decadence from the time of the Persian wars or from the death of Xerxes, or of Alexander's campaigns as a mercy killing.)[11]

There is a similar spread of responses to imperial Persian art and architecture. Again, of course, there are negative judgements. Figures such as John Macdonald Kinneir or George Rawlinson—emblematic for Sancisi-Weerdenburg of the pejorative view of Persia (1987c: 128–131)—are distinctly churlish: Kinneir (1813: 76) damning Persian sculpture (though finding Persepolis "one of... the most magnificent structures, that art has ever raised to the glory and admiration of mankind"),[12] Rawlinson finding nothing in either sculpture or architecture "indicative of any remarkable artistic genius" (1885: 317, cf. p. 380). Others complain of precisely the features of the sculpture of Persepolis that we now know, since Margaret Root's (1979) masterpiece *King and Kingship in Achaemenid Art*, to see them as reflecting an imperial ideology of calm, stability and a *Pax Persiana*. So the American Copley Amory Jr complains memorably, in 1929, of the monotony and formalism of the sculptures, and of the "bored composure" with which the Great King plunges "a dagger into rampant unicorns and lions and griffins" (Amory 1929: 68, 61).

Such negative views, in general, however, are exceptions to a rule of ecstasy: as one disappointed British traveller (Harry de Windt) admits, the reason for his disappointment at Persepolis was probably "the fact that it has been crammed down my throat, upon every available occasion, ever since I landed in Persia".[13] "Standing in the gathering twilight in front of the vast platform", the colonial official Bradley-Birt wrote (to give just one example), "the modern Western mind half fails to grasp the thought of so much splendour and antiquity" (1909: 180).[14] Again, moreover, a number of writers foreshadow trends in more recent scholarship. Far, for example, from sharing the damning judgement of Bernard Berenson on Achaemenid art, that it displayed the "originality of incompetence" (Berenson 1954: 186, cited by Nylander 1970: 148), a number of writers foreshadow the work of Carl Nylander or of Margaret Cool Root in emphasizing the extent to which Achaemenid art combined and added a twist to its various models, Greek, Babylonian or Egyptian (see esp. Root 1979, 1991; Nylander 1970). This number includes both fairly serious figures (the Orientalist Denison Ross, for whom "each element received a touch of originality at the hands of the Persians", or Curzon for whom the relationship of Persian and other art is a major issue to which he devotes a lengthy and learned discussion)[15] as well as more passing, less academic travellers: the American financial administrator A. C. Millspaugh, for example (who, with only a little self-interest, found that the Persians have always "had a rare capacity for drawing on the special gifts of other peoples without losing their own characteristics and integrity"), or the doctor Rosalie Morton (with a sentimental view of the work being done by artists brought back from foreign conquests, whose "captivity was lightened by congenial work and by comradeship, for here the genius of the then known world was brought together and flowered") (Arnold 1877: 331–332; Millspaugh 1925: 4–5; Morton 1940: 175).

Other aspects of the best modern interpretations of Persepolis are also foreshadowed. Writers as diverse as Percy Sykes or the English doctor Treacher Collins (a consultant to a Qajar prince, who sees himself as a modern Democedes of Croton, doctor to the court of Darius) both understand that the apparent sameness of Persepolitan sculpture is intentional, that it reflects in Treacher Collins's words "a oneness in composition which is exceedingly remarkable" (1896: 78–79).[16] Curzon makes the connection between the processions of the Apadana and the Panathenaia (1892: 161; cf. Root 1985). And some writers develop the broader thesis of Persian influence on Greek art and culture. "All that is Ionic in the arts of Greece is derived from the valleys of the Tigris and the Euphrates", according to Fergusson, quoted approvingly by Arthur Arnold (1877: 331–332). The American diplomat S. G. W. Benjamin sees the origins of Greek music in Persia.[17] Even George Rawlinson contemplates the possibility of Persian influence on Greek art (1885: 412). In short, the body of work that Nylander and Margaret Root were reacting against, though undoubtedly significant, represents perhaps a relatively short blip.

Many writers of this period indeed go further than modern scholars in a powerful *identification* with ancient Persia. In many regards, Persia and the Persians are often assumed to be frozen in an undeveloped state. As Sir John Malcolm, three times ambassador to the Persian court at the turn of the nineteenth century, remarks rather paradoxically in conclusion to his 1815 *History of Persia*: "Though no country has undergone, during the last twenty centuries, more revolutions than the kingdom of Persia, there is, perhaps, none that is less altered in its condition".[18] This assumption of continuity allows for the construction of an extraordinarily consistent set of ethnographic commonplaces:[19] on the one hand, humorous and quick (e.g. Rawlinson 1885: 316; Browne 1926: 309; Ross 1931: 27) and of "agreeable and prepossessing manners" (Malcolm 1815: 637–38), the Persians (or more broadly Orientals) are also deceitful,[20] vain, envious, greedy (e.g. Sykes 1915: 181–187; Anderson 1880: 274; Bassett 1886: 50), uncontrolled in the expression of their emotions[21] and, "compelled, by the nature of their government, ... alternately submissive and tyrannical" (Malcolm 1815: 637–638).

In certain areas, however, this assumption of continuity breaks down, and allows for an engagement with the ancient Persians that is unmediated (at least superficially) by contemporary experience. One such area is (ancient) Zoroastrian religion:[22] "of a more elevated character than is usual with races not enlightened by special revelation…" according to the Anglican canon George Rawlinson, a "pure spiritual monotheism".[23] This admiration for Persian monotheism is clearly in part the result of Cyrus' biblical image: "a religious sympathy seems to have drawn together the two nations of the Persians and the Jews" (Rawlinson 1885: 425; cf. Rice 1916: 11). Zoroastrianism is not, however, only a symptom of moral discrimination ("an attempt to account for the coexistence of good and evil", Ross 1931: 31), but actually a *cause* of empire. "[When] their religion with its lofty and sane ideals is taken into consideration", according to Sykes, "it is little wonder that these enlightened Aryans founded an empire and held in subjection the lower Semitic and Turanian races whose civilization they had absorbed".[24] "[The Medes and Persians] had qualities which raised them above their fellows", George Rawlinson grudgingly admits, "and a civilization, which was not, perhaps, very advanced, but was still not wholly contemptible" (1885: 315).

It is, however, more than any other area in the history of the built remains of the Achaemenid past that continuity between ancient and modern Persia is seen to have collapsed. All visitors to Persepolis and other Persian sites share an overwhelming sense of pathos. "How do the old cities sink into the earth and disappear?" lamented E. R. Durand, wife of the British Minister Sir Mortimer Durand (1902: 142). Persepolis "is a scene of utter desolation, pillars broken and cast down, columns shorn of their summits, pedestals bereft of their columns, mournful, neglected, and pathetic, yet magnificent and proud, with all the pride of a greatness that has passed away" (Bradley-Birt 1909: 183). Later he speaks of their "majesty in decay, their mute triumphant protest against the warring hand of time and man" (1909: 200–201; cf. Sykes 1902: 325). Williams Jackson, conversely, finds at Ecbatana no "trace of that solemn grandeur which is noble in its decay at Persepolis or Pasargadae" (Jackson 1906: 146, 200–201, 278).[25]

Such phrases are reminiscent of the climax of Margaret Cool Root's monograph, where the image of the four quarters singing harmonious praise to the king at Persepolis is described as "a haunting finale to the pre-Hellenic east" (1979: 311). Where they differ, however, is in their biting criticism of the modern-day Persians for failing to appreciate their heritage. "The love of travel, visiting the remains of former grandeur, and of tracing the history of ancient nations, which is so common in Europe, causes wonder in the Asiatics, amongst whom there is little or no spirit of curiosity or speculation", according to Sir John Malcolm.[26] "These people seem to take no pride and interest in their antiquities" (Baker 1876: 127). "The modern Persian, unmindful of its wonder and its beauty, still carelessly calls Persepolis by the name of the Takht-i Jamshid, the Throne of Jamshid, ascribing to the popular hero anything the origin of which is obscure of too much trouble to discover" (Bradley-Birt 1909: 181).[27] The tone of condescension becomes sharper still in the context of the tomb of Cyrus. "There is a mockery in the fact that it is now known as the Tomb of the Mother of Solomon, and is surrounded by the graves of Muslims", according to the American Benjamin Burges Moore.[28] "Such is the sepulchre of the King of Kings to-day. But let it not be imagined that its story is known to the inhabitants of the country…Always he appears to prefer legend to history and superstition to both" (Williams 1907: 231). Edward Granville Browne is apparently unique in citing Persian observations on the pathos of Persepolis (Browne 1926: 277).

The identity of the rightful inheritors of Cyrus and Darius—those who appreciate their works—scarcely needs spelling out. But this is not only a matter of artistic appreciation. The "desolation" of Persepolis is only representative of Persia's more general decline from her ancient greatness.[29] "How they have fallen from their first estate, my reminiscences woefully show", according to the English traveller George Fowler (1841: vol. II, 44–45). "The Persia of Herodotus and Xenophon was immeasurably superior to Mediaeval Persia in its attributes and is even now more respectable in its ruins" (Curzon 1892: 10). Persia, according to Valentine Baker, had "fallen through misgovernment and corruption to almost the lowest point which a once great nation can reach without dissolution" (1876: 336). Bradley-Birt takes his readers on a procession through all the great periods of Persian history before one descends with a crashing thud into the modern era:

> No country in the world can boast a prouder or more ancient history than this land of the King of Kings...Cyrus the Achaemenian, and Darius the son of Hystaspes, Shapur the Sassanian, proud conqueror of the Roman emperor Valerian, Jenghiz Khan, Tamerlane and Nadir Shah, empire builders all, Shah Abbas the Sefavi, and Fath Ali Shah, the Kajar monarch, all pass in the prime of life and splendour in one long pageant across the page of Persian history; and at the end of all the brilliant line there stands the feeble figure of the present Shah-in-Shah, the unhappy successor of the King of Kings.
>
> It is a terrible descent from the past to the present. Dishonesty and corruption have bitten deep into official life and sapped its strength...Nothing could well be more in the style of comic opera than suddenly to spring a constitution and a representative assembly on a people who for endless centuries have done nothing but obey.... A paternal despotism is undoubtedly all that Persia is fit for to-day. (Bradley-Birt 1909: 323–324)

It was, of course, paternal despotism that had been the secret of the Persians' earlier success, as a number of authors make clear. "With Orientals everything depends upon their leaders", according to the first American Minister in Persia, S. G. W. Benjamin (1887: 489). "An ordinary Oriental", comments Rawlinson in similar vein, "would have been content with such a result [merely becoming king], and have declined to tempt fortune any more. But Cyrus was no ordinary Oriental" (1885: 433; cf. 447). More often than not, however, it is the "uniform civil administration" (1885: 467)[30] of Darius that excites admiration—and identification. "Bent on settling and consolidating his Empire", according to Rawlinson, "he set up everywhere the satrapial form of government, organized and established his posts, issued his coinage, watched over the administration, and in various ways, exhibited a love of order and method, and a genius for systematic arrangement" (1885: 474).[31] The identification is even stronger, perhaps unsurprisingly, in the case of the flawed imperial hero Percy Sykes (whose history is dedicated "to British administrators in India and at Whitehall"), in particular from the kind of things he praises in the Achaemenids (many of which map neatly onto modern travellers' preoccupations):[32] the kings' construction of a network of roads, the building up of trade links, and above all the empire's vast extent: "We thus see an empire which included the whole of the known world and a good deal of territory then unknown, which stretched from the burning sands of Africa to the icebound borders of China, vast but obedient" (Sykes 1915: 180).

No matter the extent of identification, however, between these writers and Achaemenid Persia, perhaps the acid test is to ask how Achaemenid Persia measures up against the classical Greco-Roman world, with which they were of course thoroughly imbued.

In many cases, predictably, the choice between classical Greece and Persia is a fairly easy one. (Of course, it need not be a choice although it is often presented as such even in some modern scholarship.) The author of Hajji Baba, J. J. Morier, although his reaction to Persepolis was to yield "at once to emotions the most lively and the most enraptured", nevertheless finds "nothing, either in the architecture of the buildings, or in the sculptures and reliefs on the rocks, which could bear a critical comparison with the delicate proportions and perfect statuary of the Greeks"—though he adds then that this is perhaps to "[try] Persepolis by a standard to which it never was amenable" (Morier 1812: 135). Curzon mocks such comparisons—in particular, those of Persepolis with Milan cathedral and Windsor Castle—but he too thinks the Apadana staircase not as fine as the Propylaea of the Acropolis (1892: 153–154).[33] For George Rawlinson, as his famous verdict on Persian science makes brutally clear, the Persians offer little competition: "Too light and frivolous, too vivacious, too sensuous for such pursuits, they left them to the patient Babylonians, and the thoughtful, many-sided Greeks" (1885: 419).

A second group seems torn between two rival identifications. Williams Jackson, for example, becomes distracted en route from Russia to Iran by being taken to the site of the *Prometheus Vinctus*: "For a moment, Greek mythology, classic reminiscences, and thoughts of college days made me forget that the land of my quest was Iran, not Hellas" (Jackson 1906: 3). Most fascinating, in his confusion, is Percy Sykes. The purpose of his writing, he remarks in the preface to his history of Persia, is not only to be useful to his government—"by sketching the national character of a subject people"—but also to represent the "Persian point of view", both to students of Greek history and to Persians themselves, to help them to "realize more fully the splendour of their own history" (Sykes 1915: xi–xii). He justifies his writing also in terms of the influence of Persia on later civilization, but it is an influence that is channelled through the classical Greco-Roman world.[34] He reverts then also to a more conventional focus on the freedom-loving Greeks: "Nevertheless, in Hellas, were to be found a few thousand warriors who, preposterous as it might appear, were destined to repel the collective might of this vast empire..." (1915: i. 169). The Persians fought bravely in his account; he even goes so far as to say that in military terms the importance of the Persian wars had been exaggerated (the point made by Robert Graves in his poem "The Persian version" or by Olmstead in shrinking the Persian wars into a chapter entitled "Problems of the Greek frontier", but also much earlier)[35], but for Sykes, that is to forget another dimension: "the wider aspect of the case, the world aspect...from this point of view, Marathon, Salamis, and Plataea were victories not only for Greece but for mankind..."

It would be wrong, however, to conclude that histories of Persia are univocal in their ultimate adherence to the classical world. There are, moreover, at least as many anti-classical (or unclassical) voices. Henry Rawlinson certainly did not eschew his classical education but, though he travelled home through Europe a number of times, he made his first visit to Athens at the age of 49.[36] The diplomat Edward Eastwick (writing in 1864) actually ridicules Greek accounts of the Persian wars ("Greece put on her poetical spectacles") and his contemporaries' belief in them: "The real fact is, young Europe is whipped and schooled into admiration of Greece, till no one dares give a candid opinion. Otherwise, how can men in their senses affect to believe all that stuff about the invasion of Xerxes?" (1864: 26–27). The Cambridge Orientalist Edward Granville Browne begins his account of his year of adventure in Persia (the only year of adventure in his life, according to his memoirist)[37] with a rant at the failings of a classical education, its "general failure to invest the books read with any human, historical or literary interest, or to treat them as expressions of the thoughts, feelings, and aspirations of our fellow-creatures instead of as grammatical treadmills" (Browne 1926: 5–8). By contrast, by working on the Near East, he was doing the real thing.

Perhaps the best example of this independence from classical education, however, comes from the age before the decipherment of cuneiform—the author of the first full-length history of Persia in English, Sir John Malcolm (responsible for firing the 17-year-old Henry Rawlinson's interest in Persia when they travelled on the same steamer to India, cf. Rawlinson 1898: 22–24). Greek perspectives on Persia are almost entirely excluded from Malcolm's work. As he wrote to his father from Shiraz in 1800, with the exception of Alexander's conquests, there was "no fact recorded by the Greeks of which Persian historians make the least mention" (quoted in Lambton 1995: 99); he was employing every leisure hour in researches into the history of "this extraordinary country, with which we are but little acquainted". As a result of his reliance on "eastern authors" (in which he was far from exceptional amongst his contemporaries) (Malcolm 1815: x; see also e.g. Ouseley 1819–23; Price 1832), for Malcolm, for example, the tradition that Persepolis was indeed the Throne of the hero Jamshid finds no contradiction (Malcolm 1815: i. 16). On the rare occasions that Greek sources do make an appearance (in footnotes), they are invariably seen as secondary. So, in the context of the tradition that the young Zal was nurtured by a griffin, he comments in a footnote that, "It is possibly to this fable that Grecian historians allude when they relate that Achaemenes was nurtured by an eagle" (1815: i. 25).[38] Far from his being a maverick, I should say finally, Malcolm's history was enormously popular, being greeted by Sir Walter Scott, for example, as "form[ing] the connecting link between that [the history] of Greece and that of Asia" (quoted by Lambton 1995: 101).

If it is right, finally, that these early writers have in many respects been underestimated, are there not good reasons for that?

First, of course, it could not reasonably be claimed that a popular historian like Percy Sykes—let alone some of the travellers mentioned here in passing—deserve serious attention today as historians of Persia, although they may be interesting in their own right, especially when their views so often coincide with those of more serious scholars. "To each newcomer", in Curzon's encyclopaedic judgement, "the comparative rarity of his experience has been conceded as the excuse for a volume"; some, he goes on to say, are painstaking and meritorious, others "the most worthless rubbish that ever blundered into print" (1892: 12). Secondly, and more significantly, it may be that the work even of figures such as George Rawlinson or George Curzon might be considered tainted as a result of the context in which they wrote. The intense identification with Persia revealed by many writers—an identification that might reasonably be connected with the common British claim to be able to get under the skin, and so to impersonate, foreigners[39]—clearly tips over at times into a form of appropriation. Similarly, one needs only a little postcolonial sensitivity to find Sykes's claim of speaking for the Persians hard to take at face value, no matter how well motivated he may have been. Curzon's *Persia and the Persian Question*, with its geographical surveys intended to be of practical use, constituted—with two other books on India's northern and eastern flanks—a vast application for the post of viceroy of India. He is graphically open about this imperial context in his introduction: "Turkestan, Afghanistan, Transcaspia, Persia—to many these names breathe only a sense of utter remoteness or a memory of strange vicissitudes and of moribund romance. To me, I confess, they are the pieces on a chessboard upon which is being played out a game for the dominion of the world" (1892: 3–4).

This context renders conclusions that are superficially similar to current scholarship fundamentally foreign. For George Rawlinson (as for the scholars of the Achaemenid History Workshop), Cambyses' actions in Egypt are entirely sane. For Rawlinson, however, they also provide the occasion for a timeless moral: "The Oriental will generally kiss the hand that smites him, if it only smite him hard enough".[40] When British scholars understood how Persian imperial ideology drew on a variety of models, were they helped to this understanding by the similar magpie quality of British imperialism? But then no scholarship, arguably, is uninformed by such political concerns, or immune from empire building, academic or "real". As Amélie Kuhrt asked in 1991, "to what extent have we, as European scholars, claimed (and continue to claim) the Achaemenid empire for ourselves, making it a part of our own internal historical debates?" (1991: 205). Despite all their failings, and despite the context in which they wrote, in Malcolm, Curzon and even Sykes we have the ancestors of the new Achaemenid historiography.

Notes

1. I hesitate to describe it as revisionist—a term for me with no negative connotations—in the light of Amélie Kuhrt's paper in this volume.
2. And indeed to exceed them: see especially the presentation of the Cyrus Cylinder and of the Achaemenids' alleged policy of religious tolerance in the video *Persepolis Recreated* which accompanied the exhibition *Forgotten Empire*; contrast Kuhrt 1983.
3. Contrast Briant's formula (2002a: 8), "however partisan and ideological a Greek text may be, when it is located within the web of its associations, it can provide a stimulating Achaemenid reading".
4. Sancisi-Weerdenburg 1991: 2 ("Curzon did pioneering work in collecting a large number of travellers' descriptions and his lists are still a good starting point").
5. For a narrative of Curzon's travels, see Bosworth 1993.
6. See Simpson 2003: 192 for an excellent sketch of the variety of professional contexts ("This is therefore a story strongly shaped by the professional duties of civil servants, diplomats and soldiers... for whom antiquarian pursuits were a minority hobby in an overwhelming environment of heat, disease, boredom and excessive drinking"); more fully, Wright 2001.
7. "Harem intrigues" are sufficiently common in Olmstead's text to warrant an index entry.
8. Cf. Rawlinson 1885: 298 ("the causes of military success and political advance lie deeper than statistics can reach...they have their roots in the moral nature of man, in the grandeur of his ideas and the energy of his character...").
9. Jackson 1906: 26 ("Signs of weakness had already shown themselves...in the unsuccessful attempt of Darius to invade Greece, but these marks of

decadence became more and more manifest in the reigns of Xerxes and Artaxerxes, until the tottering throne of the Achaemenidae fell when Darius III [Codomannus] was conquered by Alexander the Great and afterward perished...").
10. Sykes 1922: 20 ff. ("The overthrow of the Persian empire by Alexander ranks high among the greatest achievements of man"); cf. Kuhrt 1995: 675 ("It was a remarkable achievement, and the difficulties Alexander encountered in twelve years of continuous fighting bear witness to the remarkable solidity of the Achaemenid realm").
11. Cf. Sancisi-Weerdenburg 1987*a* ("in treatises on the Persian Empire it is commonplace to assert that after Xerxes' death in 465 the whole empire gradually underwent a process of decay that made it a ready prey for the Macedonian conquests"); cf. Sancisi-Weerdenburg 1989.
12. Cf. p. 51: "In sculpture and painting, the Persians have at no time attained any degree of perfection. Even the figures at Persepolis, and other parts of the country, are deficient in taste and proportion; with the exception of some of those in the plain of *Kermanshah*, which I believe to have been executed by Grecian or Roman artists."
13. De Windt 1891: 172: "The Pyramids, Pompeii, the ancient buildings of Rome and Greece, are picturesque; Persepolis is not."
14. Cf., in an earlier period, the eulogy of Sir William Ouseley, 1819–1823: ii. 288–289.
15. See e.g. Ross 1931: 103 ("Most of the elements which went to make up these palaces were borrowed from Greek, Babylonian, and Egyptian models, but each element received a touch of originality at the hands of the Persians"), Curzon 1892 (concluding, i. 194: "while she borrowed much, she also added something of her own, enough, beyond all question, to lift her art from the rank of a purely imitative or servile school").
16. For the Democedes comparison, cf. Collins 1896: 270–271.
17. Benjamin 1887: 336–337: "I think that those who have given attention to the music of ancient Greece might gain a clearer perception of that subject by investigating the native music of Persia. Indeed it would not be surprising if it should be found that the Dorians borrowed from the Greek colonies of Asia Minor, who in turn borrowed their music from the Persians. Both were of Aryan stock. We know that neither the Persian nor the Greek of antiquity disdained to borrow customs and ideas from each other. Why then should the Greek not have borrowed music from the Persians?"
18. Malcolm 1815: 621; cf. e.g. Benjamin 1887: 169; de Lorey & Sladen 1907: vii; Anderson 1880: vii; or the illustrations labelled "The past in the present" in Olmstead 1948.
19. This catalogue of timeless vices and virtues is not, of course, absolutely consistent: appreciation of Persian wit, for example, is sometimes clearly more than merely formulaic: e.g. in the case of Browne 1926 or the letters of Edward Burgess 1942; rarely also Persian characteristics are seen as mutable, esp. by later writers such as Millspaugh 1925: 98; Merritt-Hawkes 1935: 87–88. But, for the most part, such stereotypes are replicated seamlessly, writers find confirmation of "ideas that predate travel" (see Gikandi 1996: ch. 2), and an imaginary Persia becomes authoritative. So, e.g. Hajji Baba of Ispahan (the fictional creation of J. J. Morier 1824) is noted by many writers to be "truer than much that purports to be fact" (e.g. Fowler 1841: i. 48; Mounsey 1872: iv; Williams 1907: 3; Millspaugh 1925: 23), with Sykes engineering a translation into Persian for use by the Indian government to teach Indians proper Persian, Sykes 1902: 8 n. 2.
20. E.g. Kinneir 1813: 22–23; Rawlinson 1885: 319 ("the love of finesse and intrigue [which] is congenital to Orientals"); Anderson 1880: 66–67, 233.
21. E.g. Rawlinson 1885: 319 (finding "Aeschylus' tragedy of the 'Persae'...in this respect, true to nature"); Bell 1928: 55 ("To the Englishman, tears are a serious matter").
22. Nonetheless, there are a number of ill-defined strategies for maintaining the idea of continuity. One is to hold to the racial distinction: modern-day Zoroastrians, Parsees or Guebers, are the pure Iranians and in some sources seen as more honest, hard-working, essentially Protestant than their Muslim neighbours (e.g. Price 1832: 34; Mounsey 1872: 152–153; Sykes 1898: 143; Sykes 1902: 198; cf. Bassett 1886: 316). Alternatively, other Aryans may have taken on the mantle of empire? Or there may be some hope of renaissance, whether it be broadly political (in the light e.g. of the constitutional movement and Reza Shah's coup: Rice 1916: 41, 185–186; Williams 1907: 255–257; Sykes 1910: 38, 340; Millspaugh 1925: 4–5; Merritt-Hawkes 1935: 87–88; Morton 1940: 173, 355) or religious (Islam is frequently seen as no more than a vehicle for other feelings, a "loose garment that may be fitted to any occasion without pinching", Benjamin 1887: 96; cf. Arnold 1877: 484,

23. 491—despite the lack of penetration of Christian missionaries).
23. Rawlinson 1885: 316, 444; counter-evidence to the thesis of Persian monotheism is put down to a decline from pure beginnings.
24. Sykes 1915: ch. 2; 1902: 198 pursues a similar racial distinction (adding the twist that the Bombay Parsees exemplify "the physical deterioration which India so surely produces"); cf. Ross 1931: 35; Benjamin 1887: 88.
25. Cf. Ross 1931: 6 and Amory 1929: 49 (on Pasargadae: "one solitary column bathing in a sunbeam and proclaiming more loudly than words departed and historic grandeur").
26. Malcolm 1827 ii. 236; cf. Williams 1907: 188, 215. Contrast the emotional link posited between Persians and Persepolis by Morton 1940: 173 ("This is a close, deep feeling, due to their racial identification with all that Persepolis signifies, and their belief that in their time, or in that of their children, Iran will again be great").
27. Denison Ross makes a contrast with the Greeks, 1931: 34.
28. Moore 1915: 352 (see also the captions to Burges Moore's illustrations of Cyrus' tomb and the palace of Xerxes: respectively, "Goats and children guard the tomb that Alexander entered with reverence", "the wild ass stamps over his head"—a quotation from Fitzgerald's Omar Khayyam—or the illustration of Cyrus' tomb at Williams 1907: 230–231); cf. Bradley-Birt 1909: 223, 228; Carroll 1960: 45–46 (Bisitun), 62 (Persepolis).
29. And, in the more optimistic view of some twentieth-century writers, appreciation of their heritage is envisaged as a path to "independent prosperity": see Williams 1907: 231; Merritt-Hawkes 1935: 87–88 ("The Persians come to Persepolis to gain courage to forge ahead with the modernization of their country").
30. Conversely, Sir John Malcolm finds the root of all Persia's problems in her lack of a proper civil administration, 1815: 637–638.
31. Bradley-Birt is unusually most attracted to the Sasanian kings: cf. 1909: 78, 90.
32. E.g. Sackville-West 1926: 86, 99–100 ("we are at the mercy of snow and flood, and...of limp Oriental methods"); contrast Benjamin 1887: 469 ("I heartily advise those who wish to enjoy horseback travelling and camping-out to try Persia").
33. Two other fine comparisons (not mentioned by Curzon) are between Persepolis and the Houses of Parliament (Anderson 1880: 149–151) and between Cyrus' tomb and a dog kennel (Amory 1929: 50).
34. Cf. Sykes 1922, emphasizing the influence of Zoroastrianism "on Judaism, and indirectly on Christianity" (p. 16); his emphasis (p. 4) on "how deeply Persia has influenced Europe" is undermined by the examples given: "We owe to her the peach...the orange, the lime, the pistachio nut, and possibly the vine. Of flowers, the jasmine, lilac, and narcissus not only come from Persia but have retained their Persian names, as have most of the fruits enumerated above."
35. Memorably by the diplomat Edward Eastwick, 1864: 36–37.
36. For the life of Henry Rawlinson, see esp. his brother's *Memoir*: Rawlinson 1898.
37. Denison Ross, in the 1926 edition of Browne's *A Year Amongst the Persians*, vii: "outside his year in Persia his life was singularly devoid of adventure, and in the events of that year his biographer can add nothing to what he has himself related so vividly"; see further Bosworth 1995.
38. In his later *Sketches of Persia*, Malcolm seems almost to be suppressing his classical education as a sport, disarmingly suspending discussion, e.g. of whether Persepolis was a palace or a temple ("I am much too wise to venture on speculations which have bewildered so many learned men") merely to report in Herodotean fashion a lengthy conversation, irrelevant to that narrow question, on the hero Rustam: 1827: i. 212.
39. The classic formulation of which is John Buchan's Sandy Arbuthnot, esp. in *Greenmantle* (1916). Actual attempts at impersonation in the Persian context include Henry Rawlinson's at Kum (Rawlinson 1898), Sykes's disguise as a Cossack (Sykes 1902), and Col. Charles Stewart (Stewart 1911). See, however, Fromkin 1991 for a sceptical approach, citing T. E. Lawrence ("I've never heard an Englishman speak Arabic well enough to be taken for a native of any part of the Arabic-speaking world, for five minutes"); it is notable that e.g. Stewart chose to disguise himself as an Armenian (1911: x–xi). Cf. Rawlinson's claim that neither Herodotus nor Xenophon ("neither the lively Halicarnassian, nor the pleasant but somehow shallow Athenian") "had the gift of penetrating very deeply into the inner mind of a foreign people", 1885: 421.
40. Rawlinson 1885: 433, 447; cf. Benjamin's judgement on modern Persians, 1887: 489, that "with Orientals everything depends upon their leaders".

4

Portraits of the Achaemenid Kings in English Drama: Sixteenth–Eighteenth Centuries

Parvin Loloi

Professor Briant's paper, in this collection, illustrates admirably how the histories of Alexandrian Wars initiated the concept of orientalism in the seventeenth century, which reached its peak, in Saidian terminology, in the nineteenth century. This paper will go further back in time and examine some of the legacies these early sources have left on the English stage during the great age of English drama in the early modern period. Most of the great Achaemenid rulers had plays devoted to them on the English stage in the sixteenth, seventeenth and eighteenth centuries. The dramatists' interest in these great figures took many different forms and the judgements they offered of them, explicitly or implicitly, were highly diverse. This paper also examines something of this variety in the work of a number of dramatists and considers what patterns emerge from this survey. Given the limitations of the subject, I shall largely leave undiscussed such differences as are explicable purely in terms of the changing styles of English drama during this period.[1]

Unfortunately, none of the very greatest English dramatists of the period wrote a play devoted to one of the Achaemenids. But they were not ignorant of them, and neither did they expect their audience to be ignorant of them. Thus Marlowe, in the two plays that make up his *Tamburlaine the Great*,[2] has Tamburlaine declare:

> The host of Xerxes, which by fame is said
> To drink the mighty Parthian Araris,
> Was but a handful to that we will have.
> (Part I, II.iii.15–17)

Tamburlaine is encouraged by Menaphon, who says to him:

> How easily may you with a mighty host
> Pass into Graecia, as did Cyrus once,
> And cause them to withdraw their forces home,
> Lest you subdue the pride of Christendom!
> (Part I, I.i.129–132)

When Cosroe is named as king of Persia, Ceneus announces:

> …to stay all sudden mutinies,
> We will invest your highness emperor;
> Whereat the soldiers will conceive more joy
> Than did the Macedonians at the spoil
> Of great Darius and his wealthy host.
> (Part I, I.i.150–154)

In the first part of the Shakespearean *Henry VI*,[3] King Charles, expressing his gratitude to Joan of Arc, says that when she is dead "Her ashes, in an urn more precious / Than the rich jewel-coffer of Darius, / Transported shall be at high festivals / Before the kings and queens of France" (I.vi.24–27). The Countess of Auvergne, planning to kill Lord Talbot, boasts of her anticipated success:

> The plot is laid; if all things fall out right,
> I shall as famous be by this exploit,
> As Scythian Tomyris by Cyrus' death.
> (II.iii.4–6)

But it is to less well-known dramatists that we must turn to find whole plays devoted to the Achaemenid kings.[4]

Cyrus was the titular subject of at least three English plays during the period under consideration. Attitudes to Cyrus were much influenced by knowledge of Xenophon's *Cyropaedia: or, The Education of Cyrus*. Xenophon much admired the older Cyrus (he served as a mercenary with the army of the younger Cyrus). The *Cyropaedia* presents an idealized account of Cyrus' education and of some of the events of his life. He is also the "Cyrus the King" who in the Old Testament, in the book of Ezra, commands the rebuilding of the Temple in Jerusalem. Chiefly under the influence of Xenophon, Cyrus was often presented as an exemplary ruler, characterized by his wisdom, good judgement and self-restraint. It is striking, for example, that an anonymous eighteenth-century moral treatise, *Mercy the Truest Heroism: Display'd in the Conduct of Some of the Most Famous Conquerors and Heroes of Antiquity*, should give first place to Cyrus and his treatment of the Chaldeans, telling us of Cyrus that Xenophon presents him "as an excellent Pattern to all Princes" and "describes him both while a private Man, and after he arrived to the Height of Grandeur, to have been good-natur'd, of a sweet Temper, affable, meek, merciful and forward to oblige every one" (Anon. 1746: 6). It is such a noble Cyrus who is at the centre of a play called—to give it its full title—*The Wars of Cyrus King of Persia, against Antiochus King of Assyria, with the Tragical End of Panthæa*, which was published in 1594. Its title page says that it has been "played by the children of her Majesties Chapell". Though published anonymously, it was possibly the work of Richard Farrant (c.1528–1580), a musician and a gentleman of the Chapel Royal involved in dramatic presentations at court. He is best known for establishing the early public theatre, and his interests were mainly in ancient history and myth. Indeed, he was the author of a lost play, *King Xerxes*, which was performed before Elizabeth I in January 1575.[5] *The Wars of Cyrus* is concerned with Cyrus' attraction to Panthæa and his final renunciation of her. The story is founded on an episode in the *Cyropaedia* (Xenophon is mentioned by name in one of the play's choruses—cf. Anon. 1594: C3r); it was also retold in William Painter's *Palace of Pleasure*, a collection of narratives first published in 1566. In Farrant's play we see Cyrus distributing rewards justly and behaving with exemplary religious duty; we see him initially refusing to see the beautiful Panthæa in case he should fall in love with her, believing, as he says, that "Nothing can more dishonour warriors / Then to be conquered with a womans look" (Anon. 1594: B3r). We see Cyrus' evident nobility transform the intentions of the would-be assassin (Ctesiphon), who later praises Cyrus as "milde, lovely, virtuouse, wise and bountifull, / Able to reconcile his greatest foes, / And make great princes of his meanest friends" (Anon. 1594: E4r). Another character declares of Cyrus that, "holy thoughts direct his royall deedes". (Anon. 1594: F1v)

Around a century after the publication of *The Wars of Cyrus* the same king was the subject of another play, *Cyrus the Great*, by John Banks (1630–1710). The play was Banks's third play, and was originally written in 1681. It was not produced then, however, as the actors disliked it. It was eventually produced in 1695. Even then it had only a short run of four performances, halted by the death of the actor William Smith, who was playing the role of Cyaxeres, the king of Media. The part of Cyrus was taken by the great actor Thomas Betterton. Banks's play has a subtitle, *Cyrus the Great, or, The Tragedy of Love*, which makes clear where the emphasis is placed. Again the central narrative is concerned with Cyrus and Panthæa (played by the famous Elizabeth Barry). Banks's Cyrus is somewhat prone to boast of his achievements. At one point he proclaims:

> I own it with a Pride, I have restor'd
> The World to its dear antient Liberty,
> Freed Captiv'd Nations from their Tyrant's Yoaks,
> And plac'd 'em on the Necks of barb'rous Kings,
> ...
> Made my Commands in one quick Moment spread
> Like Thunder terrible through all the City.
> (II. i. [9–12 & 14–15])

Banks's Cyrus is much less able to resist love than the Cyrus of Farrant's play. His evident generosity is soon polluted by jealousy. He struggles between the call of his kingly duty and the demands of love: "I feel my Vertue now begins to tire, / And Love Plays all the Tyrant in my Soul" (IV. i. [48–49]). Finally, duty and virtue triumph and he renounces Panthæa—a renunciation which is rewarded, as it were, by the final defeat of the Assyrians.

The play shows little or no historical awareness: Banks's general theatrical manner is very derivative—there are some distinctly un-Persian witches who appear to have strayed in from a production of *Macbeth*; there is a young girl driven mad by love who dispenses gifts in a manner very like that of Ophelia in *Hamlet*.

A third play, *Cyrus: A Tragedy* by John Hoole, was published in 1768. Hoole, a friend of Dr Johnson, derived his play, which was performed on 3rd December 1768 at the Theatre Royal, Covent Garden, from an Italian operatic original; the result is a long-winded and dramatically uninteresting version of the account in Book I of Herodotus of Cyrus' return from supposed death and actual death at the hands of Astyages, and of the relationship with his mother Mandane.

Cyrus' successor, Cambyses, is the central figure in two English plays of the period, both of considerable interest. Where Cambyses is concerned Herodotus—or accounts derived from Herodotus—did much to shape the views of his character and behaviour. Herodotus describes Cambyses as "more or less insane" (*Histories*, translated by Robin Waterfield, Oxford & New York, Oxford World Classics, p. 181), as a king who "committed mad acts...against his closest relatives... [and]...against the rest of the Persians as well" (*Histories* 183). Recounting Cambyses' arrogant cruelty, his judgement is that "everything goes to make me certain that Cambyses was completely mad; otherwise he would not have gone in for mocking religion and tradition" (*Histories* 185). The first of the English dramatic versions of Cambyses comes in Thomas Preston's *Cambises, King of Percia*, first printed in 1570. The play is a perfect example of the transition from the old morality plays to modern tragedy, mixing as it does abstraction-bearing names like Diligence and Cruelty with individual characters such as

Cambyses himself, Smerdis, Praxaspes and Sisamnes (all of whom come from Herodotus). Preston's Cambyses is compared, in the play's Prologue, to Icarus, hubristically heading for a fall:

> He in his youth was trained up, by trace of vertues lore;
> Yet (being King) did cleane forget, his perfect race before.
> Then cleaving more unto his wil such vice did immitate:
> As one of *Icarus* his kind, forewarning then did hate.
> Thinking that none could him dismay, ne none his fact could see,
> Yet at the last a fall he tooke, like *Icarus* to be.
> (Preston 1595: A2ʳ [19–20])

He revels in his cruelty—"Taking delight the Innocent, his guiltlesse blood to spil" (Preston 1595: A2ʳ [30])—until punished by "mighty *Jove*". He murders children, he commissions two men called Cruelty and Murder to kill Smerdis; he orders the death of Sisames, the judge, decreeing "draw thou his cursed skin, straight over his both eares" (Preston 1595: C2ᵛ [4387]). After Cambyses' own accidental death, the play's Epilogue concludes "the tragicall history of this wicked king" (Preston 1595: F4ᵛ [2]) with an appropriate enough prayer for Queen Elizabeth and her government:

> As duty bindes us for our noble Queen let us pray,
> And for her honourable Councel, the truth that they may use:
> To practise Justice and defend her grace each day;
> To maintain Gods word they may not refuse.
> To correct all those that would her grace and graces laws abuse,
> Beseeching God over us she may raigne long:
> To be guided by truth and defended from wrong.
> (Preston 1595: F4ᵛ [15–22])

In Preston's play, an Achaemenid king provides a kind of negative exemplar of bad and tyrannical government, just as dramatic accounts of Cyrus generally offered a positive exemplar of the virtues of good government.

In the following century, the 18-year-old Elkanah Settle, only recently become an undergraduate in Oxford, set out on a theatrical career with the composition of his *Cambyses, King of Persia: A Tragedy*. The play was completed by December 1666 and was accepted by the Duke of York's Company, managed by William Davenant, and performed on 10th January 1667. It had considerable success, playing for six nights to packed houses. According to a note at the end of the first printing of the play in 1671, some accused Settle of having plagiarized his work from Preston, but there are no grounds for this charge. Settle's rhymed heroic tragedy gives us an arrogant Cambyses who opens the play with an assertion of his power:

> The trembling World has shook at my Alarms;
> *Asia* and *Africa* have felt my Arms.
> My glorious Conquests too did farther flye;
> I taught th'*Egyptian* god Mortality:
> By me great *Apis* fell; and now you see
> They are compell'd to change their gods for me.
> I have done deeds, where Heaven's high pow'r was foyl'd,
> Piercing those Rocks where Thunder has been toyl'd.
> (Settle 1671: I, i., 1–7)

His has been a reign of "bloody Cruelties [...] / When Rapes and Murders were but common sin" (Settle 1671: 4). Though he opens the play, Cambyses does not dominate it, being absent from the stage for long spells and dying in Act IV. Settle, indeed, seems more interested in how others can (or cannot) frame successful lives in a court and country governed by a tyrant than in the phenomenon of the tyrant himself. The complex plot of the play is an elaboration on materials provided by Herodotus. Settle's Cambyses (who was played by Betterton) eventually develops a conscience of a kind, and (rather like Shakespeare's Richard III) is troubled by ghostly visions. Settle shows some historical awareness. One key scene, the last in the play, takes place before "a temple of the Sun, uncover'd according to the Antient Custome, with an Altar in the middle, bearing two large burning Tapers" (Settle 1671: 73). The play ends with the succession of Darius.

In portraying Darius himself, English dramatists were influenced by a number of sources. Herodotus, naturally, has much to say about him; other Greek writers discuss him, too. In *Phaedrus*, Plato cites Darius alongside Solon as one of the greatest of lawmakers. Greek historians of Alexander the Great, notably Quintus Curtius, naturally also discussed Darius, and many English dramatists would have been familiar with a biblical tradition of Darius. Certainly this was the case with the unidentified author of the earliest dramatic treatment. In 1565 there was published a work whose full title reads as follows: *A Pretie new Enterlude both pithie and pleasaunt of the Story of king Daryus, Being taken out of the third and fourth Chapter of the thyrd booke of Esdras*. In modern terminology, the source cited here are the third and fourth chapters of I Esdras, the first book of the Old Testament Apocrypha. For the most part I Esdras tells the story of the rebuilding of the Temple of Jerusalem under the protection of first Cyrus and then Darius (a story also told in the books of Ezra and Nehemia). The chapters of Esdras which attracted the dramatist, however, have no parallels in Ezra and Nehemia—a story about how three guardsmen debate the question of what is the strongest force in the world, in the hope that the one who proves himself wisest will be rewarded by Darius. Darius himself, disappointingly, does not feature extensively in the play, even though he gives it its title. For the most part the characters of the play are allegorical figures—with names like Charity or Iniquity—which have more to do with debates about Christian morality than ancient Persia. Most of the specifics of the play, the language of which is often very lively, are explicitly English; characters have nicknames like Nick Candlestick and John Puddingmaker. For the author of the play, the rebuilding of the temple seems to signify the religious renewal of his own world, a desire for which is expressed in specifically Protestant terms. Like Preston in his *Cambyses*, the dramatist closes with a prayer that divine guidance be extended to Queen Elizabeth and her counsellors—so that she might, metaphorically, preside, like Darius, over an act of religious rebuilding (Loloi 1999).

A different kind of moral concern and a different kind of source underlie the next dramatic treatment of Darius, in *The Tragedy of Darius* by the Scottish nobleman Sir William Alexander, Earl of Stirling, which was first published in 1603. It was one of a series of four plays—the others being devoted to Croesus, Alexander and Julius Caesar—which Alexander called *Monarchike Tragedies*. In line with that overall title, Alexander's interest is mainly in the morality of government; his main source (directly or indirectly) is Books III to V of the *Historiae Alexandri Magni / History of Alexander the Great* by the Latin historian Quintus Curtius. Alexander's play, though it works more by extended soliloquy and debate than by narrative action, deals with the consequences of the combination of what he calls Darius' arrogance—his "proud and contemptible manner"[6] in writing to Alexander—and, on the other hand, his "invincible courage".[7] These include, crucially, his betrayal by Bessus and Nabarzanes. Both sides of Darius—the arrogance and the courage—are given expression in Alexander's grandiose and stylized verse. (This is very much a play designed for reading in the study rather than for actual performance.) Alexander's Darius is a study in self-deception, of a mind "through presumption made quite blinde".[8] His Darius is used as an exemplum of the transience of all human power, and has the makings of a genuine tragic hero, not least in the extended poetic lament which opens Act IV Scene 3, Darius' pained reflections on the "stormy state of Kings [...] / The glorious height whence greatnesse grones to fall!"[9] and his dignified insistence that "I never shall wrong Majestie so farre, / As ought to doe that not becomes a king".[10] Alexander's Darius is a subtle and interesting portrait.

Rather less subtle is the portrait of the same king contained in John Crown's play, *Darius King of Persia: A Tragedy*, of 1688. Again Quintus Curtius is the main source, though here thoroughly elaborated and at times almost lost in an abundance of stage spectacle. Crown's Darius is an altogether more hysterical figure than the one we met in Alexander's play. There is an almost manic quality to his abrupt transitions of mood. His repeated loss of self-control is contrasted with the reported self-restraint and generosity of Alexander the Great. In this play, indeed, more than any of the others under discussion, we find the expression, by some of its characters, of virulent anti-Persian sentiments. The Persians are described as unfit to govern—"The Men are all devour'd by Luxury" (Crown 1688: 5). One of those who abandons Darius—Bessus—puts it thus:

> Nay, I have ever thought, a *Persian* King
> Was at the most but Master of a Mint.
> *Persia* has Gold and Jewels, but no Men;
> It has been long depopulated, all
> By Slavery, and Vice; (Crown 1688: 5)

Such Persian soldiers as there are, Nabarzanes, another character says:

> My Lord, they are all Images of Whores.
> They march into the field, rather equipp'd
> Like Ladies for a Ball, than Troops for
>   War.
>   (Crown 1688: 5)

"*Persians*" he says "can be strong in nothing but Perfumes" (Crown 1688: 19). Throughout the play Persians, with the partial exception of Darius, are presented as cowardly and as deficient in political ideas and ideals. Nabarzanes reports:

> I often talk'd to 'em of Liberty.
> Alas! They understood not what I meant,
> For in the *Persian* Tongue is no such word.
>   (Crown 1688: 35)

Darius has some redeeming qualities, but even his bravery is presented as but one of the extremes of his unstable personality.

In the last play to be considered in this necessarily brief survey, we encounter an Achaemenid monarch who appears to be entirely without redeeming qualities. In Colley Cibber's *Xerxes: A Tragedy*, of 1699 (which appears to be the only English play devoted to this particular king), we are presented with a Xerxes, after the defeats of Thermopylae and Salamis, who wallows in self-deception, believing he has inflicted glorious defeats on the Greeks (or, at any rate, trying to behave as though he has). Flatterers and sycophants are happy to indulge him in his illusions, and to be rewarded for doing so. To others he appears as merely the victim of "his drunken Fancy" (Cibber 1699: 7), as "a tainted soul" growing increasingly vicious. Coupled with his delusional behaviour is his lust, focused chiefly on Tamira, wife of Artabanus. Such pleasures he now claims to be the very purpose of life: "Why, what have Men to do on Earth / But to Indulge their Appetites" (Cibber 1699: 15). He turns to torture in a perverse attempt to get his way with Tamira, only to find that she has a dignity beyond his reach. He lies to all around him and he argues cynically for sexual promiscuity like a Restoration rake. He finds, towards the play's conclusion, a joyless emptiness in the life of power until, at the mercy of the rebels who seek to overthrow him, he tries (quite unsuccessfully) to assert his superiority to all that fate can throw at him. His final words, after being wounded in battle, are, fittingly, words of self-deception: "Ha! 'tis false! / I am not dying! No! I'm weary of the World, / And now will sleep for ever!" (Cibber 1699: 46).

From the nobility and wisdom of Cyrus to the near-madness and cruelty of Cibber's Xerxes, the dramatists of early-modern England found in the Achaemenid kings an intriguing series of studies in the morality and the psychology of empire that had clear theatrical potential. Individual dramatists naturally had their own attitudes towards the various kings they depicted, and the tastes and political situations of the times in which each dramatist worked also exerted their influence. But underlying such considerations was the dominant influence of the variety of sources on which they drew. Most treatments of Cyrus were favourable, under the influence of Xenophon's idealization of him in the *Cyropaedia*, far more favourably disposed towards a Persian monarch than was normally the case—for obvious reasons—in Greek texts. The dramatic presentation of Darius was rather more mixed, drawing, as it did, on two rather different sources: on the one hand, the generally favourable Old Testament and Apocryphal accounts and, on the other, the less benign treatments in the classical historians, from Herodotus onwards. Herodotus' account of an insanely tyrannical Cambyses is largely followed by the two dramatists who made him the central figure of a play. Cibber's portrait of Xerxes, while clearly influenced by Herodotus, actually presents an image of him that is more extreme than anything in the pages of the Greek historian.

The plays discussed here range in date from the middle of the sixteenth century to the middle of the eighteenth century. They—like contemporary writings in a number of other genres—offer clear evidence of a continuing interest in the early Persian Empire. Perhaps it is not surprising that in the very centuries in which the English were building their own great empire, their dramatists should so often have found in an earlier empire important and attractive, though often prejudiced, materials for presentation on the stage.

Notes

1. I am indebted to my husband, Glyn Pusglove, whose expert knowledge of early English literature has been of great help in preparing this paper.
2. Quotations are taken from the edition by J. S. Cunningham & E. Henson (Manchester, 1998).
3. The quotations are taken from The Arden Shakespeare edited by Andrew Cairncross (London, 1969).

4. During the period under discussion here, several plays on more or less the same themes were written in French. Among them are: Philippe Quinault, *La Mort de Cyrus, Tragédie*, in five acts and in verse (Paris, 1659); Thomas Corneille, *Darius, tragédie* (Paris, 1662); de Le Ferie, *Alexandre et Darius. Tragédie* (Paris, 1723); Anonymous, *La Mort de Xerxes, tragédie françoise* (Paris 1728; the British Library Catalogue attributes this to Molière).

5. The information on Farrant is taken from Mathew & Harrison (eds) 2004: vol. 19, 102–103.

6. *The Poetical Works of Sir William Alexander, Earl of Stirling*, ed. E. Kastener & H. B. Charlton (Edinburgh and London, 1921), p. 114.

7. *Ibid.* p. 115.

8. *Ibid.* p. 125.

9. *Ibid.* p. 195.

10. *Ibid.* p. 201.

5

Light from Aramaic Documents

Anke Joisten-Pruschke

From the nineteenth century onwards, Aramaic texts from the Achaemenid period have been regularly discovered on stone, clay and papyrus. In addition to the great discoveries from Elephantine, the correspondence of Arsames, the Persepolis Treasury Tablets and the inscriptions from Taima, Aramaic documents are still being discovered. These texts provide further insight into the administrative methods of the Achaemenids as well as detailed descriptions of their religion, culture and private life. The richness of this material considerably expands what is known from Iranian sources, namely the Elamite and Old Persian texts, and hardly any historian of Achaemenid history can ignore these primary sources. Of course this is also true for the great number of Babylonian texts of this period, and the less numerous Greek texts. Whereas continuity was maintained within the satrapy of Babylonia—Babylonian remained the administrative language, apart from some Aramaic documents and the Aramaic endorsements still present from the Assyrian period—the language changed in other parts of the Persian Empire. At some time during the reign of Darius I, Aramaic became the official language, the dominant administrative and diplomatic language, also dominating the cultural, religious and—in the west of the empire—even private correspondence. The increasing amount of Persian loan words in Aramaic, the adoption of Persian syntax seen in the letters of Arsam and other documents, and the use of Aramaic words in an Iranian context make it an unavoidable task for Iranists to study the Aramaic language.

The starting point is the southernmost Persian garrison in Egypt at Elephantine and Syene (better known as Aswan) on the opposite bank. Garrisons of the Persian military administration were located in both of these settlements. The soldiers were Arameans, Babylonians, Jews, Chwarezmians, Medians and Persians. They had intense professional, economic and private contacts. For example, the Jew Anani, son of Haggai, belonged to the military unit of the Babylonian Nabukudurri, and another Jew from Elephantine belonged to the unit of the Iranian Artabanu or Haumadata. There were also close business contacts: according to one text (P. Berlin 23000) the Egyptians Hori and Petemachis made arrangements concerning the delivery of goods and a boat. In the Sayce/Cowley G Papyrus the marriage of the Egyptian Ashor and the Jew Mibtahiah is recorded. There were temples of Bethel, Malkat-Šamin, Banit and Nabu in Syene; on Elephantine there was the main shrine of the god Khnum as well as the Yhw temple of the Jews. In the private letters of Hermopolis the Aramean Shabbethai, son of Shug, greets the temple of Bethel and of Malkat-Šamin, and at the same time he blesses the addressee Pasai in the name of the Egyptian god Ptah. Here we clearly see the image of a multicultural society with all its advantages and its inherent problems.

In the year 525 BC Cambyses conquered Egypt and made it the 6th satrapy of the Persian Empire. Thus begins—according to Manetho—the 27th dynasty of Egypt, also called the time of the "first Persian reign", during which Egypt was governed by the Achaemenids for 125 years. Most of the Aramaic-Jewish documents date from this period. They are official writings, private letters, legal documents and lists. In the following, two cases will be examined, from the corpus of Aramaic-Jewish documents, which were connected to decisions made by the empire's government.

First case: the rebellion of 410 BC on Elephantine and its effects

In the year 410 BC a rebellion took place on the Nile island of Elephantine. This rebellion was probably connected to the troubles described in the texts by Driver (especially letters Vii, Viii and X; cf. Driver 1957). In the so-called "Straßburger Papyrus" the Jews describe what happened:

> military units of the Egyptians rebelled. We did not leave our posts, and nothing was found which was destroyed by us. In the year 14 of Darius the king, when our Lord Arsam went to the king. This is the evil act which the priests of the god Khnum did in Jeb the fortress together with Vidranga, who was *fratarakar* there. They gave him silver and goods. There is a part… of the king in Jeb the fortress, they destroyed it and built a wall in the middle of the fortress… And now this wall is built in the middle of the fortress. There is a spring built in the middle of the fortress. Those priests of Khnum have blocked up this spring. (ll. 1–6, 8 = Cowley 1923: 27; Porten & Yardeni 1986: A4.5)

The following passage is only partially preserved in the Straßburger Papyrus, but Sachau-Papyrus 1,8ff. gives a detailed description of the Jewish temple's destruction:

> Then, Naphaina led the Egyptians there with the other troops. They came to the fortress of Elephantine with their weapons, broke into that temple, demolished it to the ground, and the stone pillars which were there—they broke them. Moreover, they destroyed 5 stone gateways, built out of square stone, which were in that temple. And their standing doors, and the hinges of those doors, which were made of bronze, and the roof made of cedarwood—all of this with the rest of the wooden things, which were there—all they burned with fire. The gold and silver basins and whatever was in this temple—all they took and made their own. (ll. 8–13 = Cowley 1923: 30; Porten & Yardeni 1986: A4.7)

The destruction of the temple of the god Yhw hit the nerve of the Jewish community. In the Straßburger Papyrus quoted above—the report of the Jews of Elephantine—the Jews chiefly document their innocence as Jewish mercenaries of the Persian army and stress their loyalty to the Achaemenians. Oddly enough, the blame for the rebellion is laid on the priests of Khnum, albeit with the proviso that everything had happened with the agreement of Vidranga who was the Persian *frataraka* of Elephantine whom the priests of Khnum had bribed, whereas in Sachau-Papyrus 1 and 2 only Vidranga is punished for his deeds. Neither the Khnum priests nor their punishments are mentioned. Did the report serve to open the satrap's eyes and to uncover the real culprits? Were the facts not known to the satrap? According to Sachau-Papyrus 1 and 2, the Jews of Elephantine sent a petition to the satrap Arsam as well as to the high priest in Jerusalem asking for the reconstruction of their temple. Neither Arsam nor the high priest answered them. Since the report from 410 BC was written three years had passed, when in 407 BC the Jews from Elephantine sent another petition asking for the reconstruction of their temple, this time not turning to Arsam or the high priest of Jerusalem, but now addressing the official responsible for their ethnic group, the governor of Juda—Bagohi—and asking that he might lend his support for the reconstruction of their temple of Yhw. In their petition they draw attention to three points:

1. The temple was built in the times of the Egyptian pharaohs.
2. Cambyses had not destroyed it when he had conquered Egypt.
3. The satrap Arsam was not involved in the rebellion.

For my discussion the first two points are important. The Jews refer to a long tradition and to the acceptance of the temple by Cambyses, thus attesting their loyalty to the Achaemenians from the very beginning. Those two arguments formed, as it were, a general legal basis for the existence of the temple and its reconstruction. Ingo Kottsieper does not agree with this: "Das völlige Schweigen über eine Priviligierung oder Autorisation des Tempelkultes durch die Perser zeigt erneut, dass dieser eben nur geduldet worden war und kein Recht zugunsten seiner Wiedererrichtung angeführt werden konnte" (Kottsieper 2002: 168). However, no evidence has been found so far in the Achaemenian Empire for the existence of a legal tradition of privileging or authorizing temples or temple cults. Whoever was loyal to the Persians and did not stand in the way of their conquests automatically had a right to his or her own temple and cult. Some temples were erected by direct order of the king. Among those were the Hibis temple in the oasis of El Kargeh, and the temple of Jerusalem. Other temple buildings, such as the temple of Taima, were not erected by order of the king (cf. Beyer & Livingstone 1987: 286f.). The right (of a temple) and the protection involved were given as long as the status quo remained undisturbed. As loyal mercenaries of the Persian army and as Jews from Elephantine, whose temple was already built at the time of the pharaohs and had not been destroyed by Cambyses, they had "entsprechende Privilegien" (cf. Wiesehöfer 1995: 42). This was their authorization. Therefore it is not very surprising that they were allowed to rebuild their temple. However, there was a significant restriction: "meal-offerings, and incense they shall offer upon that altar just as was done in the past" (Sachau-Papyrus 3. ll.9–10 = Cowley 1923: 32 = Porten & Yardeni 1986: A4.9). Burnt offerings were excluded from this authorization.

Generally, consideration of the priests of Khnum on the part of the Persians is assumed as a reason for the ban on burnt offerings. To the priests the sacrifice of the ram was a great sin, and the thought that their holy animal—the ram—was burnt on the altar by foreigners was inconceivable. But such an interpretation is greatly at variance with the context of the documents. Since the priests of Khnum were suspected of being involved in the rebellion one would hardly have considered them. In this case, it doesn't even matter that they were denounced by a third party, namely the Jews of Elephantine. Moreover, the thought that the high priest in Jerusalem might have acted against another Jewish temple by calling on Bagohi is not very plausible. It is just the time when the Persian Bagohi enters into—according to Sachau-Papyrus 3 with the approval of the Samaryan Delaya—the well-known agreement that had been designed to be presented to the satrap Arsam. Against the background of the then prevailing tensions between Jerusalem and Samaria, additional co-operation with the high priest in Jerusalem is quite unlikely (cf. Donner 1995: 468f.). In the meantime, when the report, the petitions and the memorandum had been sent, something must have happened which explained the absence of an answer from the satrap Arsam. The Straßburger Papyrus gives us an indication. It says: "If an investigation is made by judges, by the police and hearers who are appointed in the province of Tshetres, (it would be known) to our lord according to what we said" (Straßburger Papyrus, ll. 8–10 = Cowley 1923: 27 = Porten & Yardeni 1986: A4.5). Such an investigation had probably taken place, and this was the reason for the absence of the satrap's answer. One may even go further and assume that the investigation did not produce a conclusive result concerning the guilty party, otherwise a corresponding decision by the satrap would be known.

The Aramaic documents, however, point to the following conclusions resulting from an investigation:

1. The Jews could—as before—be regarded as loyal and reliable mercenaries.
2. No proof could be furnished for the involvement of the Khnum priests, otherwise the documents would indicate their punishment.

Nevertheless, the possibility that the Khnum priests seemed even more suspicious in the eyes of the Persians cannot be ruled out. Even Darius I insisted on his right to the confirmation of the Khnum priests of Elephantine. We know from the demotic correspondence of the satrap Pherendates, of a case in the 30th year of Darius' reign, during which the Khnum priests of Elephantine had to withdraw a candidate whom they had nominated as priest, because Darius refused his approval because he suspected him of being in contact with a rebel (Spiegelberg 1928: 604–622).

Of course the question may be asked, why did the government allow the loyal Jews to reconstruct their temple but forbid burnt offerings? More recently, some evidence has been offered by Inner Iranian sources, specifically the Persepolis Fortification Tablets (cf. Koch 1977, 1987, 1990, 1992: 276–296). From these, it seems that the Lan offering was to Ahuramazda. According to Koch this was a national offering celebrated daily in the heartland of Persia, Media and Elam; in addition to Ahuramazda, old Iranian gods, Elamite deities and the Assyrian god Adad were worshipped. According to Koch all gods were given rations of barley, wine, beer or fruit. In her post-doctoral thesis, Koch (1990) assumes that with the help of the Persepolis Fortification Texts one can divide the Achaemenian heartland into six administrative districts, and assign the locations mentioned on the tablets to the individual districts. In so doing, she believed that she could make the following observation for the distribution of the rations:

1. The Lan offering—to Ahuramazda—was the only offering made all over the Persian heartland. Only for this one there were "rations by the king".
2. The other gods were only worshipped in locally restricted regions. They were probably old-established gods.
3. In principle only barley, wine, beer and fruit were intended for offerings.
4. In the Elamite tradition h.ku-šu-kum was a meat offering. It was only made in the Elamite enclave of the third district and in the region of Elam. But here, too, only barley, wine, beer and fruit were given to the priests. Some references show that the receivers exchanged these rations for small animals. In principle, meat offerings were not provided by the government. The Elamites circumvented these regulations by exchanging the received barley for small animals and the government silently tolerated this practice.

Heidemarie Koch's theses have then been taken up to answer the question, why did the government forbid the Jews to make burnt offerings? The argument runs as follows: because the Persians really disapproved of the sacrifice of animals, or at best tolerated it, they could forbid the Jews their burnt offerings, but neither the research of Morrison Handley-Schachler (2004) nor the work of Shahrokh Razmjou (2004, 2008) has been considered. On the basis of his research Handley-Schachler simply calls the Lan offering "a general sacrifice to Magian gods" (2004: 204). The publications by Razmjou show clearly that small animals were supplied for the Lan offering too: they were slaughtered and eaten by the priests, or by the participants in the cult ceremony. Similar proceedings are assumed for h.ku-šu-kum and the meat offering of the Elamites. Clearly, it was not the killing of small animals which led to the prohibition of burnt offerings on Elephantine.

The answer as to why burnt offerings were forbidden lies in the various kinds of offerings made by the Jews themselves. There were three: mnḥh, lbwnh, and 'lwh. Mnḥh is the meal offering. It consisted of baked flour dishes to which salt, and usually oil and incense were added. Lbwnh was the smoke or incense offering which was burnt in special pans for incense, or on incense altars. The third offering 'lwh or "what rises up in smoke" was disapproved of. For this sacrifice the animal was killed, and the priest received the skin as well as a piece of the meat. The rest of the sacrificial animal was completely burnt. This method of sacrifice conflicted with everything a religious Zoroastrian believed. To him it was inconceivable to kill an animal, to let it touch the "holy fire", and on top of everything else, to burn it completely. Sachau-Papyrus 10, l.6 explicitly says: "it is a Mazdean who is set over the province" (= Cowley 1923: 37; Porten & Yardeni 1986: A4.2). A ban on burnt offerings in the newly built temple of the Jews from Elephantine was the logical consequence, according to the spirit of the ruling dynasty's religion to which the satrap Arsam and Bagohi belonged. This ban clearly shows the limits of Achaemenid religious tolerance.

The Jews' request for the re-erection of their temple took place against the background of its destruction in the cause of a rebellion. A decision for the reconstruction had thus become an official matter of major importance for the government. The government had consciously interfered with the cult of the Jews and prohibited burnt offerings because it was not compatible with a Mazdean's religious beliefs. The ban on burnt offerings could only be issued because law and order were disturbed and decisions were required from government. Had there not been a rebellion, there would probably not have been any adjustment of the cult of the Jews of Elephantine either.

Second case: Sachau-Papyrus 6 (Berlin P.13464 = Sachau-Papyrus 6, pl. 6 = Cowley 1923: 21 = Porten & Greenfield 1980: 78f. = Porten & Yardeni 1986: A4.1)

Whereas Sachau (1911: vol. 1, 36) and Ungnad (1911: 13) called the papyrus a "Sendschreiben betreffend das Passah-Fest", Cowley (1923: 60) described it as "order to keep the (Passover and) Feast of Unleavened Bread", and Porten and Greenfield (1980: 79) as well as Porten and Yardeni (1986: 54) simply headed it "Passover Letter". With substantial parts of the papyrus having been destroyed it is—admittedly—quite difficult to ascertain its content. The left and the right edges are missing, and on the front from lines 4–7 and on the reverse from lines 8–10, half of the right side of the papyrus has broken away. In spite of these difficulties the following gives an approximation of the document's context in order to ascertain what exactly the empire's government regulates in the papyrus. In order to make it easier to discuss the papyrus, the text of Sachau-Papyrus 6 and its translation precede the discourse (for the transcription, see Joisten–Pruschke 2008: 72).

Translation:

1 ... (To my brothers
2 Jedaniah) and his colleagues, the Jewish (army), your brother Hananiah. (For the) welfare of my brothers (may) the gods (seek)...
3 ...Now this year, year 5 Darius the king. From the king (letter/messenger/order) was sent to Arsam...
4 ... Now you thus count...
5 ... and from day 15 to day 21 of (Nisan)...
6 ... be pure and take heed! Work...
7 ...drink (not) and all that is leavened...
8 ... sunset to the day 21 of Nisan...
9 ...bring into your rooms and seal it in between the days...
10 ...
11 (To) my brothers Jedaniah and his colleagues, the Jewish army, your brother Hananiah.

The first thing that needs to be recorded is that Sachau-Papyrus 6 was not a document released by the Persian chancellery of the satrap, or by his order. It lacks all the characteristics of the letters of Arsam (cf. Driver 1957). Typical features of these official letters are:

1. They always start with: Mn Arsam 'l NN.
2. To the left of the letterhead—except for the letters Vi, Viii, Xi and Xiii—a reference is added.
3. After an abbreviated repetition of the sender and the addressee there is a salutation which differs in form from the one known in Elephantine.
4. After the salutation there are two possibilities: one is k't followed by an order from Arsam (letters I, Vi, Viii IX, and Xiii), the other features a first k't referring to a third

person, followed by a discourse on what was said, then another k'*t* which gives Arsam's real order (letters Ii, Iii, IV, V, Vii, X, Xii).
5. The letters always close with: arpc NN jd' ṭ'm' znh NN spr'.

All of these features are lacking in Sachau-Papyrus 6. Presumably the letter was introduced in the form typical for the Jewish community: ʾl NN followed by the person's assignment to the Jewish army, or to the Jews of the temple of the god Yhw/the god of heaven. Then the sender is mentioned, and the salutation commonly used in Elephantine follows in its longer or—as it is here—in its abbreviated version. The form of this document puts the letter firmly in the context of the Jewish community. Hananiah—a Jew—sends a letter to the chairman of the Jewish community and its members. In line 3—introduced by k'*t*—the date and the king's order to Arsam are stated, whereas the order's subject matter has not been preserved. In line 4 there is a second k'*t*, followed by details of a code of behaviour, in which the period from 15th to 21st Nisan is important. The following points should also be discussed:

1. The two k'*t* which follow each other, and their importance for the core of the content.
2. A determination of the content following the second k'*t*.
3. The part Hananiah played.

In Arsam's letters k'*t* introduces the order or the reference of a third person followed by a discourse, which is followed by yet another k'*t* together with the subsequently issued order. Sachau-Papyrus 6 does not follow this pattern: here we have a k'*t* in line 3, followed by another k'*t* after half a line in line 4. The half line contains about 35 to 38 characters, and is therefore too short to include a reference by a third person and a subsequent discourse which, according to the style of Arsam's letters, should start at this point. Likewise, the order cannot have come after the second k'*t* because the text of Sachau-Papyrus 6 goes against this. Therefore, this style must differ from the style of the Arsam letters. In Sachau-Papyrus 6 the first k'*t* is followed by the date and the order of the king to Arsam. Following the second k'*t* Jewish rules of conduct for the period from 15th to 21st Nisan are indicated. The first k'*t* is combined with a copula, that is it is emphasized by way of a new thought starting here. The k'*t* of line 4, however, is written without a copula and thus indicates a contextual relation to what was said before. This means that the order of the king and the text following in line 4 are directly connected to each other. From line 4 on, it is explained what is to be done in the time from Nisan 15th to 21st. At the beginning there are demands such as "be pure and take heed", followed by the imperative "drink not, what is leavened", and "seal for the days". Generally 'bjdh (l.6) [has been reconstructed as 'bjdh [l t 'bdw] referring to Dt.16:8 and Ex.12:16. Without mentioning the term psḥ explicitly, the content of lines 4ff. and the period of time from 15th to 21st Nisan refer to that feast. Additionally, two ostraca indicate the celebration of psḥ, but without telling us anything more about it. The ostracon Porten/Yardeni D7.6 and D7.24 have been dated to the beginning of the fifth century BC. Since Sachau-Papyrus 6 has to be dated to around 419 BC, the psḥ was already celebrated within the Jewish community of Elephantine at that time. Therefore, the order of the king cannot contain the introduction of the Passover feast. Furthermore, it is hard to believe that the Jews of Elephantine needed to be informed about the way the feast had to be celebrated. Even a new regulation of the feast from Jerusalem is unlikely, as the priests of Jerusalem would at least have enforced the new regulations together with the king, and not the king all by himself. In my opinion, an order would most likely have had to do with the mercenary service of the Jews from Elephantine, because there is a reference to the Jewish army in the salutation. Any feast, but especially Passover, means rest from work, in this case from mercenary service. This mercenary service is under the direct control either of the satrap or of the government of the empire, and can be interrupted only by those authorities. That Hananiah transmitted the king's order—which means that the king had been addressed directly—may be due to Arsam's unwillingness to comply with the Jews' wish to celebrate the Passover and all that it implied. Finally, together with the second k't everything connected to the feast is mentioned, thereby confirming all that was linked to the king's order. Thus—just as the two k't require it—the order of the king and the content of the text following the second k't would refer to each other closely.

I now examine the special part played by Hananiah. This man is not only mentioned in Sachau-Papyrus 6, but also in Sachau-Papyrus 11,7.8; it is said about him:—"(Khnum) is against us since Hananiah has been to Egypt until now". This note gives us several clues. At a certain time Hananiah had come to Egypt and he was still there when Sachau-Papyrus 11 was written; and there were particular difficulties with the priests of Khnum which Hananiah's part was linked to. This means that the function and responsibility of Hananiah must have been an outstanding one. This becomes even more obvious in his function in Sachau-Papyrus 6 when he is the transmitter of the king's order. If one searches for comparable figures whose function was—by order by the king—restricted as regards its time and content, you may find the Neith priest and senior physician Udjahorresnet. He could have been closely associated with Cambyses, and he temporarily spent some time in Elam under Darius I and was sent to Egypt with an official mission by the latter to restore "the houses of life"—the educational institutions connected to the temples. Unfortunately, Hananiah's exact orders and what he achieved are no longer available to us. In any case, for Sachau-Papyrus 6 it is that the Jews of Elephantine wanted to celebrate their feast, which meant rest from mercenary service work. It is assumed that they first sent a petition to Arsam, which he either turned down or left unanswered. As a second step, the Jews of Elephantine turned towards the king himself, who gave Hananiah special orders, among them to transmit the unrestricted permission to celebrate the Passover feast. Probably, Hananiah was associated with the king's closest surroundings—as was Udjahorresnet—and had been given these orders—again like Udjahorresnet—because of his ethnic and religious affiliations.

Under Persian rule the earlier structures remained without a break in Babylonia as well as in Egypt. In Egypt this is particularly clear in the confirmed existence of demotic administrative and legal documents. Or, as Dandamayev pointed out: "each province remained [an] independent socio-economic unit with its own social institutions, internal structures, old local laws, customs, traditions, systems of weight and measures, and monetary systems" (1999: 272). At the same time, the presence of Persian military and mercenary forces as well as Persian officials concerned with the tribute, demonstrated Persian control over the territory. It was a constant balancing act to safeguard both local autonomy and the empire's interests. Nevertheless, local autonomy could be instantly restricted or interfered with as soon as Persian rule was endangered by unrest, that is, by rebellions or conflicts. This is documented in the demotic correspondence of the satrap Pherendates, where a Khnum priest is not confirmed in his office because he is suspected of being in contact with rebels. The satrap's or the king's decisions which were called for in conflict situations also belong in this context. The dealing with the reconstruction of the temple of the Jews of Elephantine and Sachau-Papyrus 6 can be considered examples. Despite these interferences in conflict situations, demotic and numerous Aramaic documents show that it was characteristic of Achaemenian politics "to interfere as little as possible in the traditional political and social structures of their province" (Dandamayev 1999: 271).

6

All the King's Men

Christopher Tuplin

In a recent publication Thierry Petit (2004) has examined the story of Cyrus and Orontas in Xenophon *Anabasis* 1.6.1–11, detected a ritual expressive of subordination, associated that subordination with the term *bandaka* and elaborated a parallel with medieval homage rituals.[1] To test his account of the episode and its implications I shall consider the evidence for ceremonial procedure, examine *bandaka* and certain other Iranian and non-Iranian words, and assess the impact of the medieval analogy.[2] I do not pretend to provide an exhaustive account of all the issues raised by Petit's stimulating paper, and what follows is a dogmatic report on what I believe to be demonstrable rather than a thoroughly documented demonstration.

There are three phases in the story:[3] *Phase 1* Darius II gives Orontas to Cyrus as *hupekoos* (subordinate). Orontas then fights Cyrus at Artaxerxes II's behest[4] using the Sardis acropolis as a base (Xenophon *Anabasis* 1.6.6). *Phase 2* Cyrus and Orontas exchange *dexiai* (handshakes) at the end of that conflict. Orontas then revolts and damages Cyrus' land from a base in Mysia (*ibid*. 1.6.6–7). *Phase 3* Cyrus and Orontas exchange *pista* (pledges) after Orontas has come to the altar of Artemis at Sardis and persuaded Cyrus that he has repented (*ibid*. 1.6.7) but Orontas then tries to defect during Cyrus' march on Babylon (*ibid*. 1.6.1–3, 8). Our key text is Xenophon's account of the trial and execution of Orontas following this third act of disloyalty.

There are five further details: 1. Orontas is γένει προσήκων βασιλεῖ (related to the king: *ibid*. 1.6.1)—so he was related to Cyrus too, and may count as an Achaemenid; 2. the trial is conducted before the seven 'best' Persians of Cyrus' entourage including a Greek mercenary general whose report is the source of Xenophon's knowledge of the details;[5] 3. Orontas admits that Cyrus could not now believe he would again be *philos kai pistos* (friendly and loyal) to him (*ibid*. 1.6.8). So *philos kai pistos* describes his state during periods of loyalty to Cyrus; 4. condemnation to death is indicated by the seizure of Orontas' belt (*ibid*. 1.6.10); 5. as he is led away, "those who did *proskynesis* to him before, did so then", even knowing "he was about to die" (*ibid*.).

There are three ways to validate Petit's claim: A) does the *Anabasis* narrative actually suggest a ceremony? B) is there other direct evidence of such ceremonies? C) is there indirect evidence best explained by postulating such ceremonies?

A. The postulated ceremony has three elements: 1) Person A, who can be described as *hupekoos*, *bandaka*, *doulos* or *huperetes*, states a wish to serve Person B, and does *proskynesis*; 2) a mutual handshake and oath seals the relationship, in which A becomes *philos kai pistos* to B; 3) B invests A with certain perquisites, symbolized by the wearing of a belt. Various potential problems present themselves.

First of all, Petit's argument amalgamates elements from all phases of the relationship and the trial, and is therefore methodologically vulnerable.

(a) Orontas' formal statement of a wish to serve Cyrus is extracted from a combination of Darius making him Cyrus' *hupekoos* (Phase 1) and Orontas persuading Cyrus he has repented of his defection (Phase 2).

(b) We must assume not just that the Phase 2 exchange of *dexiai* is equivalent to exchanging *pista* at an altar in Phase 3 but that each implies the other, Xenophon having arbitrarily chosen to mention one in one case and then the other in the other. Xenophontic usage elsewhere allows, but does not compel, such an assumption: mutual *dexiai* are not always accompanied by oaths (cf. e.g. *Hell*.4.1.15, 31, *Cyr*.3.2.14, 4.6.10, 6.1.48, 8.4.25). And is Xenophon being arbitrary? The mention of the altar might suggest that the second reconciliation involved heavier symbols of restored trust—that is, that the phases should be distinguished not amalgamated.

(c) The only *proskynesis* in the story is that done to Orontas on his way to execution. The identity of those who did it is not stated, but the fact that condemnation to death did not deprive him of social status need have nothing to do with subordination rituals. That the putative investiture ceremony involved *proskynesis* is mere assumption and, as Herodotus (1.134) suggests that in social contexts Orontas would not do *proskynesis* to Cyrus, the assumption is disturbingly substantial.

Secondly, investiture with obligation-carrying perquisites does not figure in the *Anabasis* account. Evidence elsewhere about high-rank individuals gifting property against military or other service never says anything about the act of conferral (we hear only about it being an act of generosity, reward or honour on the part of the donor), so its inclusion in the ceremonial is heavily driven by the medieval parallel, and Orontas' belt is a doubtful help. Signalizing condemnation by grasping the belt recurs in the case of Charidemus, a Greek exile who offended Darius III during a council of friends (Diodorus 17.30.4–5), but belt-wearing characterized Persians in general (Charidemus was dressing *à la perse*), and is surely too common in Persian and Greco-Persian iconography to mark a distinctive status—unless certain belts had specific features of material, design or colour that now elude us. It is more likely that belt-seizure is an example of clothing standing for the individual: compare, for example, the story about Artaxerxes I inflicting punishment on the cloak of a malefactor, not the man himself (see Plut.*Mor*.35E, 173D, 565A, Amm. Marc.30.8.4, Dio Chrys.37.45, with Stolper 1997).[6]

Thirdly, although I shall return to terminology later, there are two points to note immediately: a) *huperetai* is certainly not relevant (*pace* Petit 2004: 181). The *huperetai* who take Charidemus away (Diodorus 17.30.5) correspond to those mentioned in other execution scenes (Plut.*Artox*.29 (Darius) and Diod.16.43 (Thettalion)) and to the anonymous οἷς προσετάχθη in the present passage, and are simply undefined servants; b) *hupekoos* is a banal term for imperial subjects, and three contexts with personal overtones—Tissaphernes' demand that Ionian cities be *hupekooi* to him (Xenophon *Hellenica* 3.1.3), Pharnabazus' prospect of making current fellow-slaves *hupekooi* (*ibid*. 4.1.36) and the *oikoi kai hupekooi* (houses/estates and subordinates) given to members of Cyrus' elite (id. *Cyropaedia* 8.6.5)—do not indicate that *hupekoos* signifies anything radically different in *Anabasis* 1.6.6. The first two belong in the ordinary dimension of imperial rule; the third is only pertinent if the *hupekooi* are satrapal courtiers—which they are not.

B. Directly parallel evidence for an investiture ceremony is elusive. One might anticipate help from Xenophon's other writings. But the vignettes in *Hellenica* and *Agesilaus* involving Otys, Spithridates, Agesilaus, Pharnabazus and his son concern political deals, marriages and Greek *xenia*-relations (Xen.*Hell*.4.1.1–40, *Ages*.3.3, 5, 5.4–5), and the chance to introduce something relevant in *Cyropaedia* is not taken. The account of royal-elite relations in Book VIII speaks only in collective terms, and the four depictions of individual bonds in the narrative (three of which involve defectors from the Assyrian camp) are disappointing. Gadatas does *proskynesis* to Cyrus (5.3.17), but there is no further formality, and the actual sealing of the pact between Pheraulas and his Sacan household manager is not described.[7] The deals of Abradatas and Gobryas with Cyrus are more interesting: there is performative language, the two men "give" themselves to Cyrus and there is an exchange of handshakes in one case.[8] But these are alliances with non-Persians, and no more validate Petit's ceremony than does the episode in *Anabasis* VII where, after talk of becoming Seuthes' brother, getting land and marrying his daughter (7.2.25,38), Xenophon gives himself and his companions as *philoi pistoi* (7.3.30)—a deal with a Thracian, in a context of Thracian-style gift-giving, and sealed by drink rather than handshakes (7.3.32). Xenophon is interested in trust and relations between ruler and ruled, but it is not clear that in *Anabasis* 1.6 he understood himself to be describing a distinctive method of embedding a distinctive relationship.[9]

As for other sources, accounts of other post-rebellion reconciliations are inadequately specific,[10] as is that of the way Cyrus made Amorges, Spitacas and Megabernes mutual *philoi*, although it involved handshakes and a curse on defaulters (Ctesias 688 F9[8]). I doubt we can reconstruct Achaemenid ceremonial from the interplay of *proskynesis* and kiss in Alexander's trial introduction of *proskynesis*—and if we did it would not match Petit's model (Plut.*Alex*.54, Arr.*An*.4.12.3–5, Chares *FGrH* 125 F14).

At the same time, Persians were not averse to ceremonial: it is readily imagined not just on the scale suggested by the iconography at Persepolis and Naqsh-i Rustam or in relation to the tantalizing "giving of earth and water" (cf. Kuhrt 1988*a*), but at an individual level of public reward for services rendered.[11] Moreover, evidence for ceremony can be thin even when formal relationships existed: for example, the direct evidence for a ritual to seal Greek guest-friendship is tiny.[12] So Petit's claim is certainly not absurd but it is not yet proved.

C. Where direct evidence is so elusive, the chances for indirect evidence are slim. Still, there are remarks to be made about terminology and other phenomena that might find illumination in terms of the relationship marked by the postulated ceremony.

On the terminological front there are words in *Anabasis* 1.6—*hupekoos, pistos kai philos*—and words found elsewhere, that have been explicitly or implicitly associated with that text, e.g. *bandaka, doulos, protoi* and *dokimotatoi*.[13] Investigation will bring still more words to our attention, but the limits are reasonably clear. On the other front pertinence is trickier. Our concern is subordination of individual to individual, so any institutional feature with that characteristic is theoretically open to review, and the scope for *petitio principii* is almost limitless. For that reason, I shall say little under this heading.[14] It is arguable (for example) that, given appropriate limits, a ritually marked relationship distinct from function-oriented office might be a useful tool in directing the loyalty of mutually equal-status elite members to the king rather than one another (Briant 2002*a*: 352; cf. 326, 332 etc.), a distinction between Persians (who could have such a link to the king) and non-Persians (who could not),[15] a neutral way of defining a satrapal court, an explanation of the way high-rank rebels could sometimes be readmitted to favour, or even an explanation of Otanes' alleged privilege of being "free" (albeit subject to the laws of the Persians).[16] But neither such propositions nor the general sense of a nexus of personal relations, property tenure and duty of service emanating from Achaemenid sources (often in social contexts where the *mores* of Cyrus and Orontas are hardly directly relevant) suffice to validate the case. On the latter point, of course, the medieval parallel might be brought to bear. Petit hesitates to move from homage ceremonies to feudo-vassalic relations (I will return to that later), but does claim the ceremony would apply between Spithridates and his 200 horsemen, who are a primary exhibit in Sekunda's (1988) explication of Xenophontic remarks about satrapal cavalry in terms of a world of dukes and knights. But Sekunda's model itself has a very modest base of direct evidence, too weak to sustain the burden of proving Petit's case as well. Another medieval issue—a general sense of rigidly hierarchical society—is something else to which I return later.

We come now to terminology. Alongside office titles (which in principle express the function of their holder)[17] and broad designations of elite non-royal Persians, the sources for Achaemenid history do offer words that locate individuals in reference to another individual. That such terminology is sometimes used both where the king is and is not a party may enhance a sense of system. But are some of these terms labels that can be formally (so perhaps ritually) bestowed, and is there a label proper to our postulated ceremony?

Bandaka is a term applied by Darius to a number of high-ranking individuals who suppressed resistance to his rule, two of whom were also among the six comrades who originally helped him to seize the throne,[18] and it is widely thought the *mot juste* for formal vassals. Sparse signs that it became a personal name in Babylonia and Lydia may not militate against this,[19] but the fact that Elamite and Akkadian translators rendered it banally as "servant" and Darius himself also used it in DB §7 of the generality of subject peoples, gives one pause.

The word only appears at Behistun. Absence of later application to individuals reflects a body of texts nearly devoid of named non-royal persons.[20] However, the other absence is deliberate. At Bisitun it is part of a formal statement of the extent and effectiveness of royal rule; later texts have such statements, but "they are my *bandaka*" is missing.[21] Perhaps it was too honourable a term for "subject" for the more authoritarian and egocentric post-Bisitun discourse, but that it was a broad term for "subject" seems inescapable. The Greek view that *all* subjects were *douloi* could thus reflect a negative translation of *bandaka* (cf. Missiou 1993) but, in any event, *bandaka* cannot uniquely denominate a distinct relationship limited enough to be feasibly enacted by ritual ceremony.

Old Persian does not offer an alternative either. *Anušiya* and *marika*, both of which are sometimes implicitly canvassed, will not do. *Marika* at the end of Darius' tomb inscription means "young man" and designates the Crown prince (Schmitt 1999). *Anušiya* appears at Behistun of supporters of Gaumata and the Lie-Kings (§§ 13, 32, 42, 43, 47, 50), Darius' henchmen (§ 68) and the army of Darius' father (§ 35). In each context the core idea (people who are on one's side) is treated differently in the other languages: their authors do not attribute the word any special status, and there is no reason for us to assign it more than narrative content. Its application indifferently to Darius' friends and enemies points the same way.

To see words as technical is a temptation when dealing with a limited corpus, but vagueness is characteristic of Old Persian. *Dahyu* (land/people) and *kara* (army/people) are notorious. *Data* has a resonance (hence import into other languages) but the traditional rendering "law" is too restricted (Briant 1999: 1135; Stolper 1993: 60f.; 1994: 340 n. 14). When Xerxes calls himself *mathišta* after Darius (XPf § 4), I hesitate to discern a technical term, given the use of the same word for Margian and Elamite rebel leaders (DB §§ 38, 71). *Marika* can designate the Crown prince (see above), but Akkadian rendering of it as "servant" and the comic poet Eupolis' rechristening of the "slave" Hyperbolus as Marikas attest less socially elevated applications (Cassio 1985). *Fratama*, found with *anušiya* in a phrase signifying "the principal supporters" of Gaumata and the Lie-Kings, has been seen as a honorific title thanks to four Elamite bureaucratic texts (PT 36, 44, 44a, PT 1957-2), but there are real problems with this (see Tuplin 2005*b*), and I doubt *fratama* ever means more than "first". The fact that a Greek cognate, *protos*, is sometimes linked with *bandaka* brings us to Greek terminology.

Protos itself can be dismissed, as can *dokimos*, *logimos*, *aristos*, *epiphanes*, *megistos*, *kratistos* and the like. Nothing suggests technical use or is distinctively Persian. Otherwise Greek texts disclose an elite society of 1) office-holders; 2) categories of birth or clear adlection such as royal relatives (real and created), benefactors, table-sharers, or wearers of purple and/or royally gifted jewellery; 3) a general group of *hoi epi thurais* ("those at the gates", i.e. courtiers); and 4) people described as *pistoi* and *philoi*. Both words appear in *Anabasis* 1.6.8, and *pistos* has been seen as a Greek equivalent for *bandaka*. That only makes sense if *bandaka* has restricted scope—which (as we have seen) is not the case—but I shall pause a moment longer on the two Greek words.

The prominence of the *philoi* and/or *pistoi* of kings or princes must be kept in proportion. The narrative of Persian history (as of any autocracy) organizes individuals in relation to powerful figures. Security is paramount, so categorization of people close to those with power as trustworthy is banal—and natural for the Greek observer. Moreover, around autocrats even normal things like friendship look deliberated: those in power must be careful about their friends. We in turn must be careful not to assume we are dealing with Persian titles or ranks. It *is* striking that we hear in quasi-formulaic terms more about the king and his friends than for example the king and his advisers. But there are no quasi-Hellenistic rankings, and categorization of especially close king-elite relations in terms of friendship could actually represent a *Greek* vision. Old Persian *dauštar* is unattested here, and (despite the impression one might initially get from the elegantly persuasive treatment of Greek views of friendship in Konstan 1997[22]) the semantics of *philos* are perfectly consonant. If so, it is not wholly banal. That the tyrant has no friends (as Greeks liked to say) but the Great King does shows they took for granted that he was a legitimate ruler, even if his subjects were *douloi*.[23] And if Greeks positively *chose* to speak of friends (rather than picking it as the least bad match for some Persian term), they detected something of the mutual support and affective bond implicit in *philos* in the otherwise unequal relationship between the king and his chief associates.

These ruminations lead two ways. On the one hand, any occasional use of *philoi* and *pistoi* as quasi-titles (and very few texts even appear to display this[24]) is a linguistic by-product of Greek interpretation, not evidence about Persian rankings, and there is no real chance of validating Petit's thesis through terminology. On the other, the vision of the king and his friends evokes a broader perspective. Our sources provide many titles and non-specific labels—and concomitant economic differentiation. But what sort of hierarchic society are we talking about? For Xenophon (in *Cyropaedia*) imperial management followed principles of military hierarchy, while the king was surrounded by a meritocratic elite entirely dependent upon him for its status: Xenophon has an agenda, but it starts from a view of reality. Herodotus' model of Persian society postulates family, phratry, clan and nation, rather broad status-distinction within the general population,[25] and a dominant king surrounded by a Persian elite within which the plainest differentiation is between Achaemenids and others (cf. Briant 1990). The first and third features are validated by Persian sources—family and phratry match Old Persian *vith* and *tauma*;[26] 'Achaemenid' is central to royal identity—and the central one should also be respected. It is not dissimilar to Darius' picture, textual and iconographic: the king is special among the creatures of Ahuramazda and Persia is special among lands of the earth, but among Persians there is just a broad distinction between courtiers and others, with special members of the former only sketchily visible (cf. Stronach 2002: 387–388). Otherwise there are those who accommodate themselves to his rule and those who fall victim to the Lie, and there are the strong and the weak. Darius has his agenda too, but it is one in which royal superiority obviates, rather than being based upon, elaborate hierarchy, and later kings did not alter it. Another lexical point comes in here. In the Bisitun text Darius says his family were *amata* (DB §3). The context calls for high status, but the word attracts from Elamite and Akkadian composers equivalents that do not meet this requirement. *Šalup* connotes no more than free status, and can be used of non-Iranians; *mar bane*, normally rendered "citizen" or "free man", is undemonstrative of significantly elite status (cf. Dandamayev 1981; Frame 1992: 230f.): Babylonian citizens included people of low socio-economic status, and one feels the author could have done better if *amata* had conveyed a vivid sense of elite rank. Use of *mar bane* for Darius' fellow-conspirators and leading supporters of Gaumata and the Lie-Kings (groups defined by visible activity not status) and to render "strong" (as opposed to "weak") confirms that it only indicates a general sense of special status.[27] *Amata* was generically descriptive not technically terminological,[28] and the society it belonged to showed rather flat elite differentiation.[29] If it is true that the Persians pictured themselves as bees,[30] this expressed the same vision; and it is possible to see how Herodotus persuaded himself that the so-called Constitutional Debate was validated by Persian sources (3.80–83, 6.43).

We have come some way from Petit's ceremony, and seen little to dispel initial doubts about his reading of the key text. What of its medieval overtones? I offer some bald assertions.[31]

Ideally, a parallel established between two independently and plainly attested contexts could be used to explore ill-evidenced aspects of Achaemenid society. In fact, the utility of the postulated parallel is compromised by the part it plays in excavating the Achaemenid ritual in the first place.[32] Another problem is that radically different discourses exist about the medieval world. Petit reflects a traditional discourse in which vassalage and feudal hierarchy were central to medieval society. But revisionism has questioned—indeed, as good as rejected—this picture (cf. Brown 1974; Reynolds 1994).[33] Cross-period comparison thus becomes complex; and doubts about the applicability of traditional discourse across a wide geographical and chronological range evoke local and temporal variations that just make complexity even more complex.

One notes a contrast in the ritual gestures—*proskynesis* and handshaking as against a special manual act (vassal's hands between lord's hands) followed by a kiss. The medieval version suggests equality (cf. Bloch 1961: 228, 446f.), the Achaemenid one difference—and this in a context that could also be modelled in a more egalitarian fashion. The ritual moment could, of course, be a suitable one to assert the alternative model, and if the ritual only operated (in Sekunda's terms) between king and duke and duke and knight, the egalitarian model might survive. But traditional discourse about feudalism has it over a larger number of levels. So the parallel is inexact, and the conclusion to be drawn unclear.

Less inexact, but troubling, is another point. Reynolds insists there is no systematic terminology for homage and the supposed feudo-vassalic system (1994: 22ff.), so the proposition that Petit's putative ritual does not map onto a stable technical vocabulary may not prove there was no ritual, but it does challenge its significance. No one is denying that rituals existed in the medieval environment, merely insisting that we should see them in a wider context of public representation of social relations. We can no more prove for Achaemenid times than medieval ones that a fixed ritual was confined to a specified situation.

Petit plays down fiefs and feudalism. This is unfair, as the putative fixed medieval ritual belongs to a larger traditional story about the fief-vassal nexus in medieval society; and his reason for dissociating Achaemenids from feudalism—that satraps' estates were not coterminous with territorial jurisdiction—makes assumptions questioned by revisionist discourse (Carolingian counts are not the only model) and may only show that Persia provides a different variety of feudo-vassal society. There is certainly an evidential gap here: the tenure of noble estates—for example the large entities within which Babylonian bow-land and *hatrus* lay (Stolper 1985)—generally eludes surviving documentation. That Sekunda (1988) postulated dukes and knights and Stolper (1985) spoke of Babylonian "manors" shows how beguiling the medieval analogy is: evidence for homage ceremonial might validate such talk—after all, Petit explicitly envisages an investiture ceremony between "duke" Spithridates and his 200 "knights". Homage *could* exist independently of fief-holding[34] but—granted solid evidence for Achaemenid homage—it might seem hypercritical to detach it from the evidence for estate-holding. Solid evidence, however, is what we do not have.

Traditional accounts of feudalism located its emergence in post-Carolingian state collapse, weak monarchy and privatized power.[35] This hardly sounds like the Achaemenid world. Anti-mutationists doubt there was any such clear-cut change during the "long tenth century" (see Barthélemy 1998),[36] while Reynolds actually affirms that the least bad fit between real conditions and the traditional feudal-vassal account came two centuries later amidst reasserted royal power and the development of bureaucracy (Reynolds 1994: 74–75, 478f.; Little & Rosenwein 1998: 111). This actually sounds more like the Achaemenid world. But there is a contrast between a medieval system in which central control was eventually reasserted by repackaging a mess of existing property relations *via* artificial legal redefinition (producing a rule-bound feudal hierarchy that is a theoretical construct-after-the-event, not the key to thirteenth-century political society) and an Achaemenid one in which existing tenure-service models are used to appropriate the fruits of victory in newly conquered territory. Revisionist discourse insists that the status of the free men (noble or otherwise) as subjects of a super-eminent king was far more important than their status as his or anyone's vassals (e.g. Reynolds 1994: 46; 1997: 259f), and that horizontal social relationships occupied as much attention as vertical ones.[37] I think this applies to the Persians too, but in an era of imperial expansion the fief–vassal nexus could still be more significant than revisionists concede even for the thirteenth century.[38]

Finally, feudalism evokes knighthood and incorporation of a warrior mentality into systems of government. The Achaemenid resonance is debatable, since it is hard to assess how far we are here dealing with a warrior society.[39] On the other hand, many reject a romance-fuelled view of medieval knighthood anyway, so the distance may not be so great after all. But reducing distance does not make a parallel. Achaemenid times reserved a far more important place for infantrymen than did the Middle Ages; Persian military ethos potentially affected a quite different functional and social variety of individuals. The world of the Immortals is radically different from that of the knight in shining armour.

In conclusion, we can say that a) the case for Petit's ceremony turns out to be quite vulnerable; b) Persian society did not work in ways implicit in any substantive version of Petit's thesis; people knew their place, but it was characteristically defined by function or in relation to the king. The perception of satraps as quasi-kings, if valid, reinforces this proposition: satrapal society is an image of royal society, not the next step of a hierarchical cascade. The Persian *ethno-classe dominante* affected some homogeneity, and it is hard to show this was a wholly misleading mask for external consumption; c) this view is not undermined by any parallel between Petit's putative ceremony and medieval *commendatio*, because *commendatio* need have no major structural role, and (more generally) because the medieval world of territorial monarchies is so far removed from the huge but unitary Achaemenid imperial state.

Notes

1. Briant (2002*a*: 623) had already written that Cyrus' closest confidants were bound to him by personal ties, symbolized by a hand-clasp before the gods (1.6.6–7).
2. Rigorous separation of medieval and Achaemenid aspects is not easy, as there is a strong link between the general claim of a subordination ceremonial and the particular claim that it structurally resembles medieval homage rituals. Petit is in some degree using a medieval parallel to justify a reading of Achaemenid evidence that might not otherwise seem warranted.
3. In each, assertion of mutual loyalty is followed by an actual or attempted breach of that relationship. In two cases his alternative loyalty is to the king; in the third this is neither asserted nor precluded.
4. ταχθείς is Xenophon's word—appropriate to positive appointment. Briant (2002*a*: 342 [where there is a mistranslation of the French original]) assumes that the move from Phase 1a to Phase 1b corresponds to Artaxerxes' perception of Cyrus as rebel—i.e. Artaxerxes takes him out of subordination to Cyrus.
5. *Ibid.* 1.6.5. The trial was attended, and intervened in, by Clearchus. Cf. Diod.15.10.2, where Greeks present at Tiribazus' trial are invoked to confirm that one could not ask Delphi περὶ θανάτου. Both cases suggest that, perhaps surprisingly, the business of the life or death of a Persian noble was not one to be conducted only among peers and behind closed doors.
6. For a different piece of belt symbolism cf. Hdt.8.120 with Lenfant 2002.
7. ταῦτα συνέθεντο is all that is said (8.3.48). Pheraulas is one of Cyrus' friends (8.3.28), who wishes (like Cyrus) to have time to devote himself to his own friends (8.3.44, 50). Pheraulas and the Sacan are said to *philein* one another (50); but does that make the Sacan one of Pheraulas' *philoi* in some sort of technical sense?
8. Abradatas takes Cyrus' right hand and says φίλον σοι ἐμαυτὸν δίδωμι καὶ θεράποντα καὶ σύμμαχον. Cyrus formally says "I accept" (cf. Agesilaus' response to Pharnabazus' son naming him *xenos*) and adds that Abradatas must σκηνοῦν σὺν τοῖς σοῖς τε καὶ ἐμοῖς φίλοις (6.1.48–49). When Gobryas joins Cyrus he says ἥκω πρὸς σὲ καὶ ἱκέτης προσπίπτω καὶ δίδωμι σοι ἐμαυτὸν δοῦλον καὶ σύμμαχον, σὲ δὲ τιμωρὸν αἰτοῦμαι ἐμοὶ γενέσθαι, καὶ παῖδα οὕτως ὡς δυνατόν σε ποιοῦμαι, and he offers Cyrus use of his fortress, tribute, military service and his daughter (4.6.1ff.). Cyrus replies ἐπὶ τούτοις ἐγὼ ἀληθευομένοις δίδωμι σοι τὴν ἐμὴν καὶ λαμβάνω τὴν σὴν δεξιάν (4.6.9—a provisional promise to help avenge Gobryas' loss). Later he visits Gobryas' fortress and decides he is reliable; he therefore "owes the promise" (5.2.8.), accepts the treasure, but not the daughter, thanks Gobryas for the chance to prove he will do no wrong and break no *sunthekai* (agreements) to misuse what Gobryas has offered, and will honour him for his good services (5.2.11). There is certainly some formality here, but it is tied to rather specific circumstances.
9. The other interesting covenant text in *Cyropaedia* is that between Cyrus and the Persians (8.5.24f.). This is a sort of bilateral defence treaty: Cyrus will intervene if someone attacks Persia or attempts to subvert its laws, Persians will help Cyrus if someone attempts to overthrow his *arkhe* or if any of the subjects rebel. At this stage Persia has its own king (Cambyses) but the situation subsists even when Cyrus is king and indeed thereafter, too. There is also an arrangement that a "member of the family" ὃς ἂ ν δοκῇ ὑμῖν ἄριστος εἶναι will carry out religious functions when the king is not in the country. This has nothing to do with personal loyalty bonds, though one might say that Xenophon's perception that the relationship of king and Persia was distinctive is probably correct: there is no satrap of Persia in *Cyropaedia* and there was probably none in reality either.
10. E.g. Xen.*An*.2.4.1, Plut.*Artox*.6.5, Diod.15.90–93, 16.46.3, 52.3, Ctesias 688 F14[38,42], 15[50, 52–53], Ael.*VH* 6.14.
11. Status marked by nature or quantity of gifts received (Briant 1990: 97f.); presumed ceremony of bestowal (*ibid.* 100). For ceremonies cf. Briant 2002*a*: 303, 307, 337, citing e.g. Esther 6:9 (Mordecai paraded through the city on a royal horse etc. with proclamations); Hdt.4.143 (the—perhaps public—comment of Darius about

Megabyzus), Xenophon, *Cyropaedia* 8.3.23 (in the context of an existing procession), Hdt.1.132.6, Strabo 15.3.17 (the present or prize for those fathering most children), Strabo.15.3.17, Arrian, *Anabasis* 7.4.7 (postulated annual wedding ceremonies at the vernal equinox).

12. Xen.*Hell*.4.1.39 (Agesilaus and Pharnabazus' son); *Il*.6.119–236 (Diomedes and Glaucus); *Od*.1.115ff (Telemachus and "Mentes"), 21.11–42 (Odysseus and Iphitus). It involves formal statement of intention, naming of the *xenos*, and exchange of gifts.

13. Briant (2002*a*: 327) brings the last pair in, *via* an association with *bandaka*.

14. I also suspect that in default of a terminological lead no compelling case could ever be made—despite what is said later about medieval parallels.

15. Power remained with the Persians (Briant 2002*a*: 349, 352).

16. Can it be a privilege not to have a status that many aspire to? Yes: consider wage-slavery.

17. Sometimes literal meaning *is* at variance with the actual status: cf. Henkelman 2003*b*: 119f. on *lipte kutira* = "garment-bearer" and other cases. But this does not in itself authorize us to postulate formally bestowed titles that only express status. Nor does Aperghis' claim that *haturmakša* and *etira* sometimes represent rank, not function (1999: 157).

18. DB §§ 25 (Vidarna), 26 (Dadarši [I]), 29 (Vahumisa), 33 (Taxmaspada), 38 (Dadarši [II]), 41 (Artavardiya), 45 (Vivana), 50 (Vindafarnah), 71 (Gaubaruva). The last two were among the original six companions (§68), but the six are not collectively called *bandaka*. Instead §68 states (in Old-Persian) that they acted with Darius as *anušiya* (variously rendered as "faithful" or "follower") or (Elamite/Akkadian) that they provided help. (The Aramaic version matches the OP one, but has no equivalent for *anušiya*.)

19. Sb 9385 r.9 (Joannès 1990*b*), Gusmani 1964: no. 14 (translated in Dusinberre 2003: 230). Eilers 1989: 683a notes that *banda-* is an element in many (later) Iranian personal names.

20. The only exceptions are Gobryas and Aspathines on the tomb façade, but they have other and grander titles, and do not appear in a narrative context.

21. Compare and contrast DB §7 with DNa §3, DPe §2, DPg §2, DSe §3, DSm §2, DSv §2 and XPh §3.

22. He treats the "King's *philos*" as a novelty of the Hellenistic world, but this is because it presupposes the relevant autocratic context, and Konstan's focus in the earlier part of his book is on the republican *polis*. (He virtually ignores the Achaemenid world—occasional citations of *Cyropaedia* are for evidence about Greek attitudes—presumably because it is a non-Greek environment; but that ignores the fact that Greek sources are describing it.) There is nothing unnatural to Greek usage or sentiment as presented by Konstan in the usage represented by "King's friend". The history of Agesilaus is also worth recalling here (cf. Cartledge 1987: 139ff.).

23. In the same way, Isocrates can recommend Diodotus as *philos* to the legitimate regent Antipater (*ep*.4). Tyrants have flatterers, but the king's flatterers are not a formulaic stereotype, even if he suffers from eunuchs and women, and dislikes unwelcome advice.

24. Xen.*Oec*.4.6 (the king sends *pistoi*—not e.g. τῶν πιστῶν τινας—to review garrisons) is sometimes wrongly cited in this context, but Xen. *An*.1.5.15, where Cyrus intervenes in a brawl σὺν τοῖς παροῦσι τῶν πιστῶν, may be a case. Most editors and/or translators also put Aesch.*Pers*. 1f (τάδε μὲν Περσῶν τῶν οἰχομένων / Ἑλλάδ᾽ εἰς αἶαν πιστὰ καλεῖται, / καὶ τῶν ἀφνεῶν καὶ ττο–λυχρύσων / ἑδράνων φύλακες, κατὰ πρεσβείαν / οὓς αὐτὸς ἄναξ Ξέρξης βασιλεὺς / Δαρειογενής / εἵλετο χώρας ἐφορεύειν) in this category. But it may just mean "we are loyal to the Persians who have gone to Greece, we are guardians of the palace, selected to mind the land because of our age" (for passive καλεῖσθαι in non-title contexts cf. *Choeph*.321, *Sept*.929). In the same play the queen regularly addresses the chorus as *philoi*, which, though commonplace in Sophocles (19 examples in 5 plays), is unusual in Aeschylus (a possible exception is fr.47a.821) and Euripides (cf. only *Alc*.935, 960). Even so, it is impossible to be sure Aeschylus was prompted by a belief that *philos* was a title.

25. His comments on kissing and *proskynesis* in 1.134 presuppose three broad groups.

26. The co-presence of the words in DB §§ 14 and 63 shows that they are not simply synonymous; since there were more kings in Darius' *tauma* than the individuals named in his direct ascent line in §2, we may infer that *tauma* is the larger unit (*contra* Herrenschmidt 1976; Briant 1990: 79; Lecoq 1997: 170). This is consistent with the use of *vith-* in words meaning "prince" (cf. Vittman 1991/92: 159 for demotic attestation in CG 31174 of *vis(a) puthra*, corresponding to *u-ma-su-pi-it-ru-ú* or *u-ma-as-pi-it-m-u* in BE 9.101, 10.15, an equivalent

27. of *mar biti*, i.e. "son of the house"). The opening of DB amounts to a persuasive definition of Darius' *tauma* as a royal family of Achaemenids (one including Cyrus and Cambyses), and Herodotus' identification of the Achaemenids as a *phretre* is his attempt to capture the special character and importance of "Achaemenid" as a category.
27. DB §§ 13, 32, 42, 43, 47, 50 (Lie-King supporters); DB §13 (Darius' helpers); DNb/XPl §2a (for OP *tunuva*, strong).
28. There is an odd resonance of the use of *azata* to mean both free and noble (de Blois 1985).
29. Rollinger 1998b: 178, n.124, commenting on DB 3, says of *mar bane* that the author had to render specifically Persian *Gesellschaftsformen* with a Babylonian terminology that was insufficient. "Das Bemühen ist allerdings spürbar, einen besonders auszeichnenden gesellschaftlichen Status zu umreissen." He does not comment on *šalup*.
30. Roscalla 1998: 97–101; cf. the assertion (Hdt.7.61.2) that in ancient times the Greeks called Persians Kephenes (i.e. drones) and an apparent allusion to the king of Assyria as a bee in Isaiah 7:18. Application of the image by Aeschylus to Xerxes in *Persae* 126-9 would reflect authentic Persian ideas, and one might also note the queen bee imagery in Xen.*Oec.* 7.17, 32–34, 38–39, which Pomeroy 1984: 240–242, 276–277 links to the Persian content of *Oec.* 4. Can any of this cast light on the bee (?) that replaces an expected winged disc on a seal-image from Babylonia (Stolper 2001)?
31. I am immensely indebted to my Liverpool colleague Marios Costambeys for assistance with historical material far outside my competence and (I am minded to think) far more complicated than most of what an Achaemenid historian usually has to contend with. Dr Costambeys bears no responsibility for any misuse of his advice of which I may be guilty.
32. It is a curious coincidence that an early piece of evidence for medieval commendation into vassalage concerns the return to submission of an erstwhile rebel, the nephew of Pippin (Reynolds 1994: 86, 98).
33. See more generally Little & Rosenwein 1998: Part 2 (Feudalism and its Alternatives).
34. Revisionist discourse is insistent upon this; but it is true in more traditional discourse as well, if you go far enough back into the early medieval period.
35. For a brief summary see Reuter 1999: 17f.; for a full exposition see Poly & Bournazel 1991.
36. Some salient points are summarized in Barthélemy 1998.
37. Hence examination of dispute resolution or dispute avoidance in (relatively) local historical documents and wider evocations of the peasant communities attract more interest than feudal hierarchy (see Davies & Fouracre 1986; Althoff 2004).
38. When Reynolds (1994: 158) says that the combination of power politics and customary law will explain the relations of subjection that most tenth–eleventh-century landowners found themselves in and that we do not need to bring grants of property on restricted terms or the personal submission of commendation into the issue, she says something that *mutatis mutandis* may apply to many people in the Persian Empire, but not necessarily to those whose property ownership derived from the *caesura* of Persian conquest.
39. Mitigation of that model in monumental royal iconography faces plenty of counter-indicators, starting with the sweeping military successes of the first half-century of the empire's existence and going on to the prominence of the horseman in non-royal funerary iconography and the presence of various armed figures on seals and coins. Fighting skills are part of the *curriculum vitae* of the elite Persian—witness Darius' tomb inscription (DNb §2g) or Herodotus' assessment of the value put on bravery and of the content of Persian education (1.136)—but can we be sure that elite Persians felt set apart primarily on that ground?

7

Cyrus and the Medes

Matt Waters

Analyses of the problems associated with the rise of Cyrus the Great and the Persian Empire are seldom original, but developments in scholarship herald continued reassessment of these problems. The determination of the scope and organization of the Median Empire is an important goal in this context for a number of reasons, not least of which is the determination of the course and extent of Cyrus the Great's early conquests. Any such undertaking requires looking both forwards and backwards from Cyrus, a historiographic necessity in light of the paucity of contemporaneous sources relevant to Cyrus' rise.

A 2001 colloquium on the place of Media in the succession of empires from Assyria to Persia resulted in the publication of the volume *Continuity of Empire(?): Assyria, Media, Persia*. The editors of the proceedings inserted the question mark plus parentheses in order to highlight a "more conciliatory" (p. viii) approach to the title, as reflective of the open state of many of the questions pursued at the conference, and thus in the published proceedings, about the Medes and Media. The overall impression one gets from reading this volume is that modern scholarship is engaged in a concerted deconstruction of the "Median Empire"—at least as traditionally defined, that is stretching from the Halys river in Anatolia through northern Mesopotamia and Iran to points eastwards, perhaps as far as Bactria. This deconstruction has resulted in a modified picture of the Medes as a loosely connected federation of tribes capable of short-term, devastating effectiveness (e.g. the overthrow of the Assyrian Empire) but as an entity with neither the structure nor the cohesion to maintain an empire in the sense of a bureaucratic, centralized, supra-regional entity.

Assyrian and Babylonian sources make a compelling case: as long as Assyrian sources pertain there is no sense of a unified Median entity. These sources offer a clear picture up to *c.* 650. There is a gap in quantity and quality of Assyrian sources for the subsequent period, not just about the Medes, but in the year 615 the Medes reappear in Babylonian sources as a major element in the overthrow of the Assyrian Empire. The Babylonian evidence also compels a reconsideration of Median reach westwards both into northern Mesopotamia and into eastern Anatolia (see Lanfranchi, Roaf & Rollinger 2003).

Such a deconstruction is by no means a unanimous view of the Medes. Although archaeological evidence supports many of the judgements based on textual sources (at least for the period up to *c*.650), there remains enough uncertainty for the period after 650 to temper negative judgements (Gopnik 2003; Kroll 2003; Roaf 2003; Sarraf 2003; Stronach 2003*b*). Consideration of the Medes as a confederation or coalition (e.g. the Mesopotamian *Umman-manda*, a term that in itself is problematic in interpretation) rather than a "traditional" empire seems well justified, but such consideration does not necessarily call for a devaluation of their importance in the Near Eastern tradition.[1] Most would argue that the Medes ought to be of central focus in the period before (and during) the rise of the Persian Empire, even if one should look elsewhere for continuity of specific trappings of an imperial organization.

Eastern Iran remains in many ways a historical cipher during this period, and that is only slowly changing.[2] There are two main problems from a historian's view. The archaeological evidence from this broad area is difficult to incorporate into a historical narrative, a problem that is compounded by its complement: the fact that we have few textual sources to supplement the archaeological evidence. The written sources for the Medes stem from points westward, mainly Mesopotamian and Greek and, after the Medes' fall, from the Persians to the south.[3]

Cyrus the Great appears in an inscription of the Babylonian king Nabonidus (r. 556–539 BC). Nabonidus describes a dream regarding the imminent threat of the Medes, who in this text are given the more generic, pejorative label *Umman-manda*, which is usually translated "horde" or the like (see n. 1). The dream assures Nabonidus that these Medes will cease to be a threat, as Cyrus, king of Anshan, will destroy their power in the third year, which is usually understood to mean 553. The Nabonidus Chronicle (ii 1–4) indicates that in the year 550/549 Cyrus defeated Ishtumegu, the Astyages of classical sources, and took Ecbatana. The dates of these two texts are not easily reconciled, though there has been no shortage of attempts.[4] These references serve as the basis of our knowledge of Cyrus' defeat of the Medes. Greek sources preserve much more expansive traditions, including some that emphasize Median treachery as a key component in Cyrus' victory.[5] The Nabonidus Chronicle also refers to the army's subversion of Astyages, but it does not preserve a developed tale such as that in Herodotus (I.108–129) about Harpagus.

The problems of a Median–Babylonian or Persian–Babylonian alliance (or in the latter case an understanding that kept Babylon out of the struggle, see Beaulieu 1989: 109) are another issue, but one whose ramifications are beyond the scope of this paper. Suffice it to note here that references to the "city of the Medes", sometimes interpreted to reflect a treaty between Nabonidus and Astyages, confuse the issue. The reading "city of the Medes" appears to be a red herring. Schaudig's edition of the text, based on two exemplars, reveals an alteration of the determinatives KUR (text 1 i 42), partially restored, and URU (text 2 i 49) before *ma-da-a-a* (i.e. the Medes). This alteration signals scribal inconsistency rather than historical significance, so the specific attribution in modern scholarship to the "city of the Medes" should be set aside.[6] The significance of Media mentioned in this passage is another matter, though it may simply be formulaic.[7]

Cyrus' importance in the Ancient Near Eastern traditions reverberated in the Greek.[8] It is obvious to anyone who has given even a cursory look into the surviving traditions about Cyrus that we are primarily reliant upon the Greeks for our information. That fact in itself is a necessary, if superfluous, starting point and must motivate any attempt to discern the progression of Cyrus' conquests. The Near Eastern tradition, in Cyrus' inscriptions or otherwise, preserves no indication of his youth and upbringing, but the import of Cyrus in history, specifically as the founder of the greatest empire to date and one that had enormous and lasting significance upon classical Greece, made his career one of great interest to the early Greek historians. Of course, these histories are of varying reliability and were themselves primarily reliant upon oral traditions. These sources have been shown, or must often be assumed, to reflect anachronistic projections backwards from the Persian Empire at its height or well-established literary motifs. The problems involved with the historical implication of these legends, as well as their origins and dissemination, are legion.

Cyrus' defeat of the Medes in the classical traditions is inextricably linked with the legends of Cyrus' birth and upbringing. There is no shortage of scholarly treatments dealing with them individually or thematically, and even in the classical sources themselves there is a great deal of variation. The birth of Cyrus is clearly in the mode of the so-called Sargon Legend—exposure of the infant, humble upbringing and eventual dominion—but particulars of his parentage show surprising disparities (see Lewis 1980: especially chs 5–7 for analysis of the type; also Kuhrt 2003). These range from Cyrus as the son of Cambyses and the Median princess Mandane to Cyrus as the son of Atradates the bandit and Argoste the goat-herder.[9] Those Greek versions that identify Cyrus as the son of Cambyses accord (at least in this respect) with Cyrus' own account, in the Cyrus Cylinder and dedicatory bricks from Uruk and Ur, that he was the son of Cambyses.[10]

Most of the Greek versions focus on Cyrus' upbringing at the Median court under Astyages. This for a long time led scholars to believe that the Persians were subject to the Medes, until Cyrus overthrew Astyages. Current scholarship for the most part rejects this approach, and the tendency has been to attribute these classical versions of Cyrus' rise as of Median origin.[11] To put not too fine a point on it, perhaps these traditions should be considered, ultimately, of Persian origin (more specifically, Cyrus' origin), modified within a Median milieu, to rationalize dynastically Cyrus' kingship over the Medes and their incorporation into the Persian Empire. The original propaganda may have undergone many modifications in its journey into the Greek traditions, but it seems a reasonable assumption that Cyrus' generally positive portrayal in these so-called "Median" legends does not by accident parallel those in other cultures and, furthermore, that Cyrus and his agents facilitated them to justify the transition to Cyrus' rule. This application of propaganda was not new and, for that matter, is not far removed from Darius I's creation of an Achaemenid dynasty linking himself to Cyrus' lineage, in order to justify his reign in turn.

The Near Eastern traditions, and by extension the Greek, are unsurprisingly slanted toward the victor's perspective, whereby Cyrus is portrayed as the favoured of the gods—of Marduk in Babylonia and of Yahweh in Judah—and the restorer of their temples and prerogatives. In both the Cyrus Cylinder and the so-called Verse Account of Nabonidus, both inscriptions commissioned by Cyrus, the impiety and neglect of Nabonidus are stressed in contrast to the rectitude and probity of Cyrus.[12] In the biblical accounts of Second Isaiah and Ezra, for example, Cyrus is a heroic, divinely favoured figure, the one who released the Jews from captivity and facilitated the rebuilding of the Temple (e.g. Yamauchi 1990: 89–92; Briant 2002a: 46–48, 884–885). The Greek tradition typically views Cyrus as an ideal ruler, a father figure, typified by Xenophon's *Cyropaedia*. Of course, Cyrus' rise endured creative licence to fit particular perspectives and aims. The legends of Cyrus in Media may be considered manifestations of a general propaganda pattern, one initiated by Cyrus.

That Cyrus' victory over Astyages marked a watershed in the history of the Ancient Near East is beyond doubt, but its particulars and its immediate ramifications one is hard-pressed to track. The Nabonidus Chronicle alludes to the victory over Astyages, an expedition against an uncertain region (apparently Urartu) in 547, and the conquest of Babylon in 539. The broken reference in the chronicle for 547 is no longer read as an allusion to Cyrus' campaign against the Lydians, but this campaign is still dated in the 540s (see Briant 2002a: 33–36, 882; Rollinger 2003: 315, n. 128; 2005a; 2008).[13] Details about Cyrus' activity before the conquest of Media and after that of Babylon, as well as a number of other unaccounted-for years during his reign, are lacking. According to Ctesias, Cyrus' victory over Astyages (and marriage to the latter's daughter Amytis) soon brought Cyrus the submission of the Hyrcanians, Parthians, Scythians and Bactrians.[14] This report, if it has any basis in historical reality, is significant both for Cyrus' rise and also for the configuration of a "Median Empire" in the mid-sixth century.

As for Cyrus' rise, the resources and manpower of north-eastern Iran would, of course, have greatly augmented Cyrus' military capabilities. Whether Cyrus' conquests were all part of a master strategy or not are unknown, but his rapid rise strikes most modern historians as no accident. It was not simply a response to external stimuli and the aptitude to take advantage of good fortune, though perhaps an element of that may be allowed.[15] Herodotus (I.153) indicates that Cyrus entrusted further campaigning in Anatolia (against the Ionians in particular) to subordinates, while he planned to handle Babylonia, the Scythians and Bactrians, and Egypt. Whether this conflicts with Ctesias' account is open to debate. Since we lack definitive complementary documentation, we simply cannot at present date (or even confirm) these campaigns against the Scythians and Bactrians. But there is nothing intrinsically problematic with this account, so historians' ingenuity—or folly—remains unfettered. Herodotus and Ctesias need not be at loggerheads here. One might argue, for example, that the initial submission of the Bactrians and Scythians was short-lived, and Cyrus had to campaign there in person to deal with subsequent problems.[16]

As for the configuration of a "Median Empire", Ctesias presupposes a close relationship between the Medes and north-eastern Iran (note Vogelsang 1992: 212–215, 303, ch. 7). Based on this alone, it may seem an arbitrary assumption that Median authority, even if one does not wish to use the loaded term "empire", extended some way eastwards beyond the north-central Zagros. That the Medes, as a military assemblage, encompassed large tracts of north-eastern Iran—reflected, for example, by the use of *Umman-manda* in Babylonian texts—is a reasonable working hypothesis (Briant 1984b: ch. 4; Vogelsang

1992: 58–68; Briant 2002*a*: 76, 892–893, 1026–1027; also n. 3 above). In the Assyrian period, we cannot with any confidence track a significant Median reach westwards. After the fall of Assyria it becomes a more open question (cf. Rollinger 2003 and Tuplin 2004*b*). The Medes' sway to the east is likewise uncertain, but the epiphenomenon seems likely. However, even if the postulate is accepted, there is no lack of difficulties. Delineation is one not insignificant problem.

Many eastern areas that appear as parts of the empire in Darius' Bisitun Inscription find little or no mention in the sources relevant to the political history of the preceding fifty years, for example, Aria, Drangiana and Arachosia, among others. That reticence may mean nothing, but it remains a question of no small import how and when these areas were incorporated, and through what means. Near Eastern textual sources are silent on this, however, and the Greek sources are even more meagre than for other matters of this period.

To complete this vicious circle a return to the related problem of how Cyrus positioned himself to overcome the Medes is in order. This problem is a manifestation of the question how and when Cyrus incorporated eastern and southern Iran, even if historically the two did not proceed in a linear manner. Cyrus' rapid rise must have an explanation very early in his reign, perhaps even in that of his predecessors. If Herodotus is correct in naming Cyrus' wife Cassandane an Achaemenid—this marriage tradition is indirectly corroborated by the Nabonidus Chronicle—then we have a window into one early Persian dynastic marriage. Consequently, there is some ground for further speculation into its political ramifications, as I have maintained elsewhere (Waters 2004). Cyrus' rise is more comprehensible if the south and east, or at least parts thereof, were incorporated earlier rather than later, that is before 550 rather than in the 540s or, even less likely, after the conquest of Babylon. The Nabonidus Chronicle (col. iii, l. 16) and the Dynastic Prophecy (col. ii 17–21) indicate that Cyrus took Nabonidus alive. Berossus noted (*FGH* 680 F10a) that the defeated Nabonidus was given Carmania by Cyrus.[17] This is not to assert that subsequent difficulties (e.g. as intimated by Herodotus I.153 and I.177) or additional conquests (e.g. the Massagetae) were not an issue. That Darius' Achaemenids had an eastern Iranian orientation (reflected in personal names as well as the emphasis in royal inscriptions on Ahura-Mazda and, to a lesser extent, on "Aryan" stock) is a piece of the puzzle (Waters 2004: 97–99; cf. Vogelsang 1992: 1–19, 214–218, and *passim*).[18]

With the dearth of information about the military and political activity (beyond Egypt) of Cambyses, it is only the relative onslaught of documentation during Darius' reign, mainly represented by the Bisitun Inscription, which sheds further light on this issue. Darius names a number of noble Persians who aided him in his seizure of power (DB §68). These or their fathers—along with similar notables, both Iranian and Elamite—would certainly have been prominent under Cyrus and Cambyses. The Achaemenids are one group for which we can track at least some of the names via the Greek tradition.

The Medes played a prominent role as rebels against Darius (DB §24–34).[19] The portrayal of rebellions in Media (under Fravartiš/Phraortes), Armenia (no leader specified—Vogelsang 1986; Rollinger 2005*b*: 24–26) and Sagartia (under Çiçantakhma) are grouped together in the same section. Both Fravartiš and Çiçantakhma claimed to have been of the family of Cyaxeres, the Mede who overthrew the power of Assyria. Cyaxeres understandably held a prominent place in the tradition, and it may be assumed (even if impossible to validate beyond this type of circumstantial argument) that his legacy outshone any of the other Median rulers, thus the rebels' identification with his family.[20] How much one may extrapolate from the arrangement of Darius' account about the breadth of Median sway is an open question.[21] However, while reading DB §24–34 to reconstruct a Media that under Astyages encompassed Media, Armenia and Sagartia seems reasonable enough,[22] the Bisitun Inscription differentiates eastern regions that many would postulate as having been under Median authority (e.g. Parthia), based on extrapolation from Ctesias and other classical sources.[23] It is difficult to reconcile these varying strands of evidence, even in a speculative enterprise.

The support of Vivana and Dadarshi, the satraps of Arachosia and Bactria, respectively, was a crucial component to Darius' success (see Briant 2002a: 64, 82, 121).[24] Other individuals, Persians and Medes, beyond the six co-conspirators listed in DB §68, also are named explicitly. As for the Medes, Darius' pronouncement is curious: "neither Persian nor Mede nor anyone of our family" (DB §13) would act against Bardiya/Smerdis. Why bother to include the Medes, even in a (presumably) rhetorical statement? One individual, Taxmaspada (DB §33), identified as a Mede, played an important role in support of Darius. The Medes appear to have been a critical factor in the formation and organization of the empire under Cyrus, and this persisted with his successors; as Pierre Briant has noted, "the Medes were apparently the only conquered peoples who acquired positions of high rank" (Briant 2002a: 81).[25] That the Medes had a special place in governing the empire is no revelation, but the rationale for this relationship is elusive.

The Greek conception of "Medism" also warrants mention in this context, though its particulars and their problems range far afield of this paper. Simply, the Greek use of the term "Mede/-ian" to qualify the Persians and the Persian Empire clearly has some historical significance, even if it is unclear what that may be (see Graf 1984; Tuplin 1994; Briant 2002a: 25–27). This phenomenon in the Greek world must have had some basis, unless one is prepared to assume that it was a literary device. That Greek traditions, again with acknowledgement to many variations, placed such emphasis on Cyrus' descent from or upbringing in the Median royal house, is significant (as discussed above). The Medes were a force with which to be reckoned, and their incorporation into Cyrus' growing power made the Persians that much more of a force, even if at a generic level this entity was still manifestly to the Greeks the "Mede". Do the Greek traditions about Cyrus' Median upbringing and descent refract facets of a historical reality or of Cyrus' propaganda? The latter should be considered a distinct possibility.

As typical of a broad, historical sweep, other problems arise. One contentious one lies in the revival of the date of Zoroaster to the late seventh–early sixth centuries, as per the traditional date of Zoroaster in the ancient and medieval tradition. This issue was divorced from the problems of Cyrus' rise when scholarly consensus during the 1980s and 1990s tended to date Zoroaster to the turn of the millennium or even earlier. A return by some scholars to the traditional date, however, lends a renewed, old urgency to the debate. The so-called "traditional date" (*c.*600) for Zoroaster is extremely problematic.[26] Darius' wholesale invocation of

Ahura-Mazda in itself is enough to demonstrate that he and his successors were adherents of a Mazdaean belief system, whether this was relatively new or not. It certainly seems new in western Iran at that time, but that is simply because it cannot be clearly tracked before Darius.[27] The correspondence of names in Darius' family to those illustrious in Avestan tradition—most prominently the name of Vishtaspa—places Darius' family in a Mazdaean setting.

Whether Cyrus' marriage to Cassandane may be taken as a manifestation of a political alliance with the Achaemenid clan is moot, but such an interpretation—a hypothetical and provisional one—allows some insight into the dynamics between early Persian families and, by extension, the backdrop to Cyrus' ability to overthrow the Medes: an empire, a confederation, an ill-organized and ill-mannered horde, or however one wishes to label it. Whatever the structure of their state (using the term very loosely), the Medes loomed large in the subsequent historiographic tradition. Cyrus' conquest of them had lasting repercussions for world history, and it is important to remember that this conquest did not occur in a vacuum.

Acknowledgements

This is a modified and extended version of a presentation given on 30th September 2005, at the World of Achaemenid Persia Conference. I would like to express my gratitude and appreciation to the conference organizers, to Mr Farhad Hakimzadeh in particular and the Iran Heritage Foundation, as well as to the University of Wisconsin–Eau Claire, for travel support. Special thanks are also due to the American Council of Learned Societies for research support.

Notes

1. On the *Umman-manda*, see Komoroczy (1977), Lanfranchi (2003), Reade (2003: 153) and Rollinger (2003: 295, n. 30); cf. Zawadzki (1988). Note also Vogelsang (1992: 215), Tuplin 2004*b*: 232–233, 242–243), and n. 21 below. For the use of the plural "kings" in biblical passages to describe the Medes, see Liverani (2003: 8–9).
2. Note the important study of Vogelsang (1992), with references, as well as Vogelsang (1998); see also Briant (2001: 69–75, 162–165) for an overview of more recent work.
3. There are no extant written sources from the Medes themselves. On the problems with the (reconstructed) Median language, see Schmitt (2003), and compare Briant (2002*a*: 24–25, 879) and Lecoq (1997).
4. For Nabonidus' inscription, see Schaudig 2001: 417, 436–437 (col. i, l. 27) and Beaulieu 1989: 108 (col. i, l. 29). For the Chronicle, see Glassner 2004: 234–235. If one account is to be favoured over the other with regard to chronology, the Chronicle generally takes precedence, since this text is viewed as more reliable than royal inscriptions. See Briant (2002*a*: 31–33, 881) for a discussion and references.
5. Consistency in the classical tradition is a chimera, as a number of different versions persisted in Herodotus, Ctesias, Xenophon and their successors (e.g. Herodotus I.95 claimed knowledge of three other stories beyond the one he relates); see Jacobs (1996: 85–90) and Briant (2002*a*: 14–16).
6. Compare, for example, Briant 2002*a*: 883–884; Jursa 2003*b*: 169, n. 2; Rollinger 2003: 303, n. 69; and Tuplin 2004*b*: 235. For the text, Schaudig 2001: 490, 497, n. 714, cf. also pp. 231–232. KUR is the determinative used in Akkadian cuneiform before the name of countries and URU that used before the names of cities.
7. Consider Briant's query on this line: "Could it not simply be that for a Babylonian (as for a Greek or an Egyptian) the generic ethnic term *Mede* also included the Persians?" (Briant 2002*a*: 100). The Nabopolassar and the Fall of Assyria Chronicle refers to a treaty between Cyaxeres and Nabopolassar (l. 29; cf. Glassner 2004: 220–221), but there is no information on how long this lasted; cf. Kuhrt 1988*b*: 122.
8. Echoes of the Achaemenids in Iranian tradition are difficult to track. See, for example, Nöldeke 1930: 4–10, 16–22; Christensen 1936: esp. ch. 4; Knauth 1975; Yarshater 1983: 366–367; Gnoli 1989: ch. 3; Shahbazi 1990; Tuplin 1997.

9. Hdt. I.107–130 and Nicholas of Damascus FGH 90 F 66, via Ctesias. For Ctesias' version, and discussion of the significance of its aspersions on Cyrus' parentage (i.e. as a reflection of a partisan of Artaxerxes II against Cyrus the Younger) see Lenfant 2004: lvii–lx, 93–99 for the text.
10. Cyrus Cylinder, l. 21. For text and translation, see Schaudig 2001: 550–556 and Pritchard ed. 1969: 315–316. Near Eastern texts leave no indication of Cyrus' mother.
11. For a discussion, see Briant (2002a: 23–24, 879); with regard to the "Median origin" of this tradition, see Briant (1984a: 74–75) and Brosius (1996: 42–43). Note also the trenchant analysis by Tuplin on these issues (1994: 251–256).
12. For the cylinder, see above n. 10. For the Verse Account of Nabonidus, see Smith (1924: 27–97) and Schaudig (2001: 563–578). For a discussion and references, see Briant (2002a: 40–44, 883–884).
13. Rollinger follows Oelsner's collation of col. ii, l. 16: ^{KUR}⌈Ú⌉-[raš-ṭu]—reading "U[rartu]" at the broken spot of the chronicle. There are other possibilities for a toponym beginning -Ú- (see Parpola 1970: 362–378), but "Urartu" best fits the context. Cyrus' campaign in this region may have precipitated his clash with Lydia.
14. Lenfant (2004: 108–109 [text], lxi [discussion] with notes); see also Briant (1984b: ch. 3) and Vogelsang (1992: 210f.). Ctesias §8 (Lenfant 2004: 112–113) also relays that Spitakes and Megabernes, the sons of Amytis and her first husband Spitamas, were made satraps of the Derbikes and Barcaeans respectively, a version that also implies Median influence on the Cyrus saga (Briant 2002a: 893), complicated as this may be. Ctesias' account of the (initial) voluntary submission of these regions parallels that of the Cyrus Cylinder's account of the submission of the western (Trans-Jordan) regions of the Neo-Babylonian Empire after Cyrus took Babylon (ll. 28–30); Schaudig (2001: 553, 556); see Briant (1984b: 36).
15. Herodotus' discussion of the Persian tribes (I.125), and the prominent place of the Pasaragadae (within which, according to Herodotus, the Achaemenid clan was foremost) are also relevant in this equation; see Briant (2002a: 18–19, 27–28, 85).
16. Compare Briant (2002a: 38–39, 883) and Francfort (1988: 170–171).
17. These sources are subject to the usual qualifications. For the Nabonidus Chronicle, see Glassner (2004: 236–237) and for the Dynastic Prophecy, see Grayson (1975: 32–33). For Berossus, see Verbrugghe & Wickersham (1996: 61), also Beaulieu (1989: 231). Note also Diodorus' notice (XVII 81) of Cyrus' receiving aid from the Aria(m)spai (alluded to also in Arrian, Anab. III.27.4–5 and IV.6.6). Of course, the chronology of these incidents described by Diodorus, if historical, is uncertain. Berossus' notice about Carmania implies only that that region was under Cyrus' control before his conquest of Babylon. See also Mallowan (1970: 8–9), Cook (1983: 29–30) and Briant (2002a: 34–40, 883).
18. Vogelsang's (1992) north–south divide in ancient Iran (see esp. 306–308) offers a useful guide to interpreting many of these historical problems. At the risk of over-simplification of Vogelsang's thesis, one might hypothesize a "Median-Scythic" north and a "Persian-Elamite" (a label Vogelsang does not use) south, with Achaemenid support of Cyrus (e.g. by way of his marriage to Cassandane) as one component that enabled Cyrus' early expansion. In this sense the term "Achaemenids" is applied somewhat anachronistically and in a broader clan perspective than Darius' dynastic usage.
19. Gaumata the magus is explicitly identified as a Mede in the Akkadian version of DB §10; see discussion and references at Briant (2002a: 100, 895–896).
20. Regardless of Astyages' place in the Median tradition, it is not surprising that a Median rebel under Darius avoided identification with the Median king defeated by Cyrus.
21. Note Rollinger 2005b: 25–27, esp. p. 27. Rollinger's emphasis on a Median confederation rather than an empire is generally compelling. This, however, does not necessarily mean that the Medes were incapable of long-range planning or strategic goals.
22. That section ends with Darius' typical summation: "This is what has been done by me in [x]," with the inclusion of the particular area; in this case notably only "Media" is named. See Vogelsang (1992: 124).
23. Note Hdt. I.134 about the Medes' hierarchy of rule: they ruled their immediate neighbours, who in turn ruled their neighbours (etc.): see Vogelsang (1992: 177).
24. Darius' father Hystaspes is also assumed to have been a satrap based on Darius' account (DB §35–36), although his exact title is not given. It is not demonstrable that the satraps Vivana and Dadarshi held their posts before Darius.

25. On the placement of Media in the Achaemenid satrapy lists and in the sculptural programme at Persepolis, see Vogelsang (1986: 131–135; 1992: 110–112, 124–125, 174–177); Briant (2002a: 172–180, 909–910); Tuplin (1994); and Rollinger (2005b).

26. For a recent reassertion of the traditional date of Zoroaster, see Gnoli (2000) with references, and note the reviews of this work by Kellens (2001) and Shahbazi (2002); note also de Jong (1997: ch. 2).

27. For a general overview, see Briant (2002a: 93–96, 894–895).

Part 2

Religion

8

The Achaemenian Practice of Primary Burial: An Argument against Their Zoroastrianism? Or a Testimony of Their Religious Tolerance?

Oric Basirov

Introduction

Many basic elements of the funerary practices in pre-Islamic Persia are often more readily perceived by starting from the wrong end. Indulging, therefore, in a 1,000-year anachronism, I would like to highlight an isolated and little-known report from a highly hostile Christian source, which goes a long way to demonstrate that the funerary practices of the ancient Iranian imperial dynasties, even those of the avowedly Zoroastrian Sasanians, do not present a solid basis for determining their faith.

The account of the "Martyrdom of Jacque" in the Acts of Christian Martyrs states that, "Yazdgird I [AD 399–420] after resuming the persecution of the Christians, suffered a lonely death" and (presumably as a divine retribution) "his body was not placed in a tomb" (Bedjan 1894: 189–200). This story, although probably apocryphal like many other examples of Christian anti-Zoroastrian propaganda, seems nonetheless to take it for granted that Yazdgird's body, under normal circumstances and contrary to the Zoroastrian funerary laws, would have been buried in a tomb and not exposed to the elements as these laws emphatically decree. It is also noteworthy that a highly partisan source such as the Acts of Martyrs, which habitually vilifies the Zoroastrian cult of exposure, not only excludes the Zoroastrian monarchs from that tradition, but also comments on royal burial as though such a forbidden practice was customary and common knowledge.

Several Iranian sources, such as Hamzah-i Isfahāni (*Tārīkh-i Payāmbarān va Shāhān* 44, n. 5; 52–53, 57; see also *Mujmil at-Twārīkh* 463–464), Tabari ([trans. 1983]: 634, 779) and especially Firdausi (*Shāhnāma*, [Persian refs. in round brackets, English refs. in square brackets]: Yazdegird I (IV.1823) [VI.393]; Cabades I (IV.2001) [VII.210]; Chosroes I (V.2216) [VIII. 65–6]; Prince Nūshzād (V.2047–8) [VII.275–6]; Bahrām-i Chūbīn (V.2443) [VIII.343]; Chosroes II and his empress, Shīrīn (V.2541) [IX.41–2]; Yazdegird III (V.2590) [IX.110]) have also recounted the death scenes of the Sasanian emperors, and the manner in which the royal remains were disposed of. This usually meant placing the embalmed body in a mausoleum rather than consigning the excarnated bones to an ossuary. The unknown author of the *Mujmil at-Tawārīkh* (a work based predominantly on the writings of Hamzah) lists 27 monarchs, giving in some cases a brief description of their places of burial, which are still archaeologically unattested. Firdausi describes the death scenes of virtually all Sasanian emperors together with many members of the royal family and court dignitaries, and gives detailed accounts of the embalming[1] and interment of four emperors, one empress, an apostate prince and a usurping general.

Indeed, this apparent exemption from the funerary laws seems to have been a royal privilege shared by at least three dynasties. Archaeological evidence demonstrates that primary burial was traditionally practised by the Achaemenians, and two classical sources suggest that Parthian emperors also followed this ritual (Dio Cassius, LXXIX.i.2; Isidore of Charax, xii: 9). This apparent royal profanity, committed by so many supposedly Zoroastrian kings, invites further investigation of the funerary practices of the time.

Law versus tradition

It is generally agreed that Zoroastrianism introduced to western Iran a mandatory funerary ritual, which involved the initial exposure of the body and the secondary disposal of the bones. However, long after the advent of the eastern faith, a significant number of western Iranians, especially their imperial dynasties, apparently continued with their traditional Scythian practice of embalmment followed by primary burial. This is evidenced, *inter alia*, by the Achaemenian monumental mausolea, which are generally identified as tombs rather than ossuaries.

Archaeological evidence, moreover, highlights the multiplicity and the eclectic nature of Persian funerary practices, rather than their adherence to a specific set of religious laws. It shows that western Iranians, whether Zoroastrian or pagan, consistently adopted several funerary customs (except cremation) from their conquered nations in the Ancient Near East. This is shown by the many diverse forms of primary burial, attested in western Iran throughout the Bronze and Iron Ages and long after the arrival of the new faith. These include a large number of fully articulated skeletal remains buried either in simple graves or in coffins. Multiple burials in both cases are by no means unusual. Coffins are either buried in the earth or neatly arranged in large subterranean vaults. Virtually all these coffins are made of terracotta and come in different shapes, sizes and decorations, and appear to have been used in a variety of ways.[2] Burials almost invariably produce grave goods of all descriptions, which occasionally include datable coins placed in the mouth, palms or on the eyelids of the corpse. Most excavations in the Iranian world have also yielded large cemeteries from the Achaemenian, Parthian and even the Sasanian periods (Schmidt 1957; Azarnoush 1975: 181–182; Balcer 1978: 86–92; Fukai & Matsutani 1977: 42–50, pls 4–6, 9/2, 10–11; 1980: 150–151; Whitehouse 1972: 65, fig. 2; 1974: 23–30, pl. XI/b–d). It is reasonable to assume that some of these burials belonged to the non-Zoroastrian peoples of Iran. This assertion, however, cannot reasonably be made for every tomb and cemetery, as the evidence is too substantial and too widespread (both geographically and chronologically) to justify the exclusion of the majority of the population of Iran from those cemeteries. In fact, such is the weight of the evidence in favour of interment, that without the prior knowledge of the laws of the *Vendidad*, the archaeological material alone could easily lead one to conclude that primary burial was the normal method of disposal of the dead in Zoroastrian Iran during Achaemenian, Parthian and even early Sasanian times.

This apparent toleration of primary burial in a supposedly Zoroastrian society, although hardly noticed by the classical or even the Byzantine writers,[3] seems nonetheless to have baffled generations of more recent scholars. Some have gone as far as calling into question the faith of the Achaemenian emperors. They see the royal tombs as a testimony to their violation of the religious laws, and a conclusive argument against their Zoroastrianism. It is not clear, however, why they seem to have targeted only the Achaemenians, and not the Parthians and Sasanians, as evidently both these dynasties did also practise primary burial. Others have tried, in a variety of ways, to reassess the traditional views on the subject and to reconcile the archaeological evidence for inhumation with the religious laws.

Attempts to rationalize burial on religious grounds

Many attempts have been made to explain or even justify primary burial within the framework of the Iranian religion. Some of these, which tend to Zoroastrianize prehistorical burial sites and grave goods, such as those found in Luristan, are beyond the scope of this paper (Ghirshman 1978: 103–104; Vanden Berghe & Ghirshman in Dandamayev 1989*a*: 21–33, 39). The Achaemenian royal tombs, on the other hand, are seen by some as representing a special concession to the members of the imperial family. As one great scholar puts it, "the person of monarch was too exalted to defile the sacred elements" (Schmidt 1970: 84). This argument cannot be reconciled with the laws of the *Vendidad*. Under an extraordinary funerary law (*Vendidād* V: 27–38, VII: 6–9; cf. Darmesteter 1880), the degree of pollution produced by the corpse is directly related to the deceased's religious and secular rank. A dead priest would therefore produce the most potent pollution, a dead king (warrior) produces only one degree less than a dead priest, and only a dead Ahrimanic creature would produce no pollution at all. This shows that, as far as the funerary laws are concerned, the person of the monarch cannot be so exalted that it does not defile the sacred elements at all.

Another, more significant, attempt to justify the royal tombs in the context of the laws of the *Vendidad*, deals with the fact that the dead were first waxed and sealed off in metal coffins and then placed in elevated sarcophagi or stone cists. It is argued that this type of burial will not cause the corpse to pollute the sacred elements (Vanden Berghe 1968: 29; Boyce 1982: 56–57). Many Zoroastrians in modern Persia bury their dead in sealed metal coffins placed in cement-lined graves using the same argument employed to explain the royal tombs (Boyce 1984*c*: 221). These arguments can again be challenged on straightforward theological grounds. Any form of primary burial seems incompatible with the mandatory ritual of "beholding the sun" (*Vendidād* VII: 45–46), and isolating an embalmed corpse in a sealed coffin would indicate an intention to preserve the polluting flesh in perpetuity.

So far, the most serious, and at least partially successful, attempt at justifying primary burial in the context of the religious laws is the reassessment of a number of "tombs" as ossuaries. The first such attempt, made more than

80 years ago, relied entirely on literary and linguistic evidence provided by Iranian and classical sources (Inostrantsev 1923: 1–28). It argued that royal Sasanian tombs were probably ossuaries, because Muslim Persian writers, being the only source of reference, have described them by the Greco-Arabic word *nāus*; and according to one of these writers, Hamzah-i Isfahāni, this word does not mean a tomb in a Muslim or Christian sense, but a Zoroastrian funerary building. Furthermore, he seems to draw a distinction between a *nāus* and a *daxma*, describing the former as a stone-coffin or an excavated rock-chamber (*Tārīkh-i Payāmbarān va Shāhān*: 44, n. 5; 52–53, 57). This is a clear description of Sasanian rock-carved ossuaries still to be seen in many parts of Persia. It is reasonable to assume, therefore, that Muslim Iranian sources did occasionally use the word *nāus* to describe a Zoroastrian ossuary, whereas a *daxma* seems to have usually meant a place of exposure.

It argued further that the Greek word ταφος, "grave", which refers to the royal Parthian tombs in Nysa and Arbela, may also have been occasionally used by the classical writers to describe Zoroastrian ossuaries, and that the earliest occurrence of this word in an Iranian funerary context is attested in the Greek text of the fifth-century BC Limyra bilingual lapidary inscription, with the corresponding word in the Aramaic text being the Zoroastrian word, *astodana* (Fellows 1841: 209, 468, pl. 36/1; Darmesteter 1888: 508–510; Bivar 1961: 120–121; Hanson 1968: 7, n. 9; Shahbazi 1975: 111–124).

This linguistically based reassessment of tombs as ossuaries was later given a degree of archaeological legitimacy when it was realized that the Limyra monument also possessed two cists, or burial pits, sunken into the respective floors of its two sepulchral chambers, neither large enough to hold a fully stretched integral adult corpse. The use of a cist rather than a *kline* usually indicates an Iranian burial (Cahill 1988: 498), and the small size of the cists would certainly increase the possibility of a Zoroastrian secondary disposal of the bones. The Limyra monument is therefore seen by some as the earliest surviving example of a Zoroastrian monumental ossuary, and this has paved the way for the reappraisal of a number of other funerary buildings as ossuaries, using the dimensions of their burial pits as the key diagnostic factor (Von Gall 1988: 561; Boyce & Grenet 1991: 83, n. 82, 102, n. 185, 105; Boyce 1982: 210–211; Shahbazi 1975: 133–134; 1987: 852). The Achaemenian mausolea in Pars are naturally excluded from this group, as their burial cists are invariably too large to justify their use as ossuaries. A few other important tombs, however, have now been reclassified by some scholars as ossuaries. The most important members of this group, the so-called "Median Rock Tombs", are generally dated to the late Achaemenian or early Hellenistic era (Von Gall 1966: 19–43; 1972: 261–283; 1988: 557–582; Boyce & Grenet 1991: 105, n. 203), and include such well-known monuments in Iraqi Kurdistan as Qizqapan (Edmonds 1934: 183–192, pls 23–27, figs 1–4; von Gall 1988: 557–558, taf. 22–29, abb. 1–7; Boyce & Grenet 1991: 101–105), Kur u Kiç (Edmonds 1934: 190–191, pl. 27, figs 5–7; von Gall 1988: 580–582, taf. 30–31, abb. 8; Boyce & Grenet 1991: 105), and Fakhrika in north-western Iran (Huff 1971: 161–171, taf. 50–53, abb. 1–7; Boyce & Grenet 1991: 82–84).

Certain additional features of these sepulchral buildings appear even more Zoroastrian. The Qizqapan monument, for example, has a relief showing two magi praying on either side of a fire-altar, which is an unquestionably Achaemenian religious iconography. Many also have convenient platforms for exposure. As a result, their reassessment as ossuaries seems to have been based on a preconception that they were built as ossuaries in the narrow sense of a Zoroastrian *astōdān*. There is no irrefutable evidence, however, to link such secondary burial exclusively with exposure. The excarnated bones, which may have once been buried in the cists of these buildings, could also have come from primary burials. In fact the ritual of post-interment, as opposed to post-exposure, secondary burial has always been widely observed by many diverse cultures throughout the world, and is still a common practice in many southern and central European countries.

It is likely that many other so-called tombs were either built with bone receptacles, or converted later to fulfil that purpose. However, only a handful of these tombs so far have been reinterpreted as ossuaries on apparently sound archaeological grounds. The relative scarcity of the surviving monumental ossuaries may be partly explained by the notable leniency of the laws regulating the final destination of the excarnated bones. Such lenient views stand in stark contrast to the seemingly uncompromising nature of the rules directing the disposal of the dead flesh. The rite of exposure is compulsory, and any freedom of choice in respect of that practice is limited to the selection of the actual place of exposure. The treatment of the desiccated bones, on the other hand, is governed by far less rigid laws. Not only a wide range of repositories are allowed for keeping the bones, but the very practice of secondary disposal is voluntary. The observance of this ritual depends on what is practically possible for the mourners in the particular circumstances (*Vendidād* VI.51).

One must also consider the fact that a ritual as avowedly sacrosanct and personal as a funeral, would compromise—if necessary—even the most inflexible funerary edicts. There are many occasions when the laws of some of the most intractable religions have been skilfully adjusted to satisfy the personal preference of the deceased and his/her relatives, or to suit the practical requirements of the time. This probably also happened to the Zoroastrians throughout their long history in western Iran, as many evidently did not feel obliged to observe a uniform funerary rite.

It seems, therefore, that the Achaemenian sepulchral monuments cannot be exclusively reconciled with the Iranian faith. One has to accept the extreme difficulty, if not the impossibility, of explaining primary burial in Zoroastrian Iran only in the context of the funerary laws of the *Vendidād*. There were probably divergent customary perceptions as to the proper method of disposal of the dead. These may have been influenced by ancient traditions inherited from their nomadic, steppe-dwelling ancestors, by special circumstances and personal choice and by a degree of religious tolerance, which did apparently prevail in Achaemenian Persia.

Religious tolerance in the Achaemenian Empire

Early Zoroastrianism in western Iran appears to have possessed a degree of tolerance in funerary matters, which was evidently still present in Achaemenian and Parthian times. The religious tolerance of these two dynasties is of course a well-known and generally accepted fact,[4] and it seems that this forbearance was sometimes demonstrated even by the clergy. This is confirmed by Arrian who, quoting the eyewitness account of Aristobulus, describes the tomb of Cyrus the Great and its permanent retinue of the officiating magi (Arrian 6.29; see also Strabo 15.3.7–8). There is no evidence, however, that the magi practised any ritual other than exposure for their own dead.

Such an attitude not only distinguishes the earlier period of Zoroastrianism from its later stage, but also sets it apart from the rigidly observed funerary laws that, until very recently, we have been familiar with in the West. The universal application of these laws is taken so much for granted, that any deviation is not only seen as a transgression but also often used as an argument to question the adherence to the relevant faith.

It is reasonable to assume that the practice of primary burial was a legacy of the pre-Zoroastrian past, which the new faith was either not yet strong enough, or perhaps still too tolerant of, to suppress. The clergy, faced with the seemingly continuous opposition of many western Iranians to the funerary laws of their eastern faith, may have been unwilling to implement those laws. This clerical dilemma may have lasted until the fall of the Parthian Empire, and even a stricter application of the funerary laws during the Sasanian period does not seem to have completely eradicated the practice of primary burial.

It is noteworthy that the apparent incompatibility of the laws of the *Vendidād* with the surviving sepulchral monuments, such as the Achaemenian royal tombs, does not seem to have been noticed by the many classical writers who have given accounts of Iranian funerary rituals. Their description of exposure and burial is often combined in the same work, sometimes even on the same page, without the writer apparently perceiving any inconsistency in Iranian funerary practices. One explanation for this may be that the early classical writers did not comprehend the concept of a compulsory and uniform funerary ritual; and neither were they familiar with any such requirement being dictated by a religion and upheld by a powerful clergy. It may not be a coincidence that it was not until the late sixth century AD, and during the domination of a particularly hostile Christian power in Constantinople, that the incompatibility of the ancient Iranian tombs with the rite of exposure was first remarked on. Agathias, who made these remarks, went on to state categorically that Medes and other early inhabitants of Persia—presumably, Achaemenians and Parthians—did not practise exposure, which he associated only with the Zoroastrian Sasanians, assuming therefore that those early dynasties were not Zoroastrian (Agathias II.23.9–10). Significantly, it has taken some western scholars more than 1,300 years to revive Agathias' implied argument against the Zoroastrianism of the great Persian dynasty, relying again mainly on the sepulchral monuments of its emperors. However, this also does not seem to present a very solid basis on which to determine the religion of the Achaemenian emperors.

The religion of the Achaemenians

Many scholars, probably the majority, take the Zoroastrianism of the great Persian dynasty as a foregone conclusion. Some would regard any alternative suggestion as unnecessary, and might even go so far as to treat it with suspicion and contempt. Indeed, in the field of Zoroastrian scholarship, one could hardly encounter a more emotive and contentious issue than this, except perhaps for the date of the Great Prophet. For a variety of reasons, these two controversies seem relentlessly linked, and sometimes even act together. Unfortunately, some of the ensuing debates have departed from academic impartiality and, even within those boundaries, are often marred by many bitter and dramatic arguments, with each side utterly unyielding and firmly entrenched. It seems that, short of a groundbreaking new archaeological discovery, there is little hope of adding any significant new evidence to the already well-aired arguments.

Those who question the faith of the emperors seem to rely almost too heavily on the Achaemenian funerary tradition of primary burial. They also point out the extreme paucity, indeed almost total lack, of any reference to Avestan material, including the very name of the prophet himself, in the royal inscriptions. Such an omission could be explained by the fact that the Achaemenian lapidary texts are imperial proclamations and were not meant to record religious literature. Moreover, the Iranian religion, before the Arab conquest, seems to have been identified more with the supreme god, rather than with the Great Prophet. Iranians naturally acknowledged Zoroaster as their prophet, but they were more inclined to refer to themselves as Mazdah-worshippers. Indeed, the term "Zoroastrian" as the sole designation of the religion does not seem to have come into common use until the Islamic period.

The traditionalists have put forward a large volume of defensive arguments, some of which, although still inconclusive and not scientifically irrefutable, seem nonetheless to be more convincing and based on firmer foundations. A selection of these is listed below:

1) Some Avestan royal names, being of eastern Iranian origin and not known in western Iranian nomenclature, are attested either in the Achaemenian inscriptions or in the Greek accounts of that dynasty. These include the name of the father of Darius the Great, which is rendered in its Avestan form of Vištāspa as opposed to Vištāsa, and which would have been used had it existed in Old Persian. Such an unfamiliar Eastern name must have been taken directly from the Avesta.

2) The word "Daiva" in the inscription of Xerxes bears the derogatory meaning of a demon, evidently ascribed to it by Zoroaster, rather than its original meaning of a deity.

3) One could detect a clear Zoroastrian influence in the Old Testament (Boyce 1982: 43–44; Smith 1963; cf. Yasna 44 & Isaiah II 40–48) and early Ionian philosophy (see Boyce 1982: 153–163, citing the works of Thales, Anaximander, Anaximenes, Heraclitus of Ephesus and Pythagoras). It is reasonable to assume that the Achaemenian conquest of the Ancient Near East must have played a significant role in introducing the Iranian religion to the Jews and the Greeks.

4) There seems little doubt about the religion of the later Achaemenians. *Alcibiades*, a work emanating from the Academy, states that Persian princes were taught "the Magian lore of Zoroaster, son of Horomazes" (*Alcibiades* I.122A). Had the early Achaemenians been pagan and later converted to Zoroastrianism, the inquisitive Greek mind would surely not have missed such a dramatic apostasy.

It is tempting to add to these arguments the fact that the Achaemenian funerary tradition, although highly eclectic, consistently avoided cremation even though it was a fairly widespread practice in many conquered territories. In Zoroastrianism, cremation is Ahriman's 13th counter-creation and "a sin for which there is no atonement" (*Vendidād* I.17).

The supreme deity of the Great Kings and the Great Prophet

As both the emperors and the Prophet clearly worshipped the same god, the question must, therefore, be asked: how did the emperors acquire their deity? Their much-invoked Wise Lord was either acquired through the medium of the Prophet, or taken directly from the pre-Zoroastrian pantheon.[5] At the same time, Ahura Mazdah is not only linked unequivocally with the great Iranian faith, but is also virtually inseparable from the Great Prophet himself. Any suggestion, therefore, that Zoroaster's ultimate source of revelation might have been worshipped independently and outside his faith runs in the face of a large and convincing body of opinion to the contrary. Nonetheless, one still has to ask the question: how did Zoroaster come to worship his god? Some believe it was the Prophet himself who both conceived and elevated an abstract concept to the exalted rank of the three great Ahuras (Konow 1937: 217–222). This conclusion is arrived at by comparing the Iranian gods with their Indian counterparts, both of which were once members of a single Indo-Iranian pantheon.

The proper name of the Iranian supreme god is Mazdah, "an ancient Aryan term denoting a mental form highly valued as an important factor in life" (Jackson 1892: 102; Benveniste 1929: 40). The Vedic equivalent of this word is another abstract concept, Medha, meaning insight, wisdom and prudence. It is argued that, as Medha was not deified in India, its Iranian counterpart, Mazdah, should also have remained, under normal circumstances, undeified. It is therefore assumed that it was Zoroaster himself who must have proclaimed Mazdah as a god, and elevated him further to the rank of the highest principle, Ahura Mazdah. Such a doctrine would indeed be in perfect harmony with the Prophet's other abstract deities, the Ameša Spenta (Konow 1937: 221).

A stronger body of opinion, however, believes that Mazdah always existed in the Iranian pantheon, and that the Great Prophet, rather than deifying an abstract concept, may have actually chosen an existing Ahura as the supreme deity of his new religion (Kuiper 1957: 86–97). This theory would have to be supported by the identification of an Indian counterpart for the Iranian Ahura Mazdah. Such a counterpart is seen by some in an existing, obscure and nameless *deus otiosus* known in the Vedic pantheon as Asura, "who is supreme". The nameless Asura is therefore regarded as having originally represented the (presumably) deified Indian Medha and as such, was probably known as Asura Medha. It is believed that such an identification of the two Indo-Iranian Asura/Ahura would be more readily explicable than the alternative deification of the abstract noun Mazdah, by Zoroaster (Thieme 1970: 404–441).

The pre-Zoroastrian existence of Ahura Mazdah in the Iranian pantheon, however, does not automatically suggest that he was ever worshipped independently and outside the Zoroastrian faith in western Iran as, for example, Mithra was. There is hardly any evidence to support this.[6] One is, therefore, inclined to accept that Ahura Mazdah, whether conceived or chosen by the Prophet, is above all a Zoroastrian deity, and when the Achaemenian emperors invoke him repeatedly in their inscriptions, they probably do so as Mazda-worshipping Zoroastrians.

Notes

1. Comparable with Herodotus' accounts of Egyptian and Scythian mummifications.

2. E.g. the adjustable clay coffins from Persepolis: Schmidt 1957: 117–123, figs 23–25, pls 87–88; the inverted clay coffins from Achaemenian-period Babylon (see "Stŭlpgräber", "turned graves"); Reuther 1926: 34, 234–245, taf. 79–84; Baker 1995: 220, pl. 16, figs 5–8.
3. For the sole but significant exception of Agathias, see below.
4. A few cases of desecration of alien tombs and temples by the Achaemenians have been either dismissed as fallacious, or rationalized as means of quelling rebellion (e.g. Boyce 1982: 72 on Herodotus' [III.16 and 38] apparently unjustified denigration of Cambyses; see also Boyce 1982: 173–177 on Xerxes' "Daiva Inscription" [Kent 1953: 151, XPh.35–41]).
5. The frequency of the invocations necessitated the adoption of three simple ideograms in Old Persian, one to render the *nsm*, and two the *gsm* of this word (see Kent 1953: 12, 165).
6. Some versions of his name in eastern Iranian languages (Middle and Modern) are used for the Sun; e.g. *urmasda* in the Khotanese Saka (Konow 1937: 219), *remazd* in Khwarezmian, and *remozd* in Sangleči (Benveniste 1960: 74). All these versions are taken as having originally referred to the Zoroastrian Ahura Mazdah, rather than to a solar deity such as Mithra.

9

Ahura Mazdā the Creator[1]

Albert de Jong

In his formidable book *Family Religion in Babylonia, Syria, and Israel*, Karel van der Toorn has highlighted the enormous impact a monarch can have on the development of religions, by suggesting that many of the characteristic aspects of the religion of ancient Israel can be attributed to the activities of the first king of Israel: Saul. Van der Toorn writes:

> Though the changes occurring under Saul's rule were first of all political, he had a major impact on Israelite religion. As the head of state he promoted his god to the rank of national god; his temple in the capital became the religious centre of the kingdom. Its priesthood, sworn to loyalty, was expected to serve the king's best interests. Priests became the civil servants of a state religion.[2]

Van der Toorn's basic idea is simple and attractive: the rise of Yahweh, the god of Israel, is explained through the importance this god, one among many in the West Semitic world, had as the family god or the personal god of Saul. The rise of Saul was accompanied by the rise of Yahweh and the novelty of the Saulide state was accompanied by the novelty of a state religion.

Scholars who work on the Ancient Near East may object to the details of van der Toorn's suggestions,[3] which I am in no position to check. Many will likely find very little in these suggestions to be excited about: the career of the god Aššur in first-millennium Assyria (and that of Marduk in first-millennium Babylonia) was so obviously connected with royal initiative, that one can easily imagine something similar happening slightly earlier in the provinces.[4]

The strange thing is, of course, that where it concerns scholarship on the religion of the Achaemenid kings, the roles have traditionally been reversed: most of the discussions—and there have been so many—have focused on the impact of the religion on the kings. The impact of the kings, or in a more general sense, of the reality of the empire, on the religion has rarely been the subject of much interest. I believe that the failure to address this problem is one of the chief reasons why the academic discussions on the religion of the Achaemenian kings show this remarkable combination of intense, passionate and often bitter debate with such an obvious lack of historical relevance. Let us not dwell on the question whether or not the kings were Zoroastrians, not even on what I suggested on a different occasion as a relevant question: What do we mean when we say they are or are not?[5] But let us dwell for a moment on one of the other favourite puzzles associated with the subject: the Achaemenian tolerance of other religions.

In and of itself, tolerance is a problematic concept,[6] for it only exists in opposition to oppression, persecution and other kinds of unfriendly behaviour. We have sufficient evidence of these kinds of behaviour in Darius' inscription at Behistūn.[7] At the same time, we have some evidence that the kings did not practise oppression and persecution all the time: that they had, in fact, enough common sense to realize that their empire would be better off if they would leave the various peoples who lived in it to their own affairs, as long as they paid their tribute and did not cause too many problems.[8]

Exactly the same strategies were current, of course, in the multi-ethnic empires that came before the Persians. The Achaemenid Empire in several ways relied on the earlier example of these empires, and the question that needs to be addressed when it comes to intolerance would be: who would have taught the Persians not to tolerate other religions? Where on earth could they have found an example for that? The answer is, of course, that there is no such example anywhere in the ancient world.[9] It seems that preconceived ideas about how Zoroastrians in general would (i.e., should) view non-Zoroastrians have caused so much surprise at the tolerance of the Achaemenian kings. In fact, this type of tolerance, based, it seems, on a sound notion of how to organize an empire, has been used occasionally to cast doubts over the extent of infiltration of Zoroastrian ideas into the Persian Empire.

Had the kings been true Zoroastrians, according to such interpretations, they would have been ruthless persecutors of others, for does not the Avesta teach that those who do not worship Ahura Mazdā worship the *daēvas* and is not the death of *daēva*-worshippers essential for the prosperity of the world?

These are the two assumptions, I believe, that underly the puzzlement over Achaemenian religious tolerance: 1) that Zoroastrianism, of whatever period and whatever region of the world, must be understood on the basis of the Avesta and the Avesta alone; and 2) that the Avesta teaches Zoroastrians to eradicate *daēva*-worship. I shall submit here that both assumptions are wrong. They are wrong because they are incomplete.

The chief advantage of the Avesta as a comparative source for the religious history of Achaemenian Persia is that it is thought to be older than the Old Persian inscriptions. I have no doubt that the Avestan texts are older than the inscriptions. I have doubts, however, concerning the use of these texts.[10] All too frequently, up to the most recent scholarship on these matters, scholars seem to assume that the Avesta is somehow similar to the Bible in Christianity, or the Qur'ān in Islam: that is, a source of guidance and inspiration, of imagery and propaganda; if not a holy book, then at least a holy text. Evidence for this kind of use of texts from the Avesta, however, is extremely late; in spite of the huge chronological gap between the two empires, the parallel with the Sasanian period is instructive enough to warrant a few comparative remarks.

We have, I believe—although many scholars believe the opposite—no reliable evidence at all for the use of the Avesta as a source of iconography or of narrative traditions before the late Sasanian period, that is before the fifth century AD. Not accidentally, I would submit, the attempts at codification of the texts, evident from the creation of the Avestan alphabet, arise at the same time as the first obvious uses of Avestan names and texts for non-religious purposes.

This is actually not limited to the pre-Islamic history of Zoroastrianism. The cognitive role of the Avesta, let us say, the use of the Avesta as a source of wisdom, guidance, stories and quotations, is rarely found among living Zoroastrians, who may cherish the concept of the Avesta (the Avesta as *fact*), its sounds and its performance in ritual. The *Pandnāmag ī Zarduxšt*, a Middle Persian catechism, famously opens with a series of questions every Zoroastrian must be able to answer when he or she has reached the age of 15. These are questions like Who am I? Where did I come from? Were the gods there before me or not? etc.[11] The answers to these questions fortunately follow, for it would be exceptionally difficult for even the most talented priest of the period to find those answers in the Avesta.

As to the second point: yes, the Avesta (and even more so the later Zoroastrian tradition) teaches the believers to despise and combat *daēva*-worshippers. It also describes them: these are wretched creatures, living in the night-time, covering themselves in human excrement and cooking and eating corpses.[12] No Zoroastrian in recorded history has *ever* assumed that his fellow countrymen who happened to worship other gods was one of these devil-worshippers. In the whole range of terms used, in later texts, for non-Zoroastrians, *dēwēsn* is never used for actual people.[13]

So, also in Zoroastrian traditions, one cannot really locate the duty to be intolerant to others. There would, at any rate, be little reason to do this during the reign of the monarchs who left us inscriptions, for the superiority of the Persian religion over the others manifested itself in the existence of the empire: Darius especially, in terms that would strike one almost as literal quotes from Ashurbanipal, often attributes his victories to the fact that he, the king, worshipped Ahuramazda, whereas his opponents did not.[14] The battle had almost been decided beforehand, for who can compete with the excellent qualities of the god of the Persians?

It is this context of praise that also undoubtedly underlies the almost fixed formula with which more than half of all royal inscriptions begin. I have to say "almost fixed" for there are a number of variations in the words. Interestingly, whereas there is a whole library of academic studies on the variations, there is very little on the basic text.[15] It is short, it is almost the first words anyone who wants to learn Old Persian masters and it is, I believe, extremely important. It is known in some recent studies as "the prayer", but I find that a very unhelpful title. These are the words:

> Ahuramazdā is the great god, who has created this earth, who has created that heaven, who has created mankind, who has created happiness for mankind, who has made NN king, one king of many, one lord of many.[16]

As I just mentioned, I think the primary context of this formula is one of praise. The excellent qualities of the god of the Persian kings are illustrated by the two things he had done in history that were of the greatest importance for the king: he had made the world and mankind in it and he had given sovereignty over the world and mankind to the king.

The most remarkable thing about this short text is its ubiquitous appearance in the royal inscriptions. For this, I believe, there are no good parallels from the vast corpus of royal inscriptions from the Ancient Near East. There are many such inscriptions, indeed, that open with a line extolling the greatness of a particular god, but these most often appear in a special context: most of these texts are building inscriptions or inscriptions commemorating the dedication of a statue; most of them are, in that sense, specifically *about* the religion.[17] This is not the case in the Old Persian corpus. In other aspects, the Old Persian royal inscriptions *do* follow Near Eastern examples, most obviously in the self-presentation of the king with the words "I am so-and-so, king of" etc.[18]

There is a need, therefore, to interpret not only the text itself, but also its regular appearance in the inscriptions, and perhaps also its striking absence from the first of these inscriptions, Darius' great inscription at Behistūn. For this last problem, I do not have any satisfactory solution. For the other questions, we should note, first of all, that the position of Ahura Mazdā as the creator of all that is good, which means all that exists, is a crucial part of Zoroastrian theology. If there is a central idea to all varieties of Zoroastrianism we know of, it is this: that every person must know who was behind the world we are in. Ahura Mazdā can be addressed and is addressed frequently as "the creator" (*dādār*), and much energy was invested throughout Zoroastrian history in highlighting this aspect.

A second, perhaps more important, point to make is this: the story of the creation of the world and its final destiny at the end of time, which is a single story that can be seen as the framework of all Zoroastrian theology,[19] is the only real Zoroastrian myth. Zoroastrianism does not really have a very elaborate mythology and Ahura Mazdā's role in the history of the world is rather limited in those texts that discuss the history of the world: he is the only actor in the work of creation, he is very active in the process of revelation, culminating in the final revelation to Zarathustra and the establishment of the religion under Wištāsp, and then he disappears from the narrative, only to reappear as the most important actor in descriptions of what is going to happen at the end of time. So, if the kings wanted to extol his virtues and to enlist his prestige to underline their right to the throne, the work of creation really is the *only* subject they could have chosen. Here we have another important difference with most of the religions of the ancient world, in which there is a much more direct and documented activity of a variety of gods in human history.

The discussion of this particular subject of ancient Zoroastrianism has been muddied by the suggestion of Jean Kellens that Ahura Mazdā was not a creator god at all.[20] This suggestion was based on a characteristically learned and detailed analysis of passages from the Gāthās in which the verb "to create" occurs and it has made quite an impression on a number of scholars. Others, fortunately, have been quick to point out that the whole exercise was futile in being based on a very particular notion of "creation" as *creatio ex nihilo*, which is currently thought to be a Christian philosophical invention of the second century AD.[21]

It is time to come to an end and I would like to end with an outline of the directions future discussions of the religious history of the Achaemenian Empire should, in my opinion, take. These directions can be summed up in two main lines of research, the first of which has already been developed considerably: this first line of research would be a comparative effort to situate the inscriptions and the other data in the context in which they belong, which is the Ancient Near East, in particular the evidence from the Neo-Assyrian, Neo-Babylonian and Neo-Elamite empires or kingdoms. This is indispensable work, for it is all we can do to counter the current trend of writing the history of Iran as something exclusively Iranian.

The second line of research involves much more speculation and will, therefore, cause controversy. As I have already indicated, a textual comparison of the Avesta with the Old Persian inscriptions at present makes little sense. More can be gained, if we try to compare the notions in the inscriptions with what we can reconstruct of the history of Zoroastrian ideas and practices. The obvious problem is that the Achaemenian data are the earliest we have. That fact, in itself, must be significant and before we do anything else, we should try to see how great the impact of the Achaemenian Empire was on the development of Zoroastrianism. Work has been done for this subject, especially with regard to the religious calendar of Zoroastrianism, which is a product of the Achaemenian Empire.[22] I have suggested that the fact that the earliest indications of a type of Zoroastrian theology in Greek literature are perhaps from the fifth and certainly from the fourth centuries BC implies that the Persian *magi* were responsible for this particular synthesis.[23] So to sum up, I think the most important and rewarding strategy of research will be this: ask not what Zoroastrianism did for the king, but ask what the king did for Zoroastrianism.

Notes

1. Since this paper was meant to be programmatic, I have kept it in its rather informal, first-person, version, adding only those references which are indispensable. Some of the points made in this paper are elaborated in De Jong forthcoming *a, b*.
2. Van der Toorn 1996: 267.
3. See, for example, Caquot 1998: 228 ("ambitieuse et très spéculative").
4. See Abusch 1999 (with references) for Marduk; Holloway 2002 for Aššur.
5. De Jong 2005: 88.
6. See, for example, Ahn 2002: 195–196, n. 25.
7. For Achaemenid cruelty and oppression, see now Lincoln 2003.
8. As I have argued in De Jong forthcoming *c*, it is, in fact, extremely unlikely that there was a specific strategy of *religious* tolerance; local life, including religious life, was left to customary law, but religion was not—it seems—singled out (or recognized) as something that stands apart from other aspects of culture.
9. With the possible—and possibly significant— example of the Neo-Assyrian Empire, which was (it must be admitted) much smaller in scope and diversity than that of the Achaemenids. See Holloway 2002: 100–159; 193–197 *et passim*.
10. De Jong 2009.
11. The best translation still is Zaehner 1956: 20–28.
12. This is the well-known image conjured up (on the basis of Pahlavi texts) by Zaehner 1955: 14. The evidence in the Avestan texts is slightly different, as is shown in De Jong forthcoming *d*.
13. The main word used for non-Zoroastrians is *an-ēr*, "non-Iranian".
14. See the text quoted in Kuhrt 1995: 500 (on Ashurbanipal's destruction of an Elamite sanctuary, punishing kings who did not worship Ashurbanipal's gods).
15. But see Herrenschmidt 1977, for the text as *fact* and for the variations.
16. Thus, for example, DNa 1–8; DE 1–11; XPa 1–6; XPb 1–11; A²Hc 1–7; A³Pa 1–8, etc.
17. See the building inscriptions assembled in Hallo 2000: 246–314.
18. DB I.1; DBa 1; DPe 1; XPa 6; A²Sd 1, etc.
19. See the discussion in Shaked 1994: 1–26.
20. Kellens 1989.
21. May 1978.
22. See Boyce 2005 with references.
23. De Jong 2005; in more detail De Jong forthcoming *a*.

10

From Gabled Hut to Rock-Cut Tomb: A Religious and Cultural Break between Cyrus and Darius?*

Bruno Jacobs

The identification of the tomb of Darius I at Naqsh-i Rustam (Fig. 10.1) is confirmed by its inscriptions. The monument is one of four huge and in external appearance essentially identical rock-cut tombs at that place. In the case of the tomb of Cyrus the Great, however, its identity is not as certain. The identification of the Gabr-i Madar-i Sulaiman (or so-called Tomb of the Mother of Solomon) at Pasargadae (Fig. 10.2) with the tomb of this king became particularly popular following Reza Shah's celebration of 2500 years of Iranian monarchy when he honoured Cyrus as his ancestor in front of this very building (Wiesehöfer 1999: 55). However, this identification is far from certain.[1] One immediate problem is that the internal space—it is just 3.11 m x 2.17 m—hardly seems large enough to accommodate the funeral goods reported in surviving sources (Arrian, *Anabasis* VI 29, 5–6; Strabo XV 3, 7).

A description in Strabo, derived from Onesicritus, refers to a ten-storey building in the top floor of which Cyrus was buried (XV 3, 7 [C 730]). This picture is in no way compatible with the Gabr, but could perhaps fit the nearby building known today as the Zendan-i Sulaiman (Fig. 10.3). The most detailed preserved descriptions, however, depend on Aristoboulos. One of these is also transmitted in Strabo, where it is said that the tomb of Cyrus was a πύργος (XV 3, 7). If one translates this as "tower" it again seems to fit better with the Zendan. Moreover Arrian, who provides the other description that goes back to Aristobulus, uses the word τετράγωνος (*Anabasis* VI. 29, 5) and, if this is understood to mean "square", it too points to a building like Zendan-i Sulaiman or Ka'aba-i Zardosht—buildings whose function is, as is well known, still unclear (Sancisi-Weerdenburg 1983*b*: 145–151).[2] However, although according to Curzon the word τετράγωνος is readily used in later Greek for isolated buildings,[3] in Arrian it refers to the substructure of the building in question, and the distinction between sub- and superstructure fits the appearance of the Gabr-i Madar-i Sulaiman better than that of the Zendan. Moreover, the stepped substructure of the Gabr (which measures 13.35 m x 12.30 m) is much closer to being a square than the superstructure, in which there is a clear distinction between narrow faces and longer sides. The mention of a στέγη, a chamber, in

92 THE WORLD OF ACHAEMENID PERSIA

Fig. 10.1 Naqsh-i Rustam: Tomb of Darius I (right) and Tomb III. (Photograph B. Jacobs)

Strabo is also plainly more appropriate to the superstructure of the Gabr than to the Zendan. Finally, the particularly low entrance of the building is something explicitly mentioned in Arrian's description (*Anabasis* VI. 29, 4–11), and in drawing attention to this, Curzon may well have hit upon an unequivocal indication that the well-known gabled hut should indeed be identified as the tomb of Cyrus (Curzon 1892: v. II, 81; cf. von Gall 1979: 271–272).

This type of grave monument was repeated several times. One example is the Takht-i Rustam (Fig. 10.4): only the lowest courses of its ashlar masonry are preserved, but it was certainly meant to be a counterpart to the tomb of Cyrus (Kleiss 1971: 157–162; Stronach 1978: 302–304), and that similarity has led to the suggestion that it was the grave of Cyrus' son Cambyses (Herzfeld 1941: 214, but see Henkelman 2003b: 113, 161). There is also another less pretentious grave of this type in the Buzpar valley, the Gur-i Dokhtar (Stronach 1978: 300–302), but also in this case all speculations about who may have been buried there are arbitrary.[4]

The critical years between the revolt of Gaumata, the death of Cambyses during his Egyptian campaign, and the moment at which Darius I could regard his efforts to consolidate his hold on power as definitely successful, are the most discussed in the whole history of the Achaemenid Empire (see now Tuplin 2005a). Nevertheless there is still no consensus on fundamental issues, such as whether Darius really did away with a usurper when he eliminated Gaumāta or whether his victim was actually

Fig. 10.2 Pasargadae: Gabr-i Madar-i Sulaiman. (Photograph B. Jacobs)

Bardiya, the younger brother of the recently deceased Cambyses.[5] There has been a similar inability to agree on whether Cyrus and Darius were blood relatives or not. It is true that at the moment most historians are probably inclined to reject Darius' representation of the facts and conclude that he did not come from the same family as Cyrus, but the question remains open.

Reflections about continuities and discontinuities between the reigns of these two men are therefore of some interest. In this context Darius' own assertion in §14 of the Bisitun inscription that he had restored the ayadanā, "places of worship", and returned confiscated property is, of course, of little significance. These actions represented a package of measures aimed at restoring the status quo in the context of efforts to return the royal house to its ancestral place,[6] and all such measures were intended to demonstrate continuity "within the dynasty", whether or not it really existed. By contrast, measures that were not part of this programme and actions that were not carried out under the immediate pressure of the events in question deserve more consideration, because they may unintentionally disclose the true state of affairs.

A whole series of facts seems to point in the direction of substantial discontinuity. For example, Pasargadae, the site not far from the old city of Anšan that was turned into the capital during Cyrus' reign, lost its status as an imperial centre under Darius. The title "king of Anshan", used by Cyrus[7] and

Fig. 10.3 Pasargadae: Zendan-i Sulaiman. (Photograph B. Jacobs)

Fig. 10.4 Takht-i Rustam. (Photograph B. Jacobs)

his predecessors, was abandoned by Darius (Waters 2004: 98). In pictorial art, changes in style and subject are plain to see. And many scholars believe a still more radical change can be perceived in the religious sphere. This is because Cyrus appeals to Marduk in the cuneiform text of the so-called "Cyrus cylinder", whereas Darius, by contrast, never tires of stressing that he owes his power to Ahuramazda, a god whom Cyrus shows no sign of having recognized. That strikes many observers as an extremely sharp break in the area of religious belief, one often interpreted as a conversion from a pagan religion to Zoroastrianism (Gershevitch 1964: 16–17; Duchesne-Guillemin 1970: 232–238; Koch 1977: 171–182).

As the funerary sphere is obviously very closely connected with the religious ideas of the deceased and his relatives, one might be inclined to suppose that the change in tomb architecture between Cyrus the Great and Darius I is a sign of this sharp break and permits us to draw conclusions about the actual relations between the two men.

Of course, one could object that in Lycia pillar tombs, house-tombs, sarcophagi and rock-cut tombs were built and used simultaneously and that there is no reason to suppose that this was the result of different religious convictions. What these different Lycian tomb forms *do* signify is, of course, still unclear: is the choice in each case connected with the social position of the owner (Zahle 1983: 142–143), political rank, or the desire for individual distinction (Keen 1995: 221–225)? In the case of Pasargadae and Naqsh-i Rustam, by contrast, all the tombs are royal, and there is no question of the different shapes being markers of divergent social status or rank. The change could, therefore, very well have had deeper significance, especially if Stronach is right to observe that the substructure of the Gabr-i Madar-i Sulaiman is in essence a miniature Elamite ziqqurat. Stronach (1997: 41) refers in this context to Choga Zanbil[8] and thus suggests that Cyrus closely continued Elamite tradition, whereas Darius and his successors behaved differently.⁹

Stronach summarizes the supposed discontinuity thus: "The changes that Darius introduced when he came to the throne were probably far more drastic than has hitherto been realised" (Stronach 1997: 50), and M. Waters (2004: 91) speaks of "a significant break" and reckons that "the full magnitude of this break has yet to be explored".

So does the change from the gable-roofed hut (or at any rate from a free-standing funerary building) to a rock tomb signal a break? We shall investigate this question by analysing the change in conjunction with the other alterations noted above as possible indicators of discontinuity. There is, of course, no *necessary* relation between a break in funerary practice and changes in other fields of religious or even of cultural life in general (Humphreys 1981: 8–9); but such a relation is possible, not to say probable, and appropriate observations in other fields may therefore provide a basis for analogous conclusions in the funerary realm.

If one compares the history of the Assyrian Empire, a change of capital city is no extraordinary process. Seizure of power by another line of the Achaemenid family could be a sufficient explanation. Consider, for example, Sargon's choice of Dur Sharrukin as his new capital: he was a younger son of Tiglath-Pileser III and, because he was not the firstborn, his legitimacy was open to question (Thomas 1993: 465–470). The move of the Urartian king Argishti I from Tuspa to Toprak-Kale has also—rightly or wrongly—been explained by the supposition that he was a usurper (Ayvazian 2005: 198). The abandonment of Pasargadae could also have arisen from a feeling that the old capital had become unlucky. The Assyrian king Sennacherib, for example, abandoned Dur Sharrukin immediately after his father's death in battle (Matthiae 1998: 59–63). Cyrus the Great and his son Cambyses both failed to return alive from their respective last expeditions—Cyrus lost his life in a battle in Dyrbaean territory east of the Caspian Sea, and Cambyses died during his Egyptian campaign, probably from blood poisoning. This may have been sufficient reason to move to a new capital.

Changes in the style and subject matter of pictorial art between Cyrus and Darius are also perhaps significant only at first sight. To demonstrate this, one should recall—briefly and with considerable simplification—a few well-known facts. The art of the Persian court was always eclectic, using existing elements, but creating something unique from them. Thus in the mythological themes decorating the door jambs of gate R and palace S at Pasargadae—all from the time of Cyrus—Assyrian and Elamite iconographic prototypes were combined, but the model for the headgear of the famous winged genius was probably Phoenician, while the relief technique followed Late Babylonian and Greek patterns (Nylander 1970: 137–138; Farkas 1974: 7–10, 83; Boardman 2000: 102–104, 124).

Because of the political crisis that overshadowed his accession to the throne and the first years of his reign, Darius I apparently felt compelled to set a new course in the choice of themes, a fresh start for which the monument at Bisitun is the only exemplar. In terms of style, iconography and subject matter, it is indebted to completely different patterns, iconography and subject matter owing much to an Old Babylonian prototype, whereas its style is essentially Greek and Assyrian (Farkas 1974: 30–37, 84; Root 1979: 194–226 [ignoring the Greek stylistic component]; Boardman 2000: 109–10).

The shift to the "Persepolis style", which took place immediately afterwards, involved another new mixture of elements. But what we find as a result at Persepolis and Susa is both style and subject matter that are closer to Pasargadae R and S than to Bisitun (cf. Farkas 1974: 54–59, 88–116; Boardman 2000: 110–11, 125–26)—an observation that has also been made by Stronach (1997: 43). In both places mythological themes are of great importance,[10] and the image on the south-eastern door of palace S may already present us with an example of the sort of gift-bearers familiar at Persepolis (Stronach 1978: 69–70, fig. 36, pl. 61a). The shift from Bisitun to Persepolis does not indicate a sharp break, and we do not have to assume that the shift from Pasargadae to Bisitun is different in this respect.

As for the presumed change in religious belief between Cyrus and Darius, this is probably just a source problem. In the case of Darius our main evidence comes from the royal residences at Persepolis and Susa and their immediate surroundings, the texts normally being drawn up in three languages, including Old Persian. In these texts the king praises and gives thanks to his personal god Ahuramazda. In the case of Cyrus, by contrast, our most eloquent testimony is the Akkadian-language cylinder text from Babylon (Eilers 1971: 161–66; Lecoq 1997: 181–85; Brosius 2000: 11–12). This belongs entirely in the Babylonian tradition, as indeed is already apparent from the object's barrel shape; and the fact that the cylinder is as a whole clearly embedded in its local environment makes Cyrus' address to Marduk completely understandable. An explicit contrast is actually drawn between Cyrus, who venerates Marduk (l. 27), and his predecessor Nabonidus, who ostensibly did not (l. 17), and we can be certain that Cyrus lost no time in grasping the hands of Marduk in order to gain legitimacy as king of Babylon. Moreover, the gods Bel and Nabu are also mentioned in the text.

By contrast, there is no recorded acknowledgement of Ahuramazda by Cyrus, but the explanation may be that there are no utterances by Cyrus that are at all comparable to those of Darius I. Recognition of Marduk and Bel did not in any case exclude veneration of Ahuramazda, as is shown by the fact that in Babylon Darius also seems to have acknowledged Bel (and perhaps other gods). This emerges from U. Seidl's recent re-examination of fragments belonging to a copy of the Bisitun monument from Babylon (1999a: 299; 1999b: 109), which shows that the accompanying text, so far as it is preserved, used the name Bel where the original at Bisitun had Ahuramazda. Since Darius called himself "king of Babylon" and thus documented his appreciation of that title, one can proceed on the assumption that he too grasped the hands of Marduk to legitimate himself (MacGinnis 1995: nos 19, 31, 43–44, 64, 78–79, 81; cf. Schmitt 1975: 385–90; 1985: 418). Both rulers, Cyrus and Darius, were thus equally persuaded that in a foreign place the local deities were powerful. The identity of the god whom Cyrus worshipped at home is therefore a completely open question, but that it was Ahuramazda as in the case of Darius, is—though certainly not attested—perfectly possible, and this clearly limits the probability of a religious break between the two royal lines.

What then, is the position in this regard in the area of funerary practices? M. Boyce did not detect a break. In her view the solidity of their construction meant that both house-tombs and rock tombs served the purpose of preventing contamination of the elements by the corpses of the deceased (Boyce 1984b: 290). Behind this assertion lay her conviction that the Persian kings were Zoroastrians. But even if we do not dismiss that premise as hypothetical and unprovable, there remains the point that massive construction is an extremely widespread characteristic of royal grave monuments—monuments that are, after all, supposed to last and to make an impression on the observer.

Independently of this objection, we must acknowledge that our interpretation of the data—in this case the divergent forms of graves—is influenced by a deep-rooted conception that life means individuality, death means its end, and a grave monument serves the purpose of compensating for that loss: there is thus always a temptation to ascribe too much value to the grave monument itself as a bastion against transitoriness and a safeguard of individuality (cf. Humphreys 1981). But the fact that all the grave monuments after that of Darius lack inscriptions and are attributed to successive rulers only by circumstantial evidence (cf. Schmidt 1970: 90, 93, 96, 99, 102; Calmeyer 1975: 110–112; Kleiss & Calmeyer 1975: 94–98), while actually remaining anonymous, is an immediate warning against such a view. And, although we cannot provide an explanation for the change from house-tomb to rock-cut tomb, these considerations are a reminder not to divorce tomb form from underlying burial practices or overvalue a change in the former without considering the latter.

What do we actually know about funerary practice in connection with the graves of Cyrus and Darius I? The relevant material is not particularly rich, but there is some archaeological evidence and this can be combined with information to be found in the secondary literature.

According to our sources interment of the body covered with wax, and exposure of the corpse to be stripped of flesh by vultures or dogs, with ensuing burial of the bones, are the most familiar procedures for dealing with the mortal remains of deceased people in the Iranian sphere. The two methods, interment and excarnation, are contrasted one with another by Herodotus and Strabo. Of the two, Herodotus is notable for surrounding what he sees as the obscure rite of corpse exposure with a certain air of mystery. He writes as follows (*History* I. 140):

> There is another practice concerning the burial of the dead, which is not spoken of openly and is something of a mystery: it is that a male Persian is never buried until the body has been torn by a bird or a dog. I know for certain that the Magi have this custom, for they are quite open about it. The Persians in general, however, cover the body with wax and then bury it.

Strabo (XV. 3, 20 [C 735]), on the other hand, puts it more briefly:

> They smear the bodies of the dead with wax before they bury them, though they do not bury the Magi but leave their bodies to be eaten by birds.

The covering with wax mentioned by these ancient authors would have had a sealing or isolating effect. It served the purpose of keeping the appearance of the corpse bearable for as long as it was visible and accessible. By modelling and the use of cosmetics it was possible to improve the look of the deceased, hide injuries and conceal flaws. Traces of greasepaint have been established in *kurgans* belonging to the Saka, but how far such treatment of corpses was commonly practised or reserved for the more privileged social strata remains a matter of speculation, as there is as yet no relevant evidence from excavations in Iran and appropriate investigations have not been set in train.[11] Archaeologically speaking, ancient conservation of a corpse is not easily proven, the more so since the sort of circumstances favourable to the preservation of relevant evidence encountered in the Siberian permafrost have not so far recurred elsewhere. In future excavations the surface upon which the body was laid ought to be scrutinized for traces. To give an example, the presence of pollen might allow one to establish the use of honey. Honey is well suited for conservation, because putrefactive bacteria do not prosper on the sugar solution.

Treatment with wax, of course, only aims at short-term preservation and is very different from embalming (be it with honey or by other means), a process that has in view the long-term conservation of the body. Unfortunately there is, as far as I can see, only one allusion to this practice, and this relates—as is only to be expected—to a king, namely Cyrus the Great and his grave at Pasargadae.

Strabo and, in more detail, Arrian give an account of the magnificent grave goods that were visible inside the tomb chamber. Apart from the *klinē* and the golden sarcophagus, Arrian mentions fabrics and garments in varied colours, swords, necklaces and earrings. All this was still there for Alexander to see when he visited Pasargadae after the conquest of Persis. After his return from the eastern realms of the empire, however, he found the grave looted (Arrian, *Anabasis* VI. 29, 9; Strabo XV 3, 7). All the valuables had been stolen, and the burglars had even tried to remove the sarcophagus. For this purpose they opened the lid and discarded the body of Cyrus. The corpse, the sarcophagus and the lid were the only things that had been left in the tomb.

Alexander entrusted Aristobulus with the restoration of the sepulchre, and also ordered that the body of Cyrus, so far as it was still intact, should be put back into the sarcophagus (Arrian, *Anabasis* VI 29, 10: Καὶ τοῦ μὲν σώματος ὅσαπερ ἔτι σῶα ἦυ). The Greek text says σῶμα ("body"), not ὄστεα ("bones")—a point which had already struck Curzon (1892: 80 Anm. 1.)—and, if it was possible after more than 200 years to speak in these terms, the body must have been in a comparatively good condition. It must, therefore, have been conserved, and that can only mean embalmed. The appropriate measures will have been taken soon after the king's death in battle, while the campaign was still going on.

It may also be possible to glean some more information from the sources about the actual process of burial, although one should remain conscious that the available tradition is of limited reliability. A warning not to overestimate it is provided by the supposed inscription on Cyrus' tomb, which is reported, with variations, in Arrian (*Anabasis* VI 29, 8), Plutarch (*Alexander* 69, 4) and Strabo (XV 3, 7. 8.), but cannot possibly be regarded as historical (Schmitt 1988: 18–25). Nonetheless, if we approach the material with due caution, what we learn is this: the

Fig. 10.5 Naqsh-i Rustam: Tomb of Darius I, the burial places in the central chamber. (After Schmidt 1970: pl. 39 B)

grave robbers tried to steal the sarcophagus as well as the grave goods but had no success because it was too big, although, as Arrian reports (following Aristobulus), parts were dented, and other parts, presumably ornaments, torn off. But if it was impossible to remove it from the grave through the door, it must have been equally impossible to bring it in that way. Hence, the sarcophagus must have been already in position before the burial and probably also before the completion of the building, and that implies that the body of the ruler was transported to the grave in some other receptacle, presumably a wooden sarcophagus.

The procedure must have been similar in the later burials at the rock-cut tombs of Naqsh-i Rustam. For in the grave of Darius three chambers, branching off from a gallery running parallel to the façade, were hewn out of the rock, and in each of them were three burial places of considerable dimensions. In all instances there are approximately rectangular cavities (Fig. 10.5) measuring about 1.05 m in depth, the floors of the gallery and of those cavities thus being exactly on the same level. The dimensions of the cavities at the upper edge are 2.10–2.11 m respectively in length and 1.05 m in width. In five of the nine burial places the inner walls project, so that the clear dimensions are now 1.92–1.93 m x 0.98 m (Schmidt 1970: 87–88, figs 31–32, pls 38–39).[12] The corpses could have been transferred into these cavities from—possibly wooden—transport receptacles. But it is also possible, as was assumed by E. F. Schmidt, that sarcophagi made of wood, metal, or wood covered in metal were placed in the cavities (Schmidt 1970: 88). The word used for the sarcophagus in the tomb of Cyrus is πύελος, which is properly a "tub", and that is a term that also suits the cavities in the rock tombs.

In spite of the change regarding the shape of the tombs there is thus no hint that the burial procedure itself altered.[13]

A marginal note is in place here about a tragic event. From the relief decoration and the inscription we can deduce a *terminus post quem* of 512 BC for the completion of Darius' tomb (Jacobs 2003: 327–331, esp. 330). The fact that his parents were both still alive when the tomb was essentially finished makes a completion before 500 BC probable. Our information that the parents were still living comes from Ctesias, who reports that they visited the tomb of their son (Ctesias F 13 [Photius p. 37a26–40a5 §19]; Lenfant 2004: 121). As was just mentioned, the construction offered room for nine burials provided for the king himself and, presumably, for close relatives. The interest of Darius' parents in the arrangements inside the tomb may have to do with the fact that they themselves numbered among the beneficiaries who were to find their final rest there in days to come. As it transpired Hystaspes and his wife had to make use of this option earlier than expected, because the Chaldaeans who hauled them up to the tomb during their sightseeing trip accidentally released the ropes when they were startled by some snakes, and so both perished.

But irrespective of where Darius' parents eventually found their final rest, the archaeological data show that the essential difference between the two types of tombs is that there is an individual tomb in one case and a family grave in the other. The presence side by side of four externally nearly identical grave monuments at Naqsh-i Rustam (see Fig. 10.1) may even betray an intention to develop the location of the royal tombs into a dynastic monument.

Let us sum up the results. Although the appearance of the tombs changed markedly, there is, as far as any statement on the matter can be ventured, no corresponding evidence regarding funeral rites. The body of the deceased ruler was brought to the grave in an appropriate portable container and was laid to rest in another container that was already on site. It follows that the burials of Cyrus and Darius are no more of an indicator that there was a sharp break between the two reigns than are the other areas in which at first sight there seemed pressing reason to suppose that there was such a break. In the debate about whether or not Cyrus and Darius were blood relatives, therefore, whatever other arguments may be used, none of these indicators can be adduced against Darius' assertion that he was related to Cyrus and thus came from the same family. Whether that assertion was actually true is, however, another question which will be dealt with elsewhere.

Notes

*My warmest thanks go to Christopher Tuplin for his assistance with the English version of this paper.

1. A detailed case for the identification of the "Tomb of the Mother of Solomon" with the tomb of Cyrus can already be found in Curzon 1892: II, 75–84. A survey of the subsequent arguments put forward *pro* and *contra* this identification is given by Stronach 1978: 24–25.
2. The view that the Zendan was a tomb was taken by Goldman 1965: 305–308; Krefter 1968: 99–100, 113.
3. Curzon 1892: II, 83.
4. There is absolutely no evidence that supports the suggestion that the younger Cyrus, the brother of Artaxerxes II, was buried there (Shahbazi 1972: 54).
5. Wiesehöfer's (1978) dissertation played an important role in stimulating discussion of this issue. A thorough synopsis of the course of the debate is presented by Rollinger 1998b: 156–176, 200–209.
6. Kellens (2002: 455–456) says that, with the restoration of the āyadanā, "il (scil. Darius) se présente comme un restaurateur".
7. A survey of Cyrus' titulatures can be found in Waters 2004: 94.
8. Cf. perhaps the Neo-Elamite tombs near Kazerun, mentioned in Potts 1999: 312.
9. Henkelman has recently emphasized the close ties of Cyrus and his predecessors to the local Elamite tradition in the heartland of the Achaemenid Empire; these are especially palpable in the use of the title "king of Anshan" (Henkelman 2003a: 187–196, esp. 193–195).
10. Mythological images at Pasargadae: the winged "genius" on Gate R, reliefs of a warrior and a lion demon in the north-west doorway (Stronach 1978: 68, fig. 34, pl. 58), and of a man in a fish-skin cloak and a rampant bull in the south-west doorway of Palace S (Stronach 1978: 68–69, fig. 35, pls 59–60). Mythological images at Persepolis: the Royal Hero fighting a lion and various monsters on door jambs in the Palace of Darius, the "Harem" and the Hall of 100 Columns (Schmidt 1953: pls 114–117, 144–147, 195–196; Walser 1980: taf. 90–96, 107). Images of mythical beings from Susa: de Mecquenem, Le Breton & Rutten 1947: pls VI:4, VII, VIII:1–2; Ghirshman 1964a: figs 191–192, 195.
11. Perhaps the burials recently found on the Kuh-i Rahmat will furnish more information about funeral customs.
12. In the other royal rock-cut tombs the dimensions of the cavities in the rock are in some cases greater, in some cases similar. Tomb II: three burial places in one chamber; the two cavities in front each measure 2.80 m in length, 1.23 m in width and 1.39 m in depth, while the one at the rear measures 2.60 m x 1.23 m x 1.39 m (Schmidt 1970: 93). Tomb III: three chambers with one burial place each, of which the outer ones each measure 2.25 m x 1.24 m x 1.30 m, while the one in the middle is a little bit wider (1.38 m) and deeper (1.42 m) (*ibid.* 96). Tomb IV: three chambers with one burial place each measuring 2.52 m x 1.30 m x 1.32 m (*ibid.* 98). At Persepolis the dimensions are as follows: tomb V: three chambers with two burial places each, whose dimensions are about 2.15 m x 1 m x 0.98–1.02 m; the cavities in the chamber on the left (at 2.20 m) are a bit longer, the front one in the chamber in the middle (at 1.10 m) somewhat broader (ibid. 102). Tomb VI: one chamber with two burial places, of which the front one measures 2.90 m x 1.20 m x 1.40 m and that at the rear 2.47 m x 1.19 m x 1.26 m (*ibid.* 106).
13. Von Gall (1979: 272–273) also makes a connection between the tombs at Naqsh-i Rustam and the tomb of Cyrus, but supposes that, whereas at Naqsh-i Rustam sarcophagi were sunk into

the cavities of the burial places, there was a *klinē* standing in the *pyelos* of the tomb of Cyrus. This idea was prompted by evidence from the Losarskata Mogila near Duvanlij in southern Bulgaria (Filow 1934: 119–126, figs. 143–150), but in that case the corpse was burnt and this surely indicates a different funeral rite from the one used for Cyrus. Moreover, von Gall's theory does not fit the description of Aristobulus in Arrian (*Anabasis* VI 29, 10), which presupposes that the body was in the sarcophagus and the *klinē* stood next to it. These circumstances were presumably known from the first visit at the grave (the one mentioned by Strabo).

11

Zoroastrianism under the Achaemenians: A Non-Essentialist Approach

Philip G. Kreyenbroek

As this paper will show, modern insights and approaches in the field of religious studies can make us view the religion of the Achaemenians in a new light. Many of the arguments that have been advanced to argue against the presence of Zoroastrianism under the earlier Achaemenids were based on premises that no longer seem convincing. A modern understanding of the transmission of religious traditions, moreover, implies that the Achaemenid period represents a crucial phase in the history of Zoroastrianism. Furthermore, we can now interpret some of the extant material in new and perhaps more illuminating ways, suggesting that Zoroastrianism may have taken root in western Iran without major conflicts with the older, traditional religion of that region.

The background to these new insights is a change of paradigm that affects many disciplines, namely the shift from a mainly deductive to a predominantly inductive approach. This means that, rather than assuming we understand the general picture and can use this knowledge to interpret details, it now seems preferable to begin with a close scrutiny of the details, using these to try and obtain a general picture.

It has to be said at the outset that we do not have sufficient data in the field of ancient Iranian studies to allow us to rely entirely on an inductive approach. Still, a result of this paradigm shift that is particularly relevant to the study of the Achaemenid period is the rejection of an "essentialist" definition of the concept of religion, that is, the assumption that each religion has an "essential" form or version, a sort of Platonic ideal, underlying and informing all actual expressions of the religion in question. An alternative approach regards the development of a religion as a dynamic process, in which the original teachings of the faith naturally play a role, but which is informed at least as strongly by the way in which believers at a given time understand reality.

Applied to ancient Iranian studies, this means that earlier scholars were forced by the cultural assumptions of their time to look first and foremost for the essence of Zoroastrianism, which they naturally tended to find in the message of Zarathustra as reflected in the *Gatha*s. The evidence of other sources was either used to help complete one's picture of the essential religion, or else to illustrate a given community's lack of understanding of what the religion truly taught. Evidence about Achaemenid religion, then, was interesting for specialists on Zoroastrianism only in so far as it confirmed existing presuppositions about that religion. Where it differed from that construct, it was considered to be un-Zoroastrian, and therefore irrelevant—a way of thinking that ensures that no essential changes can be admitted in the history of a faith, since any novel element was by definition un-Zoroastrian.

However, if one understands the development of a religion as a dynamic, ongoing process, and regards the realities of each period as equally valid as those of the earliest phase, the Achaemenid era at once comes to seem crucial. At that time the Zoroastrian tradition, which until then had presumably served villages and small communities, became the faith of the imperial family. Thus it was cast in the role of an imperial faith in a land that was remote from its country of origin. Many of the new demands on such a religion must have been unknown until then, and presumably required new beliefs, traditions and institutions, which came to be accepted as fully Zoroastrian. In other words, a new form of the Zoroastrian tradition must have developed under the Achaemenians. It was this tradition that ultimately gave rise to the later forms of Zoroastrianism that are best known to us.

Another "deductive" assumption that is often found in works on Achaemenian religion is that contacts between Zoroastrianism and the established religions of the region must have been confrontational. There are no data to suggest that this was so, however, and it seems equally plausible to assume that the acceptance of the Zoroastrian tradition in western Iran was a gradual and peaceful process. The assumption that new religions become established through conflict appears to be based on our knowledge of the history of Christianity and Islam. It is true that, like these, Zoroastrianism was a credal faith—the first instance in the Indo-Iranian tradition of a religious identity that was based on a world view (*daena*) rather than ethnicity or local culture. Zoroastrianism therefore may have been the first Iranian religion whose basic assumptions allowed it to admit newcomers on a large scale. At the same time, however, there is a conspicuous lack of evidence of religious confrontation in Achaemenid times. A contributory factor to this may have been that, unlike Christianity and Islam, early Zoroastrianism was not a scriptural faith. The sacred texts of Zoroastrianism were probably transmitted without the use of writing until well into the Sasanian period (Kreyenbroek 1996). Scriptural religions tend to regard the truth found in their sacred books as absolute, unique and exclusive. On the other hand, the present writer's experience of non-written religious traditions suggests that these tend to be "inclusive" rather than "exclusive", admitting that much has been lost since the faith first appeared, and prepared to accept that new elements, if they seem appropriate, must have been part of their religion as it originally was.

If applied to conditions in Achaemenid Iran, this could suggest that Zoroastrianism was perceived by some western Iranians as a sophisticated and prestigious alternative—rather than a rival—to the traditional western Iranian religion, with which in any case it must have had many elements in common. We cannot assume that the Achaemenians' view of what a religion was corresponded to ours. Rather than "the only way to worship God", the concept may have been understood as "the most effective way to worship God in a given society", on a par with other culturally determined phenomena such as dress or language. It may be significant in this connection that the only people who are implicitly blamed in the Achaemenian inscriptions for not worshipping Ahuramazda are certain rebellious Elamites (DB V.14–7), the Persians' fellow occupiers of the Achaemenid heartland. Darius, it might be inferred, wished or expected the inhabitants of Persia to worship Ahuramazda at least nominally, while he had no such expectations of Egyptians, Jews or Babylonians.

The most obvious reason for assuming that the Achaemenian inscriptions reflect a form of Zoroastrianism is, simply, the presence there of Ahuramazda ("Lord Wisdom"). Some scholars have held that Mazda was originally an Indo-Iranian divinity, while others reasoned that Mazda-worship (or "Mazdaism") was a common feature of ancient Iranian religious traditions, and not necessarily related to Zoroastrianism. Such theories, however, assume the existence of this divinity in Indo-Iranian, or at least pre-Zoroastrian, times, for which there is no evidence. It is true that *medha* "wisdom", like other abstract concepts, is venerated in some ancient Indian texts, but as an abstraction rather than a fully personalized divine being.[1] Grammatically, moreover, OInd. *medha* is treated as a feminine noun, which makes it seem unlikely that it was the name of a great male Indo-Iranian god. Nor do we have evidence that major new divine figures came to be worshipped among the Iranians before the time of Zarathustra.

On the other hand it seems typical of Zarathustra's theology that he developed a tradition which already existed in the Indo-Iranian religion, namely that of regarding powers that have an impact on human life (such as *mithra* "contract") as a separate category of personal divine beings, the *ahura*s (OInd. *asura*); the names of the *ahura*s typically reflect their functions. All divine beings who are invoked in the *Gathas* in fact have these characteristic traits. That a trained priest would invoke Lord Wisdom as the greatest of a group of such beings seems plausible.

The use of the name Ahuramazda in the inscriptions therefore points to the presence of Zoroastrianism as an important factor in the religious life of the early Achaemenians. The inscriptions show, moreover, that other teachings which are thought to be typically Zoroastrian, such as the central role of the opposition between Good and Evil, and the belief that the soul will be recompensed in heaven or punished in hell after death, were accepted by the Achaemenid court.[2] There is sufficient evidence, then, to show that Zoroastrianism was present in early Achaemenid Iran. If that is so, at least three religious traditions were represented there: 1) the Elamite religion; 2) the ancient Persian, "Magian" tradition; and 3) Zoroastrianism.

The question remains, how did the Zoroastrian tradition relate to the established religions of the region, notably to the western Iranian, "Magian" tradition, which had evolved from the same roots and with which it presumably had certain beliefs and practices in common? It is conceivable that the attraction of Zoroastrianism lay in its more sophisticated understanding of the world and man's place in it.[3] Thus Zoroastrianism may have been perceived as a progressive Iranian tradition, whose coexistence with local traditions was accepted as a matter of course.

It is interesting to note that when terms of Avestan origin were used in the language of the Achaemenids, they did not always have precisely the same connotations as in the Avesta. The use of the word *artavan* "righteous" for the blessed dead is a case in point. While it seems typical of Zarathustra's message that he connected the concept of "righteousness" with man's thoughts, words and actions in this life, Old Persian evidently continued the traditional Indo-Iranian usage, using the term *(a)rtavan* for those souls who lived on or near the sun after death (Kuiper 1957). This usage evidently persisted in Old Persian in spite of the court's adherence to Zoroastrianism. Another instance is the use of the word *draoga* with a strong connotation of "lying, speaking untruths" (cf. Persian *dorugh* "lie"), which is not a prominent aspect of the concept of *drug* in the Avesta. In the inscriptions of Darius, the *topos* of the rebel who shows his wicked nature by lying about his name or status occurs too frequently to be fortuitous, or to be based on historical truth (see DB IV. 2–31). It seems plausible, therefore, to assume that the most prominent of these stories, stating that the person who was defeated by Darius was not, as he claimed, Cambyses' brother Bardiya (Greek: Smerdis) but the Magian Gaumata, was in fact a brilliant fabrication, making use of the western Iranian "Zoroastrian" belief that one who lies is *ipso facto* a follower of Evil.

All this suggests that key Avestan concepts formed part of Achaemenian discourse on religion, but that they were not always understood as they were in eastern Iran. The theory that, at the time of Darius, elements of the Avestan tradition were still in the process of being assimilated by western Iranian culture, is strengthened by an imprecation found in DB IV.78, 80, where it is said: "If thou shalt behold these inscriptions and these sculptures and shalt destroy them [...] may Ahuramazda be a smiter to thee [...] and what thou shalt do, that for thee may Ahuramazda utterly destroy" (Kent 1953: 132). In other Zoroastrian writings, whether Avestan or Middle Persian, a direct association of Ahura Mazda with destructive deeds appears to be unheard of. The most plausible conclusion from this is that the Zoroastrian tradition did play a role in Achaemenian affairs, but that its development there was still at a relatively early stage.

These considerations may help us explain the Achaemenian use of the priestly title *atravaxsh* (in Elamite script: *haturmaksha*), which in Avestan usage denotes a participant in the ritual, but in Achaemenid Iran was used for a priest who had both ritual and administrative duties (as priests often did under the Sasanians). The title, meaning "one who makes the fire grow", is unknown in India and seems too specific to be a common Iranian one. It is therefore likely to be of Zoroastrian origin. Thus, in a religious landscape with three major religious traditions, we have references to three main priestly titles: the *shatin* representing the Elamite religion, the western Iranian *magu(sh)* or "Magian", and lastly the *atravaxsh*.

It would hardly be far-fetched, then, to hypothesize that what distinguished the *atravaxsh* from the *magush* was their ability to perform proper Zoroastrian rituals, with an Avestan liturgy. In other words, the term *atravaxsh* may originally have denoted a Zoroastrian priest of eastern Iranian origin, who may have been encouraged to come to western Iran in order to recite the liturgy in the sacred language of Zoroastrianism. Apart from his administrative duties the *atravaxsh* is typically associated with a ceremony known as *lan*, a term of Elamite origin, which at the time of Darius seems to have acquired the generic meaning "food offering". On the Elamite tablets of Persepolis we find references to commodities donated by the state as "offerings" (OP. *dausha* < Av. *zaothra*) for the *lan*; such offerings were often received by *atravaxsh*. In these contexts the *lan*, whose dedication is never explicitly stated, is generally mentioned together with rituals dedicated to various divine beings of Iranian or Elamite origin. It thus seems that in many localities, *lan* ceremonies were combined with services for divinities who were particularly venerated there.

The Persepolis tablets suggest that the *lan* typically entailed the offering of a single commodity, while modern Zoroastrian rituals involve the offering of at least two. This led M. Boyce (1982: 134) to state that the *lan* could not be identified with any known Zoroastrian ceremony. However, we know that the *lan* had the following significant features:

1) It involved the consecration of solid or liquid offerings;[4] with wine, beer, grain, barley, flour and fruit being frequently mentioned
2) the quantities of its offerings could vary considerably
3) the offerings were consumed after consecration
4) it could be performed by a single priest
5) it did not involve Haoma offerings, and rarely animal sacrifice[5]
6) it was performed very frequently
7) it involved no specific dedication.

It may seem strange, then, that Professor Boyce was not reminded of a ritual, which she and Dastur Kotwal have so extensively documented, namely the ceremony now known as *Dron* (Boyce & Kotwal 1971). As was described in that publication:

1) the *Dron* always involved the consecration of bread (made of grain, barley or flour), and often that of wine and fruit
2) the quantity of its offerings could vary considerably
3) the offerings were later consumed[6]
4) it could be performed by a single priest
5) it did not involve Haoma, and not usually animal sacrifice[7]
6) it was performed very frequently, in many cases daily
7) it was normally dedicated automatically to Ahura Mazda and the divinity of the day, so that the dedication need not be specified.

While it is true that the offerings for the *Dron* described in the Pahlavi literature generally include a range of commodities, the only essential offering is that of cakes (*dron*), together with a little butter. Butter could not be supplied for long periods of time, as was customary under the Achaemenians, so that this small additional offering may have been supplied by the priest or the community. The similarity between the two rituals, then, seems striking.

In later Zoroastrianism, the *Dron* service formed part of the more elaborate ceremony now known as the *Yasna*.[8] It could also be performed independently, either as an elaborate ceremony or as a short daily ritual for Ohrmazd and the divinity of the day.[9] This may explain the juxtaposition in the Persepolis tablets of gifts for the *lan*, for which no dedication is explicitly mentioned, to those of ceremonies for divinities who were the objects of local cults, and needed to be specified.

While some elements of Zoroastrian ritual may have had counterparts in the earlier western Iranian tradition, other features, notably the liturgy, must have been clearly distinct. The Zoroastrian liturgy is recited in Avestan, while traditional Magians presumably recited in their own language. There are no indications to suggest that the ancient Iranians had a sophisticated system of teaching foreign languages. It seems likely that at an early stage of the expansion of Zoroastrianism in western Iran, officiating priests were native speakers of Avestan, who may have been encouraged to settle there so that Zoroastrian ceremonies could be performed with their proper liturgy. Given the royal patronage of Zoroastrianism, which presumably resulted in an increasing need for priests who could recite the liturgy, it seems likely that some Magi also began to memorize the Avestan prayers (rather than learning the Avestan language, cf. Kreyenbroek 1996). As is well known, the term *mogh* (from OIr. *magu* "Magian") eventually came to be used for the Zoroastrian priesthood generally, which suggests that Magi gradually took over the leadership of the Zoroastrian religion in western Iran. At the same time, the *atravaxsh* families who had settled in western Iran may in time have adopted the language and customs of their new homeland. Thus the original distinctions between "Avestan" priests and Magi eventually disappeared.

Whether the Achaemenid state sponsored traditional "Magian" food offerings as well as Zoroastrian *lan* rituals remains a matter of speculation, and the use of priestly titles can do no more than help us speculate. In a few cases (see Koch 1987) the same people could be called *magush* in one document and *atravaxsh* in another; the term *lan.lirira* "performer of the *lan*" is sometimes added to the name of a *magush*; and in one case an *atravaxsh* is elsewhere called *magush lan.lirira*. On the other hand, there appear to be no references to an *atravaxsh* *lan.lirira*, which suggests that this would be a tautology, the *lan* being the essential task of an *atravaxsh*. All this would be consistent with the assumption that a Magian who had memorized the Avestan texts could be called *magush lan.lirira*, or *magush atravaxsh*, while a native speaker of Avestan was always an *atravaxsh*. It is conceivable, then, that some of the Magians who are not given the title *atravaxsh* or *lan.lirira* were western Iranian priests who still recited in their original language. This is far from certain, however, as the facts could also be explained in other ways. As Razmjou (2004) suggests, the term *magush lan.lirira* may have implied a specific ritual competence, which both *atravaxsh* and *magush* could acquire.

While much remains uncertain, a non-essentialist approach to the history of Zoroastrianism implies that the Achaemenid period was extremely significant for the further development of that religion. Moreover, if we accept that the use of certain Zoroastrian terms varied between Avestan and Old Persian, we can interpret the data of the Persepolis tablets in a way that suggests a non-confrontational expansion of Zoroastrianism through western Iran in the Achaemenid period.

Notes

1. I owe this information to my colleague, Professor T. Oberlies. See also Konow 1937.
2. It seems possible that the Zoroastrian belief in the resurrection of the dead is reflected by a remark attributed by Herodotus (III. 62) to Prexaspes, who told Cambyses: "If the dead can rise up again, expect Astyages the Mede to rise and fight against you; but if things are as they used to be, then be sure no harm will come to you from him."
3. If the contents of the Achaemenian inscriptions are taken to reflect the way the Achaemenid court understood Zoroastrianism, Darius I's statement (DNb. 11–15): "I am not hot-tempered. What things develop in my anger I hold firmly under control by my thinking power. I am firmly ruling over my own (impulses)" (Kent 1953: 140) may express a concept of startling novelty at the time, namely that man can rule over his emotions. This would be consistent with what is known of Zoroastrian teaching.
4. That is, the *dausha* or *zaothra*, see above and *Nerangestan* 47.1 (Kotwal & Kreyenbroek 2003: 198–199).
5. C f. Koch 1987: 270–71; Razmjou 2004: 106.
6. See *Yasna* 8.2.

7. See *The Pahlavi Rivayat accompanying the Dadestan i Denig* 58.76, 77 (Williams 1990), where the sacrifice of big cattle is forbidden when the *Dron* is performed without the *Yasna*, while some commentators say that all animal sacrifice is forbidden for that service.
8. The fact that the word *dauçanyasna* (< **zaothranam *yasna* "ceremony of food-offerings") is once attested (Koch 1987: 264), suggests that a "Zoroastrian" term for this or a similar ritual may already have been in circulation.
9. Compare the short daily ceremony described by Kreyenbroek (2004: 330–331) on the basis of *Nerangestan* 29.12–15, and the elaborate ceremonies and long lists of offerings found in Ner. 10 (Kotwal & Kreyenbroek 1995: 58–81).

12

The Formation of Achaemenid Imperial Ideology and Its Impact on the *Avesta*

Abolala Soudavar

1. Introduction

At the end of his conference presentation, Albert De Jong succinctly suggested, "Ask not what Zoroastrianism did for the king, but ask what the king did for Zoroastrianism." From the title of my paper, it seems that I heeded his advice even before hearing it. In reality, however, my initial goal was different: I had only wanted to explore the formation of the Achaemenid imperial ideology. Its impact on Zoroastrianism came to me from what I saw and what I read. The more I delved into it, the more I was convinced that it was Darius' kingly ideology that affected the *Avesta*, and not vice versa.

Even though my study rests on a number of controversial issues, it is my hope that the sum of my conclusions will project a coherent and acceptable scenario as to how Darius' kingly ideology unfolded, and how it impacted on Zoroastrianism.

2. Some preliminary methodological considerations

It is generally perceived that the deciphering of iconography is less precise than the deciphering of text. But the reading of an ancient and cryptic text such as the *Avesta* can be speculative and imprecise as well. It is now recognized that the *Avesta* was an orally transmitted text, which was "crystallized" in the post-Achaemenid period, perhaps gathered and organized into different chapters in Parthian or early Sasanian times, and written down not before the reign of Khosrow I (r. 531–579). A small fraction of it has been preserved as passages inserted within liturgies that were recited without necessarily being understood, the earliest copies of which were discovered in the eighteenth century and may even date to the fourteenth century (Kellens 2002: 242–43; Skjaervø 2005: 80–81). It is, to say the least, hazardous to rely solely on the conclusions made on such a text.

By contrast, Achaemenid iconography is not a copy but the original, and can be dated accurately. It is also very precise, because it is based on a vocabulary designed to enhance the projection of royal authority and legitimacy. This vocabulary was most probably developed by the same functionaries or scribes who devised the inscriptions, and goes hand in hand with their vocabulary and complements it. It is therefore wrong to treat Achaemenid iconography as mere decorative compositions. There is considerable information imbedded in it, and one must try to decipher it. In this quest, oddities play an important role. When confronted with them, one has the duty to address them and not sweep them under the carpet. One must propose a plausible explanation, and that explanation shall remain valid until disproved or unseated by a more plausible one.

3. The birth date of Zoroaster

A key question for the understanding of Darius' kingly ideology is the degree of Darius' familiarity with Zoroastrianism, or in other words, whether he was acting according to a set ideology or formulating a new one himself. It inevitably leads to the question of the maturity of Zoroastrianism and the birth date of Zoroaster, an issue that is fiercely debated between two schools of thought. The first relies on the *Avesta*, and places Zoroaster in between 1800 and 800 BC. The second argues for a birth date of 618 BC by relying on data transmitted by tenth-century documents, which specify that 258 years elapsed between the coming of Zoroaster and that of Alexander.

I subscribe to the latter because I see much confusion in the theories advanced by the proponents of the first school, and at the same time an increasing wealth of evidence in support of the second. Even though this date is not essential to my main thesis, it does help to put it into perspective. Conversely, the observations presented for my thesis will ultimately reinforce the proposition of a late date for Zoroaster.

3.1. Inconsistencies of the first school

The wide range of dates proposed by the proponents of the first school is proof enough that their methodology is inconclusive. Mary Boyce, for instance, at first proposed a date range of 1700–1500 BC based on a perceived similarity of the Avestan language with that of the Indian *Rig-Veda*, but then reduced it to 1200 BC as philologists began to gravitate around an arbitrary round figure of 1000 BC (Boyce 1984*c*: 18). The fact is, however, that the dating of the *Rig-Veda* itself is hypothetical, and while philologists such as Kellens argue about the archaic nature of the Avestan language and a linguistic hiatus between what they term as "Old" and "Young" *Avesta*,[1] none of them were ever able to propose a reliable methodology for measuring the age of the Avestan language. Philology is not an exact science and their dates are based on guesswork. A guess based on experience may be valuable, provided it is relevant. In this case it is not, because even if it is true it is not decisive. As Gershevitch has argued, the speed of language development can vary, and different dialects may evolve differently over time and space (Gershevitch 1995: 2–3). English for instance, which is an offshoot of Germanic languages, has evolved more than present-day German, and Tehrani Persian has advanced more than Afghani Persian.

Moreover, out of respect for tradition and/or to impress their followers, men of religion have always favoured an archaistic language. Thus, if one stumbles on a copy of *Divinus Perfectionis Magister* (dated 25th January 1983) by the late Pope John Paul II, one cannot declare it to be a very old document on the basis that no one spoke Latin in twentieth-century Italy. The priestly style of the *Avesta* is archaistic but not necessarily archaic or ancient.[2]

Since the measure of linguistic evolution for the *Avesta* is inconclusive, proponents of the first school sought to buttress their theory with another proposition: that the Avestan environment described a pastoral and primitive society (Boyce 1989: 62–66). But the general consensus for Zoroaster and/or the Avestan native land is somewhere in the eastern Iranian world, in a corridor that stretches from Sistān in south-west Iran, up to present-day Uzbekistan.³ In this stretch of land, most of the rural communities are still pastoral today, and primitively so.⁴ Any poet-priest from the high plateaus of this corridor will naturally derive his imagery from what he can see in his small world: a pastoral environment by day and a star-studded vivid sky by night. As for Boyce's technical twist that the Avestan people were "stone-age people with only a confused notion of the distinction between stone and metal objects", Malandra has recently demonstrated that it was without merit and based on false assumptions.⁵

In the meantime, anthropologists have discovered that the proto-Indo-Aryans, on their route to India, had settled down in the second millennium in an area that is situated between present-day Uzbekistan and northern Afghanistan, known as the "Bactria Margiana Archaeological Complex" or BMAC (Parpola 2002: 246–247). In the emblematic BMAC, the believers of the first school claim to have found the missing link that justifies their theory, even though there is absolutely no tangible link between any of the BMAC characteristics and those of the *Avesta* (Kreyenbroek 2005; Shayegan 1997). Suffice it to say that Asko Parpola, whose 2002 article in *Iranica Antiqua* represents the seminal study on proto-Indo-Iranian migrations and settlements, could not find any linkage between BMAC and the Avestan community, but instead, proposes a *c.*800 BC date for Zoroaster based on a theory that the prophet's monotheistic vision of the world must have been inspired from an Assyrian model (Parpola 2002: 246–247). The latter theory is as yet unsupported by any other evidence.

In tone and imagery, the Gāthās (i.e. the part of the *Avesta* generally attributed to Zoroaster himself) are very similar to the Gnostic lamentations of the Sufis of the eastern Iranian world, and are certainly no more "BMAC" than, for example, the *Lamentations* of the celebrated Sufi Khājeh ʿAbdollāh Ansāri (AD 1006–1089) of Herāt. As for the later *Avesta*, Y 57.27, Yt 5.13 and Yt 10.125 describe a *quadriga* (i.e. a four-horsed chariot) for Sraosha, Anāhitā and Mithra. The construction of such a vehicle not only necessitates a certain sophistication for tying up the four horses and maintaining manoeuvrability, but also presupposes the existence of a fast road or a racing circuit—such as the Circus Maximus of Rome—that warranted the use of a fast chariot.⁶ The *quadriga* is neither a stone-age vehicle nor a BMAC cart.

An early date for Zoroaster implies that Zoroastrianism left an impact somewhere, at least by the advent of the Achaemenids. To evaluate this impact one must concentrate on the important particularities of Zoroastrianism and not on secondary issues such as funerary rites that are tied to ancient tribal customs and are not Zoroastrian proper.⁷ What distinguishes the Zoroastrian creed from previous Iranian religions is the concept of the Amesha Spenta group of divinities who assist Ahura Mazdā in his various tasks, and the profession of faith in Y 12.1 (the Zoroastrianism Creed) by which the believer must declare:

> I profess myself a Mazdā-worshipper, a follower of Zarathushtra, opposing the Daevas, accepting the Ahuric doctrine, one who praises the Amesha Spentas, who worships the Amesha Spentas. (Y12.1, Boyce 1984*a*: 57)

And yet, despite Darius' 72 mentions of the name of Ahura Mazdā in Bisotun alone, no mention of the Amesha Spentas or Zoroaster ever appears in his inscriptions.

Skjaervø remarks that the Sasanians did not mention the Amesha Spentas either (2005: 52). This is true, but early Sasanian kings clearly stated that they were "Mazdyasna" believers, a word the chief priest Kerdir unambiguously qualified as a religion (*dyn*).[8] Had Zoroaster lived *c*.1000 BC, one would expect that five centuries later his religion would have been defined in a more comprehensive way than mere praise for Ahura Mazdā.

Unable to find a connection to the Zoroastrian creed in royal inscriptions, Skjaervø then relies on clay documents from Darius' treasury, in order to suggest that some of them pertained to sacrificial rations for Zoroastrian divinities, including Spenta-Armaiti (who is one of the Amesha Spentas) (2005: 53). The fact is, however, that Zoroastrian divinities were not the creation of Zoroaster's mind but had been revered a long time before him, and were only regrouped by him in a new compact pantheon. As Razmjou's article—which is Skjaervø's source in this instance—explains, Spenta-Armaiti was an Aryan divinity, and possibly a Median one, that had always been revered as the goddess of Earth; her name appeared in these ration-disbursement tablets not with the other Amesha Spentas, but in the company of ancient tribal deities such as gods of mountains and rivers and Mithra, for all of whom sacrificial ceremonies were held (Razmjou 2001: 9–12). Darius' support for the reconstruction of the Temple in Jerusalem—out of his own treasury (Ezra 6: 8)—did not make a Jew of him, nor did his support for Egyptian temples make an Amon-worshipper of him. By the same token, the support of sacrificial rites for Aryan deities, whom Skjaervø labels as "Avestan" deities, did not make a Zoroastrian of Darius.

More generally, Skjaervø's attempt to draw a parallel between the Achaemenid inscriptions and the *Avesta* confounds form with substance: the parallel that he sees is not the result of a common religious belief but is due to a common form of expression rooted in the same Iranian culture shared by the Achaemenids and the *Avesta*.[9]

Finally, as Pierre Lecoq has remarked, gods who are referred to as *yazata*s in the *Avesta* were still called *baγa*s by the Achaemenids, and the Achaemenid calendar bears no trace of Zoroastrianism (Lecoq 1997: 159, 161). Had the prophet lived some five centuries earlier, a Zoroastrian calendar would certainly have been developed by the time of the Achaemenids, and Darius would certainly have used it in Bisotun where, instead, he dates 18 events of his reign with non-Zoroastrian months. Moreover, Razmjou has recently argued that the Achaemenid calendar names all pertained to entities that were essentially Iranian or Persian, but mostly non-Avestan. While the seventh month of both the Zoroastrian and Achaemenid calendars pertained to Mithra, in the latter calendar, the month-name Baγayadish (god-worship) referred to him by the generic name of gods, that is, *baγa*. In other words, the god par excellence of the Achaemenid calendar was still Mithra and not Ahura Mazdā (Razmjou 2003: 22–24, 31–32).

3.2. Assessing the "258" figure

The 258 years mentioned by the texts measure the time elapsed between the conquest of Iran by Alexander (i.e. the death of Darius III in 330 BC) and the "Coming of Religion" that Gnoli has convincingly argued refers to the year Zoroaster envisioned his new religion, and which the mini-calendar of Zādspram specifies to have occurred at the age of 30.[10] Hence a birth date of c.618 BC.

3.3. Recent objections

In his critical review of Gnoli's recent book in favour of this date, Kreyenbroek raises three general objections in the form of questions that I believe should be answered.

Why did a "rapidly evolving civilisation" (presumably the Achaemenids) accept the message of a "near contemporary" with "ideas rooted in the Stone Age"?

If Zoroastrians had a system of recording all events in respect of the epoch-year of the "Coming of Religion", then why is it that they did not keep it alive indefinitely, and why did they switch their reference point to the "hated" Alexander's conquest of Iran?

Given that Greeks understood "effortlessly" matters pertaining to Iranian "religion and chronology", how could they confuse Zoroaster's birth date with "the origin of his spiritual being" (i.e. Zoroaster's *fravashi* which Zoroastrians believed to have come to being 6,000 years earlier)? "If the Greeks were misled in this vital point, what validity can we claim for the rest of their evidence?" (Kreyenbroek 2003: 123)

The problem with all of the above questions is that they are based on incorrect assumptions and raise inconsequential objections:

It is far from proven that Achaemenids were Zoroastrians, and even if they were, they were no different than Persians adopting Islam or Romans adopting Christianity, religions that were in no way less rooted in the "Stone Age" than Zoroastrianism.

Quoting Zoroastrian priests, Biruni produced a number of lists tabulating the reign of Iranian kings. However, one cannot conclude from these tables that Zoroastrians were in the habit of recording regnal years from the first year Zoroaster formulated his religion; neither did Christians start to tabulate regnal years from the day Jesus of Nazareth was born. Unless religious officials get entangled with the ruling power, they usually show no desire to record political events. In the case of Zoroastrians, this only happened after the advent of the Sasanians. The above-mentioned tables are clearly reconstructs from that period.[11] Furthermore, it is not always clear what event defines an epoch-year. For instance, as Taqizadeh had demonstrated, three different epoch-years were concurrently used for the Sasanian Ardashir I (r. 224–241), until one eventually prevailed over the others (Taqizadeh 1943–46: 26–30). For religion-related matters, Zoroastrian priests did not only use the year of the "Coming of the Religion" but, as we shall see, also chose other events in their prophet's life as reference points. Moreover, the adoption of Alexander's conquest of Iran as a reference date should be of no surprise to us, since cataclysms such as earthquakes, famine and the plague are commonly used by people to situate events, even within Muslim or Christian communities who have a well-defined—religion-based—calendar.

By far the most unacceptable of Kreyenbroek's assumptions is the reliability of Greek sources and the accuracy of their perceptions concerning Iranians. It is not only Aeschylus (525–456 BC) who, at an early stage of Greek contacts with Iranians, claimed that Persians saw Darius as a god (Aeschylus, *Persians*, 681), but also Greek translators of the Sasanian era who, after centuries of Iranian and Hellenic intermingling, still qualified Iranian kings as gods, a false claim which, unfortunately, most philologists and historians have accepted without question.[12] The straight answer to Kreyenbroek's last question is: Greek sources can indeed be misleading.

3.4. The reliability of the "258" figure

The reliability of a datum generally depends on three criteria: 1) that the datum is transmitted by the paramount, or relevant, tradition; 2) that it is correlated by multiple sources; 3) and that the sources are old and close to the date when events took place. The "258" figure has all of these characteristics:

(a) It was transmitted through Irano-Zoroastrian channels and not through a foreign one, and through the same oral traditions—so dear to Boyce—that present-day Zoroastrians have inherited, with the difference that this oral information was frozen in the tenth–eleventh century and set into writing, when writers such as Mas'udi and Biruni collected it from Zoroastrian priests.

(b) It is consistent under a plurality of forms: it appears as a direct quote in works by Mas'udi (d. 957) and Biruni (973–1048), who not only lived a century apart but obtained their information from different regions, the former from southern Iran, and the latter from the eastern Iranian world.[13]

It appears as an immutable time bracket for reconstructing the lost chronology of earlier history: the *Bundahishn*, for instance, fills this time bracket with a different list than Mas'udi's.[14]

Most importantly, it can be derived from the fact that it provides an explanation to a very odd historical question: why in AD 224, when the Sasanian Ardashir I ascended the throne, did he change the calendar, not in the way that the last Shah of Iran had done by moving the starting point, but by compressing history and cutting out a chunk of 206 years, which reduced the Parthian period to 266 years?

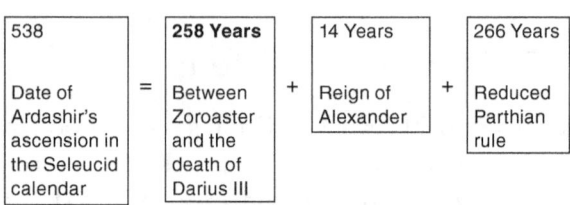

Based on arguments previously advanced by Taqizadeh and Henning, Gershevitch reasoned through a mathematical equation that it was a blind faith in this "258" figure that allowed Ardashir to promote his calendar change.[15] Only faith and dogma can trump common sense in such a way.

(c) The "258" figure was in use long before the tenth century. Indeed, since it had attained a dogmatic status by AD 224, and because dogma does not develop overnight, one could surmise that this figure was relied upon at least one or two centuries earlier, that is, close to the era of Alexander.

3.5. Avestan text in support of "258"

Upholders of the first school, however, deride any conclusion not based on the *Avesta*. But if the *Avesta* is the only valid source in this matter, then one should look at it more carefully, especially where it speaks about the birth of Zoroaster, as in stanza 13:94 of the Farvardin Yasht. This stanza celebrates the birth of Zoroaster:

> 13:94 Let us rejoice, for a priestly man is born, the Spitamid Zarathushtra.
> From now on (*iδa apąm*) ...
> From now on (*iδa apąm*) ...

and is followed by 13:95 which reads:

> 13:95 From now on (*iδa apąm*), Mithra…will promote all supreme authorities of the <u>countries</u> (*daxiiunąm*) and will pacify those in revolt.
>
> From now on (*iδa apąm*), strong Apam Napāt will promote all the supreme authorities of the countries and will subjugate all those in <u>rebellion</u>.[16]

Three observations are in order here: first, Yt 13:95 obviously refers to a political event and not a religious one; second, it situates this event shortly after the birth of Zoroaster—which gives added credibility to our assertion that Zoroastrians traditionally situated political events in relation to events in the life of their prophet and not necessarily the date of his conversion; third, the underlined words "countries" and "rebellion" imply a situation in which different nations were subjugated by one central authority, in other words, a situation within an *empire* (which must be an Iranian one as it relates to the Avestan world).

The only Iranian empire prior to the Achaemenids was of course that of the Medes.[17] This ties in perfectly with the historical data, because the Medes sacked Nineveh in 612 BC and subjugated Urartu in 610 BC, that is, within a decade after the supposed birth of Zoroaster *c*.618 BC. It also seems very logical: the new supremacy of the Medes necessitated a new source of legitimacy and a new kingly ideology; this ideology was then based on the support of two ancient Iranian deities, Mithra and Apam Napāt. Later on, Avestan priests naturally tallied this event with the birth of Zoroaster, the closest religiously significant event that they could think of.

The inescapable conclusion imbedded in these two stanzas of the Farvardin Yasht is one that supports the late date for Zoroaster and, at the same time, sheds light on the ideology of the Medes. Yet the tendency among philologists nowadays seems to be going in the opposite direction, one dictated by a dogmatic belief in a prehistoric and pastoral Zoroaster. Skjaervø, for instance, has recently translated the first two sentences of Yt 13:95 as:

> Here, henceforth, Miθra…shall further all that is foremost of the lands, and he pacifies those that are in commotion.
>
> (*iδa apąm * napā̊ sūrō fraδāt…*) Here the strong Scion of the Waters shall further all that is foremost of the lands, and he shall restrain those that are in commotion. (Skjaervø 2005: 67)

His translation has two major problems. First, despite being an adept of oral theories, he seems to be unaware that a basic tenet of oral narrations is a repetitive intonation, often marked by a string of sentences beginning with the same words. With that simple rule in mind, one immediately sees that the last two sentences of 13:94 and the first two of 13:95 are all punctuated with an "*iδa apąm*" opening, and that as a consequence, a second "*apąm*" (which constituted the first part of the name of Apam Napāt/*apąm napā̊*) has been dropped in the above sentence of the Farvardin Yasht (marked by *). Scribes who are not very literate in what they copy often think that if a word is repeated twice, one of them must be suppressed. It is a common scribal error that needs to be rectified.[18] Skjaervø's translation based on a non-rectified text thus breaks the symmetry in the missions entrusted to Mithra and Apam Napāt after the birth of Zoroaster, and by starting the last verse with "Here" has given it a geographic rather than a time-based meaning. Second, by using the words "lands" and "commotion" in lieu of "countries" and "rebellion", his translation projects a pastoral event rather than a political one. One should note, however, that what he translates as "lands" pertains to the Avestan *daxiiunąm*, the same word that Darius uses in his inscriptions to designate the people under his dominion (see below), and this unequivocally relates to inhabited political entities such as countries or nations, and not to pastoral ones.

Despite the logical implications of Yt 13:94 and Yt 13:95 in tandem, it would be reassuring if the validity of these two stanzas was somehow verified independently and through other considerations. In what follows, we shall see how on more than one occasion, text and iconography concur in upholding our interpretation of a Median kingly ideology based on the dual support of Mithra and Apam Napāt.

3.6. Iconographical evidence in support of Yasht 13:95

I first noticed the relevance of this passage when I was studying the symbolism of the lotus flower as an emblem of the aquatic deity Apam Napāt, and the sunflower as the emblem of the solar deity Mithra. My supposition was that the frequent combination of these two flowers in Iranian iconography was due to the identical roles that Mithra and Apam Napāt were given in Yt 13:95 (Soudavar 2003: 53–57). The natural course to pursue was to find out when these two emblems were first combined in the Iranian context. The iconographic evidence suggested that this happened in the late seventh–early sixth century BC.

Indeed, among all Iranian archaeological items, two groups of items bear the earliest combined lotus and sunflower motifs: the silver hoard from the Kalmākareh grotto (in Lorestān) and the glazed bricks from Bukān (in Kordestān), both discovered in the Median heartland in the 1990s and 1980s respectively (Soudavar 2003: 86–87). Based on the epigraphic peculiarities of a rhyton inscription—of a type that is found on many other silver vessels from the Kalmākareh hoard—Vallat has suggested a dating between 589 and 539 BC (2000: 29). Similarly, the complex iconography of the Bukān bricks, which is an amalgam of Assyrian and Urartian motifs mixed with indigenous Lorestān-type elements, is rendered in a style that precedes the Achaemenid stylistic standardization. Thus, the iconographical evidence shows a combination of these two flower motifs in the vicinity of 618 BC, which is consistent with our interpretation of Yt 13:95.

3.7. The prevalence of the Median kingly ideology before Darius

Historians generally shy away from defining Cyrus' religion (Briant 1996: 106–108), but the facts speak for themselves:

a) Cyrus never mentions Ahura Mazdā in his inscriptions.

b) A colossal sunflower–lotus combination (49 cm wide) is carved on his tomb (Stronach 1971: 155–158), which, as indicated before, is the symbol of the dual Median deities, Mithra and Apam Napāt (Soudavar 2005: 88).

c) Horse-sacrifice rituals of a Mithraic nature were conducted at Cyrus' tomb by his successors (Briant 1996: 106, 108).

d) As I have suggested elsewhere, Darius states in his letter to Gadatas that Mithra was worshipped by his predecessors (Soudavar 2003: 108–111).

e) Cyrus' generals had erected temples to Mithra and Anāhitā who, as the goddess of waters, became a substitute for Apam Napāt (also an aquatic deity) (Strabo XI.8.4, www.perseus.tufts.edu); Soudavar 2003: 107–111; Bivar 1998: 12–13; Razmjou 2005b: 150).

In the absence of proof to the contrary, it is safe to assume that Cyrus, and probably Cambyses,[19] adhered to the kingly ideology that the Medes had previously formulated. Therefore, Darius' ideology, based on the supremacy of Ahura Mazdā, must be regarded if not as an outright revolution, at least as a drastic change of direction. As we shall see, it was a distinct monotheistic creed with an antagonistic impetus against the Median beliefs of his predecessors.

4. Darius' kingly ideology

The noteworthy implication of a late date for Zoroaster is that Zoroastrianism as we now know, with its complicated rituals and canonical laws, had not enough time to develop between the lifetime of its prophet and the advent of Darius in the year 522 BC. Darius may or may not have known of Zoroaster and his teachings. The fact is that he does not mention either of them. Darius promoted a monotheistic ideology that exalted the supremacy of Ahura Mazdā, the god that Zoroaster also favoured, and a god that must have been popular among a certain group of Iranians. Moreover, Darius' initial fervour for Ahura Mazdā is accompanied by a total disdain for other deities. Similarly, in contrast to his devotion to Ahura Mazdā and his group of assistant divinities, the Amesha Spentas, other divine beings about whom Zoroaster speaks in the Gāthās are qualified as *daevas* or demoniac beings.

Darius' zeal in promoting Ahura Mazdā is akin to the zeal with which the Safavid Shāh Esmā'il I (r. AD 1501–1524) exalted the Imam 'Ali and promoted Shiism as the new religion of Iran in AD 1512, without really knowing what it entailed, but with a marked antagonism towards the established Sunni community of the land. It took more than a century and a half for Safavid Shiism to take shape, mostly through the intervention of foreign clerics imported from Lebanon. Similarly, Zoroastrianism may have developed through the intervention of eastern priests among a Persian elite that revered Ahura Mazdā without a full understanding of Zoroastrian precepts. And in the same way that a minority of Safavid Shiite zealots converted Iran to Shiism, and ultimately shaped their religion by adopting Sunni concepts as their own, Darius and his supporters may have paved the way for the development of a Zoroastrianism that ended up absorbing many of the existing beliefs of Iranian communities.

The more pertinent issue, however, whether one believes in a late date for Zoroaster or not, and whether he was familiar with Zoroastrianism or not, is how well founded and well established was the monotheistic ideology that Darius wished to promote.

Through a series of examples, I shall argue that, similar to Shāh Esma'il's Shiism, it was ill-defined and more antagonistic toward other Iranian religions than foreign ones, and Darius had to modify his initial stance in order to accommodate the entrenched beliefs of his own constituencies, sometimes successfully and sometimes not.

4.1. The Bisotun solar emblem

My first example is from Bisotun where in his earliest political manifesto, Darius exalted Ahura Mazdā 72 times to the exclusion of any other deity, and attributed all his achievements and victories to his support. For lack of a suitable model in the Iranian tradition, he chose a Mesopotamian symbol for the personification of Ahura Mazdā: a bearded man within a winged sphere.[20] This choice per se is not indicative of a weak foundation for Darius' brand of Mazdaism, because as the new religion of his empire it needed a universally recognizable symbol, and neighbouring Mesopotamia is where he could find one.

A sudden and tentative change of attribute for Ahura Mazdā, however, does hint at a weak foundation, and this is what Darius tried to do. After being confronted with the popularity of solar deities among his various subjects,[21] Darius decided to empower his Ahura Mazdā with solar attributes, and thus added a *solar* emblem on his hat in Bisotun (Fig 12.5). This emblem is a later addition, for there is a noticeable gap around it which separates it from the original design and which is indicative of an afterthought: a new piece of stone with a solar emblem had to be inset on top of Ahura Mazdā's hat in a previously flattened surface that would otherwise not allow the carving of an additional emblem in relief.

Two points need to be emphasized in this respect: a) this idea must have backfired because this was the first and last time that such an attribute was given to Ahura Mazdā; and b) although the easy choice for a solar emblem was the sunflower, Darius so abhorred any association with Mithra that he preferred the symbol of the Babylonian solar god Shamash with its pointed rays (Fig. 12.1) to that of a similar Iranian deity. But the idea of kingly authority reflecting solar power was too important to be readily discarded, and as we shall see, Darius found a clever way to reintroduce it in his ideological programme.

Fig. 12.1 The solar emblem of Shamash. (*Das Vorderasiatisches Museum* [Berlin, 1992], p. 189)

4.2. A new emblem for the concept of *khvarnah*

My second set of examples is from Persepolis and Susa. By the time Darius decides to erect palaces there, he is in full control of his empire, and like Shāh Esmā'il, he sheds some of that early zeal by allowing a vague reference to "all the gods" after invoking Ahura Mazdā in his DPd inscription.[22]

A more significant compromise, however, was to acknowledge the importance of the *khvarnah*, this auspicious fortune that Iranians have always considered as a necessary attribute of kingship. According to an ancient myth, the legendary king Jamshid (Yima) lost his kingship when he lost the *khvarnah*, and thereafter every Iranian king strove to show that he had become the recipient of the *khvarnah* and had not lost it. For his palaces, therefore, Darius chose a winged sphere as the symbol of the

Fig. 12.2 Two sphinxes guarding the symbol of *khvarnah*. Brick panel from Darius' palace in Susa. (Musée du Louvre, Sb 3324)

khvarnah, and placed a sphinx on each side as its guardians, in order to convey the idea that the *khvarnah* was resident there and had not departed (Fig. 12.2).[23]

There were, however, two problems with this choice: a) in keeping with his preference for foreign elements, Darius had chosen symbols that were not easily understood by his own constituency; and b) since overstated praise is essential to the Iranian culture, the projection of *khvarnah* could not be limited to a single statement but had to be repetitive in order to project abundant *khvarnah*.[24] However, the shape of the winged sphere was not suitable for a repetitive pattern, while symbols previously adopted by the Medes, namely the sunflower

Fig. 12.3 The *khvarnah* frieze. Eastern stairway of Apadana, Persepolis. (Courtesy of the Oriental Institute, Chicago. Photograph nos P 15301 and 15302)

and the lotus flower, were more suitable for a multiple showing.

To make the winged sphere symbol more understandable, it was visually associated with the lotus–sunflower combination, which filled the adjacent space (Fig. 12.3). And to render it compatible with the new imperial ideology, the creation of the *khvarnah* had to be attributed to Ahura Mazdā. Indeed, the sudden shift in the symbol of Ahura Mazdā, from the rectangular-shaped wings of the Bisotun prototype (Fig. 12.5) to more rounded ones in Persepolis (Fig. 12.6) cannot be taken lightly, and must have been dictated by an overriding consideration. The modification of such an important symbol in Achaemenid iconography—one that is generally marked by a preference for stylistic continuity and standardized icons—can only be explained by a desire to establish a visual link between the new emblem of *khvarnah* and that of Ahura Mazdā.[25] The latter was thus brought into harmony with the former to convey the idea that the *khvarnah* emanated from Ahura Mazdā. Since the Medes had associated this power with Mithra and Apam Napāt, the supremacy of Ahura Mazdā in Darius' new imperial ideology necessitated its appropriation for this deity. The easiest solution was to declare that the *khvarnah* itself was a creation of Ahura Mazdā.

The same approach is taken one step further under Xerxes. In a frieze that, similar to Figures 12.2 and 12.3, was meant to show that the *khvarnah* remained with Xerxes, and in which its winged sphere was also flanked by two guardian sphinxes and the rest of the frieze was sprinkled with lotus–sunflower combinations, we can see Ahura Mazdā standing above the winged sphere and not emerging from it (Fig. 12.4). It was clearly meant to re-emphasize that the *khvarnah* emanated from him.

In the *Avesta*, the concept of *khvarnah* is riddled with inconsistencies and oddities that only make sense if we look at them as borrowed concepts from the Achaemenid ideology rather than the other way round. First among these is the fact that each time the *khvarnah* is mentioned it is almost systematically preceded by a "Mazdā-created" label. Such overemphasis is generally an indication to the contrary.[26] Through the addition of this label, Ahura Mazdā is attributed a political power that is usually not part of religious philosophy.

Moreover, in trying to project an image of an all-powerful god, it is not only necessary to attribute creation to him but also to show

Fig. 12.4 Ahura Mazdā standing on top of the *khvarnah* symbol. Palace of Xerxes, Persepolis. (Photograph A. Soudavar)

that he can exert continuous control over the created. In the *Avesta* however, Mithra is recognized as the deity who bestows the *khvarnah* and the one who can take it back, while Apam Napāt is the one who guards it under water in its non-active phase. Ahura Mazdā does not and cannot interfere in their functions.

However, the most blatant contradiction appears in the Farvardin Yasht where Ahura Mazdā is in need of the *khvarnah* of the *fravashis* (spiritual beings) of the Righteous to achieve various functions such as protecting Anāhitā (Yt 13.4) or the Earth (which is also qualified as "Mazdā-created", Yt 13.9). In another instance, in Yt 13.12, he even states that if it were not for the help of the *fravashis*—presumably through their *khvarnah*—he would not have been able to protect the good people and beneficial animals (Dustkhāh 2002: 406–407). Logically, a god cannot be in need of what he can create. While Mazdā-created labels were added to project the omnipotence of Ahura Mazdā, all contradictions could not be ironed out. Contradictory notions were bound to appear in a manipulated or rectified text that was oral-based and not written.

4.3. The emphasis on the radiance of the *khvarnah*

A brick panel in Persepolis shows the independent conception of the *khvarnah* within a tripartite cycle: encapsulated as a pearl in its dormant and underwater phase, its rise from the water through a stack of lotus flowers and its appearance in the sky as a sunflower (see Fig. 12.7). The whole panel is surrounded by a border of triangles that emphasizes the radiance of the *khvarnah*. But according to an Iranian legend incorporated into the *Avesta*, a falcon-type bird by the name of *veraghna*, whose feathers are full of *khvarnah*, acts as

124 THE WORLD OF ACHAEMENID PERSIA

Fig. 12.5 The rectangular-shaped wings of the Ahura Mazdā symbol in Bisotun. (Photograph A. Soudavar)

a transfer agent for this auspicious fortune. It is thus that on another glazed brick from Persepolis (Fig. 12.8) we can see the *veraghna* with two encapsulated *khvarnah* spheres in its claws, surrounded by a similar border of radiating triangles.[27]

Elfenbein has suggested that the association of solar radiance with the *khvarnah* came as a result of punning on the phonetic resemblance of the first part of this word with *khvar* (i.e. sun in Old Persian) (Elfenbein 2001: 492). This is a possibility, but punning alone cannot create such a lasting and powerful attribute as the radiance of the *khvarnah*. I suspect that the emphasis that Darius put on the radiance of the *khvarnah* may ultimately have sealed its association with radiance. As we shall see, this emphasis was not only achieved through the imagery of his palaces but also through the use of a new qualifying word, *chiça*, that embodied the radiance of the *khvarnah*. The abandonment of the solar attributes of Ahura Mazdā was thus compensated by the claim of a *khvarnah* that was endowed with solar radiance.

Ironically, the emphasis on the radiance of the *khvarnah* opened the door for the reintroduction of the *khvarnah* iconography previously devised by the Medes. The problem with opening the door to ancient beliefs, especially if they are popular and colourful, is that they can overwhelm the newer ideology for which they were summoned for support. It is thus that the pearl, lotus and sunflower overwhelmed the winged-sphere symbol, as wall after wall of the Susa and Persepolis palaces was covered in them (Soudavar 2003: 103, figs 106–108).

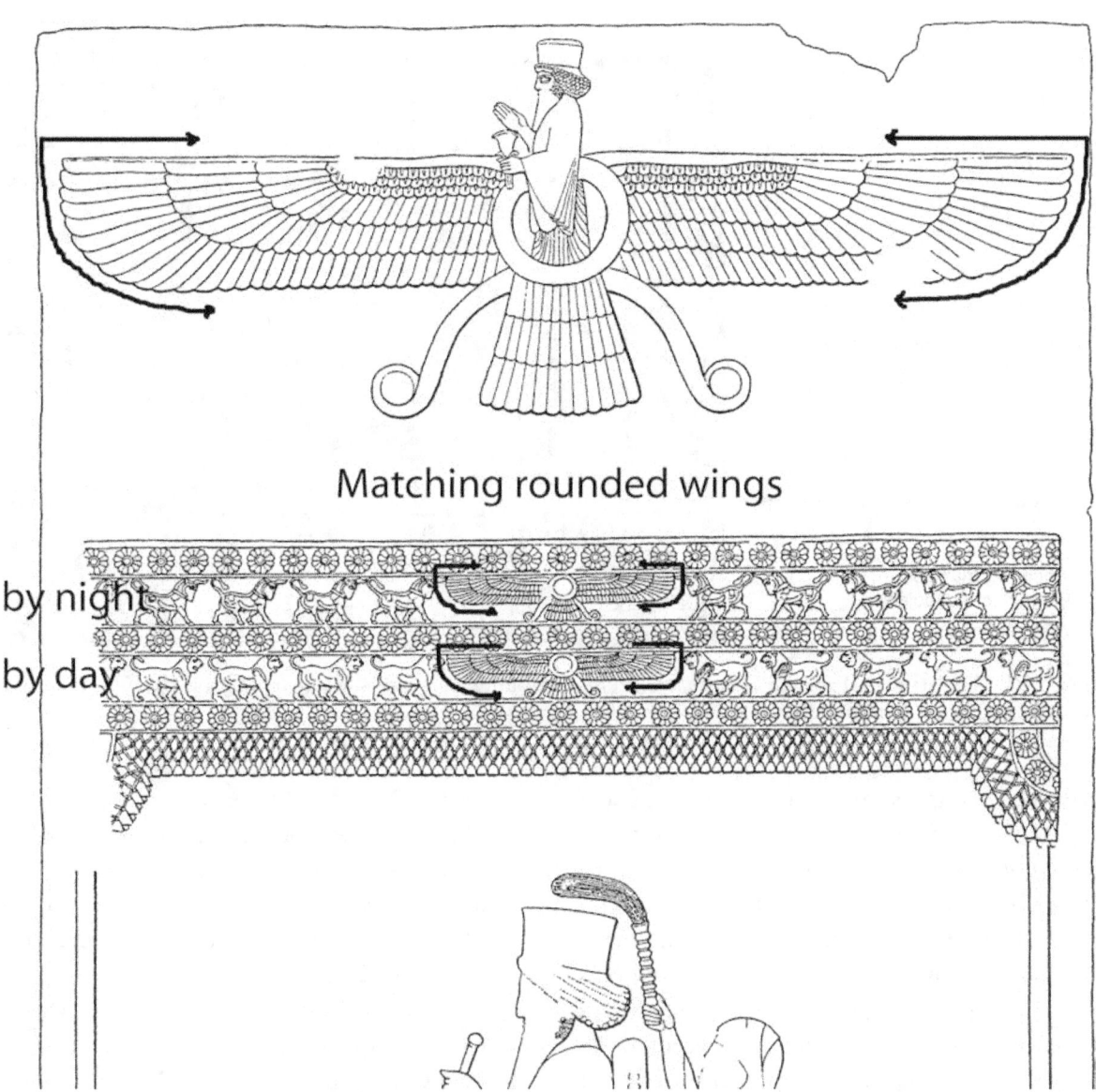

Fig. 12.6 Matching the shape of the symbol of Ahura Mazdā to that of the *khvarnah* in Persepolis. (Curtis & Tallis 2005: 76)

Similarly, there is a noticeable contrast between the Gāthās composed by Zoroaster himself, and the rest of the *Avesta* added by later priests. The Gāthās praise the supremacy of one god only, Ahura Mazdā; but subsequently, he is overwhelmed by the more colourful, and seemingly more powerful, deities of the later *Avesta*.

4.4. The support of the conspirators

Earlier on, I had surmised that the monotheistic reverence of Darius and Zoroaster for Ahura Mazdā stemmed from an ideology that must have been popular among a small

126 THE WORLD OF ACHAEMENID PERSIA

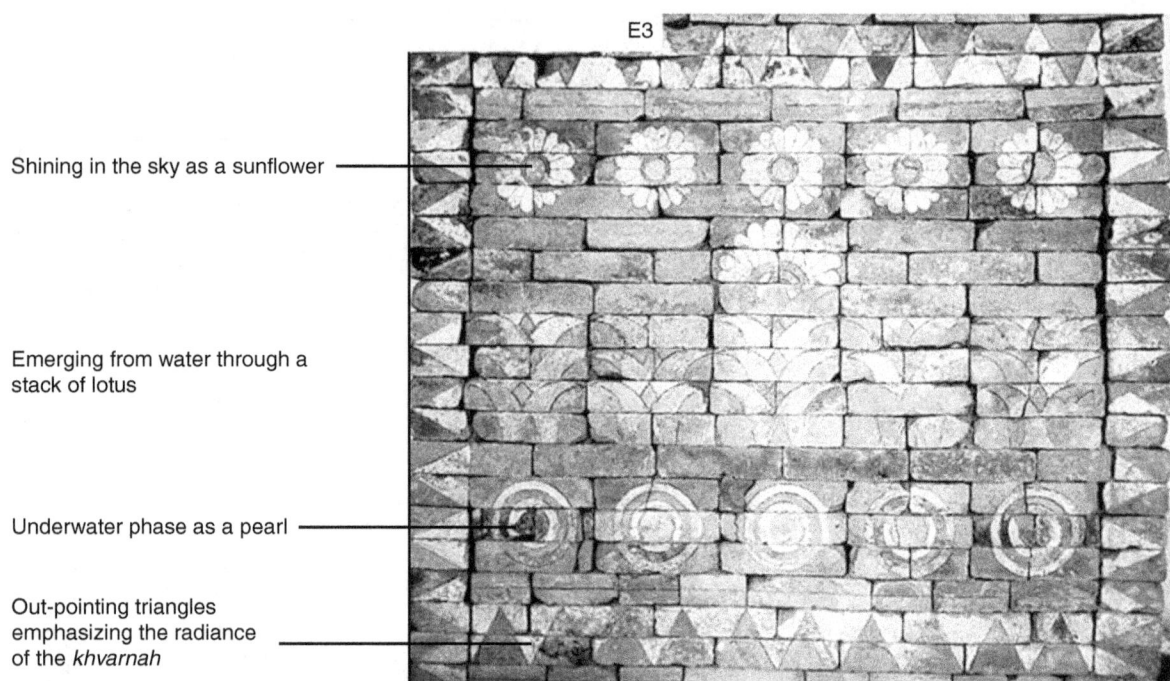

Fig. 12.7 Tripartite cycle of the *khvarnah*. Glazed brick panel, Persepolis. (Courtesy of the Oriental Institute, Chicago. Photograph no. P 58470)

group of Iranians, and it is likely that some of Darius' fellow conspirators, if not all, belonged to that group.[28] Indeed, both Herodotus and Bisotun agree that the usurper magus, Gaumata, was in control of the army and harshly suppressed any opposition (DB §13, Lecoq 1997: 191; Herodotus 2000, ii: 93 [Book III, §71]). It therefore seems logical to assume that under the cloud of terror that hung over their heads, the conspirators needed to trust each other. Their trust was probably based on common religious beliefs or affiliation.

My fourth example may reinforce this assumption. It is a silver plaque in the name of Otanes, one of Darius' co-conspirators whom Herodotus portrays as the elderly statesman who initiated the conspiracy (Fig. 12.9). It bears a cuneiform inscription deciphered by Pierre Lecoq:

I am Otanes..., I am (one) of the men in Persia. I...orders of Darius, the Great King. Darius says: *I protect the powerful (who is) just, I punish the liar (who is) a rebel.* By the support (*vashnā*) of Ahura Mazdā and with me, Darius is the Great King.[29]

Of course Otanes mentions Ahura Mazdā. But more important for our discussion is the sentence (in italics) in which Otanes is clearly challenging the Median beliefs expressed in Yt 13:95. The functions of supporting *authority* and suppressing *rebellion* are transferred from Mithra and Apām Napāt to Darius who, in effect, will act as Ahura Mazdā's deputy on earth.

But Yt 13:95 begs a question: why did the Medes need two deities to perform the same task in the first place, and why was one, for example Mithra, not enough? As Mary Boyce has explained, Iranians saw day and night as

Fig. 12.8 Symbol of *veraghna* surrounded by triangular light rays. Glazed brick, Persepolis. (Curtis & Tallis 2005: 95)

two different realms: the day came under the protection of Mithra and the night under that of Apam Napāt (Soudavar 2003: 53). This division was obviously incompatible with a monotheistic conception of the world, and had to be modified. This is what Otanes tried to achieve.

The plaque also reflects Darius' early preoccupations, and his emphasis in the Bisotun inscriptions that his orders were carried "by day and by night".[30] As deputy of Ahura Mazdā on earth, Darius had to abolish the division of time into two realms and contend that he effectively ruled both. The degree of his concern in this respect is measured by the number of lion–bull icons that were incorporated in the Persepolis visual propaganda programme.

I had suggested in a previous study that in this icon, the lion represented the sun and the bull symbolized the moon, and the whole reflected the day and night revolutions (Fig. 12.11) (Soudavar 2003: 116–120). The subsequent discovery of a seal from Sardis, with the sun and moon depicted over an intermingling lion and bull (Fig. 12.10), validates my interpretation.[31] Moreover, we can see that in placing a winged sphere in the middle of two rows, one flanked by bulls and the other by lions (Fig. 12.6), the designer of Darius' canopy was projecting that the *khvarnah* supported the king by day and by night. In so doing, the designer was still conditioned by a Median mindset by which night and day belonged to two different realms. The more clever presentation, however, was the combined lion–bull icon, which somehow blurred the separation between the two realms by presenting them as a perpetual phenomenon (Fig. 12.11). While similar icons exist in other cultures, they generally depict a lion devouring a helpless prey. The innovative approach

Fig. 12.9 Silver plaque of Otanes. (Private collection)

Fig. 12.10 The lion and bull design surmounted by sun and moon motifs. Seal from Sardis. (Dusinberre 2002: 278)

here was to depict it as a temporary and non-fatal attack of the lion, since the bull is springing back up with his head turned backwards, ready to re-engage with the lion. The artifice was meant to convey perpetuity in time.

The conclusions of Cindy Nimchuk (this volume) for the foundation plaques of the Apadana in Persepolis, bring an added vista into Darius' preoccupation with the realms of Mithra and Apam Napāt. As she argues, the choice of material for the two plaques (one in gold and the other in silver) was by design, and invoked the sun and the moon. In keeping with our analysis of the Otanes plaque and the Persepolis canopy, it seems that Darius was emphasizing that his authority—as described on the DPh inscriptions of the foundation plaques—was upheld "by day and by night". Moreover, gold Croeseids (i.e. coins from Lydia or more generally Asia Minor) were also placed in the foundation boxes along with the plaques. Of particular interest are the confronting heads of a lion and a bull on them (Fig. 12.12). It puts the lion and bull on an equal footing and confirms their role as iconic symbols for day and night, and not one as prey of the other.[32] By burying this coin, Darius was symbolically burying the Median division of the world into two realms.

Finally, the Otanes plaque shares a peculiarity with Bisotun, namely a slanted stroke placed before the first word (see top left of Fig. 12.9), which vouches for an early date of c.519 BC. Indeed, an important characteristic of the Old Persian script is the use of the slanted stroke as a word separator. This sign must initially have been conceived as a device to bracket words rather than to separate them, for we see that in Bisotun, the first word has it on both sides, that is, before and after. But Achaemenid scribes must have realized very quickly that the first stroke was superfluous and hence dropped it. To this date no inscription other than Bisotun has it. Its appearance on this plaque, therefore, attests to a date close to that of Bisotun. This early date corroborates our contention that Darius and his supporters strove from the outset to dismantle the Median ideology based on the dominion of Mithra and Apam Napāt over the realms of day and night.

4.5. *Arya chiça* in lieu of the Aryan *khvarnah*

My last example is from the trilingual Naqsh-e Rostam inscription (DNa §2) where Darius declares to be the "son of Vishtaspa the Achaemenid, Pārsā son of Pārsā, Aryan and Arya chiça". The latter—underlined—sentence has generally been translated as "Aryan and from Aryan origin".

In a forthcoming article, I argue that the Old Persian word *chiça*, its Avestic counterpart *chiθra*, as well as their progenies, all derive from a common root *chit*, which means brilliance and appearance, but to which philologists have unfortunately added unwarranted

Fig. 12.11 The lion and bull icon symbolizing the perpetual night and day revolutions, Persepolis. (Curtis & Tallis 2005: 78)

meanings such as "seed", "nature" and "origin" that can lead to a nonsense, as in the underlined sentence here: Aryan means precisely "of Aryan origin", there was no need to repeat it (Soudavar 2006a: 170–177). A Kurd would not say that he is Kurdish *and* of Kurdish origin; Clovis of France (r. 466–511) was never designated as a Frank *and* of Frankish stock. In addition, what benefit was there in claiming to be an Aryan if some of those who rebelled against Darius, such as the Medes and the Scythians, were also Aryans?

What Darius meant here was that he possessed the Aryan *khvarnah*; but because the word *khvarnah* had acquired a Mithraic connotation, he preferred to replace it with an equivalent term, hence *chiça* whose brilliance could also symbolize the radiating power of the *khvarnah*. In this trilingual inscription, neither the Babylonian scribe nor the Elamite one knew how to translate the purely Iranian idea of Aryan *chiça*, and refrained from doing it.[33] Modern philologists should have done the same.

Why did Darius do this? He did it because Yt 18.2 specifies that it is the Aryan *khvarnah* that "vanquishes the non-Aryan nations" (Dustkhāh 2002, i: 481), and Darius was claiming that he had conquered a series of nations that included non-Aryan ones:

DNa, §3—Darius the King says: By the will of Ahura Mazdā here are the nations (*dahyu*) that I conquered beyond Persia:
...the Mede, the Elamite, the Parthian, the Arian, the Arachosian, the Sattgydian,

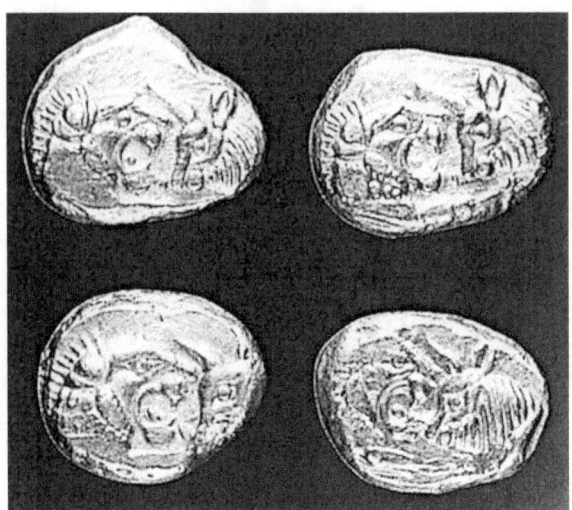

Fig. 12.12 Gold 'Croeseids' from the foundation box of the Apadana. (Curtis & Tallis 2005: 58)

the Gandharian, the Indian, the Amyrgian Scythian, the Tigrakhoda Scythians, the Babylonian, the Assyrian, the Arab, the Egyptian, the Armenian, the Cappodocian, the Lydian, the Greek, the Scythians From Beyond The Seas, the Thracian, the Aspidophores Greeks, the Libyans, the Ethiopians, the Macians, the Carians.

It should be noted that in Bisotun Darius also gives a list of nations which, although less extensive than this one, nonetheless includes non-Aryan nations. There is, however, a subtle difference in the way these two lists are introduced. In Bisotun, Darius presents a list of nations that "obeyed" him (DB §6, Lecoq 1997: 188). These were nations conquered by his predecessors, some of which had rebelled but were ultimately vanquished by Darius. Darius had restored order in the empire but as yet had not conquered any non-Aryan nation. By contrast, in the preamble to the DNa list he boasts that these were the nations "conquered" by him, among which there were non-Aryan nations such as the Thracians and the Ethiopians. The conquest of non-Aryan nations required the possession of the Aryan *khvarnah*.

The choice of *chiça* as a substitute for *khvarnah* ties well with the iconographic evidence by which Darius emphasizes the radiance of the *khvarnah* through triangular rays. By rendering the *khvarnah* luminous, he was able to claim back the solar attribute that he once tried to obtain through Ahura Mazdā. Thus, in retrospect, it was perhaps not the *Avesta* hymn composers of Elfenbein who perceived the phonetic similarity between the sun (*khvar*) and *khvarnah* (Elfenbein 2001: 492), but the imperial Achaemenid functionaries who seized upon it to build a solar imagery that kingship required. The use of the word *chiça* in lieu of *khvarnah* was to reinforce this solar imagery.

Unlike Darius' unsuccessful borrowing of a foreign solar symbol in Bisotun, the substitution of an equivalent Iranian term for the *khvarnah* had a lasting effect. It penetrated the Avestan vocabulary (Soudavar 2006a: 169–170), and reappeared as *chihr* in the ubiquitous Sasanian imperial slogan *ke chihr az yazatan*, one that was meant to portray the king reflecting the gods in their radiance and power.[34]

But the more interesting effect is how it inspired Zoroastrian priests to portray their prophet. We can see it in the Zāmyād Yasht: after the *khvarnah* flew away from Jamshid (Yima) and was hidden under water by Apam Napāt, the Turānian Afrāsiyāb (Frangrasyan) tries to recover it, but is repeatedly unsuccessful and utters each time:

> I have not been able to conquer the *khvarnah* that belongs to the Aryan nations—to the born and the unborn (i.e. now and for ever)—and to the holy Zoroaster. (Yt 5:42,

Yt 19:57, 60, 63–64, Dustkhāh 2002, i: 305, 495–96; Malandra 1993: 93–95)

In this passage, Zoraster is said to possess the Aryan *khvarnah*,[35] an auspicious power that only emanates from the Aryan nations. The problem, however, is that Jamshid's myth precedes Zoroaster because he himself alludes to it in his Gāthās (Y 32.8).[36] Therefore, it was impossible for Afrāsiyāb to have known Zoroaster and to attribute the Aryan *khvarnah* to him. The inclusion of the name of the prophet in this myth is obviously a later addition, but for what purpose?

Since time immemorial, priests have tried to increase the importance of their religion's prophet by borrowing kingly attributes and imagery. Shiites for instance used epithets such as *soltān* and *shāh* for their prophet and imams; and Christians have often portrayed Jesus seated on a golden throne, and have given him titles such as Pantocrator, and even Saviour (Greek *soter*), which was after all the epithet of Ptolemy I (r. 305–284 BC). Similarly, Zoroastrian priests seized upon the myth of Jamshid and the mention of the Aryan *khvarnah* in it to attribute the strongest form of *khvarnah* to their prophet, as Darius had also claimed. They probably invented concurrently the term Kiyānid *khvarnah*, in order to distinguish kingly *khvarnah* from the one now appropriated for Zoroaster.

5. The origins of the *khvarnah* and chronology issues

Pondering about the *khvarnah* and its relationship to Mithra and Apam Napāt, I had previously said that, "What is not clear, however, is whether these deities were chosen because of an existing association with *khvarnah* or because, as lords of daylight and night time, they were perceived as natural choices to embody the *khvarnah* cycle" (Soudavar 2003: 90). It now seems that the latter is true, and that the *khvarnah* was a tribal concept, referred to as the Aryan *khvarnah* that pre-existed the Medes. Even though in the *Avesta*, the Aryan *khvarnah* is labelled as "Mazdā-created", it clearly belonged to the Aryan nation and Ahura Mazdā had no further control over it. It was there to be claimed by a strong leader. It provided an authority beyond any bestowed by Ahura Mazdā, and thus had to be invoked separately. Several observations vouch for this assertion: there is a similar clan or tribe-related auspicious power that is invoked by other central Asian tribes, namely the Turcomans and the Mongols, in their edicts. In all of these edicts, the invocation of clan power comes after, and in addition to, a supreme deity that precedes it in their *invocatios* (Soudavar 2006*b*).

In the Gāthās, Zoroaster uses the word *khvarnah* only once and with "auspiciousness" as its meaning (Y 51.18, Dustkhāh 2002, i: 80). Had this word originally been associated with Mithra, it is doubtful that Zoroaster would have used it.

In the Zāmyād Yasht, Ahura Mazdā derives his creation powers from the *khvarnah* of the spiritual beings (*fravashis*) of the *ashavans*, a term which primarily seems to refer to the past heroes of the Aryan tribes.

In the same Yasht, when the Glory moves away from Jamshid it is simply termed as *khvarnah*, but when Afrāsiyāb wants to recuperate it, it is qualified as the Aryan *khvarnah*. This suggests that originally there was only one type of *khvarnah* and it belonged to the Aryan nations.

One may add that Lubotsky's and Parpola's recent suggestion for the etymology of *khvarnah* as being derived from Scythian *farnah* corresponding to Sanscrit *parna* (meaning "feather"), ties it more to a mythical bird than to a deity (Parpola 2002: 309–310).

This may then explain why Darius chose to rely on the concept of *khvarnah* to promote his legitimacy. The *khvarnah* was not a Median invention; the Medes had only given it a new veneer. Darius did the same by incorporating it into a monotheistic Mazdean ideology but paradoxically, by rendering it radiant and luminous, he reinforced its connection to the Iranian sun deity, Mithra. As soon as Mithra was reinstated by Artaxerxes II (r. 405–359 BC), the *khvarnah* became once again associated with it, and by extension the Median model of the solar and aquatic pair of deities was reinvigorated. In choosing to invoke Mithra and Anāhitā along with Ahura Mazdā in his inscriptions (Lecoq 1997: 269–270, 274–275), Artaxerxes II did what Iranian kings whose legitimacy was contested had to do: claim the support of Ahura Mazdā and the gods, which popular belief associated with the *khvarnah*. Thus similar to Sasanian kings such as Narseh (r. 293–303) or Khosrow II (r. 590–628), whose legitimacy had to be validated or reinstated, Artaxerxes II invoked Mithra and Anāhitā to bolster a legitimacy that had been eroded by the challenges mounted by his brother, Cyrus the younger (Soudavar 2003: 18–19, 73–78, 106–108).

Irrespective of when the Avestan hymns were composed, what is certain is that the attribution of the perpetual Aryan *khvarnah* to Zoroaster would have prevented the Achaemenid kings from claiming the same and would not have survived that era. Thus, the attribution of the Aryan *khvarnah* to Zoroaster must have happened after the demise of the Achaemenids. The obvious conclusion then is, if in the post-Achaemenid era there were additions to the *Avesta* in an archaistic style, the same could have happened earlier on, namely, the *Avesta* could have been composed by priests who favoured such a style (in the manner of Roman Catholic priests who still write in Latin). The archaistic style of the text, therefore, loses all validity for dating the time of its composition.

There is an interesting parallel between the Ābān Yasht dedicated to Anāhitā, and the Zāmyād Yasht, in that both include passages about the hidden *khvarnah* in the waters of lake Farākh-Kart (Vorou-Kasha). More interesting, however, is the difference between these two passages. In the Zāmyād Yasht, the story of the *khvarnah*, from its loss by Jamshid to its hiding in the waters of lake Farākh-Kart by Apam Napāt, is given in full detail. Then comes Afrāsiyāb, trying to recover it on his own, without seeking the help of a deity. His unsuccessful attempts lead to the utterance of the above-mentioned sentence in which he states that the Aryan *khvarnah* belongs to Zoroaster (Yt 19:57, 60, 63–64, Dustkhāh 2002, i: 495–496). By contrast, the only part of this story reported in the Ābān Yasht is about Afrāsiyāb's attempt to recover the *khvarnah* from its dormant and underwater stage. He sacrifices to Anāhitā and asks for her help. Help is denied, and as a result, he is unsuccessful. He then utters the same sentence as above (Yt 5:42, Dustkhāh 2002, i: 305).

According to Mary Boyce, the creation powers of Apam Napāt clashed with those of the supreme creator Ahura Mazdā, and he was gradually supplanted by another aquatic deity, Anāhitā (Boyce 1987: 149–150). The question is, why was there a need to supplant him at all? In a monotheistic conception of the world, was it not easier just to suppress, or ignore, problematic deities, as Darius did in his inscriptions and Zoroaster did in his Gāthās? The only plausible answer is that the need for the intervention of an aquatic deity was necessary for the *khvarnah* to emerge from its dormant stage under water. Mithra had no control over waters and therefore could not bestow the *khvarnah* unless it was released from the waters, and that was the responsibility of an aquatic deity. By emphasizing the radiance of the *khvarnah*, Darius had caused the consolidation of the position of the solar deity Mithra as the giver of *khvarnah*, and at the same time created the necessity for an aquatic counterpart for him as its keeper. The Avestan priests, who composed the Zāmyād and the Farvardin Yashts, resuscitated the Median pair of Mithra/Apam Napāt as the giver and guardian of the *khvarnah*. The Ābān Yasht, on the other hand, seems to conform better to the kingly ideology founded by Darius and subsequently modified by Artaxerxes II. Anāhitā appears in this Yasht as a powerful deity who not only controls the *khvarnah* but is also solicited by heroes as well as evil beings, to grant them their wishes. She, of course, accepts the wishes of the former but denies those of the latter. Anāhitā was thus the perfect choice for Artaxerxes to invoke alongside Mithra, because by eliminating Apam Napāt, the night and day division that Darius had so persistently fought against was avoided. At the same time, the invocation of this new pair of solar and aquatic deities projected for Artaxerxes the aura of popular legitimacy associated with the *khvarnah*. Nevertheless, Mithra's popularity posed a threat to the supremacy of Ahura Mazdā; it was safer to promote Anāhitā. She thus became the choice cultic deity of later Achaemenids and eventually, that of the Sasanians.

The Ābān Yasht therefore seems to have been composed in conformity with the directional changes instituted by Artaxerxes II and represented mainstream Achaemenid ideology, while the Zāmyād and Farvardin Yashts seem to have been composed on the fringe of the empire, or after the demise of the Achaemenids. Both were, however, modified in the post-Achaemenid era, in the passages where Zoroaster is said to possess the Aryan *khvarnah*.

6. Pārsā son of Pārsā

In a previous analysis of the genealogical identity that Darius provides in DNa (see 3.5 above), and through a comparison with Turcoman nomenclatures, I had argued that there was a structural difference in the use of the words "Achaemenid" and "Pārsā": one was repeated and the other not. If Darius' father was an Achaemenid, so was he; there was no need to repeat it. On the other hand, if the Pārsā qualification is repeated for father and son, it must point to a non-hereditary and non-permanent qualification (Soudavar 2006*a*: 171–172). I was, however, unable to suggest a meaning for Pārsā. But in light of my present analysis, I would like to suggest that, whatever the origins of the word, by the time of Darius it had acquired a religious connotation. Pārsā probably designated the group of Iranians who fanatically believed in the supremacy of Ahura Mazdā, to which Darius and his co-conspirators belonged. "Pārsā son of Pārsā" meant that both father and son adhered to the same Mazdā-worshipping group.

Several observations favour such an argument. Firstly, the modern Persian word *pārsā* means religious or pious, and I am at a loss to find any suitable etymological justification for it except as an affiliation with the term that Darius had used. Secondly, one should note that in referring to Mazdean priests who practised nightly ceremonies at the Chashmeh Sabz pond near Tus in Khorasan, Hamdollāh-e Mostowfi (d. 1335) uses the word *parsāyān*, which vouches for a pre-Islamic origin for the word *pārsā* (Mostowfi 1915: 148–149). Thirdly, in the coinage of Persis, there is for the period leading to the rise of Ardashir I, the odd representation of a ruler on the obverse, and his father on the reverse (e.g. Fig. 12.13). The combination seems to be the visual rendering of Darius' "Pārsā son of Pārsā" expression, which must have remained in use in the stronghold of the Achaemenids, present-day Fārs (which was named after the Pārsās). The Persis dynasty of rulers there were notoriously religious. The religious standing of Ardashir and his forefathers derived from their hereditary position as keepers of the temple of Anāhitā in Estakhr, and ties well with my previous assumption that the cult of Anāhitā was associated with the mainstream ideology of later Achaemenids. The home of the Pārsās thus remained the bastion of religious zealots who believed in the supremacy of Ahura Mazdā as the creator god, but whose cultic activity gravitated around Anāhitā. The hereditary religious leadership of the early Sasanians justified a "Pārsā son of Pārsā" qualification. The same may be true for the early Achaemenids.

7. Conclusion

I have tried to demonstrate that Darius began his reign with a strong monotheistic fervour but gradually had to relax it in view of the popular beliefs of his own constituency. That, in turn, much affected the outcome of Zoroastrianism, which must have had a strong monotheistic undertone at the time of the prophet, but lost it as it became more and more entangled with imperial ideology.

Initially, Darius' monotheistic fervour left no room for other deities to be invoked. It was a fervour shared by a group of supporters who all believed in the supremacy of Ahura Mazdā. To explain the activity of this group of zealots, I offered as a model the militancy of the Safavid Shāh Esmā'il and his followers. Although Henning once rebuked Hertzfeld for comparing pre-Islamic Iran with the post-Islamic era (Henning 1951: 15), I believe that the "history repeats itself" cliché is nowhere more fitting than in the Iranian context. If the young Shāh Esmā'il came out of hiding to conquer the Aq-Qoyunlu Empire that his maternal grandfather had founded, it was not to emulate Herodotus in his story of Cyrus II (who also rose to conquer the Median empire of his maternal grandfather), but because similar circumstances usually lead to similar outcomes. At the very least, the Safavid militancy model offers a possible scenario for how a small group of believers can impose their ideology on the rest of the population, an ideology that in turn will end up espousing many of the concepts and beliefs of its initial foes.

As Skjaervø has noted, there are indeed many parallels between the *Avesta* and Achaemenid ideology. But rather than proceed with his a-priori stance that "the Achaemenids had always been Zoroastrians or at some time for some reason the early Achaemenid became Zoroastrian" (Skjaervø 2005: 53), and restrict the scope of possibilities, I have allowed text and iconography to guide me in the opposite direction: the possibility of Achaemenid ideology affecting the composition of the *Avesta* and, by extension, Zoroastrianism.

Darius' kingly ideology was a forceful ideological revolution that can only be comprehended against the foil of his predecessors' beliefs. The key to this understanding is Yt 13:95, which not only explains the Median kingly ideology but provides, in conjunction with Yt 13:94, a solid clue for the birth date

Fig. 12.13 Coin of Shāpur and his father Pāpak, c.AD 210. (*Dr Busso Peus Nachf. Münzhandlung*, catalogue no. 368, lot 364)

of Zoroaster. The importance of this clue is validated by numerous iconographic as well as textual examples that show how persistently Darius tried to suppress the dual night and day realms of Mithra and Apam Napāt, that is, the very foundation of the Median kingly ideology.

Among Darius' innovative approaches was his reformulation of the concept of *khvarnah* by associating it with solar radiance, in conjunction with his emphasis on possessing the Aryan *khvarnah* (which he described as the Radiance of the Aryans). But since the same power was later on attributed to Zoroaster, we have solid proof of the partial composition of the *Avesta* in the post-Achaemenid era. This, in turn, invalidates the very foundation of the believers in an archaic and ancient *Avesta* who insist that the Avestan language was only in use c.1000 BC or earlier. Their theory is in reality a house of cards built on quicksand.

Like every other prophetic religion of the world, Zoroastrianism has been encumbered over the centuries with additions or aberrations dictated by political developments. Zoroaster's own monotheistic vision emanated from a sharp intellect which first defined "thought", and perceived the conceptual necessity of evil as the foil against which good must be measured (Gershevitch 1995: 6; Henning 1951: 46–47).

In form, his Gāthās have such a Gnostic tone that one wonders if Zoroaster should not be considered as the father of all subsequent Gnostic developments of the east Iranian world. Like all of these Gnostic ideologies, his Gāthās lament the love for the Creator, asking for guidance from him, and ultimately seeking unity with him. It is hard to imagine how such a superior intellect and pure-hearted visionary could be the author of, or inspiration for, a multi-polar *Avesta* riddled with divinities that ultimately undermine Zoroaster's monotheistic and Gnostic outlook.

Based on a stylistic analysis of text, Kellens and Pirart once suggested that the *Avesta* had more than one author (1988: 7), but more important than the authors are the main ideologues of the *Avesta*, namely, those whose ideas shaped the holy book of Zoroastrianism. If Zoroaster was the first such ideologue, then the second one was undoubtedly Darius, son of Vishtaspa the Achaemenid, Pārsā son of Pārsā, an Aryan and possessor of the Aryan *khvarnah*.

Notes

1. In 1985–87 Kellens estimated the hiatus between the older and younger *Avesta* to be four centuries (1987: 135–139). Four years later, he seems to have revised it to two centuries (1991: 14).
2. According to Kellens, the younger *Avesta* emulated the older one, at times without a proper understanding of the latter's underlying structure (1987: 139). It implicitly admits the attachment of later priests to an archaistic language.
3. Gershevitch (1995: 4–5) favours Sogdiana as Zoroaster's homeland. Grenet (2005: 29–51) projects the views of different authors on maps, all emphasizing this eastern Iranian corridor as the growth place of Zoroastrianism.
4. Fussman, for instance, characterizes the Avestan community as a "civilization of cattle breeders, marginally agricultural, with a non-lasting habitat that was unsophisticated construction wise, without any trace of urban civilization, using the horse and the cart for warfare and practicing looting raids" in order to conclude that it must have belonged to the second millennium BC (Fussman 2005: 221). Unfortunately, anyone who has witnessed Afghan raids on eastern Iran (I being one such witness) can vouch that except for the use of a gun, Fussman's definition also fits Afghan raiders of the twentieth century. His definition is in fact a perfect fit for the marauding bands of Afghans, Hezaras or Turkmen who lived a few centuries earlier and before the advent of the gun. Such a characterization is therefore not proof for assigning the Avestan community to the second millennium BC.
5. Boyce had been misled by Bailey's erroneous translation of *abgenag* (glass) as "crystal"; glass is classified in the *Bundahishn* as a metal (presumably because it is obtained through a melting process, as metals are) (Malandra 2003: 273).
6. Most mythological chariots, such as those mentioned in the *Iliad* (23, 334–348), are described as a *bigae* or two-horse chariot, but Swennen remarks that the *quadriga* is already mentioned in the *Rigveda* (Swennen 2004: 89). Whatever implication it may have for its dating, the *quadrigae* pertains to a sophisticated society and not a primitive one.
7. Francfort, for instance, demonstrates that the supposedly Zoroastrian funerary practice of leaving the dead body in the open air was practised in non-Iranian Central Asian communities and alongside burial tombs for goats or camels, which further vouches for the non-Zoroastrian nature of those communities (Francfort 2005: 276–277, 294–295; see also Kellens 2005: 45–46; Razmjou 2005b: 154).
8. "and the Mazdean religion (*dyny mzdysn*), as well as the Magians, found respect in our country" (Gignoux 1972: 187). The *Avesta* also refers to its religion in the same way: "the good Mazdean Religion" (Y 6.12, Y 16.6), "Mazdā-worshipper and a Zoroastrian" (Y 12.6).
9. The most blatant example of Skjaervø's misguided approach is his reliance on the linguistic imagery of a grasping hand to convey the notion of vanquishing, capturing and subduing an enemy (Skjaervø 2005: 71–73), which is neither a religious nor a kingly concept but stems from the normal development of a language, similar to what in English would be described as "having the upper hand". For more on the hand (*dast*) imagery in the Iranian context, see Soudavar 2003: 13–14.
10. Gnoli 2000: 156. The mini-calendar of Zādspram allows a lifespan of 77 years for the prophet (Gignoux & Tafazzoli 1993: 87); it consequently puts his death at c.541 BC.
11. See note 14, below. Kellens's objections as to the unreliability of "258" because of its connection with imaginary regnal years (Kellens 2001: 177) becomes irrelevant as per the scenario in which a religious tradition only kept dates pertaining to its own survival, and upon which regnal years of a forgotten distant past had to be suddenly transplanted in Sasanian times.
12. I refer here to the ubiquitous Sasanian political idiom *ki chihr az yazatan* and the erroneous Greek translation of the word *chihr* as "family", rather than as a reflective aura, which I have argued to be the proper meaning in Soudavar 2003: 41–47. Since the latter's publication, Panaino has independently come to the same conclusion (2004: 555–585), and Philippe Gignoux has also supported my thesis (personal communication).
13. Biruni 1377: 20: "258 years from the beginning of Zoroaster's prophethood (*zohur*) to the beginning of Alexander's era (*tārikh-e eskandar*)"; Biruni

1377: 174 and Mas'udi 1962, ii: 551: "258 years from Vishtaspa until the advent of Alexander"; Mas'udi 1962, i: 202 also states that the father of Vishtāsp, i.e. Lohrāsp, was a contemporary of Nabuchodonosor (r. 605–562 BC).

14. The "Coming of the Religion" (which supposedly occurred when Zoroaster was 30 years old) was confounded in these reconstructions with the year Zoroaster converted Kay Goshtāsp (i.e. Vishtaspa) to his cause in the 13th year of a reign lasting 120 years. Thus, the part of Kay Goshtāsp's reign included in the "258" figure is calculated by the texts as 120 minus 30. The Bundahishn (p.156) gives Kay Goshtāsp as 120−30 = 90 years, Bahman 112, Homāy-e Bahman-dokht 30, Dārā-ye chehr-āzādan ("who is Bahman") 12, Dārā-ye Dārāyān (i.e. Darius III) 14. Mas'udi (At-tanbih val-eshrāf: 85–88) gives: Kay Goshtāsp 120−30 = 90 years, Bahman 112, Khomāni 30, Dārā 12, Dārā-ye Dārāyān 14. Both lists total 258 years. One can readily see from these examples that the compilers of the regnal tables had no clue about earlier history, and reconstructed it by fitting into an orally transmitted time-bracket of 258 years the names of ancient and mythical figures, equally received through an oral tradition.
15. For a detailed reasoning see Gershevitch 1995: 6–7 and also Taqizadeh 1947: 34–38, where the latter provides a full explanation and extensive data on how the Seleucid era was equated with the tenth millennium of the Zoroaster era.
16. Dustkhāh 2002, i: 425 (see note 18 below).
17. Since the *Avesta* is about Iranian people we must look for an Iranian empire, and not, for instance, for an Elamite one.
18. Gershevitch (1959: 27) and Malandra (1971: 211) had both previously reinstated the missing *apąm* (I am indebted to Xavier Tremblay for pointing out these two references to me). It is precisely because of a better rendering of this narrative rhythm that I have relied on the Persian translation of the *Avesta* by Dustkhāh, rather than on others.
19. If Herodotus (book III, §65; Herodotus 2000, ii: 85) is to be trusted, when Cambyses asks his followers to seek revenge on Gaumata, he does it "in the name of the *gods* of [his] royal house" and not Ahura Mazdā (or Zeus in the Greek context).
20. See Soudavar 2003: 88–92 and 101 for the justification of the term "winged sphere" in lieu of a winged disc.
21. For the importance of sun gods in Anatolian and Mesopotamian cultures, see Beckman 2002: 37–40.
22. "this is what I request from Ahura Mazdā, with all the *gods*; may Ahura Mazdā, with all the *gods*, fulfill my wishes" (Lecoq 1997: 228).
23. Soudavar 2003: 23, 100. For a representation of the same on a gold ornament see Dusinberre 2003: 149.
24. For the concept of *farreh-afzun* (abundant *khvarnah*), and the multiplicity of its symbols, see Soudavar 2003:16–19, 59–62, 91.
25. This modification was only applied when the two emblems were represented together, not when Ahura Mazdā was represented alone as in Naqsh-e Rostam.
26. The strong concentration of the "Mazdā-created" label in some of the liturgies such as Y 4 and Y 6 also seems to be an attempt to attribute the creation of entities to Ahura Mazdā, when they may have been previously associated with other deities. In Y 4.10, for instance, where the "Mazdā-created Waters" are praised in the same sentence as the aquatic deity Apam Napāt (lit. Son of Waters), the label was necessary to sever the creation ties of Apam Napāt with the Waters.
27. For an embossed gold medallion of *veraghna* surrounded by a sunflower-type radiance, see Curtis & Tallis 2005: 147, fig. 185.
28. The imposition of the extreme type of Shiism after the ascent of Shāh Esmā`il to the throne was also mainly effected by a small group of supporters known as the Qezelbāsh.
29. I shall rely here on the initial text published in a sales catalogue (Lecoq 2003: 105), even though Lecoq has had more insights into it since then. The Old Persian word *vashnā* has generally been translated as "By the Grace of (a divinity)". This is why Lecoq expressed some surprise at its use by Darius himself in DPd §2 (1997: 227). The use of the same word by Otanes perhaps indicates that "support" is a better translation than "grace".
30. The "by day and by night" emphasis appears in DB §7 in three languages, and in DB §8 in the Babylonian version only (Lecoq 1997: 189).
31. The sun and moon also appear on Sasanian seals, see seals DJ3 and DJ6 in Bivar 1969: pl. 11.
32. A recent article by Cahill and Kroll attributes the creation of these Croeseids to Croesus' time (I am grateful to Cindy Nimchuk for pointing this out to me). Unfortunately I am not convinced by their arguments for the following reasons: a) I can find no justification as to why Croesus would switch from the powerful symbol of a single lion to a mixed symbolism of two confronting animals, neither winning nor losing, which somehow

diminishes the projection of power, and can only be justified with a Median-type theory advanced here (I doubt one could find a similar one in the Greek context); b) the test data is inconclusive and in any case also covers the 499 BC burning of Sardis; c) more importantly, since they emphasize that the coins were found in areas that displayed widespread fire and burning (Cahill & Kroll 2005: 595), the scenario fits the 499 event much better than the conquest by Cyrus. The latter's army may have looted the city, but it would have been uncharacteristic of Cyrus to let his army burn a surrendered city. Their main argument, that no item datable to post-*c.*550 BC was found in the debris, rests on a dating of Greek vases that, as they admit themselves, is contested by some scholars. However, the discovery of a later item is needed to destroy their theory entirely. Be that as it may, even if this type of coin was originally Lydian, for Darius it represented the symbol of day and night.

Persians were notorious for adopting foreign symbols and interpreting them in their own way.

33. DNa §2, Lecoq 1997: 219; the Elamite version simply repeats the *Ariya chiça* without attempting any translation (Dr Chlodowig Werba, personal communication).
34. See note 12 above.
35. In Yt 18, the Aryan Khvarnah is both qualified as *airiianəm x^{v}arenō* (i.e. "the Aryan *khvarnah*") and *airiianąm x^{v}arenō* (i.e. "the *khvarnah* of the Aryans"). The formula here of a *khvarnah* that is emphasized to belong forever to the Aryan nations is just a more explicit way of describing the same thing (I am indebted to Xavier Tremblay for this clarification).
36. Dustkhāh 2002, i: 80. In Vendidad 2.2, Ahura Mazdā tells Zoroaster that Jamshid was the first man to whom he talked (Dustkhāh 2002, ii: 665). The myth of Yima can in fact be traced back to the Indo-European heritage (Malandra 1983: 175).

Part 3

Gender Studies

13

The Royal Audience Scene Reconsidered

Maria Brosius

Our understanding of the presentation of women in Achaemenid art remains limited.[1] This is partly due to the scarcity of literary and archaeological sources which have come down to us, and partly due to a tradition of scholarship summarized in Ernst Herzfeld's comment that: "In Achaemenid sculpture no woman is pictured, and evidently it never became a normal subject" (Herzfeld 1941: 325). This view is predominantly based on the absence of female representations on the Persepolis reliefs,[2] where the artistic theme focuses on the king's bodyguards and courtiers as well as on the delegations of the different peoples of the empire (Root 1979: esp. ch. 6). But the art of Achaemenid palace architecture followed a particular theme within the concept of imperial ideology, expressing the most important message with regard to royal rule—the depiction of the king as the absolute, but peaceful, monarch ruling over his subjects (Root 1979: 161, 298–299, 309–311). The absence of female depictions at Persepolis has no bearing on the status of royal and high-ranking women at the Persian court or their relevance as artistic subjects in Achaemenid art.

As the, albeit few, literary and archaeological sources demonstrate, there was no restriction regarding the depiction of Persian women. According to Herodotus (7.69.2), Darius I had a statue of his wife Artystone made of gold, and archaeological finds recovered from the Persian satrapies confirm that the artistic representation of women was far from being an exceptional occurrence. Women were depicted on a variety of media, for example precious metal, ivory, tapestry and stone, on seals and on finger rings. Incense-burners and kohl tubes were crafted in the shape of women wearing Persian-style clothing and hairstyles. As these finds have now been well documented,[3] I would like to turn our attention back to the centre of Persian power, Persepolis, and discuss a seal impressed on some Persepolis Fortification Tablets. The seal, PFS 77*, is carved in Neo-Elamite style and depicts an audience scene in which an enthroned woman, attended by a female servant, receives a female visitor (Fig. 13.1).[4] By placing the image of this seal in a wider archaeological context it is argued in this contribution that specific artistic depictions of royal and high-ranking Persian women existed

Fig. 13.1 Female audience scene carved in Neo-Elamite style on PFS 77*. (With kind permission of M. B. Garrison, M. C. Root and the Persepolis Seal Project)

which were part of a recognized catalogue of Achaemenid court art. The reason why similar scenes were found outside the Persian heartland was that these images were copied and adapted by the local elite. As the Persepolis seal furthermore demonstrates, this type of court scene finds its immediate origins in Neo-Elamite culture, though further cultural connections may be found in Urartian and other Ancient Near Eastern art.

In Achaemenid court art the image of the audience scene is epitomized in the king's audience scene, a relief panel originally placed as the centrepiece of the Apadana reliefs, but later moved to the royal treasury (Fig. 13.2). The scene shows the king seated on a high-backed throne with his feet resting on a footstool. He is depicted wearing his royal regalia, the many-folded Persian dress and the crown, holding a lotus flower and a staff in his hands. The heir to the throne stands behind the king, attended by two high-ranking courtiers. Two incense-burners separate the king from the approaching visitor, a Persian noble wearing a round cap, tunic and trousers and, in a gesture of deference, bowing slightly before the king while holding his hand in front of his mouth. A similar scene is depicted in the doorways of the audience hall of Artaxerxes I, the One-Hundred- Column-Hall. It shows the enthroned king with two royal courtiers or servants standing behind him, one of whom is holding up a fly-whisk (Fig. 13.3). Similar images of such audience scenes can be found on seals from Persepolis and Dascyleium. Among the Persepolis seals, PFS 22, carved in Fortification style, depicts a seated figure with staff and lotus flower receiving a visitor led by the hand by a courtier.[5] The more elaborate court style is used for the audience scene impressed on several *bullae* from Dascyleium (Fig. 13.4).[6] In an example dated to the late fourth century BC, a combination of the different audience reliefs from the Apadana and the One-Hundred-Column-Hall has been identified on the inside of a Persian shield on the so-called Alexander Sarcophagus from Sidon (cf. Garrison 2001: 65–82, esp. 81, figs 13–14). It shows the enthroned king in the centre holding his staff (Fig. 13.5), with a servant standing behind him with a fly-whisk, while the visitor in tunic and trousers stands before the king in a deferential posture.[7]

The fact that this court scene was a recognized image of the king becomes evident in its adaptation in local dynastic art. The Harpy monument from Xanthos in Lycia is undoubtedly the most striking example of the adaptation of the Persian royal audience scene, carved on the four relief panels of the tomb.[8] The east face depicts the king enthroned on a high-back chair, holding his royal insignia, the lotus flower and staff, his feet resting on a footstool. He is receiving a male visitor in audience, whose gift, a bird, is held in the outstretched arms of a kneeling servant or courtier (Fig. 13.6a). It has been suggested that a local ruler selected this scene in order to commemorate his audience with the Persian king as one of the most significant events of his life (Borchhardt 1990: 164). The north and south sides of the tomb present similar scenes, with the enthroned ruler receiving gifts of a

Fig. 13.2 Audience relief from Persepolis. (Photograph M. Brosius)

helmet and a bird from their respective visitors (Figs. 13.6b–c).⁹

For the present discussion the most striking scene is that of the relief on the west face of the Harpy tomb, which depicts a female audience scene. While the left section of the relief shows an enthroned female with a cow and a suckling calf standing on an altar, the right section depicts a second woman seated on an elaborate high-backed throne. Her feet rest on a footstool; in her right hand she holds a lotus flower and in her left hand a bird. Before her stand three women, all of them holding up a flower in one hand. All the women wear Greek dress and hairstyle. While the complete scene is not easy to interpret and its figures are difficult to identify, it can certainly be established that the audience scene in the right section of the relief was modelled on a Persian prototype (Fig. 13.6d).

That the depiction of female audience scenes is not an exceptional occurrence is demonstrated on two reliefs from Dascyleium. The Anthemion stele shows a seated woman, accompanied by two female attendants standing behind her, one of whom appears to be holding up a fly-whisk, being approached by two women (Fig.13.7).¹⁰ The fact that these women appear to be wearing long veils places the stele close to Persian, or Persianizing, art (Bakır 2001: 174). A second stele from Dascyleium depicts a woman enthroned on a high-backed chair, with a female figure standing in front of her (Fig. 13.8).¹¹

The female audience scene is best known from an Achaemenid seal formerly in the De

144 THE WORLD OF ACHAEMENID PERSIA

Fig. 13.3 Audience relief from a doorway of the One-Hundred-Column-Hall, Persepolis. (Photograph M. Brosius)

Fig. 13.4 Audience scene on a bulla from Dascyleium. (With kind permission of Deniz Kaptan)

Clerq Collection and now in the Louvre (AO 22359) (Fig. 13.9). This seal shows a woman seated on a high-backed throne, itself elaborately crafted. Her feet rest on a footstool. The woman is dressed in the long-sleeved, many-folded Persian dress and wears a crown or diadem and a veil falling down her back. In her hand she holds a lotus flower. The image bears a striking resemblance to the royal audience scene. There can be no doubt that she is a high-ranking Persian woman who holds the lotus flower as a mark of her status,[12] and whose feet, like those of the king, are not allowed to touch the ground (Athenaeus 12.514). As in the king's audience scene, a large incense-burner standing before her separates the enthroned figure from her female visitor, a woman in Persian dress, wearing a mural crown and a bobbed hairstyle; a veil is hanging down her back. She holds an object in her left hand (a lotus flower?). A third female figure, also in Persian dress and veil, offers a bird to the seated figure. The smallest of the three women, she is a female servant who hands the offering on behalf of the woman visitor. Yet this scene has repeatedly been interpreted as depicting an offering to a seated goddess (Amiet 1977: 821; Spycket 1980: 44). If "ordinary" women could not be depicted in Persian art, then such prominent figures must be female deities. Accordingly, the present of the bird had to be a religious offering, rather than an act of gift-giving. But this interpretation makes matters rather more complicated than they are. It supposes not only that the Persians made statues of their gods, an assumption for which we have no evidence whatsoever, and which is even contradicted by Herodotus (1.131.1) but also, by extension, that such statues would be put up in a sacred space, such as a temple. Yet there is no evidence that the Achaemenids

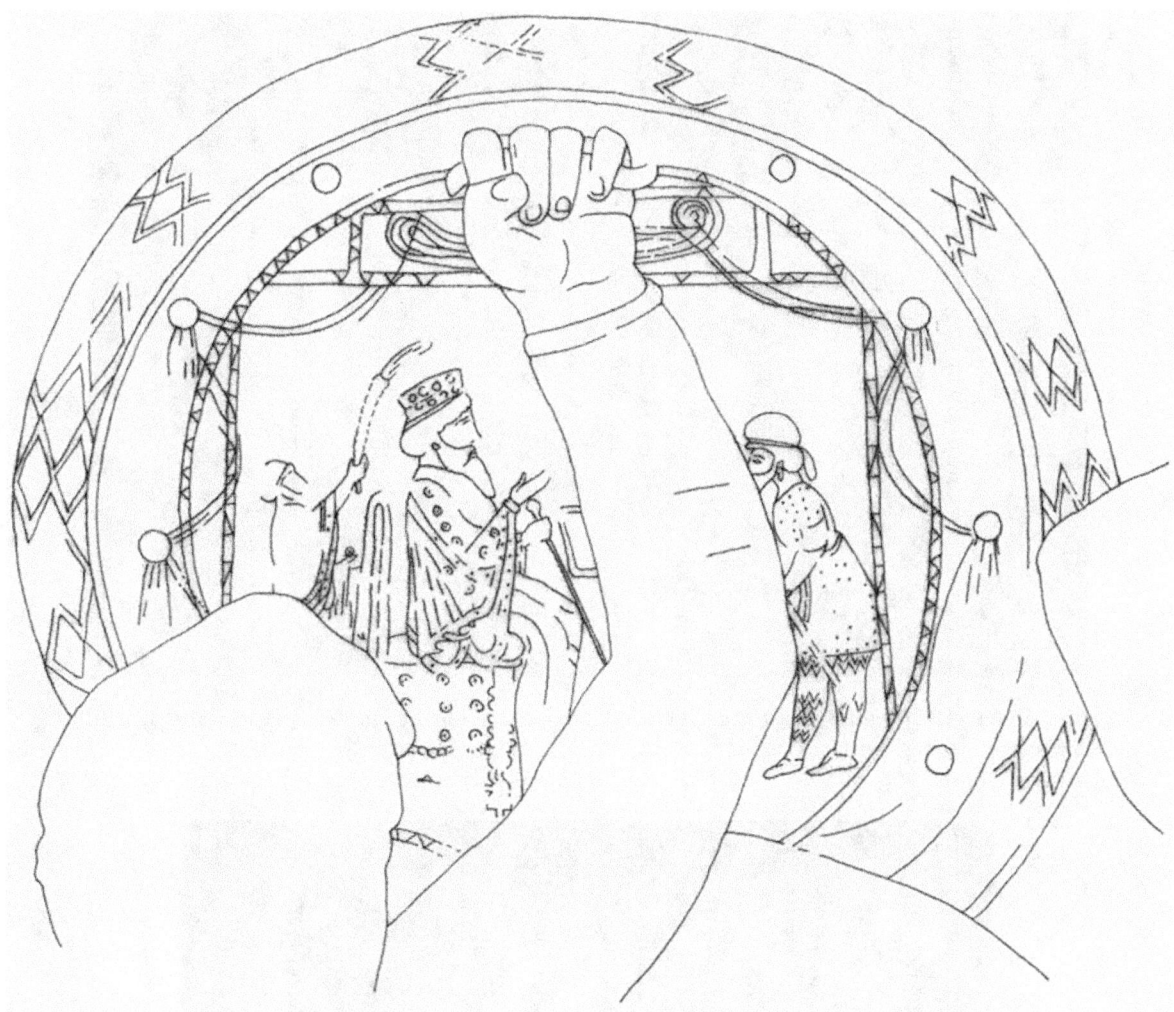

Fig. 13.5 Audience scene on the inside of a Persian shield on the so-called Alexander Sarcophagus. (Drawing by Marion Cox)

built temples in which to worship their gods; on the contrary, they performed religious rites in open-air sanctuaries, and in front of fire altars. Furthermore, a religious interpretation of the Louvre seal implies that such bird offerings were made, yet according to the Persepolis Fortification texts, sacrificial animals included mostly sheep and goats, as well as horses.[13]

The enthroned female of the Louvre seal bears no attribute that would allow her to be identified as a divinity. The crown signifies her status as a high-ranking woman, and is well attested as a headdress for royal women in the Ancient Near East. An excellent example for the Achaemenid period comes from the relief plaque from Egypt, which depicts a crowned Persian lady (Moorey 1988*b*: pl. 59), and the depiction of four crowned Persian women on the carpet from Pazyryk standing before a fire altar.[14] We can surely envisage that royal women of different rank, for example

Fig. 13.6a Harpy tomb, east face. (With kind permission of the Trustees of the British Museum)

Fig. 13.6b Harpy tomb, north face. (With kind permission of the Trustees of the British Museum)

The Royal Audience Scene Reconsidered **147**

Fig. 13.6c Harpy tomb, south face. (With kind permission of the Trustees of the British Museum)

Fig. 13.6d Harpy tomb, west face. (With kind permission of the Trustees of the British Museum)

Fig. 13.7 Female audience scene on the Anthemion stele, Dascyleium. (After Tomris Baktr 2001)

the king's mother and the king's wife, wore crowns.[15]

If we compare the female audience scene of the Louvre seal with the scenes depicted on the Harpy tomb, we find a striking similarity—an enthroned royal or high-ranking figure receiving a bird as a gift offering. Yet by identifying one scene as a divine scene and the other as a monarchical one, we are applying different measures of interpretation, evidently depending on whether the scene depicts a female or a male figure. It seems that the main reason for identifying the seated woman on the Louvre seal as a goddess stems from the misconception that women were not depicted in Achaemenid art, which excludes the possibility that this image represents a royal woman in a courtly scene. The difficulty in this case must be that the depiction of a female audience scene would without any doubt signify that royal or high-ranking Persian women indeed held an official, public status at court. It would also indicate that artistic motifs existed which were recognized themes in royal representational art. While the religious interpretation of the scene on the Louvre seal has to be dismissed, together with the examples discussed above, it provides strong evidence for the fact that royal women were depicted in

Fig. 13.8 Female audience scene on a funerary stele from Dascyleium. (With kind permission of Pierre Briant)

art and the suggestion that they did indeed hold audiences.

To support this argument further I would like to turn to seal PFS 77* from Persepolis (Fig. 13.1) (Brosius 1996: 86).[16] The seal shows a woman with a bobbed hairstyle seated on a throne. An incense-burner separates the enthroned figure from her female visitor, who also wears a long dress and a bobbed hairstyle. She is smaller than the seated figure, undoubtedly an indication of her lower rank. Both are holding an object (a bowl or a stylized flower?). Behind the enthroned figure stands a female servant

Fig. 13.9 Female audience scene on the Persian seal from the De Clerq Collection, Louvre. (Drawing by Marion Cox)

holding a fly-whisk above her head. None of the women wears a crown. The image is reminiscent of the king's audience scenes from the Persepolis reliefs.

What makes this scene invaluable for our discussion is not only the fact that it is carved in Neo-Elamite style,[17] but also that it bears an Elamite inscription which identifies the seated female figure. The seal and inscription together provide, in my view, indisputable evidence that this scene depicts a high-ranking woman, not a goddess, and that this represents a court scene. The inscription reads "MUNUS Seraš DUMU Hubanahpina", "(the) woman Seraš, of (the) man Hubanahpi", and identifies the enthroned female as a high-ranking lady of the court. Thus, this Neo-Elamite seal from Persepolis holds the key to the way we ought to interpret the female audience scene. It provides a vital piece of evidence to support the argument that non-divine women were depicted in art belonging to the Persian period, and specifically, that they were presented in scenes related to courtly themes.[18]

The fact that the seal is Neo-Elamite comes as no surprise, as the Persians' adaptation of Elamite art and culture is well attested, not least through M. C. Root's fundamental study (1979; cf. Brosius 1996: 87). Apart from the Neo-Elamite seals used in the administration of Persepolis, Root identified the hand-over-wrist gesture, exemplified in the thirteenth-century statue of queen Napir-asu, queen of Untash-Gal, from Susa,[19] and the rock relief of the local ruler Hanni and his queen at Shekaft-e Salman near Malamir, as a gesture which was adapted in Persian art, evidenced in the high relief figure of a Persian woman (see above p. 148). Yet what is important to point out is the fact that the scene on PFS 77* provides a direct antecedent for the royal audience scenes from Persepolis (although, of course, the audience or presentation scene can be traced back to much earlier periods). It also provides a historical context for the Persian audience scene on the Louvre seal as well as for the scene on the stele from Dascyleium. The fact that this motif was adapted by the Persian elite and recognized as an image that depicted kings as well as royal and high-ranking women, is of considerable historical significance. It adds to our understanding of Achaemenid art as well as of the Persian royal court.[20]

If we accept this view it alters the way we think about status and official rank of women at the Persian court. Based on PFS 77* the images on the seals depict actual events and would be identified as such by the viewer, or the reader, of the seals. This artistic motif originates in Achaemenid court art, and its adaptations can be found in the Persianizing art of the empire, exemplified in scenes such as depicted on the Anthemion stele and even the Harpy tomb. A more difficult problem to address is, under what circumstances did royal or high-ranking women hold audiences,[21] and who were the women allowed to approach them?

I would like to take this discussion one step further by arguing that the corpus of court art, which included the female audience scene, also included the depiction of women in banquet scenes. Banqueting was a courtly pursuit, which found its artistic expression as part of the "official" representations of the king and his court. It is best known from Aššurbanipal's banqueting scene from the North Palace at Nineveh, dating to c.650 BC (BM 124920; cf. Winter 1976: fig. 6). The relief shows the king reclining on a couch, the queen seated beside him on a high chair. Both are holding drinking bowls. In the Achaemenid period the image of the banqueting royal couple can be found on several artefacts from the Achaemenid realm, suggesting that the motif of the banqueting couple was adapted into Persian art. Notably it is carved on a funerary stele from Dascyleium dated to the fourth century BC, in which the lower panel depicts a reclining man and a woman, wearing Persian dress and a crown and veil, seated next to him on a chair.[22] The woman has the typical bobbed hairstyle and is wearing round earrings, a crown and a veil. Both figures are holding up drinking bowls. The scene is framed by two servants (one male, one female?). A rather Hellenized representation can be seen on an ivory plaque from Demetrias, showing a reclining Persian in tunic, trousers and the soft felt cap with cheek flaps. He appears to be receiving a drinking cup from a woman standing or seated behind his couch. Each figure is attended by a male or female servant respectively (Boardman 2000: fig. 5.83b). Banquets were significant occasions at the Achaemenid court and could range from small events, which included only the king, the king's mother and the king's wife,[23] to several hundred, if not thousand, guests. The imagery found in the few examples mentioned here is all the more important because they depict actual scenes that occurred at the royal (and satrapal) court. The Dascyleium stele and the plaque from Demetrias are versions of a motif that, like the audience scene, will have derived from the corpus of Achaemenid court art.[24]

Notes

1. The question of female representation in Achaemenid art has previously been discussed in a chapter of my doctoral thesis (Brosius 1991), which was only summarily included in the subsequent publication (Brosius 1996: 84–87). This paper offers a more detailed examination of one particular image referred to in this chapter, the audience

or presentation scene, depicted on PFS 77*. My interest in this image has been re-ignited by recent discussions of the royal audience scene by Deniz Kaptan (1996, 2002) and Mark Garrison (2001), as well as a workshop on ancient courts, which forced me to think more consciously about the position held by royal women within the hierarchy of the Achaemenid court (Brosius 2007).
2. On this problem see also the comments made by Sancisi-Weerdenburg 1983a: 22.
3. Some of the objects depicting women have been documented in Chester G. Starr's articles on Greeks and Persians (1975, 1977), J. Boardman's (1970a) book *Gems and Finger Rings*, as well as a brief article by A. Spycket (1980); cf. also Moorey 1988b: esp. pls 59–60, 78b–d, 82. For the female figures engraved on gold plaques cf. Dalton (1964) and Rudenko (1970) for the finds from Pazyryk. Daems (2001) adds nothing new and disappoints in its incompleteness and lack of critical analysis.
4. I am very grateful to Margaret Cool Root and Mark Garrison who allowed me to discuss PFS 77* here prior to its publication in the forthcoming volume of their Persepolis Seal project (Garrison & Root in preparation).
5. For a photograph and a drawing of the image see Garrison 2001: 65–82, esp. 81 with figs 13–14.
6. See Kaptan 1996: 259–271; 2002: esp. pls 47–59. Cf. also Miller 2003a: 301–302, 305; cf. Hrouda 1991: 426.
7. Although obscured by the soldier's arm, it must be assumed that the scene includes incense-burners that separated the king from his visitor (cf. von Graeve 1970; for a drawing of this scene see Boardman 2000: fig. 5.63).
8. See Zahle 1975: esp. pls VI–VIII, X; Borchhardt 1990: 164–165. Cf. also Miller 2003a: 306–307; Ghirshman 1964a: 349: figs. 444, 425. For a further example see the relief of the Nereid monument from Xanthos which also depicts a Hellenized version of the Persian ruler enthroned, wearing the upright tiara, behind him a courtier standing holding his parasol, followed by three other courtiers. The king is being approached by two visitors (cf. Borchhard 1990: 167). According to Philostratus (*Imagines* 2.31) a Greek painting showed an audience scene between the Great King and Themistocles (cf. Hofstetter 1978: 173).
9. Arguments for Elam's considerable political and cultural influence on Achaemenid Persia have been convincingly put forward by P. Miroschedji, who analysed the peaceful acculturation of the Persians (1985) and, most recently, by W. Henkelmann (2003a). For Urartian parallels of this scene see below, n. 18. For early Mesopotamian examples see Irene Winter's discussion on the presentation scene on Ur III seals (Winter 1986: 253–258, pls 62–64).
10. The incense-burner, seemingly standing between the two female visitors, allowed T. Bakır (2001: 174) to suggest that the scene depicts a funerary ceremony. But equally it can be argued that the incense-burner is part of a courtly audience scene, where its appearance is well attested.
11. I wish to thank Pierre Briant for drawing my attention to this unpublished find from Dascyleium and for allowing me to use his photograph of the stele for this publication.
12. Cf. van Loon 1986: 245–52. See also the discussion on the lotus flower by Irene Winter (1976: 25–54, esp. 45).
13. Cf. Moorey 1988a; also Hallock 1969 for the Fortification texts relating to religious rites, and Handley-Schachler 1992.
14. Cf. Starr 1975: pl. XXIIIB. In the scene the two women standing closer to the altar are taller than those standing behind them, probably indicating the different rank between them. In contrast to the smaller women the taller ones wear long veils. They also hold a lotus flower in their hands, whereas the others are depicted with a bundled rope or a piece of textile in one hand, while the other hand rests on the wrist of the former. The same gesture is being made by the royal courtier standing behind the king and the heir to the throne in the royal audience scene of the Apadana. For crowns worn by Near Eastern queens see the stele of Aššuršarrat (wearing a mural crown) illustrated in Börker-Klähn (1982, vol. 1: 217, vol. 2: pl. 227), and Naqia/Zakutu (wearing a rounded headdress) on the stele of Esarhaddon (1982, vol. 1: 213–214, vol. 2: pl. 220).
15. It is highly likely that the wives of satraps, who often were daughters of the king, also wore crowns. For an example, see the crowned female on the funerary stele from Dascyleium (Moorey 1988b: pls 81–82).
16. The seal appears on PF 800–802 which attest grain rations for Manukka, and PF 1029 and PF 1030 which record rations for *šuttezza* workers, who in one case are identified as workers of the woman Irdabama (cf. Brosius 1996: 129–144).
17. It is not the only Neo-Elamite seal found in Persepolis, as we know from the seal of Cyrus I and the seal of Irdabama (PFS 51; cf. Brosius 1996: 129). This fact has implications for our

understanding of the origins of this scene, which we immediately associate with Darius I, but has much older predecessors.

18. For a further example of a Persian seal depicting a scene reminiscent of the female audience scene see J. Lerner (this volume). Two depictions of a female audience scene can be found on a pectoral and a medallion from Toprak-Kale, Urartu, both dated to the mid-seventh century BC. Both objects show a woman seated on a throne receiving a female visitor. Again, this scene has invariably been interpreted to represent a goddess receiving a gift from a female offerant, but no element in this scene suggests that we are dealing with a deity. These objects could well be placed within a recognized artistic theme and represent a queen or high-ranking woman holding an audience. Cf. Meyer 1970: 137; Riemschneider 1966: pl. 28 (medallion).
19. See Root 1979: fig. 66. Cf. Amiet 1966: figs 280, 421. Cf. also the thirteenth-century ivory statuette from Choga Zanbil depicting a woman wearing an Elamite dress and using the same hand-over-wrist gesture (Amiet 1966: 361, fig. 268 = Louvre Sb 5089).
20. Removed from the formal setting of the audience scene is the scene of Persians in council, depicted on an ivory plaque from Demetrias in northern Greece (cf. above p. 150).
21. One can, for example, think of the royal women's responsibility to act as mediators between the king and members of the Persian nobility (cf. Brosius 1996: 116–122).
22. See Özgen & Öztürk *et al.* 1996: 46, fig. 87b; cf. p. 47 for the wall painting of a reclining Persian from Karaburum; cf. Moorey 1988*b*: pls 81–82; cf. Dusinberre 2003: 93–95, fig. 36.
23. Cf. Heracleides of Kyme FGrH 689 F2; Plut. *Art.* 5.5.
24. See also the funerary stele from Çavuşköyü (Starr 1977: pl. X), which depicts a similar banqueting scene in the lower panel.

14

An Achaemenid Cylinder Seal of a Woman Enthroned

Judith A. Lerner

Introduction

It has often been observed of the art of the Achaemenid period that, compared with those from other periods of Iranian art, representations of women are rare.[1] None occurs in official or in monumental art. Those that are known are primarily small scale (seals, ivories, metalwork) and come mainly from western and north-western parts of the empire—Babylonia, Syro-Palestine, Egypt, Asia Minor and Armenia[2]—but also from its easternmost extent, Bactria and the north-west of the Indian subcontinent.[3] Examples from the empire's heartland are even less common.[4] Achaemenid-style female images are also found beyond the boundaries of the empire, as on the tapestry fragment used to border the saddlecloth that was discovered in one of the Scythian tombs at Pazyryk, Siberia (Fig. 14.6) (Rudenko 1970: 296–297, fig. 139, pl. 177); and on the intaglio of a gold ring from a fourth-century tomb at Pydna, Macedonia (Fig. 14.3) (Paspalas 2000: 532: fig. 2, 548–555).[5] To judge by their garments, headdresses and hairstyles, most of these images are of high-born women and not of goddesses. A likely exception is the seated woman on what is the best-known female representation from the period, the chalcedony cylinder seal in the Louvre that was part of the De Clercq collection and is without provenance (Fig. 14.2).[6] More will be said about this figure's identity, but for now it is only necessary to recall the seal's composition: to the left in its impression, a woman in the wide-sleeved Achaemenid robe and wearing a low tiara covered by a long veil sits in a high-backed chair; she is approached by two figures, also in Achaemenid dress, a youngster bearing an offering of a bird and a woman holding a bucket and wearing a dentate tiara with pendant ribbons; between them is a footed incense-burner.

The Buffalo Museum cylinder seal

To this corpus of Achaemenid female images should now be added a small rock crystal cylinder seal in the Buffalo Museum of Science (Fig. 14.1), which is part of a collection of more than 200 seals assembled over 60 years ago by a founder of the Museum, Chauncey J.

Fig. 14.1 Modern impression of cylinder seal C16496, in the Buffalo Museum of Science, Buffalo, New York. (By kind permission of the Buffalo Museum of Science)

Hamlin (1881–1963).[7] Carved in a schematic manner with simply rendered yet volumetric forms, and with each of the three main compositional elements isolated from the others, the seal shows a figure clad in the long Achaemenid robe, seated on a chair, behind which an attendant, also in the Achaemenid robe, stands with a fly-whisk and a towel; to the right (in front of the seated figure) is a footed incense-burner with a chained lid. This combination of elements echoes that of the enthronement scenes at Persepolis, specifically those in the door jambs of the southern wall of the Hall of a Hundred Columns on which the Achaemenid king appears, not in audience, but in an imperial display accompanied only by an attendant with fly-whisk and towel (Fig. 14.4) (Schmidt 1953: pls 98–99, 104–105). But the seal displays a major difference: the enthroned figure is not the Great King but a woman. She clearly has breasts and is spinning; in place of the flower that the king holds in his left hand, the woman holds a distaff; and instead of the long staff that the king supports in his right hand, she grasps the thread from which a spindle hangs. The attendant behind her is also female. She, too, has breasts and her hair is in the short bouffant style worn by the men and some of the women of the period; her headgear, however, is unusual: a tight-fitting cap with a long "pigtail" or tassel at the back. The seated woman's hair is not visible as it is covered by a head cloth, wrapped like a turban.

The subject matter of the Buffalo seal poses tantalizing questions about the diffusion

Fig. 14.2 Modern impression of cylinder seal AO 22359, Musée du Louvre, Paris. (After Spycket 1980: pl. XXV, 7)

of royal imagery across the Persian Empire, the interconnections between the "imperial core" (with its workshops influenced by royal or official patronage) and provincial and even more peripheral areas (with workshops catering to satrapal and local elites' needs), as well as the relationship between seal ownership and seal iconography. The imagery of the Buffalo seal departs from all other Achaemenid glyptic depictions of seated women by using the visual *topos* of an enthroned ruler, an attendant with a fly-whisk, and a footed incense-burner.

To propose answers to these questions, we will first consider related female representations and enthronement imagery, followed by specific details of the Buffalo seal and, in conclusion, speculate where and for whom such a seal might have been made.

Related female representations, thrones and enthronement

Among the most common portrayals of women in Achaemenid-period glyptic art are those that show them seated, holding a flower or a bird and a flower (see nn. 2–3). These images draw nothing from Achaemenid "official" art. The women are generally solitary, as

Fig. 14.3 Drawing of the design on a gold ring from the north cemetery at Pydna, Macedonia. (After Paspalas 2000: 532, fig. 2)

if caught in a private moment; there is no hint that an audience with one or more personages is about to take place.

It should be noted that a woman in audience does occur in an Achaemenid context, on seal PFS 77*, known from impressions on several of the Persepolis Fortification Tablets.[8] As shown in the composite drawing in Figure 14.5, she holds a bowl and is attended by a standing woman who wields what is probably a fly-whisk, while another woman approaches her, proffering a bowl; between this last person and the seated woman is what may be an incense-burner. The Elamite inscription identifies the seal's owner as a woman. Although it sealed early fifth-century documents, the style of the seal marks it as earlier in date, made well before its use on the tablets. As such it may be related to seals of this earlier period that show a seated personage holding a bowl, accompanied by an attendant with a fly-whisk

Fig. 14.4. East jamb of the east doorway, southern wall, Hall of a Hundred Columns, Persepolis. (Drawing by Ann Searight)

or fan.⁹ However, while the Buffalo seal might be considered a continuation of this imagery, I believe that it derives instead directly from the enthronement scenes at Persepolis: the isolation of each of the figures on the Buffalo seal gives it an almost hieratic grandeur that is lacking on the earlier seal. Furthermore, the spinner's chair with its high back renders it more throne-like than the low-backed seat on the earlier seal, PFS 77*. Most other seated women sit on backless or low-backed chairs. The spinner's chair has a higher back, suggesting a throne, and is in this way similar to the chairs of the De Clercq and Pydna seals (Figs 14.2–3).¹⁰ The seemingly mundane activity of spinning is carried out on a chair more appropriate to a formal or public display, such as an enthronement.

Turning to the enthronement scenes at Persepolis, we find quotations and abbreviations across the Persian Empire from the early fifth century to the end of Achaemenid rule, with two prime examples being a seal design reconstructed from several *bullae* found at the Phrygian satrapal seat at Dascylium (Kaptan 1996) and the painting of the king in audience, which decorated the inside of a Persian warrior's shield on the so-called Alexander Sarcophagus from Sidon (Stronach 2002; Boardman 2000: 182, fig. 5.63). These examples adhere strictly to royal artistic conventions: the subject is the enthroned king and his temporal power. The Buffalo seal also follows these conventions but has transformed an icon of royal authority into a domestic image. How do we explain this phenomenon of feminizing an imposing and majestic male representation? Who is this woman and how and where did such a seal come to be carved? Some observations on specific details of the seal may provide some answers.

Elements of the seal: identity and provenance

First, the seal almost certainly belonged to a woman. Although men owned seals bearing female figures, most are goddesses.¹¹ The absence of a crown or more elaborate headdress identifies the lady on the Buffalo seal as mortal and hence strengthens the likelihood of female ownership. Although the lady sits as if enthroned, no one comes into her presence as, for example, the queenly figure and child or youth on the De Clercq cylinder. Her activity is private and personal; and it is a quintessentially female pursuit. Indeed, in the Ancient Near East (as well as in the West) the distaff and spindle are uniquely female attributes, and a woman spinning a universal symbol of womanhood. Females holding the distaff and spindle appear on funerary monuments that belonged to women from at least the early first millennium BC,¹² although the distaff and spindle are mentioned in earlier texts in association with Inanna-Ishtar, as well

Fig. 14.5 Composite drawing of PFS 77*. (Courtesy of M. B. Garrison, M. C. Root and the Persepolis Seal Project)

as with the Sumerian goddess Uttu, both a divine weaver and a paradigm of the married woman.[13]

The footed incense-burner with chained lid that stands in front of the spinner recalls the paired censers placed before the Great King in his audience and enthronement scenes, where they may refer to some ritualistic function—as indeed might have been the use of the single incense-burner on the De Clercq cylinder seal.[14] But such objects may also have had a more profane use, such as scenting the audience chamber in order to intensify the awe of the royal presence,[15] and a domestic purpose in non-royal contexts. As an example of domestic usage, a "bronze censer" is listed as part of a mid-sixth-century Babylonian woman's dowry, although whether it was a floor model is not known (Roth 1989/1990: 18–19, 26 = Akkadian *maqtaru*). In Achaemenid times incense-burners of the footed type, their lids chained to the stand upon which the container sits, were in use at least in the western part of the Achaemenid Empire where they were coveted as precious objects (Kaptan 1996: 262, and for references).[16] Footed incense-burners appear on several Achaemenid seals with figures of commoners, both male and female, the former clad in the Median trousers and jacket, the latter garbed in the long Achaemenid-style robe: a cylinder in the Louvre on which a man, wearing a high-domed hat and seated on a stool receives another man who wears the same headgear, with the incense-burner

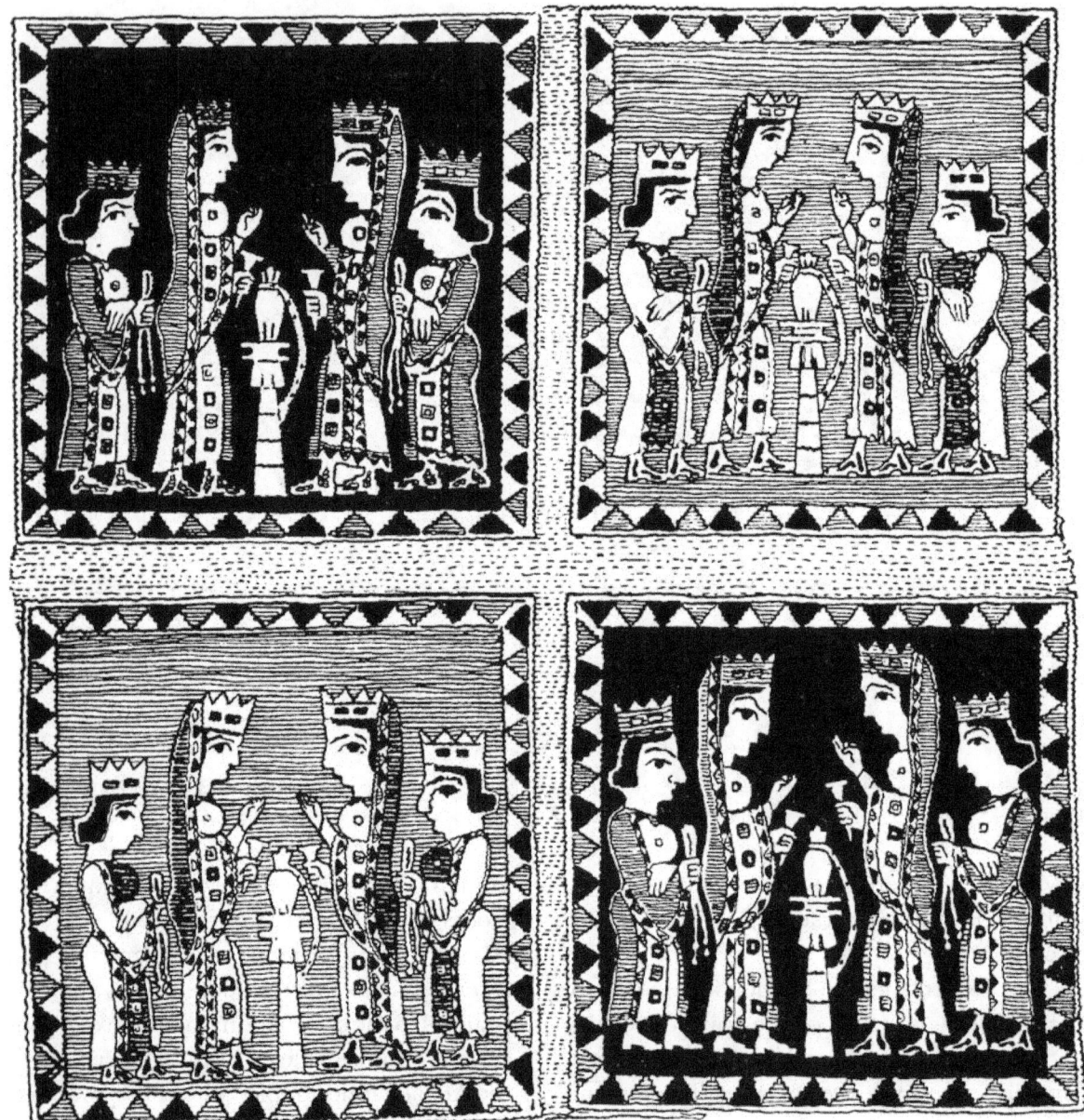

Fig. 14.6 Drawing of one of the woven fabrics that formed the saddlecloth from Kurgan 5, Pazyryk. (After Rudenko 1970: 297, fig. 139)

between them (Collon 1987: no. 659); a conical stamp seal in the British Museum on which a man is sitting on a low-backed chair holding a lotus flower and raising what might be a cup before a footed incense-burner (Curtis & Tallis 2005: no. 209 = BM 115523); an impression from Nippur of a man on a high-backed chair, holding a lotus flower and a cup, sitting opposite a horse, with the incense-burner between them; and finally, a silver ring in the

Getty Museum showing a woman, her hair in a long braid, seated on a stool, holding a phiale and facing an incense-burner (Spier 1992: 67, no. 136).[17] The incense-burner on the Buffalo seal, then, seems to reflect this private usage, although it might also have a devotional aspect, as the inclusion of the lotus and flowers and drinking cups on the seals just cited suggests.

Such seemingly personal and domestic features on the Buffalo seal—the spinning woman, the servant with a fly-whisk, the footed incense-burner—link it to what P. R. S. Moorey identified as "that repertory of élite domestic scenes on stamp seals...showing women holding flowers or both a bird and a flower, that may illustrate...acts of devotion to a goddess" (Moorey 2002: 207–208). Moorey was referring to the stamp seals associated with the western part of the Achaemenid Empire, although, as evidenced by the rings in the Oxus Treasure and seals from north-west India, similar imagery (and style) are also found in its eastern part. However, at this point in our discussion, the homely task of spinning may also refer to the seal owner's devotion to a particular divinity. Thus, the spinning woman on the Buffalo seal appears as a private individual, albeit surrounded by ostensibly royal trappings, pursuing a feminine task that has some religious or devotional allusion—not unexpected for a personal seal.

To return to our speculation on how and where the seal came to be made, we must take a closer look at the lady's and her attendant's headwear. Women in Achaemenid-period glyptic, metalwork and sculpture, if they are not wearing a crown or tiara, are either bareheaded with a long braid falling down the back, or wear a low cylindrical or beret-like cap, which is sometimes covered by a veil (and see also the female images cited in nn. 2–4). This first type of headgear is worn by the standing woman on the De Clercq seal (Fig. 14.2), its dentate top indicating her royal status which is further emphasized by the long diadem ribbons that fall down her back. A distinctly different type of prestige headdress is worn by the seated woman she approaches: a low fluted tiara covered by a veil. This fluting is, to my knowledge, unique among female depictions of the period and, I believe, is an indication of the seated woman's divine identity, most likely Anahita.[18]

Also unique among female depictions is the turban-like cloth covering the Buffalo lady's head. To my knowledge, the only other turbans that occur in the art of the period are those worn by two of the subject peoples on the base of the statue of Darius: Persians and Arians, the latter from the eastern part of the empire.[19] Both of these figures are beardless, but they are certainly intended to be male as are all the other subject peoples who are carved on the base.[20] Despite a turban being worn by two males and its absence from other female representations, turbans may well have been a feminine fashion of the time. In describing the preparations required of the women who were to share the king's bed, Pierre Briant (2002a: 282) cites those carried out by Judith as she prepares to join Holofernes: after bathing and anointing herself and prior to putting on her best garment, her sandals and her jewellery, she dresses her hair and wraps a turban around it (*Judith* 10:3–4).[21] A composition of the second century BC, *Judith* may nonetheless reflect feminine fashion of a slightly earlier time. The word *mitra*, used in the Greek text for Judith's head covering, has been translated variously as "tire", "tiara", "headband", "fillet", "snood" and "turban", but in her Song of Triumph (16:8), Judith describes binding or tying up her hair which could suggest that she wrapped it in a cloth to effect a turban.

In contrast, the attendant's cap with its "tail" or long tassel hanging from its top is not unique, although it is distinctive. At first glance it recalls that of the small figure offering the bird on the De Clercq seal, but this figure is meant to be a boy or youth; although of an earlier time and place, his hairstyle (rather than headdress) recalls the long lock worn by young princely figures in Levantine art.[22] Instead, the headdress that best matches the attendant's is the one worn by the woman buried in Kurgan 5 at Pazyryk (Rudenko 1970: 97–98, 104, pl. 66.A). Made of wood, the hat is characterized by an opening on top to receive the wearer's hair, which was braided and wrapped around an artificial plait of horsehair. Although this way of dressing the hair was likely to be a local Saka style, it may have emulated hairstyles or headgear that was fashionable in at least some areas within the Persian territory. (It bears mentioning that Kurgan 5 contained several items of Achaemenid Persian origin or inspiration, the most notable being the carpet with its Persepolitan imagery, as well as the saddlecloth with the paired women, cited at the beginning of this paper [Fig. 14.6] and with which I shall conclude.)

Conclusion

What can we make of this seal with its borrowings from royal iconography? Who would have commissioned it and where would that individual have lived? Its small size and cursory carving suggest that it belonged to a private individual—surely a woman. Based on style and certainly imagery, I propose that it is a product from the periphery of the Achaemenid Empire since it seems to me unlikely that a seal showing a woman in this regal manner, transformed into a universal symbol of womanhood by the act of spinning, could have been made in some more central region. This phenomenon brings to mind the woollen tapestry that was combined with two other textile fragments to fashion the saddlecloth found in Pazyryk Kurgan 5, in as much as this object demonstrates a clear misunderstanding of Achaemenid artistic conventions (Fig. 14.6) (Rudenko 1970: 296–297, fig. 139, pl. 177.c; Lerner 1991: 10–12). The greater height of the woman standing closest to the footed incense-burner has been correctly recognized as indicating her higher social status, confirmed by the veil that falls down her back and the flower she holds, while the shorter woman, who grasps a towel, is seen as her servant or attendant (Azarpay 1994: 180; Moorey 2002: 207). Yet both women wear dentate tiaras, an inappropriate headdress if the shorter one is a servant. This dissonance has been explained as a way of indicating that the shorter woman is a young princess (e.g. Abdullaev & Badanova 1998: 208), but it seems unlikely that she would then grasp a towel, which would be unsuitable to her status (Lerner 1991: 11, nos 33–34).[23] Rather, such misunderstanding of Achaemenid visual conventions could easily occur in a peripheral area.[24]

For its part, the Buffalo seal does not misunderstand the visual conventions of Achaemenid royal iconography so much as *deliberately transform* it from a statement of masculine authority to an essential image of womanly power, signalled by the throne-like chair, the attendant with a fly-whisk and towel, the footed incense-burner and the unmistaken symbols of womanhood, the distaff and spindle. Themes such as the royal audience and enthronement were well known throughout the empire and influenced local artistic output, which adapted the style and schema to local tastes, as we have already seen demonstrated by the Dascylium seal (Kaptan 1996; Stronach 2002: 389). But the royal audience scene, as Deniz Kaptan has noted about this seal, is "the illustration of the ideology of loyalty to the Great King" and, as such, seals such as this one were used by the local satraps "to stress their obedience to the central administration in Persia" (Kaptan 1996: 267–268).

It seems unlikely that an individual would choose to represent herself in this fashion unless she were at some remove from the purview of a central authority; and, indeed, I believe that our spinner is not divine but mortal, perhaps a member of the local elite. Despite her "enthronement", her lack of appropriate headdress marks her as human, although showing herself spinning may refer to her affiliation with a particular goddess.[25] In sum, the liberties taken with the imagery of this seal, along with the nature of its style, suggest a provincial origin, well on the periphery of the Persian Empire—perhaps, by analogy with some of the Pazyryk finds, in one of its eastern reaches, such as Aria, Bactria or Sogdiana.[26]

Notes

1. Some have been included in Aurelie Daems's iconographic survey (2001: 42–46); see also Brosius 1996: 85–86; Spycket 1980: 43–44; 1981: 399–401.
2. *Babylonia*: figurines from Tell Imgharra and Kish (Culican 1975: pls XVII:5C; XVIII:6, XIX:7, XXIII:10A); *Syro-Palestine*: the bone cosmetic container or handle bought in Aleppo and now in the Ashmolean Museum, Oxford (Moorey 2002: 215, fig. 5); the bronze caryatid censer from Amman (Khalil 1986: 104, pl. 16) and the ampullae termed "Syro-Achaemenid" (Culican 1975); *Egypt*: a limestone plaque of a standing woman carved in high relief (Cooney 1965: 44–46, pl. XXVI, figs 7–8); *Asia Minor*: the misnamed "Greco-Persian" seals that show standing and seated women (Boardman 1970*a*: nos 854, 862, 876, 879–880, 891–892, 903, 950, 990, figs 283, 294, 297–298 (for a critique of this term, see Gates 2002), and the stele from Ergili/Dascylium (Starr 1977: 84, pls IX and XI); *Armenia*: the three women represented on the rim of the gilded silver rhyton from Erevan, one of which John Boardman notes is "an exact translation of the Persian-dressed figures on the [Greco-Persian] seals" (2000: 187, fig. 5.68).
3. Plaques and metal finger-rings from the group of objects known as the "Oxus Treasure" (Dalton 1964: 102, pl. 15: nos 103–104) and the two seated ladies with dentate tiaras and pigtail or diadem tie in the Peshawar Museum, collected by Sir John Marshall in the North-West Frontier Province in the early twentieth century (Callieri 1997: cat. 4.1 and 4.2), most of which bear a strong stylistic relationship with the seals attributed to the western part of the empire. Curiously, we have no seals in this style that can be attributed to the heartland of the empire, that is, from Iran itself.
4. In contrast to most of the evidence for female representations—particularly those in glyptic art—these examples are from archaeological contexts, notably Susa (Amiet 1972*a*; also Spycket 1980: pls XXI, fig. 1, XXV, fig. 8), although a rare example is the seal ring from Pydna in Macedonia (Fig. 14.3) to be discussed later. Few other female representations occur in archaeological contexts; except for the stele from Dascylium and figurines from Babylonia, mentioned in note 2, the others are accorded a western provenance based on style or material. I consider the beardless blue head from Persepolis and the head from Masjid-i Suleiman to be male (contra Spycket 1981: 400–401) and plan to include them in a forthcoming article on an unfinished limestone head in the Arthur M. Sackler Museum, Harvard University.
5. The ring or wreath that she grasps in her right hand along with a flower and the position of her left hand, raised and holding a phiale, recall the pose of the crowned goddess—on an Assyrian seal in the British Museum (BM 132161) from ninth- to seventh-century BC Nimrud—who sits on a high-backed chair, holding a ring in her left hand and raising her right arm with the hand in an open gesture, no doubt a distant model for this late seal.
6. Louvre, AO 22359 (former De Clercq Collection, 385).
7. C16496; length: 29 mm; diameter: 18.2 mm. The seal was purchased from a dealer in 1941 and a photograph of its impression was published by

Ingholt (1944: 11, fig. 30 and p. 12). I am grateful to Samuel M. Paley for bringing the Hamlin seals to my attention and for inviting me to publish this and the other Iranian seals of the first millennia BC and AD in the collection in the planned catalogue that he and Erica Ehrenberg are editing; I am also grateful to Katherine Leacock of the Buffalo Museum of Science for permission to publish the seal here. Finally, I am indebted to Rudolph H. Mayr for his skilful photography of its impression.

8. I gratefully acknowledge the generosity of Mark B. Garrison and Margaret Cool Root in making available their composite drawing of this seal impression (to appear in Garrison & Root, in preparation).

9. However, these compositions mainly show men, and the fly-whisk resembles a rectangular fan (as in *La Fileuse*); furthermore, the fan- or fly-whisk-bearer faces a seated personage. Garrison observes that this seal's stylistic resemblance to PFS 93*—the Elamite-inscribed seal that names a Cyrus of Anshan, son of Teispes, which, when used was an heirloom—probably makes PFS 77* an heirloom as well (Garrison 2006).

10. One should also note the high-backed chair of exuberant design, on which sits the woman, wearing a dentate tiara and most likely a goddess, on the felt wall hanging from Kurgan 5 at Pazyryk (Rudenko 1970: pl. 154). The visual analogy with the De Clercq seal leads us to the suggestion later in this paper that the De Clercq seal represents a goddess with her worshippers, while the Pydna seal may not depict a divinity. Further speculation about these two seals, both so appropriate to the Buffalo seal, is made later in this paper.

11. Writing about "the feminine in glyptic art" in Mesopotamia, Zainab Bahrani notes that, "seals bearing images of Ishtar could be owned by men as well as by women" (Bahrani 2001: 134). A fourth-century BC example is the chalcedony cylinder found at Gorgippa (ancient Anapa) in south Russia and now in the State Hermitage Museum, showing the Achaemenid king standing before a goddess (Ishtar) who is mounted on a lion; although it is not inscribed, it seems most likely that the seal belonged to a man, probably within the royal circle or who served in an official capacity (Boardman 1970a: pl. 878). As Bahrani points out, "other than the identity of a worshipper in a presentation scene, there is no direct correlation, or rule, regarding the subject matter depicted on the seals and the gendered identity of the seal owner". This observation applies to the De Clercq seal, which must have been owned by the standing queenly figure, as well as to other seals of the Achaemenid period. Indeed, seals known to have belonged to women display images that are also found on men's seals; thus, on the Persepolis Fortification Tablets, the seal of Queen Irtašduna (known to Herodotus as Artystone), a wife of Darius (PFS 38), depicts a heroic encounter (Garrison 1991: 7, figs 6–7), while that of the high-ranking Irdabama (PFS 51) shows a hunt on horseback (1991: 4–5, figs 3–4) (Irdabama's seal was probably made in the seventh century BC and was thus an heirloom when she used it).

12. Well-known examples are the Syro-Hittite funerary reliefs from Marash and Zinjirli in north Syria (Bonatz 2000: pls XII–XIV, XX and XXI); such depictions of women continue into the first and second centuries AD with the many funerary reliefs from Palmyrene tombs (Tanabe 1986). Another well-known example, perhaps a votive relief, is the Neo-Elamite fragment from Susa (Muscarella 1992*b*). Women spinning and engaged in other weaving activities occur much earlier on seal impressions from fourth-millennium Choga Mish in Iran; these, however, look like workshop scenes without a religious or other symbolic meaning (Collon 1987: nos 627–630).

13. For an early discussion of the spindle (along with the hair clasp) as a symbol of womanhood and the attributes of Inanna-Ishtar, see Hoffner 1966, especially pp. 229–331. For Uttu, who, in the myth *Enki and the World Order*, is put in charge by her husband Enki of "everything pertaining to women", see Frymer-Kensky 1992: 23. In addition to this signification in Mesopotamia, the same meaning is given to the spindle along with the distaff in Ugaritic, Hittite, biblical (viz. the virtuous woman of Proverbs 31:19) and Greek texts; for this last, recall Penelope as well as Circe and Calypso at their looms. Since these objects are divine attributes, some scholars have posited that the Syro-Hittite reliefs depict a goddess, but in such contexts it seems more likely that these women are not divine but depictions of the deceased. Both Harry Hoffner (1966) and Elena Rova (2008) cite the association of spindles and distaffs with specific funerary rituals (I am grateful to Elena Rova for sharing her paper with me prior to its publication, as well as a related paper, Cottica & Rova 2006). Likewise, the seated spinner on the Susa relief is not a goddess, although she could be an acolyte of one since she sits before

a table heaped with what may be divine offerings. (Note what appears to be the edge of a garment in the lower right, indicating that some figure was originally opposite her on the other side of the table.)
14. Censers (*thymiatēria*) are included by the second-century AD author Athenaeus in his inventory of the banquet paraphernalia sent to Alexander by Cleomenes, who was in charge of the financial administration of Egypt (cited by Briant 2002a: 296). This is not the place to discuss the terminology associated with incense-burners (*turibula*) and censers; suffice to say that in this paper, we are referring to a burner used for incense composed of a bowl-shaped receptacle with a conical cover that rests on an upwardly tapering stand.
15. Goldman (1991b: 180–181), who terms this type of covered floor stand for burning incense a *turibulum*, notes its earlier appearance in the seventh-century BC relief of Aššurbanipal's banquet as well as a later parallel in early Islamic times when those about to be brought into the presence of the Caliph perfumed themselves from incense-burners brought into the waiting area.
16. See also Miller 2003a: 306, pl. III, for an Achaemenid-style incense-burner on a sixth-century Clazomenaean hydria; and, for actual silver-footed incense-burners found in Anatolian tombs of the period, Özgen & Öztürk *et al.* 1996: 113–116, nos 71–72.
17. Legrain 1925: no. 984: behind him is an outstretched hand, identified by Legrain as "a Phoenician attribute...an emblem of blessing or offering" (p. 353).
18. If this is the case, the De Clercq and the Anapa seals may represent two rare and early depictions of the goddess. That the enthroned woman on the De Clercq seal may be Anahita is suggested not by her long veil, which some mortal women wear over their dentate tiaras (e.g. the wife of the deceased on the Dascylium stele, cited in n. 2, and one of the ivory statuettes from Susa, cited in n. 4) but by the fluting of her headdress, which, albeit anachronistically, is similar to the fluting at the base of the crown worn by the goddess Anahita in the investiture relief at Naqsh-i Rustam of the Sasanian king Narseh (293–302 AD); this fluted border is echoed in Narseh's crown on his coinage, while on the relief the full height of his crown is fluted (see Göbl 1960 and Shahbazi 1983: pl. 26, for a good view of this female figure, although Shahbazi rejects this traditional identification as Anahita). Moorey (1979: 224) also identifies the seated lady as Anahita because of the bird, "the traditional emblem/offering to Ishtar/Anahita/Aphrodite", and not because of the decoration of her tiara, which he describes (as have virtually all the many authors who have written about this seal) as "dentate". Briant (2002a: 253–254) concurs with this identification as Anahita, and adds a seal impression on the Persepolis Treasury tablets (PTS 91) and a finger-ring from the Oxus Treasure showing a woman seated on a low-backed chair, wearing a crown and holding a flower and a ring—although there are actually two such women depicted in similar fashion (Dalton 1964: nos 103–104, pl. 16, figs 52–53) and less convincing as divine images.
19. Roaf 1974: 94–97, 106–107, pl. XXXI–1 and 4, who notes that the style of this headgear "is not immediately familiar".
20. To explain why the Persian is beardless, Roaf suggests that, "since the statue was made in Egypt where beards were a sign of barbarism, the artist may have made a concession to Egyptian spectators by showing the Persian without a beard" (1974: 96). But that does not explain the Arian's lack of a beard, especially when on the tomb reliefs the Arian is bearded, as is the Persian. It is noteworthy that clean-shaven or beardless males in Achaemenid art—in addition to other subject peoples, the Arabians, Nubians and Egyptians—are servants, possibly eunuchs, but also princes, such as the heads from Persepolis, Bard-i Nashandeh and the Sackler Museum (see n. 4); an interesting exception is the linchpin cast in the form of a beardless male wearing a flat-topped cap that was found at Persepolis (Curtis & Tallis 2005: no. 403).
21. My thanks to Lisbeth S. Fried for her help with this passage in the Septuagint.
22. My thanks to Dominique Collon for pointing out this parallel and the difference between the headdress of the attendant on the Buffalo seal and that of the small figure on the De Clercq seal. The best-known example of a royal child wearing this long braid is the small figure of the king, shown as the god's child, on the "Baal au Foudre" stele from Ras Shamra, now in the Louvre Museum, AO 15775 (http://biblelouvre.free.fr/images/M/L/L-BaalFoudre-Det2.jpg).
23. Even though the towel is grasped so as to form a loop in the manner of the king's chamberlain on the Treasury relief and by the attendant with the king in the doorways of the Hundred Column Hall (Schmidt 1953: pls 119, 121, and fig. 4 for

the Treasury relief, and pls 98–99 and 105 for the Hundred Column Hall) and so must indicate a specific item of court paraphernalia, in contrast to the towels that are carried by attendants in the palaces of Darius and Xerxes, their more mundane function is indicated by the way they are held—lying across the outstretched palm of the attendant (Schmidt 1953: pls 149 [Darius], 179–181, 183–184 [Xerxes], and 193–194 [the "Harem"]). Interestingly, the attendant on the Buffalo seal holds the towel in this fashion.

24. The provincial or peripheral character of the tapestry was noted by Bernard Goldman on the basis of the "singularity" of the footed incense-burner depicted on it (1991*b*: 179). Johanna Zick-Nissen had attributed the tapestry to Anatolia (1966: 580) and, although it could have travelled the great distance beyond the eastern bounds of the empire to the Altai where it was then cut up to construct the saddlecloth, I believe that its origin within the eastern part of the empire is more likely; indeed, its design may be identified, as has the carpet from the same kurgan, on the basis of the red dye used in the carpet, "as a provincial (Central Asian) interpretation of the fashionable Achaemenid court style" (Böhmer & Thompson 1991: 34).

25. In a Greek context, Aphrodite, the goddess of love and procreation, is shown spinning in her capacity as a goddess of fate on funerary monuments of the fifth century (see Suhr 1969: 151–154; also Barber 1994: 236–238, on the "particularly Greek" "notion of female deities creating a life by spinning a thread" and who restores the Venus de Milo as "standing in the typical position for spinning thread in the Greek manner"). Typically in these depictions, there is little in the way of dress, headgear or demeanour to differentiate Aphrodite from images of mortal women engaged in a similar pursuit (Boardman 1970*a*: 219). I am grateful to Despina Ignatiadou who, after my paper, raised the possibility that the lady on the Buffalo seal could be a goddess despite the absence of an appropriate-looking headdress and, subsequently, for drawing my attention to the occurrence of the "Spinning Aphrodite" in Greek glyptics by sharing her publications of a glass seal from a fourth-century female burial at Pydna. However, in a Near Eastern/Iranian context, I believe that the absence of a tiara or some more elaborate headdress than a turban marks our lady as mortal, and by analogy with the funerary monuments in Near Eastern contexts that show a woman spinning (see n. 12 above).

26. In his discussion of the Pydna ring, Paspalas (2000: 549) reaches a similar conclusion about the combination of the female figure and throne type, "as one that craftsmen closer to the center of the empire kept strictly apart".

15

The Big and Beautiful Women of Asia: Picturing Female Sexuality in Greco-Persian Seals

Lloyd Llewellyn-Jones

It is commonly recognized that seals and seal imagery were important features of Persian cultural and political expression; as such Herodotus correctly ascribed seals a common usage throughout the Persian Empire (Hdt. 1.195). Seals were small, and the subjects carved on them in intaglio were only readily intelligible in impression on clay or wax. They, or at least their impressions, conveyed authority and could sanction action and expenditure since they belonged to individuals (but also to offices) who can be identified as royalty, satraps, civil servants and merchants. While the seal itself remained with the owner, the objects sealed by merchants, officers of state or royalty could travel far and wide: the seal impressions discovered at Persepolis and various sites throughout the length and breadth of the Achaemenid Empire eloquently demonstrate how far they actually did travel. It can be argued, therefore, that the seals come close to providing us with the universal iconographic medium that we need for the study of common imagery within the vast geographic layout of the Persian Empire and that seal imagery is, consequently, of tremendous importance to the historian of the Achaemenid period, since the iconography often reveals—in terms of style and decoration—the widespread cultural contacts made within the empire, especially with regard to Egypt and the eastern Mediterranean.

This paper does not attempt to trace the sweeping chronological, geographical or stylistic changes within the iconographic make-up of the seals, but focuses instead on the specifics of iconography within the gems' pictorial schema. Specifically, the following aims at analysing images of women found on what are commonly termed Greco-Persian seals, a series of distinctive scaraboid seals and gemstones which date to the period of the early to mid-fifth and fourth centuries BC and are generally thought to have their origins in workshops in Anatolia, that is, in the Persian satrapies of Asia Minor.[1] John Boardman has meticulously examined the manufacture and use of the Greco-Persian seals and has suggested several important hypotheses for our understanding of the iconographic make-up of the gems: their source of origin, for example, has been suggested partly by their distribution, which occurs mainly within Anatolia itself (although they also travelled far west to Italy, north to the Black Sea and east into Central Asia and India). The Greco-Persian seals are predominantly Greek-style finger-rings carved with images that may, in stylistic inspiration, be singularly Greek, homogeneously Persian or an amalgamated Greco-Persian style, and are crafted for the most part in blue chalcedony, the most popular material for seal carving in the Greek mainland studios too.[2]

Furthermore, Boardman suggests that while it is not viable to say whether any of the Greco-Persian seals were *specifically* cut by Greek artists, the style and, in particular, the choice of subject matter can be said to have been inspired by both the work of Greek craftsmen and the themes of Greek art (Boardman 1994: 44). Consequently, it is obvious that the seals belong to a heavily Hellenized environment and that they were, more than likely, created for and utilized by the Persian and Persianizing courts of Achaemenid Asia Minor or even by the dignitaries of the semi-independent kingdoms of Anatolia, and perhaps even the luminaries of the Syro-Phoenician coastal city-states (Boardman 2000: 152–174).

Certainly an examination of the iconographic layout of individual seals reveals important factors that contribute to Boardman's thesis: in battle scenes between Persians and Greeks, for example, the Greeks are always shown as the vanquished foe. In one case a Persian cavalryman lances a naked Greek (Boardman 2001: pl. 881; cf. 1994: 45 pl. c = Rome, Villa Giulia),[3] while in another the Great King himself kills a naked hoplite representing, perhaps, the king's rule over the entire Greek people (or at least his anticipated hold over the western Greeks) (Boardman 2001: pl. 849; once Arndt, A1410). Such precise images make the ideological, cultural and political sphere of the gems obvious to understand, certainly if we compare the seals to the more familiar Greek-made artefacts (Attic vases in particular), which highlight Greek military success over Persians and sometimes emphasize the point by equating martial prowess with sexual aggression and physical domination of the weak and effeminized *barbaroi*.[4]

Whilst the ideology of Persian political, military and cultural superiority predominates in the theme of the seals, nevertheless in terms of artistic style and flavour there is a heavy Greek influence, with foreshortened human and animal figures, some three-quarter faces, some frontal faces, and realistic renditions of poses, anatomy and dress. It has been noted that some of the Greek subjects show a highly developed familiarity with Greek myth, suggesting a direct Greek intervention. One seal impression, possibly found in India, shows the naked demigod and hero Herakles resting his right foot on the carcass of the Nemean lion, while the nymph Nemea offers him sustenance from a jar as Eros, the god (or personification) of desire, flies overhead to crown the nymph with a garland (Fig. 15.1a) (Boardman 2001: pl. 856 = London, BM, Walters no. 524). This curious seal, depicting the uncommon subject of the great Greek hero, might be either considered a direct Greek import, the work of a Greek craftsman in Anatolia or the work of a local Persian or Anatolian artist picking up on the Greek styles commonly seen in the monumental and minor arts of Achaemenid Asia Minor as well as on objects imported from mainland Greece (Boardman 1964: 84–109; 1994: 21–48; 2000).[5] For Boardman the Herakles seal is emphatically "an example of a gem offering an unfamiliar variant on a common story, and the more interesting for its being a Greek work in the Persian Empire" (2001: 311; cf. also 1969: 596; 1994: 46–47).[6] If the distinctly laissez-faireist subject matter on many Greco-Persian seals is also inspired by examples from Greek artworks, this will impact on our perceptions of the decidedly Hellenized behaviour of the patrons who actually commissioned the seals. Without doubt the scenes on the gems—of Persian women with their menfolk, their children and their dogs, or even of Persians relaxing, drinking and dancing—are very much in the spirit of Classical Greek art but decidedly not of Persian art where such plebeian subjects are rare. As Boardman makes clear:

> The Greek artists invented a number of motifs which must have appeared startling to Persians in the provincial western courts, who had been used to the more formal treatment of divine or royal motifs on their seals. The innovations reflect not only the utterly different atmosphere of Greek art, with its realism and observation of natural forms and action, but also to some degree the real influence of the Greeks and their "civilising" of the newcomers from the east. Dogs scratching themselves or animals coupling must have been as common sights in Persia as in Greece but it took Greeks to find subjects like this suitable for portrayal. No doubt in Persepolis too Persians leaned on their spears while their women played with their children and their dogs, but these were not the motifs for an easterner's art. (2001: 324)

The seals' images clearly reflect on the pleasures of life in the satrapal courts of Asia Minor and have a certain "hint of the Raj" about them, showing Persians "somewhat corrupted by the Hellenized natives" (Boardman 2000: 170). This in itself makes the cultural interplay of the iconographic schema—namely the blend of artistic and cultural influences—on the seals unique and exciting: do we have in the seals a Greek view of Persian culture or is it Persians reviewing themselves through Greek iconographic conventions?

Given the rich cultural and iconographic crossover encountered in the Greco-Persian gems, I believe it is viable to use a methodological framework for decoding the iconography of the seals based on the type of scholarship recently formulated for the reading of the iconography of Greek minor arts, in particular Attic vase paintings. Recent scholarly approaches to the study of the representation of Athenian women, for example, are undoubtedly of use in unlocking the gender-loaded codes of the seals' imagery too, since both genres systematically share so many artistic and cultural devices and schemes. [7]

For example, much attention has been given to the idea of a Greek pot having several consecutive narrative meanings, and that the handling and revolving of a vase or cup in the user's hands can trigger a narrative sequence encoded on the object—a narrative which is sometimes deliberately and clearly rendered by an artist, but one that is more often left ambiguous and open to the viewers' individual interpretations.[8] Interestingly, a sense of narrative can be read into certain seals from Anatolia too, certainly in those multi-surfaced gems classified as "pyramidal" or "pendant" seals that, like a Greek vase, allow the viewer to rotate the object and to construct a story. On one example (a four-sided carnelian pendant seal), a seated man (a satrap?) is approached by an armed guard, then by a woman holding a *rhyton* and a garland, and finally by a shorter (and possibly younger) girl holding a *rhyton* and a *phiale*. The standing figures—perhaps representing members of the satrap's family or court—all face and process towards the seated man, requiring us to revolve and view the seal in a certain order (cf. Boardman 2001: 317, fig. 294; once Arndt).[9] Of course, most Greco-Persian seals are flat scaraboid seals with all conception of narrative necessarily contained on one side of the intaglio. Nonetheless, the iconographic composition is often rich, and scenes can be densely packed with incident and detail.

This is particularly true of scenes of women who, remarkably, feature prominently in the Anatolian-made gems, certainly when contrasted with the paucity of images we have of women from the Iranian heartland.[10] It is to the rich and remarkable iconography of Greco-Persian women that I now turn my attention. I will begin by examining some scenes which share a common Greco-Persian cultural theme (in terms of iconographic representation) suggesting a fluid interdependence of subject matter and sources of inspiration, before moving on to examine the body-image in the representation of the women in more detail.

Images of lone women in Persian dress form a high percentage of the seals' iconographic make-up, suggesting perhaps that there was a ready market for female jewellery in the form of seals or at least that the female figure was a popular one with clients, either male or female (Fig. 15.1b).[11] Females seated on a variety of low stools or chairs are common; some wear crowns, diadems or tiaras, perhaps indicating a noble status.[12] Occasionally a seated woman wears a veil and interacts with figures around her. One interesting gem is carved on both sides with images clearly echoing Athenian genre scenes (Fig. 15.1c): the front of the gem depicts a woman playing the harp—an iconographic trope of both the Near East and of Greece—whilst in the company of her pet Maltese dog, which is, incidentally, the pet par excellence of Athenian women too, and certainly the most popular type of pet depicted in the so-called "gynaikaion scenes" on Attic vases.[13] The back of the gem represents her in the company of a diminutive figure (a child or slave) whilst holding a bird on her hand. From the scale it looks like a rook or even a hawk, but this is unlikely; the artist has simply scaled up a pet songbird, which is utilized in the same way as is found in the Greek images (Fig. 15.1d).[14] What we have in these scenes is, as in Attic gemstones and vase painting, an idealized and overtly romanticized take on life within the "women's quarters".

There are several scenes on the gems, which, like their Attic pottery counterparts, could be classified as "domestic", although using such a tag is not without its problems.[15] What can be said with confidence, however, is that such scenes are a wholly Greek genre and rendered in a very Greek manner, with—most typically—a man in the company of a single woman. Both subjects, however, are dressed in Persian costume. The woman, for her part, is often the active partner in the scene, ministering to her male partner's needs and providing him with comfort by offering him an unguent bottle or a *phiale* of wine (Fig. 15.1e). In one scene a man stands at ease with his arm around the waist of a woman "in a pose of un-oriental familiarity" (Boardman 2001: 316 and pl. 891 = London BM 436). The iconography strongly suggests that marital harmony is being emphasized in the seals, an idea which is given impetus by other scenes of mother–child relationships, which also come to the fore, in ways that clearly echo Greek "family" genre scenes.[16]

The most interesting of the "domestic" scenes shows a woman offering a cup to an armed man who stands opposite her, a spear in his hand (Fig. 15.1f). Such an image can readily be compared to the so-called "Departure of the Warrior" scenes commonly found on

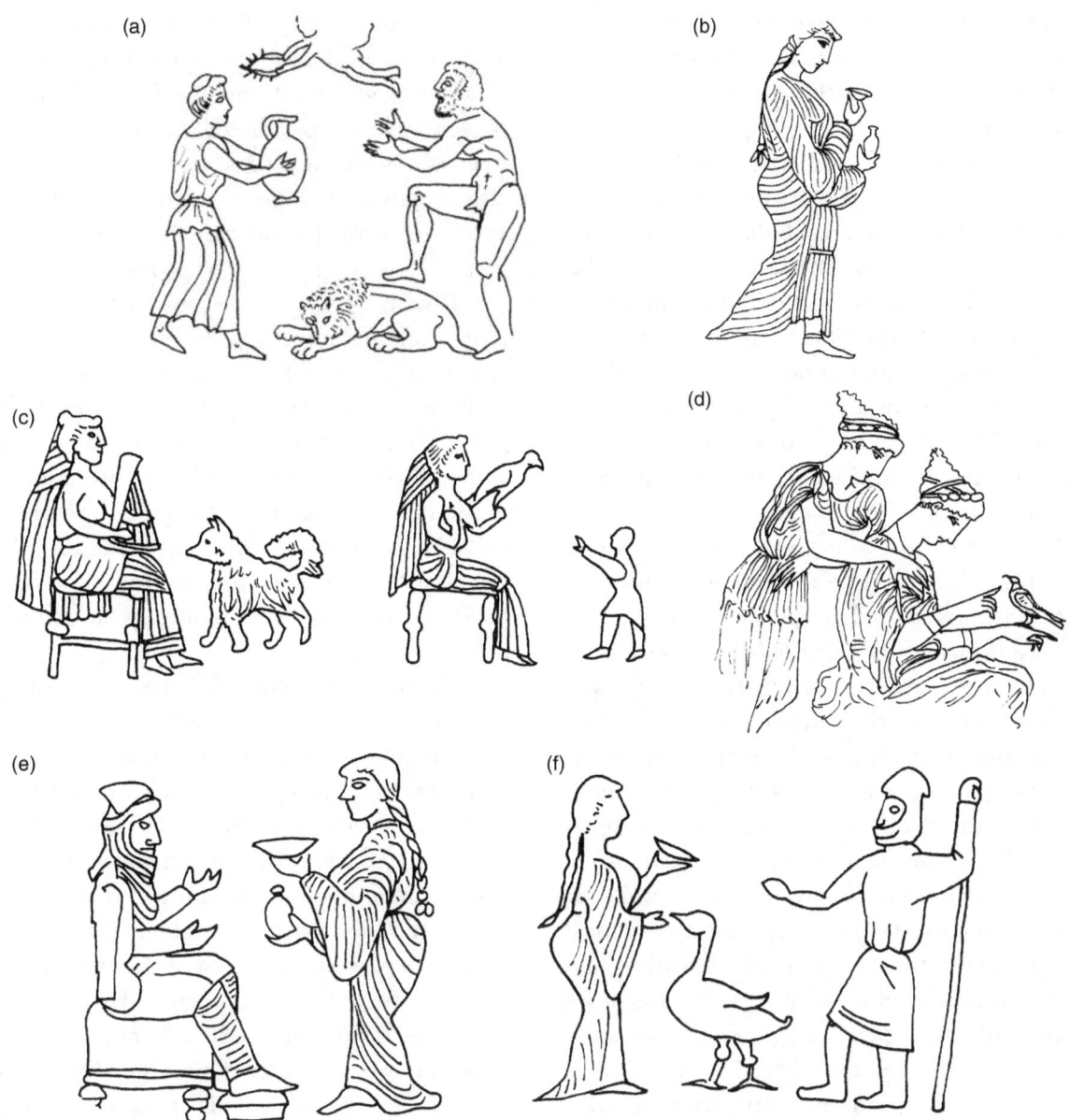

Fig. 15.1 (a) Herakles and the Nymph Nemea. (After Boardman 2001: pl. 856). (b) Woman in Persian dress. (After Richter 1956: pl. 133). (c) Woman with harp and Maltese dog, and reverse image of woman with bird and child (or slave). (After Boardman 2001: pl. 964). (d) Women with a songbird. (Detail taken from an Attic *epinetron* by the Eretria Painter). (e) Woman administering to a seated man. (After Boardman 2001: 880). (f) The Departure of the Warrior, Greco-Persian style. (After Boardman 2001: pl. 892)

Greek black- and red-figure pots from the Late Archaic period through to the late fifth century BC (Reeder 1995: 154–160; Llewellyn-Jones 2003: 100, fig. 109). The scene typically shows a heroized young warrior (sometimes a mythical figure) armed and ready to leave the domestic sphere for military action. He is sent off to war by close members of his family in different line-ups according to the artists' composition of the scene. The soldier's mother and father are frequently represented, but it is more usual for the artist to depict the farewell between a husband and wife, recalling classic moments of Greek epic poetry where, for instance, Hector of Troy bids farewell to his wife Andromache for the last time before he meets his death on the battlefield (Homer *Iliad* 6. 467–474). [17] In the Departure of the Warrior scenes the wife, with her head lowered in modesty, often extends a ritual *phiale* towards her spouse; he gazes at her mournful beauty and clutches his weapons as he prepares to leave. These scenes often include detailed symbolic devices such as a goose, swan or heron standing at the middle of the composition in between the married couple. The presence of the waterbird (which is not always portrayed in a true naturalistic scale) transcends any pretence at rendering an accurate "daily life" scene and suggests that the artist is drawing on the symbolic aspect of the bird which, according to Sian Lewis's perceptive readings of the Departure Scenes, is there to announce the constancy of the woman who waits at home while her man is away from the domestic sphere fighting (Lewis 2002: 163–166). The symbolism of such a scene certainly becomes apparent on an item like a seal, since such gems were the personal items of individuals who might wear them on a daily basis. It is difficult to assign a gender to the owner of a seal bearing such an image, but one might interpret its symbolic value in two ways: either it is the forget-me-not of a soldier on duty or it is a love token for the wife at home. The theme of separation and constancy applies in both cases.[18]

What we have here, of course, is a very Greek depiction of the bond between a husband and wife and not necessarily a Persian take on marriage at all. After all, Greek writers remind us that among Persian royalty and nobility (who form the core of these images), polygamy was practised, although in the Greco-Persian material evidence we do not see any images of a single man with a number of attendant wives to confirm the idea.[19] On the gems, Greek monogamy is the norm.[20]

Having considered some of the common representational themes found in Attic vase painting and the Anatolian seals, I want to turn now to some specifics of the iconography, namely the body-image of the women of Asia Minor. I will decode the use made of the female body shape in the gems by comparing its representation with examples found in Greek art and employing the methodologies used for reading vase paintings and minor arts.

If, then, we reconsider the image of the nymph Nemea on the Herakles seal from the Punjab (Fig. 15.1a), we note that she is represented in a typically Greek style: her body is well proportioned; she is slim-hipped and full-breasted; she wears an arm-exposing linen *chiton*; her hair is bound up in a fillet. She resembles, to all intents and purposes, many such women on Greek gemstones or pottery of the Classical period. Turning now to a sole figure of a Greco-Persian woman, however, we see several notable differences (Fig. 15.2a). In terms of dress, the woman wears an Achaemenid court robe: a large bag-shaped tunic made, it appears, from pleated linen which is caught into a sash at the waist and pulled out of the band to create elegant "sleeves".[21] The skirt of the garment is folded in such a way that pleats are brought forward to a central waterfall of cloth. A small train follows the figure, but the skirt is pulled up enough in front to reveal soft slippers or boots. She wears a very un-Greek hairstyle of a single plait or braid hanging low down her back and intertwined with tassels or pompoms. This hairstyle is not attested in any visual source other than the Greco-Persian seals, where it features predominantly.[22]

The most striking feature of the image, however, is the woman's physical build. Women on the Greco-Persian gems are uniformly buxom, with full breasts and, most noticeably, very large buttocks, which are given particular emphasis by the drapery of their robes that seem to cling to their ample fat. This steatopygic fatness is the most notable feature of the representation of women in the Greco-Persian gems although, interestingly, steatopygia is not attested in any of the (albeit scarce) representations of women elsewhere in the empire. Two beautiful Achaemenid ivory female figurines from the Phoenician coast, for example, cup their small breasts in their upraised hands, but their figures are decidedly lacking in curves otherwise (Caubet & Gaborit-Chopin 2004: 78, pl. 82; Stucky 1985). The woman adopting the hand-over-wrist gesture on a limestone plaque now in Brooklyn has full breasts but is not fat (Brosius 1996: 85), while the three female figures depicted on a cylinder seal "audience scene" are wearing Achaemenid court robes, the drapery of which is arranged in the same style as on the Greco-Persian gems (Amiet 1977: 440, pl. 821; 456; Briant 2002*a*: 253, fig. 37b).[23] Yet apart from some emphasis on the breasts, the figures' buttocks and hips are depicted flat and decidedly lacking in curves.

What, then, do the existing images suggest about the physical make-up of real Persian or Anatolian women? Steatopygia, of course, is an unusual accumulation of fat in and around the buttocks of women.[24] It was famously common among the Hottentots of Central Africa where it is regarded by them as a mark of beauty and fertility, since the condition begins in infancy and is fully developed on the first pregnancy. The discovery of the infamous Neolithic figures in stone and ivory (the so-called ice age "Venus" figurines) has been used to support the theory that a similar steatopygous race once existed in Asia and Europe, although there is no evidence for this and thus it cannot be used to propose that all Anatolian women of the Classical period were steatopygic.

What the "Venus" figurines do indicate, however, is that at the very least the steatopygic trait was revered and desirable in a woman. Likewise, while the Greco-Persian seal images tell us very little about the reality of the physical appearance of the women of Hellenized Persia, in terms of gender ideology they are loaded. Women with large buttocks are a feature of Greco-Persian gems alone. In some of the Greco-Persian examples, the obsession for a large build is so pronounced that in the iconography the buttocks almost form a shelf suggesting that these images must attest to a localized fetish for the ample, Rubenesque, woman where beauty is expressed through fleshy abundance and fatness denotes fertility (Figs 15.1b, 15.1e, 15.1f, 15.2a & 15.2b). Even the Greek Hippocratic corpus makes that association, highlighting for us the dichotomy between the physical reality of women's lives at the heart of the Greek world and the artistic ideal that the community created.[25] Robert Garland has suggested that judging from the scarce osteo-archaeological evidence, plus our knowledge of the somewhat inactive and secluded lives of many women of various *poleis*, most Greek women would have had a tendency to run to fat and that it is only an artistic conceit that depicts them slim-hipped, flat-bellied and boyish (Garland 1995: 120; also Llewellyn-Jones 2002: 193–194, n. 24).

Fig. 15.2 (a) Woman in Achaemenid court robe with lotus and flowers. (After Boardman 2001: pl. 879). (b) Woman in Persian dress with floral wreath. (After Boardman 2001: pl. 903). (c) Fat youth. Detail taken from an Attic red-figure *krater*. (After Clark 1956: fig. 17). (d) *Coitus a tergo*: woman with mirror. (After Boardman 2001: pl. 298). (e) Greek style sex scene between a Persian man and woman. (After Boardman 2001: pl. 862). (f) *Coitus a tergo* with a clothed man and a woman with mirror. (After Boardman 2001: pl. 1065)

In the Greek artistic sphere, a figure must not be too fat or too thin, since this causes imbalance and complication of line. In *The Nude*, Kenneth Clark alludes to a figured vase from the mid-fifth century BC on which four men are represented: on one side two buff athletes are shown throwing the discus and javelin; they are muscular and solid and lithe. On the other side, separated from the action, is a fat young man with a big belly seen in profile, turning his back on the games (Fig. 15.2c) (Clark 1956: 24, fig. 17). Next to him is a skinny youth facing the athletes, but seeming to pull away as far as he can from the action. The reading of the jar is unambiguous, as least as far as Clark is concerned: both fat and thin are at odds with the ideal of vigorous male beauty.

But what of women? On the whole, Greek artists tend to depict women with slight builds. In one titillating scene for instance, two women are shown anointing their bodies with perfume; they are lithe, almost masculine in the outlined contours of their bodies, almost boyish in the narrowness of their hips and the flatness of their stomachs (Kilmer 1993: pl. R207). It has often been noted that the vision of the ideal female body in Greek art (prior to the late fourth century BC) takes the ephebic body as its model and simply adds rudimentary breasts to the torso to create the biological sex of the figure (Llewellyn-Jones 2002). Nevertheless, other images of women, especially in the short-lived genre of blatantly pornographic vase paintings of the Late Archaic and Early Classical periods, are ample in their fatness. It has been suggested that these women are old prostitutes, denigrated by society and misused and abused by groups of their young clientele, who are frequently shown in an orgiastic frenzy beating them with slippers or simultaneously penetrating them orally and anally (Kilmer 1993: 104–07, pl. R518). However, nothing specifically suggests that sexual humiliation is the theme of these images or of the real-life practice behind the representation. Might these scenes not be the ultimate male erotic fantasy of mature women actively participating in lively sex, their fatness adding to their sex appeal? Throughout most of human history, fat has been thought to be the best feature of the female body, the most desirable and beautiful stuff of all.[26]

Maybe the Greek women of Persian Ionia, or the Persian women who settled in Asia Minor, operated under a set of rules in which big was beautiful. From the seal images we can say with confidence that cultural taste aspired to that body-image and artists were therefore content to depict them as ample. Nonetheless, it is worth recalling Xenophon here, as he plunged deeper into the Persian Empire during his mercenary career, being concerned that, "if we once learn to live in idleness and luxury, and to consort with the beautiful and big (*kalai kai megalai*) women of these Medes and Persians, we may, like the lotus-eaters, forget our way home" (*Anabasis* 3.2.25).

But what is actually meant here by Xenophon's term *megalai*? Recently, scholarship has come to the conclusion that Xenophon cannot be talking about the beautiful *fat* women of Asia, but the beautiful *tall* women. For Christopher Tuplin, "the women are *megalai* not because they are fat...but because height is a mark of beauty and of presence appropriate to an imperial people", while Robin Lane Fox suggests that no Greek mercenary would want to be reminded of the short dumpy woman he left at home and that therefore, to Greek eyes, the women of Asia were uniformly tall and beautiful (Tuplin 2004a: 156; Lane Fox 2004: 202). Something more than—and less than—scholarship is at work here. For, judging from the iconographic representations, height is not the issue at all; if these gems show us the kind of women that local ideology found beautiful, then the women Xenophon was encountering in Asia were fat and beautiful—and not just fat, but *really* fat, ample indeed; for that is the correct reading of *megalai* in this context. The argument that only height can give these women sex appeal or dignified presence devalues the beauty of the soft fleshy bodies depicted in the seals and tells us more about the contemporary taste in female physique than Classical taste in body-image. It must also be remembered that Xenophon was not describing the physically active women of the Scythians alluded to in the Hippocratic *Airs, Waters and Places*, but the refined ladies of the Anatolian satrapies whose daily regime extended little beyond the rigours of weaving on a loom.[27]

The secret of sex appeal, it has been suggested, lies at the waist, or to be more specific, the waist–hip ratio calculated by dividing the waist measurement by the hip size: the smaller the waist in relation to the hip, the more desirable a woman is seen to be. The waist is one of the distinguishing human features since no other primate has one—or, as Klein succinctly puts it, "a fat ass makes us human" (1996: 37). In the seals, the belting of the Achaemenid female robe and the organization of its pleats emphasizes such a diminutive waist and glories in the swell of the breasts and, most obviously, the buttocks and hips. By their physiques the women of the Greco-Persian seals are defined as undeniably sexual. The women of Asia are beautiful because they are big.

It is well recognized that representations of the sexes in Greek art exploit the architectural and erotic possibilities of the curve at the buttocks and hips (cf. Stewart 1997: 86–97). Blatantly erotic vase paintings, however, go one step further and fetishize the posterior in order to show anal intercourse between a man and woman (Kilmer 1993: 44–45, n. 35, 82–86, 114–117, 182–183; see also Stewart 1997: 161–167). In the Greco-Persian seal imagery there are similarly a few intimate scenes of a Persian and his lover—be she wife, concubine or whore—in the same act and, given the obvious penchant for fleshy buttocks in Achaemenid Anatolia, it is no surprise to find a similar fetish for *coitus a tergo* (Fig. 15.2d) (Boardman 2001: pl. 298 = Munich A 1432 [missing]; pl. 906. Paris BN 1104). In the Near East such scenes, so frequently found in Assyrian and Babylonian contexts, have often been interpreted as having a religious significance, but the Greco-Persian scenes are decidedly secular, reminiscent of many such examples in the Attic repertoire.[28]

However, only one sex scene is depicted in an overt Greek style: a large bed accommodates a young couple in the midst of lovemaking (Fig. 15.2e). The young woman with large breasts, and wearing her hair in a simple plait, reclines on a pile of cushions and supports her weight on her arms while her legs (with their slippered feet) are hooked over the shoulders of her lover who grips her behind her knees and kneels on the bed in order to penetrate his lover's vagina (see Boardman 2001: pl. 862 = Boston *LHG* 63). There is a certain realistic innovation here, since the kneeling position of the youth is not usual even in Greek representations, but as Boardman notes, the girl's legs in the air recall Lysistrata's injunction to her followers to "lift their Persian slippers to the ceiling" (2001: 311; see also Ar. *Lys.* 229).

The debate over the secular or sacred context of the sex scenes can impact on our understanding of both the Greek and Greco-Persian examples: what exactly is the sexual act being practised here: anal or vaginal intercourse? What, if any, are the repercussions of either sexual act as to the status of the woman represented? Is she a wife or a prostitute? In many of the seal representations, the penetrated woman holds a mirror and often glances backwards at her lover, leading Boardman to surmise that these scenes are "thoroughly secular" (2001: 317). But how then are we meant to interpret the mirror? Is it a woman's symbol designating her as housewife or as whore? On one seal a man remains fully clothed while penetrating a naked woman (Fig. 15.2f) (2001: pl. 1065 = Malibu, J. Paul Getty Museum 85. AN. 370.26). Do the clothes indicate that he is visiting a professional woman or is he initiating an intimate act of lovemaking at home?

Despite some ostensibly unanswerable questions, it is hoped that this brief investigation into the images of women and gender on the Greco-Persian seals will augment our understanding of the complex intercultural relations clearly in operation in the Classical period. Recent and important work on the Athenian use of Persian imagery in art and other forms of fashionable Persica has forced us to reconsider our understanding of Greco-Persian socio-cultural relations, especially in terms of gender ideology (see, most importantly, Miller 1997). An examination of the seals from Achaemenid Asia Minor can only further demonstrate that the cultural interaction was indeed a two-way process, with the Persians adopting and adapting Greek artistic styles and scenes to their own specifications as readily as the Greeks adapted Persian art, architecture or items of dress. As such, a study of the Greco-Persian imagery of gender works in harmony with and expands on the ongoing analysis of the Greek writings on Persian women, and develops the groundwork already undertaken on the representation of women in gender ideology in the indigenous art and literature of Greece.

Notes

1. For an investigation of Greco-Persian seals, their chronology and imagery see Richter 1956; d'Amore 1992; Boardman 1980: 106–107; 1994: 42–46; 2000, 2001; Dusinberre 1997; Kaptan 2002 (who opts to use the term "Persianizing" over "Greco-Persian"); von der Osten 1931. For a discussion of the function of seal images generally see Merrillees 2005; Garrison 2000. On the Anatolian satrapies and the cultural interactions of the province see Kaptan 2003; Bakır *et al.* 2001; Casabonne 2004a; Dusinberre 2003.
2. See comments in Boardman 2001: 303–327. Of course, the cylinder had long been the preferred seal type for Mesopotamia, ideally used to seal rectangular inscribed tablets. But in the Classical period, and in the empire rather than in the Persian heartland itself—where the cylinder remained popular—sealing was more regularly done of rolled papyrus, requiring only an imprint over a knot (*bulla*). For this, a stamp seal or finger-ring was more suitable, although a cylinder could be used. For comments on the increasing popularity of stamp seals in the Classical period see Merrillees 2005: 15.
3. For a further example see also Boardman 2001: pl. 1062 (New York, Rosen Collection); the style is almost entirely Greek.
4. For a good discussion of Greek military/sexual dominance over the eastern barbarians see Cartledge 1998. See further discussion in Hall 1989.
5. For a good discussion of Attic vases in the Achaemenid Empire see de Vries 1977.
6. The iconographic image of Herakles in this pose with an attendant nymph is only otherwise known from a *metope* at Olympia and from a sealing from Ur. See Boardman 1994: 325 n. 56.
7. For interpretations of women in Attic art see especially Lewis 2002; Blundell 2002; Reeder 1995; Llewellyn-Jones 2002, 2003.
8. For the use of narrative on Attic vases see Lissarrague 1987, 2000; see also Stansbury-O'Donnell 1999; Small 2003.

9. However, other Anatolian cylinder, pyramidal, pendant or cube seals show no real sense of narrative at all; they simply display a series of unconnected human figures, male and female, Greek and Persian. See Boardman 2001: 315, fig. 289, pls. 861, 876, 906.
10. On the rarity of images of Achaemenid women in Iranian art see Brosius 1996: 84–87; Root 2003b: 27–29.
11. Women standing alone: Boardman 2001: pl. 283 = New York, Met. 133; pl. 854 = Berlin F 181; pl. 879 = BM 434 (this is also presented as colour pl. 2). The same image is depicted by Goldman (1991a: pl. 26; pl. 903 = BM 433). For this image see also Goldman 1991a: pl. 25; Richter 1956: 34, no. 133 & pl. 133. See further Goldman 1991a: pls 24, 28, 27, 31.
12. See for example Boardman 2001: col. pl. 4 = BM 436; pl. 966. Cambridge; pl. 990 = Munich A 1421. For the same image see also Goldman 1991a: 96, fig. 32; Boardman 2000: 155, pl. 5.3 = from the Oxus Treasure; von der Osten 1931: fig. 103 = New York Met. 86.11.43. For the Oxus Treasure woman see also Goldman 1991a: 87, fig. 5. The woman on the Oxus Treasure ring wears a mural crown that, from central Iranian sources, appears to be the headdress of royal Achaemenid women and has its origins in Assyrian royal iconography. However, it is difficult to assign this figure as a royal female and the ring probably depicts a court lady, suggesting that the crenellated crown was worn by female royalty and nobility. In this I follow Daems 2001: 46.
13. Boardman 2001: pl. 964 = Boston 03.1013. Front. See also Goldman 1991a: pl. 23. For the image of the female harpist on seals from the Greek mainland see Boardman 2001: pl. 600 = Leningrad and pl. 472 = unknown location. For debates surrounding the Attic "women's room" scenes see Lewis 2003: 130–171; for the Maltese dog in Attic art see Lewis 2003: 19–20, 159–161.
14. Boardman 2001: pl. 964 = Boston 03.1013. Back. For Greek seal images of women with pet birds (or symbolic-magical birds like the iunx) see Boardman 2001: pl. 759 = Tarentum. Red-figure *epinetron* by the Eretria Painter. Athens, National Museum 1629. On songbirds as pets see Lewis 2003: 161–163.
15. See Lewis 2003: 135–138 on the problem of using the term.
16. Boardman 2001: pl. 891 = London, BM 436 (reverse). It depicts a woman holding a lotus bud and offering a toy (a rattle?) to a young child. For comparative scenes in Attic art see Lewis 2002: 14–20; Garland 1995: 144; Neils & Oakley 2003.
17. For the role of the mother in the scenes see Lewis 2003: 38–42.
18. Boardman (1980: 105) argues that, "the subjects [on the seals and gemstones] are mainly explicable by the probability that the gems were worn by women". I would prefer a more fluid interpretation as to the sex of the owners, wearers and, indeed, users of the seals.
19. See, for example, Ktesias 44; Hdt. 1.135. See further Brosius 1996: 35–37.
20. Only once, around 413 BC did the Athenians permit men to take two wives. This was a pragmatic solution to the fact that as so many young Athenian men had died during the Sicilian disaster there was a surplus of unmarried Athenian women. For details see Ogden 1999: xxvi–xxvii.
21. A good discussion of the Achaemenid female robe is provided by Goldman 1991a.
22. Most women in Achaemenid art either wear veils (which obscure the hair) or else adopt the "pageboy" coiffure of tight curls and ringlets. See Daems 2001: 44.
23. See further Brosius & Lerner, this volume.
24. Steatopygia is a genetic trait that seems to have been widespread in Eurasia during the icy Pleistocene until around 10,000 years ago. It is a way of storing fat reserves (energy) for hard times. Steatopygous mothers had a better chance of surviving through winter with their children. On the image of steatopygia see Gilman 1986. For the "Venus" figures and their relationship to the bodies of real women see Duhard 1990, 1991.
25. For the issue of fatness in Greek medical thought see Pinault 1993.
26. On the issue of fat beauty see Klein 1996; Braziel & LeBesco 2001.
27. *Airs, Waters, Places* 19–21. See comments in Pinault 1993.
28. For Near Eastern evidence and debates see Leick 1994: 50, pl. 6 and Assante 2002: figs 1–3. For the Greek artistic evidence and debates see Younger 2005: 123–125.

Part 4

Art and Architecture

16

The Social Dimensions of Babylonian Domestic Architecture in the Neo-Babylonian and Achaemenid Periods[1]

Heather D. Baker

Introduction

The aim of this paper is to use the written documentation from first-millennium BC Babylonia, in combination with other data, to develop a framework within which we can better understand the archaeological evidence for modifications to domestic dwellings. This issue is of interest for a number of reasons. First, it has a direct bearing on our understanding of the organization of the household, and of how people lived. Second, and related to the first point, it has implications for identifying activity areas within the house and relating them to their social context. In particular, we have to consider whether any specialist activity areas are replicated among the different units or whether they are retained in communal use once a house is divided up. Third, there have been a number of interesting recent studies of Mesopotamian domestic architecture which have focused on "permeability", that is, on patterns of circulation within the house (e.g. Brusasco 1999/2000, 2004). Clearly, physical alterations to the house can affect circulation patterns radically, but such modifications may be under-represented in published accounts, especially those of earlier excavations. Fourth, living densities, and especially variations in them, may shed light on differences in social status; they also, of course, have implications for demographic studies. Finally, while my focus is on first-millennium BC Babylonia, some of the considerations raised here may have implications for the interpretation of excavated houses from other periods and areas.

The configuration and typology of the Neo-Babylonian houses have been treated in a recent, comprehensive study by Miglus, to which the reader is referred for further details (1999: 177–213). Essentially he divided the houses into single-courtyard houses and multipartite ones, the latter group including double houses and houses of more complex layout. Although Miglus was primarily concerned with houses from the first half of the first millennium BC, in practice of course there was continuity between the periods of Neo-Babylonian and Persian rule, in housing just as in other aspects of daily life. This continuity, combined with the frequent absence of precise dating criteria, means that it is not possible for us to subdivide the period for the purposes of the present study.[2]

Houses are not only attested through excavation but also through a wealth of cuneiform economic documents from first-millennium BC Babylonia.[3] A preliminary attempt to compare the excavated houses with those documented in the texts, and to reconcile discrepancies between the two sets of data, has been made by Baker (2004: 56–62), and a more detailed study of urban properties in general is currently being prepared by the same author (Baker forthcoming). The principal characteristics of the documentation relevant for the present purposes will be considered in further detail below.

Background

The basic starting point for examining the relationship between Mesopotamian houses and their inhabitants has to be the seminal work of Stone on this subject (1981, 1987).[4] In studying the excavated residential districts of Old Babylonian Nippur, she was able to match up one particular house (House I in the TA area), and the alterations made to it, with the changes in its ownership as documented by tablets actually found in the house. However, among the abundant material from first-millennium BC Babylonia there is not a single instance where we can match up a particular excavated house with cuneiform tablets relating to it, so we have to operate on a somewhat more abstract level. Nevertheless, using Stone's study as a point of departure, and taking into account the abundant written evidence for the family and the household, it is possible to make some progress in addressing this issue.

In spite of the wealth of documentary evidence for the Neo-Babylonian household and family, there is as yet no synthesis available comparable to Postgate's excellent overview for the earlier period (1992: 88–108). However, many detailed, specialist studies on aspects of family matters have been published in recent years (see especially Wunsch 1995/96). Patterns of residence will be dealt with in further detail in Baker forthcoming.

Our basic problem is to delineate more precisely the developmental cycle of the household and to attempt to identify the likely effects of the household's transformation on the archaeological record. First it is necessary to review the definitions of the terms that are central to any discussion of residence patterns, following the work of Laslett (1972). "Household" is intended to signify a "co-residential domestic unit"; as such it can include not only family members but also resident slaves, lodgers, and so on. A "Simple Family Household" consists of a "Conjugal Family Unit" (married couple or widowed person with offspring), with or without slaves. An "Extended Family Household" consists of a conjugal family unit with the addition of one or more relatives other than offspring, with or without slaves. Finally, a "Multiple Family Household" includes two or more conjugal family units, which are connected by kinship or marriage.

In speaking about the developmental cycle of the household, therefore, I am essentially referring to its transformation from one of the aforementioned states to another. We might expect that normally such a transformation would be triggered by one or more significant life events, such as the death of the head of the household, or the marriage of a son. According to Schloen (drawing on the work of Saller), we might expect that around two-thirds of households would have been in the nuclear family stage at any one time, that is, two-thirds would have been of the Simple Family Household type (Schloen 2001: 125).

The scenario envisaged by Schloen for the Levant is likely to have applied to Babylonia also, because there too the early death of the parents would tend to keep the numbers of joint family households rather low. This is borne out by a recent study of Neo-Babylonian demography by Gehlken, who found that around half of the male temple personnel in his sample worked together with their father for up to five years, and thus the opportunities for both father and adult male sons to live in the same household were restricted (Gehlken 2005: 103).[5] In any case, the textual evidence indicates that residence was essentially virilocal, with adult males tending to form their own household upon marriage. In reality, of course, anomalous situations abounded, hence the stress placed in more recent studies upon the household "cycle", which admits of a chronological element, rather than upon a static "norm" of nuclear family-based residence patterns. It has to be borne in mind that there is an inherent bias in our documentation towards the recording of anomalous situations, because these were the very cases which invited careful regulation in order, for example, to protect the vulnerable and to forestall the prospect of future litigation. Such is the case with the Neo-Babylonian tablets dealing with the rights of widows, which have been studied recently by Roth (1991/93; see below for further discussion).

The starting point: Nippur, TA House I

Before we turn to the first-millennium evidence it is worth looking more closely at Stone's analysis of TA House I. The scenario can be summarized as follows: upon the death of their father, four brothers divided up House I between themselves according to their respective shares, with the oldest son taking a preferential share. Within a relatively short period of time a series of adjustments were made, with the end result that the youngest son, Enlil-galzu, was left owning part of the original house, and the remainder of it came into the possession of one of two brothers who owned the house next door (House H). During this process a number of physical alterations were made to the original house:

1) A new entrance from the street was created in locus 155 (see Fig. 16.1c) because Enlil-galzu, the owner of this part of the house, no longer had access to the original entrance in locus 157 since that room was now owned by an unrelated individual, Ipqu-Enlil.

2) The original entrance in locus 157 was now blocked up (see Fig. 16.2a) because that room had been acquired by Enlil-galzu, whose own part of the house already had an entrance (locus 155, see above).

3) The doorway between locus 157 and locus 173 was now blocked up (see Fig. 16.2b) because those rooms were now owned by different, unrelated parties.

4) The doorway between locus 179b and the central courtyard, locus 152b, was now blocked up (see Fig. 16.2b) to give Enlil-galzu, owner of the north-western part of the house, sole use of the courtyard.

5) The wall between locus 179b and locus 179a was demolished (see Fig. 16.2b) to make one large room.

6) A doorway between the newly created room locus 179a/179b and House H locus 180 was created, thereby adding loci

182 THE WORLD OF ACHAEMENID PERSIA

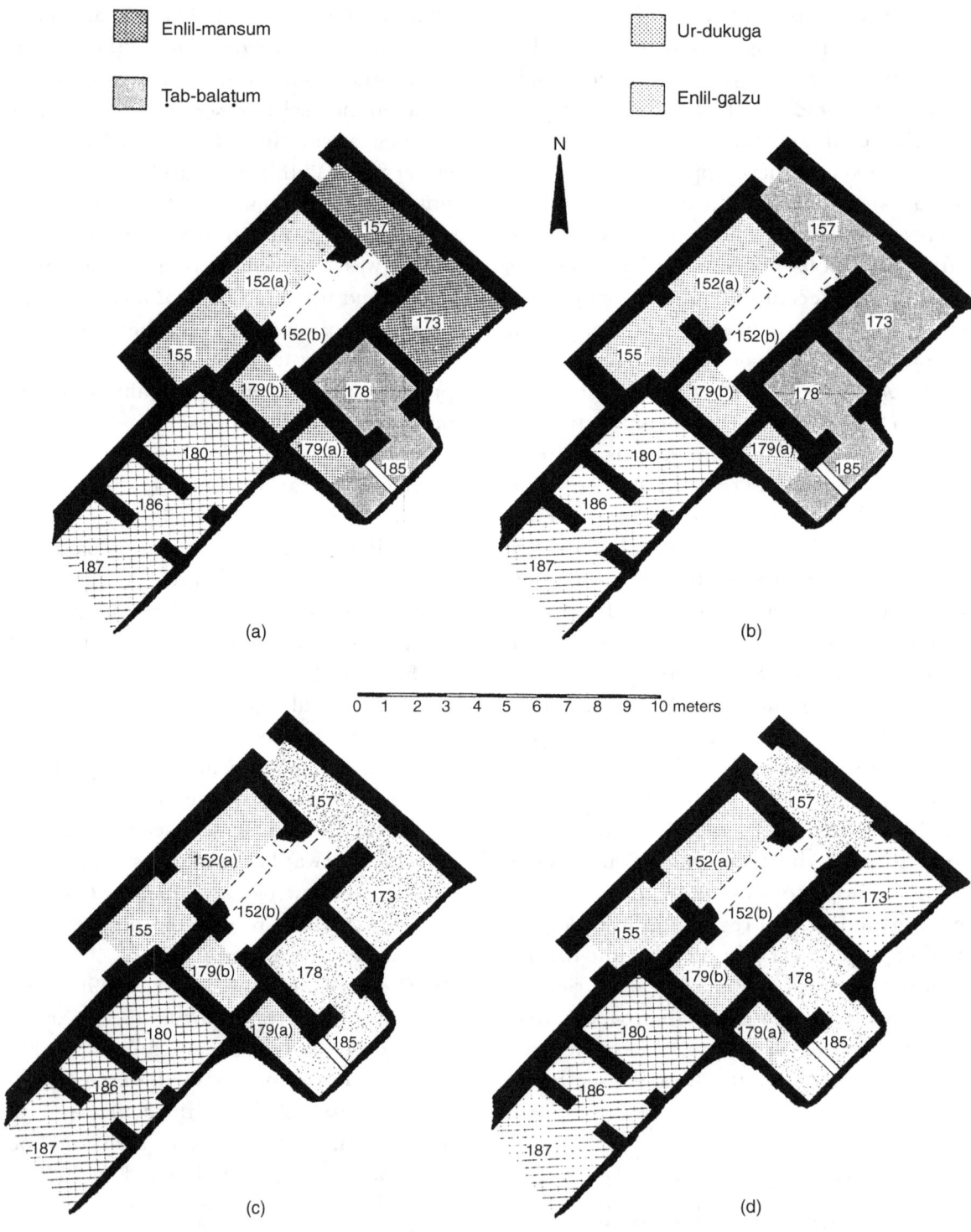

Fig. 16.1 Ownership changes of TA House I. (After Stone 1981: Fig. 2)

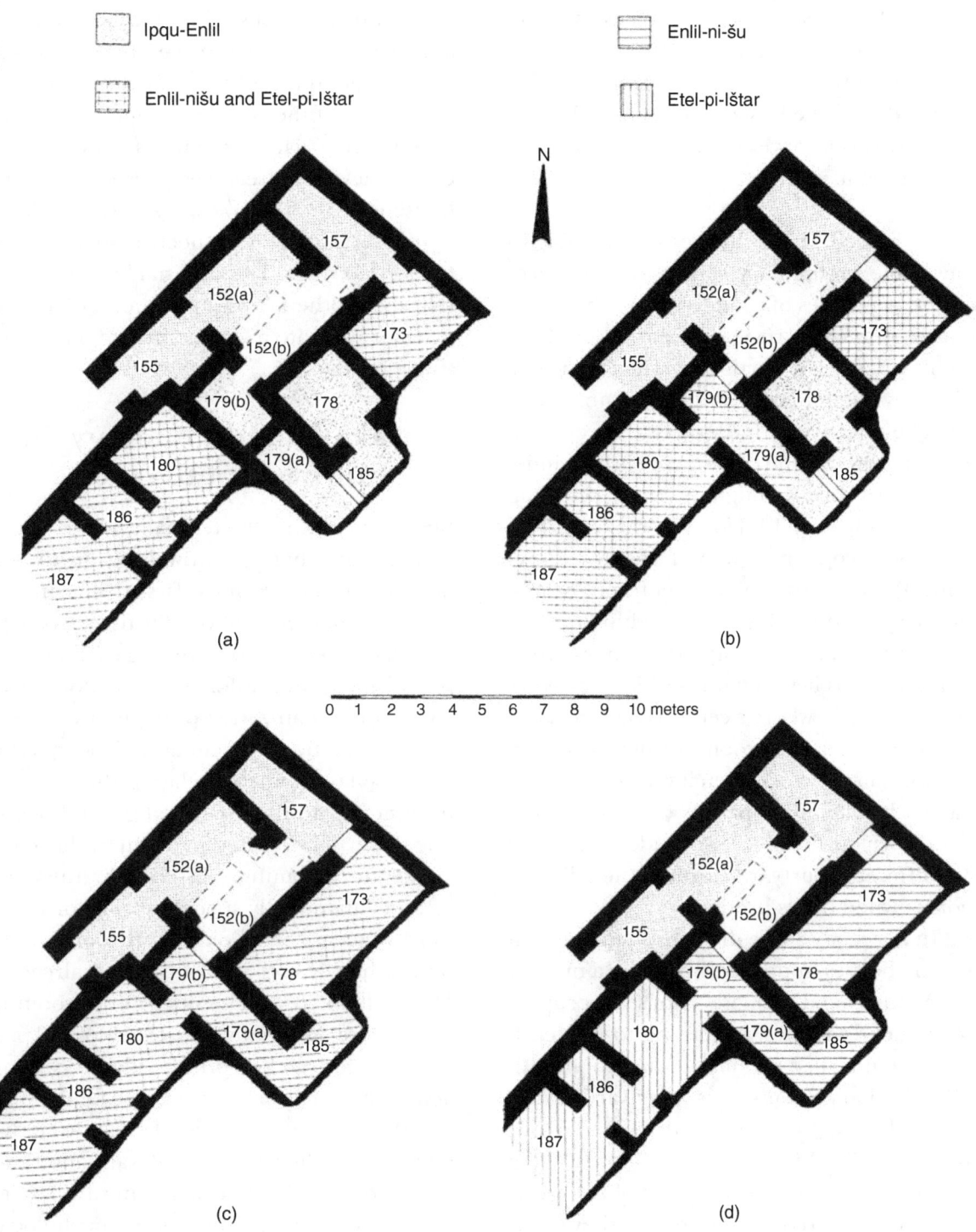

Fig. 16.2 Ownership changes of TA House I ctd. (After Stone 1981: Fig. 3)

179a/179b, 185, and 178 to House H next door (see Fig. 16.2b).
7) The wall between locus 178 and locus 173 was demolished (see Fig. 16.2c), thereby creating one large room and adding locus 173 to House H.

On the basis of these changes it is possible to draw some preliminary conclusions concerning the principles of modification, which will be useful to us in reviewing the first-millennium evidence. In particular, when what was originally a single courtyard house came to be owned by unrelated individuals, there was a tendency towards the creation of entirely independent units, as we might expect. According to the example of TA House I, this could be done by a combination of measures, especially: 1) making a separate entrance where necessary (and blocking up a redundant second entrance); 2) blocking up any doors which communicated between units which were now separate; and 3) where a central courtyard was enclosed by suites of rooms owned by different, unrelated parties, then it was reserved for sole use by one of the parties (in this case the new owner on the south-west side had access to a different courtyard through the adjacent rooms owned by his brother).

In her study Stone distinguished between "linear" houses, supposedly housing a nuclear family unit, and "square" houses occupied by extended families. According to her, each nuclear family had one main living room with 1–2 subsidiary rooms plus courtyard space. So, in theory, the four brothers could just about have lived in the space (House I) that they inherited from their father, sharing the central courtyard of the house, but they chose not to do so. It is worth reminding ourselves at this point that evidence of ownership does not necessarily equal evidence of residence (the renting of houses and parts of houses is amply attested). Since three of the four heirs quickly relinquished their shares in House I, it follows that they were not dependent on the paternal house for the purpose of dwelling—either they had already established their own households, or they were assisted in doing so by converting their respective shares of the house into silver. The original "square" house that the brothers inherited together had been transformed into a "linear" house owned by a single brother.

Akkadian terminology for the parts of the house

Before examining the textual evidence for the division and sharing of dwellings in the first millennium BC, we must first review in brief the Akkadian terminology for the parts of the house, since our understanding of these terms provides essential information as to how the layout and organization of the house was conceptualized by its occupants. The question of house layout and of relating the Akkadian terminology to the excavated ground plans is one that will be treated in detail by the author (Baker forthcoming). Essentially, there is a lack of functionally specific terms for rooms: words such as "bedroom", "bathroom", and so on are hardly ever used (as noted already by Miglus 1999: 227). The question of room use is therefore essentially an archaeological problem and, for our period, the identification of activity areas/room function has tended to be based upon the presence of specific fixtures and fittings, the treatment of walls and floors, and (more rarely) objects left in situ. Modern techniques, such as the micromorphological analysis of floor deposits, which have much to contribute to this problem, have yet to be applied at the sites that are the subject of the present study (for a brief introduction to such techniques see Matthews 2003: 174–76).

I have suggested elsewhere that this absence of functionally specific terminology concerning the house reflects conventions of record keeping: individual bathrooms or bedrooms were unlikely to be sold on their own, and when they formed part of a larger complex there was no reason to refer to them by name (Baker 2007: 71). The terms for parts of the house which occur most frequently in the documents are those for the courtyard (*tarbaṣu*) and the individual "wings" which enclosed it and which were designated according to the four points of the compass (*bīt šūti, bīt iltāni, bīt amurri, bīt šadî*).[6] In fact the very occurrence of these terms for the courtyard and its surrounding suites almost always reflects the fact that the context concerns a house being divided or shared in some way. Again, when a house is treated as a whole, there is rarely any need to refer to its constituent parts by name.

Textually attested scenarios for the division and/or shared use of houses

Before we address the question of shared ownership and use of houses, we should first briefly consider issues of residence in general. As mentioned above, residence at this period was virilocal, with the husband normally establishing his own household upon marriage. There is one textual reference to a wife living in the loft above an annexe that is rented out by her husband (Strassmaier 1897: no. 25). However, one should be extremely wary of drawing from this single case any conclusions about the segregation of women.

Upon the death of the head of the family, such houses as he owned would be apportioned among his heirs. According to Roth, his widow had no automatic right of continued residence within the marital home (1991/1993: 25f.). The husband, in anticipation of his death, might assign to his wife a house or part of a house, either (unusually) as an outright gift with full title, or as a lifetime interest, that is, where the widow had no right to dispose of the property in question, which reverted to the husband's heirs upon her death. Alternatively, the widow might have recourse to her own dowry property: either she might live in the house assigned to her as part of this dowry,[7] or she could rent a dwelling by drawing on the income from her dowry. If the widow was left without adequate means of support then she could seek legal redress by making a claim against her husband's heirs.

In one case a man bequeathed to his widowed mother a house, and it is stated in his "testament" that his two sons would live in the house with her for as long as she lived (Baker 2004: 139–141, no. 59);[8] presumably title to the house would pass to his sons and heirs after her death, although this is not explicitly stated. The man's mother was to provide dowries for her two daughters, his sisters, out of her own dowry. The circumstances suggest that the man was currently living in a household made up of himself, his widowed mother, his two sons (who were probably unmarried and had not yet formed their own households), and his two unmarried sisters—although explicit evidence for co-residence, apart from the aforementioned post-mortem provisions, is lacking. The absence of any mention of the man's wife indicates that she had already died; it is likely that the man's mother played a part in caring for her motherless grandsons. In any case this tablet provides ample illustration, if such were needed, of the complexity of the family cycle.

The written evidence for the splitting up of houses comes in a variety of forms, and the nature of the available documentation varies over time. The sale of parts of houses, which are clearly identifiable as such, is almost entirely restricted to the Hellenistic period. Whether this represents a real trend towards the more frequent sale of smaller house units at this time is doubtful. The sale of small "houses" is well attested in earlier centuries (Baker 2004: 62), and at least some of these must represent parts of traditional courtyard houses rather than complete houses in their own right. It seems likely therefore that the difference is one of phrasing: before the Hellenistic period the properties which are the subject of sale contracts tended to be called by the generic term *bītu* rather than by one or more of the terms which explicitly refer to a house sector (e.g. *bīt šūti, tarbaṣu*, etc.) and which are commonly found in sale contracts of the Hellenistic era.

In the case of the division of inheritance, we have to distinguish between those documents that concern the apportioning of complete, adjacent houses between the heirs, and those which deal with the splitting up of single properties. Cases belonging to the former category are interesting for the study of patterns of residence within neighbourhoods but are outside the scope of the present work. Inheritance documents referring to the division of single houses are especially numerous in the Hellenistic period, but this may be because records of inheritance division in general are relatively well represented among the late corpus.

The leasing of parts of houses is attested in a handful of documents from the sixth century BC. In contrast to the sale and inheritance documents, such lease contracts are entirely absent from the Hellenistic corpus. However, this almost certainly reflects a change in record-keeping practices rather than the actual situation, since other kinds of lease documents are also lacking and it is well established that certain kinds of legal contracts dropped out of the cuneiform record at this time (Doty 1977: 323–330).[9] Finally, there are a number of miscellaneous documents that refer in passing to houses being shared between different parties.

We have to extract from the written evidence the range of possible scenarios for the shared ownership and use of houses in order to provide the context for examining the archaeological evidence. There are a number of points that should be borne in mind. First, as we observed above, evidence of ownership is not the same as evidence of residence. The renting of houses or parts of houses was very common and we should not assume that a person acquiring a house or part of a house by whatever means actually intended to live in it. To give one example, a marriage contract from Borsippa written in 494 BC records a dowry that included a part of a house measuring approximately 61 m^2, given by a mother to her daughter (Krückmann 1933: no. 2, written in Borsippa in 499 BC).[10] According to the tablet the two women were obliged not to obstruct one another's access. However, we know from another document that the daughter did not subsequently live in her share of the house herself, but rented it out to a third party.[11]

Second, a house could be divided between different parties "on paper", without any corresponding physical alteration to its layout. For example, in the initial stages of the history of TA House I at Nippur, while the house was still entirely owned by the brothers, there were no evident internal alterations made to it (see Fig. 16.1a–b). It was only after part of it had been acquired by an "outsider" that modifications to the fabric were made. In this connection it is interesting to note that in the Cairo

Geniza documents shares in houses seem even to have functioned as monetary units, with fractions as small as 1/48 being recorded (Goitein 1969: 89; 1983: 82–83).

A third point is that, judging by the documentary evidence, the need to physically divide up a house is likely to have varied with social status and wealth. In the Neo-Babylonian period not only the wealthiest but even middle-income families usually owned more than one urban property. If whole houses could be distributed among the heirs upon inheritance, then the question of sharing and/or physically splitting up a house need not have arisen. For example, in the case of a well-known tablet, which records the division of the enormous estate of Itti-Marduk-balāṭu of the Egibi family, sixteen houses were divided between his three sons (Strassmaier 1897: no. 379, written in Babylon in 508 BC). The oldest son, Marduk-nāṣir-apli, received seven houses in Babylon and three in Borsippa, while his two younger brothers took four houses in Babylon and two in Borsippa as their joint share. In another case of inheritance division the oldest son received seven slaves, a main house (bītu rabû), another house, and a field, while his younger brother took three slaves, a plot of unbuilt land, and some arable land as his share (Weisberg 1980: no. 348 (written in Uruk in 591 BC), and the duplicate tablet: Jakob-Rost & Freydank 1978: no. 86). This theory—that physical modifications to houses may be correlated with social status—is one that we should be able to test against the archaeological record, by determining whether the more humble dwellings more often betray more traces of internal modification than grander ones.

In our texts the term bītu often refers only to part of a house, and not to a whole house of the traditional plan. As in other periods of Mesopotamian history, bītu has many shades of meaning and can signify a single room or suite of rooms. There was a tendency to keep whole houses within the family wherever possible (Baker 2004: 62), and quite often the sale of complete houses can be linked with conditions of hardship. This is the case, for example, with a number of sales of substantial houses from Kutha recorded in tablets of the later Achaemenid period (see Jursa 2003: 56).

These facts raise the question of how we can determine when a document concerns a bītu that represents only part of a typical courtyard house. In fact it is not always clear, but there may be some clues, for example when a specific part of a house, e.g. a bīt šūti, is mentioned, or when the area is less than $c.90$ m², which is the smallest attested size for a courtyard house at this period (Baker 2004: 62).

In the light of the arguments advanced above, we can put forward four possible scenarios for residence within a traditional Babylonian courtyard house. Three of these involve relatives living together, either as 1) a Simple Family Household; 2) an Extended Family Household; or 3) a Multiple Family Household. In the fourth case we have to consider the possibility of courtyard houses being shared by different family households that were not related to one another. As we saw above, the case of TA House I at Nippur suggests that in such circumstances houses would tend to be remodelled in order to form separate units. However, we cannot exclude the possibility that courtyards were sometimes shared between unrelated family units, especially since we have textual evidence from the first millennium for the renting of parts of houses as well as whole houses.

According to the written sources, when different parties (whether related or not) occupied a courtyard house, they shared the use of the courtyard itself, and also of the (privately owned) exit passageway if the house was not directly accessible from a public street. The owners or occupiers referred to in the documents are almost always men. We have to assume that these were typically adult male heads of their own households, but we are not given any details about the size and composition of their own families. Since most of the tablets that refer to the sharing of houses record the division of inheritance, the parties concerned are de facto related to one another. References to more than three such parties sharing a house are rare.

One document written in Uruk in 551 BC describes the division of a house between a man's three grandsons and his son, their uncle (Dougherty 1920: no. 114; cf. San Nicolò & Petschow 1960: no. 6). As I understand the text, the house is of the double courtyard type.[12] The main courtyard house (*bītu rabû*) is divided between the oldest grandson and his youngest brother. The so-called "outer court" (*tarbaṣu bābānû*), which is a little smaller in area, is divided between the middle grandson and his uncle, each of whom is to have two of the four suites of rooms surrounding the courtyard. In the case of the main house the respective shares of the two brothers are not specified. I suggest that this is because the youngest brother was not yet adult and thus there was no question of his establishing his own household.

The archaeological evidence for house modification

It is possible to propose a number of potential scenarios for alterations to a house plan, reflecting different circumstances. First, the main entrance could be relocated as a response to physical changes in the immediate environment. For example in the case of House II in the Merkes quarter of Babylon, a new entrance was needed when the building of House III next door prevented the use of the old one (Reuther 1926: 93). Second, modifications could be made which changed the internal circulation pattern more radically from the inside, by the blocking up of existing doors and/or the opening up of new ones (and perhaps also involving a change in the location of the main entrance or entrances) according to the requirements of the occupants;[13] in this case the perimeters of the house were left intact. The earlier stages in the transformation of TA House I at Nippur represent an example of this situation (Stone 1981: figs 2A–3A; see Figs 16.1a–2a). Third, we may be dealing with modifications that actually changed the perimeter of the house, thereby either expanding or reducing the area that it occupied. Expansion may have been accomplished either by incorporating part of a neighbouring property into the house or by building on adjacent unbuilt land. For example, TA House H was expanded at the expense of House I by the acquisition and incorporation of several loci (see above). Conversely, TA House I itself was diminished in area by this process. Alternatively, a reduction in area may result from the partial abandonment of a house. This is said to have been the case, for example, with Building B, Level I, in the WC-2 area at Nippur (Armstrong 1989: 38, 305, fig. 60); the author dates this level to *c.* 600 BC. Note in this connection that we also have occasional textual references to a part of a house plot being derelict or unbuilt. For example, one tablet from Uruk (written in 555 BC) which refers to "a built north(-facing) wing and south(-facing) wing and the remainder of the house, which is to be torn down and rebuilt" (Dougherty 1923: no. 398, ll. 5–6). Another tablet (written in Uruk in 589 BC) concerns "a built house with its door-jambs fixed in place, and the north(-facing) wing (which) is unbuilt" (Keiser 1918: no. 127).[14] Finally, a fourth scenario involves the blocking up of doorways prior to abandonment. This was presumably intended to protect the fabric of the house until such time as the owners could return to it, or perhaps to prevent harm to children and animals who might stray into the ruins. Such a case has been observed for Building A, again in the WC-2 area at Nippur, according to Armstrong's interpretation (1989: 30).

Apart from the examples cited above, physical alterations to Babylonian houses of the first millennium BC have been quite rarely observed. Some 46 excavated houses from the first half of the first millennium BC have been catalogued by Miglus (1999: 307–314). However, in most cases the published accounts do not give sufficient detail for the purposes of this study. For example, Woolley reports modifications to Neo-Babylonian houses at Ur (1962: 46), but there is no detailed description or plan of the alterations. In fact the houses at Ur were so badly preserved that in many cases doorways to rooms could not be located. It has been observed that some houses at Uruk were very long-lived and were rebuilt many times (e.g. Lenzen 1963: 15–16), but a detailed description of any internal modifications which might have been made has not been published. At Tell al-Lahm (ancient Kissik) in the westernmost house in Sounding 7, the main entrance into Room 1 had been blocked (Safar 1949: 159); however, it is difficult to interpret such an alteration in the absence of a complete ground plan. For the present, then, we have some usable data from the cities of Babylon, Isin, and Nippur.

In the case of the Merkes quarter of Babylon,[15] internal modifications to house layout are very rarely recorded. The quality of the excavations and final publication suggests that they would have been reported if present, and therefore the lack of reference to them is likely to represent the actual state of affairs. This, I believe, reflects the fact that these houses represent high status dwellings of the kind whose owners, as we have seen, were less subject to the kinds of pressures that might have led to divided or shared occupancy.[16]

In the case of Isin, the excavators of the Neo-Babylonian house in the sounding of Nordabschnitt III reported that in a later phase of occupation, which may be of Achaemenid date, two doorways were blocked up (see Figs 16.3a–3b): the doorway between the central courtyard 4 and the reception room 6, and the doorway between room 9 on the north-east side of the courtyard and room 12, which was situated at the north-east end of the "reception room" and accessible from it (Ayoub 1981: 51–53, plan 7). These alterations effectively divided the house into two parts: the suites of rooms to the north-west and north-east on the one hand, and those to the south-west and south-east on the other. Both sectors had access to the courtyard and via that to the exit, which was most likely located in the northern corner of the building. It seems likely that room 9, which has been interpreted as a kitchen and which was now accessible only from the courtyard, was used by both sets of occupants; it is notable that no ovens were found in the southern sector, according to the published plan. The blocking of the doorway from the courtyard into what would previously have been the main living room (Room 6) of the house is unusual since this opening would have constituted an important source of light and air. (This doorway is not shown on the original excavation plan; its approximate location is reconstructed in Fig. 16.3a.)

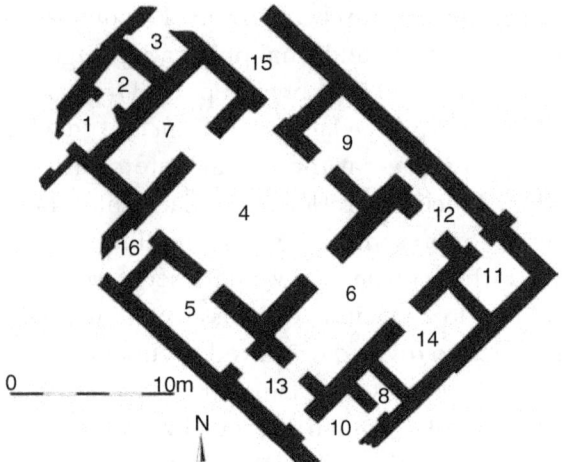
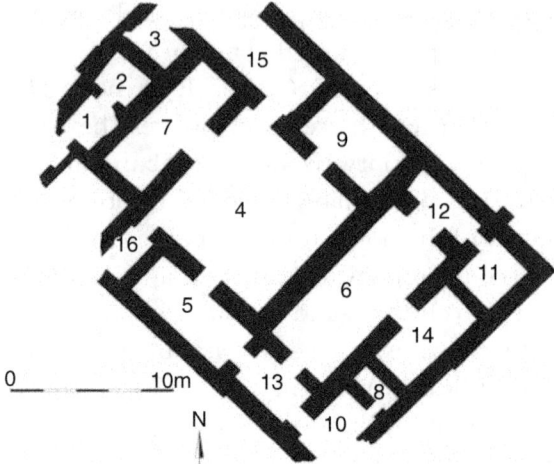

Fig. 16.3a Isin, house in Nordabschnitt III, earlier phase.

Fig. 16.3b Isin, house in Nordabschnitt III, later phase.

Turning to Nippur, some of the modifications observed in Buildings A and B in the WC-2 area have already been mentioned above. In fact quite a number of alterations were made here between Levels II and I. These changes are documented in a preliminary report by the excavators (Gibson, Zettler & Armstrong 1983: 184–190; a more detailed account of the excavations can be found in Armstrong 1989: 23–47). I shall summarize them here because they reveal some striking characteristics that are relevant to the questions I am addressing. Although the walls of Level I were generally built upon the stubs of the Level II walls, the presence of wind-blown aparna between them attests to an intervening period of abandonment.

The layout of the house known as Building A in Level II is shown in Fig. 16.4a. At some point in Level II, according to the excavators' plans, a couple of doorways were blocked up, between loci 130 and 131, and between loci 133 and 134. It is unclear how these changes, which would apparently have left loci 130 and 134/148 without means of access, are to be interpreted, unless the blocking took place prior to the temporary abandonment which followed Level II.

Significant alterations to the plan of the house were made in Level I, as can be seen in Fig. 16.4b. The vestibule, locus 119, now led only into the courtyard since the doorway into former locus 134/148 was now blocked up. This latter room was now converted into two separate rooms, loci 120 and 127, with a door communicating between them. The north-westernmost room of this pair, locus 127, now communicated with the room to the north-east via a new doorway. This latter room, locus 108, was a new long room fashioned out of what had previously been loci 130 and 131. Thus it is possible to discern two discrete suites of rooms: 120/127/108 on the south-west and north-west sides of the courtyard, and 141/138/139 on the south-east side. The main entrance (via vestibule 119), central courtyard 111, and kitchen 110 remained equally accessible to both suites.

In Level II the house had had a secondary exit opening via locus 135 onto an open area, a kind of "backyard". In Level I this area was now built over. In the absence of a

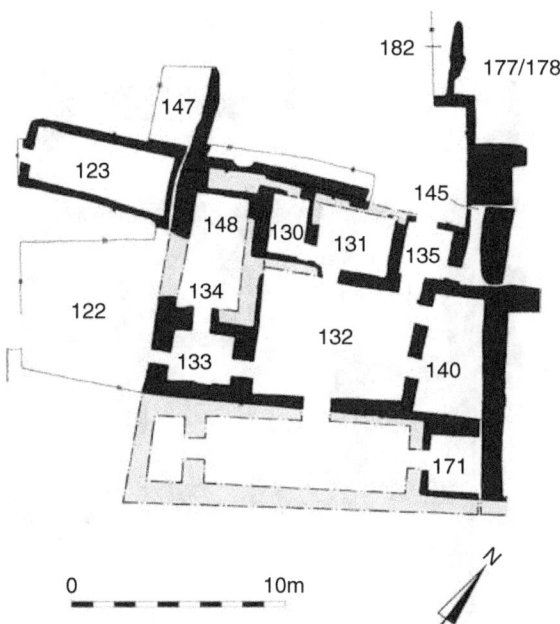

Fig. 16.4a Nippur, WC-2, Building A in Level II.

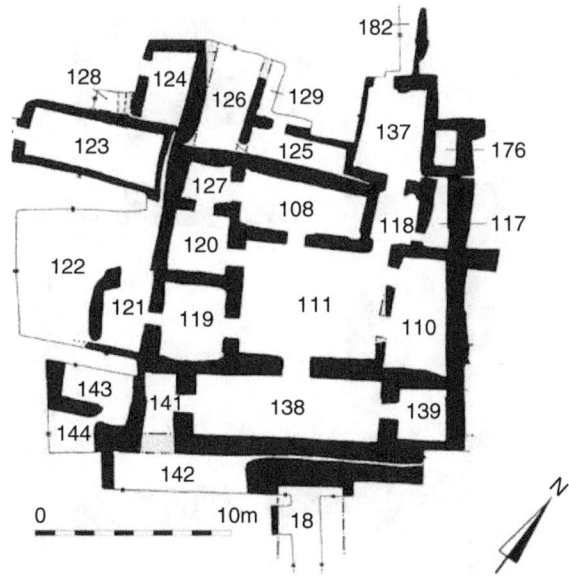

Fig. 16.4b Nippur, WC-2, Building A in Level I.

complete ground plan it is difficult to interpret the remains here. However, the new rooms were accessible from Building A via locus 118, which implies that they represent an extension of that house. It is possible (but not certain) that this extension represents the conversion of Building A into a house of the "double courtyard" type; at any rate the dimensions, location, and shape of locus 129, in so far as they are preserved, are reminiscent of a courtyard.

As mentioned above, several doorways within Building A were blocked up at the very end of Level I, prior to abandonment. These include: the doorways between the central courtyard (locus 111) and loci 120, 108, and 118; the doorway between loci 124 and 128, and perhaps also the main entrance leading from locus 121 into locus 119.

The adjacent house, Building B, also witnessed significant changes in its layout in Level I compared with its previous state. The plan of the house in Level II is shown in Fig. 16.5a, and the Level I changes are illustrated in Fig. 16.5b. Originally the house had been accessed via an entrance from the street leading through loci 163 and 162 to the central courtyard, locus 155. In Level I the rooms in this north-western corner were now made into part of a separate suite: the main entrance was relocated to the north-eastern corner of the courtyard, and the doorway which had led from locus 162 to the courtyard was now blocked up by the end of a wall projecting into the courtyard itself. Thus the suite of rooms on the north-west side formed by loci 161, 307, and 308 could now only be reached via locus 177/178, an open area at the western corner of the building. On the south-west side the room formerly known as locus 116 was now accessible only via locus 112 since the doorway between it (as locus 115) and the courtyard was now blocked up. Locus 112 was now no longer used as a kitchen as it had been in Level II (as locus 114).

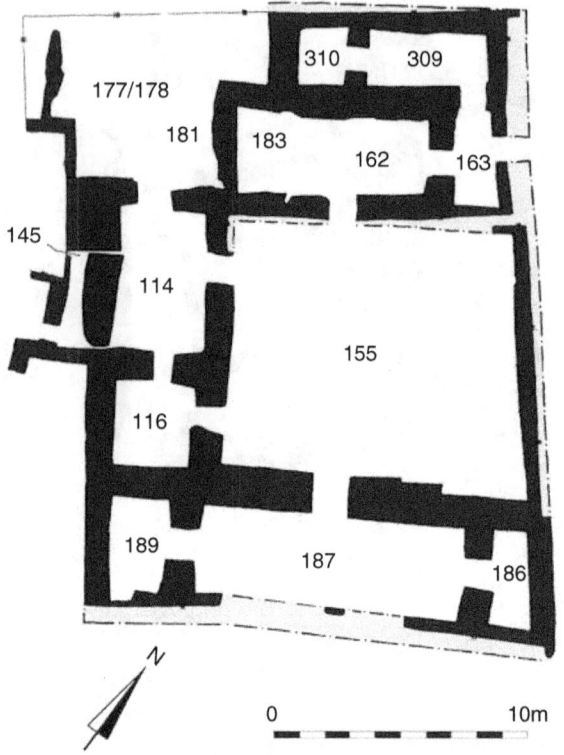

Fig. 16.5a Nippur, WC-2, Building B in Level II.

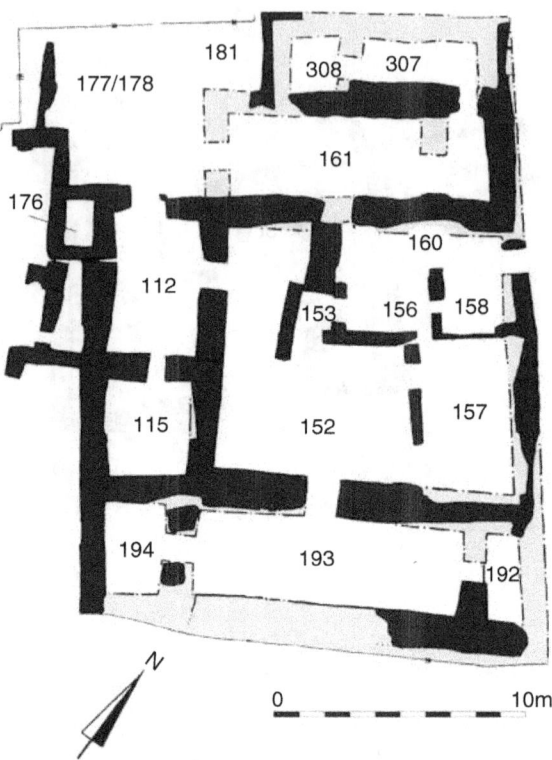

Fig. 16.5b Nippur, WC-2, Building B in Level I.

By these modifications the house was apparently divided into two suites of rooms: those on the north-west and south-west sides of the central courtyard (loci 112, 115, 161, 308 and 307, with apparently exclusive use of the open area loci 177/178 and 181), and those on the south-east side (loci 192/193/194). The situation in the central courtyard is complicated since various phases of insubstantial walls were identified. At one point a vestibule, locus 158, was formed within the courtyard to accommodate the relocated main entrance. A kitchen area, locus 157, has also been identified.

Finally, it is worth noting that other areas of Nippur have also produced evidence for modifications to residential buildings. This is especially true of the TA area whose stratigraphy has been recently re-evaluated by Armstrong (1989), where it is possible to trace the development of several houses through successive phases of occupation. However, for reasons of space I must restrict my analysis to the three examples discussed above.

In all three of the cases examined it is possible to detect modifications whereby the houses in question were altered in order to create two relatively independent suites. In the first two instances, with the Isin house and with WC-2 Building A at Nippur, there are striking similarities in that the courtyard, kitchen, and main entrance seem to have been retained in common use by both sets of occupants. In the case of WC-2 Building B the main entrance, which had originally served the whole house, had to be moved since the suite in which it was located was now part of a separate unit. The partitioning of the courtyard during at least part of the Level I occupation may represent an attempt to create different sectors within that open space for use by the different parties occupying the two suites. Interestingly, one effect of the walls which formed the vestibule 158 and the adjacent locus 156 seems to have been to shield the main entrances to both suites (i.e. the doorways leading into loci 193 and 112), preventing visitors in the vicinity of the entrance from having any direct line of sight into these suites. It is not clear whether locus 157, said to have been a kitchen, served only the occupants of the nearby rooms on the south-east side of the courtyard; the occupants of the western suite may have relied on other facilities (the open area loci 177/178 was equipped with an oven in Level II, at least). We can conclude that in at least two out of our three case studies, cooking facilities seem not to have been replicated within the different suites but rather one kitchen was kept in common use.

Summary and conclusions

The archaeological evidence for modifications to houses in first-millennium BC Babylonia is not yet so extensive as to permit an exhaustive treatment of the subject at hand on the basis of the excavation data alone. In any case, as I hope to have shown, it is fruitless to attempt to interpret such evidence without taking into consideration the very rich contemporary textual sources that inform us about the family, about the household cycle, and about patterns of residence. In bringing to bear on the problem these abundant documentary sources it is possible to define far more precisely than has hitherto been attempted the range of contexts in which physical alterations to Babylonian houses might have been made. It has been suggested that certain specific kinds of modification might be expected to correlate with certain stages in the household developmental cycle. For example, the courtyard tended to be reserved for the use of those who were related to one another, and unrelated parties owning adjacent rooms would tend to be denied access to it. So, if the original house-owning family unit contracted and part of the courtyard house was acquired by "outsiders", separate units tended to be created. However, there remains the possibility that the courtyard was shared by unrelated parties when different parts of a courtyard house were rented out. It has also been argued that the phenomenon of house alteration is likely to correlate with social status, a claim which seems so far to be borne out by the evidence to hand. Finally, in the course of this study a "typology" of the various kinds of physical modification has been proposed, ranging from simple changes in the location of the main entrance(s), through to changes which affected the internal circulation pattern more profoundly, to those which altered the actual perimeter of the house, either by enlarging its size or reducing it. Such changes are of interest not only because they inform us about the living conditions of the occupants, but also because when viewed at a level beyond that of the individual household they may shed light on the longer-term development of entire residential districts. At the neighbourhood scale, urban development may be reflected in myriad changes of the kind I have been discussing.

It is hoped that the ideas put forward here have contributed to our understanding of the relationship between house and household, and that they may in the future be tested on other data sets from ancient Mesopotamia.

Notes

1. The research, which is the subject of this paper, was conducted under the auspices of the START Project on "The Economic History of Babylonia in the First Millennium BC" funded by the Fonds zur Förderung der Wissenschaftlichen Forschung (Austria).
2. In his house-by-house catalogue Miglus (1999: 307–314) indicates post-Neo-Babylonian occupation where identified.
3. For a general introduction to the economic documents see Jursa 2005.
4. Note the comments made in the reviews of Stone's work by Charpin (1989) and Postgate (1990), as well as the more recent studies on this general theme with regard to Old Babylonian housing, e.g. by Charpin (1996, 2003) and Feuerherm (2007).
5. Gehlken also revised substantially downwards (to *c.*20 years or even below) the average age at first marriage for men at this period, which had previously been estimated at *c.*29 years (see Roth 1987: 737).
6. Respectively "south(-facing) wing", "north(-facing) wing", "west(-facing) wing", and "east(-facing) wing". For the translation "south(-facing) wing" etc. rather than the conventional "south wing" see Baker 2008.
7. According to Roth (1991/93: 26, n. 109), at least one eighth of dowries included an urban house plot. Since the wife normally resided in the marital home established by her husband, such a property would have generated rental income for her.
8. The tablet was written in Babylon in 542 BC.
9. Doty argues that sales of slaves and arable land ceased to be recorded on cuneiform tablets following the imposition of certain taxes early in the reign of Antiochus I.
10. The tablet has been edited by Joannès 1989: 166–168.
11. The Istanbul tablet L 1652 (written in Borsippa in 491 BC), edited by Joannès 1989: 246–247.
12. The interpretation presented here differs from that of Miglus 1999: 227.
13. In this connection it is interesting to note the existence of two rituals to be performed when a house wall was broken through in order to form a new doorway; see Ambos 2004: 63, 128–129.
14. An edition of this tablet can be found in San Nicolò & Petschow 1960: no. 10, where the translation differs slightly from that offered here.
15. See Reuther 1926: 77–122 (with the corresponding illustrations in the Tafelband) for a detailed description of the Neo-Babylonian houses.
16. The high status of these houses compared with others of the same period is evident, for example, in their greater than average size, the quality of their construction and fittings, and the fact that adjacent houses never shared party walls but rather each had their own separate external wall.

17

Why Columned Halls?

Hilary Gopnik

Since their construction, the columned halls of the Achaemenid Empire have stood as icons of Persian artistic accomplishment. The still soaring columns at Persepolis with their elaborate capitals have defined the space that now constitutes the ruins of the site for generations of visitors, just as they must have defined the space of the original monuments. Margaret Miller has suggested that the columned hall so symbolized the Persian imperial presence that, when the Athenians wanted to demonstrate visually their own newfound imperial aspirations as victors over the Persians, it was to this form that they turned as the most evocative image of Achaemenid power. The construction of a columned hall, the Odeion of Pericles on the Athenian acropolis, even though the form made little functional sense in this context, can be seen as a deliberate attempt by the Athenians to co-opt the imperial imagery of the Persian kings (Miller 1997: 218–242). In spite of the overwhelming impact of this distinctive building-type on both modern and ancient readings of Persian culture, surprisingly little discussion has centred on the way in which columned halls may have functioned as architectural environments. In this paper I will attempt to place the columned hall within the context of architectural theory by tracing the development of the peculiar articulation of space that is created by multiple rows of columns in a confined area, and I will examine how and why this form may have become the archetypal Persian architectural device.

Although the nature of the columned halls at Persepolis has formed part of the western notion of Persia for centuries, comparisons for this architecture were originally sought in Greek forms (see for example Byron 1982: 138). With the discovery of the columned buildings at Hasanlu (Fig. 17.1) and the subsequent excavation of columned halls at Tepe Nush-i Jan (Fig. 17.2) and Godin Tepe (Fig. 17.3) in the 1950s and 1960s, however, it was felt that the Achaemenid columned halls had been given a distinctively regional pedigree that could account for the development of the form. What's more, the connection of Godin and Nush-i Jan with Media closely matched the classical sources, and a Median inspiration for a part of Achaemenid architecture seemed established. Frankfort's 1953 comment in *Art and Architecture* that nothing

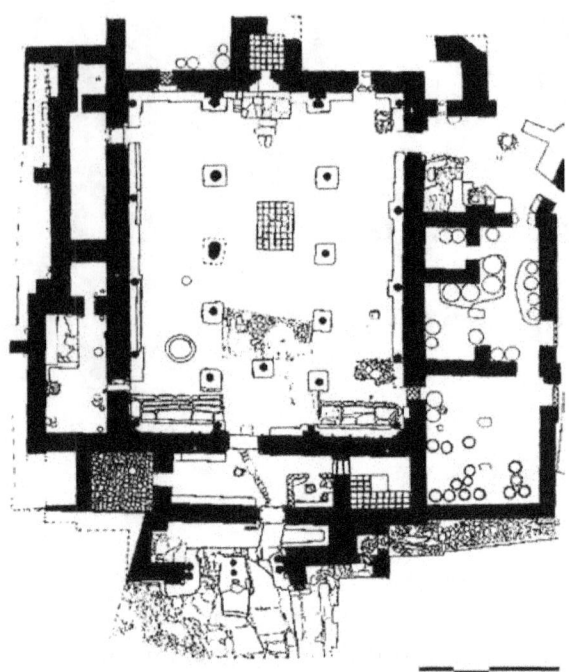

Fig. 17.1 Plan of Hasanlu Burned Building II. (After Young 1966: fig. 1)

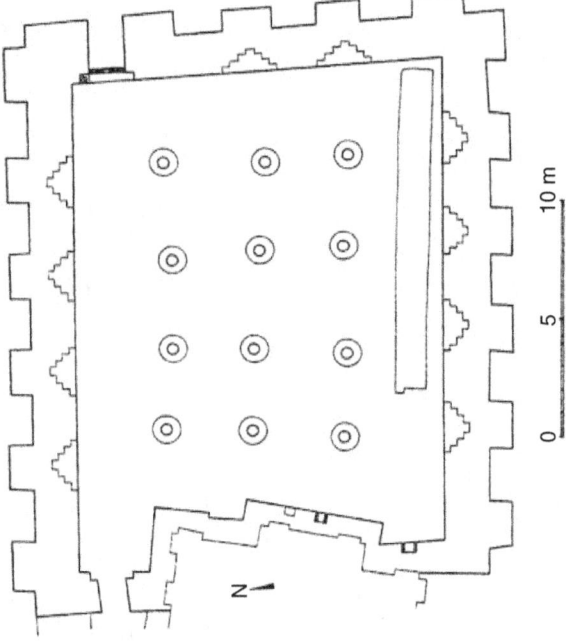

Fig. 17.2 Plan of Columned Hall at Nush-i Jan. (After Stronach & Roaf 2007: fig. 7.1)

was known of the origin of pillared halls could be responded to in the 1996 edition revised by Roaf and Matthews with a note on these Median sites (Frankfort 1996: 355).

However, the recent discovery of columned halls at the sites of Muweilah (Magee 2001) (Fig. 17.4) and Rumeilah (Boucharlat & Lombard 2001) (Fig. 17.5) in south-eastern Arabia, dating between the ninth and seventh centuries BC, and the partial excavation of a columned building from Kerkenes Dag in Anatolia (Summers 2002) probably dating to the seventh century, have complicated the unilinear model of a line of succession from Hasanlu to Persepolis. Instead it appears that there were several threads of technological, cultural, and perhaps sociological innovations leading in different directions through time and space, but ultimately culminating in the Achaemenid Apadana.

Cuyler Young has pointed out that the buildings at Hasanlu and the main hall at Godin shared some basic important features that seemed to define the columned hall form (Young 1994) (Figs 17.1 and 17.3). These features include benches running along the sides of the walls, a hearth, a "seat of honour", an anteroom and perhaps a stairway off the anteroom (well documented at Hasanlu, but only conjectural at Godin). These features are notably absent at Nush-i Jan (Fig. 17.2), but it has been argued that this may be because of the unique function of that site as a ritual centre (Stronach & Roaf 2007: 198). The Arabian sites exhibit these features only as a platform (perhaps for an incense-burner found nearby) at Muweilah (Magee 2001: 123) (Fig. 17.4), and an exterior stairway at Rumeilah (Boucharlat & Lombard 2001: 216) (and then only in phase 2). The hall at Kerkenes has not been excavated sufficiently to ascertain its contents. The

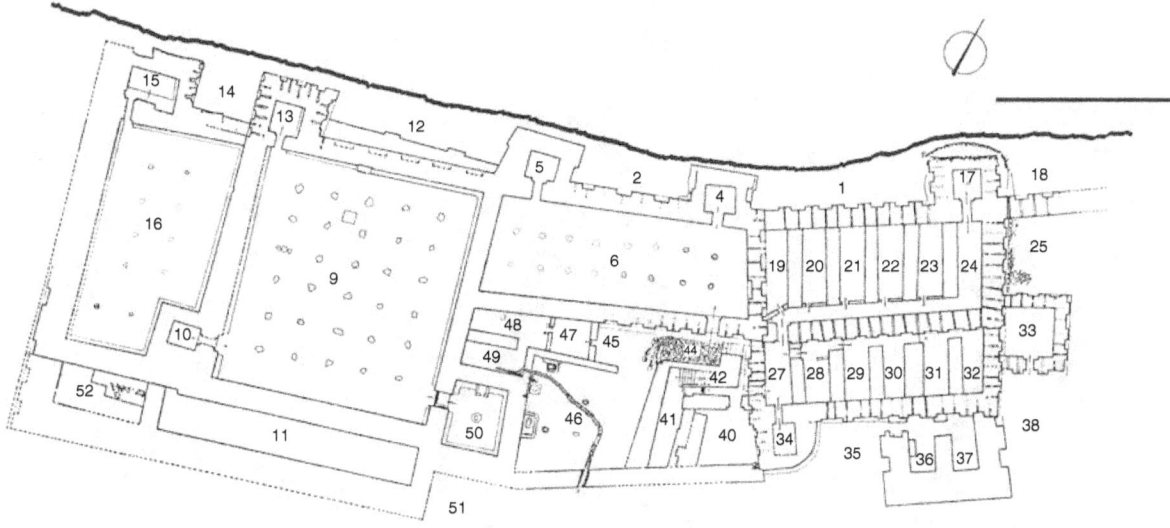

Fig. 17.3 Plan of Godin Period II: 2.

columns from Muweilah, Rumeilah, Godin, and Nush-i Jan all have similar bases, with a flat stone set into the floor level (and judging from the irregular nature of the stones probably invisible when the room was in use), and smaller stone, mud brick, or mud plaster forming a surround around them. One very notable feature present at Godin as well as at both Arabian sites is a small room with an entrance off the main hall with a single column near its centre. At Godin this ancillary room is fitted with benches and a seat of honour, mirroring the features of the main hall (Gopnik & Rothman 2010: 309) (Fig. 17.6).

If all of these columned halls share some common features, in terms of architectural form, the multi-rowed columned halls of central Iran and south-eastern Arabia can be distinguished from the two-rowed halls of Hasanlu, Kerkenes, and Ziwiye. In all the multi-rowed columned halls, column bases are laid out in even rows such that no dominant aisle or axis is created by the columns themselves. In the Hasanlu columned halls (Fig. 17.1), and probably at Kerkenes, the middle aisle is wider than the side aisles, creating a marked axis down the centre of the structure, across the hearth and towards the seat of honour at the back of the room, thereby also clearly creating a central space and two subsidiary ones. Cuyler Young has pointed out that this layout may be related to the Anatolian megaron, which it closely resembles (Young 1966) and indeed the appearance of megaron-like structures at Kerkenes along with one or more two-rowed columned halls would seem to confirm the connection between the two forms (Summers 2003). The apparent seventh-century date of the two-rowed hall at Kerkenes suggests that the distinction between the multi-rowed and two-rowed columned hall types is geographic and/or cultural rather than chronological as had previously been supposed. In other words it is probably mistaken to think of the multi-rowed form as having evolved from Hasanlu, but instead that there were a number of distinct but related architectural traditions in the first half of the first millennium BC that made use of columns to create a large,

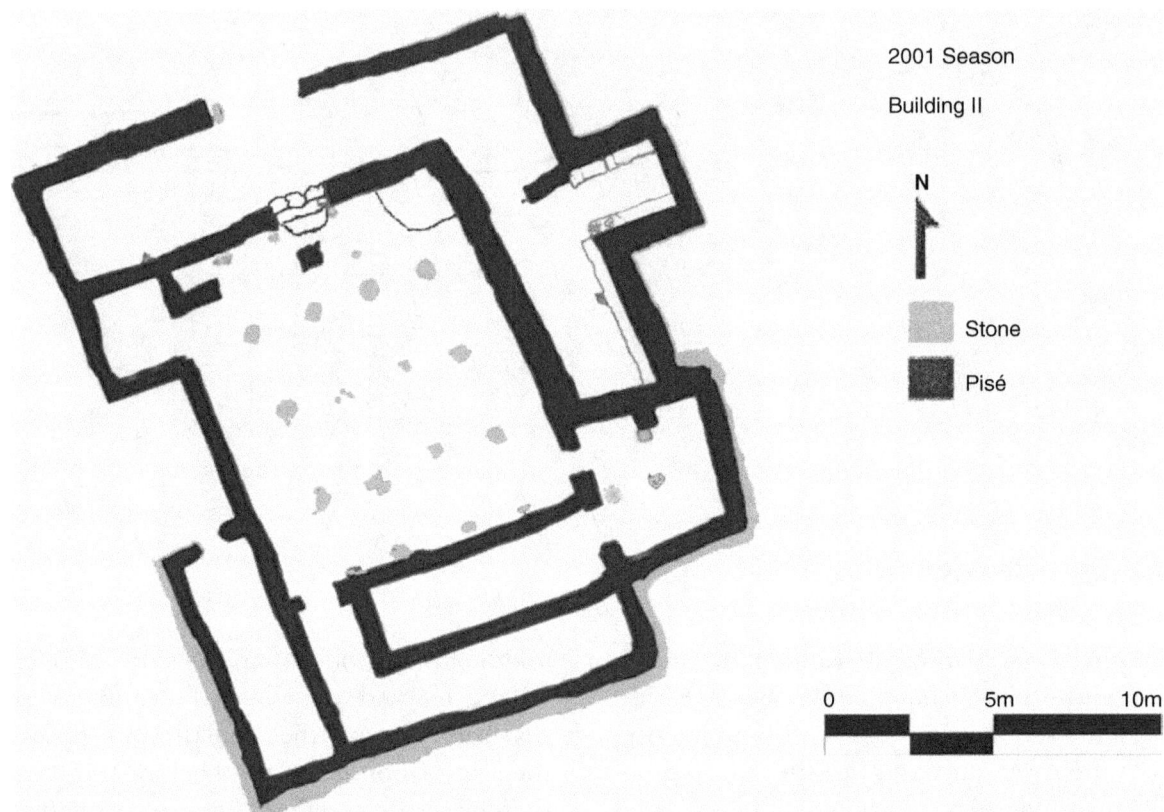

Fig. 17.4 Plan of Building II at Muweilah. (After Magee 2003: fig. 2)

enclosed, roofed space. Whatever its origins it would appear that the multi-rowed columned form took on a unique set of cultural implications, such that, at least as excavated to date, with the notable exception of Persepolis, no single site can boast more than a single multi-rowed columned hall. The two-rowed form on the other hand seems to be used as a more or less standard plan for large buildings in sites where it occurs.

The contents of the few pre-Achaemenid multi-rowed columned halls that have been excavated suggest a common social role for these buildings as centres of power although the very variable nature of the remains indicates that both the source and the expression of that power were site and area specific.

The Iron Age occupation of Godin can be divided into two broad phases: the main occupation phase when the large elite structure with storage rooms and columned hall was in use, and a subsequent reoccupation of the building by pastoralists, who took advantage of the massive wall stubs that remained after the roof had collapsed in many places, to construct a small house and stable (Gopnik 2003). The main building at Godin was thoroughly emptied before its abandonment, leaving only a few garbage dumps in the furthermost reaches of the magazine hallways, but we can nonetheless reconstruct from these scanty remains some patterns of use (for a detailed account of the functional distribution of ceramics at

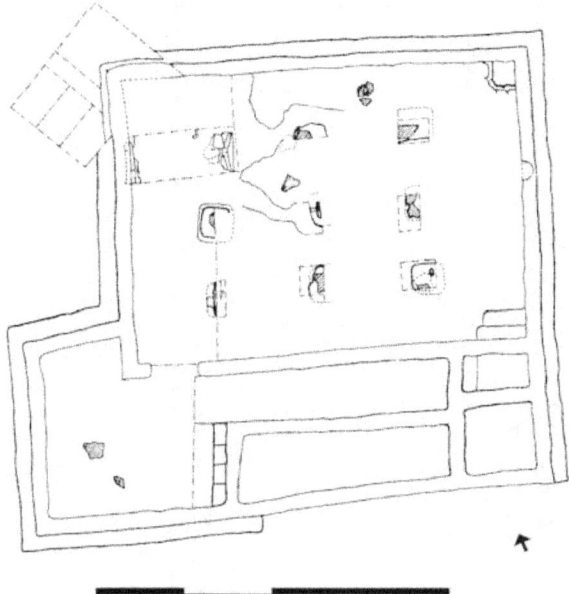

Fig. 17.5 Plan of Building G (phase 3) at Rumeilah. (After Boucharlat & Lombard 2001: fig. 7)

Godin, see Gopnik 2005). The proportion of fine wares discarded in these refuse heaps was much higher while the columned hall was in use than in the subsequent pastoralist settlement and, even more importantly, the distribution of functional types was very different in the two phases of occupation. The proportion of all sizes of bowls in the assemblage is much higher in the garbage dumps that accumulated while the elite building was occupied, with smaller bowls, probably used as drinking bowls, dominating the assemblage. Unlike in the subsequent pastoralist occupation, where only the crudest wares were used for large serving vessels, the occupants of the columned hall building used fine ware bowls with a wide range of diameters, reflecting the complexity of food service in this elite edifice.

At Rumeilah, a similar distribution of bowls, drinking vessels and serving vessels was found including an assortment of bowls with graffiti of unknown significance incised into the slip, bridge-spouted serving vessels and a distinctive type of footed cup, all types that are not found in any quantity elsewhere at the site (Boucharlat & Lombard 2001: 218). At Muweilah as well, ceramic vessels connected with serving and eating predominate, including 40 bridge-spouted vessels apparently stored or stocked in the small single-columned room that all three sites have in common. At Muweilah, however, there was also evidence of bronze-working, which appears to have taken place in the ancillary rooms rather than the central hall, and the storage of imported iron weapons and blades, again found in the ancillary rooms (Magee 2003: 184, 189).

The pattern of evidence indicates that all of these structurally very similar multi-rowed columned halls were connected with the local elites of the area. The range of activities taking place in these structures almost certainly differed from site to site, extending from the storage to the production of elite goods. Their central-columned rooms and adjoining single-columned annex, however, all seem to have been used primarily for eating and drinking on an impressive scale.

It would appear then that the fundamental notion of a columned hall, as well as some specific features, were widespread in western Iran by the ninth–seventh centuries and certainly well before Cyrus commissioned the construction of palace P at Pasargadae. It is also becoming increasingly evident that columned halls were not exclusively associated with an ethnic or political group such as the Indo-Europeans or Medes but were instead part of a new architectural expression of social position. The appearance of the form in south-eastern Arabia almost certainly indicates that it was also present in south-western

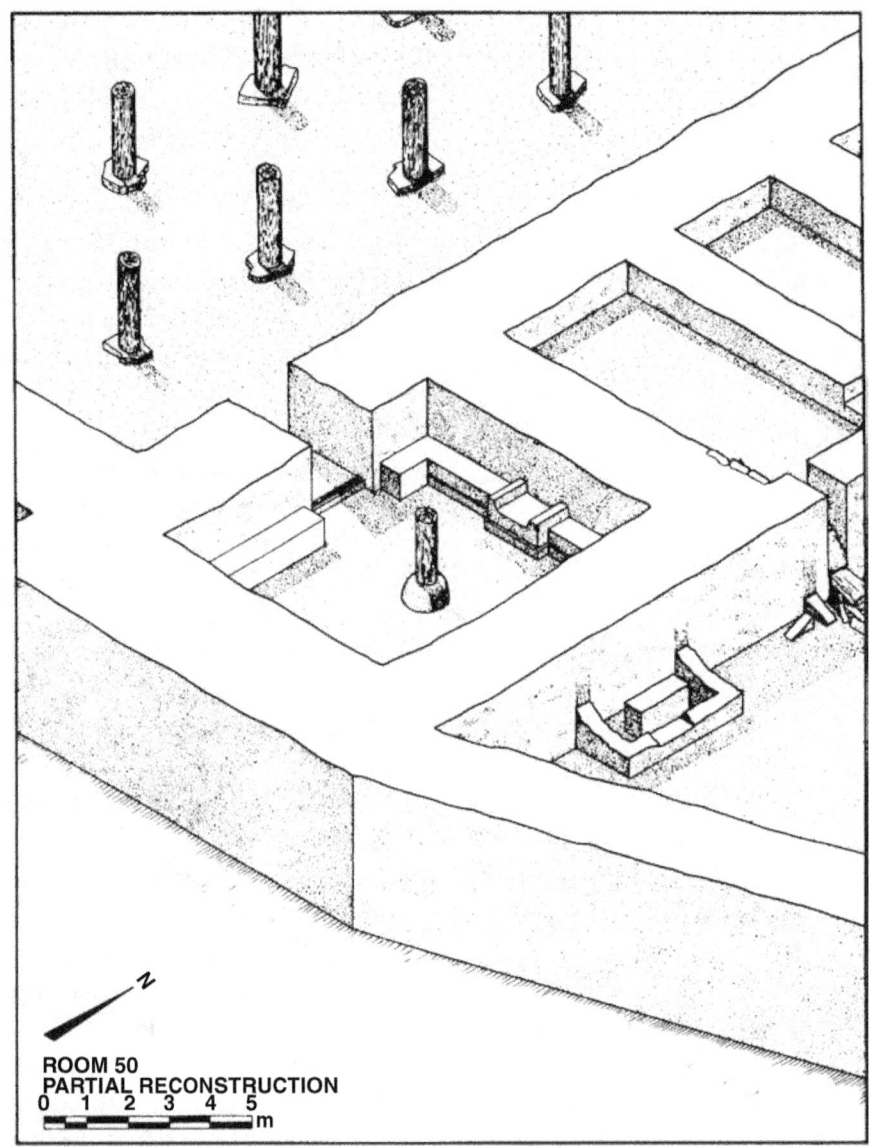

Fig. 17.6 Reconstruction of Room 50 at Godin Period IIa.

Iran with which the Arabian sites had close and persistent trade contacts. Further excavation may well reveal this missing part of the pattern.

The use of columns was not, of course, reserved for this building tradition. The isolated use of free-standing and engaged mud-brick columns is found throughout Mesopotamian architecture. Columns appear as early as the Ubaid period (at Tell el-Ouelli) but are used most notably as a decorative device on the façades of temples (for instance at Uruk, Tell al-Rimah, and Tell Leilan), and also occasionally in a colonnade (Uruk and Kish).[1] Wooden posts were probably used more extensively to support wooden balconies or reed roofing, but they were certainly not a major component of the monumental architectural tradition. In the north, the Syrian *bit hilani* made effective use of columns for defining entrances (Frankfort 1996: 282–290), and at Hattusha the Hittites used roof-bearing columns in storage rooms and entrance porticoes, but there is no extant example of more than two rows of columns in any one structure (Bittel 1970). Although Naumann reconstructed a multi-rowed columned audience hall on the second floor of building D at Hattusha there is very little evidence to support this reconstruction, which seems to rely in part on a parallel with the later Iron Age halls (Bittel, Naumann & Beran 1957: 10ff). In Urartu, columns continued to be used as roof supports, but as at Hattusha, while columns are sometimes used along a stretch of a corridor, storeroom or portico, there is—and this is actually quite surprising given the apparent ease with which the form is eventually adopted—no well-documented instance of an enclosed room with a roof supported by regularly spaced multiple rows of columns, a columned hall in our terms. The few structures of this kind that were once thought to be Urartian in date have now all been convincingly demonstrated to belong to the later Achaemenid occupations of Urartian sites.[2]

Going further afield, the reluctance to use this form seems to be widespread. The most obvious examples of hypostyle halls in the Near East are found in Egyptian temples, but here the central axis is well marked and all important, and the whole hall marks a transition from the outside world to the inner sanctum of the temple (Philips 2002: 260–261), assuming a very different role from the free-standing isolated columned halls of Iron Age Iran. From the little evidence we have for Egyptian palaces, columns, while abundant, are used either to define axial corridors or as porticoes and peristyles associated with courtyards, and not in multiple rows to roof large enclosed spaces (Philips 2002: 237–239, 242–244, figs 484, 496). The North Palace at Amarna does feature a columned hall, but here it is an evident allusion to the temple form, with an emphasis on a central axis leading to an inner sanctum, in this exceptional case apparently a throne room.

The use of columns as transitional forms between exterior space and regulated interiors is in fact one of the most widespread applications of the columnar form worldwide. It is seen in the *bit hilani* of north Syria in the Near Eastern context, but even more extravagantly and widely developed in the classical world where the columned portico or peristyle becomes the defining architectural feature of most public structures.[3] The vertical pattern of a row of columns with its alternation of dark and light, space and structure, seems to define the transition between a sunlit exterior and dark interior perfectly. The architectural theorist Christopher Alexander lists a columned portico bridging a courtyard and interior as one of his 232 universal forms of architectural design (Alexander, Ishikawa & Silverstein 1977), and Grant Hildebrand (1999: 26–27) argues that humans are inherently attracted by the "edge of the forest" effect created by a double row of columns with a view of a more open expanse. In the modern context, the loss of the columned portico was singled out by the postmodernist movement to illustrate the poverty of modernist architecture, and many postmodernist buildings feature a prominent, if sometimes ironically proportioned, columned entrance.[4]

It is therefore certainly neither the notion nor the engineering ability to use columns to support a roof that is either new or distinctive in Iron Age Iran and Arabia. If the pattern of even columniation seen in the Iron III and Achaemenid columned halls was merely an expedient to roof a large area, we need to ask not so much where it came from, but why it is resorted to comparatively rarely in the architectural history of the Near East or, indeed, worldwide.

Since the very first treatises on architectural theory, architects have argued that one fundamental role of architectural design is to marry the requirements of structure and space.[5] As humans, our experience of an enclosed environment, whether man-made or natural, seems to be deeply involved in our understanding of the interplay between these two features. Mud-brick architecture tends to emphasize space over structure. The whitewashed interiors of most Mesopotamian monumental buildings lead the visitor from space to space along well-defined axes that tend to minimize attention drawn to the structure itself. Painting or carved relief on the walls served further to mask their weight-bearing function. Such architectural features as monumental doorway figures, however, were deliberately placed to emphasize structure at important points of transition such as the entry to a throne room: "In architecture, monsters are always located in the joint between architectural elements...the margins of the built environment determine the phenomenon of the spatial environment, and they are the locus where the transformation of space takes place" (Frascari 1991: 21). Columns, whether actually structural or not, are often used as such markers of structural elements.

The columns of the columned porticoes of Hasanlu (Fig. 17.1) are not there to hold up a roof but rather to mark the transition into the upcoming columned space. Once past the portico, the visitor is led into the main hall through the anteroom doors deliberately placed on an angle, so that the perception of the clearly defined main axis of the hall can only function upon entry to the room. Inside, there is no ambiguity of space or directionality, but instead the visitor is immediately presented with the central focus of the room, the seat of honour to its rear. The columns not only clearly divide the space into one main area and two subsidiary ones, they serve as transitional elements to highlight the passage from the side benches—probably a position of secondary importance or for waiting—to the central aisle and interaction with the central figure.

In the multi-rowed columned halls of the Iron Age, the evenly spaced pattern of columns impedes the creation of such a division of space. Although the seat of honour and hearth create an axis of sorts, architecturally there is no emphasis on this axis. At Godin the uneven number of files of columns seems intended, in fact, deliberately to thwart the creation of a central axis, as not even the seat of honour and hearth are centrally placed (Fig. 17.3). There is now no defined transition between the side benches and central space, or even a clear orientation for the room at all. Used in this way columns become an emblem of pure structure. They do not mark a transition, create an internal space, or lead a visitor through a corridor. What's more, they draw attention to themselves instead of to the space around them. Architectural theorist Robert Venturi points out that, in opposition to a pier or wall, "the column form results from its dominant, precise function as a point support. It can direct space only incidentally in relation to other columns or elements".[6] The even placement of the columns along all axes in the multi-rowed columned halls precludes any such direction of space, even in relation to the other columns.

The lack of a central axial direction to these rooms, however, does not lessen the importance of the raised seat of honour, with which, with the addition of a wooden chair or throne, the power figure would be raised vertically in a space where, through the structural emphasis on the soaring columns, verticality is emphasized more than any other dimension. What this emphasis on the multiplication of the column does instead is create a many to one—instead of a focused one on one—encounter with the central figure. If the function of these halls was ritual gathering and feasting, then it may well have been that visually emphasizing the large number of celebrants may have been as important as focusing on the power figure. This effect of multiplication would be created by the disorienting multi-axiality of the rooms, which precludes any attempt at judging quantities in space, and would therefore be a particularly effective architectural device for a structure designed explicitly for large public displays of strength in numbers.

In fact the architectural tradition that makes the most extensive use of the multi-rowed, evenly spaced hypostyle hall is the early congregational mosques, where the multiplication of columns and repressed axiality are used not only to distinguish these structures from Christian churches and their focal altars, but also to emphasize the large numbers of participants in the congregation: "Arab interiors [of early congregational mosques] were an indeterminate sequence of pillars and aisles. A sensation of monotony overcame the beholder, giving him the impression of a structure with no center and no ends" (Pereira 1994: 267). In most later hypostyle mosques axiality was restored either by widening the mihrab aisle or aligning arches to emphasize the files running parallel to the qibla.[7] In seventeenth-century India, Shah Jahan ordered the construction of open-sided hypostyle audience halls, which Ebba Koch argues were directly inspired by the ruins at Persepolis, but here again the central aisle leading to the throne is widened so that the passage to the king is emphasized (Koch 1994: 134–165).

The negation of axiality to create commonality, possibly in fact inspired by the Persian columned halls and congregational mosques, was used to great effect by Frank Lloyd Wright in one of the only deliberately hypostyle modern western designs. The "Great Work Room" of the SC Johnson Wax building in Racine, Wisconsin, built in 1938, was one of the first "open plan" white-collar workspaces. Wright felt that the gathering of workers together in a single area, punctuated only by regularly spaced dendriform columns would create a kind of sacred communal space, "as inspiring a place to work in as any cathedral ever was in which to worship" (Wright 1994: 181). Interestingly, hierarchy was maintained here also in the vertical dimension by the construction of a glass-floored platform to house executive offices.

It is significant in this regard that at Godin the small single-columned room that opens directly off the main hall (Fig. 17.6), and that appears to be a regular feature of columned halls to judge by its recurrence at both Muweilah (Fig. 17.4) and Rumeilah (Fig. 17.5), is elaborately fitted with benches and a seat of honour, as if to accommodate the reception of a single individual. Since no columns occur in *any* of the other houses at either of the south-eastern Arabian sites, it seems unreasonable to suggest that this single column was used merely as an expedient to span a larger space with roof beams. Given Median technical expertise with a variety of mud-brick vaults and roofing struts as preserved at Nush-i Jan

(Stronach & Roaf 2007: 188–189; Roaf, this volume) and Godin (Gopnik & Rothman 2010: 320), the use of single columns in these relatively small rooms is further evidence that the column must have taken on a significance beyond its technical function as a roof support.[8]

The emphasis on the structural component of columns by Iron Age builders in Iran and Arabia, demonstrated by their apparent reluctance to place them so as to define internal spaces, may have not only served to emphasize the numbers of celebrants by refusing to divide the crowd, it may in fact have held a metaphoric reference to the subjects themselves. In a number of recent works the metaphoric and symbolic role of the column in the classical and neo-classical traditions has been explored by architectural historians.[9] The interpretation of a columnar support as a metaphor for a human figure was pervasive in the classical world as evidenced not only by the use of caryatids and their male counterparts, telamones (both of which, interestingly, were said by Vitruvius to represent Persians or supporters of the Persians [1.1.5]), but more profoundly by a supposed relationship between the proportions of the orders and the male and female figure (Vitruvius 4.1). In the Euripidean tragedy *Iphigenia at Taurus* (1.1.45–50) the heroine has a dream in which she sees her brother Orestes in the form of the central column of her father's house:

> Only one column left upright in all
> My father's house. But that one stood alive,
> A man with bright brown hair and
>   breathing lips.
> And then against my will my hand went
>   out,
> As it does toward strangers here
>   condemned to die,
> And touched his forehead with this fatal
>   water—
> And with water of my tears, because I knew
> The dream was of Orestes and his end.
> The pillar of a family is the son.[10]

John Onians has suggested that the columns of the Parthenon itself may have been a metaphoric reference to the Athenian phalanx that had so convincingly defeated the Persians at Marathon (1999: 43).

The Persians clearly shared this metaphorical reading of a supporting figure. Their affection for architectural metaphor is amply demonstrated by both the door jamb reliefs at Persepolis and the reliefs on the tombs at Naqsh-i Rustam, in which the subject regions of the empire are symbolically presented as the supports for the throne platform.[11] The fact that in the inscription at Naqsh-i Rustam Darius specifically refers to this visual pun is an indication of the remarkable self-consciousness and pervasiveness of the metaphor in Persian visual culture:

> If now thou shalt think that "How many are the countries which King Darius held?" look at the sculptures (of those) who bear the throne, then thou shalt know, then shall it become known to thee: the spear of a Persian man has gone forth far; then shall it become known to thee: a Persian man has delivered battle far indeed from Persia.
> (Kent 1953: 138)

The juxtaposition of a depiction of architectural columns below the throne supporters whose capitals clearly mirror the arm positions of the throne bearers, as seen particularly from the removed position of a visitor to the monument, suggests that the metaphorical reference to individuals, in particular the subjects of the king, could be extended specifically to architectural columns of the type used at Persepolis. The appearance on the northern door jambs of the Hundred Column Hall at Persepolis of 100 guards bearing vertical spears that clearly are meant to mirror the 100 columns of the hall is further evidence that the equation of an architectural column with a supporter of the power of the king was a well-accepted trope in the Achaemenid visual vocabulary.

The suggestion that in the Iron Age multi-rowed columned halls, the columns themselves may have been visual referents for the subordinates to the figure of power is not meant to imply that this is a simple or univalent symbol. That architectural forms, like any visual culture, can have multiple and complex meanings is amply demonstrated in the context of Christian sacred spaces for which we often have detailed texts to parse their meaning. In the early Christian Lateran Baptistery in Rome, for instance, the 12 ground-level columns are meant to invoke the 12 apostles, while the sequence of their capitals (Composite, Ionic and Corinthian) are direct allusions to the Roman visual vocabulary of triumphal monuments (Onians 1988: 62–63). Magee has suggested to me that at Muweilah the "forest" of date-palm wooden columns of the columned hall may have been intended as an image of an oasis, a very powerful and evocative image in a desert environment. Similarly, it is clear that the zoomorphic capitals at Persepolis are meant to invoke the power of the apotropaic mythic beast that populates Achaemenid imagery. Like any complex artistic tradition, Iron Age architecture was intricately tied to the cultural systems that created it, and any attempt to understand these systems must acknowledge the complexity of their representational worlds. As Margaret Root has suggested so forcefully, the most distinctive feature of Achaemenid art is the creation of an artistic programme through ordered repetition and multiplicity of similar forms (Root 1979: 309–311). The pre-Achaemenid multi-rowed columned hall and its ability to evoke the whole through the many, and order through multi-dimensionality, may have been an early and persistent expression of this aesthetic.

Notes

1. For an overall discussion of columns in the Near East see Stronach & Roaf 2007: 186–188.
2. For a dating of the columned halls at Erebuni and Armavir to the Achaemenid period see Ter-Martirossov 2001 (*contra* Kanetsyan 2001); for a dating of the columned halls at Altıntepe and Cımın Tepe to the Achaemenid period see Summers 1993.
3. The only well-attested examples of roofed evenly spaced columned halls in the sixth–fourth centuries BC in the classical world are the Odeion of Pericles discussed above and the Telesterion at Eleusis. The unusual design of the latter building seems to have been uniquely associated with the ritual activities of the mystery cult that it housed. See Shear, Jr 1982: 128–140.
4. For a discussion of postmodernist use of classical forms see Gerlernter 1995: 277–285.
5. In Vitruvius' terms of *firmitatis* (soundness) and *utilitatis* (utility), "The principle of soundness will be observed if the foundations have been laid firmly and if whatever the building materials may be they have been chosen with care but not with excessive frugality. The principle of utility will be observed if the design allows faultless unimpeded use through the disposition of the spaces, and the allocation of each type of space is properly oriented, appropriate and comfortable" (Vitruvius 1.3.2).
6. Venturi 1977: 35, with specific reference to the columns in Santa Maria in Cosmedin, Rome.
7. For a discussion of the development of the mosque form and its relationship to the function of the buildings as gathering places see Hillenbrand 1994: 31–128.
8. For a review of the prior development of mud-brick vaulting in Mesopotamian architecture see Oates 1990.
9. See for example Onians 1988; Rykwert 1996.

10. *Iphigenia at Taurus* (1.1.45–50), translated by Richmond Lattimore (Chicago, 1956).
11. Margaret Root has traced the origin of these "atlas" figures in Egypt and Mesopotamia in her groundbreaking book *The King and Kingship in Achaemenid Art* (1979: 149–161). One pertinent addition to this review is the appearance in Egypt of symbolic depictions of architectural columns bearing uplifted arms in the same pose (Philips 2002: 262).

18

A Reassessment of Brick Motifs and Brick-Building Techniques at Achaemenid Susa

Sabrina Maras

Introduction

In the nineteenth century, a number of intrepid European and British travellers visited the ancient site of Susa in south-western Iran, although they failed to note the site's archaeological potential (Chevalier 1997b: 34).[1] In 1851 the Englishman W. K. Loftus made a visit and took a great enough interest in the remains of the once-great Elamite and Persian capital city to return and excavate between 1853 and 1854 (Curtis 1993; 1997a). His efforts produced some of the first decorative brick fragments from the Achaemenid-period palace of King Darius I (c.522–486 BC). After a substantial break of 30 years from the time of the initial soundings carried out by Loftus, the French became involved in the site's excavations from 1884 to 1886, with Marcel and Jane Dieulafoy (Chevalier 1997b: 34) discovering the Persian archer brick fragments (André-Salvini 2000: 19). It was almost half a century after Loftus's initial discovery of Achaemenid-period decorative brick friezes at Susa that, in 1897, the French mining engineer Jacques de Morgan returned to excavate at the site under the auspices of his government's newly created Délégation scientifique française en Perse—a project which was provided with an unprecedented amount of funding for any French archaeological project of the era (Chevalier 1992: 16). Some 15 years later, in 1912, the Délégation saw its dissolution under the resignation of de Morgan, after which his collaborator, Roland de Mecquenem, took over excavations at Susa for an additional quarter of a century until 1946, locating the moulded, unglazed "fantastic animal" friezes from the palace of Darius among other finds (André-Salvini 2000: 21). Research at the site changed hands once more to Roman Ghirshman until 1967 and, finally, to Jean Perrot until the latter part of the twentieth century (Chevalier 1997a: 16).

During the century or so of French excavations at Susa, thousands of decorative bricks and brick fragments were uncovered, and many were brought to Paris to be reconstructed, preserved and studied at the Musée du Louvre. Although a substantial number of the bricks excavated at Susa remain at the site, the significant brick corpus at the Louvre has given art historians a wealth of information regarding brick manufacturing techniques used in ancient Persia during the Achaemenid period. Until recently, a not negligible quantity of the Achaemenid brick fragments housed at the Louvre were still in need of assessment—a task undertaken by the present author during two successive research periods at the museum between 2001 and 2002. This paper is an account of new information gleaned from the aforementioned decorative bricks and brick fragments, and the resulting reassessment of both brick-building techniques and use of iconographic motifs at Achaemenid Susa, specifically during the reign of Darius the Great.

Susian brick friezes

The rich repertoire of decorative brick friezes found to correspond to Achaemenid Susa include heraldic sphinxes, Darius' royal archers or "Ten Thousand" and a number of both glazed and unglazed moulded baked or sun-dried bricks depicting winged bulls, striding lions and winged griffins (see Harper 1992: 226, 229, figs 155, 157). Most of these friezes were painstakingly reconstructed from thousands of brick fragments actually found reused in later levels (Caubet 1992: 224). Only the lion frieze was discovered nearly intact, with a length of more than 4 m (Labrousse 1972b: 122; André-Salvini 2000: 20). The bricks were recovered from within or near the palace[2] on the Apadana mound, but not in the Apadana area itself (Muscarella 1992a: 217). A number of bricks bearing geometric or floral motifs were also found scattered over the Apadana mound (1992a: 217).

Brick friezes may have been placed both inside the palace or out in the courtyards, as both weather-resistant glazed, baked bricks and more fragile unglazed, sun-dried bricks were used for similar renditions of the same themes (although, *pace* Muscarella's suggestion that the two types of brick resemble each other in exact detail (1992a: 240), enough variations exist to suggest that different moulds were indeed used for their execution). The sizes of the bricks also varied (at least three brick sizes have been observed by the present author within the body of glazed and unglazed brick material at the Louvre), which further supports architecturally varied placement, such as over doorways or other areas of smaller surface.[3] Nevertheless, identical iconography (in the form of winged bulls, griffins and striding lions) does appear to some extent in both the glazed, moulded bricks and the plain, unglazed moulded bricks (Caubet 1992: 224). Subtle but visible variations in the details of the moulded forms are discernible enough to conclude that both glazed and unglazed friezes were desired for the embellishment of the royal city. Although colourless, the friezes created from the unglazed, moulded bricks are nevertheless visually striking—the delicately moulded curls, manes and feathers of the various beasts subtly throw shadows of texture on the brick panels, creating a three-dimensional effect which might have played well with the variations in both daylight and lamplight within the palace courtyards or rooms. A lack of glaze by no means signified a less agreeable visual encounter for the king and his entourage. Both the glazed and unglazed bricks should be viewed as intentional in terms of the aesthetics of Darius' visual programme.

Brick origins and parallels

Although the palace complex was connected to a columned hall or Apadana—notably a non-Mesopotamian architectural feature[4]—the palace of Darius itself, where most of the brick fragments and friezes were found, appears to have been based on a standard

Assyro-Babylonian palace plan (Muscarella 1992: 216), built around three successive courtyards (Amiet 1992: 13). In fact, comparisons with the palace of Nebuchadnezzar II (604–562 BC) at Babylon suggest the latter was a prototype of sorts (Amiet 1992: 13). Furthermore, the decor of the palace itself also echoed what has been construed as Babylonian in inspiration—glazed and moulded brick friezes such as those found in the Ishtar Gate or Processional Way at Babylon (Caubet 1992: 224).

Architectural and decorative parallels between Babylon and Susa, such as the use of similar—but not identical—brick-building materials in the construction of the palaces of the two capital cities, and Darius' incorporation of so-called "Babylonian" iconography into his own palace friezes, have led scholars to identify the source of inspiration for the Persian king's south-west Iranian palace as ultimately originating from Babylon. Supporting this assertion has also been Darius' very own claim in the Susa Foundation Charter (Dsf 3k: 49–55) that, "the men who wrought the baked brick, those were Babylonians" (Kent 1953: 142). This could suggest Darius' dependency on Babylonian artistic and architectural expertise to create both his palace plan and its glazed and moulded brick embellishment (Sauvage 1998: 148). But did the Babylonians really make the brick, as Darius stated in his royal proclamation, or could there have been other invisible hands behind the artistry of Darius' royal palace at Susa?

The response to this question is less than a resounding affirmation of Babylon as the sole source of inspiration for the resulting Achaemenid capital. As will now be demonstrated, there may have been a more indigenous origin for the inspiration of the brick decor at Susa yet, in contrast, a more universal origin for both its manufacture and eventual execution into decorative friezes. These alternative, non-Mesopotamian origins become apparent when one examines the history of decorative brick traditions in the Ancient Near East, the actual material composition of the bricks at Susa, the iconography of Susa's friezes within a specifically south-west Iranian world view and, most importantly, the telling brick-masons' marks found on a number of bricks, which point to individuals or teams of brick-masons from areas of the Persian Empire much further afield than Susiana or nearby Babylon.

Brick-making traditions

Baked brick was a comparatively easily made or procured—although not necessarily cheap[5]— alternative to rarer materials for construction and architectural decoration in stone-poor regions such as Mesopotamia. Moulded brick decor initially seems to have appeared at the site of Uruk during the Kassite period, specifically at the Ishtar temple built by Karaindash in c.1415 BC (Sauvage 1998: 26). Textual evidence also suggests the use of glazed bricks in Mesopotamia during the Middle-Assyrian period from the reigns of Adad-nirari I (1307–1275 BC), Aššur-reš-iši (1133–1116 BC) and Tiglath-Pileser I (1115–1077 BC) (Sauvage 1998: 29; Moorey 1994: 315). In addition, from the ninth century BC onwards, we have material evidence in Assyria for the use of predominantly flat glazed bricks as tiles within friezes.[6, 7]

In Babylonia, by contrast, moulded and glazed brick decor[8] followed the traditions of Babylonian relief sculpture. This has led scholars to suggest that Babylon had an independent tradition of baked brick-making from that of Assyria, where the preference seems to have been for flat glazed bricks as opposed to moulded types (Moorey 1994: 318), although one should make a note of the flat glazed bricks used in the initial stages of Babylon's seventh–sixth-century BC brick decor. But the use of decorative brick for architectural purposes was not solely the domain of Assyria or Babylonia. Their Mesopotamian traditions seem to have run parallel to that which was already developed in Elam (Moorey 1994: 318).

Elam

Indeed, in south-west Iran there existed a tradition of glazed and moulded baked bricks as early as the mid-fourteenth century BC, as expressed through the glazed tiles from Haft Tepe (Malbran-Labat 1989: 283; Sauvage 1998: 31; André-Salvini 2000: 18). At Susa itself, the tradition began at least in the Middle Elamite II period (in the twelfth century BC),[9] and then reappeared in the Neo-Elamite period (c. eighth–seventh century BC), seemingly continuing a tradition that may perhaps be called indigenous (Muscarella 1992a: 217; André-Salvini 2000: 18).

More evidence that would point to an independent Elamite tradition of brick manufacturing is found in the material composition of the bricks themselves. A number of studies have shown that Achaemenid bricks were manufactured from a different formula than the earlier clay bricks of neighbouring Mesopotamia, using a mixture of sand and lime (Caubet 1992: 223; Muscarella 1992a: 217; Moorey 1994: 319). In fact, as early as the twelfth century BC in Elam, this siliceous brick material was being used to formulate the bricks used in palace structures (Malbran-Labat 1989: 283; Muscarella 1992a: 217).[10] This same formula was used not only at Achaemenid Susa for the decorative brick friezes, but also at Persepolis (Muscarella 1992a: 217; Haerinck 1997: 30), and—most tellingly—at Achaemenid Babylon (Muscarella 1992a: 217; Haerinck 1997: 30). With a long tradition of moulded and glazed brick decor already well established in the area of south-west Iran, running parallel to that of Mesopotamia, Elam's contribution to Achaemenid Susa's palace friezes should be recognized.[11]

Iconography

One more aspect of the Susian brick friezes, which has evoked Babylon to some extent, is the iconography used in the brick designs. While certain echoes of Babylon consciously (and one could say purposefully) appear in the visual schema at Susa, taken in the full context of Susa's visual programme these echoes are only a small portion of the symbols chosen to express royal power at the Persian capital. For example, the striding lion can hardly be disputed as a direct reference to either Babylon itself (as expressed on the Processional Way at Babylon), or at least to traditional Mesopotamian iconography which has always relied heavily on the image of the lion to represent concepts such as royal power.[12] The image of the winged bull presents a similar theme—images of bulls figure prominently in the art of many cultures of the Ancient Near East, and are thought to represent concepts such as unmitigated power, fertility or, as at Babylon, perhaps the representative of the god Adad (Oates 1979: 153).

But the clever replacement of what may represent an Elamite-inspired griffin[13] for the Babylonian "Mushushu" dragon inserts what would have been a distinctly Elamite iconographic component (and, moreover, one well-known to the populace of Susiana)

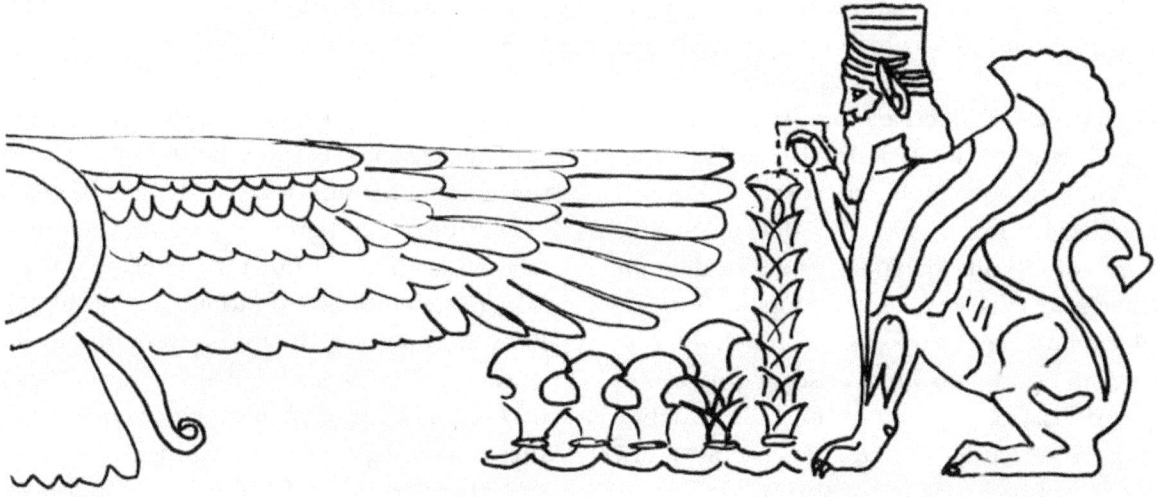

Fig. 18.1 Reconstruction of a sphinx with raised paw using Susa Brick [SB] 22075 fragment.

to the "Babylonian" storyboard, thus beginning what I consider to be a subtly imposed programme of visual assimilation of the many cultures within the Persian Empire into one recognizable artistic *koinê*, ultimately expressed in the multicultural "one nation under Ahuramazda" identity of Darius' Achaemenid superpower.

Taken into the larger context of the Susian visual programme, the Babylonesque "fantastic animals" are only a point of political reference within this visual dialogue, which includes very un-Babylonian archers, sphinxes, winged disks (Curtis 1993: 10, 55, pl. 20b, glazed brick no. 105) and Persian tribute bearers. The visual programme executed through brick friezes at Persian-period Susa additionally mirrors images seen later executed in stone at Persepolis (for example, Fig. 18.1, which is reconstructed from several brick fragments located by the author in the Louvre corpus).[14] These brick-frieze fragments establish further evidence to support the concept that there existed at Susa in the late sixth century BC the beginnings of a preconceived Achaemenid visual programme, which would eventually be executed so fully in stone at Persepolis. The choice of iconography used in the brick friezes appears to have been less random than specific. Any visual mention of Babylon within this iconographic programme would be secondary to the main purpose of Darius' political message conceived in brick— the integration of a vast empire under his rule.

It is evident that taking into account, 1) the parallel tradition of architectural brick decor in Elam; 2) the evidence for the use of siliceous brick in the region of Elam from the twelfth century BC onwards; and 3) the assimilation of Babylonian iconography into a multicultural visual programme which included Elamite iconography (among others), Babylon cannot claim sole—or even primary—responsibility for the inspiration behind the glazed brick decor manifested at Achaemenid Susa. One must look towards Elam as an artistic and political power that was as influential in the minds of the Persians of the late sixth century BC as ancient Babylon had ever been. In a brilliant coup of visual propaganda, Darius manifested his control over the two former political powers—Elam and Babylon—by integrating their distinctive symbols into his own Achaemenid artistic vision.

How should one interpret, therefore, the declaration made by Darius in the Susa Foundation Charter mentioning the Babylonians as key contributors within his palace building plan? As Carl Nylander so aptly noted, a "too literal use of this text is hazardous. The ultimate aim and function of the Foundation Charter was not a precise and truthful recording of the particulars of the construction process" (1975: 317). It is also clear from administrative documents found at Persepolis that there are inconsistencies between Darius' claims in the Foundation Charter and those who actually produced the work.[15] One might therefore ask, who really wrought the bricks at Susa?

Brick-masons' marks

Evidence which may tell us something about the brick-masons is the various brick-masons' marks extant on the flat surfaces of the Susian bricks (Labrousse 1972b: 104)—at times found on the top, at times below or on the sides of the bricks. The marks are of four different types,[16] executed as either a scratch made on a pre-baked brick; a small, glazed character; a painted mark (Loftus 1855: 435); or a mark in relief (personal observation). The marks vary from numerical fitters' marks (Curtis 1993: 8) to alphabetic symbols to indeterminate signs, and there is a great variety in the corpus. As to the purpose of the brick-masons' marks—comparisons with those found on Neo-Assyrian and Neo-Babylonian bricks suggest that the Susian marks could have served several different functions.

In Assyria, brick-masons' or fitters' marks have been found on glazed brick panels from Nimrud (Curtis 1993: 10) and Khorsabad (Reade 1963: 39–40). Fitters' marks were used in Assyria to join brick to brick, but were not as commonly used as at Babylon, occurring only when the design on the brick-face was not sufficient for panel reconstruction (Reade 1963: 40; Moorey 1994: 320). At Babylon, however, the marks were ubiquitous, as seen in the sets of courses of seven bricks used to create the glazed brick façade of the throne-room at Babylon dating to the time of Nebuchadnezzar II (Reade 1963: 40). Two kinds of marks could be used: numerical strokes would denote the course within which the brick resided (such as one stroke for row 1, two for row 2, and so forth),[17] or various geometric shapes could be used to denote the placement within the course of the brickwork (Reade 1963: 39). It has been suggested that the bricks were partially baked before reaching the painter (Reade 1963: 40). The fitter's marks were possibly added while the bricks were put into or taken out of position within the frieze design, before actual glazing (Moorey 1994: 320).

Although studies have shown that some brick-masons' or fitters' marks at Susa are similar to those found in Assyria (at Nimrud and Fort Shalmaneser) and Babylonia (Labrousse 1972b: 122; Curtis 1997a: 40), and probably served the function of positioning marks (André-Salvini 2000: 16), some of these marks may nevertheless have also denoted either groups of artisans or individuals.

If one compares, for example, the way stonemasons' marks were used at Persepolis, Susa and Pasargadae, a large number of the symbols denote an actual mason's identifying mark as opposed to a simple positioning mark. It has been posited that the marks found at

Persepolis in varying locations, such as on foundation tablets, column bases, column capitals and other areas (Roaf 1983: 90), identified either an individual worker (Schmidt 1953: 161) or a gang (Nylander 1975: 317–323; Roaf 1983: 93). This would act as a practical record-keeping device for the purposes of accountability, and evidence at Susa does suggest that at least six teams or groups of individuals were used for the non-decorative brick structures at the capital city, differentiated by five different signs (Labrousse 1972b: 104). Although speculative, this same system could very well be applicable to the glazed, moulded brick friezes at the site. If this is the case, what can the marks tell us about the groups or individuals producing the bricks?

Significantly, there exists a similarity between the Persepolitan stonemasons' marks and contemporary alphabets, including Lydian (Nylander 1970: 87), Aramaic and South Arabian scripts, as noted by various scholars (for a full analysis of the various views, see Roaf 1983: 93). Nylander suggested that stonemasons' marks found in the bases of the Apadana foundations at Susa were connected with Ionian and Lydian craftsmanship, and accordingly the marks could be connected with "Anatolian" workmen (Nylander 1975: 322). Nylander further posited that local stonemasons (meaning those inhabiting the region of Fars in the sixth century BC, and, one could presume, Elamites, Persians and others co-mingling in the region)[18] were involved in the stonework at Pasargadae, as indicated by "errors and signs of lack of routine"—in other words, the work was not as clean as that performed by experienced stonemasons (Nylander 1970: 144). Further evidence that local workmen were involved in construction at Pasargadae is evidenced through the suggested Median term for stonemason, *karnnuvaka* (1970: 144).

If nothing else, the example of the stonemasons' marks found at the three major Achaemenid cities gives a clear picture that the individuals or groups working the stone were of mixed cultural identities. This is a significant detail in terms of allocating responsibility for the manufacture of the glazed and moulded brick friezes of Achaemenid Susa. Again, one can suggest a somewhat integrated workforce. In Achaemenid Iran, construction methods would appear to have been adapted to take advantage of the full workforce available—regardless of cultural affiliation or regional identity. In a political system based on a universal ideology of inclusiveness (i.e. belonging to the empire), all artisans could in essence be "equal", and must have enjoyed unprecedented freedom in terms of the exchange of knowledge and skills.

In terms of identifying Babylonian brickmasons at Susa, there is simply not enough evidence to sustain a purely Babylonian workforce.[19] Interestingly, Loftus maintained the Aramaic origin of a number of Susian brickmasons' marks (Loftus 1857: 398; Curtis 1993: 8). As Aramaean was the lingua franca of the Achaemenid Empire (at least in the written, if not spoken, word), this would not seem so unusual (Briant 2002a). However, new unpublished marks have recently come to light, which considerably expand the association of the Susian brick-masons' marks with not only the Aramaic but possibly also the Lydian, Lycian, Semitic and South Arabian alphabets. These marks may well represent a motley crew of brick-masons, which may or may not include Babylonians.

The following chart (Fig. 18.2) of brick-masons' marks recently observed by the author in the Louvre brick corpus contains previously unpublished symbols.[20] These marks are comparable with a variety of marks found not

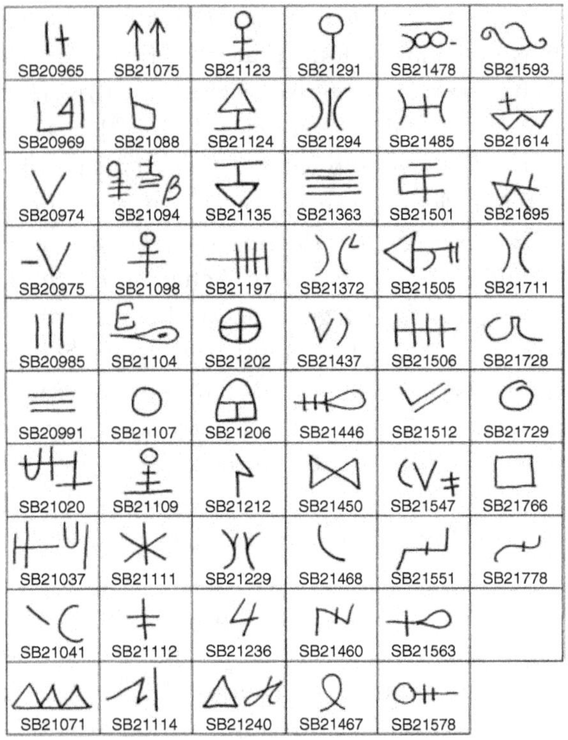

Fig. 18.2 Chart of Susa brick-masons' marks as observed by the author.

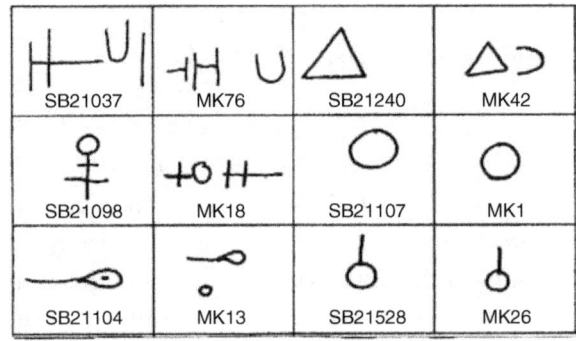

Fig. 18.3 Comparative chart of Susa brick marks [SB] with those of the Tall-i Takht at Pasargadae [MK]. (MK76, MK18, MK13, MK42, MK1 and MK26 are after Stronach 1978: fold-out 1)

only in various geographic locations within the mid- to late sixth–fifth-century BC period of the Persian Empire but also, surprisingly, on such disparate media as stone, coins and pyramidal stamp seals. Their astounding variety represents another aspect of the voluntary or imposed artistic and cultural integration within the Achaemenid Empire, which reflects a nation mixed in races, languages and ideals unified under one overarching identity.

For example, comparisons of these newly identified brick-masons' marks with the stonemasons' marks from the Tall-i Takht at Pasargadae (Fig. 18.3) show a number of close similarities (such as SB21037 with MK76; SB21098 with MK18; SB21104 with MK13; SB21094 with MK3), as well as several identical matches (SB21240 with MK42; SB21107 with MK1; and SB21528 with MK26; refer to Stronach 1978: fold-out 1). Some stonemasons' marks from the Tall-i Takht have been identified as Ionian or Lydian (Stronach 1978: 21–22), which would then potentially signify an eastern Greek origin for some of the brick marks, and thus brick artisans or overseers, at Susa. Further evidence to support this cultural exchange comes in the form of several bricks from Susa (SB20974, SB21240 and SB21202) which bear linear marks such as those found on masonry at Sardis (cf. Boardman 2000: 118, fig. 3.38a).

There also exist a number of similarities between the Susian brick-masons' marks (such as SB21468, SB21291 and SB21450) with stonemasons' marks at both Susa and Persepolis (Fig. 18.4), published by Nylander (1975: 6, pl. XXXIV). This may either demonstrate the possibility that a stone artisan could additionally manufacture moulded decorative bricks, or that the methods used for accounting and identifying stone masonry were seen as sufficiently adaptable to brick-making.

Many of the marks found on the moulded bricks from Susa still need identifying. Some may be alphabetic. Parallels are found between a number of Susian brick-masons'

Fig. 18.4 Comparative chart of Susa Brick [SB] marks with those found on stone at Susa and Persepolis. (The latter are after Nylander 1975: 6, pl. XXXIV)

marks and alphabetic symbols in the Lydian, Lycian, ancient South Arabian and both North and South Semitic alphabets. For example, SB21551, SB20974 and SB21202 may be Aramaic (cf. Millard 1962: 46), but SB21202 (Fig. 18.5a) also mimics a Greek symbol (cf. Diringer 1968: 306, fig. 19b). The following marks (Fig. 18.5b) appear Lycian: SB21075, SB21104, SB21451 and SB21299 (see Diringer 1968: 330, fig. 19.29.c). And finally, at least two marks (Fig. 18.5c) may be of a South Arabian script (SB21291 and SB21450) (cf. Diringer 1968: 146, fig. 12.5), although this is a tentative suggestion that requires further study.

Some parallels are also seen between the brick marks and the devices used as "personal identity markers" on Anatolian pyramidal stamp seals of the Achaemenid period—SB21468 and SB21291 (Fig. 18.6a) are similar to linear devices published by Boardman (1970b: 23, fig. 3, nos 1, 7, 13); and with some countermarks found on Achaemenid-era coins (Fig. 18.6b), such as SB21098, SB21075, and SB21711 (1970: 24, fig. 4), and SB21563 from an Anatolian

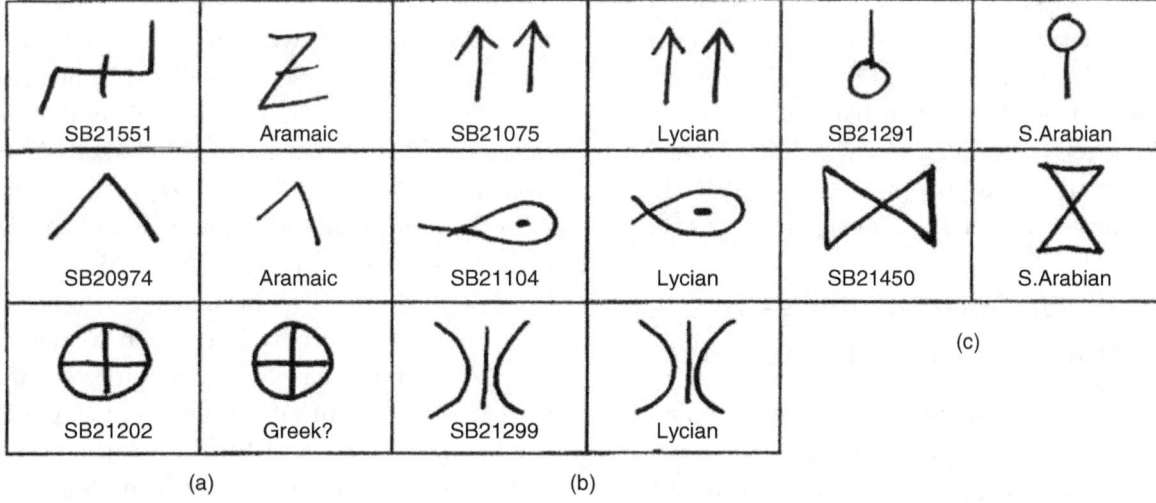

Fig. 18.5 Comparative chart of Susa brick marks [SB] with Aramaic, Greek (a), Lycian (b) and Ancient South Arabian (c) alphabetic characters.

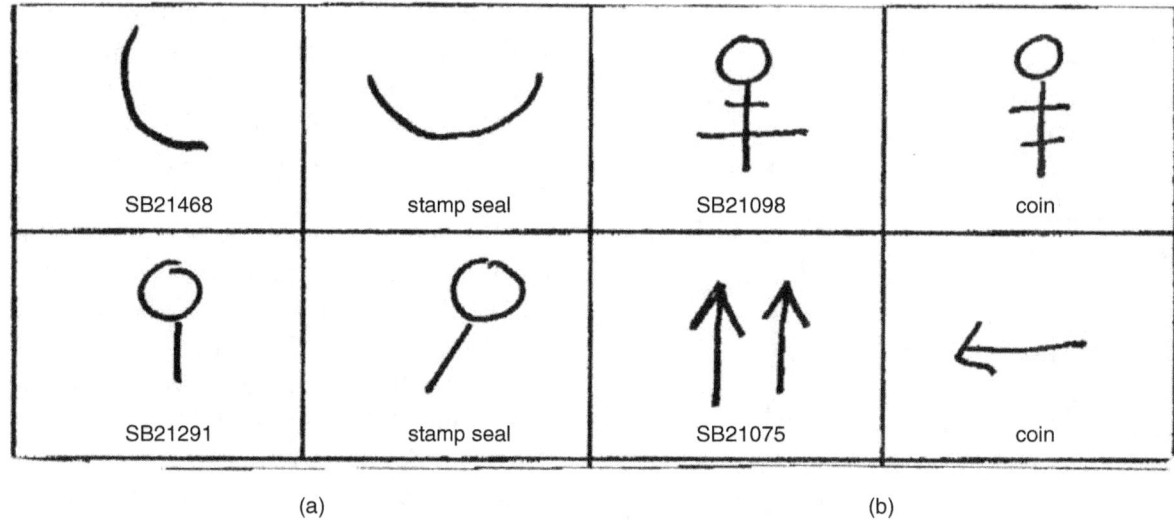

Fig. 18.6 Comparative chart of Susa Brick [SB] marks with personal devices on stamp seals (**a**) and coins (**b**) of the Achaemenid period.

coin (Boardman 2000: 118, fig. 3.38c)—all devices used to identify actual individuals. Could this signify such a use for the similar brick-masons' marks? Or are the marks simply random? It seems possible that, with these aforementioned parallels in mind, the brick-masons' marks could represent individuals or groups, or even correspond to cultural affinity. These issues are as yet unresolved, but the brick-masons' marks can tell us something about those involved in the actual *chaîne opératoire* of brick-frieze construction, which may ultimately explain at least the need for such a variety of marks, as opposed to one succinct, repetitively used corpus of signs.

The *chaîne opératoire*—brick manufacturing techniques

It took a rather complex process to create the decorative brick friezes found at Susa. There were at least eight steps involved in manufacture, which included: 1) mixing the straw, mud or other material necessary for the bricks (in the case of the Susian bricks, sand and lime) (Labrousse 1972b: 119); 2) placing the mixture into moulds; 3) a firing process which, if the bricks were to be glazed, included being fired up to three times (Caubet 1992: 223). For the bricks that were purely terracotta, a second 1 cm-layer of fine paste different in clay from the main body of the brick was added to create finely sculpted details (Bourgeois 1992: 285; André-Salvini 2000: 17). After initial baking, the bricks were 4) laid out horizontally once more (Labrousse 1972b: 120); 5) painted with the glaze; and 6) rebaked. After the final baking, the bricks would then have to be 7) transported to the palace location, to be 8) reassembled (Sauvage 1998: 76–77).

For each step in the brick manufacturing process, there may have been a specialist. In Mesopotamia, there were titles for the workers involved in all the different stages of brick-making—those who "work the earth with a hoe, the dirt specialist, transporter of dirt, brick worker, maker of cooked bricks, cooker of bricks, brick-mason", and so on (see

Salonen 1972: 169–174; also Sauvage 1998: 79). In Assyria, for royal structures, so much manpower was needed that prisoners of war would supply the necessary hands (Sauvage 1998: 81). In the Neo-Babylonian period, groups of 10, 50 or 100 people could be organized into troops or general workers, with whom specialized masons or architects would work (Joannès 1982: 26–44; Sauvage 1998: 80). For certain jobs, there were also private entrepreneurs (Joannès 1989: 128, 134). Sauvage has suggested (1998: 38) that certain brick-masons' marks were possibly marks of the property of the entrepreneurs or brick-makers working for royal constructions. These marks may very well have represented groups of artisans, or the chief supervising the work. In sixth-century BC Persia, a similar entrepreneurial system may have been in place, although this remains unknown. With such a division of labour necessary for decorative brick manufacture, it would seem essential for each team to have its own identifying symbol, or for the chief artisan to mark his work for reasons of payment or professional accountability.

Additional evidence exists to counter the idea that the Susian brick-masons' marks were purely for fitting the bricks within a frieze. Curiously, some of the decorative bricks from Susa carry no mason's marks at all. Furthermore, a number of the bricks with identical iconographic motifs have non-identical masons' marks (cf. SB21111 and SB21114, both representing the same section of the crown of the archer's head with braid; and SB21505 and SB21512, identical robe with lance sections; each brick carries a different mason's mark). Conversely, identical masons' marks are found on bricks bearing different frieze sections (such as SB21124 sleeve edge vs. 21135 robe section). Another oddity relates to the different ways the markings were executed—on sections of identical motifs different types of markings are used, such as a glazed marking on SB21506 vs. a marking in relief on SB21528, both depicting the same section of hanging cordons. This seeming randomness in the placement of the marks would go contrary to their use as fitters' marks. There seems to be no clear evidence yet that all the brick marks found on the decorative bricks from Susa served one sole purpose, and it is probable that a quantity of the marks were actually for the purposes of accountability.

Conclusion

Although we cannot ascertain that the brick-masons' marks corresponded to an individual or a group of a particular cultural affiliation, their rich variation demonstrates that, as for stonemasons at the Achaemenid capital cities, the manpower used both to make the bricks and to construct the brick friezes which graced the walls of Darius' palace at Susa was representative of the synthetic nature of the empire. Those who wrought the bricks may have included Babylonians, but it seems just as likely—considering the evidence presented by the iconography and material composition of the bricks, in conjunction with the rather multicultural origins of the brick-masons' marks—that those who wrought the bricks for Darius were artisans of the Persian Empire hailing from a number of provinces such as Elam, Lydia, Anatolia or perhaps even brought in from more far-flung regions of trade and contact such as South Arabia.[21] The bricks of Darius' palace not only visually proclaim the power of the Persian Empire, but also reflect the masterful integration of its many people within the Achaemenid artistic *koinê*.

Acknowledgements

The author wishes to thank Mme Annie Caubet of the Département des antiquités orientales of the Musée du Louvre for her generosity in permitting full access to the collection of Persian materials in the Réserve Visconti, as well as her kind permission to publish the material mentioned in this paper. Many thanks are also due to Beatrice André-Salvini and Nicole Chevalier for their kindness and support during my many research visits to the Louvre; also to Noémi Dauce and Jean Nguyen for their long hours of assistance and companionship while sorting the seemingly inexhaustible brick fragments; and last, but not least, to Professor David Stronach for his inspiration and guidance.

Notes

1. These included H. C. Rawlinson (Curtis 1997a: 36) and Austin Henry Layard in 1841, who pronounced the ruins "of little interest" (Chevalier 1997b: 34).
2. For the suggested placement of the various friezes within the palace complex of Darius, see Muscarella 1992a: 217.
3. As already noted by Caubet, some fragments bear figures on a smaller scale, with a height of 9 rows of bricks as opposed to 17. She has also suggested that smaller tiles of 13x13x14 cm were probably used to adorn stairways, doors and windowsills (Caubet 1992: 224).
4. As discussed by Dr H. Gopnik (this volume), the columned hall in the early to late Iron Age occurred in various geographic contexts in the Near East, from north-west and south-west Iran to south-east Arabia, but appears to be quite non-existent in the central Mesopotamian architectural koinê.
5. Baked brick could be two to five times more expensive in Neo-Babylonian times than sun-dried brick (Sauvage 1998: 84). Due to the high cost of fuel, making kiln-fired bricks was so expensive that their use was minimized when possible (Moorey 1994: 306).
6. The oldest was found at Assur from the temple of Anu and Adad in the form of a fragmentary orthostat, dating to Tukulti-Ninurta II's rule (c.890-884 BC) (Moorey 1994: 315; Andrae 1925: pl. 7; Reade 1963).
7. Bricks were glazed on one face to be used in a fashion similar to tiles, or on one or two adjacent sides, but rarely did they carry relief (Sauvage 1998: 29). Note, however, that the use of moulded or shaped glazed bricks has been reported at Nineveh (Moorey 1994: 317) and at Nimrud (Postgate 1973: 193).
8. Examples such as the Ishtar Gate and Processional Way, all attributed to Nebuchadnezzar II in the sixth century BC (Moorey 1994: 318).
9. In Elam, the first inscribed glazed bricks or tiles date to Untash-Napirisha (1340–1300 BC) and from Shilhak-Inshushinak (1150–1120 BC) (Sauvage 1998: 31).
10. The first were made for Untash-dingir.gal (see Amiet 1966: n. 261; Malbran-Labat 1989: 283).
11. As previously suggested by Moorey (1994: 319), who attributed this to the possibility that Egyptian technology had already influenced Achaemenid craftsmen by the reign of Darius.
12. One need only note the Neo-Assyrian lion-hunts of Ashurnasirpal II (883–859 BC) at Nimrud and those of Ashurbanipal (668–c.627 BC) at Nineveh (Reade 1998b: 39, 72–79), which figure so prominently in association with the Assyrian king, to confirm a royal fascination with the beast.
13. I would like to thank my colleague Javier Alvarez-Mon for this observation. His forthcoming paper, "Elamite rings of power", explores this subject in more depth.
14. One should also note Labrousse 1972b: fig. 35, which illustrates Susian brick fragments (also personally observed) depicting the lower body of a bull being attacked by a lion, such as that found in stone on the Persepolis Apadana staircase.
15. Nylander observed that a number of administrative documents found at Persepolis demonstrate that "not only Ionian and Sardians were used for stone working, nor only Egyptians and Sardians for work on wood" (1975: 317; see also Cameron 1948; Hallock 1969).
16. As personally observed by the author. I would also like to thank Noémi Dauce from the Ecole du Louvre for corroborating this detail at the 2005 conference in London. She has also noted brick-masons' marks executed in relief in her own work on the material, which it is hoped will be published in her thesis.
17. See Reade (1963) for a complete description of the process.

18. For a full study on the acculturation process between the Elamites and the Persians, refer to Henkelman's (2003*a*) excellent and thorough paper on the subject.
19. J. Canby has questioned the Babylonian contribution based on the material composition of the bricks themselves (1979: 316).
20. However, it must be remembered that this list, which significantly expands the known corpus of brick-masons' marks published by Loftus in the 1850s, is by no means complete. These marks are extracted solely from a partial sampling of the glazed and moulded archer brick series.
21. Where stonemasonry—and thus presumably stonemasons—existed during the Iron Age. See Magee (2005*b*) for evidence of trade and exchange between south-east Arabia and Iran in the Iron II period.

19

Empire Encapsulated: The Persepolis Apadana Foundation Deposits[1]

C. L. Nimchuk

Cambyses, son of Cyrus and ruler of the Persian Empire, died in 522 BC, igniting a fight for the throne that lasted over a year; when the dust settled, Darius, son of Vishtaspa, was Great King, King of Kings. One of the many tasks to which Darius turned was the construction of the city of Persepolis (Parsa) as the centre of his realm. Certainly the most imposing and impressive building at Persepolis was the Apadana, with its staircase that truly seemed to depict the entire world bringing offerings of tribute to the king. Let us now move forward approximately 2,500 years.

In 1933, Darius' city was being excavated by Ernst Herzfeld, with Friedrich Krefter appointed as the excavation architect. In mid-September 1933, Krefter was in charge of the excavation while Herzfeld was away from the site. Krefter had noticed a depression in the north-western corner of the Apadana, and thought the depression might indicate robbed foundation inscriptions. Following this line of reasoning, on 18 September 1933 he had the workers explore the north-eastern corner, in case this corner held a deposit of inscriptions. Krefter's hypothesis was correct, as there was indeed a deposit.[2]

The north-east deposit held a stone slab placed atop a square stone box and lid. Within the box were two inscribed metal tablets, one silver, one gold; each was inscribed with the same trilingual text (DPh). Six coins were found beneath the box, four gold coins of the lion-and-bull Croeseid type, one silver griffin tetradrachm from Abdera, and one silver turtle stater from Aegina.[3]

On 20 September, excavations in the south-eastern corner of the Apadana revealed another, similar deposit, with a square stone box, two inscribed metal tablets (one gold, one silver) inside the box, and four gold and two silver coins underneath.[4] The four gold coins were again the lion-and-bull Croeseid type. The silver coins were Cypriot double-sigloi: the coin with an obverse lion head was from an unknown Cypriot mint; that with the obverse bull and reverse eagle head was possibly from Paphos. Another Cypriot silver coin (?Lapethus mint) was later recorded in the same area.[5] This latter coin has created problems in understanding the deposits, since it was recovered after the initial excavation.[6]

Given the report of the depression in the north-west corner of the Apadana, and the two intact deposits in the north-east and south-east corners, along with the Achaemenid tendency to symmetry and mirror imaging (again witnessed in the Apadana staircase reliefs), it is logical that there would have been four foundation deposits in the Apadana, one at each corner.[7]

Discussion of the Apadana deposits has generally focused on dating issues, for example, the use of the deposits to fix the probable dates of the coins or to examine whether the coins and inscription provide clues to the date of the tablets and the work on the Apadana.[8] In contrast, little focus has been aimed at understanding the foundation deposits as a whole. Here I wish to examine the elements included with and excluded from the deposits by Darius. After all, Darius carefully crafted visual and verbal statements of his world view for particular audiences; as such, the foundation deposits of the premier building on the Persepolis platform must have played a part in the message.[9]

The Apadana foundation deposits have several elements in common with Mesopotamian (particularly Neo-Assyrian) traditions and practices, such as the stone boxes, tablets made of precious material (often inscribed), miscellaneous precious objects, and the arrangement of these objects in layers.[10] Three aspects, however, set the Apadana deposits apart: the DPh text does not mention the deposit itself, instead referring to Darius and the extent of the empire; Mesopotamian deposits rarely, if ever, include coins; and the material contents themselves (only gold and silver for the tablets and precious objects, without other metal or stone tablets or plant material) are unusual.[11] I propose that Darius made deliberate choices of inclusion and exclusion for the deposits, expressing particular and conscious messages to select audiences. The deposits were meant to sanctify, legitimate and protect the king, the Apadana and the realm, as well as offer a lasting commemoration to Darius himself.

The DPh text [12]

The trilingual DPh text was recorded in Old Persian, Elamite and Late Babylonian (the three official languages associated with Darius' inscriptions).

> Darius, Great King, King of Kings, King
> of Lands/Peoples, son of Vishtaspa
> an Achaemenid. Declares Darius
> the King: This (is the) kingship which I
>   hold—
> from the Saka who (are) beyond   5
> Sugdu (Sogdiana), from there as far as
>   Kush,
> from Hind (Sind), from there as far as
>   Sparda—
> (the kingship) which Ahura Mazda, the
>   greatest
> of the gods, granted to me.
> Let Ahura Mazda protect me and my
>   house.[13]   10

"This (is the) kingship which I hold—from the Saka who (are) beyond Sugdu (Sogdiana), from there as far as Kush, from Hind (Sind), from there as far as Sparda" (lines 4–7). Here, Darius obliquely lays out the royal Mesopotamian statement of all-encompassing rule, that is, rule of the four quarters or corners of the world. Instead of the traditional generic claim that he is "king of the four quarters", Darius has consciously named his four quarters or corners, thereby making the empire spatially tangible. The naming of the four quarters creates liminal regions that separate internal and external; passing from the internal (empire) to the external (non-empire) means passing from order to chaos (and the unknown). Darius has crafted a simple yet elegant statement that makes tangible the empire. In so doing, he has emphasized his own accomplishments: through the aid of Ahura Mazda, he has consolidated and strengthened the empire, bringing order to the lands and peoples; thus, he has obeyed the will of Ahura Mazda; further, his success reinforces Ahura Mazda's choice of him as king, providing evidence of his worthiness.[14]

The physical inscriptions that delineate the four quarters were located under two corners of the Apadana, with the high probability of one originally having been under each corner. These physical inscriptions acted as anchors for the metaphysical corners of the empire, aligning the four quarters (existing both in the text and hundreds of miles away) to the four corners of the building on which were carved representatives of the diverse lands encompassed by the four quarters.[15] The inscriptions do not explicitly mention the foundation deposits or the Apadana building, yet the rhetoric highlights the symbolic connections between the empire, the deposits and the Apadana.

Others have noted that the Persepolis platform, at the heart of the empire, is aligned to the solstices. During the summer solstice the sun rises in the north-east (the region of the Saka), and sets in the north-west (Sparda); during the winter solstice the sun rises in the south-east (Hind/Sind) and sets in the south-west (Kush). The DPh text, thus, records the physical extent of the empire, the four quarters, according to solstice sunrises and sunsets, thereby also metaphorically implying the royal Mesopotamian claim to rule from the rising to the setting sun. The Apadana itself follows this orientation, with the diagonal formed by the north-west and south-east corners aligned to the sunset of the summer solstice.[16] The summer solstice marks the longest period of daylight in the year, representing in Mazdaean terms the prominence of Light over Darkness, the Truth over the Lie.[17] Darius, through the alignment of the platform and buildings, and the construction of the DPh text, has consciously set his empire into both Mesopotamian royal traditions and a Mazdaean cosmological system.

It is noteworthy that, in material terms, each of these four quarters was also linked with the metal gold. Sparda (Lydia), with its capital Sardis, was known for the gold taken from the Pactolus river; this region was further linked to the wealth of Croesus, the king of Lydia conquered by Cyrus; and the Lydians were credited with being the first to mint coins in both gold and silver (Hdt. 1.14, 50–52, 54, 92–94; 5.101). Kush (Nubia) held importance as a source of gold throughout much of Egyptian history, and Darius received annual "gifts" from the Kushites (Ethiopians), including gold (Hdt. 3.97, 114).[18] India (Hind/Sind) was the only region to have its taxes reckoned in gold instead of silver (Hdt 3.94–95, 98, 102–106).[19] Given the previous three correspondences, the listing of the Saka beyond Sogdia rather than Bactria as the north-eastern representative seems surprising, since Bactria was generally associated with gold in the Achaemenid period.[20] The naming of the Saka, however, does follow the pattern: the region of the Saka beyond Sogdia ranged into the Altai Mountains, a rich source of gold; and Saka (or Scythian) tombs show evidence of much decorative goldwork.[21]

Darius, by delineating the physical expanse of the empire, bestows both order and prosperity. The naming of the four quarters marks the boundary between order and chaos, empire and non-empire. At the same time, the resources found in liminal regions represent the prosperity brought to the empire by the institution of order.[22] The inscription itself, the use of precious metals and the ceremony focused around the deposits proclaimed Darius' success to both the divine and the human spheres.

Darius consciously crafted particular messages for particular audiences. A foundation deposit, by its very nature, implies a divine audience. Yet, we must keep in mind that the establishment of a foundation deposit was not a hidden and secret act, but one that took place in public, whose ceremonial celebration would have been layered with symbolic and metaphoric significance and witnessed by much of the court.[23]

Gold and silver, tablets and coins

As noted, the deposits' concentration on gold and silver is unusual; neither the tablets nor the precious objects were composed of any other material. There is no indication from earlier Mesopotamian deposits that the materials used were specifically, as opposed to generally, designated.[24] Darius' choice of gold and silver as the material for the tablets and the objects, to the exclusion of all other materials, must have been deliberate.

It was common in the ancient world for rulers to exchange gifts of gold and silver objects, and for rulers to present such gifts to other humans and divinities.[25] The choice of gold and silver for the tablets thus serves both as a gift object of substantial value and as the medium for the message from the Great King (Darius) to the Greatest of the gods (Ahura Mazda).

What about the gold and silver coins? Why did Darius choose to include coins (and only coins)? And why did he choose these specific coins in these amounts? Coinage implies the control of economic resources, in this case gold and silver. Darius claimed the political control of the lands associated with gold and silver resources, as noted above with the DPh inscription. Darius could also claim control of the technology associated with minting through his political control of Sparda (Lydia). From a Persian perspective, coins were extraordinary, an innovative way to keep gold and silver.[26] The inclusion of coins in the deposits, therefore, expands Darius' achievements from control of the political (land) and economic (resources) to the technological (minting process) as well. The coins can be seen, as with the tablets, as both message and gift: Darius has accomplished even more in fulfilling Ahura Mazda's will, and has presented tokens of this fulfilment.

The composition of the deposits raises the question of the proportion of gold coins to silver. As already noted, symmetry plays a part in the structure of the Apadana. If each corner of the Apadana held a foundation deposit (as suggested above), and the two missing deposits had the same composition as those extant, we would expect to have four gold coins in each deposit. In addition, we have four quarters of the empire named in the DPh text that mark the liminal shift from order to chaos (at the ends of the empire); the association of these regions with the solstices; and the link between the four named quarters and the resources of gold and (to a lesser extent) silver. These elements add up to a tidy symmetry and parallelism. The four gold coins in each deposit may thus evoke the four quarters and their resources. Such nuanced detail bespeaks Darius' deliberation in composing the deposits.

The number of silver coins and their relationship to the gold is more problematic, not least because of the third coin in the southeastern deposit. If it was intrusive, the two extant deposits would have each included two silver coins, half that of the gold, with some corresponding significance unknown to us presently. If the coin was not intrusive and was indeed part of the deposit, the three silver and four gold would total seven coins (a significant numeral in the Mazdaean belief system).[27] If this pattern held true, it would mean a silver coin was missing from the northeast deposit.[28] Each proposition provides one answer and raises more questions; we cannot look to other deposits for confirmation of either option, and at this point must simply note the questions.

A second important consideration is that of the coin types. The choice of gold Croeseids parallels and reinforces Sparda as a quarter associated with gold (and coinage!), again resonating and iterating multiple levels of control. Darius certainly could have included silver Croeseids in the deposits, yet he chose not to.[29] What, then, are we to infer from the silver types Darius did choose to incorporate? Michael Vickers has postulated that the silver coins dated to late in Darius' reign and were meant to be symbolic of his political control of the regions where the coins were minted.[30] Margaret Root, in contrast, has suggested that the silver coins could have represented Darius' wish and intention, early in his reign, to control the regions associated with the silver coins.[31] Antigoni Zournatzi (2003: 11–19) has pointed out that commercial relationships (and thus indirect control), rather than direct political control or the wish for such, may underlie the choice of silver coins.[32]

Mazdaean religion and the Apadana deposits

It seems inconceivable that Darius would design and inter the foundation deposits of the Apadana without due and considered reverence. Therefore, can we better understand the specifics of the Apadana deposits—their physical locations, the stone boxes, the use of gold and silver tablets and coins—through a consideration of the Mazdaean belief system? I think we can.

The Mazdaean system tells of seven stages of creation: a stone sky; water; earth; plant; cattle; man; and fire. In Mazdaean worship, these creations are represented in the offering ritual: earth was the ritual precinct; water and fire were present in vessels; a pestle and mortar represented the stone of the sky; the *haoma* pressed by the mortar and pestle signified plant creation; cattle were symbolically present in terms of the sacrificial animal or its products; and man was represented by the priest.[33]

Deity	Creation
Khshathra (Vairya)	Sky of stone
Haurvatat (Apam Napāt, Varuna)	Water
(Spenta) Armaiti	Earth
Ameretat	Plants
Vohu Manah	Cattle
Spenta Mainyu	Just man
Ahura Mazda	
Asha (Vahishta)	Fire
(Mithra)	

The Apadana foundation deposits embody these seven stages of creation, metaphorically linking the creation of the Apadana, Persepolis and the empire with the creation of the world.

Fire and water were especially important elements in the Mazdaean religion. Darius is portrayed standing in front of a fire altar at Naqsh-i Rustam;[34] and Herodotus (along with other Greek authors) tells us of the reverence the Persians had for fire and water (Hdt. 1.131–132). In the Old Iranian pantheon, Ahura Mazda occupied the primary position as "lord of wisdom". Two subordinate deities (Ahuras) were Varuna (guardian of oaths; lord of the "truly spoken word", i.e. Truth) and Mithra (guardian of covenants, i.e. associated with Loyalty).[35] Water was associated with Apam Napāt (Varuna) and Fire with Mithra.[36] These elements were considered "pure", and could also purify; thus, the water ordeal and fire ordeal were used to reveal the truth (i.e. purify) in accusations of breaking oaths or covenants.[37]

The sun and moon are also important celestial and cosmological aspects of the Mazdaean religious system.[38] Prayers are regularly recited to the Sun and Mithra, to the Moon, and to the Waters and Fire.[39] Within the Zoroastrian monthly calendar, days 9–12 are dedicated to Fire, Waters, Shining Sun and the Moon, respectively.[40] The grouping of days 9–12 in the calendar forms a foursome that can divide into two pairs: Fire/Sun (days 9/11) and Waters/Moon (days 10/12). The *Arda Viraz Namag*, in relating a metaphysical visit to heaven and hell, preserves a tradition in which the star station represents "good thoughts", the moon station "good words" and the sun station "good acts".[41] "Good words" are related to oaths, and thus Apam Napāt (Varuna), the guardian of oaths and the deity whose realm is the Waters; "good acts" relate to covenants, and thus Mithra, who is guardian of covenants and whose realm is Fire.[42]

This brings us back to the metals, gold and silver. The association of gold with the sun ("golden sunlight") and silver with the moon ("silvery or white moonlight") is a truism, for good reason. Given the significance of sunrises and sunsets in the orientation of Persepolis, the Apadana and the empire as a whole, it would be singularly appropriate to have the metals associated with these "lights" carrying the message of Darius to Ahura Mazda, who is associated with "Light", "Good", "order" rather than "darkness", "chaos", the "Lie".[43]

To project the cosmological symbolism further, gold may represent not only sunlight and the sun, but also the elemental Fire. By the same token, silver may represent not only moonlight, but Water.[44] The gold and silver thus can metaphorically embody two sacred elements and their associated deities; as such, the gold and silver would sanctify the physical and metaphysical spaces of building and empire through their associations with the purity of fire and water (neither of which would have been able to be physically maintained in a deposit under a building).[45]

This could also explain the puzzle of the gold and silver coins—the coin types and metals reverberate symbolically and rhetorically on both geopolitical and ideological levels. The gold coins are from Sparda, a land-based portion of the empire, and the direction in which the sun sets during the summer solstice. The silver coins are from coastal locales that are in a relationship with Persia, if not vassals.[46] To extend further, ancient concepts of the world conceived of the earth surrounded by or floating on water.[47] The gold coins are symbolic of the extent of the lands held, from sunrise to sunset, and the silver coins symbolic of the water encountered at the ends of the earth, in essence "from sea to sea". Through the gold and silver coins, we have a reiteration of the sacred Mazdaean fire and water elements, as well as an echo of the Achaemenid "earth and water" symbols of submission to the king.[48] Darius again has reinforced his claim to control the entire world.

Taken as a whole, the deposits and their associated rituals would have symbolically re-enacted the stages of Creation, a powerful statement of imperial creation, since these deposits would have been placed early in the construction of the Apadana, the core building on the citadel of the capital city, the heart of the empire, an empire that Darius had forged anew. Earth was represented by the foundation area (bricks and earth) in which the deposits were set (and by the geographic origin of the Croeseids); water was represented by the silver metal of the tablets and coins, and the geographic origins of the latter; fire was represented by the shining gold of the tablets and coins; the sky of stone was represented by the stone box that surrounded the tablets. What about the plants, animals and man? According to the Mazdaean traditions, they would have been part of the ceremony marking the depositions; they would not have needed a permanent place in the depositions, since the first-created plant, animal and man were sacrificed in the process of Creation.[49]

Aspect of Creation	Deposit Representation
Sky	Stone box
Fire	Gold (tablets, coins)
Water(s)	Silver (tablets, coins)
Earth	Area of foundation
Plant	Part of ritual ceremony
Cattle	Part of ritual ceremony
Just man	Priest (part of ritual)

The Apadana foundation deposits are more than a means to date the coinage, the building or the exact extent of the empire at various points in Darius' reign. The Apadana building and its deposits, through the materials, objects and texts, were associated with the creation of the world and the empire: the Apadana anchored and embodied the empire, and the deposits sanctified the creation of the kingdom, as well as commemorating it, through the symbolic elements of divine creation. The composition of the deposits shows deliberate care in the choice of media and messages, care taken by Darius as king and creator.

Notes

1. This paper draws on research presented by the author (in press). I wish to thank the University of Illinois at Springfield for support in attending the conference, and everyone who gave me feedback on this research, both in Toronto and in London.
2. Mousavi 2002: 224–230. See the Oriental Institute website for a photograph of the deposit: http://oi.uchicago.edu/OI/MUS/PA/IRAN/PAAI/IMAGES/PER/APA/1B9_72dpi.html.
3. Schmidt 1957: 110, 113–114. The four Croeseids are Persepolis 28–31, the silver tetradrachm from Abdera is Persepolis 36, and the silver stater from Aegina is Persepolis 27. See the Oriental Institute website: http://oi.uchicago.edu/OI/MUS/PA/IRAN/PAAI/IMAGES/PER/MF/5A2_72dpi.html.
4. Mousavi 2002: 230. Herzfeld's (1938b: 413–414) reporting of the contents of the deposits is somewhat confused, stating that the deposits were found in 1934, and implying that there were four silver coins in each deposit, although photos of only four silver coins in total (rather than eight) appear in the publication.
5. Schmidt 1957: 110, 113–114. The south-east gold Croeseids are Persepolis 32–35, the double-siglos of unknown Cypriot mint is Persepolis 37, the Cypriot double-siglos possibly from the Paphos mint is Persepolis 38, and the problematic Cypriot coin is Persepolis 39.
6. Schmidt later found the coin while excavating in the deposit area. He acknowledged that the coin might not belong to the deposit, but treated it as if it did (1953: 70, 79; 1957: 110). The style and dating issues of this coin have been discussed by Root (1988: 2–3) and Kagan (1994: 38–39). Traditionally, the (?)Lapethus coin has been dated later than the other two silver coins in the deposit. Kagan has argued that this coin could be dated prior to c.500 BC; given the location of the find, he has strongly supported inclusion of the coin in the deposit (p. 38). Clearly, the circumstances of the finding and reporting of the third silver coin

raise more questions than answers regarding the deposit. See further below.
7. Fragments of stone boxes similar to those from Persepolis were found at Susa; they may have served a similar function as foundation boxes (Mousavi 2002: 230).
8. The list of scholarship on the dating of the Apadana deposits is lengthy. For an introduction to the scholarship, see e.g. Vickers (1985); Root (1988, 1989); Kagan (1994: 17–52); and Jacobs (1997).
9. See Root (1989: 38–43) and Bejor (1974: 735–740) for holistic discussions of the nature and meaning of the Apadana foundation deposits. For Darius' world view, messages and audience, see Margaret Root (1979, 1988, 1989) and Nimchuk (2001).
10. See Ellis (1968) for Mesopotamian deposits, their elements and their structure; note that many of the Mesopotamian deposits are associated with temples, which is not the case with the Apadana.
11. The famous, earlier instance of coinage in a foundation deposit is in the Artemision at Ephesus, for which see Bejor (1974: 740, n. 25). The date of the beginnings of coinage production is much discussed, as is what constitutes a "coin". At the time of Darius' accession, coinage was still a recent concept, particularly separate species of gold and silver coins. See Nimchuk (2002: 55–79).
12. In the interests of time and space, I here present conclusions drawn from my previous analysis of the text, for which see Nimchuk (2005).
13. Translated by the author.
14. Darius' inscriptions reveal a strong concern over order and the accomplishment of Ahura Mazda's will; see the Bisitun (DB) and Naqsh-i Rustam (DNa, DNb) texts in Kent (1953: 116–134, 137–140).
15. Root (1989: 39–43) discusses the representation of the extent of the empire in the DPh text (with focus moving outward from the centre) and in the images (with focus moving inward towards the centre); both representations reveal the central power of the king.
16. See George (1979) for the alignment of the Persepolis platform and the buildings on the platform.
17. George (1979: 196–197).
18. Baines & Malek (1980: 20).
19. Note that gold is listed as a resource found at the liminal edges of the known world: India, Kush (Ethiopia), northern Europe (where griffins guard the gold, Hdt. 3.116, 4.27). See also Fleming (2002).
20. Darius' palace at Susa was adorned with gold from Bactria and Sardis (DSf §3h in Kent 1953: 144).
21. The Altai mountain region supplies both alluvial and mined gold. For the recent find of an intact sixth–fifth-century BC Scythian tomb with thousands of pieces of goldwork, see the Deutsches Archäologisches Institut website at http://www.dainst.org/index_596_en.html; for a public report, see the *New York Times* article of 9 January 2002 by John Varoli, "Scythian Gold from Siberia said to Predate the Greeks" (accessed online at http://www.nytimes.com/2002/01/09/arts/design/09GOLD.html). For Assyrian and Achaemenid influence on Scythian art, see Reeder (1999: 49–50).
22. Silver is present in natural gold deposits, and as such is associated with gold; see Ramage & Craddock (2000: 10–11).
23. Ellis (1968: 5–34, especially p. 31); Bejor (1974: 739–740). As with grave burials, the deposition of the tablets and coins would remove them from the human realm (Bejor 1974: 738).
24. See Ellis (1968: 131–140).
25. For the use of gold and silver Archers as gifts in the reign of Darius, see Nimchuk (2002: 67–71).
26. For a discussion on the technology of gold refining and coin production, see Ramage & Craddock (2000).
27. The significance of the number seven is exemplified in the seven stages of Creation, and the divine Heptad of Ahura Mazda and six junior deities; see Boyce (1984a: 10, 12–14). Note that the Bisitun text (DB §68–69) reveals this same structure with Darius and the six nobles who helped him kill Gaumata.
28. See above for discussion of the possibly intrusive coin. A third possibility is that there were meant to be progressive numbers of silver coins, e.g. one, two, three and four, and the two excavated deposits were in the middle of the sequence. Given the symmetrical and mirror-imaging structures of the Apadana, such sequencing, although possible, seems less obviously logical.
29. Both gold and silver Croeseids would have been easily accessible to Darius. Scattered silver Croeseids were found in the Persepolis Treasury building during excavations, presumably scattered in Alexander's sack of the city. See Schmidt (1957: 110–114) for the loose silver Croeseids (Persepolis 1–4, 6–7) excavated in the Persepolis Treasury.

30. Vickers (1985: 4–9, esp. p. 6).
31. Root (1988: 4–5).
32. These locations are economically associated with silver (pp. 16–19). My thanks to Professor Margaret Miller for recently bringing this work to my attention.
33. Boyce (1984a: 9–10, 13, 27–29).
34. See Schmidt (1970: 84–86, plates 19, 22).
35. Boyce (1984a: 9).
36. Yasht 19 in Boyce (1984a: 29–30). Apam Napāt ("Son of the Waters") is also known by Ahura Berezant (1984a: 29). Apam Napāt has been associated with Varuna, for which see Boyce (1984a: 9, 29–30).
37. Boyce (1984a: 29–30—introduction to Yasht 19; p. 64—introduction to *Vis u ramin*, sections 54–55).
38. Abolala Soudavar has suggested that the lion and bull in the art of Persepolis represent day and night, thus the sun and moon as the sources of light for day and night; see his contribution in this volume.
39. Boyce (1984a: 3). See Yashts 5 (p. 33), 6 (pp. 31–32), 10 (pp. 27–29). The sun is itself part of the creation of Fire, and is associated with Mithra (p. 10); it, too, has the ability to purify (Yasht 6, pp. 31–32).
40. Boyce (1984a: 19).
41. Boyce (1984a: 86).
42. Note that the upper register relief of the tomb of Darius also depicts—to the right of the winged disc figure of Ahura Mazda above the fire altar—a disc with an emphasized lunate crescent in the lower portion. This disc is level with the torso of Ahura Mazda, with the head of the deity at a higher level; see Schmidt 1970: pls 19, 22 (tomb of Darius) and 49 (tomb of Artaxerxes I, which shows the lunate disc more clearly). Schmidt thought the perplexing image represented a crescent moon and the vague reflected outline of the remainder of the moon, and suggested it might be associated with Mithra (Schmidt 1970: 85). I suggest that the lunate disc represents both the sun and the moon, superimposed into one image. Thus, the image would represent the Old Iranian gods Ahura Mazda, Mithra and Apam Napāt. Ahura Mazda, as the supreme Ahura, is both visually larger and higher than the lunate disc by reason of the expanse of wings and the depiction of the torso and head, although the discs themselves are at approximately the same level. This would be a singularly appropriate image to appear on the tomb, since the DNb inscription emphasizes that Darius is greatly concerned with his "good words" and "good acts" (see Kent 1953: 138–140).
43. Yasna 30 in Boyce (1984a: 35). The rebel kings in the Bisitun text are associated with the "Lie" (DB §44–64), and are therefore opposed to and brought under control by Darius and Ahura Mazda (e.g. §8, 11–14, 52–56), for which see Kent (1953: 116–135) and Nimchuk (2001: ch. 2).
44. Stars are also associated with water in the Mazdaean system, as for example the star deity Tishtrya is equated with Sirius, the Dog Star, and is revered because of the association with rain; see Boyce 1984a: 32 (Yasht 8). This does not negate an association of water and the moon.
45. For the close connection between fire and water, see Boyce (1985: 148–150).
46. Zournatzi 2003: 11–19.
47. For the ancient Iranian concept of the world, see Boyce 1984a: 16–17, and 45–50 (from the Greater Bundahishn).
48. Kuhrt (1988a). As Kuhrt argues, earth and water were meant to establish a superior–inferior relationship (the Persians, of course, being the superior party) and to underscore the seriousness of the oaths sworn; the specifics of the type of relationship itself would vary according to circumstances (pp. 94–99). See also Zournatzi (2003: 11–16).
49. Boyce 1984a: 10. The plants and animals would have been part of the sacrificial elements, while "man" would be represented by the priest and participants.

20

Persepolis: A Reinterpretation of Palaces and Their Function

Shahrokh Razmjou

Introduction

From the very beginning, early travellers and visitors to Persepolis referred to the buildings as palaces, as it seemed to them that this was clearly what they were. After archaeological excavations began at Persepolis, archaeologists assigned names and functions to the different buildings. Archaeologists working at the site, Herzfeld in particular, named the palaces after the architectural features of each building. They used terms such as "Apadana", "Tripylon Gate", "100 Columns Hall", "Harem" and so forth. Xerxes' "Gate of All Countries" became known as the "Gate of All Nations".[1] There was a particular problem with buildings that had no name, such as the Great Columned Hall. Neither the foundation inscription nor the monumental inscriptions mentioned its name. On the other hand, some buildings which did have a name, for example the Tachara, had no clear function. Herzfeld therefore had to name them himself and he continued to interpret them according to the architectural form of each building. After him, Schmidt and others made little change to his ideas, and continued to call the buildings and spaces after Herzfeld. Today many of these interpretations are problematic and need revision.

The Great Columned Hall

When Herzfeld excavated the Great Columned Hall at Persepolis he called it the "Apadana".[2] The word he used was mentioned in later Achaemenid texts on column bases from Hamadan from the time of Artaxerxes II (A2Ha, A2Hb; see Kent 1953: 155). He translated the word as "Columned Hall" simply because it occurred on inscribed column bases.[3] He regarded the hall as "the public part of a royal palace" (Schmidt 1953: 70; Herzfeld 1941: 352). Afterwards the term was used to refer to massive columned halls in general but the size of the column bases in Hamadan is actually small compared with the Great Columned Hall at Persepolis.[4] All evidence of Apadanas shows that they all had small columns, not huge ones. And if *apadana* simply means "columned hall", then why were other columned halls not called "Apadana"?

In a Treasury text from Persepolis, a columned hall is referred to as *i-a-an-(na)*.[5] The

Fig. 20.1 A column torus from Ecbatana (Hamadan) mentioning Apadana and Anahita, British Museum. (Courtesy of the Trustees of the British Museum)

meaning of this word is "great door", that is, a court and audience hall, the same meaning as the Safavid word *alighapou*.[6]

In his own inscriptions, Artaxerxes refers to establishing an Apadana by the favour of Ahuramazda, Anahita and Mithra (A2Ha; see Kent 1953: 155). The names of Anahita and Mithra only appear together in Achaemenid royal texts from the time of Artaxerxes II. Other sources report that he founded a temple for Anaïtis in Hamadan where he erected statues of her.[7] The only evidence for architectural activities by Artaxerxes II in Hamadan is his inscriptions about building an Apadana.

The word *apadana* in Old Persian cuneiform was usually read with an "a" at the beginning and not a long "ā" (Fig. 20.1). Kent has analysed the word as apa + dāna (1953: 168). The first sign can be read with a long ā as there are other words in Old Persian starting with a long ā and using the same sign. For example, we note words such as *āyadana* or *Āθar*. In that case, we can read the word *apadana* as *āpadāna* and the word would then mean "place of waters". If we read the word as *āpadāna*, and some scholars believe that this is possible, then we suggest that it can be a term for a temple of Anahita, the goddess of all waters. This is also supported by data from classical sources. Usually the name Apadana appears together with the names of Anahita and Mithra. It is interesting that the name of Anahita on its own only appears in those texts that are about establishing an Apadana. In the occurrences of the same name in Mesopotamia, there is also a connection with a temple of Artemis, who is a female deity and a parallel to the Iranian Anahita, goddess of all waters.[8] As confirmation of this connection, we can refer to Plutarch's report about Aspasia, appointed by Artaxerxes II as a priestess of Artemis of Ecbatana, who bears the name of Anaïtis.

In Elamite, the name Apadana is written as Hapadanu and there is no reference to a columned hall. The Fortification texts mention "water" as a sacred item that receives rations.[9] In the same ritual payment texts, there is also evidence of religious payments to sacred places called Hapidanu or Hapidanush that can be compared with Hapadanu. They may be related to Apadana or they may even be the same.

Until now, there is no evidence for any Apadana at Persepolis, but this name was given to the Great Columned Hall and to every columned hall in general by archaeologists after Herzfeld. The word *apadana* is always connected with water. In Nisa texts, the word is used for a wine storage area, which is in fact a place for storing liquids.[10] There is also a reference to this word in the Old Testament.[11] Although the passage is unclear and is obscured in translation, the original name and its relation to water in the sentence is convincing. Some scholars have also suggested a possible connection between this word and a place for water (e.g. Lecoq 1997: 115).

Tachara and Hadish

One of the buildings in the inscriptions of Darius was called Tachara and a nearby palace was called Hadish by its founder, Xerxes. Herzfeld saw the Tachara as the private palace of Darius and Hadish as the private palace of Xerxes. Both names were translated by Herzfeld as "palace",[12] but in fact the Tachara is a small building and not suitable for the residence of the great king.

Some people have suggested that the images on the door jambs of the northern rooms of the Tachara palace (and side rooms of the Hadish) indicate a bathroom, as the individuals shown on the reliefs carry towels and perfume (e.g. Dutz & Matheson 2000: 70-71; Basiri 1946: 35; Mostafavi & Sami 1955: 37) (Fig. 20.2). This idea was rejected, as there was no evidence for any bath in that location.[13] The other reason for calling the palace a residential palace is based on the images of figures in Persian and Median dress walking up the stairs and carrying food, vessels, liquids and small cattle in the Tachara (also in the Hadish). They have been identified as servants carrying food for the royal table (Herzfeld 1941: 268; Wilber 1969: 102; Sami 1970: 33; Ghirshman 1964a: 192) (Fig. 20.3). This interpretation is problematic, as some of these figures are armed and it is difficult to believe that armed kitchen attendants would have been allowed to enter the private palace of the king (Fig. 20.4).[14] They carry live animals and must be a part of a ceremonial procession that took place there. They are also shown carrying covered vessels and leather bags, and prepared food. The covered vessels indicate that it was not important to show the contents, but the procession and the number of participants were important. Obviously live animals could not have been consumed alive by the royal family. They needed to be killed, prepared, cleaned and boiled, fried, baked, stewed or roasted. However, there is no space for such activity inside the palace and a kitchen cannot be identified. In fact a location for a kitchen does not exist and even if there *was* a kitchen, the smell, noise and smoke would not be suitable for a palace. The building is not big enough to provide space for such activities, and as the so-called kitchen would have been just a door away from the main hall it would have been impossible to prevent the noise, smell and smoke from reaching it.

The other problem is the headdress of these figures. Those with the long pleated Persian dress have a pleated headdress and those with the Median tunic and trousers have a one-piece headdress. In both cases, the chin is covered and the mouth and nose could be covered if necessary. We are familiar

234 THE WORLD OF ACHAEMENID PERSIA

Fig. 20.2 Individuals on a door jamb of the Hadish Palace, Persepolis. (Photograph S. Razmjou)

Fig. 20.3 Individuals carrying food to the Hadish Palace. (Photograph S. Razmjou)

with these figures from the Oxus Treasure (Fig. 20.5) and Daskylion. In a famous relief from Daskylion, two individuals are shown in Median dress, one clearly beardless, holding bundles (*barsom*s) in front of a shrine. They have headdresses that cover the mouth and nose (Briant 2002a: 245–246) (Fig. 20.6) and they are priests performing a ritual ceremony. The heads of two sacrificed animals can be seen in front of the shrine. There are a number of parallel images on seals and seal impressions, all showing people in similar types of dress performing a ritual ceremony (Briant 2002a: 244, figs 33/a, 33/c–f; 249, fig. 35/b). In the images from the Oxus Treasure, priests are sometimes shown wearing a short sword while performing a ceremony (Fig. 20.7).

There is also the evidence of figures in Persian dress, who appear on seal impressions from Persepolis. In one example, the king appears in front of a fire altar performing a ceremony (Schmidt 1957: 27, pl. 7, seal no. 23) (Fig. 20.8). On the opposite side is a figure in Persian dress with a pleated headdress. The question is, do such figures represent priests or servants? To answer this we need to refer to Mary Boyce:

priests customarily wore white, whereas "warriors" peacocked it in reds and

236 THE WORLD OF ACHAEMENID PERSIA

Fig. 20.4 A man carrying a small animal and armed with a short sword, Hadish Palace, Persepolis. (Photograph S. Razmjou)

purples and other brilliant hues. So presumably if the paint had not worn off the ancient sculptures, priests and nobles would be instantly distinguishable, even when dressed in clothes of the same style. (1982: 21)

There is a statement by Plutarch that confirms Boyce's suggestion:

> Why do women in mourning wear white robes and white head-dress? Do they do this, as men say the Magi do, arraying

Fig. 20.5 Detail of a man carrying a vessel, Hadish Palace, Persepolis. (Photograph S. Razmjou)

themselves against Hades and powers of darkness, and making themselves like unto Light and Brightness? (Plutarch *Moralia* IV. 26; trans. Babbitt 1972: 47)

It is therefore important to prove the existence of white on those headdresses. At Persepolis almost all of the original colours have disappeared through rain and wind but at Susa there are glazed bricks which show the same scene. These bricks fortunately have their colours preserved. Amongst these bricks there is a fragment which shows a clean-shaven man with the same headdress painted

Fig. 20.6 Daskylion, two Magi holding *barsoms* in front of a shrine and sacrificed animals, Archaeology Museum of Istanbul. (Drawing by Ann Searight)

in white (Curtis & Razmjou 2005: 90, no. 54) (Fig. 20.9).[15] It is interesting that another type of headdress in the same collection is shown in a dark (black?) colour.[16] White and black headdresses for priests continued in later periods. The "Median" headdress is shown in yellow: perhaps it relates to the rank of the priests or the material they used for their headdresses. Persian priests were of a higher rank and always appeared before the Medes.

Being shaven is also a sign of priesthood. It is an Ancient Near Eastern tradition for Egyptian, Assyrian and Elamite priests. On seals, priests are shown without a beard, and the same applies at Persepolis. Half of the figures walking up the staircases are shown

Fig. 20.7 A gold plaque showing a man with a bundle and sword, Oxus Treasure, British Museum. (Drawing by Ann Searight)

without a beard, and in Susa all Persians with the distinctive headdresses discussed above are clean-shaven. The figures in the northern rooms of the Tachara are clean-shaven and the grand priest Kartir in the Sasanian period is also always clean-shaven (Fig. 20.10). The figure that appears on the

Fig. 20.8 Seal impression on a clay label from the Treasury archive (seal no. 23), Persepolis, National Museum of Iran. (Photograph S. Razmjou)

Fig. 20.9 Glazed brick from Susa, showing a clean-shaven man in a white headdress, Musée du Louvre. (Photograph S. Razmjou).

famous audience scene behind the crown prince and in front of the royal weapon holder is clean-shaven as well and has been identified as a "towel-bearer" (Schmidt 1953: 165) (Fig. 20.11). However, a towel-bearer was probably not important enough to stand in front of the royal weapon holder. He wears a pleated headdress, and on the same scene when shown from the left, he has a tasselled scarf on his left shoulder, which falls down his back.[17] Clean-shaven figures on stone reliefs from Susa are shown with the same tasselled scarf (de Mecquenem 1947: 84, fig. 53/10). This could be a sign of higher-ranking priests. In a drawing from the Safavid period, a Magus is shown in front of a fire altar in Istanbul (Homayoun 1970: 311, pl. 134.I) (Fig. 20.12). He is clearly clean-shaven and has a tasselled scarf on his back. John Usher, a British traveller in the nineteenth century, described Yazidi priests and their white cloths and tasselled scarves (1865: 417). Even today, Zoroastrian and Armenian priests in special ceremonies use a scarf hanging from their shoulders.[18] Unfortunately, the meaning is no longer known.

The unusual figure representing a Persian depicted on the plinth of the statue of Darius from Susa is presumably a Persian priest (Roaf 1974: 94–96) (Fig. 20.13). He is clean-shaven and has the headdress and a scarf. Because he is shown from the left side, the scarf is shown with tassels.[19]

These clean-shaven figures also appear with other religious icons that confirm the ritual connection. Another stone fragment from Susa shows a person with the same headdress, but with a *padam* (a religious mouth cover) worn under his chin (Razmjou 2005b: no. 199) (Fig. 20.14).

The appearance of these figures with the same headdress holding a fly-whisk behind the king's throne is not in contradiction of their duties. As we know from ancient texts, fighting *khrafastra*s—or harmful creatures, including insects, created by the evil spirit—was a religious duty for priests (De Jong 1997: 338, 341). Herodotus describes the same ceremony practised by the priests:

But the Magians kill with their own hands every creature, save only dogs and men; they kill all alike, ants and snakes, creeping and flying things, and take much pride

Fig. 20.10 Grand priest, Kartir, Naqsh-e Rajab (Photograph S. Razmjou)

Fig. 20.11 A clean-shaven man with a pleated headdress, Audience Scene, Treasury Hall, Persepolis. (Photograph S. Razmjou)

therein. (*Histories* 1.140; trans. Godley 1981: 179–181; De Jong 1997: 339)

This act was therefore religious and had a ritual concept. The clean-shaven person wearing a priestly headdress cannot be identified as a simple servant, but as a priest with certain duties. We know from Greek sources that Persian kings were accompanied by Magi,[20] but the Greeks usually thought that these clean-shaven attendants to the king were eunuchs.

The name of Tachara was translated as palace, but the word still exists in other related cultures.[21] In the Caucasus region that had close cultural relations with the Persians, the word is still in use. There is a word in Old Armenian, *tājār* (*dājār*), meaning temple or sacred place. After Christianity became the official religion of Armenia, this name was adopted for part of a church or a type of shrine that only priests were allowed to enter to perform a ceremony (see Razmjou 2002; 2008). In Georgia, which was an important region in the Achaemenid period, the word *tadzari* (*tachri*) is used for sacred places. It means any temple, including pagan, Zoroastrian, Christian or Buddhist. It is still used in modern Georgian and can also be found in medieval Georgian manuscripts.[22] The Tachara word with its original meaning

Fig. 20.12 A sixteenth-century engraving showing a clean-shaven Magus in front of a fire altar in Istanbul. (Homayoun 1970: 311, pl. 134. I)

Fig. 20.13 A figure representing a Persian on the plinth of the statue of Darius from Susa, National Museum of Iran. (Photograph S. Razmjou)

was still in use in the Sasanian period, and there is a word in Sasanian texts, *uzdes-tachār*, which means "temple of idols" (Wüst 1966: 127).

To return to the figures on the staircases, we note that the textile that appears in their hands cannot be a towel. It probably had a religious significance.[23]

If we suggest that these individuals were priests and not servants, the palace would then appear to have been a place for ritual activities or a "palace-temple". The food would be regarded as offerings and the animals would be brought for sacrifice. There are texts about offerings of small animals in the Persepolis Fortification Tablets (Razmjou 2004: 104–105).

However, a place would be needed to sacrifice these animals, and the palace was not suitable for such a task. What was needed was a separate area for sacrifice and the author has identified one outside the Tachara (Razmjou 2002; 2008) (Fig. 20.15). This building was added to the palace at the same time as the figures with the animals, during the reign of Xerxes. At this time, the function of the palace was changed into a sacred place for sacrificial ceremonies, perhaps as shown on a seal from the Ashmolean Museum (Moorey 1979: 222, fig. 3/B). At that time the name of the palace

Fig. 20.14 A stone fragment from Susa showing a clean-shaven man with a pleated headdress and *padam* worn under his chin. (Curtis & Tallis 2005: 157, no. 199)

was changed to Hadish. In fact, it was Xerxes who changed the function of the Tachara and renamed it Hadish.

Xerxes' main Hadish became much bigger than the former Tachara. The second Hadish had many images of individuals carrying animals, including some small cattle, into the palace. Clearly Xerxes wanted to stress the great number of offerings, an increase from previous times.

Hadish is also translated as "palace" (Schmidt 1953: 30, 41), and there is no other equivalent in later Persian. But an equivalent term was used by the Romans, namely *aedes*. This is a kind of temple with a sacrificial function. Inscribed fragments of a column base from Xerxes' Hadish refer to a Tachara (Schmitt 2000: 75, 97). This suggests that a Tachara could be part of a bigger Hadish, but more evidence is needed to confirm this.

In Babylonian and Elamite translations of Old Persian texts, there is no reference to a temple, which is strange, but we should remember that these terms all had different meanings. Temples in general were called *āyadana* in Old Persian.[24] In the Babylonian version of the Bisitun inscription, the equivalent for this word is "É. MEŠ *šá* DINGIR. MEŠ" (houses of the gods) (Schmidt 1953: 33; von Voigtlander 1978: 17, line 25). When the Elamite and Babylonian texts refer to Tachara, they use the same Persian word, but in their own pronunciation. There was probably no equivalent to this word in Elamite and Babylonian. I believe it is difficult to continue to describe the Tachara and Hadish as residential palaces as they have a strong religious significance.

The Treasury

The Treasury was a place where artefacts were preserved. Perhaps because there was no obvious stone structure and because it was buried under the mud from the mountain, it did not attract treasure hunters. The building contained different types of valuable material. According to the tablets found here, the name seems to be correct, but this is misleading in terms of the function of the building. Usually a treasury is a place for financial activities and payments of money and for storing valuable material for administrative purposes, which this building is not.

The financial evidence found in the Treasury Hall comes in the shape of the Treasury tablets, which date from the time of Darius to the early reign of Artaxerxes I, between 492 and 460 BC (Cameron 1948: 1). They were stored there for about 150 years and no other texts were written after that time. In fact, they belong to an archive and are not related to this particular building.

Some other objects are not valuable artefacts, but were deposited there because of their

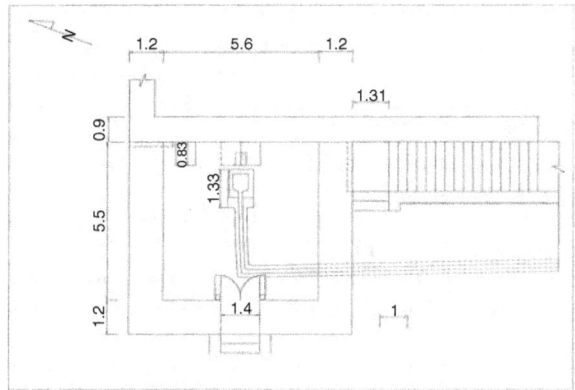

Fig. 20.15 The sacrificial room, on the north-west corner of the Tachara Palace, Persepolis. (Drawing by S. Razmjou and P. Sookiasian)

importance, for instance the collection of pestles, mortars and plates, made of green chert (Bowman 1970: 1; Schmidt 1957: 53). They were inscribed, showing that they were used in a ritual ceremony. After being inscribed they were stored in the Treasury and were never used again. Some other objects have historical and cultural value, such as a small inscribed stone vessel of Ashurbanipal, marble vessels of the pharaohs Nekhau and Amasis from Egypt's 26th dynasty, and fragments of stone vessels inscribed in Hittite hieroglyphics (Schmidt 1957: 84). There is also a Greek statue of a sitting woman and a Neo-Elamite inscribed plaque, as well as Babylonian objects with the name of Nebuchadnezzar II, and Persian Achaemenid artefacts.[25] In addition, massive reliefs of Xerxes' audience scene were kept here. They were originally placed in the courtyard.

The Treasury Hall at Persepolis was therefore a place for depositing jewellery, figurines, parts of chariots (such as lynchpins), used ritual objects, 150-year-old texts, obsolete and even damaged reliefs,[26] and artefacts from old cultures and other countries, not only under the Persian rule, but also from cultures outside the empire, including Hittite, Assyrian, Babylonian, Elamite, Egyptian, Ionian, Greek and so forth. Today, such a place, holding different artefacts from different countries, different cultures and from different periods, would be a museum. In my opinion, the Treasury Hall of Persepolis was not a financial or administrative centre but a royal archive used to deposit and store objects. It was an early kind of museum located in the royal complex and belonging to the Persian kings.

The Harem (?)

This building is in the south of the platform and is known today as the Harem of Xerxes. In his report, Herzfeld referred to this building as the South-Eastern Palace (Krefter 1971: 17) but Schmidt preferred to call it a harem (1953: 255). The plan of the building and its dimensions are the same as those of the Tachara.

What are the reasons for this name? 1. The building is on a lower level, almost surrounded by neighbouring buildings, and is therefore less accessible. 2. Unlike the Tachara, one entrance is missing, which has been interpreted as limiting access to it. 3. There are some small L-shaped compartments on one side of the building. However, I do not see sufficient reason to call the palace a harem.[27] Schmidt (perhaps following Herzfeld) may have been inspired by the harems of the Ottoman Sultans. The lack of one entrance cannot be seen as evidence for such an interpretation. I believe the additional rooms were made for temporary use and were not women's quarters. This area was also easily overlooked by the neighbouring garrisons, towers and fortifications and therefore would not have been a suitable place for the residence of royal women. Krefter once suggested the name "Second Tachara", which seems to be more correct (1971: 17). There are no inscriptions giving the name of this building and the foundation inscription found by Herzfeld, which is written by Xerxes (XPf), saying that he was chosen by his father as successor to the throne, does not support the idea that the building was a harem.

Conclusion

In my opinion, there were no residential areas on the platform at Persepolis; the rooms were probably used for short periods by special guests. It is possible that these rooms were used on a temporary basis by the king and his officials or by some dignitaries, or even by envoys before and after an audience ceremony. Persepolis was more than the ceremonial centre of the Persian Empire. It was used by the kings for official meetings and as a place where they also performed ritual ceremonies. Changing old perspectives about Persepolis can provide us with an opportunity to reinterpret the site and the finds in a more accurate way, which will help to increase our knowledge and understanding of the Achaemenid Persian Empire.

Notes

1. Xerxes originally called this palace-gate *duvarθim visadahyum*, meaning "Gate of All Lands" (or Countries). See XPa, Kent 1953: 148; Schmitt 2000: 68.
2. The idea of calling columned halls "Apadana" seems to have been used before Herzfeld. Dieulafoy called smaller columned buildings "Apadana", such as the so-called Harem at Persepolis, which he referred to as "the small Apadana". See Krefter 1971: 17.
3. From the *torus* and column bases found in Hamadan and Susa. See Herzfeld 1941: 227; Schmidt 1953: 70, n. 3.
4. For the column bases of Hamadan, see Knapton, Sarraf & Curtis 2001: 101–102.
5. This is a translation given by Cameron. Persepolis Treasury texts 79, 83; see Cameron 1948: 194, 198.
6. For a translation of this word, see Giovinazzo 1989: 205–206.
7. Berossus, *Artoxerxes* 27.3; Knapton, Sarraf & Curtis 2001: 100.
8. I am grateful to Prof. C. Tuplin who kindly informed me about different references in classical texts
and ancient sources to Apadanas in the Middle Euphrates and Habur valleys. The name is used for structures that are a short distance from a stream or river, and there is a connection with a temple of Artemis.
9. The unpublished text PF-NN 1064 (K2). In the text it is written "A. lg." meaning water.
10. E.g. in text no. 74 from Nisa, the named person is in charge of the delivery of wine from an Apadana = '*pdn*. See Diakonoff & Livshits 2001: 15. In another text, no. 816, there is a reference to a vineyard called Old Apadana = 'TYQ '*pdn*, *ibid*. 73f. For a translation of '*pdn* in Nisa texts, see *ibid*. 185.
11. "He will pitch his royal tents (=Apadana) between the seas at the beautiful holy mountain." (Daniel 11: 45).
12. Schmidt 1953: 30, 41; the translation "winter-palace" is by Herzfeld 1941: 232.
13. See, for example, Tajvidi 1976: 140, n.
14. The delegations shown on the staircases of other palaces are in contradiction to Greek stories mentioning that no one was allowed to carry a weapon in front of the king. See e.g. Collins 1974: 148.
15. This piece is kept in the Musée du Louvre.
16. The fragment is on display in the Louvre. See de Mecquenem 1947: fig. 27/2.
17. This relief was found in the Treasury Hall at Persepolis and is still *in situ*.
18. As I myself have witnessed, some Zoroastrian priests today still hang scarves around their necks. In some ceremonies the scarf is draped over one shoulder.
19. Although the headdress is similar to those worn by other people, they are not the same. Even today, the headdresses of some Muslim priests can be easily mistaken for local traditional headdresses. Such similarity in ancient times is mentioned by Strabo: "In summer they (the Iranians) wear a purple or vari-coloured cloak, in winter a

vari-coloured one only; *and their turbans are similar to those of the Magi* [my italics]; and they wear a deep double shoe" (Strabo, *Geography* 15.3.19–20, trans. Jones 1966, p. 183).
20. E.g. Pliny says the Magi accompanied Xerxes in Greece (Briant 2002*a*: 267).
21. In modern Persian this word no longer has its original meaning.
22. I owe this information to J. Gagoshidze and K. Khimshiashvili who kindly informed me about the term.
23. In a Persepolis Fortification Tablet, there is a reference to those who were looking after the royal tombs. They are called "garment-bearers" (Henkelman 2003*b*: 108). This could also be a vestment. Here the appearance of the textile together with incense-burners inside the palace door jambs seems to be significant.
24. Kent translates the word as "sanctuary". See Kent 1953: 169.
25. These finds are published in Schmidt 1957.
26. The relief, now in the National Museum of Iran, was damaged in the Achaemenid period during the move to the Treasury Hall.
27. For a discussion of this question see Shahbazi 2004: 163.

21

The Role of the Medes in the Architecture of the Achaemenids[1]

Michael Roaf

*Dedicated to the memory of Cuyler Young and
Ann Britt and Giuseppe Tilia*

It has long been accepted that some fundamental aspects of the architecture of Achaemenid Persia were borrowed from the Medes. In recent years, however, the evidence for the history of the Medes has been subjected to detailed re-examination and this has led some scholars to a radical reassessment of the nature of the Median state and its role in the formation of the Achaemenid Empire. It is, therefore, timely to reconsider whether the easy assumption that Achaemenid architecture owed much to the Medes can still be upheld. In this paper I review some of the similarities (as well as noting some of the differences) between the surviving remains of Median architecture at Tepe Nush-i Jan and at Godin Tepe and those of Achaemenid architecture. While it is most likely that these parallels are the result of Median influence on the Persians, the absence of architectural evidence for the immediately pre-Achaemenid period in Media, Persia and neighbouring regions means that other sources for these features cannot be excluded.

The extent of ancient Media is now the subject of controversy. The traditional view, based on statements given in Herodotus' *Histories*, is that by 550 BC the king of the Medes ruled an empire stretching from central Turkey to the Indus valley (see, for example, Diakonoff 1985 [=Lanfranchi, Roaf & Rollinger eds 2003: 399 fig. 1]; Kessler 1991; Roaf 1990: 203, slightly modified in Roaf 1995: 57, fig. 23). Since the veracity of Herodotus' account of Median history started to be seriously questioned in the 1980s (Helm 1981; Sancisi-Weerdenburg 1988, 1994; Young 1988, 1992), there has been an increasing number of scholars who have proposed that the extent of Median rule between the fall of Assyria and their defeat by Cyrus was much smaller than had hitherto been believed. This culminated in several contributions in the proceedings of a conference that took place in 2001, in which the very existence of a united Median kingdom was doubted (Lanfranchi, Roaf & Rollinger 2003; for further discussion see 2003: 397–406). According to this revisionist approach the Medes were nothing more than "bands of nomads", to repeat Heleen Sancisi-Weerdenburg's assessment (1988: 198), and the territory over which these tribes roamed in the sixth century was not much different from the territory settled by the Medes according to eighth-century Assyrian texts.[2]

If this extreme position, which is held by some very distinguished scholars, is correct, one might question whether the Medes could have exerted any influence over the Achaemenids in any respect and especially in architecture; but, as recently stressed by Shahrokh Razmjou (2005a), the Medes and Media are treated as one of the two most important peoples and regions after Persia in the inscriptions of Darius.[3] The primacy of the Medes is also evident in the Achaemenid reliefs, in which the Medes are shown directly after the Persians when Persians are illustrated, or in the first place in the absence of Persians (Roaf 1983: 130, fig. 131). Furthermore, in the so-called Susa Charter (DSf) Medes are explicitly mentioned among the craftsmen who contributed to the construction of Darius' palace in Susa. "The goldsmiths who wrought the gold, those were Medes and Egyptians [...] The men who adorned the wall, those were Medes and Egyptians."

It is, therefore, in my opinion, a worthwhile enterprise to attempt to assess possible Median influence on Achaemenid architecture, even though we are hampered by the lack of certainty in our knowledge of the location of ancient Media. For this reason I restrict my remarks to the excavated remains from two sites which are acknowledged by most scholars to have been situated in ancient Media and I will not take into account the evidence from other sites such as Baba Jan (Goff 1977) or Ozbaki (Majidzadeh 1999, 2000; see also the website on Ozbaki), which have, with some justification, been suggested as Median. The two sites that I will discuss are Tepe Nush-i Jan and Godin Tepe, both situated close to the later Median capital Hamadan and both occupied in the seventh century BC, and possibly earlier and later.[4] Tepe Nush-i Jan is a hilltop sanctuary excavated by David Stronach with four exceptionally well-preserved buildings constructed out of sun-dried mud bricks (Stronach & Roaf 2007). The Median building at Godin Tepe is situated on top of an ancient tell and was excavated by Cuyler Young (Young 1969; Young & Levine 1974). Here a single mud-brick building with several columned halls was extended in several phases.

The evidence for Achaemenid architecture comes from three main sites: Pasargadae founded by Cyrus and possibly completed under Darius (Stronach 1978), Susa built by Darius (Harper, Aruz & Tallon 1992), and Persepolis started by Darius and largely completed in the reigns of his son and grandson (Schmidt 1953; Roaf 1983: 150–59; 2004).[5] The buildings at these sites survive largely as the stone substructures of the walls. At Persepolis and at the neighbouring site of Naqsh-i Rustam (Schmidt 1970), the tomb façades give an impression of the elevation of an Achaemenid palace and the remarkable Ka'bah-i Zardusht at Naqsh-i Rustam (a later copy of the less well preserved Zendan-i Sulaiman in Pasargadae) still survives up to the roof.

When comparing these examples of Achaemenid architecture with Nush-i Jan and Godin Tepe we are not comparing like with like. Achaemenid architecture is imperial and monumental on an entirely different order to the surviving remains of Median architecture (Fig. 21.1). The surviving remains of Achaemenid architecture are for the most part stone while the Median buildings have walls of mud brick.

In my review of possible Median features in Achaemenid architecture I will follow the chronological development of the buildings at Tepe Nush-i Jan.[6] The first building constructed at Nush-i Jan was the isolated tower-like Central Temple, which was still standing to a height of some 7 m. The façade was buttressed and the mud-brick walls were

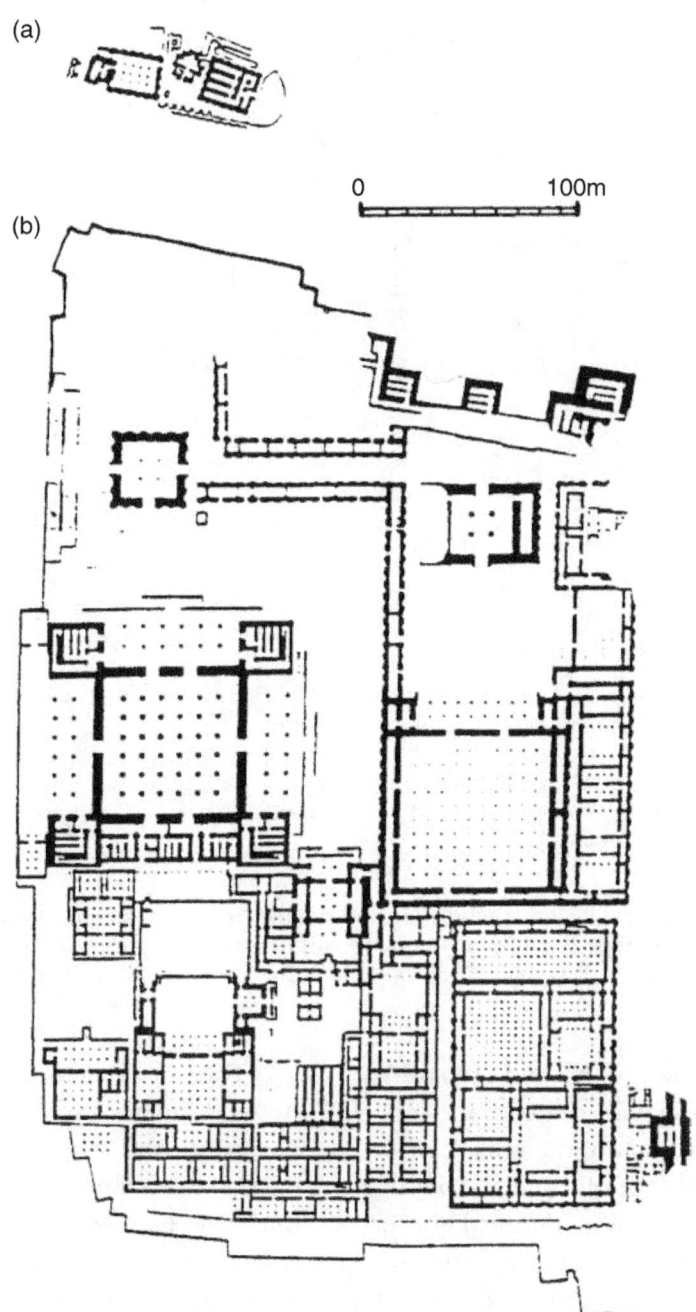

Fig. 21.1 Plans of the excavated buildings at Tepe Nush-i Jan (**a**) and on the citadel terrace at Persepolis (**b**). The plans are reproduced at the same scale and show the difference in conception between the modest Median hilltop sanctuary and the vast imperial Achaemenid project of which the citadel formed only a part. (After Stronach & Roaf 2007: fig. 1.11 on p. 57)

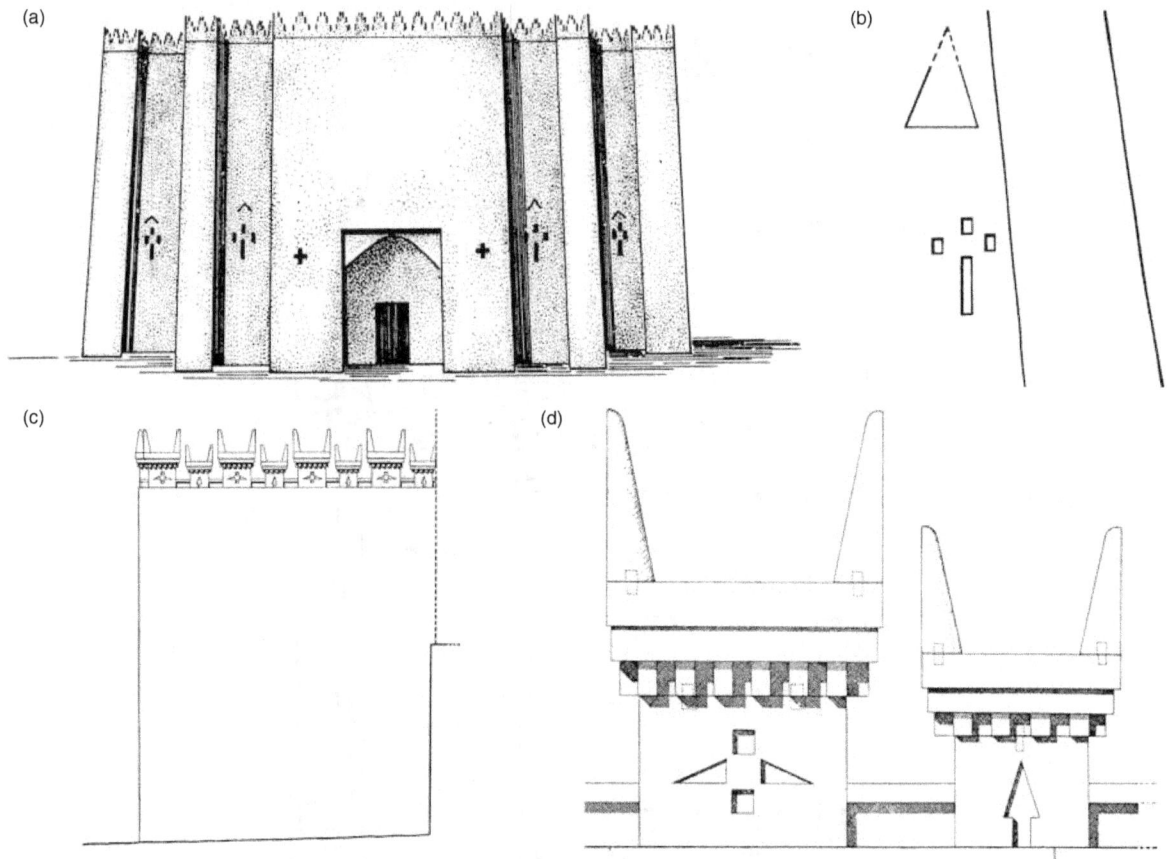

Fig. 21.2 Wall decorations. Reconstruction (**a**) and detail (**b**) of the wall decoration of the south façade of the Central Temple at Tepe Nush-i Jan compared with the reconstruction of the elevation (**c**) and detail (**d**) of the horned parapet at Persepolis. Not to scale. (After Stronach & Roaf 2007: fig. 2.5 on p. 72; Tilia 1969: figs 5–6)

decorated with triangular and cross-like designs (Fig. 21.2). These designs are reminiscent of the decoration of the horned parapet by Palace H at Persepolis (Tilia 1969: figs 5–6). They are definitely not identical but certainly seem to belong to the same tradition.

The central room of the Nush-i Jan temple also had wall decorations consisting of crosses and elaborate niches (Fig. 21.3). The niches are stepped and have rows of hanging dentils. Even more elaborate niches were found in the Columned Hall at Nush-i Jan. Somewhat similar dentils decorate the horned parapet at Persepolis.

These two elements, rows of dentils and stepped niches, are found on the Ka'bah-i Zardusht and the Zendan-i Sulaiman in Pasargadae. Since stepped niches are also found in Urartu, such wall decorations may have been more widely distributed than the surviving evidence suggests.

The mud-brick altar in the Nush-i Jan temple has a stepped top. The same shape is found in the fire altars shown on Achaemenid royal tombs and in actual examples in stone or mud brick.

An unexpected discovery at Nush-i Jan was the use of curved moulded mud struts

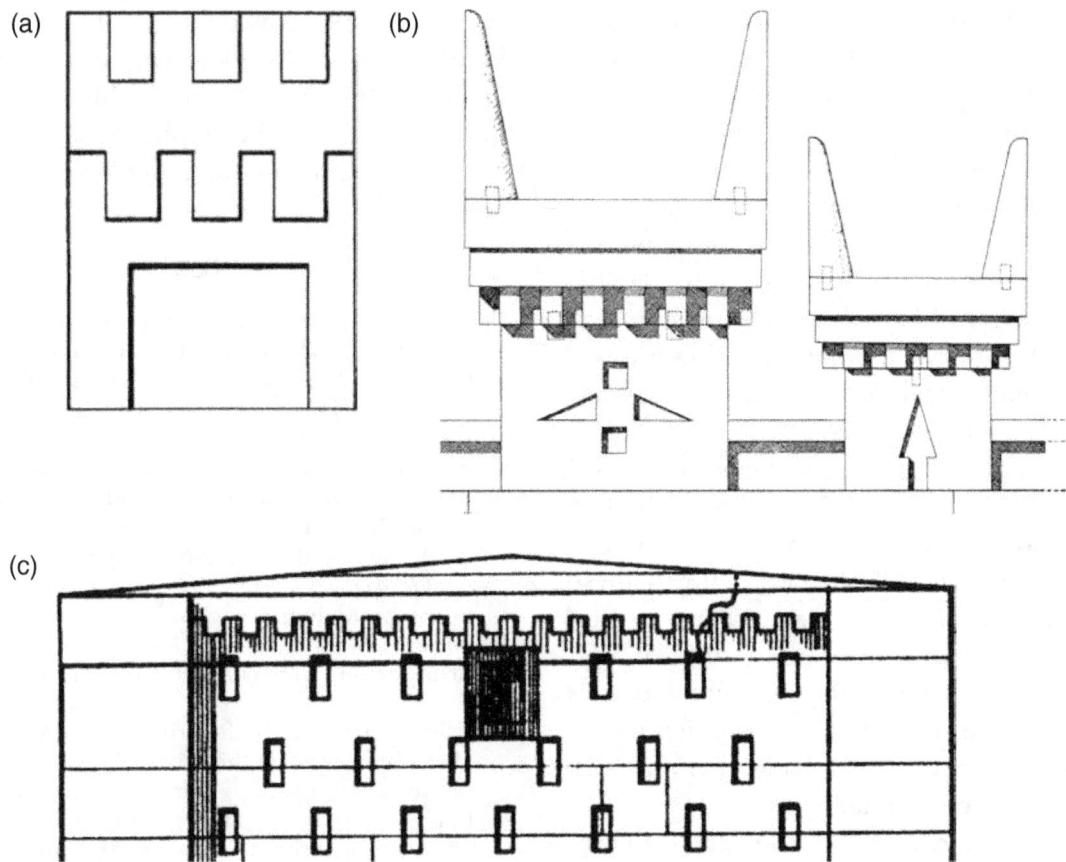

Fig. 21.3 Niches and dentils. Niche with dentils in the Central Temple at Tepe Nush-i Jan (**a**), dentils on the horned parapet at Persepolis (**b**), and niche and dentils on the Zendan-i Sulaiman at Pasargadae (**c**). Not to scale. (After Stronach & Roaf 2007: fig. 2.14 on p. 86; Tilia 1969; Stronach 1978)

to roof the anteroom of the temple. This method of roofing was used in other buildings at Nush-i Jan and at Godin Tepe. The same technique is also found at Persepolis in the fortification wall and the substructure of Palace D (Tajvidi 1976; personal observation). In the current state of our knowledge it is reasonable to suggest that mud vaulting struts were a Median invention that was adopted by the Persians.[7]

At Nush-i Jan a sequence of buildings was constructed. These included The Old Western Building, probably a second temple, the Fort consisting of a series of long magazines, and a columned hall. These buildings were built on platforms. At Persepolis too platforms were constructed for individual buildings.[8]

Another feature of the Fort at Nush-i Jan was the presence of arrow slots: the only complete example had a triangular top. Numerous arrow slots of this shape were found at Godin Tepe. Extensive use of arrow slots is found in Achaemenid architecture, both in the fortifications and also in the decoration of the buildings and other objects. We cannot, however, claim that the Achaemenids must have adopted the use of arrow slots from the Medes, as arrow slots were probably very widely distributed throughout the Near East: similar arrow slots were uncovered in the fortification walls at Ashur (Andrae 1913: fig. 186), which date to the seventh century BC or earlier and were thus contemporary with the Median buildings at Tepe Nush-i Jan and Godin Tepe.[9]

In a later phase at Nush-i Jan the buildings were surrounded by a wall with an arcade of arches and into the space between the two temples a Columned Hall was inserted. This Columned Hall had three rows of four columns. At Godin Tepe there were several columned halls including one with five rows of six columns.

Columned halls have been found on many other pre-Achaemenid sites in western Iran and Urartu: these have only two rows of columns.[10] The distinction between these halls and the Median ones with more than two rows of columns is an important one. And indeed the inspiration for the columned halls with multiple rows of columns, which are so typical of Achaemenid architecture may well be derived from Media.[11]

To conclude, despite the very different character of the known examples of Median and Achaemenid architecture, there are some striking similarities.[12] In particular, there are similarities in the way the walls were decorated with geometric shapes and stepped niches and dentils. And in this connection one may remember the statement in the Susa Charter that the Medes "adorned the wall". The stepped form of Achaemenid fire altars may also have been inspired by the Medes.

The most significant inheritance was probably the adoption of the columned hall with multiple rows of columns. One cannot, however, be certain that these features were not part of a wider tradition and the possibility that they were not adopted from some other tradition cannot be ruled out. It is particularly problematic that we have so little evidence for the period between the fall of Assyria and the rise of the Persians in Media, Persia, and neighbouring regions. If we knew more about architecture in Iran immediately before Media was incorporated into the empire of Cyrus, some of these uncertainties might be resolved.

Notes

1. The text presented here follows closely the talk given at the conference, with some alterations to take account of subsequent criticisms. References and illustrations are reduced to a minimum. As I stated at the meeting, much of the information in this paper is derived from discussions with David Stronach and will be found in the publication of the architecture of the major buildings of the Median settlement at Nush-i Jan (Stronach & Roaf 2007), which supersedes the accounts given in the preliminary reports. The majority of the possible borrowings from Media that appear in Achaemenid architecture were listed in Roaf 2003: 16.
2. In his contribution to the British Museum meeting Matt Waters rejected this minimalist view concerning the north-eastern extent of Median domination (Waters, this volume). Christopher Tuplin (2004b) has also proposed that Median domination extended into Anatolia.
3. It might appear that Media was listed in the tenth position in the list of countries in the Darius Bisutun inscription (DB) but in this case the countries other than Persia are divided into two geographical groups, the first headed by Elam contains the eight countries to the west and south, and the second headed by Media contains the 14 countries to the east and north; and so Media effectively follows Elam as it does in the early inscription at Persepolis (DPe). In other lists Media follows Persia. In non-Persian traditions, such as Egyptian, Greek, and Jewish, Medes are closely associated with Persians (for references see Tuplin (1994) although I do not find his interpretation entirely convincing).
4. For discussions of the dating see Stronach & Roaf 2007; Gopnik 2003; Curtis 2005a.
5. Additional architectural information comes from sites such as Borazjan (Dashtestan), Babylon (Haerinck 1997), and Dahan-i Ghulaman. Regrettably Ehsan Yaghmaee was unable to attend the conference at which he would have described the recent exciting discoveries made at Borazjan.

6. Further illustrations can be found in Stronach & Roaf 2007.
7. Mud vaulting struts have also been identified in pre-Achaemenid Tell Jemmeh in Israel (Van Beek 1983: 17–18; 1987: 78–85; 1993: 670–672). It may be that this technique was taken to Israel by Medes who had been deported by the Assyrians. Although various vaulting techniques are known in Assyrian buildings (Novak & Schmid 2001), these do not include the use of vaulting struts. Mud vaulting struts are more widely distributed in the Achaemenid period and later (for discussion see Huff 1990; Stronach & Roaf 2007: 190–191).
8. Assyrians also constructed buildings on platforms. In Assyria, however, several buildings were normally constructed on one platform. An exception is the Nabu Temple in Khorsabad, whose platform was connected to the citadel platform by a bridge (Loud & Altman 1938). A building on what looks like a platform made of ashlar stone blocks can be seen on a relief depicting Harhar in western Iran from Room 2 in the Palace of Sargon II (r. 721–705 BC) in Khorsabad.
9. In the northern fortification wall and in the fortification on the Shah Kuh, as decoration of the walls of the Treasury, at Persepolis, and on stone and glazed merlons from Susa (Curtis & Tallis 2005). They also decorate the incense burners and butts of spears at Persepolis.
10. The columns in these buildings were placed on flat stones and the lower parts were protected by plastered brick surrounds, which, after they were plastered have a bell-shaped profile reminiscent of the stone Achaemenid bell-shaped column bases.
11. For further discussion and the new discovery of early columned halls with multiple rows of columns in south-east Arabia see the contribution of Hilary Gopnik (this volume) which includes references to the relevant literature. The earliest Achaemenid halls have only two rows of columns: the first with multiple rows are Palace P at Pasargadae and Dasht-i Gohar near Persepolis (Tilia 1974, 1978: 73–80), which may have been built early in the reign of Darius or possibly in the reign of Cambyses. The Median form might not have been introduced until after the reign of Cyrus.
12. Most of these parallels are between Median buildings built in the seventh century BC and buildings dating to the reign of Darius or later. This may be an accident of discovery since very little architecture is preserved from the reigns of Cyrus and Cambyses.

22

Changes in Achaemenid Royal Dress

N. V. Sekunda

Introduction

The purpose of this paper is to suggest that the royal dress worn by the Achaemenid monarchs changed over time, which I have argued briefly elsewhere (Sekunda & Chew 1992: 3–4, 11, 12–13). The principal feature of the earliest known form of royal dress was the Elamite Royal Robe. At some point this form of dress was changed for another, such as we see represented in the Persepolis reliefs, whose principal feature was the "Achaemenid robe". At a later period this was exchanged for items of royal dress, which had originally been worn by the Median kings. The principal item in this final form of royal dress was a long-sleeved purple tunic with a central, vertical white stripe. These forms of royal dress did not evolve one from the other; they were rather the result of radical changes, presumably for political reasons of which we are not completely aware.

Royal dress of Median style

We know from a number of classical literary sources that the principal feature of Persian royal dress during the fifth and fourth centuries was a long-sleeved purple tunic with a white stripe down the centre. There are a whole host of references to this in a number of publications, and it is not the aim of this paper to gather all the evidence together once again.

The most detailed description of late Achaemenid royal dress comes in a passage of Curtius (3.3.17–19) describing the review of the army, which took place near Babylon before the battle of Issus. Curtius probably wrote during the age of Augustus, but he undoubtedly used a contemporary Greek source, ultimately based on an eyewitness account of the parade. This was probably the memoirs written by Patron the Phocian, a Greek mercenary general in Persian service. I have used the translation of John C. Rolfe in the Loeb series:

> The attire of the king was among all other things noteworthy for its luxury: it was a purple tunic with a white centre in it, a cloak of gold ornamented with golden hawks, which seemed to attack each other with their beaks; from a golden belt, with which he was girt woman-fashion, he had hung an *akinaka*, the scabbard of which was

a single gem. The Persians call the king's cap a *kidaris*; this was bound with a blue band with a white distinction.

The Greek lexicographers Hesychius and Photius (*s.v. sarapis*) tell us that the king's tunic with its white stripe down the centre was called the *sarapis*, while Pollux (7.58) informs us that the name for the common Persian sleeved tunic was *kapuris*. However, a fragment of Democritus of Ephesus preserved in Athenaeus (12.525d), describing the luxurious oriental dress of the Ephesians, mentions their *sarapeis* of quince-yellow, purple, white, and even sea-purple; so it is possible that *sarapis* was also used as a name for the Persian tunic in general.

Arrian (*Anabasis* 4.7.4, 6.29.3) confirms that the Persian hood, which he calls a *kitaris*, was not normally worn upright except by the king (6.29.3). The word tiara, which appears frequently in the sources given to the Persian hood, may be Greek in origin. Therefore, when writing in English, it is safest to call this garment a hood.

The description of the king wearing his tunic girt "woman-fashion" (*muliebriter*) may mean that the king, riding in his chariot, wore his tunic falling straight to the knees under his belt. This is in opposition to the common Greek style of wearing the tunic girt up, with the belt tied over an "overfold" bringing the tunic well above the knees to facilitate riding a horse.

Ancient Greek preserves the word *kandys* for the sleeved Median cloak, invariably worn draped over the shoulders with the sleeves hanging unoccupied, with the arms free underneath the cloak. This type of garment continued in use until modern times (Knauer 1978; Linders 1984). According to Widengren (*Arctica* (Uppsala) XI: 235, 237), the word is connected with the Renaissance Polish word *kontusz* given to the outer coat, and can be traced back to an original Iranian *kantuš*. Sir Harold Bailey suggested a derivation from the Iranian *kan* "to cover" with the suffix *tu*, and so giving *kan-tu* "covering" (Thompson 1965: 122, n. 13). The *kantuš* was worn as a cloak, tied at the neck, with the arms free under the cloak, and not inserted into the sleeves.

The description of Achaemenid royal dress preserved in Curtius is the most complete one that has come down to us in the classical literature. Other descriptions, although briefer, are entirely in agreement with that of Curtius. For example Xenophon (*Cyr.* 8.3.13) describes the Persian king as wearing an upright hood, a purple tunic with a white centre, scarlet *anaxyrides* (or trousers), and an all-purple *kantuš*.

Furthermore, the description of Persian royal dress given by the classical sources is supported by the classical representational evidence. The most detailed of these is the image of Darius III in the "Alexander Mosaic" from Pompeii (Fig. 22.1).

The only element of Achaemenid royal dress neither described in the sources, nor shown in the representations are the shoes. In his play *Persai* (660), Aeschylus has the ghost of Darius wearing crocus-yellow shoes, but we do not know if this is correct, as it cannot be checked against any representational evidence.

The *arštibara*

The king's person was protected by a bodyguard of 1000 "spearbearers", *doryphoroi* in Greek or *arštibara* in Old Persian. Somewhat earlier in the same passage describing the review of the army outside Babylon before the

Fig. 22.1 Darius III as shown in the Alexander Mosaic. (Photograph N. V. Sekunda)

Issos campaign (Curtius 3.3.15), in a section which is rather difficult to understand, we are told that after the "Kinsmen" marched "The *Doryphoroi*, as they call the formation next to these, who alone are allowed to wear the royal dress" (*Doryphoroe vocabantur proxim his agmen, soliti vestem excipere regalem*). Essentially this means that the "spearbearers" also wore the long-sleeved purple tunic with a central white stripe.

Below the chariot of Darius a Greek mercenary is shown running out of the way to escape being crushed by the wheels of the chariot. In front of him he holds his bronze-faced hoplite shield, knocking over all who find themselves in his way. In front of the hoplite shield a Persian is shown being knocked to the ground, perhaps symbolic of the fall of the empire. He puts up his arms against the hoplite shield and his face is shown reflected in its bronze surface. The Alexander Mosaic has survived better in some parts of its surface area than in others. The Mosaic had already been destroyed in some areas by root damage at the time of its discovery. After excavation it was further damaged in other places. Consequently areas of mosaic have become detached from their original locations and have been put back in the wrong place. In other places areas of damage have been inexpertly repaired. The figure of this Persian is one area where large sections of mosaic are no longer in their original place.

We can clearly see the purple tunic, although the place where the central white stripe would have been reflected in the

Fig. 22.2 Persian "spearbearer" shown in the Alexander Mosaic. The area of the mosaic below the black line has been incorrectly located and originally belonged elsewhere. (Photograph N. V. Sekunda)

bronze face of the shield is now filled with a piece of mosaic not in its original place, which features an animal shape. Clearly this Persian is a "spearbearer" (Fig. 22.2). The edge of the cuff of the tunic is decorated with a dog-tooth band of alternating triangles of purple and white. Round his head the young, clean-shaven Persian wears a hood of material that appears to be gold. Round his neck he wears a twisted metal torque. The clothing worn on the lower body of the "spearbearer" is not shown on this representation.

A "spearbearer" is also shown in a second, independent, representational source. This is the so-called Alexander Sarcophagus, which was used for the burial of King Abdalonymous of Sidon. Much of the original polychrome decoration of the sarcophagus has now disappeared, but it can be studied thanks to Winter's plates (1912). The "spearbearer" (Fig. 22.3) is shown in that work in plate 8. The purple of the tunic and its central white stripe are clearly shown. In this figure the colours of the trousers have also been preserved, yellow with a single line of scarlet diamonds in a thin band of colour preserved just below the tunic-hem. Traces of blue are also preserved on the shoes. If the dress of the "spearbearers" were an exact copy of the dress of the king, then this would contradict the information of Aeschylus that the king wore crocus-yellow shoes. There may, however, have been minor variations between the dress of the king and the "spearbearers", such as in the colours of the shoes. If the dress of the "spearbearers" replicated all the garments of the monarch exactly, we could restore the *anaxyrides*, or trousers, worn by

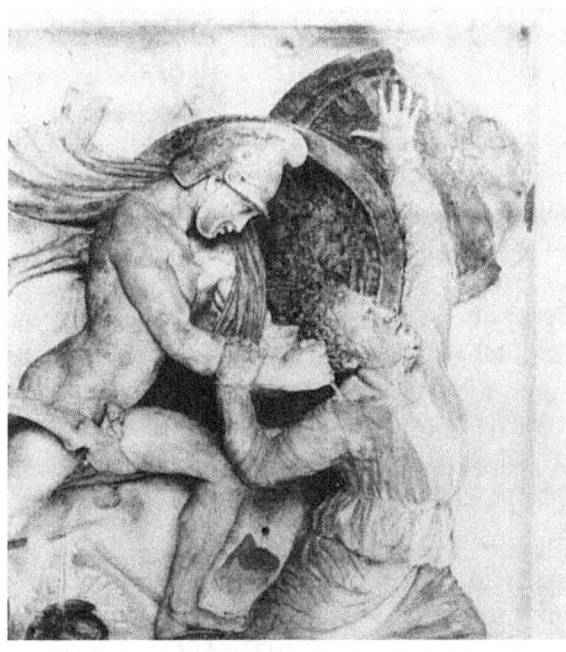

Fig. 22.3 Persian "spearbearer" shown on the Andalonymous Sarcophagus. (After Winter 1912: pl. 8)

the king as being of scarlet and yellow lozenges, rather than simply scarlet as described by Xenophon, and the boots as being blue.

The Book of Esther (8:15) mentions the Jew Mordechai leaving the presence of king Artaxerxes II, having found royal favour, in "royal dress" of violet and white, wearing a great golden crown and a cloak of fine linen and purple. This passage indicates that "royal dress" could be awarded as a gift by the king either to an individual or to the "spearbearers", it seems, en masse.

The adoption of Median dress

Herodotus (1.135; 7.62.1), writing at some time towards the end of the fifth century, tells us that the Persians had adopted Median dress instead of their own. This is confirmed by Xenophon (*Cyr.* 1.3.2) who adds that the Persians' purple tunics, their sleeved cloaks, and the bracelets about their wrists, were all Median in origin.

Elsewhere Xenophon (*Cyr.* 8.1.40) attributes the change to the reign of his semifictional hero Cyrus the Great. In another passage, Xenophon (*Cyr.* 8.3.1) tells us that before starting out on the first "Royal Procession" Cyrus summoned to himself those of the Persians and of the allies who held rank and distributed Median cloaks to them. This was the first time the Persians had worn the Median cloak.

We do not know how credible Xenophon's information is. Presumably Xenophon, like Herodotus, knew or had heard that the type of dress currently worn by the Persians had originally been Median, but I do not believe he had any genuine knowledge of when this change had taken place. This does not necessarily mean that Xenophon had himself "invented" Cyrus the Great as the person who had exchanged Persian dress for Median. If the change had taken place at the turn of the sixth and fifth centuries, then reliable knowledge of when the change had really taken place may have been lost in the intervening generations. The Persians themselves may have come to believe that Cyrus the Great introduced the change, either through the failure of collective memory, or as the result of a deliberate policy of sanctioning change by ascribing it to the most authoritative figure in Persian history.

Persians are not shown in the Greek representational evidence currently available to us before the first two decades of the fifth century, that is, from the first clashes of the Athenians with the Persians at Marathon (490) or the conflicts of Xerxes' invasion of Greece (480/479). Persians are exclusively shown in Median dress from the very beginning. The

260 THE WORLD OF ACHAEMENID PERSIA

Fig. 22.4. The ghost of Darius I as shown on an Attic vase in Tübingen.

earliest depiction in Greek representational evidence of a Persian king wearing Median royal dress known to me is on an Attic vase in the Institute of Archaeology of the University of Tübingen (E.67, *CVA* Germany 54, pl. 2645) painted about 440 (Fig. 22.4). It depicts a scene from Aeschylus' play *The Persians*, in which the ghost of King Darius is summoned back from the underworld. The purple tunic with a broad white stripe running vertically down the front is quite clear.

Royal dress as shown in the Persepolis reliefs

If we look at the earlier representational evidence from Persepolis, we get a completely different picture of Achaemenid royal dress. Although both soldiers and courtiers may be shown wearing what is recognizably Median dress, the king is never shown dressed in this way. He is always shown wearing what has come to be known, in our modern archaeological jargon, as the "Achaemenid robe". This is a capacious robe tightly gathered with a belt at the waist, with long but full sleeves, and falling down to the ankles, not to the knees. On his head the king never wears a Median hood, but rather a crown, which may take a number of forms (cf. von Gall 1974). He never wears a cloak of any form. The Persian monarch can appear similarly dressed in representations on Achaemenid sealstones, jewellery, and other forms of Achaemenid art, not exclusively on Persepolitan relief sculpture.

The colours of the "Achaemenid robe" worn by the king can be established, at least in outline, thanks to a number of sources. Traces of polychrome decoration have survived in a number of examples of Persepolitan sculpture. Sufficient polychrome detail has survived to enable us to restore the colours of the robe worn by the crowned and bearded male figure within the "winged disc" symbol that appears in a number of places at the palace.

The "winged disc" symbol appears in two forms, either simply as a winged disc, or as a winged disc with a human figure shown within the disc. It used to be thought that the symbol represented the Iranian supreme deity Ahuramazda. Shapur Shahbazi (1974; 1980) and then Peter Calmeyer (1979) have both suggested that the winged disc without any human figure represents the "Fortune" or *khvarnah* of the Iranians, while the disc with the human figure represents the "Fortune" of the monarch. Their arguments are most convincing. Later Jamzadeh (1982) identified the symbol with royal glory (see also Kaim 1991). In either case it follows that the human figure shown in the winged disc, representing the "Fortune" of the king or his "glory", wears the robes of the king. Consequently it is possible to use this representation as a basis to restore the royal "Achaemenid robe" in colour.

A watercolour sketch of an example of the human figure within the winged disc symbol from the "Hall of a Hundred Columns" was made by Ernst Herzfeld. Although this sketch was only published in monochrome, the original sketch is preserved in the Herzfeld Archives of the Freer Gallery of Art, Washington, DC. Here I repeat the description of the sketch made by Judith A. Lerner (1971: 23–24). The crown of the figure was gold, while the robe was red decorated at the hemline with a border of red lions on a blue background. The sleeve of the robe had a border decorated with identical figures, although all traces of colour have gone. The rest of the surface is covered with round incised designs, which probably represent appliqués.

Lerner (1973) compared the colours of this watercolour to those preserved on a fragmentary relief showing the human figure within the winged disc in the possession of the Fogg Art Museum, Cambridge, Massachusetts. This relief had originally come from one of the door-jambs of the southern wall of the "Hall of a Hundred Columns", whence it had been removed between 1840 and 1878 (Lerner 1971: 20). It entered the Museum collection as part of the Grenville L. Winthrop Bequest, and was cleaned in 1965 prior to its permanent exhibition. Lerner (1971: 24) observed that there were differences in detail between the colours used in the watercolour and on the relief, although the polychrome preserved on the robe of the human figure was predominantly red, with details in blue. This conforms to the general outline of polychrome preserved in the Herzfeld sketch and, given that Herzfeld's sketch may have been somewhat simplified, it is possible to reconcile the two sources.

Further source material became available when Ann Britt Tilia published her observations on the preserved polychrome at Persepolis. Polychrome traces were observed on the clothing of the figure within the "winged disc" symbol on the western jamb of the northern doorway in the Council Hall at Persepolis, and a tentative reconstruction (Tilia 1978: pl. B) of the figure was offered. The robe is red with blue hems decorated with red lions. Both sides of the borders are edged with a band of material decorated with a dog-tooth design, consisting of white triangles at the top and alternating red and white triangles at the bottom. The robe is decorated with round appliqués of white and blue, differing in detail between the uppermost part of the tunic and the middle one. Furthermore, "It has been possible to establish that the royal costume was decorated in the same manner as that worn by the figure in the winged ring above the throne scene. On the eastern jamb of the western doorway traces of red pigment remain on the robe of the king" (Tilia 1978: 44).

Tilia had made use of Lerner's work for the reconstruction of the upper portions of the "Achaemenid robe" worn by the figure in the winged disc. She also made use of a further watercolour by Herzfeld (Tilia 1978: 56), which was only published somewhat later by Calmeyer (1989: pl. 1). This watercolour records the colours that were once preserved on the lower part of a relief on the eastern jamb of the northern doorway of the Council Hall, which had been buried before excavation, thus preserving the polychrome decoration. The lower part of the robe is also red, although not decorated with appliqués, with a double border running down the centre of the front of the robe, and a single border at the bottom of the robe. As was the case with the upper portions of the Royal Robe, these lower borders are likewise coloured blue and are decorated with red lions. Both sides of the border are edged with a band of material decorated with a dog-tooth design, of white triangles at the top and alternating red and white triangles at the bottom. Herzfeld showed the king's shoes as blue, but some difficulty exists with this detail of the watercolour, for during her examination of the extant sculpture, Tilia (1978: 56) found clear traces of red, where Herzfeld had painted blue. If Herzfeld is to be believed it could be that the blue, now disappeared, had been painted on top of the red. Red is often used as a base colour in ancient painting. It seems likelier, however, that the blue shoes are a mistake. Whether blue or red, the boots are not the crocus colour as recorded by Aeschylus for the period when the Achaemenid monarch wore Median dress.

The only major element of information that is missing now for a plausible restoration of the dress of the king at the time, are the details of the appliqués applied to the upper portions of the robe. I have elsewhere attempted a reconstruction of the overall appearance of the appearance of the king as recorded at Persepolis (Sekunda & Chew 1992: pl. A1). I used the detailed view of the costume worn by the figure of King Xerxes I (Fig. 22.5) in the main hall of the Harem building, northern doorway, western jamb, as observed by Tilia (1978: 54, fig. 6), as well as her colour reconstruction. Two sets of roundels decorate the king's tunic. Those on the upper sleeve represent a circle filled with a cross consisting of four lotus-flowers, alternating with four lotus-buds, all around a central boss. Those on the rest of the tunic show a tree of life sitting upon a crescent (moon?) within a border of lotus-blossoms. Lerner's work being unavailable to

Fig. 22.5 The costume worn by the figure of King Xerxes I in the main hall of the Harem building. (After Tilia 1978: 54, fig. 6)

me at the time, I suggested that the roundels might have been white against a blue background, as shown in Tilia's reconstruction. I now incline to the belief that it is more likely that the appliqués would have been gold discs sewn onto the robe.

"Court Style" and "Vernacular Style"

We now see that the dress worn by the king as depicted in the Persepolis reliefs has no connection whatsoever with the Greek literary or representational evidence, which is *only* relevant to the fifth and fourth centuries, after the change to Median dress. It follows that we should never refer to the Greek literary evidence when we discuss the dress of the king, or for that matter Persian dress in general, as shown on the Persepolis reliefs.

The type of dress and equipment shown on the Persepolis reliefs, and on the brick reliefs from the Achaemenid palaces of Susa and Babylon, are only valid for the last decades of the sixth century. During this period a canon of representational art was developed, which may be called Achaemenid "Court Style", which then survived unchanged until the last days of the empire.

Thus the façade of the Royal Tomb built by Artaxerxes III shows "spearbearers" dressed and armed in a manner identical to that of the "spearbearers" of Darius I (Fig. 22.6). Indeed, traces of blue paint have been found on the shoulder of the tunic and on the cap of one of these figures, as has been recorded (Tilia 1978: 43, fig. 2c). This could be the remains of a blue hem on the arm of the "Achaemenid robe", and could, in turn, serve as evidence that during the earlier period—as later—the "spearbearers" wore the same dress as the king.

This does not represent contemporary reality, nor does any other figurative art executed in "Court Style" during the fifth and fourth centuries. The change to Median dress had taken place a long time before this figure was carved. Alongside this "Court Style" is another style of representational evidence which seems to reflect contemporary reality, generally—but misleadingly—called "Greco-Persian" art, but which would more aptly be termed "Vernacular Style".

The reason for the change from the "Achaemenid robe" to the Median trousers and tunic is not known. Apart from any aesthetic consideration, riding must have been extremely difficult when wearing the traditional "Achaemenid robe", which the Median tunic and trousers made easier. Changes in

Fig. 22.6 Figure of a "spearbearer" from the façade of the tomb of Artaxerxes III. (After Tilia 1978: 43, fig. 2c)

royal dress are, however, rarely made for practical considerations.

Cyrus and Cambyses in Babylon

The so-called "Nabonidus Chronicle", a cuneiform document dealing with the history of Babylonia, records an investiture ceremony of Cambyses in Babylon. It is possible to maintain that the investiture ceremony was an annual event, but I follow the interpretation of the investiture ceremony as having taken place once only for each ruler. In this case it will have taken place on 15th March 538 BC, following the capture of Babylon by Cyrus in 539, and inaugurating the period of co-regency of Cyrus and Cambyses in Babylon.

> When on the 4th day (of Nisannu) Cambyses, the son of Cyrus, went to E-ningidar-kalamma-summu, the official of the Sceptre House of Nabû (or of the *šangû*-priest of Nabû?) [*gave him*] the Sceptre of the [Land]. When [*Cyrus*] came, in Elamite attire he [took] the hands of Nabû [...] lances and quivers *he picked* [*up, and*] with the crown-prince [he *came down*] into the courtyard. He (*or possibly* they) went back [*from the temple*] of Nabû to E-sagil. [He/they libated] all before Bēl and the Son of [...].

I am most indebted to Andrew George, whose collation of the tablet and translation I have given above. The Nabonidus Chronicle is fragmentary at this point, and previous interpretations of the ceremony have been flawed by misleading readings of the text. George (1996: 380) comments on the passage as follows:

> The detail that was most noteworthy for the chronicler was evidently the fact that someone involved in the ceremony wore Elamite clothing. The identity of this person is lost at the end of l.25. Previous commentators have assumed it was Cambyses, but the way the text is formulated makes this improbable. The narrative seems to imply that this person joined the ceremony after Cambyses had been presented with the sceptre, but then played the leading part: as I read it, he took the hand of Nabû and led him in procession—presumably from his cella in E-ningi-dar-kalamma-summa—to the temple's courtyard, with the crown-prince, Cambyses, in attendance. Probably Elamite clothing means Persian dress; either way, it is hard to see who else but Cyrus himself would have accompanied Nabû and Cambyses in this ritual and been permitted to dress for it in such a manner.

For the purpose of this paper, it is not important whether it was King Cyrus who was wearing Elamite dress, as seems more probable, or the Crown prince, Cambyses. It seems most unlikely, however, that Persian dress, which I would understand to mean the "Achaemenid robe", would be described as Elamite. I therefore propose that the "Achaemenid robe" was only adopted as Achaemenid royal dress at some date subsequent to 538, and prior to that date Achaemenid royalty had worn the Elamite Royal Robe.

The Elamite Royal Robe

The Elamite Royal Robe was a long garment, reaching to the ankle, open at the right side, where it was decorated with a border of rosettes and a long fringe. In general the robe is not dissimilar to a garment of a similar shape worn not only by Elamites but also by other Ancient Near Eastern peoples. As an example we might cite the cloaks worn by the Assyrian general and the Elamite women in an Assyrian relief (Madhloom 1970: pls XXXVIIIb, LII, 2). It does seem to be distinguished, however, by the specifics of its decoration, and also by the contexts where it is worn. The most significant feature is the band of rosettes behind the fringed hem of the garment. A number of representations of the Elamite king wearing the Elamite Royal Robe have been preserved.

To take the penultimate example first, in an Assyrian relief depicting the death of Tempt-Humban-Inshushinak (Teuman) in the battle fought on the Ulai River in 653 (Fig. 22.7), the Elamite king is wearing a long robe open at the right side and decorated with a border of rosettes and a long fringe. It should be noted that only the king wears this robe, and no other Elamite shown on the relief does. It is therefore worn to distinguish the king from his subjects: it is the "Elamite Royal Robe". On his head the Elamite king wears a bonnet held in place with a band tied around the forehead, with the ends hanging free behind the neck.

On a stele that the next and last but one king of Elam, Atta-hamiti-Inshushinak (653–648 BC), set up to himself, the king is also shown wearing a robe with this distinctive decoration (Hinz 1972: 157, pl. 32). Only the upper part of the torso is preserved, but it is covered in a robe crossing the shoulders and ending in a fringe, and then in a series of highly decorated borders, the last one of which is rather narrow and is divided into boxes decorated with small rosettes in the middle. The round bonnet the king wears on his head has a peak projecting above the eyes. Then comes a wide band, decorated with rosettes, securing the bonnet in place. The band seems to be tied at the back, the loose ends falling over the hair hanging behind the neck (see Calmeyer 1976: 57–58).

Of particular interest to us studying the dress of the Achaemenid kings, is a further example of sculpture, demonstrating that the wearing of the Elamite Royal Robe was not confined to the ruler of the principal Elamite kingdom, but was adopted by subordinate kings too.

Fig. 22.7 The Elamite king Tempt-Humban-Inshushinak (Teumman) shown at the battle of the Ulai River in 653, in an Assyrian relief now in the British Museum. (Photograph N. V. Sekunda)

Fig. 22.8 Relief of the Elamite Hanne at Kūl-i Farah. (After Perrot & Chipiez 1890: fig. 473)

During the reign of Shutruk-nahhunte II (717–699 BC), a vassal of the Elamite king named Hanne built up a small kingdom in the eastern mountain province of Ayapir. His court appears to have been closely modelled on that at Susa. The plain of Mālamīr lies 150 km to the north-east of Susa, and contains four groups of rock-reliefs, one being located at Kūl-i Farah. A relief carved in this gorge (Vanden Berghe 1959: 61, pl. 90b; 1963: 25–28 (with earlier bibliography) pl. x–xi), about 1 m high and 1.70 m wide, shows the prince performing a sacrifice to the god Tirutir. A 24-line inscription carved over the relief clarifies the action depicted (Fig. 22.8).

The ruler is facing right with his arms crossed over his belt in prayer. On his head, although damaged, he clearly wears a hat over his hair, tied around the head at the bottom with a band. Behind him stand two other figures, one above the other. Above stands his minister Shutruru dressed in a tunic with a wide belt reaching to the knee. He carries a quiver on his back and holds a bow out before him in his left hand. Beneath stands Shutrurura (?) the cup-bearer of the royal court, wearing a complex robe reaching down to the ankles, seemingly consisting of a number of pleated horizontal layers separated by bands. His arms are crossed across his chest in the same gesture as the monarch. In front of the king are two further carved groups. Above are shown three musicians, wearing simpler plain robes reaching the ankle and secured at the waist by a belt. The musicians all carry musical instruments, probably different types of harp. The lower carving shows a sacrifice. A priest in a short tunic stands in front of a small altar. In front of him three men bring forward an ox to be sacrificed. Above him are shown the decapitated bodies and heads of three rams, while another man brings forward a horned goat to be sacrificed.

The king is distinguished from all the other figures by his dress. He wears a cloak crossed over at the shoulders and falling in two layers, one layer falling to the hip, and the other to the ankle. Under the upper layer of the cloak he wears a sort of fringed apron, worn over the lower layer of the cloak. The upper layer of the cloak is secured at the waist by a belt. All edges of the cloak finish in a border consisting of square boxes containing rosettes, and a fringe of tongues of material. According to Hinz (1972: 143) this cloak is "a sartorial invention, it appears, of the Elamites". Once again in this relief, only Prince Hanne wears this robe and it clearly marks him out from all other figures as wearing the Elamite Royal Robe.

A second relief from Mālamīr, also published by Vanden Berghe (1963: 33–34, no. 5), shows a male figure standing and facing right with his hands held out in front of him in a gesture of adoration. On his head he wears a round bonnet secured by a headband. Perhaps the ends of the headband can be observed to the rear of his hair. He wears a long robe reaching to the ankles and secured at the waist by a belt. At the shoulder and down the length of the robe are what appear to be rows of fringes, although it has to be admitted that this relief is much eroded. The relief does not have an inscription so the personage involved cannot be identified. If we presume him to be royal, however, we may have a further example of the Elamite Royal Robe being worn.

The Elamite Royal Robe may have been used in the second millennium BC. A haematite cylinder seal from the Old Elamite II period (Amiet 1980: 137, pl. V, no. 7) shows three figures. At the right stands a male warrior god with his right foot symbolically placed on a mountain and a sceptre in his right hand. In front of him stands a bareheaded male figure, wearing a robe reaching down to the ankle with a long fringe at the bottom and down the folded side of the tunic. Behind him stands, according to the publisher, the goddess Lama, wearing a crown and a robe consisting of horizontal layers of pleated material, with her hands held before her in a gesture of adoration. The figure in the centre could be a king wearing the Elamite Royal Robe. Admittedly the rosettes are not shown on the border but this could be explained by the small scale of the piece. This interpretation must, however, remain uncertain. Fortunately it is not crucial to our argument to know whether the Elamite Royal Robe was worn before the first millennium or not.

We can certainly say, on the basis of the representational evidence listed above that, in the seventh century BC the distinguishing feature of the Elamite Royal Robe was not its shape, or even its fringe, but rather the border of rosettes. The Elamite Royal Robe was worn not only by the king of Elam, but also by the rulers of Elam's satellite states.

At the beginning of the seventh century BC the Elamite state was, in fact, a federation of states of which Anshan was a member. King Kutir-Nahhunte II (693–692 BC) was the last known Elamite ruler to use the title "Great King of Anshan and Susa", which suggests that control of Anshan was lost at about this time. Texts relating to the destruction of Elam by Ashurbanipal in c.646 BC mention a king of Parsuwash named Kurash. This individual can perhaps be identified with Cyrus I, the grandfather of Cyrus the Great. The great-grandfather of Cyrus the Great, Teispes, seems to have been the first Achaemenid king to have used the title "King of Anshan", and it was presumably under his reign that Anshan first came under independent Achaemenid rule (Hansman 1985: 31–34). It would, indeed, be perfectly reasonable to assume that Teispes and his successors modelled their courts along the lines of other Elamite courts, including the one at Susa. If so it is only natural to assume that, like Hanne in the relief from Kūl-i Farah, he wore the Elamite Royal Robe as part of his insignia.

Bearing all these factors in mind, it seems that the first Achaemenid kings, down to at least 538, wore the Elamite Royal Robe. In this context we shall turn to the winged figure carved on Gate R at Pasargadae.

Fig. 22.9 The winged figure from Pasargadae Gate R. (After Stronach 1978: fig. 25)

268 THE WORLD OF ACHAEMENID PERSIA

Fig. 22.10 The Ker Porter engraving of the Winged Figure from Pasargadae Gate R.

The winged figure from Pasargadae, Gate R

The relief has been heavily damaged, and the details are difficult to see, so I have chosen to show here the drawing of the winged figure as published by David Stronach (1978: fig. 25) (Fig. 22.9).

A great amount of discussion has surrounded this figure, and it is not the purpose of this article to review all the differing interpretations. For a fuller description of the object itself and for a review of the different interpretations the reader is referred to the definitive work of Stronach (1978: 47–55). Three possible ways of interpreting the figure seem to exist. It might be a god, it might be a king, and therefore Cyrus himself, or it might be something in between. I shall confine myself to making the following points:

(1) The figure wears the Elamite Royal Robe. This was first noted by Dieulafoy (1893: 49 ff) and has subsequently been accepted by most commentators on the relief. This would seem to give the relief some royal significance. If it is a god then it is presumably a king of the gods, if it is a mortal then it is presumably a king, and if it is something "in between" it is something royal which is "in between".

(2) If the figure represents a mortal, then it should represent Cyrus himself. Such an interpretation seems to be ruled out by the fact that the figure is winged, which can hardly be a mortal attribute.

An inscription is known to have once stood above the winged figure in Gate R and is recorded in early drawings of the relief, for example in the Ker Porter engraving reproduced here (Fig. 22.10). It runs "I, Cyrus the King, an Achaemenid". Below the two lines of Old Persian (at the top) the inscription is repeated in one line of Elamite and then in one line of Babylonian. It was once held that the figure must represent Cyrus because he is labelled with this inscription. It has since been pointed out, however, that the inscription is not unique, either to this doorway or to this particular figure. Two other examples of the same inscription still survive engraved on stone antae at Pasargadae, and two further examples of this same inscription (CMa in Kent's categorization) are known to have once flanked the south-west portico of Palace S. These inscriptions are now known to have been retrospectively inscribed by Darius at a later date (Stronach 1990). They did not label anything. As far as one can tell they were inscribed on undecorated architectural members and are to be considered "building inscriptions" in the tradition of Mesopotamian building inscriptions of this type. Thus, although the inscription is in the first person, the inscription is to be understood as meaning "I, Cyrus the King, an Achaemenid (built this)". They can be compared to the trilingual inscription DSc, which runs "I, Darius the Great King, King of Kings, King of countries, son of Hystaspes, an Achaemenid" and is preserved in two examples each written on the base of a column. Consequently the inscription cannot be used to support the argument that the winged figure is a portrait of Cyrus himself.

(3) The figure wears what I believe may possibly be a helmet, rather than a cap, surmounted by a crown. This crown is referred to as a triple *'atef*-crown or a *hmhm*-crown, ultimately of Egyptian derivation but also widely known in North Syrian or Phoenician iconography. Stronach (1978: 50) describes it as follows:

Resting on the long twisted horns of the Abyssinian ram (*Ovis longipes palaeo-egyptiacus*), between two opposed uraei each of which supports a small sun disc, the main part of the headdress consists of three bunches of reeds, each surmounted by a solar disc and each set against a background of ostrich feathers. Three solar discs with concentric circles mark the bottom of the reed bundles…

Given the date of the relief, it would be reasonable to suppose that the crown has passed into Achaemenid iconography via the agency of North Syrian or Phoenician art, or rather court practice, rather than directly from Egypt. This has been the general assumption of most scholars who have dealt with the relief. Furthermore, Stronach (1978: 52) has noted the free association of crowns of this type with four-winged figures, which is a feature of Syro-Phoenician art. Barnett (1969: 416–19) had previously demonstrated that crowns of this type are found associated with a number of divinities in Syro-Phoenician art.

Barnett believed the relief represented the Phoenician god Ba'al-Aliyan entering the building to bless it or blessing those who enter it. In support of this view he suggested that after the conquest of Babylon and the west in 539 the local princes might have sought to flatter Cyrus by equating him with one of their local gods. However, as has been pointed out by Stronach (1978: 54), "a cursory comparison reveals striking differences in dress, coiffure, pose and physiognomy"; "Is it possible, however, to honour a god by representing him in a costume other than his own or by asking him to perform duties that have no connection with his role?"

The eclectic features of the figure need to be stressed. The other "apotropaic" reliefs found decorating the gateways at Pasargadae are directly borrowed from Assyrian art (cf. Kawami 1972). Although "the ultimate Assyrian ancestry of the four-winged genius is equally clear" (Stronach 1978: 51) there are differences in pose, dress, and coiffure from its Assyrian prototypes (cf. Stronach 1997: 43). The robe is Elamite and the crown is Syro-Phoenician. It represents the very beginning of known Achaemenid relief art, at the very point when it arises out of elements drawn from different cultural circles. Logically, if the figure does represent a god, then it should represent an Iranian god for whom a completely new attempt is being made to create a fresh representational identity. Given the kingly attributes of the Elamite robe, the figure could represent the chief god and thus Ahuramazda. This might not be completely impossible in theory, for we know little about the religion of the early Achaemenids, but it does seem most unlikely given their later practices with regard to depicting (or more possibly not depicting) this deity. I think, therefore, that we should reject the proposal that the figure represents a god.

In support of his argument Barnett noted a passage in Ezekiel (28:2) where the prince of Tyre says "I am a god; I sit throned like a god on the high seas" which implies that the king of Tyre associated himself to some degree with a local god. Barnett's argument is not quite clear at this point, but he seems to be saying that the winged figure from Pasargadae Gate R wears the crown of the god Ba'al because the Syro-Phoenician princes equated Cyrus with that deity. However, we could turn this argument on its head.

If a number of the Syro-Phoenician princes claimed divine attributes, it is possible, even probable, that they wore the appropriate divine crown as part of their royal regalia. Thus the Syro-Phoenician version of the Egyptian *hmhm*-crown may have been worn by a number of local rulers as well as their gods, and like the Elamite Royal Robe, it is possible that the *hmhm*-crown may be not so much a symbol of divinity as a symbol of kingship. It is therefore possible that the crown was adopted by Cyrus in 539 as a crown of kingship, following the submission of the kings of Syria and surrounding regions.

(4) The figure has four wings. As has already been noted, this feature would seem to give the figure a status other than human. Herzfeld, supported by Stronach (1978: 54), thought the figure a representation of a "genius" rather than a personality. The stance, to be sure, is borrowed from Mesopotamian art, but the symbolic meaning of the iconography is not. We should avoid a too Mesopotamo-centric approach, and should interpret the winged figure from what we know of Iranian belief systems. As Shahbazi (1974: 141) noted in a similar context "It can be shown that [...] similar representations could have different connotations for different people".

A more plausible approach, in my opinion, would be to interpret the winged figure from Pasargadae Gate R as an early form of the king's *khvarnah*, or "Fortune". In later Persepolitan art, when the Achaemenid "Court Style" had more fully emerged, the figure of the spirit appears within a winged disc. Here, because the disc has not yet appeared in the symbolism, the wings are attached to the spirit itself. Thus the wings suggest that it is the king's *khvarnah* that is depicted, and not the king himself. In the later depictions of the king's *khvarnah* at Persepolis the figure of the spirit wears the Royal "Achaemenid robe". Here, at Pasargadae, the king's *khvarnah* wears the Elamite Royal Robe, which was, as I have suggested above, worn at this period by the Achaemenid king himself.

Therefore I would argue that down to 538, the Achaemenid kings wore the Elamite Royal Robe as part of their royal dress. This was replaced by the "Achaemenid robe" as royal dress at some point after 538, but before work started on the Persepolis reliefs.

The human figures surviving from the reliefs of Palace P at Pasargadae are dressed in the "Achaemenid robe". A trilingual inscription "Cyrus, the great king, an Achaemenian" has been carved on the folds of the skirt of one of these figures, on the right-hand jamb of the north-west doorway of Palace P at Pasargadae. If this can be regarded as a label (Stronach 1978: 95) rather than a building inscription, it follows that the change in dress came between the completion of Gate R and the start of work on Palace P. It was once thought that Palace P was constructed during the reign of Cyrus, but Stronach (1978: 100) has demonstrated that Palace P was built during the reign of Darius, possibly during the last decade of the sixth century. It follows that Cyrus is shown anachronistically dressed in the "Achaemenid robe" in these reliefs, some time after the change from the Elamite Royal Robe had taken place.

It would, therefore, be tempting to attribute this change to Darius I. Recent work (Stronach 1997; Potts 2005b) has stressed the Elamite, or rather non-Iranian character of the Achaemenid state under Cyrus and Cambyses. Although Darius aimed to legitimize his assumption of the throne by claiming, possibly falsely, common descent with Cyrus the Great, he was also keen to emphasize the Iranian nature of his rule. He "recast a number of powerful visual symbols in order to express a new, more separate 'Persian identity' in the character of Achaemenid kingship" (Stronach 1990: 199). It is quite possible that the "Achaemenid robe" was worn as Persian traditional dress at the time, and this may have been why it was adopted as the new form of Achaemenid royal dress.

Further references to Achaemenid royal dress

There are a further two passages relevant to Achaemenid royal dress known to me in the Greek sources which should be mentioned.

Firstly, Arrian (*Anabasis* 6.29.6) tells us that Cyrus' body lay in a golden sarcophagus. Placed on it was a *kantuš*, and beside tunics of Babylonian workmanship, were Median *anaxyrides* (trousers) and "hyacinth-dyed" (i.e. a shade of dark blue) garments together with some of purple and other colours, and neck-torques, *akinanka* (daggers), and earrings of gold set with jewels. The items of clothing mentioned in this passage could be gifts from different regions of the empire, rather that the garments worn by the king: surely too many to be worn together at any one time. Otherwise one would have to accept that Cyrus wore at least one version of royal dress, which was Median. Another possibility is that the garments may have been placed in the grave of Cyrus by a later ruler, at some time well after the king's death.

Secondly, Plutarch tells us in his *Vit. Artax.* 3.2 that, on the death of a monarch the new king would travel back to the ancient capital of Pasargadae to receive his initiation from the royal priests. There he would enter the sanctuary of the "goddess of war", take off his clothing, and put on the clothes Cyrus the Great wore before becoming king. He would eat fig-cake and pistachios and drink a cup of sour milk. Then further secret mysteries would be performed before his investiture was complete. This passage seems to refer to the clothes Cyrus wore as a commoner, and not to some other form of royal dress worn before the Elamite Royal Robe was adopted.

Conclusion

The main purpose of this paper has been to show that there was at least one fundamental change in Achaemenid royal dress. At some point around the turn of the sixth and fifth centuries the Achaemenid robe was replaced by Median royal dress. The unanimity of the Greek literary and representational sources, and our complete inability to reconcile them with the Persepolitan reliefs, seems to rule out any other interpretation.

A secondary goal has been to gather the evidence suggesting that earlier in the sixth century the Achaemenid monarch may have worn an earlier form of royal dress, which included the Elamite royal robe. The evidence for this is less convincing. It is based on one representation and one fragmentary text. The robe worn by the winged figure from Pasargadae Gate R is very close to that worn by the Elamite king Tempt-Humban-Inshushinak (Teuman) on Assyrian reliefs. On the other hand, there are significant differences between the robe worn by these two figures and those worn by other Elamite monarchs. Furthermore, other figures, not necessarily royal and not necessarily Elamite, wear fringed robes very close to the type we call "The Elamite Royal Robe". Further work on the representational evidence is necessary. Nevertheless, as things stands at the moment, the argument advanced above seems to reconcile the evidence best.

Part 5

Archaeology

23

The Passing of the Throne from Xerxes to Artaxerxes I, or How an Archaeological Observation Can Be a Potential Contribution to Achaemenid Historiography

Kamyar Abdi

Introduction

Interdisciplinary research plays a relatively minor part in the study of the Achaemenid Persian Empire. Chiefly dominated by historical, philological, art historical and sometimes strictly archaeological studies, exploration into various aspects of the Achaemenid Empire seldom applies theoretical and methodological concepts from affiliated fields to a given question, despite the potential insights they may offer. This paper is a heuristic attempt to demonstrate the potential contribution a particular archaeological concept—context of discovery—may be able to offer to some aspects of Achaemenid historiography.

The importance of context

Archaeological context (i.e. the accurate provenance of an artefact discovered in an archaeological matrix) has progressed in the past few decades to one of the few universally accepted concepts in archaeology (cf. Schiffer 1987). Close attention to archaeological context, its detailed recording during the course of excavations and its crucial role in post-excavation interpretations has for some time become an integral part of the field training of any archaeologist, regardless of which theoretical school he/she may hail from. The unanimous emphasis on archaeological context is based on the basic and irrefutable principle that the place of discovery plays a crucial role in inferences drawn from a find, whether a ubiquitous domestic item such as a potsherd or a unique item such as a royal bas-relief or inscription. Finds can provide direct information about their function and significance when discovered in their primary context. Alternatively, a non-primary context, while useful in determining patterns of use and discard, is of lesser value in establishing the cultural or historical significance of a find.

In this paper, I will argue that an observation on the context of two important finds from Persepolis—the Treasury Reliefs and copies of the Daivâ Inscription—can potentially shed some light on circumstances surrounding the passing of the throne from Xerxes to Artaxerxes I, the political environment within which it occurred and its impact on the imperial policy of the Achaemenids.

The passing of the throne from Xerxes to Artaxerxes I according to classical sources

According to Diodorus (11.69), Xerxes was assassinated in early August 465 BC by Artabanus, the captain of the royal bodyguard, who plotted to take over the throne. Artabanus was led at night by Mithradates (the king's chamberlain) into the king's chamber where he killed Xerxes and then set out after the king's three sons: Darius, Hystaspes and Artaxerxes. According to Ctesias (29–30) and Diodorus (11.69.1–5), Artaxerxes, deceived by Artabanus into believing that Xerxes was assassinated by the Crown prince Darius, killed his own brother. Artabanus then tried to kill Artaxerxes but was instead killed by Artaxerxes, who then defeated his other brother Hystaspes, the satrap of Bactria, and ascended the throne. Artaxerxes I was recognized as the new king as far away as Elephantine by 2nd or 3rd January 464 BC. His first year on the throne is estimated to have begun on 13th April 464 (Neuffer 1968).

The finds

Two important finds from Persepolis date to around the time the above-mentioned events were unfolding in the Achaemenid court: the Treasury Reliefs and the Daivâ Inscription.

The treasury reliefs

Two almost identical reliefs were discovered in the spring of 1936 during the Oriental Institute of the University of Chicago excavations under Erich Schmidt at the Treasury complex (Schmidt 1939: 17, 20, fig. 11). Of the two reliefs, the better-preserved copy, some 6 m long, was transported to the newly established Iran Bâstân Museum, where it is still on prominent display (Fig. 23.1). The second, less well-preserved copy was set up for display in its place of discovery in the Treasury (Fig. 23.2).

The porticoed courtyard where the reliefs were discovered is part of the Treasury complex, a large and extensive series of buildings occupying the south-eastern corner of the Persepolis platform. Schmidt initially identified the part of the Treasury where the reliefs were found as the office of the commander of the king's bodyguards (Old Persian *hazarpat*, Greek *chiliarch*) (Schmidt 1939: 25). Building on Schmidt's argument, Junge argued (1940: 25) that this must be the office of the *hazarpat*, because as the highest official of the court he was also the chief of the royal treasury and therefore must have held office in the Treasury. Junge therefore argued that the reliefs were gifts of honour from the king to *hazarpat*, which he set up in his office. Olmstead, who believed that the king displayed on the relief is Darius (see below) identified the *hazarpat* of this time as Takhmaspâda, a Mede (Olmstead 1948: 217), but Hinz argued that it was impossible for a Mede to have been the commander of the royal bodyguards which consisted exclusively of Persians (Hinz 1969: 68). Schmidt later argued that the Median dignitary in the relief might have been the royal treasurer, who in the latter years of Darius, was a certain Baradkâma, a name that can be either Median or Persian (Schmidt 1953: 169, n. 66). Ghirshman (1957: 227), who concurred with Schmidt's opinion about the identification of the Median individual, nonetheless pointed

Fig. 23.1 The southern Treasury Relief now in the Iran National Museum.

out that the porticoed courtyard in which the reliefs were discovered was built by Darius as a temporary throne room while he was awaiting construction work at the Apadana to be completed (Ghirshman 1964b: 205), and thus may not have been intended as the office of the *hazarpat*.

Most important is the subject matter of the Treasury relief. It is what can be called an audience scene (Fig. 23.3), earlier examples of which are to be found from the time of the Neo-Assyrian empire at sites such as Tell Barsip (Stronach 2002). It shows the Achaemenid king seated on a throne and holding a staff in his right hand and a flower or flower-like object in his left hand. Another individual—most probably the Crown prince, considering his Persian robe, headdress and royal-style beard—of the same size as the king is standing behind him, also holding a flower or flower-like object. Behind him are four other smaller individuals, beginning with one in a hooded outfit and holding a folded towel. Schmidt believed that this individual was beardless—and therefore a eunuch—and may have been the lord chamberlain or the royal cupbearer (Schmidt 1953: 169). A. Shapur Shahbazi also argued that the individual was a eunuch and suggested that he may have been the royal chamberlain (Shahbazi 1976: 153). Behind the hooded individual is a man in Median outfit and cap, presumably the royal weapon-bearer as he is carrying an axe. Behind him, and outside what appears to be the pillars of a baldachin, are two soldiers in Persian outfits holding spears.

In front of the king and behind two objects generally assumed to be incense-burners (Melikian-Chirvani 1993) is an individual in Median outfit bending slightly forward and holding the palm of his hand before his mouth, a posture generally assumed to be a gesture of deference before royalty (Frye 1972). The identity of this individual has been the subject of some discussion, leading to debates surrounding the function of the porticoed courtyard mentioned above: Schmidt believed that he was the commander of the king's bodyguards (Schmidt 1953: 168, 169; see also Junge 1940), whereas Ghirshman

Fig. 23.2 The eastern Treasury Relief *in situ* at the Treasury complex, after restoration. (After Tilia 1972: pl. XCVII, fig. 7)

argued that he was the grand master of ceremonies (Ghirshman 1964b: 205). Hinz, on the other hand, believed him to be the master of the royal household ("der Hofmarschall") (Hinz 1969: 68). Behind this individual and behind the pillars of the baldachin, are two more soldiers in Persian outfits, one with a spear and the other with an object that may have been a situla.

Most important is the identity of the two central figures in the Treasury reliefs, namely, the king and the prince: until the early 1970s scholars were unanimous in identifying the king as Darius and the individual standing behind him as the Crown prince Xerxes (cf. Schmidt 1939: 21; 1953: 168; Herzfeld 1941: 256; Olmstead 1948: 217; Ghirshman 1957: 276; 1964b: 205; Hinz 1969: 63), but a discovery in the late 1960s cast some doubt on this identification. Then engaged in conservation work at Persepolis, Ann and Giuseppe Tilia noticed that the two Treasury Reliefs were originally set up on the central panels of the eastern and northern stairways of the Apadana, but that they were later relocated to the Treasury and in their place was installed the relief showing alternating Persian and Median guards (Tilia 1972: 191–98).

Ann Tilia continued to maintain that the king was Darius, but argued that the reliefs were removed by Artaxerxes I simply because of a change in the New Year ceremony (1972: 129). A number of other scholars also continued to maintain the original identification of the king and the Crown prince as Darius and Xerxes (cf. Farkas 1974: 53, 117; Root 1979: 94–95; Porada 1979a), but the revelation that the reliefs were not in their primary context prompted a number of scholars to rethink the identity of the main figures, and to explore alternative interpretations of the reliefs and their historical significance.

The first scholar to tackle the Treasury Reliefs in light of the recent discovery was Richard Frye who suggested that the king was not Darius, but Xerxes, and the Crown prince his eldest son Darius (Frye 1974). This view was also advocated by the late Shahbazi (1976). Frye argued that once in power, Artaxerxes I removed the reliefs from view, as they were distasteful reminders of his murdered father and elder brother and especially of the feeling of remorse that he may have experienced after killing his brother Darius and later realizing his innocence (Frye 1974).

A technical detail came to support the revisionist hypothesis, as Hubertus Von Gall pointed out that the king must have been Xerxes, for Darius always wore a dentate crown (Von Gall 1974: 151), but the argument based on the crown alone failed to convince some other scholars (cf. Root 1979: 93; Roaf 1983: 131). The revisionist hypothesis has also been criticized by Cahill who points out (1985: 386) that even in the Treasury the reliefs were displayed prominently (but of course, not publicly), and argues that the

Fig. 23.3 Reconstruction of the eastern Treasury Relief. (After Tilia 1972: fig. 3)

removal of the reliefs should be attributed to major changes in ceremonies carried out at Persepolis.

While the debate on the identity of the king and the Crown prince on the Treasury Reliefs and the reason(s) for their removal is far from over, the fact remains that an observation regarding the context of the Reliefs, and the realization that they are not in their primary context, prompted some scholars to rethink the identification of the main figures represented.

However, the Treasury Reliefs are not the only monuments from the transitional period from Xerxes to Artaxerxes I that were removed from their primary context. Another, equally important monument lost its primary context and wound up in a non-primary context.

The Daivâ Inscription

A year earlier, on 26th June 1935, the Oriental Institute expedition found seven stone slabs in the Garrison Quarters—a group of structures to the south-east corner of the Persepolis terrace (Schmidt 1939: 11–12). These slabs were set up on their edges as the facing of a bench in Room 16 (Fig. 23.4). Four of these seven slabs—three in Old Persian and one in Babylonian—turned out to be virtually identical to another text found in 1931 by Ernst Herzfeld in the so-called "Harem" complex (Herzfeld 1932). The other three slabs—two in Old Persian (PT3 142 and PT3 143) and one in Babylonian (PT3 141)—bore a rather different text that led to them being labelled as the "Daivâ Inscription" (Herzfeld 1936; Kent 1937). In the meantime, excavations in Room 5 at the Garrison Quarters yielded a fragmentary slab inscribed with the same text in Elamite (PT3 337). This slab seemed to form part of a door sill of late Achaemenid date, but may, as the other ones, have been part of a bench of an earlier level (Schmidt 1939: 12). The missing fragment of this slab was discovered in 1957 by Ali Sami during excavation and conservation work in the same area (Cameron 1959).

In 1961, a third Old Persian copy of the Daivâ Inscription was discovered during excavations at Pasargadae by the British Institute of Persian Studies under David Stronach (1965: 19). This copy had been used in the construction of a drain in trench K on Tall-i Takht (Fig. 23.5) (Stronach 1978: 151–152).

The discovery of the first four copies of the Daivâ Inscription at Persepolis soon led to a series of publications. The initial report of the discovery in *The New York Times* (9th February 1936), *The University of Chicago Magazine* (28/4 (1936): 23–25), *The Illustrated London News* (22nd February 1936: 328) and *Archiv für Orientforschung* (11 (1937): 91) was followed by a number of more thorough studies by Ernst Herzfeld (1936; 1938a: 27–35), Ronald Kent (1937; 1943: 302–306; 1953: 150–152), Hans Hartman (1937: 145–160), Isidore Lévy (1939), Arthur Christensen (1941) and Jean de Menasce (1943).

In principle, the Daivâ Inscription is a typical royal Achaemenid text, apart from a few remarkable exceptions in its subject matter. Like other royal inscriptions, the Daivâ Inscription begins with the king (Xerxes) introducing himself and his lineage, and continues with the praising of Ahurâ Mazdâ followed by a list of lands under the king's control. Henceforward begins the unique feature of the Daivâ Inscription, where Xerxes presents an account of how he suppressed a rebellion (in unspecified lands) after he became the king and (again, in unspecified lands) put an end to worship of a certain category of deities described as the *Daivâ*, in places called the *Daivadâna*, and how he replaced the worship of the *Daivâ* with the worship of Ahurâ Mazdâ. The Daivâ Inscription concludes with typical praising of Ahurâ Mazdâ and prayers for his blessing.

The exact date when the Daivâ Inscription was composed seems to depend on the reference in the text to the Ionians of the west coast of Asia Minor and the mainland Greeks. In his early publications, Herzfeld argued that the reference to "Ionians who dwell in the sea" in the Daivâ Inscription included the Greeks of the west coast of Asia Minor and, accordingly, dated the Daivâ Inscription to between 486 and 480 BC (Herzfeld 1936: 64–65). Herzfeld later stated that the mainland Greeks do not seem to be mentioned in the text, and the text must thus be dated to between 479 and 472 BC, that is, between the year the Achaemenids lost control over mainland Greeks and the year Pausanias was driven from Byzantium (Herzfeld 1947: 396). Herzfeld finally settled on 478 BC as the date of composition (Herzfeld 1968: 351). This date approximately corresponds with Kent's date of 479 BC, who, nonetheless, believed that the mainland Greeks are in fact mentioned in the text (Kent 1943: 304–305).

Ever since its discovery, the text and historicity of the Daivâ Inscription and what Xerxes meant by *Daivâ* and *Daivadâna* in this peculiar inscription have occupied students not only of the Achaemenid Empire but also of ancient Iranian studies in general, as well as related fields. Herzfeld, who first published the text, argued that it relates to an uprising led by the Magi of Media, and the *Daivâ* were the pre-Zoroastrian deities whose temples—the

Fig. 23.4 Seven stone slabs, including three copies of the Daivâ Inscription, being excavated in the Garrison Quarters. (After Schmidt 1939: fig. 9)

Fig. 23.5 A copy of the Daivâ Inscription reused in the construction of a drain on Tall-i Takht at Pasargadae. (After Stronach 1978: pl. 122b)

Daivadâna—in Media, Persia and Susiana in Iran were destroyed by Xerxes (Herzfeld 1936: 27, 74–77; 1947: 401). Kent (1937: 305) and Hartmann (1937: 159), on the other hand, argued that the Old Persian version mentions only one rebellious land and only one place where the *Daivâ* were worshipped. Levy drew on a correlation to Herodotus (*History* VIII.85) and suggested that by *Daivadâna* Xerxes was referring to the Athenian temples (Lévy 1939).

While Lévy's correlation of *Daivadâna* with the Athenian temples appealed to scholars in the classical fields (cf. Hignett 1963), some Iranists, following Herzfeld, tried to discover Xerxes' motivations for the compilation of the Daivâ Inscription in the Iranian world. For instance, Albert Olmstead suggested that Xerxes was referring to Bactrian or other eastern Iranian deities (Olmstead 1948: 231–32). Richard Frye also argued for cults in eastern Iran, for example, in Kerman, or more likely Elamite cults in Fars and western Iran (Frye 1984). This, according to Frye, was motivated by a deliberate attempt by Xerxes to "de-Elamitize" and "Iranicize" the cultural and religious character of Persia proper (Frye 1984: 172). Lecoq too recently re-emphasized that in XPh Xerxes was referring to the heretic Iranians (Lecoq 1997: 172).

Another group of Iranists has also sought an Iranian origin for the Daivâ Inscription, attempting, concurrently, to address broader issues, especially the religious orientation of the Achaemenids in general and Xerxes in particular. Ugo Bianchi used the absolute negative use of the word *Daivâ* in the Daivâ Inscription to argue that the Achaemenids were indeed Zoroastrians, pointing out the special emphasis placed on Xerxes' attempt to replace old Iranian deities such as Indra, with Ahurâ Mazdâ (Bianchi 1977). In the same framework, but with a slightly different approach, Mary Boyce argued that in the Daivâ Inscription, Xerxes was referring to the destruction of a place of worship in Iran for warlike beings condemned by Zoroaster (Boyce 1982: 175). According to Mohammad Dandamayev (1976: 226) these deities were Mithrâ and Anâhitâ. Roman Ghirshman identified one such *Daivadâna* at Tappeh Nush-i Jan (Ghirshman 1976).

Perhaps the most enduring hypothesis on the historicity of the Daivâ Inscription was first put forward by Hans Hartmann

(1937: 139). Drawing upon a reference in Herodotus (*History* I.183), Hartmann argued that the *Daivadâna* mentioned in the Daivâ Inscription was in fact the Bel-Marduk temple in Babylon which, according to Herodotus, was destroyed by Xerxes after it rose in rebellion early in his reign. In the following years, Hartmann's proposition was advocated by a number of scholars in one way or another (see Nyberg 1938: 364–66; Duchesne-Guillemin 1962: 156; Widengren 1968: 138; Herrenschmidt 1980: 326). This hypothesis, in turn, has led to the discrediting of Xerxes as a megalomaniac despot with erratic behaviour and no tolerance for the belief systems of his subjects, especially their religion (Zaehner 1961: 154; Burn 1962: 317).

In recent years, however, the *Daivadâna* = Bel-Marduk temple correlation and, consequently, the personality of Xerxes have been subject to a revision. Amélie Kuhrt and Susan Sherwin-White (1987), in particular, present a review of the pertinent written sources, concluding not only that the *Daivadâna* in the Daivâ Inscription cannot be identified with the Bel-Marduk temple in Babylon, but also that Xerxes' attitude towards Babylonian deities and temples is rather different from what classical sources, especially Herodotus, portray.

Following the same trend in Achaemenid historiography, Heleen Sancisi-Weerdenburg put forward the argument that the Daivâ Inscription does not reflect any historically specific event or action, but merely indicates the royal ideology of the Achaemenid dynasty (Sancisi-Weerdenburg 1989: 551, 557). In other words, according to this view, the Daivâ Inscription is a royal proclamation stressing that rebellion against the empire, in any form and by anyone, is sacrilegious and equal to worshipping false gods instead of Ahurâ Mazdâ, and thus will be punished by the empire. This view of the Daivâ Inscription is also adhered to in one way or another in the most recent reviews of Achaemenid history (see Briant 1996: 567–70; Wiesehöfer 1996: 47–55).

In another paper, I proposed a different interpretation for the Daivâ Inscription (Abdi 2006). I argued that what Xerxes was trying to state in the Daivâ Inscription is that after he came to power, in some corners of the empire there were places of worship in which religious activities were carried out that included burning dead matter on a fire (i.e. burnt offerings) as some sort of sacrifice. What Xerxes tried to do was to stop this alarmingly un-Zoroastrian practice, and to instruct participants in these activities on the proper, that is, Zoroastrian, way of offering sacrifice to fire. Xerxes' efforts, however, were not very successful in an empire as vast and ethnically and religiously diverse as that of the Achaemenids. His instructions were therefore mostly ignored and his edict (i.e. the Daivâ Inscription) was discarded after his death.

In my paper, apart from factual examples to support my interpretation of the Daivâ Inscription, I stressed the archaeological context of the multiple copies of the Daivâ Inscription and how—as outlined in the introduction to this paper—this archaeological observation is important in reconsidering the subject matter and historical setting of this peculiar inscription. Let us begin by looking at the archaeological context of various copies of the Daivâ Inscription. In total five copies of the Daivâ Inscription have been discovered so far: two Old Persian, one Babylonian and one Elamite version from Persepolis, and one Old Persian version from Pasargadae. These numbers roughly correspond with the quantity of different versions of other royal Achaemenid inscriptions. The important fact here is that, unlike most other royal Achaemenid inscriptions that are found *in situ* (i.e. in the place they were displayed or ritually deposited), every copy of the Daivâ Inscription discovered so far comes from a non-primary context. As mentioned earlier, at Persepolis three copies were used as part of a bench in Room 16 in the Garrison Quarter (Fig. 23.4), and the fourth copy in Room 5 in the same area formed part of a door sill of late Achaemenid date, which may, as the other ones, have been part of a bench of an earlier level. The only copy of the Daivâ Inscription found at Pasargadae also comes from a non-primary context and exhibits a similar pattern of reuse, as it was used in the construction of a drain in trench K on Tall-i Takht (Fig. 23.5).

This fact is of paramount importance from an archaeologist's point of view. It means that, sometime after its composition, but not before the end of the Achaemenid period (as indicated by its place of discovery, dated to later in the Achaemenid period), the Daivâ Inscription lost its symbolic significance, was removed from its primary context (i.e. where it was originally meant to be placed or displayed) and discarded.

However, the life cycle of an item, even a unique item such as the Daivâ Inscription, does not come to an end with its entry into the archaeological context. Many items are reclaimed and reused in a different context that has little or no relation to their original context. This is clearly seen in the case of the discarded copies of the Daivâ Inscription, which were later reclaimed, and with no consideration for their ideological significance were reused in a completely different context (i.e. as pieces of masonry in insignificant construction work).

Discussion

An explanation as to why the Daivâ Inscription and the Treasury Reliefs were removed from their primary context would warrant an exploration of the broader developments of the Achaemenid Empire from the time Darius took power. Darius, a shrewd military man raised in the tumultuous years of early empire building, proved to be a pragmatic ruler like the founder of the empire, Cyrus the Great. He soon realized that in order to rule the diversity of people that formed the Achaemenid Empire in peace and harmony, he would have to introduce a policy of cultural tolerance. Thus, people were allowed to carry on with their beliefs and practices as long as they paid their tribute on time and demonstrated their obedience to the imperial authority.

Xerxes, on the other hand, was born a prince, and as such, experienced a radically different upbringing. In his childhood, he must have received substantial teaching in Zoroastrianism, which—among many other topics—included instructions on proper the procedure for making a sacrifice to fire that he, once he had assumed the throne, tried to implement in the empire through edicts such as the Daivâ Inscription. Xerxes was, however, probably alone in his crusade, scarcely able to find similarly pious individuals to share his devotion to Zoroastrian instructions on a trivial religious practice or who cared as much about a fairly insignificant matter which had little bearing on the smooth operation of the empire. Soon this and other ill-fated actions (the failed Greek expedition and the loss of Persian lives, for example) led to growing discontent among the Persian nobility, culminating in his assassination in 465 BC.

Xerxes' son and successor, Artaxerxes I (465–425 BC), on the other hand, was a different man. He is unanimously hailed by Greek authors as a capable and skilful king and a valiant warrior (see Plutarch, *Artoxerxes* 1.1) who restored the empire to its former glory and to political and military dominance. He reconquered Egypt by putting down the Libyan rebel Inarus, signed the peace treaty of Callias with the Athenians, and last but not least, in an unprecedented show of mercy, gave refuge to Themistocles, his father's greatest opponent. However, not to short-change his father on religious matters, Artaxerxes I institutionalized Zoroastrianism as the official religion of the empire, as evidenced by the reformation of the imperial calendar at around 441 BC with months named after the leading Zoroastrian deities (Taqizadeh 1938; Bickerman 1967). The religious regulation Xerxes was trying to enforce became irrelevant and the decree was withdrawn and discarded, probably shortly after its author met his demise. With the Daivâ Inscription no longer serving its function, it found its way into its archaeological context. Perhaps at this point, certain individual(s) stationed at Persepolis reclaimed the discarded inscriptions and used them in constructing a bench in the Garrison Quarters. Other copies of the inscription found their way into equally unusual places elsewhere in the Garrison Quarters, the Harem building and in a drainage channel on the platform at Pasargadae, a degrading location unattested for any other royal inscription of the Achaemenid period.

For Artaxerxes, if we trust Greek sources about his dignity, seeing the image of his murdered father and that of his older brother killed by his own hands on prominent display was too much to bear, and not such a prudent idea to begin with in a court ripe with political intrigue. He therefore ordered the Treasury Reliefs to be removed from their highly visible location on the Apadana stairways and transported to the privacy of a courtyard in the Treasury.

Conclusion

While this paper's input into the debates surrounding the significance of the Treasury Reliefs or the Daivâ Inscription and their contribution of the Achaemenid historiography—especially for the transitional period from Xerxes to Artaxerxes I—may be modest, the fact remains that the main point raised in the paper, namely, the importance of archaeological context and the distinction of primary versus non-primary context in drawing inferences from archaeological finds, including unique discoveries, has been illustrated quite effectively. The lesson to be learned is that a better understanding of the intricacies of the Achaemenid period requires an interdisciplinary approach drawing from the theoretical and methodological repertoire of all the related fields.

24

Cultural Transition in Iranian Azerbaijan through the Iron Age III–Achaemenid Period Based on Recent Archaeological Survey and Excavations (Abstract)

Bahram Adjerloo

The development of the Achaemenid Empire in the north-west part of the Iranian plateau is still problematic. How was the Median kingdom affected by the rise of the Achaemenid Empire? What are the cultural characteristics of the Achaemenid period in Iranian Azerbaijan? Did the same Iron Age III cultural characteristics continue in the Achaemenid period?

Recent surveys in the Qaradaq region, Marand plain and eastern districts of Lake Urmia have reconstructed an Urartian landscape of the eighth–seventh centuries BC. However, a recent survey in the Mughan plain has not yet revealed any ancient material related to the sixth–fourth centuries BC. A stratigraphic sounding at Tepe Shiramin, south of Tabriz, did not reveal any cultural assemblage of the Median kingdom or that of the Persians. Recent excavations at Ziviyeh and Qalaychi, however, show that if we accept the cultural assemblages of Ziviyeh and Qalaychi as belonging to the Manaean culture, we will have to review Hasanlu IVB as a Manaean level. Is it, therefore, possible to relate Hasanlu IVB to the Medes? Historically, the Median kingdom was very large. If Hasanlu IVB was originally Median, why is there no cultural assemblage similar to Hasanlu IVB on the east side of Lake Urmia?

The archaeological data from Tepe Shiramin and the Blue Mosque of Tabriz, both on the east side of Lake Urmia, are not comparable to Tepe Hasanlu IVB–III. Also, archaeological surveys in the Ardebil–Mughan plain focusing on the Median–Achaemenid period do not provide any further information.

Results of recent archaeological investigations in the Lake Urmia basin demonstrate three very broad periods. These are as follows: prehistoric period (up to $c.850$ BC), the Urartian period (up to $c.650$ BC) and the post-Urartian period (after $c.650$ BC).

The settlement pattern in the Urartian period is very different to that of the post-Urartian period: for instance, Urartian settlements are more numerous and are sited on the plain or next to the hills. They are also larger than the post-Urartian settlements which are placed in the hills and highlands.

Survey evidence suggests a shift in the subsistence patterns from agriculture to stock living, although further research is required.

Archaeological investigations have not identified the material culture of the Medes and Persians in the Lake Urmia basin, Mughan plain and Qaradaq region during the post–Urartian period. Moreover, there are no ancient inscriptions or other written sources.

The Hasanlu II and post-Urartian Bastam cultural assemblage have not been found on the east side of Lake Urmia nor in the Ardebil–Mughan plain. Thus, the archaeological data does not explain how the Median kingdom was replaced by the Achaemenid Empire. In addition we cannot yet define the cultural characteristics of the Achaemenid period in Iranian Azerbaijan.

This research suggests that it is necessary to change our ideas and interpretations regarding the Achaemenids in the north-west Iranian plateau.

25

Archaeological Evidence for Achaemenid Settlement within the Mamasani Valleys, Western Fars, Iran

Alireza Askari Chaverdi, Alireza Khosrowzadeh,
Bernadette McCall, Cameron A. Petrie,
D. T. Potts, Kourosh Roustaei, Mojgan Seyedin,
Lloyd Weeks and Mohsen Zaidi

Introduction

Our knowledge of the archaeology of the Achaemenid period in south-west Iran has been dominated by research undertaken at the royal capitals at Susa, in lowland Khuzestan, and at Pasargadae and Persepolis, in highland Fars. However, these sites are in excess of 500 km apart and are each situated in distinctive environments, and we know little about the area that lies in between.[1]

There have been several attempts to identify the regions and locations between Persepolis and Susa that are mentioned in the Persepolis Fortifications archive (e.g. Mostafavi 1963, 1967; Hinz 1961; Hallock 1978; Koch 1986, 1990, 1992; Aperghis 1996, 1998, 1999; Tuplin 1998). However, a comparison of the different reconstructions shows that in each case, different routes have been favoured, and specific toponyms have been attributed to different areas.[2] A key component that is typically lacking from attempts to establish secure identifications of these locations is archaeological substantiation. This is partially due to the fact that only a limited amount of archaeological investigation has been carried out on the actual routes between Susa and Persepolis.

The landscape between Khuzestan and the Kur River Basin is dominated by the often sharply folded ridges of the Zagros Mountains. At intermittent points throughout the range, there are alluvial plains, which are suitable for settlement (Miroschedji 2003: 18; Petrie, Askari Chaverdi & Seyedin 2005: n.14).[3] However, much of the intervening land between these plains is not cultivable, and there are only a limited number of routes that link the plains and provide access through the range (Speck 2002: 16–18, 142ff; also Stein 1940: 11ff.). The archaeological fieldwork that *has* been carried out in these plains, and particularly along the routes themselves, has primarily consisted of rapid rather than systematic surveys (e.g. Stein 1940: 11ff.), and there has been little in the way of controlled excavation.

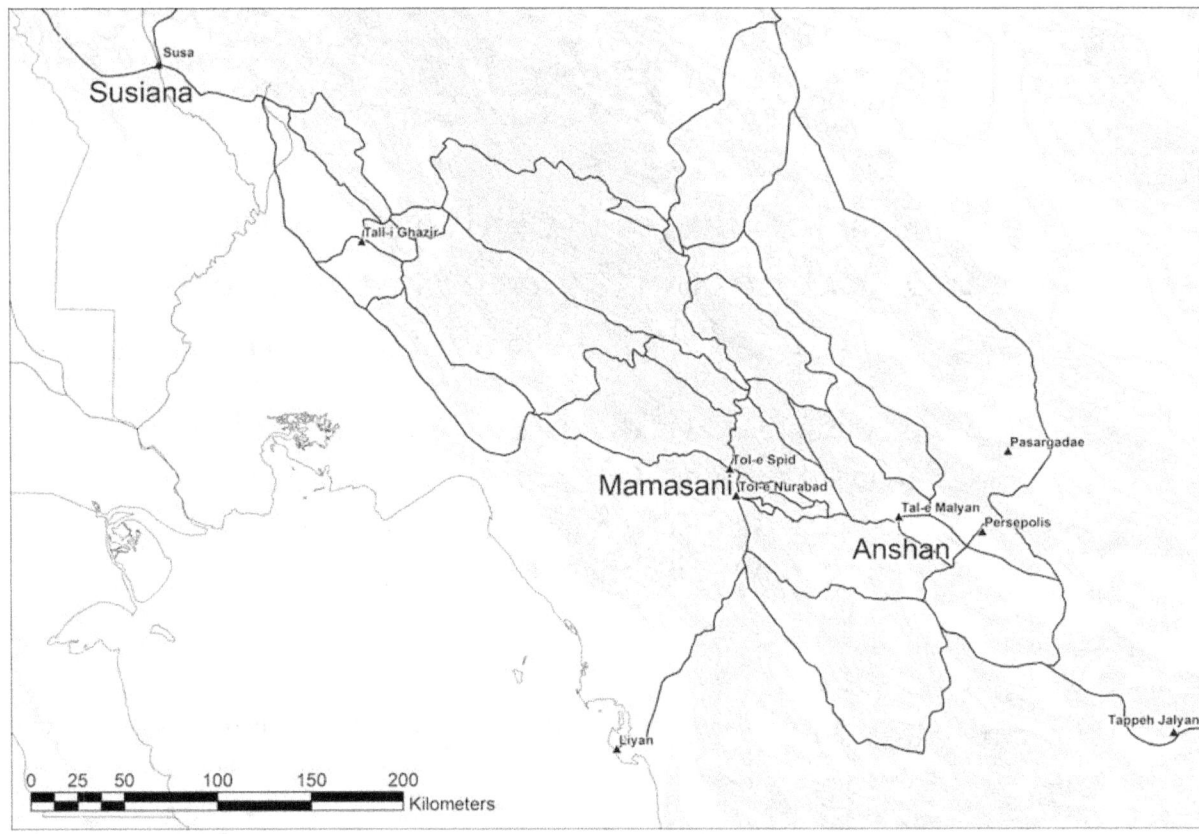

Fig. 25.1 Map of south-western Iran, showing the locations of Susa, Persepolis and Tol-e Spid and Tol-e Nurabad. The main routes through the south-western Zagros are indicated by solid black lines.

The Mamasani region

In January 2003, a collaborative project between the Iranian Centre for Archaeological Research of the Iranian Cultural Heritage and Tourism Organization and the University of Sydney directed by Professor Daniel Potts and Mr Kourosh Roustaei, commenced a research programme focusing on the Mamasani District of western Fars, which has long been recognized as one of the more important regions on the main route between Persepolis and Susa (e.g. Herzfeld 1907, 1928; Stein 1940: 27ff.).

The Mamasani District is situated approximately 400 km south-east of Susa and 150 km west of Persepolis, and sits between c.880 and 980 m above sea level. It is comprised of a series of long, fertile intermontane valleys, which connect via narrow passes to form a component of one of the main north-west to south-east routes between Susa and Persepolis (Fig. 25.1).

Perhaps the first archaeologist to take an interest in the region was Ernst Herzfeld, who first visited Mamasani in 1905 (1907: 87ff.), and again in 1924 (1926, 1928: 82–85, 1935). During his brief stays he documented the rock reliefs at Kurangun that have since been dated to the Old and Neo-Elamite periods, and recorded an inscribed brick from the settlement mound of Tol-e Spid that attests to the construction of a temple at the site during the Middle Elamite period. He also visited the Achaemenid site of Tappeh Servan (Jinjan), the post-Achaemenid rock-cut tomb of Da-u Dukhtar and the early Sasanian tower of Dum-e Mil.

The strategic location of Mamasani led Herzfeld to propose that it was a possible location for the region of Huhnur, which is referred to in Mesopotamian Ur III period texts as the Key or the Bolt to the land of Anshan, which was the ancient capital of Fars (Herzfeld 1968: §146; Hansman 1972). He also asserted that it was a possible location of the "Persian Gates", which were seized by Alexander on his way to Persepolis in 330 BC (Herzfeld 1968: §146). Sir Aurel Stein passed through the region in 1935, and visited a number of the same sites (1940: 27–48), and Stein's claim that the "Persian Gates" were located in the Tang-i Khas (1940: 11–27), immediately to the east of Mamasani, has since been widely accepted (e.g. Herzfeld 1968: §146; Hansman 1972: 118; Bosworth 1980: 324–329; MacDermott & Schippman 1999).

The field research that has thus far been carried out by the Mamasani Archaeological Project team consisted of test soundings at the two sites: Tol-e Spid and Tol-e Nurabad. In addition, a regional survey of two of the Mamasani valleys, which are known locally as Dasht-e Rustam-e Yek and Dasht-e Rustam-e Do, was also conducted. This field research was carried out over two six-week seasons in 2003, with a subsequent one-month study season in 2004 (see Potts *et al.* 2006; Roustaei, Alamdari & Petrie 2006; Weeks *et al.* 2006; Petrie, Askari Chaverdi & Seyedin 2006; Zaidi, McCall & Khosrowzadeh 2006).

Tol-e Spid

The site known as Tol-e Spid is the tallest preserved site on the Fahliyan Plain, which is known locally as the Dasht-e Rustam-e Yek. Some time after the 1970s the site was extensively damaged by bulldozers and ploughing, and what remains covers approximately 2 ha. Much of this is quite low, rising only 3–4 m above the surrounding plain. In stark contrast, the highest point of the site rises abruptly to a height of 16 m, and the steepness of the sides of this eminence suggests that much more of the mound must once have been preserved to such a height, and the mound itself may have been somewhat larger. From the top of the mound, it is possible to see the location of the relief at Kurangun and also Tappeh Servan, and these both lie within 5 km of the site (Petrie, Askari Chaverdi & Seyedin 2006).

The northern face of the high part of the mound has been cut so that there is a vertical section that stands 12 m above the lower parts of the mound. During the two seasons in 2003, a preliminary stratigraphic sounding was excavated down this upright section. This sounding revealed that the mound was comprised of at least 24 separate phases of occupation, and the ceramic material and radiocarbon determinations collected from this sequence of deposits indicate that the site as a whole was occupied from at least 4000 BC up to *c.*50 BC. The uppermost 12 phases comprise 5 m of deposit, and are almost all characterized by structural remains and the appearance of a generally conservative ceramic assemblage that has parallels with the so-called Late Plain Ware assemblage of the Kur River Basin, which is best dated to the Late Achaemenid and post-Achaemenid periods (Petrie, Askari Chaverdi & Seyedin 2006).

The earliest Achaemenid period deposits are those of Phase 12. The deposits that lie immediately below Phase 12 are particularly difficult to interpret. Phase 14 is unlike any of the other phases known from the sounding, being a thick and consistent layer of intentionally deposited clay and degraded mud-brick fill. Immediately above this, Phase 13 is marked by a series of fill layers of pebbles and chalk, which have been cut by a sequence of pits. There is no substantial deposition between Phase 13 and the mud-brick structure of Phase 12. However, while the Phase 13 deposits are marked by mixed material with the latest material dating to the second millennium BC, Phase 12 presents diagnostic ceramics that date to the mid-first millennium BC. This suggests that there was a significant change in the cultural assemblage between these two phases. It appears most likely that the site was abandoned some time before the mid-first millennium BC, and the Phase 12 structures represent a major reoccupation (Petrie, Askari Chaverdi & Seyedin 2006).

After initial construction, the Phase 12 wall appears to have been rebuilt once before being abandoned. The deposits above the remains of the Phase 12 wall do not appear to have been levelled, as they are directly overlain by the pebble pavement, which follows the sloping ground surface created by the destroyed wall.[4] The sequence of structures that comprises Phases 10–1 displays evidence for regular rebuilding, and the structures of several phases follow the same wall alignments, and often show signs of the reuse of wall stubs. This suggests that there was a considerable amount of remodelling of the structures taking place at the site without protracted periods of abandonment between any of these phases (Petrie, Askari Chaverdi & Seyedin 2006).

The uppermost 12 phases at Tol-e Spid comprise in excess of 5 m of deposit and with the exception of a small number of previously unattested vessel forms, there appears to be a general continuity of vessel fabrics and forms throughout the sequence. Phase 12 is marked by the presence of a small number of clay versions of the distinct Achaemenid tulip bowl, including examples that appear to have imitation gadroons. Also present was a distinctive grey-ware bridge spout, which is made in a fabric that is distinct from the remainder of the assemblage. A number of the complete vessels that appear in the later phases show clear parallels to Achaemenid/Late Plain Ware forms from Persepolis, but are typically smaller in size (Petrie, Askari Chaverdi & Seyedin 2006).

Out of the total of ten radiocarbon dates for the Tol-e Spid sequence, four have been collected from Phases 12 to 1. The probability range for the radiocarbon determination from Phase 12 (Wk13985: L.3063—800–200 BC) predominantly falls between 550 and 350 BC, suggesting that this phase dates to the Achaemenid period proper, and may well date towards the beginning of the appearance of Late Plain Ware. The radiocarbon determinations from Phase 10 (Wk13986: L.3050—390–170 BC) and Phase 5 (Wk13987: L.3024—400–170 BC) are virtually identical, and suggest that these phases should be dated to the Late Achaemenid or post-Achaemenid periods. The determination from Phase 3 (Wk13988: L.3009—370–50 BC) appears almost certainly to date to the post-Achaemenid period (Petrie, Askari Chaverdi & Seyedin 2006).

The number of separate structural phases that date between $c.550$ and 50 BC indicates that rebuilding or remodelling episodes were taking place at the site with considerable regularity during the later first millennium BC. In one respect, the assemblages from Phases 12 and 11 at Tol-e Spid appear to be the earliest well-dated Achaemenid assemblages yet identified in Fars; the evidence for continuity of ceramic forms from the Late to the post-Achaemenid periods correlates well with the evidence for the Kur River Basin and Pasargadae (Boucharlat 2003; Sumner 1986; Stronach 1978). However, where the assemblages are viewed as a whole, there are several clear changes in the types of imported wares, and also in some of the vessel forms, which indicates that with further excavation it may be possible to differentiate between Achaemenid and post-Achaemenid assemblages.

Tol-e Nurabad

Approximately 10 km to the south of Tol-e Spid is the Dasht-e Nurabad, which is dominated by the imposing mound of Tol-e Nurabad. This site is preserved to a height in excess of 24 m, and covers an area of $c.9$ ha. The excavation of a sounding into the upper levels has revealed a sequence of deposits that appear to date to the late second and first millennium BC. However, only small quantities of ceramic material were recovered from these deposits, and this has made it particularly difficult to date them using relative parallels. Phases B9–B6 contain material that appears to be Middle or possibly Neo-Elamite in character. It *is* possible that some of the material from these phases actually dates to the Neo-Elamite period, but the size of the ceramic assemblage and the continuity of vessel forms from the Middle to the Neo-Elamite periods in Khuzestan makes it difficult to differentiate between the two (Weeks *et al.* 2006).

Phases B5 and B4 are characterized by substantial mud-brick architecture and the associated ceramic material indicates that both are most likely Achaemenid in date. The presence of such deposits at the site is confirmed by the collection of characteristic Achaemenid tulip bowl fragments on the surface of the mound.

Phases B3–B1 have parallels to Late or post-Achaemenid ceramics (Weeks *et al.* 2006).

As for Tol-e Spid, there is clear evidence for Tol-e Nurabad being occupied during the Middle Elamite period, but at present it is not yet possible to comment on whether or not Tol-e Nurabad was occupied between $c.1000$ and 500 BC. The ceramic evidence is by no means clear-cut, and this will only be clarified by further excavation.

Achaemenid and post-Achaemenid settlements in Mamasani

Survey results

Concurrent with the excavations conducted at Tol-e Spid and Tol-e Nurabad, a preliminary survey was carried out in Dasht-e Rustam-e Yek and Dasht-e Rustam-e Do, which are the two northernmost plains in the Mamasani District. A total of 51 sites were recorded during this survey.

No occupation that might be dated unequivocally to the first half of the first millennium BC has yet been identified. This is partially due to the absence of deposits from the stratigraphic soundings that can clearly be dated to this period.[5] However, evidence for occupation during the Middle Elamite or Qaleh period (i.e. $c.1400$–1000 BC) was identified at 16 sites during the survey (Zaidi, McCall & Khosrowzadeh 2006).[6]

Achaemenid period occupation was identified at as many as 17 sites, several of which are large multi-period mounds that are situated close to reliable water sources and remain relatively visible in the landscape. It is notable that 12 of the 17 sites that were occupied during the Achaemenid period also appear to have been occupied during the Middle

Elamite/Qaleh period. Therefore, there does not appear to be a significant discontinuity between the location of the last Elamite phase of occupation thus far identified, and the earliest Achaemenid phase, despite the chronological separation of the two phases. While this might be indicative of a deliberate choice by Achaemenid period inhabitants to reoccupy old mounds, it also serves to highlight the sites that might contain evidence for early first-millennium BC occupation that has not been identified on the surface. Post-Achaemenid occupation was identified at as many as 12 sites. All of the sites occupied during the post-Achaemenid period had been occupied during the Achaemenid period (Zaidi, McCall & Khosrowzadeh 2006).

In addition to the mound sites that have evidence for occupation during the Achaemenid and post-Achaemenid periods, four highly distinctive sites with architectural remains have been identified at Mamasani, three of which are in the survey area, while the other lies south of the modern town of Nurabad.

Tappeh Servan (Jinjan)

The site of Tappeh Servan or Jinjan was initially identified by Herzfeld and also visited by Stein. It is situated on the southern side of the Rud-e Fahlian, approximately 4,700 m to the south-west of Tol-e Spid (Herzfeld n.d., 1926: 258; Stein 1940: 37). It is marked by the presence of a number of column bases which resemble those from the Apadana at Persepolis, although on a much smaller scale (Fig. 25.2). This suggests that the structure was built during or after the reign of Darius I.

A very brief excavation at the site was carried out in 1959 by a Japanese team, who succeeded in recording all of the visible column

Fig. 25.2 *In situ* column base at Tappeh Servan.

bases, exposing some associated floor surfaces and illustrating a selection of pottery from the site, but they were not able to uncover a coherent plan of the structure (Atarashi & Horiuchi 1963). Stein claimed that two different sizes of column bases were visible, but the Japanese excavators were only able to differentiate one size (1963: 14; after Stein 1940: 34–36). The excavators agreed with Herzfeld that this was a royal pavilion, and suggested that it was a component of the Achaemenid highway between Persepolis and Susa (Atarashi & Horiuchi 1963: 14; after Herzfeld 1926: 258).

This site was revisited during the recent survey (Zaidi, McCall & Khosrowzadeh 2006), and excavations commenced in 2007 and continued in 2008 and 2009. The remains of a multi-phase complex incorporating a monumental Achaemenid pavement and portico have been exposed at the site, and are the focus of ongoing research (Potts *et al.* 2007; Potts *et al.* 2009).

Tappeh Pahnu

A second site with evidence of stone column bases was visited during the survey. This site,

Fig. 25.3 Column bases removed from a ploughed field at Tappeh Servan.

known locally as Tappeh Pahnu, is situated slightly over 17 km to the north-west of Tappeh Servan, and lies close to the centre of Dasht-e Rustam-e Do. The area where the columns were found is now no longer recognizable as a site per se, as it has been heavily ploughed. However, one plain column base remains *in situ* in a field, while a number of other bases are now collected together in the village adjacent to the site. These columns occur in two distinct sizes, with the larger examples being similar in size to those from Tappeh Servan. However, the columns from Tappeh Pahnu do not show the same elaborate carving. With the exception of one column that shows some signs of fluting, the Tappeh Pahnu columns appear to be either unfinished or deliberately left smooth (Zaidi, McCall & Khosrowzadeh 2006) (Fig. 25.3).

It is not yet possible to offer a clear date for the remains at Tappeh Pahnu, but on the basis of the ceramics found in the ploughed field, it is most likely that the site was occupied in the Achaemenid and possibly also in the post-Achaemenid periods.

In addition to the architectural evidence at Tappeh Servan and Tappeh Pahnu, remains of a third structure are said to have been discovered at Tol-e Gach Garan-e Ka Khodada (Askari Chaverdi, personal communication), which is located about 5 km to the south of Tal-e Nurabad. Although these remains have not been seen firsthand by any of the authors, column bases and capitals that are similar to the Achaemenid types seen at Tappeh Servan were evidently visible at the site.

Da-u Dukhtar

Lastly, it is worth mentioning the rock-cut tomb of Da-u Dukhtar, which is situated at the western edge of the Mamasani region. The tomb is cut high on a vertical rock face, and has four engaged columns on the façade, reminiscent of the Achaemenid royal tombs at Naqsh-i Rustam and Persepolis (von Gall 1993). Herzfeld (1935: 35) initially proposed that this was the tomb of Teispes or Cyrus I, and while this attribution was accepted for some time (Stein 1940: 47; also see von Gall 1993), Stronach has effectively argued that the tomb should be dated to somewhere between the late fifth and third centuries BC (1978: 304; see also von Gall 1993).[7]

The presence of a tomb in Mamasani that is so obviously modelled on the Achaemenid royal tombs at Naqsh-i Rustam and Persepolis is highly significant for what it suggests about political power and spheres of control in Fars during the post-Achaemenid period.

Mamasani in the Achaemenid and post-Achaemenid periods

This evidence for Achaemenid and post-Achaemenid occupation in Mamasani emphasizes the region's importance. At present, the period between the Middle Elamite and Achaemenid occupations at both Tol-e Spid and Tol-e Nurabad remains an unknown quantity, yet this period is in many ways critical to understanding the processes of acculturation that were taking place in Fars between the Elamite and Persian populations during the early first millennium BC, and also for understanding the origins of Achaemenid power in the region (Henkelman 2003a; Stronach 2003a; Alvarez-Mon 2004). The carving of additional figures on the Kurangun rock relief during the Neo-Elamite period does, however, indicate that it is more than likely that the region was inhabited during this period.[8]

The identification of distinctive Achaemenid levels at Tol-e Spid and Tol-e Nurabad, the discovery of Achaemenid period ceramic material on the surface of 17 archaeological sites, and the evidence for specific Achaemenid period structures at Tappeh Servan and Tappeh Pahnu emphasize that there were important social, political and economic dynamics in operation in the Mamasani region during this period. However, the work that has thus far been undertaken has only scratched the surface and further excavations of the upper levels at Tol-e Spid and Tol-e Nurabad, and new soundings at various other sites are likely to provide a completely new insight into the cultural processes that were in operation in the Mamasani region in the later first millennium BC.

In terms of attempting to interpret the structures at Tappeh Servan and Tappeh Pahnu, the idea that there were royal way stations and potentially storehouses along the route between Persepolis and Susa is of particular interest (Koch 1986, 1990; Tuplin 1998; Aperghis 1998, 1999).[9]

The structure at Tappeh Servan has traditionally been interpreted as being a royal pavilion, way station or regional storehouse such as those discussed by Aperghis (1998, 1999).[10] It is not yet possible to establish the function of Tappeh Pahnu. In any case, both structures are likely to have been important components on the royal route between Susa and Persepolis, and in the taxation and administration of the Mamasani region. If the structure at Tol-e Gach Garan-e Ka Khodada is in fact similar, then this is also likely to have served a similar function. It is particularly noteworthy that each of these sites is situated in a different valley. They lie 17–18 km apart from each other and each is located away from the other major sites on the respective plain (Herzfeld 1926: 258; Atarashi & Horiuchi 1963: 13).[11] The distance between each structure correlates well with the expected distance between stations and storehouses (Koch 1986, 1990; Aperghis 1999; Tuplin 1998: 106), and also suggests that there may have been multiple routes through Mamasani that were used for travel between different sites (Fig. 25.4).

While the possibility that these sites were way stations or storehouses is provocative, it must be put into context of the known routes through this part of Iran. There have been various discussions of the main routes through the southern Zagros, but a study of the routes between Susa and Persepolis by Henry Speck (2002) throws into question many prevailing assumptions. Having spent several years in the 1970s exploring these routes on the ground, Speck has assessed the classical texts that relate to Alexander's seizure of the Persian Gates, and presented a somewhat radical interpretation of the routes.

The traditional interpretation of Alexander's route has been primarily based on Stein's initial proposal (1940; see e.g.

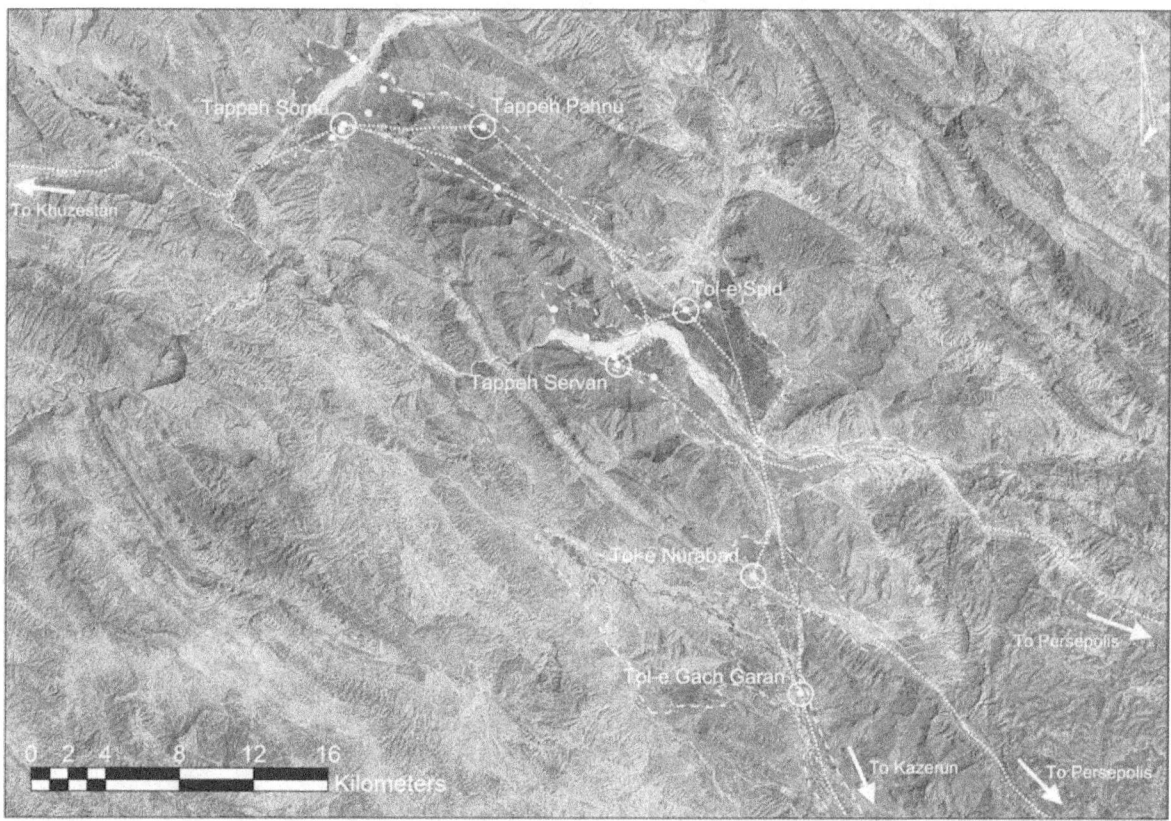

Fig. 25.4 Map of the plains of Mamasani, showing the location of the major sites discussed in the text, and possible routes of egress through the region.

Herzfeld 1968: §146; Hansman 1972: 118; Bosworth 1980: 324–329; MacDermott & Schippman 1999: 294), which envisaged that Alexander split his force in the Mamasani region and sent Parmenio to Persepolis via Kazerun, while he advanced to the Persian Gates, which lay in the Tang-i Khas, to the east of Mamasani (Stein 1940: 11–27). However, drawing on historical accounts of people who travelled from Bushire to Shiraz (e.g. Curzon 1892), Speck has proposed that the route via Kazerun and the Dasht-e Arjan was not viable in the Achaemenid period. He also suggests that a route via Firuzabad involved too much of an extensive detour to the east for it to have been used as the royal route (Speck 2002: 142ff.).

In contrast to the prevailing view, Speck has proposed that the Persian Gates were located in the elevated Beshar Valley, close to the modern town of Yasuj (2002: 16–18, 142ff.). While he does not agree that Mamasani was the location of the Persian Gates, he does suggest that the main winter route between the lowland and highland capitals lay through this region (Speck 2002: 16–18, 142ff.), and this would suggest that the structures at Tappeh Servan and Tappeh Pahnu were almost certainly on the main royal route through the south-western Zagros. If Speck's reinterpretation of the routes through the southern Zagros is correct, then a complete re-evaluation of the geographical information contained in the Persepolis Fortification archives will be required, and this will benefit enormously from systematic archaeological surveys of the intermontane valleys that lie on these routes.

Notes

1. This paper is the product of ongoing collaborative research between the Iranian Centre for Archaeological Research (ICAR) of the Iranian Cultural Heritage and Tourism Organization (ICHTO) and the University of Sydney, which is directed by Professor Daniel Potts and initially Mr Kourosh Roustaei. None of this work would have been possible without the support and encouragement of Mr Seyed Mohammad Beheshti, the former Director General of the ICHTO, Mr Jalil Golshan, Deputy Director of the ICHTO and Dr Massoud Azarnoush, the Director of the ICAR. The other authors of this paper were involved in the excavation of the sounding at Tol-e Spid (Askari-Chaverdi, Petrie and Seyedin), the excavation of the sounding at Tol-e Nurabad (Khosrowzadeh, Weeks and Zaidi) and the surface survey carried out in Dasht-e Rustam-e Yek (Khosrowzadeh, McCall and Zaidi). This paper makes use of material that has now been published in a project monograph (Potts & Roustaei 2006). The authors would like to thank the organizers of the conference *The World of Achaemenid Persia*, for accepting this paper, and delegates who asked questions during the session and afterwards. This paper was completed while Cameron Petrie was the Katherine and Leonard Woolley Junior Research Fellow at Somerville College Oxford (2003–2006) and the Research Fellow in South Asian Archaeology at the Department of Archaeology, University of Cambridge (2005–2010).
2. In trying to interpret these documents, there are certain fundamental assumptions that must be made about the point of origin for some journeys, the actual routes taken, the distance between locales and the time taken to travel those distances, which make secure identification of specific locations difficult (see Potts 2005*a*). In some instances, fundamental information that has been used as key components of some analyses, such as the distance between Susa and Persepolis, is often incorrect (e.g. Tuplin 1998: 104–105).
3. For the location of some of these plains, and the archaeological investigations that have thus far been conducted see http://web.arch.ox.ac.uk/archatlas/web/contributions/Petrie/RoutesandPlains.htm
4. The deposits overlying the pavement were densely compacted and showed signs of burning, which was presumably an aspect of the use of this part of the site at this time.
5. Without comparative material from these soundings, it is difficult to identify such material on the surface of other sites. Evidence for settled occupation dating to this period is virtually unknown in the Kur River Basin (Sumner 1994; Carter 1994; Boucharlat 2003: 262), so there is also an absence of comparative material in the surrounding regions. Although Neo-Elamite vessel forms are known from Susa (Miroschedji 1981), and have been identified on sites and in graves at Tal-i Ghazir in Ram Hormuz (Carter 1994), no such forms have yet been identified in Mamasani. One of the authors of this paper (McCall 2009: 203–203) has undertaken detailed study of the survey ceramics from Mamasani using more recently available comparanda from Chogha Zanbil (Mofidi Nasrabadi 2007), and has argued that up to six sites have evidence for a Neo-Elamite presence.
6. This correlates with the evidence from Tol-e Spid (Phases 14–13) and Tol-e Nurabad (Phases B9–B6).
7. Although there are the remains of a number of stone structures visible at the base of the rock face, the ceramic evidence from the surface suggests that these buildings date to the Early–Middle Islamic period *c*.ninth–eleventh centuries AD (Whitcomb 1991). As noted in Zaidi et al. 2006, these structures were revisited in 2003 and no evidence of ceramics earlier than the Islamic period was found.
8. More recent work on the reliefs at Kurangun has indicated that the main panel was carved in the *sukkalmah* period (Vanden Berghe 1984, 1986; Seidl 1986; Miroschedji 1989), and additional figures were added during the Neo-Elamite period (Vanden Berghe 1984, 1986: 162–163; Henkelman 2003*a*: 189; *contra* Seidl 1986; Miroschedji 1989). Potts has recently argued that the main deity shown on the relief can be identified as a conjunction of Inshushinak/Ea/Napirisha while the female deity is Kiririsha (Potts 2004). This relief, taken together with the brick from Tol-e Spid attesting to the construction of a temple to Kilahshupir at this site, which is less than 4 km from Kurangun attests to a protracted Elamite heritage for this region—spanning at least from *c*.1900 BC up to *c*.700 BC (Vanden Berghe 1986: 162–163).

9. Using evidence from the Persepolis Fortification texts, Tuplin has argued that the royal way stations at Parmadan should be located at Fahliyan (1998: 106). However, Tuplin's calculations are based on incorrect estimations of the distance between Persepolis and Susa. He proposes that the distance via Kazerun is 850 km and the distance via the Persian Gates is 750 km (1998: 104). However, these distances are incorrect by in excess of 200 km in each instance, which encourages us at least to question his attributions. In contrast, Aperghis has proposed that Parmadan should be located at Kazerun (1999: 154), and he does not identify Fahliyan per se. Instead, he suggests that Shullakke should be located at Nurabad (1999: 154). It has also been argued that it is possible to establish the underlying ethnicity of the populations of certain regions involved in the Persepolis Fortification network on the basis of whether Elamite or Persian months were being used (e.g. Razmjou 2004; after Hallock 1969). While this is entirely possible, it might also be a simple reflection of the ethnicity of the individual doing the recording, and the fact that it was acceptable to use either system at this stage of Darius' rule.
10. As a result of a comprehensive analysis of the PF texts using a database, Aperghis has proposed that there is evidence that a large number of the texts (over 25 %) are receipts at storehouses of commodities supplied by producers, that these producers are linked with both royal estates and holdings of Persian nobles and commoners, and that the produce that was being collected was a form of taxation on the populace of Persis and Elam, which was entrusted to a Supply Officer who might have jurisdiction over several supply houses (Aperghis 1998, 1999: 157–161). One particular individual who appears to have been active in the area close to the border between Elam and Persis is Irtuppiya, between Hidali and Kurdushum, including Hunar, Zakzaku, Shullakke and Liduma (Aperghis 1999: 181–182).
11. It is interesting that the columned structure at Tappeh Servan appears to have been established in a part of the Dasht-e Rustam-e Yek that had not previously been settled, but one that was in direct line of sight of the relief at Kurangun. Boucharlat has noted that there appears to have been an area in the immediate neighbourhood of Persepolis where there was an absence of settlement, possibly as a result of the king having intentionally emptied out this zone so that it could be used for the military and agricultural activities needed to support his court (2003: 262). Perhaps similar principles of isolation were in operation in relation to the royal way stations?

26

A Review of Research and Restoration Activities at Parsa-Pasargadae: Analysis, Evaluation and Future Perspectives

Mohammad Hassan Talebian

Introduction

This paper is a review of the activities carried out by the Parsa-Pasargadae Foundation in the period 2002–2005.[1] Some 190 years have passed since the beginning of archaeological activities at Persepolis. These initial works include investigations by Herbert Weld (Blundell) on behalf of the British Museum in 1892 (Weld Blundell 1893), and the systematic excavations conducted by Ernst Herzfeld and Erich F. Schmidt during the 1930s (Herzfeld 1929–30, 1934; Schmidt 1953, 1957, 1970). These were followed by restoration measures carried out from the 1950s onwards. The Ministry of Culture and Archaeological Organization later directly supervised excavation programmes through the Institute of Achaemenid Research and with the assistance of the Italian Organization of IsMEO (Sami 1967; Tilia 1972, 1978; Mousavi 2002; Shahbazi 2004). Finally, after an interval of over two decades, the Parsa-Pasargadae Research Foundation resumed scientific activities in 2002. The aim of these was to implement improved conservation and the investigation of the wider cultural landscape of the Persepolis–Pasargadae region through the use of various new scientific techniques, and with the additional aim of seeking cooperation with our non-Iranian colleagues.

A short glance at research programmes carried out in this region prior to 2002 reveals the fact that most projects were mainly focused on well-known archaeological monuments and sites (particularly Persepolis) or on cultural–historical issues which are ultimately related to them from structural, visual, and functional perspectives. It means that no research has yet been carried out which takes into account the region's cultural landscape or its integral identity. Consequently, most of the authorities' attention was mainly concentrated on those same monuments and sites, but ignored those other seemingly less important ones, which in some cases have been destroyed because of development projects. A coherent strategy for the Parsa-Pasargadae landscape therefore seemed a necessity due to the extension of the concept of cultural

Fig. 26.1 Aerial view of the extended buffer zone of Persepolis.

heritage in recent years with its emphasis on the cultural context. There follows a brief survey of archaeological researches and restoration projects that have been carried out in the Parsa-Pasargadae region.

Archaeological investigations in the cultural landscape of Parsa-Pasargadae

As mentioned above, excavations and restoration activities have long concentrated on the major Achaemenid sites of Persepolis and Pasargadae. Consequently, the investigation, documentation, and publication of many ancient settlements in the general region of Pasargadae-Marvdasht have been neglected. However, these sites are often very important, consisting of mounds or *tepes* covering periods of occupation from the prehistoric period onwards and including settlements, graves and forts. Urban and industrial developments have unfortunately sometimes led to irreparable damage to these archaeological sites. For this reason one of the basic goals of the Parsa-Pasargadae Research Foundation has been to preserve the integrity of the entire cultural landscape. Initially we focused on gathering scientific documentation. We mapped the area extending from Pasargadae to Persepolis, including the Marvdasht plain, by 1:3000 and 1:8000 aerial photography, so as to facilitate a clearer understanding and

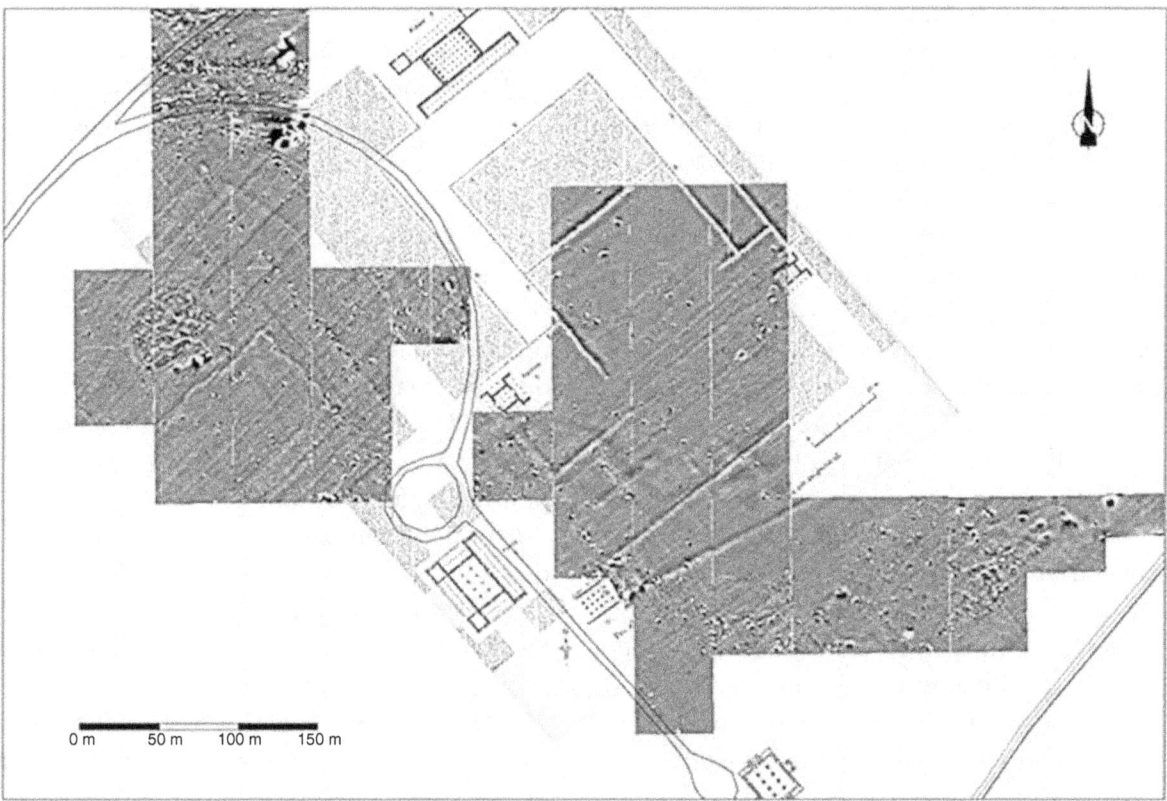

Fig. 26.2 Area covered by a geophysical survey showing irrigation canals and architectural elements at Pasargadae.

control of archaeological remains not visible to the naked eye. In addition, we extended the buffer zone of Persepolis by purchasing 52.5 ha of nearby land (Fig. 26.1). Finally, we used modern technology, such as geophysical surveys, in a wide range of functions and places. For instance, some 47.3 ha of the field next to the Persepolis platform have been carefully measured and investigated by the matrix method in order to clarify the relationship of the palace remains and the plain itself.

The measurement was first conducted on the southern side, from north of the residential quarter south of the platform and extended to the south and west of it, along the Pardis (the area of the Royal Tents). In some places modern installations, such as electric cables, water pipes, and power posts prevented a clear understanding of the buried structures, a fact that underlines the urgency of restricting such elements in future. However, traces of construction were visible in the area to the west of the South Residential Quarter and south of Pardis (Persepolis South). These probably belong to ancient water canals used to irrigate the gardens on this site but we hope to conduct further excavation in this area in order to clarify this problem.

We continued these investigations around historical mounds that are constantly threatened by agricultural developments. For example, the area to the north of the "Fratadara Temple" revealed architectural elements, and the North Residential Quarter to the north of the platform (Persepolis North) showed structural remains and extensive settlements.

Geophysical survey indicated buried metal furnaces, and stones fused with metal proved the use of such installations in this area. In addition, two parallel walls could be traced running to the north of the platform and extending all the way to the mountain behind. Again, we hope to clarify these fortifications around the platform by conducting excavations in the near future.

In the same spirit, a geophysical survey of the Pasargadae area was undertaken by our team, together with Professor Rémy Boucharlat of the French National Research Centre. It resulted in the identification of previously unknown architectural elements next to the Zendan-e Soleyman and other places, the tracing of irrigation canals, and determining the exact relationship between the palaces and the garden area (Fig. 26.2).

Another aspect of our investigation has been concerned with tracing and cleaning the underground water canals of the Persepolis platform, which have long been clogged up. This was done not only to prevent future flooding of the site but also to understand the entire system. The water system of Persepolis consisted of underground channels, which directed the accumulated water away from the platform in the direction of the area beyond. Many previous investigators, including Herzfeld, Ali Sami and Ali Hakemi, had already investigated these water channels, but the entire system remained poorly understood until now.

In 2003 some 600 m of these water channels were carefully cleaned by our archaeological and restoration team (Figs 26.3–26.4). Further cleaning was conducted between the large, stepped tunnel in the area east of the 100 Column Hall, all the way to the southeast of the Treasury, and in the water channels between the 100 Column Hall and the Treasury, as well as in a small part of the water channels situated on the northern area of the 100 Column Hall and in the vicinity of

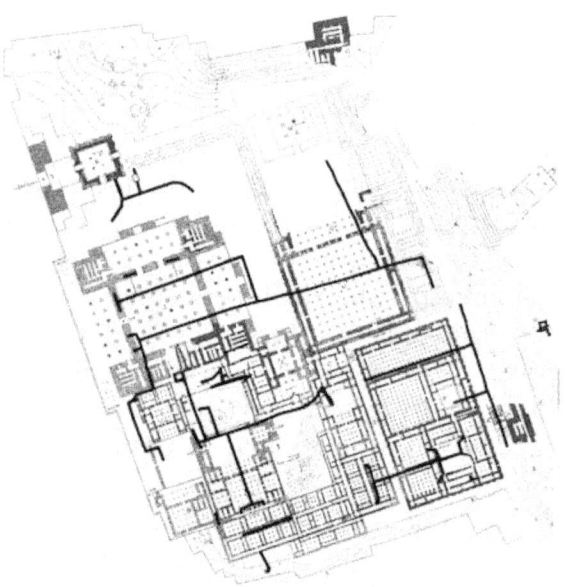

Fig. 26.3 Map showing the underground water channels at Persepolis.

Fig. 26.4 Underground water channel at Persepolis.

the so-called Unfinished Gate. These investigations produced a large number of sherds (totalling 2,024), which probably belong to the Achaemenid and post-Achaemenid periods. These finds are now cleaned and preserved in the Centre for Documents at Persepolis. In 2004 cleaning of the water channels continued south-east of the Treasury and extended all the way to the south wall of the platform. It was during these excavations that we found a pool-like basin in the south-eastern area: this had received the water, allowed it to settle and then redistributed sediment-free water beyond the platform to the South Residential Quarter from where the channels continued as open channels at ground level. Considering the fact that there is a water reservoir in the South Residential Quarter, we can clearly see the relationship between this quarter and the palace area. The discovery of the key to the puzzle of the water system at Persepolis enables a similar explanation of the previously puzzling water system and water basin at Chogha Zanbil (Ghirshman 1968). We hope to continue our investigation in the southern part of the platform at Persepolis and clear out the debris accumulated since the 1930s, in order to reveal the entire south platform wall and recover a large number of stone fragments and other valuables hidden beneath the debris.

Another goal of the Parsa-Pasargadae Research Foundation has been to facilitate the co-operation between our teams and non-Iranian experts and institutions. The best example of such co-operation has been achieved in the investigation of the Tang-e Bolaghi region. The area between Pasargadae and Persepolis is mainly covered by the Bolaghi gorge and plain. It is formed by the Pulvar river, which leaves the south-western tip of the Pasargadae plain through a narrow gorge and joins the main Kor river south-west of the Marvdasht plain. A dam under construction[2] in the southern sector of the Bolaghi plain will soon submerge an area covering some 12 km. It was therefore urgent to investigate the historical remains as soon as possible. The northern part of Bolaghi is so narrow that the Achaemenids had to cut narrow roads into the rock on either side of the river (Fig. 26.5).

The French National Centre for Scientific Research (CNRS) has been co-operating with us for several years, first in the geophysical surveys mentioned above and lately in the rescue excavations at Tang-e Bolaghi. In these excavations three other European institutions are working with us on several sites: an Iranian–Italian team supervised by Dr P. Callieri of the University of Bologna; an Irano-Polish group supervised by Dr Barbara Kaim of the Warsaw University, and an Iranian–German team led by Dr Barbara Helwing of the German archaeological institute. These excavations followed a speedy but thorough survey of the archaeological sites of Tang-e Bolaghi,

Fig. 26.5 The northern side of the road cut into the rock at Tang-e Bolaghi valley.

which resulted in the identification of nearly 130 sites by a team led by Mr M. T. Ataie. Of these, 24 were deemed necessary for rescue excavations, as can be seen from the satellite image of the Kor river basin.

There are also mounds within the banks in the lower area, dating from the prehistoric period up to the late seventeenth century. A site with the remains of stone-faced walls was excavated by the Irano-Italian team: it evidently represented an Achaemenid village, and the finds included a pottery storage jar and a tripartite bronze arrowhead. Most recently this group discovered a grave containing a body buried in the crouched position, accompanied by a pottery vessel. This clearly dates from an earlier period, in all probability belonging to the Bakun culture.

The Franco-Iranian team has investigated rock-cut roads as well as two cemeteries. One, dating from the Safavid period, contained many close-set graves dug into layers containing Sasanian walls and a plastered basin, as well as fragmentary column tori and bases of the Achaemenid period. The other cemetery contained graves covered with loose stones. Seven were excavated: five had been thoroughly pilfered but two contained intact skeletons, one of which was accompanied by grave goods evidently of Sasanian date. The team also dug some trenches in the "stone road", but the results are not yet clear.

The Polish–Iranian team has excavated a site with Sasanian architectural remains and pottery, including large jars, and investigated a related cemetery, although this had been previously looted. The German–Iranian team excavated two sites, which produced surface pottery of historic date overlying earlier cultural remains belonging to prehistoric periods. Most importantly, one site revealed levels of Bakun A, with painted pottery of exceptional workmanship as well as evidence of pottery kilns.

Observations concerning preservation and restoration at Parsa-Pasargadae

The main goal of preservation at cultural heritage sites today is to maintain their cultural integrity and identity with due respect to their environmental and natural position. This has been followed from the outset by the Parsa-Pasargadae Research Foundation, which has therefore focused on preservation rather than traditional methods of restoration. Here we present four types of remains, each of which is subject to different sources of deterioration, and each demands a distinct way of prevention of decay:

1. Those that have been exposed to weathering;
2. Those that have been unearthed and subjected to a new but different environment;
3. Those that have been subjected to harmful human intervention;
4. Those that have been subjected to traditional methods of "restoration".

Below are some examples of these four types.

1.1. The Gate of All Nations

This building has remained exposed from antiquity, and weathering and environmental corrosion have left clear traces on its walls. Most importantly, traces of water erosion, veins and breaks in the stone, and flaking in different parts are quite visible. However, a comparison with its state as seen in old drawings and photographs shows little difference, except in those places where restoration has been carried out. It seems that such restoration attempts have kept this monument in fairly good condition, and to some extent has prevented any major flaking and breaks arising from freezing of the stone in winter.

1.2. The sculptured façade on the northern Apadana staircase

This area has also been for the most part exposed to natural elements. Erosion and environmental damage are clear on the stone. In addition, remains of human damage, such as axe-blows, are also very visible on the surface, some dating from remote antiquity. Comparison with old drawings suggests that most damage has been done by moss and grey lichens growing along the upper part of the staircase.

The second problem concerns remains that have been excavated and then exposed. These are represented by four examples.

2.1. The lower part of the sculptured façade on the eastern Apadana staircase

This sits directly on the ground. Ascending seepage of water and flaking of the surface has caused a good deal of erosion on this monument since its discovery by Ernst Herzfeld. In addition, the violent exposure to the elements after lying hidden inside soft earth for over 2,000 years has made acclimatizing difficult. Even the application of a wax covering on the surface during the 1940s and 1950s has not helped in any way, and has actually led to further deterioration of the stone. The setting of the blocks directly on the ground means that water has been able to pass through the stone, freeze, and expand or alter its texture, causing massive surface flaking. Other causes of erosion have been the great disparity between day and night temperatures, and the weak nature of the stone or its inability to breathe.

2.2. The inscriptions of the eastern Apadana staircase

These texts, inscribed on soft stone, are directly set on the ground and as with the first example, they have been exposed to all corroding elements such as water seepage, internal expansion, surface flaking, and wax-covering treatment. Comparison with earliest photographs shows that they have suffered greatly.

2.3. The upper register of the sculptured façade on the eastern Apadana staircase

The position of the blocks set well above the ground has prevented natural erosion caused by dampness, and the restoration and filling of the huge gap in the middle of the register are so well executed that they have strengthened the core of the monument. Comparison with older photographs shows that in this case the present condition of preservation is quite satisfactory.

2.4. The middle register of the sculptured façade on the eastern Apadana staircase

Here surface flaking and dampness have been fairly limited by the application of a wax covering, but constant touching by visitors has caused deformation in the colour and texture of the stone. Sweat and salt applied to the surfaces by hand touching could further damage

Fig. 26.6 Wooden cover to protect the eastern staircase of the Apadana Palace at Persepolis.

the stone. For this reason we have taken measures to prevent visitors from approaching too close to the stairway façade.

These examples clearly demonstrate that the condition of erosion depends on the position of the monument and the degree of its exposure to various decaying agencies. Therefore, each case demands a careful study and a distinct method of prevention and arrest of corrosion. What is now practised in the Parsa-Pasargadae cultural region is a close investigation of causes, the prevention of decay, and less traditional restoration. This is being done by clearing ancient water canals, both those that are above the ground, even around the royal tombs, and those that are underground; by carrying rainwater from the platform area in the way the original builder intended it is hoped that this will reduce dampness, surface flaking, and the growth of algae, etc. We are also monitoring each change through photography and other documentation, and we are controlling the human-effected damage by directing visitors along well-defined safe paths and preventing them from touching the sculptured façades. These paths have been covered with wooden planks resting on soft spongy materials, and thus they do not put pressure on the underlying stone floors. They also match the colour and texture of the surrounding area and therefore cause little intrusion. This is especially useful in the spring when the largest numbers of visitors assemble on the platform (Fig. 26.6).

Conclusion

The goal of the Parsa-Pasargadae Research Foundation is to include a clear understanding of the environmental systems and to take into account the entire cultural landscape, better to appreciate its integrity and authenticity. To help us reach these goals we have assembled teams of geologists, preservation and restoration experts, archaeologist, architects, environmentalists, and even philologists. We have also taken measures to safeguard the monuments from further industrial and urban developments. Our efforts to co-operate with non-Iranian colleagues and institutions have proved fruitful, and the community as a whole has begun to appreciate and support us. A perfect proof of this is the recent announcement by the company building the Sivand Dam that it is ready to limit the extent of its work to give us time to save more sites, either permanently or by rescue excavation.[3] I hope this trend will continue in the future.

Notes

1. I would like to start express my gratitude towards the authorities of the British Museum and the Iran Heritage Foundation who have made this gathering possible. I hope that this will be the first of many gatherings that unite our efforts in serving the cultural heritage of ancient Iran.
2. The construction of the dam is now completed and the area is flooded.
3. See n.2 above.

27

The Achaemenid Army in a Near Eastern Context

Nigel Tallis

Despite the significance accorded the Greco-Persian wars in Greek literary-historical and artistic sources, the Achaemenid Persian army has received little attention in comparison with studies in Greco-Roman military history. This part of my paper will focus on some of the new possibilities for locating the Achaemenid army within the wider framework of Near Eastern military practice and tradition through the exploration of new evidence for military ritual and drill.

One of the most vivid and compelling pieces of writing to survive from the ancient world must be Herodotus' description of Xerxes the Achaemenid bridging the Hellespont and crossing with his army to bring retribution to the Greeks.[1] Such accounts, woven into these literary narratives of conflict by Ancient Greek and Roman writers, have been part of our own historical tradition since at least the Renaissance. These stories, with their mythic themes of resistance and power, were so rich and compelling as tales of high adventure that they have been accepted and absorbed, adopted and remoulded countless times to suit other circumstances and other ages.[2] Their lure was such that the complex interactions over some 200 years between the Achaemenid Persian Empire and its westerly neighbours are today almost wholly remembered in popular culture as conflict between "Persians" and "Greeks". While modern studies increasingly demonstrate the subtleties involved in the relationships between centre and periphery, both within and without the empire,[3] it is these vivid stories that continue to have popular appeal.

Thus, the irony of this account is that it cannot avoid providing a brief glimpse of a quite different army to that intended. Not a rabble of unwilling conscripts under the whip (a motif of regular army discipline itself deliberately misrepresented), but an ordered, technologically advanced army with a core of fully professional and drilled soldiers, quite unlike the amateur "warriors" of the Greeks.[4]

This is how Herodotus describes Xerxes and his army marching across the bridge of boats into Europe in 480 BC:

When they had done this they crossed over, the foot and horse all by the bridge nearest to the Pontus, the beasts of burden and the service train by the bridge towards the Aegean. The ten thousand Persians, all wearing garlands [*stephanos*], led the way, and after them came the mixed army of diverse nations. All that day these crossed; on the next, first crossed the horsemen and the ones who carried their spears reversed; these also wore garlands. After them came the sacred horses and the sacred chariot, then Xerxes himself and the spearmen and the thousand horse, and after them the rest of the army. Meanwhile the ships put out and crossed to the opposite shore. But I have also heard that the king crossed last of all. (Hdt 7.55)[5]

Herodotus describes how this event was recorded as a painting[6] and it seems possible that he actually evoked this scene either through seeing this or one very like it or, more intriguingly, he understood the appropriate rituals and drills for solemn events fraught with dangers, real and supernatural.[7]

Two pieces of evidence now indicate how this may have been possible:

The two badly abraded relief fragments illustrated here (BM 124923, BM 135204) from the North Palace at Nineveh (Figs 27.1a and 1b), show a scene in three registers representing infantry in the Assyrian army marching to the right, perhaps in three columns. In the

(a)

(b)

Figs 27.1a and b Part of a relief panel in two fragments (BM 124923: lower; BM 135204: upper) from the North Palace at Nineveh of Ashurbanipal, probably representing events of 653 BC. This shows part of a scene in three registers representing infantry in the Assyrian army marching to the right. Four Assyrian guardsmen carrying reversed spears are shown in the central register marching towards three priests wearing fishtail hats who greet them—one of whom holds a lotus-shaped holder and a cloth, the second a cloth only and the last nothing. The Assyrians are flanked in the registers above and below by marching Elamite archers wearing garlands. (Figure 1b by Ann Searight) central register there is a file of four Assyrians (although for the left-most only a hand and spearhead is preserved) marching towards three priests wearing fishtail hats. They have long, square-cut beards and hair bunched on the shoulders secured with a corded headband, as often shown on Assyrian guardsmen when not in battle dress (e.g. Barnett *et al.* 1998: 385c, pl. 312; Barnett & Forman 1960: pl. 61, BM 124850). They are barefoot and wear short-sleeved tunics and kilts with a long vertical fringe and a broad waist belt beneath a narrow sword-belt.

Over their left shoulders they carry short spears at the slope, reversed and with the spearheads pointing downwards. The spearheads have a deep socket with an angular blade and a pronounced mid-rib. The shafts have a plain rounded butt with a loop or tassel around the shaft a short distance from it. This is another significant detail. Although ninth-century chariot spears and the javelins carried by cavalry may have what appear to be streamers or tassels at this point (which may also be throwing-loops as well as identifying marks, e.g. Barnett & Forman 1960: pl. 27, BM 124553), it seems likely that in this case these features are throwing-loops. They are in exactly the place where Assyrian soldiers are shown holding their spears when in an overhead "striking" position (which appears unsuitable as a balanced and secure hold for a thrusting spear) and King Ashurbanipal records that heavy *azmarû* spears of this type could be thrown (Luckenbill 1926–27, ii: 986; Streck 1916: 256.I.22).[8]

In the two registers above and below the file of Assyrians there are files of marching archers, with Elamite-style quivers, hairstyles and dress (with kilts hitched up at the front). They also wear feather or floral crowns or garlands in their headbands.

Due to the presence of Elamites, and on the basis of the feather or floral crowns suggesting the fluted caps on guardsmen from the Persepolis reliefs, Barnett proposed that these troops were auxiliary archers from Persia. Barnett also suggested that all these fragments with garlanded figures were from "Room S" in the North Palace at Nineveh, while admitting the artistic styles of the individual fragments differed quite significantly.[9] He also described them as "Persian auxiliary bowmen" in the Assyrian army, although he noted that, while one group were probably Elamites, it was not clear that any of the others were Persian and that other, more plausible, ethnic attributions had been proposed for some (Barnett 1976: 55).

It seems most likely that the scene shown is a ceremonial parade either at Nineveh or near Arbela following the great Assyrian victory over the Elamites at the river Ulai in 653 BC.[10]

The Assyrian guards do not wear garlands in this fragment, but similar guardsmen do in other surviving pieces.[11] It is possible that the fluted caps shown worn by Persian nobles and guardsmen (see e.g. Curtis & Tallis 2005: nos. 27–32) might be an evolved, stylized form of ceremonial floral garlands but that is not the significance of these fragments. The garlands most likely indicate a ritual or celebratory aspect to the content, but the key detail is that the Assyrian guardsmen are depicted marching with reversed spears in the manner described by Herodotus for "the ones who carried their spears reversed", 1,000 elite spearmen, "picked men like the others", who marched in advance of the king.[12] The relief is too fragmentary to determine much of the order of the procession approaching the priests, but it is clear that the Assyrian guards with reversed spears are at the head.

It is also notable that these fragments of soldiers wearing garlands in a ceremonial victory parade include priests and apparently a flute-player,[13] particularly in view of the wearing of garlands and music in Greek military ritual: "Early next morning Agesilaus ordered Gylis, the polemarch, to draw up the army in battle order and to set up a trophy, and to command every man to wear a wreath in honour of the god and all the flute-players to play" (Xenophon *Agesilaus* 2.24).

In fact, rituals involving the reversal of the natural or the normal, particularly relating to dangerous activities, battle, death or the supernatural are not difficult to find (even ignoring numerous representations of deliberately reversed weaponry in Ancient Near Eastern art).[14] For example, the Hittite text of the fifteenth century BC detailing a number of drills and ceremonies for the royal guard (Güterbock & van den Hout 1991: 38–39) describes the proper procedures and circumstances for both reversed and upright spears in the same ceremony and also notes the division of the guards into different grades of spearman, including "gold spearmen" (cf. the division of the Persian royal bodyguards into grades of golden and silver "pomegranate-bearers" and "apple-bearers").[15] The fragmentary end of the tablet, which Güterbock suggested concerned the guards bringing food to the king states: "But a spear-man [takes] a spe[ar], but the bronze (blade)[of the sp]ear is tu[rned] down" (ibid.: 39; IBoT I 36, §58, 47).

For large groups to perform these rituals effectively requires practice and established procedure (as indicated by the Hittite texts, although oral tradition would be adequate). In a military context this means drill. It is possible that the details of reversal in these rituals are both practical (perhaps relating to the specifics of weapons' drill, and ease of use of the weapon in a confined space), and may in addition relate to proximity, with weapons, to the king and to aspects of funerary ritual (which may of course involve strands of all these elements, for which the Tatarli paintings provide conspicuous evidence).

The existence of these evidently closely related elite army rituals over wide geographical areas, and their persistence over time, deserves further investigation, but for the moment their significance is as an indicator of a pervasive and now highly visible aspect of a tradition of military ritual and drill in the Ancient Near East.

Notes

1. Unless otherwise stated, Greek texts are after the various Loeb editions.
2. This process would appear to have reached a nadir in the 2007 film *300*, whose advocates sought to escape criticism for its curiously skewed themes, authoritarian undertones and lurid, ultra-violent content by claiming it was merely fantasy. This largely computer generated epic was a close adaptation of a comic book, which was itself based directly on a 1962 Hollywood film of the Cold War (*The 300 Spartans*), which was loosely based on the battle of Thermopylae.
3. For recent studies on the interactions with local elites within the western empire see, for example, Dusinberre 2003.
4. For a good modern summary of ancient Greek warfare see van Wees 2004: 89–93.
5. This is a culmination of two preceding passages in Herodotus describing the expeditionary forces' order of march, with two other descriptions of this practice, and associated with other rituals (a "punishment" or sacrifice; the presence of the sacred chariot):

    With that reply, he [Xerxes] immediately ordered those who were assigned to do these things to find the eldest of Pythius sons and cut him in half, then to set one half of his body on the right side of the road and the other on the left, so that the army would pass between them. This they did, and the army passed between. First went the baggage train and the beasts of burden, and after them a mixed army of all sorts of nations, not according to their divisions but all mingled together; when more than half had passed there was a space left, and these did not come near the king. After that, first came a thousand horsemen, chosen out of all Persians; *next, a thousand spearmen, picked men like the others, carrying their spears reversed*; and after them ten horses of the breed called Nesaean, equipped most splendidly. Behind these ten horses was the place of the sacred chariot of Zeus, drawn by eight white horses, with the charioteer following the horses on foot and holding the reins; for no mortal man may mount into that seat. After these came Xerxes himself in a chariot drawn by Nesaean horses [...] In this way Xerxes rode out from Sardis; but whenever the thought took him he would alight from the chariot into a carriage [*harmamaxa*]. Behind him came a thousand spearmen of the best and noblest blood of Persia, carrying their spears in the customary manner; after them a thousand picked Persian horsemen, and after the horse ten thousand that were foot soldiers, chosen out of the rest of the Persians. One thousand of these had golden pomegranates on their spear-shafts instead of a spike [i.e. a round ferrule instead of a butt-spike], and surrounded the rest; the nine thousand who were inside them had silver pomegranates. *Those who held their spears reversed also carried golden pomegranates*, and those following nearest to Xerxes had apples of gold. (Hdt. 7.39–41) (author's italics).

An overview of Assyrian sacred chariots (also with "white" draught horses) is now conveniently in Reade 2005: 16–19.

6. Hdt 4.88: "After this, being pleased with his bridge of boats, Darius made a gift of ten of everything to Mandrocles the Samian, the architect of it; Mandrocles took the first-fruits of these and had a picture made with them, showing the whole bridge of the Bosporus, and Darius sitting aloft on his throne and his army crossing; he set this up in the temple of Hera, with this inscription: 'After bridging the Bosporus that teems with fish, Mandrocles dedicated a memorial of the floating bridge to Hera, having won a crown for himself, and fame for the Samians, doing the will of King Darius.' This memorialized the builder of the bridge." (See Borchhardt 2002: 93–94).

7. Hittite rituals for an army facing defeat, involving passing through the severed parts of a sacrificial victim, on occasion human (*KUB* 17.28; *CTH* 730 iv 44–55), are also mirrored in Herodotus (Hdt. 7.39, see above), where a similar ritual is performed by the Achaemenid army. This may reflect specifically local Anatolian customs, either because a significant proportion of the troops present were in fact raised locally, or because the Persians wished to placate local divinities, or perhaps because Herodotus, traditionally from Halicarnassus, knew that such a ritual would be appropriate for his narrative. Herodotus explains this as punishment for Pythius the Lydian, who sought to keep back one of his sons (the victim) from service in the royal army. If Herodotus and his intended audience knew that this ritual was perhaps associated with the warding-off of military defeat then the episode may have been fabricated to foreshadow the eventual Persian "defeat". Alternatively it may reflect Herodotus' rationalization of a significant ritual reported to him, perhaps as a response to an ill omen for the army (most likely the immediately preceding eclipse of Hdt 7.38), which he did not understand. For this episode as a purification ritual known also in Macedon see Evans 1988: 139; in Boeotia, Plutarch *Moralia* 209d.

A useful summary of work concerning Assyrian royal and public ritual is in Porter 2004: 259–260, n. 5. The definition of ritual used (2004: n. 6, "a relatively fixed set of symbolically charged elements, such as words, images, music, or actions, that are performed at fixed intervals or on fixed occasions, that may be religious in implication but are not necessarily so, and that are performed before a considerable number of people who are capable of having some impact on the political life of their state or community") is apt in this case, considering the key importance of the military to the political life of ancient states and the practical role that shared ritual plays in military life in terms of group identity, unit cohesion and drill. However, see also Porter 2005: 5–6 for the difficulties in defining "ritual".

8. Note that in DNc (Kent 1953: 140), Old Persian *arštibara*, "spear-bearer" (with *aršti-* "spear" having a root in Sanskrit to "rush, push", Kent 1953: 172) has *aršti-* translated as *azmarû* in the Akkadian version. Significantly, Xenophon notes that the Persian spear of cornel wood (*palton*), stronger and more wieldy than the longer Greek spear (*doru*), was ideal for both throwing and thrusting "by the skilful" (Xenophon, *Horsemanship* 9.1.11). Throwing-loops and nocks, of different design, are clearly shown far earlier on javelins of the Early Dynastic period (cf. the javelins shown in the chariot-quiver of Eannatum

of Lagash on the "Stela of the Vultures"), and archaic Greek warfare featured both javelins and throwing-loops (van Wees 2004: 169–170, n. 12 [previous study]; near-identical depiction of Neo-Assyrian striking pose, fig. 21B, pl. XVIII etc).

9. Subsequently, two of these fragments have been assigned, based on style and material, to scenes relating to the aftermath of the Ulai battle in the Southwest Palace (Reade 2005: 21; Barnett *et al.* 1998: nos. 415–416).

10. For a brief overview of military ritual and ceremonial in terms of "triumphs", see now Reade 2005: 19–22 (also Reade 1967: 43, n. 7; 1976: 100). If the fragments attributed to the Southwest Palace are indeed to be associated with the Ulai battle reliefs then the victory parade, or episodes from it, was represented in both palaces. Alternatively, more than one victory may be represented.

11. Assyrian guardsmen, garlands, (chariot) and parasol, Barnett 1976: pl. LXII (Istanbul 6338), assigned to the Southwest Palace, Room XXXIII (BB) in Barnett *et al.* 1998: 415; archers (from Carchemish? See Wäfler 1975: 216–231, pl. LXII [BM 124924]); garland worn by a musician in a garden, Barnett 1976: pl. XIV (BM 118916); feather (or floral?) crests of divine crowns, Barnett 1976: pl. XXXVIII. See also Barnett *et al.* 1998: 312, pl. 320, drawing of slab 10, Room XXII (XX), Southwest Palace, Nineveh, where "a celebration after the battle is probably shown". Assyrian "auxiliary" archers and spearmen with garlands in their headbands and around their helmets, and a beardless figure in a long robe carrying a (perhaps significant) upright plaited object, possibly an unlighted torch. Reade suggests (2005: 22) this may be a triumphal entry into Nineveh with captives from Babylonia and possibly Arabia.

12. See Henkelman 2002, where *arštibara* are attested with missions of some responsibility, comparable to those of Assyrian royal bodyguards (*ša qurbûti*) in Sargonid texts. For a summary of classical texts relating to Persian royal guardsmen, *melophoroi* or "apple-bearers" (including Xenophon, Heraclides, Aelian, Curtius, Arrian, Athenaeus and Hesychius), see Briant 2002*a*: 261–262. Since the conference in 2005, the mid- to late fifth-century BC painted figural decoration from the tomb at Tatarli has been published in greater detail. This includes a remarkable scene of infantry spearmen marching with reversed spears behind a royal (?) chariot, in a funeral procession, as part of an army returning from campaign against unidentified Saka. They are not shown with garlands, but are in "Median" battledress, with cap and broad stripes down the front of the tunic and apparently led by a standard bearer. Summerer & von Kienlin 2007: 80, 87; Summerer 2007: nos. 1–2/3–30.

13. Istanbul 6339, Barnett 1976: 56, pl. LXX (J), attributed to the Southwest Palace, Room XXXIII (BB) in Barnett *et al.* 1998: no. 416, pl. 320.

14. For possible reversed spears (rather than gateposts) in a ritual context on seals see e.g. Collon (1987: no. 814).

15. Indicated by the gold or silver spherical ferrules on the butts of their spears (see Curtis & Tallis 2005: no. 51 and Hdt 7.41 [n. 5 above]). Where the ferrules have openings cast into them (as shown in art and found in excavated examples, Moorey 1980: 61, fig. 10, no. 181) it might be so as to give a whistling effect when thrown rather than being purely decorative. The ferrules themselves may have been designed better to balance the spear for throwing, since arrow-length darts, clearly throwing weapons, with rounded ferrules (rare for the Assyrian period, where spike ferrules, if any, are usual) are clearly shown carried in the quivers of seventh-century BC Assyrian chariots (Barnett & Forman 1960: 56 [lower, a pair being carried to the chariot], 60–61 [visible in the quivers]).

28

The Origins of the Achaemenids (Abstract)

Sima Yadollahi and Abbas Yalvaee

In spite of the narratives of Herodotus about the Achaemenids, and in spite of the many surveys and excavations carried out during the last century, and in spite of the fact that the first Achaemenid cuneiform inscriptions were deciphered more than one and a half centuries ago, our understanding of the origins of the Achaemenids still remains problematic. Migration routes traditionally proposed by some archaeologists and scholars are the north-east and north-west of Iran and even the region of Fars. This paper will suggest an alternative interpretation by considering some new aspects of this issue:

- During the second millennium BC some populations with Indo-European elements that began to appear in the south-east of Anatolia and north of Syria were exposed to Aramaic and Assyrian contacts. Some of them had frequent confrontations with the Assyrians during the late second and a considerable part of the first millennia BC. Finally, they were defeated by Sargon II in the late eighth century BC.
- The Assyrians routinely exiled their active enemies in large groups from and to different parts of the Near East, affecting the population composition of these regions. Some Indo-European populations could have been among the groups and tribes transferred by the Assyrians.
- The Achaemenids were quick to adopt Aramaic writing and language and some other artistic and cultural elements from the Levant and Egypt, which may not be well explained by the traditional hypotheses.
- Achaemenid cuneiform has some elements in common with Urartian cuneiform, but it does not originate from Elamite or Assyrian cuneiform.
- Indo-Iranian and Achaemenid names found in south and south-western Iran cannot be traced in the relatively numerous inscriptions (Assyrian, Babylonian and Elamite) of the late eighth and the seventh century BC at least until about 630 BC.
- Neither in the north-east and north-west (ancient Parsua) of Iran nor in the province of Fars (southern Iran) have any reliable Achaemenid archaeological remains been discovered that could be associated with the times prior to the establishment of the dynasty.

- The word "Parsua", according to some linguists, has no Indo-European roots but derives from Akkadian.
- It is probable that for political and military reasons the Achaemenids were among those groups exiled by the Assyrians from the north of Syria and the south-east of Anatolia to the neighbouring regions of Babylonia and Elam. It is suggested that such an event might have taken place during 740–640 BC.

29

Excavations in Dashtestan (Borazjan, Iran) (Abstract)

Ehsan Yaghmaee

This paper reports on recent important excavations near Borazjan in the Dashtestan region in the province of Bushehr in south-west Iran. In 1978 the author surveyed the Dashtestan area and discovered the remains of 21 palaces. Excavations were conducted at two sites, Sang-e Siah and Bardak-e Siah.

The most recent excavation at Sang-e Siah, located 12 km north of Borazjan, was in 2005 and lasted for two months. The Achaemenid palace at this site has a central hall with porticoes on four sides. This main hall measures 24.40 m x 20.50 m and has 16 column bases. Each column base has black stone at the bottom and white stone in the middle and at the top. There are 16 column bases in the north, south, and west porticoes respectively (arranged in two rows), and 28 column bases in the east portico, again in two rows. Parts of the column capitals such as eagle's eyes, feathers, and lion's teeth, all of limestone, were also found. The walls of the main hall were of mud brick which had been plastered and painted green.

Bardak-e Siah is north-west of Borazjan and is surrounded by palm groves. Excavations at this site were in 1978 and 2005 and still continue. Here there is another Achaemenid palace. The main hall has doorways in the east, south and west walls. The north side has not yet been excavated. The column bases in the main hall again had black stones at the bottom and white stones in the middle and at the top. The tori were white. The stone door-jambs in the east and west doorways are small but the door-jambs in the south doorway are large and finely constructed. Here were found four large stone fragments on one of which is part of a bas-relief of Darius the Great. Also near the southern doorway we found part of a cuneiform inscription. This may be the Achaemenid city of Tamukan.

Part 6

Seals and Coins

30

An Analytical Investigation on the Coin Hoard of the Oxus Treasure (Abstract)

Mehdi Daryaie

Coins are more precisely datable than any other archaeological materials and thus offer a primary source for the study of social, economic and political history. Thus they should be an ideal cultural material for comparative analysis. However, although coins serve as a valuable source of information, their interpretation is not always straightforward. In this respect one of the most important archaeological discoveries in Iranian archaeology, the Oxus Treasure which was found between 1877 and 1880 on the north bank of the Oxus river (now known as the Amu Dar'ya) in modern Tajikistan, is the subject of focus in this paper. It is unknown who originally discovered the Oxus Treasure and it is thought that the treasure was found over several occasions.

In this paper, the main focus will be on the coins within the treasure. Were all these coins circulated? Are there any forgeries in the collection? How can we detect fakes? The Oxus Treasure is a large collection of ancient Iranian metalwork now housed in the British Museum. The treasure consists of approximately 180 gold and silver objects such as: gold bracelets and armlets, gold discs, rings, vessels, earrings and pendants, a gold sword scabbard, two model gold chariots, several silver and three gold statuettes, two stone cylinder seals, about 50 decorated small, thin gold plaques and numerous gold beads. Museum records indicate that the hoard was also originally associated with around 1,500 coins; however, only approximately 200 of these coins can presently be identified in the Museum's collection as belonging to the Oxus Treasure.

The contents of the hoard range in date from the sixth to the second century BC. While the coins vary in date, the majority of the metal objects are from the Achaemenid Dynasty (550–330 BC).

A coin hoard is a combination of coins which archaeologically or numismatically convey a historic message. The total number of the coins, their fabric and their denomination are important factors in the content of the hoard and therefore its interpretation. Additionally, the function of the coin hoard will be examined. What type of coin hoard was the Oxus Treasure? According to the coin hoard distribution pattern, most of the Persian coins (darics and sigloi) were found in the western satrapies mainly in Asia Minor and it is quite odd that the Oxus hoard contained darics and sigloi. Were they circulated in the northeastern satrapies such as Bactria? If not, how did they reach this area? Was it through military campaigns or trade exchange?

A few other questions will also be discussed, including previous research on Oxus coins, the probable date of hoard burial, and the question of whether there are any fakes in the coin hoard. If so, then the application of SEM and XRF analyses would be essential. Finally, after studying 200 pieces of the Oxus coin hoard, it was concluded that there are no forgeries in the British Museum coin collection.

31

Anatolian Crossroads: Achaemenid Seals from Sardis and Gordion

Elspeth R. M. Dusinberre

Seals can provide a unique entry into understanding ancient societies: used by individuals or offices for ratification, identification and ornamentation, they functioned simultaneously as official insignia and indicators of personal taste.[1] The differences and similarities between the Achaemenid seals found at the satrapal capital of Sardis and the large but second-tier city of Gordion are therefore especially interesting. This paper considers the seals from Sardis and Gordion, exploring their shapes, sizes, materials, style, iconography and findspots. It situates them in their historical, political and geographic contexts to examine the Achaemenid Empire itself and the different ways in which Achaemenid hegemony affected different types of sites.

Seals and society in Achaemenid Anatolia: a study in contrasts

Most of the seals from Sardis are pyramidal stamp seals and rings and are of such high-prestige materials as gold and chalcedony. The great majority reflect imperial Achaemenid iconography and were produced in one of the so-called "Greco-Persian" styles. They were excavated from tombs of elite Sardians.[2] The seals from Gordion, by contrast, come in a wide variety of shapes and materials, including a fairly large number in glass. A significant number were imported from places far to the east, west and south. They exhibit a tremendous variety in artistic style and imagery. Most of them were found reused in post-Achaemenid domestic and work contexts.[3]

The seals from Sardis demonstrate the cohesion of the Achaemenid elite and the overwhelming adoption of Achaemenid ideology at this satrapal capital. The lack of pre-Achaemenid seals from Sardis and the preponderance of high-status ones in the Achaemenid period reiterate the importance of the Achaemenid administration at this satrapal headquarters. The seals from the once-important city of Gordion depart radically from the pre-Achaemenid Phrygian corpus of seals at the site. They suggest a change in administrative practice during the Achaemenid period. They also demonstrate that Achaemenid ideology and practices penetrated to less administratively significant sites in the empire as

Fig. 31.1 Sardis, Gordion, Anatolia and surroundings. (After Dusinberre 2005)

well as to sites of such satrapal significance as Sardis.

Sardis

Sardis had been the capital of Lydia and retained its administrative importance under Achaemenid hegemony, becoming the satrapal seat of Sparda and a primary centre for Achaemenid government in western Anatolia. Its seals reflect its importance in the empire in some particularly interesting ways. At Sardis we repeatedly see an important phenomenon: official imperial iconography rendered in a local style, with local tastes and preferences perhaps reflected in the selection of imperial images. The large number of seals found—34 of them—is partly a reflection of the enormous number of tombs excavated at Sardis (well over 1,000). It is interesting, in light of such large numbers, that there have been to my knowledge no seals at all found at Sardis that predate the Achaemenid period. The Sardian seals were found in graves of the elite.[4] Interestingly, it is impossible to discern the ethnicity of a seal's user at Sardis—choice of image and artistic style are not indicators of Persian or Lydian or other background. Instead, seal users (the elite) show remarkable conformity of taste in seal imagery, demonstrating an artistic koine that linked the elite at Sardis across ethnic background to imperial authority. Thus users embedded themselves in an artistic framework that

Fig. 31.2 IAM 4523, from Sardis: lion and bull combat. (After Dusinberre 2003; © Istanbul Archaeological Museums)

Fig. 31.3 IAM 4522, 4581, 4523, 4520: pyramidal stamp, cylinder seal, "weight-shaped" seal, and ring with stone bezel. (After Dusinberre 2003; © Istanbul Archaeological Museums)

reinforced their own goals or sense of authority and power.

The seals excavated at Sardis demonstrate a variety of choices available in shapes and materials.[5] The most popular shape is the pyramidal stamp seal, of which there are 15. Of the nine rings with sealing faces, three are of pure gold, with gold bezels, and six have stones carved in intaglio, generally set on a swivel so the sealing surface could be turned towards or away from the finger. Three seals are roughly cylindrical squat stamps that are wider at the top than at the bottom—sealing—surface. Three are cylinder seals. The remaining two seals are suspended from a bracelet and a necklace. The most common material of which the pyramidal stamp seals are made is blue chalcedony, a particularly beautiful and translucent stone. The ring bezels, by contrast, are generally made of carnelian, when they are not of gold.[6]

All the seals excavated at Sardis have settings that show they were worn on the body in a visible spot, such as a necklace or a wrist chain, or perhaps pinned to a garment: they were not kept out of sight in a pocket or purse. Many seals have particularly beautiful suspension devices, with elaborate attention paid to the qualities that enhance their value as adornments. The highly visible nature of the seals underscores their importance as indicators of individuality: not only the image carved on a seal but also its very form could convey messages about the person using it, and the fact of choice between different shapes and styles at Sardis is a crucial one.

The seals excavated at Sardis demonstrate that multiple artistic styles existed concurrently at this satrapal capital, but most of them are carved in one of the styles commonly called "Greco-Persian".[7] The seals from Sardis carved in this style are almost all linked with imperial Achaemenid iconography and indeed often with iconography associated with high status.[8] They provide compelling support for the suggestion that this style should be seen not as any kind of ethnic indicator, but rather as a newly crafted style designed to indicate the elite status of the user in the Achaemenid hierarchy.[9]

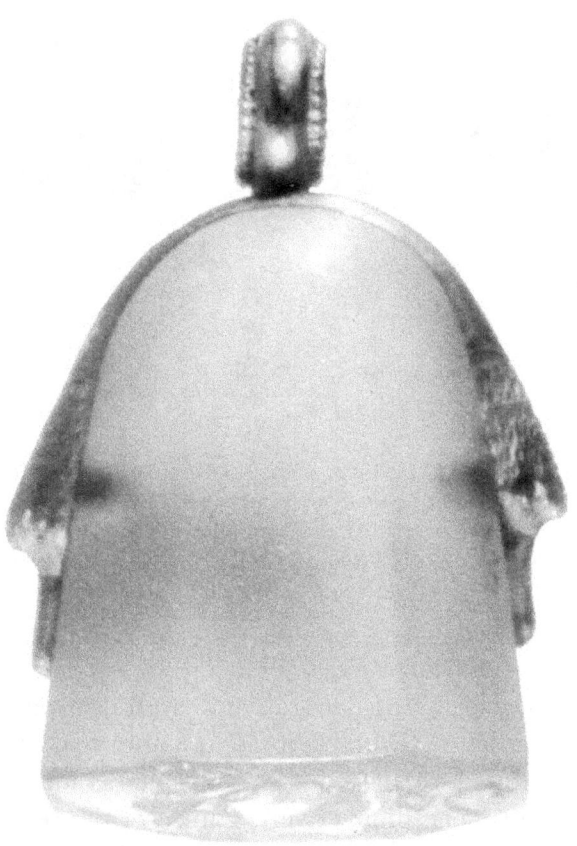

Fig. 31.4 IAM 4641. A suspension device in the shape of ducks' heads clasping a blue chalcedony pyramidal stamp seal. (After Dusinberre 2003; © Istanbul Archaeological Museums)

The seals from Sardis demonstrate the cohesion of the Achaemenid elite and the adoption of Achaemenid imperial ideology at this satrapal capital. At Sardis, we repeatedly see an important phenomenon: official iconography rendered in a specific style, with local tastes and preferences perhaps reflected in the selection of imperial images.[10] This provides support for the suggestion that we rename this style at last. I would like to suggest "Achaemenid hegemonic" as a name that is neither ethnically nor geographically situated but rather emphasizes the meaning of this style in its various and fluid socio-political contexts.

The iconography of the seals from Sardis carved in "Achaemenid hegemonic" style forms an internally consistent set of images. Favoured are lions: five seals show single lions, one shows a lion and a bull, one a heroic combat with a lion, one an archer scene with a lion, and one a heroic control scene with lions.[11] Two seals show winged lions in heraldic groupings.[12] This predilection for lions is found in sculpture from Sardis dating to the Achaemenid period, but it also reflects the large numbers of lions that appear on the Persepolis Fortification seals. That prototypical Achaemenid beast, the lion-griffin, is also popular, including in scenes that involve the Achaemenid hero-king figure: three seals show single lion-griffins, one shows a heroic combat scene with a lion-griffin, and one shows a heroic control scene with lion-griffins.[13] Other composite animals featured are bearded winged crowned sphinxes, a goat-sphinx, and a human-headed bird.[14] A bull and a boar complete the list of animals carved in this stylistic category.[15] As has been seen, scenes involving the Persian hero figure are present, with two heroic combats, two scenes of heroic control, and one archer scene.[16] The last remaining seal carved in "Achaemenid hegemonic" style shows the king enthroned.[17] These images thus overwhelmingly incorporate images favoured in Iran, and many of them display exceptionally powerful and high-status central images indeed.[18]

If, as I have argued elsewhere, the style should be seen as a newly composed and socially symbolic art of empire, it demonstrates at Sardis the network of artistic and socio-political connections that united the Persian, and Persianizing, elite.[19] This polyethnic group at Sardis clearly had different options to choose from when patrons had

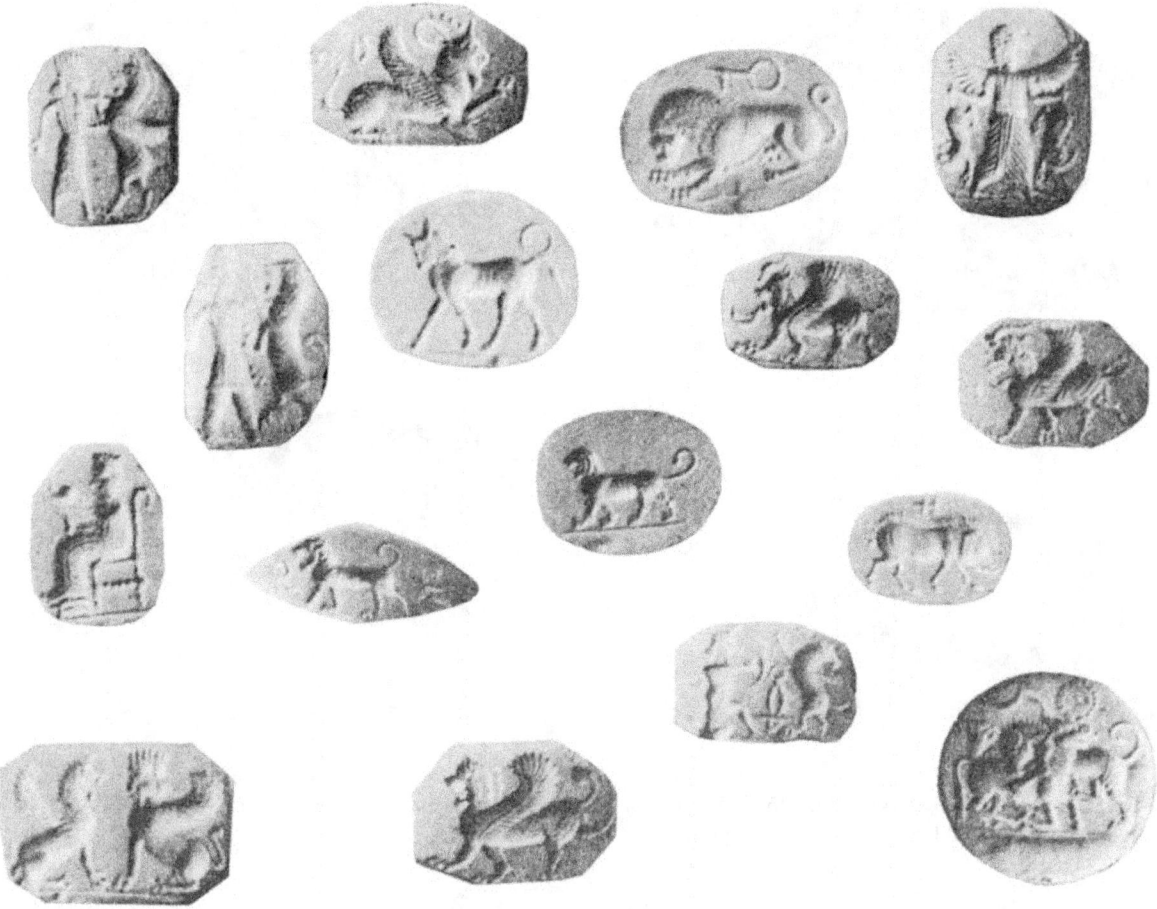

Fig. 31.5 Seals from Sardis: modern impressions. (After Curtis 1925: pl. 11)

their seals made; the preponderance of this style, carved primarily on stamp seals made of glorious semi-precious stones, is significant. The observation takes on added significance when we consider the tremendous adherence within this style to iconography that links Sardis directly to the Achaemenid heartland and to Achaemenid imperial iconography. The seals of Sardis thus become a real citation of power, an affirmation of connections to the Achaemenid elite across the empire expressed in a style that can be linked to the new regime and its supporters. In addition, the great beauty of the seals themselves suggests they were meant to be seen as well as used, that this was a message to be proclaimed aloud.

Gordion

Gordion saw very different circumstances during the time of Achaemenid hegemony, and its seals offer fascinating insights into what life in this large and thriving city might have been like.[20] Archaeological evidence at the site shows it had been conquered by the Lydians not long before the arrival of the Achaemenid armies; its role as capital of Phrygia had already ended. It is therefore particularly interesting to note that the city prospered under Achaemenid

Fig. 31.6 IAM 4579, 5134, 4591, 4525. Details of selected images in "Achaemenid hegemonic" style. (After Dusinberre 2003; © Istanbul Archaeological Museums)

rule, expanding to its greatest size during this time and seeing an increase in evidence for interaction with other peoples both within and outside the borders of the Achaemenid Empire.[21] Moreover, architectural remains demonstrate the construction of at least one large elaborate house with painted walls at this time and a building that was decorated with colourful mosaics.[22]

In the Achaemenid period, the use of seals at the site exploded. From the time of the Achaemenid Empire, as many as 29 seals and impressions were recovered from excavated deposits at Gordion, a tremendous increase over earlier numbers. It is important to note that most of the Achaemenid period seals from Gordion were found in Hellenistic period deposits—the number is probably too great to be accounted for by residual finds from casual loss and suggests that a number of Achaemenid tombs may perhaps have been found and looted during the Hellenistic period.

Unlike the earlier eras at Gordion, when the few seals made were crafted from local materials, during the Achaemenid period the stuff from which the seals were made is remarkably varied. Materials include glass, bone, ivory, agate, lapis lazuli, chalcedony, faience, rock crystal, meerschaum and more. They come from everywhere, from as far east as Afghanistan and as far south as Egypt, from the wildly banded agate found near Sardis, and from the heartland of the Achaemenid Empire itself. It seems thus that the Achaemenid presence at Gordion led to

Fig. 31.7 Gordion Seals 100, 246, 44, 187, and 153. (After Dusinberre 2005; © Gordion Archaeological Project)

greatly increased mobility of glyptic artefacts and possibly artists and patrons, so that the raw materials available for seals (not to mention the seals themselves) were suddenly vastly more varied than they had been.

Perhaps one material, glass, may serve as a case study for the importance surrounding this observation. Workshops across the empire produced not only seals of hard stone but also examples in glass. Those glass and glass paste seals from Gordion with Achaemenid imagery are predominantly of traditional Mesopotamian shapes: a cylinder and pyramidal stamp seals, with one scaraboid thrown in.[23] Three further glass scaraboids have strongly Hellenizing imagery. Thus more than a fifth of the Achaemenid seals from Gordion are made of glass, and they show that the artists drew on overtly Achaemenid imagery and Near Eastern shapes and also on strongly Greek imagery and shapes. There is some overlap, so that Achaemenid imagery might show up on Hellenizing shapes. The glass is of different colours, including blue, green and clear. Whether they were purchasing seals hot off the glass press at Gordion itself, using imports from elsewhere or travelling to distant lands themselves to bring seals to Gordion with them, people at Gordion clearly had a wide range of options and possibilities for personal selection in glyptic shape and image, even within this one material category.

The iconography that decorated the Achaemenid period seals was as varied as the materials available for use. Instead of the striations and nondescript imagery that characterize some of the sealstones from the pre-Achaemenid period and many of those from the post-Achaemenid period, the seals dating to the Achaemenid period at Gordion have instantly recognizable and often highly idiosyncratic imagery. Some of the more glamorous imported sealstones include an Achaemenid period Neo-Babylonian-style worship scene on a chalcedony conical stamp seal, an Egyptian faience scarab and a spectacular red agate cylinder carved in "Achaemenid hegemonic" style with an Achaemenid worship scene. It is highly unusual for Anatolia, in that it is inscribed in Aramaic: "Seal of Bn', son of Ztw, (something else)".[24]

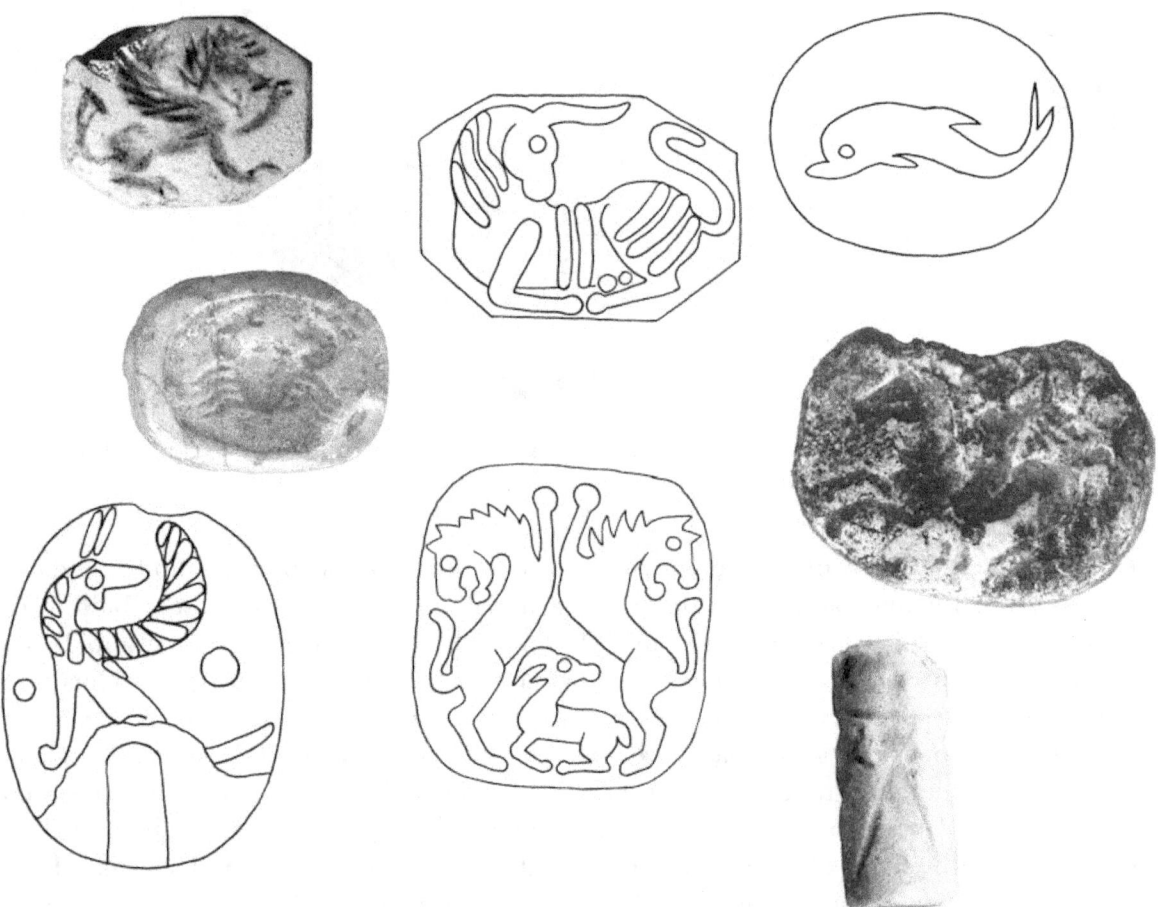

Fig. 31.8 Gordion Seals 56, 188, 44, 90, 112, 192, 205, 75. A selection of glass seals from Gordion. (After Dusinberre 2005; © Gordion Archaeological Project)

These seals have precise parallels elsewhere in the Achaemenid Empire and situate Gordion solidly in the middle of glyptic practice throughout the empire. This statement gains additional strength from a series of other seals found at Gordion, including a lapis lazuli scaraboid with pacing lion, and various pyramidal stamp seals representing composite monsters such as griffins. They give an idea of an Achaemenid administration at Gordion, a taste for Achaemenid imagery. The cylinder seal in "Achaemenid hegemonic" style, Seal 100, with its strongly Achaemenid imagery and Aramaic inscription, may even demonstrate the presence of ethnic Persians at the site, who brought not only their government and its tools with them but also language, religion and aesthetics.

Two sealings that date to the Achaemenid period may add to our sense of the artistic variety in Achaemenid glyptic at Gordion. One clay tab is an isolated impression left by a cylinder seal with an Achaemenid goat hunt on it, Achaemenid in imagery, shape and style.[25] A further little sealing is an impression left by a bezel ring, preserving a surprisingly sensuous image of a nude female. It is Greek in concept, execution and form.[26] The Achaemenid period seals and sealings from Gordion thus attest to the tremendous variety of glyptic

Fig. 31.9 Gordion Seals 100, 73, 246. "Achaemenid hegemonic" cylinder, Neo-Babylonian-style worship scene, and Egyptian scarab. (After Dusinberre 2005; © Gordion Archaeological Project)

Fig. 31.10 Gordion Seals 156 and 272. (After Dusinberre 2005; © Gordion Archaeological Project)

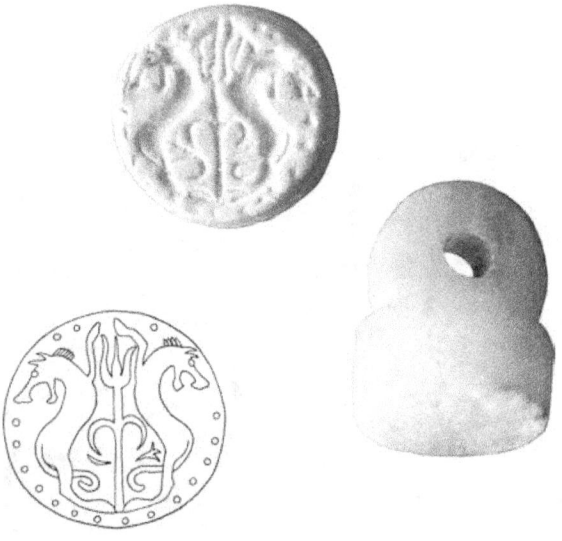

Fig. 31.11 Gordion Seal 187. (After Dusinberre 2005; © Gordion Archaeological Project)

imagery and materials imported from elsewhere in and beyond the empire.

Even the seals that seem to have been made at Gordion or that show Phrygian artistic influence are more varied in the Achaemenid period and show more outside influence than they had before this time. So, for example, Seal 187 is a variation on a standard Phrygian shape, but with heraldic lions as a central vegetal element in a very strongly Achaemenidizing manner.[27]

One large grey cylinder is a real tour de force, with Phrygianizing animals participating in a standard Achaemenid chariot hunt scene, complete with a woven basket on the chariot and with a winged disc hovering overhead.[28] Its style links it to Phrygian production, but its imagery is wholly Achaemenid. It is clear that the variety of iconography and form characterizing the seals imported during the Achaemenid period influenced local carvers even as it had its impact on patrons of glyptic art.

A last little stamp is a particularly vibrant and unusual seal from Achaemenid Gordion, of a style not seen elsewhere that may be local.[29] It is a scaraboid of a jet-black stone carved with a scene showing a chariot drawn by two horses, in which stands the king under a parasol with a charioteer and an attendant behind him. The rearmost figure holds a spear. Although Achaemenid glyptic abounds with chariots, the images are almost all hunt scenes carved on cylinder seals. The Gordion seal thus shows the chariot rendered on a different form, a

Fig. 31.12 Gordion Seal 199. (After Dusinberre 2005; © Gordion Archaeological Project)

Fig. 31.13 Gordion Seal 150. (After Dusinberre 2005; © Gordion Archaeological Project)

stamp seal, and with different imagery than was common in the heartland. Some aspects of its style link it to Phrygian precedents. It may represent new local developments, incorporating local traditions of sealing practice and artistic style.

Concluding remarks

The Achaemenid period thus saw some real differences in the seals that have been excavated at the two sites. Satrapal Sardis, seat of Achaemenid administration, was the home of 34 seals made of elegant semi-precious stones, often with elaborate silver or gold mountings. A majority of these seals was carved in "Achaemenid hegemonic" style, drawing directly on images from the Persian heartland that were full of imperial ideological resonance. Gordion, a large site of secondary importance but with impressive new buildings constructed during the Achaemenid period, has produced 29 seals and sealings. They demonstrate a wider range of materials, styles and imagery than do the seals from Sardis—like the Sardian seals, these ones draw enthusiastically on the imagery of the Achaemenid heartland, but seal users at Gordion also selected seals sporting Greek, Egyptian and other images.

The seals demonstrate the close connections that bound together the Achaemenid elite at its ruling centres. They also demonstrate the overwhelmingly strong impact of Achaemenid hegemony on second-tier cities in the empire. The numbers and variety of seals at Gordion show its inhabitants took to seal using with verve, and they seem to have incorporated many aspects of Achaemenid administrative practice into their lives. The numbers and types of seals at Sardis show that its ruling elite were using seals not just to effect the practices of Achaemenid administration, but also to signal, to proclaim, their membership in that elite. Thus the seals of the two sites point to and underscore some of the differences between their roles in the empire. But the seals also demonstrate the extent to which Achaemenid practices and ideologically charged iconography penetrated to multiple levels of society and multiple types of local social organization throughout the empire.

Notes

1. I would like to thank the British Museum, the Iran Heritage Foundation, and the University of Colorado for making the conference at which this paper was delivered, and my participation in it, possible. Some of the ideas discussed here are also included in Dusinberre 2009.
2. For the seals from Sardis, see Dusinberre 1997, 2003: 158–171, 264–283.
3. For the seals from Gordion, see Dusinberre 2005: 12–14, 24–26, 30, 49–69.
4. For the Sardian tombs of the Achaemenid period, see Dusinberre 2003: 128–57 and 239–63; for the tombs in general see McLauchlin 1985.
5. Pyramidal stamp seals: IAM 4521, 4522, 4525, 4527, 4528, 4578, 4579, 4580, 4589, 4591, 4592, 4641, 4642, 5133, 5134; weight-shaped seals: 4523, 4524, 4590; cylinder seals: 4532, 4581, 4643; rings with gold bezels: 4548 (bezel undecorated), 4585, 4636, 4637; rings with stone bezels: 4519, 4520, 4632, 4633 (sealing surface of scarab undecorated), 4634, 4635, 4639; bracelet: 4518; necklace: 4640.
6. Stone identifications drawn from Curtis 1925.
7. As Gates emphasizes (2002: 119), the fact that many of the "Greco-Persian" seals are unprovenanced has previously crippled much intelligent discussion of the style. Even of those "Greco-Persian" seals used by Moorey in his discussion of ritual and worship on Achaemenid seals (1979), only that from Gordion has an excavated context. A similar situation describes the few inscribed "Greco-Persian" seals, of which most are inscribed in Lydian (Boardman 1970b). In order to understand the significance and impact of the style, it is essential to develop a discussion based on those seals with proven context. We are fortunate indeed that a seal from Gordion (Seal 100: see Dusinberre 2005, 2009), and the seals from Sardis, allow us to weave this discussion into the ongoing discourse being developed by such scholars as D. Kaptan, working with the Daskyleion sealings, and J. E. Gates, working with the Persepolis sealings (see Kaptan 2002; Gates 2002).
8. For the status of at least one seal user at Sardis, see the arguments in Dusinberre 1997.
9. Dusinberre 1997: 109–15; 2003: 158–71, 264–83.
10. For the Sardian tombs of the Achaemenid period, see Dusinberre 2003: 128–157, 239–263; for the tombs in general see McLauchlin 1985.
11. IAM 4636, 4585, 4634, 4639, 4580, 4523, 4589, 4591, 4578.
12. IAM 4525, 4579.
13. IAM 4528, 4642, 5134, 4527, 4581.
14. IAM 4581, 4579, 4641, 4521.
15. IAM 4520 and 4632.
16. IAM 4589, 4527, 4581, 4578, 4591.
17. IAM 4524.
18. See Dusinberre 1997.
19. See esp. Dusinberre 1997.
20. See a discussion and overview in Dusinberre 2005, with references.
21. Voigt & Young 1999.
22. See Dusinberre 2009, with references.
23. The glass seals illustrated here are a selection of those excavated at Gordion. Seal 56 is Dusinberre 2005: cat. no. 49, Seal 188 is cat. no. 52, Seal 44 is cat. no. 48, Seal 90 is cat. no. 46, Seal 112 is cat. no. 51, Seal 192 is cat. no. 53, Seal 205 is cat. no. 35, and Seal 75 is cat. no. 50. See Dusinberre 2005 for comparanda.
24. Dusinberre 2005: cat. nos 38 (Neo-Babylonian style), 36 (scarab), 33 (cylinder). Comparanda for Seal 73 include: Porada 1948: nos 795a, 797, 798, 804–808; von der Osten 1934: nos 470–97; Nunn 2000: no. 260; Moorey 1980: no. 470; Ornan 1993: fig. 39; Avigad 1997: no. 826; Root 1998: 257–261; 2003a; Ehrenberg 1999: nos 34–56, nos 43, 53; Ehrenberg 2001: 188–189; Bregstein 1993: nos 215–257; Legrain 1925: nos 965–68; Legrain 1951: nos 656–663; Kaptan 2002: DS1. Comparanda for Seal 246 include: Teeter & Wilfong 2003: no. 136; Hayes 1959: 87; Keel 1997: 606; Walters 1926: no. 157; Teeter 2002: fig. 12.6; Blinkenberg 1931: nos 1457–1458; Petrie 1886: pl. 37, no. 11; 1888: pl. 8, no. 30. For Seal 100, see Dusinberre 2009.
25. Dusinberre 2005: cat. no. 55. Comparanda include Root 1991, 2003a: 9; Bregstein 1993: nos

145–169; Nunn 2000: no. 270. See the discussion in Dusinberre 2005.
26. Dusinberre 2005: cat. no. 56. Comparanda include Konuk & Arslan 2000: nos 195–258; Moorey 1980: 85; Legrain 1925: pl. 36ff.; Woolley 1962: nos 701ff.; Boardman 1970*b*: 322; Richter 1920: no. 36; Spier 1992: 34, no. 52; Boardman 2001: nos 710, 711, 861; Osborne 1912: 317, 340; Richter 1968: no. 237. See the discussion in Dusinberre 2005.
27. Dusinberre 2005: cat. no. 40. Comparanda include examples from Boehmer 1977, 1978; Bregstein 1993: no. 318–320; Legrain 1925: nos 846–847; Garrison & Root in prep: PFS 90. See the discussion in Dusinberre 2005.
28. Dusinberre 2005: cat. no. 34. Comparanda include Garrison 2000: figs 29–30; Herbordt 1992: 98–122; Boardman & Moorey 1986: esp. figs 12, 19, 22; Buchanan 1966: no. 686. See the discussion in Dusinberre 2005.
29. Dusinberre 2005: cat. no. 39. Comparanda include Garrison 1991: 7–10, 20; Garrison & Root 2001: 83–85 and *passim*; Buchanan & Moorey 1988: no. 521; Kaptan 2002: DS 67, DS 68 and DS 85; Bregstein 1993: no. 195; Briant 2002*a*: 607–608. See the discussion in Dusinberre 2005.

32

Archers at Persepolis: The Emergence of Royal Ideology at the Heart of the Empire*

Mark B. Garrison

I. Introduction

The crowned archer has long been recognized as a central motif in the ideology of kingship of the Achaemenid Persian period (Fig. 32.1). Most famously, the four types of Achaemenid coinage of imperial ("regal") issue all carry on their obverse a figure in Persian court dress who wears a crown and either holds (types I, III and IV) or shoots (type II) a bow (Figs 32.2a–b).[1] This study will seek to explore and expand the semantic contexts/content of archer imagery in the imperial coinage of type I and type II via the rich storehouse of images preserved in the seal impressions on tablets from the Persepolis Fortification archive (509–493 BC).[2] Well over 100 distinct seals from the PFS corpus show what I shall call "archer imagery".[3] Only a handful of the archer images from the PFS corpus have as yet appeared in print.[4] It is hoped that this study may serve as a preliminary introduction to this evidence and its importance for our understanding of archer imagery as it appears in the reign of Darius I. This study will also attempt to broaden the contexts in which we consider this archer imagery via other glyptic imagery from the PFS corpus showing related ideological concerns. An examination of this glyptic evidence may allow us not only to identify the iconographic heritage from which the imagery on the archer coins of type I and type II emerged, but also to expand our understanding of the semantic significance of the motif both within the rather narrow context of official Achaemenid royal ideology and within the general context of Persian culture in the late sixth century BC in south-western Iran.

I have elected to focus on how the imagery from the PFS corpus may broaden and enrich our understanding of the imagery of coins of types I and II exclusively. These two types, owing to their chronological priority, apparently short period of issuance and distinct imagery, have often been addressed separately from the coinage of types III and IV (e.g. Stronach 1989: 259–261; Root 1989; Nimchuk 2002; Le Rider 2001: 125).[5] Because of their chronological priority and distinctive imagery, the coins have figured prominently in attempts to understand the development of royal ideology early in the formative reign of Darius I.

Fig. 32.1 Achaemenid imperial coin types. (After Stronach 1989: fig. 1)

Fig. 32.2 (a) Siglos of type I (BM example). (b) Siglos of type II (BM example)

Many difficult and highly contested aspects of the coinage qua coinage, for example, the relationship to the Croesids, chronology, location of mints, monetary function/policy, circulation, relationship of the daric and siglos etc., will not be addressed in any substantial way in this study.[6]

II. Semantic context and content

Critical to any understanding of the significance of the imagery that appears on the coins of types I and II is knowing to whom this imagery was addressed. Of all questions surrounding these artefacts, the question of the intended audience is, perhaps, the most perplexing.[7] The issue is intimately linked, of course, with the questions of the function(s) of these objects (coinage, bullion, tokens of imperial favour, medium of conspicuous display of Darius' splendour and role as donor, etc.) and where in the Achaemenid world they were used. All or substantial parts of the traditional explanation of these artefacts, coinage meant to pay Greek mercenaries in western Asia Minor, has recently come under some criticism (e.g. Briant 2002a: 409, 934–935; Vargyas 2000; Nimchuk 2002). Unfortunately, the question of audience cannot be answered in a definitive manner owing to the almost total lack of archaeologically meaningful contextual information. The hoard evidence, by its very nature, is singularly uninformative as regards audience (Carradice 1987: 79, table A). The remarkable occurrence of an archer coin of type II used to seal several tablets from the Fortification archive represents one exceptional circumstance where the archaeological context is in fact quite rich (Root 1988, 1989). Here clearly we see an archer "coin" in action, being used to seal administrative tablets. Of the audience within the context of the Fortification archive, we are, by the standards of ancient art, reasonably well informed (see Garrison 2000: 155–156).

I doubt that anyone, even the most enthusiastic glyptic specialist would, however, suggest that the primary function of the type II archer coins was sphragistic. The occurrence of this coin used as a seal in the Fortification archive surely highlights (again), however, the critical role that the imagery played. While the object qua object had intrinsic value (bullion), the applied imagery added value (and I speak here not in the sense that the image function as a guarantor of value beyond that of the actual mass of metal, i.e. as coinage, but as a conveyor of messages, as a mode of communication, concerning themes/ideas central to the Achaemenid imperial project in the heart of the empire). In this sense, my own tendencies are to see these artefacts, the coins of types I and II, as first and foremost conveyors of meaning. If this is correct, then the intended audience can hardly have been Greek mercenaries, who would have cared little about what was on the metal, only on its purity and weight, but high-rank/status individuals whose loyalty, either new or old, was a central concern of the Achaemenid king. In this light, these artefacts function then as vehicles of cultural/political (re)affirmation rather than as vehicles of cultural/political persuasion. The goal of the imagery is not to convince, but to signal loyalty/affiliation; its arena of circulation is not exclusively western Asia, but elites within (potentially) the empire as a whole.[8]

In order to assess more fully the semantic contexts and contents of the imagery of the coins of types I and II, I turn now to the evidence from the PFS corpus.

III. Archers at Persepolis: imagery of type I coins and the PFS corpus

The type I coin (Figs 32.1–2) and its imagery are without a doubt the most provocative and interesting of all the Achaemenid imperial coin types. There is a general consensus that 1) the half-figure represents some aspect of Achaemenid kingship and that 2) type I is the earliest of the types.[9] As is often mentioned, type I is documented to date only in silver (siglos), and is very rare.[10] Its imagery is the most distinct of the four types. A half-figure dressed in the Persian court robe and wearing a long beard and a dentate crown faces right. He holds in his left hand a stringed bow, the string face pointing towards the half-figure. In his right hand he holds two arrows. The figure is rendered in profile. The carving is exceptionally deep and well modelled.

Several features distinguish the type I image from all other types. Firstly, the type to date is documented only in silver, whereas the other types occur in both sigloi and darics. Secondly, the figure is only a half-figure, shown from approximately the waist up, unlike the other types, which show a full figure. Thirdly, the half-figure is rendered in a true profile, whereas the other types are all a combination of frontal and profile perspective.[11] Fourthly, the carving is exceptionally deep and well modelled, much richer than the carving in any of the other types.

Stronach (1989: 264–269), Root (1989: 43–50) and Nimchuk (2002: 63, 65) have examined in some detail the imagery of type I. Stronach, following earlier commentators, noted the strong Assyrianizing aspects to the type I imagery, especially the compositional device of a half-figure (related to the half-figure of Aššur/Šamaš in a winged disc), and the stylistic and iconographic connections with the rock relief at Bisitun.[12] For Stronach, these observations were first and foremost of chronological significance, although he does raise again—only to dismiss—the intriguing suggestion, initiated by Seyrig (1959) and Naster (1962, 1964), that the half-figure of type I, on analogy with the half-figure of the god Aššur/Šamaš in a winged disc, was divine (Stronach 1989: 266–268).[13] For Stronach the half-figure of the king on the type I coins was derived from a traditional Mesopotamian depiction of kingship.[14] Within the Achaemenid context, the type I image was meant to project several messages: the emphasis of a more assertive "Persian identity" and a less tolerant policy towards the subject peoples (following the revolts at the beginning of Darius' reign); the linking of Darius' rule with Assyrian royal power; the emphasis of the bow as the "Iranian national arm" and "salient emblem of kingship"; the projection of an undisguised militant message directed particularly to Ionians (following the Ionian revolt).[15] Root (1989: 43–44) has suggested that the type I image was "derived from a narrative representational and actuality context of royal display".[16] The reduction of the scene to simply the half-figure in the coins of type I carries with it numinous qualities, perhaps related to an Achaemenid "oriens" ceremony. While the bow and arrows functioned as symbols of authority and military power, the overall message of the type I (and type II) archer bespoke a "quintessentially Persian, Achaemenid, manifestation of imperial power" (Root 1991: 16). Nimchuk (2002: 65–66, 70) stresses the calmness of the type I image as expressive of ideas of order and strength (the bow and arrow conveying a military aspect of this strength). The image functions to establish Darius' legitimacy as king, his metaphorical presence wherever the coins circulate, and the prosperity of orderly rule.

The seals from the PFS corpus greatly enrich the visual and semantic contexts in which to contemplate the imagery of the type I archer. While no one seal in the PFS corpus provides an exact compositional match to the type I image, there are numerous stylistic elements, compositional types and iconographic details that seem directly relevant to discussions of the imagery of the type I archer.

Many examples of type I archer coins are rendered in a carving style that is well modelled, stressing volumetric mass. These qualities are emphasized especially by the deep-profile shoulder and full volumetric rendering of the sleeve of the upper part of the court garment. I am especially struck by the very close stylistic connections between the type I archer and a small group of seals rendered in the Court Style in the PFS corpus. I here illustrate PFS 11* (Figs 32.3a, 4a), one of four seals from the PFS corpus carrying a trilingual (Old Persian, Elamite and Babylonian) inscription naming Darius.[17] All four of these seals naming Darius are carved in the Court Style. PFS 11* represents a rather rarer version of the Court Style that stresses deep volumetric masses in its carving.[18] The style is strikingly similar to that seen in the type I archers. The likelihood that seal carvers and coin die carvers might often have been the same individuals has been frequently noted.[19] The close stylistic relationship between the type I archer and PFS 11* would suggest that the very workshop(s) from which the type I imagery arose are probably to be located in the region of Persepolis.[20]

A quiet, calm, timeless quality infuses both the type I archer and the royal figures in PFS 11*. In both PFS 11* and the type 1 coin, the royal figure is ambiguously poised between mortal/divine, in the seal image via the magical doubling of the royal figure and the semblance of these figures to the half-figure in the winged ring, in the coin image via the emphasis only on the upper part of the torso of the royal figure and its isolation.

As in PFS 11*, the iconographic details of dress, beard, hairstyle and crown of the type I archer are deeply entrenched in court imagery as preserved in glyptic from the imperial centre. Here, again, those seals cut in the Court Style especially provide important comparative material from the middle to late years of the last decade of the sixth century BC. Stronach (1989: 264–265) interpreted the variation in the rendering of faces and dentate crowns in coins of type I as reflecting a considerable period of experimentation and evolution. The fact that one sees a good deal of variation in the rendering of details of hair, beard, crowns and faces in seals rendered in the Court Style in the PFS corpus may suggest that the issue is not a chronological one, but artistic (workshops/artists).

Perhaps the most important contribution that the seals from the PFS corpus may add to the discussion of the imagery of the type I archer concerns the enigmatic half-figure aspect of the archer. As mentioned, the half-figure aspect of the type I archer has for many years generated considerable commentary owing to its potential relationship to the half-figure emerging from the winged element/disc, seen both in the Assyrian and Achaemenid period. While the winged ring/disc without a human figure is by far the more common in the PFS corpus, there are many examples of the half-figure emerging from the winged ring/disc (as PFS 11* illustrates). Of course, more examples of such an entity do little directly to clarify the nature of the half-figure in the type I archer coins. It does, however, drive home the powerful visual connection between the half-figure and the numinous.

One particular type of archer scene from the PFS corpus may also be relevant to the discussion. There exists a substantial number of archer scenes in which the archer is a composite human–animal creature.[21] Despite the variety of animal elements used in these creatures, their basic constitution is almost always the same: a human head, arms and torso (from the waist up) combined with an animal body and legs. Often the creatures are winged. These scenes are rendered in various styles, but most commonly it is the local carving style, the Fortification Style.[22] PFS 78 (Figs 32.3b, 4b) is a particularly striking and evocative example. Here, the archer consists of the human upper torso combined with a winged scorpion body. The creature has a long beard with horizontal striations, a rounded mass of hair at the back of the neck and wears a *polos*-like headdress. The hairstyle and beard of the archer are very similar to that seen in Court Style seals. The creature shoots towards a winged lion; between the archer and the winged lion there is a lion couchant.[23] In the terminal field a bird sits above a floral device. The modelling is deep and active in the human torso. Another example, PFS 118 (Figs 32.3c, 4c), the style of which I have discussed in another context, shows a human torso combined with a bird body, tail and legs; a scorpion tail and stinger curls upward behind the creature.[24] The archer here shoots towards a rampant lion. PFS 306 (Figs 32.3d, 4d) may stand as one among many examples in the PFS corpus of the archer welded onto a winged lion

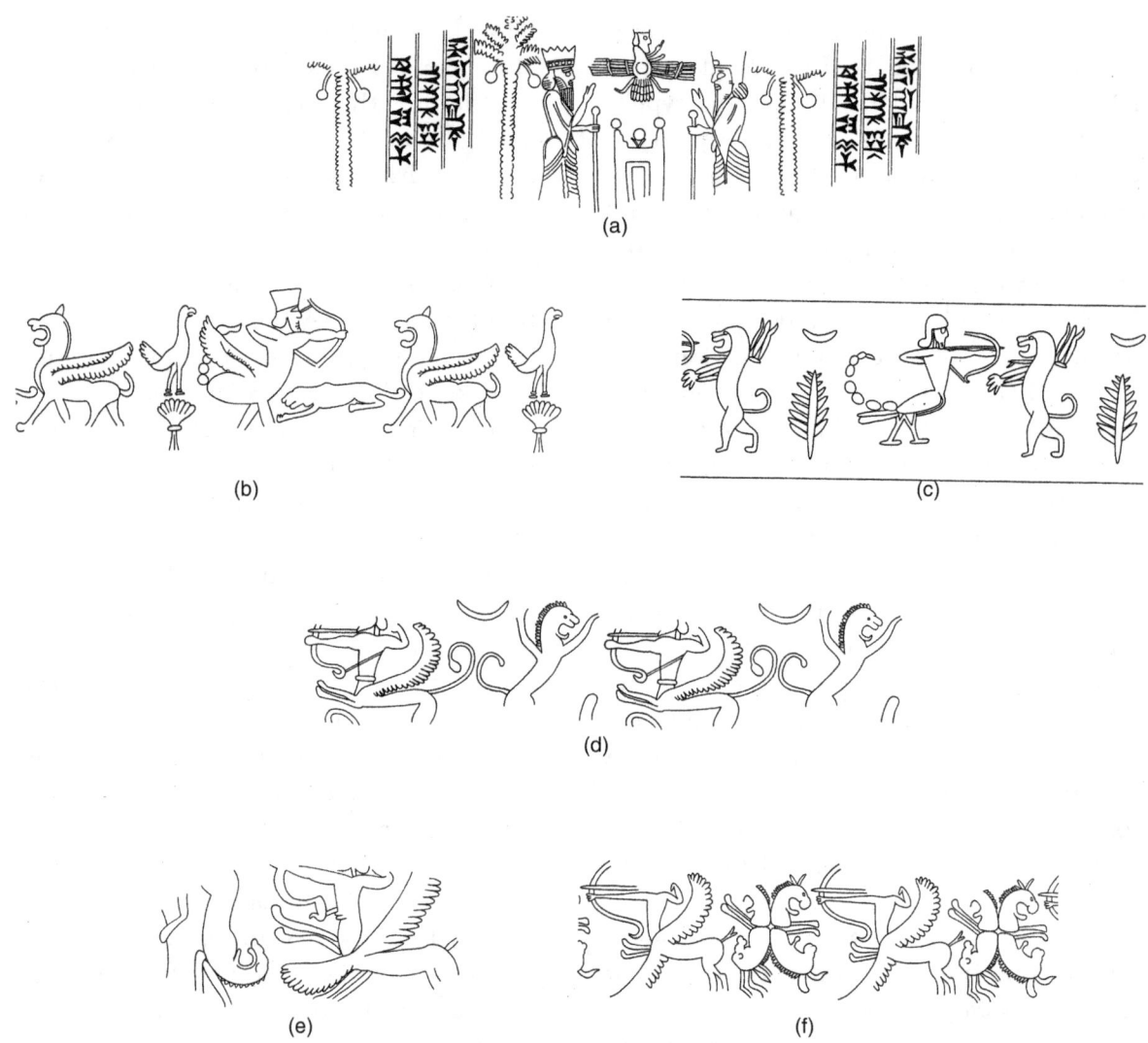

Figs 32.3a–f Collated line drawings of seal impressions from the Persepolis Fortification archive: (a) PFS11*, (b) PFS 78, (c) PFS 118, (d) PFS 306, (e) PFS 250, (f) PFS 537.

body. As is sometimes the case with these creatures, there is also a set of animal forelegs. Not uncommonly, the archer creature in PFS 306 also wears as belt. PFS 250 (Figs 32.3e, 4e) is another particularly evocative example where the archer creature is winged, this time with two wings indicated. It appears to have two sets of animal forelegs! The inverted lion immediately to the left suggests a particularly complex composition in the part of the seal that is not preserved. The preserved bow end in PFS 250 seems to be a duck-head. PFS 537 (Figs 32.3f, 4f), one of the most striking designs in the whole of the archer corpus, shows the archer combined with a winged bull or caprid body (again, with a set of animal forelegs and two wings), shooting towards a whirligig of animal protomes. A handful of these scenes showing a composite archer takes on a heraldic quality by having two archers confront each other,

Figs 32.4a–f Seal impressions from the Persepolis Fortification archive: **(a)** PFS 11* on PF 1813 (le), **(b)** PFS 78 on PF 402 (rev), **(c)** PFS 118 on PF 2005 (rev), **(d)** PFS 306 on PF 221 (rev), **(e)** PFS 250 on PF 1549 (le), **(f)** PFS 537 on PF 292 (rev).

as seen in PFS 540 (Figs 32.5a, 6a), where the archer creatures appear to have winged lion bodies; note, again, the second set of animal forelegs on the archer creature on the left. PFS 1174 (Figs 32.5b, 6b) may preserve fragments of a similar composition, with the addition of a central focal element consisting of a star set into a circle; only one archer creature is in fact preserved. The carving of this seal is exceptionally sharp. Finally, on PFS 715 (Figs 32.5c, 6c) the human torso of the archer is grafted onto a bird in flight; a set of animal forelegs also occurs. The archer also appears to wear a double belt, an iconographic feature often associated with the hero in scenes of heroic encounter.[25]

The appearance of scenes involving composite archer creatures in the PFS corpus is

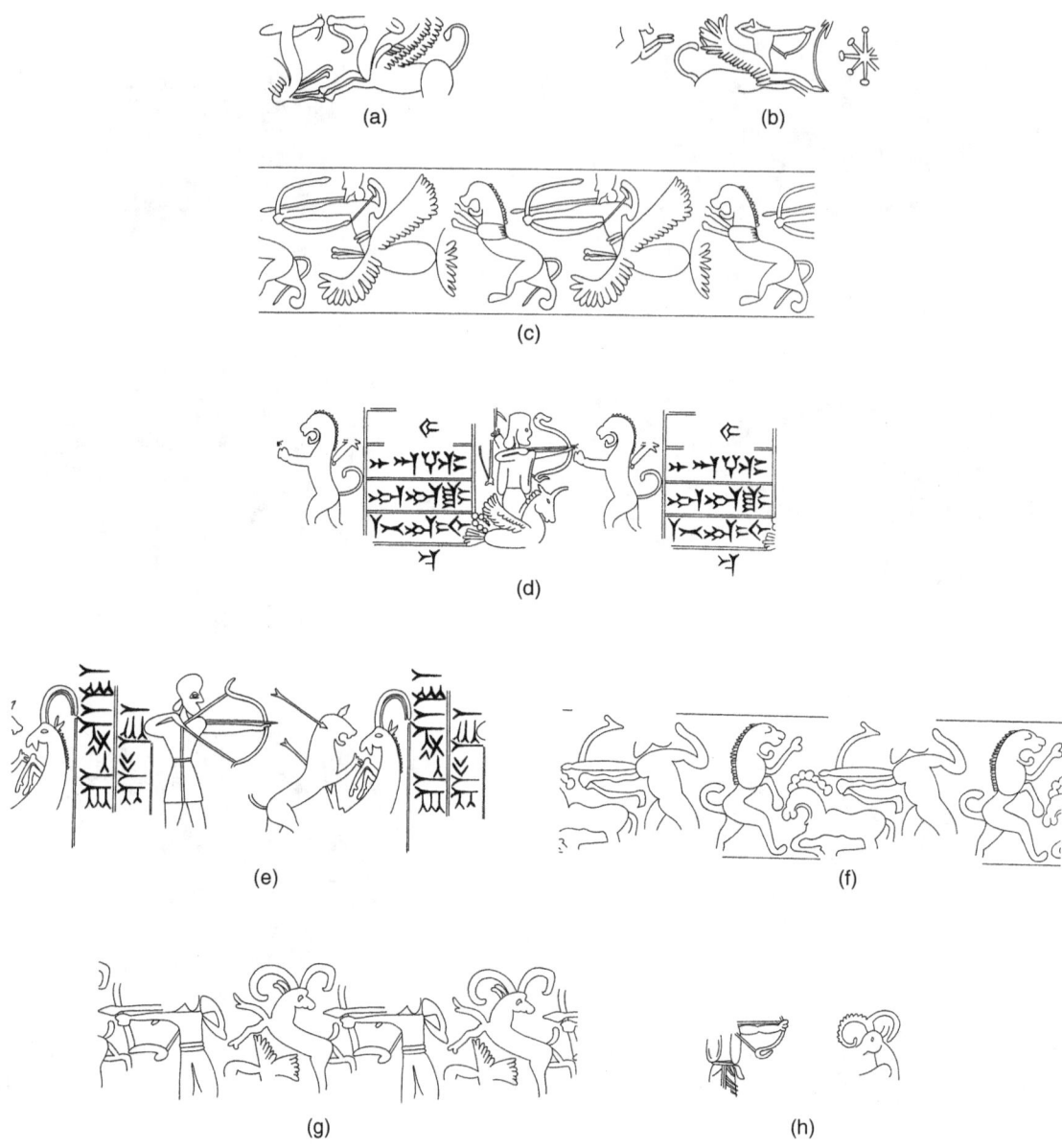

Figs 32.5a–h Collated line drawings of seal impressions from the Persepolis Fortification archive: **(a)** PFS 540, **(b)** PFS 1174, **(c)** PFS 715, **(d)** PFS 261*, **(e)** PFS 35*, **(f)** PFS 722, **(g)** PFS 700, **(h)** PFS 1568.

quite unexpected. They seem to reach back and reference designs, few in number, found on Middle Assyrian and Kassite Babylonian glyptic and Kassite *kudurrus*.[26] I say reach back because the composite archer creature seems rarely found in Neo-Assyrian or Neo-Babylonian art.[27] The composite scorpion archer also evokes the scorpion-man of both Assyrian and Babylonian art of the first millennium BC. The seals with composite archer creatures are not, however, Assyrian and/or Babylonian heirlooms, but are firmly entrenched stylistically in workshops documented in the PFS corpus. The potential narrative traditions from which the

Figs 32.6a–h Seal impressions from the Persepolis Fortification archive: **(a)** PFS 540 on PF 295 (rev), **(b)** PFS 1174 on PF 1224 (ue), **(c)** PFS 715 on PF 488 (rev), **(d)** PFS 261* on PF 1225 (rev), **(e)** PFS 35* on PF 1733 (rev), **(f)** PFS 722 on PF 494 (le), **(g)** PFS 700 on PF 471 (rev), **(h)** PFS 1568 on PF 1854 (re).

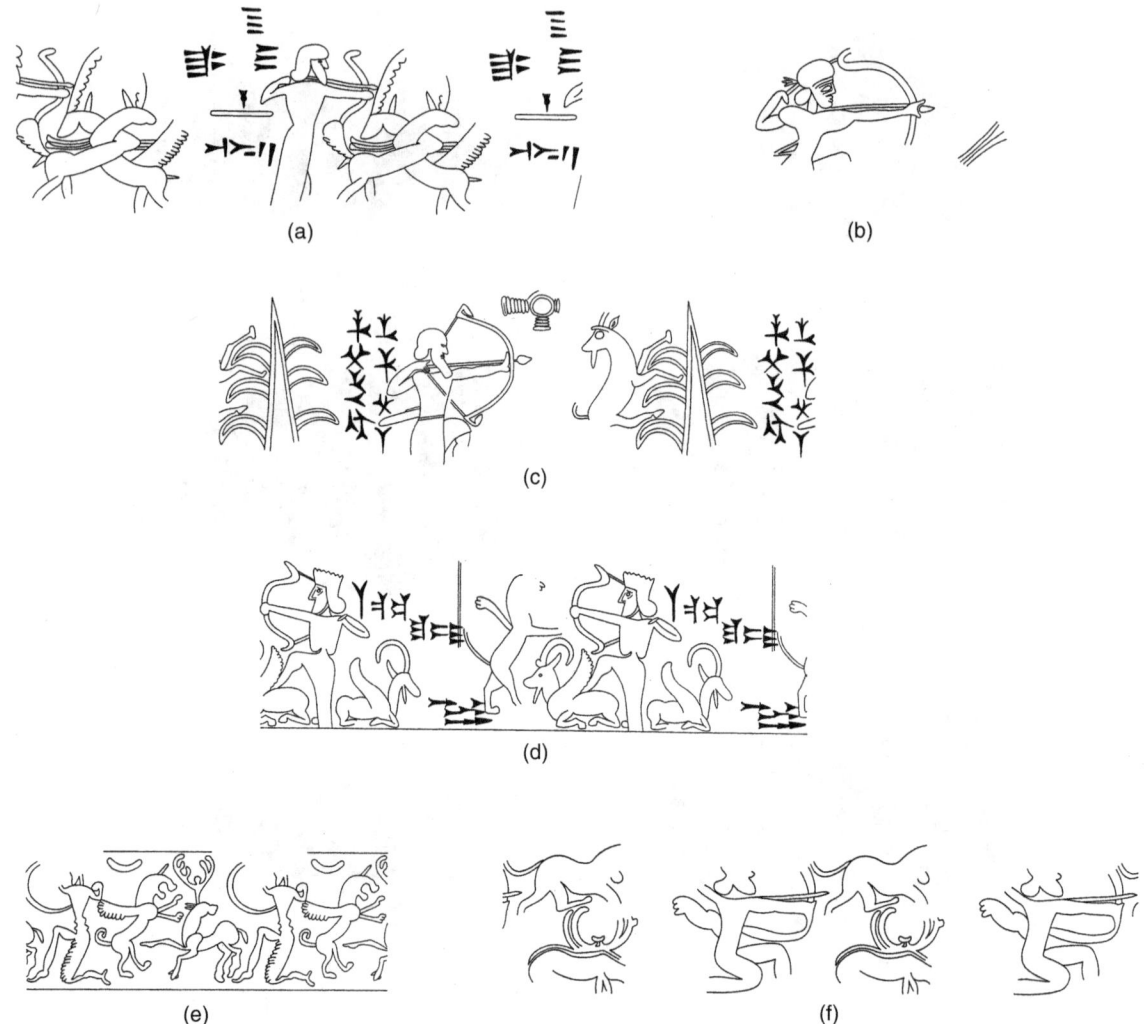

Figs 32.7a–f Collated line drawings of seal impressions from the Persepolis Fortification archive: **(a)** PFS 425*, **(b)** PFS 137, **(c)** PFS 115*, **(d)** PFS 390*, **(e)** PFS 182, **(f)** PFS 730.

scenes emerged are, of course, completely lost to us. The central point to be made within the context of our discussion of the type I archer is, however, not the probable mythological/narrative tradition behind such creatures, but the new context in which to contemplate the human half-figure; that is, in addition to the often-made link between the half-figure of the type I archer and the half-figure in the winged ring/disc, we now have a potentially evocative visual/narrative field in which to consider the type I archer. In the broadest perspectives, these composite archer creatures are clearly of a fantastical, numinous world, thus reinforcing the view that the half-figure is a potent signifier of numinous character.

I would also stress that these scenes of composite archers in the PFS corpus enrich our consideration of the half-figure in the winged ring/disc itself. In the case of PFS

Figs 32.8a–f Seal impressions from the Persepolis Fortification archive: **(a)** PFS 425* on PF 119 (rev), **(b)** PFS 137 on PF 1115 (le), **(c)** PFS 115* on PF 2033 (rev), **(d)** PFS 390* on PF 88 (rev), **(e)** PFS 182 on PF 568 (rev), **(f)** PFS 730 on PF 501 (rev).

715 (Figs 32.5c, 6c), where the human torso is attached to a bird in flight, we are—literally—transported into the upper realms of the half-figure in the winged ring/disc.

This linkage of association, half-figure of the type I archer, half-figure in the winged ring/disc and composite human–animal archers, may find its synthesis in the remarkable seal

Figs 32.9a–f Collated line drawings of seal impressions from the Persepolis Fortification archive: **(a)** PFS 141, **(b)** PFS 71*, **(c)** PFS 286, **(d)** PFS 977, **(e)** PFS 128, **(f)** PFS 305.

Figs 32.10a–f Seal impressions from the Persepolis Fortification archive; (a) PFS 141 on PF 95 (le), (b) PFS 71* on PF 280 (rev), (c) PFS 286 on PF 160 (le), (d) PFS 977 on PF 867 (rev), (e) PFS 128 on PF 74 rev, (f) PFS 305 on PF 481 (ue).

PFS 261* (Figs 32.5d, 6d). This scene shows the waist and upper torso of a human archer rising up from the back of a fantastical bull-headed (?) bird body with a scorpion tail. The archer shoots at a rampant lion at right. The archer is loaded with royal paraphernalia. He wears the court garment, sleeves pulled up to reveal his arms, shoots a duck-headed bow and wears a quiver and extra bow on his back. He appears to have a short beard and *polos*-like headdress. An Elamite panelled inscription names one Šati-dudu, son of Tardumannu.[28]

The design is particularly dense and nuanced in its semantic, referencing multiple aspects of kingship and divinity. Bow, quiver, arrows, court garment and panelled inscription are quintessential elements of kingship as found not only in glyptic from Persepolis, but also in monumental relief at Bisitun and Naqsh-i Rustam.[29] The archer's confrontation with a lion, while not literally depicted in monumental reliefs at Persepolis, recalls, however, the hero's confrontation with lions documented in the reliefs from the Palace of Darius;[30] similar scenes are amply documented as well in the heroic encounter scenes from the PFS corpus.[31] The confrontation with lions is, of course, a traditional preserve of Assyrian (and earlier) kings. The composite creature from which the archer on PFS 266* emerges (or of which he is part) has multiple referents. The distinctive and sharp profile of the bull's head vividly evokes the composite capitals on many structures at Persepolis (i.e. royal architecture par excellence); thus, we are in the realm of the multi-faceted roles that these creatures play as conveyors of concepts of protection, linkages to imperial architecture of the Assyrian period and, potentially, mythological narratives. The multiple animal forms in the composite creature, bull, bird and scorpion, draw upon various Assyro-Babylonian divine referents.[32] Finally, the archer and composite creature together in PFS 261* appear to reference simultaneously two distinct traditions regarding divinity: the deity who rises/is elevated (e.g. Aššur/Šamaš in the winged ring/disc) and the deity who stands on the back of an animal/creature.

To this group of scenes featuring the half-figure just discussed, that is the half-figure of PFS 261*, the half-figure of the type I archer, half-figure in the winged ring/disc and composite human–animal archers, we ought to add also the crowned half-figure found within a circle as preserved, for example, on PTS 16 and PTS 17 (dating to the reign of Xerxes) from the Treasury archive.[33] Dressed in court garments and often crowned, all of these various manifestations of the half-figure compel us to consider what appears to have been the multidimensional nature of the visual semantics of Achaemenid kingship. Regarding specifically the image of the half-figure, there appear to be at least two major dimensions. The first is addressed via gesture and iconography, and is itself multidimensional; for example, some of these half-figure types are "pacific" (e.g. the half-figure in a circle holding a flower, the half-figure in a winged ring/disc), others are potentially pious (e.g. PFS 11*) and/or militant (e.g. type I archer), while others are openly aggressive (e.g. composite archer creatures in the PFS corpus). The second is addressed by the very nature of "half-figure-ness" itself, where the overarching semantic is the numinous.[34] While many of these concepts are deeply rooted in the visual imagery of Achaemenid kingship at the time of Darius I, the type I archer seems to express in a most direct and unambiguous manner the numinous aspects of that kingship.[35]

In closing this section on the type I archer, I would like again to stress what I take to be the critical importance of the rising/uplifted qualities of the half-figure in most of its iterations (the type I archer, the archer in PFS 261* [Figs 32.5d, 6d], the half-figure in the winged ring/disc, the composite bird-man archer in PFS 78 [Figs 32.3b, 4b], and the half-figure found within a circle). This quality of "ascension" appears to have been one of the central semantic concerns of Achaemenid imagery. It finds expression not only in the various manifestations of the half-figure that we have explored here, but also in the use of atlantid figures, both in glyptic and monumental relief at Naqsh-i Rustam and Persepolis.[36] Indeed, this concept of ascension is deeply embedded in the very structure of both the rock-cut reliefs at Bisitun and Naqsh-i Rustam, where the imagery is lifted up onto the vertical face of the rock, and the site of Persepolis itself, where the terrace, podia, inverted floral column bases and the animal-protome capitals constitute a series of elements that successively lift the architecture up away from the surrounding Marv Dasht plain.[37]

The half-figure of the type I archer, thus, rather than being a deviant form, is part of a considerable constellation of imagery and concepts that seek, at the heart of the empire, to address various aspects of the numinous qualities of Achaemenid kingship.

IV. Archers at Persepolis: imagery of type II coins and the PFS corpus

Of the type II coin and its imagery there is a general consensus that 1) the crowned figure represents some aspect of Achaemenid kingship and that 2) type II appeared after type I and before type III.[38] Type II occurs in silver (siglos) and gold (daric), but the daric is exceptionally rare.[39] Its imagery appears to mark a rather dramatic break with the imagery of type I (Figs 32.1–32.2). A full-length figure dressed in the Persian court robe and wearing a long beard and a dentate crown faces right in a kneeling position (often described as a knielauf, but this is questionable). The sleeves of the upper part of the garment are pulled up to reveal the bare arms; the hem on the lower part of the garment has also been pulled up to reveal the forward leg below the knee. The figure appears to be barefooted. The archer pulls back the arrow on a stringed bow (often with duck-head finials). On his back there is a quiver full of arrows. The lower part of the body is rendered in profile; the upper part of the body appears to be foreshortened slightly, but for the most part is frontal.

As with type I, Stronach (1989: 264–269), Root (1989: 43–50; 1991: 15–17) and Nimchuk (2002: 63, 65) have examined in some detail the imagery of type II. Stronach appears to attribute to the type II archer many of the same semantics that he sees in type I, that is the emphasis of a more assertive "Persian identity"; a less tolerant policy towards the subject peoples; the emphasis of the bow as the "Iranian national arm" and "salient emblem of kingship"; and the projection of an undisguised militant message directed particularly to Ionians.[40] For Stronach, however, the militant message is the overriding one (well-stocked, open quiver, ready for battle, urgent pose emphasized by the pushed-up sleeves and skirt pulled up to reveal the forward leg). He also places the type II coin image within what he identifies as a second "style", appearing in *c.* 500 BC and reflecting a "new, more relaxed, more consciously 'heroic' style" that portrayed the king as a "super-hero" (Stronach 1989: 271–272). Root (1989: 45–46; 1991: 16–17) has placed the type II archer firmly within the glyptic imagery from the PFS corpus, suggesting that the kneeling archer has been lifted "out of the narrative context of this cylinder seal format" and isolated "within the circular space defined by the coin surface" (Root 1989: 45). The referents would have been the "king as valiant hunter", an age-old Mesopotamian tradition, "controlled domain", a specifically Iranian concept (1989: 46), and "the prowess and military power of the Persian king" (Root 1991: 17). At the same time, the type II archer is also seen to derive from an "actuality context of royal display" (as the type I archer) and an attempt to appeal to a western audience (Root 1989: 47, 49–50).[41] Nimchuk (2002: 64, 66), following Stronach, also stresses the "aggressive attitude" of the type II archer, representing the king as both hunter and protector (as Root). For her the type II archer is "aggressive but also incorporating" in that all subjects may be addressed (2002: 66).

As with the type I archer, so too with the type II archer: no one seal in the PFS corpus provides an exact compositional match. The lack of an occurrence of an isolated archer (i.e. an archer shown without a quarry) in the centre of the empire has troubled many commentators (see the remarks of Stronach 1989: 270–271) and has been, perhaps, one of the primary motivations for scholars looking to the West for contemporary parallels. I have no difficulty with the lack of an exact compositional parallel for the type II archer in Persia. Because an isolated archer does not occur in either monumental relief or glyptic does not mean that it did not originate, or circulate, within the same semantic contexts as relief and glyptic. Indeed, the lack of an isolated archer in relief and glyptic may even have been consciously planned. As preserved, each of the three major vehicles for the dissemination of the visual imagery of Achaemenid kingship, monumental relief, glyptic and coinage, while employing the same visual vocabulary, clearly has its own distinctive syntax.[42] Thus, as with the type I archer, the most critical part of the analytical process is to understand the vocabulary and syntax of each of these vehicles within the broader semantic field that, as a whole, they represent.

Developing the suggestion of Root (1989: 45) that the kneeling archer has been lifted "out of the narrative context of this cylinder seal format", several compositional types that may bear directly on the type II archer are to be found in the PFS corpus. One type shows the standing archer who shoots at a predator (almost always a lion) attacking another animal. PFS 35* (Figs 32.5e, 6e) is one of the most interesting of this type. Here an archer dressed in a thigh-length skirt shoots at a lion attacking a caprid. The movement of the lion away from the archer is unusual, the position of the caprid on its back unique; the arrows in the back of the lion also are rare, and give the scene a highly narrative flavour.[43] PFS 722 (Figs 32.5f, 6f), rendered in the local Fortification Style, is a beautiful example of a triangular composition with the lion facing the archer while an animal lies in the lower field between the two.[44] The revival of this "protection imagery" is particularly interesting within the Persepolitan environment. The theme is almost non-existent in Neo-Assyrian glyptic.

The PFS corpus contains a relatively large number of scenes of the standing archer shooting at an isolated animal/creature. As is generally the case in all of the compositional types, we see a variety of carving styles. Prey can either be lions/leonine creatures or various caprids, bovids or cervids. PFS 700 (Figs 32.5g, 6g) is an example of a particularly busy composition where the archer shoots at a horned creature that moves away from him. A bird in flight fills the field below the upraised forelegs of the animal. The archer wears a double-belted Assyrian garment. PFS 1568 (Figs 32.5h, 6h), although only partially preserved, is a striking design. The archer, shooting at a horned animal moving away from him, wears a court robe that shows exceptionally detailed rendering of the belt and folds on the lower part of the garment; the depiction of the pushed-up sleeves of the upper part of the garment in two pendant swags of drapery, one on either side of the torso, is not common, but it is a distinctive feature in an interesting group of seals that seem to have been made by the same hand.[45] PFS 1568 appears, however, to be from a different hand working in a more modelled style of carving.[46]

Although relatively few in number, the scenes of a standing archer shooting at heraldic or crossed animals/creatures are all carefully executed. I have selected only one example for illustration, PFS 425* (Figs 32.7a, 8a). The archer shoots towards a pair of winged, horned creatures whose necks are intertwined. The intertwined animal/creatures are also found in combination with other types of scenes and as a compositional device alone.[47] They deserve careful and detailed study in the future.

Owing to its formal characteristics, those scenes in which the archer either raises his forward leg or kneels are clearly of direct relevance to the discussion of the type II archer. The archer raising his forward leg is seen in a variety of compositions, including the "protection" scene, shooting isolated animals/creatures and shooting towards heraldic or crossed animals/creatures. There are to be found within the compositions that have the archer with raised leg some true masterpieces of glyptic art, such as the beautifully modelled PFS 137 (Figs 32.7b, 8b) and the monumental PFS 115* (Figs 32.7c, 8c). The latter is an exceptional design showing an archer, dressed in a belted, Assyrian garment, shooting towards a rampant caprid before a schematic tree.[48] In the upper field is a winged disc.[49] The degree of modelling, detailed carving and the spaciousness of the scene are rare even within the PFS corpus where large seals carved in a virtuosic modelled style of carving can be found.[50] The emphatic verticals of the composition also relate the seal to the large, Court Style royal-name seals of Darius I, PFS 7* (Cat. No. 4), PFS 113* (Cat. No. 19) and PFS 11* (Figs 32.3a, 4a) and PFUTS 18*.[51] The inscription, still under study, is Akkadian and appears to be two personal names written logographically. The composition seems inspired by a small group of Middle Assyrian seals where a kneeling archer shoots towards a rampant animal and tree.[52] The rendering of the tree on PFS 115* is, however, distinctly non-Middle Assyrian, and I see little stylistically to suggest a Middle Assyrian date for the seal. The rarity of Akkadian/Babylonian inscriptions in the PFS corpus coupled with the carving style may suggest, nevertheless, that PFS 115* is a true heirloom seal, rather than some archaizing piece.[53]

PFS 390* (Figs 32.7d, 8d) shows a variant on this compositional type where the archer raises his forward leg to place it on the back of a winged caprid couchant. A similar creature faces in the opposite direction behind the archer. The archer, wearing the court robe, dentate crown and pointed beard, shoots towards a rampant lion.[54] While the archer has much of the traditional accoutrements of the royal figure in Court Style seals, the carving is clearly Fortification Style. The scene in fact grafts onto the archer with raised leg what are essentially pedestal creatures. These creatures, whose numinous role in Achaemenid glyptic has been addressed (Dusinberre 1997), are commonly found in the PFS corpus.[55]

Kneeling archers constitute a significant percentage of the total number of archer scenes within the PFS corpus. Currently, some 55 of the approximately 126 archer scenes from the PFS corpus, some 44 per cent, show a kneeling archer. This statistic in and of itself compels us to resituate the type II archer in a decidedly Persepolitan context. The kneeling archer scenes from the PFS corpus are rendered in a variety of styles and occur in the following compositions: 1) shooting towards a predator (generally leonine) attacking another animal (generally caprid or bovid, often winged), the "protection imagery"; 2) shooting towards an isolated animal/creature; 3) shooting towards heraldic or crossed animals/creatures. The scenes with the kneeling archer tend to be rather active and crowded, and there are even a few examples with a lively, narrative flavour. In the protection scenes the predator is often disposed in an especially creative manner in the upper field of the composition. It is interesting that the Court Style and iconography associated with the Court Style (e.g. court robe, dentate crown, half-figure in the winged disc, date palm, bulls, human-headed bulls, panelled inscriptions, etc.) are very rare in scenes with the kneeling archer.[56]

PFS 182 (Figs 32.7e, 8e), rendered in the local Fortification Style, is a nice example of a dynamic protection scene. Here the archer shoots towards a rampant winged lion that threatens a stag. The stag moves to the left, but turns its head back to the right towards the archer. The archer appears to wear an abbreviated version of a double-belted, Assyrian garment with elaborate fringing over the back leg. By ranging from the top to the bottom of the field while in a kneeling pose, the kneeling archer dominates the visual field in a manner very different from the other types of archers. PFS 730 (Figs 32.7f, 8f), another Fortification Style carving, is an interesting variant where the lion is placed in the upper field above its victim. The archer himself is winged, not an uncommon phenomenon among the kneeling archers in the PFS corpus, and appears to wear a version of the Assyrian garment. The elaborate horns on the animal below the lion are not easily comprehended with regard to species. PFS 141 (Figs 32.9a, 10a) shows another version of the protection scene. Here the archer, who has an animal tail and wears an elaborately fringed garment that leaves the forward leg exposed, shoots at a rampant lion attacking a horned animal. The two dominant verticals of the composition, lion and archer, here come face to face, the archer almost touching the forelegs of the lion, while the victim is squeezed into the lower field between the two.

PFS 71* (Figs 32.9b, 10b) is one of the few kneeling archers to exhibit aspects of royal/court iconography. As mentioned above, the seal occurs also in the Persepolis Treasury tablets, there labelled PTS 33*.[57] The broad and modelled animal forms, the abstractly rendered paw of the forward foreleg of the rampant lion and the distinctive treatment of the facial details of the archer find no ready parallels in the fully developed Court Style as represented by the royal-name seals of Darius I. So, too, the narrative qualities of the scene, the dead lion with arrows in its body in the lower field, the rampant lion with two arrows in its body and the open and full quiver on the back of the archer, strike a very different tone from the quiet, timeless scenes preserved in the royal-name seals. The star and crescent in the upper field are other features that are not normally associated with scenes cut in the Court Style. The archer wears, however, the court robe with sleeves pulled up to reveal the bare arms. The garment is belted and there appears to be a knife in the belt. The large panelled inscription in the terminal field is also a feature of many Court Style seals.[58] The seal then, while carved in a modelled style, is imbued with Court Style iconography. The archer himself in PFS 71* offers one of the closest parallels, in pose and iconography, to the kneeling archer of type II coinage.[59]

PFS 286 (Figs 32.9c, 10c) is another rare example of a lively, narrative mode of presentation in scenes that have a kneeling archer. Here the archer shoots towards a caprid that has been hit by an arrow in the back of its neck; its forelegs have collapsed as the animal falls to the ground. The broad and flat forms of the human figure are documented in other seals from the PFS corpus, while animal forms appear to be mainstream Fortification Style. The emphasis on the large, elaborate horns of the animal is a feature found throughout the PFS corpus regardless of compositional type or style. PFS 977 (Figs 32.9d, 10d) is another lively scene carved in the Fortification Style. The archer, wearing a fringed garment, shoots towards an elaborately horned animal (antelope?) that bounds away from the archer while turning his head back towards him. A long-necked bird (vulture?) flies towards the animal in the field immediately before it.

Finally, there are two interesting examples of the kneeling archer shooting towards a heraldic group. Both are carved in the Fortification Style. In one, PFS 128 (Figs 32.9e, 10e), the archer, wearing a double-belted Assyrian garment, shoots towards a pair of crossed lions. In the upper terminal field there is a star. The other, PFS 305 (Figs 32.9f, 10f), partakes of both the heraldic group and the protection imagery. The archer shoots towards a pair of lions posed heraldically over an animal marchant.

V. Conclusion

This very preliminary overview of archer imagery as preserved in the PFS corpus has revealed an exceptionally rich and diverse visual tradition for the scene in glyptic at the heart of the empire. One of the major conclusions to emerge from this overview is how firmly the imagery of the archer coins of types I and II are grounded in this glyptic imagery. The archer imagery on these coins then must be contextualized within a much broader semantic field wherein the archer is articulated in a variety of poses, dress and headdresses. He is sometimes winged, and generally shoots at lions, caprids and bovids, often of a fantastical, winged nature. Thus, while the use of an actual type II archer coin (PFS 1393s) to seal the transaction on PF 1495 is a rather rare phenomenon, since the sealing matrix was a coin rather than a seal, the imagery on that coin—a kneeling archer—is, nevertheless, right at home in the centre of the empire.

The glyptic evidence from Persepolis does not, of course, negate the critical role that abstract concepts associated with the bow (and arrows) may have played in expressions of Achaemenid kingship at the time of Darius I. Those concepts were both deeply entrenched in earlier expressions of kingship in Elam and Assyria and, potentially, declarations of specifically Iranian ideas of kingship. The glyptic evidence from Persepolis does, however, dramatically document the powerful hold that the shooting archer imagery had in the visual repertoire in south-western Iran in the late sixth century BC.

Specifically, I have suggested that the type I archer is to be contextualized, stylistically, iconographically and conceptually, within the court-mandated glyptic programme. The emphatic "half-figure-ness" of the type I archer seems also to be intimately related to various glyptic imagery wherein the half-figure is stressed: the figure emerging from the winged ring/disc; composite human/animal archer creatures, several of which are winged or actually in flight; crowned half-figure found within a circle; and, in the case of PFS 261*, an archer rising out of the back of a fantastical winged creature. All of these images seem to express concepts of "ascension" that appears to have been one of the central semantic concerns of Achaemenid imagery.

The kneeling shooting archer of the type II coin imagery is part of a much larger repertoire of shooting archers from Persepolis. While these scenes preserved in the PFS corpus clearly filled a variety of semantic notions, I would isolate two aspects of this semantic field as particularly critical for our consideration of the type II archer. The first aspect is that of protection. The revival of the scene of the archer who shoots at a predator attacking another animal in the PFS corpus is really quite striking, given the fact that the imagery is almost completely absent in Neo-Assyrian and Neo-Babylonian glyptic. It suggests a conscious looking backward into earlier periods to revive a theme long associated with a role intimately linked with ancient notions of kingship. The second aspect is that of the pose of the kneeling archer. Appearing in almost half of the shooting archer scenes from Persepolis, the kneeling archer was clearly the preferred visual expression of the shooting archer as a concept. The variety of scenes in which the kneeling archer appears suggests that we ought to be open to multiple levels of reading depending upon context. It seems noteworthy, however, that many of the scenes involving the kneeling archer are dynamic and busy ones, some even having narrative qualities. The kneeling archer of the type II coin thus may be actively invoking the concept of dynamic movement/action. This is of interest not least of all because dynamic movement/action is not a prominent feature of monumental relief of the time of Darius. Thus, the kneeling archer of the type II coinage may then have been selected to express an aspect of Achaemenid kingship distinct from that in monumental relief.[60]

Notes

*I would like to express my thanks to the Iran Heritage Foundation, and especially to Farhad Hakimzadeh, for their efforts in presenting the conference. In London at the British Museum I am especially appreciative of the assistance provided by John Curtis and St John Simpson. For matters related to the study of the seals from the Fortification archive I thank yet again Margaret Cool Root, Matthew W. Stolper, Wouter Henkelman, Annalisa Azzoni, Beth Dusinberre, L. Magee and L. Garoutte. Abbreviations follow the conventions established in Garrison & Root 2001: xv–xvi; "PFS corpus" designates the complete corpus of seals that occur on the PF tablets (i.e. those tablets published in Hallock 1969; the seals that occur on those tablets are the ones that fall under the publication scope of the Persepolis Fortification Tablet Seal Project, see Garrison & Root 2001: 1). PFUTS is the siglum used to identify seals that occur on the uninscribed tablets from the Fortification archive (see Garrison 2008).

1. The archer coinage has generated a substantial body of scholarship over the last 100 years. Carradice (1987), owing to its importance for the chronology of the coin issues, and Le Rider (2001: 123–205), owing to the depth and clarity of his exposition of the issues, mark watersheds. For other introductions and surveys of scholarship, see e.g. Root 1979: 116–118; 1988, 1989, 1991: 15–17; Harrison 1982: 14–38; Stronach 1989; Descat 1989; Alram 1993; Henkelmann 1995–96; Descat 1995; Briant 2002a: 409, 934–935; Dusinberre 2000; Vargyas 2000; Nimchuk 2002; Konuk 2003. For bibliographic updates to Briant 2002a: see Briant 1997: 82–83; 2001: 129. Although I am concerned with the archers of types I and II, I follow the subdivisions of types III and IV suggested by Stronach (1989: 258–261, fig. 1).

2. For the background on the Persepolis Fortification archive, see Garrison & Root 2001: 1–32; Briant, Henkelman & Stolper 2008.

3. By this descriptive phrase I include both figures that shoot a bow and arrow (what others have termed a "hunt scene" or a "contest scene") as well as figures that hold a bow and/or arrow(s). Seals from the PFS corpus showing archer imagery will be published in Garrison & Root, in preparation.

4. For previously published comments on a few select seals that bear archer imagery from the archive, see Root 1991: 15–16, figs 1–2 and Garrison 2000: 134–141. Famously, among the seals preserving

archer imagery from the PFS corpus, is an impression of an actual type II archer coin (see Root 1988, for its initial publication; the coin is generally cited in any discussion of coinage of types I and II).
5. The exact dates of issuance of the coins of types I and II are, of course, still hotly disputed; see Le Rider 2001: 128–133, for a summary of opinions. In brief, the temporal boundaries are set by Darius' accession to the throne, 522 BC, and the now well-known occurrence of a type II coin to seal PF 1495, the transaction of which is dated to the 12th month of year 22 of Darius I, i.e. early in 499 BC (see Root 1988).
6. These questions have recently been thoroughly surveyed by Le Rider 2001: 41–121 (electrum coinage of the Lydian kings), 123–178 (Achaemenid coins of types I and II).
7. Briant (2002a: 934) on the problem of royal coinage: "despite numerous recent contributions on the subject..., I remain perplexed due to the breadth and complexity of the problems raised by such studies."
8. For similar stress on the ideological functions of the coins, see Root 1991: 15–17; Briant 2002a: 934–935; Vargyas 2000: 35–39, 43 (on the daric);Dusinberre 2000: 164–164; Nimchuk 2002; note also the remarks of Le Rider 2001: 79. Nimchuk 2002: 66–67, has expressed most strongly the communicative role of archer coins of types I and II, articulating a two-fold hierarchy of audiences: 1) Persian elites; 2) local, non-Persian elites, in particular, those of Lydia. Note the comments of Root (1991: 15–16) on the imagery of the coins of types I and II expressing a distinctive heartland message. For convenience, I shall continue to reference these artefacts as coins, although my argument assumes that in fact they did not function as such in the modern understanding of the term. The fact that the archer coins functioned exceptionally well as vehicles of communication can be seen in the ancient Greek literary sources (frequently discussed; from this perspective see, especially, Dusinberre 2000: 164–165: "signifiers of the might of the Persian king").
9. The precise date of its appearance is, however, still hotly contested; opinions have been surveyed most recently by Le Rider 2001: 128–133. The application of the type II archer coin (almost universally thought to have appeared after type I) on PF 1495 in early 499 BC provides a secure *terminus ante quem* for the first appearance of type I (see Root 1988).
10. See Vargyas 2000: 35–36, n. 17, on a possible daric of type I. Carradice 1987: 79, table A counts 99 sigloi of type I found in hoards, 98 of which come from the remarkable Çal dağ hoard.
11. The upper torso of the type II archer and the type IIIb can sometimes be rendered in a manner that evokes a profile shoulder, but it is certainly not anything like that seen on the type I archer.
12. For Stronach (1989: 265) the telling details for the connection of the coins of type I to Bisitun are the plain sleeve, the diagonal pleats at the top of the lower part of the garment and, in some examples, the similarity in facial details to the half figure in the winged ring at Bisitun.
13. Calmeyer (1979b: 307–308) also opted for a divine reading of the image. See also, recently, Dusinberre 2000: 165.
14. Stronach 1989: 267–268. The predecessors that Stronach cites are all full-length figures of Assyrian kings, suggesting that he is foregrounding simply the aspect of the ruler's holding the bow and/or arrows and not the half-figure per se.
15. Stronach 1989: 264–269. The linking of the ideological messages of the type I coins to events in Ionia seems now rather unlikely, given the securely dated appearance of a type II coin in early 499 BC (see above, n. 9).
16. The half-figure of the king would have been the manner in which most people would have actually viewed the king as he rode by in a chariot.
17. The other royal seals are PFS 7* (Cat. No. 4) and PFS 113* (Cat. No. 19) and PFUTS 18 for the royal-name seals of Darius see Garrison in press d.
18. Discussed more fully in Garrison 2000: 141–42 and Garrison, in press d.
19. E.g. Root 1989: 45; Kaptan 2000: 213–216.
20. As already noted by Root 1989: 45.
21. Potentially described as a "centaur-archer," but the term is problematic in this context given that none of the animal bodies of such creatures from the PFS corpus may be identified securely as equine.
22. Regarding the Fortification Style, see the summary introduction in Garrison & Root 2001: 18.
23. An animal lying between the archer and his primary target, a feature that adds a narrative-like character to the scene, is a rare compositional type in the PFS corpus. PFS 71* (the same seal as PTS 33*) and PFS 35*, are probably the most striking examples of this type of scene (both seals are discussed in more detail below).

24. Garrison 1991: 16–17; 1996: 40–42, for the artist.
25. See the list of occurrences in Garrison & Root 2001 (belt, sv.)
26. For Middle Assyrian and Kassite glyptic, see the list of occurrences in Seidl 1989: 176–177. For the *kudurrus*, see Seidl 1989: 177.
27. Seidl (1989: 177) lists only one example of composite archer creatures in Assyro-Babylonian glyptic (Porada 1948: no. 749, unprovenanced). See now also Collon 2001: no. 65, which is also unprovenanced and could, I think, easily date down into the Achaemenid period.
28. I give the complete reading of the inscription in Garrison 2000: 140, and further analysis in Garrison, in press *c*.
29. Most recently Nimchuk 2002: 64–65, on the importance of the bow as an emblem of Achaemenid kingship.
30. Schmidt 1953: pl. 146.
31. Garrison & Root 2001: 501–502 (lion, sv.)
32. See various dictionary entries in Black & Green 1992, as well as the recent analytical articles of Breniquet 2002: 157–165 and Scurlock 2002.
33. Schmidt 1957: 24–25, pl. 6, for PTS 16 and PTS 17, interpreted as representations of Ahuramazda. These seals are also discussed by Moorey (1978: 146–148), Calmeyer (1979*b*: 307–308) and Stronach (1989: 267), the first two opting for reading the figures as deities.
34. As Root 1989: 48.
35. This visual rhetoric of kingship is thus very different from the textual rhetoric of Bisitun and Naqsh-i Rustam, where the stress is, for the most part, on the very particular relationship between Darius the legitimate (and human) king and the god Ahuramazda. On the considerable commentary on the royal inscriptions of Darius from Bisitun and Naqsh-i Rustam, see the introductory survey in Briant 2002*a*: 124–128, 170–171, 210–213, 900–901 and 913; detailed commentary on both text and visual imagery may be found in Root 1979: 131–226.
36. I explore the use of atlantid figures more fully in Garrison in press *a*, *b*; in preparation. For monumental reliefs, see the analyses by Root 1979: 147–161.
37. I pursue this line of thought in more detail in Garrison in press *a*. The concept of ascension in monumental relief has been carefully explored in Root 1979: 131–161.
38. As with type I, the precise date of the first appearance of type II is still much debated. See the comments above, nn. 5 and 9.
39. Le Rider 2001: 142–143, counts five known darics of type II. See Vargyas 2000: 35–37, on the function of the type II daric.
40. Stronach 1989: 264–272.
41. The type II archer is seen to have appealed to the West owing to its multicultural evocations, in particular, of the bow-shooting Herakles and spear-throwing Athene, resulting in a marriage of the ideas of Persian king as primeval royal hunter, archetypal western hero and Olympian contestant (Root 1989: 49–50). Vargyas 2000: 36–38, tracks some of the scholarship that has developed from this suggestion. Vargyas (2000: 38) himself sees the change from type I to type II as reflecting changed political circumstances, from a period where legitimacy was the main concern (i.e. early, immediately after the revolts of 522/21 BC, type I coinage representing "Darius is the legitimate king") to one where the nature of Achaemenid kingship was paramount (later, during the middle years of Darius I, type II coinage representing the "power of the Achaemenid king").
42. I explore this observation in more detail in Garrison in press *a*.
43. See also the comments below regarding PFS 71*, and above regarding PFS 78.
44. The horned creature in the lower field appears to have a leonine facial profile.
45. Discussed in Garrison 1991: 39–40.
46. PFS 1568 is one of the few seals that I would identify as Court Style among this thematic group.
47. See Garrison & Root 2001: 512 (crossed animals or creatures, s.v.), for examples occurring in heroic encounters. Garrison 2006 discusses the isolated crossed/intertwined animals scene type in more detail within the context of what has been traditionally identified as late Neo-Elamite glyptic.
48. Owing to the caprid's rampant pose and the rigidly symmetrical tree, I read the caprid and tree within the tradition of the heraldic scene rather than simply as an isolated animal at which the archer shoots.
49. The seal is also found on a PF-type tablet in a private collection (Jones & Stolper 2006: 16–18). The impression of PFS 115* on that tablet clearly preserves an animal in the field between the archer and the rampant caprid. This animal is not preserved in any impression from the PFS corpus, and thus is not included in the composite drawing published here as Fig. 32.7c.
50. The now well-known PFS 16* (Cat. No. 22) seems stylistically related to PFS 115*.

51. For the royal-name seals of Darius, see above, n. 17.
52. See Matthews 1990: nos 311–314, 352 and 424; in the last two seals the archer is standing. Note the remarkable Middle Assyrian seal applied to a tablet dating to the reign of Darius I published by Ehrenberg 1999: no. 217. She notes that the inscription on the seal appears to be a later addition, perhaps Late Babylonian (which, as she and others use the term, is not synonymous with Neo-Babylonian).
53. Although more study on all aspects of this important seal is needed.
54. The Elamite inscription is too poorly preserved to be read. There appear to be traces of a vertical panel for an inscription immediately to the left of the rampant lion; the panel is, however, not aligned with the preserved signs, although this may be due to distortion in the application of the seal. Overall, the inscription does not seem to fit well into the space, suggesting some type of addition/modification.
55. See Garrison & Root 2001: 522 (pedestal animal(s)/creature(s), s.v.), for examples occurring in heroic encounters.
56. Of course, the Court Style as a phenomenon is rare in the PFS corpus as a whole.
57. Schmidt 1957: 30–31, pl. 10, for PTS 33*. The seal carries an Aramaic inscription of which the first three lines are preserved: ḤTM□/□RTWR/ZY BR: "Seal of Artavardiya son of....". This reading departs from that given by Bowman in Cameron 1948: 92 (followed by Schmidt 1957: 31; cf. however, Hallock 1977: 133, n. 13). The individual who uses PFS 71* in the Fortification archive is Irdumartiya, the Elamite rendering of Old Persian Artavardiya. Hallock (1997: 129) identified this Irdumartiya/Artavardiyah as one of the "helpers of Darius" mentioned in the Bisitun inscription (Kent 1953, iii: 41–42). Note also Koch 1990: 65 and 231, identified as the "Hofmarschall" in the years 26–27, after Parnaka; Aperghis 1999: 164, the probable "commander" of Shiraz. The occurrences of PFS 71* on PF 280 (year 14, 508/7 BC) and PF 1830 (4th and 5th months of year 15, 507 BC) are some of the earliest dated examples of emphatic court iconography in the PFS corpus.
58. The inscription in PFS 71* is, of course, in Aramaic rather than Elamite or, in the case of the royal-name seals, trilingual. Garrison (2006) explores in more detail the Elamite and Aramaic inscriptions in the PFS corpus.
59. See above, n. 57, on the date of the earliest occurrences of PFS 71* in the PFS corpus.
60. See also the comments above on the distinctive characteristics of the visual programmes in monumental relief, coinage and glyptic at the time of Darius I. The kneeling pose could, conceivably, be a militant/aggressive expression on Darius' part (as Stronach 1989: 264–269; Nimchuk 2002: 66) and/or a reference to age-old concepts of the king as hunter (as Root 1989: 46; 1991: 16) or protector (see above).

33

Clay Tags from Seyitömer Höyük in Phrygia

Deniz Kaptan

In the 1990s the staff members of Afyon and Eskişehir Museums in Turkey published a series of reports about the rescue excavations of a large mound in Phrygia, 26 km to the north-west of Kotiaeion (modern Kütahya) (Aydın 1991; Topbaş 1993, 1994; İlaslı 1996) (Fig. 33.1). Among the excavated artefacts were four clay tags bearing seal impressions. This paper addresses the preliminary results of our study of the tags, in particular the seal image SHS 3 showing an Achaemenid martial scene.[1]

The mound is named after the nearby town of Seyitömer, well known for the coal mining enterprise of the Department of Coal Mines of Turkey, which in fact funded the salvage excavations in the hope of its complete removal so that the approximately 15 m-thick seam of coal could be mined. When the funding ended after several seasons of excavations, the General Directorate of Monuments and Museums of Turkey overturned the proposition of the Department of Coal Mines and made a decision in favour of the preservation of Seyitömer Höyük. As a consequence the mound at present stands majestically in the middle of an open coalmine pit and awaits further archaeological exploration.

Although this region is still not very well known in Achaemenid studies, there are Achaemenid period-related stelai and tumulus burials within a radius of 100 km around the site. Among these sites are Altıntaş, Seyitgazi (Nakoleia), the Midas City and the vicinity of Aizanoi.[2] The site was continuously inhabited from the Early Bronze Age to the late Roman period, but so far none of the finds have revealed the ancient name of the settlement.[3]

The quantity of the Seyitömer Höyük tags is relatively small, but in the record of seal impressions from western Asia Minor during the Achaemenid period, they constitute a significant group after the several hundred *bullae* found in Daskyleion, the satrapal seat in Hellespontine Phrygia (Akurgal 1956; Kaptan 2002). So far only two sealings, each from a different archaeological context, have been reported from Gordion, once the capital city of the Phrygians (Dusinberre 2005: 69–71, cat. nos 55–56).

Archaeological context

The tags come from two separate archaeological contexts. One showing a bird-headed feline

Fig. 33.1 North-western Asia Minor. (Adapted from Kaptan 2002, i: Map 2)

creature (SHS 2.1) and the other a gorgon-like representation (SHS 1), they were excavated in trenches in the north-western sector of the mound (Aydın 1991: 195, pl. 12). In 1993 two others, one bearing a second impression of the seal showing the bird-headed feline creature (SHS 2.2) and the other representing a Persian victory scene (SHS 3) were found together in trench G-14, reportedly just below the Hellenistic period levels in the north-eastern sector of the mound (İlaslı 1996: 3–4). The architecture of this area to which these two sealings were related was disturbed due to a destructive fire, but multiple depressions of wooden posts, each about 15–20 cm in diameter, could still be observed on the floor. The adjacent trenches revealed fortification walls and chambers with plastered walls, which at some sections were preserved up to 1.5 m high.[4] It is difficult to comment on whether or not this description can imply the presence of a storage area or indicate some economic activity that took place just behind the fortification walls, although the presence of tags in this location is a reminder that in the Ancient Near East sealings and tablets can be found in rooms close to or within the fortification system, and designated as "service areas" near the entry to the city (Khachatrian 1996: 365–366; Manukian 1996: 371–372, fig. 1, pl. 77; Root 1996: 6–7; Garrison & Root 2001: 23–34). It is noteworthy that the earlier report, dated a year before the sealings were unearthed, actually

Fig. 33.2 Back of Kt 9400. Kütahya Museum. (Photograph D. Kaptan)

Fig. 33.3 SHS 2.2 on Kt 9400. Stamp seal impression. Kütahya Museum. (Photograph D. Kaptan)

mentions that precisely in this area a total of 15 pithoi arranged in rows (G-14 alone yielding 8 of the pithoi) were excavated and then subsequently removed (Topbaş 1993: 3–4, pl. 6.a–b). Several pits containing a rich assemblage of Greek and late Phrygian pottery and charcoal were also excavated. It is therefore tempting to suggest that the tags might have been associated with this storage area, which was excavated a year earlier on the same spot. Further investigation of the stratigraphy of the mound and pottery analysis of this area may help to unravel this puzzle.[5]

Shape and description of the tags

The Seyitömer tags are flattened lumps of clay with a maximum height of 2.50 cm. Three of them are round and the fourth, bearing the impressions of SHS 3, is ovoid and 3 cm wide. The maximum thickness is 0.9 cm. The fingerprints and markings of the palm of the individual who shaped the soft clay and pressed the seal are visible on each tag, in particular on the backs of Kt 9400 and Kt 8309 (Fig. 33.2). Seal impressions appear on both faces of the other two tags (SHS 3.1 and SHS 3.2 on Kt 9401; SHS 1.1 and SHS 1.2 on Kt 9047). String holes have been observed on Kt 8309 and Kt 9047. No other markings other than fingerprints appear on any of the tags.

Colour changes, pits and cracks on the surface of Kt 9401 indicate intensive exposure to fire, most probably due to the conflagration that damaged the occupation level where the tags were found (Figs 33.4–33.5).

Functions

Two of the sealings (Kt 8309 and Kt 9047) found in the north-western sector of the mound bear string holes indicating that they were suspended

364 THE WORLD OF ACHAEMENID PERSIA

Fig. 33.4 SHS 3.1 on Kt 9401. Cylinder seal impression. Kütahya Museum. (Photograph D. Kaptan)

Fig. 33.5 SHS 3.2 on Kt 9401. Cylinder seal impression. Kütahya Museum. (Photograph D. Kaptan)

from some object.[6] As no marking other than fingerprints has been observed, we have no clue about what kind of items they were.

Those found at G-14 in the north-east bear no string holes (Figs. 33.2–33.5). They seem to be new additions to the miscellany of bits of clay bearing seal impressions—often referred to as "visiting cards" or "trial pieces"—that have been found throughout all periods and the function of which has so far not been convincingly explained (Collon 1987: 119; Herbordt 1992: 68). Kt 9400 and Kt 9401 were perhaps used for accounting purposes, such as tokens. The sealed tag may have been left with an official when an item was taken away or brought in. They could also have been used as a kind of authorization device sent by someone whose message would be delivered orally by the bearer of the seal impression.[7]

Seal impressions

Three seals were used on the tags. Kt 9047 bears the image of the same stamp seal, SHS 1, on both faces. It shows a nude winged figure holding two lions by their tails. Snakes and animal ears emerge from the frontally represented head. The image, which resembles a series of representations on archaic Greek and Phoenician seals, seems to be a combination of the Near Eastern nude hero, Bes and the Greek gorgon (Boardman 1968: 27–44, nos 38, 49, 53; Spier 1992: 54, nos 103–104). The second seal image, SHS 2, appears on two tags (Kt 8309 and Kt 9400). The seal must have been a stamp, most probably the round bezel of a ring. The seal impression, which shows a horned bird-headed feline striding left on a plain ground line, one forepaw raised over a plant (SHS 2.2, Pl. 2), is reminiscent of griffin representations on some of the "Greco-Persian" seals (e.g. Boardman 1970a: pls 842, 957–958).[8] The overall rendition of the image with its elongated limb seems to be close to works in Phrygia when compared with the Pazarlı painted terracotta plaques, presumably dated to the sixth century BC (Koşay 1941; Akurgal 1955: 72–78; Mellink 1984: 171;

The Museum of Anatolian Civilizations [n.d.]: 184–185). Perhaps what we see on SHS 2 is an outcome of the same tradition that prevailed in the Persian period.

SHS 3 and the martial scene

The last seal, SHS 3, was a cylinder and it was rolled twice on Kt 9401. The measurements reveal that the cylinder rolled on the tag had an approximate height of 2 cm. Its diameter was about 1 cm. The cylinder was rolled on each face of the tag. The process of rolling the seal twice on soft clay was probably not easy, as fingerprints appear over one of the seal impressions (SHS 3.1) which was presumably produced first (Fig. 33.4). A complete roll had originally appeared on the other side (SHS 3.2), but the right half was subsequently damaged by fire and chipped off (Fig. 33.5). Thanks to the duplication of the image we are able to obtain a composite drawing of the entire scene (Fig. 33.6). The scene on SHS 3 represents a spear-wielder facing an archer and a fallen warrior between them.

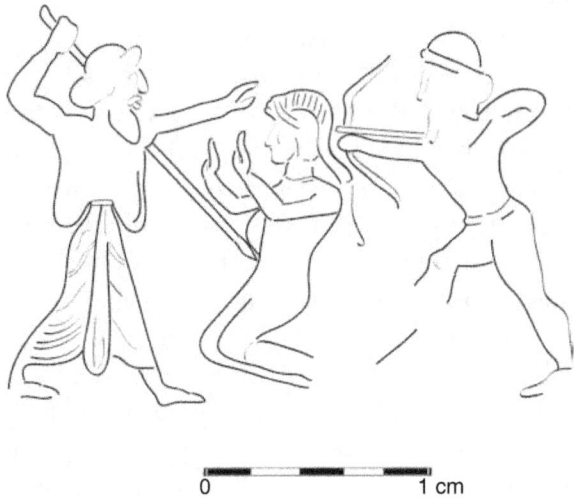

Fig. 33.6 Composite drawing of SHS 3. Scale 3:1 (Drawing D. Kaptan)

On the left of the scene, the seal impression shows a striding man, facing right with the body depicted frontally and clad in the Persian court robe, with the sleeves pushed up revealing bare arms. Diagonal folds and a vertical central fold of the lower garment are well defined. He has a long beard rounded at the tip and a rounded coiffure on the forehead and at the back above his neck; he is possibly wearing a thin band over his head. Facial details such as the smoothly bulging cheek, lips and part of the moustache are well preserved on the impression. As he is about to thrust his spear he also raises his left hand to seize his opponent by the head. This opponent, represented in the centre of the scene, is a defeated warrior facing left, in a Greek helmet with a crest. He is shown in full profile on his knees with raised hands and arms bent. He seems to be naked. His shield, rather small in size, is shown in the background behind him. Framing the scene on the right is a striding archer who aims his bow across the fallen victim towards the spear-wielder. This figure is in a rather poor state of preservation and can only be observed on SHS 3.1. He has a beard and rounded coiffure resting at the back of his neck; he is possibly wearing a domed headdress or a fillet. The outline of his bare-looking legs presents him as a muscular warrior.

Despite the damage on the right portion of seal impression SHS 3.2, the remaining part of the design offers a few clues about the carving style of the seal. Among them, the victor in Persian court robe is the best preserved and reveals a smooth relief quality particularly on the face, which shows slightly bulging cheek and lips and a prominent nose. These stylistic qualities are reminiscent of a royal-name seal image from Daskyleion, DS 4, representing the audience of the king, and two seals from Russia, the inscribed Moscow Artaxerxes cylinder and the Zvenigorodsky cylinder, both representing a Persian victory scene.[9] The preserved folds of the lower garment also indicate that the engraver worked carefully and was at ease with the rendition of the Achaemenid image. His defeated opponent displays a rather awkward pose as his legs overlap and his arms bend. His hands, however, are remarkably expressive. Both of them are directed towards the victor, palms facing him, and each shown as a thick dynamic line with the thumbs bent over. This rendition also brings to mind the same Daskyleion seal, DS 4, mentioned above.[10] The representation of the usher's hand covering his mouth on DS 4, perhaps in a gesture of respect to the king, strikingly resembles that of the defeated opponent's on SHS 3. These are not knob or fork-like hands as seen on many Achaemenid koine and Persianizing seals but rather more carefully represented fingers and thumb in profile.

Figures in Achaemenid costume triumphing over enemies generally appear in two basic settings in Achaemenid glyptic. In one, they are in battle scenes, in which the victor is shown in the midst of a fight that he is winning, and the inevitable victory is furthermore postulated by various components in the scene, such as the winged disc hovering above and dead bodies lying on the ground wearing the same attire as the Persian's main opponent. These scenes do not represent combat in a real sense; they seem to emphasize Persian superiority over the enemy who is going to be inevitably defeated. Representations of this type on seals were found in various areas of the empire.[11] The other type shows the final stage of the victory when the enemy is completely defeated, captives taken and all tied to the same rope.[12] These scenes bear a thematic resemblance to the Behistun relief on which "the lie-followers" were shown captured and tied together with one rope (Sarre 1923: pl. 3 (centre); Root 1979: 58–61, 183–226; Jacobs 2002: 354–355, fig. 1; Curtis & Tallis 2005: pls 4, 6). On the seals the victor either leads them and/or he plunges his spear into a kneeling figure. A seal image, PTS 28, on several *bullae* from the Treasury and sealings found in a jar from the Fortifications of Persepolis contributes to this subject (Schmidt 1957: 10–11, pl. 9 (PT 4 948, 865, 330); Tajvidi 1976: pls 140–142; Curtis & Tallis 2005: 231, no. 424). In the representation the Achaemenid victor, who leads three captives tied by a rope attached to his belt, spears a kneeling warrior in a Greek helmet while grabbing him by the arm.

SHS 3 shares features with both of these representational types. Like the fallen warrior on PTS 28 the Persian's victim on SHS 3 also wears a Greek helmet, but on this seal he faces his foe and raises his arms imploringly toward him. This gesture is rather reminiscent of the Behistun relief where the chief of the rebels stretches out his arms towards Darius who crushes him with his foot. On SHS 3 the emphasis on the further exertion of power is expressed by the position of the victor's left arm, raised over the defeated warrior's head. Similarly, in the heroic encounter scenes the Persian hero often stretches out his left arm to grasp the horn or forelocks of the creature in order to further pacify it.[13] SHS 3 is not the only seal that shows this kind of contact between the victor and his opponent. There are a number of seals showing that seal cutters working in western Achaemenid and Greek styles used this pattern widely (Boardman 1970a: pls 849, 851, *infra* nn. 26–28). For example, a fragmentary Daskyleion seal (DS 64) depicts a defeated warrior wearing a Greek helmet and shield as the victor grabs him by stretching out his left hand (Kaptan 2002, i: 88, 140–141; 2002, ii: pls 87–88, 195–196). An Aramaic inscribed cylinder in the Bibliothèque Nationale, Paris, cut in the Greek style, shows the victor in trousers and tunic seizing the frontally depicted naked warrior by the head (Boardman 2000: pl. 5.7). A seal from Caria, also in the Greek style, depicts the same theme: the victor in Achaemenid costume and the defeated warrior on his knees in profile shown in a similar posture to that on SHS 3 (Boardman 1970*a*: 310, pl. 849; Zazoff 1983: pl. 39.6). Above all it appears that a few seals with archers scenes from the corpus of Persepolis Fortification Tablets bear the most impressive compositional similarities to SHS 3. In these scenes the aggressor on the left and the victim in the middle are animals, not humans. Among them, PFS 722 represents the closest compositional structure that shows a lion on hind legs, and an archer drawing his bow across the ibex. (Personal communication with M. C. Root; Garrison & Root 2001: 43; Garrison & Root in preparation.) The outcome of a significant transition in the iconography seems to be on display on SHS 3.

SHS 3 also shows thematic links to some of the Greco-Persian reliefs and funerary art from Asia Minor, for example the paintings from the burial at Tatarlı (Summerer 2007), and the recently published Çan sarcophagus from a tumulus burial on the Granicus plain (Sevinç *et al.* 2001: 396–397). One of the long sides of the painted sarcophagus shows a triumphant horseman clad in Persian riding attire thrusting his spear into a fallen warrior sprawled under a tree. The authors note the iconographic associations of the scene, in particular the armour of the horseman, to a seal design from Persepolis Treasury, PTS 30. The Seyitömer seal image provides further evidence that thematic parallels of the representation on the Çan sarcophagus were available on seal images at home in Asia Minor.

The Seyitömer Höyük seal, SHS 3, is a new contribution to the Achaemenid seal corpus. Stylistically it stands close to the western Achaemenid koine seals, such as DS 4 and the Moscow Artaxerxes seal and Zvenigorodsky seal.[14] Elsewhere, I have discussed how seals as portable objects could be viewed as a great source for the transmission of Achaemenid elements and potential models because they travelled with their owners and their designs on clay travelled even farther (Kaptan 2007). The discovery of a seal like SHS 3 shows that Achaemenid seals were circulating even in the rural parts of Anatolia and that Achaemenid imagery was available in a broad spectrum. The Seyitömer tags also reveal that Achaemenid koine works could be expected in the region at any site that has levels from the classical period. The seal impressions on clay found in Phrygia and Hellespontine Phrygia possibly represent only a very small fraction of what was available to people during the Achaemenid hegemony, but they present sufficient evidence that sphragistics could contribute significantly to our knowledge of the diffusion of Achaemenid imagery in Asia Minor.

Notes

I am grateful to Metin Türktüzün, the Director of the Kütahya Museum, and Ahmet İlaslı, of the Afyon Museum. My project on the seals of the Achaemenid period in the museums of Turkey has been generously supported by the Iran Heritage Foundation and the Soudavar Memorial Foundation.

1. The abbreviation SHS is used for the Seyitömer Höyük Seal. Each seal is given a number, followed by the number of the seal impressions. For example the abbreviation SHS 1.2 indicates the second seal impression of Seyitömer Höyük Seal No. 1. The abbreviation 'Kt' followed by a four-digit number refers directly to the tags. These

are the inventory numbers given by the Kütahya Museum.
2. Altıntaş stele: Pfhul & Möbius 1977–1979: no. 75. Aizanoi/Akalan tumulus: Arman 1998. Surveys based on classical sources regarding the region and the Persians: Sekunda 1991: 130–136; Tuplin 1989: 236–237.
3. Mitchell (1993: 181) notes the difficulty of archaeologically and epigraphically distinguishing one settlement from another in the upper Tembris valley: "As in north-east Lydia, these heavily rural market towns show virtually nothing to distinguish themselves from the larger *komai* or *katoikiai* of the region."
4. The excavators note that the fortification system was first built during the Early Bronze Age and then restored and reused during the succeeding periods. The Bronze Age period walls, which appear to be preserved up to 5 m, were made of mud brick reinforced with wood. Wood samples taken from the Early Bronze Age levels have been included in the Aegean Dendrochronology Project (see Kuniholm 1996; http://www.arts.cornell.edu/dendro/).
5. The field notes of the excavations and the other finds from the corresponding levels will be studied in the future.
6. Henkelman, Jones & Stolper (2004: 45–48) pose critical questions about the functions of sealed tags and "anepigraphic" Persepolis Fortification Tablets and sealing practices.
7. Gibson (2001/02) suggests that this kind of function could be a possibility for the sealings excavated at prehistoric Hamoukar; cf. also Dusinberre 2005: 70.
8. Floral designs appear before animal representations on a few gold signet rings from the North Black Sea area tombs (e.g. Chertomlyk) dated to the late fifth and early fourth centuries BC (Boardman 1970a: pls 700–701), but stylistically the image on SHS 2 seems not to have much in common with the representations on these rings.
9. a. DS 4: Kaptan 2002, i: 113–115; 2002, ii: 50–55, pls 47–59.
   b. The Moscow Artaxerxes cylinder: Strelkov 1937: fig. 2; Nagel 1963: no. 5; Root 1979: 122, 182, pl. 34b; Kaptan 2002, i: 87, n. 363.
   c. The Zvenigorodsky cylinder: Ward 1910: no. 1049; Root 1979: 182, n. 2; Zazoff 1983: 168, fig. 48a; Boardman 2000: 159–160, pl. 5.6; Kaptan 2002, i: 87–88.
10. *Supra* n. 9 a; cf. Kaptan 2002, ii: pls 54, 59.
11. E.g. DS 63–64 from Daskyleion: Kaptan 2002, i: 87–88, 140–141; 2002, ii: 86–88, pls 192–196. The seal of Arshama from Egypt: Boardman 2000: 174, pl. 5.21. A cylinder in the Hermitage: Zazoff 1983: 168, fig. 48c. A cylinder from the Oxus Treasure: Sarre 1923: pl. 52 centre; Collon 1987: no. 574; Boardman 2000: 160, pl. 5.5; Merillees 2005: 70, no. 66; Curtis & Tallis 2005: no. 413. A cylinder in the British Museum: Collon 1987: no. 747; Merillees 2005: 69, no. 65; Curtis & Tallis 2005: no. 415.
12. See the Artaxerxes cylinder and the Zvenigorodsky cylinder above n. 9 b–c. There are a few more seals showing a similar composition: Ward 1910: nos 1048, 1052; Root 1979: 182, n. 2 b–c.
13. E.g. DS 3 in Kaptan 2002, i: 55–58; 2002, ii: 5, pls 9–46; PFS 584, PFS 859, 1264s in Garrison & Root 2001: 297–304.
14. *Supra* n. 9.

34

The Archer Coins: A Closer Examination of Achaemenid Art in Asia Minor

Yannick Lintz

Introduction

Within the ambit of Achaemenid studies, there are few areas that have been more debated than that of coinage. Since the earliest studies by Barclay Vincent Head of the British Museum (1877) and by Ernest Babelon of the Bibliothèque Nationale de France (1893), there have been many publications on the subject. This question is probably one of those which are considered to have been fully explored, and one in which new theories might be thought to do nothing else but present old theories in a different guise. I have therefore attempted here to sketch out a kind of historiographic analysis of the question. The term "historiographic" is perhaps somewhat of an exaggeration, but moving beyond the diversity of the approaches taken by numismatists, historians, and art historians, I think it is interesting to look more closely at the reasoning and methodology adopted by these different specialists in the elaboration of their vision. What sources did they use, and what were their preconceptions? Moreover, taking into consideration the earliest publications of 1877 and 1893, one can distinguish a chronological sequence which spans almost 120 years. Over such a period of time, I think it is permissible to ask questions both with reference to the historical vision pertaining to certain epochs, and to particular historical schools of thought. The aim of such a study is not to present an exhaustive critical study of all the works published on Persian coinage since the end of the nineteenth century, and through this to take sides in a historiography of the Achaemenid Empire. Rather, I should simply like to analyse here some of the approaches that form the core of the study of these coins, which I consider to have been markers in this history, and which therefore present a certain vision of Achaemenid history. These theories can take sides on questions of style, or technique, or the chronology of these pieces as they can reveal political, economic, or cultural realities. In a second section, I should like to reflect in a brief summary on questions of methodology which are perhaps more pertinent to this subject than in other areas of study within the Achaemenid history. It would be presumptuous of me to pretend that I am presenting an innovatory approach, which might allow for the presentation of a new vision of the subject.

In all cases, I find that the vision of each of these different approaches remains relatively isolated one from the other. The numismatic expert does not pretend to be an art historian. His or her area of study is the production technique of the coins, their chronology and diffusion, whilst at the same time scrupulously noting all the individual marks on the hundreds of coins within a hoard or collection. The art historian, on the other hand, is working on the interpretation of the representations on these coins. The coins are of interest to him or her, only in as far as they are the support for an image: it is the image that he/she studies, that is the type, and not the object in its individual material reality. The historian uses the image in order to deduce realities of a political or cultural order. And in this manner, one could continue to enumerate the particular visions of each specialist, which is why I believe a methodological analysis is interesting before, perhaps, renewing the debate. For this reason, I will begin by asking these methodological questions, sphere by sphere, in order to be able in the end to draw a general overview of analysis of this coinage.

A few references in the history of the study of "archer" coinage

One could trace these references from a chronological point of view, observing in effect that there are moments of increased activity in the debate at certain points in history between the end of the nineteenth century and the present day. Taking into consideration the date of approximately 50 publications on this precise subject, three distinct periods of increased interest in the subject appear. The first roughly covers the period between 1880 and 1910, characterized by the publication of the catalogues of Persian coinage in the great European public collections. The end of the 1950s and the beginning of the 1960s see the publication of many archaeological studies on the subject, notably those by Robinson (1958), Noe (1949, 1956), Schmidt (1957) and Herzfeld (1938b).[1] And finally, right at the end of the 1970s, and especially during the 1980s and 1990s, there emerges a literature dealing with much more theoretical aspects of the question. The most representative authors of this third period are Margaret Cool Root (1988, 1989, 1991) and David Stronach (1989).

The first catalogues of Persian coins or the history of Persian kings

The two works by Head and Babelon cited earlier, mark the starting point of the interest in Persian coins.[2] These two figures, both curators—one of coins at the British Museum and the other in the Cabinet des monnaies et médailles in the Bibliothèque Nationale de France—took on the huge task of compiling the catalogue of the most important European collections of Greek coinage. Their work is inscribed within the antiquary tradition that was alive in Europe as early as the seventeenth century, and which saw certain scholars defending the study of living antiquity rather than simply that of texts. In 1664, Spanheim is the founder of numismatics as well as epigraphy, as an essential method of study for the history of antiquity, when he states: "Coins are in some way more concrete, less prone to corruption thanks to the quality of their material as well as to the simplicity of their art; and because of the number of places in which they are found, and their quantity and variety, they greatly outrank any other source of information" (Spanheim 1673: 14). He is not content with simply collecting the coins and then presenting them to connoisseurs, he also reflects on a way in which to use them as a critical tool. A generation later, Francesco Bianchini attempts to carry out the same task for images, defending the use of their analysis alongside that of the texts. He defines his method: "If I see the relief of the Arch of Titus which represents him on his chariot, if I read the inscription which was added by the Senate, if I look at the antique medals on which he is represented in the attire of a conqueror, these images make a much more profound impression on the soul because they not only attract the eyes by their texture and design, but because they insinuate themselves into the spirit with their evident signs of antiquity, which serve as a testimony to that which is represented" (1747: 20–21). Head and Babelon, in their study of Persian coinage at the end of the nineteenth century, organize their research on these two principles: numismatics and comparative iconography as methods of investigation for history.

If we examine the work of Ernest Babelon in more detail, we see that his study inscribes itself within the catalogue of Greek coins of the Bibliothèque Nationale. His study forms part of the catalogue of Greek coins. In contrast to Head at the British Museum or Lenormant in France at an earlier epoch, his innovatory approach at the time was to organize his classification according to a vision of the Persian Empire and its different satrapies or local dynasties inside the empire, rather than from an analysis of the Greek coinage of Asia Minor, of which the regal coins depicting the archer are one category. One should note however, that the corpus of published works on Persian coinage, which corresponds to the catalogues of the great European numismatic collections, is still today classified as part of the Greek collections. The minting of coinage in the world of antiquity is still regarded exclusively as a western phenomenon, and the eastern kingdoms involved in the minting of coins (Phoenicia, Cyprus, and the cities in Asia Minor) all did so within the boundaries of their contacts with the West. Babelon, in his catalogue, chooses to classify the coins according to the kings, tracing their history from the rule of Darius I to that of Darius III. He thus forces himself to find individual characteristics in these portraits, allowing the identification of the various kings. In this he is following in the footsteps of Charles Lenormant (the father of François), basing himself as he did on an exhaustive examination of physical details, which often lead to a somewhat subjective and arbitrary classification. Charles Lenormant explained thus his method of attribution: "The heads of the figures represented on these coins (the darics) are of two distinct types...One of the kings has a very prominent aquiline nose, whilst the other has a regular profile. The coins with a straight-nosed figure are the more common of the two, and can therefore be considered to represent the portrait of Xerxes; we believe that the coins showing a king with an aquiline nose depict Darius" (1849: 135). Babelon uses the same principles. For other portraits, he bases himself on written historical sources. This is his description of Cyrus II the Younger: "represented as a running archer, kneeling, on the right. He is beardless and has long hair" (Babelon 1893: 11). In his introduction (1893: xv), he justifies this attribution by specifying that Cyrus was 22 or 23 when he died, and that the Greeks (he cites Herodotus VII, 61 and IX, 22) gave him the epithet *Younger*. We could systematically pick up on the more or less random criteria used by him in this classification of the kings, which today seems to us somewhat whimsical. Nevertheless, it seems to me that his minutely detailed descriptions of the physiognomies and the attire are still of great interest to us and worthy of interpretation.

The theories of the numismatist-archaeologists or the archaeologist-numismatists, at the end of the 1950s

Head and Babelon's theses in the classification of Persian coinage, based on the succession of reigns found in Greek authors, were used until 1958 (i.e. for almost 80 years!), at which point Robinson (1958: 187–193) comes forward with a convincing system of classification and succession of types. He adopts a new system of classification based on the aspect and gestures of the archer-king. With this method, he distinguishes four types in which the king, advancing towards his right, is bearded, crowned[3] and wearing the regal robes (*kandys* in Greek).

Type 1: the king is shown half-length, holding a bow in his left hand and two arrows in his right.
Type 2: the king is shown full-length, shooting with his bow and carrying a quiver on his shoulder; both knees are bent, as though running, but on his knees.
Type 3: the king holds a spear in his right hand and a bow in his left hand; many examples also show him with a quiver on his shoulder.
Type 4: the spear in group 3 is replaced by a dagger.

Robinson's system of classification marks the end of a vision of Achaemenid history based on references from Greek authors, and moves towards a material analysis of the object in the light of archaeological discoveries in Asia Minor and Iran. Thus, in numismatics, a certain number of monetary hoards are discovered and then published in their totality. In 1951, the hoard of Baraklı (ancient Smyrna) was brought to light, which today is in the archaeological museum in Izmir and includes four sigloi on which the archer is represented. In 1956, Noe published two hoards, one known as the Smyrna hoard, discovered in 1945 and consisting of almost 300 pieces, and that of Çal dag discovered in 1948 (almost 700 pieces). In 1987, Carradice listed 42 hoards containing archer coins (sigloi or darics) (1987: 79). Since then, many hoards have been published (Alram 1993; Aydemir 1997; Carradice 1998*a*; 1998*b*; Konuk 2002).[4] This considerable archaeological documentation, of the order of several thousand pieces, is therefore regularly the object of typological classification following the model proposed by Robinson. With time, numismatists have refined this system of classification with the introduction of variants within each type. In 1987, Carradice (1987: 78) defined two variants within group 3, taking up the position of Kraay (1977: 193–194) who ascertains within the framework of the study on the Asyut hoard, that some of the type 3 coinage differs in that there are two pellets present beside the beard. In this sense, these coins can be considered as a first variant. One should note that this purely formal distinction has yet to be interpreted. The second variant within group 3 is subdivided by Kraay and Carradice into two chronologically distinct groups (the early model and the late one). This chronological distinction, which assumes an evolution in style, is not the object of a very precise commentary. It is not easy to see in these two groups that are so different in the representation of garment and physiognomy, a simple chronological evolution. The same comment can be made for the distinction made within type 4 of a late version compared with an earlier one. In 1989, Stronach (1989: 260–261) proposed another classification for the variants in type 3, in which he distinguished three and not two groups, with a chronological subdivision for the second group, similar to that of Carradice. The essence of his argument is based on the relative chronology of the dates or periods of circulation of these coins. This chronological study is in effect possible, in the study of hoards for example, because the coinage can be compared with the other pieces in the hoard for which the fabrication and circulation dates are known. And what becomes of the coins showing the young beardless king that Babelon attributed to Cyrus the Younger? They do not fit within the types defined by the numismatists in the wake of Robinson. Carradice mentions them in his study of 1987, specifying: "This identification was always questionable, and certainly needs support from other evidence. A comparison with other darics suggests to me that the type may have been re-cut from a regular, bearded type 3 royal-archer" (1987: 77). This hypothesis seems tenuous to me. Examination of the three examples from this series in the collection of the Bibliothèque Nationale de France does not show solely removal of material; there is also evidence of "additional" material compared with type 3 (the hair is longer and the garment thicker).

Another aspect studied by these different authors is the question of the location of the production workshops. For the moment, there are only theories. As Georges Le Rider says, "it is logical to think that it was at Sardis that the first coins with the archer-king (those representing him at half-length) were minted, and I would willingly attribute the production of types 2 and 3 to the same workshop" (2001). He continues his hypothesis by specifying that another centre of production should be envisaged for type 4, perhaps Daskyleion. These hypotheses are taken on board by Carradice (1987: 85) who uses for example the study of the punches, in order to explain the different production sites for one model. All these theories are based on deductions made from a comparison of formal elements, but in no instance are they based on archaeological discoveries revealing traces of workshops. They go back to fundamental principles of this science, which consist in typological classification. The extensive research carried out recently has brought to light a considerable corpus of pieces, which renders both the classification and the theories more precise.

Iconography and coinage, or how we can define Achaemenid art through numismatics

The question posed by Babelon and others as to the identity of the figure represented on each coin, has been transformed into an enquiry into the nature of the character represented. As early as 1966, Henri Seyrig propounded the question as to the nature of the archers: royal or divine? In 1971, Schlumberger contradicted this proposition on the strength of the analysis of the headdress, which, according to him, is typical of the royal tiara described by Greek authors. In 1979, Margaret Cool Root made a firm stand for the figure represented being the king. She states: "I think there is no doubt that the archers on Achaemenid coins are meant to represent the king at least to the extent of symbolizing the concept of Kingship" (1979: 117). In chapter 8 of her

Fig. 34.1 Archer coins of the Persian Empire (Type 1). (Bibliothèque Nationale)

Fig. 34.2 Archer coins of the Persian Empire (Type 2). (Bibliothèque Nationale)

work, she argues her point by developing a comparison between the reliefs of Persepolis and an analogy with Assyrian iconography. This debate is ongoing (Casabonne 2004b). In its own way it asks the more general question of the message of the image:[5] God or king, the image does not have the same meaning. It is clearly evident that this kind of approach, very theoretic, is more firmly anchored to a comparison by analogy of concepts, rather than to

Fig. 34.3 Archer coins of the Persian Empire (Type 3). (Bibliothèque Nationale)

Fig. 34.4 Archer coins of the Persian Empire (Type 4). (Bibliothèque Nationale)

a comparison of individual objects. One reasons at length on the image as an ensemble of meaningful signs, bearers of a cultural meaning such as language. This technique, which became the norm in the history of art in the wake of Panofski's theories (1957, 1959), undoubtedly allows one to reflect in a new way on Achaemenid history, on the political and cultural dimensions of this empire within a broader geographic and chronological vision.

Within this framework, the archer coins are integrated in the corpus of images which represent the royal hero. The principal debate born of this type of analysis is concerned with the degree or the character of the oriental culture (Assyrian, Elamite, Achaemenid) contained within these images, to the detriment of the Greek character sustained by others. Numerous studies reflect this research into the notion of a Greco-Persian style (Boardman 1970*a*: 302–327; 1970*b*; Root 1989: 43–49; Stronach 1989: 264–278; Dusinberre 1997: 99–130; Vargyas 2000: 33–46; Kaptan 2000: 213–223). The two underlying questions are: who conceived the model; and for whom? Research on the style implies reflection on the cultural history of the Achaemenid Empire. On the basis of images found on coinage associated with the depiction of other images of royal heroes, the aim is to understand the nature of Achaemenid royal power, and the modalities of the exercise of this power on the people. Margaret Cool Root and others such as Pierre Briant (1996: 420–421) analyse the different modalities of the exercise of power through these representations. Root states: "The central imperial policy of the Achaemenids exerted its powerful force in a direction that was dynamic—but not at all in the sense of aiming toward a goal of cultural pan-Persianism. Its pragmatic goals involved military power and control of vast resources and wealth. Its symbolic methods of facilitating these goals involved a rhetoric of unity in the maintenance and even nourishment of cultural diversity" (1991: 6). It is in this context of a "patrimonial kingdom" as Root might say (1991: 4), that one can compare the representation of the kneeling, running archer with those representations of Herakles, which evoke the image of the hero throughout the eastern Mediterranean.

Methodological remarks in the form of an evaluation

This brief evaluation of the different types of studies, which have been carried out since the end of the nineteenth century on the regal coinage with archers, allows one to draw some methodological conclusions.

The contribution of archaeology

Archaeology is essential to answer questions of chronology, conditions of production, and diffusion and the first and last of these can be addressed through archaeological discoveries in Asia Minor and in Iran. However, questions pertaining to the conditions of production, that is the workshops, their location, and organization, still largely remain to be established. One way forward is through further archaeological discoveries. One can also hope that scientific analysis of the chemical composition of the metals contained in the coinage, such as those carried out at Sardis (Cowell & Hyne 2000), will be developed further. As it is the case with all scientific investigation carried out on the composition of materials, this type of research will become significant if there is a sufficient body of examples. One might in this way be able to classify the coins according to their material composition, and then compare these results with the iconographic types.

The contribution of numismatics

The methods of classification employed by numismatists always have the advantage of minutely detailed examination and description: face, reverse, and countermarks. The combination of these now allow one to make some interesting deductions, for instance in chronological studies. A perspective opened up by Konuk (2000) in his study on the coinage from Caria, seems to me to be of interest. By studying a type of local coinage during the Achaemenid time, he attempts to evaluate the degree or type of Persian influence within a restricted regional context. Casabonne (1996) has also developed this type of study for Cilicia. The study of satrapic coinage could also lead to progress in our knowledge of regal coinage.

The contribution of art history

The studies carried out on the seal images of Persepolis by Garrison and Root, as well as the corpus of Achaemenid seals and seal images of Asia Minor published recently, allow one greatly to enlarge the corpus of images, leading to a better comprehension of the cultural meaning of each one (cf. Garrison & Root 1998; Kaptan 2002; Dusinberre 2005).

Another aspect that could be explored would be that of the sources of inspiration used by the artists making coinage in Asia Minor. This local heritage of images is regularly referred to for seals. One cannot stop oneself from also imagining Greek models for types 3 and 4 of the coinage. The figures running on their knees within a circular format are typical of Greek images found within medallions on archaic Greek drinking bowls.

It is not a question of deducing examples of imitation; the various specialists regularly demonstrate the complexity of these issues of influence. But a comparative and detailed study could reveal interesting information.

To conclude, a rapid examination of this "historiography" of the study of Persian coinage reveals a real research dynamic. The constant renewal within this area of study is due first of all to the considerable volume of publications of a newly discovered corpus of coinage and seals (hoards, private collections, unpublished museum collections). Furthermore, the specificity of these coins allows the confrontation of several disciplines, which individually cannot but refine their methods over time.

Notes

1. The works of Herzfeld in this field precede the articles previously quoted, but Robinson for example uses Herzfeld's arguments in different studies on Achaemenid coinage.
2. In France, a first study of the "archer" coins was made by the archaeologist and numismatist François Lenormant (1873).
3. There have been some attempts to give a chronological framework to Achaemenid crowns, on the basis of supposed differences between those of Darius I, Xerxes and Artaxerxes I (see Roaf 1983: 131–133; Calmeyer 1977).
4. This last collection is not a hoard, but a private collection including 18 sigloi. These coins were bought in the area of Izmir and we might therefore suppose that they come from this area.
5. A very interesting analysis is developed about images as media in Uehlinder (2001). We can mention for example Boardman (2000) and Garrison (2000).

35

The Frataraka Coins of Persis: Bridging the Gap between Achaemenid and Sasanian Persia

Vesta Sarkhosh Curtis

Introduction

It is a matter of great interest to see to what extent Persian motifs survived on coins of the local kings of Persis after the collapse of the Achaemenid Empire in 331 BC. Did Achaemenid iconography, as known from Persepolis and the coins of the Persian kings and satraps, disappear with the arrival of Alexander and the Seleucids only to be revived with the Sasanian dynasty in AD 224, or is there evidence of a continuation of Achaemenid iconography in the early Hellenistic period?

Evidence of Achaemenid-style art in the early Hellenistic period comes from the rock tombs and reliefs at Qizqapan, Sikavand and Dukan-i Davud in Iraqi and Iranian Kurdistan. Here, scenes of worship show male figures either on their own or in front of a fire altar (Fig. 35.1; Herzfeld 1941: 204, fig. 313; Ghirshman 1964a: figs 111, 115, 117). The costume of these worshippers is similar to that of priests in Achaemenid art. They wear a soft hat with earflaps and a neck-guard and the mouth is covered. Such outfits are known from Achaemenid reliefs at Persepolis, Susa and Daskyleion, as well as Achaemenid seals and gold plaques and figurines from the Oxus Treasure (Moorey 1988c: figs 41–44a, 45; Curtis & Tallis 2005: figs 40, 50, 54, 198–199, 200, 213, 236, 258–259). Figures in worshipping pose and carrying the sacred *barsom* bundles also appear on two post-Achaemenid reliefs below the Terrace at Persepolis, which were discovered by Ernst Herzfeld in 1923/4 (1929–30: 2, 33, fig. 55) (Fig. 35.2).

Evidence for the survival of Achaemenid motifs also comes from coins of the Frataraka kings of Persis, the dynasty that ruled in and around Persepolis after the collapse of the Achaemenid Empire. The coins, which were already known from collections in the late eighteenth and nineteenth centuries, consist of silver tetradrachms, drachms and silver fractions (Figs 35.3a–j). The tetradrachms and some drachms show on the obverse the head of the local king wearing the so-called satrapal hat, a soft hat in the Achaemenid style with earflaps, neck- and mouth-guard. On the reverse there is a male worshipping figure, probably a king, standing in front of a building, sometimes holding a bow. The winged symbol, probably the *khvarnah/khvarrah* or Kingly Glory/Fortune, familiar from Achaemenid art, often

Fig. 35.1 Qizqapan relief in Northern Iraq. (From Edmonds 1934: 186, fig.1)

Fig. 35.2 Frataraka reliefs, Persepolis. (From Herzfeld 1941: pl. LXXXVI)

appears above the building. Occasionally, the reverse of these coins shows a seated king holding a sceptre. This motif is known from fourth-century BC satrapal silver fractions from Samaria, such as that of Mazaios (c.361–333 BC), showing the seated great king holding a sceptre in his left hand and a flower (?) in his right hand (Fig. 35.3i). The reverse shows a winged figure holding perhaps a diadem in his right hand, or sometimes a rider figure (Fig. 35.3j; Boardman 2000: 5.55, 5.56; Curtis & Tallis 2005: fig. 362). At Persepolis, the seated king holding a sceptre appears for example on the two enthronement reliefs of Xerxes originally from the Apadana and the relief of Xerxes on the door-jamb of the main hall of the Central Building (Fig. 35.4; Moorey 1988c: figs 29, 30). The king holding a bow is found on the rock relief at Bisitun, and on tomb reliefs at Naqsh-i Rustam and Persepolis (Fig. 35.5; Moorey 1988c: figs 12–13, 38). The royal archer also appears on Achaemenid darics and sigloi (Curtis & Tallis 2005: figs 318–326). A seated figure wearing a Median-type costume and holding a bow is shown on coins of the satrap Datames/Tarkamuwa from Tarsus (Fig. 35.3k-l). Here, the Achaemenid winged symbol is also present.

There is no doubt that the motifs on the Frataraka coins of Persis are drawn from Achaemenid iconography, but it is not clear when these coins were struck; their date has long been disputed. Dates that have been suggested range from c.300 BC to 140 BC for the early Persis coins which, according to their "Irano-Aramaic" inscriptions, were struck by the *Frataraka, pltk'*, the local rulers or governors of Persis. The word *frataraka* derives from Old Persian *fratara/fraθara*, meaning before, ahead of us (Skjærvø 1997: 102; cf. New Persian *fara*). The exact meaning of this is disputed.[1]

In terms of the survival of Achaemenid traditions, the date of the coins is obviously crucial, as it will show: a) whether there was a continuation of pre-Hellenistic iconography in the early Seleucid period; or b) whether there was a total breakdown of Persian authority and identity in the former Achaemenid heartland before there was a renaissance of certain Achaemenid traditions with the arrival of the Parthians. The purpose of this paper is to review the evidence for the date of these coins and to bring the results of recent studies, which are predominantly of a numismatic nature, to the attention of archaeologists and historians.

Fig. 35.3 (**a–f**) Frataraka silver tetradrachms (British Museum); (**g–h**) silver drachm (British Museum); (**i–j**) silver fraction of Mazaios from Samaria (British Museum); (**k–l**) silver stater of Tarkamuwa (Datames), Tarsus mint (British Museum); (**m–r**) Frataraka silver tetradrachms, Persepolis hoard (National Museum of Iran); (**s–t**) silver trophy tetradrachm of Seleucus I from Pasargadae (British Museum); (**u–v**) Frataraka silver tetradrachm (Classical Numismatic Group, Mail Bid Sale 69); (**w**) Frataraka silver tetradrachm (cf. fig. 3a), rotated to show undertype (British Museum); (**x–y**) Frataraka silver drachm (National Museum of Iran). Not to size.

Fig. 35.4 Audience relief from Persepolis. (Photograph S. Razmjou)

Fig. 35.5 Tomb relief of Artaxerxes at Persepolis. (Photograph S. Razmjou)

Persis coins and excavations

The British Museum's collection of coins of Persis (Figs 35.3a–h) was published in 1922 by G. F. Hill. In his important introduction to the *Catalogue of the Greek Coins of Arabia, Mesopotamia and Persia*, Hill (1922: clx–clxxxii) gives a summary of the study and interpretation of these coins up to his time, and refers to earlier publications, including those of the numismatist Alotte de la Füye in 1906. Hill recognized (1922: clxx) four main series within the coinage of Persis and suggested a starting date of c.250 BC for the tetradrachms (see below).

Then, in 1932 Herzfeld found some coins of Persis at Persepolis. He refers to them in connection with Greek dedicatory inscriptions found below the Terrace:

> In those inscriptions occur the oldest identifications of Zoroastrian deities with Greek gods. The date is, according to the type of the script, style of sculptures and some coins found in the ruins, very shortly after the time of Alexander. (Herzfeld 1934: 232)

About nine years earlier, in the same location, Herzfeld (1929–30: 33, fig. 55) had found below the Terrace at Persepolis the two stone reliefs referred to above (Fig. 35.2). He rightly compared them with the coins of Persis and dated them to about 250 BC. In *Iran in the Ancient East* Herzfeld described the reliefs as follows:

> In the temple at the foot of the Terrace of Persepolis are the stone jambs of a

window, on which a prince and his wife are pictured [...]

Effaced as the figures are, the prince can be identified from his coins as one of the first *frātadāra* of Istakhr, a dynasty which began probably shortly after 300 BC. The place of the sculpture, inside the jambs, is the traditional location for sculptures at Persepolis. The attitude—right hand raised, left holding the barsom, the sacred wand—is an attitude of prayer, as we know from the Median tombs, Dukkān-i Dāūd and Sakawand, and also from the gold plates of the Oxus Treasure. [...]

The opposite stone does not show, as in Persepolis, the mirror reflection of the prince, but a picture of his queen, the first and only lady at Persepolis—a subject that is strictly avoided in official Achaemenid art. Her attitude is the same. The dress is a long undergarment that reaches down to the ankles, and a cloak or shawl. The drapery is indicated by timid lines roughly engraved. As works of art the frātadāra sculptures are pathetically poor, a relapse into primitive methods. The refined low-relief at Persepolis is lost; the figures are but a flat, dead surface with interior design engraved, standing out from a slightly deeper ground-plane. (Herzfeld 1941: 286, pl. LXXXVI)

Herzfeld never published an excavation report, but E. F. Schmidt gave a summary of Herzfeld's excavations in *Persepolis I*, using Herzfeld's field catalogue and plan of the building. Schmidt also published photographs of the two reliefs (1953: pls 17/A–C), but does not refer in his report to coins found during Herzfeld's excavations. Like Herzfeld (1934: 232; 1941: 275), Schmidt (1953: 56) described engraved stone votive objects with dedicatory Greek inscriptions, which identified Zoroastrian deities with Greek gods.

Herzfeld's coin hoard (*IGCH* 1797)

The coin hoard that Herzfeld found below the Terrace at Persepolis was published by Edward Newell in *The Coinage of the Eastern Seleucid Mints from Seleucus I to Antiochus III* in 1938 and is also listed in Thompson, Mørkholm and Kraay's *An Inventory of Greek Coin Hoards* (*IGCH* 1797). According to Newell (1938: 159–160, n. 28) the hoard was discovered "during the campaign of 1934–5, about a quarter of a mile to the north of the great Palace terrace. It lay on the floor of a small room belonging to some insignificant building which had been erected after the destruction of the palace itself". It is clear from his account that he either did not know or did not think it was important to record more precise details of the find spot. Newell wrote (1938: 159–160, n. 28) that these coins were "in possession of Riza Khan Pahlevi, Shah of Iran. Photographs of these coins are preserved in the library of the American Numismatic Society and in the Oriental Institute of Chicago".

The tetradrachms are described as follows:

Professor Herzfeld's hoard [...] consisted of the following varieties:

1 Tetradrachm of Seleucus I, victory and trophy type, in good condition.

1 Tetradrachm of Bagadat, type Brit. Mus., Pl. xxviii, 7, in fine condition.

1 Tetradrachm of Oborzos, type Brit. Mus., Pl. lii, 10, in fine condition.

7 Tetradrachms of Autophradates I, Brit. Mus., Pl. xxix, 5–6, in very fine condition. (Newell 1938: 159–160)

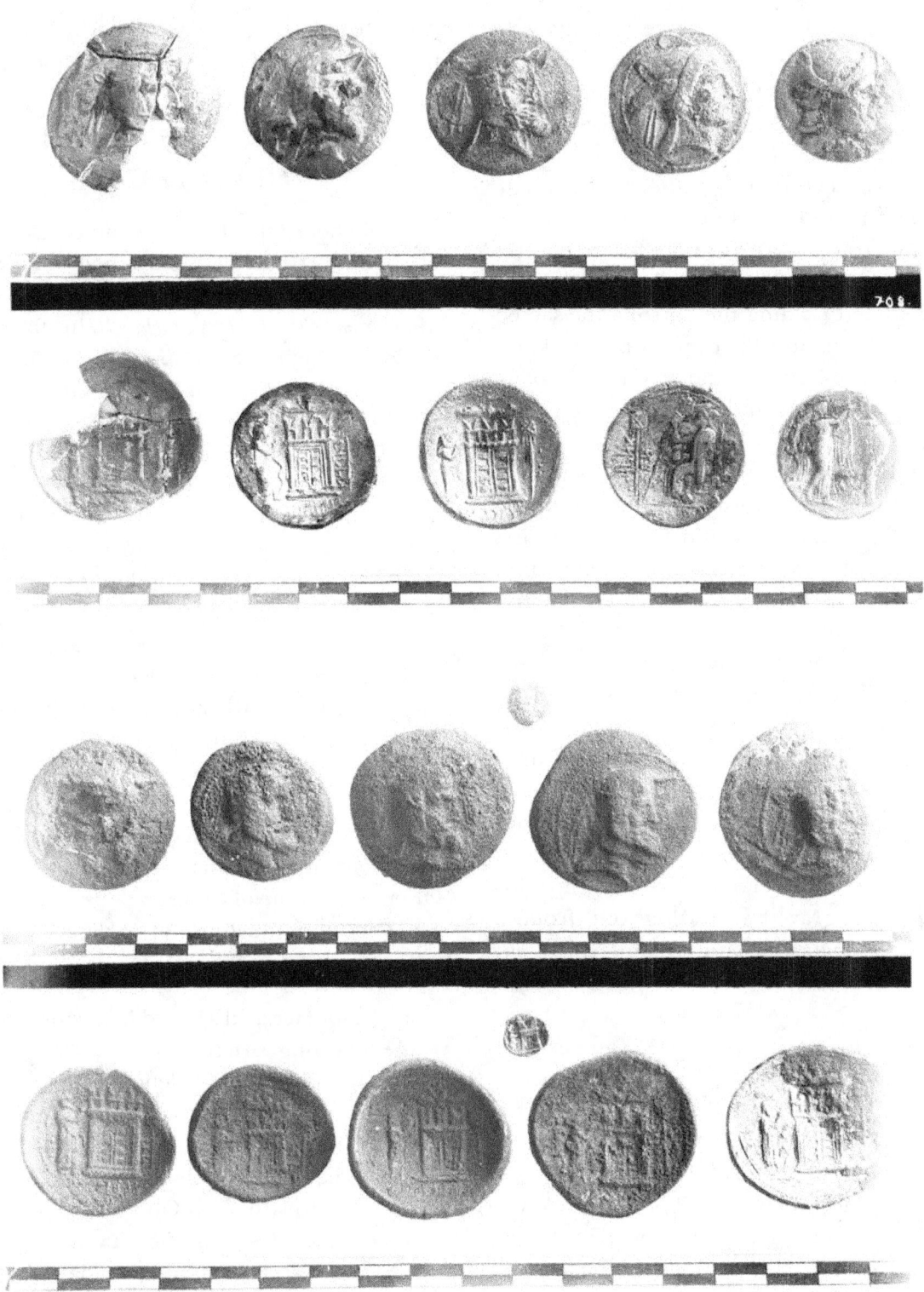

Fig. 35.6 Herzfeld's Persepolis Hoard. (Photograph courtesy of the American Numismatic Society, New York)

Altogether, then, the Herzfeld hoard from Persepolis consisted of ten tetradrachms, including one of Seleucus I. At some point the entire hoard must have been presented to Reza Shah, who then deposited the coins at the Golestan Palace in Tehran. From there they were transferred to the Iran Bastan Museum (Muzeh Melli/National Museum of Iran). The Bagadad tetradrachm and the Seleucid trophy coin listed by Newell and clearly recognizable on photographs of the Persis hoard in the Oriental Institute of Chicago (Fig. 35.6), are today no longer among the Herzfeld coin hoard in the National Museum of Iran in Tehran (Figs 35.3m–r, x–y). They disappeared from the gallery in a major theft in 1991 (SH 1370). Of the ten tetradrachms, only three Frataraka tetradrachms in the present Tehran collection can be matched up with the photographs in the Oriental Institute of Chicago.[2]

Dating the coins of Persis

Hill (1922: clx–clxi) divided the coinage of Persis into four series, covering the period c.250 BC to the early third century AD. The first series consisted of the tetradrachms of the Fratarakas, some drachms and silver fractions (1922: clxiv–clxx, pls XXVIII.7–XXIX). The title Frataraka is used on coins of Persis only for the first series. The second series consisted mostly of drachms and also smaller denominations (1922: clxx–clxxii, pls XXX–XXXII.4). In Hill's third series the drachms have a new design on the reverse, where a fire altar and worshipping figure are surrounded by inscriptions (1922: clxxii–clxxiv, pls XXXII.5–XXXIV.5). The influence of Parthian coins is unmistakable (cf. Wroth 1903; Sellwood 1980). The final fourth series (Hill 1922: clxxiv–clxxii, pls XXXIV.6–XXXVII) is also Parthian inspired, but sometimes shows busts on both obverse and reverse. In the second to fourth series the kings of Persis use the royal title *MLKA/shah*.

In 1986 Michael Alram analysed the coins of Persis in detail and came to the conclusion that the tetradrachms of the Fratarakas and all the drachms from Persis formed a homogeneous group, which ran without interruption from probably the beginning of the second century BC to the early third century AD. He saw all the coins of Persis as evidence for growing Parthian influence in the former Achaemenid Empire at a time when Seleucid power was fading (Alram 1986: 163). Parthian presence in Mesopotamia and south-western Iran began around 140 BC. According to Alram (1986: 162–163), both the iconography of the coins and the fact that the names Ardaxšir and Vadfradad are found on both tetradrachms and the later drachms, suggest that all the kings of Persis belonged to the same dynasty. Alram sees a clear continuity in the coinage, which according to him, would not be possible if we were to accept the traditional date of the early third century BC for the Frataraka coins.

Alram's proposal of a late date for the entire coinage of Persis was then used by Josef Wiesehöfer to support his historical analysis of Persis.[3] In *Die "dunklen Jahrhunderte" der Persis* (1994), Wiesehöfer argues that no sign of unrest or independence in Persis can be found in classical sources for the time of Seleucus I to Antiochus III. A so-called successful policy of the early Seleucids guaranteed them the full support of the local dynasts (Wiesehöfer 1994: 60). Like Alram, he would not date the beginning of the Frataraka issues and Bagadad's coins to the end of the third century/beginning of the second century BC (1994: 120). He has recently confirmed his date of second century BC for the coins of the Frataraka rulers of Persis (Wiesehöfer 2007: 40, 44–47). The Frataraka Vahbarz, whose tetradrachms are known, is identified as the Oborzos, who according to Polyaenus (VII, 39–40) slaughtered 3,000 *katoikoi* or military settlers in revenge for the killing of 3,000 Persians (Sherwin-White & Kuhrt 1993: 29; Wiesehöfer 1994: 101). Wiesehöfer (1994: 119) regards the coinage of Vahbarz and Vadfradad I as an indication of a revolt against the Seleucid overlords and sees Vadfradad I as the last Frataraka, the successor to Vahbarz, and probably "the man whom the Seleucid king Demetrius II asked for assistance against the Parthian king Mithradates I in 140 BCE" (Wiesehöfer 2007: 42).

A late date is also preferred by Pierfrancesco Callieri (2001: 102, 107) who equates the beginning of Frataraka rule in Persepolis with the end of Seleucid supremacy in the region, that is, *c*.200–180 BC. In a more recent article Callieri argues once again in favour of the early second century BC for the beginning of Frataraka rule (2004: 99–100) and writes that "this new chronology rests on actual evidence, and not only on *argumenta e silencio*" as the high chronology did (2004: 99).

Potts (2007) and Haerinck and Overlaet (2008) also opt for a late date for the Frataraka coins. Mary Boyce and Frantz Grenet (1991: 116 and n. 257), on the other hand, have suggested an early date around the middle of the third century BC for the Frataraka coins.

Evidence for an early dating: trophy coins and overstrikes

Evidence for an early dating of the Frataraka coins is the presence of a trophy coin[4] of Seleucus I in Herzfeld's coin hoard. Trophy coins were also excavated by Stronach (1978: pls 177–180), three being found in Hoard I in 1962, and eight in Hoard II in 1963. These were probably minted at Persepolis (Kritt 1997: 135, pl. 33A–C; Houghton & Lorber 2002: 77; Müseler 2005–06: 80–82, fig. 1).[5] No Frataraka coins are known from the excavations at Pasargadae (Jenkins 1978: 185–198). A trophy coin was also found in the excavations of Istakhr, near Persepolis (Miles 1959: 19, no. 1, pl. 1), together with later drachms of Persis, but no Frataraka coins. A hoard that appeared on the US coin market in 1986 included trophy drachms and tetradrachms, together with one tetradrachm and five drachms of the Fratarakas (Kritt 1997: pl. 34).

The trophy coin of Seleucus I shows on the obverse the profile of a young male helmeted figure with attributes of the Greek Dionysus. The reverse depicts a fully draped standing Nike, holding a wreath in her raised hand and about to place it on a trophy of arms beside her (Fig. 35.3s–t). The name of Seleucus appears to the left and the title ΒΑΣΙΛΕΩΣ (king) on the right. The royal title was only adopted by Seleucus I in 305 BC, which suggests that the trophy coins could not have been struck before this date (Newell 1938: 157, 160–161; Houghton 1980: 8–9). Seleucus I died in 280 BC.

Dietrich Klose (2005: 93–103) has discussed in great detail the coins of Persis and has come to the conclusion that the tetradrachms of the Frataraka date to the beginning of Seleucid rule in Iran. He has shown convincingly that tetradrachms of Bagadad were struck over coins of Seleucus I (305–281 BC). The lion's mane of Herakles that appeared on Seleucus' coins is still clearly visible beneath (Klose 2005: 94). He has also pointed to close links between the iconography of the

Persis coins (e.g. headgear, costume and worshipping pose) and reliefs at Persepolis and Naqsh-i Rustam, and refers to the post-Achaemenid tomb relief at Qizqapan (2005: 96). Like Klose, Wilhelm Müseler (2005–06: 83, fig. 5) regards this reuse of Seleucid coins as a pointer for an early Hellenistic date. This chronology has been re-emphasized in the catalogue of a collection in the Munich Coin Cabinet (Klose & Müseler 2008: 11).

The above observation is also supported by an examination of the British Museum's collection of Frataraka coins (1915.0108.10; 1856.1201.1; 1874.0715.487, see Figs 35. 3a, 6).[6] Here, the lion's mane of Herakles on the undertype is clearly visible, together with the nose, lips, chin and neck, and in one case there are even traces of the lion paws tied under the chin.

A drachm in the Tehran collection, which is not part of the Herzfeld hoard, also reveals traces of the Herakles undertype on the obverse (Fig. 35.3x, y). The reverse shows signs of a possible undertype, but this is not clear and it could be the result of a double striking. This coin is probably a drachm of Vadfradad/ Authophradates. These understrikes, which are common on early Frataraka coins, do not appear on the coins of the later series.

Oliver D. Hoover (2008: 213), who has also analysed the Frataraka coins as overstrikes on Seleucid undertypes, suggests in his detailed and important numismatic examination, that the Frataraka coins were struck sometime before 295 BC and continued until shortly after 281 BC. Furthermore, Hoover's research on overstrikes has convincingly produced a revised regnal sequence for the Frataraka rulers. He has shown, contrary to general opinion, that Bagadad (Bagadates/Baγdād or Baγadād) was not the first Frataraka ruler of Persis (2008: 213).

A tetradrachm of Bagadad was struck on an undertype, which is associated with issues of Seleucus I from Ecbatana after *c*.295 BC (Hoover 2008: 213 and no. 31; 226). But another tetradrachm of Bagadad, which appeared on the market in June 2005, shows as its undertype traces of headgear with earflap and mouth-guard, typical of the Frataraka coins (Fig. 35.3u; 2008: 213–214, n. 28; *CNG* Mail Bid Sale 69, lot 766, 8th June 2005). The undertype on the reverse shows part of the building also typical of Frataraka coins and not a Seleucid or Alexandrine reverse type (Fig. 35.3v). As there are no known coins of Bagadad wearing a soft hat with forward peak and mouth-guard, this coin must have been struck on the coin of another Frataraka ruler who preceded Bagadad.

If we were to accept that Bagadad was not the first ruler of the Frataraka dynasty, then this would explain why only coins of Ardaxšir/ Artaxerxes I and Vahbarz/Oborzos, who each appear with a soft hat with forward peak and mouth-guard, earflaps and neck-guard, were found together with trophy coins of Seleucus I in the 1986 hoard published by Brian Kritt in 1997 (see above). This important observation by Hoover (2008: 214) is crucial for the chronology of the early rulers of Persis.

An obverse die link for coins of Vahbarz/ Oborzos and Ardaxšir/Artaxerxes I shows that these two Fratarakas were consecutive rulers (Alram 1986: 166–167; Hoover 2008: 213–214). Hoover has discovered that tetradrachms of Vahbarz were also struck on an earlier Persis undertype, which strongly suggests that Vahbarz/Oborzos was not the first ruler of the Frataraka dynasty of Persis (see *CNG* Mail Bid Sale 69, lot 770, 8th June 2005). The first Frataraka ruler of the Persis dynasty, therefore, may have been Ardaxšir/Artaxerxes I at the beginning of the third century BC, who struck tetradrachms as a "Seleucid official" (Hoover 2008: 214). He suggests that the Frataraka dynasty began sometime before 295 BC, starting with Ardaxšir/Artaxerxes I, who was succeeded by Vahbarz/Oborzos. The last two Frataraka rulers were Vadfradad I and Bagadad. The rule of Vadfradad I must have continued until at least 281 BC because of the Antiochus I (281–261 BC) undertype identified on a coin of Vadfradad I. Hoover has shown that coins of Vadfradad/Autophradates were struck over: a) a Susa trophy coin of Seleucus I; and b) over a horned horse-head tetradrachm of Antiochus I commemorating his father Seleucus I (Hoover 2008: 227, nos. 32–33). This suggests that Vadfradad/Autophradates of Persis was in power in or soon after 281 BC when Seleucus I died, and Vadfradad continued to reign after Antiochus I succeeded his father, Seleucus. A later date than that of Antiochus I is unlikely, as otherwise one would have expected the tetradrachms of Persis to have been struck over the coins of Seleucid rulers after Antiochus I (281–261 BC). The reigns of the last two Fratarakas, Bagadad and Vadfradad, coincide with the period when Seleucus I was preoccupied in Anatolia in 282–281 BC (2008: 215).

Hoover has suggested (2008: 215) that Bagadad may have succeeded Vadfradad, but this is not certain. An Aramaic graffito naming *bgdt* (Bagadad) on a coin of Vadfradad supported this order (2008: 215). However, the publication of a tetradrachm of Vadfradad I overstruck on a Bagadad tetradrachm shows that Bagadad could not have succeeded Vadfradad (Klose & Müseler 2008: 87, no. 2/18). Taking these two pieces of conflicting evidence into consideration, one could argue, as Hoover now suggests (personal communication, April 2009), that these two Fratarakas may have been contemporary rivals.

It is also worth emphasizing that Bagadad's coins (Figs 35.3e-h) show two important differences compared with other Frataraka coins:

1) Bagadad wears his headgear in a different manner to the others. While all other Fratarakas have their ears and chin covered on the obverse of their coins, coins of Bagadad on the obverse show his face uncovered. The earflaps and chin-guard are tucked in at the top beneath a wide band. His headgear also lacks the usual forward peak that we find on coins of Ardaxšir, Vahbarz and Vadfradad (Figs 35.3a–d, m–r, w–y). By contrast, on the reverse of Bagadad's coins depicting a worshipping scene, the king stands with his hands upraised and fingers outstretched. He wears a headgear with forward peak and his ears and chin are covered.

2) On the reverse of some tetradrachms and fractions, Bagadad is shown seated on an Achaemenid-style throne, again wearing a headdress, which leaves his face bare (Fig. 35.3f). This is a royal investiture scene and not a religious scene. If we were to assume, as suggested by Hoover, that Bagadad and Vadfradad were possibly contemporary contenders for the throne of Persis, then Bagadad may have purposely chosen a portrait, which differentiated him from that of the other Fratarakas. In addition, his choice of an investiture scene, closely copying Achaemenid satrapal coins and the reliefs of Darius and Xerxes from Persepolis, may have had a political purpose: to emphasize his legitimacy as the chosen dynast, whose portrait was distinctively different from that of his rival. But like all the other Fratarakas, Bagadad portrayed himself in religious worshipping scenes on the reverse of some of his coins.

Finally, on coins of Vadfradad (Fig. 35.3d) we find on the reverse a winged Nike-type figure holding a wreath or diadem over the head of the worshipping king, who holds a bow in his left hand and has his right hand raised with fingers outstretched. A winged figure appears on top of the building and a banner is shown on the far right. All the symbols and the presence of the Nike figure behind the king give a message that the main figure, the worshipping king Vadfradad I, enjoys divine support. The parallel with trophy coins of Seleucus I (Fig. 35.3s–t) is noticeable here (see also Klose & Müseler 2008: 32, no. 27).

Conclusion

We have seen that there is a striking resemblance between the iconography of the tetradrachms of Persis and Achaemenid iconography, as known from reliefs, seals (Figs 35.3e–h, o–p) and other small objects.

The costume of the worshipping figures on the tetradrachms, consisting of the Median belted tunic worn over trousers with vertical folds, and the long-sleeved coat, is similar to Achaemenid-period costumes as seen on seals and reliefs. Such Median-type outfits are shown on Achaemenid seals with religious scenes (Fig. 35.7; Curtis & Tallis 2005: 158–159, no. 200; 160, no. 209), votive plaques of the Oxus Treasure (2005: 164, no. 213), as well as Achaemenid-period reliefs from Persepolis (2005: 82, no. 40; 85, nos. 47, 48). The Median-type outfit of the Fratarakas with the long-sleeved tunic and a girdle-like belt ending in two long ties, reminds us—as mentioned above—of the seated figure on the reverse of the Datames/Tarkamuwa coin (*c*.378–372 v) (Fig.35.3l). The fact that the Fratarakas shown in worshipping scenes always have a chin-guard while standing in

Fig. 35.7 Achaemenid seal. (British Museum 89528)

worshipping pose, which partly covers the mouth and is comparable to a *padam*, suggests that the scenes depicted are of a religious nature.[7] The royal figure wearing a similar outfit to priests does not, however, have to be a holy person or a priest-king, but could be just a worshipper, or as de Jong (2003: 201) suggests, the guardian of the shrine.[8] A strong link with Achaemenid iconography is also provided by the presence of other symbols on the reverse of the Frataraka coins, such as the winged figure, the *khvarrah*, the long staff and the bow (Figs 35.3c–h, m–r, x–y).

The structure on the reverse of the tetradrachms, in front of which a worshipping figure stands, has been linked with Achaemenid buildings, such as the Zendan-i Sulaiman at Pasargadae and the Ka'bai Zardusht at Naqsh-i Rustam (Stronach 1966: 219; Callieri 1998: 29–33). The similarities are indeed very close and it seems very likely that these or similar buildings are represented. However, it is not impossible that there were also other buildings of this type in the vicinity of Persis, some of them perhaps dating to the post-Achaemenid period. Thus, Ann Britt Tilia found horn-shaped stone fragments—parapet ornaments—on top of the Terrace at Persepolis, near Palace H (Tilia 1969: fig. 5; Haerinck & Overlaet 2008: 210–211, pl. 8). These are similar to the horns on top of the buildings shown on the coins. Thus, the buildings shown on the coins might represent later versions of the type of buildings at Zendan-i Sulaiman and Naqsh-i Rustam. These buildings are probably religious, as indicated by the fact that the figure worshipping in front of the building always has his chin covered, which suggests that he wears a *padam*.[9] It is even possible that there may have been a fire altar inside the building, thus accounting for its prominence on the coins. The buildings on these coins have been discussed in recent articles by Potts (2007) and Haerinck and Overlaet (2008). Potts agrees that the Frataraka buildings "must have been inspired" by the Ka'ba and Zendan, as well as by tomb reliefs at Naqsh-e Rustam, but following the late dating of Alram and Wiesehöfer, he thinks that "at least 250 years separated the earliest Frataraka from the latest monument at Naqsh-i Rustam", and therefore it was not known by the Frataraka what the original purpose of the buildings would have been. We think this is unlikely. Like Potts, Haerinck and Overlaet (2008) follow a late date for the Frataraka coins, but do not see any connection with Ka'ba-i Zardusht or Zendan-i Sulaiman. Instead, they point to representations of altar shrines on Roman coins, all dating from the first and second centuries AD, where there was a fire altar inside the shrine. They also suggest that the doors of the building on the Frataraka tetradrachms opened outwards[10] and that the altar shrine, which is shown on the early coins of Persis, is then replaced on the later Persis coins by an altar. There are clearly chronological difficulties in accepting any connections between these Roman parallels and the building on the Frataraka coins. Even if we followed Alram's date of the early second century BC for the beginning of the Frataraka coins—which I do not accept for the reasons given above—the Ara Pacis and the shrines on the first- and second-century AD Roman coins are far removed in date from the Frataraka coins.

There is strong numismatic evidence for Seleucid undertypes being used by the early rulers of Persis, which favours a Seleucid date of the early third century, soon after the collapse of the Persian Empire and the beginning of Seleucid rule over Iran. It is during this early period, when Seleucus I and his son Antiochus I were preoccupied with external threats. Seleucus was fighting Lysimachus in the west and Antiochus faced internal revolts and at the same time the Ptolemys were advancing into Seleucid territories. During this period, the Frataraka rulers of Persis produced a coinage, which drew inspiration from the now conquered, but not too distant, Achaemenids. At the same time, they introduced Hellenistic symbols, such as the crowning Nike, as seen for example on trophy coins of Seleucus I which were struck after 305/4 BC (Fig. 35.3s–t; Houghton & Lorber 2002: pl. 11, nos. 195–196), as well as the Nikephorus type of Seleucus I and Antiochus I (Houghton & Lorber 2002: pl. 7, no. 119.8c; pl. 18, no. 321.1).

The religious iconography of the Frataraka coins, which used symbols of the Iranian *khvarrah* or divine glory, as well as the Hellenistic Nike, suggests a glorification of the past in Persis during a short period after the collapse of the Achaemenid Empire and before the consolidation of Seleucid power in the region. For a brief period Persis was able to reuse Seleucid coins to mint its own local coinage, but this period of relative freedom was short-lived, as tetradrachms and drachms naming the Frataraka cease after Vadfradad I and Bagadad. A different type of coinage is produced in Persis under Vadfradad II (?) (Fig. 35.8a-b; Alram 1986: pl. 18, nos. 546–550), which is related to the Frataraka coinage with regard to the iconography and minting technique, but also shows distinct differences,[11] particularly with the loss of the title Frataraka. From the time of Vadfradad III[12] (Fig. 35.8c-d) the coin portraits change drastically and the resemblances with Parthian coins of Mithradates I and II are unmistakable (Fig. 35.8g-h; Alram 1986: nos. 561–563), which indicates that the series with Parthian-type coin portraits could not have started before 140 BC. All the later drachms are struck in the Parthian tradition and show a strong link with Parthian iconography (Figs 35.8c–f, i–j). In the Parthian fashion, the local king of Persis is MLK'/*shah*. On these later coins of Persis, the fire altar takes a more prominent position (Fig. 35.8e–f). Worshipping scenes continue, but the building is soon replaced by a fire altar, which may represent the royal fire associated with the local king of Persis. This is not, as suggested by Haerinck and Overlaet (2008: 218) because in the Parthian period the kings of Persis had control over the priests, but because the fire shown is associated with the king shown on the obverse. This is the fire of the king and as such continues into the Sasanian period.[13]

The portraits of the later Persis kings on the obverse (Figs 35.8c–f, i–j) are stylistically very similar to the Parthian overlords and the iconography seems to be derived directly from Parthian prototypes (Figs 35.8g–h, k–l). Astral symbols were popular on Parthian coins (Figs 35.8k–n). Although worshippers in front of a fire altar were occasionally shown on the reverse of Parthian copper coins (Fig. 35.8n, p), they were not as popular as other motifs, such as the seated archer or the enthroned king (Fig. 35.8h; Curtis 2007: 420, figs 9–10). The Sasanians, who originated from Persis and came to power at the beginning of the third century AD, used the motif of the fire altar as the most important symbol for the reverse of their coins (Figs 35.8q–t). The royal fire or fire of the king is combined with another royal symbol on coins issued by the new ruling dynasty in Iran.

Acknowledgements

I am grateful to the organizers of the conference for inviting me to give a paper, in particular Dr John Curtis. I am indebted to my colleagues in the Department of Coins and Medals and the National Museum of Iran, for their help, support and suggestions:

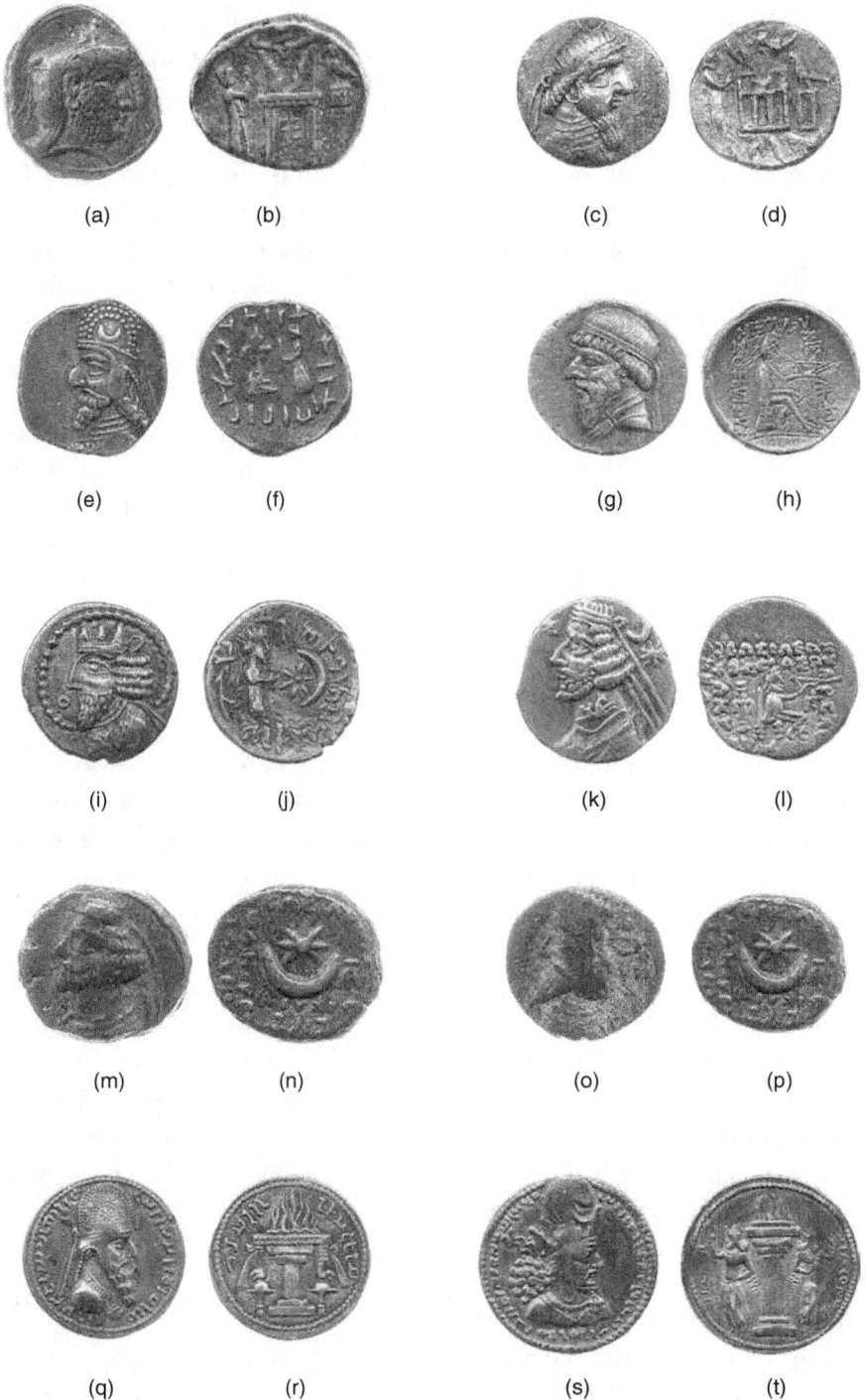

Fig. 35.8 (a–b) silver tetradrachm, Persis (British Museum); (c–f) silver drachms, Persis (British Museum); (g–h) Parthian silver drachm, Mithradates I (British Museum); (i–j) silver drachm, Persis (British Museum); (k–l) Parthian silver drachm, Orodes II (British Museum); (m–n) Parthian bronze coin, Orodes II (British Museum); (o–p) Parthian bronze coin, Artabanus II (British Museum); (q–r) Sasanian silver drachm, Ardashir I (British Museum); (s–t) Sasanian silver drachm, Shapur I (British Museum). Not to size.

in London, Joe Cribb, Amelia Dowler and Richard Abdy; in Tehran, Mr Mohammad Reza Kargar, former Director of the National Museum of Iran, Mrs Elahe Askari, former Head of the Department of Coins and Seals, Mrs Zahra Jaffar-Mohammadi, former Head of International Exhibitions and Ms Zohreh Basseri, Curator of Parthian and Sasanian Coins at the National Museum of Iran and Head of the Coins and Seals Department.

I much indebted to Dr Oliver Hoover for sending me his article, while in preparation, and for allowing me to refer to his suggestions and our discussions. I am also grateful to Dr Shahrokh Razmjou for all his suggestions, references and the long discussions we have had; and to Dr Andrew Meadows, my former colleague and now Deputy Director of the American Numismatic Society in New York. Above all, this paper would not have materialized without the help and input of my colleague Dr Elizabeth Pendleton.

My thanks also go to Richard Hodges, who scanned the Persis coins in the National Museum of Iran in November 2006.

Abbreviations

IGCH M. Thompson, O. Mørkholm & C. M. Kraay, *An Inventory of Greek Coin Hoards*. New York, The American Numismatic Society, 1973.

CH IX A. Meadows and U. Wartenberg, *Coin Hoards*, vol. 9. *Greek Hoards*. London, Royal Numismatic Society, 2002.

CNG *Classical Numismatic Group, Inc.*, Lancaster, PA and London.

Notes

1. For the readings of the title *frataraka/fratadara/fratakara*, see e.g. Naster 1968; Wiesehöfer 1994; Skjærvø 1997; Panaino 2003. This word is now read as *frataraka*, which is known from Achaemenid-period papyri found in Elephantine, Egypt, originally meaning "who is before, ahead of, prior, superior" (Skjærvø 1997: 102). The inscriptions of the early tetradrachms give the ruler's name, followed by *prtrk' zy 'lhy' (frataraka i bayān)*, which has been interpreted in a variety of ways by scholars: Frataraka of the gods, Frataraka of the dead kings of divine descent (for a detailed discussion see Panaino 2003). Recently, Soudavar (2006a: 163–164) has suggested "deputy of gods (on earth)". Sometimes, a patronymic, *br* (son of), is added to the end of the inscription. For example, some tetradrachms of Bagadad (*bgdt*) mention that he is the son of Bagawart (*bgwrt*) (Alram 1986: 165, no. 511; Klose & Müseler 2008: 18, 34, nos. 2/1, 2/3). Some coins of Ardaxšir (*'rtxštr(y)*) and Vahbarz (*whwbrz*)—both tetradrachms and drachms—(Alram 1986: 166–167, nos. 520, 526; Klose & Müseler 2008: 34, 36, nos. 2/7, 2/11) add after the personal name of the Frataraka, the phrase *br prs*, i.e. son of a Persian (see also Skjærvø 1997: 101, 102, table 3.1). A similar reference to a "Persian" lineage is also found on Darius' inscription at Naqsh-i Rustam. Here, the Achaemenid king describes himself as an "Achaemenian, a Persian, son of a Persian [...]" (Kent 1953: DNa: 138, para. 2, 8–15). The epithet "son of a Persian" is not just a reference to the name of the region of Persis/Parsa (Müseler 2005–06: 87), but it emphasizes the Persian identity of the Frataraka (Klose 2005: 96; Klose & Müseler 2008: 25).
2. The photographs were kindly tracked down and scanned by Richael Witschonke at the American Numismatic Society.
3. An early chronology had been suggested by Ruth Stiehl in 1959.
4. The registers of the Department of Coins and Seals of the National Museum of Iran list four Seleucid trophy coins, D.K. no. 2540, described as from "Persepolis", two of which disappeared in the theft of 1991/1370.
5. Trophy coins have been associated with the mint of Persepolis, Susa and recently again Persepolis (see Newell 1938; Houghton 1980; Kritt 1997; Houghton & Lorber 2002).
6. Hill (1922: 197), for example, had also recognized that Frataraka tetradrachms were struck on other earlier coins.
7. Wiesehöfer (1994: 131–135) sees a difference between the satrapal headgear and the priestly

headgear. Furthermore, he does not see the depiction of a *barsom* as an indication that the figure shown must be a priest.
8. The royal and religious significance of the coin images has also been noted by de Jong (2003: 192, 201) when discussing the reverse of these coins, particularly in connection with the sword, sceptre and banner (Avestan *drafša*/Middle Persian *drafš*/New Persian *derafš*). It is interesting that in the Pahlavi Vendidad the *drafš* is interpreted as a symbol of divine glory—the *xwarrah/khvarrah*—just like the winged figure, the bird on top of the standard (de Jong 2003: 193–195).
9. A distinction between the priestly tiara and the satrapal headgear, as suggested by Wiesehöfer (1994: 131–134), should be treated with caution.
10. There is no reason to believe that the doors of the building on the early Persis coins opened outwards. Near Eastern doors usually open inwards, especially if there are decorated panels on the doors, as traditionally they would be visible when entering the building.
11. For example, the introduction of the bird on both obverse and reverse, as well as the fabric of the coins, are different compared with the Frataraka coins.
12. As suggested by Klose and Müseler (2008: 47), coins resembling Mithradates I may be attributable to a new ruler, Vadfradad IV.
13. For example, see also coins of Ardashir I and II, Shapur II and III and Bahram IV and Yazdgird I (Göbl 1971: pls 1, 7, 8, 9).

Part 7

Gold, Silver, Glass, and Faience

36

Technological Aspects of Selected Gold Objects in the Oxus Treasure

Barbara R. Armbruster

Works concerned with Achaemenid jewellery or Ancient Near Eastern gold in general often focus on style and iconography whereas technological matters are rarely considered (Amandry 1958; Rehm 1992; Musche 1992). However, there are some notable exceptions. A remarkable appendix in an exhibition catalogue on ancient art takes the method of manufacture, state of conservation and the elemental composition of some significant Achaemenid jewellery into account (Arnold 1996). The publication of the "Lydian Treasure" includes remarks on the manufacture of the metalwork and a number of goldsmith's tools (Özgen & Öztürk *et al.* 1996). In addition, technical notes have been published dealing with jewellery found in the Achaemenid tomb on the "Acropole" at Susa (Harper, Aruz & Tallon 1992: 245–251).

This paper is a study of a small number of exceptional Achaemenid gold objects and discusses their methods of manufacture. It is proposed that lost wax casting and the use of the lathe were important techniques in vessel production, as well as plastic shaping and joining techniques used in the manufacture of jewellery. These observations were based purely on visual examination of some of the jewellery and vessels in the Oxus Treasure in the British Museum. The specific pieces examined are the famous pair of bracelets with terminals in the form of winged griffins and two vessels, namely, a plain hemispherical bowl and a jug with lion's head handle. The aim is to illustrate the high standard and specialization of Achaemenid precious metalworking and to discuss the types of materials and tools used in the goldsmith's workshop.

The Oxus Treasure is the most important collection of Achaemenid goldwork. It consists of about 180 gold and silver items (excluding coins) and is generally dated to the fifth–fourth centuries BC. The hoard was discovered in the late 1870s on the bank of the Oxus River in central Asia and bequeathed by A.W. Franks to the British Museum in 1897 (Dalton 1964; Curtis 1997*b*, 2004). The Oxus Treasure is suggestive of the sumptuousness of Achaemenid art.

The bracelets with griffin terminals

British Museum, ME 124017: Wt. 397.1 gm, H 128 mm, W 115.7 mm, Hoop diam. 14.3 mm,

Fig. 36.1 Bracelet, Oxus Treasure. (Photograph B. Armbruster)

Fig. 36.2 Detail: side and wings and cast recesses. (Photograph B. Armbruster)

T tube *c.*1.5 mm, T base metal wings 0.7–0.9 mm, T strips of cells 0.12 mm, Depth of wings cells 1.5–2 mm, Depth of depressions 1.6 mm

Victoria & Albert Museum, 442-18 (ME Loan 1155): Wt 395.5 gm, H 124 mm, W 117 mm, Hoop diam. 13.3 mm, T hoop *c.*1.3–1.6 mm, T base sheet of wings 0.85–0.9 mm, T strips of cells 0.12 mm

The large bracelets are composed of an open-cuff body, a pair of griffin terminals and inlays (Fig. 36.1). The component parts, both the cast elements and worked sheet gold, were individually manufactured and then joined (Armbruster 2005). These outstanding bracelets exemplify the taste for massive jewellery with monumental and ornamental characteristics. The fantastic creatures that adorn their extremities have a bird of prey's head and wings, a lion's body and forepaws and a goat's horns and legs. The griffin motif is well known in Near Eastern and Central Asian art, and its origins go back to Bronze Age iconography (Hayashi 2000; Rehm 1992: 40–47). The griffins have attributes of sculpture and serve as forceful sculptural counterpoints to the plain character of the hoop. Despite the figurative design and elements of naturalism with anatomical details they have an otherwise ornamental quality. The eagle's head and the lion's body have stylized parts referring to jowls, muscles and anatomical lines. The open hoop of each bracelet is kidney-shaped rather than oval or round. They retained their original shape except for a hole in one of the cuffs. This damage seems to have been intentionally made after the discovery of the treasure, probably to check whether the hoop was solid or hollow, and several authors have since considered the central part of the hoop to be solid (Dalton 1964: 32; Mitchell 1989: 28; Palazzo Venezia 1993: 104, no. 112).

The griffins were originally inlaid with coloured stones, glass or glazed composition, now lost. O. M. Dalton mentions a lazulite fragment left in one compartment and it seems that a few of the smaller inlays survived (Dalton 1964: 34; Curtis & Tallis 2005:

139). There is a remarkable arrangement of cells in bands and curved patterns mimicking the outline of a bird's feathers and wings (Fig. 36.2). Such feather patterns are common in Achaemenid art, not exclusively goldwork.

The particular fashion, an open cuff with animal terminals and an in-swing opposite the terminals, is characteristic of a group of Achaemenid bracelets which were normally made in matching pairs (Musche 1992: 279–280; Rehm 1992: 47–49). The kidney shape was thought to be of functional origin preventing the bracelet from breaking when opened (Amandry 1958: 11; Rehm 1992: 48) but there is no convincing argument for this suggestion. The most prominent examples of the kidney-shaped bracelets include bracelets said to be from Iran with winged caprid terminals, the lion-headed bracelets excavated at Susa, an ibex-headed pair decorated with filigree from Pasargadae and another piece from Karlsruhe, the latter with terminals representing a caprid head in a lion's mouth and said to have been found in Greece (Arnold 1996: 51, no. 20; de Morgan 1905; Stronach 1978: pl. 160; Amandry 1958: 12, pls 10, 12). A pair of golden bracelets with kidney-shaped hoop and lion-protome terminals from the "Lydian Treasure" has comparable stylistic elements to this group of Achaemenid jewellery (Özgen & Öztürk et al. 1996: 178–179, no. 130).

Such bracelets are represented on depictions on stone reliefs from Persepolis and glazed brick panels from Susa (Pope 1938: pl. 93A; Curtis 2005c: 133, fig. 51; Caubet & Muscarella 1992). The Persepolis reliefs show delegations of Lydians and Sakā bringing kidney-shaped bracelets with animal terminals as tributes or gifts to the king. In this case the pairs of large bracelets are not worn as jewellery but held in both hands, with the griffin terminals standing upright. They, like the Oxus bracelets, appear to be objects of ostentation or gifts rather than personal ornaments (Curtis 2005c: 133). On the other hand, the Susa glazed bricks and the evidence of a pair of kidney-shaped bracelets found *in situ* in the Susa tomb confirm that smaller versions of these gold bracelets were worn on the wrist.

Lost wax casting

The hoop of the bracelets appears to be cast since no solder seam is visible and the wall of the tube has a considerable thickness—about 1.7 mm. The tubular cuff and the head are hollow castings but the relief hindquarters, ears, horns, mane and forepaws are solid. There are cast recesses for champlevé inlay on the griffin's head, body and tail. The tubular hoop, forepaws, head, ears and horns, including the deep settings, were cast over a clay core by the lost wax process (Armbruster 2001). The relief parts of the surface of the hoops as well as the griffin's wings, details of the head and the cloisons are solid casts that were also modelled in wax (Fig. 36.3). In some places evidence of working the wax with tracers and scrapers is recognizable. Rough surfaces resulting from the casting process remain on the crest, which imitates beaded wire, and on the neck and unfinished edges (Fig. 36.4).

Lost wax casting is a method whereby a model is made in wax, with wax rods attached to keep channels open in the mould for the flow of metal and gases. The wax model and the rods are completely encased in clay and dried until the clay is hard. Then the mould is heated so that the wax flows out of the channels, leaving a hollow ceramic mould (Fig. 36.5) (see Wübbenhorst & Engels 1989: 14). In the case of hollow objects, the wax is modelled over a clay core and pins (chaplets) are pushed through the wax into the core. These serve to

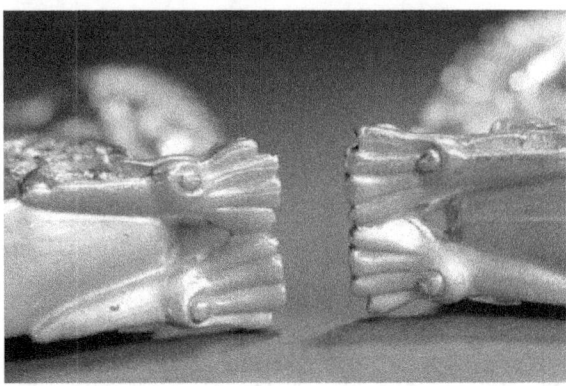

Fig. 36.3 Relief parts modelled in wax, then cast. (Photograph B. Armbruster)

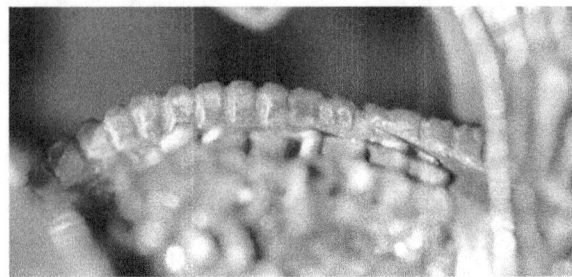

Fig. 36.4 Detail: crest. (Photograph B. Armbruster)

hold the clay core in place while the molten metal is poured into the cavity (Fig. 36.6). Gold melted in a crucible is poured into the hollow mould. After solidification of the cast metal the mould is destroyed in order to extract the piece and the casting channels are cut off.

Plastic shaping

Finishing of the raw casts was carried out partly by plastic shaping techniques. The smooth surface of undecorated parts indicates that they were polished. The cast metal surfaces of the bracelets and the elements of relief were reworked by chasing (see Armbruster 2003). Tool marks from punches and chisels used for chasing and chiselling the surface and corners of the cells after casting are recognizable (Fig. 36.7). The clay core remained in place, hidden within.

For the production of sheet metal and wires an ingot was worked with hammer and anvil (see Nicolini 1990: pl. 217). Rectangular-sectioned wire was used for the wing's frame (Fig. 36.2). Strips for the wings and additional cloisons were cut from a thin hammered sheet. Pliers were used for bending the sheet strips into cloisons.

Worked sheet elements that are fixed in place are present on the frame and back of the wings as well as in cell clusters. The edge of a thin plate clearly shows how it was adapted to the outline of the wing (Fig. 36.8).

Joining and repairs by soldering

Although separately manufactured, the component parts are joined together so masterfully as to appear to be a single piece. Soldering was used for mounting and joining the different constituent pieces for the wings and several cloison clusters. Soldering was carried out by using a gold alloy with a lower melting point than the base metal. The various elements were assembled, and small particles of solder applied and fused in the heat of a furnace.

The cast settings have very thin cast bottoms measuring about 0.5 mm, which were reworked with punches and often cracked. Several instances of damage can be detected. One of the bracelets needed repair during its manufacture (Fig. 36.9). A small gold sheet was soldered to the floor of one recess on the hip in order to close a casting fault.

Another joining technique detected on the bracelets uses so-called jeweller's stitches, which are described below.

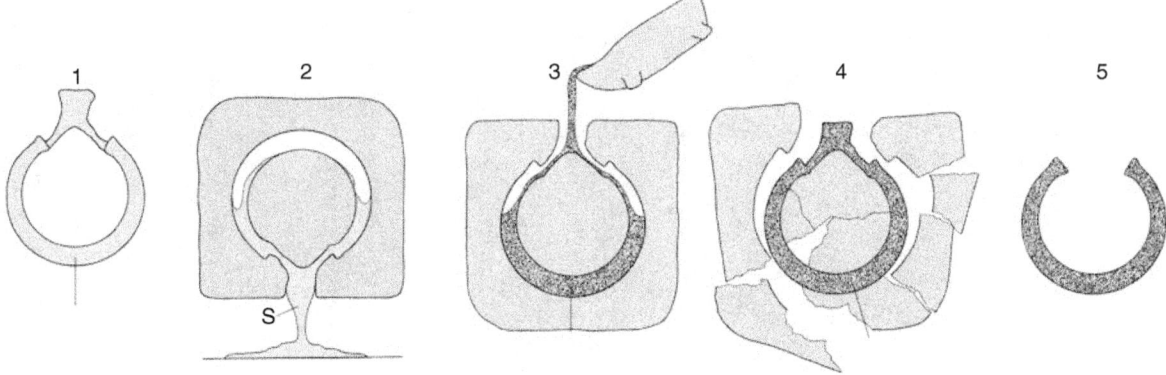

Fig. 36.5 Lost wax casting. (After Wübbenhorst & Engels 1989)

Incrustation

Apart from the wings, the hollows of the square and rounded settings were all prepared as negative forms in wax, cast and finished. In the case of the Oxus bracelets none of the recesses indicates their production by carving or chiselling in the metal, or deep chasing, as proposed by Dalton (1964: 33). The bracelets attest to three methods of manufacturing. Some recesses were created by carving in the wax model before casting. They were reworked after casting by means of plastic shaping (Fig. 36.7). This is the case for the inlay compartments without any subdivided cells on the legs, horns and the front part of the head, as well as for the oblong sunk panel, which was composed of several individual depressions representing the tail.

Other settings were cast as described above, but subdivisions added. These cloisons consist of thin sheet-metal elements mounted by soldering. Bent gold strips forming the cloisonné cells were soldered vertically onto a base sheet in the shape of the desired inlay. This ensemble was then inlaid in the compartment and mechanically fixed by gold chips gouged from the walls, the so-called jeweller's stitches (Fig. 36.10). With a sharp engraver or chiselling tool several deep incisions were made on the inner compartment wall, creating a sharp spur. The gouged spur was then bent into a hook that pinned down the fine sheet insert (Fig. 36.11). Fixing by means of stitches is a mechanical join. Jeweller's stitches for fixing decorated back plates have already been demonstrated for Celtic filigree (Whitfield 1987: 81). This second method of making cloisons was applied to the incrustations on the neck, side and back of the head, the breast and the rectangular hollow on the back of the griffins. The cloisonné panels of both griffins' chests are missing on one bracelet, but remains of the jeweller's stitches are still in place.

The third variety of setting was used exclusively for the wings. They are worked separately from the cast hoop by fashioning a base plate with a thick rectangular-sectioned wire forming the soldered rim of the setting. The wings were themselves fixed to the cast bracelet by soldering. The final work consisted of filling the large wing-shaped depression with small cell elements. As in the second method, fine gold strips were bent in the shape of feathers and large quantities of these elements were attached by soldering them onto a separate wing-shaped sheet (Figs 36.2, 8). The ensemble was finally fixed in the depression

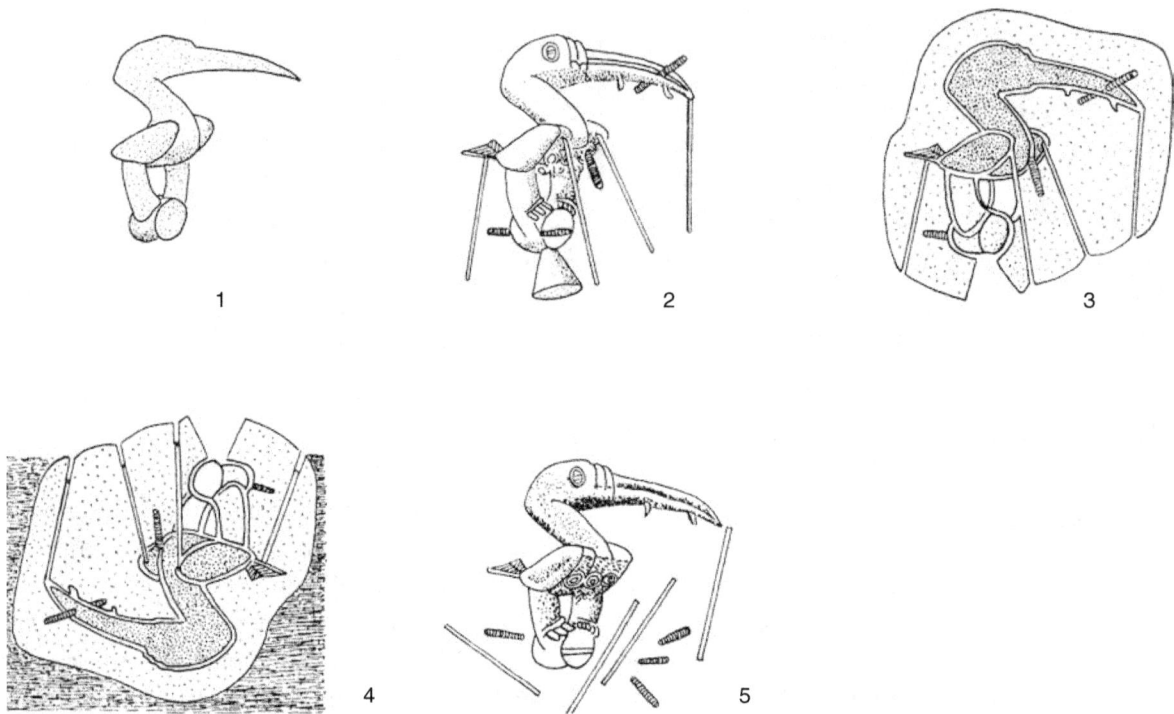

Fig. 36.6 Lost wax casting with clay core. (After Easby 1974)

by means of jeweller's stitches cut in the rim of the wing (Fig. 36.10).

Coloured materials used for polychrome inlays in Achaemenid goldwork are turquoise, lapis lazuli, carnelian, onyx, rock crystal, blue and white vitreous paste and some mother-of-pearl. The inlay material had to be shaped according to the outline and height of the settings. It seems that a black substance, probably bitumen, was in some cases applied as a bedding material and adhesive (Arnold 1996: 54–55). The preference for delicate intricate ornamental detail with polychrome designs is characteristic of a particular style of Achaemenid jewellery.

Discussion

Comparable goldwork to the complex Oxus bracelets is represented in the Musée du Louvre and the Miho Museum. Two tubular bracelets, one with seated duck terminals and the other with duck's head terminals, are prominent examples of elaborate polychrome cloisonné inlays (Arnold 1996: nos 21–22; Seipel 1999: 68–69, nos 30–31). They are exclusively created with this means of decoration, the coloured cells representing the feathering of the bird, which contrasts with the plain surface of the hollow hoop. The representation of feathers is comparable to the inlays of the Oxus griffins' wings (Fig. 36.2).

A pair of omega-shaped bracelets with winged caprid terminals said to be from Iran, are richly decorated with inlays of carnelian, turquoise, lapis lazuli and vitreous paste (Arnold 1996: 51, no. 20; Seipel 1999: 67–68, no. 29). One terminal from each bracelet is missing. They are the best-known parallels to

Fig. 36.7 Detail: tool marks in recesses. (Photograph B. Armbruster)

Fig. 36.8 Detail: edge of a thin plate. (Photograph B. Armbruster)

the bracelets with griffin terminals but differ in their representation of caprids as fantastic creatures, their all-over decorated cuff body and the fact that their tubing appears to be strengthened by a copper lining. However, they have much in common, including the hollow terminals with cast recesses, the outline of the animal bodies as terminals, the hindquarters incorporated in the ornamental design of the hoop and especially the concept of the wings. The wings are made from a frame with an inserted thin plate with cloisonné cells outlined, as on the Oxus bracelets. They appear to have been created within the same workshop tradition.

A richly ornamented pectoral with rectangular plaque pendant in the Miho Museum also appears to have been manufactured in the same workshop as the bracelets with winged caprid terminals as well as the polychrome jewellery from the Susa tomb (Seipel ed. 1999: 65–67; Williams 2005: 111, pls 9–11). Several stylistic features and motifs on this outstanding piece coincide with the aforementioned gold ornaments and all combine champlevé and cloisonné inlays.

Two gold bracelets with lion's head terminals found in the Achaemenid tomb on the "Acropole" at Susa have a kidney shape with an in-swing opposite the terminals and a polychrome design similar to the Oxus bracelets. A significant proportion of the champlevé and cloisonné inlays of lapis lazuli, turquoise and mother-of-pearl survived (Harper, Aruz & Tallon 1992: nos 172–173; Curtis & Tallis 2005: 174–176, figs 268–270). The terminal of the gold torc with lion's head terminals and ribbed hoop from the same tomb is made in two sections joined at the neck and held in place by a pin. Some inlays of lapis lazuli, turquoise and mother-of-pearl remained in place. The bracelets and torc are decorated with cast champlevé and sheet-work cloisonné cells, the latter being soldered to separate thin gold plates and then attached to the torc. In addition to the bracelets with griffin terminals, two spiral gold bracelets or torcs and a bracelet with lion's head terminals from the Oxus Treasure are also closely comparable to

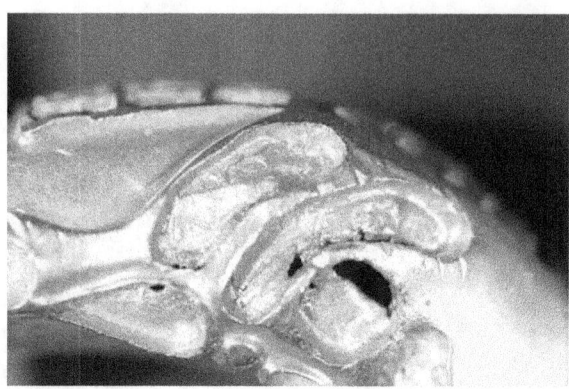

Fig. 36.9 Repair: soldered sheet. (Photograph B. Armbruster)

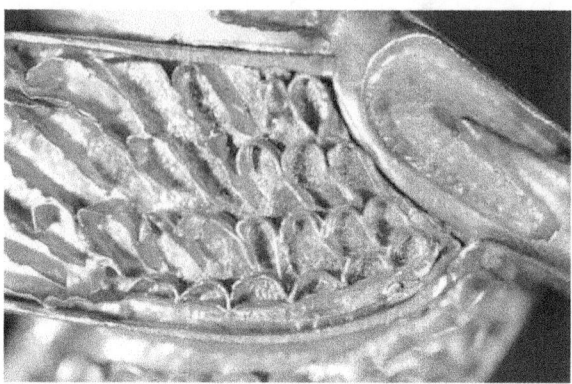

Fig. 36.10 Jeweller's stitches. (Photograph B. Armbruster)

the Susa jewellery (Curtis & Tallis 2005: nos 155–156, 160).

A tubular neck ring with mythical beast terminals is preserved in the Siberian Collection of Peter the Great in the Hermitage Museum (Schiltz 1994: 382, fig. 302; Minns 1913: 272, fig. 188). The piece in the shape of an overlapping ring is fashioned in two parts joined with a pin on the back. Some turquoise elements remain in the champlevé on the goat's horns. The panels with delicate cloisonné work imitating the tufts of the lion's mane are technically and stylistically very close to patterns on the Oxus bracelets and to the other previously mentioned jewellery with cloisonné inlay. The shape of the horns, the crest and the recesses are so similar that they appear to be manufactured in the same workshop as the ones from the griffin's terminals on the Oxus bracelets (Fig. 36.12).

Luxury tableware

The Oxus Treasure contains five precious metal vessels, including two plain bowls and a jug in gold, and two decorated shallow bowls, one of gold and one of silver. Luxury tableware reflects the Achemenid taste for precious vessels used in banquets (Dalton 1964: 8–9; Simpson 2005). The present case study concerns the plain hemispherical bowl and the horizontally fluted jug with handle terminating at the top in a lion's head (Fig. 36.13). In the author's opinion both reveal details of lost wax casting processes using rotary tools for the preparation of the wax model.

Comparable objects are represented in the so-called "Lydian Treasure" from İkíztepe. Among the silver vessels are a plain hemispherical bowl (height 52 mm, 219.2 gm), and a jug with horizontal fluting and a handle with a stylized bird's head (height 188 mm) (Özgen & Öztürk et al. 1996: 74, 102, nos 11, 52; von Bothmer 1984: 28, 33, nos 33, 38): both have very similar shapes to the Oxus vessels. These authors note that the jug is raised in sheet gold but the weight relative to the dimensions of the jug might instead indicate casting. Other silverware from the "Lydian Treasure", such as an oinochoe with lion's head handle and a lydion with a squat spherical body, bear similar horizontal fluting (Özgen & Öztürk et al. 1996: nos 12, 63). This is also the case for a gold bowl with two animal handles found in a rich Sarmatian burial at Novocherkask and now in the Hermitage Museum (Sulimirski 1970: pl. 43).

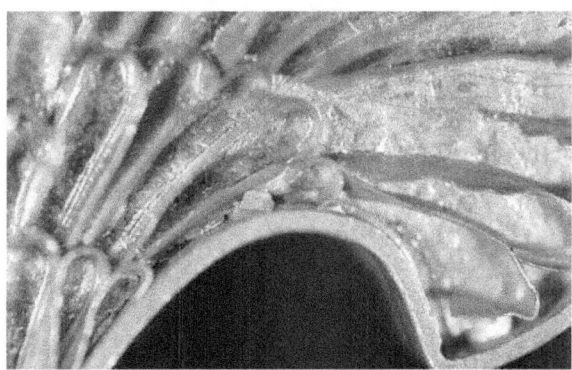

Fig. 36.11 Gouged spur (stitch). (Photograph B. Armbruster)

Fig. 36.12 Detail: griffin's horns. (Photograph B. Armbruster)

The Apadana reliefs at Persepolis also depict comparable vessels offered to the king. A Bactrian delegation brings hemispherical bowls, and Lydians and Armenians carry vessels with animal-headed handles.

Bowl

British Museum, ME 123921, H. 67 mm, Diam. 99 mm, Thickness 1.7 mm, Wt. 306.5 gm

The undecorated hemispherical bowl has a plain surface. The outside and inside are entirely smooth and highly polished (Fig. 36.13, left) (Dalton 1964: 9, no. 20, pl. 3; Curtis & Tallis 2005: no. 99). It is cast by the lost wax technique. The wax model was manufactured over a clay core and using a lathe, as will be explained below with the jug. This bowl has a central point at the external bottom indicative of the use of a lathe (Fig. 36.14).

Jug

British Museum, ME 123918, H. 130 mm, Diam. 86.5 mm, Thickness 1.7–1.9 mm, Wt. 368.5 gm

The jug with animal-headed handle has a fluted body and flared rim (Dalton 1964: 8, no. 17, pl. 7; Curtis & Tallis 2005: no. 125) (Fig. 36.13, right). The oviform body, which narrows towards the flat base is encircled with horizontal fluting reaching from the shoulder to the base. The jug's slightly concave neck is plain and expands conically to the rim. The handle has a polygonal section. Its upper terminal is fashioned as a naturally sculptured lion's head biting the rim and the extremity below represents a circular rosette (Fig. 36.15–16). The rim forms an open spout opposite the handle.

The jug reveals a high standard of craftsmanship. It is considered by this author also to be cast using the lost wax technique. The thickness and weight relative to height are typical of a cast vessel. Tool marks and surface structure of the jar indicate the use of a lathe and rotary motion for fashioning the wax model. On the centre of the underside a central point indicates where it was fixed to the turning spindle of a lathe (Fig. 36.17). Another kind of centring point can be seen on some decorated vessels that are raised and chased in sheet metal (Simpson 2005: 108, nos 101–104). In this case the point is indicative of the use of a pair of compasses marking the centre of the inner part of the vessel for outlining and tracing the decoration.

Fig. 36.13 Hemispherical bowl and jug with lion's head handle, Oxus Treasure. (Photograph B. Armbruster)

Fig. 36.14 Centring point. (Photograph B. Armbruster)

For manufacturing the hollow-cast object, a clay core was first worked on the axes of the lathe, using cutting tools such as scrapers, chisels or other kinds of blade (Armbruster 1995). After completely drying the clay core, a layer of wax was applied and worked on the lathe. The horizontal fluting which decorates the jug was also worked in the wax. The outer shape with parallel ribs reflects this way of preparing a perfectly regular wax model using a rotating spindle. The wax model was joined to wax channels and covered by several layers of tempered clay to form the casting mould. After drying, the clay mould was heated to melt out the wax. Then the cavity was filled with molten gold. Once the cast had cooled, the clay mould was broken, the clay core extracted and the casting channels cut off. After casting, the outer surface was worked with a very fine abrasive such as ash and partly polished. The outside bottom is smooth and polished, but the turning point of the lathe can still be seen. The inner surface was neither smoothed nor polished, and it still bears traces of the rough metal surface of the cast (Fig. 36.18).

The jug's handle was cast using the lost wax technique. The octagonal section and decorated terminals of the handle were prepared in the wax model. After casting, the handle was polished and details of the decoration were then executed with chasing tools. The rosette was reworked with a tracer (Fig. 36.16) (cf. Lowery, Savage & Wilkins 1971). After the body of the jug had been cast by the lost wax method, the separately manufactured handle was attached. The extremity with lion's head biting the rim was fixed by soldering, whereas the lower part was riveted at the end with a traced rosette. A hole had to be drilled in the jug's body for the rivet, which was presumably fixed at the back of the rosette by soldering. The rivet was hammered down on the inside of the jug. The rosette was also fixed by soldering on the outside of the vessel, so that there is a double means of attachment at this point.

The goldsmith's workshop

The outstanding bracelets and vessels from the Oxus Treasure reflect the sophisticated technical knowledge of the Achaemenid period. The goldsmiths must have been specialized professionals with high levels of artistic and practical skill. Several fine metalworking techniques were combined and executed in a predetermined sequence of steps.

Fig. 36.15 Jug handle: lion's head biting the rim. (Photograph B. Armbruster)

Fig. 36.16 Jug handle: rosette. (Photograph B. Armbruster)

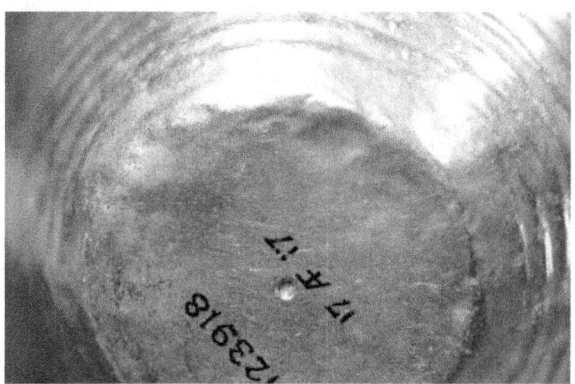

Fig. 36.17 Bottom of jug: centring point. (Photograph B. Armbruster)

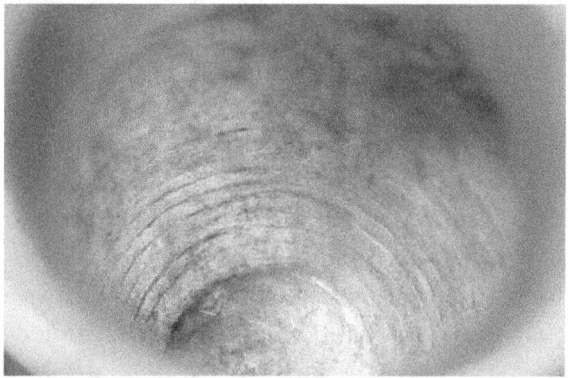

Fig. 36.18 Interior of jug: raw cast surface. (Photograph B. Armbruster)

The bracelets represent one of the most difficult manufacturing achievements of the Oxus Treasure apart from the miniature chariot.

The workshop that produced such elaborate gold jewellery must have been well equipped, highly specialized and presumably installed close to and controlled by the court. Tool marks and surface textures, as well as the form and decoration of the objects under consideration, indicate that the equipment included the following items: a furnace with bellows, clay crucibles, clay moulds and crucible tongs needed for melting and casting in lost wax. Grinding stones and abrasives were used for smoothing and polishing the cast surfaces, and for fashioning the small coloured inlays. Chasing and reworking the cast settings and the relief decoration was done using punches, chisels and engravers. For the manufacture of sheet metal and square-sectioned wire, hammers and anvils of stone, bronze or iron were required. Pliers were used to bend strips, sheets and wire. Dividing sheet metal into strips or other shapes was carried out by means of a hammer and chisel with a sharp cutting edge. Soldering was done in the furnace using a gold alloy with a lower melting temperature than the base metal. Measuring tools such as dividers and rulers were used during the manufacturing process for dimensional accuracy.

The goldsmith's workshop manufactured various kinds of fine metal vessels, including cast bowls and jugs as well as hammered bowls. This must have required equipment for casting, including a furnace with bellows, crucibles and tempered clay for manufacture of moulds just as in the case of the jewellery. In addition, a lathe with turning spindle was required for turning the vessel's clay core and the wax model. The equipment for making hammered sheet vessels with chased decoration comprised hammers, anvils and stakes for shaping the vessel, and punches and chisels for chasing and tracing.

Concluding remarks

The gleam of precious metal and the sheer beauty of ancient gold should not make us forget that goldwork at its best is not just a personal ornament or tableware but a piece of art and craft, and one which allows a glimpse into the technology of a particular period. Goldwork depends on various factors: the availability of the raw material, the tools and techniques and the ability and knowledge of the craftsman. Although symbolic merits and the framework of traditional design certainly have a heavy influence on style, the type of craftsmanship available limits the creativity and the execution of form and decoration.

The complex world of Achaemenid gold technology can only be touched on briefly and the organization of the craft, the economic implications of metalwork, the provenance of the raw material and the symbolic value of gold ornaments and vessels lie beyond the scope of this paper. Nevertheless, the following conclusions can be drawn from this study. There are numerous features and traces on ancient gold objects, which record the actions of their makers even where their tools have not survived. Rotary tools and lost wax casting were combined in the production of Achaemenid tableware. These have not previously been associated with Achaemenid gold vessel production. Moreover examination of the griffin bracelets revealed new information about hollow casting, cast recesses and worked sheet gold, and the use of jeweller's stitches for attaching cloison panels.

The study has outlined some of the technical know-how of Achaemenid artisans and the important technological level achieved in their arts and crafts. It emphasizes the skilfulness of the goldsmiths, as well as their specialization, technical virtuosity and sophisticated knowledge. The ideas suggested in this paper are designed to emphasize the importance of a technological approach for the classification of metal artefacts, and to encourage further research in the history of ancient metalwork.

37

From Susa to Egypt: Vitreous Materials from the Achaemenid Period

Annie Caubet

Summary

A general survey carried out of the evidence for production of vitreous faience and other materials at the Musée du Louvre on the occasion of a temporary exhibition has emphasized the differences and interaction between the products of Egypt and the Ancient Near East. The Achaemenid or Persian period was a time of strong interactions between these two cultures. It was during this period that some of the most perfect vitreous artefacts of antiquity were produced. They were remarkable for their technical innovations, for their eclectic styles, for the variety of types and for their wide dissemination. In this context, the discoveries at Susa are unique. The glazed brick decoration of Darius' palace is spectacular and the tableware, jewellery, amulets and statuettes related to cult practices display a high level of perfection; they also provide a good chronological framework for similar objects found in the Levant and in Egypt.

Introduction

During the Persian Achaemenid period, the glass industry achieved a high level of perfection: this has emerged from the work done on the collections at the Louvre, which have been systematically analysed as part of a catalogue of the faience and glass from the Ancient Near Eastern collections, while a temporary exhibition organized at the Louvre in 2005 has enabled an appraisal of the techniques practised in the eastern Mediterranean, Asia Minor and Egypt in antiquity (Caubet & Bonnefois Pierrat 2005). Against this backdrop, the discoveries at Susa play a particularly important role: the abundance and variety of objects, the continuity over a long period and nearly 6,000 years of history have turned the contents of this metropolis into works of reference.[1] This is especially notable for the production of glass in the Persian period, which can shed new light on similar artefacts found in the Levant and Egypt.

This paper groups together under the term of glass industry the different techniques using sand, lime and alkali in order to produce either "faience" (a misnomer but a convenient term to describe objects made of glazed silica paste), "frit", glass or glazed clay objects.[2] These different categories have undergone a variety of applications. The most spectacular and most famous from the Persian period is the architectural decoration at Susa, with the frieze of archers and mythological monsters. Excavations by Jacques de Morgan and Roland de Mecquenem on the Apadana site have uncovered many other types of objects including tableware, amulets and statuettes.

Architectural decoration

During the establishment of Persian power at Susa, the city was entirely redesigned around a new centre, the Apadana, which was erected on a terrace separated from the rest of the settlement by a ditch. This vast palace complex comprises two separate sections, the columned hall with stone bases and capitals and the Mesopotamian-type palace organized around a series of courtyards providing light to the rooms. This second complex has a façade made of brick with figured decoration and borders of abstract decoration. The destruction of the palace by Alexander the Great led to the scatter and reuse of materials used in the original decoration. The early reconstruction of this figured decoration begun by Dieulafoy and de Mecquenem (1947) has continued without any radical change (Labrousse 1972a; Tallon 1997; Daucé & Nguyen 2003). The palace of Susa displays an imagery comparable to that of Persepolis, but with differences that are not only due to the use of different materials, such as stone at Persepolis and brick at Susa.

Several types of brick can be seen at Susa and each type presents a different decorative repertoire.

1. Silica paste and polychrome glazed bricks were utilized for two types of decoration: flat motif decoration (type 1–1) and moulded relief decoration (type 1–2). The flat motifs (1–1) include some small figures representing archers (in which the head of the archer is two courses of brick high), processions of servants or tributaries and abstract decoration (staircases, scrolls and components of niches or windows, etc.). The moulded reliefs (1–2) were used for the lion frieze of the west court, for the friezes of mythological animals (winged bull, lion, lion-griffin) and pairs of sphinxes, and especially for the "large" archer frieze (in which the head is three courses of brick high). Two of these archers were shown at the exhibition *Forgotten Empire* in London in 2005, including a recently reconstructed one (Fig. 37.1).[3]

2. Bricks of moulded clay were utilized for a large set of friezes representing mythological beasts, that is, a winged bull, a lion and lion-griffin, similar to those produced in silica brick relief (1–1), with the difference that the anatomical details, such as the fur, muscles or feathers, were created solely using moulding or carving and without using colours.

Judging by the number of fragments recovered, these two types of brick were probably used for creating large murals which adorned the façades of courtyards. Two other brick techniques are attested by a very small number of reconstructed fragments:

3. A few clay bricks coated in lime plaster.[4]

4. Bricks made of unglazed grey silica paste, possibly imitating the grey limestone at Persepolis, can be identified as elements of servants or tributaries.[5]

These different technical categories and variations in the decoration are probably indicative of the presence of artists with varying expertise, possibly of different ethnic origin. They have contributed to the achievement of an innovative ornamental

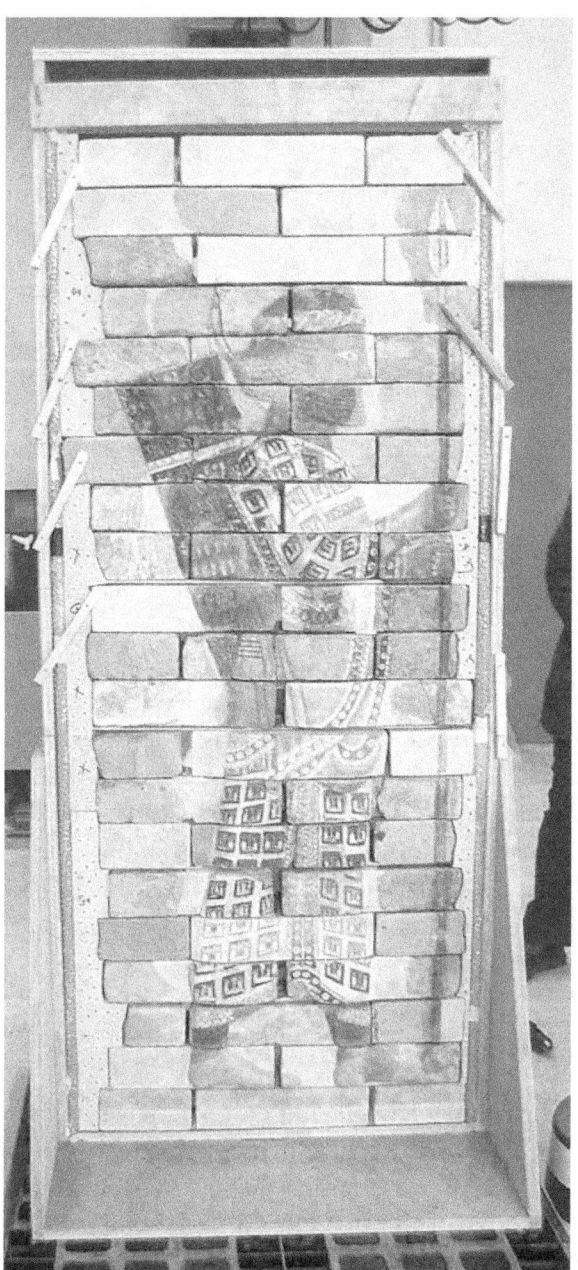

Fig. 37.1 Archer Sb 23,177 during reassembly in the summer of 2005.

and architectural programme. The unique composite and distinctive style, provided by elements that were borrowed and adapted to suit different requirements, is characteristic of Achaemenid art.

At Susa, the use of glazed brick to decorate official buildings and monuments originates in the Middle Elamite period (Amiet 1976; Caubet 2003). This type of decoration, known in second-millennium Egypt and Mesopotamia, remained popular with the great empires of the first millennium BC, including Assyria (Reade 1963; 1995), Babylon (Nunn 1988; Marzahn 1993) and Susa itself, where the Neo-Elamite dynasty continued the tradition of its second-millennium predecessors (Amiet 1967). What distinguishes the glazed decoration at Susa from its first-millennium Mesopotamian equivalent is the continuity in the use of a traditional process inherited from artists from the Middle Elamite period and who used silica paste bricks whereas in Assyria and Babylonia the coloured glazes were applied to moulded clay bricks, which were also used to produce unglazed decorations. In Babylon, the decorative repertoire was limited to the repetition of isolated motifs depicting animals (both real and mythological) and divine symbols and characterized by the absence of human figures. It may therefore be to a Babylonian tradition that we must attribute all the Achaemenid clay moulded relief decoration (type 2) at Susa representing composite lions and monsters. Thus, the architectural decoration from the Persian period at Susa attests the presence of many parallel traditions, either inherited from the Elamite period or borrowed from Babylon; the new imagery, which only partially parallels that at Persepolis, was made possible using revived manufacturing techniques and expertise.

Tableware

The Persian period has yielded a considerable amount of faience tableware. Again the techniques vary. The production of silica paste vessels, inherited from Elamite traditions, continued but polychrome vessels were not as popular.[6] By contrast, the period saw the development of a technique which had appeared in the previous period in Elam and Mesopotamia, namely the application of glaze to wheel-thrown clay vessels. This technique represents a significant advance because by throwing on the wheel a greater quantity of vessels could be produced but the application of silica glaze on clay requires a perfect knowledge of the mechanical properties of the components in order to make the surface and the body adhere. During the Seleucid and Parthian periods glazed clay vessels replaced glazed silica faience and became the preferred fine tableware in Mesopotamia and Iran (Caubet & Pierrat-Bonnefois 2005: 174ff). However, it remained unknown in the Levant and Egypt, which retained the old tradition of silica faience until the end of antiquity.

The repertoire of shapes is the same for both techniques, and was inspired by that of metal tableware, with a preference for carinated bowls and bowls decorated with oval lobes or gadroons (Fig. 37.2) (Pierrat & Caubet-Bonnefois 2005: nos. 407, 422). Most importantly, this repertoire became thoroughly global and it is very difficult, if not impossible, to identify pieces as being from Iran, the Levant or Egypt. The emblematic form is the rhyton or drinking horn with a mouthpiece in the shape of an animal's head, which is found all over the empire, in various materials and especially glass (Caubet & Pierrat-Bonnefois 2005: nos. 415–418 and 423 for a set from Egypt).

Vessels used for worship form a separate category, which is well represented in faience and using common forms of Egyptian origin: a good example is the libation vase with an

Fig. 37.2 Gadrooned bowl, green faience, Egypt. (Musée du Louvre AE 11059)

elongated body and narrow neck supporting a thick horizontal mouthpiece (Caubet & Pierrat-Bonnefois 2005: no. 10 from Susa and no. 383 from Egypt). The mouthpiece was often manufactured separately and added on: when the neck is missing, the object has sometimes been wrongly interpreted as a "baluster" (Curtis & Tallis eds 2005: no. 81). Several examples of these vessels have been found at Susa, of identical shape but in different colours, in blue or green faience and blue Egyptian frit.

Amulets

The amulets displaying either magic symbols, such as the Eye of Horus, or protective animals and god-demons obviously derive from Egyptian tradition. They have been imported to the Middle East or copied locally since the Bronze Age, and are generally difficult to date. The examples found in Iran allow the precise dating of examples from the Levant and Egypt. Thus the Achaemenid period favoured a particular type of Eye of Horus in the form of a large double-sided plaque, generally light green in colour. It is almost impossible to distinguish between examples from Homs, Egypt, Persepolis (Curtis & Tallis eds 2005: no. 264), Susa (de Mecquenem, Le Breton & Rutten 1947: 46–47, fig. 24; Caubet & Pierrat-Bonnefois 2005: nos. 410–411) or the Levant, as can be seen from an amulet (Fig. 37.3) recovered from Homs.[7] Similarly, the amulets in the shape of a lion's head or of the god-demon Bes found at Susa are characteristic of this global art of the Persian period, strongly influenced in this case by Egyptian traditions.

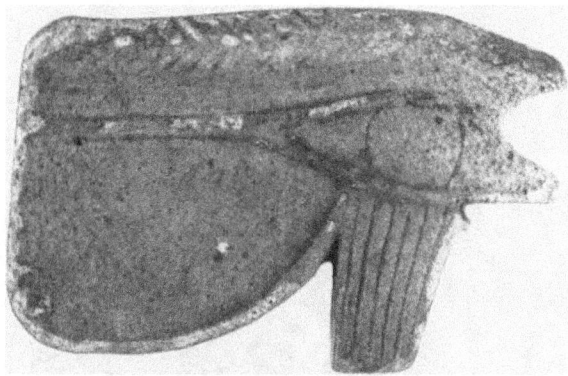

Fig. 37.3 Eye of Horus, green faience, Homs or its environs. (Musée du Louvre AO 4531)

Statues and statuettes

The misshapen god-demon Bes, who appeared in Egypt and the Levant at the time of the New Kingdom, reappeared in the Persian period. He is featured on various types of objects, pendant amulets (see above), statuettes and moulded vases. Compared with ancient examples, the figure from the Persian period underwent subtle stylistic changes, particularly noticeable in the softening of the lines of the face: the creature has lost its fearsome leonine characteristics and appears more benign, the beard and hair are arranged in a very refined way and the numerous curls are arranged symmetrically. Again, very similar examples were found at Susa, the Levant and Egypt (Caubet & Pierrat-Bonnefois 2005: nos. 414 from Susa, and 425 from Egypt). The statuette discovered in Amrit (Fig. 37.4) near Tartus, ancient Tortosa, is characteristic of this group (see Longpérier 1882: pl. XIX/1; Perrot & Chipiez 1890: 65, fig. 21; Heuzey 1923: 66, no. 197).[8] It is shown supported by an Egyptian dorsal pillar and rests on a small base; it was made, to quote Heuzey's description, "dans un moule à deux pièces; cependant elle n'est pas proprement moulée en creux, mais percée verticalement de part en part d'un trou cylindrique, communiquant avec une autre ouverture circulaire, pratiquée au revers du pilastre" (Heuzey 1923: 66). The white silica paste is very fine although the glaze has gone, leaving only traces of concretions due to burial; the eyes are inlaid. The long beard ends in a coil, showing a decorative arrangement that is exactly reflected in the amulets of Susa and Persepolis (Curtis & Tallis eds 2005: no. 263); similar "drop-shaped" eyebrows meet over the nose in a kind of finial underneath which is a triple fillet: this detail is similar to the stylized lotus on stone architecture (e.g. on the sphinx relief [Curtis & Tallis eds 2005: no. 46] or on the cornerstones of the parapet of the Tachara palace [Curtis & Tallis eds 2005: no. 39]), and is a striking manifestation of the "cross-disciplinary" and distinctive type of the decorative Achaemenid repertoire which ranges from the miniature to the monumental, from stone to goldworking or pottery and covers a vast geographical area.

The earthenware statuettes of Bes are a manifestation of an apposite mix of Egyptian and Asian elements, which also characterizes the stone statue of Darius discovered at Susa. The beautiful fragment representing a female figure (Fig. 37.5) supported by a

Fig. 37.4 a–c Statuette of Bes from Amrit near Tartous, acquired in 1860. (Musée du Louvre AO 25952)

dorsal pillar is probably entirely Egyptian.[9] A fragment of Egyptian hieroglyphics on the pilaster can be read as "priest".[10] The fine cream-coloured paste and the pale blue matt glaze, the quality of the surviving fragments (the thighs moulded within an invisible tunic, the hand resting on the forward left leg) make one long to see the remainder of the sculpture. It is estimated that it measured about 50 cm, roughly three times smaller than life size: this is exceptional for a faience statuette; the size alone represents a tour de force and attests the extremely high technical level attained by the artisans of the Persian period.

Conclusions

Several features emerge from this overview: the architectural decoration at Susa is entirely original, albeit within a local tradition and nothing of this kind has been found elsewhere in the empire. By contrast, the tableware and small moulded glass, faience and frit objects have a global character with strong similarities to objects found in Iran, Egypt and the Levant. It is virtually impossible to identify the origin of these works, probably because of the policy of interchange between artists from different regions of the empire. The architectural decoration at Susa, in all its complexity, and the glass objects of all types are distinguished by a high level of technical and aesthetic perfection that makes them immediately identifiable as belonging to the Persian period.

Appendix

Note on the reassembly of the archer Sb 23,177

Thousands of brick fragments representing the different techniques mentioned above have been excavated on the tell of the Apadana at Susa, some of which had already been identified by W. K. Loftus (Curtis 1993; 1997a), and further excavations are still uncovering them on a regular basis. According to the agreement between Iran and France, some of the finds of earlier excavations were given to the Louvre. In Paris, a first reconstruction of the fragments discovered by Marcel Dieulafoy was carried out (Tallon 1997). The first restoration formed the basis for a second one, from the elements found during the excavations by Jacques de Morgan and then by Roland de Mecquenem. A series of panels depicting isolated archers was then reassembled, several of which are today on long-term loan in various museums in Berlin, New York and London.[11]

These restorations have utilized virtually all the complete bricks in the collection. However, there remained a large number of interesting fragments. From 1994, a stocktake and identification exercise was initiated by students training in the Département des Antiquités Orientales.[12] This survey enabled the selection of fragments for the reconstruction of an archer dressed in a rosette

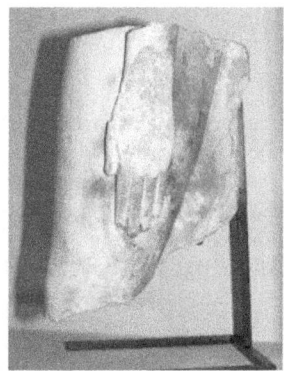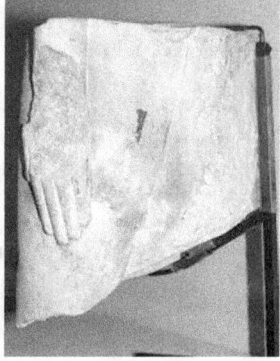

Fig. 37.5 Female statue, pale blue faience. Susa, Donjon excavation, 1933. (Musée du Louvre Sb 10214 = AE 33880)

decorated tunic (Sb 21965; Demange 2000: no. 270; Caubet & Pierrat-Bonnefois 2005: no. 290; Curtis & Tallis 2005: no. 52, reproduced but not shown in this exhibition). The reconstruction was carried out in 2000 by restorers Sandrine Gaymay and Marie-Christine Nollinger, under the scientific guidance of Agnès Benoit. The figure is made of 18 courses of brick, from the feet to the tip of the spear and the end of the bow. In 2004–2005, another archer was reconstructed by the same restorers who were assisted by Jeanne-Marie Sornay-Setton, again under the direction of Agnès Benoit.[13] As with the first reconstructions, the missing elements were cast from other panels and discreetly coloured. The faces of the last two archers were reconstructed as no original fragments existed. The face, right hand, back foot and some parts of the tunic of the archer dressed in the tunic decorated with a fortress were supplemented by modern casts. The fortress motif depicts three towers on a small hill, that is, two white towers flanking a round yellow tower with black merlons. As no equivalent fragment could be found, the brick chosen for the skirt at the level of the knee has a slightly smaller fortress motif, with two white towers framing a blue tower.

Notes

1. According to the successful survey conducted by Amiet (1988).
2. For definitions, manufacturing methods and production history see Moorey 1994.
3. The first (no. 51) is displayed in the British Museum and is on long-term loan from the Louvre. The other object shown in London (Sb 23177), an archer facing right wearing a tunic with a fortress motif on a white background, is in fact not the one reproduced in the exhibition catalogue as no. 52 (Sb 2965, archer facing right, tunic with rosettes on a yellow background); see the appendix on the reconstruction executed in 2004–2005.
4. E.g. the warrior's veiled head (Harper, Aruz & Tallon 1992: no. 161).
5. E.g. the hand holding a lid (Harper, Aruz & Tallon 1992: no. 165).
6. The examples reproduced in Curtis & Tallis (eds 2005: nos. 130–131) are probably from the Neo-Elamite period, not from the Persian Achaemenid period: see numerous examples in the tombs at Susa (de Miroschedji 1981).
7. Louvre, AO 4531. H. 6.5; L. 9; Thickness 4.4 cm. From a batch of 38 amulets brought back from "Homs and its environs" by Father Ronzevalle (Caubet & Pierrat-Bonnefois 2005: 126).
8. Louvre, AO 25952. H. 20.2 cm. From the necropolis of Amrit and acquired from Pérétié in 1860.
9. Louvre Sb 10214 (AE = 33880), preserved height 14.5 cm. Excavations by de Mecquenem (1933), "Keep", found in the rubble under the Sasanian palace (report by de Mecquenem, Archives of the Département des Antiquités Orientales, 1933, pp. 7–8). According to the Egyptian department, where the object is kept, it is a statue of a goddess, perhaps a lion-headed goddess, parallels of which are kept in the reserve collections of the Cairo museum. This information was kindly provided by Geneviève Pierrat-Bonnefois and Sylvie Guichard.
10. According to the inventory sheet Sb 11214 produced by Pierre Amiet.
11. See Daucé & Nguyen 2003 for the history of these reconstructions.
12. Aude Mantoux and Elodie Paillard, assisted by Sophie Marchegay and Laura Battini; see Mantoux's report (1994); also Sabrina Maras, a student at UCLA; finally, see the fourth-year paper (2003) by two students at the Ecole du Louvre, Noémie Daucé and Jeanne Nguyen.
13. Sb 23177, unpublished. My thanks to Agnès Benoit for this information.

38

Prestige Drinking: Rhyta with Animal Foreparts from Persia to Greece (Abstract)

Susanne Ebbinghaus

Monumental sculpture and architecture are the main visual expressions of Achaemenid Persian royal and imperial ideology. Portable objects, such as seals, coins and metalwork, may illustrate how imperial concepts spread throughout the empire, and how they were received and modified on a local level. This paper takes a closer look at the evolution of a characteristically Achaemenid vessel type, the rhyton with animal foreparts, and follows its distribution within and beyond the borders of the Persian Empire.

It will be argued that the origin of the rhyton with the animal foreparts, whose shape combines elements of the animal-headed cup, the zoomorphic vessel and the drinking horn, has to be sought in sumptuous plates created for the Achaemenid court in the later sixth century BC. A comparison with earlier forms of animal-headed vessels, notably the Neo-Assyrian examples, will help to better understand the function and peculiar iconography of the Achaemenid rhyta. Through their use as ritually charged drinking vessels and prestigious gifts, the habit of drinking from rhyta spread among the local elites of the empire, signalling at the same time allegiance to the Great King and the drinker's high status. It seems that the trickle-down effect was slow at first, but where rhyta were embraced by broader sections of the population, modifications of form, iconography and function become more visible and indicate the adaptation of the vessel type to local needs. A brief overview of the occurrence of rhyta in Anatolia, Cyprus, the Levant, Egypt, Scythia, Thrace and Greece will shed some light on the workings of cultural interaction in the period of Achaemenid Persian rule.

39

Achaemenid and Greek Colourless Glass

Despina Ignatiadou

Ancient art and technology owe much to a series of attempts to create substitutes of precious materials. The manufacture of colourless glass in pre-Roman antiquity must be seen as an attempt to imitate rock crystal, the most precious material on earth. The substitute was desirable as the original was not simply difficult to obtain, especially in large pieces, but also presented flaws that sometimes rendered it useless for carving. As the substitute was a technological innovation it was greatly admired and also considered very precious. In the case of glass many people could not tell the difference between the original and the substitute, or did not bother to, so these continued for a long time to be named with the same word.

The first peak period for the production of colourless glass vessels is in Assyria of the eighth–seventh centuries BC. The production seems to have lasted for less than two centuries and came to an end before the establishment of the Achaemenid Dynasty (von Saldern 1970). In the dark period that followed, the craft was probably kept alive by artisans making colourless beads and other small items. This usually happens with the dark periods in the production of most materials, as of course materials are not re-invented again and again.

In the Achaemenid period, vessel making is revived but the date and place of the revival is not clear. There is a general impression that this happened in the fifth century BC but existing evidence is not strong at all. Vessels made during the Achaemenid period are mainly of open shapes and as such were used for libations or drinking, unlike the coloured narrow-mouthed glass containers for keeping perfumes and other substances, although examples of these are known (Barag 1985). Although there are also some undecorated examples, most are decorated in what is known as the International Achaemenid Style (Melikian-Chirvani 1993), which was also used as decoration for vessels made of other precious metals. This style combines leaf decoration of several types, sometimes complemented by grooves, almonds and omphaloi.

The first colourless glass vessel of the classical period to be studied individually was the *phiale* from Ephesus, unearthed in the foundation of the Hellenistic Artemision. It is decorated with two grooves and 24 relief lanceolate leaves.

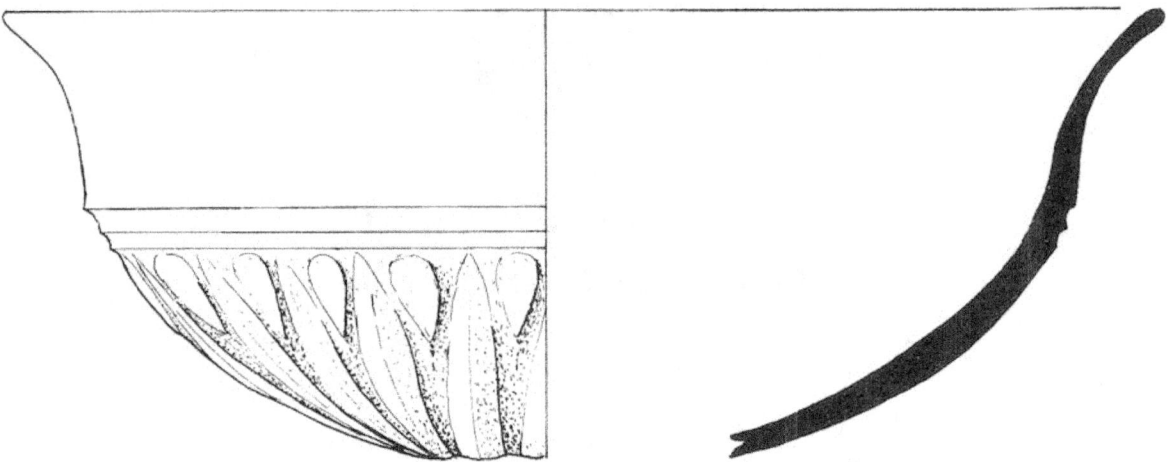

Fig. 39.1 Colourless glass *phiale* from Ephesus. (After Barag, 1985: no. 46)

Between the tips of the leaves there are small almonds (fig. 39.1). In 1937 Fossing's comments on this vessel marked the beginning of the comparisons with Achaemenid metalwork and the connection to a passage from Aristophanes on glass drinking cups in the Persian court. Similar glass vessels had not yet been discovered, so Fossing compared it with metal ones and placed the find in the context of the Achaemenid production of luxury items. Moreover, as the shape of the vessel did not exactly match that of metal ones, he did not go much further than discussing matters of decoration.[1] Different views were later expressed—Rostovtzeff (1941, i : 539) suggested a Phoenician or Egyptian origin, von Saldern (1959: 41) ascribed it to an industry either in Mesopotamia or in western Iran, the Aegean or on the Syrian coast, whereas Harden (1969: 58) preferred a Mesopotamian origin—but Fossing's view prevailed, as he was a pioneer and serious researcher of ancient glass working. His views functioned as a basis for the attribution of every similar vessel to Achaemenid glass working and also to an arbitrary early dating, sometimes as early as the middle of the fifth century BC.

The Hellenistic Artemision was built on the site of the archaic Artemision, on an extended platform, 2 m above the previous level. The extension was supported by massive piers and the glass was found together with other small finds "in the rammed earth which filled the interstices between the Hellenistic piers, built inwards to support the steps and external columns of the latest temple" (Hogarth 1908: 27–29, 313, 318, no. B.1). This was clearly a late classical stratum but Hogarth considered the finds to be "debris of votive offerings, dedicated in the course of the two centuries during which the Croesus temple existed". In 1908, at the time of the publication, the fourth century BC was probably not considered a *comme il faut* period, as he describes the glass as being of "Fine fabric, worthy of the 5th century". The old temple was destroyed by fire in 356 BC but we do not know when the later temple was founded. All we know is that Alexander the Great found the temple to be unfinished in 334 BC and this is the *terminus ante quem* for the manufacture of the vessel.

Several unprovenanced glass vessels were later compared to the Ephesus *phiale* and consequently dated to the end of the fifth or the beginning of the fourth century BC.[2] I consider this early date unlikely and I think that the Ephesus *phiale* is a creation of the middle of the fourth century BC. Its shape is not a forerunner of the handleless *skyphos* but a distinct one that evolved independently.

In 1957 Schmidt's publication of the glass finds unearthed in the Treasury of Persepolis appeared, and this only enhanced views on the Persian origin of the vessels of this type. Colourless glass vessels identified there include, among others, a bowl with relief almonds and perhaps also an *omphalos*, an animal-head beaker and a beaker with vertical fluting (perhaps belonging together), a bowl with horizontal grooves, the animal-shaped end of a jug handle, and some relief fragments (one with a palmette, the other with a rosette). In the publication it is clearly stated: "the place of origin (of the almond bowl) must be sought in one of the western lowland provinces, for we have no clues for the manufacture of glass vessels on the Iranian plateau during this period". As far as the other vessels are concerned, they are thought to be "Persians' booty from Egypt", or "Mesopotamia too may be considered as a possible source of glassware discovered at Persepolis". As a matter of fact the latter was also indicated by the results of chemical analysis carried out on one fragment (Schmidt 1957: 3, 91–93, 127–135, pls 66–67, 70). The views of the author were ignored and since then tens of glass vessels, most of them not comparable to the Persepolis ones, were identified as Persian. Fukai expressed reservations. In his treatise on Persian glass he wrote that, "the place where these vessels were actually made cannot be determined, but I suspect that it was the Mesopotamian region, not the Iranian highlands" (Fukai 1977: 18–20). Doubts were also expressed by Oliver Jr (1970) and Grose (1989: 80–81). As it was conjectured that the Persepolis finds were deposited in the Treasury long before it was destroyed, vessels compared to those were arbitrarily dated even to the fifth century BC. However, as also in the case of the Ephesus bowl, the only certain fact is that the Persepolis glass antedates the destruction of the site in 330 BC.

The Persian character of the Persepolis finds, and the early dating, was also based on the appearance of vessels on the Apadana staircase reliefs. However, two very important factors are constantly overlooked. First, no exact, and sometimes even approximate, parallels are depicted. Second, the depicted vessels are offered as gifts to the Great King by delegations from the satrapies. The Ionians are offering handleless *skyphoi*, the Bactrians beakers and calyx cups, and the Syrians, Medians and Armenians are carrying amphorae (Walser 1966; Calmeyer 1993; Tourovets 2001).

The main argument for the early dating of the Persepolis finds was based on a passage from the Acharnians of Aristophanes. Ambassadors to the Persian court were forced to drink wine from glass vessels: Ξενιζόμενοι δὲ πρὸς βίαν ἐπίνομεν ἐξ ὑαλίνων ἐκπωμάτων καὶ χρυσίδων ἄκρατον οἶνον ἡδύν (Aristophanes, *Acharnenses*, 73–75). This passage is quoted in every text concerning classical or Achaemenid glass, since the word *hyalos* is of course thought to mean glass.[3] But it is not so.

Greek lexicographers and etymologists consider the word *hyalos* to derive from the verb *hyein* (to rain): glass is therefore something that looks wet in the sense of bright or clear.[4] The word is used to describe all transparent or bright substances. Aëtius attests that the word was used by Philolaus the Pythagorian in the fourth century BC and by Ion Chius to describe the sun as glassy, and the moon as glassy clear, meaning bright.[5] Aristotle uses it to describe the behaviour of the light.[6] Hippocrates and Pollux use it to describe the humours of the body; thus are described urine, and the tunics of the eye.[7] Aristophanes again, in his *Clouds*, uses it for an apparent crystal ball used to light fire from sunrays. Strepsiades asks Socrates whether he has seen the beautiful transparent stone by which they kindle fire and he answers: you speak of the glass? [8] Herodotus refers to it in the description of burial customs in Egypt. There the dead are buried in sarcophagi made of glass, probably a kind of translucent stone.[9] Later, Diodorus describes how in Ethiopia they pour molten glass over the dead, referring probably to some kind of lake.[10]

We must therefore be very cautious when citing ancient authors, as the word *hyalos* and its derivatives are used throughout classical antiquity to describe every transparent or translucent material, including glass, glaze, crystal, gems, lake and also amber.[11] It is especially misleading to verify the meaning of terms by relying on the later scholiasts. Those usually explain the terms based on the technological know-how of their time when man-made glass was easily distinguished from natural rock crystal and each material was described in only one word.[12] In the fifth century BC, however, only rock crystal can be called *crystallos* (because it resembles ice and is considered hard) and *hyalos* (because it is transparent).[13] Coloured glass was at that time called *lithos chyte* (poured stone)[14] or *kyanos* (if it was blue), and colourless glass probably did not exist at all. It is therefore most probable that the Persian cups mentioned by Aristophanes were made of rock crystal.

To summarize, what is today identified as Achaemenid Persian glass included the Persepolis finds (which were never attributed to Persian workshops), the Ephesus bowl and other vessels from Asia Minor and Greece (not clearly connected to the Persian heartland) and several vessels from the art market named as Persian on very insecure grounds. As for the dating, all we have are vessels that were simply made before 330 BC, which is the *terminus ante quem* for the destruction of Persepolis and 334 BC for the visit of Alexander to Ephesus.

It is evident that colourless glass of the Achaemenid period is not necessarily also Persian and the two terms are not synonymous. On the contrary, it seems probable that the production of such glass took place only in the satrapies, mainly the west ones. In this sense this kind of glass is correctly termed Achaemenid when found within the geographical and chronological boundaries of the empire. But what about the numerous Greek finds? Are those to be considered Achaemenid too?

One hundred and ten colourless glass vessels of the Achaemenid period survive, either whole or in fragments. Of these, 87 have a secure or fairly secure provenance. The numbers favour Greece but we must be cautious as Greece has been more systematically excavated and consequently there are more finds.

Almost all the vessels are dated to the fourth century BC. The exceptions are a bowl from Babylon found in a sixth-century BC burial (von Saldern 1970: fig. 41, no. 46), a bowl found in Ihringen, Germany, in a burial of the fifth century BC (Wedepohl 2003: 47–48) and two alabastra dated to the sixth–fourth centuries BC, one from Ravenna, Italy, and the other from Athlit, Israel (von Saldern 1970: fig. 49, nos 54, 54a). The Greek finds are concentrated in Macedonia and Rhodes and there are another four vessels from other parts of Greece. The two Greek groups differ in character, as does the Anatolian group.

Most of the 14 Rhodian finds are very small *phialai*, 10–13 cm in diameter, but there are also three calyx cups and one *alabastron*. Four of the *phialai* are of a type not found outside Rhodes; these have not yet been thoroughly studied but seem to belong to an early local production influenced by Achaemenid aesthetics. The other vessels follow the International Achaemenid Style. They present similarities to the Macedonian and the Anatolian finds. The researcher Pavlos Triantaffyllidis correctly attributed some of them to a Rhodian-Carian workshop, as Rhodes was under Carian rule at the time of the production, and thus we could consider the case of Rhodes as an Achaemenid production (Triantaffyllidis 2000; Ignatiadou 2004: 182).

In Macedonia some vessels are of similar style but they appear in a larger variety of shapes. There is a preference for drinking cups, such as the calyx cup, and the handleless *skyphos* (which later evolve into the Hellenistic mould-made bowl), and many vessels represent these shapes. Unlike Rhodes, *phialai* are almost completely absent. But what is really important is that vessels are only part of a large production of colourless glass items. At that time, in the third quarter of the fourth century BC, the Macedonians were playing board games with both colourless and coloured game counters. The ladies wore colourless glass rings. Men and women used seals made of colourless glass bearing intaglio representations of gods. And wooden couches used in banquets were decorated with colourless glass inlays forming sophisticated compositions and placed over gold foil. Many of these couches supported the bodies of their dead owners during cremation or within graves. The wood has disappeared but their decoration has survived and we are fortunate to have the

Table 39.1 Findspots of colourless glass vessels of the Achaemenid period

Colourless glass vessels of the Achaemenid period: 110 of known provenance: 87	
Greece	37
Asia Minor	24
Persia	10
Scythia	5
Colchis	2
Cyprus	2
Babylonia	2
Italy	2
Cyrenaica	1
Germany	1
Israel	1

Table 39.2 The three major regional groups of colourless glass vessels of the Achaemenid period

Colourless glass vessels of the Achaemenid period			
Greece (Late classical period)	37	Macedonia	19
		Rhodes	14
		Thrace	1
		Attica	1
		Arcadia	1
		Aetolia	1
Asia Minor	24	Caria	12
		Phrygia	6
		Black Sea	2
		Ionia	1
		unprovenanced	3
Persia	10	Persepolis	10

remains from almost 100 pieces of furniture. I have no doubt that this is a local production, especially as it is concentrated over one generation and within the area of central Macedonia. It is well situated in the frame of artistic production of the area. Shapes and decoration have parallels in other materials. It does not appear anywhere else in Greece, or indeed anywhere else. As a matter of fact it is a unique phenomenon for the classical period and can only be compared to the peak of the Assyrian production of colourless glass of the eighth–seventh century BC (Ignatiadou 2001; 2002).

The distribution of the Anatolian finds is also instructive. Some 21 of the 24 finds have an exact provenance. Caria leads with 12, mainly from Halicarnassus (Ignatiadou 2004). The other finds are from Mylasa (Erten Yağci 1995) and Caunus (Roos 1972: pl. 62:1, 10; 1974: 17–18, no. 40, pls 3, 14). Then comes Phrygia with six vessels published from Gordion, and more are soon to be published by Janet Jones (von Saldern 1959; Jones 2005). The southern Pontic coast is represented by two vessels from Amisos (Akkaya 1997). Strangely, Ionia has only yielded a single find, namely the Ephesus bowl discussed above. I would expect many more, but I think this is due to the fact that the Ionian cities were excavated at a time when small finds were considered rather unimportant and therefore probably not retained. However, there is still hope of discovering fragments in old boxes. It is also a pity that classical layers of Ionian cities are not currently excavated.

Among the finds from the burial chamber of Maussollos in the Mausoleum at Halicarnassus were the remains of eight colourless glass vessels. They can be considered typically Achaemenid in shape and decoration. Two are tall calyx cups decorated with long petals. One is probably a bowl. Four are beakers decorated with horizontal grooves. Their bottoms do not survive, so we do not know whether they were plain or ended in animal-heads. I suspect this at least for the smallest one, which is too narrow for a beaker. One grooved vessel has very thick walls and its diameter is large to be a beaker. It is identified as an animal-head *situla*, since fragments were also found that curve irregularly and these seem to belong to a ram's head. The vessels were probably made in western Anatolia and their composition is identical to that of the glass found on both sides of the Aegean. We can be sure that they were grave goods in the burial of Maussollos who died in 353/352 BC so this is our new *terminus ante quem* and the earliest secure terminus we can establish today (Ignatiadou 2004).

All the colourless glass vessels that exist today have been attributed to a vaguely unified Achaemenid glass production. I believe the finds from Greece and the Greek colonies, or areas influenced by Greek aesthetics, form a distinct sub-group.

I prefer to call this group Ionian rather than Achaemenid although this may be a little unjust to the neighbouring satrapies of Lydia, Phrygia and Caria, which are also possible candidates for the beginning of the production. The formation of the International Achaemenid Style owed much to the contribution of the satrapies. Although the lotus decoration is an inheritance from earlier periods and neighbouring Egypt, *omphaloi* and almonds have their roots in Phrygia, the rosette in central Anatolia and the grooves in Lydia or Phrygia (Melikian-Chirvani 1993). However, I believe we can see the Ionian element in the shapes of the vessels. Although some popular shapes, like the bowls, did not originate in Ionia, their evolution betrays the influence of the Ionian artistic environment. We must not consider these vessels as purely Achaemenid, as the cultural character of Ionia is clearly distinct from that of other areas of the empire. My attribution to Ionian workshops is not based on geographical provenance but on the importance of cultural influences.

The first scholar to suggest an Ionian origin for some so-called Achaemenid vessels was Byvanck-Quarles van Ufford (1970: 133; 1991), only to be ignored by most other researchers. In 1989 Grose, who always managed to say so much in a few words, wrote on the colourless glass vessels: "within the Mediterranean their distribution coincides with the Macedonian and Greek commercial spheres, which makes it difficult to determine whether these table wares were made in the Persian heartland or in one of the western Persian satrapies, or even in a Greek community outside the empire", and he concluded that the glass *phiale* in the Toledo Museum of Art "may be the product of an early Hellenistic glass industry operating in the eastern Mediterranean, rather than a true Achaemenid vessel manufactured in Persia" (Grose 1989: 81).

To conclude, what we know today about the production of colourless glass vessels in the Achaemenid period is that:

- the finds are distributed mainly on both sides of the Aegean and the Black Sea coast;
- the differences in the larger local groups indicate the existence of several local workshops;
- there are no secure grounds to date the beginning of the production to the fifth century BC;
- most of the vessels have been found in contexts of the fourth century BC, the earliest secure one being that of the Maussolleion, just before the middle of the century;
- and as the numerous Macedonian finds are dated later than this, one of the west Achaemenid satrapies is the most probable candidate for the production of the first vessels.

Notes

1. British Museum, GR 1907.12-1.542. Fossing 1937: fig. 1; 1940: 83–84, fig. 54; Barag 1985: 68–69, fig. 4, pl. 5, with an extended bibliography; Pfrommer 1987: 7, Anm. 389, 540.
2. They are mainly deep *phialai* or wide handleless *skyphoi*: **1.** Museum für Kunst und Gewerbe, Hamburg, inv. no. 1973.103 (von Saldern 1975: 37–38, figs 1–2; 1995: 66, no. 1, dated to the end of the fifth–beginning of the fourth century BC). **2.** Kunstmuseum, Düsseldorf, inv. no. P. 1973.12 (von Saldern 1975: 38, figs 3–4, dated to the end of the fifth–beginning of the fourth century BC). **3.** Hermitage Museum, inv. no. E 529, received in 1894 from the Academy of Sciences (Oliver Jr 1970: 12–13, fig. 8; von Saldern 1975: 39; also Kunina 1970: 255–256, no. 47, ill. 27, dated to the end of the fifth–beginning of the fourth century BC). **4.** Metropolitan Museum of Art, inv. no. 69.11.6 (Oliver Jr 1970: 9–10, figs 1–2).
3. All ancient Greek and Latin sources on glass can be found in Trowbridge 1930. All excerpts from ancient passages included in this text are from Musaios 1.0d-32, 1992–1995.
4. Trowbridge 1930: 22. The word appears first in a poem of the sixth century BC by Corinna: (Phrynichus, *Eclogae*, 280,3: καὶ Κόριννα τὸν ὑάλινον πόδα θήσεις).
5. Aetius, *De placitis reliquiae*, 349, 21–22: Φιλόλαοσ ὁ Πυθαγόρειος ὑαλοειδῆ τὸν ἥλιον; Aetius, *De placitis reliquiae*, 356, 21–22: Ἴων σῶμα τῇ μὲν ὑαλοειδὲς διαυγές, τῇ δ' ἀφεγγές.
6. Heron, *Definitiones*, 135,10,7–10: φέρεσθαι γὰρ πᾶν φῶς κατ' εὐθείας γραμμὰς ὅσα δὲ διαφαίνεται δι' ὑέλων ἢ ὑμένων ἢ ὕδατος, κατὰ κεκλασμένας, τὰ δὲ φαινόμενα ἐν τοῖς κατοπτρίζουσι κατὰ ἀνακλωμένας [γωνίασ].
7. Hippocrates, *Coa praesagia*, 146, 2–3: οὔρου πυώδεος καὶ ὑαλώδεος; Pollux, *Onomasticon*, 2,70,3: τὰ μέρη δὲ τῶν ὀφθαλμῶν χιτῶνας ἐκάλεσαν οἱ ἰατροί...τῷ δὲ τρίτῳ φακοειδεῖ καὶ κρυσταλλοειδεῖ καὶ ὑαλοειδεῖ.
8. Aristophanes, *Nubes*, 766–768: St. ἤδη παρὰ τοῖσι φαρμακοπώλαις τὴν λίθον ταύτην ἑόρακας, τὴν καλήν, τὴν διαφανῆ, ἀφ' ἧς τὸ πῦρ ἅπτουσι; Σω. τὴν ὕαλον λέγεις.
9. Herodotus, *Historiae*, 3, 24, 1–7: τελευταίας ἐθεήσαντο τὰς θήκας αὐτῶν, αἳ λέγονται σκευάζεσθαι ἐξ ὑάλου...ἔπειτα δέ οἱ περιστᾶσι στήλην ἐξ ὑάλου πεποιημένην κοίλην (ἡ δέ σφι πολλὴ καὶ εὐεργὸς ὀρύσσεται).
10. Diodorus Siculus, *Bibliotheca Historica*, 2,15,1.2–2.1: ταριχεύσαντες γὰρ τὰ σώματα καὶ περιχέαντες αὐτοῖς πολλὴν ὕελον ἱστᾶσιν ἐπὶ στήλης, ὥστε τοῖς παριοῦσι φαίνεσθαι διὰ τῆς ὑέλου τὸ τοῦ τετελευτηκότος σῶμα, καθάπερ Ἡρόδοτος εἴρηκε.
11. During the same period other relevant terms are also used, like *krystallos* (meaning "ice", for rock crystal or glass) and *lithos* (meaning "stone", for rock crystal and gems). The other two terms for

glass are *kyanos* (meaning "blue") and *lithos chyte* (meaning "poured stone"). The former is earlier and is used for lapis lazuli and its substitute blue glass.

12. Pausanias describes a painting of the fourth century BC by Pausias in the Tholos of Epidaurus. Methe (Drunkenness) was depicted as a woman drinking from a cup, which was so transparent that one could see her face through the glass (Pausanias, *Graeciae descriptio*, 2, 27, 3, 5–8: γέγραπται δὲ ἐνταῦθα καὶ Μέθη, Παυσίου καὶ τοῦτο ἔργον, ἐξ ὑαλίνης φιάλης πίνουσα ἴδοις δὲ κἂν ἐν τῇ ῥαφῇ φιάλην τε ὑάλου καὶ δι' αὐτῆς γυναικὸς πρόσωπον). To Pausanias, in the second century AD, the word *hyalos* did mean glass; he was familiar with glass vessels that were widely produced and called *hyalina*. This does not necessarily mean that the much older painting depicted a vessel made of glass and not crystal (Stern 1999: 42, fig. 21).

13. In antiquity, glass and rock crystal are both perceived as transparent materials, but differing in other aspects; glass is soft and warm, crystal is hard, cold and clearer. Galenus, the physician of the second century AD, when describing the tunics of the eye clearly states that doctors call "glass like" the softer tunic and "crystal like" the harder one, due to their respective resemblance to glass and crystal: Galenus, *De placitis Hippocratis et Platonis*, 7, 5, 26.1–27.6: εὑρήσεις γὰρ ὑπὸ τοῖς χιτῶσιν ἔνδον ὑγρὰ σφαιροειδῆ διττά, τὸ μὲν οὕτω μαλακὸν οἷαπέρ ἐστιν ὕαλος ἡ μετρίως λυθεῖσα, τὸ δ' οὕτω σκληρὸν οἷος ὁ μετρίως παγεὶς κρύσταλλος. ὀνομάζεται δ' ὑπὸ τῶν ἰατρῶν ὑαλοειδὲς μὲν τὸ μαλακώτερον, κρυσταλλοειδές– δὲ τὸ σκληρότερον ἀπὸ τῆς πρὸς ὕαλόν τε καὶ κρύσταλλον ὁμοιότητος, οἷς οὐ νον ταῖς συστάσεσιν, ἀλλὰ καὶ ταῖς χροιαῖς ἔοικεν ἀκριβῶς γάρ ἐστι καθαρὰ καὶ διαυγῆ καὶ λαμπρά. Other similar passages in Trowbridge 1930: n. 55.

14. The term *lithos chyte* also appears in Herodotus describing crocodiles adorned with gold and blue glass in Egypt, cf. Herodotus, *Historiae*, 2, 69, 5–7: Ἐκ πάντων δὲ ἕνα ἑκάτεροι τρέφουσι κροκόδειλον, δεδιδαγμένον εἶναι χειροήθεα, ἀρτήματά τε λίθινα χυτὰ καὶ χρύσεα ἐς τὰ ὦτα ἐνθέντες. Glass produced in Egypt was almost exclusively coloured and we can therefore be sure that *lithos chyte* in this case means coloured glass. Egyptian terminology is similar. There has never existed an Egyptian word for glass, where it was instead called "poured turquoise" (poured lapis lazuli), or "poured stone" (Schlick-Nolte 2001: 30).

40

Documentary Aspects of Persepolis and the Oxus Treasure (Abstract)

Shapur Shahbazi

Ever since its accidental discovery in 1877, the Oxus Treasure has remained one of the most informative sources for our understanding of Achaemenid art. No doubt the 180 items recovered on the banks of the Bactros (Balkh) constitute only a portion of a treasure that once adorned a shrine, perhaps the famous Temple of Anahita in Bactria, but they provide us with documentary aspects of Iranian life and culture to a degree unmatched except by the Persepolitan bas-reliefs. Both Persepolis and the Oxus Treasure illustrate in the "royal style" of art various Iranian costumes, masterpieces of metalwork and jewellery, and offer clear evidence of Iranian beliefs and rituals. What is represented on stone at Persepolis is seen in gold and silver plaques and jewellery of the Oxus Treasure. The most valuable items of the latter are the representation of the *barsom*-holding priests (Magi) in "Median" costume, the figure of an eagle with outstretched wings (symbolizing royal power and armed forces), an ornamented gold sheath for the Persian short sword (the *akinakes*), and a pair of torques. All of these have parallels at Persepolis. Together, they have enabled scholars to evaluate other objects from sites in Bulgaria, Syria, Palestine, Egypt, Siberia and India, and attribute them to the Persian period. They have provided us with tools to document certain aspects of Zoroastrian traditions, Iranian military equipment and the best evidence to date for "royal art", which was the zenith of Ancient Near Eastern art directed and patronized by Achaemenid Persia.

Apart from the well-known objects of the Oxus Treasure and Persepolitan reliefs, I shall illustrate some Persepolitan bowls, torques, bricks and stone which have not been sufficiently studied before, and which go a long way to furthering our understanding of the documentary aspects of the two mutually complementing sources: Persepolis and the Treasure of the Oxus.

41

Achaemenid Silver, T. L. Jacks and the Mazanderan Connection

St J. Simpson, M. R. Cowell and S. La Niece

Introduction

In 1935 the third in a series of international blockbuster exhibitions on Persian Art opened at the State Hermitage in St Petersburg. It is claimed to have had a staggering total of 25,000 objects displayed in 84 rooms of the Hermitage and included "an entire gallery ... given to Achaemenid art, the most complete and well balanced to be seen anywhere today, particularly notable for the sumptuous silver and gold vessels that give an idea of the opulence of the great kings" (Pope 1935, quoted by Gluck & Siver 1996: 290). Among these were two silver lobed bowls and a gilt-silver rhyton in the form of a bridled horse head. These are said to have been discovered in Mazanderan province of northern Iran, and were part of an important but since dispersed collection of Iranian antiquities then belonging to Mr Thomas Lavington Jacks (1884–1966). The rhyton was acquired by the Metropolitan Museum of Art at the end of the Second World War, but the two silver bowls passed through different private collections until they were separately acquired by the British Museum in 1997 and 2006 and are currently displayed together in the new Rahim Irvani gallery for Ancient Iran. This is the first detailed publication of these two objects, and includes new compositional analyses and a detailed examination of their manufacturing techniques. It also offers an opportunity to discuss their previous history and the evidence for their alleged provenance of Mazanderan.

T. L. Jacks

Jacks was an important figure in early twentieth-century Anglo-Iranian business relations (Fig. 41.1). Born on 19th November 1884, the son of Richard H. Jacks, a bank manager with Capital and Courier Bank in Melksham, he was educated at Trowbridge and at Wellingborough Grammar School where he boarded from January 1899 to August 1901. He does not appear to have flourished either academically or at sports at Wellingborough and he appeared low on the list of results in the December 1900 examinations.[1] In October 1909, aged 25, Jacks joined the Anglo-Persian Oil Company (APOC) as an Oil Assistant in Muhammara (Fig. 41.2). His first year evidently was a difficult one. A Company appraisal in

Fig. 41.1 Thomas Lavington Jacks (1884–1966). (© BP; reproduced by permission)

Fig. 41.2 T. L. Jacks (right) with John D. Black (standing), C. A. Walpole (left) and N. Ramsay (centre). (© BP; reproduced by permission)

January 1910 stated that he "is very green", followed in September by a statement "replace Jacks"; yet by July 1911 it was recommended "that Mr Jacks be retained until, at least we can assure you that he is incapable of rising" (BP Archive, BP 67702).

This trust was repaid in full. Ferrier's (1982: 592) history of BP describes him as "Confident and competent, well groomed and an accomplished polo player, he emerged after the war as a strong personality". Ten years later Jacks was promoted to Assistant Manager (1917–1920), later rising to Joint General Manager responsible for refining operations and based at Abadan (1923–1925), with J. A. Jameson, stationed at Masjid-e Sulaiman, being responsible for the oil fields and Arnold Wilson being responsible as Managing Director charged with liaison with Government and the APOC Board of Directors (Fig. 41.3). In 1925 Jacks overhauled the administration of the Company's operations in Iran and in the same year was awarded a CBE on the king's birthday, 3rd June (*Supplement to The London Gazette* no. 33053, 3rd June 1925: 3778).

Wilson left Iran in 1926 following his appointment as Managing Director of the D'Arcy Exploration Company, a subsidiary of the APOC. Wilson had "got on well enough with Jameson, who was much the same temperament as A.T., and who, in his office at Mesjid-e-Suleiman, was at a considerable distance from A.T.'s masterful eyebrows and dominating aura. He got on less well with Jacks, next door to him in Abadan, and a man less after A.T.'s own heart than the robust and rumbustious Jameson" (Marlowe 1967: 264).

Jacks "was impressive in appearance and cut a dashing figure in the Persian capital with his attractive wife [Elsie Sheridan Stevens] and his hospitality. He soon enjoyed a favourable social reputation among both the members of the foreign colony and Persians" (Ferrier 1982: 596). It was against this background that Jacks developed his collection in Tehran during the late 1920s and early 1930s. This was a period of a booming local antiquities market following the development of the agricultural, housing and transport infrastructure, and stimulated by the creation of new patronage in Tehran and abroad. The collection appears to have been carefully selected and spanned the third millennium to the Safavid period. It included a mid-/late third millennium spouted bronze vessel of western Iranian type,[3] a mace-head of similar date,[4] several canonical "Luristan bronzes",[5] two Achaemenid silver bowls and a horse-head rhyton (discussed below), Sasanian stamp seals,[6] Early Islamic and Seljuk glazed wares,[7] Islamic metalwork,[8] and Safavid silks.[9] This collection was clearly well known to Pope who referred to two pieces in his *Introduction to Persian Art* (1930: 66, 85) which was published in 1930, but whether Pope himself played a role in its formation, either directly or as a middleman, is uncertain (cf. Muscarella 2000: 9; Gluck & Siver 1996: 18, 258).

Fig. 41.3 T. L. Jacks as Chairman with Mr J. A. Jameson crossing the Zuhreh river by ropeway in 1926. (Naft, November 1928, 15; reproduced by permission of BP)

Jacks was promptly promoted to the newly created post of Company Resident Director in Tehran, a position which he enjoyed until he retired (Fig. 41.4). The purpose of this post was to facilitate closer dialogue between the Company and the Persian government, a role which Jacks evidently succeeded in fulfilling. He played an influential role in the protracted negotiations for a new convention to replace the lucrative D'Arcy Concession which the Persian Government had cancelled unilaterally in November 1932; and he continued to reform management within the Company (*Who was Who* 1972: 586; Ferrier 1982; Bamberg 1994; Longhurst 1959: 78).[2]

During 1930 Jacks became closely involved with his former colleague Arnold Wilson, chairman of the organizing committee, in helping facilitate the highly influential Second Exhibition on Persian Art in London which was opened by King George V at Burlington House on 7th January 1931.[10] Indeed it was through Jacks that the entire transportation costs of the Iranian loaned material were financed by the APOC.[11] Jacks personally loaned 13 objects to this exhibition. These included six Luristan bronzes, which were

Fig. 41.4 T. L. Jacks (centre right) as Resident Director with His Royal Highness the Crown Prince of Persia (centre), Honorary President of the Red Lion and Sun Society, at the presentation ceremony of a travelling dispensary by the Anglo-Persian Oil Company, the Gulistan Palace, Tehran, Saturday 25th February 1928. The group consists of (left to right): Colonel Buzarjumihri, Acting Director of Tehran Municipality; Mr Uvaisi, member of the Committee of the Red Lion and Sun Society; Mr L. Lockhart; Mr Ahi, member of the Committee of the Red Lion and Sun Society; Mostafa Khan Fateh; H. E. Mumtaz ed Dowleh; Mr R. E. Balfour; Dr Amir Khan A'lam, His Majesty's Physician; HRH the Crown Prince of Persia; Mr T. L. Jacks; H.E. Pahlov-Nejad, Lord Chamberlain to HRH the Crown Prince; Mr F. S. Greenhouse; Dr Hakim ed Dowleh; Colonel Ala-Mir. (Naft, May 1928, 5; reproduced by permission of BP)

among the first publicly exhibited finds from this region as the Luristan cemeteries had only been discovered in 1928 (Muscarella 1988: 34) and none were by this stage displayed as such in museums such as the British Museum. Jacks' other loaned pieces consisted of Safavid silks, but noteworthy by their absence are the two Achaemenid silver bowls and rhyton which Jacks subsequently included in a loan to the Third Exhibition on Persian Art which opened in St Petersburg on 12th September 1935 (Pope 1935: 30).[12]

The reason for this is uncertain but may reflect their acquisition by Jacks between 1930 and 1935 when they were exhibited in the Persian Art exhibition at the Hermitage and during which year he took early retirement, resigning from the Board of Directors of the Anglo-Persian Oil Company on 8th May of that year. Jacks returned to England to live at Meadow Lake, Sandown Avenue, in the pleasant Surrey village of Esher, but continued to play an active role in the East India and Sports Club at 16 St James' Square, London

SW1. Founded in 1849 and originally composed of the East India, Devonshire, Sports, and Public Schools Clubs, this underwent several changes of name during the 1920s until it finally assumed its present name. As with other expatriates lacking a London home, Jacks presumably used this club as a base. The members were from "the Armed Forces, civil servants, and businessmen, mostly with an Asiatic background or with interests in India or the Middle or Far East. They were, on the whole perhaps, a conventional, conservative, slightly philistine body of men, intent on the preservation of British imperial interests, and accustomed to look on the British Establishment with a sort of impotent contempt from the outside" (Marlowe 1967: 287; cf. also Nevill 1969: 254–55; Forrest 1982).[13] Jacks died on 13th December 1966 in a nursing home at 36 Abbey Road, Chertsey and was buried six days later in Plot 132 at Long Ditton Lawn Cemetery near Kingston upon Thames, bequeathing his considerable savings to his wife (who died in the same year), Walter Cyril Jacks, his surviving brother (of Warren End Cottage, Crowborough), George Browne, his housekeeper and chef, Alfred Bartlett, his butler, and his club.[14]

Achaemenid silverwares from the Jacks collection

It appears that Jacks had disposed of at least part of his collection at the time of his retirement some 25 years before his death, and the three Achaemenid silver objects therefore have slightly different histories.

By 1940 the first of the two bowls (henceforth Bowl A) under discussion here entered the collection of the prominent collector and dealer Joseph Brummer, thus was exhibited under Brummer's name at the Fourth Exhibition of Persian Art which was held at the Iranian Institute in New York that year (Ackerman 1940: 317 = case 31A). Brummer had trained as a sculptor under Rodin and maintained a passion for ancient sculptures and *objets vertu* until his death in 1947 (anon. [*c*.1943]: 16; Parke-Bernet Galleries 1949: vol. II, 30, no. 127). His collection was subsequently privately offered to selected museums and individuals, followed by a public auction in 1949; a large portion was then acquired by the Metropolitan Museum of Art as part of its drive to expand its collections after the Second World War (Hoving 1975: 118; Tomkins 1970: 316). This bowl remained unsold in the 1949 auction but was bought in by Joseph Brummer's younger brother Ernest (1891–1964) who had jointly run the Brummer Galleries in Paris (opened 1906) and New York (opened 1914). Ernest Brummer died in 1964 and a portion of his collection, including this bowl, was auctioned in London that year (Sotheby's 1964); the remaining nucleus was finally dispersed by his widow Ella Brummer through auction in Zurich in October 1979 (Galerie Koller 1979). The present bowl was included in the earlier of these two sales and was sold for £3,000 (Sotheby's 1964: 68–69, lot 165). It subsequently entered the private collection of Amschel Rothschild. Following his premature death in July 1996, it was acquired by the British Museum in 1998 as a private treaty sale organized through Christie's and purchased with the generous assistance of the Art Fund, the British Museum Friends and the Friends of the Ancient Near East (Fig. 41.5).[15]

In 2006 the British Museum acquired the second lobed bowl (Bowl B), again with the generous support of the Art Fund, the British Museum Friends and the Friends of the Ancient Near East (Fig. 41.6). Since

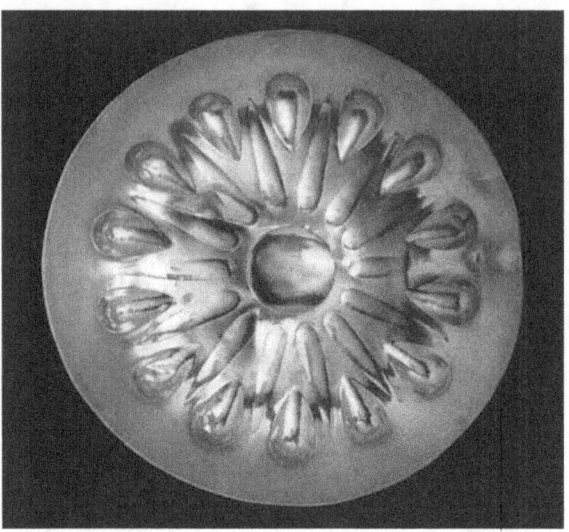

Fig. 41.5 Top view of silver Bowl A (British Museum 1998, 0117.1).

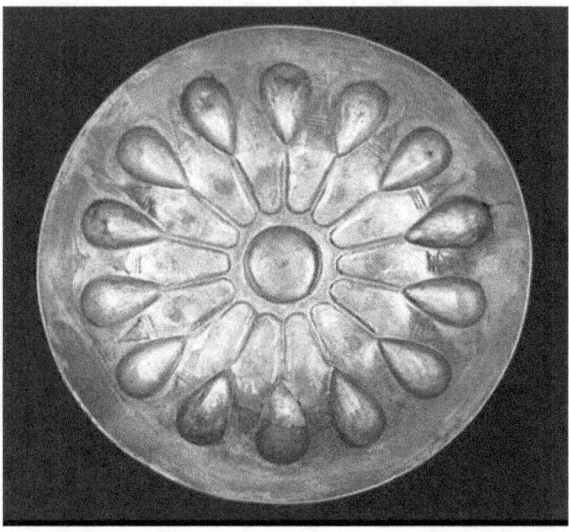

Fig. 41.6 Top view of silver bowl B (British Museum 2006, 0706.1).

being part of the Jacks collection this bowl had entered the ownership of Pope, who was the first to illustrate it (Pope 1938: vol. I, 371, vol. IV, pl. 120A). It was subsequently listed by Luschey in his corpus of Achaemenid *phialai* (1939: 41–42, no. 9a), mentioned in *Parnassus* (February 1940: 34), and exhibited in 1940 at Johns Hopkins University in Baltimore and the Fourth Exhibition of Persian Art in the Iranian Institute in New York, by which time it had entered the collection of Joseph Brummer (Ackerman 1940: 317 = case 31B). Following Brummer's death it was sold at auction for US$1,052 in 1949 (Parke-Bernet Galleries 1949: vol. II, 30, no. 127). It was later republished by Amandry (1956: 12, n. 2) when it was exhibited at the Exhibition of Persian Art in Rome the same year and recorded as being in the collection of Fahim Kouchakji (Rome 1956: 138); it remained in private ownership until it was offered to the British Museum as a private treaty sale through Christie's in 2005 (Simpson & La Niece 2006).

In addition to these two fine bowls, Jacks also possessed a gilt silver rhyton in the form of a bridled horse's head decorated below the rim with a row of birds. This was likewise said to be from Mazanderan (Pope 1935, 1938: vol. I, 355, vol. IV, pls 110A–B). Details of the harness, notably the bar-shaped cheek pieces ending in horses' hooves and "boars' tusk" fittings on the strap crossings, closely resemble those depicted on Apadana reliefs at Persepolis and this object has periodically been illustrated in discussions of Achaemenid art (Wilkinson 1949; Svoboda 1956: 36, fig. 9; Schmandt-Besserat ed. 1978: 81, no. 101; Muscarella 1980: 30, pl. X: fig. 6; Moorey 1985: 26, 30; Pfrommer 1993: 67, n. 815). This rhyton was exhibited at the Hermitage in 1935, and again sold by Jacks to Joseph Brummer (Ackerman 1940: 322), from whom it was later acquired by the Metropolitan Museum of Art (MMA 47.100.87, Rogers Fund, 1945), listed by Muscarella (1980) as a classic piece of Achaemenid craftsmanship and, like the two bowls, is unquestionably genuine.[16]

Scientific examination of the two silver bowls in the British Museum

Bowl A (1998,0117.1) is shallow with a plain rim, low omphalos and 14 embossed tear-shaped lobes, between each of which was engraved a plain elongated petal (Fig. 41.7). The vessel measures 30.7 cm across, 4 cm high, weighs 952 grams and has a filled capacity of 1.92 litres. It was formed through hammering a single sheet which measures 2 mm in thickness at the edges. There are centring marks on the interior and exterior, and there are two lightly scratched letters in the centre of the omphalos on the underside.

Bowl B (2006,0706.1) has a similar form to the first, measures 26.7–27.1 cm across, 3.0 cm high, weighs 669.5 grams and is decorated with 14 radiating lotus stamens with the petals chased on the underside (Fig. 41.8). It has a filled capacity of 1.35 litres. It was again formed through hammering a single piece of sheet which measures 2 mm in thickness at the edges. There are centring marks on the interior and exterior, and there is a deeply scored mark resembling a noughts and crosses grid across the centre of the omphalos on the underside (Fig. 41.9).

Richter (1950) proposed that lobed *phialai* were made by hammering into a matrix or by casting, possibly in clay moulds, and the late P. R. S. Moorey (1980: 30) cites an unpublished clay mould of this type which was found in Iraq. Punches with tear-shaped ends were sometimes used to create lobes of precisely the same shape and size, and an actual punch of this type was reportedly found at Ikiztepe in Lydia (Özgen & Öztürk *et al.* 1996: 61, 229, no. 219). However, in the present cases, radiographic examinations carried out in the Department of Conservation & Scientific Research at the British Museum confirm manufacture by hammering, namely by raising and sinking (repoussé). This was a typical technique for other similar Achaemenid silverware. The thickness of the body of the bowls shows concentric changes, with the centre portion—approximately defined by the centre circle of the design—being thinnest. The thickness gradually increases outwards, to the start of the deeply lobed design, and then decreases somewhat to the outside edge of the lobes. The edges of both bowls are further thickened. The lobes themselves are much thinner than the adjacent body areas which is consistent with the heavy working and stretching required in forming these (Fig. 41.10). There is no evidence for ancient repairs or joins, although there is a modern silver patch repair to one of the lobes on Bowl B with a composition close to that of the modern sterling standard of 92.5 per cent silver. The visual appearance of fracture surfaces at a point where there was maximum working is typical of the effects of embrittlement in ancient silver (Wanhill 2003). Residual hammer marks are clearly visible on the deep lobes of the design on the upper surface of Bowl A. There is damage to the vessel, with some deep dents near one edge and a fracture in one of the lobes. The underside, particularly on the raised areas of the lobes, shows a slightly granular structure which may be due to re-crystallization at points of maximum stress. The edges of the fracture in the lobe are also very granular and consistent with embrittlement effects on ancient silver. Although centring marks have been interpreted elsewhere as evidence for turning (e.g. Armbruster, this volume), in the present case it seems that they were related to the marking out of the design.

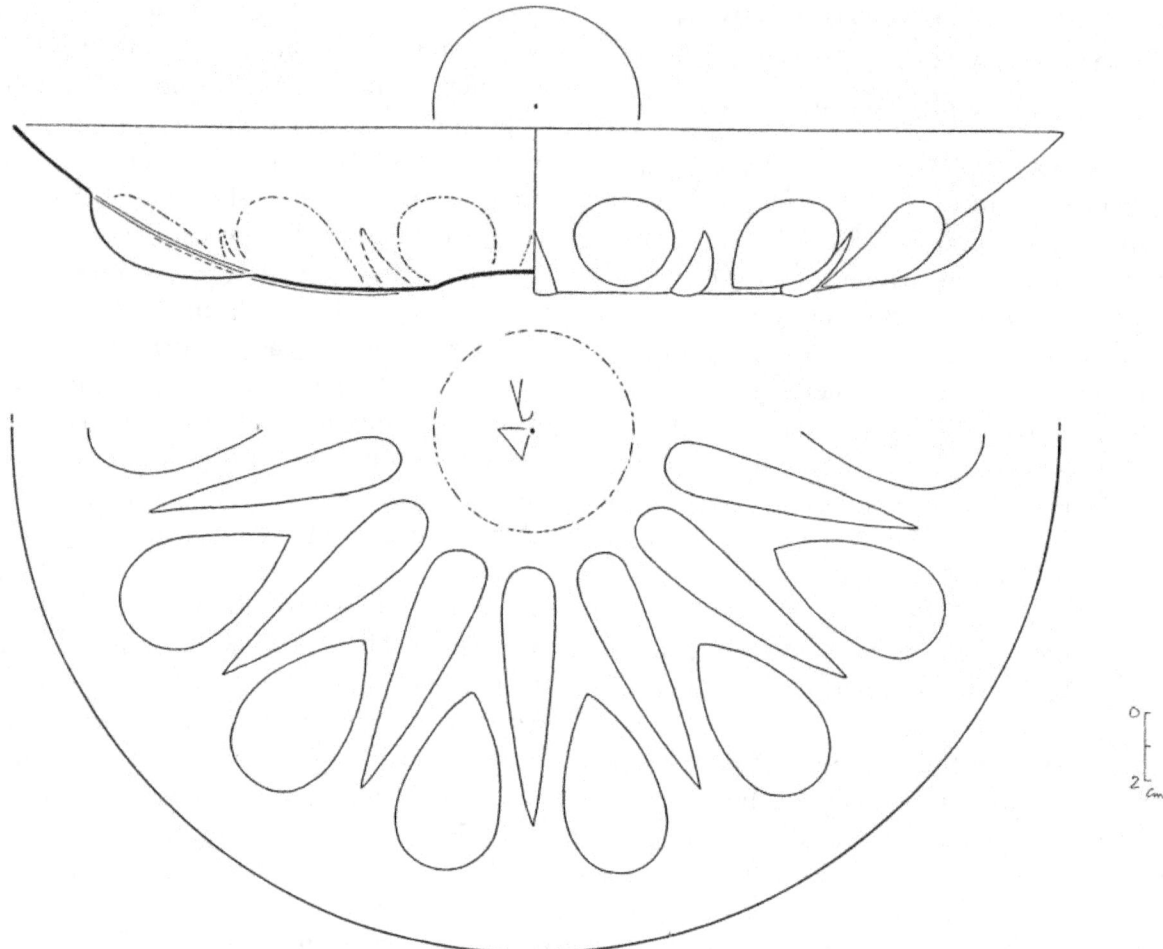

Fig. 41.7 Profile and underside of Bowl A (1998,0117.1). (Drawing by Ann Searight)

The lobes and flutes of the design have been carefully outlined by chasing.

There are features, particularly on the underside and rim of Bowl A, which are consistent with corrosion attack. The apparent preferential attack on the underside suggests that it may possibly have been buried face down or at least that the upper surface was protected in some way. Moreover, closer examination of the corrosion patterns on the underside suggest that the centre may have been shielded by another object measuring some 23–25 cm across as the outer lobes were consistently damaged and the corrosion appears to be heavier around the rim. However, all the bowl surfaces have been heavily cleaned since their original discovery, and there are no residues of any original corrosion.

Both bowls were analysed by X-ray fluorescence (XRF) on both sides. The analyses were carried out non-destructively, that is without surface preparation such as abrasion or cleaning, and since XRF is a surface method of analysis, the results must be regarded as approximate or semi-quantitative.

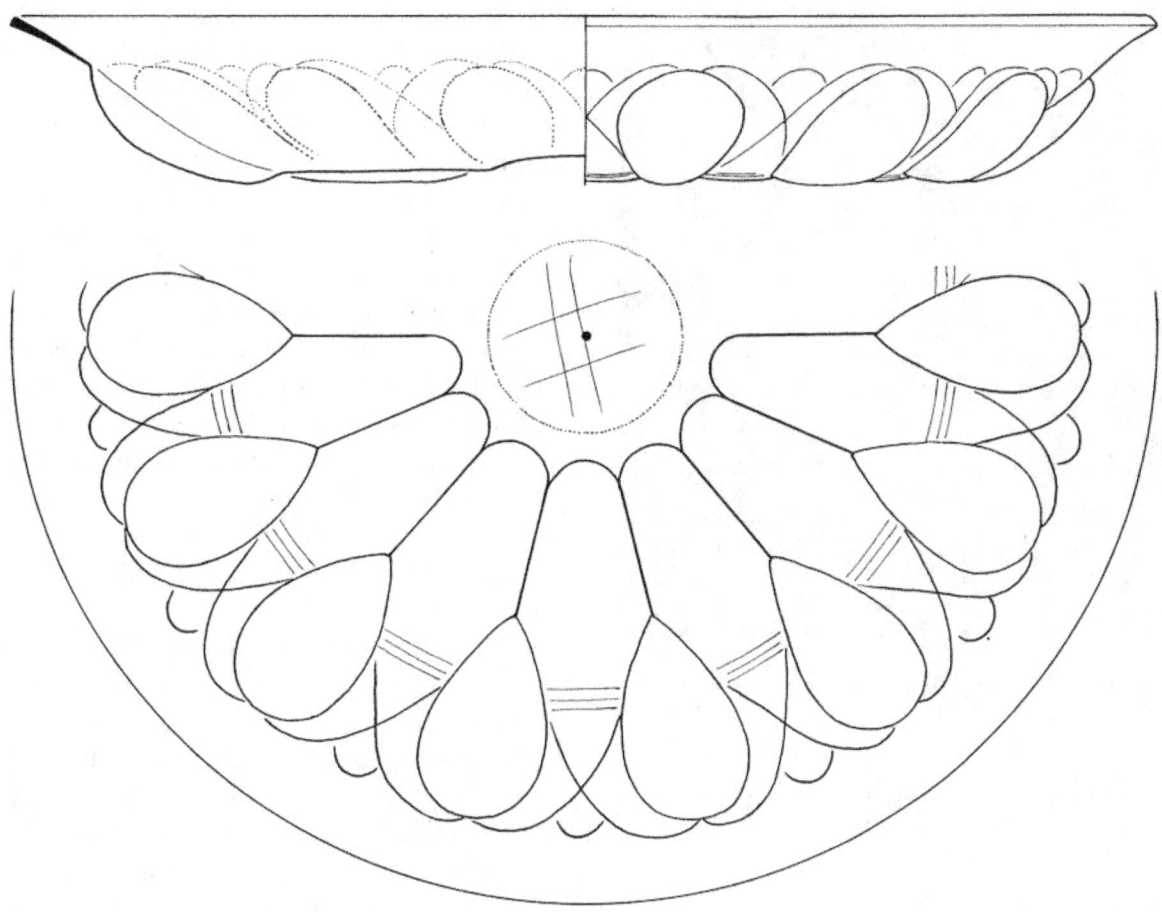

Fig. 41.8 Profile and underside of Bowl B (2006,0706.1). (Drawing by Ann Searight)

The compositions, an average of several similar analyses, are as follows:

	Bowl A	Bowl B
Silver	97–98%	97–98%
Copper	1.5–2%	1–2%
Gold	0.1–0.2%	0.3–0.4%
Lead	0.2–0.3%	0.2–0.3%

The precision or reproducibility of the XRF analysis is +1–2 per cent relative for silver and +5–20 per cent for copper, gold and lead. The accuracy cannot be clearly defined because the analysis was non-destructive and corrosion or surface enrichment effects may cause some systematic errors. There may be a small overestimation of the silver and gold and a corresponding underestimation of the copper. There is good agreement between the composition of this bowl (a high silver content with traces of gold and lead) and that of other Achaemenid silver published by Curtis, Cowell & Walker (1995), Gunter & Jett (1992) and Hughes (1984, 1986). However, it should be noted that the composition of Achaemenid silver is not specifically characteristic and that it is generally similar to most ancient silver in having traces of gold and lead (e.g. Strong 1979: 215–216). Hence the composition of

Fig. 41.9 Detail of scratched mark on the underside of Bowl B (2006,0706.1).

these bowls is consistent with Achaemenid silver.

Discussion and comparanda

Both bowls belong to the same general class of shallow lobed bowls or *phialai*, yet they differ in detail. Bowl B belongs to a canonical type of Achaemenid shallow lobed bowl, exemplified by that bequeathed to the British Museum by A. W. Franks in 1897 and probably from the site of Altıntepe near Erzincan (Dalton 1964: 44, pl. XXIII, no. 180). This type is usually dated to about the fifth century BC although it may have continued slightly later. However, Bowl A may be slightly later, perhaps dating within the fourth century BC, as the restrained nature of the decoration is a more stylized form of the lobes. Similar elongated petals depicting a sunburst occur on the interior of a silver bowl found in a grave at Panderma which has been attributed a late fourth century date (Erdmann 1967: pl. 5B); the same motif recurs on the top of Philip of Macedon's gold burial larnax and three gold discs found in the Great Tomb at Vergina (Andronicos 1981: 26–27). This decoration becomes progressively more heavily stylized on later Seleucid and Parthian bowls (Gunter & Jett 1992: 80–82, no. 5).

A common feature of ancient silver is the presence of marks or inscriptions, usually regarded as designating ancient ownership. It is likely that such marks have been overlooked on other pieces, particularly where the bowls have been heavily cleaned or if the marks themselves were later deliberately effaced in antiquity. In the present case, both bowls have ancient marks deliberately scratched in the centre of the underside. In the case of Bowl A this consists of two signs, the first resembling a letter or the curly "Y" device found on Achaemenid coins (cf. Boardman 1998: 4). On Bowl B the mark more closely resembles a modern noughts and crosses grid. This is the first time this particular mark has been recorded on Achemenid silver but there is no doubt that it is ancient. Ancient graffiti, varying from one or two letters or a monogram to a full name, recur on the undersides of a number of vessels—particularly bowls—in the so-called Lydian Treasure which derives from a looted tomb at Ikiztepe (Özgen & Öztürk *et al*. 1996: 33, 93–94, 98, 103–106, nos 40–42, 46, 54, 56, 59–60). A Western Aramaic inscription was also scratched on the underside of an Achaemenid silver mesomphalic *phiale* decorated with a lotus-leaf design and in the British Museum (Shefton 1993: 180–181, 199: n.11, fig. 9 = BM 134879). However, it might be added that none of these bowls possess the miniature stamped control marks found on the four lobed bowls said to be from Hamadan and now divided between Tehran,

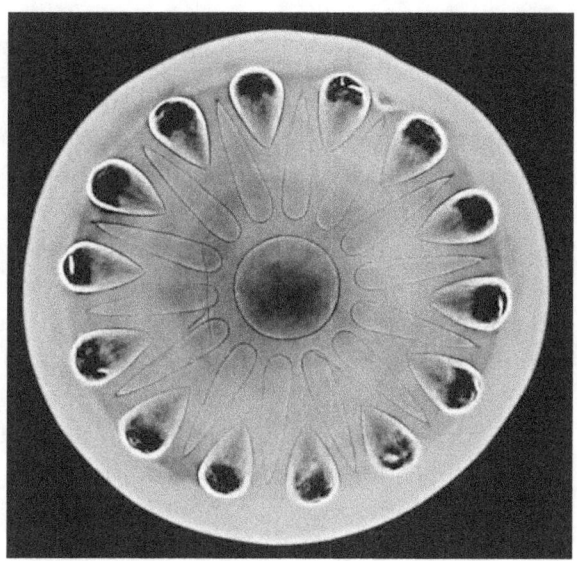

Fig. 41.10 Radiograph of Bowl A (1998,0117.1).

London, Washington and New York (cf. Curtis, Cowell & Walker 1995; Gunter & Root 1998: 13–15, fig. 2).

The addition of ownership marks—whether scratched or punched—is not surprising as silverwares were prized for aesthetic and prestige reasons. However, they were also valued for their high metal content and use as currency in financial transactions, either through the weight of the complete vessel or through subdivision by cutting off pieces suitable as "small change" (Zournatzi 2000). It is not surprising to therefore occasionally find hoards of Achaemenid silver, either in the form of complete vessels or a mixture of complete vessels, coins, ingots and vessel fragments (so-called *hacksilber*). Excavated findspots of such hoards include Babylon (Reade 1986*b*) and might be extended to include other groups of silver or gold plate such as the "Oxus Treasure" or the group of four silver bowls with inscriptions of Artaxerxes I (r. 465–425 BC) which have a combined weight of 600 *sigloi* at 5.44 g (Curtis, Cowell & Walker 1995; Gunter & Root 1998; cf. Vickers 1996: 55). There is a slowly growing body of metrological data for this period and the weight of Bowl A corresponds to 170 *sigloi* on an average of 5.6 g within the fifth century and later standard range of $c.5.40–5.67$ g (cf. Vickers 1991; Vickers & Gill 1994: 46–52).

The Mazanderan connection

Both bowls are said to have been discovered in Mazanderan province, which is located between Gilan and Gurgan. The physical geography of this region consists of a narrow but densely settled and cultivated plain sandwiched between dunes and marshes along the coast and densely forested mountains to the south. Mazanderan and Gurgan may have been grouped together as the Achaemenid province of Varkana but few archaeological sites of this period have been identified (Vogelsang 1992: 20–25). Further west, within Gilan province, illicit and archaeological discoveries demonstrate the existence of a distinctive local culture during the Early Iron Age of the late second and early first millennia BC. Most of these known sites consist of hillside cemeteries but a dense pattern of villages and other settlements is attested from the coastal plains. The local ceramic tradition suggests a conservative material culture employing handmade burnished wares which continue into the Parthian period and some of the ceramic forms are inspired by toreutic. The existence of a distinct Iron IV (Achaemenid period) material culture assemblage within Gilan is confirmed by many of the finds from the excavations at Ghalekuti by the Japanese Archaeological Mission to Dailaman (Haerinck 1989). Iranian excavations have confirmed Moorey's suggestion of a north-west Iranian provenance for a very distinctive type of pottery lamp found in the Achaemenid cemetery at Deve Huyuk (Moorey 1980: 24–26, fig. 5, nos 62–64). The recent discovery of a looted Achaemenid cemetery at Dashli Yar (Dowsaran), some 45 km north-west of Zanjan, with gold jewellery closely paralleled with that from Pasargadae, Susa and Akhalgori, suggests that there was a wealthy local clientele in Gilan at this period (Sarkhosh Curtis & Simpson 1998: 188–189).

The rapid development of loose or false provenances for objects appearing on the Iranian art market is a well-known problem. The use of "Hamadan", "Giyan", "Hissar", "Ziwiye", "Luristan", "Gilan", "Amlash", "Nishapur" and now "Jiroft" typically begin as descriptions for regionally or even chronologically distinctive groups of cultural material but soon become used to become convenient "catch all" phrases embracing objects from less fashionable regions or modern workshops (e.g. Muscarella 1977, 1980; Gunter & Root 1998). Nevertheless, regular finds of hoarded metalwork have been reported from Mazanderan since the late nineteenth century. In addition to the two bowls and rhyton discussed above, a third Achaemenid *phiale* on which "a horse in Sasanian style has been subsequently engraved on the interior" was also said to have been "found in Mazanderan, and now [is] in the Tehran market" (Pope 1938: vol. I, 370, n. 3). Finally, von Bothmer (1961: 10, pls 15, 101, no. 45) illustrates a circa second century BC inscribed Parthian gilt-silver bowl which was reportedly found in this region and was formerly in the collection of Herzfeld (cf. Strong 1979: 109). A number of Sasanian and later silver items have also reportedly been found here. As early as the 1890s a small metal hoard was apparently discovered which included a Late Sasanian gilt silver strainer-vase decorated with scenes of vintaging and which is said to have been found together with a plate showing a banqueting scene "in a copper vase in Mazanderan, Persia, in 1893" (Dalton 1964: 65; cf. Smirnov 1909: distribution map, nos 66, 86 = BM 124094 & 1963,1210.3). The commencement of construction of the Trans-Iranian Railway in 1927 which served east Mazanderan and Gurgan, as well as new roads to and along the coast and widespread clearance of forest in advance of cultivation, resulted in a number of other chance finds. A fifth–sixth century mirror-cover in the Muzeh Melli in Tehran was reportedly discovered in 1938 during construction of a road across the Elburz mountains between Kharaj and Chalus, and a silver plate in the same collection was reportedly found in Mazanderan prior to 1948 (Harper 2000: 52; cf. *Illustrated London News*, 21st August 1948, 215). In addition, a further six Sasanian silver bowls are reported as chance finds from this region, three of which were said to have been discovered by chance by the Tehran railway line near Sari in November 1954 (Vanden Berghe 1959: 7, pl. 7a–d). More recently, construction work near Sari led to the discovery of some 40 or more identical unpublished sheet bronze trough-spouted bowls, socketed spearheads, axeheads and adzes which had apparently been deposited together in a single hoard.[17]

Conclusions

The lack of information about the circumstances of discovery of the British Museum bowls prevent us from understanding more about their context although it is possible they derive from a hoard as lobed bowls have not yet been found in funerary contexts (where shouldered drinking bowls were a more popular form of grave-good). Nevertheless, object-based studies have independent value and in this case add to the small body of authenticated and scientifically researched Achaemenid silverware from Iran. This is an important point as much remains to be understood about regional variability in the crafts. Vessels are carried by as many as 10 of the 23 Delegations shown on the Apadana reliefs at Persepolis. Among these are amphorae with plain or fluted bodies and opposing plain or zoomorphic handles, one of which sometimes doubles as a short open spout. Pairs of horizontally fluted or plain beakers, and fluted or plain shouldered drinking-bowls are also shown, whereas attendants carry stemmed bowls covered with plain hemispherical lids or bowls, or pairs of plain hemispherical bowls, sometimes one placed over the other. Two canonical forms are curiously absent, however, namely the lobed bowls and rhyta. Thus depictions alone do not help us reconstruct the range of types in circulation. Much research has focused on silverwares from Anatolia and it will be instructive to re-examine in future the manufacturing techniques of pieces from other parts of the empire, and to develop a more comprehensive understanding of their metrology. Moreover, the function of these bowls is also unclear. The identical inscriptions on the four Artaxerxes silver lobed bowls refer to them being "saucers" or "wine-drinking vessels", and Phyllis Ackerman (1940: 317) once commented that they "were balanced on the palm of his hand, holding it with his fingers over the far edge, and lowering it to rest on his forearm...Wine in the hollows made dark pools against the lighter tones over the shallower surfaces"—yet these vessels are far from suited to drinking. Unlike the shouldered bowls which can be comfortably held with one hand and tipped to the mouth when filled as far as the carination, the lobed bowls scatter their contents uncontrollably when tipped in a similar manner. It is therefore much more likely that they doubled as easily stackable serving dishes and examples of conspicuous wealth. Not for nothing did Xenophon remark about the Persians that "If they possess a great number of cups, they are proud of possessing them" (*Cyropaedia* VIII.8,18).

Notes

1. We are grateful to Mr Neil Lyons, Honorary Secretary of the Old Wellingburian Club at The School, Wellingborough for this information.
2. We are indebted to Michael Gasson and Caroline Hughes at the BP Archive at the University of Warwick for their assistance in researching Jacks' career and for generously arranging for the photographs reproduced here. Our thanks also to Janet Wallace, former Archivist in the British Museum, and Joanna Bowring in the Central Library of the British Museum, for their help in investigating additional sources.
3. Royal Academy 1931*b*: 10, case 13L: not illustrated; Pope 1938: vol. IV, pl. 62A.
4. This was deposited in the Department of Oriental Antiquities (now Department of Asia) in the British Museum on 24th February 1953 and forwarded for opinion to the Department of Western Asiatic Antiquities (later Ancient Near East, now Department of the Middle East), where it was photographed and returned on 13th March that year (WAA deposit book entry 733, q.v. "Luristan bronze"); it was not acquired and both this and other pieces in the Jacks collection were dispersed on the market.
5. Royal Academy 1931*b*: 9, 15–17, 19, cases 13B, 13XX, 21B, 21N, 21CC: not illustrated; Pope 1938: vol. IV, pls 61D–E.
6. Pope 1938: vol. I, 790, 791: fig. 271d, 800: fig. 276b, 801, vol. IV, pls 256L, S, JJ, NN, 255NN.
7. Pope 1930: 66; 1938: vol. I, 678, vol. II, 1583, 1611–1612, 1618: n., 1630, vol. VI, pls 193A, 618B, 726B.
8. Pope 1938: vol. VI, pls 1283A–B, 1381. The tripod lamp-stand has been cited as a close parallel for a lamp-stand of Khurasan type in the Victoria & Albert Museum which has been attributed a tenth–twelfth century date (Melikian-Chirvani 1982: 53–54, n. 3 = inv. no. 1417–1903; cf. also Allan 1976: vol. II, 708, Lampstand A/2).

9. *ILN* 17.1.31, 88: lower left; Royal Academy 1931*b*: 171: case 301H; Pope 1938: vol. III, 2082: n. 2, 2113, 2125, 2200 n. 2, vol. VI, pls 1050A, 1076A, 1085.
10. E.g. Gluck & Siver 1996: 186. Further records of this exhibition unfortunately do not survive at the Royal Academy of Arts; for this information we are very grateful to Mark Pomeroy, Archivist at the Royal Academy.
11. Gluck & Siver 1996: 9; cf. Majd 2003: 44, 52, n. 37.
12. The first of these silver bowls is said to have been previously exhibited at the Hermitage as early as 1906 but this cannot be confirmed, and is more likely to be a conflation of the date of opening of the Brummer gallery in New York and the date of the exhibition in St Petersburg (cf. Parke-Bernet Galleries 1949: 30, no. 127).
13. A formal written enquiry to the club concerning Jacks did not yield any further information as all membership details are considered confidential. The club's published history does not record Jacks (Forrest 1982).
14. We are grateful to Marilyn Tickell of Elmbridge Borough Council for information relating to Jacks' burial. The grave plot was purchased by his executor Mr Henry Crawford Maclellan of 4b Fredericks' Place, Old Jewry, London EC2. An announcement of the funeral and a brief obituary appeared in *The Times* (15th December: 14g).
15. For preliminary announcements of this acquisition see Simpson 1998*a–b*, 1999.
16. Our thanks to Dr O. W. Muscarella for his comments on this piece.
17. These unpublished finds are currently held in Gorgan museum and we are very grateful to Mr Ghorban Ali Abassi for kindly showing these to one of the authors in May 2004.

Part 8

Regional Studies

42

Achaemenid Arabia: A Landscape-Oriented Model of Cultural Interaction

Björn Anderson

In the late sixth century BC, the Achaemenid Persian Empire replaced the Neo-Babylonian Empire as the dominant hegemonic structure in the Near East, controlling a vast territory stretching from Egypt to Turkey to Afghanistan. Arabia, too, was counted by the kings as part of their domain, as evidenced by the appearance of Arabians in lists and depictions of subject peoples. Our understanding of Persian–Arabian interaction is limited, however, by a scarcity of secure archaeological evidence and a series of often vague textual and inscriptional references. To be sure, recent work has clarified matters to some degree, but the fact remains that traditional archaeological and historical data is, at least at present, far too incomplete to comfortably address the problem.[1] In this paper, I propose to incorporate a landscape-based approach to the question, looking for clues as to how the spatial character of north-west Arabia may have influenced, if not dictated, the nature of Achaemenid presence in Arabia, as well as the empire's effects upon the Arabians themselves. I suggest that traditional demarcations of territory, especially in regard to hegemony, are misleading when applied to Arabia, that it is a landscape, which by its very nature divides itself into individual parcels that must be separately engaged. While the Achaemenid kings may have counted Arabia among their holdings, in actual fact they only controlled a small percentage of the region in any direct sense, turning to alternative strategies for the remainder.

Examination of the landscape's role in shaping cultural interaction is particularly relevant with reference to Arabia, for its sweeping sand deserts, searing heat and rugged mountain ranges are highly evocative aspects of its character in popular imagination. Expeditions of European travellers in the nineteenth and early twentieth centuries reinforced the image of an alien, inhospitable geography (cf. Doughty 1888; Brünnow & von Domaszewski 1904; Jaussen & Savignac 1909; Musil 1927; Musil & Wright 1930; Philby 1957). This characterization persists today, as both films and literature frequently employ the motif of the forbidding desert. The western perception of Arabia is an outside view, one fuelled by generations of preconceptions. To Greek and Roman eyes, the desert was often an "other", a place where the familiar gave way to the exotic. It was a land apart, a borderland where habitable gave way to uninhabitable. Mythical creatures, fantastic flora, societies with unusual customs and other elements of the bizarre are often associated with the desert in classical literature and artistic representation.[2] This differentiation extended into a dichotomy between civilized and uncivilized, whereby nomadic tribes were often characterized as savage or uncultivated (Shaw 1982, 1983). The pervasive colonialist division between East and West owed much to this classical legacy, and exercised a considerable influence on the development of twentieth-century thought (cf. Dyson 1985; van Dommelen 1998; Gosden 2001).

Such was the classical approach to desert landscapes at large. When they engage Arabia, however, a strange contradiction is apparent. As an inhospitable desert landscape, inhabited by nomads, it has similarities to North Africa, which was characterized by the Romans in especially barbaric terms. But descriptions of the Arabian people, in sources such as Herodotus, Diodorus and Strabo, show groups such as the Nabataeans exhibiting a certain degree of cultural refinement. While this largely positive portrayal may owe in part to a perceived Hellenization, it also reflects a classical awareness of the antiquity of the region, one where the great empires of the past had been in operation. Arabia was, to the outsider, therefore heavily mythicized, as much a fiction as a reality.

At this juncture, it is important to clarify what is meant by the problematic phrase "Arabia". As it is used today, the term applies to the entire Arabian Peninsula and Jordan. In antiquity, however, the borders of Arabia shifted considerably, depending on the particular perspective of the viewer. In some cases, it stretched from Syria to Yemen, including the Negev and at times the Sinai. In others, it was more restricted. Part of the difficulty arises from the term "Arab", which seems not to have had any uniform definition. Indeed, in many uses it seems to be a convenient byword for nomad, with little attention paid to the particular space these Arabs may have occupied.[3] To be sure, this complicates our analysis, as we cannot always be certain to whom the ancient sources refer when they speak of the Arabs or Arabians.[4] In this inquiry, I am specifically considering north-west Arabia, which I define as that part of southern Jordan known in biblical parlance as Edom and the area of Saudi Arabia called the Hejaz, which stretches north and west from the vicinity of Medina, as well as the Negev desert of modern Israel. This is not an entirely arbitrary division, for this region (which comprised much of the later kingdom of Nabataea) was—with a few expeditionary exceptions—the south-eastern extent of imperial power, whether Neo-Babylonian, Achaemenid or Roman.[5]

Were it not for its strategic importance, it is entirely possible that north-west Arabia would have slipped the notice of the great Near Eastern powers, including the Achaemenid Empire. After all, it was not a particularly fertile landscape, and transit was difficult and often dangerous. But the demand for precious aromatics, particularly frankincense, myrrh and cassia, which were produced in South Arabia, made the area a significant trade centre. The easiest overland route from Yemen to the Mediterranean ran through the Hejaz, and it was the primary means of conveyance until the formalization of Roman shipping routes in the second century AD.

These luxury aromatics were highly prized throughout the ancient Mediterranean and Near East, and there is evidence that they were transported north as early as the beginning of the second millennium BC. They could sell for quite high prices, at least four times the cost of cultivation and transportation during the Roman Empire, and control of the trade routes was therefore of significant interest to major regional powers. Herodotus (3.97) states that, "The Arabians rendered a thousand talents' weight of frankincense yearly". Whether or not he is exaggerating the amount of this tribute/gift, we can nevertheless derive from his statement that this was a large-scale operation.[6]

Geography

In a broad sense, Arabia is classified as desert. As a whole, the region receives less than 100 mm annual rainfall, and is mainly comprised of sweeping sands and rugged mountain ranges. Closer inspection, however, reveals a landscape of considerable diversity. Northwest Arabia is broken up into several ecological sub-regions, as defined by topographic barriers (mountain ranges) or relative environmental conditions. As this paper is concerned with the impact of landscape in shaping cultural interaction, it is important to consider these sub-regions in closer detail (Fig 42.1).

Edom, meaning "red land", is a plateau of semi-desert and shrub-land, bordered to the west by the Wadi Arabah and to the south and east by the Arabian desert. The terrain is generally rugged, especially in the Shara mountain range in the vicinity of Nabataean Petra. Owing to its proximity to the Gulf of Aqaba and the Mediterranean Sea, Edom receives greater annual rainfall than areas further inland, and the steep cliffs and ravines allow for limited agriculture, especially when catchment systems are employed.[7] The quality of soil is generally poor, on account of the large amount of wind-blown sand that is carried into the area, and in antiquity nomadic or semi-nomadic strategies were generally more prevalent there than was sedentary habitation, which was largely restricted to the better-watered areas north of Petra.

South of Edom, the Arabian Massif rises some 2,500 m from the sea, forming a large and often impassable coastal range. To the western side of this range, deep ravines (wadis) carry water to a narrow strip of land between the mountains and the sea, and in certain places it is suitable for agricultural development. These fertile areas are not contiguous, however, as they are broken up by arid stretches where runoff does not collect. Inland, the Arabian Massif gives way to the al-Hisma depression, a sandy landscape stretching from Jordan's Wadi Rum southwards to Meda'in Saleh. The depression is narrower in the south than in the north, with the result that a greater proportion of rainwater drainage is concentrated into a smaller area. This lends to fertile soil and several significant oases, where settlements emerged.[8])

To the east of the depression lies first a resumption of the Arabian Massif, and then the vast sand desert (the Great Nafud) that characterizes much of north-eastern Arabia. These deserts may be crossed, with difficulty, by camels but it is important to note that horses are not capable of making the journey. The Wadi Sirhan, which runs from north-eastern Jordan southwards to al-Jawf, did serve as an important ancient linkage through these regions, but the principal access to the Hejaz (and beyond it, to South Arabia) was via the al-Hisma depression.

This examination of North Arabian topography and environment reveals a diverse landscape rather than a single monolithic desert expanse. In this arid climate, access to water is obviously the principal characteristic

448 THE WORLD OF ACHAEMENID PERSIA

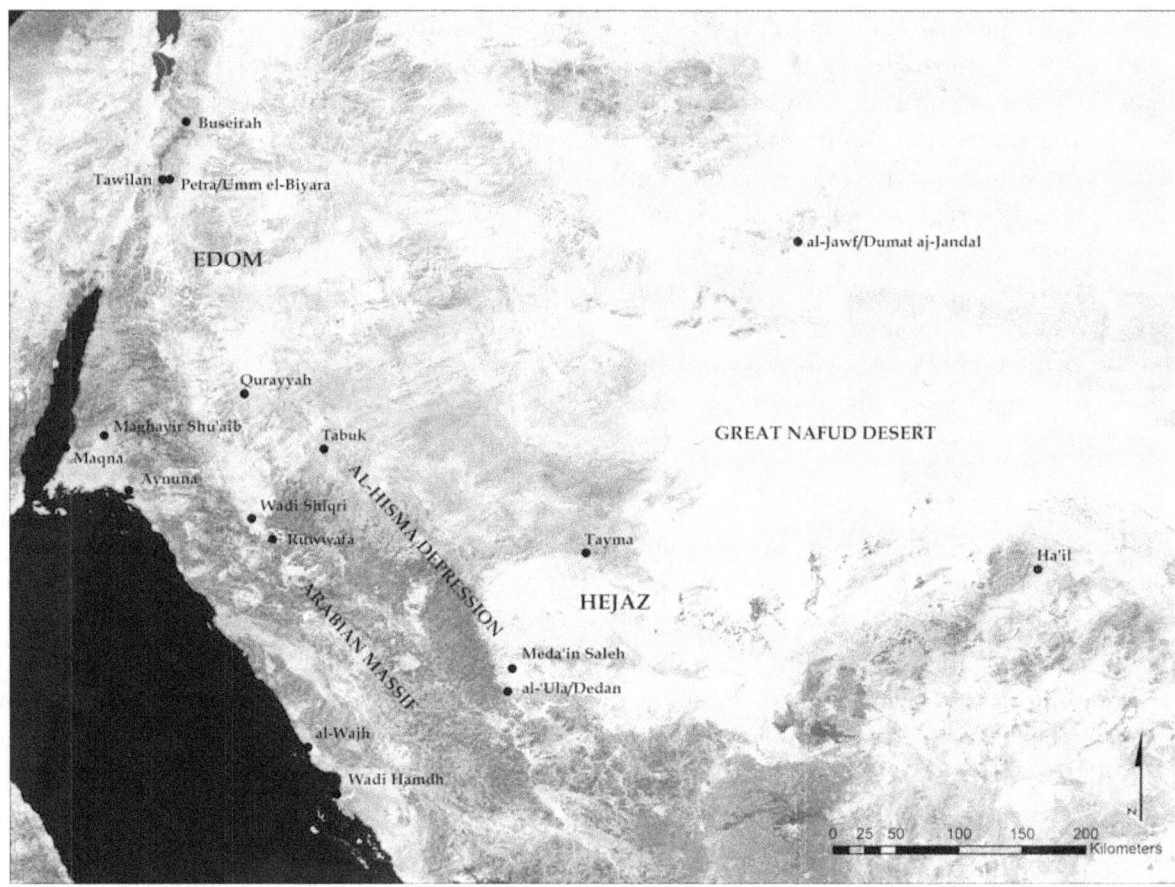

Fig. 42.1 North-west Arabia. (Satellite photograph with place names by B. Anderson)

determining habitability, and settlement was restricted by this variable. Indeed, Breton (1999: 18) terms Arabia a "hydraulic culture", inasmuch as access to springs and oases was the primary factor in shaping relations between and within nomadic and sedentary groups. Owing to the distribution of water, there is often considerable distance between sedentary populations, and the Arabian Massif serves to separate the coastal settlements from those in the Hisma. Between the settlements are large stretches of empty space, and considering them in terms of islands in the midst of a sea is not inappropriate.[9] In this sense, the landscape should not be seen as a single unit, but instead as a series of small enclaves which largely operate independently, with nomads and caravans serving in the capacity of ships, bringing news, trade items and occasionally military forces.[10]

North-west Arabia in the Pre-Achaemenid period

The growth of the great Mesopotamian empires of the Iron Age ushered in increased contact between north-west Arabia and the wider Levant. While the archaeological record is scanty, especially in the Neo-Assyrian period, the prominent placement of Arabians in Neo-Assyrian and Neo-Babylonian royal annals provides valuable information.[11] As early as 853 BC, we find historical evidence of "Arabs" (a problematic identifier, as noted above): an Arabian contingent took part in the campaign led by Syria and Anatolia against Shalmaneser III.[12] The Assyrians fought several campaigns against the "Arabs", at times pushing as far south as Tayma.[13] Bawden suggests that the frequency with which the Assyrian and Babylonian Empires conducted campaigns against Arabia may be indicative of local resistance to incursion, although it seems more likely that the remoteness and inaccessibility of certain areas made consistent control of the region untenable. We might well inquire into the reason why these Mesopotamian empires maintained such interest in Arabia, especially in light of the difficulty experienced in administering it. Bawden, no doubt correctly, ascribes it to economic factors (Bawden, Evans & Miller 1980: 71–72). As stated above, there is evidence that the immensely profitable trade in aromatics, which was to colour so much of the region's history, was already active at the end of the second millennium BC and Neo-Assyrian incursions into Arabia may well have been occasioned by a desire for direct control of the trade routes.[14]

Tayma paid tribute to the Assyrians as early as 736 BC, according to the records of Tiglath-Pileser III (Bawden, Evans & Miller 1980: 71). This large settlement in northern Arabia is particularly significant, as it was here that the Neo-Babylonian king Nabonidus took up residence from 555–544 BC (Kuhrt 1995: 600–607; Eichmann, Hausleiter & Schaudig 2006). Nabonidus built a palace, a temple and several other structures in the city as he developed the worship of his patron god Sin.[15] It is during his reign that scholars date the destruction of the Edomite capital Buseirah, an event that marked the end of the existence of Edom as a political entity.[16] Parr (1982) has suggested that the Edomites of Buseirah fled south to Dedan on the basis of ceramic similarities between the two sites, but this remains an unresolved issue.[17]

Achaemenid Arabia: internal and external evidence

Following the collapse of the Neo-Babylonian Empire at the hands of Cyrus the Great in 539 BC, the administration of the entire Near East fell into the hands of the Achaemenid Persian Empire. Persian administration was, by and large, characterized by the presence of satrapies, local capitals responsible for security, taxation and other logistical matters. Were north-west Arabia to align with what we might consider standard Achaemenid practice, such an expansive and economically significant area would surely fall under the satrapal aegis. But there is no material evidence of a satrapy south or east of Gaza, although Buseirah, Dedan and Tayma have been suggested as potential locations (cf. Weippert 1987: 102; Bartlett 1990: 29; Knauf 1990: 203). While this may owe in part to the fact that much of Saudi Arabia is as yet underexposed archaeologically, or again to the difficulty in tracing Achaemenid settlement or recognizing specifically Persian material culture, it may also be the case that this particular area was engaged differently, owing in no small part to the character of its landscape.[18]

Our information on Achaemenid presence in north-west Arabia is scanty, at least in the south of the region. To the north, we are on somewhat surer footing. At Tawilan (near Petra), a cuneiform business document was discovered, which documents the business dealings of a local entrepreneur while in Syria.

Importantly, this text is dated in the accession year of an Achaemenid monarch, and is thought to have been brought to Tawilan rather than written there.[19] Weippert suggests that the recorded transactions may have taken place in the context of an Achaemenid satrapy, although he is rightly cautionary on the basis of such fragmentary evidence. Even so, the proximity of the economically and ceremonially important satrapy in Egypt would have called for development of way stations and garrisons along the routes linking it to Persia, and we can expect that Persians were not an unfamiliar sight at the north-western extremes of the region in question.

In the heart of the Hejaz, however, there is little secure archaeological or historical evidence that bears witness to an Achaemenid presence. Most significant perhaps is the inscription from Dedan, dating to the Persian period, which mentions a "governor" at the site (Winnett & Reed 1970: 115ff.). On the surface, this seems to suggest clear evidence of Achaemenid administration, but Graf has argued against such a reading. Noting that the term (a local variation of a standard Aramaic word) was already in use in the Neo-Babylonian period in Arabia, he suggests that it does not refer to the contemporary situation but may rather be a "vestige of Nabonidus' ten-year sojourn at Tayma" (Graf 1990a: 48–50).

Our clearest indication of the character of Persian relations with north-west Arabia is found in the Iranian heartland of the empire, where Arabians appear in a variety of contexts. The Fortification Tablets from Persepolis bear witness to Arabian travellers in Persia. PF 1477 identifies the subject as Arabian, and the same name appears (without ethnic epithet) on PF 1539.[20] PF 1507 documents 12 Arabians who receive flour; PF 1534 accounts for the distribution of their beer. These texts likely originated in the same place, perhaps Kurdušum. The texts thus show Arabians on the move, travelling and trading in the Achaemenid heartland.

The Persepolis Fortification Tablets attest to an Arabian named Išbakatukka travelling to see the king with small groups of other Arabians through the Persepolis region under court authorization in 500 BC. These non-polemical Persian primary sources recording food disbursements are crucial evidence. They testify to significant give and take between Arabians and the courtly/administrative activities of the vast Achaemenid realm in commercial contexts, and the fact that they were allotted food suggests that they were employed by the empire (Retsö 2003: 239). This supports the idea of secondary administration through local agents, as discussed below.

The seal used by Išbakatukka on these documents is carved in a local Persepolitan style known as the "Fortification Style" (Garrison 1988, 1991; Garrison & Root 2001: 18) (Fig. 42.2). This suggests that Išbakatukka was very well integrated within the Persepolis cultural sphere, where he surely commissioned his seal. The mainstream stylistic qualities of the seal of Išbakatukka, in the context of Persepolis seals used by people of varying station and identity criss-crossing the empire on crown business, attest to the place of elite Arabians within this empire. This particular Arabian was well established in the workings of the imperial bureaucracy (trusted with discretion on behalf of the king), and he was familiar enough with the culture in Persepolis to commission a seal in the local style popular in court circles there.

In Achaemenid art, too, Arabians are important figures. They are prominent in the royal tomb reliefs at Naqsh-i Rustam, and can also be identified on the register of tribute-bearers on the eastern staircase of the Apadana at Persepolis. On the latter, the Arabian delegation is shown leading a camel to the king.[21] (Fig. 42.3) The context of the relief suggests that the camel is a gift, as is the vessel borne by the central figure in the delegation (Calmeyer 1993).[22] This stands as further evidence of Arabia's membership in the empire.

On the tomb of Artaxerxes III at Persepolis, the Arabian envoy wears a special necklace, which Schmidt interprets as a "torque of honour" in conjunction with its appearance on other figures from lands known to enjoy favoured status in imperial administration (Schmidt 1970: 111–116). If this is correct, it may be surmised that it would have been ceremonially bestowed by the king in the royal audience hall, the Apadana, further evidence of high-level visits by Arabian dignitaries to Persia.[23] Surely they would have been entertained in grand style during their stay, witnessing entertainment and rituals selected by the court. These important Arabian figures were likely tribal leaders, tied by kinship and descent to the prominent families.

With the exception of the Persepolis Fortification Tablets, the majority of the archaeological evidence discussed so far points to a small group of elites. Court officials and royalty were the only members of society to call upon the king at his palace, although in this case we are probably dealing with tribal leaders. This likely represented only a minute fraction of Arabian travel in Persia. Herodotus notes that the Arabians rendered 1,000 talents of frankincense as yearly tribute, and while his figure is surely exaggerated, it suggests that regular commercial exchange of aromatics was undertaken via the empire's extensive trade network (Herodotus, *Hist.* 3.97).[24] There must have been a steady stream of Arabian visitors on various errands: payment of tribute, commercial activities and audiences with the kings. North-west Arabia was therefore clearly part of the Achaemenid Empire; the remaining question is how this inclusion worked out in actual practice.

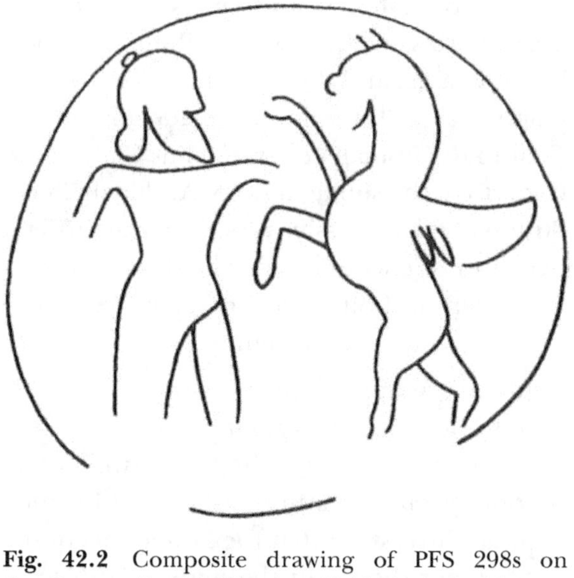

Fig. 42.2 Composite drawing of PFS 298s on the Persepolis Fortification Tablets, belonging to Išbakatukka the Arabian. (Courtesy of M. B. Garrison, M. C. Root, and the Persepolis Seal Project)

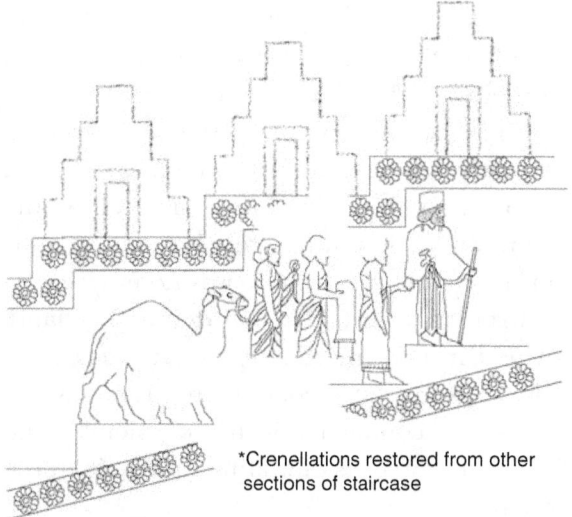

*Crenellations restored from other sections of staircase

Fig. 42.3 The Arabian Delegation on the east staircase of the Apadana at Persepolis. (Drawing B. Anderson)

Towards a landscape-oriented model

Recalling the discussion outlined above, where it was suggested that Arabia's geography divides the region into a series of isolated enclaves whose location is above all determined by access to water, the application of a standard territory-based hegemonic model is inappropriate. After all, much of the space in north-west Arabia was effectively empty of habitation, and the establishment of a satrapy to control it would therefore have been somewhat superfluous. The local priorities for the Achaemenid Empire, as they had been for those that preceded it, were to safeguard the trade in luxury aromatics and ensure that the region remained under official subjugation. The first of these aims would have been effectively achieved through the placement of garrisons and officials at the main caravan stops along the main trade route through the al-Hisma depression.[25] It would have been impossible for merchants successfully to bypass these sites, and indeed even one or two strategically placed posts would be sufficient to collect tariffs and oversee the importation of these highly desired goods.

The second priority, that of regional security, would have been a more difficult problem to resolve. A show of force at the main way stations might repel frontal assaults on these points, but there was no easy way to control or secure the broader desert landscape through traditional military measures. Diodorus Siculus, epitomizing Hieronymus of Cardia, comments on the problems faced by Seleucid armies operating in Arabia in the fourth century BC:

"They are exceptionally fond of freedom; and whenever a strong force of enemies comes near, they take refuge in the desert, using this as a fortress; for it lacks water and cannot be crossed by others, but to them alone, since they have prepared subterranean reservoirs lined with stucco, it furnishes safety" (Diod. 19.94.6, tr. R. M Geer).

The Seleucid general Demetrius eventually besieged the Nabataeans, presumably at Petra, and in a telling dialogue, the Nabataean envoy offers a peace settlement:

We therefore beg both you and your father to do us no injury, but after receiving gifts from us, to withdraw your army and henceforth regard the Nabataeans as your friends. For neither can you, if you wish, remain here many days since you lack water and all the other necessary supplies, nor can you force us to live a different life; but you will have a few captives, disheartened slaves who would not consent to live among strange ways. (Diod. 19.97.4–5, tr. R. M Geer)

While the dialogue is undoubtedly reconstructed by Diodorus/Hieronymus, the message is certainly apposite, inasmuch as the nomads operate in an otherwise inaccessible area where straightforward military conquest is inadvisable, and the gains from such a campaign slight. This point was made abundantly clear to the Roman general Aelius Gallus, who undertook the subjugation of Arabia in 23 BC. Strabo and Dio Cassius report on the difficulties Gallus encountered, wandering lost in the desert without food or water. Dio's brief account is particularly telling:

At first Aelius encountered no one, yet he did not proceed without difficulty; for the desert, the sun, and the water (which had some peculiar nature), all caused his men great distress, so that the larger part of the army perished...In the midst of this trouble the barbarians also fell upon them. For hitherto they had been defeated whenever they joined battle, and had even been losing some places; but now, with the disease as their ally, they not only won back their own possessions, but also drove the survivors of the expedition out of the country. (Cassius Dio, *Hist. Rom.*, 53.29.3–8, tr. E. Carey, H. Foster)[26]

Such encounters with the nomads are not restricted to the post-Achaemenid period, as Neo-Assyrian annals and reliefs recall both conflict and resolution with nomadic groups operating in north-eastern Arabia (cf. Weippert 1987; Reade 1998*a*).[27] By and large, empires recognized that it was easier and more efficient to negotiate contractual agreements with nomadic groups, employing them as agents, rather than attempt to pacify them by force. The illustration of the desert as a sea, dotted by island settlements, is again relevant; if we distance ourselves from pejorative connotations, we may consider the nomads in terms of pirates, specialists in their environment who could appear and disappear at will, and were notoriously difficult to capture.

Given the space that separated major caravan sites in north-west Arabia, often over 100 km, it would have been impossible to secure the entire roadway. For this reason, at least in more historically accessible periods, caravans were generally accompanied by a large contingent of guards (Breton 1999: 69).[28] Even so, the risk of a nomad ambush was ever-present. In order to approach a greater degree of security, it was necessary to incorporate the nomads into the power structure, to give them incentives for cooperation. Enlisting them as agents enabled the Achaemenids to manage the area successfully, if indirectly, and provided the nomads with greater autonomy. This likely explains the role of Išbakatukka and the other Arabians who were allotted supplies in Persepolis; their employment by the state may well have been linked to their role as agents.[29]

According to this model, Achaemenid hegemony in Arabia was a limited notion, largely determined by the character of the landscape. Garrisons and administrative officials were stationed in places where sedentary habitation was possible. In the broad expanse between these localized centres, the Persians were only nominally present, acting through the agency of allied nomadic groups. In exchange for their services, the Arabians were counted among the empire's tax-exempt clients. While there is some difficulty sorting out exactly how this tax exemption worked, as the Arabians still gave yearly "gifts", it nevertheless seems to be the case that the open desert lay under this secondary form of administration.[30]

Arabia may not have experienced the same imperial presence as more heavily populated regions, such as Asia Minor or Egypt, but it was nevertheless an active member of the empire. Arabians came and went to Persepolis on regular errands, both commercial and official, and as the seal of Išbakatukka bears witness, they became well versed in local Iranian expressions of identity. The pervasive and peripatetic nature of Achaemenid rule, which entailed so much travel to and from different parts of the empire, surely presented the Arabians with regular reminders of the administrative and ideological system within which they were counted as subjects. Nomadic agents, working to patrol the desert and collect tribute, would necessarily have interacted with imperial officials on a regular basis, and thus even nomads in the desert would have been exposed to Persians and Persian-ness.

What impact did these connections have on the development of Arabian cultural identity? While evidence to answer such a claim is sparse, we may look for clues in the later history of the region, especially the Nabataean kingdom that established itself following the dissolution of Achaemenid hegemony in the late fourth century BC. The Nabataeans seem to have emerged at least in part from the sedentarization of elements of the Qedarite confederacy, the primary group operating in the area during the Achaemenid period, and the Nabataean royal line was likely descended from its elite families. If we recall the visits of Arabian emissaries to Persepolis during the reign of Artaxerxes III discussed above, we may surmise that these same elites who visited the Great King and observed the lifestyle and ideology of the court were themselves active in the formation of Nabataea as a political entity. This exposure to the workings of the court and their inclusion in it would surely have influenced their own expressions of identity, and it is not unreasonable to suppose that notions of their dignified standing as guests of the Great King affected interactions within their own local sphere of influence.[31]

Notes

1. Graf 1990b and Knauf 1990 are important contributions to the question at hand, and should be consulted in particular for details on the epigraphic record.
2. See e.g. Herodotus *Hist.* 3.102, Strabo *Geog.* 16.4.16, as well as the famous Nile Mosaic from Pompeii, which shows a progressively fantastic scene as one moves further into the desert and away from the Mediterranean.
3. In deference to this issue, the term "Arabians" is generally preferred and is used here throughout.
4. For a recent and comprehensive approach to this problem see Retsö 2003. Also consult the review by Bowersock (2004).
5. To be sure, there was an Achaemenid presence in South Arabia, especially Oman, but this was effectively cut off from north-west Arabia on account of the intervening desert, and much of the Persian trade with Oman involved direct shipments to and from south Iran. For further discussion, see Dr Potts's contribution to this volume and Potts 1990: 378, 94–400; Briant 2002a: 761. For a discussion of the (admittedly scant) evidence of Persian presence in Yemen, see Simpson ed. 2002: 126–127 and Curtis 2005b: 51.
6. Indeed, the typical caravan in historic times ranged from 1,000 to 2,500 camels, as well as several hundred merchants, guides and guards. For a discussion see Breton 1999: 69.
7. Examples of such systems are ubiquitous in the Nabataean period. For a discussion see Oleson 1995.
8. For a more detailed discussion of the environmental setting see Parr, Harding & Dayton 1969: 196–198.
9. On trade and interaction along desert corridors see Smith II 2005.
10. For a discussion of the social, cultural and economic implications of island interaction in Bronze Age Greece see Broodbank 2000.
11. Bennett discusses the evidence in Jordan, which she calls "hardly overwhelming" (1982: 182). Note the presence of Midianite ceramics in north-west Arabia, which do seem to reflect Neo-Assyrian, Egyptian or more generally "Levantine" stylistic influences (see Bennett 1982: 181–187; Parr 1982: 129–131).
12. The king of Damascus, Adad-idri (Ben-Hadad) and the leader of Hamath, Irkhuleni (Hittite: Urhilina) are recorded as the generals of the coalition against Assyria. See *Cambridge Ancient History* 3.1 393; Eph'al 1982: 6.
13. The Akkadian and biblical sources referring to the region and/or people of "Arabia" are discussed by Eph'al (1982: 29–71). For the evidence at Taymā see Bawden, Evans & Miller 1980: 71–72; Eichmann, Hausleiter & Schaudig 2006.
14. For the presence of incense-burners (as indicators of the incense trade) see Shea 1983; Fowler 1984. Such burners continued to be produced for centuries, e.g. the second-/third-century AD examples published by Hassell (2002). Archaeological evidence from the Neo-Assyrian period is difficult to evaluate, but the annals of Tiglath-Pileser tell us that following the defeat of Šamsi, queen of the Arabs in 733 BC: "Gold, silver, camels, she-camels, all kinds of spices, their tribute as one [they brought] before me (and) kissed my feet" (Eph'al 1982: 36). For a newly discovered inscription on the deeds of Ita'amar, who is listed in Assyrian records as paying tribute in 715 BC, see Nebes 2007. On the definition

14. of "spices", cf. Sauer, who defines it in an Arabian context as: "such aromatics as frankincense and myrrh, stacte (myrrh oil), cinnamon bark, nard, etc" (Sauer & Blakely 1988: 111 n.1; cf. also Groom 1981).
15. A stone plaque/cube found at the site is particularly telling in terms of cultural interaction, showing mixtures of Egyptian, Arabian and Mesopotamian iconography (Bawden, Evans & Miller 1980: 85).
16. Naturally, this does not mean that the Edomites disappeared as a population. Most likely a remnant remained settled in towns and villages, while others surely nomadized. For a discussion of this process see Anderson 2005: 24–25.
17. Parr also makes the alternative suggestion that Dedan was part of "greater Edom" or Teman. For this discussion as well as an account of the Khuraybah pottery see Parr 1968/1969, 1982.
18. It is tricky to determine the presence of a satrapy on the basis of archaeological evidence, as they did not always call for major local changes, as discussed by Briant (2002a: 76–79) and Meadows (2005).
19. The king is identified only as Darius, and there is insufficient evidence to determine his identity more closely (Weippert 1987: 102).
20. For a discussion (in conjunction with sealing) see Hallock 1969; Garrison 1988.
21. The identification of the camel-leading delegation as Arabian is suggested by Schmidt (1953: 84). The identification of many of the groups is based on comparisons with the labelled throne-bearers from the royal tombs at Naqsh-i Rustam; however Schmidt notes that the "Arabians" on the Apadana are not conclusively identifiable (1953: 89). Alternatives (including the Babylonians) have been proposed.
22. On the problems associated with "gifts" and "tribute", see below, n. 27.
23. For a contrary reading of the visual evidence, which suggests that the later tomb reliefs are standard imitations of Darius' original propaganda rather than reflections of the contemporary fourth-century situation, see Retsö 2003: 238–239.
24. For a discussion of the inflation of Achaemenid tribute figures reported in Herodotus see Fleming 2002. Obviously, 1,000 talents (28.6 tons) of frankincense per year is an impossible sum.
25. This Achaemenid policy is hardly unique. Similar approaches to the desert can be seen under Roman, Sasanian and Ottoman rule (see e.g. Bowsher 1986).
26. See also Strabo *Geog.* 16.4.23–24, where the disaster is ascribed to the Nabataean administrator Syllaeus. As I have argued elsewhere, this attribution of blame likely results more from Gallus' position as Strabo's patron than a diabolical Nabataean plot, and indeed Syllaeus may himself have been lost (see Anderson 2005: 77–79).
27. For a wider discussion on empire/nomad relations see Lancaster & Lancaster 1992; Khazanov 1994; Haiman 1995; Bienkowski & van der Steen 2001.
28. Such a policy is not unique to antiquity. For a discussion of Ottoman relations with nomads and deserts, including the establishment of garrisons along the Hajj route, see Hütteroth & Abdulfattah 1977: 34; Lewis 1987: 28; Kennedy 2007: 42–49.
29. For further discussion of this question see Knauf 1989, 1990; Graf 1990a, 1990b.
30. There has been much discussion over the identification of Arabs as "gift-givers" (as opposed to tribute-payers) in Herodotus *Hist.* 3.97. Given the amount (1,000 talents of frankincense) and frequency (annual) of the "gifts" rendered in Herodotus' account, is there really a difference between *dôrea* and *phoros*? And what reprisal might be expected if the gift were not presented? For discussion of the "voluntary guise" of ancient gift-giving see Mauss 1954: 1–7; Root 1979: 227–229; Eph'al 1982: 208; Graf 1990b: 138–139; Gunter & Root 1998; Briant 2002a: 69.
31. For further discussion of Nabataean revivals of the Achaemenid legacy see Anderson 2002, 2005.

43

Because of the Dread Upon Them

Lisbeth S. Fried

According to Ezra 3:2–3, one of the first acts of the returnees from Babylon, after they had settled in their towns, was to set up the sacrificial altar to YHWH on its original site. The reason given is "the dread of the 'peoples of the lands' that was upon them":

> Then Jeshua son of Jozadak, with his fellow priests, and Zerubbabel son of Shealtiel with his kin set out to build the altar of the God of Israel, to offer burnt offerings on it, as prescribed in the Law of Moses the man of God. They set up the altar on its foundation, because of the dread of the peoples of the lands that was upon them, so he offered burnt offerings upon it to YHWH, morning and evening. (Ezra 3:2–3)

These verses can be approached in two basic ways. One is to assume their historicity and attempt to determine who the Jews were afraid of, and why, and if their fears were well founded. The second approach is to regard the passage as a simple creation of the biblical author with no historical validity at all. Commentators typically take the latter position. Because they find no disputes in Haggai or Zechariah, whose prophecies are securely dated to the same period, most commentators assume that the conflicts in Ezra are not historical. They assume they were composed by the biblical author either to account for the long period of temple building—22 years, from the 1st year of Cyrus to the 6th year of Darius I, that is, 538–516 BC (e.g. Clines 1984: 72; Bedford 2001)—or to reflect tensions at the time of composition (e.g. Williamson 1985). As Hugh Williamson states (1985: 45), "it is both a mistake of method, and a misunderstanding of the writer's intention, to use this passage…for the purpose of historical reconstruction". In spite of this warning, some commentators who agree that the passage is not historical still assume that conflicts existed between the "peoples of the land" and the returnees (Clines 1984: 72–83; Grabbe 1998: 133, 136–38). Even if the events are not historical, it is important to understand the world view of the biblical writer according to whom such conflicts existed. The world view of the writer has historical value itself, even if the events per se did not occur. Accordingly, this paper asks first who the "peoples of the lands" were that the writer had in mind, and second if it makes historical sense for the Jews to have been in dread of them at the time of the return.

The "peoples of the lands"

What did the biblical writer have in mind when he referred to the "peoples of the lands"? What does the term mean? This phrase in all of its configurations occurs 81 times in the Hebrew Bible, but the plural appears only in 24 of them. I have previously discussed the singular form of the term (Fried 2006). The singular form always refers to the aristocracy, the elites who control and administer an area. This may not be the meaning of the plural, however. The plural term occurs in two forms: "the peoples of the land" and "the peoples of the lands", as here in Ezra 3:3. The plural forms appear only in exilic and post-exilic texts. Some 16 of the 24 occurrences are in Ezra-Nehemiah and Chronicles.[1] Another five are in post-exilic additions to Deuteronomy (Deut. 28:10) and the Deuteronomic history (Josh. 4:24; 1 Kings 8:43, 53, 63). A typical example is 1 Kings 8:53, "For you have separated them [i.e. your people Israel] from among all the peoples of the earth [lit. "land"], to be your heritage, just as you promised through Moses, your servant, when you brought our ancestors out of Egypt, O Lord God". The remaining three include Esther 8:17:

> In every province and in every city, wherever the king's command and his edict came, there was gladness and joy among the Jews, a festival and a holiday. Furthermore, many of the peoples of the land [here, Persia] professed to be Jews, because the fear of the Jews had fallen upon them.

Ezekiel (31:12), a lament over Assyria:

> Foreigners from the most terrible of the nations have cut it [i.e. Assyria] down and left it. On the mountains and in all the valleys its branches have fallen, and its boughs lie broken in all the watercourses of the land; and all the peoples of the earth [lit. "land"] went away from its shade and left it.

The third is a late expansion to Zephaniah (3:20):

> At that time I will bring you home, at the time when I gather you; for I will make you renowned and praised among all the peoples of the earth [lit. "land"], when I restore your fortunes before your eyes, says YHWH.

In all these texts, the reference is to non-Judeans/non-Israelites. This is also true of its use in Chronicles. The speech put in the mouth of the Rab Shekah by the Chronicler is typical:

> Do you not know what I and my ancestors have done to all the peoples of the lands? Were the gods of the nations of those lands at all able to save their lands out of my hand? (2 Chronicles 32:13)

Here, as elsewhere in Chronicles, the referent is always non-Judeans/non-Israelites. The plural form also occurs eleven times in Ezra-Nehemiah (Ezra 3:3; 9:1, 2, 11; 10:2, 11; Nehemiah 9:24, 30; 10:28, 30, 31). In these texts, the reader is never told whom the term refers to except that "their abominations are like those of the Canaanites, the Hittites, the Perizzites, the Jebusites, the Ammonites, the Moabites, the Egyptians, and the Amorites" (Ezra 9:1), that is, like those of the ancient enemies of Judah and Israel. These are the peoples with whom the Hebrews shared the land of Canaan at the time of the settlement. The peoples mentioned are those from areas that later became the Persian satrapies of Egypt, Cilicia and Beyond the River. Of the texts in Ezra-Nehemiah, the referent is clearest in Nehemiah 9:30:

> Many years you were patient with them, and warned them by your spirit through your prophets; yet they would not listen. Therefore you handed them over to the peoples of the lands.

The reference here and in all these texts appears to be to the non-Israelite/non-Judean peoples who dominated Israel from the time of her settlement in Canaan. This is the referent in the Deuteronomic history, in Chronicles, in Ezra-Nehemia and elsewhere. They are the peoples who lived around the Persian province of Yehud, often within the historical land of Israel. The authors of Ezra-Nehemiah, and the author of Ezra 3:3, use the plural forms of the term in the same way that all the biblical authors have used them. There is no indication anywhere that the authors of Ezra-Nehemiah, or of Ezra 3:3, employed a meaning different to that of other biblical writers. Grabbe (1998: 138) agrees that the biblical author considers the "peoples of the land/s" to be foreigners, non-Judeans. Nevertheless, he argues that they were not "really" foreigners, but descendants of Jews who never were deported. This is an odd statement from one who denies that the section is at all historical (1998: 133).

In this paper, I seek to determine first if there were—historically speaking—non-Judeans/non-Israelites in the area traditionally considered the land of Israel, and second if it would have made sense historically for the Jews to have been afraid of them in the early years of the return. If the answer to both questions is in the affirmative, then there is no need to posit, as Grabbe does, that the "real" referent of the term is the descendant of Jews who had not been deported.

Yehud's borders and her neighbours

Yehud's borders

Excavations, coins and seals have been used to determine the boundaries of Persian Yehud. Seal impressions in both Aramaic and Hebrew with the name Yehud have been found in several Persian-period sites, with over half of them from Ramat Rahel. The others are Gezer, Nebi Samuel, Tell el-Fûl, Bethany, Husan, Tell en-Nasbeh, En-Gedi, Mosah, Jericho and Jerusalem (Stern 2001: 548). The distribution of these seals (plus the distribution of Persian-period Yehud coins) provides a way to determine the boundaries of Persian Yehud—if used cautiously. The presence of a seal or coin may result from travellers, rather than indicate provincial boundaries (Lemaire 1990: 36; Carter 1999: 89–90). The south-westernmost point in which Persian Yehud stamp impressions or coins have been found is Beth-Zur (Khirbet et-Tubeiqah), about 32 km south of Jerusalem (Reich 1992; Carter 1999: 154; Funk 1993).

The south-east corner of Persian Yehud is En-Gedi (Tel Goren), *c*.1,300 km west of the Dead Sea and *c*.40 km south-east of Jerusalem. Jar handles were found there stamped with *yh*, *yhd* and *yhwd* seals (Mazar 1993). Small amounts of Persian-period pottery were also found. A significant amount of Attic pottery enables the site to be dated positively to the fifth and fourth centuries when it was temporarily abandoned (Mazar 1993; Carter 1999: 158–159). Excavators indicate a prosperous Persian period settlement.

Mizpeh (McCown *et al.* 1947; Zorn 1993, 1994, 1997; Zorn *et al.* 1994) and Jericho

(Kenyon 1983: 113; Carter 1999: 162; Stern 2001: 548) are the northernmost cities in which Persian period *yh(w)d* stamp seals have been found. Accordingly, the line from Mizpeh to Jericho was likely the northern border of the province. This excludes both Bethel and Ai. The easternmost extent of Yehud, based on stamp seal impressions, is the city of Jericho. The eastern border of the province continued south to Netophah, to Tekoa and as far as En-Gedi. The south-westernmost site to reveal *yehud* stamp seals was Beth-Zur. Drawing a line from Beth-Zur northward to Mizpeh includes all the sites listed in Ezra 2 except for Ono, Lod and Hadid, which likely belonged to Phoenicia. The boundaries outlined here (Beth Zur to Mizpah to Jericho to En-Gedi) delimit a very small Yehud, some 840 km².

The Arab kingdom of Qedar

Archaeological evidence reveals the presence of non-Judean/non-Israelite peoples living in the historic land of Israel at the time of the Jewish return from Babylon. South of Persian Yehud lay the Arab kingdom of Qedar, which included the Sinai, the Negev and the Arabah south to the Gulf of Aqaba/Elat (Lemaire 1994). Inscriptions dating to the fifth century reveal an Arab kingdom of Qedar stretching from at least Dedan in western Arabia across to the Nile Valley and north as far as the southern border of Yehud (Rabinowitz 1956; Winnett 1937: 50–51). This is confirmed by an additional inscription found at Lachish and dated to the end of the sixth or the beginning of the fifth century BC (Lemaire 1974). The inscription reads "Altar of incense of 'Iyš ben Mahli the king (*hmlk*)". Both names are well-known Semitic, Arab names. Lemaire reasons that the name could not refer to a Judean king.

At this time there was no king of Judah and the names of the descendants of David who might have posed as kings are known from the biblical text. The Edomite kingdom which might also be a likely candidate did not exist after the sixth century as it was wiped out by the Babylonians (Stern 2001). It seems that in the absence of a significant Judean population in the Babylonian period, the Arab Qedarite kingdom had expanded north to the southern border of Judah and had established its capital at Lachish (Lemaire 1994). Level I at Lachish is dated to the Persian period, the fifth and fourth centuries, after which the site was evidently abandoned. Excavations revealed a Persian-period palace built in a combination of Achaemenid and North-Syrian architectural styles (Wright 1955; Ussishkin 1993). It seems to have been the royal residence of a ruler of the Arab kingdom of Qedar. This kingdom would have extended from the southern border of Yehud as far as the Nile Valley, across to the Mediterranean south of Gaza, and eastwards at least as far as Dedan (see also Graf 1990b).

Samaria

Judah's northern border was the province of Samaria, or Shomron in Hebrew and Aramaic. This area is attested as a province with its capital at the city of Samaria (Roman Sebaste) from 722 BC when the northern kingdom of Israel fell to the Assyrians (Stern 2001: 49–51). Assyria fell to the combined forces of Babylon and Media in 612 and in 604 the Neo-Babylonian rulers began to cement their hold over the former Assyrian provinces in the Levant. The officials in Samaria who had been appointed by Assyria must have transferred their loyalty to the new ruler without a battle, as there are no destruction levels to indicate the beginning of Neo-Babylonian rule (2001: 319).

After a long period of sharp decline during the Assyrian and Neo-Babylonian periods, intensive settlement is noted again in the Persian period (Finkelstein 1993: 1313–14; Zertal 1990, 1993: 1312). Half of all the Persian-period sites were concentrated within a 10 km radius around the city of Samaria (a phenomenon equivalent to the settlement around Jerusalem in the Persian province of Yehud). A second area of concentration was the Dothan Valley, and 80 per cent of those sites were newly founded in the Persian period. The Wadi ed-Daliyeh papyri (Gropp 2001) dating to the period just before the Alexandrine conquest of Samaria reveal people with YHWHistic, Edomite, Arabic, Moabite, Phoenician, Babylonian and Persian names indicating the mixed ethnic population of the Persian province of Samaria.

Yehud's eastern and western borders

The easternmost extent of Yehud was the city of Jericho, judging by the distribution of stamp seal impressions. Across the river lay the kingdom of Ammon in the northern part of present-day Jordan. Excavations in Jordan reveal that the Ammonites continued in Ammon after the destruction of Jerusalem and into the Persian period (Herr 1993, 1999; Lipschits 2004). It does not appear that they were deported. South of Ammon was probably the Arab kingdom of Qedar.

The western border of Yehud was Phoenicia. The funerary inscription of the Sidonian king Eshmunezer II (mid-fifth century) suggests that the entire northern coastal plain was placed under Sidonian, that is Phoenician, control, and was outside the jurisdiction of Yehud. South of the Phoenician coast were the coastal cities of Philistia. Four of the five cities of biblical Philistia were also prominent in the Persian period—Ashdod, Ashkelon, Gath (Tell es-Ṣafi) and Gaza. Although the southern coastal area continued to be known as Philistia, excavations at Ashdod and Ashkelon reveal that it too was inhabited by Phoenicians who had replaced the Philistines (Stern 2001: 407–412).

It must be concluded from the above that there were indeed non-Judeans/non-Israelites in the area traditionally considered the land of Israel. To the peoples listed here must be added the Persian and Babylonian officials and their families residing in the capital cities, as well as the many soldiers and their families garrisoned in the cities and throughout the countryside (see Briant 2002a and Fried 2004 for discussions of Persian imperial administrative practices). Since it is established above that the term "peoples of the land/s" refers to non-Judeans/non-Israelites, and since it is shown that there were non-Judeans/non-Israelites in the area traditionally considered the land of Israel, it is reasonable to conclude that these foreign peoples were the referent for the term. The question remains, however, whether it would have been reasonable to be in dread of them.

A dread upon them

The Greek writers emphasize the safety of the provinces, stressing that Persian garrisons were established in every large city and were dispersed as well as concentrated in strategic locations throughout the countryside. They point out, moreover, that the empire was crisscrossed by a network of roads that were all well guarded (Briant 2002a: 357–387). Xenophon states that, for example:

In Cyrus' province it became possible for either Greek or barbarian, provided he were guilty of no wrongdoing, to travel fearlessly wherever he wished, carrying with him whatever it was to his interest to have. (*Anabasis* 1.9.11–12)

Herodotus gives numerous humorous anecdotes to illustrate how scrupulously the roads were guarded. The first portrays Harpagus the Mede when he wished to contact Cyrus secretly in Persia:

(Because) the roads were guarded, there was only one way he could think of to get a message through to him: this was by slitting open a hare, without pulling off the fur, and inserting into its belly a slip of paper on which he had written what he wanted to say. He then sewed up the hare, gave it to a trusted servant, together with a net to make him look like a hunter, and sent him off to Persia with orders to present the hare to Cyrus, and to tell him by word of mouth to cut it open with his own hands, and to let no one be present while he did so. The orders were obeyed. Cyrus received the hare, cut it open, found the letter inside and read it. (*History* I. 123–24)

More amusing is Herodotus' report on Histiaeus' effort while in Susa to contact his nephew Aristagoras in Miletus.

(Histiaeus) was in difficulty about how to get a message safely through to him (Aristagoras) as the roads from Susa were watched; so he shaved the head of his most trustworthy slave, pricked the message on his scalp, and waited for the hair to grow again. Then, as soon as it had grown, he sent the man to Miletus with instructions to do nothing when he arrived except to tell Aristagoras to shave his hair off and look at his head. The message found there was, as I have said, an order to revolt. (*History* V.35)

In contrast to this testimony of the Greek historians, modern scholars have assumed that the soldiers who accompanied Nehemiah on his journey from Susa to Judah (Neh. 2:9) did so for his protection, not to man the citadel in Jerusalem (e.g. Myers 1965: 98, 100; Fensham 1982: 163; Blenkinsopp 1988: 216).[2] According to Blenkinsopp (1988: 216), "provision of an armed escort, together with guides and travel rations, was standard procedure". Blenkinsopp cites the Persepolis Fortification Tablets as his source for his statement that the provision of an armed guard was standard practice for wayfarers. The tablets provide lists of rations for travellers stopping at waypoints for the night; they receive a day's ration to supply them until the next night at the next waypoint. These archives show that there were very few large parties, suggesting that, contrary to Blenkinsopp's assumption, it was not the custom to travel with a guard.

Herodotus is the basic source for knowledge about the common occurrence of travellers and of the safety of the roads. His portrayal of the Royal Road describes any main thoroughfare throughout the Persian Empire (Tuplin 1987: 110, n. 6). To quote Herodotus: "For this, indeed, is what the road is like. All along it are Royal Stages and excellent places to put up; and, as it is all through inhabited country, the whole road is safe" (*History* V: 52). Thus, travel was safe and the most that the traveller had to fear was unwanted police surveillance (*History* V: 35, VII: 239). The cavalry accompanying Nehemiah came not to provide an armed escort for him, but to man the citadel at Jerusalem (Hoglund 1992: 210).

If each bend in the road was as scrupulously monitored as the Greek writers and the

Persepolis Tablets imply, how realistic would it have been for the returnees to have been in dread of their neighbours, the "peoples of the lands"? Does not the safety of the roads imply safety in the empire generally? To answer this question, I examine areas in the empire where conflict occurred to determine the causes of the conflict and the nature of the Persian response to it.

Anatolia

One area of persistent conflict was Anatolia, an area divided into numerous satrapies whose borders fluctuated. Herodotus is replete with examples of the rivalry and competition among the neighbouring satraps that this fluctuation elicited. For example, Mitrobates, ruler (ἄρχου) of Dascylium, taunted Oroetes, viceroy of (ὕπαρχος) of Sardis, for not taking the island of Samos, just outside his doorstep. In reply, Oroetes killed both the taunter, Mitrobates and his son, as well as Polycrates, ruler of Samos. He thus brought Samos as well as Dascylium under his control (*History* III: 127). At the news of Polycrates' death, Maeandrius, vice-regent of Samos, called an assembly of the townsfolk to proclaim isonomia (*History* III: 142). That he was not actually announcing a democracy, in Herodotus' opinion at least, is witnessed by the response that Herodotus puts in the mouth of one in the audience: "Nay, but who are you to rule over us, being a low-born and a rascal".

Maeandrius soon rebelled against the Persians, who retaliated by killing everyone on the island and turning it uninhabited over to Syloson, Polycrates' nephew (*History* III: 145–149). Whether or not the Samosans had welcomed the revolt, they were all killed.

Rivalry, jealousy and brinkmanship among satraps were a major cause of the Ionian Revolt too, which lasted over seven years. Darius had given Histiaeus an area in Thrace as a reward for loyalty. Megabazus, commander of the Persian European armies, complained to Darius that he had given Histiaeus a Greek, forests enough for shipbuilding and silver mines large enough to commission armies. Darius could soon expect a revolt. Darius assented and brought Histiaeus with him to Susa, handing over Thrace (with the mines and the forests) to the accuser, Megabazus.

In response to this ill treatment of his uncle, Aristagoras, Histiaeus' nephew, convinced the cities of Ionia to rebel. The Persians retaliated against the rebellion by destroying each of the towns that participated in the revolt. Herodotus reports on the fate of one of the towns, Miletus:

> Most of the men were killed by the long-haired Persians; the women and children were made slaves, and the temple at Didyma, both shrine and oracle, was plundered and burnt...After that, the captive Milesians were brought to Susa. King Darius did them no further hurt, but settled them by the sea called Red, in the city called Ampe, whereby flows the Tigris as it issues into the sea. The Persians themselves occupied the land in the immediate neighbourhood of the town, and the rest of the cultivated region which belonged to it, and made over the mountainous parts of the interior to the Carians of Pedasus...In this way Miletus was emptied of its inhabitants. (*History* VI: 19–20, 22)

Whether or not the inhabitants agreed to the revolt, the men in the cities were slain, and the rest, with the women and children, deported to Susa. The Ionians were not the only deportees in the Persian Empire. Herodotus mentions the Eretrians, who were deported to a village outside Susa (*History* VI: 120); and Deodorus knows of Boeotian and Carian deportees living in other villages near the Persian capital (Diodorus XVII. 110.4–5).

The Great Satrap's Revolt also reveals the effect of the persistent rivalry and competition among the satraps. In 367, Ariobarzanes, satrap of Dascylium, was commended for effectively increasing the prestige and power of the Great King. He had cemented Persian control of the southern Troad and had extended it across the strait into the European portions of the Hellespont. This positive view of Ariobarzanes changed the next year, however, when Autophradates became satrap of neighbouring Lydia. The latter did not take kindly to the southern Troad, traditionally part of Lydia, being in the hands of Dascylium, and said a few words to the king about all the land in Ariobarzanes' possession. The king accordingly declared Ariobarzanes a rebel, and ordered Autophradates and Mausolus to attack him by land and by sea respectively (Weiskopf 1989: 42–43). The result was war, deaths and deportations.

Egypt

In addition to the Greek histories, we have several archival Aramaic documents from Persian-period Egypt. One letter from Arsames, satrap of Egypt at the end of the fifth century (TAD A.6.10), indicates the prerogatives of the satrap in the Persian Empire:

> From Arsames to Nakhthor.
>
> And now, formerly, when the Egyptians rebelled, then Samshek, the former official, strictly guarded our domestic staff and goods in Egypt so that there was not any decrease in my estate. Moreover, from elsewhere he sought domestic staff of craftsmen of all kinds and other go[o]ds in sufficient numbers and made (them over) to my estate.
>
> And now, thus have I heard here, that the officials who are [in Low]er (Egypt) are being diligent during the troubles (?). They are strictly guarding the domestic staff and goods of their lords. Moreover, they are seek[ing] others from elsewhere and add[ing (them) t]o the estate of their lords. But you are not doing so.
>
> Now, even formerly I sent (word) to you about this: "You, [be] diligent. Strictly guard m[y] domestic staff and good[s] so that there will not be a[n]y decrease in my estate. Moreover, from elsewhere seek domestic staff of craftsmen of all kinds in sufficient numbers and bring them into my court, and mark them with my brand, and make (them over) to my estate just as the [for]mer officials had been doing."
>
> Thus let it be known to you: if there be any decrease in the domestic staff or in my other goods and from elsewhere you do not seek and you do not add to my estate, you will be strictly called to account and a harsh word will be directed at you.
>
> [Ar]taḥaya knows this order. Rashta is the scribe. (TAD 6.10)

Apparently during the "troubles", that is, during a rebellion in Lower Egypt, many of Arsames' officials were able to guard his estates there, and so prevent slaves from fleeing (cf. TAD 6.3). Arsames warns Nakhthor, the addressee, that he must do the same, and strictly guard Arsames' domestic staff and his goods. Not only that, he must add to them! He must actively seek out craftsmen, bring them to the satrapal court, mark them with Arsames' brand, and then deliver them to Arsames' estates. In other words, Nakhthor is to look for craftsmen, find them and enslave them. This is reminiscent of the passage in 1 Samuel 8, which warns against the power of the king. Perhaps this passage does not describe the Judean king, but the Persian one![3]

> "You shall solemnly warn them, and show them the ways of the king who shall reign over them." So Samuel reported all the words of YHWH to the people who were asking him for a king. He said, "These will be the ways of the king who will reign over you: he will take your sons and appoint them to his chariots and to be his horsemen, and to run before his chariots; and he will appoint for himself commanders of thousands and commanders of fifties, and some to plough his ground and to reap his harvest, and to make his implements of war and the equipment of his chariots. He will take your daughters to be perfumers and cooks and bakers. He will take the best of your fields and vineyards and olive orchards and give them to his courtiers. He will take one-tenth of your grain and of your vineyards and give it to his officers and his courtiers. He will take your male and female slaves, and the best of your cattle and donkeys, and put them to his work. He will take one-tenth of your flocks, and you shall be his slaves." (1 Samuel 8:9–17)

Archives from the Nile Island of Elephantine in Egypt also provide an intimate look into the life of the ordinary person during the Persian occupation. In spite of the ubiquitous presence of Persian garrisons, brigandage appears to have been a constant threat. A Demotic letter (EPE C4) dated to the 36th year of Darius I (5th October 486; Month of Payni, Day 17), warns the recipient not to leave a shipment of grain unguarded on the wharf for fear of bandits, but to bring it immediately to the storage facility in the house of Osirouer (Uṣer–wer):

> I said to him, "The grain, if it is deposited on this ground, without the men who will carry it to Egypt being present, then the brigands who are on the mountain will come for it by night (and) steal it." We are used to seeing the brigands when they are on the mountain on the southern side opposite us. Artbanu is used to seeing them as well. It usually happens that they sit opposite us by day, but there is (a) long distance between us (and) between them. The grain, if it is brought down without armed men to guard this grain, (then) the brigands will come for it by night (and) they will take it away.
>
> If it is pleasing for his lord, the grain, if it is to be taken away to the house of Osireouer, cause (word) to be sent to Artbanu not to cause it to be brought to the ground [=off the quay, i.e. inland] (rather) cause it to happen (that) the grain which can be brought down in one load (be) that which will be brought down from the quay. Cause the men to guard the remainder sitting on the quay. (EPE C4)

Most important to the well-being of any community is the assurance of just courts of law. Greek writers portray the exemplary conduct of the Persian judges. Herodotus reports (*History* V: 25; VII: 194) that Cambyses had cut the throat of one royal judge and flayed off all his skin because he had been bribed to give an unjust decision. He reports that Darius crucified another judge for the same offence (*History* VII: 194). The letters from Elephantine present the opposite picture, however. Bribes were the rule and judgments depended on them. One letter is particularly illustrative (TAD 6.10). (Unfortunately, only the right-hand side is preserved.)

> To my lords Jedaniah, Mauziah, Uriah and the garrison, [yo]ur servant [PN]. [May all the gods] seek after [the welfare of our lords at all times. It is well with us here.
>
> Now, every day which...he complained to the investigators. One Zivaka complained to the investigator...we have, inasmuch as the Egyptians gave them a bribe. And from the (time which?)...which the Egyptians before Arsames, but they act thievishly.
>
> Moreover, [the Jews arrived from?] the province of Thebes and say thus: Mazdayasna/A Mazdean is an official of the province...we are afraid inasmuch as we are fewer by two.
>
> Now, behold, they favoured.... If only we had revealed our presence to Arsames before, then something like this would not have [happened to us....] He will report our affairs before Arsames. Pisina pacifies us [lit. our presence]. [Whatever] you find—honey, castor oil, string, rope, leather skins, boards [send us, since] they are full of anger at you.
>
> Pasu son of Mannuki came to Memphis and...and the investigator. And he gave me silver, 12 staters and [I am] happy with it...Hori gave me when they detained him because of the pitcher. Tiri...said: 'at the order of the king and they detain them. And the damage (caused to) Arsames and the compensation (due to) Djeh[o...] and Hori whom they detained.
>
> On the sixth day of Phaophi the letters arrived...we will do the thing.
>
> To...my lords, Jaadaniah, Mauziah, y[our] se[rvant....] (TAD 6.10)

The image in the letter is of bribed and capricious judges. Whatever the difficulty may have been, satisfaction was evidently not achieved at Elephantine, the local level, because the case was referred to Thebes as a higher level of the administration. The judgment went against the letter-writer there because, as he states, "the Egyptians gave them a bribe", so the case was appealed to the next level again—the satrap. The Iranian, Pisina, was willing to go to Memphis and to Arsames to present their case to him, so goods for the bribes were requested. Pasu son of Mannuki, a Babylonian, had provided the letter-writer with 12 staters for the bribes, but this was evidently not enough. The letter-writer asks Jedaniah and his colleagues at the garrison to send whatever they have, to add to the bribe. To the mind of the letter-writer, those bringing the largest bribe had the strongest chance of a favourable outcome.

Another example of the effect of bribes on inter-ethnic relations appears in a letter in the Jedaniah archive from Elephantine (TAD A4.5):

> [Several lines missing]
> ...we grew/increased,
> detachments of the Egyptians rebelled. We did not leave our posts, and nothing damaging was found among us.
>
> In the 14th year of Darius the [Ki]ng, when our lord Arsames went to the king, this is the evil act which the priests of Khnum, the god, did in the capital of Yeb [i.e. Elephantine] in league with Vidranga who was *frataraka* here. They gave him silver and goods. There is part of the king's store-house which is in Yeb the *bîrtā'*, they demolished it and built a wall in the middle of the *bîrtā'* of Yeb.
>
> [About three lines missing]
>
> And now that wall [stands] built in the midst of the *bîrtā'*. There is a well which was

built in the midst of the *bîrtā'*, which did not fail to give the garrison drink. Whenever they would be [garrisoned?] there, they would drink water from [th]at well. The priests of Khnub the god stopped up that well.

If inquiry be made of the judges, police, and investigators who are appointed in the province (*medinta*) of Tshetres, it will be kno[wn] to our lord in accordance with this which we say.

Moreover we are separated...
[Three lines missing]
VERSO
(d/r)ḥpny' which are in Yeb the *bîrtā'*...we grew/increased...was not found in...to bring meal-offer[ing]...[or] to offer there to Yhw the g[od] [sacrifices?]...in which...but a brazier...the אשרנא they took [to make them their] own...

If it please our lord...much...we from the garrison...[If it] please our lord, may an order be issued...we. If it please our lord,...[let] them [pro]tect the things which...to [rebuild] our [temp]le which they demolished. (TAD A 4.5)

Dated to 410 (the 14th year of Darius II), the letter reveals the tense state of affairs between the priests of Khnum and those of Yhw, as well as the power that the governor had to adjudicate between them. According to the letter, the priests of Khnum had given the governor, Vidranga, money and valuables. In turn, he permitted the Khnum priests to build a covered walkway to their temple. In the process, they tore down part of the royal storehouse, blocked up the garrison's well, and vandalized the temple of Yhw. As a result it became unfit for service, and the Jews were unable to bring offerings to their god.

In the opinion of the letter-writer, the governor permitted this destruction only because of the gifts of silver and other goods that the priests of Khnum had brought him. Whether or not the perception was accurate, that was the perception. The conflict between the priests of Khnum and those of Yhw points to the role of the Persian administration in adjudicating between rival ethnic groups. Parties resolved conflicts by appealing to whoever could influence those in command, and gifts and bribes routinely accompanied the appeal. That the Jews offered their own gifts to Arsames is revealed in another letter (TAD A4.10).

Your servants—Jedaniah son of Gemariah by name, 1
    Mauzi son of Nathan by name, 1
    Shemiah son of Haggai by name, 1
    Hosea son of Jathom by name, 1
    Hosea son of Nattum by name, 1
all told five persons, men of Syene, who are in Yeb the citadel—thus say: "If our lord...and our temple, the one of Yhw the god, be rebuilt in Yeb the citadel as formerly it was built—and sheep, ox, and goat (as) burnt offering are (n)ot made there, but (only) incense (and) meal-offering—and should our lord make a statement [about this, afterwards] we shall give to the house of our lord si[lver...and] barley, a thousa[nd] *ardabs*." (TAD A4.10).

The situation on the Nile Island of Elephantine is typical of the situation everywhere in the empire. A Persian garrison (composed of men and their families brought in from distant parts of the empire) erected a temple to their god on a site dedicated to the local god of the Nile, Khnum. The local priests finally succeeded in convincing (bribing?) the local governor to allow them to tear down the intruding sanctuary. In this case the local populace prevailed, but there is no assurance that that would always be so. The Lycian populace at Xanthus had to suffer the intrusion of a temple to the alien Carian god King Kaunos when a Persian garrison was installed there composed of ethnic Carians (Metzger 1979; Fried 2004: 140–54).

Sidon

The rivalry and competition among the satraps of Asia Minor and between the different ethnic groups on the Nile Island of Elephantine is also visible among the governors of the provinces of Beyond the River. According to the funerary inscription of Eshmun'ezer, King of Sidon in the last years of Darius I, land in Beyond the River was added to the borders of Sidon in return for favours done the Great King.

> The Lord of Kings [i.e. the Achaemenid ruler] gave to me [i.e. to Sidon] Dor and Jaffa, the mighty lands of Dagon, which are in the Plain of Sharon, in accordance with the important deeds that I did. We added them to the borders of the country so that they would belong to Sidon forever. (ANET 662)

The lands that the Persian king had given to Sidon must have been taken from someone else. This transference of land from one provincial governor to another—as from one satrap to another—could only result in competition and rivalry among them.

Judah

Nehemiah's memoir, assumed by even minimalist biblical scholars to be genuine (e.g. Grabbe 1998), provides additional information about life in Beyond the River during the Persian occupation. Nehemiah was sent as governor of Judah in 445 with a mandate to rebuild the city wall. His attempt to build it was immediately met with accusations of rebellion against the king (Nehemiah 2:19).

> But when Sanballat the Horonite [Governor of Samaria] and Tobiah the Ammonite official [Governor of Ammon], and Geshem the Arab [King of the Qedarite Arab Kingdom] heard of it, they mocked and despised us, saying, 'What is this that you are doing? Are you rebelling against the king?' (Nehemiah 2:19)

It is true that we learn this only from Nehemiah, and Grabbe has accused him of paranoia (1998: 167), yet these accusations of rebellion by the governors of the provinces roundabout Judah are consistent with what seems to have occurred elsewhere in the empire. After Nehemiah completed the city wall, these governors of the neighbouring provinces again threatened to accuse Nehemiah of rebellion (Nehemiah. 6:5–7).

> Sanballat for the fifth time sent his servant to me in this way with an open letter in his hand.[6] In it was written, "It is reported among the nations—and Geshem also says it—that you and the Judaeans intend to rebel; that is why you are building the wall; and according to this report you wish to become their king.[7] You have also set up prophets to proclaim in Jerusalem concerning you, 'There is a king in Judah!' And now it will be reported to the king according to these words. So come, therefore, and let us confer together." (Nehemiah 6:5–7)

Nehemiah does not report why they were out to do him in. It may be that any change in the status quo provoked uncertainty, suspicion, jealousy, and resentment among neighbouring governors and satraps whose only recourse was to accuse the newcomer of rebellion. The governors of the peoples of the neighbouring provinces are the leaders of the "peoples of the lands".

The first years of the return

According to Ezra 3:2–3, Jeshua, the High Priest, and Zerubbabel, governor of Judah, set up the altar of the God of Israel in its place because they were afraid of the peoples of the lands. No year is given, but reference to Jeshua and Zerubbabel suggests the second year of Darius I (Hag.1:1) 520. There is little information relevant to Judah in this period. Nevertheless, it is possible that the rivalry among the satraps discussed in the Greek writings, the interethnic hostilities revealed in the Elephantine letters, the suspicions with which the governors of Beyond the River greeted Nehemiah, and the competition hinted at in the funerary inscription from Sidon, were all experienced as well by the returnees from Babylon. According to Ezra 6, Tattenai, vice-satrap of Beyond the River in the reign of Darius I, went to Jerusalem to investigate the temple building project there. Evidence reviewed above suggests that he was very likely responding to complaints, and that these would have been accusations of rebellion from the other governors of Beyond the River. If the governors of the neighbouring peoples were accusing Judah of rebellion, we may well conclude that the threat from the peoples of the lands was real, and the dread of them appropriate.

Notes

1. Chron. 5:25; 2 Chron. 6:33; 13:9; 32:13, 19; Ezra 3:3; 9:1, 2, 11; 10:2, 11; Nehemiah 9:24, 30; 10:28, 30, 31.
2. This is also implied in Williamson's (1985: 176) translation, "The king had sent army officers and cavalry to accompany me". The Hebrew says: "The king sent army officers and cavalry with me".
3. The literature on the so-called Deuteronomist, the presumed author of this text, is enormous. He is usually assigned to the exilic period, but for various reasons I assign him to the Persian period (Fried 2002).

44

Xerxes and the Tower of Babel

A. R. George

Introduction

Among the great sites of ancient Persia the best known to visitors to Iran are certainly Persepolis and Pasargadae in the province of Fars, with their wonderful ruins of stone palaces and tombs built by the kings Cyrus and Darius. A less prominent place on the itinerary of archaeological sites is occupied by the ancient city of Susa in the plain of Khuzistan. Susa is its Greek name; the Elamites called it Shushun, the Babylonians knew it as Shushin, later Shushi(m) and Shushan, the Achaemenid Persians as Shusha. Its present name, Shush-i Daniel, combines the ancient toponym with that of the prophet Daniel, who (legend has it) saw in Shushan a vision of a ram and a goat that foretold the eclipse of Persia by Alexander of Macedon. Susa is vastly older than Pasargadae and Persepolis: it has a history going back well into the fourth millennium and was the lowland capital of a succession of independent states in the third and second millennia. Among these states was the Elamite kingdom of Shutruk-Nahhunte and his sons, Kutir-Nahhunte and Shilhak-Inshushinak, twelfth-century monarchs well known as conquerors of Babylon.

The French excavations at Susa, led by Jacques de Morgan at the turn of the nineteenth century, uncovered the citadel, palaces and temples of Achaemenid and Elamite kings. On the citadel (today often termed the acropolis) they also turned up an abundance of important ancient artefacts, including many not of local origin but from Susa's western neighbours in Mesopotamia (Harper 1992). Foremost among these were stone monuments of the Old Akkadian kings, Sargon, Manishtushu and Naram-Sîn, published by Fr Vincent Scheil in early volumes of *Mémoires de la Délégation en Perse*. The best known of them is certainly the great limestone stele of Naram-Sîn that depicted this king's defeat of the mountain-dwelling Lullubi people and was originally set up in Sippar on the Euphrates (Scheil 1900: 53–55). An added caption in Elamite reveals that Naram-Sîn's stele was taken to Susa by Shutruk-Nahhunte as spoils of war after his invasion of Babylonia, a period of hostilities that led to the fall of Babylon in 1157 BC. Another famous Babylonian monument found at Susa but originally from Sippar is the great stele of Hammurapi of Babylon, inscribed with the laws that so impressed twentieth-century Europe (Scheil 1902: 11–162). The probability is that this and many of the other early Mesopotamian artefacts found at Susa were taken there as booty at about the same time as Naram-Sîn's stele, during the period of Elam's short-lived hegemony over Babylonia.

Such booty-taking was part and parcel of conquest. It is well known that Babylonian kings themselves accumulated in and around their palace statues and other objects looted from conquered peoples (Koldewey 1990: 162–169; Unger 1931: 224–228; Klengel-Brandt 1990). The exhibition at the British Museum that gave occasion for the conference whose proceedings appear in this volume included a stone bowl of Ashurbanipal, the last great king of Assyria (668–c.630). Its inscription shows that it once belonged to the Assyrian king's palace, but was excavated in the royal treasury at Persepolis (Schmidt 1957: pl. 49/1a–d; Curtis & Tallis 2005: no. 117). It was probably taken from Nineveh as loot when the Assyrian capital fell to the Babylonians and Medes in 612 BC. How it ended up in Persian ownership is a matter for speculation, but its presence in the treasury speaks for the Achaemenid kings' interest in the products of Mesopotamian royal power. A still more pertinent example of booty-taking comes from the time when Babylonia fell under the control of the Persian Empire. Many precious objects were removed from their proper locations in Babylonia to Persepolis and there also became part of the royal treasury (Schmidt 1957: 57–63). Especially noteworthy are several fine beads, cylinder seals and other votive objects originally presented to Babylonian temples by royal benefactors in the seventh and sixth centuries.

The eye-catching monuments of third- and second-millennium Mesopotamia from Susa are not the only Babylonian objects that de Morgan found there. Less conspicuous as works of art, but noteworthy nevertheless, are three objects from a much later period: a damaged clay cylinder (Fig. 44.1) of Nebuchadnezzar II, who ruled the Babylonian empire in the sixth century BC (604–562), and a marble vase and stone slab bearing labels of the same king's household (Langdon 1905/1906). Unfortunately no exact provenances are recorded but since the cylinder fragment was already discovered in 1900, the citadel is the likely find spot. The citadel of Susa was obviously not the original location of these objects. The vase and slab can be presumed without more ado to have been pillaged from the palace at Babylon, but the presence in Susa of the cylinder fragment presents a larger problem.

Nebuchadnezzar's cylinder fragment

The principal use of Neo-Babylonian cylinders was to bear pious texts reporting royal building work, typically of temples, city walls

Fig. 44.1 Nebuchadnezzar II's cylinder fragment from Susa, Sb 1700. (Courtesy Musée du Louvre)

and other monumental construction projects. These building inscriptions often indicate that the cylinders on which they were written were intended for embedding at regular intervals deep in the foundations and superstructure of the buildings in question. Archaeology confirms this, for a good few cylinders have been found intact in hollow spaces in walls, untouched since their deposit and revealed only by archaeologists dismantling the building.

The text written on the cylinder found at Susa records Nebuchadnezzar's completion of Etemenanki, the ziggurat of the god Marduk at Babylon. This building was the enormous temple-tower that most accept inspired the biblical legend of the Tower of Babel. No spectacular ruin remains of the ziggurat of Babylon, for it was levelled in antiquity, but its foundations reveal it to have risen from a base 90 metres square. Ancient sources allow for approximate reconstructions of how it once looked (Schmid 1990). Just recently a stele of Nebuchadnezzar II came to light that includes a depiction of the tower in profile, which, even allowing for idealization, leaves no doubt as to the building's general appearance. It was a stepped pyramid consisting of six storeys with the sanctuary of Marduk making a seventh at the summit (see provisionally Schøyen 2007, and my drawing in Levy 2008: 31).

At least 12 exemplars of this king's Etemenanki cylinder have survived, including that found at Susa (tabulated in Da Riva 2008: 19–20, C41.1–12). None of them is complete. The fact that they are all broken can be explained as a result of the building's eventual demolition. Three exemplars (now in Philadelphia) were bought from dealers in London and Baghdad in the years 1888–1889 and are without secure provenance (CBS 33, 1125 and 1785). This was a time when people from the villages near Babylon were digging out the remaining courses of baked bricks of the ziggurat's mantle for use as building material, and it seems likely that the Philadelphia cylinders came to light as a result of their excavations. Four further exemplars were excavated at Babylon between 1899 and 1913: (a) one at the north-west corner of the ziggurat's mud-brick core, in a pit left by the villagers; (b) another in Homera, the mound of rubble from the ziggurat's superstructure dumped in north-east Babylon by Alexander of Macedon and his successors; (c) a third (represented by two fragments) in disturbed contexts in the ruins of the palace complex (Qasr, Hauptburg); and (d) a fourth recovered from modern fill in the courtyard of the temple of Ninurta in the southern part of the city (Berger 1973: 295–296; the find spot of the last mentioned is more accurately reported by Koldewey 1911: 31, "im modernen Schutt"). An eighth exemplar is a fragment that came to light during Iraqi work at Babylon in the late 1970s (Al-Rawi n.d.: 23–24, Babylon 105–A).

What was an exemplar of Nebuchadnezzar's ziggurat cylinder doing in Susa? The discrepancy between the intended location of the cylinder and its actual provenance is a key issue in this paper, and for that reason I have conducted a statistical analysis of the find spots of 386 cylinders left by Neo- and Late Babylonian kings and other builders. Certainly there are more that have escaped attention and, of course, very many more that remain *in situ*, but the figure is an appreciable sample that will give a trustworthy picture. The data of this investigation are too extensive to include in this paper, but a brief summary of the pertinent results is instructive. Only 28 (7 per cent) of the 386 cylinders were certainly found at any distance from the buildings for which they were intended, including the four exemplars of Nebuchadnezzar's ziggurat cylinder noted above as found elsewhere in Babylon; only 7 of the 28 seem certainly to have been excavated in cities where they did not belong, including the piece from Susa. Most of these 28 are fragments from very disturbed contexts and were probably removed there at some later date after the ruination of the buildings in which they had originally been buried. Exemplary are the pieces of Nebuchadnezzar's ziggurat cylinders found in Homera, Qasr (Hauptburg) and the temple of Ninurta. These are best understood as chance survivals of broken pieces dispersed to secondary locations after the demolition of the tower, whether in antiquity or later. Fragments of baked brick from the ziggurat's mantle ended up likewise strewn all over the city. The demolished remains at Homera were no doubt a resource much used by later builders happy to find there huge quantities of good-quality baked bricks ready-made and waiting, for reuse whole or for recycling as hardcore.

Some have maintained that duplicates of cylinders were kept in archives as records (e.g. Ellis 1968: 112–113). The archaeological evidence for the retention of archival copies of cylinders (as opposed to draft texts on tablets) in the Neo-Babylonian period is slim, and not at all compelling for the period before Nabonidus (555–539). This king's antiquarian interests are well known and might have given rise to small collections of cylinders in the temple of Shamash at Sippar and, less certainly, the Hauptburg at Babylon. Nabonidus seems to have worked on the wall that surrounded the precinct of the ziggurat (Schaudig 2001: 474–475; George 2007: 88–89), but there is no reason to believe that he touched the superstructure of the tower itself; that being so, no cylinder embedded in the ziggurat could have found its way into his possession.

The data collected in my study of the provenances of Neo-Babylonian cylinders indicate that the number of cylinders that appear never to have been put to the use for which they were intended is very small indeed. With specific regard to the cylinder fragment found at Susa, the chances are very remote that it was kept at another location in Babylon, for example in one of the palaces. Very much more probably the cylinder was originally embedded in the brickwork of Babylon's ziggurat and remained there until the surrounding brickwork was dismantled. Consequently it becomes important to examine how this seemingly insignificant object might have found its way from a location inside Etemenanki to its final resting place in Susa. To address this problem further it is necessary to consider the history of Etemenanki. In doing so, the evidence of archaeology, cuneiform documentation and later tradition will be adduced, but it is the archaeological record that is most eloquent.

The destruction of Etemenanki

The history of the ziggurat of Babylon in the mid- to late first millennium BC is known in outline (George 2007). Heavily damaged by Sennacherib of Assyria when he laid waste to Babylon in 689, the tower was partially rebuilt by his successors, Esarhaddon and Ashurbanipal, and completed after the fall of Assyria by Nabopolassar and Nebuchadnezzar II of Babylon. According to later Greek historians, the structure was levelled by Alexander of Macedon in preparation for a rebuilding that never took place (Strabo, *Geographica* XVI 1; Arrian, *Anabasis* VII 17). Instead the site lay abandoned until a large building was erected on it, probably in the Sasanian period (Schmidt 2002: 283–290). Cuneiform records seem to confirm the general truth of the Greek historians' assertion but suggest that the work of levelling was prolonged long after the great conqueror's death. They document the clearing of debris from the site of Marduk's cult-centre not only in the time of Alexander but also under his successors: Philip Arrhidaeus, Alexander IV, Seleucus I and the Crown Prince Antiochus (see in more detail George 2007: 91). The levelling of the tower was no small task and must have been undertaken only because the building was already irremediably ruined. The question arises, was it ruined by erosion over time or by a more deliberate aggressor? The answer lies in archaeology.

When the levelled stump of the ziggurat at Babylon was laid bare by local people in the 1880s, they removed the baked bricks that faced it in order to reuse them, leaving only a mud-brick core surrounded by a pit and surmounted by the vestiges of Sasanian and later structures. The first German expedition to Babylon surveyed the remains in 1913 but it was not until the autumn of 1962 that a second expedition, led by Hansjörg Schmid, examined the pit and core with a modern archaeological eye for architecture and stratigraphy. In the summer of that same year the Assyriologist Franz Böhl published an influential article on the Babylonian revolts led by native insurgents against the Achaemenid emperor, Xerxes I (Böhl 1962). There he asserted that, after suppressing the revolts, the vengeful Persian desecrated the cult-centre of Marduk and partly demolished it. In this Böhl was relying not on Babylonian or Persian sources, but on the reports of Xerxes' destruction of Babylonian temples by late Greek and Roman authors, principally Diodorus, Strabo, Arrian and Aelian.

Whether or not Schmid knew of Böhl's article at the time of his excavation I do not know, but he certainly relied on it when writing up the results of his excavation (Schmid 1981, 1995). He had found stratigraphic and structural evidence for deliberate damage to the ziggurat's superstructure, and sought to explain it. The damage consisted of an irregular depression in the southern façade of the ziggurat reaching well into the mud-brick core and plunging deep below the height to which the rest of the structure was levelled (Schmid 1995: 76, pls 32–33, plan 6) (Fig. 44.2). Since the damage reached the mud-brick core it presupposed the prior destruction at ground level of the baked-brick mantle along a fair stretch of the building's southern façade and of the three staircases that abutted that façade. This destruction was not the work of natural dilapidation but of human intervention. To Schmid it seemed that whoever had damaged the ziggurat had done so to prevent easy access to its superstructure, and had wanted to render it unusable. In his analysis, the resulting hole had been repeatedly washed by the floodwaters of the Euphrates while the rest of the structure still stood. The annual flood slowly undermined the tower so that, eventually, rebuilding was impossible and it had to be demolished. The original damage that permitted the ingress of water would then have preceded the building's levelling by many years and so occurred well before Alexander's conquest of the Persian Empire. Adopting Böhl's reconstruction of the history of Babylon in the early fifth century, Schmid identified Xerxes I as the culprit.

Not long after the publication of Schmid's preliminary report in 1981, Böhl's reading of history was shot down. The first salvo was fired by Amélie Kuhrt and Susan Sherwin-White, who pointed out that the accounts of Greek and Roman historians were tendentious and partisan, in that they

Fig. 44.2 The irregular depression that Hansjörg Schmid discovered in the southern façade of the ziggurat in 1962. The depression is clearly visible in the curved strata that interrupt the brickwork of the ziggurat's core (left and right) and underlies later, more level strata, including brickwork probably of Sasanian date (middle). The broad water-filled ditch in the foreground is where the baked-brick mantle once stood; it gives some idea of the depth of solid brickwork that originally fronted the core. (Reprinted from Schmid 1995: pl. 33a)

deliberately sought to contrast Greek civilization with Persian tyranny, and so were unreliable as historical sources (Kuhrt & Sherwin-White 1987). Without native evidence for the destruction of Babylonian temples under Xerxes, the Greek accounts carried no weight. When Schmid repeated his accusation against Xerxes in his final report (Schmid 1995), he elicited a hostile reaction among ancient historians, who criticized his adherence to Böhl's discredited reconstruction of history. But they offered no alternative explanation for the archaeological evidence that Schmid reported.

It is indeed difficult to find an explanation for the huge hole Schmid found in the ziggurat's side that does not attribute it to deliberate violence. The damage sustained by the mud-brick core could not have occurred without the prior destruction of a long section of the baked-brick mantle. This mantle faced the core to a thickness of between 13 m at its deepest point below ground and 18 m at a point 5.5 m higher than that (Schmid 1995: 56, 75). In addition, the thickness of the mantle of the southern façade was supplemented by the width of the abutting staircases, so that here the depth of baked brick measured as much as 25.5 m on the horizontal plane (1995: 75). As Schmid saw, no natural force can have penetrated such a mass of baked brick bonded with bitumen; damage resulting in a hole in the core can only be attributed to human intervention, but when and in what circumstances?

The strata that covered the hole in the core were similar in composition to those that overlay the levelled areas of the core, being notably free of fragments of mud brick (Schmid 1995: 76). They indicate that the depression was cleared out at the same time as the core was levelled, during work that removed the debris to another place leaving nothing behind. Therefore the hole was made either at the time of levelling or some time before. The contrast between the rest of the mud-brick core carefully levelled to a uniform height and the irregular depression in its southern side makes it highly improbable that the hole was made by the tower's eventual levellers, that is, by Alexander and his successors. Since they planned a rebuilding, it made sense to level the core to form an even platform suitable to take the new brickwork. It would not have been sensible to excavate a deep pit on one side. Finally, had the hole been made after the core was levelled, for example by treasure-hunters, fragments of mud brick from the excavation would have littered the strata around the hole's edges. Schmid found no sign of any such disturbance. The intervention represented by the hole thus occurred after the completion of the structure under Nebuchadnezzar II (*c*.590) and, so it seems, well before the mid-fourth century.

In this period the most plausible event to occasion violence against Babylon's most prominent building remains the suppression of one or other of the fifth-century revolts led in the cities of north Babylonia by the pretenders Bel-shimanni and Shamash-eriba. It is now certain that these revolts took place in the reign of Xerxes, probably both in his second year, 484 (Waerzeggers 2003/2004). As Schmid explains, the location of the damage, on the tower's south façade, points to the concomitant ruination of the tower's staircases. The destruction wrought on the tower was not only a symbolic attack on Babylonian religious and political identity. A more pragmatic reason would be strategic, as Schmid understood: with its staircases demolished the building was rendered temporarily useless as a place of refuge and defence. In human history many armies commanded to squash rebellions have smashed prominent religious buildings not only as a display of force but also to flush out resistance.

Xerxes and the "tomb of Belos"

The discovery of the hole in the tower's side led Schmid also to reconsider a legend told by Ctesias and Aelian. Ctesias was writing in the early fourth century BC, less than 100 years after Bel-shimanni's revolt. Aelian flourished nearly 600 years later. The story they relate tells how Xerxes visited (Ctesias) or broke open (Aelian) the "tomb" of Belitanas (Ctesias) or Belos (Aelian), that is, Marduk as Bel of Babylon. Schmid concluded that the story was based on a true event—the making of the hole in the ziggurat's side—but did not pursue the matter further (1981: 134–136).

The temple-tower of Babylon was often identified as a tomb by classical historians, not only on account of its superficial resemblance to the familiar Egyptian pyramid but perhaps also because of the persistence of the story related by Ctesias and Aelian. The legend tells in detail how Xerxes found inside the "tomb of Belos" a corpse lying in a sarcophagus full of oil, accompanied by a stele holding a text that enjoined its discoverer to replenish the sarcophagus with oil. When Xerxes tried to do so, he found he could not. This story is reminiscent of a much older tale told about two prominent figures of Mesopotamian legend, Adapa and Enmerkar, which survives only as a fragment (Picchioni 1981: 102–109; Foster 2005: 531–532). King Enmerkar desecrated a tomb 9 cubits deep, destroying its entrance but failing to find a corpse. Pierre Briant has noted that the "motif of a king violating sepulchres is very widespread" (Briant 2002a: 963). Thus Ctesias and Aelian's story may owe something to a motif of native folklore; but I have shown elsewhere that it reports many details that recall genuine Neo-Babylonian ritual practice (George 2007: 90–91). The argument is summarized in the following paragraph.

Inscribed cylinders of the kind discussed earlier were a minimal foundation deposit; on important occasions grander gestures were made. Statues of royal builders could be built into the brickwork, like the stele of Ashurbanipal in Babylon and Borsippa that depict him in canephorous pose (Ellis 1968: 24–25; Reade 1986a: 109). Or they might be buried deeper in the structure. Nabonidus is reported to have found a damaged statue depicting Sargon of Akkade in the foundations of Ebabbarra at Sippar (Lambert 1968/1969: 7 ll. 29–36), but it is unclear whether the statue was part of some very ancient foundation deposit; it might have been cast aside when broken and later incorporated in the structure as fill. An explicit instance, however, of the formal deposition of a statue in the structure of a building occurs in the case of the ziggurat of Babylon. Nebuchadnezzar's father, Nabopolassar, records in his own Etemenanki cylinder that he "fashioned representations of [his] royal likeness bearing a soil-basket, and positioned them variously in the foundation platform" of the ziggurat (BE I 84 ii 57–61, ed. Weissbach 1938: 42). In the first millennium, run-of-the-mill cylinders were placed in simple baskets and buried in hollows in walls, but we know that important stone monuments were given more elaborate treatment. They were interred in lidded terracotta boxes known as *tupshennu*, like the one used to bury the stone tablet of Nabû-apla-iddina as part of an elaborate foundation deposit beneath the temple of Shamash at Sippar (Woods 2004: 28, fig. 3, 34–35). Finally, it is a commonplace injunction in the building inscriptions of Neo-Assyrian kings of Babylonia for a future builder to secure a blessing by anointing foundation statues and inscriptions with oil. This detail completes a picture of authenticity. A human image in a box, an admonitory inscription, a rite involving oil: the Greek story preserves these salient elements of Babylonian foundation deposits and the rituals associated with them.

The suggestion, then, is that the story of Xerxes and the tomb of Belos is not only based on truth but retains some accuracy in matters of detail. In other words, while in this story the narratives of Ctesias and Aelian are essentially literary, they have some historical basis. With the archaeological evidence for the building's destruction in mind, it is legitimate to use the story, as Schmid did, to suggest that a Persian ruler, probably Xerxes, did indeed damage Marduk's cult-centre at Babylon, specifically by demolishing the baked-brick staircases on the ziggurat's south façade. I further propose that during this work the demolition teams came across at least one composite foundation deposit, comprising a royal statue in a box and an inscribed object calling for the ritual pouring of oil. Perhaps it was one of the foundation deposits left by Nabopolassar, as described in his cylinder inscription, perhaps it included the very stele of Nebuchadnezzar II that depicts him in front of the ziggurat (awaiting publication, see above), or perhaps it was a legacy of earlier building work by Esarhaddon or Ashurbanipal. The inscription was deciphered with the aid of local informants, and the Persian king, or his representative, was duly summoned to conduct the appropriate ritual. The event became distorted in the retelling, acquiring an element of the supernatural and the literary motif of the ill-starred ruler. The stone statue glistening with oil in its terracotta box turned into a human corpse miraculously preserved in a crystal sarcophagus. The blessing in the inscription turned into a signal of royal doom that could not be averted.

Conclusion

The reassertion of the essential truth of the Greek story of Xerxes and the "tomb of Belos" brings us back to our place of departure, the problem posed by the inscribed clay cylinder intended by Nebuchadnezzar for the temple-tower of Babylon but found instead at Susa. The cylinder's provenance has also been overlooked as evidence for the building's history. We have seen that it was almost certainly originally buried deep in the tower's structure. In the absence of an exact archaeological provenance I cannot prove that it was not recovered from the ziggurat's ruins by Alexander or his successors at the time of the building's demolition and then taken to Susa, but equally I cannot imagine a reason for any of them taking it there. In the light of the results of Schmid's careful fieldwork it is more sensible to attribute the cylinder's removal to Xerxes, the mighty destroyer of the Tower of Babel. I suggest that it fell out of the ziggurat's brickwork as his men proceeded in their demolition of the tower's staircases. It was then presented to the authorities, who had it sent back to Susa as dramatic proof of a job well done. There Nebuchadnezzar's cylinder joined other items of booty from Babylonia, in a stark display of Persian hegemony over a more ancient land.

The exhibition that occasioned this volume included a piece that throws up a neat parallel. This was a sixth-century bronze weight inscribed in archaic Greek with a dedication to Apollo of Didyma (Haussoullier 1905; Curtis & Tallis 2005: no. 445). It was originally the property of the famous sanctuary of Apollo near Miletus in Ionia, but it was excavated far from there, on the citadel of Susa. Historians agree that the weight surely fell into Persian hands either when, in 494 BC at the end of the first Ionian revolt, Miletus was sacked and the temple of Didyma was emptied of its valuables and burnt (Herodotus VI 9, cited by Briant 2002a: 494), or 15 years later when the same temple was looted in the aftermath of the Persians' defeat at Mycale (Ctesias §27, cited by Briant 2002a: 535). Even more certainly than the cylinder of Etemenanki, Apollo's weight was taken to Susa as booty of war.

Nebuchadnezzar's Susa cylinder seems a mundane thing but it would not have been the first such object to have been removed from its original location by conquerors. In this way a cylinder deposited by Warad-Sîn of Larsa in the wall of Ur in 1825 BC (middle chronology) turned up in Babylon after Samsuiluna had captured Ur 85 years later and dismantled its wall. And a cylinder embedded by the Babylonian king Merodach-baladan II (721–710) in the temple Eanna at Uruk was found in the northwest palace at Kalah (Nimrud), the Assyrian capital of Sargon II (721–705), who gained control of Uruk in 710 and subsequently continued work on the temple (see Radner 2005: 236–240). Following their recovery both these cylinders evidently served as models for subsequent royal inscriptions. But, in a land where there was no interest in emulating Babylonian building inscriptions, that was hardly the destiny of Nebuchadnezzar's cylinder. What, then, did this object mean to Xerxes?

In the Ancient Near East the collection of looted objects provided conquerors with concrete symbols of supremacy over defeated peoples and kings. In accumulating trophies of victory in their palaces, the great kings of Persia displayed the same penchant for the symbolism of triumph that was shown before them by Shutruk-Nahhunte of Elam and several kings of Babylon. Objects with labels of royal ownership or other royal inscriptions (like Nebuchadnezzar's cylinder) made the transfer of power and prestige particularly explicit, for to ancient minds name and self were indistinguishable. The ownership of conquered kings' names, in the guise of looted inscriptions, in some sense gave power over the very personae of those kings, and over the countries they had ruled.

Sometimes, but not always, the transfer of power to the conqueror was emphasized by the deliberate mutilation of looted statues and erasure of inscriptions (on this topic see recently Bahrani 2003: 149–184). As Karen Radner shows in her book *Die Macht des Namens*, the preservation of a predecessor's name was part of the business of securing legitimation, while the expunging of an enemy's name was a demonstration of contempt (Radner 2005). In the treatment of objects taken as booty both activities can be seen, so that some such artefacts were preserved entire, but others defaced or smashed. Conquerors thus had an ambivalent attitude to the monuments of the vanquished. This brings us to the sorry state of Nebuchadnezzar's Susa cylinder, which survives as just a fragment. It might have been broken accidentally, either as it came out of the ziggurat or later in Susa. Or it might have been deliberately smashed by the victorious Persians as an act symbolic of their triumph over Babylon and their scorn for the great name of Nebuchadnezzar.

Sceptics will remark that the foregoing reconstruction of what happened at Babylon in 484 BC is founded on circumstantial evidence and hearsay. Admittedly, it lacks the decisive evidence that would make it incontrovertible. I present it here as an hypothesis: a reading of history that in my mind makes the most coherent sense of all the information that we have at our disposal, archaeological and documentary, historical and literary. It is for others, if they can, to come up with better explanations for that information.

45

"Judges of the King" in Achaemenid Mesopotamia[1]

Shalom E. Holtz

In his monumental history of the Persian Empire, Pierre Briant studies the case of Babylonia under the first two Achaemenid kings, Cyrus and Cambyses, and reaches the following conclusion about the effect of the Achaemenid conquest:

> It is clear that neither Cyrus nor his son wished…to bring about a total disruption of existing conditions. Many institutions known from their time find their antecedents in the Mesopotamian imperial structures of the previous centuries. In other words, the transformations did not necessarily result from suppression or destruction of the existing institutions, but more often and doubtless more efficaciously came about by gradually adapting these institutions to the new structure outlined by the conquerors. (Briant 2002a: 70)

This conservative trend in Achaemenid imperial policy continued even during what Briant calls the "radical acceleration" toward administrative unification under Darius I. Briant himself notes that "the unification of administrative practices on an imperial scale does not imply a loss of traditions" and that "the conquest and dominion played out on two levels… unification and maintenance of diversity" (2002a: 507).

According to Briant, then, Mesopotamia's transition from rule by Neo-Babylonian kings to Achaemenid emperors was not as dramatic as one might expect. Even though the region was now subject to new royal authorities, many institutions continued to function as they had in earlier times under native kings. Even the government of Darius I, which did much to unify administrative practices, did not completely obliterate the native traditions of the populations it governed. Instead, according to Briant, the Achaemenid rulers maintained local diversity within the broader context of the empire.

The purpose of the present study is to illustrate, and thus add support to, Briant's conclusions by examining one particular office: the office of *dayyānu ša šarri*, Akkadian for "judge of the king".[2] By collecting references to this office in cuneiform sources, the present study will trace the history of the institution of "judges of the king" in Mesopotamia and demonstrate that it survives the transition from Neo-Babylonian to Achaemenid kings. To do so, the present study will begin by considering some of the limitations of the available evidence. It will then briefly describe the office of *dayyānu ša šarri* under the Neo-Babylonian kings just prior to Cyrus' conquest. Then, it will document the survival of this office under the Achaemenid Empire by surveying the available evidence from this period.

I. Nature of the evidence considered

The evidence presented in the present study comes from the abundant corpus of cuneiform legal documents composed in Achaemenid Mesopotamia. These documents come from archives once kept in Mesopotamian cities including Babylon, Borsippa, Sippar, Uruk and Nippur.[3] The cuneiform documents themselves attest the survival of native Mesopotamian traditions under Achaemenid rule. Even while the empire wrote official documents in Aramaic on leather or papyrus, scribes in Mesopotamia continued to write legal documents in cuneiform, as they had for almost 3,000 years.

Some reflections on the limitations of the present study are in order. There are two main limitations, one resulting from the sources themselves and the other imposed by the present study. The cuneiform sources themselves limit the present study of the administration of justice, and of any legal question, for that matter, for a number of reasons. Foremost among these is the fact that legal affairs in Achaemenid Mesopotamia were not always recorded in cuneiform on clay tablets. During the period in question many, if not most, legal documents were probably written in Aramaic on papyrus or leather. These latter materials deteriorate under normal archaeological conditions (apart from exceptional environments in Egypt, the Dead Sea and Afghanistan), so that these Aramaic documents are now lost. Although clay tablets survive, this does not mean that all the cuneiform legal tablets ever written are available to the scholarly community. Some tablets have yet to be excavated or rediscovered in museums, while others were probably destroyed even in antiquity.[4] Furthermore, the picture is severely limited by the fact that more than half of the nearly 13,000 tablets estimated to exist come from only two temple archives: the Eanna at Uruk or the Ebabbar at Sippar (Jursa 2005: 2). These temples were, of course, not the only places where justice was administered. The existence of private archives offers a glimpse of other adjudicatory venues and mitigates this bias towards temples, but only to a certain extent. In sum, one must always wonder if the study of cuneiform archives in Achaemenid Mesopotamia provides a comprehensive picture of the legal situation at that time.

The second limitation to the present study is, as noted above, self-imposed: by singling out one office, the *dayyānu ša šarri*, the survey will not consider other authorities that play a judicial role but do not have the title "judge". These include such authorities as city governors, temple officials, assemblies and even the king himself. Although the study will reach some conclusions about the legal system in Achaemenid Mesopotamia, a complete description is beyond its purview.[5]

II. The office of *dayyānu ša šarri* in the Neo-Babylonian period

With these limitations in mind, the discussion can turn to the office of the *dayyānū ša šarri*, "the judges of the king". Documenting the survival of the office of *dayyānu ša šarri* into the Achaemenid period must begin with a description of this office in the Neo-Babylonian period, just prior to Cyrus' conquest. Before turning to the judges themselves, however, it is useful to consider the ideological connection between the king and the judges that is expressed in the title.

This connection can be traced back to the very beginnings of Mesopotamian royal ideology. For the Neo-Babylonian period, a prime expression of this royal ideology is found in a literary text, which Wilfred G. Lambert calls "Nebuchadnezzar, King of Justice". The text praises the king as follows:

> He was not negligent in the matter of true and righteous judgment, he did not rest night or day, but with council and deliberation he persisted in writing down judgments and decisions arranged to be pleasing to the great lord, Marduk, and for the betterment of all the peoples and the settling of the land of Akkad. He drew up improved regulations for the city, he built anew the law court. (Lambert 1965: 8)[6]

According to this text, the king is directly involved in sustaining the system of justice—he promulgates decisions and regulations and maintains the courts. It seems that this association between the king and justice gave rise to the Akkadian title *dayyānu ša šarri*, literally "judge of the king". The title alone expresses an ideological association between the king and the courts. It also raises the possibility that there was some practical connection between the royalty and the judiciary, perhaps through the appointment process. However, the Akkadian title leaves the definition of this practical connection open to speculation and, unfortunately, the available evidence does not shed much additional light on this question.

Having briefly considered the ideological underpinnings of the title *dayyānu ša šarri*, the discussion can now return to survey the attestations of the title in the Neo-Babylonian period. Numerous Neo-Babylonian legal documents refer to groups of individuals designated *dayyānu ša šarri* ("judges of the king"), usually written with the Sumerograms ^{lu2}DI.KU$_5$.MEŠ *ša*$_2$ LUGAL. More frequently, however, instead of the generic *šarri* ("king"), the documents name the king in the title, such as *dayyānu ša Nergal-šarra-uṣur* ("judges of Neriglissar") or *dayyānu ša Nabû-nā'id* ("judges of Nabonidus").

The best-attested Neo-Babylonian "judges of the king" are the judges of Neriglissar and Nabonidus who served in Babylon. They are the subjects of an extensive study by Cornelia Wunsch in which she assembles all the available references to them (2000: 557–597). Wunsch studies a group of "judicial documents" ("Richterurkunden") that describe the participation of judges of Neriglissar or judges of Nabonidus in the adjudication of disputes and in land sales. The names of the particular judges appear at the end of these documents, with the title *dayyānu* ("judge") following each name (2000: 558). Wunsch compiles all these names into a directory of all the judges of Neriglissar and Nabonidus in Babylon, including the judges' seals, and lists the dates of each judge's service. By studying this information, Wunsch arrives at a detailed description of the office of "judge of the king" in Babylon during the Neo-Babylonian period.

Wunsch observes that individual judges of Neriglissar and Nabonidus in Babylon did not hear cases alone. Instead, cases were heard by "judicial councils" ("Richterkollegien"), which consisted of several judges and sometimes included other officials, as well (2000: 568 and the chart on pp. 570–571). Based on the judges' family names, she concludes that the members of these councils came from economically influential families that are well attested in business documents from the period (2000: 568). Usually, judicial councils included only one representative of any particular family. Wunsch also determines that there was a strict hierarchy within these councils based on seniority; a judge could advance only with the departure of a more senior judge (2000: 572).

III. The office of *dayyānu ša šarri* under Achaemenid kings

Wunsch's work on the judges of Neriglissar and Nabonidus is the starting point for the present discussion of the survival of the *dayyānu ša šarri* under the Achaemenid kings. The discussion will begin with Wunsch's evidence from Babylon and will then turn to consider other evidence from the same city, followed by evidence from other cities.

Wunsch herself documents the continuity of the office in Babylon by showing that three men, named ^{m}Nabû-balāssu-iqbi, ^{m}Rīmūt-Bēl and ^{m}Nabû-etel-ilāni, began their careers with the designation "judges of Nabonidus", and continued their careers as "judges of Cyrus" in Babylon (cf. 2000: 573). Even though a new, foreign king had come to power, these three "judges of the king" retained their position.

Wunsch draws her evidence from the prosopography of the so-called "Richterurkunden", documents that end with a record of the names of the judges. Other legal documents that Wunsch does not consider, also attest to the survival of the office of *dayyānu ša šarri* in Babylon. For example, a summons written in Uruk and dated to 18 Šabāṭu, year 1 of Cyrus (30 January 538 BC) requires a certain individual to come and "argue a case" before the judges of the king. The relevant section reads as follows:

a-di U$_4$ 15-*kam*$_2$ *ša*$_2$ ITI BAR$_2$ ^{m}PN$_1$ *it-ti* ^{m}PN$_2$ ^{lu2}ŠA$_3$.TAM E$_2$.AN.NA *u* ^{m}PN$_3$ ^{lu2}SAG.LUGAL ^{lu2}EN *pi-qit-ti* E$_2$.AN.NA *a-na* TIN.TIR^{ki} *il-la-kam*$_2$-*ma di-i-ni* ... **ina pa-ni** ^{lu2}**DI.KU$_5$.MEŠ** *ša*$_2$ **LUGAL** *i-dab-bu-ub*

"By 15 Nisannu, ^{m}PN$_1$ shall go with ^{m}PN$_2$, *šatammu* of the Eanna and ^{m}PN$_3$, the *ša rēš šarri* administrator of the Eanna to Babylon and argue a case **before the judges of the king.**"[7]

The summoned individual (^{m}PN$_1$) must come to Babylon together with two officials of the Eanna temple, the *šatammu* and *ša rēš šarri*, to "argue a case" before the judges of the king. Unlike the examples cited by Wunsch, this summons does not name the judges of the king before whom the case is to be argued. It does, however, provide additional evidence for the survival of the office of *dayyānu ša šarri* in Babylon during the reign of Cyrus.

The evidence presented thus far has been limited to tracing the history of the office of *dayyānu ša šarri* in Babylon from the Neo-Babylonian period into the Achaemenid period. The evidence from outside Babylon shows that the office survives the transition to Achaemenid rule there as well. In the Neo-Babylonian period, judges of Nabonidus and Neriglissar are known from several other cities (e.g. Wunsch 2000: 567, n. 32). Although there is not yet sufficient evidence to trace any of these judges' careers through the transition from Babylonian to Achaemenid rule, the available evidence shows that the institution of *dayyānu ša šarri* itself does survive this transition. The evidence comes from the two large temple archives of the Ebabbar at Sippar and the Eanna at Uruk.

In Sippar, a text dated to 21 Ayaru, year 8 of Cyrus (25 May 531 BC) records the activities of an adjudicating council that met there. The lines that narrate the actual activities are broken,[8] but the concluding lines that contain the names of the council read as follows:

i-na EŠ.BAR [*di-i-ni*] MU.MEŠ
[^{m}]^{d}EN-TIN-*iṭ* ^{lu2}E$_2$.MAŠ UD.KIB.NUN^{ki}
^{md}EN-PAP ^{lu2}**DI.KU$_5$ LUGAL** A-*šu$_2$ ša$_2$*
^{md}NA$_3$-A-MU A ^{md}30-DINGIR
^{md}NA$_3$-PAP ^{lu2}**DI.KU$_5$ LUGAL** A-*šu$_2$ ša$_2$* ^{m}*ha-za*-[X]-DINGIR
^{m}*ri-mut* ^{lu2}UMBISAG A-*šu$_2$ ša$_2$* ^{md}EN-GI A ^{m}IM-*šam-me-e*

"At the decision of this [case]:
^{m}Bēl-uballiṭ, the *šangû* of Sippar;
^{m}Bēl-nāṣir, **the judge of the king**, son of ^{m}Nabû-apla-iddin descendant of Sîn-ilī;
^{m}Nabû-nāṣir, **the judge of the king**, son of ^{m}Haza-[X]-ili;
^{m}Rīmūt, the scribe, son of ^{m}Bēl-ušallim descendant of Adad-šammê. (Cyr 301:11–14)

Two members of the adjudicating council, ^{m}Bēl-nāṣir and ^{m}Nabû-nāṣir, have the title *dayyān šarri*.[9] They demonstrate that, as at Babylon, the title continued to be used well into the reign of Cyrus.

The archives of the Eanna attest to "judges of the king" at Uruk as well. One summons written at Uruk on 18 Šabāṭu, year 5 of Cyrus (15 February 533 BC) reads as follows:

U$_4$ 7-*kam$_2$ ša$_2$* ITI ŠE MU 5-*kam$_2$* ^{m}*kur-aš$_2$* LUGAL TIN.TIR^{ki} LUGAL KUR.KUR ^{m}PN$_1$ *a-na* UNUG^{ki} *il-la-kam$_2$-ma di-i-ni*... **ina pa-ni** ^{lu2}**DI.KU$_5$.MEŠ** *ša$_2$* **LUGAL** *i-dab-bu-ub*

"On 7 Addaru, year 5 of Cyrus, king of Babylon, king of the lands, ^{m}PN$_1$ shall come to Uruk and argue a case...**before the judges** of the king."[10]

As in the summons cited earlier in the discussion, this summons also requires the summoned individual (^{m}PN$_1$) to "argue a case" before the judges of the king. However, instead of requiring the individual to appear in Babylon, this summons requires him to appear in Uruk to argue his case. The "judges of the king", before whom the case would be argued, would be in Uruk, rather than in Babylon.

Further evidence for the office of *dayyānu ša šarri* at Uruk during the reign of Cyrus comes from the record of a legal decision written at Uruk, recently published by David B. Weisberg as OIP 122, 38.[11] The text dates to 16 [+] Du'ūzu, year 9 of Cyrus (7 [+] July, 530 BC). It begins with a record of the plaintiff's statement, which is introduced as follows:

^{m}PN$_1$ ^{lu2}*za-ku-u$_2$ ša$_2$* ^{d}INNIN UNUG^{ki} *a-na* ^{lu2}**DI.KU$_5$.MEŠ** ^{m}*ku-ra-aš$_2$* **LUGAL TIN.TIR^{ki} LUGAL KUR.KUR** *iq-⌈bi⌉ um-ma*...

"^{m}PN$_1$ a *zakû* of Ištar of Uruk said thus to the **judges of Cyrus king of Babylon, king of the lands**..."[12]

In addition to this notice, the seal of one of these judges of Cyrus appears on the right and, according to Weisberg's restoration, the left edge of the text. The legend, written in cuneiform, gives this judge's name, ^{m}Bau-ēreš, followed by his title, *dayyānu*. This same judge's name, probably followed by the same title, *dayyānu*, also appears in the text itself, among the names of the officials in whose presence the tablet was written. After the narration of the proceedings in court and the decision, the text reads as follows:

i-na ma-har ^{md}***ba-u$_2$-APIN-eš*** ⌈^{lu2}DI.KU$_5$⌉[X.X.X] ^{m}DA-^{d}AMAR.UTU DUB.SAR A ^{m}⌈DU$_3$⌉-*eš*-[DINGIR] ^{md}*ba-u$_2$*-APIN-*eš* ^{lu2}*si-*

pi-ri ša₂ ᵐ*gu-ba-ri* ˡᵘ²NAM TIN.TIRᵏⁱ *u₂ e-⌈bir⌉* [ID₂] *ṭup-pi ša-ṭir*

"(This) tablet was written in the presence of **ᵐBau-ēreš, the judge** [...]ᵐIle"i-Marduk, the scribe, descendant of Eppeš-[ili], and ᵐBau-ēreš, the parchment-scribe of Gobryas, satrap of Babylon and the Transeuphratene district."[13]

In both the seal legend and the notice at the end of the text, the name of ᵐBau-ēreš is followed by the title *dayyānu* ("judge"). The title does not include the term *ša šarri* ("of the king") even though it is clear from the document's opening lines that the judges are indeed "judges of the king". The use of the abbreviated title *dayyānu* conforms with the usage Wunsch observes in documents from the reigns of Nabonidus and Neriglissar: the names of "judges of the king" are usually followed by the title *dayyānu*, rather than by the longer title *dayyānu ša šarri* (cf. Wunsch 2000: 558).

The decision record only discussed dates near the end of the reign of Cyrus. The career of the judge ᵐBau-ēreš as a *dayyānu ša šarri* apparently does not end when Cambyses succeeds Cyrus to the Achaemenid throne. Tracing his career during the reign of Cambyses must begin with the examination of excerpts from three legal records written in Uruk at that time. These three excerpts document the career of two judges, one named ᵐBau-ēreš and the other named ᵐRīmūt. The first comes from the record of a decision reached on 12 Addaru, year 3 of Cambyses (22 March 526 BC):

ina ITI ŠE MU 3-*kam₂* ᵐ*ri-mut u₃* ᵐ*ba-u₂*-APIN-*eš* ˡᵘ²DI.KU₅.ME...*i-na ṭup-pi iš-tu-ru-ma*

"In Addaru, year 3, **ᵐRīmūt and ᵐBau-ēreš the judges** wrote in a tablet..."[14]

In this text, two men, one named ᵐBau-ēreš and another named ᵐRīmūt, have the title *dayyānu*. A judge named ᵐRīmūt also appears in the following excerpt from a text written in Uruk earlier in the same year, on 24 Du'ūzu, year 3 of Cambyses (11 July 527 BC):

ᵐPN₁ *ša ina ma-har*ᵐ*ri-mut*ˡᵘ²DI.KU₅ LUGAL *u* ᵐDA-ᵈAMAR.UTU ˡᵘ²UMBISAG *iq-bu-u₂ um-ma*...

"ᵐPN₁, who said thus before **ᵐRīmūt the judge of the king** and ᵐIle"i-Marduk, the scribe..."[15]

In this second example, the man named ᵐRīmūt is specifically designated as a *dayyān šarri*. This designation lends support to Hans Martin Kümmel's restorations of the following excerpt from a third text written in Uruk on 30 Addaru of the same year (9 April 526 BC):

ᵐPN₁ *u₃* ᵐPN₂ ᵐPN₃ *u₃* ᵐPN₄ *a-na* ᵐPN₅ ˡᵘ²ŠA₃.TAM E₂.AN.NA ᵐPN₆ [ˡᵘ²SAG.LUGAL ˡᵘ²EN *pi-qit*] E₂.AN.NA *u₃* ᵐ*ri-mut u₃* ᵐ*ba-u₂*-KAM₂ [ˡᵘ²DI.KU₅.ME] LUGAL *iq-bu-u₂ um-<ma>*

"ᵐPN₁ and ᵐPN₂, ᵐPN₃ and ᵐPN₄ said thus to ᵐPN₅ *šatammu* of the Eanna, ᵐPN₆ [the *ša rēš šarri* administrator] of the Eanna and **ᵐRīmūt and ᵐBau-ēreš the [judges] of the king**."[16]

In this third excerpt as it is restored by Kümmel, two men, one named ᵐRīmūt and the other named ᵐBau-ēreš, have the title *dayyān šarri*. Since all three documents come from the same place and almost the same time, it seems safe to conclude, as Kümmel has, that the proper names in all the documents refer to the same two judges—ᵐRīmūt and ᵐBau-ēreš—even though the names occur without filiation.

The three excerpts just examined have shown that a man named ᵐBau-ēreš served as a "judge of the king" during the reign of

Cambyses. Based on this, it seems reasonable to suggest that the "judge of the king" named ᵐBau-ēreš is the same Bau-ēreš as the judge of Cyrus in OIP 122, 38. If this suggestion is correct, then the career of ᵐBau-ēreš provides another example of a "judge of the king" surviving the change of monarchy, this time from Cyrus to Cambyses. Of course, this example is much less striking than Wunsch's examples of "judges of the king" surviving the change from Babylonian to Achaemenid rule. Nevertheless, the career of ᵐBau-ēreš demonstrates that even under Cyrus and Cambyses the office of *dayyānu ša šarri* remained as it had been under the Neo-Babylonian kings: despite the connection to the king implied by the title, changes in the monarchy seem to have had little effect on the office.

The discussion until this point has considered some of the evidence for the office of "judge of the king" during the reigns of Cyrus and Cambyses. It will now turn to some of the available evidence from the reign of the next Achaemenid king, Darius I. In particular, it will examine two examples of legal texts that are worded in a manner similar to that of other texts already examined. The first is the ending of a debt note drawn up in Babylon on 18 Šabāṭu, year 6 of Darius I (25 February 515 BC). The text states:

ina ma-har ᵐᵈNA₃-*na-din*-ŠEŠ ᵐEN-*šu₂-nu* ᵐ*ba-ga-'i-in* ᵐ*na-din* ᵐᵈ30-SIG₅-*iq* ᵐ*ap-la-a u* ᵐᵈNA₃-ZI-*tim*-URI₃ ˡᵘ²DI.KU₅.MEŠ ᵐMU-ᵈNA₃ ˡᵘ²*si-pi-ri u₂-il₃-ti e-let*

"The note was drawn up before ᵐ**Nabû-nādin-ahi,** ᵐ**Bēlšunu,** ᵐ**Baga'in,** ᵐ**Nādin,** ᵐ**Sîn-mudammiq,** ᵐ**Aplaya and** ᵐ**Nabû-napištim-uṣur, the judges** and ᵐIddin-Nabû, the parchment scribe."[17]

This notice indicates that the note was drawn up before seven men who all bear the title *dayyānu*. It may be compared with the concluding lines of OIP 122, 38, which are cited earlier, in the discussion of the "judges of the king" at Uruk. Both texts name the judges among those "before (*ina mahar*) whom" the text was written.

The second text from the reign of Darius 1 is an excerpt from the beginning of the record of a decision pertaining to a piece of property. This text states as follows:

PN₁ *a-na ma-har* ᵐKI-ᵈNA₃-TIN *u₃* ˡᵘ²*ki-na-at-te-šu* ˡᵘ²DI.KU₅.MEŠ *a-na muh-hi* E₂ *šu-a-tim… a-na di-i-ni tu-te-lu-'-ma*

"PN₁ came to court before ᵐ**Itti-Nabû-balāṭu and his colleagues, the judges,** regarding that house…"[18]

Like the opening lines of OIP 122, 38, quoted earlier, these lines introduce the complaint of the plaintiff (ᶠPN₁). To state her case, she "comes to court before ᵐItti-Nabû-balāṭu and his colleagues, the judges". Although only one judge, ᵐItti-Nabû-balāṭu, is named, the term "his colleagues" (ˡᵘ²*ki-na-at-te-šu₂*) indicates that he was not the only judge who heard this case. Rather, the term apparently refers to a judicial council, like the ones that functioned during the reigns of earlier kings.

Both of the examples from the reign of Darius attest only to the use of the title *dayyānu*, rather than the term *dayyānu ša šarri*. As of the present writing, I am unaware of any references to the title *dayyānu ša šarri* that may be dated to the reign of Darius. One may, therefore, question the continuation of the office of *dayyānu ša šarri* during this time. However, it has already been noted that under earlier kings, the shorter title designates the names of individuals who are actually "judges of the king". Assuming that the title continues to be used in the same way, one may argue that the office of *dayyānu ša šarri* continues even under Darius I.

IV. Conclusions

The survey of the cuneiform evidence just undertaken has traced the institution of *dayyānu ša šarri* from the Neo-Babylonian period into the Achaemenid period. It has demonstrated that in Mesopotamia, apparently, the *dayyānu ša šarri* continued to hear cases well into the reign of Darius I. The office of *dayyānu ša šarri*, then, is another example of how the Achaemenid kings maintained local institutions while building their vast empire.

The office of *dayyānu ša šarri* is significant in its own right because it is an example of the survival of a pre-Achaemenid institution under Achaemenid rule. The significance of this survival grows even more when one considers the role played by those who held the office. As all the examples quoted earlier show, these individuals administer justice by trying cases and rendering legal decisions. To all appearances, the laws they follow are the norms that had been in place for centuries before the Achaemenid conquest. On the local level, at least, these judges maintain the rule of law. To some degree, it seems that the Achaemenid emperors left this important function in the hands of local Mesopotamian authorities rather than seeking to impose a new legal order. Of course, in the case of the *dayyānu ša šarri* this is not so surprising. No doubt the existence of a local judicial system associated with the king served the administrative needs of the emperors. They could easily adopt it and incorporate it into their system of government.

By way of conclusion, the case of the *dayyānu ša šarri* in Mesopotamia should be considered within the broader context of the administration of justice in other parts of the Achaemenid Empire. The present discussion has pointed to the Mesopotamian "judges of the king" as evidence for the Achaemenid kings' maintenance of a native judicial system, and, more broadly, for the survival of the Mesopotamian legal tradition. Evidence from elsewhere in the Achaemenid Empire shows a similar maintenance, and possibly an active cultivation, of local legal traditions. A brief Demotic text from Egypt describes how Darius I convenes a commission to codify and translate Egyptian laws. This example from Egypt has long been associated with what is perhaps the most famous example of the Achaemenid preservation of native legal traditions: the Hebrew Bible's description of Ezra's mission to the province of Judea.[19] Artaxerxes I orders Ezra to appoint "magistrates and judges" who are to judge the Judean populace and inform them of the laws of their God. In issuing this order and authorizing the punishment of disobedient subjects, the king gives royal backing to the laws of Judea. The judges Ezra appoints are, of course, from a later time than any of the Mesopotamian *dayyānu ša šarri* discussed in the present article. Nevertheless, the Judean judges, like the *dayyānu ša šarri* in Mesopotamia, illustrate the generally tolerant Achaemenid policy toward local legal institutions.

The present study has demonstrated that the office of *dayyānu ša šarri* survives the transition to Achaemenid rule in Mesopotamia. It thus provides additional specific support for Briant's general conclusions about the Achaemenids' maintenance of local diversity within their empire. One may reasonably conclude, then, that when it came to the rule of law, the Achaemenid emperors saw no need to "reinvent the wheels of justice" which had been turning efficiently for centuries.

Notes

1. This paper was read at the conference "The World of Achaemenid Persia" at the British Museum on 29 September 2005. In preparation for the conference, a preliminary version of this paper was presented at the Judah Goldin Memorial Seminar in Hebrew Bible and Related Fields held at the University of Pennsylvania on 20 September 2005. The present final version has benefited from the comments of the participants in the Goldin Seminar. Aaron Koller read and commented on a written draft. I thank them all and, of course, assume responsibility for any shortcomings. Abbreviations in the references to cuneiform sources and in the list of works cited follow Reiner & Roth 1999: ix–xxvii. Dates follow Parker & Dubberstein 1956.
2. The term *dayyānū ša šarri* might also be translated "royal judges". The present paper does not use this translation to avoid confusion with the native Persian royal judges, mentioned, for example, in Herodotus III.31. See the discussion in Briant 2002a: 129–130, 510.
3. For a general discussion of this material see Jursa 2005.
4. For a discussion of what documents in a cuneiform archive survive to the present day, see Baker 2004: 5–6.
5. For a discussion of this subject see Oelsner, Wells & Wunsch 2003: 915–920.
6. For more on Mesopotamian royal ideology, see Seux 1980/83, especially the discussion of *šar mīšari* on pp. 163–165.
7. AnOr 8, 37: 1–8. A similar summons (YOS 7, 31: 1–10) requires the summoned individual to go to Babylon from Uruk and argue his case *ina bīt dīni ša šarri*, "in the king's court of law".
8. In terms of form, the text closely resembles Wunsch's "Richterurkunden". It is classified as a "sworn deposition" in Bongenaar 1997: 18, n. 40.
9. Note that the title here and in some of the other examples below occurs without the particle *ša*. The absence of this particle does not indicate a different title.
10. AnOr 8, 50: 1–9.
11. For earlier editions and discussions of this text, see Weisberg's commentary in OIP 122, p. 73.
12. OIP 122, 38: 1–3.
13. OIP 122, 38: 46–50. Note that among all these officials, only one, ᵐBau-ēreš, has the title *dayyānu*, even though the plural forms in the opening lines of the document and the subsequent narrative clearly indicate that more than one judge was present. Based on this discrepancy, one may suggest that the two scribes also served as "judges of Cyrus", or that other, unnamed judges participated in the proceedings. Deciding between these two possibilities requires additional research beyond the scope of the present paper.
14. YOS 7, 161: 7–11. For more on this text and the decision in it, see San-Nicolò 1932: 341–342.
15. YOS 7, 159. For more on this text, see von Bolla 1941: 113–120.
16. YOS 7, 137: 10–14. Restorations follow Kümmel 1979: 136 n. 198.
17. BE 8/1, 107: 19–21.
18. Dar. 410: 4–7. The present reading follows the edition in Wunsch 1993: II, no. 353 (pp. 293–294). For discussion of the situation surrounding this text, see 1993: II, 71.
19. Ezra 7:25–26. For a recent discussion of this subject, including references to earlier literature, see Steiner 2001. For a different understanding, see Fried 2001.

46

Xerxes and the Babylonian Temples: A Restatement of the Case[1]

Amélie Kuhrt

In 1941 Cameron published an article on Darius I and Xerxes in Babylonia using Babylonian evidence. Böhl in 1962 presented additional arguments and more evidence strengthening and amplifying Cameron's article. From then on it was accepted that Babylonia revolted twice in Xerxes' reign: 484 (= RY 2) and 482 (= RY 4) respectively. Xerxes' response to the revolts was to destroy the great Marduk sanctuary in Babylon and loot its cult statue. This meant that the annual New Year festival of Babylon, which had become a crucial element in the legitimization of those claiming power in the preceding 250 years, could no longer be performed.[2] This loss of legitimacy by the Persian kings in Babylonian eyes was marked by the omission of the title "king of Babylon" from the royal Persian titulary from 482 on. A further humiliation for Babylonia was an administrative rearrangement whereby the huge Neo-Babylonian imperial territory, previously a single province, was divided into two: "Babylon" and "Across-the-River". This reconstruction was rooted in an image derived from the accounts of classical writers, beginning with Herodotus 1.183, into which Babylonian and Persian evidence was made to fit—to which it was, indeed subordinated.

In a paper published in 1987 by Kuhrt and Sherwin-White, it was demonstrated that not one element of the evidence used to construct this picture stands up to scrutiny and that the Cameron–Böhl presentation of the fate of Babylon and its temples must be rejected. Over the last 15 years, this has become the established view. In a recent important article, Caroline Waerzeggers (2003/2004) has presented an analysis of Babylonian archives (primarily from Borsippa and Sippar) and shown that a major administrative, social, and economic restructuring, inevitably involving temples and cults, took place in Babylonia in the years immediately following 484.

In the light of Dr Waerzeggers's work, I have noticed a tendency to label the new orthodoxy of the last 15 years or so as a "revisionist" view of Achaemenid rule in Babylonia. The implication is that we should now return to the pre-1987 position and put our trust once again in the Greek accounts of Xerxes' destruction of temples in Babylon. Is that or can that, indeed, be the case?

A fundamental point to make is that the 1987 article did *not* present a "revisionist" view of Achaemenid history. It did *not* try to approach Xerxes' actions in Babylonia from a new angle thus creating a hypothesis to set against, and test, the prevailing one—it was simply a demonstration that the evidence used earlier either did not exist or was deficient. Let me run through the main points quickly:

(a) Nowhere does Herodotus say that Xerxes removed the cult statue (Gr. *agalma*) of Bel-Marduk, even less that he destroyed any temple in Babylon. He *is* described as guilty of an act of sacrilegious pillage—removal of a precious statue (Gr. *andrias*)—but nothing else. In fact, Herodotus describes Esangil, Etemenanki, and the Marduk statue *intact* and personally viewed by him, using the present tense. We may have our doubts as to whether Herodotus actually ever visited Babylonia (Rollinger 1993; Kuhrt 2002) but, in as much as his account has been the lynchpin of the portrait of Xerxes as the destroyer of Babylon's central and most prominent cult, we have to acknowledge the inescapable fact that he never said anything of the kind.

(b) Support for Xerxes' drastic action was sought by Cameron, followed by Böhl, in the omission of the "king of Babylon" title after 482. There was, in fact, at the time one text in Berlin (Ungnad 1908: no. 118) that did not fit his reasoning, dated as it is to Xerxes' regnal year 6+x, which should probably be emended to RY 8, that is, 478. This Cameron dismissed as a scribal error, although it is not a particularly easy one to explain. In the 1980s, two important groups of Babylonian texts were published, one in the Ashmolean Museum (McEwan 1984), the other from the German excavations at Uruk (Kessler 1984). Both contained documents dated to the reigns of Xerxes (486–465) and his successor, Artaxerxes I (465–424/3). Examination of the titulary showed that Xerxes had continued to be assigned the "king of Babylon" element sporadically throughout his reign. Three Artaxerxes I documents showed that his successor, too, had still used it occasionally. The latest document known so far, in which it appears, dates from 441 (Rollinger 1998a; 1999). The evidence shows, quite incontrovertibly, that while there was an evolution in the formulation of Achaemenid royal titles in Babylonia, there is no abrupt, decisive change that could be linked with a political event.

(c) As the Marduk cult statue continued to be in Esangil, there is no reason to assume cessation of the New Year festival in Babylon. What is *likely* is that royal participation was rare after the end of the Neo-Babylonian Empire, if indeed it ever occurred. The only documented instance of an Achaemenid king taking part is its rather unusual performance by both Cyrus and Cambyses five months after the Persian conquest of Babylonia (Grayson 1975: 7, iii 24–28).[3] Although there is some (slight) evidence for continuation of the festival itself,[4] the next *certain* instance of a *king* acting in the ceremony occurs in 205 (i.e. over 300 years later), when Antiochus III celebrated it on completion of his triumphant eastern campaign (Sachs & Hunger 1989: no. 204; cf. Sherwin-White & Kuhrt 1993: 130–131). Clearly, royal participation in Babylon's New Year festival had ceased to be the decisive barometer of social and political well-being that it had become in the centuries of contested control over the country by Assyrians, Chaldaeans, and Babylonians. But that change in emphasis seems to have begun already in Cyrus' reign and continued right through into the Hellenistic period—there is no evidence of any subsequent Achaemenid king or Alexander (the much vaunted "restorer") ever performing it. However, all without exception were recorded and remembered in Babylonia as recognized, legitimate kings of the region.

(d) When exactly the reorganization of the Babylonian province took place, we do not know. The latest evidence for the territory undivided is, at present, 486, the final year of Darius I (Stolper 1989). The earliest evidence for a governor of the separate province of Babylon is Gubaru (Gobryas) in 420, although he was probably preceded in this position by Artareme attested in 431 (Stolper 1985).

This, in summary, is what the evidence *is*. It is not an alternative approach to, or revisionist image of, Xerxes. It is a *correction* of the earlier picture, which was based on a careless reading of Herodotus combined with incomplete Babylonian evidence and an implicit wish to make very disparate types of material harmonize with a presumed "knowledge" of Xerxes' actions, policies, and character (Sancisi-Weerdenburg 1989/2002). The faultiness of that procedure cannot be subject to argument—there is not a shred of evidence to support it.

And this is not changed by Dr Waerzeggers's brilliant article, as she herself would be the first to admit. What her study shows, most valuably, is that a fundamental change in Babylonia's social and political framework took place in Xerxes' second regnal year, namely, 484. In that year there were two overlapping revolts in Babylonia (including Babylon itself): one was very short-lived, perhaps no more than two weeks, the other lasted three months. They were confined to the north of the region. After 484, the archives of the old established urban elites, who had controlled the highest positions in city government and the temples (including Uruk in the south), cease. The archives that continue belong, in Waerzeggers's words, to individuals from "a different stratum of society, one that may be described in political terms as pro-Persian and in economic terms as dependent on the presence of the Persian nobility", people like the members of the Murashu family attested a little later. In other words, what the evidence shows in not a destruction of cults—there is sufficient evidence to show that they continued—but a breaking by the Achaemenid authorities of the concentration of power in the hands of a powerful, traditional "aristocracy". This would, of course, have necessitated a thoroughgoing restaffing of temples, although the scanty evidence does not allow us to be more precise. Significantly, no such fundamental change can be documented in the southern cities of Uruk and Ur. What is striking here is that, whereas previously the top posts in, for example, the Uruk sanctuary had been monopolized by old families based in Babylon, they are replaced by *local* people early in Xerxes' reign.

It is tempting to associate these far-reaching changes with other administrative reforms, such as the provincial reorganization.[5] All the evidence for these changes clusters around the end of Darius I and early Xerxes period, although chronological certainty eludes us, as does the precise sequence of events. Were the revolts in 484 sparked by this major bureaucratic reorganization, led by the groups most closely affected in northern Babylonia? Or were they part of the response by the Persian authorities to the revolts? This remains impossible to decide either way at the moment.

The much-trumpeted, oft-repeated claims that a whole bevy of classical historians tell us that Xerxes destroyed temples in Babylon are in fact, false. Their testimony is rather general, often confused and internally contradictory. Herodotus, as we have seen, says nothing of the kind. The only other contemporary historian who is likely to have had some access to knowledge of Persian history is Ctesias (Jacoby 1923/1958: 688 F13[26]; Lenfant 2004: 124), who mentions a revolt of Babylon in Xerxes' reign—the *only* one to do so—but *no* destruction. The Aelian passage, frequently cited as an independent source, in fact derives from Ctesias (see Lenfant 2004: 128 [F13b*]). While it mentions Xerxes performing a ritual in Babylon (perhaps in a temple, but that is uncertain) and obtaining a bad omen, he says nothing about any destruction (however cunningly one might try to read that into it). Berossus (Jacoby 1923/1958: 680 F10a), in the early third century, has Cyrus destroy Babylon's walls, which were (according to Herodotus 3.159) destroyed by Darius I at the end of a revolt, although he has described them previously (Herodotus 1.178–181) in the present tense, as though they were still standing in his day—which, indeed, they were and well beyond (Rollinger 1993). Diodorus once has the ziggurat ruined by the passage of time, and elsewhere (D.S. 2.9.9; 17.112.3) he says it was destroyed by unspecified "Persians"; while Justin (*Epitome* 12.13.6) has Alexander restore interrupted festivals, but says nothing about any physical destruction or when that interruption occurred. Only Strabo (16.1.5), nearly 500, and Arrian nearer to 700, years later link Xerxes' name with a destruction of sacred structures in Babylon, although neither mentions a removal of Marduk's statue.

Moreover, Arrian presents the Babylonian priests anxious to induct Alexander, on his entry in 331, into the intricacies of the correct cult of Babylon's supreme god—impossible if the statue were not *in situ* and the sanctuaries in ruins, while Strabo hedges his statement with *hos phasin* "so they say", suggesting he is quoting popular rumour rather than a reliable source.

While there is not, and never has been, any evidence whatever for Xerxes (or Persian) destruction of Babylonian temples and cults, apart from this ambiguous material, we now have material that allows us to begin reassessing his reign constructively as a time of profound change, marked by a considerable tightening of the Achaemenid grip on its imperial territories. Xerxes is emerging, more and more, as one of the most important architects of a stable and successful Persian Empire.

Notes

1. This is the text of the talk I gave in October 2005 in response to Andrew George's paper, published here. An expanded and updated version is being submitted as a contribution to the Festschrift for M. W. Stolper.
2. For a recent discussion of the festival, see Bidmead 2002.
3. Note the important new reading, based on collation, of these lines by Andrew George (1996: 379–380).
4. Possibly in the reign of Darius I: Ungnad 1908: no. 89; cf. Unger 1931: 150, n.1; and during the revolts in the reign of Xerxes: Böhl 1962: 110–114.
5. But note that, contrary to Joannès 1990*a*, there is now evidence for the continuation of the old Babylonian office of *šākin tēmi*, see Waerzeggers 2003/2004: 178, Addendum.

47

The Role of Babylonian Temples in Contributing to the Army in the Early Achaemenid Empire

John MacGinnis

In the early autumn of Darius year 4 (518 BC) a band of soldiers made their way back to Babylonia from duty overseas in the service of the Achaemenid army. Their home was the ancient city of Sippar and we know about their return from a brief entry in an administrative text—*CT 57* 82—now preserved in the cuneiform collections of the British Museum. Lines 6–8 read, laconically:

> 38 shekels of silver for šamaš-iddin and his horsemen who have come back from Egypt.

This is typical of the nature of the sources at our disposal—the texts do not deal with military matters per se but are accountancy documents generated by the temple bureaucracy. Who was šamaš-iddin, who were his men, and how did it come about that they found themselves doing a tour of duty in Egypt?

To address these questions we can start by taking a look at the Babylonian background of this scene. Babylonia was at the centre of the Achaemenid Empire and an immensely wealthy country. To a large degree this wealth was generated by a network of cities positioned along the river and waterways. Each of these had a temple complex at its heart: Babylon had Esagila, the temple of the supreme god Marduk; Nippur had the Ekur temple of the god Enlil; Borsippa housed the Ezida of the god of writing Nabû, and so on. There were many others—we will talk about two more shortly—not to mention the innumerable smaller settlements. The temples themselves were self-governing to a degree—though there were royal inspectors and occasional state directives—and also had responsibilities in governing their local districts. There was a hierarchical difference between cities that were ruled directly by an appointed governor—*šakin ṭēmi*—where the temple also had its own separate chief administrator with the title *šatammu*, and those where the head of the temple was at the same time the chief of local government with the title *šangû*.

Two cities of particular interest to us are Uruk with its Eanna temple to the goddess Ištar, in the south of Babylonia, and Sippar with its Ebabbara of the sun god šamaš in the north. The significance of these two places is that in both cases they were the sites of major excavations in the late nineteenth and early twentieth centuries which, along with large-scale exposure of the temple complexes themselves, yielded cuneiform tablets in huge numbers—in the case of Uruk by the thousands, in the case of Sippar tens of thousands. I should mention that in both cases excavations have resumed from time to time—particularly at Uruk—and the flow of information is ongoing. Both archives start in the Neo-Babylonian period and run into the early Achaemenid period and, to date, there are no other excavated temple archives on anything like their scale, although there are scattered texts from other sites.[1] The archives cover all manner of administrative matters and now, more than 100 years after their excavation and after a long and at times disjointed publication history, they are beginning to tell their story. I will focus on Sippar, not least because the vast majority of the Ebabbara archives are here in London, forming the 30,000 tablets registered in the "Sippar Collections" of the British Museum, with tens of thousands more pieces awaiting processing.

Clearly these temples represented significant economic forces in their own right. A recent estimate calculates that the Ebabbara had around 3,000 men, women and children directly under its control (MacGinnis 2004), and that does not include the many independent artisans and farmers who leased land privately. And the Ebabbara was at the small end of the scale; the Eanna of Uruk was substantially larger, perhaps by a factor of 3–5. It is therefore not surprising that the temple communities had obligations to the state, including the supply of manpower. This encompassed workers for corvée duty as well as recruits for the army as such.

Manpower

Infantry

We are in a position to make some remarks on the manpower provided. What type of soldiers did the Ebabbara field, and where did they come from? The bulk were infantry, which is to say archers. These were the backbone of the Babylonian army and we know about archers in Sippar from innumerable texts detailing payment of rations, issues of clothing and provision of weapons. The last enables us to say that they were equipped with bows, bow-cases, arrows (between 40 and 60 each) and daggers, and might also be provided with donkeys for their baggage.

As regards the pool from which the archers were drawn, there were three principal sources:

1. Temple dependants (*širku*s)
2. Free citizens (*mār banê*)
3. Holders of a bow-fief (*bīt qašti*)

Temple dependants

The first of these, the temple dependants, may have included both a small professional cadre for whom archer duty was the principal occupation, as well as those drawn from the ranks of the Ebbabara's *širku*s at large. It would also include the subset of shepherds issued with bows to defend themselves and their flocks. In all probability all *širku*s were liable for bow service, subject to age and fitness. As the majority of *širku*s were engaged in agricultural occupations (farmers, shepherds and gardeners) this is the main source. Occasionally this is clearly articulated in the texts.

Free citizens

The second source of archers was the free citizens (*mār banê*). As Jursa has shown in his research on the archives of Bēl-rēmanni and Nidinti-Marduk, free citizens were liable to perform bow service (Jursa 1999). We do not know what the precise legal basis of this service was; Jursa suggested that it may have arisen either as a result of urban tax obligations or because it was a duty incumbent on all citizens (Jursa 1999: 109). On the whole the service seems to have been commuted into payments in silver, apparently at a rate of 1 mina per year, though this may not have exempted the individuals concerned from the performance of occasional civic duties.

Holders of a bow-fief (bīt qašti)

Thirdly we have to consider bow-fiefs. Fiefs were integral to the state system of raising troops in Babylonia. We do not know exactly when bow-fiefs were instituted—or re-instituted—in Sippar, but the time of the earliest attestation has been progressively pushed back from Cambyses to Nabonidus to Nebuchadnezzar. Perhaps the deeper origins go back to the Middle Babylonian period or even before. In the case of Sippar, the texts at our disposal say very little about the military aspect of fiefs, presumably since they were handled by a separate branch of the administration in either the temple or the royal palace in Sippar (whose existence we know of but whose archives have not been recovered). What little evidence we have deals with the collection of dues or other managerial matters. We have no direct evidence of whether or how the troops supplied by these fiefs were incorporated into an integrated command for the region. Interestingly enough, we do have one example of a fief owned by a Persian—called Artumazza—from the first year of Darius (BM 54107 = MacGinnis, forthcoming: no. 7).

Organization

Moving on to organization, the main body of temple archers was divided into *eširtus*—decuries—of shepherds, farmers and gardeners. Each decury was headed by a *rab eširti*.

In theory we would expect the *rab eširti*s to have been in charge of ten men, but this is in fact not always the case and may rarely have been so. Note, for example, that the ledger of temple staff *CT 56* 664 lists four archers, and that the companies of archers detailed in BM 55136+ are comprised of units of four men (MacGinnis, forthcoming: no. 5). It may be that the theoretical order of the temple archers was of an *eširtu* of eight men comprising two units of four, with the actual strengths commonly falling below even this. By contrast it is noteworthy that according to the one document which is complete enough to judge by (BM 43300, cf. Jursa 1999: 233), the decuries of free citizens really did consist of ten men and were not short-staffed. The man in direct overall command of the temple archers was called the *rab qašti*.

As for the total number of archers that the temple could field, we can give no definitive answer although we can hazard some guesses. An important text to consider is *CT 56* 481+, a list of agricultural workers, 120 in all, of whom 17 are (serving as) archers. This represents a levy of about 14 per cent. Recent work on the total numbers of *širāku* dependent on the Ebabbara suggests that there may have been around 1,300 adult males (MacGinnis 2004: 36).[2] A levy of 14 per cent on 1,300 would yield a force of 182, which may be towards the upper limit of what the Ebabbara could field. More commonly, it is noteworthy that the number 50 occurs repeatedly in issues of equipment and it may be that this was the standard size of the body of troops routinely fielded by the Ebabbara.

To give some comparative data, texts from Uruk variously give figures of 50 and 70 archers (*YOS 6* 116.8, 151.9, *YOS 7* 154; *VS 6* 202). One text from Borsippa deals with 300 *širku*s sent to Aššur as archers. During the

Šamaš-šum-ukīn revolt Uruk raised 500 or 600 archers to go to the aid of Ur, while on another occasion mention is made of 1,000 archers stationed in Ur (Frame 1992: 244). In the case of the fief system around Nippur in the later Achaemenid period, a recent estimate is that the maximum number of archers this might have supported was 2,000 (van Driel 2002: 321). The problem with these figures is that they come from a variety of periods and also obscure different recruitment patterns, but overall they are probably reliable enough in giving us an idea of the size of units involved.

Considering all of this together it is probable that, resourced from its own *širku*s, the Ebabbara could field between 50 and 100 archers in normal circumstances, and perhaps double that in times of greater demand. Added to this would be the archers drawn from the decuries of free citizens and those supplied by bow-fiefs; we have no estimates for the numbers involved in either of those categories. Of course, in times of utter emergency it may be imagined that the entire able-bodied (male) population was called up.

The tasks for which the archers were needed fall into three main areas: (a) duties in support of temple activities; (b) participation in state works projects; and (c) participation in military campaigns of the king.

Duties in support of temple activities included:

- guarding the temple precinct and general police duties
- protecting labourers performing earthwork
- guarding the temple flock
- accompanying movements of materials, cultic equipment and revenue
- accompanying merchants and caravans from Sippar
- accompanying carpenters sent to Lebanon to fell cedar
- rounding up fugitive *širāku*.

Cavalry

The second arm of the Babylonian–Achaemenid army was the cavalry. The temple maintained a stable and a body of horsemen. As regards numbers, no text gives any direct indication of the number of horses in the stables, but BM 60366 lists eight horsemen (MacGinnis, forthcoming: no. 12), while the quantities in *Dar.* 253 are evidently for 12 men even though only 3 are named. I would estimate that this figure of 12 approaches the upper limit of the cavalry fielded by the Ebabbara.[3]

Chariotry

The third branch of the army was chariotry. The evidence for chariotry raised in the district of Sippar is sketchy. Babylonian chariots in this period had a three-man crew: the commander (*mār damqa*), the driver (*mukīl appāti*) and the "third man" (*taslūšu*) whose job was to protect the other two. All three of these are mentioned in the administrative documents, although the *mār damqa* is only attested in the early Neo-Babylonian phase of the archive. There are no direct references to military chariots in the texts from Sippar (though there are numerous references to the ceremonial chariot of Šamaš). We might reasonably expect to find clues in the texts dealing with items manufactured and repaired by the carpenters, leatherworkers and smiths, but the reality is that there is no record of temple artisans working on military chariots. This might be taken to imply that the chariots were not actually based at the temple. One plausible alternative location where they might have been based would be the royal palace in Sippar, mentioned earlier. As for numbers of chariots, it is very difficult to make any estimation at all. Fielding a chariot was an expensive business and it may be that the temple itself had limited liability—if no one else, perhaps just the *qīpu* had a chariot. Alternatively, an upper limit might be suggested by the maximum number of *tašlīšu*s attested, that is, about 14.

Manufacture of weapons

The weapons themselves could be manufactured by temple craftsmen: we have evidence that they were involved in the production of bows (both Akkadian and Cimmerian, with appropriate arrows), as well as spears and daggers.

Equipping

The supply by the temple to its personnel of the clothing, arms and provisions for undertaking service abroad is designated by the term *rikis qabli*. Essentially, the term was used for the provisioning and equipping of men sent out from Sippar to do service further afield. The term is also found occasionally in contexts which are not obviously military, for example the *rikis qabli* of the "carpenters of Lebanon" who were probably sent to fetch cedars from the Lebanon mountains.

A good example of *rikis qabli* is in a text from the end of the reign of Cambyses, which records the issue of 11 jerkins, 11 pairs of sandals, 33 litres of oil, 66 litres of cress, 66 litres of salt, 11 water bottles, and 11 caps to 6 farmers and 5 shepherds of šamaš (MacGinnis 1998). They appear to have been despatched to the *rab ummi* (an army commander) and the witnesses included the *ša muhhi sūti* and a shepherd (Rēmūt-ilani). The presence of the *ša muhhi sūti* is illuminating: he was a private tax farmer overseeing a large concession of temple land, and his presence here underlies the agricultural background of the manpower and the fact that there was a negotiated path by which these requisitions to the army were made.[4]

Another text giving a good illustration of the equipment involved is BM 68702, also from the reign of Cambyses (BM 68702 = MacGinnis, forthcoming: no. 51). It records the issue of 50 blankets, 50 jerkins, 10 sacks, 5 saddlebags, some donkeys (the number is missing but presumably 5), 50 water bottles, 50 quivers, 50 bows, 50 lances, 50 caps, 50 pairs of sandals, as well as oil, salt and cress. Apparently the 50 men were accompanied by 5 equids, that is 1 per 10 men—evidently a further manifestation of the decury system.

Areas of deployment

Where were these troops sent? We have seen already that Egypt was one destination but as far as our evidence goes this is out of the ordinary. More typical are the cases where we hear of troops being sent to Elam (MacGinnis 2002), and more recently Stefan Zawadzki (2003) has been assembling evidence from the time of Nebuchadnezzar for deployments against Tyre. One major way in which the temples benefited from such campaigns was in being presented with prisoners of war. In the Chaldean period the Ebabbara received a donation of 43 prisoners of war from Egypt, and there is also evidence for individuals of Cilician origin who may also have come to the temple as prisoners.[5]

The archives yield some evidence for the years in which campaigns took place, or at least in which there was a mobilization.

A key word here is *madaktu*, to be translated as either "call-up" or "levy camp", and a number of texts enumerate troops, livestock or provisions sent to the *madaktu*. Very specific is the record of "rations of the month of Abu of the men who went to the army" (ŠUK.HI.A iti NE [šá l]úERIM.MEŠ šá a-na ú-mu il-li-ku, BM 61015.rev.5–6[21]) (MacGinnis, forthcoming: no. 45). We also have dates from the texts dealing with *rikis qabli*, the issue of weaponry, and call-up for bow service. Taken together these sources suggest military activity in the following years:

Cambyses

2   BM 62472 (MacGinnis, forthcoming: no. 21)
8   BM 64707 (MacGinnis 1998)
9   BM 68702 (MacGinnis, forthcoming: no. 51)

Darius

2   *Dar.* 46
3   *CT* 55 286
4   *CT* 57 82, BM 64637 (MacGinnis, forthcoming: no. 2)
8   *Dar.* 234
9   *Dar.* 253
16   BM 63847 (MacGinnis, forthcoming: no. 33)

How long did the men serve away from home in the case of a military call-up? We cannot say for sure, but the norm may have been to serve a year and then return home while fresh troops were rotated in; we note in passing that this was the practice in the Median army according to Diodorus (Diod. Sic. II 24.6). Some confirmation for this comes from BM 78828 (Nebuchadnezzar year 28) which records issues to carpenters of the king going off to join him on campaign, presumably as military engineers (MacGinnis, forthcoming: no. 35). On the other hand, there are also indications that three-month deployments may have been the norm. The evidence for this was reviewed by van Driel (2002: 228f., 261), who comments that in an agrarian society a lack of a time limit would be virtually impossible.

Chain of command

This is an area where there is still work to do. Previously I have suggested the following chain of command for the troops under the Ebabbara (MacGinnis 1997: 186).

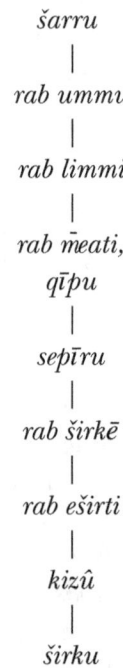

šarru
|
rab ummu
|
rab limmi
|
rab meati, qīpu
|
sepīru
|
rab širkē
|
rab eširti
|
kizû
|
širku

I would not now say that this is necessarily wrong, but there is room for refinement. One area of uncertainty concerns how the *qīpu* (and his Aramaic-writing deputy the *sepīru*) fitted into the main hierarchy. De facto the *qīpu*s would, in a major mobilization, have been in command of hundreds of men, hence it seems likely that they would have slotted in alongside the *rab meāti*. Another question is how the *rab qašti* related to the *rab širkē*. More generally, there is the problem that overall the Babylonian army is unlikely in reality to have been divided into the neat uniform multiples of ten that the titles suggest. It is more probable that each temple, province, group of fiefs and so on will have contributed its own regiment and that these units will have maintained their integrity when brought under central command. These observations also apply to the units of cavalry and chariotry.

A further question surrounds the role of the *šangû*. How did he fit into this structure? And the most important question remains: how and to what degree were the archers drawn from the ranks of *širku*s—who were under the immediate direction of the *rab qašti*—co-ordinated with the forces generated from other sources (free citizens, bow-fiefs)? As yet we have no answer to that.

Conclusions

To summarize our findings for Sippar, we have found that the Ebabbara could routinely field bodies of up to 50 archers out of its own *širku*s, occasionally 60, and it may be guessed that in times of heightened demand it might be triple that number. The head of these archers was the *rab qašti*. In addition to this there were individuals liable to bow service as a result of their title to bow-fiefs. We have no reliable information on how many individuals were so encumbered. And in addition to these it appears that free citizens were organized into decuries for archer duty as a result of tax and/or social classification. In this case too we have no reliable information on the numbers involved. The temple is found fielding up to 12 cavalry. As for chariotry, the evidence is sparse but it is noteworthy that all three members of a chariot crew—*mār damqa, mukīl appāti, tašlīšu*—are mentioned in the texts in one context or another, and there is scattered evidence for chariot fiefs in the environs of Sippar, but we are not really in a position to estimate the number of chariots involved. It is possible that the temple itself only deployed one chariot, which would probably then have been the chariot in which the *qīpu* led the force, but it may also be that the unit was more extensive and that we are simply missing the relevant documentation. Weaponry could be manufactured and repaired by temple craftsmen.

There are a few possibilities for comparing our finds with data from other sources. Pictorial representations of Babylonian soldiers are not common but they do exist, if admittedly from a period slightly earlier than the one under consideration. For instance, Babylonian soldiers may be seen in scenes from the North Palace of Ashurbanipal at Nineveh wearing kilts and headdresses, armed with bows, quivers and sometimes scabbards.[6] In the record of Herodotus—slightly later than the period under consideration—the Assyrians (did this mean Babylonians?) wore linen corsets and were armed with bronze helmets, shields, spears, daggers and studded wooden clubs (Herodotus vii.60, 63; cf. Strabo xv.3.19). Attempting to correlate these descriptions with the data from the Neo-Babylonian texts results in a reasonable if not watertight fit. As Joannès (1982: 16) has pointed out, the record of Herodotus corresponds pretty well with what we know from the cuneiform texts, and suggests that the soldiers of Babylon were already "armée à la Perse" in pre-Achaemenid times.[7] One element missing in our temple documentation is the shields—unless this is the real meaning of the word *ṣallu* (otherwise translated as "skin"). There also seems to be no mention of scabbards and neither is there any mention of Herodotus' clubs. Nevertheless, following Bongenaar, we may present the following for the lexicography of the equipment of the Neo-Babylonian soldier:

qaštu	bow
šiltāhu	arrow
lulītu	arrowhead
garru	another type of arrowhead
tillu	bow case or quiver
namāru	another word for quiver
šalṭu	Cimmerian bow case
azmarû	lance
paṭru	dagger
ṣallu	shield
karballātu	headdress
šir'am	jerkin
tuk.kur.ra	blanket
šibbu	belt
mēšenu	sandals
nūṭu	water bottle
šaqqu	sack
ukāpu	saddlebag

In the case of the headdress (*karballātu*) and jerkin (*šir'am*) it is not clear whether or not they were partially armoured, for example, with metal plates. Most probably this was a technical possibility. However, in the case of the Ebabbara, the lack of any evidence for smiths making pieces for these items suggests they did not contain metal plates.

Lastly, I would stress that a number of sources contributed to the formation of the Babylonian wing of the Achaemenid army. In addition to the contingents from the temple/urban polities, contingents were also drawn from the Chaldean tribal structure, from subject dominions (e.g. the Assyrians) and from mercenaries. So our evidence from Sippar, interesting as it is, can only form a small part of the picture.

Notes

1. For an exemplary review of the archives of the Neo-Babylonian period, see Jursa 2005.
2. 1,300 is a rounding up of the average of 1,079 and 1,486.
3. A category of particular interest is the workers designated *šušānu*. They may have been cavalry support, i.e. grooms. It is possible that juridically they were tied to enfeoffed land in the same way that *ikkaru* were tied to temple land. Accordingly, it is plausible that *šušānū* were tied to horse-fiefs. If so, this would be the only hint we have of horse-fiefs around Sippar.
4. In essence, the farmers—*ikkaru*—were semi-free dependants tied to the land. Prior to the fourth year of Nabonidus the transfer of agricultural *širku*s to bow service was relatively straightforward. Subsequently, following the introduction of the *fermes générales*, it was a duty of the *rab sūti/ša muhhi sūti* involved to supply the corresponding manpower as required. Another clear articulation of this is in the lease contract *BRM 1* 101, edited by Jursa: Šamaš-kaṣir son of Nabû-mukīn-apli subcontracts from the *rab sūti* Bulṭāya son of Marduk-erība a concession to farm half of the temple's land; one of the stipulations is that Šamaš-kaṣir will give the *rab qašti* half of the farmers and gardeners which Bulṭāya is required to provide for bow duty.
5. There was a Village of the Cilicians (Alu Ša Humāya) near Sippar (Jursa 1998: 92), the existence of which might suggest a sizeable number of individuals, but the indications in the administrative material do not necessarily suggest more than six. Note that according to Dandamayev (2005: 224) the temples would have had a limited ability to absorb large numbers of prisoners of war as slaves.
6. I would like to thank Julian Reade for drawing my attention to these depictions.
7. Of course, it might be more logical to say that the Persians were "armée à l'assyrien"!

48

West of the Indus—East of the Empire: The Archaeology of the Pre-Achaemenid and Achaemenid Periods in Baluchistan and the North-West Frontier Province, Pakistan

Peter Magee and Cameron A. Petrie

Introduction

The monuments uncovered at Pasargadae, Persepolis and Susa and associated royal inscriptions provide a wealth of data concerning the subject peoples of the Achaemenid Empire. In assessing these, it is paramount to consider that they are largely propagandistic documents that detail only one side of a process of imperialism and economic exploitation. Of particular note are the early inscriptions of Darius I that not only provide an overview of the empire but also emphasize how he managed to consolidate the boundaries of the imperial system at a time of political strife. The Far Eastern reaches of the empire, for example, are codified into a series of manageable satrapies called Thatagush, Gandhara and Hindush. Scholars have often interpreted the entry of these place names into the historical record as evidence that prior to the accession of Darius these regions were poorly organized and/or lacked economic or political organization (e.g. Wheeler 1962). In this paper we explore how recent archaeological excavations in Pakistan (Fig. 48.1) provide an alternative understanding of the pre-Achaemenid levels of complexity in these regions, and the manner in which the Achaemenid kings ruled subjects in these far-flung eastern satrapies. By exploring the pre-Achaemenid archaeology of this region we can recast the inscriptional data in a manner that gives voice to those who inhabited regions far from the imperial centre.

Epigraphic evidence for Achaemenid satrapies in South Asia

Inscriptions primarily recovered from imperial capitals that date from the reign of Darius I onwards indicate that there were three provinces located along the eastern frontier of the Achaemenid Empire in what is today South Asia: Gandhara, Thatagush

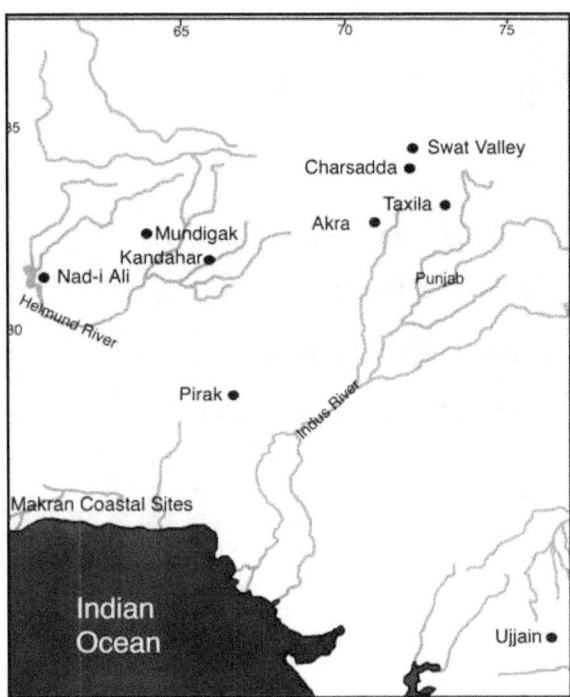

Fig. 48.1 Map showing the main sites mentioned in the text.

and Hindush (reviewed in Vogelsang 1992: 94–179; also Magee *et al.* 2005). The commemorative Bisitun inscription, which was carved between *c.*520 and 518 BC (Schmitt 1990: 299–300), lists Gandhara and Thatagush amongst the provinces that Darius inherited when he seized the throne in 522 BC (DB:—§6. 1.12–17—Kent 1953: 117–119; also Lecoq 1997: 187–214). Thatagush is also listed as one of the provinces that rebelled against the new king (DB:—§20. 2.5–8—Kent 1953: 121–123) and was the location of one of the three battles in the ensuing campaign against rebellious forces in the eastern provinces of the empire (Fleming 1982; Bivar 1988: 200; Vogelsang 1990: 100; 1992: 127–129). However, the date of the initial annexation of Gandhara and Thatagush remains uncertain. Recent assessments of the classical sources that relate Cyrus the Great's expedition to Central Asia agree that he marched through Arachosia in southern Afghanistan, destroyed the city of Capisa (modern Begram), and then campaigned into Bactria between 539 and 530 BC, when he died somewhere in the north-east of his newly expanded empire (Francfort 1988: 170; Bivar 1988: 198–199; Vogelsang 1992: 187–189).[1] The arrangement of the eastern provinces in a number of Darius' royal inscriptions has been taken to indicate the existence of close relationships between Baxtrish (Bactria) and Gandhara (Vogelsang 1990: 99–100), and between Harauvatish (Arachosia) and Thatagush, and this might indicate that Gandhara and Thatagush were annexed at the time that Cyrus secured Arachosia and Bactria. Whether or not this is the case, Darius considered them to be part of his empire in 522 BC.

It has been argued that Hindush is analogous with modern Sind (e.g. Bivar 1988: 202–204), although there are no excavated remains that support this suggestion. Hindush is notably absent from the Bisitun inscription, but it does appear on all but one of Darius' other surviving inscriptions, including two of the so-called Foundation Charters from Susa that do not mention either Gandhara or Thatagush (see Magee *et al.* 2005: 713, n.16). Hindush also appears with Thatagush among the 24 "fortress cartouches" inscribed on either side of the base of a statue of Darius, recovered at Susa in 1972, and both are represented on the so-called Canal Stelae from Egypt (Stronach 1972; Roaf 1974; Vogelsang 1992). Bivar has suggested that Hindush was annexed in 515 BC, following the reconnaissance of the Indus River by Scylax of Caryanda undertaken in 517 BC (1988: 201–203; after Herodotus IV: 44; also Vogelsang 1990: 101–104).

Archaeological investigation of the South Asian satrapies

Archaeological research in western Pakistan relevant to the timeframe of these "events" has more often than not focused on attempting to correlate the historical and archaeological records.

The Peshawar and Swat Valleys

Sir Mortimer Wheeler's (1962) excavations at the Bala Hissar at Charsadda in 1958 provided the first well-stratified archaeological sequence in the region. Although he initially proposed that there was no substantial occupation at the site before the Achaemenid period, reanalysis of Wheeler's sequence (Dittman 1984; also Vogelsang 1988) and renewed excavations at the site (Ali *et al.* 1998: 6–14; Young 2003: 37–40; Coningham 2004; Coningham & Ali 2007) have shown that the earliest known levels date to the mid-second millennium BC, and that it is the only site in the Peshawar Valley that might have an unbroken sequence of occupation from *c.* 1400 to 50 BC (Dittmann 1984: 159, 193). The recent excavations at the Bala Hissar have aimed at confirming the timing of the site's foundation (Ali *et al.* 1998: 6–14; Young 2003: 37–40; Coningham 2004; Coningham & Ali 2007), but have produced little in the way of new results that are directly relevant to the Achaemenid period.

In the Swat Valley to the north of Charsadda, Italian and Pakistani archaeologists have been conducting research since the late 1950s. The excavations at necropolises, including Kherai (Stacul 1966*b*: 261–74), Loebanr, Katelai, Butkara (Salvatori 1975: 333–51) and Timargarha (Dani 1967: 22–40), have revealed a sequence of cultural material, which Italian researchers have separated into numbered phases (Swat I–VII) (Tusa 1979: 675–90).[2] Dani labelled this assemblage the "Gandharan Grave Culture" (1967: 22–40). The investigation of affiliated settlement sites such as Aligrama and Ghaligai (Stacul 1967; Stacul & Tusa 1977) has contextualized this grave sequence by revealing associated domestic assemblages.

There is a general agreement that the Swat/Gandharan Grave sequence as a whole can be dated from the late third through to the end of the first millennium BC. However, there is controversy over the relative dating of the phases and the absolute dating of the entire sequence, and no single site has been excavated that provides a complete sequence (contrast Stacul 1966*a*: 37–79 with Dani 1967: 24–40; see Dittman 1984).

Sir Aurel Stein (1929: 40, 47) was the first to identify the site of Bir-kot-ghwandai as Bazira, a city which, according to Arrian (*Anabasis* IV: 27–8), was captured and fortified by the Macedonians during Alexander's conquest of Swat. Excavations at such a site had the potential to anchor the Swat sequence to a specific Achaemenid historical context, and work began with the aim of establishing the validity of Stein's identification (Filigenzi & Stacul 1985: 436). Callieri thought he was initially able to provide validation due to the discovery of a fortification wall during excavations (Callieri 1990: 676; Callieri, Filigenzi & Stacul 1990: 164; see also Callieri *et al.* 1992), but on the basis of numismatic finds, it has been established that this wall could not have been constructed until the Indo-Greek period in the second–first centuries BC (Olivieri 1996: 50). In fact, Olivieri (1996: 50) has gone so far as to say, "the information provided by the excavation to date is not yet sufficient to prove categorically that the archaeological site of Bir-kot-ghwandai actually corresponds to the Bazira mentioned by Alexander's historians".

The research that has been conducted in the Peshawar and Swat Valleys has provided an opportunity to understand more fully the cultural context upon which Achaemenid control (if we can think of it in those terms) was exercised. The so-called Gandharan Grave Culture clearly represents a distinctive material culture horizon found at a diverse range of settlements and employed in burial customs. It is bounded on the west by the Swat Valley, to the north by Chitral, and to the east distinctive Gandharan ceramics have been found at Hathial, adjacent to the early historic city of Taxila, which was located on the Bhir mound (Allchin 1982).[3] We will return below to the issue of how the spread of Gandharan material culture can be understood in reference to the Achaemenid annexation.

Akra and the Bannu Basin

Between 1985 and 2001 a research team comprised of members currently at Bryn Mawr College, the British Museum, the Institute of Archaeology (UCL), the Pakistan Heritage Society and the University of Cambridge conducted archaeological research in the Bannu basin, which lies south of Peshawar in the North West Frontier Province.[4] The basin is a small topographically defined region to the east of the Sulaiman Range, and is separated from the Gomal plain in the south and the Indus River and plain to the east by a series of substantial ranges.

In 1995, the project turned its attention to the site of Ter Kala Dheri (TKD), located about 5 km to the south of Bannu city on the banks of an ephemeral stream known locally as the Lohra nullah (Khan, Knox & Thomas 2000). This settlement appears to have once been quite large, and while it may have originally stretched along the bank of the nullah at a width of 400 m, it is now almost entirely destroyed by erosion and intentional destruction (Khan, Knox & Thomas 2000: 81). Here excavations revealed in situ floor deposits associated with a previously unknown assemblage of hand-made ceramic forms, characterized by black on red geometric decoration on a brown ground (Khan, Knox & Thomas 2000: 83, 86–89). This distinctive ceramic material was labelled Bannu Black on Red Ware, and two radiocarbon determinations from the stratified layers containing this new assemblage indicated a probable date in the early first millennium BC (Khan, Knox & Thomas 2000: 89–91). As we have noted elsewhere, the closest technological, morphological and stylistic parallels for Bannu Black on Red Ware are to be found in the early Iron Age (so-called Yaz Depe I) cultures of south-west Central Asia (Magee et al. 2005).

Following the preliminary excavations at TKD, attention was focused on the large mound of Akra, which is located about 7 km downstream (Fig. 48.2). Between 1995 and 1998, three separate topographic surveys were carried out indicating that the total preserved area of Akra might be around 80 ha (Khan et al. 2000a: 46). Two main archaeological zones at Akra can be delineated, using the Lohra nullah as an arbitrary boundary. Area A on the left side of the nullah consists of a large mound that has been extensively damaged by modern digging. The upper surface is now predominantly flat, but it is punctuated by several outcrops of cultural deposit, the largest of which rises about 15 m above the preserved mound surface and about 35 m above the surrounding plain. On the right bank of the stream Area B consists of several mounds that have been damaged by levelling for modern fields and erosion caused by the course of the nullah. These mounds vary in

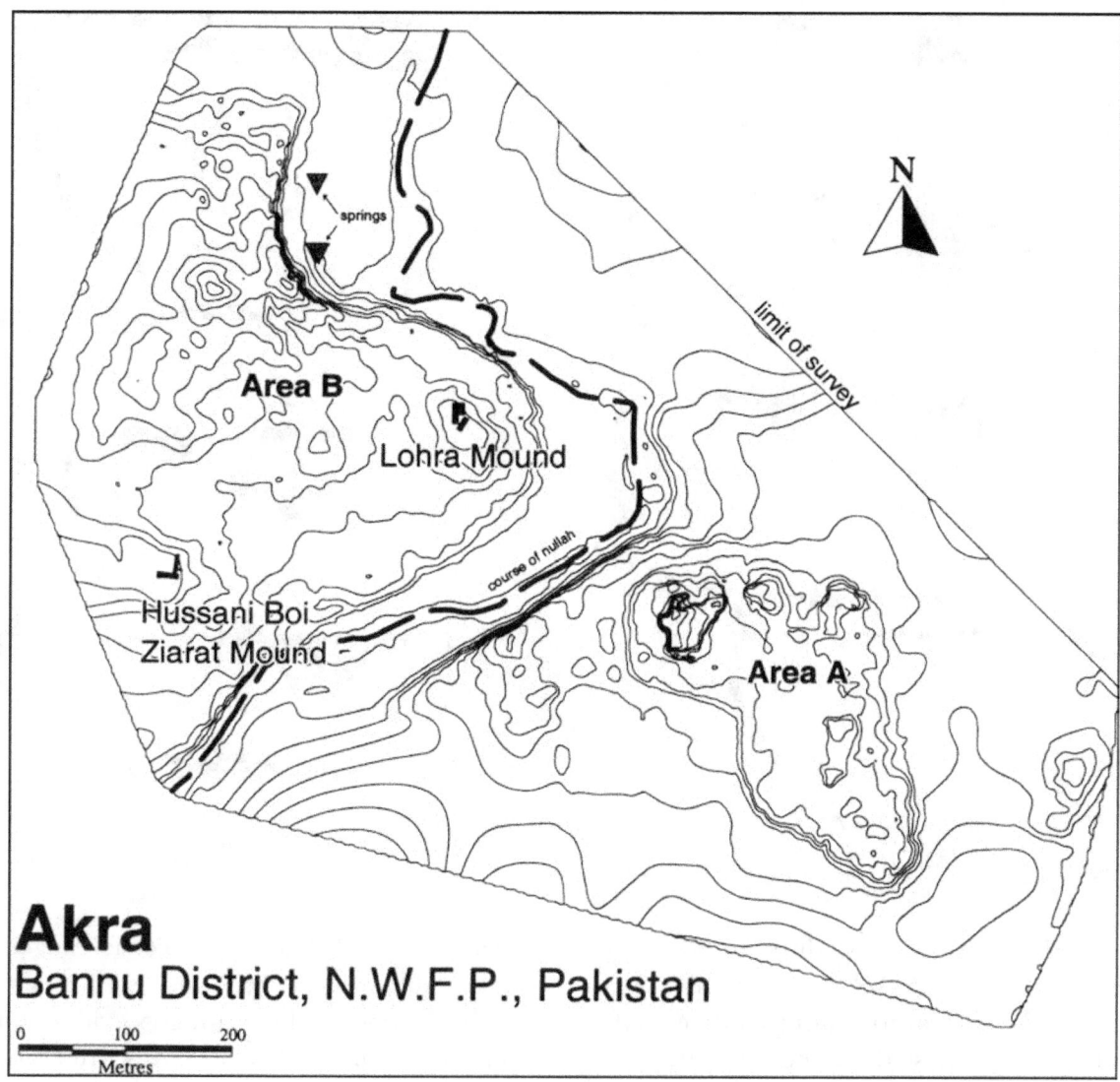

Fig. 48.2 Topographical plan of Akra.

size and height, and rise between 14 and 20 m above the surrounding plain.

In the initial reconnaissance of Akra in 1995, it was observed that fragments of the distinctive Bannu Black on Red Ware (Fig. 48.3) like those found at Ter Kala Dheri were also visible on the surface of the mounds on the right bank of the nullah (Area B). Between 1996 and 2000, excavations were carried out on three different mounds in Area B with the aim of confirming the early first-millennium BC dates suggested for Bannu Black on Red Ware at Ter Kala Dheri; defining the stratigraphic position of this ware in relation to other occupation at the site; and providing some data on the extent and size of the settlement during the first millennium BC. The excavations that have been carried out include a shallow sounding (Chigkamar mound [hereafter CGK]), a deep stratigraphic probe (Lohra mound) and

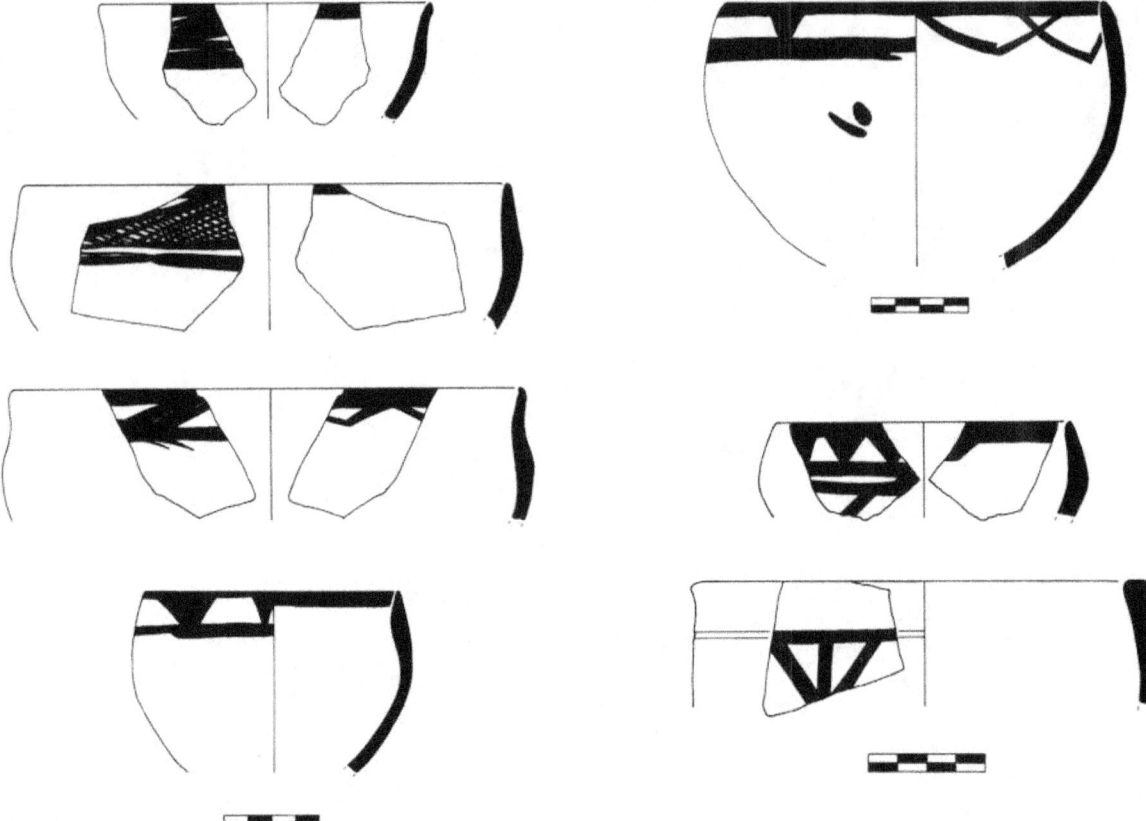

Fig. 48.3 Bannu Black on Red Ware from Akra.

an open area excavation (Hussaini Boi Ziarat Dherai [hereafter HBZD]). An intensive programme of radiocarbon dating confirmed the chronology suggested by the excavations at TKD: that is, Bannu Black on Red Ware dates to the first half of the first millennium BC, and this suggests that Akra was occupied from at least c.900 BC onwards. It is estimated that the settlement comprised nearly 30 ha of occupation during this timeframe.

Excavations in Area B also provided an assemblage (labelled Assemblage 1) that postdated the Bannu Black on Red Ware (Fig. 48.4). Typological comparisons with material from Iran and Afghanistan, including the distinctive tulip bowl, suggested a dating between 600 and 300 BC for this assemblage (Magee et al. 2005: 724–725; Petrie, Magee & Khan 2008).[5] As we have discussed in more detail elsewhere, this dating provides some archaeological confirmation for the argument, hitherto based on epigraphic and historical data, that Akra might be the capital of the Achaemenid satrapy of Thatagush (Magee et al. 2005: 732–737).

Excavations and surveys in Baluchistan

While the Neolithic and Bronze Ages in the Kachi plain and/or the coastal zone of Baluchistan have been well studied through the excavation of Mehgarh, Pirak and sites such as Miri Qalat and Shahi Tump, considerably less

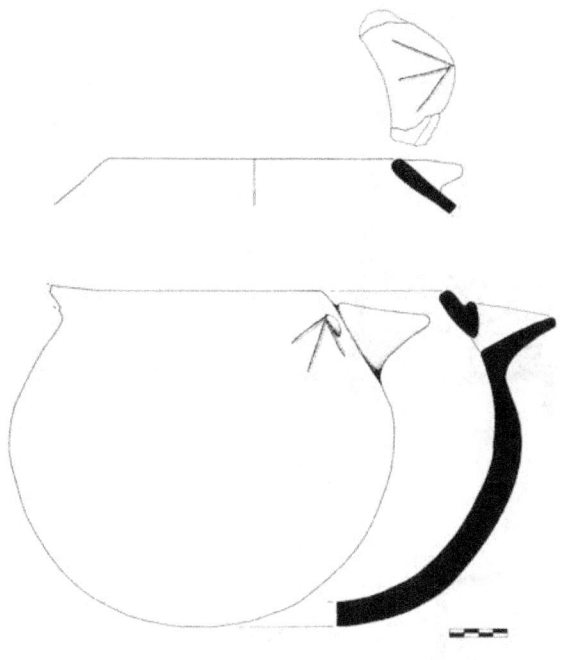

Fig. 48.4 Spouted vessel from Akra.

Table 48.1 Recalibrated Pirak Period IIIA radiocarbon determination (OxCal 3.10, using IntCal 2004; Reimer *et al.* 2004)

Code	C14 date	2 sigma Radiocarbon Likelihoods	Relative contribution to probabilities
Ly 1643	2970±140	1495–1474 BC	.013
		1461–890 BC	.961
		881–836 BC	.026

attention has been focused on the Iron Age. The exceptions are the later levels at Pirak, survey material collected in the Kachi plain and some recently excavated but poorly stratified material from the Makran coast.

The site of Pirak (Fig. 48.5) is of singular importance for understanding developments in the late third and second millennium BC in this region (Jarrige & Santoni 1979; also Enault 1979). In the uppermost levels of the excavation, a distinctive phase of occupation was characterized by both new architecture constructed on top of existing Period II buildings and new ceramic types. The beginnings of this period, which was labelled Period III by the excavators, was dated solely on the basis of one radiocarbon date (Ly 1643), which originated from the first phase of occupation (Period IIIA) (Jarrige & Santoni 1979: 335).[6] When this date is recalibrated using the latest calibration curve (see Table 48.1) it suggests that Period III began sometime after 1500 BC. There is a high probability, however, that this terminus post quem can be brought down to *c*.1460 BC, and it is notable that the mode of this probability distribution falls between 1250 and 1150 BC.

Characteristic of the early phases of Period III is the continued use of bichrome geometrically decorated ceramics (Fig. 48.6), which first appeared in limited quantities in Period I and are diagnostic of Period II (Fig. 48.7). In the original publication, the excavators noted that this decorative style represented continuity from earlier traditions but with the introduction of new forms, especially skeuomorphs of metal forms, different styles of decoration appeared (Jarrige & Santoni 1979: 53). In contrast to this claim of continuity, Santoni (1980) subsequently suggested that this ceramic bears a "striking resemblance" to Iron Age material from Tillya Tepe. However, even the most cursive examination of material from both these sites suggests that these comparisons are tendentious at best. In fact, the style of decoration evident at Pirak has few parallels except for the use of geometric patterns that would find parallels with most painted archaeological ceramics.

The question of how far into the first millennium BC the occupation at Pirak continues and whether or not the site was occupied during the Achaemenid annexation of Pakistan remains vexed. We are reliant on the

Fig. 48.5 Plan of Period III structures at Pirak. (After Enault 1979: fig. 18)

published radiocarbon dates to answer this question since few other regional assemblages are either well dated or present meaningful comparandae. When they are recalibrated, the highest probability distribution for the three additional Pirak Period III radiocarbon determinations is between c.1300/1200 BC and 760 BC, with two of the three falling between 1130 and 760 BC (Table 48.2).[7] At the least, these determinations indicate that occupation occurred after 1300 BC, but they do not necessitate the conclusion that the site was occupied until as late as 760 BC, although this remains a possibility.[8]

Santoni's (1980) arguments dealing with the date of several phases of occupation at the nearby site of Dur Khan in the Kachi plain have much relevance here. Dur Khan is a multi-tell site for which an extensive surface collection indicated several potentially different phases of occupation. Santoni's Phase I, represented by Tells B, C and D, was marked by ceramics and other artefacts such as shell bracelets that were in part paralleled by the last phases of Pirak (1980: 298–299). Santoni concludes, "Cependant, certain caractères nous obligent à placer ce matériel dans un horizon chronologique plus tardif, probablement postérieur mais consecutif à la période IIIC de Pirak" (1980: 299; also Vogelsang 1988: 112); however, her arguments in favour of dating this phase to after Pirak IIIC are unclear. Specifically, it is not clear how it was possible to assign a surface collection of ceramics for which there is no stratigraphic control to a phase of occupation posterior to that encountered at another site.

Phase II at Dur Khan is represented in the artefact assemblage from Tell A. In describing the ceramics from the site, Santoni draws parallels to material from both the Bala Hissar at Charsadda and Bhir mound at Taxila (1980: 299–300). Much importance is placed on these parallels and her observation that typical Phase II shapes are found elsewhere in association with Northern Black Polished Ware: "qui n'apparaît pas avant 500 ou 400 av. J.C." (1980: 300). This would place Tell A at Dur Khan firmly within the Achaemenid and subsequent periods and thus single it out as one of the few sites that could be firmly identified as such in Baluchistan. However, research conducted since Santoni's paper casts doubt on the specifics of these conclusions. The dating of Northern Black Polished Ware is still very much open to question, its presence cannot be used as an indicator of the specific timeframe of the Achaemenid period (Magee 2005a: 43; after Verardi 2002). In addition, systematic re-analysis of the material from Charsadda by Dittman (1984) has pushed back the dating of most layers at this site by several centuries and this seems to be confirmed for the earliest levels by the recent soundings by the Pakistani–British team from the Universities of Peshawar and Bradford.[9] This is of some importance for the overall dating of Pirak and Dur Khan since, according to Santoni, the dating of Phase II at Dur Khan from 600 to 400 BC facilitates the dating of Phase I from 900 to 600 BC, as Pirak IIIC ends at c.900 BC (Santoni 1980: 301). It is clear, however, that these arguments are constructed on a lack of firm chronological data, either in absolute or relative terms, and one can only conclude that no compelling evidence exists for intensive human settlement in the Kachi plain in the centuries just prior to the Achaemenid annexation of this area.

Elsewhere in Baluchistan, recent research has identified several archaeological assemblages that potentially date to the first millennium BC. Of particular interest here is the so-called Durrah-i Bust assemblage (Fig. 48.8), which is characterized by a coarse grog-tempered ware with distinctive appliqué decoration (Besenval & Sanlaville 1990: 89, fig. T) and dated to Period V of the Miri Qalat sequence on the Makran coast. Franke-Vogt (2001: 268–270) has convincingly drawn parallels between this material and the appliqué ware from her surveys in south-eastern Baluchistan. She concludes on the dating of this related assemblage:

> Although the stratigraphic sequences at Rana Ghundai, Periano Ghundai and Dabar Kot are far from clear, Stein and Fairservis arrive at dates for these wares, including the Appliqué, from the Indo-Scythian to the Sasanian period. Although this proposal may well come close to the truth, the highly hypothetical nature of this comparative construct must be kept in mind. If this date is correct, this would correspond to period VII (Indo-Sasanian) in Makran. Although the Durrah-i Bust assemblage of period V, which begins at an unknown date before Alexander the Great and lasts until the second century BC also includes sherds with appliqué, pinched and rope decorations, the floral-like patterns of our Appliqué are not attested to. The later date appears more likely, but a more precise proposal than from the later 1st millennium BC to the first few centuries of the 1st millennium AD is not yet possible. (2001: 270)

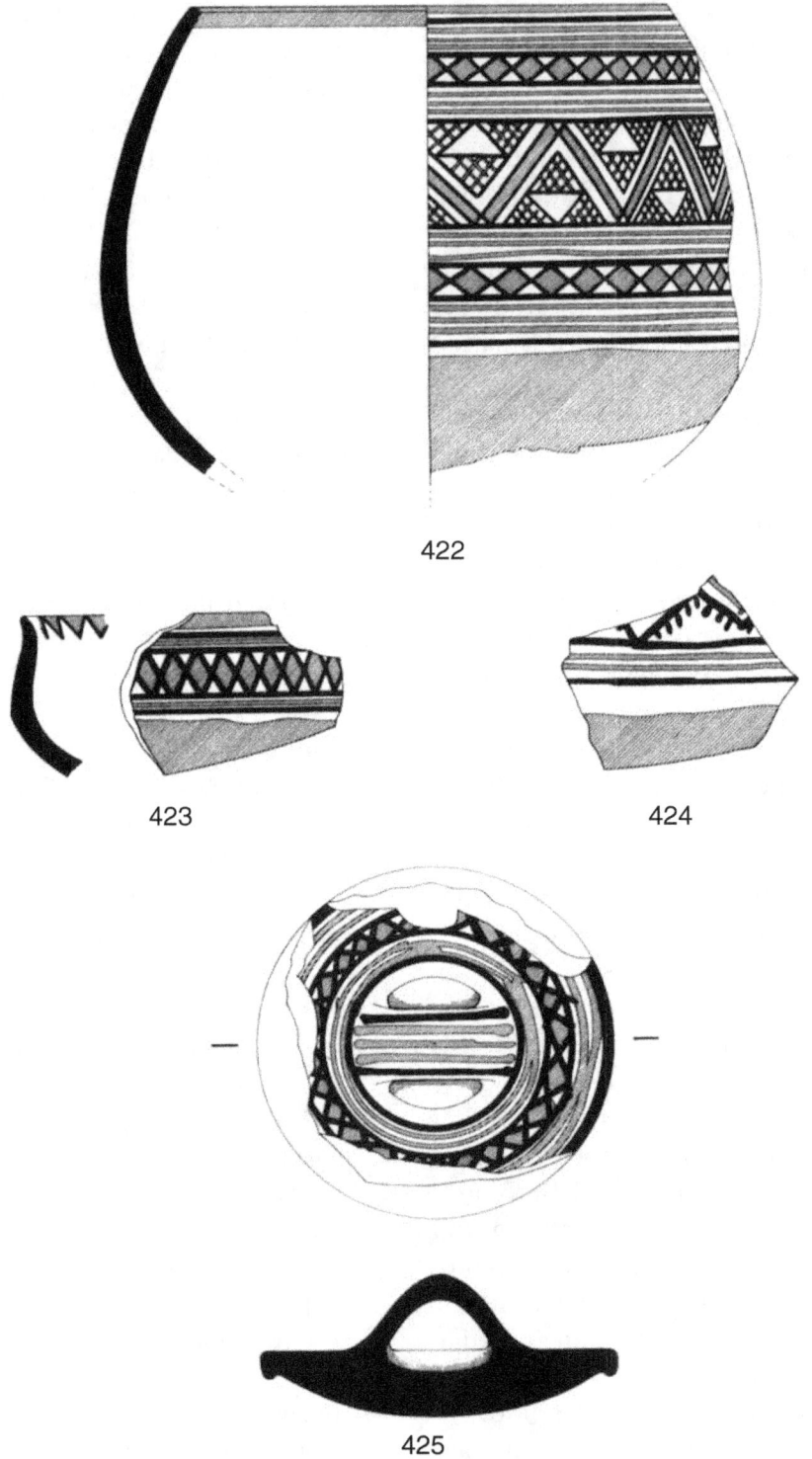

Fig. 48.6 Bichrome vessels from Pirak IIIC. (After Enault 1979: fig. 77)

West of the Indus—East of the Empire **513**

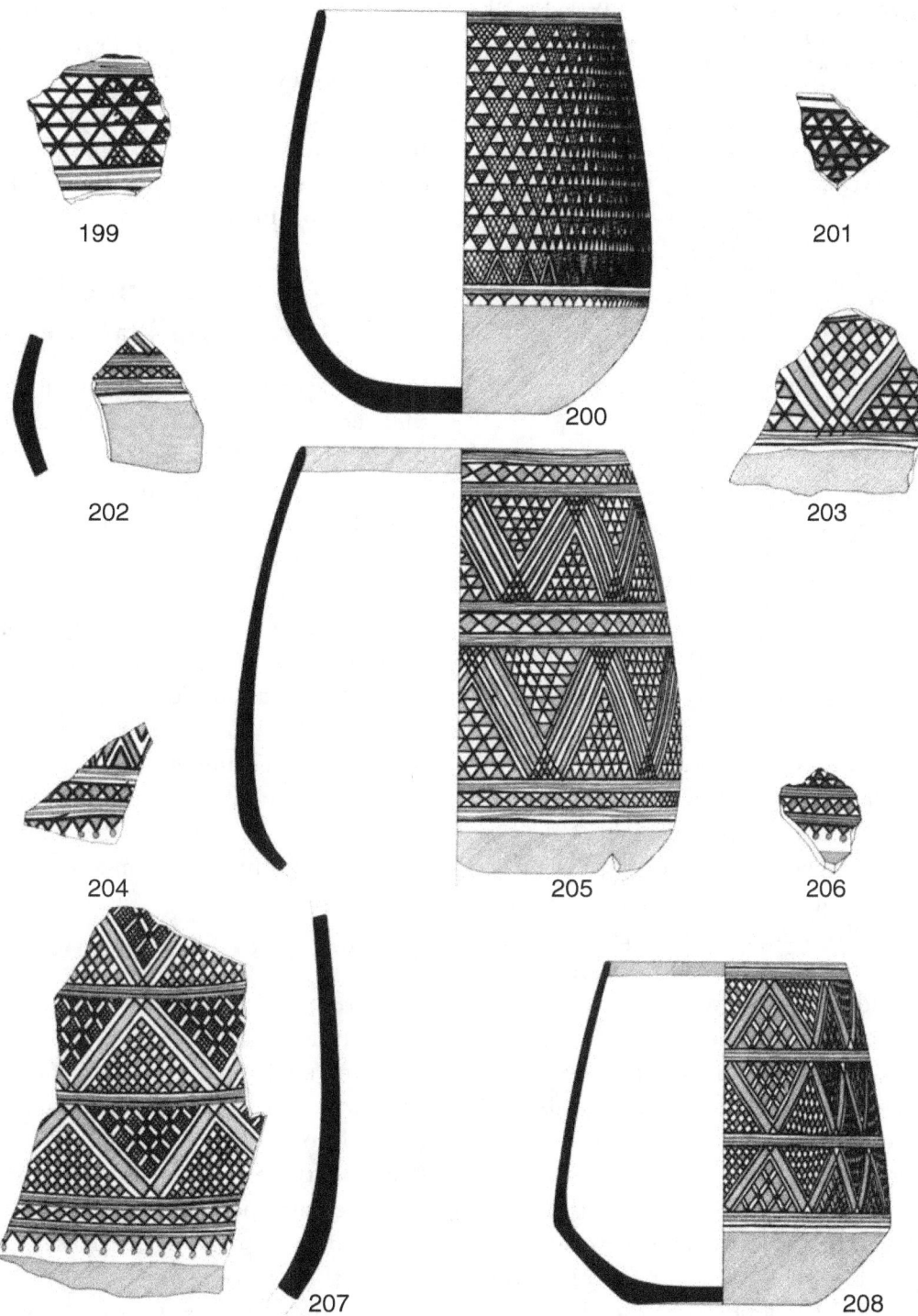

Fig. 48.7 Bichrome vessels from Pirak II. (After Enault 1979: fig. 51)

Table 48.2 Recalibrated Pirak Period III radiocarbon determinations (OxCal 3.10, using IntCal 2004; Reimer et al. 2004)

Code	C14 date	2 sigma Radiocarbon Likelihoods	Relative contribution to probabilities
Tf 1108	2725±105	1254–1244 BC	.003
		1212–1198 BC	.006
		1193–1138 BC	.025
		1133–758 BC	.914
		685–659 BC	.012
		646–585 BC	.026
		585–543 BC	.016
Tf 1109	2780±125	1372–1356 BC	.005
		1354–1340 BC	.004
		1318–760 BC	.977
		681–667 BC	.004
		626–623 BC	.001
		613–593 BC	.006
		575–563 BC	.003
Tf 861	2735±105	1256–1239 BC	.006
		1213–1196 BC	.008
		1194–1136 BC	.030
		1134–759 BC	.923
		683–665 BC	.008
		637–589 BC	.017
		580–553 BC	.009

Clearly, there is not only much that is unknown about the dating of these assemblages but the extent to which they are chronologically and/or culturally linked is also open to question. The recent publication of the Iron Age assemblage from the site of Tepe Yahya in south-eastern Iran does provide, we believe, some resolution of the chronological placement of, at least, the Durrah-i Bust assemblage (Magee 2004: 52). Several sherds that are comparable in decoration (Fig. 48.9) and, it would seem, paste were found in Period II at Tepe Yahya (2004: 52, figs 15–16), and judging by the assemblage that was available for the publication, such types were not found in the earlier Period III deposits at the site. Tepe Yahya Period II is dated from 500 to 250 BC by numerous radiocarbon dates and ceramic comparandae (2004: 73–75). This raises the possibility that the many sites that Stein, Fairservis, Besenval and Franke-Vogt have surveyed on which Durrah-i Bust and related assemblages were found might date to the Achaemenid period. Only more detailed excavations and independent dating will confirm this most tentative suggestion.

Pre-Achaemenid regionalization

In drawing this evidence together it is apparent that the archaeological picture of pre-Achaemenid western Pakistan is a complex one in which no single site can be used to order artefactual assemblages throughout the region. Moreover, we suggest that one of the most important aspects of the archaeological data is the apparent regionalization of pre-Achaemenid archaeological assemblages. Distinct regional assemblages can be identified in Gandhara, Bannu and Baluchistan. When we consider the Achaemenid imperial texts in light of the distribution and chronology of these regional facies, a different picture of the mechanisms of Achaemenid annexation emerges.

The valleys of Gandhara

We have noted above that Gandharan material culture of the first half of the first millennium BC is spread across the Swat and Peshawar Valleys and to the east across the Indus into the northern Punjab at Taxila. However, the extent to which it is possible to recreate any aspect of the economic, political or social configuration of this society is limited by the lack of extensive settlement excavations. Inasmuch as the spread of ceramics is indicative of economic interaction, it is abundantly clear that the Gandharan culture is bounded in a way that is highly suggestive of the existence of an economic interaction sphere that excludes neighbouring regions. This is most evident in the distribution of Wheeler's so-called Soapy Red Ware, a distinctive ceramic found in the basal layers of Charsadda and reported from the Hathial Ridge at Taxila. This pottery appears in minute quantities outside the east–west zone defined from the Swat Valley to the northern Punjab. For example, at Akra in the Bannu basin where contemporary layers were extensively excavated, only two Soapy Red Ware sherds were discovered in an assemblage made up of many thousands of diagnostic sherds (see Khan *et al.* 2000*a*: fig. 7; see also n. 3). Clearly, geographical considerations are part of the feedback mechanism that would codify this economic zone: east–west communication routes from the northern Punjab to the Peshawar region are facilitated by the ancient trade route that has its contemporary manifestation in the Great Trunk Road; whereas communication to the south of this line, particularly in the North West Frontier Province, is limited by the imposing ridges of the Salt Range.

How do we reconcile the existence of this economic zone with the establishment of the Achaemenid satrapy of Gandhara? There seems little doubt that the ancient city of Pushkalavati was one of the primary satrapal capitals of Gandhara (Wheeler 1962: 3; Ali *et al.* 1998: 2–3), a city that we have noted above was already established by *c.*1000 BC, and continued to be occupied throughout the first millennium BC. Therefore, it would appear that the Achaemenids encouraged, or acquiesced to, existing settlement structures in the region rather than reorganizing them to their own devising.

How the city of Taxila fits into this system, in either its first manifestation on the Hathial Ridge, or its second manifestation as the Bhir mound, is unclear. One possibility is that the pre-Achaemenid Gandharan economic zone was split at the end of the sixth century BC into a western sphere under Achaemenid control (the satrapy of Gandhara), while the area east of the Indus developed into a separate entity that was free of Achaemenid control. It has been argued that the earliest material from the Bhir mound has a "strongly Gangetic flavour" (Allchin & Allchin 1982: 314–315; Vogelsang 1988: 107–108; Allchin 1995: 131). It is also worth noting that in the *Mahabharata*, Janamejaya the king of Hastinapura conquers Taxila (cf. Sharif 1969: 9), and the reporting of such an attack in the epic might conceal a tradition relating to the Gangetic orientation of the city. The establishment of the Bhir mound at some stage in the fifth century BC (Vogelsang 1988: 108; Chakrabarti 1995: 175) may well mark, therefore, the beginning of a geopolitical bifurcation between Taxila and Charsadda. Such a suggestion clearly lies in the realm of high conjecture until more quantified data are available for all relevant sites.

The Bannu Basin

Just as the Gandharan material culture is sharply delineated in its distribution, the distinctive material culture of pre-Achaemenid Bannu seems to have specific influences and geographical limitations. The two most characteristic ceramics are Bannu Black on Red Ware and globular spouted vessels. At Akra, both these distinctive forms account for somewhere between 25 per cent and 50 per cent of the ceramic corpus from pre-Achaemenid Iron Age layers. When this material was first uncovered, no parallels from Iron Age South Asian sites presented themselves, and to ascertain the extent to which this ceramic was

516 THE WORLD OF ACHAEMENID PERSIA

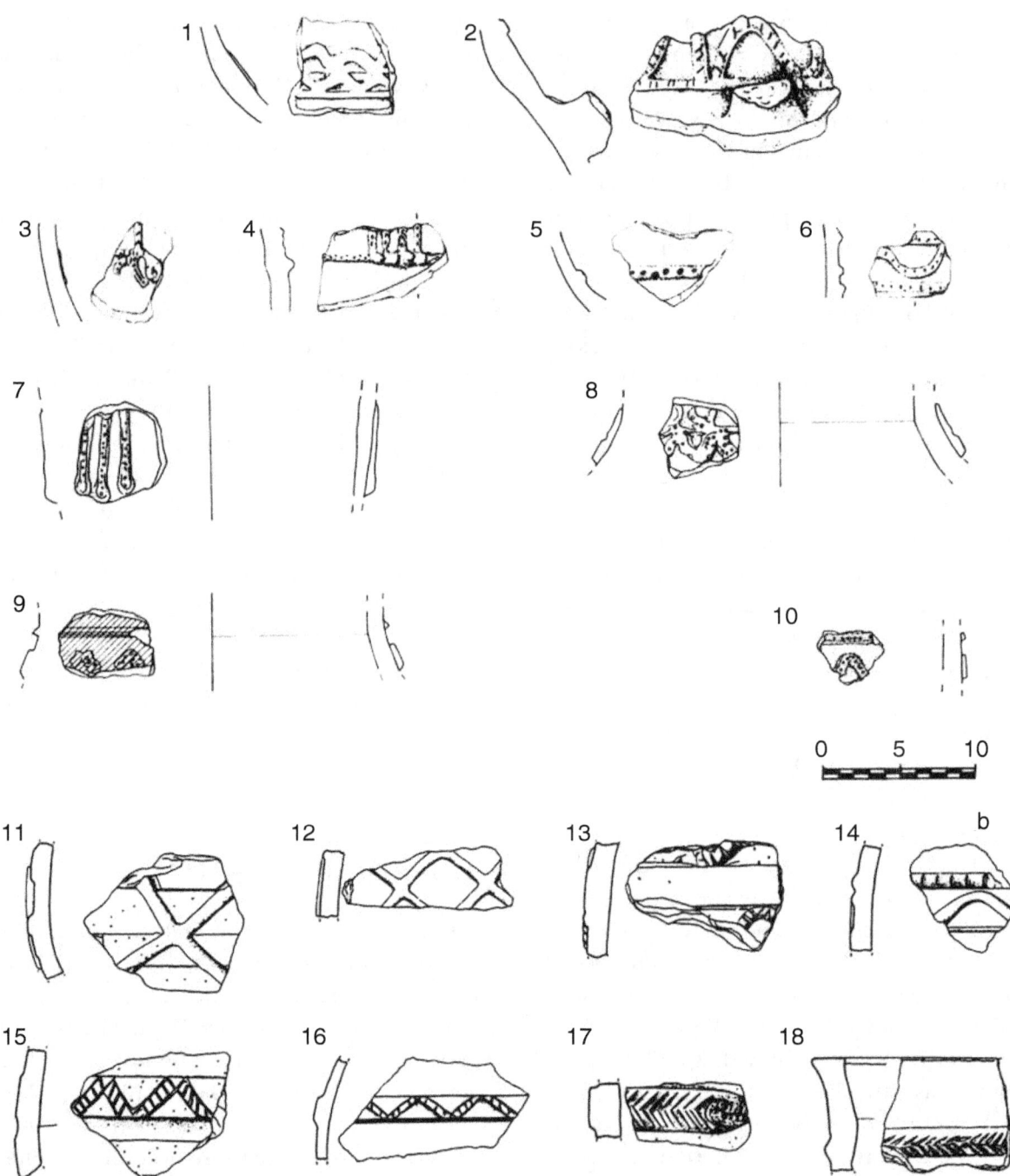

Fig. 48.8 Durrah-i Bust assemblage and appliqué ware from Sind. (After Franke-Vogt 2001: fig. 12)

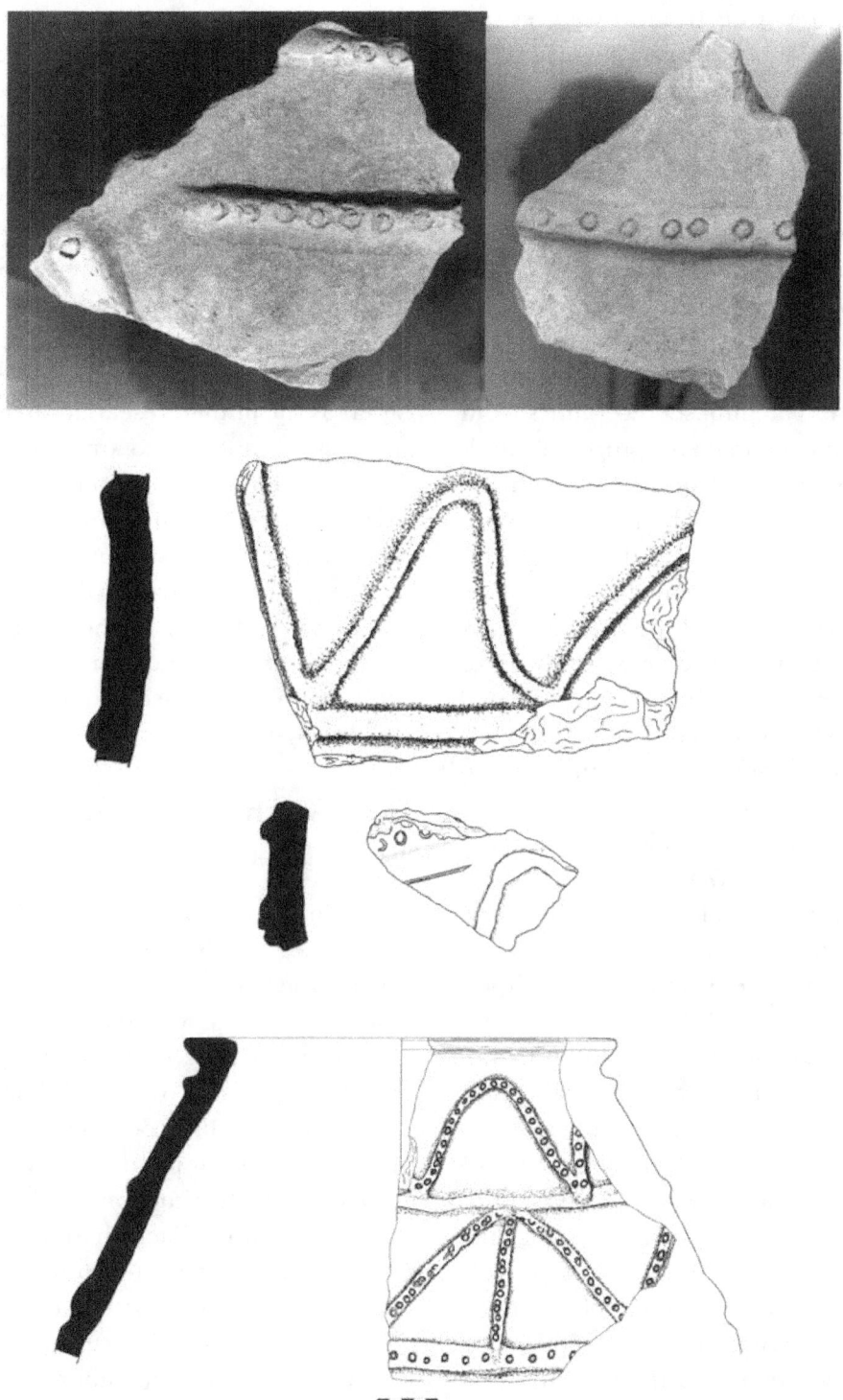

Fig. 48.9 Durrah-i Bust related sherds from Tepe Yahya. (After Magee 2004: figs 5.16, 5.27)

found but not reported from other sites, an intensive study of Wheeler's ceramics from the site of Charsadda was undertaken. This material is stored at the Lahore Fort and a complete analysis of it failed to reveal a single sherd of Bannu Black on Red Ware. It is perhaps inconceivable, given its painted character, that such material would not have been kept.

To the south of Bannu in the Kachi plain the most complete exposure of Iron Age remains comes from Pirak IIIC and Dur Khan, as noted above. The published ceramics from both these sites contain no recognizable parallel either to Bannu Black on Red Ware or the globular spouted vessels. The painted ceramics from Pirak Period IIIC are decorated with bichrome geometric patterns that cover most of the vessel (Enault 1979: fig. 77), which is quite unlike the monochrome, sparsely decorated Bannu Black on Red Ware. Similarly, Pirak IIIC spouted vessels do not contain the distinctive false spout that is found on the Akra examples.

There is compelling evidence, therefore, that just as for the Gandharan economic sphere, the economy of Akra and its hinterland was limited to the Bannu basin. As noted above and elsewhere, the inspiration for Bannu Black on Red Ware is to be found in the early Iron Age/Jaz Depe I cultures of south Central Asia (Magee et al. 2005). Why this influence is most clearly manifested in the Bannu Basin and not the Peshawar Valley or Kachi plain is not known. The excavations at Akra and the limited amount of regional survey conducted in the Bannu Basin provide some insights into aspects of regional organization in the pre-Achaemenid period. Akra is the largest settlement in the region and is located, just like Charsadda, near a snow-fed river system. Smaller settlements located in Akra's hinterland, such as Ter Kala Dheri and the thirteen other sites in the basin that have also been identified with Iron Age and later occupation, suggest the existence of some type of settlement hierarchy.

What is certain is that Achaemenid power extended into this system by the late sixth century BC. As we have argued elsewhere and also noted above, there is compelling evidence that Akra and the Bannu Basin can be identified with the Achaemenid satrapy of Thatagush (Magee et al. 2005: 732–737), but as far as the limited research can indicate, this process did not lead to any fundamental shift in settlement organization or economic life ways. There are no monumental Achaemenid period fortifications at new settlements such as are found at Dahan-I Ghulaman (Scerrato 1966) for example, further to the west. Just as in Charsadda, therefore, the Achaemenid policy in Bannu appears to be of acquiescence to local systems rather than alteration.

The Kachi Plain and the Makran

The similar trajectory for the Peshawar and Bannu regions does not, however, apply to the area of the Kachi plain. As we have noted above, there is evidence for a distinctive material culture in the late second and early first millennium BC at the sites of Pirak IIIC and Dur Khan. The distinctive bichrome decorated pottery of Pirak IIIC has few parallels outside the region, thus echoing the situation with both Soapy Red Ware and Bannu Black on Red Ware. However, unlike the situation in Bannu and Peshawar, this distinctive occupation does not appear to preface continued occupation through the early to mid-first millennium BC and into the Achaemenid period. Rather, these sites are abandoned and no new sites certainly datable to the Achaemenid period have yet been noted in this region. The Durrah-i Bust and related assemblages that have been observed further towards the coast are intriguing in this regard. The very tendentious evidence for their chronology suggests that they may be dated to this period and thus be considered as evidence for increasing coastal occupation.

Monsoonal variation and settlement dislocation

Palaeoclimatic evidence may be key in understanding the sharply contrasting trajectories of settlement growth between areas of the North West Frontier Province and the northern inland plains of Baluchistan. Varved sediments in the Oxygen Minimum Zone of the coast of Pakistan have indicated a decline in both summer and winter monsoon patterns around 1000 BC (Lückge *et al.* 2001; see also von Rad *et al.* 1999*a*, 1999*b*; Sirocko, Garbe-Schönberg & Devey 2000). This arid phase continues until nearly the last quarter of the first millennium BC. Pirak and Dur Khan are located in an area of considerably less rainfall than both Bannu and Peshawar and spate irrigation was most likely derived from the nearby Nari River. Today, the failure of a monsoon is devastating for the inhabitants of the Kachi plain because the largest input into the Nari river system is precipitation associated with both the winter and summer monsoon; snowmelt in the Toba Kakar range contributes only a small proportion. With a declining winter and summer monsoon, traditional patterns of spate irrigation would have been insufficient and long-term intensive agriculture would have been impossible.

It is precisely the interplay between rainfall and snowmelt riverine irrigation that would have made areas such as Peshawar and Bannu more inhabitable during this period. While these regions would have also suffered from declining rainfall, the main rivers that feed these valleys (the Kabul and Kurram respectively) are derived largely from snowmelt in the Afghan hills. The Peshawar Valley has the additional advantage of also being watered by the Swat and Indus Rivers, which rise in the Himalaya. It almost seems counter-intuitive to the non-climatologist that a decline in the summer and winter monsoons may be linked to increased snowfall in these highlands, but the argument is best summed up by Lückge *et al.* (2001: 275):

> The variability in the intensity of the monsoon may be linked to Eurasian/Tibetan snowcover as suggested by Dickson, Barnett *et al.* and Meehl. High (low) snowfall and the subsequent expanding (retreating) of the snow cover lead to changes in the albedo which results in the weakening (strengthening) of the monsoonal circulation. As demonstrated by Dey and Bhanu Kamar Barnett *et al.*, Meehl and Yang reduced surface heating in spring could be responsible for a delayed onset of the monsoon resulting in below average monsoonal rainfall.

These climatic challenges would account for the very different cultural and settlement trajectories experienced by the Kachi plain on the one hand and the Bannu and Peshawar regions on the other. In the latter, increased irrigation potential based on snowmelt-fed rivers would have provided the basis for increased economic centralization. Akra appears to represent just such a system: large, stone-constructed buildings are located along the edge of a stream that is fed by snowmelt. The ability to control canal irrigation would have been an important feature of any political control. It is intriguing to note that similar systems have been described as being located along river systems and canals in the Jaz Depe I culture (Biscione 1981; Francfort 1988: 169, 181–193; Briant 2002a: 752–753; also Stein 1905: 6) to which we have already alluded as an influence on the Bannu Black on Red Ware tradition. In contrast, the Kachi plain would have experienced increased subsistence stress and perhaps a move towards coastal environments in which food sources are guaranteed.

Nevertheless, it is clear from Achaemenid royal inscriptions that the satrapy of Hindush was an important one and that it must be located in some region of southern Pakistan (see Bivar 1988: 202–204; Vogelsang 1990: 101–102). As noted above, while Hindush is not mentioned in the Bisitun inscription, it does feature in all but one of the surviving inscriptions of Darius (see Magee et al. 2005: 712–713; n. 15), and it is the most commonly appearing eastern satrapy in the Persepolis Fortification Texts (Magee et al. 2005: 713, n. 24; Vogelsang 1992: 167–169). An important difference between Hindush and Gandhara and Thatagush is evident here: whereas travel from Susa to Gandhara was made via Arachosia (modern Kandahar), travel to Hindush appears to have been officiated from Hindush itself. This gives rise to the suggestion that travel to Hindush occurred via a southerly route through Kerman and towards Baluchistan (Magee et al. 2005: 713, after Vogelsang 1990: 102). A location for Hindush on the Baluchistan coast would not only make sense in light of the shifting settlement patterns noted above but would also jibe with this historical evidence. Indeed, the similarities between aspects of the Durrah-i Bust assemblage and Achaemenid period ceramics from Tepe Yahya in Kerman might be a reflection of increased economic contact between these regions. One notable issue that must be taken into consideration with this interpretation is that Hindush is listed as a supplier of ivory in the foundation charters from Susa (see Magee et al. 2005: 713, n. 16). This suggests that the province had ready access to a supply of the raw material, which is not impossible for the Baluchistan coast, but fits more logically with a location on the lower Indus.

Conclusion

Today, our knowledge of the South Asian satrapies of the Achaemenid Empire is dramatically different to what it was certainly 50, but also as little as 20 years ago. While we now have some unequivocal archaeological substantiation for an Achaemenid presence in certain regions, it is also clear that much of our knowledge is clouded by inadequate archaeological field research, and repeated re-analyses and reinterpretations of a number of key but flawed data sets.

The excavations that have been conducted at the Bala Hissar at Charsadda and the Hathial and Bhir mounds at Taxila have revealed clear evidence for cultural and economic interaction between these two major centres from the beginning of the first millennium BC onwards. However, it is also apparent that changes in orientation took place during the mid-first millennium BC, with Charsadda being drawn within the limits of the Achaemenid Empire. Similar to the situation at Charsadda, the recent excavations at Akra have also revealed clear evidence for a degree of contact and interaction with, and some form of dominance by, the Achaemenid Empire in the mid- to late first millennium BC. But there is also abundant evidence for socio-economic complexity in the Bannu Basin in the early first millennium BC, which predates any contact with the Achaemenids, and manifests itself using a distinctive material cultural assemblage that appears to have been influenced by Central Asian types. Although we now have clear archaeological evidence for interaction between these "eastern" areas and the Achaemenid centres of power far to the west, there appears to have been little in the way of direct influence and overt cultural control. What is certain is that many questions remain as to the nature of the interaction between the two, and these will only be answered by further fieldwork at sites like the Bala Hissar and Akra.

In contrast to the evidence from the northern regions, the evidence for Achaemenid period occupation in Sind and Baluchistan has been far harder to isolate. This potentially reflects differences in the nature of interaction with the Achaemenid heartland, and the types of cultural affiliations that were made possible via communication by routes across the south of the Iranian plateau and Gedrosia, rather than via Seistan and Afghanistan. However, with our increased awareness of diachronic changes in the patterns of monsoonal rainfall, we now have a clear line of evidence that might account for the apparent sparsity of mid- to late first-millennium BC settlement in Sind and the inland areas of Baluchistan. As for the Peshawar Valley and the Bannu Basin, it is clear that there are a number of key sites in Baluchistan, such as Dur Khan, which may well have evidence for occupation during this period and for which we have an acute need for further investigation.

The recent research carried out on the archaeology of the Iron Age in South Asia is casting new light on our understanding of the processes of post-Harappan urbanism and complexity. Assumptions that the inhabitants of the North West Frontier and Baluchistan were incapable of such developments without the hand of Achaemenid overlords are now untenable. However, it is also clear that in the early first millennium BC these regions were engaging with populations in Central Asia and the Ganges. Understanding the processes of cultural development in this period, establishing what precisely made these regions so attractive to the Achaemenids, and what if any impact there was from imperial control remain topics for future research.

Notes

1. This is based primarily on Herodotus (I 169, 201–216); but also Pliny (*Natural History*: VI, XXIV, 92), Arrian (*Anabasis* III 27.4) and Quintus Curtius (VII.3.1). In contrast, Briant (2002*a*: 38–40) maintains the order presented by Herodotus, implying that Cyrus campaigned to Central Asia before and after his victory in Babylon in 539 BC.
2. The list of excavated Gandharan grave sites has recently been expanded with the excavations conducted by the Directorate of Archaeology and Museums NWFP at Parwak in Chitral (Ali & Zahir 2005: 135–182; Ali, Hemphill & Zahir 2005: 183–226).
3. It is also worth noting that there are "vague" parallels between the Gandhara Grave assemblage and vessels excavated from graves at Gumla (Period V and VI) and Hathala (Pattern A) in the Gomal Valley (Dani 1970/71: 40, 56, 162–163, fig. 37; also Dittman 1984: 156, 179–183).
4. In addition to the authors of the present paper, the members of the Bannu Archaeological Project include Professor Farid Khan of the Pakistan Heritage Society, Mr Robert Knox, formerly Keeper of the Department of Asia at the British Museum, Professor Ken Thomas of the Institute of Archaeology University College London and Dr Justin Morris of the British Museum. When the field research at Akra was carried out, Professor Peter Magee was a postdoctoral research fellow in the Department of Archaeology at the University of Sydney, and Dr Cameron Petrie was a postgraduate student in the Department of Archaeology at the University of Sydney.
5. Dittman (1984: 189) noted that the tulip bowls recovered from Wheeler's Ch. I levels 28–22 are all shallow in form, and therefore argued that they are most akin to the "Late Achaemenid (and

later) form". According to his relative chronology, their appearance at Charsadda dates to the fourth and third centuries BC (1984: tables 3 and 5). The tulip-bowl forms that have been recovered from Akra include both deep and shallow variants (see Magee *et al.* 2005: fig. 16. C–D). If Dittman's chronological reasoning is followed, then the presence of these forms suggests that the site may have been occupied during both the Achaemenid and Late Achaemenid periods. This is also seemingly confirmed by the presence of bowls with offset rim, which have been dated to 600–300 BC (see Magee *et al.* 2005: 724), and painted S-carinated rim bowls, whose form and decoration have been dated to the Early Achaemenid period (Dittman 1984: 189, also fig. 10.3). However, in what constitutes an attempted rebuttal of Dittman's analysis, Vogelsang (1988: 104) subsequently argued that the tulip-bowl form should be dated to the Post-Achaemenid period in South Asia, and that Dittman's chronology has been pushed too early. In support of this argument Vogelsang cited three lines of evidence: lotus bowls, which occur in Ch. I 22–20 (but not tulip bowls, which occur in Ch. I 28–22; Wheeler 1962: 40–41), are also found at Shaikhan Dheri (Dani 1965–6: fig. 20.5–9), which was founded in the second century BC; "baroque ladies", which only occur in Ch. I 22–19 (Wheeler 1962: 40, 104ff), are also found at Shaikhan Dheri (Dani 1965–6: 48–57); and the Iranian carinated bowl form continues to be used into the second and first centuries BC in parts of the east (Vogelsang 1988: 104; citing Haerinck 1983: carte 8). However, there are fundamental flaws in Vogelsang's argument, based on circular reasoning and misleading use of evidence, and this ends up providing clear support for Dittman's revised sequence and the dating of the tulip bowls. Firstly, the lotus-bowl form, which is actually present in various deposits at both the Bala Hissar (Ch. I 22–20, Ch. II 9, Ch. IV and Ch. V; Wheeler 1962: 40–41) and Shaikhan Dheri (Dani 1965–6: Greek Period, fig. 20.5–9; and also Scytho-Parthian and Kushana periods, fig. 42.1–8), is most likely derived from the earlier tulip-bowl form, which is not present at Shaikhan Dheri. Based on Vogelsang's own reasoning, the tulip bowl must therefore date prior to the second century BC. Secondly, while there is a clear chronological overlap between the appearance of "baroque lady" figurines and lotus bowls at Charsadda (Ch. I 22–20; Wheeler 1962: 105) and Shaikhan Dheri (both appear in Greek, Scytho-Parthian and Kushana levels; Dani 1965–6: 48–57), it is only in Charsadda Ch. I 22 that tulip bowls and "baroque lady" figurines appear together (Wheeler 1962: 40, 105). The fact that this figurine type continues into the Kushan period deposits at Shaikhan Dheri suggests that it does not have a tight chronological range, and there is little to suggest that it has a strong association with the tulip bowl. Thirdly, if read closely, Haerinck (1983: 22, n. 35, 182, 215) actually argues that the carinated (i.e. tulip) bowl form originates in the Iron III period in Iran, and continues to be used into the second century in some regions, including Seistan and Peshawar. However, the examples from Qal'eh-i Sam in Seistan that are illustrated are dated to the fourth and third centuries BC (Haerinck 1983: 212–214), and the suggestion that the form continues into the second century BC in the east appears to be based entirely on Wheeler's initial relative chronology (see Haerinck 1983: 214). If Haerinck had had access to Dittman's at that time unpublished paper, one can only assume that he may well have modified some of his correlations. Therefore, on the basis of the evidence presented by Vogelsang, there is thus no valid reason to refute Dittman's arguments about a fourth- and early third-century BC date for the Late Achaemenid tulip bowls at the Bala Hissar, and the dates that have been proposed for these forms and Assemblage 1 at Akra.

6. These samples were analysed at the University of Lyon (Jarrige & Santoni 1979: 335).
7. These samples were analysed at the Tata Institute of Fundamental Research in Bombay (Jarrige & Santoni 1979: 335–336).
8. It is worth noting that the extended 2-sigma probability range of each of these determinations is a product of the fact that the large errors for each date mean that the probability distributions fall on both sides of a very large plateau in the radiocarbon calibration curve, which has an impact on all determinations that fall within the early to mid-first millennium BC.
9. As noted above (n. 5), Vogelsang (1988) has argued that Dittman has pushed some of the chronological phases too early, and that they should in fact be dated to the first millennium BC (1988: 106). However, the arguments presented there suggest that Vogelsang's doubts may be somewhat unjustified.

49

Achaemenid Interests in the Persian Gulf

D. T. Potts

Introduction

The extent of Achaemenid interest in and control over the Persian Gulf are topics that have been debated for decades (compare Schiwek 1962 and Salles 1990). In this essay I shall focus on five domains that warrant scrutiny in any discussion of Achaemenid relations with the inhabitants of the islands and Arabian littoral of the Persian Gulf. These include the evidence of an Achaemenid presence 1. on Bahrain; 2. in mainland eastern Arabia; and 3. in the Oman peninsula; plus 4. the identification of the islands of the XIVth satrapy; and 5. the role of the Persian Gulf as an information highway linking India and Mesopotamia in the Achaemenid period.

Bahrain

We shall begin with Bahrain, ancient Dilmun, because chronologically speaking this was potentially the first important Persian Gulf possession to be acquired by Cyrus after the capitulation of Babylon. The evidence for this is indirect. In the 11th year of Nabonidus, an official in Dilmun titled $^{lú}bel\ p\bar{\imath}h\bar{a}ti$ is attested in a document from Babylon (Ungnad 1908: no. 81). If this is understood literally, then the official would have been the administrator or governor of a province (Akk. $p\bar{\imath}h\bar{a}tu$). In the opinion of some scholars, Dilmun became de facto a part of Cyrus' empire with the fall of Babylon. Such a view has led Jean-François Salles, for example, to state in 1998 that the Achaemenids "had a governor in Bahrain" (Salles 1998: 53). Rather than debating the validity of this deduction, I suggest that instead we briefly examine the archaeological evidence of occupation on Bahrain in the Achaemenid period, more particularly the evidence from what was undoubtedly the political and cultural centre of the island, the great mound of Qalat al-Bahrain.

This we are in a position to do thanks to the detailed publication by Flemming Højlund and Helmuth Andersen of the Danish excavations in the Late Dilmun palatial building, formerly referred to as the "palace of Uperi" (Fig. 49.1), an allusion to one of the kings of Dilmun mentioned in Neo-Assyrian sources. In fact, much of the occupational evidence from this monumental building, which incorporated several walls from a much older

Fig. 49.1 View of the Iron Age "palace of Uperi" on Qalat al-Bahrain. (Photograph by the author taken in 1983)

palace of the early second millennium BC, has been dated on ceramic grounds to the Achaemenid period, or periods IVc–d in the Qalat sequence.

One of the types present in the building, moreover, is the so-called "Achaemenid bowl", recently discussed at length by Beth Dusinberre in its Lydian context (1999, 2003: 172–195).[1] As at Sardis, the Achaemenid bowls on Bahrain had no local precursors, suggesting the shape was introduced. That shape, however, was widespread across the Achaemenid Empire, yet the Qalat examples were locally manufactured, judging by their typically Bahraini paste. Finally, these bowls were attested in domestic contexts on the Qalat, as well as in the so-called palace. But does this evidence suggest that Achaemenid bowls were introduced into the local ceramic repertoire by Persians, Persians who arrived on Bahrain to administer it, perhaps even a Persian satrap and his entourage living in the Late Dilmun palace?

There is at least one ancillary piece of evidence that must be considered in the context of attempting to answer this question. A glass seal (Fig. 49.2) with an Achaemenid "court style" contest scene showing a royal hero grappling with a winged bull was found just above the plaster floor in room B6 of the palace (Fig. 49.3). Even if it is considered provincial by the scholar who published it (Kjærum 1997: 164), it is still a significant find which could be interpreted as a sign of Achaemenid administration, since generally similar seals were used on Persepolis Treasury and Fortification Tablets (Garrison & Root 2001: pls 274–275, 279f, 280h, 285h).[2] At the same time, it is also true that such seals were employed by the Murashu family to seal their private, economic texts at

Nippur (Zettler 1979). Hence, the possibility must be entertained that the seal, and by extension, the palatial residence, were those of a wealthy merchant family, not necessarily an Achaemenid satrap.

Another counter-argument to the proposal that the Late Dilmun palace on Bahrain might have housed an Achaemenid satrap is furnished by the Achaemenid bowls themselves. The 8 examples shown here (Fig. 49.4) were among 29 vessels representing 9 different types which were discovered, carefully buried in (largely decomposed) cloth bags beneath the floors of Rooms A8 and B12 in the palace, containing the remains of snakes—both the sea snake (*Hydrophis lapemoides*) and the rat snake (*Hierophis* [or *Coluber*] *ventromaculatus*). Although these burials definitely date to the Achaemenid period, the presence of such ritual snake deposits in the palace strongly suggests that it was not inhabited by Zoroastrians.[3] Indeed, Herodotus specifically states (1.140) that "Magi with their own hands kill everything except dogs and people; in fact, they turn it into a major achievement and indiscriminately kill ants, snakes, and anything else which crawls on the ground or flies in the air". This may well be an allusion to the killing of creatures known as Avestan *khrafstra*/Pahlavi *khrafstar* created by Angra Mainyu. As Albert de Jong has noted, "The snake (Av. *azi-*) is perhaps the main representative of the *khrafstras*. Killing it removes great sins and pollution" (de Jong 1997: 340). Much later, in the sixth century AD, Agathias (*c.* 532–580) reported on an annual festival called "the removal of evil", at which, "they kill a multitude of reptiles, and all other wild and desert-living animals and bring them to the Magi, as though as a sign of piety. In this way they think that they are doing what pleases the good god, but that they hurt and offend Arimanes [Ahriman]" (*Histories*

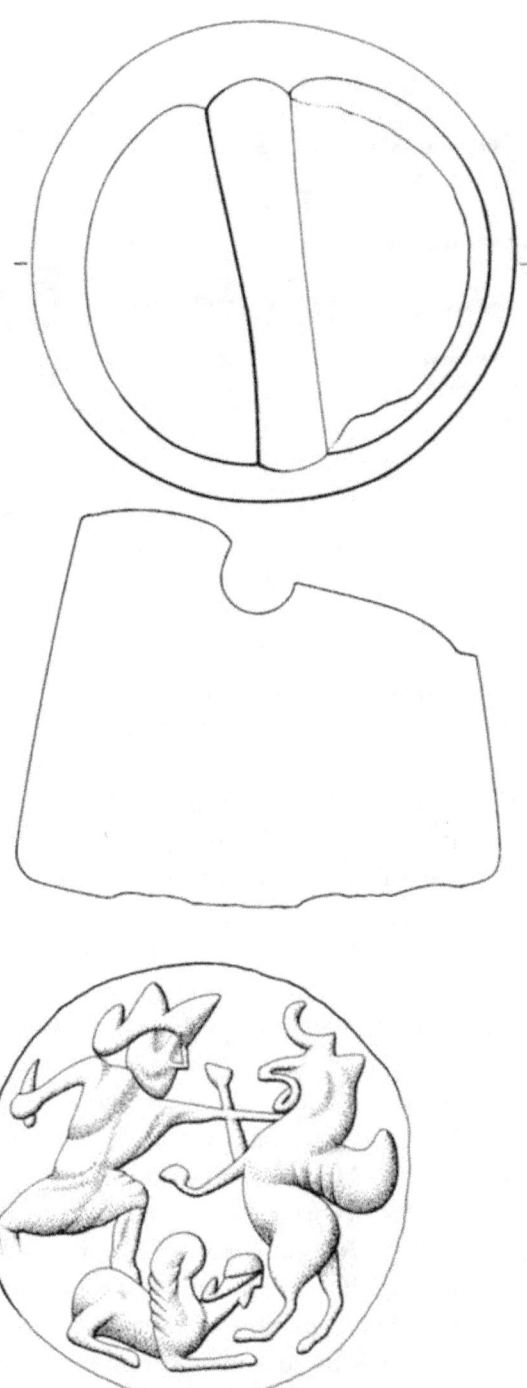

Fig. 49.2 Glass seal from Qalat al-Bahrain. (After Poul Kjærum, "Stamp-seals and stamp-seal impressions", in Flemming Højlund and H. Hellmuth Andersen, *Qala'at al-Bahrain*, vol. 2: *The Central Monumental Buildings* [Aarhus, 1997], fig. 734)

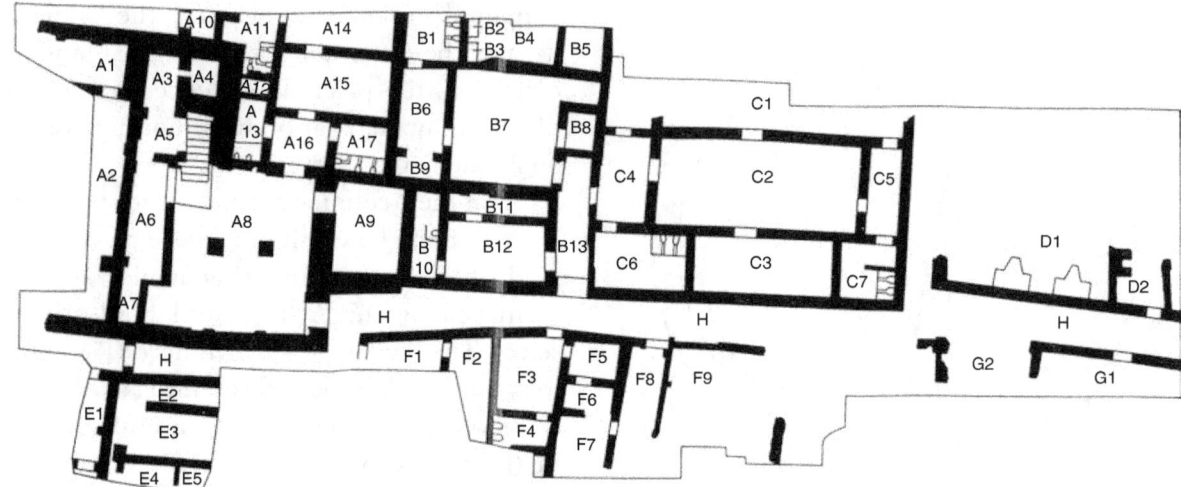

Fig. 49.3 Plan of the palatial building on Qalat al-Bahrain. (After Flemming Højlund and H. Hellmuth Andersen, *Qala'at al-Bahrain*, vol. 2: *The Central Monumental Buildings* [Aarhus, 1997], Plan 3)

2.24; cf. de Jong 1997: 341). This attitude, if indeed it existed in the Achaemenid period, hardly matches the careful burial of snakes in cloth bags and bowls beneath the floors of the palace at Qalat al-Bahrain. Unless the practice was a heterodox, folk-religious, non-Zoroastrian one introduced from Iran, it would seem unlikely to have been the cultural signature of an Achaemenid satrap.[4]

On the other hand, esoteric knowledge moving in the opposite direction, from India to the West, could perhaps explain the otherwise mysterious snake sacrifices on Achaemenid Bahrain. Ophiolatry—the worship of snakes—is considered "one of the most conservative features of worship all over South Asia" (van den Hoek & Shrestha 1992: 57). Snakes—*nagas* or *sarapas*—are semi-divine beings variously considered lords of a subterranean world, bringers of rain and guardians of the house, who must be propitiated and who embody the cycle of life and death (Vogel 1972; Sinha 1978). When travellers from Hindush (Fig. 49.5) went to Persepolis, it is perfectly possible that many will have sailed up the Persian Gulf, and travelled up to Fars from Liyan (near Bushehr and Reshahr), rather than undertaking the arduous journey entirely overland through Baluchistan and Kerman. In traversing the Persian Gulf, Indian religious concepts and esoteric lore may well have been transmitted between the East and the West, and cult practices like the snake veneration seen on Bahrain may be one reflection of such contact.

During the Achaemenid period, moreover, Indian mathematical astronomy was enriched by Mesopotamian methods and parameters, according to David Pingree (1974). The *Jyotisavedanga*—a manual for determining the mean times for performing Vedic sacrifices bound to specific times of day, months or seasons—is dependent on Mesopotamian sources of the seventh and sixth centuries BC, including MUL.APIN, while the Pāli *Dīghanikāya*, a Buddhist text of the fourth or third century BC, contains astral omens derived from the lunar, solar and atmospheric

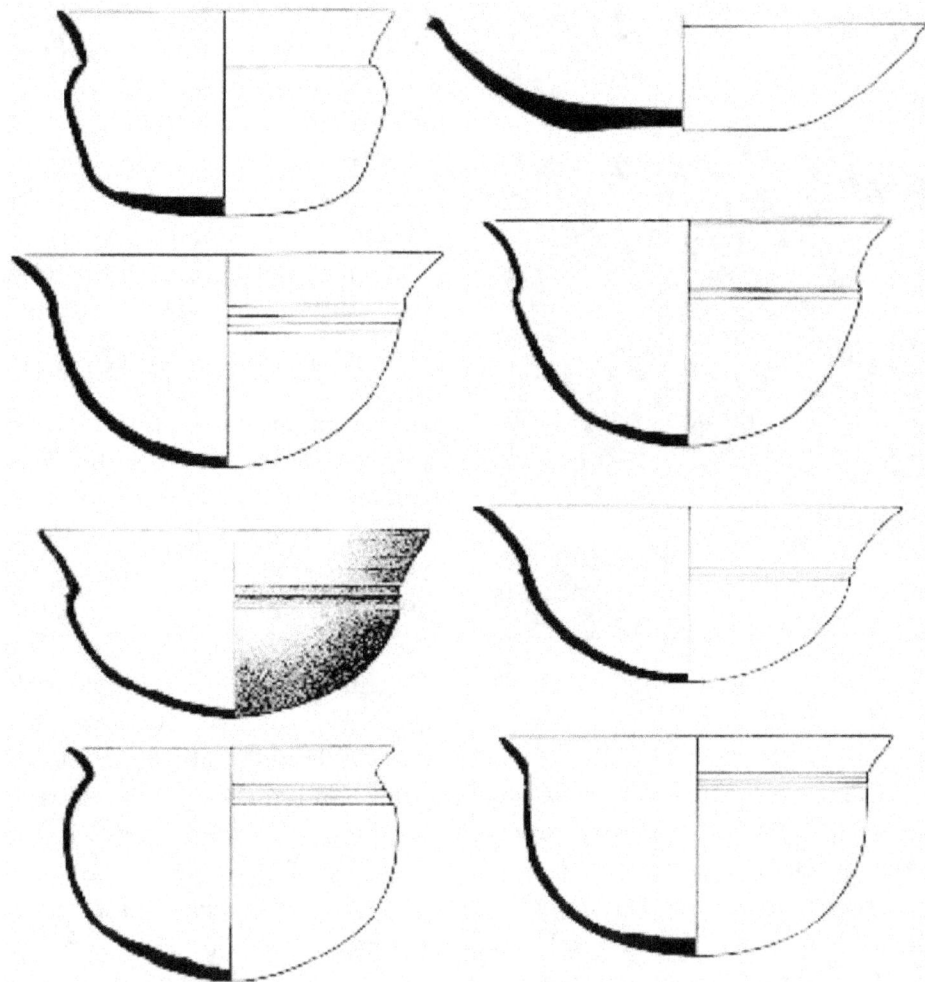

Fig. 49.4 Selection of Achaemenid-style bowls containing snakes excavated by the Danish expedition in the palatial building on Qalat al-Bahrain. (After Flemming Højlund and H. Hellmuth Andersen, *Qala'at al-Bahrain*, vol. 2: *The Central Monumental Buildings* [Aarhus, 1997], figs. 678, 682, 666, 667, 647, 658, 674 and 630)

sections of *Enūma Anu Enlil*; and the later Sanskrit *Gargasamhitā* contains omen material from both *Enūma Anu Enlil* and *šumma ālu*, which Pingree feels "must have entered India during the Achaemenid period" (1982: 618). Political conditions in the Persian Gulf during the Achaemenid period amounting to a *pax Persica* may have contributed significantly to these interchanges.

Before concluding this discussion of Bahrain, it is worth recalling a suggestion made in 1979 by the late Kilian Butz with respect to the toponym Ti-li-man or Ti-ri-ma-an in the Persepolis Fortification texts (PF 19, 202, 389, and 1882). Butz hypothesized that Ti-li-man might be an Elamized variant of Tilmun, the Akkadian form of Dilmun, and hence an indication that this region was part of the Persian Empire (Butz 1979: 361, n. 278). While the suggestion has found few adherents, it is nevertheless true that, according to Yaqut's (1179–1229) geographical dictionary,

Fig. 49.5 Head of an Indian from the Persepolis stairway reliefs. (Photograph D. T. Potts)

the name of the main town on Bahrain was Tarm (Wüstenfeld 1874: 183), a form which is reminiscent of Tirimanna (and note the alternation between the liquids *l* and *r* poses no problem, cf. *Tylos/Tyros* in Greek and Latin sources, and Bowersock 1986: 399) and, interestingly, Herzfeld had already suggested this might be an "Iranian form of Tilmun" (1968: 62, n. 3). A toponym Tarm near Qazvin was also known to Yaqut, who presumed that the superior type of cotton called "Tarmi" must have come from one or other of these places. But already in 1875 Alois Sprenger had suggested that, as cotton was unlikely to have been cultivated around Qazvin, the appellation "Tarmi" most probably referred to Bahrain (Sprenger 1875: §153) where cotton was indeed cultivated in the early fourteenth century according to Ibn Batutta (Gibb 1958: 409, f. 246), and where the Greek natural philosopher Theophrastus recorded its presence in his *Historia Plantarum* (4.7.7–8), a work which preserves the scientific observations of Androsthenes, one of the companions of Alexander of Macedon. Indeed, cotton has been recovered more recently on Bahrain in Achaemenid contexts by the French archaeological mission directed by Pierre Lombard (Tengberg & Lombard 2001: 167–181).

Mainland eastern Arabia

In his publication of the hieroglyphic cartouches on the base of the Egyptian statue of Darius, discovered by the French mission on the Apadana mound at Susa (DSab) in December 1972, Jean Yoyotte compared no. 19 with Demotic *hagor*, the designation used for the Arabs of north-western Arabia (as in Hegra, the Nabataean name of Medain Salih) (Kervran *et al.* 1972; cf. Yoyotte 1974: 181–183). In 1990 David Graf suggested that *hgl* instead was a reference to north-eastern Arabia, that area which today lies within the Eastern Province of Saudi Arabia (1990b: 143–145).

A toponym *hgr*, written in South Arabian letters, occurs on the coinage of Harithat, issues which the late Danish numismatist Otto Mørkholm thought, following Adolph Grohmann and Hermann von Wissman, derived from the general area of Hofuf (the largest oasis in eastern Saudi Arabia), in contrast to René Dussaud who identified Hagar with Dumat al-Ğandal, the Jawf oasis in the north Arabian Nafud.[5] Subsequently, and most importantly for Graf's argument, Walter Müller proposed that Gerrha, the name of a major trading entrepôt in north-eastern Arabia mentioned in numerous Greek and Latin sources, was nothing but a Graecized version of Aramaic *hagara*, itself derived from the name *han-Hagar in the local Hasaitic dialect of pre-Islamic north-eastern Arabia (according to von Wissmann 1982: 29, n. 21a). It is by this tortuous route that Graf's hypothetical interpretation of the toponym *hagor* on the base of Darius' Egyptian statue came about, an interpretation which led Salles to make a second bold claim with respect to the Achaemenids in the Persian Gulf, namely that they "were active also in the Gerrha kingdom" (Salles 1998: 53). Unfortunately, in contrast to Bahrain, there is no archaeological evidence to support the identification of an Achaemenid horizon in north-eastern Arabia. Furthermore, the attribution of Harithat's coinage to eastern Arabia is tenuous, and it is by no means clear that Graf's interpretation of the toponym on Darius' statue is superior to Yoyotte's original suggestion.

The Oman peninsula

Despite the commonly held, traditional view that the Achaemenid province of Maka lay in the region of Makran (Eilers 1983: 101–119), there is compelling evidence to identify Old Persian *Maka* with Royal Achaemenid Elamite *Makkash*, Akkadian *Makkan* and Sumerian Magan, that is, the Oman peninsula. Without reviewing the archaeological evidence from the third millennium which bears on this issue, I would just reiterate the point that in the trilingual Achaemenid royal inscriptions, the Akkadian equivalent of OP Maka is *Qadê/Qadû*, a name which appears in a now lost inscription (the so-called Ishtar slab, from Nineveh) of Assurbanipal's, recording the Assyrian king's receipt of tribute from Pade, king of Qadê, who dwelt in the town of Iskie. Twenty-five years ago I suggested that the Neo-Assyrian toponym Iskie must be identical with Arabic Izki, considered in Omani oral tradition to be the oldest town in Oman (Potts 1985*a*, 1985*b*). Subsequently, François de Blois noted a number of references to "Arabs" or "Arabians"—Elamite *har-ba-a-be*—from Makkash in the Persepolis Fortification texts (de Blois 1989). Despite the fact that it is not inconceivable for there to have been Arabs on the Makran coast, I am still persuaded by the evidence of Iskie/Izki that the Achaemenid references to Maka indeed refer to the Oman peninsula, and nothing suggests that Neo-Assyrian Qade should be located in Makran.

Moreover, the Myčians or Mačiya, that is the inhabitants of Maka, appear on the base of Darius' statue from Susa, and on one of the grave reliefs at Persepolis, wearing a short sword slung over one shoulder (Fig. 49.6), very much like those used in the Iron Age in Oman (Potts 2001: 50). Although common in Iron Age graves in the Oman peninsula, such swords have yet to be discovered anywhere in south-eastern Iran or Pakistani Makran.

Islands of the XIVth satrapy

When discussing Darius' satrapal reforms, Herodotus tells us that the inhabitants of the islands in the Erythraean Sea, along with the Sagartians, Sarangians, Thamanaeans, Utians and Mycians, were reckoned to be part of the XIVth satrapy (*Histories* 3.93). In Book 7.80, when naming the contingents that fought with Xerxes at Doriscus, Herodotus again refers to "the tribes who had come from the islands in the Erythraean Sea to take part in the expedition". To these references we may add Arrian 3.8.5 who lists "the tribes bordering on the Erythraean Sea" among the army of Darius III at Issus. Whereas Herodotus offers no locational information on these islands, Arrian gives us quite a bit in his report on the voyage of Nearchus from the mouth of the Indus River to Susa in 325/324 BC.

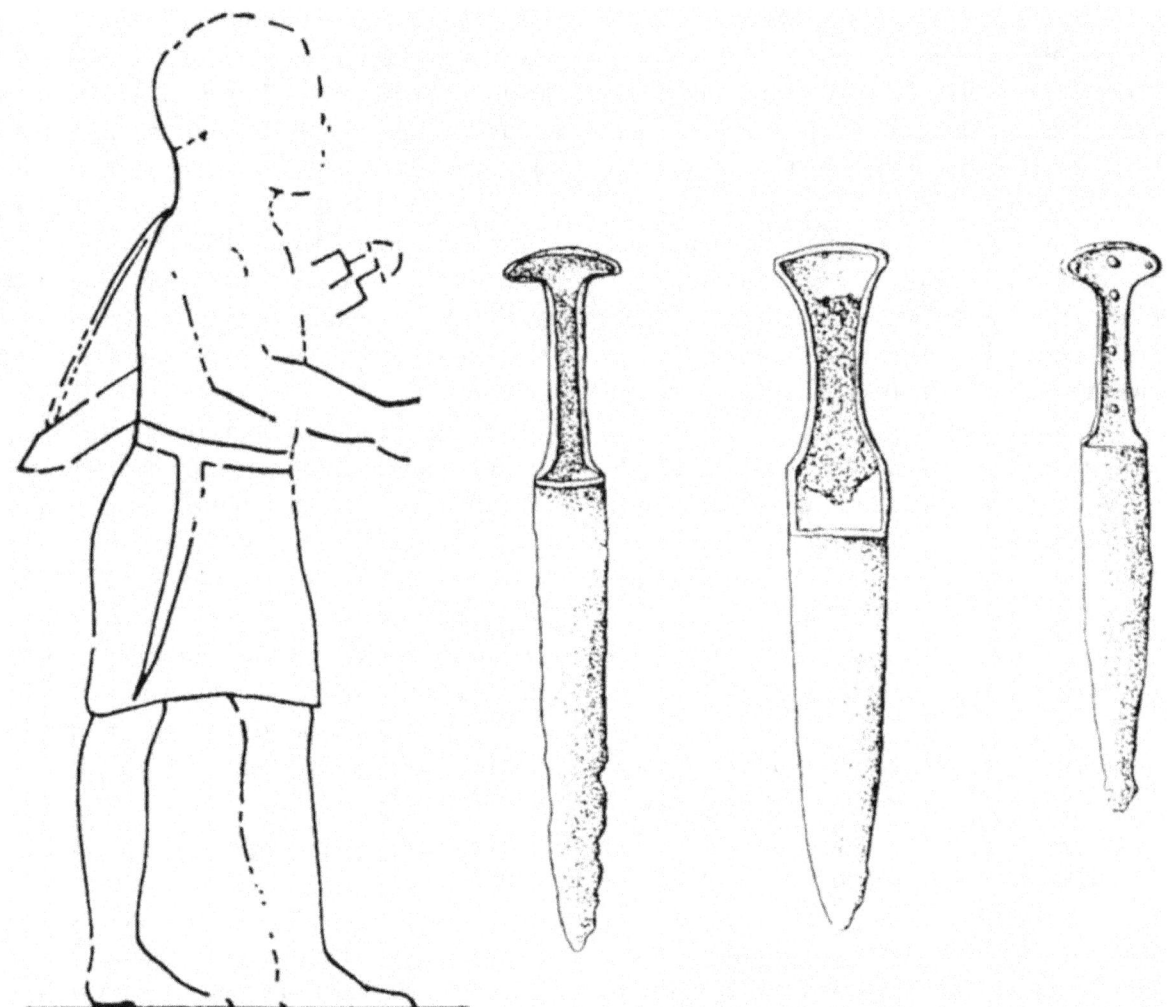

Fig. 49.6 Figure of a Mačiya shown with comparable Iron Age short swords. (After D. T. Potts, "Before the Emirates: an archaeological and historical account of developments in the region c. 5000 BC to 676 AD", in I. Al Abed and P. Hellyer (eds), *United Arab Emirates: A New Perspective* [London, 2001], fig. 14)

Scholars have worked on this material since Bourguignon d'Anville published his ground-breaking article on the historical geography of the Persian Gulf in 1764, and consequently most of the islands named by Arrian have long since been identified (see Potts in press). For present purposes we can ignore the first two islands—Karnine and Nosala—which were located outside the Persian Gulf proper, off the coast of Baluchistan, and begin with "a rugged and deserted island" called Organa (*Indika* 37.2), identified by most scholars with Hormuz. This is followed by a mixture of inhabited and uninhabited islands. Some of these have been identified via the survival of comparable name forms in Arabic or Persian, while others have been identified simply on the grounds of the stated distance from the previously named island (Fig. 49.7). These include

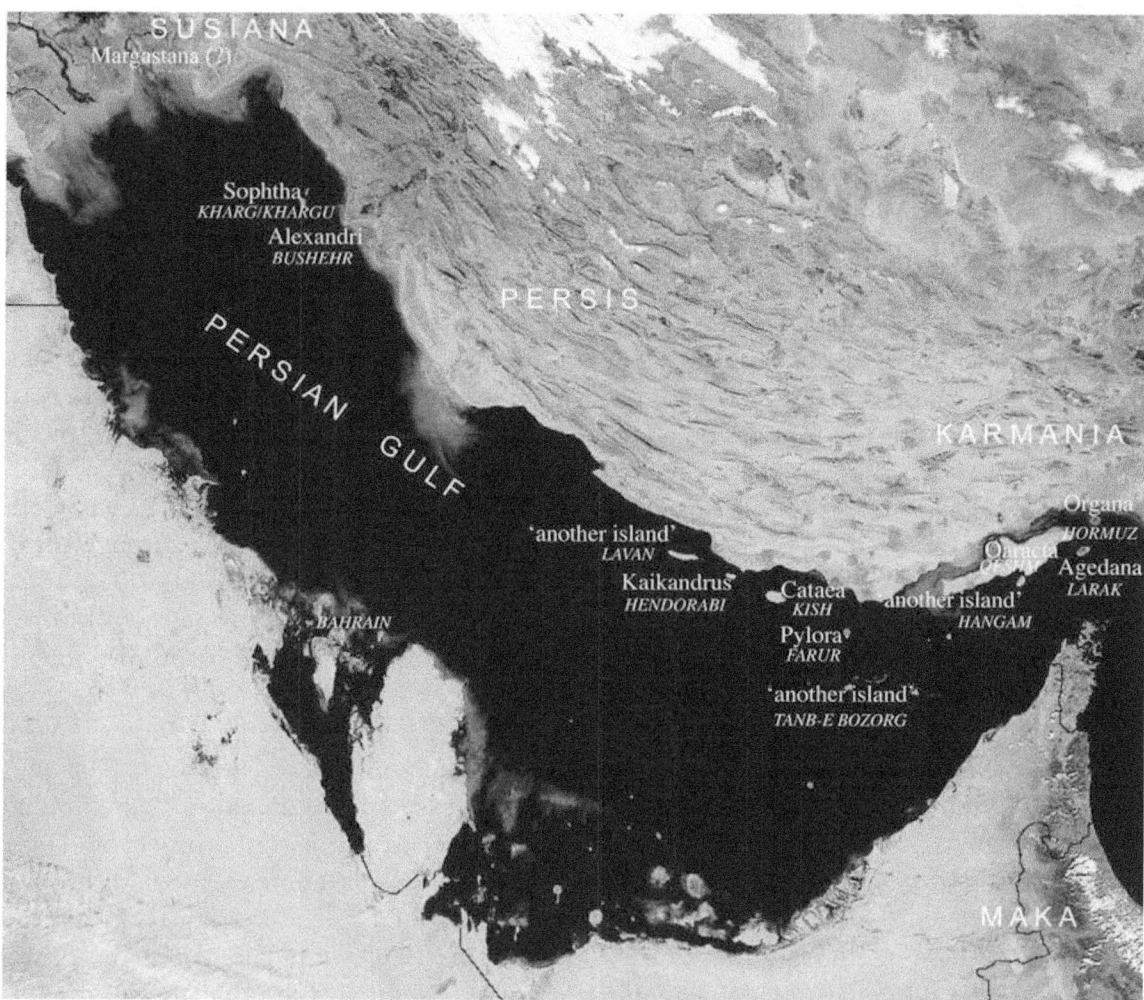

Fig. 49.7 Map of the Persian Gulf showing the locations of the main islands mentioned in the account of the voyage of Nearchus. (After D. T. Potts, "The islands of the XIVth satrapy", in press)

Oaracta (*Ind.* 37.2) = Qeshm; "another island" (*Ind.* 37.4) = Hangam; "another island" (*Ind.* 37.7) = Greater Tunb; Pylora (*Ind.* 37.8) = Farur; Cataea (*Ind.* 37.10) = Kish; Kaikandrus (*Ind.* 38.2) = Hendorabi; "another island" (*Ind.* 38.3–4) = Lavan; and the unidentified Margastana (*Ind.* 41.2).

Obviously the mere fact that Nearchus mentions these islands does not tell us that they all were counted amongst the islands of the Erythraean Sea for tax purposes, and clearly some were uninhabited and therefore of no interest to the Achaemenid administration. But at least one of these—Oaracta— deserves closer scrutiny.

Arrian (*Ind.* 37.2) describes Oaracta as a "large, inhabited island […] Vines and datepalms grew there, and it produced corn; its length was 800 stadia. The *hyparch* of the island, Mazenes, sailed with them as far as Susa as a volunteer pilot. They said that in this island the tomb of the first ruler of this territory was shown; his name was Erythras, and hence came the name of the sea."

Even in antiquity there were conflicting theories as to why the Erythraean Sea was so called, and I shall not enter into this debate here. Rather, I wish to focus on the reference to the *hyparch* of the island, Mazenes. To begin with, however, let me state that the identification of Oaracta with Qeshm is assured thanks to the survival of the toponym Burkhut or Brocht on the island in medieval geographical sources (Nimdihi, Samarqandi, Ja'fari, Ibn Magid) and in Portuguese sources (Pedro Teixeira), a point already recognized by Bourguignon d'Anville in the eighteenth century. The village of Kusheh in the interior of the island has a shrine to a Shaykh al-Barkeh or Barkh which Aubin took to be a reflex of the ancient name, associating it also with the *nisbeh* of the Zoroastrian sailor al-Brukhti, from Siraf, who is mentioned in the anonymous tenth-century *Livre des merveilles de l'Inde* (Aubin 1973: 102).

The presence of a *hyparch* on Qeshm in the late Achaemenid period is interesting, not merely in light of the question raised here concerning the extent of Achaemenid political control over the Persian Gulf, but in light of Herodotus' remarks that, alongside the indigenous inhabitants of the region, there were the *anaspastoi*, the "dispossessed". Twice, Herodotus (3.93 and 7.80) refers to the islands in the Erythraean Sea as places "where the Persian king settles the people known as the dispossessed". While Schiwek questioned the very idea that the Achaemenid kings would have sent prisoners to the Persian Gulf islands (1962: 17), there is no *a priori* reason to dispute the practice of using islands like Qeshm for the internal exile of political opponents or high-ranking Persians who fell from grace.

Strabo preserves an anecdote not related by Arrian but attributed to Nearchus, which may throw some light on this. Describing the island of Ogyris, said to be 2,000 stadia from Karmania, the identification of which has been made unconvincingly with Hormuz, by Bunbury (1879: 550); Masira, by Sprenger (1875: 100) and Schiwek (1962: 75); and Larak, by Goukowsky (1974: 122, n. 54), Strabo writes that Nearchus "was shown around Ogyris, by Mithropastes, the son of Aristes, which latter was satrap of Phrygia; and that the former was banished by Darius, took up his residence in the island, joined them when they landed in the Persian Gulf, and sought through them to be restored to his homeland" (*Geog.* 16.3.5). The banishment of Mithropastes by Darius III is thought by Brian Bosworth and others to have been a result of his father, Aristes, committing suicide following Alexander's victory at Granicus in 334 BC (Bosworth 1996: 66; cf. Goukowsky 1974: 122; Salles 1998: 116). This act ruined Mithropastes' prospects and he was "dispossessed". Ten years after Mithropastes was banished to the Persian Gulf, Nearchus and his fleet came along. Further, Strabo writes, "Nearchus says that they were met by Mithropastes, in company with Mazenes; that Mazenes was *hyparch* of an island in the Persian Gulf; that the island was called Oaracta; that Mithropastes took refuge, and obtained hospitality, in this island upon his departure from Ogyris" (*Geog.* 16.3.7).

In general, the title *hyparch* was used for governors of sub-regions within satrapies. That there were such sub-regions within the Persian Gulf, that is within the XIVth satrapy, is suggested by Arrian who says that, upon landing at Harmozia on the mainland, presumably near Minab, Nearchus met an unnamed *hyparch* who is called "hyparch of the country" at *Indika* 34.1, and "hyparch of the province" at *Indika* 36.1. Quite possibly, Mazenes, the *hyparch* of Oaracta, was simply the head man of the island, answering to a higher Achaemenid official at Harmozia. Oaracta was described by Nearchus as large, inhabited, a place where vines and date palms grew and corn (wheat/barley) was produced. It may well have been the most populous island in the lower Persian Gulf at the time. It is difficult not to think that Bahrain, which Nearchus did not visit, would have been even more populous. Perhaps its Late Dilmun palace was home to another *hyparch*, though not necessarily an ethnic Persian, judging by the snake sacrifices beneath the palace floors.

The Persian Gulf as an information highway

In conclusion, it is obvious that the Persian Gulf has always linked the lands around it—Mesopotamia, Iran, eastern Arabia and the more distant peoples of the Indian subcontinent. Indeed, on the Chalouf stele (DZc) Darius enunciated an expression of the linkage between Iran and distant Egypt via the "sea which comes from Persia" (Lecoq 1997: 248). For the maritime-oriented peoples living around it, the Persian Gulf has been a bridge, making it far easier and faster to reach the opposite shore by boat than, for example, to travel inland, whether up onto the Iranian Plateau or into the desert heart of Arabia, by foot or on donkey or camel. In the Achaemenid period, when a *pax Persica* prevailed in the Persian Gulf, the populations of the coast and islands between India and Babylonia were almost certainly not bypassed by the cultural stimuli moving in all directions throughout this part of the empire, but a great deal more research remains to be done on this important topic before we can truly claim to understand the role of the Persian Gulf at this time.

Notes

1. These are often referred to as "tulip bowls" (cf. Magee *et al.* 2005: 725).
2. While the seals that made these impressions were used by officials, they were also employed by lower-ranking messengers. Thus, the Bahrain example does not necessarily relate to someone as high-ranking as a satrap.
3. On the religion of Darius and his successors, see now Skjærvø 2005.
4. During the discussion following my lecture, Prof. Philip Kreyenbroek compared, in a very general way, snake worship on Bahrain with folk religious practices amongst the Muslim Yezidis of northern Iraq, suggesting that the existence of such unorthodox traits need not conflict with the orthodoxy of their practitioners, whether Muslim or Zoroastrian. This is a valid point, cf. Russell 1994: 190: "There are a number of orders, nominally Shi'ite, which incorporate older religious practices and beliefs, not necessarily with any dogmatic consistency, and some of these elements may derive from the worship of Mithra. But secret societies behave in similar ways in many cultures, employing ordeals, sacrifices, and grades of advancement." Whether the snakes on Bahrain should be connected with Mithraic mysteries is impossible to say.
5. For the history of this entire discussion, with full references to earlier opinions, see Potts 1991: 106–109; 1994: 81–82.

50

Integration of Foreigners—New Insights from the Stela Found in Saqqara in 1994*

Melanie Wasmuth

In autumn 1994 the National Museums of Scotland Expedition excavated a funerary stela at North Saqqara, which is part of the necropolis of ancient Memphis (Fig. 50.1).[1] It was used among other stone slabs to cover a burial of unknown date.[2] It is now on display in the Egyptian Museum in Cairo under the number JE 98807. The owner of the stela, a man called Djedherbes, is of mixed parentage, his father being a Persian by the name of Artama and his mother an Egyptian by the name of Tanefrether. His filiation is given both in the hieroglyphic and the demotic inscription. Many aspects of the stela were discussed in the original publication, but I hope that a detailed iconographical analysis of the stela can reveal further insights into the exceptional combination of cultural influences evident on the stela.[3]

Before going into the iconographical details I would like to show how typical or untypical the stela is compared with the corpus of Late Egyptian funerary stelae. The corpus of funerary stelae in Egypt during the Late Period consists of two distinct sets of stelae following different traditions. On the one hand, a large corpus of funerary stelae is known which purely follows the Egyptian tradition. They will be referred to as Late Egyptian funerary stelae. On the other hand, there do exist stelae with non-Egyptian elements, which tend to be inscribed, at least partly, in foreign languages and in many cases the owner of the stela is presented as of foreign origin. The most important sets of stelae with foreign elements are those with Carian, Aramaic and Phoenician elements. They will therefore be referred to as Carian, Aramaic and Phoenician stelae in Egypt.

The general structure of the stela of Djedherbes is representative of the Late Egyptian funerary stelae, which tend to be of similar size and proportions (Fig. 50.2)[4]—the stela of Djedherbes measures roughly 30 × 40 × 10 cm (about 12 × 16 × 4 inches). The rounded top decorated with a winged sun disc is typical for the Late Egyptian funerary stelae. The lower part tends to be divided into two parts of roughly the same dimensions. The most common type is divided into a figurative scene in the top half and a hieroglyphic inscription in the lower part; nevertheless stelae with two or more figurative registers or with a single one are also

Fig. 50.1 Stela of Djedherbes, Cairo, Egyptian Museum, JE 98807. (Based on Mathieson *et al.* 1995: fig. 3 and pl. v)

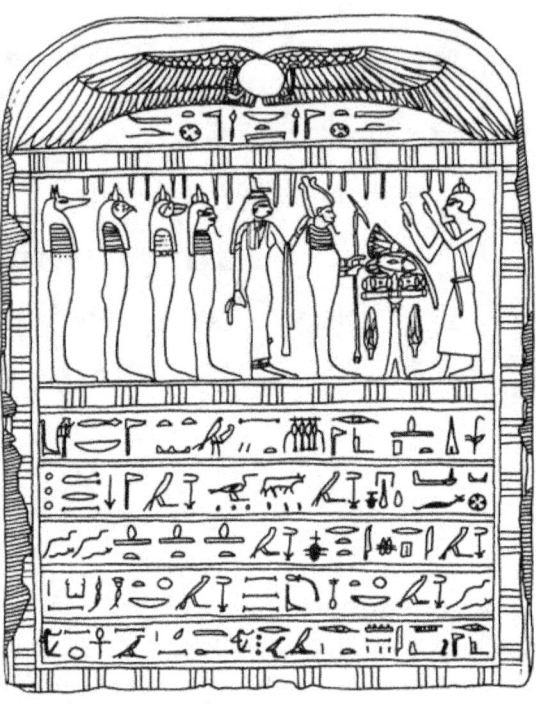

Fig. 50.2 Stela of Iretkherru from Thebes, 25th dynasty; Paris, Louvre T V 4. (Based on Munro 1973: fig. 12, pl. 3)

well attested. The different parts are usually framed by more or less elaborate bands, which in the case of the stela of Djedherbes hold the inscriptions.

Although both scenes depicted frequently occur in Egyptian art, they are not common motifs for Late Egyptian pre-Roman stelae. The upper register shows an illustration of Spell 151 from the Book of the Dead (for a typical Egyptian illustration cf. Fig. 50.3); this funerary text is usually written on a papyrus scroll and placed in the sarcophagus of its owner.[5] In pre-Hellenistic Egypt, the vignette can also be found in wall decorations of funerary chambers[6] and on coffins.[7] Close parallels to the depiction on the stela of Djedherbes can be found on cartonnage mummy cases,[8] though they are mostly of unknown provenance and usually dated to the Ptolemaic Period. Furthermore, the motif is known from shrouds[9] and stelae,[10] most of which are of Roman date.

In the lower register the owner[11] is depicted in front of an offering table; this scene is common in the decoration of the accessible chambers of Egyptian private tombs from the Old until the early New Kingdom (Fig. 50.4) as well as on stelae of the same periods.[12] In later periods the scene may still be found on the inside of coffins,[13] while it is replaced by scenes showing the deceased offering before the gods in contemporary private tombs and on the Late Egyptian funerary stelae.

Thus, although the general structure and contents of the stela of Djedherbes are Egyptian, there are many details that seem

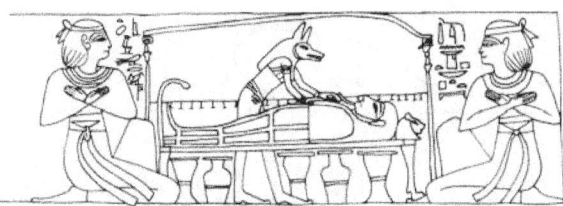

Fig. 50.3 Coffin of Khonsu from Deir el-Medineh, 19th dynasty; Cairo, Egyptian Museum, JE 27302. (Simplified drawing based on Saleh, Sourouzian & Liepe 1986: cat. 216)

foreign. Some of them I would like to analyse in greater detail.

As already mentioned, a winged sun disc is a very typical feature of a Late Egyptian funerary stela, though the Egyptian variant has no feathered tail, but uraei, and sometimes drops of water (dew) fall from the sun disc.[14] On the other hand, the winged sun disc with a feathered tail is a typical element of Achaemenid art,[15] but it is also found on Aramaic stelae from Egypt[16] (Fig. 50.5).

Another foreign element, which most probably derives from Persian art, is the style of the lion bier, which looks quite like a real lion due to its prominent stylized muscles. In contrast, the Egyptian lion bier in all pre-Ptolemaic examples is depicted as an item of furniture though decorated with a lion's head, paws and tail (cf. Fig. 50.3); also, the animal tends to be illustrated with no or only slight indications of the muscles. Closer parallels for the way the musculature is depicted on the stela of Djedherbes can be found in Persian art, especially the lions in the Hall of 100 Columns at Persepolis.[17]

Although the prominent stylization of the muscles and the general character of the lion bed is close to the lions in Persian art, the pose of its tail is not: in Achaemenid art, the lion's tail may face upwards or downwards, but is never coiled between the legs. This is also atypical for Egyptian art, where the tail of the lion bed turns upwards. Parallels for the posture of the tail on the stela of Djedherbes can be found in Hittite and especially in the Neo-Hittite art in the border area of modern Turkey and Syria.[18] Similar depictions can be seen on two unprovenanced Aramaic stelae from Egypt (Figs 50.6 and 50.7).[19]

Another detail untypical of Egyptian art is the depiction of the feet: on Egyptian paintings and reliefs usually only the outline of the foot is depicted, omitting the individual toes (cf. Fig. 50.4), although in periods in which a more naturalistic way of illustration is aimed at—for example, during the Amarna Period—the toes may be carefully carved.[20] In the Late Period, the depiction of the individual toes becomes more frequent[21]—probably because of foreign influences as for instance from Assyria or Persia,[22] where the individual toes are always depicted. But the usual Egyptian way of depicting feet before the Ptolemaic Period is still without indicating the toes.[23]

As is the case with the lion bed, several elements of different origin are combined in the depiction of the deceased in the lower register. The general character of the throne is Persian, as a comparison with the throne of Darius I in the Apadana[24] of Persepolis reveals; on the other hand, the covering of the backrest with a thick cloth (or thin mattress) derives from Egyptian art.[25] Until the New Kingdom the deceased official sits on a stool covered with a thick cloth (cf. Fig. 50.4), although during the Late Period this feature is reserved for the gods.[26]

In the depiction of the deceased himself elements from Persian and Neo-Hittite art can be detected. As the comparison with the depiction of Darius I on the Apadana of Persepolis clearly shows, Djedherbes is depicted as a Persian in a way very similar to the Achaemenid kings in the Persian

Fig. 50.4 Offering scene in the tomb of Sennefer, Thebes, TT 96, 18th dynasty. (Simplified drawing based on Lange & Hirmer 1983: pl. 23)

Fig. 50.5 Figurative scenes of the Stela of Akhatabu and Abbā from Saqqara, fourth year of Xerxes' reign; formerly in the Egyptian Museum in Berlin, inv. no. 7707, lost during the Second World War. (Based on Vittmann 2003: fig. 47)

homeland. The depiction of seated individuals holding a cup is not common in Achaemenid art, but the motif is known from seals.[27] The composition has also very close parallels in the funerary stelae of the Neo-Hittite art, where the deceased is usually depicted seated, holding a cup and often a lotus flower as well, in front of an offering table (Fig. 50.8).[28] On the other side of the table there often stands a single adorant, but scenes with two offering tables and several adorants are known as well.[29]

The offerings on the table in front of the deceased follow the Egyptian tradition, though they seem to be partly misunderstood: a misinterpreted version of the different kinds of bread is shown, on top of which a goose is deposited (cf. Fig. 50.2).[30] The particular type of table depicted was not normally used for an offering table: the typical Egyptian offering table from the Old Kingdom onwards and still in the Late Period is a single-footed table (Figs 50.2 and 50.4). On the other hand, there are several objects of similar construction, such as cases for wigs or jewellery,[31] and it therefore seems probable that this particular construction was in use for tables in daily life. The similar structure of the offering table on the Aramaic stela of Tabi (Fig. 50.6) may be

Fig. 50.6 Figurative scenes of the stela of Tabi of unknown provenance, probably fourth century BC; Carpentras, No. T 134334. (Based on Vittmann 2003: fig. 48)

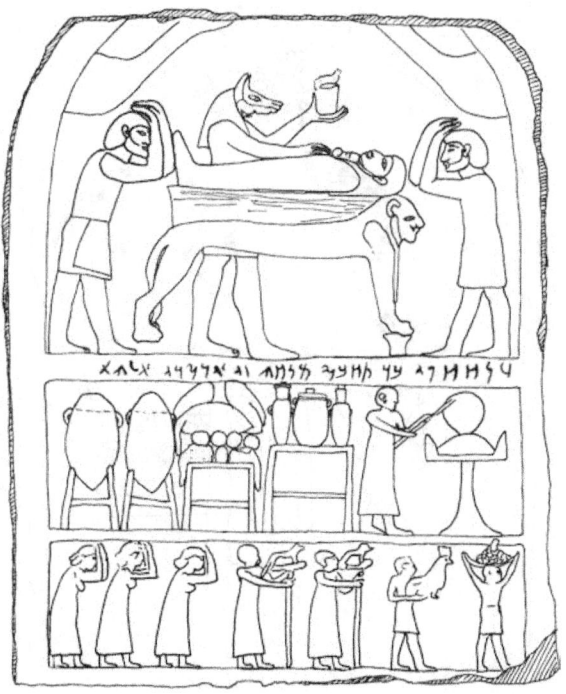

Fig. 50.7 Stela of Ankhhapi of unknown provenance and the date is not established; Vatican, Museo Egizio, inv. no. 22787. (Based on Vittmann 2003: fig. 49 and pl. 12)

explained in the same way. The second offering table has parallels in Neo-Hittite art[32] and also in the art of the Aramaeans in Egypt (Fig. 50.7).

Another non-traditional Egyptian element can be found in the dress of the adorants: the left one wears a wide-sleeved, long girdled dress with a fringe at the bottom, while the right one wears a long girdled dress without a fringe and with long, narrow sleeves. On the Late Egyptian funerary stelae the male adorants are mainly depicted in a loincloth, more rarely in a wrap-around garment with a fringe at the bottom and a prominent vertical fringe in front, neither of which is depicted on the stela of Djedherbes. A narrow-sleeved long wide dress with a fringe at the bottom but without a girdle is characteristic of the depiction of Egyptians in Persia. As this is also not the way the garments on the stela of Djedherbes are depicted, various interpretations are possible.[33]

As we have seen, the foreign elements on the stela derive from several different cultures: in some cases the closest parallels can be found outside Egypt, in other cases they are on the stelae of foreigners in Egypt. In many respects the closest parallels in composition and style can be found among the Aramaic stelae from Egypt, but certain elements are better matched in others.

The closest parallels for the illustration of Spell 151 of the Egyptian Book of the Dead on stelae before the late Ptolemaic Period as well as for several details can be found among the Aramaic stelae from Egypt. I would like to recall the stela of Akhatabu and Abbā (Fig. 50.5), which is the earliest dated example of a variant of Spell 151 on

Fig. 50.8 Stela from Zincirli, late eighth century BC; Berlin, Vorderasiatisches Museum, VA 2995. (Based on Bonatz 2000: C46, pl. 17)

a stela, and the stelae of Tabi (Fig. 50.6) and of Ankhhapi (Fig. 50.7) with similar depictions. The latter stela also shows parallels with the posture of Isis and Nephthys, the amphorae, the pose of the lion's tail and the second offering table.

The only examples in Egypt in which the figures cross the division line between different registers, as do the headdresses of Isis and Nephthys in the upper register of the stela of Djedherbes, can be found among the Carian stelae (Fig. 50.9), where from the late seventh century onwards Egyptian religious scenes are usually combined with depictions of the "prothasis scene".[34] The closest example for a depiction of a foreigner in his specific dress and hairstyle seated on a chair in front of an offering table comes from the Phoenician tradition

Fig. 50.9 Carian stela from Saqqara, 525–510 BC; London, British Museum, EA 67235. (Based on Vittmann 2003: figs. 86 a–b)

(Fig. 50.10).[35] So far unparalleled features of the stela of Djedherbes are the depiction of a Persian on a private funerary stela from Egypt, the combination of Spell 151 with a scene depicting the deceased receiving offerings on offering tables and the integration of features from several different cultural traditions.

Fig. 50.10 Detail of the stela of Khahap from Saqqara, third century BC; Berlin, Ägyptisches Museum, inv. no. 2118, lost during the Second World War. (Based on Vittmann 2003: fig. 33)

I would like to propose that the stela of Djedherbes is evidence of a workshop for the manufacture of funerary stelae for foreign residents, where the different ethnic groups living in Memphis could order funerary stelae on which indications of their ethnicity were carved. The adoption of scenes from the Egyptian funerary cult suggests that these foreigners were closely assimilated into Egyptian culture although they retained certain characteristics of their original culture. The quantity of Aramaic elements on the stela of Djedherbes makes it probable that it was produced in a workshop in which Aramaic traits were commonly used. The other foreign elements show that at the time when the stela of Djedherbes was crafted the different ethnic groups did not have separate workshops, but artists familiar with the styles of different cultures had handed their craft to a generation who had learned at least from Egyptians, Aramaeans, Phoenicians and Carians, and probably Persians as well.

The stelae from the late sixth century still combine Egyptian elements with those of a single ethnic group. In the fifth century when Egypt was under direct Persian rule it would have been surprising if a Persian, who to judge by the lack of titles was not a high official, was depicted in a way similar to the Achaemenid king. Therefore a date from the very late fifth or more probably the fourth century BC when Egypt was no longer part of the Persian Empire seems to be indicated. As discussed in Mathieson *et al.* (1995),[36] the vessels give a *terminus ante quem* to the Ptolemaic Period. It is then likely that Djedherbes lived in the intermediate period between the first and the second Persian domination of Egypt, in the first half of the fourth century BC.

Notes

*I would like to thank Michael Roaf, who read an earlier draft of this article, for his valuable contributions regarding contents and language. All the illustrations presented are drawn by the author.

1. Mathieson *et al.* 1995: 23–41.
2. Mathieson *et al.* 1995: 23.
3. This paper only shows some preliminary results, while a more detailed discussion is now presented in my doctoral thesis (Wasmuth 2009: 281–349).
4. Cf. the stela of Iretkherru from Thebes (25th dynasty) (Munro 1973: fig. 12, pl. 3 = Paris, Louvre T V 4).
5. E.g. the papyrus of Ani from Thebes (19th dynasty) (Hornung 1990: fig. 77 = British Museum, BM 10470).
6. E.g. in the tomb of Nakhtamun in Deir el-Medineh (19th dynasty); Bruyère 1926: fig. 108.
7. E.g. on the coffin of Khonsu from Deir el-Medineh (19th dynasty) (Saleh, Sourouzian & Liepe 1986: cat. 216 = Cairo, Egyptian Museum, JE 27302).
8. E.g. on a cartonnage mummy case in the Egyptian Museum in Cairo without an inventory number.
9. E.g. the shroud probably from Akhmim (Parlasca 1966: pl. 13/2 = Boston Museum, inv. no. 50.650).
10. E.g. the stelae from Edfu (Munro 1973: fig. 86, pl. 24 = Egyptian Museum in Cairo, CG 22050) and from Thebes (Munro 1973: fig. 76, pl. 21 = British Museum, BM 8486). In Mathieson *et al.* 1995: 40f. these two stelae are presented as evidence for this scene being common on Egyptian funerary stelae; both are, however, significantly more recent than the stela of Djedherbes which is dated by its

excavators to the first Persian domination over Egypt (525–401 BC).

11. The unconventional combination of figures in the bottom register does not allow a definite identification of the seated and standing figures in the offering scene. As no Persian private funerary art is known, and while the scene itself has very close parallels in indigenous Egyptian art as well as in those of foreigners in Egypt, it seems likely that the composition follows the Egyptian conventions. It is unknown in Egyptian art for the owner of a stela to make an offering to somebody other than the gods, therefore the identification of the seated figure as the father Artama seems unlikely (as proposed in Mathieson *et al.* 1995: 38f.). On the other hand, in earlier Egyptian examples the focus for the offerings is the deceased, as is the case on the contemporary stelae of foreigners in Egypt, e.g. on the stela of Khahap (Vittmann 2003: fig. 33 = Berlin, Ägyptisches Museum, inv. no. 2118, lost during the Second World War).
12. E.g. in the tomb of Ptahhotep in Saqqara from the 5th dynasty (Lange & Hirmer 1983: pl. 70); in the tomb of Sennefer in Thebes from the 18th dynasty (Lange & Hirmer 1983: pl. 23); on the stela of Antef from Abydos from the 12th dynasty (Saleh, Sourouzian & Liepe 1986: cat. 92 = Cairo, Egyptian Museum, CG 20535).
13. E.g. in the coffin of Ankhefneferu from Thebes from the early 22nd dynasty (Niwiński 1988: pl. 24 = Cairo, Egyptian Museum, inv. no. 23.11.16.3).
14. E.g. on the stela of Neskhonsu from Thebes from around 350 BC (Munro 1973: fig. 47, pl. 13 = Paris, Louvre, E 15565).
15. As already stated in Mathieson *et al.* 1995: 28.
16. One example is the stela of Akhatabu and Abbā from Saqqara from the fourth year of Xerxes' reign (Vittmann 2003: fig. 47 = previously in the Egyptian Museum in Berlin, inv. no. 7707, lost during the Second World War).
17. E.g. Walser 1980: fig. 89. Further parallels from the art of the Medes and the Persians are given in Mathieson *et al.* 1995: 28.
18. E.g. a lion sculpture from Zincirli from the eighth century BC (Akurgal & Hirmer 1978: pl. 132 = Ankara, Archaeological Museum, no inv. no.).
19. Stela of Tabi of unknown provenance, probably fourth century BC (Vittmann 2003: fig. 48 = Carpentras, No. T 134334); stela of Ankhhapi of unknown provenance and the date is not established (Vittmann 2003: pl. 12 = Vatican, Museo Egizio, inv. no. 22787).
20. E.g. on the lid of an inlaid chest of Tut-ankh-Amon; from Thebes (18th dynasty) (Saleh, Sourouzian & Liepe 1986: cat. 188 = Cairo, Egyptian Museum, JE 61477).
21. E.g. on a relief fragment from the 26th dynasty tomb of Mentuemhat (Aldred 1990: figs 185, 221 = William Rockhill Nelson Gallery of Art, Atkins Museum of Fine Arts, Kansas City, no. 48.74).
22. Cf. the lion-hunt of Assurbanipal (Strommenger & Hirmer 1962: pl. 255 = British Museum, BM 118914) or the relief fragments from Palace S in Pasargadae (Stronach 1978: pl. 58a–b)
23. Cf. Munro 1973. Although the parallel from the Tjanofer reliefs—which date from the fourth century BC—which is already mentioned in Mathieson *et al.* 1995: 29; 28, nn. 5, 11, is close, this is not a general "Late Period stylistic feature" (1995: 29), but only an occasional one.
24. Walser 1980: fig. 41; the obvious parallel to the depiction of the Great King in Persepolis is already mentioned in Mathieson *et al.* 1995: 30.
25. Although there is a Persian tradition of covering the royal throne with a thick cloth, as can be seen on seal impressions from Daskyleion (Kaptan 2003a: DS 4, 50–55, pls 47–59), the method of depiction is much closer to the different examples in Egyptian art. Possibly the above-mentioned seal, which was inscribed, "I am Artaxerxes…" (Kaptan 2003a: 50), shows the same Egyptian feature incorporated into Persian art.
26. E.g. on the stela of Neskhonsu from Thebes from the 25th dynasty (Munro 1973: fig. 7, pl. 2 = Cairo, Egyptian Museum, A 9916 & T 27/1/25/18).
27. E.g. on a rock crystal cylinder seal (Boardman 2000: 160, fig. 5.8 = Zurich University, 1961).
28. E.g. on a stela from Zincirli from the late eighth century BC; Berlin, Vorderasiatisches Museum, VA 2995 (Bonatz 2000: C46, pl. 17).
29. E.g. on a stela which is supposed to come from the area between Tell Kazane and Harran from the late eighth or early seventh century BC (Schachner & Bucak 2004: Çiz 1 & 2, 669f. = Urfa, Archaeological Museum, inv. no. unknown).
30. Another close parallel is the stela of Pa-ir-jah from Abydos from the 25th dynasty (Munro 1973: fig. 104, pl. 29 = Cairo, Egyptian Museum, JE 21970). Here the conical loaf in the middle is already depicted more like a jar than a loaf of bread and the circle-shaped loaves are depicted in a similar way, as on the stela of Djedherbes.
31. E.g. the cases for wigs and jewellery from the tomb of Yuya and Thuju at Thebes, from the

32. 18th dynasty (Quibell 1908: pls 48, 45 = Cairo, Egyptian Museum, CG 51119 & CG 51117).
32. E.g. a stela from the area of Carchemish, from 750–700 BC (Bonatz 2000: C41, pl. 16 = Munich, Prähistorische Sammlung, no inv. no.).
33. Contrary to the statement in Mathieson *et al.* 1995: 31, the identification of the dresses on the stela of Djedherbes with the Egyptian wraparound garments and the garments worn by the Egyptians on the Persian reliefs is not certain, as they all differ in characteristic details.
34. E.g. the Carian stela from Saqqara in the British Museum (Vittmann 2003: fig. 86a = EA 67235; drawing in Kammerzell 1993: fig. 30)—dating from around 525–510 BC (1993: 144). The Carian stelae from Saqqara are already mentioned in Mathieson *et al.* 1995: 29, as parallels for the crossing of the division line between registers, though I cannot agree with a contemporary dating of the Carian stelae and the stela of Djedherbes, as argued below.
35. The stela of Khahap from Saqqara from the third century BC (Vittmann 2003: fig. 33 = Berlin, Ägyptisches Museum, inv. no. 2118, lost during the Second World War).
36. Mathieson *et al.* 1995: 33.

51

Enemies of Empire: A Historical Reconstruction of Political Conflicts between Central Asia and the Persian Empire[1]

Wu Xin

In the discourse of the history of the Achaemenid Empire, one fundamental but little understood issue is the nature of the political relationship between the Persian imperial power and its provinces in the east, particularly those located in modern-day Central Asia.[2] This issue has important ramifications because it has been believed that, prior to the establishment of their political power in south-western Iran, the Persians were closely related to the pastoralist societies of Central Asia (Young 1988; Vogelsang 1992). Some scholars further suggest that the eastern ties of the Persians must have played a significant role in shaping the state organization, political decisions and artistic expressions of the Achaemenid Empire (Frye 1989). If these assumptions are indeed correct, one logical question would be whether the people of Central Asia were treated differently from the people from other regions within the empire during the Achaemenid period. The answer is clearly negative if we rely on the information given by the Persian royal inscriptions and the official art excavated from the imperial heartland in south-western Iran. Created by the king and his court to serve the ideological needs of the empire, the royal inscriptions and relief programmes, except for that carved by the great king Darius on the rock surface at Behistun in the late sixth century BC, are basically limited to delineating the boundaries of the empire by visually and verbally listing the different ethnical groups incorporated within the empire (Root 1979). The other Persian sources, mainly comprising administrative records preserved on the clay tablets excavated from Persepolis, show that Central Asia was well integrated into the imperial administrative system during the early fifth century BC,[3] but they contain no information on the political interactions between Central Asia and the Achaemenid imperial enterprise.

The contemporary or later classical textual sources, upon which the traditional Achaemenid historiography has relied heavily, are similarly not very informative about the political affairs that occurred in the empire's eastern provinces. Only a few records by classical authors refer to upheavals related to the

Fig. 51.1 Rock relief at Bisitun. (From Harper *et al.* 1992)

east. These accounts include short descriptions of: 1) the campaign of Cyrus against the Massagetae, some nomadic tribesmen inhabiting the land to the east of the Caspian Sea, in 545–539 BC;[4] 2) a revolt of Cyrus the Younger's son Tanaoxares (or Bardiya in the Behistun Inscription), who was the *despotes* of the Bactrians, the Choresmians, the Parthians and the Carmanians, against Darius between 522 and 519 BC (Briant 2002*a*: 96–106; Vogelsang 1992: 212); 3) a dispute between Xerxes and his brother Ariaramnes, who held a position in Bactria, in 486 BC;[5] 4) a revolt by Masistes, brother of Xerxes and probably satrap of Bactria, in 479 BC (Herodotus IX: 108–113); and 5) an upheaval of "Bactria with its satrap, another Artabanus", who seceded from Artaxerxes I's rule upon the new king's accession in 465 BC.[6] These incidents entered the Greek sources because they all concerned the establishment of the Persian royal lineage and the transfer of power from one king to another. The events, except for Cyrus' campaign against the Massagetae, have been interpreted as reflections of mere dynastic struggles within the Persian royal house rather than political encounters between the Achaemenid central power and the local inhabitants of Central Asia (see Briant 2002*a*: 524, 570). For more information on the political roles of the north-eastern provinces within the Achaemenid Empire, we must turn our attention to other sources.

This paper proposes that we should consider using a class of seals bearing representations of warfare as a potential source to gain insight into the political interactions between Achaemenid central power and the people residing in Central Asia. The battle scenes depicted on these seals, some of which were likely based on real historical events, serve as important evidence that the people living in Central Asia were indeed treated specially but in a negative sense, as strong enemies of the empire. An examination of the iconography on the battle seals and of the social functions of the battle imagery suggests that the Central Asians, especially the Sogdians and

Fig. 51.2 Photograph and line drawing of the seal of Kuraš of Anšan, son of Teispes, PFS 93 on PF 694. (From Persepolis Fortification Archive, Courtesy Mark Garrison)

Sakas who occupied the strategic location of the north-eastern frontier of the empire, must have caused some serious problems that may have undermined the stability of the empire. The problems caused by the east, which the Persian king and the surrounding ruling class had to face, were probably no less troublesome than those caused by the Greeks in the west.

Representations of warfare in Achaemenid art

Representations of battles and their aftermaths are quite common in Persian art. During the Achaemenid period the iconography of warfare appeared on monumental reliefs, personal decorations and particularly on seals. In fact, battle imagery occurs more often on seals of the Achaemenid period than of any of the previous periods in the history of the Ancient Near East.[7] The Achaemenid battle scenes, like their Neo-Assyrian and Neo-Elamite predecessors, can be divided into two broad categories based on their modes of representation. The first category comprises scenes showing in an iconic mode the aftermaths of battles, as represented by the Behistun relief, which depicts the victorious Persian king Darius trampling a defeated enemy while leading a file of captives who are chained together by a rope (Fig. 51.1).

The second category contains depictions of ongoing battles shown in a narrative mode. Representations of this category follow the model adopted for the human combat scene on the famous heirloom seal of "Kuraš of Anšan, son of Teispes".[8] The seal is preserved on a number of clay tablets from the Persepolis Fortification Archive (Garrison 1991). It depicts a warrior on horseback attacking an enemy on foot. The latter, while fleeing, turns his head back towards his antagonist and raises his hands in a supplicating gesture. Corpses of the defeated are shown scattered (or piled up) on the ground (Fig. 51.2).

The battle scenes represented in iconic mode are usually similar, and sometimes almost identical, in iconographic and compositional design, following closely the Behistun prototype. This uniformity leaves very little space for each scene to be unique. Compared with the generic appearance of the scenes in iconic mode, the battle images depicted in narrative mode display much more variation in iconography and composition, suggesting that each representation is unique. This larger variation results partially from depicting the various moments on the battlefield and partially from the different scales of the pictorial narratives, which sometimes represent a complete story but more often depict a reduced version of it. On the reduced versions, the result of the battle is often only hinted at rather than fully shown. The battle image on the Kuraš seal represents such an example. The different stages of the battle were abbreviated and represented by the dashing human figures and the piled-up corpses of the defeated on the ground. The doomed destiny of the warrior on foot is indicated by his supplicating gesture.

The human combat scenes depicted on a cylinder seal that belongs to the so-called "Oxus Treasure" at the British Museum shows a fuller version of the battle narrative. The seal represents in two scenes a warrior in Elamite dress fighting enemies wearing tight coats with cut-away fronts and knee-length boots, the typical garment worn by individuals from Central Asia. These two scenes, separated from each other by a vertical line in the middle, represent two successive episodes of a military engagement (Fig. 51.3). The first episode, on the left, represents an ongoing duel: the Elamite warrior strikes his antagonist with a spear while being threatened by the dagger held by his enemy. The representation on the right depicts the outcome of the incident on the left: the Elamite warrior has thrust his spear into the body of his enemy; the latter, now wounded, half-kneels, his arm held by his comrade, who raises his hand and begs for mercy. The final victory of the

Fig. 51.3 Cylinder seal and modern impression from the Oxus Treasure. (British Museum 124015)

Elamite is, again, not explicit but is indicated by the increased number of enemy corpses and the supplicating gesture of his adversary. The necessary elements for "pictorial narrative", namely "time and space", are logically demonstrated through the different "actions" described in the two separate scenes.[9]

The Achaemenid battle seals can also be divided into three groups based on the geographic association of the defeated: the first group comprises numerous depictions of military conflicts between the Greeks and the Persians;[10] the second group consists of only three seals, which bear almost identical scenes showing Persian heroes leading captives clad in Egyptian garments;[11] and the third group constitutes no less than 17 depictions of battles against individuals belonging to the different ethnic groups resident in Central Asia. Given the large territorial extent of the Achaemenid Empire, the Persians must have been engaged with many different political and ethnic groups inside and outside the empire. The fact that only three groups of people are represented as enemies, however, suggests that the images on the battle seals contain some historic information, perhaps ranging from a generic reflection of the adversarial relationship or a reflection of actual military engagements between the Achaemenid enterprise and its external and internal enemies.

The images on the first group of seals also appear on Greek painted pottery. The scenes, despite the broad range of styles and the different media, have been associated with the background of the lengthy Greco-Persian wars that occurred in the first quarter of the fifth century BC. Additionally, it has been argued that the battle scenes depicted on the Greek painted pottery of the early fifth century BC are mostly historical rather than merely motifs. The representations on the second group of seals have frequently been cited as visual evidence of the military campaign(s) against the Egyptian revolts during the reign of Artaxerxes I around 465–462 BC and/or of Artaxerxes III in 380s BC (Chileyko 1925: 19; Dandamayev 1976: taf. V.A.; Briant 2002a: 574–577, 652–665; Stolper 2001: 111). Battle images on the third group of seals, most pertinent to this paper, have neither been treated as a coherent group nor been used consistently as evidence to shed light on the political interactions between the Persian power and the people who lived in the east. We should be able to draw similar conclusions from the seals of the third group, that is to say the images depict real conflicts between the Persian Empire and the people of Central Asia because, if we suppose that the images from the first and second groups of seals are depictions of real scenes from documented historical events—namely the Greco-Persian wars and the Egyptian campaign(s)—then why would the battle scenes on the third group of seals not depict images from conflicts with Central Asians?

The following section will first survey the iconography of the seals belonging to this third group. It will then discuss the issues related to the reasons why these seals are qualified as objects carrying historical information. Finally, it will offer my conclusions on the political conflicts between the Achaemenid imperial enterprise and the local inhabitants, mainly Sogdians, Choresmians and some Saka groups of Central Asia, and my thoughts on Achaemenid historiography.

The third group of battle seals comprises at least ten unprovenanced examples scattered in different museums and private collections: this includes eight actual seals; two seal designs preserved on clay sealings;[12] and at least seven examples of seals preserved on clay *bullae* and tablets excavated from Persepolis in south-western Iran, Nippur in Mesopotamia and Daskyleion in Anatolia.

On these seals, the participants are usually clearly identified through their specific ethnic attributes. The defeated all wear Central Asian garments: tight long-sleeved coats, each with a cut-away lower front edge; loose trousers and boots; and usually bonnets with knobs on the top and earflaps fastening under the chin. This attire is typically worn by the Sogdians, the Choresmians and certain Saka groups on Achaemenid monumental reliefs (Fig.51.6).[13] The victors, also clearly identifiable by their garments and weapons, are warriors associated with the Achaemenid

Fig. 51.4 PTS 30 on clay *bulla* PT4 655, 470–469 BC, from the Persepolis Treasury. (From Schmidt 1957: pl. 9)

Fig. 51.5 Modern impression from a cylinder seal, Bibliothèque Nationale. (From Collon 1987: 744)

enterprise. They are either Persians or their representatives from the ethnic groups closely related to or allied with the head nation of the empire, including primarily the Medes and Elamites and occasionally also groups from Central Asia.

Among the excavated examples, a seal that shows a Persian hero in Achaemenid court robe locked in hand-to-hand combat with a Sogdian or a Saka warrior represents possibly the earliest example within the corpus.[14] The seal, preserved through impressions on a number of clay *bullae* from a context described as the "Persepolis Fortifications" might have been carved as early as the reign of Darius.[15] Images of three additional seals with representations of battles against Central Asians, also preserved on clay *bullae* and tablets, were recovered from the Persepolis Treasury.[16] Among these the best-preserved sample, PTS 30, is dated to 470/469 BC based on the texts that it sealed (Fig. 51.4).[17] The image shows on the left a warrior wearing a round helmet and a vest of leather or metal scales—typical Persian battle attire—poised to attack his opponent with a spear. While guarding himself with a shield, the latter fights against the Persian soldier using a mace or battleaxe, weapons characteristically used by people on the Central Asian steppe. He wears what is likely to be a tight tunic and possibly also the baggy trousers similar to those worn by the two Central Asian figures on a well-known cylinder from the Bibliothèque Nationale (BN seal). The latter depicts a pair of warriors in Persian battle attire fighting two individuals wearing typical Central Asian garments.[18] On PTS 30, the result of the battle is not explicitly indicated but the impending defeat of the Central Asian warrior is already suggested by his delayed reaction: while he has just raised his battleaxe to defend himself, the spear of the Persian antagonist has already reached him and is about to be thrust into his body. This same narrative tactic is also employed on the BN seal, but the latter has a composition that is more complicated and reflects a battle of a larger scheme (Fig. 51.5). The representation depicts a group combat. The pair in the middle is shown locked in close combat and

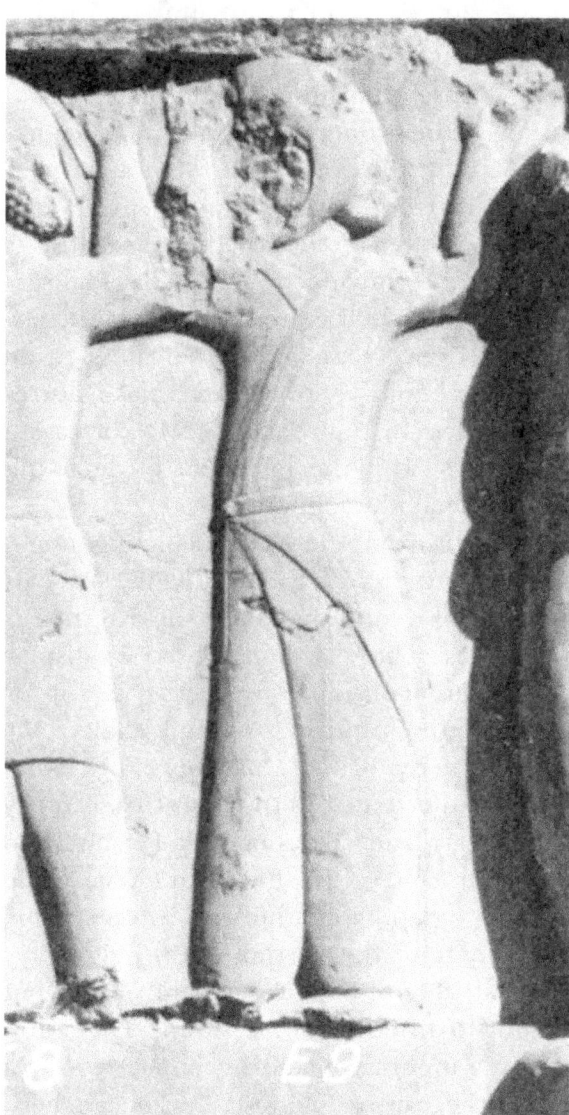

Fig. 51.6 A Central Asian figure as a throne-bearer on the east jamb of the throne hall at Persepolis. (From Schmidt 1953: pl. 110, E14)

Fig. 51.7 PTS 29 on clay *bulla* PT4 830, from the Persepolis Treasury, c.485–467 BC. (From Schmidt 1957: pl. 9)

each warrior is also threatened by an archer from his opponent's side.[19]

The representation on another seal from Persepolis, PTS 29, shows another battle duel.[20] The figure to the left is clad in the familiar Central Asian attire; the figure to the right wears a vest similar to that on PTS 30 and on the seal at the Bibliothèque Nationale. Through this vest the figure is associated with Achaemenid military power. A triangular flap extending below his waist betrays, however, that he is also wearing a tunic beneath his vest armour. If this observation is correct, the figure would represent a person from Central Asia fighting on behalf of the Achaemenid Empire.[21] As on PTS 30, the outcome of the battle is only suggested rather than described. The ultimate victory of the Achaemenid warrior is indicated by the corpse on the ground and by the slightly higher position of his head in the image field, being closer to the upper edge of the seal (Fig. 51.7).

Another seal, belonging to Aršama, a Persian prince and the Satrap of Egypt under Artaxerxes I (reigned 465–425 BC), shows a Median warrior fighting a Central Asian. The seal, preserved through its impression on a number of sealings allegedly from Egypt,[22] can be broadly dated to 453–403 BC, based on the cross-referencing of the inscription carved on the seal (which reads "Seal of [Arsames] son of [the] ho[use]"; Driver 1957) with known historical events and personal names that were contemporary to them in Egyptian, Babylonian and Greek sources.[23] On this seal, the outcome of the battle is quite clearly pronounced: the figure in Median garb strikes the neck of his antagonist with a spear. The latter strives to halt the spear with his right hand while simultaneously raising his left arm in a plea for mercy. The corpses of three vanquished Central Asian soldiers on the ground indicate that the Median warrior has in fact fought with an entire troop rather than with only one individual and announce that the battle is about to be concluded (Fig. 51.8). The seal carver gives much more attention to the victorious figure than to the defeated. Aside from his ethnic identity, the facial features of the Median figure are clearly portrayed, apparently with the intention of depicting his personal physiognomy.

Apart from the seals depicting ongoing combat, there are also a number of seals within this group that show the aftermaths of battles. These aftermath scenes display the different instances of victors taking or transporting captives. A small chalcedony cylinder in the British Museum (BM 132505), which can be dated to the early fifth century BC on a stylistic basis, depicts a Persian hero locked in close combat with an enemy while leading a captive bound with a rope.[24] The opponents of the Persian hero, judging by their attire, are both from Central Asia but belong to different ethnic groups. The figure wearing a pointy headdress appears to be a Saka; the captive behind the Persian hero represents a Sogdian or Bactrian/Parthian. According to classic sources, these people had formed alliances fighting against the

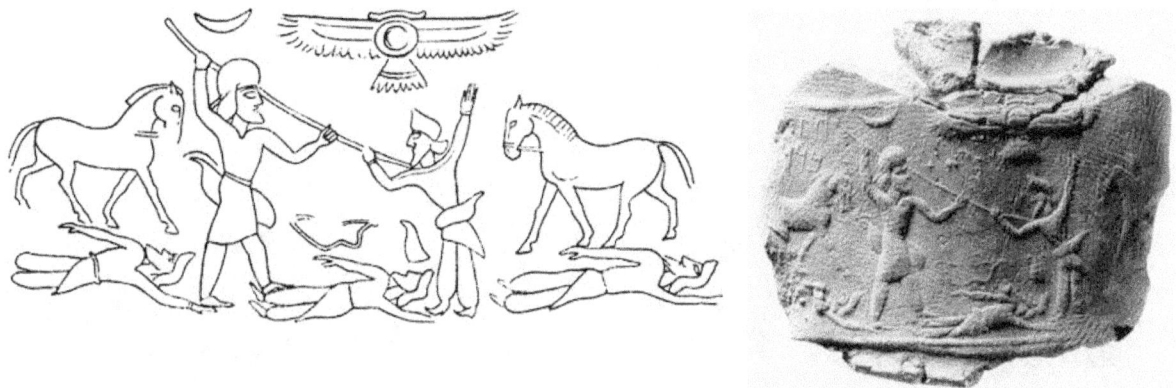

Fig. 51.8 Photograph and drawing of the seal of Ašama, satrap of Egypt, Bodleian Library, Oxford. (Photograph Boardman 2000: fig. 5.21, line drawing Moorey 1978: 149, fig. 8)

Persians. While the Sogdian (or Bactrian/Parthian) has already been taken captive, the Saka is still actively fighting the Persian hero (Fig. 51.9).

A depiction of the final phase of struggle of the defeated is seen on a seal preserved on two clay tablets from the Murašu Archive from Nippur. The seal belonged to Minû-ana-Bēl-dānu, son of Tahhua, an "inspector". The tablets are dated respectively to 418 and 414 BC.[25] The representation on the seal shows a victorious Persian, clad in a dentate crown and folded court robe, confronting three Central Asian opponents (Bregstein 1993: 586, cat. 189; Stolper 2001: 105, CBS 1594). Two of the defeated have already been taken captive. The third one is about to be subdued by the Persian hero. He is still trying to protect himself with his right hand but his left hand, which holds a double curved Scythian bow, is already dangling behind him. He has apparently no power left to strike back (Fig. 51.10).

The next stage represented on the battle seals is the transportation of the captives. A depiction of this appears on an Achaemenid heirloom seal preserved on a few *bullae* from Artachate in Armenia and on the seal of Ribat impressed on three clay tablets from the Murašu Archive. The depiction on the seal from Artachate follows the design on the Behistun relief and resembles many examples in the first and second groups.[26] It shows a file of five Central Asian captives, possibly Choresmians or Sogdians, tied together with ropes around their necks and led by a much larger figure, who wears a folded skirt and carries a quiver on his shoulder (Fig. 51.11).[27] Compared with the generic captive transportation scene on the Artachate seal, the representation on the seal of Ribat is much more detailed and specific.[28] The seal, belonging to an administrator at Nippur, was preserved on three tablets dated 424–418 BC.[29] The representation shows two Central Asian captives, hands bound together behind their backs, being driven from behind by a horseman wearing typical Persian equestrian attire, a knee-length tunic, trousers and a soft hood.[30] The horseman is in turn followed by a man in a Persian court robe (Fig. 51.12) (Bregstein 1993: 591, cat. 194).

The above surveys show that battle scenes are represented differently on each seal, to reflect the different ethnic identities of the participants, as well as capturing different moments within the course of the battle.

Fig. 51.9 Cylinder seal and modern impression, British Museum 132505.

Fig. 51.10 Clay tablet, with the impression of the seal of Minû-ana-Bēl-dānu, from the Murašu Archive, Nippur, Babylonian Section, Museum of Archaeology and Anthropology of the University of Pennsylvania (CBS 1594).

Using battle seals as sources for historical reconstruction: problems and possibilities

It has been suggested by Stolper and others that some of the Achaemenid battle seals may have been individually commissioned to commemorate historic events.[31] But in order to better understand the historical implications of the battle images, we need a more systematic approach to these seals and to study them within a broader theoretical framework.

In the Ancient Near Eastern context, representations of battles or warfare are generally symbolically and historically significant. Depictions of warfare on a monumental scale are usually used as important sources of evidence for reconstructing the history of the Ancient Near East. The function of the pictorial narratives (in both iconic and narrative modes) in the Mesopotamian context is, as repeatedly argued by Winter, "exactly as historical narrative in text" (1981: 2; 1985: 12). But on the question of whether we can use the battle imagery on seals for the same purpose, opinions differ significantly. Some scholars consider the battle images, especially those on seals bearing inscriptions, as visual illustrations of the historical accounts mentioned in textual sources,[32] regardless of the fact that the inscriptions are usually personal names and have nothing to do with the images beside them. Others believe that these images are merely "motifs", noting that the battle images on seals are not accompanied by explanatory inscriptions; that the gesture of the opponents and composition of the images on the battle scenes resemble closely those represented on the hunting scenes, which are apparently

Fig. 51.11 Photograph of a clay *bulla* from Artachate, Armenia. (From Ter-Martirossov 1996: 222, no. 210a)

ahistorical;[33] and that the battle representations are often formed by visual passages that are fixed formulas, as indicated by the similar poses or gestures of the combatants on different seals and by the corpses scattered on the ground.

There is no question that some of the images depicted on seals are indeed mere "motifs" rather than specific visual documentations of real historical events. This is especially true for those images manufactured outside Persia or outside the Achaemenid court workshops.[34] That some battle imagery was used as "motif" does not contradict the possibility that the battle images on other seals are based on true historical events. The reasons for rejecting the historical content of the battle seals are equally problematic.

First, the main social purpose of a seal is different from that of an official monument; similarly, the imagery on a seal functions quite differently from that on monumental reliefs. We should therefore not expect a seal to bear any explanatory inscription as on such official monuments as the victory stele of Naram-Sin or the Behistun relief. The lack of an inscription does not disqualify a seal image from bearing historic information.

Second, despite the compositional and stylistic similarities between battle and hunting imagery, the nature of the relationship described by a battle representation and a hunting scene differ fundamentally. Hunting imagery shows the domination of humankind over natural forces and can be mythical or fictitious. A battle scene is much more complex. It describes the adversarial relationship between the respective institutions represented by the contestants. Since warfare represents a serious human condition occurring on the level of a state or other political organization, representations of warfare, either verbal or visual, require the legitimization of the political institutions involved in the affair, and are consequently historically specific. There are indeed instances in which the result of a battle or a war was fabricated, but the fabrication of the result at least proves the occurrence of the battle.[35]

Third, the use of visual formulas does not necessarily mean that the historic referent behind the image is unspecific, nor does it contradict the interpretation of the battle scenes as real historical events. On the contrary, in a given visual language the messages that the images intend to convey are usually encoded in fixed sets of visual tropes. The repeated visual formulas on the Achaemenid battle seals function as codes for storing, conveying and transmitting messages, that is, the victory of the Achaemenids over their enemies.

However, to be qualified as a source for historical reconstruction, the battle seals do need to meet certain criteria. The primary requirement is that the images depicted on the seals must be specific and unique. This

556 THE WORLD OF ACHAEMENID PERSIA

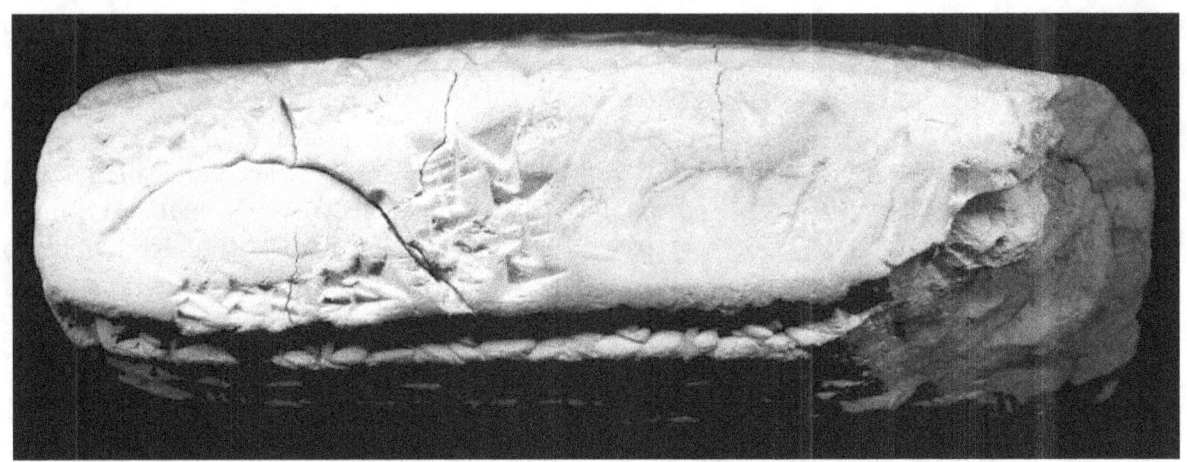

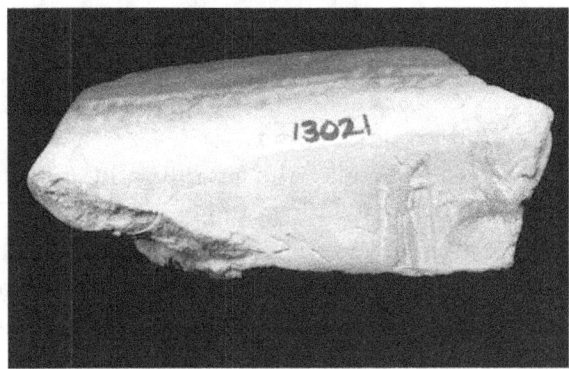 

Fig. 51.12 Photograph and composite drawing of the seal of Ribat, on clay tablets, from the Murašu Archive, Nippur, Babylonian Section, Museum of Archaeology and Anthropology of the University of Pennsylvania, CBS 5364 and 13021. (Photograph courtesy Babylonian Section, University of Pennsylvania, line drawing by the author, based on Legrain 1925)

is due to the nature of the process of history-making. As correctly argued by many scholars, history is a conscious construction that is based on the fabrication and manipulation of a series of chosen events that "occurred" in the past (White 1981; Winter 1981, 1985). Within the process of history-making, the "occurrence" of the event is typically presented to the audience through verbal and/or visual narratives. The historicity of the events is usually rendered through a "correct" and coherent description of the "actors" involved in the events and of the specific time and place within which the actions took place. The historical "truth" embedded in the narratives is usually legitimized and guaranteed by some high level of authority, such as the king or the state, and notably also by gods in the Ancient Near Eastern context. Subsequently, in order to represent an "actual historical event", the narrative must provide enough detailed information, such as the social and physical attributes of the participants in the event, so that they can be clearly identified as historically real. The more specific and precise these details, the higher the level of "historicity" the representation *intends* to project. Meanwhile, the narrative should also contain information that distinguishes the event as a unique incident by representing a special moment that occurred in a specific time and space. Within the same corpus, or in the same cultural/historical context, the more "moments" the seal images represent, the more chances there are that each image refers to a specific event.

With a few exceptions, which include the representations on the cylinder seal from Artachate and on a few stamps from, or allegedly from, Anatolia,[36] the images on seals showing battles against Central Asians do show the qualities of being specific and unique. On these seals, the heroes are clearly identified through their ethnic markers and sometimes also through their particular physiognomy. For example, the detailed depictions of the facial features of the Median victor on the seal of Ašama, especially his thick lips, and of the Persian hero on PTS 30, particularly his heavy eyelids, suggest that the artists had the intention of defining the figures by their physical characteristics.

The uniqueness of each seal in the third group of battle scenes is also apparent in the different moments that the seals represent, ranging from the stage when the victory is not yet determined, as captured on PTS 29, to the final struggles of the defeated, as depicted on the seal of Minû-ana-Bēl-dānu and BM 132505; from the moment when the vanquished sought mercy on the seal of Aršama, to the final victory on the battlefield, as preserved on the Oxus Seal; and finally, the transportation of captives, as shown on the seal of Ribat and on the seal from Artachate. The representation of the different moments on these seals is certainly based on the deliberate choices of the artists and their patrons, and suggests the attempt to recreate real moments on the battlefield.

The historical background of battle representations in Achaemenid art

Being specific and unique is not enough to qualify the images on the battle seals as "historically accurate" scenes. A consideration of the historical backdrop against which the Achaemenid battle seals were created, as well as of the social function of the representations of the human combat scenes in the particular Persian cultural milieu, could help us to further determine whether the battle images on these seals can be considered as visual documentation of real historical occurrences. Most of the battle scenes in the third group are on large cylinder seals with high levels of craftsmanship, indicating that the seals were carved in workshops perhaps surrounding the royal court and were used by the Achaemenid social elite. As elite objects, the images on the seals must have reflected the Persian elite ideology, which is centred on gaining privilege and royal favour by demonstrating before the Great King the distinctive capabilities of the individuals who are the subjects of the Persian king.[37] According to Greek authors, during the Greco-Persian war the Persian king usually sat on a platform observing his troops in battle; he would order the clerks to write down the names and origins of those who fought distinctively and reward them accordingly afterwards (see e.g. Herodotus VIII: 85, 90). If this information is accepted as valid, the rewarding of those worthy warriors must have taken place in certain ceremonies, during which martial victories and the bravery of those who participated in battle were publicly celebrated.[38] It would not be surprising if some of the heroes and possibly also their family members commissioned certain artefacts to commemorate these celebratory events and the royal favour that attended them, bestowed in the form of gifts and perhaps also higher social status. Within such a historical framework, an artefact carrying a battle scene would be an appropriate commemorative piece, for the hero being portrayed would be immediately associated by the audience with the person who had commissioned the work. To further strengthen the association, the patron probably required the battle scene to reflect the unique individual features of the hero depicted and the specific fighting moment for which he was rewarded.

As mentioned above, battle scenes were also depicted on media other than seals. The ambitious design on the Oxus Seal suggests that the image was originally intended to adorn a space much larger than a seal surface. The representation, despite its small size, reflects a high level of monumentality, which is no less powerful than that on the stele of Naram-Sin and on the Assyrian palace reliefs. The grandiose composition of the scenes on the Oxus Seal, along with the vertical line used to divide the two successive episodes on the seal—a rare element in glyptic art—indicates that the image on this seal must have originally been designed to decorate the surface of a wall or of some other perishable material, such as wood or textile.[39] If this is true, the commemorative nature of the image is clear. In fact, a painted marble sarcophagus from a late fourth-century BC burial near Çan in Anatolia offers an actual example of depicting battle scenes on a monumental scale (Sevinç *et al.* 2001; Kaptan 2003). The battle was represented on one side of the sarcophagus. It shows a horseman in typical Persian battle attire engaging a Greek warrior in combat against a rocky backdrop.[40] The examination of the image depicted on the sarcophagus surface and the result of the anthropological analysis of the skeletal remains of the body interred inside the burial suggests that the representation was probably based on a real event that the deceased had participated in and possibly died as a result of.[41] In addition to the funerary monuments,[42] images of battle were also used to decorate personal luxury items.[43] Once created, these artefacts, whether seals, funerary reliefs or personal decorations, served as reminders of the heroes' past glory and as mementos of the king's favour, regardless of whether the heroes actually commissioned the artefacts or whether they were commissioned by others. As a by-product, these artefacts are tokens of history defined and remembered by the Achaemenid social elite whose heroic past is proved by the king or other powerful authorities. Among these artefacts, the seals, which had a semi-official nature and represent a Persian perspective, should be treated as visual documentation of the political conflicts between the empire and its enemies, and should consequently be treated as evidence useful to the reconstruction of the political history of the Achaemenid Empire.

Reconstruction of historical aspects based on battle representations on seals of the third group

The above analysis of the iconography of the Achaemenid battle representations and of the social background against which the battle images were made, suggests that the images on the majority of the seals of the third group were carved based on real historical events. Created to serve an ideological purpose for the Achaemenid elite, the images depicted on the seals nevertheless offer us valuable information for the investigation and reconstruction of the political interactions between the Achaemenid central institution and the people from Central Asia, providing evidence either confirming or belying the scraps of information given by classical authors.

As mentioned at the beginning of this paper, among the preserved classical texts only five accounts are relevant to the political or military encounters between the Achaemenid kings and people related to Central Asia. Of these five accounts, three record events occurring after Darius' consolidation of the empire in the late sixth century BC and before the second quarter of the fifth century BC, and all concern problems related to Bactria.[44] The incidents come down to two, if we accept Briant's argument that the two accounts of the revolts against Xerxes in fact refer to the same event. That is to say, apart from the Central Asian campaign of Cyrus, we have only two textual references documenting political events related to Central Asia, and these are specific to Bactria. In addition to their brevity these references are vague. They do not clarify the nature of the conflicts, namely whether they were purely power struggles inside the Persian royal house, or whether they were encounters between Achaemenid central power and the people who inhabited the north-eastern corner of the empire.

The battle seals of the third group, taken as a corpus, present a scenario that is quite different from the one suggested by the textual evidence. With one possible exception,[45] all of the battle seals of this group were carved after the reign of Darius. The corpus contains seals carved from the beginning to the end of the fifth century BC. On most of the seals, the defeated can be identified either as Sogdians or as Sakas. Some of the battles depicted on these seals might have been related to the Bactrian revolts recorded in written sources, during which the Sogdians and Sakas were probably allies of the Bactrians. However, it is equally possible that the representations on these seals in fact documented military conflicts that are not preserved in the textual records. For example, the late fifth-century BC dating for the Ašama seal and for the two Murašu seals suggests the battles depicted on these may have nothing to do with the incidents mentioned by classical authors, but may refer instead to some other historical events unknown from historical records. The representations on these seals suggest that an adversarial relationship characterized at least some of the interactions between the Achaemenid Empire and some of the ethnic groups of Central Asia during the second half of the fifth century BC. In addition, the recurrent appearance of the Sogdians and Sakas on the battle seals suggests that these groups must have been among the major opponents of the empire throughout the entire fifth century BC.[46]

A few additional observations can be made when we compare the three groups of seals defined based on the geographical origins of the defeated. First, most of the scenes showing battles against the Greeks were carved outside Persia and bear images that are generic, and therefore cannot be used as evidence for reconstructing historical events. Second, the almost identical images on the three seals depicting warfare related to Egypt suggest that the images on these seals were probably derived from one common visual source, and that they therefore referred to the same single historical incident. Third, the images of battles against Central Asians are mostly unique. If each unique battle image represents a historical occasion, the number of incidents recorded on the third group of seals is no less than that for the first group. If we rely on the battle seals as a means of reconstructing Persian history, one conclusion we can draw is that the challenges presented by the Central Asians to the Persian king and the surrounding ruling class were no less significant than those brought by the Greeks.

Finally, the examination of seals bearing scenes of battles against Central Asians suggests one way of reconstructing the long-standing conflicts between the Achaemenid central institution and the peoples living in the north-eastern edge of the empire, whose historical significance in Persian historiography has been almost completely overshadowed by the Greco-Persian wars and by the revolts elsewhere in the western empire. In addition, the glyptic evidence allows us to re-evaluate some of the fundamental issues of Achaemenid historiography, such as whether the Persians were conscious about their history and, if they were, how their historical consciousness manifested itself without the use of written narratives.[47] Given the fact that no narrative account written by the Persians has been found to date, aside from the Behistun inscriptions, we cannot know for certain whether the Persians relied on oral transmissions rather than written records to commemorate and immortalize their history (Briant 2002a: 127), or whether they kept their history through narrative accounts written on such perishable material as papyrus and leather.[48] We can be confident, however, that pictorial narrative was certainly one of the channels the Persian elite adopted to commemorate their glorious personal history which, when put together, represents a collection of social memory that reflects one of the Persian approaches to the past. The battle seals, as carriers of Persian social memory, should be treated as another source for historical information and deserve further scholarly attention.

Notes

1. I owe much to Holly Pittman and Karen Sonik at the University of Pennsylvania for kindly commenting on and editing this paper. I am also thankful to Adam Brin for reading through the draft of this paper.
2. The term "Central Asia" refers here to Afghanistan, Turkmenistan, Uzbekistan, Tajikistan, Kyrgyzstan and Kazakhstan.
3. This is mainly based on the travel texts from the Persepolis Fortification archive. The accounts on the travel tablets reveal that certain locations in the eastern provinces (including Areia, Bactria, Kandahar, Barrikana, Arachosia, Kerman and India) were in contact in varying degrees with the central administration during the first half of the fifth century BC. Compared with trips to/from the western provinces, many more trips between the imperial heartland and the eastern provinces are documented on the Persepolis Fortification Tablets. But only two accounts concern trips to and from Central Asia (Hallock 1969). For a list of the travel groups to or from the destinations in the eastern provinces, see Wu 2005. Classical accounts and recently published Aramaic administrative documents reported to have come from Bactria suggest that Bactria continued to be a part of the Persian administrative system until the end of the empire (Shaked 2004).
4. The place is referred to by some scholars as the modern Araxes, or Aras River in modern Azerbaijan (Vogelsang 1992: 183). The campaign ended with the Persian king being killed by the Massagetae (Herodotus I: 214). For an analysis of the event see Dandamayev 1989b: 90 and Vogelsang 1992: 183.
5. Justin (II: 10.1–11) and Plutarch (see Briant 2002a: 524).
6. The war seems to have involved not only Bactra, the seat of the satrap of Bactria (modern-day Balkh in Afghanistan) but also probably all the north-eastern provinces of the empire, i.e. the "High Country" or the "Upper Satrapies". The war ended with "the surrender of all Bactria" to the victorious Artaxerxes. Modern historians identify the rebel Artabanus as Artaxerxes' brother Hystaspes, who was then the satrap seated at Bactra in Bactria (Briant 2002a: 570).
7. However, the battle motif still constitutes only a small portion of the image repertoire of the Achaemenid glyptic designs (Ward 1910; Collon 1987).

8. The name of the person is generally associated to the grandfather of Cyrus the Great (see Hansman 1972; Amiet 1973; Garrison 1991; Briant 2002a: 90). The seal is regarded as an example of Neo-Elamite art by Amiet (1972b), but as an example of Proto-Achaemenid art by Garrison (1991).
9. For theories on visual narrative in the Ancient Near Eastern contexts, see Winter 1981, 1985.
10. For example, PTS 28 from Persepolis (Schmidt 1957). For examples of battle scenes on seals and on other media found in Anatolia, see Kaptan 2002: 74–76.
11. This includes three almost identical chalcedony cylinder seals, one in the State Hermitage Museum in St Petersburg (Menant 1885: 168, fig. 147, pl. IX), one in the Pushkin Museum of Art in Moscow (Chileyko 1925: 17; Dandamayev 1976: taf. V, XIV), and the third, unpublished, one in The Metropolitan Museum of Fine Art. For a classical reference on the Egyptian campaigns of Artaxerxes I and Artaxerxes III, see Briant 2002a: 574–577, 652–565. The Moscow seal has drawn more attention because it bears the name of Artaxerxes. For an early date (Artaxerxes I) of this seal, see Chileyko 1925: 19 and Stolper 2001: 111; for a later date (Artaxerxes III), see Strelkov 1937: 20, Root 1979: 122; and Schmitt 1981: 36, fig. 5, SA3b.
12. These include six cylinder seals and two stamp seals. They include two chalcedony seals from the British Museum, another chalcedony cylinder in the Bibliothèque Nationale, a fragment of a cylinder from the Newell Collection (von der Osten 1934: pl. XXXI/453; Stolper 2001: 108–109), a cylinder from the Foroughi Collection (Porada 1979b: 83, fig. 45), another in the Morgan Library, and two stamp seals allegedly from Anatolia (Boardman 1970a: 882, 883). Those preserved on sealings refer to the seal of Ašama, satrap of Egypt, which was preserved on a few sealings found in an archive in Egypt and is currently housed in the Bodleian Museum at Oxford, and to a seal impressed on two clay labels: one on a clay tablet in the Dutch Institute for the Near East (NINO) in Leiden (LB 894), the second in the Département des Antiquités Orientales in the Musée du Louvre (AO 29963) (Stolper et al. 2004).
13. See for example, the throne-bearers (no. 17 on the left wing, nos. 18, 20, 28 on the right wing) on the Throne Hall at Persepolis (Walser 1966b: 62, 63).
14. But the dating of the seal is not very clear in the initial publication. The bullae were discovered in an excavation by Tadjvidi in 1971–72 (Rahimifar 2005: 10, pls 16, nos. 6552–4, 6556–8, 6560, 6561, 6562, 6563, 6564, 6574, 6578, 6581). The Persian hero seems to be wearing a Persian crown.
15. The bullae are recorded as among the "sixty clay labels or bullae from Persepolis fortifications" (Rahimifar 2005). It is not clear whether they initially belonged to the same Persepolis Archive, which was excavated by Schmidt and was dated to the reign of Darius in year 16–28 according to the administrative inscriptions on the tablets from the archive.
16. This includes three seals preserved on clay bullae and tablets from the Persepolis Treasury (Schmidt 1957: pl. 9/nos. 29–31).
17. The seals are impressed on two tablets: PT4 655 concerns payments for six artisans between 19th June and 16th August 470 BC; PT4 1014 mentions payments to 23 woodworkers between 13th December and 9th March 469 BC (see Schmidt 1957: 29–30; Cameron 1958: 134–135, 137).
18. The cylinder was acquired by the Bibliothèque Nationale in 1857 from the Paolin Collection (see Cunningham 1883: 259, pl. XXI; Ward 1910: 328).
19. Scenes depicting group combat also occur in the poorly preserved impressions of a seal used at the Persepolis Treasury and on the fragment of a cylinder seal in the Newell Collection (Schmidt 1957: 30, PTS 31; Wu 2005: 67–68; von der Osten 1934: pl. XXXI/453; Stolper 2001: 108–109). Bearing the inscription of a Persian royal name in a cartouche, the seal is variously attributed to the reign of Artaxerxes I or Artaxerxes III (Stolper 2001: 108–109; Schmitt 1981: 34). It depicts two warriors in the typical Achaemenid round battle helmet and Persian robe slaying two Central Asian warriors. The composition contains two pairs of figures: the one on the left shows a Persian warrior about to cut his enemy's neck using a knife; the pair on the right depicts another Persian figure thrusting a spear into his enemy's shoulder. On this seal, the victory of the Persian heroes is clearly emphasized.
20. Schmidt 1957: 30. The seal was probably carved during the early years of Xerxes, probably between 485 and 467 BC, based on its association with other dated seals or tablets from the Persepolis Treasury. The seal was impressed on five labels, on two of which PTS 5 also appeared and on one of which it appeared with PTS 8. Both PTS 5 and PTS 8 are associated with Xerxes, with PTS 5 bearing the inscription "Xerxes the Great King" and PTS 8, the seal of Artasyras, being

inscribed with the name of Xerxes. The *terminus post quem* of PTS 29 is thus likely to be 485 BC, the first "regnal year" of Xerxes. Furthermore, as PTS 29 was first impressed on a tablet dated to 467 BC, it may be reasonably concluded that the cylinder was carved in the period between 485 and 467 BC (see Wu 2005: 66).

21. This is not the only case that shows military conflict between two Central Asian groups. Another example but with a composition depicting a military engagement on a much larger scale is depicted on an inlaid gold torque in the Miho Museum in Japan. The victors are clearly wearing Persian battle helmets and vests as well as Central Asian "cut-front" tunics (see Arnold ed. 1996: 19).

22. The definite origin of the documents is, however, unknown (see Driver 1957: 1). This seal is reconstructed from several sealings currently housed at the Bodleian Library, Oxford (see Driver 1957; Moorey 1978).

23. Briant 2002a: 577, 586. For the documents relating to Aršama's Babylonian estates, see Driver 1957: 88–89; Stolper 1974: 95–96 and 1985: 16, 23.

24. The battle image on this seal is interpreted by some scholars as a representation of the triumph of Darius over the Sakâ Tigraxaudâ in 519 BC (Dandamayev 1989b: 140).

25. The seal was impressed on CBS 5144 and 1594. On CBS 5144, it was used as a witness seal in a text concerning taxes. The tablet is dated to 418 BC, the 5th Year of Darius II. On CBS 1594 the name is mentioned as one of the witnesses on a contract to sell a slave woman in the 9th year of Darius II (414 BC) (see Clay 1904: 101; Stolper 2001: 103–107).

26. This seal is among a few Achaemenid heirloom seals impressed on *bullae* from an archive of sealings at a site founded in 180 BC by the Armenian king Artashes I (see Khachatrian 1996: 365–367, pl. 73/5a–b, 6, 10; Ter-Martirossov 1996: 222, no. 210a–b).

27. It is more likely that the captives are Choresmians rather than Sogdians because their headdresses have domes in the centre of the head. The headdresses worn by the Sogdians, as shown consistently on monumental reliefs, have their tips rising up right above the forehead. The figure leading the captives could not be confidently determined based on the publications; the unclear quality of the images may have resulted from the poor condition of preservation of the sealings.

28. Bregstein 1993: 586, cat. 189; Stolper 2001: 105, CBS 1594. Identified also as the son of Šamašaja, Ribat was probably a business administrator at Nippur. For his administrative role, see Donbaz *et al.* 1997: 121.

29. The sealed tablets PBS13021, 5437, 5364, are dated respectively to 419 BC and 424 BC in the 36th and 41st years of Artaxerxes I (464–424) and in 418 BC in the 6th year of Darius II (423–405). For the date of 13021, see Stolper 1974; for 5437, see Hilprecht *et al.* 1898: 107; for 5364, see Clay 1912: 130.

30. This attire is shown on many Achaemenid seals and on Greek vase paintings (see for example, Boardman 1970a: figs 904, 905, 925–928).

31. Stolper has also suggested that the battle seals may have been individually commissioned to commemorate certain historic events (2001: 108).

32. For example, a seal from Moscow that shows a Persian hero leading a file of Egyptian captives has been interpreted as either a commemoration of the victory of Artaxerxes I over the Lybian Inarus, who had led the rebellious troops of Egyptians and Lybians (Briant 2002a: 215), or a seal from the reign of Artaxerxes III, who also campaigned in Egypt, for it bears an inscription that reads: "I am Artaxerxes the Great King" (Dandamayev 1976: Taf. V. A.). For the earlier date of this seal see Stolper 2001: 111 and Chileyko 1925: 19. The date of the two seals from Moscow and St Petersburg has long been a subject of debate. The Moscow seal has drawn more attention because it bears the name of Artaxerxes. For an early date (Artaxerxes I) of the Moscow seal, see Chileyko 1925: 19 and Stolper 2001: 111; for a later date (Artaxerxes I), see Strelkov 1937: 20, Root 1979: 122 and Schmitt 1981: 36, fig. 5, SA3b. Strelkov also suggests that the St Petersburg seal had served as a prototype of the Moscow seal, and dates the St Petersburg seal to the reign of Artaxerxes I.

33. For a comparative study of hunting scenes in Mesopotamia, Anatolia and Greece, see Miller 2003b: 23–43.

34. It has been argued that in Anatolia some "Achaemenid seals…seem to have contributed to the theme selection of the 'Greco-Persian' seals" (Kaptan, personal communication).

35. For example, in the records of a battle fought between the Egyptians and the Hittites at the city of Qadesh (located on the Orontes River in modern Syria), both sides proclaimed the final victory. Apparently, one side faked the result of the battle.

36. This refers to one stamp preserved on sealings from Daskyleion (Kaptan 2002: 207, figs 257–298) and two stamp seals allegedly from Anatolia (Boardman 1970a: 882, 883). The representation shows a battle between two groups of horsemen. The horsemen to the right, or the defeated, can be associated with Central Asia by their garments. The iconography and style of these seals are so similar that it is highly likely that they represent a popular seal "motif" in Anatolia.
37. For the king's subjects, the necessity of distinguishing oneself before the Great King, or being judged by him, was expressed both in Persian royal inscriptions and in classical sources. In an Old Persian inscription carved on the façade of his rock-cut tomb at Naqsh-i Rustam, the Great King Darius claims that "(DNb. 24–27) what a man does or performs (for me) according to his (natural) powers, (therewith) I am satisfied, and my pleasure is abundant... (50–52) O subject, very much make known (of what) kind you are, of what kind your ab[ilities, of what] kind your conduct" (Kent 1953: 140; DNb ll. 16–27; ll. 50–52).
38. The Persian kings were famous for their generosity in giving gifts to the people who gave good service. For a systematic compilation of the classical sources on this issue, see Sancisi-Weerdenburg 1986; Briant 2002a: 302–315.
39. Wall paintings have been found at Dahan-i Gulaman in Seistan, an Achaemenid period urban settlement of the sixth to fifth centuries BC (Sajjadi 2007). A wooden beam in Munich, which bears a representation of a large battle composition, offers an actual example of battle imagery painted on wood. The beam was possibly originally from a painted Lycian tomb of the mid-fifth century BC near Tatarlı in Turkey. The representation shows a generic representation of a military encounter between a Persian army led by the king and a group of warriors from Central Asia or the Eurasian steppe. The beam was probably looted from the tomb and is now in the Archäologische Staatssammlung in Munich, Germany (Summerer 2007: 2, 26). Felt hangings and woollen items in Achaemenid style were discovered from the nomadic kurgans at Pazyryk in the Altai Mountains in Southern Siberia (Russia) (Rudenko 1970: pl. 177).
40. There is another figure behind the horseman. The figure is interpreted in the original report as the "henchman" of the Persian warrior (Sevinç et al. 2001: 398–399), but the apparently similar garment and battle attire that equip both the figures on foot make this interpretation dubious and suggest that they may both be Greeks.
41. The anthropological analysis of the skeletal remains of the interred body shows that the deceased was a young man in his twenties, who had been badly injured falling from a horse on his left side a few years before his death (Sevinç et al. 2001).
42. Another example of the funeral monument is a wooden beam in Munich. But this battle scene, as correctly argued by Summerer, should be considered as "motif" rather than "historical" because of the generic nature of the representation (2007).
43. This is exemplified by the battle images depicted on the pendant of a gold torque at the Miho Museum (Bernard & Bernard 2002) and on a gold circular object allegedly acquired from Siberia in the eighteenth century by the Russian Tzar Peter the Great that is currently housed in the State Hermitage Museum in St Petersburg.
44. According to the Greek authors, Bactria enjoyed a special status within the Persian Empire since the Great Achaemenid kings were attached closely to Bactria. When we come to the Achaemenid reliefs, however, the Bactrians did not stand out at all. The situation is similar in the Persian written sources (Stolper, personal communication).
45. This refers to the example preserved on a number of *bullae* from the Persepolis Fortification excavated by Tadjvidi in 1971–72 (Rahimifar 2005).
46. The Sakas and the Sogdians seem also to have been treated as allies from time to time. Their special status within the empire is reflected in both classical and Persian sources. For example, on the Apadana relief, the Sogdians and pointed-hatted Sakas are depicted wearing weapons in the King's Palace, whereas the same types of weapon (*akinakas*) are carried by other delegations as gifts to the king.
47. Sancisi-Weerdenburg, based on her study of the structure of the Achaemenid royal inscriptions, that written narrative accounts documenting specific historical events were basically unnecessary for the Persians (1999: 109–110).
48. Momigliano, who has based his analysis on the information provided by the Hebrew Bible and Greek authors, argues that the Persians had their own royal chronicles or "an account of their ancient affairs" written either in Persian or in Aramaic on leather documents (Momigliano 1990: 6; see Diodorus Siculus II, 33, 4).

Bibliography

Abdi K., 2006. "The 'Daiva' inscription revisited", *Nāme-ye Irān Bāstān / International Journal of Ancient Iranian Studies* 11/12: 45–74.

Abdullaev K. & Badanova E., 1998. "Bactrian dress in the Achaemenid period", *Mesopotamia* 33: 189–218.

Abusch T., 1999. "Marduk", pp. 543–549 in K. van der Toorn, B. Becking & P. W. van der Horst (eds) *Dictionary of Deities and Demons in the Bible*, 2nd edn. Leiden.

Ackerman P., 1940. *Guide to the Exhibition of Persian Art.* New York.

Agathias, 1975. *The Histories* (transl. J. D. Frendo), *Corpus Fontium Historiae Byzantinae* IIA.

Ahn G., 2002. "'Toleranz' und Reglement. Die Signifikanz achaimenidischer Religionspolitik für den jüdisch-persischen Kulturkontakt", pp. 191–209 in R. G. Kratz (ed.) *Religion und Religionskontakte im Zeitalter der Achaimeniden.* Göttingen.

Akkaya M., 1997. "Mezardaki Pontos Hazinesi", *Atlas* 48 (Mart): 130–133.

Akurgal E., 1955. *Phrygische Kunst.* Ankara.

———, 1956. "Les Fouilles de Daskyleion", "Kyzikos ve Ergili Araflıtırmaları", *Anatolia* 1: 20–24, 43–51.

Akurgal E. & Hirmer M., 1978. *Die Kunst der Hethiter.* Munich.

Aldred C., 1990. *Egyptian Art in the Days of the Pharaohs 3100–320 BC.* London.

Alexander C., Ishikawa S. & Silverstein M., 1977. *A Pattern Language.* New York.

Ali I. & Zahir M., 2005. "Excavation of Gandharan graves at Parwak, Chitral, 2003–2004", *Frontier Archaeology* 3: 135–182.

Ali I., Hemphill B. & Zahir M., 2005. "Skeletal analysis of Gandharan graves at Parwak, Chitral (2003–2004)", *Frontier Archaeology* 3: 183–226.

Ali T., Coningham R., Ali-Durrani M. & Khan G. R., 1998. "Preliminary report of two seasons of archaeological investigations at the Bala Hissar of Charsadda, NWFP, Pakistan", *Ancient Pakistan* 12: 1–34.

Allan J. W., 1976. "The metalworking industry in Iran in the early Islamic period". D.Phil. thesis, University of Oxford.

Allchin B. & Allchin R., 1982. *The Rise of Civilisation in India and Pakistan.* Cambridge.

Allchin F. R., 1982. "How old is the city of Taxila?", *Antiquity* 56/216: 8–14.

———, 1995. "Early cities and states beyond the Ganges Valley", pp. 123–151 in F. R. Allchin (ed.) *The Archaeology of Early Historic South Asia.* Cambridge.

Alram M., 1986. *Nomina propria Iranica in nummis. Iranisches Personennamenbuch.* Vienna.

———, 1993. "*Dareikos* und *siglos*: Eine neuer Schatzfund achaimenidischer *sigloi* aus Kleinasien [mit einem metrologischen Beitrag von St. Karwiese]", *Res Orientalis* 5 [Circulation des monnaies, des marchandises et des biens]: 23–50.

Al-Rawi F. N. H., (n.d.). "New historical documents from Babylon", *Sumer* 41 (*c.*1981): 23–26.

Althoff G., 2004. *Family, Friends and Followers: Political and Social Bonds in Medieval Europe.* Cambridge (transl. C. Carroll). (First publ. as *Verwandte, Freunde und Getreue* [Darmstadt 1990].)

Alvarez-Mon J., 2004. "Imago Mundi: Cosmological and ideological aspects of the Arjan Bowl", *Iranica Antiqua* 39: 203–237.

Alvarez-Mon J., forthcoming. "Elamite rings of power", in J. Alvarez-Mon (ed.) *Elam and Persia*. Winona Lake, IN.

Amandry P., 1956. "Vaisselle d'argent de l'époque achéménide (collection Hélène Stathatos)", pp. 12–19, pls I–IV in *Memorial Festschrift of G.P. Ekonomu, volume AE 1953/54*. Athens.

———, 1958. "Orfèvrerie achéménide", *Antike Kunst* 1: 9–23.

Ambos C., 2004. *Mesopotamische Baurituale aus dem 1. Jahrtausend v. Chr*. Babylonische Archive, Bd. 3. Dresden.

Amiet P., 1966. *Élam*. Auvers-sur-Oise.

———, 1967. "Éléments émaillés du décor architectural néo-élamite" (with an appendix by M. Lambert), *Syria* 44: 27–51.

———, 1972a. "Les ivoires achéménides de Suse", *Syria* 49: 167–91, 319–37.

———, 1972b. *Glyptique susienne*. Paris.

———, 1973. "La Glyptique de la fin d'Elam", *Arts Asiatiques* 28: 3–32.

———, 1976. "Disjecta Membra Aelamica: le décor architectural en briques émaillées à Suse", *Arts Asiatiques* 32: 13–28.

———, 1977. *L'art du Proche-Orient: L'art et les grandes civilisations*. Paris.

———, 1980. "La glyptique du second millénaire en provenance des chantiers A et B de la ville royale de Suse", pp. 133–147 in M.-J. Steve, H. Gasche & L. De Meyer, "La Susiane au deuxième millénaire: à propos d'une interprétation des fouilles de Suse", *Iranica Antiqua* 15: Annex 4, 49–154.

———, 1988. *Suse, 6000 ans d'histoire*. Paris.

———, 1992. "An introduction to the history of art in Iran", pp. 2–15 in P. O. Harper, J. Aruz & F. Tallon (eds) *The Royal City of Susa: Ancient Near Eastern Treasures in the Louvre*. New York.

Amory Jr. C., 1929. *Persian Days*. Boston and New York.

Ampolo C., 1997. *La formazione della moderna storiografia sugli antichi Greci*. Torino.

Anderson B., 2002. "Imperial legacies, local identities: references to royal Achaemenid iconography on crenelated Nabataean tombs", *Ars Orientalis* 30 (*Medes and Persians: Elusive Contexts of Elusive Empires* ed. M. C. Root): 163–206.

———, 2005. "Constructing Nabataea: identity, ideology, and connectivity". PhD dissertation, University of Michigan.

Anderson T. S., 1880. *My Wanderings in Persia*. London.

Andrae W., 1913. *Die Festungswerke von Assur*, WVDOG, 23, 2 vols. Leipzig.

———, 1925. *Coloured Ceramics from Assur*. London.

André-Salvini B., 2000. "Le décor en briques polychromes du palais de Darius Ier à Suse dans les collections du Louvre", *Coré* 9 (Nov.): 16–26.

Andronicos M., 1981. *Thessalonike Museum: A New Guide to the Archaeological Treasures*. Athens.

Anon., [1943]. *Connoisseurs of the World, Being an International Biographical Dictionary of Connoisseurs, Collectors, and Patrons of Art*. London.

———, 1594. *The Warres of Cyrus King of Persia, against Antiochus King of Assyria, with the Tragic ille ende of Panthæa*. London.

———, 1728. *La Mort de Xerxes, tragédie française*. Paris.

———, 1746. *Mercy the Truest Heroism: Display'd in the Conduct of Some the most Famous Conquerores and Heroes of Antiquity; Cyrus, Alexander, Julius Caesar, Augustus, Flavius Vespasianus, Titus, M. Antoninus, Alphonsus, King of Arragon, &C*. London.

Aperghis G. G., 1996. "Travel routes and travel stations from Persepolis". MA dissertation, University of London.

———, 1998. "The Persepolis Fortification Tablets— Another Look", pp. 35–62 in P. Briant, A. Kuhrt, M. C. Root, H. Sancisi-Weerdenburg & J. Wiesehöfer (eds) *Achaemenid History XI: Studies in Persian History: Essays in Memory of David M. Lewis*. Leiden.

———, 1999. "Storehouses and systems at Persepolis", *Journal of the Economic and Social History of the Orient* 42: 152–193.

Arman F., 1998. "Akalan'da bir Lydia Geleneği", *Atlas* 69 (Aralık): 20.

Armbruster B. R., 1995. "Rotary motion—lathe and drill. Some new technological aspects concerning Late Bronze Age goldwork from southwestern Europe", pp. 399–423 in G. Morteani & P. Northover (eds) *Prehistoric Gold in Europe, Mines, Metallurgy and Manufacture. NATO Advanced Research Workshop on Prehistoric Gold in Europe, Seeon Sept. 27–Oct. 1, 1993*. NATO ASI Series E: Applied Sciences 20. Dordrecht, London and Boston.

———, 2001. "Metallguß", pp. 632–635 in H. Beck, D. Geuenich & H. Steuer (eds) *Hoops, Reallexicon der Germanischen Altertumskunde* 19. Berlin and New York.

———, 2003. "Punze, Punzieren", pp. 602–607 in H. Beck, D. Geuenich & H. Steuer (eds) *Hoops, Reallexicon der Germanischen Altertumskunde* 19. Berlin and New York.

———, 2005. "Technological aspects of the Oxus Treasure bracelets", pp. 135–136 in J. Curtis & N. Tallis (eds) *Forgotten Empire: The World of Ancient Persia*. London.

Armstrong J., 1989. "The archaeology of Nippur from the decline of the Kassite Kingdom until the rise of the Neo-Babylonian Empire". PhD dissertation, University of Chicago.

Arnold A., 1877. *Through Persia by Caravan*. New York.

Arnold D. ed., 1996. *Ancient Art from the Shumei Family Collection*. Catalogue of exhibition held at the Metropolitan Museum of Art, 20th Jun.–1st Sept., 1996. New York.

Assante J., 2002. "Sex, magic and the liminal body in the erotic art and texts of the Old Babylonian Period", pp. 27–52 in S. Parpola & R. M. Whiting (eds) *Sex and Gender in the Ancient Near East*. The Neo-Assyrian Text Corpus Project, Part 1. Helsinki.

Atarashi K. & Horiuchi K., 1963. *Fahlian I: the Excavation at Tape Suruvan, 1959*. Tokyo University Iraq-Iran Archaeological Expedition Reports Institute for Oriental Culture. Tokyo.

Aubin J., 1973. "Le royaume d'Ormuz au début du XVIe siècle", *Mare Luso-Indicum* 2: 77–179.

Avigad N., 1997. *Corpus of West Semitic Stamp Seals* (revised and completed by B. Sass). Jerusalem.

Aydemir P., 1997. *Museo de Izmir 1. Ripostigli di Monete Greche*. Milan.

Aydın N., 1991. "Seyitömer Höyük Kurtarma Kazısı 1989", pp. 191–203 in *I. Müze Kurtarma Kazıları Semineri, 19–20 Nisan 1990 Ankara*. Ankara.

Ayoub S. A. S., 1981. "Nordabschnitt III 1977 (5. Kampagne)", pp. 51–53 in B. Hrouda *et al. Isin-Išan-Bahriyat II. Die Ergebnisse der Ausgrabungen 1975–1978*. Munich.

Ayvazian A., 2005. "Observations on dynastic continuity in the Kingdom of Urartu", *Iranica Antiqua* 40: 197–205.

Azarnoush M., 1975. "Hamadan", *Iran* 13: 181–182.

Azarpay G., 1994. "Designing the body: human proportions in Achaemenid art", *Iranica Antiqua* 29: 169–184.

Babelon E., 1893. *Catalogue des monnaies grecques de la Bibliothèque Nationale: Les Perses achéménides*. Paris.

Bahrani Z., 2001. *Women of Babylon: Gender and Representation in Mesopotamia*. London.

———, 2003. *The Graven Image. Representation in Babylonia and Assyria*. Philadelphia.

Baines J. & Malek J., 1980. *Cultural Atlas of Ancient Egypt*. Oxford and New York (revised 2000).

Baker H. D., 1995. "Neo-Babylonian burials revisited", pp. 209–220 in S. Campbell & A. Green (eds) *The Archaeology of Death in the Ancient Near East*. Oxbow Monograph, 51. Oxford

———, 2004. *The Archive of the Nappāhu Family*. Archiv für Orientforschung Beiheft 30, Vienna

———, 2007. "Urban form in the first millennium BC", pp. 66–77 in G. Leick (ed.) *The Babylonian World*. London.

———, 2008. "The layout of the ziggurat temple at Babylon", *NABU* 2008/2: 37–38, no. 27.

———, forthcoming. *The Urban Landscape in First Millennium BC Babylonia*.

Baker V., 1876. *Clouds in the East: Travels and Adventures on the Perso-Turkoman Frontier*. London.

Bakır T., 2001. "Die Satrapie Dascyleion", pp. 169–180 in T. Bakır *et al.* (eds) *Achaemenid Anatolia*. Leiden.

Bakır T., Sancisi-Weerdenburg H., Gürtekin G., Briant P. & Henkelman W., eds, 2001. *Achaemenid Anatolia*. Leiden.

Balcer J. M., 1978. "Excavations at Tal-i Malyan. Part 2: Parthian and Sasanian coins and burials (1976)", *Iran* 16: 86–92, pls I–II.

Bamberg J. H., 1994. *History of the British Petroleum Company*, Vol. 2: *The Anglo-Iranian Years, 1928–1954*. Cambridge.

Banks J., 1696. *Cyrus the Great, or the Tragedy of Love*. London.

Barag D., 1985. *Catalogue of Western Asiatic Glass in the British Museum*, vol. 1. London.

Barber E. W., 1994. *Women's Work: The First 20,000 Years: Women, Cloth, and Society in Early Times*. New York.

Barnett R. D., 1976. *Sculptures from the North Palace of Ashurbanipal at Nineveh (668–627 BC)*. London.

Barnett R. D. & Forman W., 1960. *Assyrian Palace Reliefs and their Influence on the Sculptures of Babylonia and Persia*. London.

Barnett R. D., Bleibtreu E. & Turner G., 1998. *Sculptures from the Southwest Palace of Sennacherib at Nineveh*. London.

Barthélémy D., 1998. "The year 1000 without abrupt or radical transformation", pp. 134–147 in L. Little & B. Rosenheim (eds) *Debating the Middle Ages: Issues and Readings*. Oxford (material reprinted and translated from idem *La société dans le comté de Vendôme de l'an Mil au XIVe siècle* [Paris 1993].)

Bartlett J. R., 1990. "From Edomites to Nabataeans: the problem of continuity", *Aram* 2: 25–34.

Basiri H., 1946. *Rāhnamāy-e Takht-e Jamshid (Guide to Persepolis)* (in Persian). Tehran.

Bassett J., 1886. *Persia: The Land of the Imams: A Narrative of Travel and Residence 1871–1885*. New York.

Bawden G., Evans C. & Miller R., 1980. "The archaeological resources of ancient Tayma: preliminary investigations at Tayma", *Atlal* 4: 69–106.

Bayle P., 1697. "Macédoine (Alexandre le Grand roi de)", *Dictionnaire historique et critique*. Amsterdam (reprinted Paris, 1820, Vol. 10, pp. 5–19).

Beaulieu P. A., 1989. *The Reign of Nabonidus, King of Babylon, 556–539 B.C.* New Haven.

Beckman G., 2002. "'My Sun-God', reflections of Mesopotamian conceptions of kingship among the Hittites", pp. 37–43 in A. Panaino & G. Pettinato (eds) *Ideologies as Intercultural Phenomena.* Milan.

Bedford P. R., 2001. *Temple Restoration in Early Achaemenid Judah.* Leiden.

Bedjan P., 1894. "Martyrdom of Jacque", *Acta Martyrum et Sanctorum.* Paris.

Bejor G., 1974. "La presenza di monete nei depositi di fondazione dell'*Apadana* a Persepoli", *Annali della Scuola Normale di Pisa* (ser. 3) 4/3: 735–740.

Bell G., 1928. *Persian Pictures.* London (with introduction by E. Denison Ross) [originally published anonymously as *Safar Nameh: Persian Pictures: A Book of Travel,* 1898].

Bennett C.-M., 1982. "Neo-Assyrian influence in Transjordan", *Studies in the History and Archaeology of Jordan* 1: 181–187. Amman.

Benveniste E., 1929. *The Persian Religion According to the Chief Greek Texts.* Paris.

———, 1960. "Le dieu Ohrmazd et le démon Albasti", *Journal Asiatique* 248: 65–74.

Berenson B., 1954. *Aesthetics and History.* Garden City, NY.

Berger P.-R., 1973. *Die neubabylonischen Königsinschriften.* Kevelaer/Neukirchen-Vluyn; Alter Orient und Altes Testament [AOAT], 4/1.

Bernard P. & Inagaki H., 2002. "Un torque achéménide avec une inscription greque au musée Miho (Japon)", pp. 207–210 in *Catalogue of Treasures of Ancient Bactria.* Shigaraki, Japan.

Besenval R. & Sanlaville P., 1990. "Cartography of ancient settlements in central southern Pakistani Makran: new data", *Mesopotamia* 25: 79–146.

Beyer K. & Livingstone A., 1987. "Die neuesten aramäischen Inschriften aus Taima", *Zeitschrift der Morgenländischen Gesellschaft* 137: 285–296.

Bianchi U., 1977. "L'inscription 'des daivas' et le Zoroastrisme des Achéménides", *Revue de l'histoire des religions* 192: 3–30.

Bianchini F., 1747. *La istoria universale provata con monumenti e figurate con simboli.* Rome (originally published 1697).

Bickerman E. J., 1967. "The 'Zoroastrian' Calendar", *Archiv Orientální* 35: 197–207.

Bidmead J., 2002. *The Akitu Festival: Religious Continuity and Royal Legitimation in Mesopotamia.* Gorgias Dissertations, Near Eastern Studies 2. Piscataway, NJ.

Bienkowski P. & van der Steen E., 2001. "Tribes, trade, and towns: a new framework for the Iron Age in Southern Jordan and the Negev", *Bulletin of the American Schools of Oriental Research* 323: 21–47.

Biruni, Abu-Rayhān, 1998–1999/1377. *Āthār-ol-Bāqiyya.* (transl. A. Dānā-Seresht). Tehran.

Biscione R., 1981. "Centre and periphery in late protohistoric Turan", pp. 203–213 in H. Härtel (ed.) *South Asian Archaeology 1979.* Berlin.

Bittel K., 1970. *Hattusha.* New York.

———, Naumann R. & Beran T., 1957. *Boğazköy III: Funde aus den Grabungen 1952–1955.* Berlin.

Bivar A. D. H., 1961. "A 'satrap' of Cyrus the Younger", *Numismatic Chronicle* (7th series) 1: 119–127.

———, 1969. *Catalogue of the Western Asiatic Seals in the British Museum, Stamp Seals, II The Sassanian Dynasty.* London.

———, 1988. "The Indus Lands", pp. 194–210 in J. Boardman, N. G. L. Hammond, D. M. Lewis & M. Oswald (eds) *Cambridge Ancient History Volume IV: Persia, Greece and the Western Mediterranean c. 525–479 B.C.,* 2nd edn. Cambridge.

———, 1998. *The Personalities of Mithra in Archaeology and Literature.* New York.

Black J. & Green A. 1992. *Gods, Demons and Symbols of Ancient Mesopotamia: An Illustrated Dictionary.* London.

Blenkinsopp J., 1988. *Ezra-Nehemiah, a Commentary.* Philadelphia.

Blinkenberg C., 1931. *Lindos: Fouilles de l'acropole 1902–1914.* Vol. 1: *Les petits objets.* Berlin.

Bloch M., 1961. *Feudal Society.* London (transl. by L. A. Manyon; first published as *La société féodale,* Paris 1939/40).

Blundell S., 2002. "Clutching at clothes", pp. 143–169 in L. Llewellyn-Jones (ed.) *Women's Dress in the Ancient Greek World.* Swansea and London.

Boardman J., 1964. *The Greeks Overseas: Their Early Colonies and Trade.* London.

———, 1968. *Archaic Greek Gems: Schools and Artists in the Sixth and Early Fifth Centuries B.C.* London.

———, 1969. "Three Greek gem masters", *The Burlington Magazine* 111/799: 587–596.

———, 1970a. *Greek Gems and Finger Rings.* London and New York.

———, 1970b. "Pyramidal stamp seals in the Persian Empire", *Iran* 8: 19–46.

———, 1980. "Greek gem engravers", pp. 101–125 in E. Porada (ed.) *Ancient Art in Seals.* Princeton.

———, 1994. *The Diffusion of Art in Classical Antiquity.* London.

———, 1998. "Seals and signs: Anatolian stamp seals of the Persian Period revisited", *Iran* 36: 1–13.

Boardman J., 2000. *Persia and the West: An Archaeological Investigation of the Genesis of Achaemenid Art*. London (German edn, 2003).

———, 2001. *Greek Gems and Finger Rings: Early Bronze Age to Late Classical*, 2nd edn London.

Boehmer R. M., 1977. "Siegel phrygischer Zeit", *Zeitschrift für Assyriologie und vorderasiatische Archäologie* 67/1: 78–84.

———, 1978. "Weitere Siegel aus phrygischer Zeit", *Zeitschrift für Assyriologie und vorderasiatische Archäologie* 68/2: 284–292.

Böhl F. M. T. de Liagre, 1962. "Die babylonischen Prätendenten zur Zeit des Xerxes", *Bibliotheca Orientalis* 19: 110–114.

Böhmer H. & Thompson J., 1991. "The Pazyryk carpet: a technical discussion", *Source. Notes in the History of Art* 10/4: 30–36.

Bonatz D., 2000. *Das syro-hethitischen Grabdenkmal*. Mainz.

Bongenaar A. C. V. M., 1997. *The Neo-Babylonian Ebabbar Temple at Sippar: its Administration and its Prosopography*. Leiden.

Borchhardt J., 1980. "Zur Deutung lykischer Audienzszenen", pp. 7–12 in H. Metzger (ed.) *Actes du colloque sur la Lycie Antique, Istanbul 1977*. Paris.

———, 2002. "Narrative Ereignis- und Historienbilder im mediterranen Raum von der Archaik bis in den Hellenismus", pp. 8–136 in M. Bietak & M. Schwarz (eds) *Krieg und Sieg: Narrative Wanddarstellungen von Altägypten bis ins Mittelalter*. Vienna.

———, ed., 1990. *Götter, Heroen, Herrscher in Lykien*. Vienna.

Börker-Klähn J., 1982. *Altorientalische Bildstelen und vergleichbare Felsreliefs*, 2 vols. Mainz.

Bossuet J. B., 1681. *Discours sur l'histoire universelle* (new edn: Paris, 1691).

———, 1770. *Histoire universelle depuis les commencements du monde jusqu'à présent, traduite de l'anglais d'une société de gens de lettres*. Amsterdam and Leipzig (nouvelle édition revue et corrigée considérablement).

Bosworth A. B., 1980. *A Historical Commentary on Arrian's History of Alexander*, vol. 1 *(Commentary on Books I–III)*. Oxford.

———, 1996. *Alexander and the East: The Tragedy of Triumph*. Oxford.

Bosworth C. E., 1993. "The Hon. George Nathaniel Curzon's travels in Russian Central Asia and Persia", *Iran* 31: 127–136.

———, 1995. "E. G. Browne and his *A Year amongst the Persians*", *Iran* 33: 115–122.

Boucharlat R., 2003. "The Persepolis area in the Achaemenid Period: some reconsiderations", pp. 260–265 in N. F. Miller & K. Abdi (eds) *Yeki bud, yeki nabud: Essays on the Archaeology of Iran in Honour of William M. Sumner*. Los Angeles.

Boucharlat R. & Lombard P., 2001. "Le bâtiment G de Rumeilah (oasis d'Al Ain). Remarques sur les salles à poteaux de l'âge du fer en péninsule d'Oman", *Iranica Antiqua* 36: 213–238.

Bourgeois B., 1992. "Conservation report", pp. 281–286 in P. O. Harper, J. Aruz & F. Tallon (eds) *The Royal City of Susa: Ancient Near Eastern Treasures in the Louvre*. New York.

Bowersock G. W., 1986. "Tylos and Tyre: Bahrain in the Graeco-Roman world," pp. 399–406 in Shaikha Haya A. al Khalifa & M. Rice (eds) *Bahrain through the Ages: the Archaeology*. London.

———, 2004. "Review of Jan Retsö, *The Arabs in Antiquity*", *American Historical Review* 109: 293.

Bowman R. A., 1970. *Aramaic Ritual Texts from Persepolis*. Chicago.

Bowsher J., 1986. "The frontier post of Medain Saleh", pp. 23–29 in P. Freeman & D. Kennedy (eds) *The Defense of the Roman and Byzantine East: Proceedings of a Colloquium held at the University of Sheffield in Paril 1986*. British Institute of Archaeology at Ankara, 8, BAR International Series, 297. Oxford.

Boyce M., 1975. *A History of Zoroastrianism*, vol. 1: *The Early Period*. Leiden and Cologne.

———, 1982. *A History of Zoroastrianism*, vol. 2: *Under the Achaemenians*. Leiden and Cologne.

———, 1984a. *Textual Sources for the Study of Zoroastrianism*. Manchester (reprinted Chicago 1990).

———, 1984b. "Persian religion in the Achaemenid Age", pp. 279–307 in W. D. Davies & L. Finkelstein (eds) *The Cambridge History of Judaism*, vol. 1: *Introduction; The Persian Period*. Cambridge.

———, 1984c. *Zoroastrians: Their Religious Beliefs & Practices*. London.

———, 1985. "Apam Napāt", *Encyclopaedia Iranica* II: 148–150

———, 1989. "Avestan People", *Encyclopaedia Iranica* III: 62–66.

———, 2005. "Further on the calendar of Zoroastrian feasts", *Iran* 43: 1–38.

Boyce M. & Grenet F. (with a contribution by R. Beck), 1991. *A History of Zoroastrianism*, vol. 3: *Zoroastrianism under Macedonian and Roman Rule*. Leiden and Cologne.

Boyce M. & Kotwal F. M., 1971. "Zoroastrian *baj* and *dron*", *Bulletin of the School of Oriental & African Studies* 34/1: 56–73; 34/2: 298–313.

Bradley-Birt F. B., 1909. *Through Persia: From the Gulf to the Caspian*. London.

Braziel J. E. & LeBesco K., eds, 2001. *Bodies out of Bounds: Fatness and Transgression*. Berkeley, CA.

Bregstein L. B., 1993. *Seal Use in Fifth Century B.C. Nippur, Iraq: A Study of Seal Selection and Sealing Practices in the Murashu Archives*. PhD dissertation, University of Pennsylvania.

Breniquet C., 2002. "Animals in Mesopotamian Art", pp. 145–68 in B. J. Collins (ed.) *A History of the Animal World in the Ancient Near East*. Handbook of Oriental Studies, 1.64. Leiden.

Breton J.-F., 1999. *Arabia Felix from the Time of the Queen of Sheba: Eighth Century B.C. to First Century A.D.* (transl. by A. LaFarge). Notre Dame, IN.

Briant P., 1984a. "La Perse avant l'empire: un état de la question", *Iranica Antiqua* 19: 71–118.

———, 1984b. *L'Asie Centrale et les royaumes proche-orientaux du premier millénaire*. Paris.

———, 1990. "Hérodote et la société perse", pp. 69–104 in G. Nenci (ed.) *Hérodote et les peuples non grecs*. Geneva; Entretiens sur l'Antiquité classique, 35.

———, 1996. *Histoire de L'Empire Perse de Cyrus à Alexandre*. Paris.

———, 1997. "Bulletin d'histoire achéménide (I)", *TOPOI*, Suppl. 1: 5–127.

———, 1999. "L'Histoire de l'empire achéménide aujourd'hui: l'historien et ses documents", *Annales HSS* 5 (Sept–Oct): 1127–1136.

———, 2001. *Bulletin d'histoire achéménide II*. Paris.

———, 2002a. *From Cyrus to Alexander: A History of the Persian Empire* (transl. by P.T. Daniels). Winona Lake, IN.

———, 2002b. "History and ideology: the Greeks and Persian decadence", pp. 193–210 in T. Harrison (ed.) *Greeks and Barbarians*. Edinburgh.

———, 2003a. *Darius dans l'ombre d'Alexandre*. Paris.

———, 2003b. "La tradition gréco-romaine sur Alexandre le Grand dans l'Europe moderne et contemporaine: quelques réflexions sur la permanence et l'adaptabilité des modèles interprétatifs", pp. 161–180 in M. Haagsma, P. den Boer & E. M. Moormann (eds) *The Impact of Classical Greece on European and National Identities*. Amsterdam.

———, 2005a. "Milestones in the development of Achaemenid historiography in the time of Ernst Herzfeld (1879–1948)", pp. 263–280 in A. Gunter & S. Hauser (eds) *Ernst Herzfeld and the Development of Near Eastern Studies 1900–1950*. Leiden and Boston.

———, 2005b. "Alexander the Great and the Enlightenment: William Robertson (1721–1793), the Empire and the road to India", *Cromohs* 10. (http://www.cromohs.unifi.it/10_2005/briant_robertson.html)

———, 2005c. "'Alexandre et l'hellénisation de l'Asie': l'histoire au passé et au présent", *Studi Ellenistici* 16: 9–69.

———, 2006a. "Retour sur Alexandre et les *katarraktes* du Tigre: l'histoire d'un dossier. (Première partie)", *Studi Ellenistici* 17: 9–67.

———, 2006b. "Montesquieu, Mably et Alexandre le Grand: aux sources de l'histoire hellénistique", *Revue Montesquieu* 8: 151–185.

———, 2007a. "Alexander and the Persian empire, between 'decadence' and 'renewal': history and historiography".

———, 2007b. "Montesquieu et ses sources: Alexandre, l'empire perse, les Guèbres et l'irrigation", *Studies on Voltaire and the Eighteenth Century* 6: 243–262.

Brisson B., 1590. *De Regio persarum principatu libri tres*. Paris.

Broodbank C., 2000. *An Island Archaeology of the Early Cyclades*. Cambridge.

Brosius M., 1990. "Two views on Persian history in eighteenth century England", pp. 79–89 in H. Sancisi-Weerdenburg & J. W. Drijvers (eds) *Achaemenid History V: The Roots of the European Tradition*. Leiden.

———, 1991. "Royal and Non-royal Women in Achaemenid Persia (559–331 BC)." D.Phil. thesis, University of Oxford.

———, 1996. *Women in Ancient Persia (559–331 BC)*. Oxford.

———, 2000. *The Persian Empire from Cyrus II to Artaxerxes I*. The London Association of Classical Teachers, 16. London.

———, 2007. "New out of old? Court and court ceremonies in Achaemenid Persia", pp. 17–57 in A. Spawforth (ed.) *The Court and Court Society in Ancient Monarchies*. Cambridge.

Brown E. A. R., 1974. "Feudalism: The tyranny of a construct", *American Historical Review* 79: 1063–1088.

Browne E. G., 1926. *A Year Amongst the Persians: Impressions as to the Life, Character and Thought of the People of Persia. Received during Twelve Months' Residence in that Country in the years 1887-1888 by EGB. With a Memoir by Sir E. Denison Ross*. Cambridge (originally published 1893).

Brünnow R. & von Domaszewski A., 1904. *Die provincia Arabia*. Vol. 1. Strasburg.

Brusasco P., 1999/2000. "Family archives and the social use of space in Old Babylonian houses at Ur", *Mesopotamia* 34/35: 3–173.

———, 2004. "Theory and practice in the study of Mesopotamian domestic space", *Antiquity* 78/299: 142–157.

Bruyère M. B., 1926. *Rapport sur les fouilles de Deir el Médineh (1924–1925)*. Cairo.
Buchanan B., 1966. *Catalogue of Ancient Near Eastern Seals in the Ashmolean Museum I: Cylinder Seals*. Oxford.
Buchanan B. & Moorey P. R. S., 1988. *Catalogue of Ancient Near Eastern Seals in the Ashmolean Museum III: The Iron Age Stamp Seals (c.1200–350 BC)*. Oxford.
Bunbury E. H., 1879. *A History of Ancient Geography*, vol. 1. London.
Burgess C. & Burgess E., 1942. *Letters from Persia. Written by Charles and Edward Burgess 1828–1855.* (edited by Benjamin Schwartz). New York.
Burn A. R., 1962. *Persia and the Greeks*. New York.
Bury R. de, 1760. *Histoire de Philippe et d'Alexandre le Grand, rois de Macédoine*. Paris.
Butz K., 1979. "Ur in altbabylonischer Zeit als Wirtschaftsfaktor", pp. 257–409 in E. Lipinski (ed.) *State and Temple Economy in the Ancient Near East*, vol. 1. Leuven.
Byron R., 1982. *The Road to Oxiana*. New York (first edition, London 1937).
Byvanck-Quarles van Ufford L., 1970. "Les bols hellénistiques en verre doré", *Bulletin Antieke Beschaving* 45: 129–141.
———, 1991. " 'Achämenidischer Beche' ou 'bols ionien à panse arrondie'?", *Bulletin Antieke Beschaving* 66: 159–163.
Cahill N., 1985. "The treasury at Persepolis: gift-giving at the city of the Persians", *American Journal of Archaeology* 89: 373–389.
———, 1988. "Taş Kule: A Persian-Period tomb near Phokaia", *American Journal of Archaeology* 92/4: 481–501.
Callieri P., 1990. "Archaeological activities at Bir-Kotghwandai, Swat: A contribution of the study of the pottery of early historic age from the NWFP", *South Asian Archaeology 1987*: 675–692.
———, 1997. *Seals and Sealings from the North-west of the Indian Subcontinent and Afghanistan (4th century BC–11th century AD): Local, Indian, Sasanian, Graeco-Persian, Sogdian, Roman*. Naples.
———, 1998. "A proposito di un'iconografia monetale dei dinasti del Fars post-achemenide", *OCNUS* 6: 25–38.
———, 2001. "L'Iran nel periodo macedone e seleucide", pp. 101–111 in *Antica Persica. I tesori del Museo Nazionale di Tehran e la ricerca italiana in Iran*. Rome.
———, 2004. "Again on the chronology of the Tall-e Takht at Pasargadae", *Parthica* 6: 95–100.
Callieri P., Filigenzi A. & Stacul G., 1990. "Excavation at Bir-kot-ghwandat, Swat: 1987", *Pakistan Archaeology* 25: 163–192.

Callieri P., Brocato P., Filigenzi A., Nascari M. & Olivieri L. M., 1992. *Bir-kot-ghwanfai 1990–1992. A Preliminary Report on the Excavations of the Italian Archaeological Mission, IsMEO*. IsMEO, Supplemento n. 73 agli Annali-IUO, 52/4. Naples.
Calmeyer P., 1975. "Zur Genese altiranischer Motive, III: Felsgräber", *Archaeologische Mitteilungen aus Iran* (N.F.) 8: 99–113.
———, 1976. "Zur Genese altiranischer Motive, IV: 'Persönliche Krone' und Diadem", *Archäologische Mitteilungen aus Iran* (N.F.) 9: 45–63.
———, 1977. "Vom Reisehut zu Kaiserkrone", *Archäologische Mitteilungen aus Iran* (N.F.) 10: 182–185.
———, 1979a. "Fortuna-Tyche-Khvarna", *Jahrbuch des Deutschen Archäologischen Instituts* 94: 347–365.
———, 1979b. "Zur Genese altiranischer Motive: VI Toxotai", *Archäologische Mitteilungen aus Iran* (N.F.) 12: 303–313.
———, 1989. "Die roten Schuhe", *Archäologische Mitteilungen aus Iran* 22: 133, pl. I.
———, 1993. "Die Gefässe auf den Gabenbringer-Reliefs in Persepolis", *Archäologische Mitteilungen aus Iran* 26: 147–160, taf. 43–50.
Cameron G. G., 1941. "Darius and Xerxes in Babylonia, IV: Xerxes and the Babylonian revolts", *American Journal of Semitic Languages* 58: 319–325.
———, 1948. *Persepolis Treasury Tablets*. Oriental Institute Publications [OIP], 65. Chicago.
———, 1958. "Persepolis treasury tablets old and new", *Journal of Near Eastern Studies* 17/3: 161–176.
———, 1959. "The 'Daiva' Inscription of Xerxes in Elamite", *Die Welt des Orients* 2: 470–476.
Canby J. V., 1979. "A note on some Susan bricks", *Archäologische Mitteilungen aus Iran* (N.F.) 12: 315–320.
Caquot A., 1998. Review of Van der Toorn 1996. *Bibliotheca Orientalis* 55: 225–229.
Carradice I., 1987. "The 'regal' coinage of the Persian Empire", pp. 73–95 in *Coinage and Administration in the Athenian and Persian Empires*. BAR International Series, 343. Oxford.
———, 1998a. "Two Achaemenid hoards", *Numismatic Chronicle* 158: 1–23.
———, 1998b. "The Dinar hoard of Persian sigloi", pp. 65–81 in R. Ashton & S. Hurter (eds) *Studies in Greek Numismatics in Memory of Martin Jessop Price*. London.
Carroll M., 1960. *From a Persian Tea-house*. London.
Carter C. E., 1999. *The Emergence of Yehud in the Persian Period: A Social and Demographic Study*. Sheffield.
Carter E., 1994. "Bridging the gap between the Elamites and the Persians in southeastern

Khuzistan", pp. 55–95 in H. Sancisi-Weerdenburg, A. Kuhrt & M. C. Root (eds) *Achaemenid History VIII: Continuity and Change. Proceedings of the Last Achaemenid History Workshop, Apr. 6–8, 1990—Ann Arbor, Michigan*. Leiden.

Cartledge P., 1987. *Agesilaos and the Rise of Sparta*. Baltimore.

———, 1998. "The *machismo* of the Athenian Empire—or the reign of the *phaulus*?", pp. 54–67 in L. Foxhall & J. Salmon (eds) *When Men Were Men. Masculinity, Power and Identity in Classical Antiquity*. London.

Casabonne O., 1996. "Présence et influence perses en Cilicie à l'époque achéménide—iconographie et représentation", *Anatolia Antiqua* 4: 121–145.

———, 2004a. *La Cilicie à l'époque Achéménide*. Paris.

———, 2004b. "Le Grand Roi ou Dieu?", *ARTA* 2: on www.achemenet.com

Cassio A., 1985. "Old Persian Marika, Eupolis *Marikas* and Aristophanes *Knights*", *Classical Quarterly* (N.S.) 35: 38–42.

Caubet A., 1992. "Achaemenid brick decoration", pp. 223–225 in P. O. Harper, J. Aruz & F. Tallon (eds) *The Royal City of Susa: Ancient Near Eastern Treasures in the Louvre*. New York.

———, 2003. "Le temple d'Inshushinak de Suse et l'architecture monumentale en 'faïence'", pp. 325–332 in T. F. Potts, M. D. Roaf & D L. Stein (eds) *Culture Through Objects: Ancient Near Eastern Studies in Honour of P. R. S. Moorey*. Oxford.

Caubet A. & Gaborit-Chopin D., 2004. *Ivoires de l'Orient ancien aux temps Modernes*. Paris.

Caubet A. & Muscarella O. W., 1992. "The Achaemenid brick decoration", pp. 223–241 in P. O. Harper, J. Aruz & F. Tallon (eds) *The Royal City of Susa: Ancient Near Eastern Treasures in the Louvre*. New York.

Caubet A. & Pierrat-Bonnefois G., 2005. *Faïences de l'Antiquité. De l'Egypte à l'Iran*. Exposition dossier musée du Louvre.

Chakrabarti D. K., 1995. *The Archaeology of Ancient Indian Cities*. Delhi.

Chardin J., 1711. *Voyages en Perse et autres lieux de l'Orient*. Amsterdam (3 vols; reprinted 1730).

Charpin D., 1989. "Un quartier de Nippur et le problème des écoles à l'epoque paléo-babylonienne", *Revue d'Assyriologie* 83: 97–112.

———, 1996. "Maison et maisonnées en Babylonie ancienne de Sippar à Ur", pp. 221–228 in K. R. Veenhof (ed.) *Houses and Households in Ancient Mesopotamia*. Leiden.

———, 2003. "La politique immobilière des marchands de Larsa à la lumière des découvertes épigraphiques de 1987 et 1989", pp. 311–322 in J.-L. Huot (ed.) *Larsa: travaux de 1987 et 1989*. Institut Français d'Archéologie du Proche-Orient, BAH, 165. Beirut.

Chaybany J., 1971. *Les voyages en Perse et la pensée française au XVIIIè siècle*. Tehran.

Chevalier N., 1992. "The French scientific delegation in Persia", pp. 16–19 in P. O. Harper, J. Aruz & F. Tallon (eds) *The Royal City of Susa: Ancient Near Eastern Treasures in the Louvre*. New York.

———, 1997a. "La mission en Perse de Jacques de Morgan", pp. 12–17 in N. Chevalier (ed.) *Une Mission en Perse: 1897-1912*. Paris.

———, 1997b. "La découverte de la Perse antique par les voyageurs français au début du XIXe siècle", pp. 24–35 in N. Chevalier (ed.) *Une Mission en Perse: 1897–1912*. Paris.

Chileyko W., 1925. "'Pechat' Tsar Artakserksa", *Zhizn Muzeya* 1 (May): 17–19.

Christensen A., 1936. *Les gestes des rois dans les traditions de l'Iran*. Paris.

———, 1941. *Essai sur la démonologie iranienne*. Copenhagen.

Cibber C., 1699. *Xerxes, A Tragedy, As it is Acted at the New Theatre in Little Lincoln's-inn Fields*. London.

Clark K., 1956. *The Nude: A Study in Ideal Form*. Princeton.

Clarke M.-L., 1945. *Greek Studies in England (1700-1830)*. Cambridge.

Clay A. T., 1904. *Business Documents of Murashu Sons of Nippur: Dated in the Reign of Darius II (424–404)* (BE x), Philadelphia.

———, 1912. *Business Documents of Murashu Sons of Nippur: Dated in the Reign of Darius II*, (PBS II i), Philadelphia.

Clines D. J., 1984. *Ezra, Nehemiah, Esther*. The New Century Bible Commentary. Grand Rapids, MI.

Collins E. T., 1896. *In the Kingdom of the Shah. The Journey of a Medical Man through Persia*. London.

Collins R., 1974. *The Medes and Persians*. London.

Collon D., 1987. *First Impressions: Cylinder Seals in the Ancient Near East*. London.

———, 1995. *Ancient Near Eastern Art*. London.

———, 1996. "A hoard of sealings from Ur", pp. 65–84 in M.-F. Boussac & A. Invernizzi (eds) *Archives et Sceaux du Monde Hellénistique*. BCH Supplément 29.

———, 2001. *Catalogue of Western Asiatic Seals in the British Museum. Cylinder Seals V. Neo-Assyrian and Neo-Babylonian Periods*. London.

Condillac É. B. de, 1775. *Cours d'étude pour l'instruction du Prince de Parme*, vol.5. Parme.

Coningham R., and Ali I., 2007. *Charsadda. The British-Pakistani Excavations at the Bala Hisar*. BAR S1709. Oxford.

Coningham R. A. E., 2004. "The Bala Hisar of *Charsadda*: an exhibition in ten parts", http://www.brad.ac.uk/archsci/depart/resgrp/southasia/charsadda/

Cook J. M., 1983. *The Persian Empire*. London.

Cooney J. D., 1965. "Persian influence in Late Egyptian art", *Journal of the American Research Center in Egypt* 4: 39–48.

Corneille T., 1662. *Darius, tragédie*. Paris.

Cottica D. & Rova E., 2006. "Fuso e rocca: un percorso fra Occidente e Oriente alla ricerca delle origini di una simbologia", pp. 291–322 in D. Morandi Bonacossi, E. Rova, F. Veronese & P. Zanovello (eds) *Tra Oriente e Occidente. Miscellanea in onore di Elena Di Filippo*. Padua.

Cowell M. R. & Hyne K., 2000. "Scientific examination of the Lydian Precious Metal Coinage", pp. 169–174 in A. Ramage & P. Craddock (eds) *King Croesus' Gold: Excavations at Sardis and the History of Gold Refining*. Archaeological Exploration of Sardis, 11. London.

Cowley A. E., 1923. *Aramaic Papyri of the Fifth Century B.C.* Oxford.

Crown J., 1688. *Darius; King of Persia. A Tragedy. As it is Acted by Their Majesties Servants*. London.

Culican W., 1975. "Syro-Achaemenian Ampullae", *Iranica Antiqua* 11: 100–112.

Cunningham A., 1883. "Relics from ancient Persia in gold, silver and copper: third notice", *Journal of the Asiatic Society of Bengal* (52): 258–260.

Curtis C. D., 1925. *Sardis XIII. Jewelry and Gold Work*. Rome.

Curtis J. E., 1993. "William Kennett Loftus and his excavations at Susa", *Iranica Antiqua* 28: 1–55.

———, 1997a. "Les fouilles de W. K. Loftus à Suse", pp. 36–45 in N. Chevalier (ed.) *Une Mission en Perse: 1897–1912*. Paris.

———, 1997b. "Franks and the Oxus Treasure", pp. 230–249 in M. Caygill & J. Cherry (eds) *A. W. Franks. Nineteenth-century Collecting and the British Museum*. London.

———, 2004. "The Oxus Treasure in the British Museum", *Ancient Civilizations* 10/3–4: 293–338.

———, 2005a. "The material culture of Tepe Nush-i Jan and the end of the Iron Age III Period in Western Iran", *Iranica Antiqua* 40: 233–248.

———, 2005b. "The Archaeology of the Achaemenid Period", pp. 30–49 in J. E. Curtis & N. Tallis (eds) *Forgotten Empire: The World of Ancient Persia*. London.

———, 2005c. "Jewellery and personal ornaments", pp. 132–136 in J. Curtis & N. Tallis (eds) *Forgotten Empire: The World of Ancient Persia*. London.

Curtis J. E. & Razmjou S., 2005. "The Palace", pp. 50–55 in J. Curtis & N. Tallis (eds) *Forgotten Empire: The World of Ancient Persia*. London.

Curtis J. E. & Tallis N., eds, 2005. *Forgotten Empire: The World of Ancient Persia*. London.

Curtis J. E., Cowell M. R. & Walker C. B. F., 1995. "A silver bowl of Artaxerxes I", *Iran* 33: 149–53, pls XXVI–XXVIII.

Curtis V. S. & Simpson St J., 1998. "Archaeological news from Iran: Second report", *Iran* 36: 185–194.

———, 2007. "Religious iconography on ancient Iranian coins", pp. 413–434 in J. Cribb and G. Herrmann (eds) *After Alexander: Central Asia before Islam*. Oxford and New York.

Curzon G., 1892. *Persia and the Persian Question*. 2 vols. London and New York.

D'Ablancourt N. P., 1646. *Les Guerres d'Alexandre par Arrian*. Paris.

———, 1972. *Lettres et préfaces critiques* (ed. R. Zuber). Paris.

Daems A., 2001. "The iconography of pre-Islamic women in Iran", *Iranica Antiqua* 36: 1–150.

Dalton O. M., 1964. *The Treasure of the Oxus with Other Examples of Early Oriental Metal-work*. (rev. edn.). London.

D'Amore P., 1992. "Glittica a cilindro achemenide: linee di uno sviluppo tematico-cronologico", *Contributi e Materiali di Archeologia Orientale* 4: 187–267.

Dandamayev M. A., 1976. *Persien unter den ersten Achaemeniden*. Wiesbaden.

———, 1981. "The neo-Babylonian citizens", *Klio* 63: 45–49.

———, 1989a. *The Cultural and Social Institutions of Ancient Iran*. Princeton.

———, 1989b. *A Political History of the Achaemenid Empire (Politicheskaia istoriia Akhemenidskoi derzhavy)*. Leiden and New York.

———, 1999. "Achaemenid Imperial Policies and Provincial Governments", *Iranica Antiqua* 34: 269–282 (Neo-Assyrian, Median, Achaemenian and other studies in honour of David Stronach).

———, 2005. "Freedom and slavery in the Ancient Near East during the Neo-Babylonian and Achaemenid periods", pp. 217–227 in R. Rollinger (ed.) *Von Sumer bis Homer: Festschrift für Manfred Schretter*. Alter Orient und Altes Testament [AOAT], 325. Kevelaer and Neukirchen-Vluyn.

Dandamayev M. A. & Lukonin V. G., 1989. *The Culture and Social Institutions of Ancient Iran*. (English edn. by Philip L. Kohl with the assistance of D. J. Dadson). Cambridge and New York.

Dani A. H., 1965–66. "Shaikhan Dheri excavation 1963 & 1964 seasons (in search of the second city of Pushkalavati)". *Ancient Pakistan* 2: 17–214.

———, 1967. "Timargarha and the Gandharan grave culture", *Ancient Pakistan* 3: 22–90.

———, 1970/71. "Excavations in the Gomal Valley", *Ancient Pakistan* 5: 1–77.

D'Anville B., 1764. "Recherches géographiques sur le golfe Persique, et sur les bouches de l'Euphrate et du Tigre", *Mémoires de littérature, tirés des registres de l'Académie Royale des Inscriptions et Belles-Lettres* 30: 132–197.

Da Riva R., 2008. *The Neo-Babylonian Royal Inscriptions: An Introduction*. Guides to the Mesopotamian Textual Record, 4. Münster.

Darmesteter J., transl., 1880. *The Zend-Avesta, Part I: The Vendîdâd*. Sacred Books of the East, IV. Oxford.

———, transl., 1888. "L'inscription araméenne de Limyra", *Journal Asiatique* 8/12: 508–510.

Daucé N. & Nguyen J., 2003. *Recherche sur les briques achéménides de Suse en terre cuite à décor mythologique*, Monographie de 4ᵉ année de l'Ecole du Louvre, manuscrit, archives du Departement des Antiquites Orientales.

Davies W. & Fouracre P., eds, 1986. *The Settlement of Disputes in Early Medieval Europe*. Cambridge.

de Blois F., 1985. "'Freemen' and 'nobles' in Iranian and Semitic languages", *Journal of the Royal Asiatic Society*: 5–15.

———, 1989. "Maka and Mazun", *Studia Iranica* 18: 157–167.

de Jong A., 1997. *Traditions of the Magi: Zoroastrianism in Greek and Latin Literature*. Leiden.

———, 2003. "Vexilologica sacra: searching the cultic banner", pp. 191–202 in C. G. Cereti, M. Maggi & E. Provasi (eds) *Religious Themes and Texts of Pre-Islamic Iran and Central Asia. Studies in Honour of Professor Gherardo Gnoli on the Occasion of his 65th Birthday on 6th December 2002*. Wiesbaden.

———, 2005. "The Contribution of the Magi", pp. 85–99 in V. S. Curtis & S. Stewart (eds), *Birth of the Persian Empire*. London.

———, 2009. "The culture of writing and the use of the Avesta in Sasanian Iran", pp. 27–41 in E. Pirart & X. Tremblay (eds) *Zarathushtra entre l'Inde et l'Iran. Etudes indo-iraniennes et indo-européennes offertes à Jean Kellens à l'occasion de son 65e anniversaire*. Wiesbaden.

———, forthcoming *a*. "Religion at the Achaemenid court", in B. Jacobs & R. Rollinger (eds) *Der Achämenidenhof*. Stuttgart.

———, forthcoming *b*. *Les quatre phases de la religion mazdéenne. Quatre leçons au Collège de France*. Paris.

———, forthcoming *c*. "Iranian connections in the Dead Sea Scrolls", in J. J. Collins & T. Lim (eds) *The Oxford Handbook to the Dead Sea Scrolls*. Oxford.

———, forthcoming *d*. "Iran", in D. Frankfurter & H. S. Versnel (eds) *Brill's Guide to Ancient Magic*. Leiden.

de Le Ferie, 1723. *Alexandre et Darius. Tragédie*. Paris.

de Lorey E. & Sladen D., 1907. *Queer Things about Persia*. London.

de Mably G. B., 1749. *Observations sur les Grecs*. Genève.

———, 1766. *Observations sur l'histoire de la Grèce ou des causes de la prospérité et des malheurs de la Grèce*. 2nd edn. Genève.

———, 1778. *De l'étude de l'histoire, à Monseigneur le duc de Parme*, nouvelle édition revue et corrigée. Maastricht and Paris (reprinted as *Oeuvres complètes de l'abbé Mably*, XII, Lyon, 1796, pp. 1–318).

———, 1783. *De la manière d'écrire l'histoire*. Paris (reprinted as *Oeuvres complètes de l'abbé de Mably*, XII, Lyon, 1796, pp. 321–500).

de Maillet B., 1735. *Description de l'Égypte contenant plusieurs remarques curieuses sur la géographie ancienne et moderne de ce païs, sur les monuments anciens, sur les mœurs, les coutumes, et la religion des habitants, sur le gouvernement et le commerce, sur les animaux, les arbres, les plantes etc..., composée sur les mémoires de M. de Maillet, ancien consul de France au Caire, par M. L'Abbé Le Mascrier, enrichi de cartes et de figures*. Paris.

Demange F., ed., 2000. *La Mésopotamie entre le Tigre et l'Euphrate*. Tokyo.

De Mecquenem R., 1947. "Contribution à l'étude du palais achéménide", pp. 1–119 in R. De Mecquenem, L. Le Breton & M. Rutten. *Archéologie Susienne*. Mémoires de la Mission Archéologique en Iran, 30. Paris.

De Mecquenem R., Le Breton L. & Rutten M. 1947. *Archéologie Susienne*. Mémoires de la Mission Archéologique en Iran, 30. Paris.

de Menasce P. R. J., 1943. "Observation sur l'Inscription de Xerxes a Persepolis", *Vivre et Penser* 1943: 124–132.

de Morgan J., 1905. "Découverte d'une sépulture achéménide à Suse", *Mémoires de la Délégation en Perse* 8: 29–58, pl. 5.

de Pauw M., 1768. *Recherches philosophiques sur les Américains ou mémoires intéressants pour servir à l'histoire de l'espèce humaine*, I. Berlin.

Descat R., 1995. "Darius Iᵉʳ et la monnaie", *Annali Istituto italiano di numismatica* 42: 9–20.

Descat R., ed., 1989. *L'Or perse et l'histoire grecque*. Revue des Études Anciennes, 91. Paris.

Deutsches Archäologisches Institut, "Arzhan—Eine skythische Fürstennekropole in Tuva, Südsibirien. Vollständige Freilegung des Kurgans Arzhan 2 mit einem unberaubten Fürstengrab (6./5. Jh. v. Chr.)". http://www.dainst.org/index_596_en.html

de Vries K., 1977. "Attic Pottery in the Achaemenid Empire", *American Journal of Archaeology* 81/4: 544–548.

de Windt H., 1891. *A Ride to India across Persia and Baluchistan*. London.

Diakonoff I. M., 1985. "Media", pp. 36–148 in I. Gershevitch (ed.) *Cambridge History of Iran Volume 2: The Median and the Achaemenian Periods*. Cambridge.

Diakonoff I. M. & Livshits V. A., 2001. *Parthian Economic Documents from Nisa: Texts I*. Corpus Inscriptionum Iranicarum Pt. II, vol. II. London.

Dieulafoy M., 1893. *L'acropole de Suse, d'après les fouilles exécutées en 1884, 1885, 1886*. Paris.

Diringer D., 1968. *The Alphabet: A Key to the History of Mankind*, vol. 2. London.

Dittmann R., 1984. "Problems in the identification of an Achaemenid and Mauryan horizon", *Archaeologische Mitteilungen aus Iran* 17: 155–193.

Dodds M., 1929. *Les récits de voyages sources de l'Esprit des Lois de Montesquieu* (reprinted Genève, 1980).

Donbaz V. & Stolper, M. W., 1997. *Istanbul Murašû Text*. Leiden.

Donner H., 1995. *Geschichte des Volkes Israel und seiner Nachbarn in Grundzügen*, vol. 2: *Von der Königszeit bis zu Alexander dem Großen*. Göttingen.

Doty L. T., 1977. "Cuneiform archives from Hellenistic Uruk". PhD thesis, Yale University.

Dougherty R. P., 1920. *Records from Erech, Time of Nabonidus (555–538 B.C.)*. Yale Oriental Series, Babylonian Texts 6. New Haven.

———, 1923. *Archives from Erech, Time of Nebuchadnezzar and Nabonidus*. Goucher College Cuneiform Inscriptions, 1. New Haven.

Doughty C. M., 1888. *Travels in Arabia Deserta*. Cambridge.

Driver G. R., 1957. *Aramaic Documents of the Fifth Century B.C.* Oxford.

Duchesne-Guillemin J., 1962. *La religion de l'Iran ancien*. Paris.

———, 1970. "Zoroaster und das Abendland", pp. 217–252 in B. Schlerath (ed.) *Zarathustra*. Wege der Forschung, CLXIX. Stuttgart.

Duhard J.-P., 1990. "Le corps féminin et son language dans l'art paléolithique", *Oxford Journal of Archaeology* 9/3: 241–255.

———, 1991. "The shape of Pleistocene women", *Antiquity* 65: 552–561.

Durand E. R., 1902. *An Autumn Tour in Western Persia*. London.

Dusinberre E. R. M., 1997. "Imperial style and constructed identity: a "Graeco-Persian" cylinder seal from Sardis", *Ars Orientalis* 27: 99–129.

———, 1999. "Satrapal Sardis: Achaemenid bowls in an Achaemenid capital", *American Journal of Archaeology* 103: 73–102.

———, 2000. "King or God? Imperial iconography and the 'Tiarate Head' coins of Achaemenid Anatolia", *Annual of the American Schools of Oriental Research* 57: 157–171.

———, 2003. *Aspects of Empire in Achaemenid Sardis*. Cambridge.

———, 2005. *Gordion Seals and Sealings: Individuals and Society*. University of Pennsylvania Museum of Archaeology and Anthropology Monographs, 124, Gordion Special Studies, 3. Philadelphia, PA.

———, 2009. "Circles of light and Achaemenid hegemonic style in Gordion's Seal 100", pp. 87–98, pl. 11 in N. D. Cahill (ed.) *Love for Lydia: A Sardis Anniversary Volume Presented to Crawford H. Greenewalt, Jr*. Archaeological Exploration of Sardis, 4. Cambridge, MA and London.

Dutz W. F. & Matheson S. A. 2000. *Parsa (Persepolis)*. Tehran.

Dyson S. L., 1985. *Comparative Studies in the Archaeology of Colonialism*. BAR International Series, 233. Oxford.

Easby D. T., 1974. "Early metallurgy in the New World. New World archaeology". *Scientific American*: 249–256.

Eastwick E., 1864. *Three Years' Residence in Persia*. London.

Edmonds C. J., 1934. "A tomb in Kurdistan", *Iraq* 1: 183–192, pls XXIII–XXVII.

Ehrenberg E., 1999. *Uruk: Late Babylonian Seal Impressions on Eanna-Tablets*. Ausgrabungen in Uruk-Warka, Endberichte 18. Mainz am Rhein.

———, 2001. "Urukaean seal impressions at Yale", pp. 185–196 in W. W. Hallo & I. J. Winter (eds) *Seals and Seal Impressions. Proceedings of the XLVe Rencontre Assyriologique Internationale. Part II: Yale University*. Bethesda, MD.

Eichmann R., Hausleiter A. & Schaudig H., 2006. "Archaeology and epigraphy at Tayma (Saudi Arabia)", *Arabian Archaeology and Epigraphy* 17: 163–176.

Eilers W., 1971. "Der Keilschrifttext des Kyros-Zylinders", *Festgabe deutscher Iranisten zur 2500 Jahrfeier Irans*. Stuttgart.

———, 1983. "Das Volk der Maka vor und nach den Achämeniden", pp. 101–119 in H. Koch &

D. N. MacKenzie (eds) *Kunst, Kultur und Geschichte der Achämenidenzeit und ihr Fortleben*. Archäologische Mitteilungen aus Iran, Ergänzungsband 10. Berlin.

———, 1989. "Banda. i. the term", *Encyclopedia Iranica* III: 682–683.

Elfenbein, J., 2001. "Splendour and Fortune", pp. 485–496 in *Philologica et Linguistica. Historia, Pluralitas, Universitas, Festschrift für Helmut Humbach zum 80. Geburtstag am 4. Dezember 2001*. Trier.

Ellis R. S., 1968. *Foundation Deposits in Ancient Mesopotamia*. Yale Near Eastern Researches, 2. New Haven.

Enault J.-F., 1979. *Fouilles de Pirak*, vol. 2: *Étude Architecturale et Figures*. Fouilles de Pakistan, 2. Paris.

Eph'al I., 1982. *The Ancient Arabs: Nomads on the Borders of the Fertile Crescent, 9th-5th Centuries B.C.* Jerusalem.

Evans A. S., 1988. "The story of Pythius", *Liverpool Classical Monthly* 13: 139.

Farkas A., 1974. *Achaemenid Sculpture*. Leiden.

Fellows C., 1841. *An Account of Discoveries in Lycia; Being a Journal Kept during a Second Excursion in Asia Minor*. London.

Fensham F. C., 1982. *The Books of Ezra and Nehemiah*. Grand Rapids, MI.

Ferrier R. W., 1982. *History of the British Petroleum Company*, vol. 1: *The Developing Years 1901–1932*. Cambridge.

Feuerherm K., 2007. "Architectural features of Larsa's urban dwelling B 27 and division of inheritance", *Journal of Near Eastern Studies* 66: 193–204.

Filigenzi A. & Stacul G., 1985. "Excavations at Bir-kot Ghwandai", *East and West* 35/4: 430–439.

Filow B. D., 1934. *Die Grabhügelnekropole bei Duvanlij in Südbulgarien*. Sofia.

Finkelstein I., 1993. "The southern Samarian hills survey", pp. 1313–1314 in E. Stern (ed.) *The New Encyclopedia of Archaeological Excavations in the Holy Land*, vol. IV. Jerusalem.

Firdausī, 1905–25. *The Shāhnāma of Firdausī*. London (trans. A. G. & E. Warner; 9 vols) (Tehran 1956, ed. M. Dabīrsiāghi, 6 vols in Persian).

Fleming D., 1982. "Achaemenid Sattagydia and the geography of Vivana's campaign (DB III, 54-75)", *Journal of the Royal Asiatic Society* 2: 102–122.

———, 2002. "Achaemenid Indian gold", pp. 95–101 in W. Ball & L. Harrow (eds) *Afghan and Islamic Studies Presented to Ralph Pinder-Wilson*. London.

Forrest D. M., 1982. *Foursome in St. James's: The Story of the East India, Devonshire, Sports, and Public Schools Club*. London.

Fossing P., 1937. "Drinking bowls of glass and metal from the Achaemenian time", *Berytus* 4: 121–129.

———, 1940. *Glass Vessels before Glass Blowing*. Copenhagen.

Foster B. R., 2005. *Before the Muses. An Anthology of Akkadian Literature*. 3rd edn. Bethesda, MD.

Fowler G., 1841. *Three Years in Persia; With Travelling Adventures in Koordistan*. London.

Fowler M. D., 1984. "Excavated incense burners", *The Biblical Archaeologist* 47/3 (Sept): 183–186.

Frame G., 1992. *Babylonia 689–627 B.C.: A Political History*. Leiden.

Francfort H.-P., 1988. "Central Asia and Eastern Iran", pp. 165–193 in J. Boardman, N. G. L. Hammond, D. M. Lewis & M. Oswald (eds) *Cambridge Ancient History*, vol. 4: *Persia, Greece and the Western Mediterranean c.525–479 B.C.* 2nd edn. Cambridge.

———, 2005. "La civilization de l'Oxus et les Indo-Iraniens et Indo-aryens", pp. 253–328 in G. Fussman (ed.) *Āryas, aryens et Iraniens en Asie centrale*. Publications de l'"Institut de civilisation indienne, 72. Paris.

Franke-Vogt U., 2001. "The Southern Indus Valley during the later 2nd and 1st millennia B.C.", pp. 247–290 in R. Eichmann & H. Parzinger (eds) *Migrations und Kulturtransfer. Der Wandel vorder- und zentralasiatischer Kulturen im Umbruch vom. 2. zum 1. vorchristlichen Jahrtausend*. Bonn.

Frankfort H., 1996. *The Art and Architecture of the Ancient Orient* (with notes by M. Roaf & D. Matthews). New Haven.

Frascari M., 1991. *Monsters of Architecture: Anthropomorphism in Architectural Theory*. Savage, MD.

Fried L. S., 2001. "'You shall appoint judges': Ezra's mission and the rescript of Artaxerxes", pp. 63–89 in J. W. Watts (ed.) *Persia and Torah: The Theory of Imperial Authorization of the Pentateuch*. SBL Symposium Series, 17. Atlanta, GA

———, 2002. "The high places (bāmôt) and the reforms of Hezekiah and Josiah: An archaeological investigation", *Journal of the American Oriental Society* 122: 437–465.

———, 2004. *The Priest and the Great King: Temple-Palace Relations in the Persian Empire*. Biblical and Judaic Studies from the University of California, San Diego, 10. Winona Lake, IN.

———, 2006. "The 'am ha'aretz in Ezra 4:4 and Persian imperial administration", pp. 123–145 in O. Lipschits & M. Oeming (eds) *Judah and Judaeans in the Achaemenid Period*. Winona Lake, IN.

Fromkin D., 1991. "The importance of T. E. Lawrence", *The New Criterion* 10 (Sept), http://www.newcriterion.com/archive/10/sept91/fromkin.htm

Frye R. N., 1972. "Gestures of deference to royalty in ancient Iran", *Iranica Antiqua* 9: 102–107.

———, 1974. "Persepolis again", *Journal of Near Eastern Studies* 33: 383–386.

———, 1984. "Religion in Fars under the Achaemenids", pp. 171–178 in *Orientalia J. Duchesne-Guillemin emerito oblata*. Acta Iranica, 23. Leiden.

———, 1989. *Central Asian Concept of Rule on the Steppe and Sown. Ecology and Empire: Nomads in the Cultural Evolution of the Old World*. Proceedings of the Soviet-American academic symposia in conjunction with the museum exhibition, "Nomads: Masters of the Eurasian Steppe", Los Angeles.

Frymer-Kensky T., 1992. *In the Wake of the Goddesses: Women, Culture and the Biblical Transformation of Pagan Myth*. New York.

Fukai S., 1977. *Persian Glass*. New York, Tokyo and Kyoto.

Fukai S. & Matsutani T., 1977. "Preliminary report of survey and soundings at Halimehjan, 1976", *Orient* 13: 41–60.

———, 1980. "Preliminary report of survey and soundings at Halimehjan, 1978", *Orient* 16: 149–172.

Funk R. W., 1993. "Beth-Zur", pp. 259–261 in E. Stern (ed.) *The New Encyclopedia of Archaeological Excavations in the Holy Land*, vol. 1. Jerusalem.

Fussman, G., 2005. "Entre fantasmes, science et politique: l'entrée des Āryas en Inde", pp. 197–233 in G. Fussman (ed.) *Āryas, aryens et Iraniens en Asie centrale*. Publications de l'"Institut de civilisation indienne, 72. Paris.

Galerie Koller, 1979. *The Ernest Brummer Collection. Ancient Art*, vol. 2. Zurich.

Garland R., 1995. *The Eye of the Beholder. Deformity and Disability in the Greco-Roman World*. London.

Garrison M. B., 1988. "Seal Workshops and Artists in Persepolis: A Study of Seal Impressions Preserving the Theme of Heroic Encounter on the Persepolis Fortification and Treasury Tablets (Volumes I–III)." PhD dissertation, Classical Art & Archaeology, University of Michigan.

———, 1991. "Seals and the elite at Persepolis: Some observations on early Achaemenid Persian art", *Ars Orientalis* 21: 1–29.

———, 1996. "The identification of artists and workshops in sealed archival contexts: The evidence from Persepolis", pp. 29–51 in M.-F. Boussac & A. Invernizzi (eds) *Archives et sceaux du monde hellénistique. Archivi e sigilli nel mondo ellenistico. Torino, Villa Gualino 13–16 Gennaio 1993*. Bulletin de Correspondance Hellénique Supplément, 29. Athens.

———, 2000. "Achaemenid iconography as evidenced by glyptic art: Subject matter, social function, audience and diffusion", pp. 115–163 in C. Uehlinger (ed.) *Images as Media. Sources for the Cultural History of the Near East and the Eastern Mediterranean (1st Millennium B.C.E.)* Orbis Biblicus et Orientalis [OBO], 175. Freiburg.

———, 2001. "Anatolia in the Achaemenid period. Glyptic insights and perspectives from Persepolis", pp. 65–82 in T. Bakır et al. *Achaemenid Anatolia*. Leiden.

———, 2006. "The 'Late Neo-Elamite' glyptic style: A perspective from Fars", *Bulletin of the Asia Institute* 16: 65–102.

———, in press, *a*. "Visual representation of deities and demons in Achaemenid Iran: Old problems, new directions", in C. Uehlinger & F. Graf (eds) *Iconography of Deities and Demons in the Biblical World. Volume I: Pre-Hellenistic Periods, Introductory Essays*. Leiden.

———, in press, *b*. "Atlantids", in C. Uehlinger & F. Graf (eds) *Iconography of Deities and Demons in the Biblical World. Volume I: Pre-Hellenistic Periods, Introductory Essays*. Leiden.

———, forthcoming. "The seal of Cyrus the Anšanite, son of Teispes (PFS 93*): Susa—Anšan—Persepolis", in J. Alvarez-Mon (ed.) *Elam and Persia*. London.

———, in preparation. "The seals of Zisšawis".

Garrison M. B. & Root M. C., 1998. "Persepolis seal studies: an introduction with provisional concordances of seal numbers and associated documents on fortification tablets 1-2087", *Achaemenid History* 9. Leiden.

———, 2001. *Seals on the Persepolis Fortification Tablets*, vol. 1: *Images of Heroic Encounter*. Oriental Institute Publications [OIP], 117. Chicago.

———, in preparation. *Seals on the Persepolis Fortification Tablet*, vol. 2: *Images of Human Activity*. Chicago.

———, forthcoming. *Seals on the Persepolis Fortification Tablets*, vol. 3: *Animals, Creatures, Plants, and Geometric Devices*. Chicago.

Gast J., 1787. *The History of Greece from the Accession of Alexander of Macedon till its Final Subjection to the Roman Power*. 3 vols. London.

Gates J. E., 2002. "The ethnicity name game: What lies behind 'Graeco-Persian'?", *Ars Orientalis* 32: 105–132.

Gehlken E., 2005. "Childhood and youth, work and old age in Babylonia—a statistical analysis", pp. 89–119 in H. D. Baker & M. Jursa (eds) *Approaching the Babylonian Economy. Proceedings of the START Project Symposium Held in Vienna, 1–3 Jul. 2004.* Alter Orient und Altes Testament [AOAT], 330. Münster.

George A. R., 1996. "Studies in cultic topography and ideology: Review of B. Pongratz-Leisten, Ina Shulmi Irub", *Bibliotheca Orientalis* 53/3–4: 363–395.

———, 2007. "The Tower of Babel: Archaeology, history and cuneiform texts", *Archiv für Orientforschung* 51 (2005/06): 75–95.

George J., 1979. "Achaemenid orientations", *Akten des VII. Internationalen Kongresses für Iranische Kunst und Archäologie, Archäologische Mitteilungen aus Iran Ergänzungsband* 6. 196–206. Berlin.

Gerlernter M., 1995. *Sources of Architectural Form: A Critical History of the Western Design Theory.* Manchester.

Gershevitch I., 1959. *The Avestan Hymn to Mithra.* Cambridge.

———, 1964. "Zoroaster's own contribution", *Journal of Near Eastern Studies* 23: 12–38.

———, 1995. "Approaches to Zoroaster's Gathas", *Iran* 33: 1–30.

Ghirshman R., 1957. "Notes iraniennes VII: à propos de Persépolis", *Artibus Asiae* 20: 265–278.

———, 1964. *Persia. From the Origins to Alexander the Great.* London (reprinted 1978; French edition, 1964).

———, 1968. *Tchoga Zanbil (Dur Untash): II Temenos, temples, palais, tombes.* Mémoires de la Délégation Archéologique en Iran, 40. Paris.

———, 1976. "Les Daivadâna", *Acta Antiqua Academiae Scientiarium Hungaricae* 24: 3–14.

Gibb H. A. R., 1958. *The Travels of Ibn Battuta, A.D. 1325–1354*, vol. 2. Cambridge.

Gibson McG., 2001–2002. "Hamoukar, 2001–2002 Annual Report", at http://oi.uchicago.edu/OI/AR/01-02/01-02_Hamoukar.html

Gibson McG., Zettler R. L. & Armstrong J. A., 1983. "The southern corner of Nippur: excavations during the 14th and 15th seasons", *Sumer* 39: 170–190.

Gignoux P. & Tafazzoli A., 1993. *Anthologie de Zādspram.* Studia Iranica, Cahier 13. Paris.

Gikandi S., 1996. *Maps of Englishness: Writing Identity in the Culture of Colonialism.* New York.

Gillies J., 1786. *The History of Greece, its Colonies and Conquests from the Earliest Accounts till the Division of the Macedonian Empire in the East, Including the History of Literature, Philosophy, and the Fine Arts.* 2 vols. in-4° London. (repr. 1 vol., London, 1831).

Gillies J., 1789. *A View of the Reign of Frederick II of Prussia with a Parallel between that Prince and Philip II of Macedon.* London.

———, 1807. *The History of the World, from the Reign of Alexander to that of Augustus, Comprehending the Latter Ages of European Greece, and the History of the Greek Kingdoms in Asia and Africa, from their Foundation to their Destruction, with a Preliminary Survey of Alexander's Conquests, and an Estimate of his Plans for their Consolidation and Improvement.* London.

Gilman S. L., 1986. "Black bodies, white bodies: Toward an iconography of female sexuality in late nineteenth-century art, medicine, and literature", in H. L. Gates Jr. (ed.) *Race, Writing and Difference.* Chicago.

Giovinazzo G., 1989. "Présence babylonienne dans les textes économiques de Persépolis", *Annali dell'Istituto Universitario Orientale* 49: 201–207.

Glassner J. J., 2004. *Mesopotamian Chronicles.* Atlanta, GA.

Gluck J. & Siver N. eds, 1996. *Surveyors of Persian Art.* Costa Mesa, CA.

Gnoli G., 1989. *The Idea of Iran: An Essay on its Origin.* Serie orientale Roma, 62. Rome.

———, 2000. *Zoroaster in History.* Biennial Yarshater lecture series, 2. New York.

Göbl R., 1960. "Investitur im sasanidischen Iran und ihre numismatische Bezeugung. Zugleich ein Beitrag zur Ikonographie der Göttin Anāhita", *Wiener Zeitschrift für die Kunde des Morgenlandes* 56: 36–51.

———, 1971. *Sasanian Numismatics.* Braunschweig.

Goff C., 1977. "Excavations at Baba Jan. The architecture of the East Mound, Levels II and III", *Iran* 15: 103–140.

Goitein S. D., 1969. "Cairo: an Islamic city in the light of the Geniza documents", pp. 80–96 in I. M. Lapidus (ed.) *Middle Eastern Cities.* Berkeley, CA.

———, 1983. *A Mediterranean Society. The Jewish Communities of the World as Portrayed in the Documents of the Cairo Geniza, Vol. IV: Daily Life.* Berkeley, CA, Los Angeles and London.

Goldman B., 1965. "Persian fire temples or tombs?", *Journal of Near Eastern Studies* 24: 305–308.

———, 1991a. "Women's robes: The Achaemenid era", *Bulletin of the Asia Institute* (N.S.) 5: 83–103.

———, 1991b. "Persian domed turibula", *Studia Iranica* 20: 179–188, pls XVII–XX.

Gopnik H., 2003. "The ceramics from Godin II from the late 7th to early 5th centuries B.C.", pp. 249–267 in G. Lanfranchi, M. Roaf & R. Rollinger (eds) *Continuity of Empire (?) Assyria, Media, Persia.* Padua.

Gopnik H., 2005. "The shape of sherds: function and style at Godin II", *Iranica Antiqua* 40: 249–269.

Gopnik H. & Rothman M., 2010. *On the High Road : A History of Godin Tepe, Iran*. Costa Mesa and Toronto.

Gosden C., 2001. "Postcolonial archaeology: Issues of culture, identity, and knowledge", pp. 241–261 in I. Hodder (ed.) *Archaeological Theory Today*. Cambridge.

Goukowsky P., 1974. "Les juments du Roi Érythras", *Revue des Études grecques* 87: 111–137.

Grabbe L. L., 1998. *Ezra-Nehemiah*. London.

Graf D. F., 1984. "Medism: the origin and significance of the term", *Journal of Hellenic Studies* 104: 15–30.

———, 1990a. "The Origin of the Nabataeans", *Aram* 2: 45–75.

———, 1990b. "Arabia during Achaemenid times", pp. 131–148 in H. Sancisi-Weerdenburg & A. Kuhrt (eds) *Achaemenid History IV: Centre and Periphery*. Leiden.

Grayson A. K., 1975. *Babylonian Historical-Literary Texts*. Toronto.

Greenewalt C. E., 1972. "The Acropolis", pp. 15–29 in A. Ramage "The fourteenth campaign at Sardis", *Bulletin of the American Schools of Oriental Research* 206 (Apr.): 9–39.

Grell C., 1995. *Le Dix-huitième siècle et l'antiquité en France (1680–1789)*. 2 vols. Oxford.

Grenet F., 2005. "An archeologist's approach to Avestan geography", pp. 29–51 in V. Sarkhosh Curtis & S. Stewart (eds) *Birth of the Persian Empire*. London.

Groom N. St J., 1981. *Frankincense and Myrrh: A Study of the Arabian Incense Trade*. London, New York and Beirut.

Gropp, D. M., 2001. "Wadi Daliyeh II: The Samaria Papyri from Wadi Daliyeh", pp. 1–123 in E. Tov (ed.) *Discoveries in the Judaean Desert 28*. Oxford.

Grose D. F., 1989. *The Toledo Museum of Art. Early Ancient Glass: Core-formed, Rod-formed, and Cast Vessels and Objects from the Late Bronze Age to the Early Roman Empire, 1600 B.C. to A.D. 50*. New York.

Grosrichard A., 1979. *Structure du sérail. La fiction du despotisme asiatique dans l'Occident classique*. Paris.

Grundy G. B., 1901. *The Great Persian War and its Preliminaries. A Study of the Evidence, Literary and Topographical*. London.

Guerci L., 1981. "Lingue storico della Grecia e di Roma", *Rivista Storica Italiana* 93/1: 615–679.

Gunter A. C. & Jett P., 1992. *Ancient Iranian Metalwork in the Arthur M. Sackler Gallery and the Freer Gallery of Art*. Washington DC.

Gunter A. C. & Root M. C., 1998. "Replicating, inscribing, giving: Ernst Herzfeld and Artaxerxes' silver *phiale* in the Freer Gallery of Art", *Ars Orientalis* 28: 1–40.

Gusmani R., 1964. *Lydisches Wörterbuch: mit grammatischer Skizze und Inschriftensammlung*. Heidelberg.

Güterbock H. G. & van den Hout T. P. J., 1991. *The Hittite Instruction for the Royal Bodyguard*. Chicago.

Haerinck E., 1983. *La Céramique en Iran pendant la période Parthe (ca. 250 av. J.C. à ca. 225 après J.C.): typologie, chronologie et distribution*. Iranica Antiqua, Supplement II. Gent.

———, 1989. "The Achaemenid (Iron Age IV) period in Gilan, Iran", pp. 455–474 in L. de Meyer & E. Haerinck (eds) *Archaeologia Iranica et Orientalis. Miscellanea in Honorem Louis Vanden Berghe*. Gent.

———, 1997. "Babylonia under Achaemenid rule", pp. 26–34 in J. Curtis (ed.) *Mesopotamia and Iran in the Persian Period: Conquest and Imperialism 539–331 B.C.—Proceedings of a Seminar in memory of Vladimir G. Lukonin*. London.

Haerinck E. & Overlaet B., 2008. "Altar shrines and fire altars? Architectural representations on Frataraka coinage", *Iranica Antiqua* 43: 207–233.

Haiman M., 1995. "Agriculture and nomad-state relations in the Negev Desert in the Byzantine and early Islamic periods", *Bulletin of the American Schools of Oriental Research* 297: 29–53.

Hall E., 1989. *Inventing the Barbarian. Greek Self-Definition through Tragedy*. Oxford.

Hallo W. W., ed., 2000. *The Context of Scripture 2: Monumental Inscriptions from the Biblical World*. Leiden.

Hallock R. T., 1969. *Persepolis Fortification Tablets*. Oriental Institute Publications [OIP], 92. Chicago.

———, 1977. "The use of seals on the Persepolis Fortification Tablets", pp. 127–133 in M. Gibson & R. D. Biggs (eds) *Seals and Sealing in the Ancient Near East*. Bibliotheca Mesopotamica, 6. Malibu, CA.

———, 1978. "Selected Fortification Texts", *Cahiers de la Délégation Archéologique Française en Iran* 8: 109–134.

Hamzah-i Isfahani. *Tarikhi-i Payambaran va Shahan*, trans. J. Sho'ar, Tehran 1989.

Handley-Schachler M., 1992. "Achaemenid religion, 521–465 B.C.". DPhil. thesis, University of Oxford.

———, 2004. "The Lan ritual in the Persepolis Fortification Texts", pp. 195–204 in P. Briant, A. Kuhrt, M. C. Root, H. Sancisi-Weerdenburg & J. Wiesehofer (eds) *Achaemenid History XI—Studies in Persian History: Essays in Memory of David M. Lewis*. Leiden.

Hansman J., 1972. "Elamites, Achaemeneans and Anshan", *Iran* 10: 101–125.

———, 1985. "Anshan in the Median and Achaemenian Periods", pp. 25–35 in I. Gershevitch (ed.) *Cambridge History of Iran Volume 2: The Median and the Achaemenian Periods*. Cambridge.

Hanson R. S., 1968. "Aramaic funerary and boundary inscriptions from Asia Minor", *Bulletin of the American School of Oriental Research* 192 (Dec.): 3–11.

Harper P. O., 1992. "Mesopotamian monuments found at Susa", pp. 159–182 in P. O. Harper, J. Aruz & F. Tallon (eds) *The Royal City of Susa: Ancient Near Eastern Treasures in the Louvre*. New York.

Harper P. O., 2000. "Sasanian silver vessels: The formation and study of early museum collections", pp. 46–54 in J. E. Curtis (ed.) *Mesopotamia and Iran in the Parthian and Sasanian Periods: Rejection and Revival c. 238 BC—AD 642—Proceedings of a Seminar in memory of Vladimir G. Lukonin*. London.

Harper P. O., Aruz J. & Tallon F., eds, 1992. *The Royal City of Susa. Ancient Near Eastern Treasures in the Louvre*. New York.

Harrison C. M., 1982. "Coins of the Persian Satraps." PhD dissertation, University of Pennsylvania (= UMI Ann Arbor, # 8307320).

Hartmann H., 1937. "Zur neuen Inschrift des Xerxes von Persepolis", *Orientalische Literaturzeitung* 40: cols. 145–60.

Hassell J., 2002. "Cuboid incense-burning altars from South Arabia in the collection of the American Foundation for the Study of Man: Some unpublished aspects", *Arabian Archaeology and Epigraphy* 13: 157–192.

Haussoullier B., 1905. "Offrande à Apollon Didyméen", pp. 155–165 in J. de Morgan *et al. Recherches archéologiques, deuxième série*. Mémoires de la Délégation en Perse, 7. Paris.

Hayashi T., 2000. "East–west exchanges as seen through the dissemination of the griffin motif", pp. 253–265 in C. Balint (ed.) *Kontakte zwishen Iran, Byzanz und der Steppe im 6.–7. Jahrhundert*. Varia Archaeologica Hungara, 10. Budapest.

Hayes W. C., 1959. *The Scepter of Egypt*, vol. 2: *The Hyksos Period and the New Kingdom*. New York.

Head B. V., 1877. *The Coinage of Lydia and Persia from the Earliest Time to the Fall of the Dynasty of the Achaemenids*. London.

Heeren A. H. L., 1824. *Ideen über die Politik, den Verkehr und den Handel der vornehmsten Völker der alten Welt*. 4 vols. Göttingen.

———, 1833. *Historical Researches into the Politics, Intercourse, and Trade of the Principal Nations of Antiquity*. (2 vols; transl. from the German) Oxford.

———, 1840. *A Manual of Ancient History Particularly with Regard to the Constitutions, the Commerce and the Colonies*. 3rd edn (transl. from the German, corrected and improved). Oxford.

Helm P. R., 1981. "Herodotus' *Mêdikos Logos* and Median History", *Iran* 19: 85–90.

Henkelman W., 1995–96. "The royal Achaemenid crown", *Archäologische Mitteilungen aus Iran* 28: 275–293.

———, 2002. "Henkelman, Exit der Posaunenbläser". *On lance-guards and lance-bearers in the Persepolis Fortification archive*. http://www.achemenet.com/ressources/enligne/arta/pdf/2002.007.pdf

———, 2003a. "Persians, Medes and Elamites: Acculturation in the Neo-Elamite period", pp. 181–231 in G. Lanfranchi, M. Roaf & R. Rollinger (eds) *Continuity of Empire (?) Assyria, Media, Persia*. Padua.

———, 2003b. "An Elamite memorial: the šumar of Cambyses and Hystaspes", pp. 101–172 in W. Henkelman & A. Kuhrt (eds) *Achaemenid History XIII: A Persian Perspective. Essays in Memory of Heleen Sancisi-Weerdenburg*. Leiden.

———, 2006. "The other gods who are. Studies in Elamite–Iranian acculturation based on the Persepolis Fortification Texts". PhD thesis, Leiden.

Henkelman W. F. M., Jones C. E. & Stolper M. W., 2004. "Clay tags with Achaemenid seal impressions in the Dutch Institute of the Near East (NINO) and elsewhere", *Arta* 2004.001: 1–66.

Henning W. B., 1951. *Zoroaster, Politician or Witch-doctor?* London.

Herbordt S., 1992. *Neuassyrische Glyptik des 8.–7. Jh. v. Chr., unter besonderer Berücksichtigung der Siegelungen auf Tafeln und Tonverschlüssen*. State Archives of Assyria Studies, 1. Helsinki.

Herder J.-G., 1784/91. *Ideen zur Philosophie des Geschichte des Menschheit*. 4 vols. Riga and Leipzig.

———, 1787. *Persepolis, eine Muthmassung*. Gotha.

———, 1827. *Idées sur la philosophie de l'histoire de l'humanité*. (French transl. by Edgar Quinet). Paris.

Herr L., 1993. "Whatever happened to the Ammonites?", *Biblical Archaeology Review* 19/6: 27–35, 68.

———, 1999. "The Ammonites in the late Iron Age and Persian period," pp. 219–237 in B. MacDonald and R. W. Younker (eds) *Ancient Ammon*. Leiden.

Herrenschmidt C., 1976. "Délégations de l'Empire et concepts politiques de Darius Ier d'après ses inscriptions en vieux-perse", *Studia Iranica* 5: 33–65.

Herrenschmidt C., 1977. "Les créations d'Ahuramazda", *Studia Iranica* 6 (1977), 17–58.

———, 1980. "La religion des Achéménides; état de la question", *Studia Iranica* 9: 325–339.

Herzfeld E. E., 1907. "Eine Reise durch Lūristān, Arabistān und Fārs", *Petermanns Mitteilungen* 53: 49–90.

———, 1926. "Reisebericht", *Zeitschrift der Deutschen Morgenländischen Gesellschaft* 80 (N.F. 5): 225–284.

———, 1928. "Drei Inschriften aus persischem Gebiet", *Mitteilungen der Altorientalischen Gesellschaft* 4: 81–86.

———, 1929–30. "Rapport sur l'état actuel des ruines de Persépolis et propositions pour leur conservation avec 30 planches et 1 carte", *Archäologische Mitteilungen aus Iran* 1: 17–63.

———, 1932. *A New Inscription of Xerxes from Persepolis*. Studies in Ancient Oriental Civilizations [SAOC], 5. Chicago.

———, 1934. "Recent discoveries at Persepolis", *Journal of the Royal Asiatic Society*: 226–232.

———, 1935. "Archaeological History of Iran", *The Schweich Lectures of the British Academy*. London.

———, 1936. "Xerxes" Verbot des Daiva-Cultes", *Archäologische Mitteilungen aus Iran* 8: 56–77.

———, 1938a. *Altpersiche Inschriften*. Berlin.

———, 1938b. "Notes on the Achaemenid coinage and some Sasanian mint-names", pp. 413–426 in *Transactions of the International Numismatic Congress*. London.

———, 1941. *Iran in the Ancient East. Archaeological Studies Presented in the Lowell Lectures at Boston*. London, Boston and New York.

———, 1947. *Zoroaster and his World*. Princeton.

———, 1968. *The Persian Empire: Studies in the Geography and Ethnography of the Ancient Near East*. Wiesbaden.

———, n.d. *Notebook N-84*. Freer Gallery of Art, Arthur M. Sackler Gallery Archives, Ernst Herzfeld Papers.

Heuzey L., 1923. *Catalogue des figurines antiques de terre cuite. Figurines orientales. Figurines des îles asiatiques*. Paris.

Hignett C., 1963. *Xerxes' Invasion of Greece*. Oxford.

Hildebrand G., 1999. *Origins of Architectural Pleasure*. Berkeley, CA.

Hill G. F., 1922. *Catalogue of the Coins of Arabia, Mesopotamia and Persia*. London.

Hillenbrand R., 1994. *Islamic Architecture: Form, Function and Meaning*. Edinburgh.

Hilprecht H. V., Hilprecht C. & Albert T., 1898. *Business Documents of Murashu Sons of Nippur: Dated in the Reign of Artaxerxes I (464–424 B.C.)*. Philadelphia.

Hinz W., 1961. "Zu den Persepolis-Täfelchen", *Zeitschrift der Deutschen Morgenländischen Gesellschaft* 110: 236–251.

———, 1969. *Altiranische Funde und Forschungen*. Berlin.

———, 1972. *The Lost World of Elam, Re-creation of a Vanished Civilization* (transl. by Jennifer Barnes). London.

Hoffner H. A., 1966. "Symbols for masculinity and femininity. Their use in Ancient Near Eastern sympathetic magic rituals", *Journal of Biblical Literature* 85: 327–334.

Hofstetter J., 1978. *Die Griechen in Persien: Prosopographie der Griechen im Persischen Reich vor Alexander*. Berlin.

Hogarth D. G., 1908. *Excavations at Ephesus: The Archaic Artemisia*. London.

Hoglund K. G., 1992. *Achaemenid Imperial Administration in Syria-Palestine and the Missions of Ezra and Nehemiah*. SBL dissertation Series, 125. Atlanta, GA.

Holloway S. W., 2002. *Aššur is King! Aššur is King! Religion in the Exercise of Power in the Neo-Assyrian Empire*. Leiden.

Homayoun G. A., 1970. "Iran in Historisch-Geographischen Werken Europäischer Gelherter im 16 Jht", *Archäologische Mitteilungen aus Iran* 3 (N.F.): 309–316, taf. 131–144.

Hoover O. D., 2008. "Appendix 5: Overstruck Seleucid coins", pp. 209–230 in A. Houghton, C. Lorber & O. Hoover (eds) *Seleucid Coins. A Comprehensive Catalogue Part 2: Seleucus IV through Antiochus XIII*. 2 vols. New York and Lancaster, PA.

Hornung E., 1990. *Das Totenbuch der Ägypter*. Zürich and Munich.

Houghton A., 1980. "Notes on the early Seleucid victory coinage of 'Persepolis'", *Schweizerische Numismatische Rundschau* 59: 5–14, pls. 1–2.

Houghton A. & Lorber C., 2002. *Seleucid Coins. A Comprehensive Catalogue*, vol. 1: *Seleucus I through Antiochus III*. Lancaster, PA and London.

Hoving T., 1975. *The Chase, The Capture: Collecting at the Metropolitan*. New York.

Hrouda B., 1991. *Der alte Orient: Geschichte und Kultur des alten Vorderasien*. Munich.

Huff D., 1971. "Das Grab von Fakhrikah", *Istanbuler Mitteilungen* 21: 161–171.

———, 1990. "Fertigteile im iranischen Gewölbebau", *Archäologische Mitteilungen aus Iran* 23: 145–160.

Hughes M. J., 1984. "Analyses of silver objects in the British Museum", pp. 58–60 in J. Curtis (ed.) *Nush-i Jan III: The Small Finds*. London.

Hughes M. J., 1986. "Analysis of silver and gold items found in a hoard at Babylon", *Iran* 24: 87–88.

Humphreys S. C., 1981. "Introduction : comparative perspectives on death", pp. 1–13 in Humphreys, S. C. and King, H. (eds), *Mortality and Immortality : The Anthropology and Archaeology of Death*. London.

Hütteroth W. D. & Abdulfattah K., 1977. *Historical Geography of Palestine, Transjordan, and Southern Syria in the Late 16th Century*. Erlangen.

Ignatiadou D., 2001. "Glass and gold on Macedonian funerary couches", *Annales du 15ᵉ Congrès de l'Association Internationale pour l'Histoire du Verre* 15: 4–7.

———, 2002. "Colorless glass in late Classical and early Hellenistic Macedonia", *Journal of Glass Studies* 44: 11–24.

———, 2004. "Glass vessels", pp. 181–202, nn. on pp. 239–241 in J. Zahle & K. Kjeldsen (eds) *The Maussolleion at Halikarnassos, Subterranean and Pre-Maussollan Structures on the Site of the Maussolleion, the Finds from the Tomb Chamber of Maussollos*. Reports of the Danish Archaeological Expedition to Bodrum, 6. Copenhagen.

İlaslı A., 1996. "Seyitömer Höyüğü 1993 Yılı Kurtarma Kazısı", pp. 1–18 in *Kurtarma Kazıları Semineri, 24–26 Nisan 1995 Didim*. Ankara.

Ingholt H., 1944. "World famous cylinder seals reflect 3,000 years of history", *The Magazine of the Buffalo Museum of Science* 25 (Oct.): 2–12.

Inostrantsev K. M., 1923. "On the ancient Iranian burial customs and buildings", *Journal of the K. R. Cama Oriental Institute* 3: 1–28.

Isidore of Charax, 1989. *Parthian Stations* (transl. W. S. Schoff). Chicago.

Jackson A. V. W., 1892. *An Avestan Grammar*. Stuttgart.

———, 1906. *Persia Past and Present. A Book of Travel and Research*. New York.

Jacobs B., 1987. *Griechische und persische Elemente in der Grabkunst Lykiens zur Zeit der Achämenidenherrschaft*. Jonsered.

———, 1996. "Kyros der Grosse als Geisel am medischen Königshof", *Iranica Antiqua* 31: 83–100.

———, 1997. "Eine Planänderung an den Apadana-Treppen und ihre Konsequenzen für die Datierung der Planungs- und Bebauungsphasen von Persepolis", *Archäologische Mitteilungen aus Iran* 29: 281–302.

———, 2002. "Achämenidische Kunst—Kunst im Achämenidenreich, Zur Rolle der achämenidischen Großplastik als Mittel der herrscherlichen Selbstdarstellung und der Verbreitung politischer Botschaften im Reich", *Archäologische Mitteilungen aus Iran und Turan* 34: 345–396.

———, 2003. "Die altpersischen Länder-Listen und Herodots sogenannte Satrapienliste (Historien III 89–94)", pp. 301–343 in R. Dittmann, C. Eder & B. Jacobs (eds) *Altertumswissenschaften im Dialog—Festschrift für Wolfram Nagel*. Alter Orient und Altes Testament [AOAT], 306. Münster.

Jacoby F., 1923/1958. *Die Fragmente der Griechischen Historiker*. Berlin and Leiden.

Jakob-Rost L. & Freydank H., 1978. *Spätbabylonische Rechtsurkunden und Wirtschaftstexte aus Uruk*. Vorderasiatische Schriftdenkmäler der Staatlichen Museen zu Berlin, 20 (N.F. 4). Berlin.

Jamzadeh P., 1982. "The winged ring with human bust in Achaemenid art as a dynastic symbol", *Iranica Antiqua* 17: 91–99, pls I–II.

Jarrige J.-F. & Santoni M., 1979. *Fouilles de Pirak*, vol. 1: *Texte*. Fouilles de Pakistan, 2. Paris.

Jaussen A. & Savignac R., 1909. *Mission archéologique en Arabie*. Paris.

Jenkins G. K., 1978. "Coins", pp. 41–52 in D. Stronach, *Pasargadae*. Oxford.

Joannès F., 1982. *Textes économiques de la Babylonie récente*. Paris.

———, 1989. *Archives de Borsippa. La famille Ea-ilûta-bâni. Etude d'un lot d'archives familiales en Babylonie du VIIIe au Ve siècle av. J.-C.*. Geneva.

———, 1990a. "Pouvoirs locaux et organisations du territoire en Babylonie achéménide", *Transeuphratène* 3: 173–189.

———, 1990b. "Textes babyloniens d'époque achéménide", pp. 173–180 in F. Vallat (ed.) *Contributions à l'histoire de l'Iran. Mélanges offerts à Jean Perrot*. Paris.

Joisten-Pruschke A., 2008. *Das religiöse Leben der Juden von Elephantine in der Achämenidenzeit*. Wiesbaden.

Jones J. D., 2005. "Glass vessels from Gordion. Trade and influence along the Royal Road", pp. 101–116 in L. Kealhofer (ed.) *The Archaeology of Midas and the Phrygians. Recent Work at Gordion*. Philadelphia.

Junge, P. J., 1940. "Hazarpatiš", *Klio* 33: 13–33.

Jursa M., 1998. *Der Tempelzehnt in Babylonien vom siebenten bis zum dritten Jahrhundert v. Chr.* Alter Orient und Altes Testament [AOAT], 254. Münster.

———, 1999. *Das Archiv des Bēl-rēmanni*. Leiden.

———, 2003a. "Spätachämenidische Texte aus Kutha", *Revue d'Assyriologie* 97: 43–140.

———, 2003b. "Observations on the problem of the Median 'empire' on the basis of Babylonian sources", pp. 169–179 in G. Lanfranchi, M. Roaf & R. Rollinger (eds) *Continuity of Empire (?) Assyria, Media, Persia*. Padua.

Jursa M., 2005. *Neo-Babylonian Legal and Administrative Documents: Typology, Contents and Archives*. Guides to the Mesopotamian Textual Record, 1. Münster.

Kagan J. H., 1994. "An archaic Greek coin hoard from the Eastern Mediterranean and early Cypriot coinage", *Numismatic Chronicle* 154: 17–52.

Kaim B., 1991. "Das Geflügelte Symbol in der Achämenidischen Glyptik", *Archäologische Mitteilungen aus Iran* 24: 31–34, pls 7–10.

Kammerzell F., 1993. *Studien zu Sprache und Geschichte der Karer in Ägypten*. Göttinger Orientforschungen, Reihe 4, Ägypten. Wiesbaden.

Kanetsyan A., 2001. "Urartian and Early Achaemenid palaces in Armenia", pp. 145–154 in I. Nielsen (ed.) *The Royal Palace Institution in the First Millennium B.C.: Regional Development and Cultural Interchange between East and West*. Monographs of the Danish Institute at Athens, 4. Athens and Aarhus.

Kaptan D., 1996. "The Great King's audience", pp. 259–271 in F. Blakomer et al. *Fremde Zeiten. Festschrift für Jürgen Borchhardt zum sechzigsten Geburtstag am 25. Februar 1996: dargebracht von Kollegen, Schülern und Freunden*. 2 vols. Vienna.

———, 2000. "Common traits on seals and coins of the Achaemenid period in an Anatolian context", pp. 213–223 in O. Casabonne (ed.) *Mécanismes et innovations monétaires dans l'Anatolie achéménide, numismatique et histoire. Actes de la table ronde internationale d'Istanbul 22–23 mai 1997*. Varia Anatolica 12. Istanbul.

———, 2002. *The Daskyleion Bullae: Seal Images from the Western Achaemenid Empire [Achaemenid History 12]*. 2 vols. Leiden.

———, 2003. "A glance at Northwestern Asia Minor during the Achaemenid period", pp. 189–202 in W. Henkelman & A. Kuhrt (eds) *A Persian Perspective. Essays in Memory of Heleen Sancisi-Weerdenburg*. Leiden.

———, 2007. "A channel of communication: Seals in Anatolia during the Achaemenid period", pp. 275–289 in O. Casabonne & İ. Delemen (eds) *The Achaemenid Impact on Local Populations and Cultures in Anatolia*. Istanbul.

Kawami T. S., 1972. "A possible source for the sculptures of the Audience Hall, Pasargadae", *Iran* 10: 146–148.

Keel O., 1997. *Corpus der Stempelsiegel-Amulette aus Palästina/Israel von den Anfängen bis zur Perserzeit*. Orbis Biblicus et Orientalis [OBO], 13. Freiburg and Göttingen.

Keen A. G., 1995. "The tombs of Lycia—evidence for social stratification?", pp. 221–225 in S. Campbell & A. Green (eds) *The Archaeology of Death in the Ancient Near East*. Oxbow Monographs, 51. Oxford.

Keiser C. E., 1918. *Letters and Contracts from Erech Written in the Neo-Babylonian Period*. Babylonian inscriptions in the collection of James B. Nies, 1. New Haven.

Kellens J., 1987. "Quatre siècles obscurs", pp. 135–139 in B. Gray (ed.) *Transition Periods in Iranian History. Actes du Symposium de Fribourg-en-Brisgau, 22–24 Mai 1985*; Studia Iranica, cahier 5.

———, 1989. "Ahura Mazdā n'est pas un dieu créateur", pp. 217–228 in C.-H. de Fouchecour & Ph. Gignoux (eds) *Etudes irano-aryennes offertes à Gilbert Lazard*. Paris.

———, 2001. "Zoroastre dans l'histoire ou dans le mythe? À propos du dernier livre de Gherardo Gnoli", *Journal Asiatique* 289/2: 171–184.

———, 2002. "L'idéologie religieuse des inscriptions achéménides", *Journal Asiatique* 290: 417–464.

———, 2005. "Les *Aiiriia*- ne sont plus des Āryas: ce sont déjà des Iraniens", pp. 233–252 in G. Fussman (ed.) *Āryas, aryens et Iraniens en Asie centrale*. Publications de l'Institut de civilisation indienne, 72. Paris

Kellens J. & Pirart E., 1988. *Les textes vieil-avestiques. Volume I: Introduction, texte et traduction*. Wiesbaden.

Kennedy D. L., 2007. *Gerasa and the Decapolis: A "Virtual Island" in Northwest Jordan*. London.

Kent R. G., 1937. "The Daiva-Inscription of Xerxes", *Language* 13: 292–305.

———, 1943. "Old Persian texts", *Journal of Near Eastern Studies* 2: 302–306.

———, 1953. *Old Persian: Grammar, Texts, Lexicon*. 2nd edn (first published 1950). New Haven.

Kenyon K. M., 1983. *Excavations at Jericho IV*. London.

Kervran M., Stronach D., Vallat F. & Yoyotte J., 1972. "Une statue de Darius découverte à Suse", *Journal Asiatique* 260: 253–266.

Kessler K.-H., 1984. "Duplikate und Fragmente aus Uruk", *Baghdader Mitteilungen* 15: 261–274.

———, 1991. *Tübinger Atlas des Vorderen Orients* map B IV 13.

Khachatrian Z., 1996. "Archives in Artashat", pp. 365–370 in M.-F. Boussac & A. Invernizzi (eds) *Archives et Sceaux du Monde Hellénistique*. BCH Supplément, 29.

Khalil L.A., 1986. "A bronze caryatid censer from Amman", *Levant* 18: 103–110.

Khan F., Knox J. R. & Thomas K. D., 2000a. "Ter Kala Dheri: the site, excavations, artifacts and chronology", pp. 81–100 in F. Khan, J. R. Knox, P. G. Magee & K. D. Thomas, with a contribution by C. A. Petrie *Akra: The Ancient Capital of Bannu, North West Frontier Province, Pakistan.* Islamabad.

Khan F., Knox J. R., Magee P. G. & Thomas K. D., with a contribution by Petrie C. A., 2000a. *Akra: The Ancient Capital of Bannu, North West Frontier Province, Pakistan.* Islamabad.

Khan F., Knox J. R., Magee P., Petrie C. A. & Thomas K. D., 2000b. "Preliminary report on the fourth season of excavation at Akra, North-West Frontier Province, Pakistan", *Journal of Asian Civilisations* 23/2: 105–136.

Khazanov A. M., 1994. *Nomads and the Outside World.* 2nd edn. Cambridge.

Kilmer M., 1993. *Greek Erotica.* London.

Kinneir J. M., 1813. *A Geographical Memoir of the Persian Empire, Accompanied by a Map.* London.

Kjærum P., 1997. "Stamp-seals and stamp-seal impressions", pp. 160–164 in F. Højlund & H. H. Andersen (eds) *Qala'at al-Bahrain Vol. 2. The Central Monumental Buildings.* Jutland Archaeological Society, 30. Aarhus.

Klein R., 1996. *Eat Fat.* New York.

Kleiss W., 1971. "Der Takht-i Rustam bei Persepolis und das Kyros-Grab in Pasargadae", *Archäologischer Anzeiger*: 157–162.

Kleiss W. & Calmeyer P., 1975. "Das unvollendete achaemenidische Felsgrab bei Persepolis", *Archaeologische Mitteilungen aus Iran* (N.F.) 8: 81–98.

Klengel-Brandt E., 1990. "Gab es ein Museum in der Hauptburg Nebukadnezars II. in Babylon?", *Forschungen und Berichte* 28: 41–46.

Klose D. O. A., 2005. "Statthalter, Könige, Rebellen", *Numismatisches Nachrichtenblatt* 54 (Mar.): 93–103.

Klose D. O. A. & Müseler W., 2008. *Statthalter und Rebellen Könige. Die Münzen aus Persepolis von Alexander dem Grossen zu den Sasaniden*, Staatliche Münzsammlung München.

Knauer E. R., 1978. "Towards a history of the sleeved coat. A study of the impact of an ancient eastern garment on the West", *Expedition* (Fall): 18–36.

Knauf E. A., 1989. "Nabataean origins", pp. 56–61 in M. M. Ibrahim (ed.) *Arabian Studies in Honor of Mahmoud Ghul: Symposium at Yarmouk University, Dec. 8–11, 1984.* Wiesbaden.

———, 1990. "The Persian administration in Arabia", *Transeuphratène* 2: 201–217.

Knauth W., 1975. *Das altiranische Fürstenideal von Xenophon bis Ferdousi.* Wiesbaden.

Knapton P., Sarraf M. R. & Curtis J., 2001. "Inscribed column bases from Hamadan", *Iran* 39: 99–117.

Koch E., 1994. "Diwan-i Amm and Chihil Sutun: the audience halls of Shah Jahan", *Muqarnas* 11: 134–165.

Koch H., 1977. *Die religiösen Verhältnisse der Dareioszeit—Untersuchungen an Hand der elamischen Persepolistäfelchen.* Göttinger Orientforschungen, III. Reihe: Iranica, 4. Wiesbaden.

———, 1986. "Die Achämenidische Poststrasse von Persepolis nach Susa", *Archaeologische Mitteilungen aus Iran* 19: 133–147.

———, 1987. "Götter und ihre Verehrung im achämenidischen Persien", *Zeitschrift für Assyriologie und vorderasiatische Archäologie* 77: 239–278.

———, 1990. *Verwaltung und Wirtschaft im persischen Kernland zur Zeit der Achämeniden.* Wiesbaden.

———, 1992. *Es kündet Dareios der König...: Von Leben im persischen Großreich.* Kulturgeschichte der Antiken Welt, 55. Mainz am Rhein.

Koldewey R., 1911. *Die Tempel von Babylon und Borsippa.* Wissenschaftliche Veröffentlichungen der Deutschen Orient-Gesellschaft, 15. Leipzig.

———, 1990. *Das wieder erstehende Babylon.* 5th edn, ed. B. Hrouda. Munich.

Komoroczy G., 1977. "Umman-manda", *Acta Antiqua Academiae Scientiarum Hungaricae* 25: 43–67.

Konow S., 1937. "Medhâ and Mazdâ", pp. 217–222 in *Jhâ Commemoration Volume: Essays on Oriental Subjects.* Oriental Series, 39. Poona.

Konstan D., 1997. *Friendship in the Classical World.* Cambridge.

Konuk K., 2000. "Influences et éléments achéménides dans le monnayage de la Carie", pp. 171–184 in O. Casabonne (ed.) *Mécanismes et innovations monétaires dans l'Anatolie achéménide, numismatique et histoire. Actes de la table ronde internationale d'Istanbul 22–23 mai 1997.* Varia Anatolica 12. Istanbul.

———, 2002. "The Muharrem Kayhan Collection", *Sylloge Nummorum Graecorum, Turkey 1.* Numismatica Anatolica, 1. Istanbul.

———, 2003. "L'Asie Mineure aux époques archaïque et classique", pp. 113–132 in C. Alfaro Asins (ed.) *A Survey of Numismatic Research (1996–2001).* Madrid.

Konuk K. & Arslan M., 2000. *Ancient Gems and Finger Rings from Asia Minor: The Yüksel Erimtan Collection.* Ankara.

Koşay H. Z., 1941. *Pazarlı Hafriyatı Raporu. Les Fouilles de Pazarlı.* Ankara.

Kottsieper I., 2002. "Die Religionspolitik der Achämeniden und die Juden von Elephantine", pp. 150–178 in R. G. Kratz (ed.) *Religion und Religionskontakte im Zeitalter der Achämeniden.* Veröffentlichungen der Wissenschaftlichen Gesellschaft für Theologie, 22. Gütersloh.

Kotwal F. M. & Kreyenbroek P. G., 1992/1995/2003. *The Hêrbedestân and Nêrangestân.* Studia Iranica, Cahiers 10, 16, 30. Paris.

Kraay C. M., 1977. "The Asyut hoard: some comments on chronology", *Numismatic Chronicle* (7th series) 17: 193–194.

Krefter F., 1968. "Achaemenidische Palast- und Grabtüren", *Archaeologische Mitteilungen aus Iran* (N.F.) 1: 99–113.

———, 1971. *Persepolis Rekonstruktionen*. Berlin.

Kreyenbroek P. G., 1996. "The Zoroastrian tradition from an oralist's point of view", pp. 221–237 in H. J. M. Desai & H. N. Modi (eds) *K. R. Cama Oriental Institute, Second International Congress Proceedings*. Bombay.

———, 2003. Review of *Zoroaster in History* by Gh. Gnoli, *The Journal of Iranian Studies* 36/1: 121–124.

———, 2004. "Ritual and rituals in the Nêrangestân", pp. 317–332 in M. Stausberg (ed.) *Zoroastrian Rituals in Context: Studies in the History of Religions*. Leiden.

———, 2005. *The Zoroastrian World-View and its Echoes in Christianity and Islam* (Rothko Chapel lecture, Houston, Jul. 2005), ww.rothkochapel.org/explore.htm

Kritt B., 1997. *The Seleucid Mint of Susa*. Lancaster, PA.

Kroll S., 2003. "Medes and Persians in Transcaucasia: archaeological horizons in north-western Iran and Transcaucasia", pp. 281–287 in G. Lanfranchi, M. Roaf & R. Rollinger (eds) *Continuity of Empire (?) Assyria, Media, Persia*. Padua.

Krückmann O., 1933. *Neubabylonische Rechts- und Verwaltungstexte*. Texte und Materialien der Frau prof. Hilprecht collection of Babylonian antiquities, 2–3. Leipzig.

Kühne H., 1988/89. "Report on the excavation at Tall Šeh Hamad/Dur Katlimmu 1988", *Les Annales Archéologiques Arabes en Syrie* 38/39: 142–157.

Kuhrt A., 1983. "The Cyrus cylinder and Achaemenid imperial policy", *Journal for the Study of the Old Testament* 25: 83–97.

———, 1988a. "Earth and water", pp. 87–99 in A. Kuhrt & H. Sancisi-Weerdenburg (eds) *Achaemenid History III: Method and Theory*. Leiden.

———, 1988b. "Babylonia from Cyrus to Xerxes", *Cambridge Ancient History* 2nd edn, vol. 4: 112–138. Cambridge.

———, 1991. "Concluding remarks", pp. 203–205 in H. Sancisi-Weerdenburg & J. W. Drijvers (eds) *Achaemenid History VII: Through Travellers' Eyes*. Leiden.

———, 1995. *The Ancient Near East, c. 3000–300 B.C.* 2 vols. London and New York.

———, 2002. "Babylon", pp. 475–496 in E. J. Bakker, I. J. F. de Jong & H. van Wees (eds) *Brill's Companion to Herodotus*. Leiden.

Kuhrt A., 1983, 2003. "Making history: Sargon of Agade and Cyrus the Great of Persia", pp. 347–361 in W. Henkelman & A. Kuhrt (eds) *A Persian Perspective: Essays in Memory of Heleen Sancisi-Weerdenburg*. Achaemenid History, XIII. Leiden.

Kuhrt A. & Sancisi-Weerdenburg H., 1987. "Introduction", pp. ix–xiii in H. Sancisi-Weerdenburg & A. Kuhrt (eds) *Achaemenid History II: The Greek Sources*. Leiden.

Kuhrt A. & Sherwin-White S., 1987. "Xerxes' destruction of Babylonian temples", pp. 69–78 in H. Sancisi-Weerdenburg & A. Kuhrt (eds) *Achaemenid History II: The Greek Sources*. Leiden.

Kuiper F. B. J., 1957. "Avestan Mazdā", *Indo-Iranian Journal* 1: 86–95.

———, 1959. "Review of U. Bianchi, *Zamân î Ohrmazd*", *Indo-Iranian Journal* 3: 212–216.

Kümmel H. M., 1979. *Familie, Beruf und Amt in spätbabylonischen Uruk*. Abhandlungen der deutschen Orient-Gesellschaft, 20. Berlin.

Kuniholm P. I., 1996. "The prehistoric Aegean: Dendrochronological progress as of 1995", *Acta Archaeologica* 67: 327–335; http://www.arts.cornell.edu/dendro/.

Kunina N., 1970. *Ancient Glass in the Hermitage Collection*. St Petersburg.

Labrousse A., 1972a. "La charte de foundation du palais de Darius Ier", Thèse manuscrite (archive du Département des antiquités orientales, Musée du Louvre, Paris).

———, 1972b. *Rapport de fin de première année de 3ème cycle. Thème: la charte de Suse*. Musée du Louvre, Départment des antiquités orientales. Paris.

Lambert W. G., 1965. "Nebuchadnezzar, king of justice", *Iraq* 27: 1–11.

———, 1968/1969. "A new source for the reign of Nabonidus", *Archiv für Orientforschung* 22: 1–8.

Lambton A. K. S., 1995. "Major-General Sir John Malcolm (1769–1833) and *The History of Persia*", *Iran* 33: 97–109.

Lancaster W. & Lancaster F., 1992. "Tribal formations in the Arabian Peninsula", *Arabian Archaeology and Epigraphy* 3: 145–172.

Lane Fox R., 2004. "Sex, gender, and the Other in Xenophon's Anabasis", pp. 184–212 in R. Lane Fox (ed.) *The Long March. Xenophon and the Ten Thousand*. New Haven.

Lanfranchi G., 2003. "The Assyrian expansion in the Zagros and the local ruling elites", pp. 85–89 in G. Lanfranchi, M. Roaf & R. Rollinger (eds) *Continuity of Empire (?) Assyria, Media, Persia*. Padua.

Lanfranchi G., Roaf M. & Rollinger R., eds, 2003. *Continuity of Empire (?) Assyria, Media, Persia*. Padua.

Langdon S., 1905/1906. "Les inscriptions de Nebuchadnezzar trouvées à Suse", *Zeitschrift für Assyriologie* 19: 142–147.

Lange K. & Hirmer M., 1983. *Ägypten. Architektur–Plastik–Malerei in drei Jahrtausenden.* München Sonderausgabe. Munich.

Laslett P., 1972. "Introduction: the history of the family", pp. 1–89 in P. Laslett (ed.) with the assistance of R. Wall, *Household and Family in Past Time.* Cambridge.

Lecoq P., 1997. *Les inscriptions de la Perse achéménide.* Paris.

———, 2003. Sales Catalogue of *Archéologie* by Piasa, Paris: Drouot 17–18 Mar. 2003, p. 105 (lot 443).

Legrain L., 1925. *The Culture of the Babylonians from their Seals in the Collection of the Museum.* Publication from the Babylonian Section, University Museum, University of Pennsylvania, 14. Philadelphia, PA.

Legrain L., 1951. *Ur Excavations X: Seal Cylinders.* London.

Leick G., 1994. *Sex and Eroticism in Mesopotamian Literature.* London.

Lemaire, A., 1974. "Un Nouveau roi Arabe de Qedar", *Revue Biblique* 81: 63–72.

———, 1990. "Populations et territoires de Palestine à l'époque perse", *Transeuphratène* 3: 31–74.

———, 1994. "House of David restored in Moabite inscription", *Biblical Archaeology Review* 20/3: 30–37.

Lenfant D., 2002. "Pourquoi Xerxès détacha sa ceinture", *Arta* 2002.004 (www.achemenet.com).

———, 2004. *Ctésias de Cnide: La Perse; L'Inde; Autres Fragments* (texte établi, traduit et commenté par D. Lenfant). Collections des Universités de France/Association Guillaume Budé. Paris.

Lenormand C., 1849. *Trésor de numismatique. Rois grecs.* Paris.

Lenormant F., 1873. "Monnaies royales de la Lydie", *Annuaire de la Société Française de Numismatique* 4: 171–211.

Lenzen H. J., 1963. "Die Wohnhäuser des ersten vorchristlichen Jahrtausends", *Uruk Vorläufiger Berichte* 19: 15–16.

Le Rider G., 2001. *La naissance de la monnaie. Pratiques monétaires de l'Orient ancient.* Paris.

Lerner J. A., 1971. "The Achaemenid relief of Ahura Mazda in the Fogg Art Museum, Cambridge, Massachusetts", *Bulletin of the Asia Institute of Pahlavi University, Shiraz* 2: 19–35.

———, 1973. "A painted relief from Persepolis", *Archaeology* 26/2 (Apr.): 116–122.

———, 1991. "Some so-called Achaemenid objects from Pazyryk", *Source. Notes in the History of Art* 10/4: 8–15.

Lévy I., 1939. "L'Inscription triomphale de Xerxes", *Revue historique* 185: 105–122.

Levy J., 2008. *Lost Cities of the Ancient World.* London.

Lewis B., 1980. *The Sargon Legend: A Study of the Akkadian Text and the Tale of the Hero who was Exposed at Birth.* American Schools of Oriental Research dissertation series, 4. Cambridge, MA.

Lewis D., 1990. "Brissonius: De regio persarum principatu libri tres (1590)", pp. 67–78 in H. Sancisi-Weerdenburg & J. W. Drijvers (eds) *Achaemenid History V: The Roots of the European Tradition.* Leiden.

Lewis N. N., 1987. *Nomads and Settlers in Syria and Jordan, 1800–1980.* Cambridge.

Lewis S., 2002. *The Athenian Woman. An Iconographic Handbook.* London.

Lincoln B., 2003. *Religion, Empire, and Torture. The Case of Achaemenian Persia, with a Postscript on Abu Ghraib.* Chicago.

Linders T., 1984. "The Kandys in Greece and Persia", *Opuscula Atheniensia* 15: 107–114.

Linguet S.-N.-L., 1769. *Histoire du siècle d'Alexandre.* 2nd edn. Paris.

Lipschits O., 2004. "Ammon in transition from vassal kingdom to Babylonian province", *Bulletin of the American Schools of Oriental Research* 335: 37–52.

Lissarrague F., 1987. *Une flot d'images. Une esthétique du banquet grec.* Paris.

———, 2000. *Greek Vases: The Athenians and Their Images.* New York.

Little L. & Rosenwein B., 1998. *Debating the Middle Ages: Issues and Readings.* Oxford.

Liverani M., 2003. "The rise and fall of Media", pp. 1–12 in G. Lanfranchi, M. Roaf & R. Rollinger (eds) *Continuity of Empire (?) Assyria, Media, Persia.* Padua.

Llewellyn-Jones L., 2002. "A woman's view? Dress, eroticism and the ideal female body in Athenian art", pp. 171–202 in L. Llewellyn-Jones (ed.) *Women's Dress in the Ancient Greek World.* Swansea and London.

———, 2003. *Aphrodite's Tortoise: The Veiled Woman of Ancient Greece.* Swansea.

Loftus W. K., 1855. "On the excavations undertaken at the ruins of Susa in 1851–2", *Transactions of the Royal Society of Literature of the United Kingdom* (Second Series) 5: 422–453.

———, 1856. "Warkah: its ruins and remains", *Transactions of the Royal Society of Literature of the United Kingdom* (Second Series) 6: 1–64.

———, 1857. *Travels and Researches in Chaldaea and Susiana; with an Account of Excavations at Warka,* the *"Erech" of Nimrod, Shush, "Shushan the Palace" of Esther, in 1849–52*. London.

Loloi P., 1999. "A dramatic version from the Apocrypha: King Daryus and the Book of Esdras", pp. 31–40 in S. Coelsch-Foisner (ed.) *Elizabethan Literature and Transformation*. SECL Studies in English and Comparative Literature, 15. Tübingen.

Longhurst H., 1959. *Adventure in Oil. The Story of British Petroleum*. London.

Longpérier A. de, 1882. *Musée Napoléon III. Choix de monuments pour servir à l'histoire de l'art en Orient et en Occident*. Paris.

Loud G. & Altman C. B., 1938. *Khorsabad, part 2. The Citadel and the Town*. Oriental Institute Publications [OIP], 40. Chicago.

Lowery P. R., Savage R. D. A. & Wilkins R. L., 1971. "Scriber, graver, scorper, tracer: notes on experiments in bronzeworking technique", *Proceedings of the Prehistoric Society* 37: 167–182.

Luckenbill D. D., 1926–27. *Ancient Records of Assyria and Babylonia*. 2 vols. Chicago.

Lückge A., Doose-Rolinski H., Khan A. A., Shulz H. & von Rad U., 2001. "Monsoonal variability in the northeastern Arabian Sea during the past 5000 years: geochemical evidence from laminated sediments", *Palaeogeography, Palaeoclimatology, Palaeoecology* 167: 273–286.

Luschey H., 1939. *Die Phiale*. Bleicherode am Harz.

McCall B. K., 2009. "The Mamasani Archaeological Survey : Epipalaeolithic to Elamite Settlement Patterns in the Mamasani District of the Zagros Mountains, Fars Province, Iran." PhD thesis, University of Sydney.

McCown C. C. et al., 1947. *Tell en-Nasbeh Excavated Under the Direction of the Late William Frederic Badè*. Berkeley, CA.

MacDermott B. C. & Schippman K., 1999. "Alexander's march from Susa to Persepolis", *Iranica Antiqua* 34: 282–308.

McEwan G. J. P., 1984. *Late Babylonian Texts in the Ashmolean Museum*. Oxford Editions of Cuneiform Texts [OECT], 10. Oxford.

MacGinnis J., 1995. *Letter Orders from Sippar and the Administration of the Ebabbara in the Late Babylonian Period*. Poznán.

———, 1997. "*Kizû's* of the Ebabbara", *Revue d'Assyriologie* 91: 81–87.

———, 1998. "BM 64707 and *rikis qabli* in the Ebabbara", *Wiener Zeitschrift für die Kunde des Morgenlandes* 88: 177–183.

———, 2002. "Working in Elam", pp. 177–182 in C. Wunsch (ed.) *Mining the Archives: Festschrift for Christopher Walker on the Occasion of His 60th Birthday*. Dresden.

———, 2003. "A *corvée* gang from the time of Cyrus", *Zeitschrift für Assyriologie* 93/1: 88–115.

———, 2004. "Servants of the Sun God: Numbering the dependents of the Neo-Babylonian Ebabbara", *Baghdader Mitteilungen* 35: 27–38.

———, forthcoming. *Arrows of the Sun: Armed Forces in Sippar in the First Millennium BC*. Dresden.

McLauchlin B. K., 1985. *Lydian Graves and Burial Customs*. PhD dissertation, University of California at Berkeley.

Madhloom T. A., 1970. *The Chronology of Neo-Assyrian Art*. London.

Magee P., 2001. "Excavations at the Iron Age settlement of Muweilah 1997–2000", *Proceedings of the Seminar for Arabian Studies* 31: 115–130.

———, 2003. "Columned halls, power and legitimisation in the southeast Arabian Iron Age", pp. 182–191 in D. Potts, H. al-Naboodah & P. Hellyer (eds) *Archaeology of the United Arab Emirates: Proceedings of the First International Conference on the Archaeology of the U.A.E.* London.

———, 2004. *Excavations at Tepe Yahya, Iran 1967–1975. The Iron Age Settlement*. American School of Prehistoric Research Bulletin, 46. Cambridge, MA.

———, 2005a. "Mind the gap: The chronology of Painted Grey Ware and the prelude to early historic urbanism in northern south Asia", *South Asian Studies* 20: 37–44.

———, 2005b. "The chronology and environmental background of Iron Age settlement in Southeastern Iran and the question of the origin of the qanat irrigation system" [*Proceedings of the International Conference "The Iron Age in the Iranian World" at Ghent, 17–20 Nov. 2003*] *Iranica Antiqua* 40: 217–232.

Magee P., Petrie C. A., Knox R., Khan F. & Thomas K. D., 2005. "The Achaemenid Empire in South Asia and recent excavations at Akra in Northwest Pakistan", *American Journal of Archaeology* 109: 711–741.

Majd M. G., 2003. *The Great American Plunder of Persia's Antiquities 1925–1941*. Lanham, MD, New York and Oxford.

Majidzadeh Y., 1999. "Excavations at Ozbaki: first preliminary report 1998", *Iranian Journal of Archaeology and History* 13 (autumn/winter): 57–81 (in English and Persian).

———, 2000. "Excavations at Ozbaki: second preliminary report 1999 (The Ozbaki Fortress)", *Iranian*

Journal of Archaeology and History 14/2 (spring/summer), 4: 38–49 (in English and Persian).

Malandra W. W., 1971. "The Farvardin Yast, Introduction, Text, Translation, and Commentary". PhD thesis, University of Pennsylvania, Philadelphia.

———, 1983. *An Introduction to Ancient Iranian Religion*. Minneapolis.

———, 2003. "Gōhr i Asmān, a problem in Avestan cosmology", pp. 266–274 in S. Adhami (ed.) *Paitimāna, Essays in Iranian, Indo-European, and Indian Studies in Honor of Hans-Peter Schmidt*. Costa Mesa, CA.

Malbran-Labat F., 1989. "Les briques inscrites de Suse (époque pré-achéménide)", *Syria: Revue d'art oriental et d'archéologie* 66: 281–309.

Malcolm J., 1815. *A History of Persia*. 2 vols. London.

———, 1827. *Sketches of Persia* (published anonymously). 2 vols. London.

Mallowan M. E. L., 1970. "Cyrus the Great (558–539 B.C.)", *Iran* 10: 1–17.

Manukian H., 1996. "Les empreintes d'Artachate (antique Artaxata)", pp. 371–373 in M.-F. Boussac & A. Invernizzi (eds) *Archives et Sceaux du Monde Hellénistique*. BCH Supplément 29.

Marlowe C., 1590. *Tamurlaine the Great* (ed. J. S. Cunningham & E. Henson, 1998). Manchester.

Marlowe J. [pseud.], 1967. *Late Victorian: the Life of Sir Arnold Talbot Wilson*. London.

Marzahn J., 1993. *La Porte d'Ishtar de Babylone*. Mayence.

Mas'udi, Abol-Hasan ʿAli b. Hosayn. 1962. *Les prairies d'or*, vol. II (transl. C. Pellat). Paris.

Mathew H. C. G. & Harrison B., eds, 2004. *Oxford Dictionary of National Biography*. Oxford.

Mathieson I. J., Bettles E., Davies S. & Smith H. S., 1995. "A stela of the Persian period from Saqqara", *Journal of Egyptian Archaeology* 81: 23–41.

Matthews D. M., 1990. *Principles of Composition in Near Eastern Glyptic of the Later Second Millennium B.C.* Orbis Biblicus et Orientalis [OBO], 8. Freiburg and Göttingen.

Matthews R., 2003. *The Archaeology of Mesopotamia. Theories and Approaches*. London and New York.

Matthiae P., 1998. *Ninive—Glanzvolle Hauptstadt Assyriens*. Munich.

Mauss M., 1954. *The Gift: The Form and Reason for Exchange in Archaic Societies* (transl. I. Cunnison) Glencoe, IL.

May G., 1978. *Schöpfung aus dem Nichts. Die Entstehung der Lehre von der Creatio ex Nihilo*. Berlin.

Mazar B., 1993. "En-Gedi", pp. 399–405 in E. Stern (ed.) *The New Encyclopedia of Archaeological Excavations in the Holy Land*, vol. 1. Jerusalem.

Meadows A. R., 2005. "The administration of the Achaemenid Empire", pp. 181–209 in J.E. Curtis & N. Tallis (eds) *Forgotten Empire: The World of Ancient Persia*. London.

Melikian-Chirvani S., 1982. *Islamic Metalwork from the Iranian World, 8th–18th Centuries*. London.

———, 1993. "The International Achaemenid Style", *Bulletin of the Asia Institute* (N.S.) 7: 111–130.

Mellink M. J., 1984. "The native kingdoms of Anatolia", pp. 164–177 in J. Boardman (ed.) *The Cambridge Ancient History, Plates to volume III. The Middle East, The Greek World and the Balkans to the Sixth Century B.C.* Cambridge.

Menant M. J., 1885. *Recherches sur la Glyptique Orientale*. Paris.

Merrillees P. H., 2005. *Catalogue of the Western Asiatic Seals in the British Museum, Cylinder Seals VI. Pre-Achaemenid and Achaemenid Periods*. London.

Merritt-Hawkes O. A., 1935. *Persia. Romance and Reality*. London.

Metzger H., 1979. *Fouilles de Xanthos 6: La stèle trilingue du Létôon*. Paris.

Meyer G. R., 1970. *Altorientalische Denkmäler im vorderasiatischen Museum zu Berlin*. Leipzig.

Miglus P., 1999. *Städtische Wohnarchitektur in Babylonien und Assyrien*. Baghdader Forschungen, 22. Mainz am Rhein.

Miles G. C., 1959. *Excavation Coins from the Persepolis Region*. Numismatic Notes and Monographs, 143. New York.

Mill J., [1817]. *A History of British India* (abridged and with an introduction by W. Thomas, published 1975, Classics of British Historical Literature). Chicago and London.

Millard A. R., 1962. "Alphabetic inscriptions on ivories from Nimrud", *Iraq* 24: 41–51.

Miller M. C., 1997. *Athens and Persia in the Fifth Century B.C. A Study in Cultural Receptivity*. Cambridge.

———, 2003*a*. "Greco-Persian cultural relations", *Encyclopedia Iranica* XI: 301–319.

———, 2003*b*. "Art, myth and reality: Xenophantos' Lekythos", pp. 19–47 in E. Csapo & M. C. M. Csapo (eds) *Poetry, Theory, Praxis: The Social Life of Myth, Word and Image in Ancient Greece (Essays in Honour of William J. Slater)*. Oxford.

Millspaugh A. C., 1925. *The American Task in Persia*. New York and London.

Minns F., 1913. *Scythians and Greeks: A Survey of Ancient History and Archaeology on the North Coast of the Euxine from the Danube to the Caucasus*. Cambridge.

Miroschedji P. de, 1981. "Fouilles du chantier de la Ville Royale II à Suse (1975–1977). I: Les niveaux élamites", *Cahiers de la Délégation Archéologique Française en Iran* 12: 9–136.

Miroschedji P. de, 1985. "La fin du royaume d'Anshan et de Suse et la naissance de l'empire perse", *Zeitschrift für Assyriologie* 75: 265–306.

———, 1989. "Review of Ursula Seidl, 'Die elamischen Felsenreliefs von Kurangun und Naqš-e Rustam'", *Syria* 66: 358–362.

———, 2003. "Susa and the highlands: major trends in the history of Elamite civilisation", pp. 17–38 in N. Miller & K. Abdi (eds) *Yeki bud, yeki nabud: Essays on the Archaeology of Iran in Honour of William M. Sumner*. Los Angeles.

Missiou A., 1993. "ΔΟΥΛΟΣ ΤΟΥ ΒΑΣΙΛΕΩΣ: the politics of translation", *Classical Quarterly* (N.S.) 43: 377–391.

Mitchell S., 1993. *Anatolia, Land, Men and Gods in Asia Minor, Vol. I: The Celts and the Impact of the Roman Rule* (reprinted 2001). Oxford.

Mofidi Nosrabadi B., 2007. *Archäologische Ausgrabungen und Untersuchungen in Choga Zanbil*. Münster.

Momigliano A., 1952. *George Grote and the Study of Greek History (An Inaugural Lecture Delivered at University College London)*. London.

———, 1990. *The Classical Foundations of Modern Historiography*. Berkeley.

———, 2004. *Persian Letters.* new edn (transl. with an introduction and notes by C. J. Betts). Harmondsworth.

Montesquieu, 1989. *The Spirit of Laws.* (transl. and ed. A.-M. Cohler, B.-C. Miller & H.-S. Stone). Cambridge.

Moore B. B., 1915. *From Moscow to the Persian Gulf. Being the Journal of a Disenchanted Traveller in Turkestan and Persia*. New York.

Moorey P. R. S., 1978. "The iconography of an Achaemenid stamp-seal acquired in the Lebanon", *Iran* 16: 143–154.

———, 1979. "Aspects of worship and ritual on Achaemenid seals", *Akten des VII. Internationalen Kongresses für Iranische Kunst und Archäologie, München 1976* (Archäologische Mitteilungen aus Iran Ergänzungsband 6): 218–226. Munich.

———, 1980. *Cemeteries of the First Millennium B.C. at Deve Hüyük, near Carchemish, Salvaged by T. E. Lawrence and C. L. Woolley in 1913 (with a Catalogue Raisonné of the Objects in Berlin, Cambridge, Liverpool, London and Oxford)*. BAR International Series, 87. Oxford.

———, 1985. "The Iranian contribution to Achaemenid material culture", *Iran* 23: 21–37.

———, 1988a. "Religion and rulers", pp. 45–50 in J. Boardman, N. G. L. Hammond, D. M. Lewis & M. Oswald (eds) *Cambridge Ancient History Volume IV: Persia, Greece and the Western Mediterranean c. 525–479 B.C.* 2nd edn. Cambridge.

———, 1988b. "Aspects of life and crafts", pp. 51–94 in J. Boardman, N. G. L. Hammond, D. M. Lewis & M. Oswald (eds) *Cambridge Ancient History Volume IV: Persia, Greece and the Western Mediterranean c.525–479 B.C.* 2nd edn. Cambridge.

———, 1988c. "The Persian empire", pp. 1–94 in *Cambridge History of Iran, Plates to Volume IV*. Cambridge.

———, 1994. *Ancient Mesopotamian Materials and Industries. The Archaeological Evidence*. Oxford (reprinted 1999, Winona Lake, IN).

———, 2002. "Novelty and tradition in Achaemenid Syria: the case of the clay 'Astarte plaques'", *Iranica Antiqua* 37: 203–218.

Moorey P. R. S., Bunker E. C., Porada E. & Markoe G., 1981. *Ancient Bronzes, Ceramics and Seals. The Nasli M. Heeramaneck Collection of Ancient Near Eastern, Central Asiatic and European Art*. Los Angeles.

Morier J. J., 1812. *A Journey through Persia, Armenia and Asia Minor to Constantinople in the years 1808 and 1809*. London.

———, 1824. *The Adventures of Hajji Baba of Ispahan in England*. 3 vols. London.

Morton R. S., 1940. *A Doctor's Holiday in Iran*. New York and London.

Mostafavi M. T., 1963. "Quelques étapes de la route royale achéménide entre Suse et Persépolis", pp. 16–18 in K. Atarashi & K. Horiuchi (eds) *Fahliyan I: The Excavation at Tape Suruvan 1959*. Tokyo.

———, 1967. "The Achaemenid Royal Road: post stations between Susa and Persepolis", pp. 3008–3010 in A. U. Pope & P. Ackerman (eds) *A Survey of Persian Art, Vol. XIV: New Studies 1938–1960, Proceedings of the IVth International Congress of Iranian Art and Archaeology, Part A, Apr. 24–May 3 1960*. Oxford.

Mostafavi S. M. T. & Sami A., 1965. *Takht-e Jamshid (Persepolis)*. Shiraz.

Mostowfi H., 1915. *The Geographical Part of the Nuzhat-al-qulūb* (ed. G. Le Strange). Leiden.

Mounsey A. H., 1872. *A Journey through the Caucasus and the Interior of Persia*. London.

Mousavi A., 2002. "Persepolis in retrospect: Histories of discovery and archaeological exploration at the ruins of ancient Parseh", *Ars Orientalis* 32: 209–251.

Munro P., 1973. *Die spätägyptischen Totenstelen*. Ägyptologische Forschungen, 25. Glückstadt.

Muscarella, O. W., 1977. "Unexcavated objects and Ancient Near Eastern art", pp. 153–207 in

L. Levine (ed.) *Mountains and Lowlands, Essays in the Archaeology of Greater Mesopotamia*. Malibu, CA.

———, 1980. "Excavated and unexcavated Achaemenid art", pp. 23–42, pls V–XIX in D. Schmandt-Besserat (ed.) *Ancient Persia: The Art of an Empire*. Malibu, CA.

———, 1988. "The background to the Luristan bronzes", pp. 33–44 in J. Curtis (ed.) *Bronze-working Centres of Western Asia c. 1000–539 B.C.* London.

———, 1992a. "Achaemenid art and architecture at Susa", pp. 216–219, 227–241 in P. O. Harper, J. Aruz & F. Tallon (eds) *The Royal City of Susa: Ancient Near Eastern Treasures in the Louvre*. New York.

———, 1992b. "No. 141. La Fileuse [Lady Spinning]", pp. 200–201 in P. O. Harper, J. Aruz & F. Tallon (eds) *The Royal City of Susa: Ancient Near Eastern Treasures in the Louvre*. New York.

———, 2000. "The pope and the bitter fanatic", pp. 5–12 in A. Alizadeh, Y. Majidzadeh & S. M. Shahmirzadi (eds) *The Iranian World: Essays on Iranian Art and Archaeology presented to Ezat O. Negahban*. Tehran.

Musche B., 1992. *Vorderasiatischer Schmuck von den Anfängen bis zur Zeit der Achaemeniden (ca. 10.000–330 v. Chr.)*. Handbuch der Orientalistik. Siebente Abteilung. Kunst und Archäologie. Erster Band. Der Alte Orient. Zweiter Abschnitt. Die Denkmäler (ed. B. Hrouda). B–Vorderasien. Lieferung 7. Leiden, New York, Copenhagen and Cologne.

Müseler W., 2005–06. "Die sogenannten dunklen Jahrhunderte der Persis", *Jahrbuch für Numismatik und Geldgeschichte* 55/56: 75–103.

Museum of Anatolian Civilizations (n.d.), *A Guide Book*. Ankara.

Musil A., 1927. *Arabia Deserta, A Topographical Itinerary*. New York.

Musil A. & Wright K., 1930. *In the Arabian Desert*. New York.

Myers J. M., 1965. *Ezra-Nehemiah*. Anchor Bible Commentary. New York.

Nagel W., 1963. "Datierte Glyptik aus Vorderasien", *Archiv für Orientforschung* 20: 125–140.

Naster P., 1962. "Les sicles persiques à la demi-figure dans leur contexte numismatique et archéologique". *Bulletin de la société française de numismatique* 17: 170–171.

———, 1964. "De la représentation symbolique du dieu Assur aux premiers types monétaires aché-mémides", pp. 10–11 in A. A. Kampman & J. P. M. Van der Ploeg (eds) *Comptes rendus de la 11ᵉ rencontre assyriologique internationale*. Leiden.

———, 1968. "Note d'épigraphie monétaire de Perside: fratakara, frataraka ou fratādara?", *Iranica Antiqua* 8: 74–80.

Nebes N., 2007. "Ita'mar der Sabäer: Zur Datierung der Monumentalinschrift des Yita'mar Watar aus Sirwah", *Arabian Archaeology and Epigraphy* 18: 25–33.

Neils J. & Oakley J. H., 2003. *Coming of Age in Ancient Greece. Images of Childhood from the Classical Past*. New Haven.

Neuffer J., 1968. "The accession of Artaxerxes I", *Andrews University Seminary Studies* 6: 60–87.

Nevill R., 1969. *London Clubs: Their History and Treasures*. London.

Newell E. T., 1938. *The Coinage of the Eastern Seleucid Mints*. New York.

Nicolini G., 1990. *Techniques des ors antiques. La bijouterie ibérique du VIIe. au IVe. siècle*. Paris

Nielsen I., ed., 2001. *The Royal Palace Institution in the First Millennium B.C.: Regional Development and Cultural Interchange between East and West*. Monographs of the Danish Institute at Athens, 4. Athens and Aarhus.

Nimchuk C. L., 2001. "Darius I and the Formation of the Achaemenid Empire: Communicating the Creation of an Empire". PhD dissertation, University of Toronto.

———, 2002. "The 'Archers' of Darius: coinage or tokens of royal esteem?", *Ars Orientalis* 32: 55–79.

———, 2005. "The Persepolis Apadana foundation deposits", *Bulletin of the Canadian Society for Mesopotamian Studies* (Festschrift in Honour of T. Cuyler Young, Jr.) 40 (Sept.): 33–38.

Niwiński A., 1988. *21st Dynasty Coffins from Thebes: Chronological and Typological Studies*. Theben, 5. Mainz am Rhein.

Noe S. P., 1949. "Hoard evidence and its importance", *Hesperia [American School of Classical Studies at Athens]*, Supplement 8: 235–242.

———, 1956. "Two hoards of Persian sigloi", *American Numismatic Society Numismatic Notes and Monographs* 136: 23–24.

Nöldeke T., 1930. *The Iranian National Epic* (transl. L. Bogdanov). Bombay.

Novak M. & Schmid J., 2001. "Zur Problematik von Lehmziegelgewölben: Konstruktionstechniken und Verfahren zur Analyse am Beispiel von Gewölbebauten im Roten Haus in Dur-Katlimmu/Magdalu", *Baghdader Mitteilungen* 32: 205–253.

Nunn A., 1988. *Die Wandmalerei und der glasierte Wandschmuck in Alten Orient*. Handbuch der Orientalistik. Leiden.

Nunn A., 2000. *Der figürliche Motivschatz Phöniziens, Syriens und Transjordaniens vom 6. bis zum 4. Jahrhundert v. Chr.* Orbis Biblicus et Orientalis [OBO], 18. Freiburg.

Nyberg H. S., 1938. *Die Religionen des alten Iran.* Leipzig.

Nylander C., 1970. *Ionians in Pasargadae, Studies in Old Persian Architecture.* Uppsala Studies in Ancient Mediterranean and Near Eastern Civilizations, I. Uppsala.

———, 1975. "Anatolians in Susa—and Persepolis (?)", *Acta Iranica* 6, Deuxième Série, Hommages et Opera Minora Vol. III: 317–324.

Oates D., 1990. "Innovations in mud-brick: decorative and structural technique in ancient Mesopotamia", *World Archaeology* 21: 388–406.

Oates J., 1979. *Babylon.* London.

Oelsner J., Wells B. & Wunsch C., 2003. "Neo-Babylonian period", pp. 911–974 in R. Westbrook (ed.) *A History of Ancient Near Eastern Law*, 2 vols, vol. 2. Leiden and Boston.

Ogden D., 1999. *Polygamy, Prostitutes and Death. The Hellenistic Dynasties.* Swansea and London.

Oleson J. P., 1995. "The origins and design of Nabataean water-supply systems", *Studies in the History and Archaeology of Jordan* 5: 707–719. Amman.

Oliver Jr. A., 1970. "Persian export glass", *Journal of Glass Studies* 12: 9–16.

Olivieri L. M., 1996. "Notes on the problematical sequence of Alexander's itinerary in Swat: a geo-historical approach", *East and West* 46/1–2: 45–78.

Olmstead A. T., 1948. *History of the Persian Empire.* Chicago.

Onians J., 1988. *Bearers of Meaning: The Classical Orders in Antiquity, the Middle Ages, and the Renaissance.* Princeton.

———, 1999. *Classical Art and the Cultures of Greece and Rome.* New Haven.

Ornan T., 1993. "The Mesopotamian influence on west Semitic inscribed seals: A preference for the depiction of mortals", pp. 52–73 in B. Sass & C. Uehlinger (eds) *Studies in the Iconography of Northwest Semitic Inscribed Seals.* Orbis Biblicus et Orientalis [OBO], 125.

———, 2002. "The queen in public: Royal women in Neo-Assyrian art", pp. 461–477 in S. Parpola & R. M. Whiting (eds) *Sex and Gender in the Ancient Near East.* The Neo-Assyrian Text Corpus Project, 2. Helsinki.

Osborne D., 1912. *Engraved Gems: Signets, Talismans and Ornamental Intaglios, Ancient and Modern.* New York.

Ouseley W., 1819/1823. *Travels in Various Countries of the East; More Particularly Persia.* 3 vols. London.

Özgen I. & Öztürk J. et al., 1996. *The Lydian Treasure: Heritage Recovered.* Istanbul.

Palazzo Venezia, 1993. *Oxus. Tesori dell'Asia Centrale.* Rome.

Panaino A., 2003. "The baγān of the Fratarakas: gods or 'divine' kings?", pp. 265–288 in C. G. Cereti, M. Maggi & E. Provasi (eds), *Religious Themes and Texts of Pre-Islamic Iran and Central Asia. Studies in Honour of Professor Gherardo Gnoli on the Occasion of his 65th birthday on 6th December 2002.* Wiesbaden.

———, 2004. "Astral characters of kingship in the Sasanian and the Byzantine worlds", pp. 555–594 in *La Persia e Bisanzio, Atti dei Convegni Lincei 2001, Roma.* Rome.

Panofsky E., 1957. *Meaning in the Visual Arts.* New York.

———, 1959. *Studies in Iconology.* London and New York.

Parke-Bernet Galleries 1949. *The Notable Art Collection Belonging to the Estate of the Late Joseph Brummer, Public Auction Sale, Part I (Apr. 20–23 at 2 p.m.), Part II (May 11–14 at 2 p.m.).* New York.

Parker R. A. & Dubberstein W. H., 1956. *Babylonian Chronology 626 B.C.–A.D. 75.* Providence, RI.

Parlasca K., 1966. *Mumienporträts und verwandte Denkmäler.* Wiesbaden.

Parpola A., 2002. "Pre-Proto-Iranians of Afghanistan as initiators of Sāta tantrism: on the Scythian/Saka affiliation of the Dāsas, Nuristānis and Magadhans", *Iranica Antiqua* 37: 233–324.

Parpola S., 1970. *Neo-Assyrian Toponyms.* Alter Orient und Altes Testament [AOAT], 6. Kevelaer and Neukirchen-Vluyn.

Parr P. J., 1968/1969. "The Nabataeans and North-West Arabia", *Bulletin of the Institute of Archaeology (University of London)* 8/9: 250–253.

———, 1982. "Contacts between North West Arabia and Jordan in the late Bronze and Iron Ages", *Studies in the History and Archaeology of Jordan* 1: 127–133. Amman.

Parr P. J., Harding G. L. & Dayton J. E., 1969. "Preliminary survey in N.W. Arabia, 1968 (Part 1)", *Bulletin of the Institute of Archaeology (University of London)* 8/9: 193–241.

Paspalas S., 2000. "On Persian-type furniture in Macedonia: the recognition and transmission of forms", *American Journal of Archaeology* 104/3: 534–560.

Pereira J., 1994. *Islamic Sacred Architecture: A Stylistic History.* New Delhi.

Perrot G. & Chipiez C., 1890. *Histoire de l'Art dans l'Antiquité*, vol. 5. Paris.

Petit T., 2004. "Xénophon et la vassalité achéménide", pp. 175–200 in C. J. Tuplin (ed.) *Xenophon and his World*. Historia, 172. Stuttgart.

———, 1888. *Tanis II, Nebesheh, and Defenneh*. London.

Petrie C. A., Askari Chaverdi A. & Seyedin M., 2005. "From Anshan to Dilmun and Magan: the spatial and temporal distribution of Kaftari and Kaftari-related ceramic vessels", *Iran* 43: 49–86.

———, 2006. "Excavations at Tol-e Spid", pp. 89–134 in D. T. Potts & K. Roustaei (eds) *The Mamasani Archaeological Project Stage One: A Report on the First Two Seasons of the ICAR-University of Sydney Expedition to the Mamasani District, Fars Province, Iran*. Tehran.

———, Magee P., and Khan M. N., 2008. "Emulation at the edge of the empire: the adoption of non-local vessel forms in the NWFP, Pakistan during the mid-late 1st millennium BC". *Gandharan Studies* 2 : 1–16.

Petrie W. M. F., 1886. *Naukratis I*. London.

Pfhul E. & Möbius H., 1977/1979. *Die Ostgriechischen Grabreliefs I-II*. Mainz am Rhein.

Pfrommer M., 1987. *Studien zu alexandrinischer und grossgiechischer Toreutik frühhellenisticher Zeit*. Archäologische Forschungen, 16. Berlin.

———, 1993. *Metalwork from the Hellenized East. Catalogue of the Collections of the J. Paul Getty Museum*. Malibu, CA.

Philby H. St J. B., 1957. *The Land of Midian*. London.

Philips J. P., 2002. *The Columns of Egypt*. Manchester.

Picchioni S., 1981. *Il poemetto di Adapa*. Assyriologia, 6. Budapest.

Pinault J. R., 1993. "Women, fat and fertility: Hippocratic theorizing and treatment", pp. 78–90 in M. DeForrest (ed.) *Woman's Power, Man's Game. Essays on Classical Antiquity in Honor of Joy K. King*. Wauconda.

Pingree D., 1974. "The Mesopotamian origin of early Indian mathematical astronomy", *Journal for the History of Astronomy* 4: 1–12.

———, 1982. "Mesopotamian astronomy and astral omens in other civilizations", pp. 613–631 in H.-J. Nissen & J. Renger (eds) *Mesopotamien und seine Nachbarn* vol. 2. Berliner Beiträge zum Vorderen Orient, 1. Berlin.

Pliny, 1989. *Natural History Books III–VII*. Loeb Classical Library (transl. H. Rackham). Bury St Edmunds

Plutarch, 1972. *Plutarch's Moralia IV*, Loeb Classical Library (transl. F. C. Babbitt, 1972). London.

Poly J.-P. & Bournazel E., 1991. *The Feudal Transformation 900–1200*. (Translation by C. Higgit of *La mutation féudale Xe–XIIe siècles* [Paris 1980].) New York and London.

Pomeroy S. B., 1984. "The Persian king and the queen bee", *American Journal of Ancient History* 9/2 [1990]: 98–108.

Pope A. U., 1930. *An Introduction to Persian Art since the Seventh Century A.D*. London.

———, 1935. "Ancient Persian art: Animal sculpture in gold and electron", *Illustrated London News* (2 Mar.): 1.

Pope A. U., ed., 1938. *A Survey of Persian Art from Prehistoric Times to the Present*. Oxford.

Porada E., 1948. *Corpus of Ancient Near Eastern Seals in North American Collections. Vol. I: The Collection of the J. Pierpont Morgan Library*. The Bollingen Series, 14. New York.

———, 1979a. "Some thoughts on the audience reliefs of Persepolis", pp. 37–43 in G. Kopcke & M. B. Moore (eds) *Studies in Classical Art and Archaeology in Honour of P. H. Von Blankenhagen*. Locust Valley, NY.

———, 1979b. "Achaemenid art, monumental and minute", pp. 57–96 in E. Yarshater & R. Ettinghausen (eds) *Highlights of Persian Art*. New York.

Porten B. & Greenfield J. C., 1980. *Jews of Elephantine and Arameans of Syene. Aramaic Texts with Translation*. Jerusalem.

Porten B. & Yardeni A., 1986. *Textbook of Aramaic Documents from Ancient Egypt, Vol.1*. Winona Lake, IN.

Porter B. N., 2004. "Ritual and politics in Assyria: Neo-Assyrian Kanephoric stelai for Babylonia", pp. 259–274 in *Hesperia Supplements*, Vol. 33, *ΧΑΡΙΣ: Essays in Honor of Sara A. Immerwahr*. Athens.

———, 2005. "Interactions of ritual and politics in Mespotamia", pp. 1–6 in B. N. Porter (ed.) *Ritual and Politics in Ancient Mesopotamia* (American Oriental Series 38). New Haven.

Postgate J. N., 1973. *The Governor's Palace Archive*. London.

———, 1990. "Archaeology and the Texts—Bridging the Gap", *Zeitschrift für Assyriologie* 80: 228–240.

———, 1992. *Early Mesopotamia. Society and Economy at the Dawn of History*. London and New York.

Potts D. T., 1985a. "The location of Iz-ki-e", *Revue d'Assyriologie* 79: 75–76.

———, 1985b. "From Qadê to Mazûn: Four notes on Oman, c. 700 B.C. to 700 A.D.", *Journal of Oman Studies* 8: 81–95.

———, 1990. *The Arabian Gulf in Antiquity*, vol. 1: *From Prehistory to the Fall of the Achaemenid Empire*. Oxford.

———, 1991. *The Pre-Islamic Coinage of Eastern Arabia*. Copenhagen.

———, 1994. *Supplement to the Pre-Islamic Coinage of Eastern Arabia*. Copenhagen.

Potts D. T., 1999. *The Archaeology of Elam: Formation and Transformation of an Ancient Iranian State*. Cambridge.

———, 2001. "Before the Emirates: An archaeological and historical account of developments in the region c. 5000 B.C. to 676 A.D.", pp. 28–69 in I. Al Abed & P. Hellyer (eds) *United Arab Emirates: A New Perspective*. London.

———, 2004. "The numinous and the immanent: Some thoughts on Kurangun and the Rudjhaneh-e Fahliyan", pp. 143–156 in K. von Folsach, H. Thrane & I. Thuesen (eds) *From Handaxe to Khan: Essays Presented to Peder Mortensen on the Occasion of his 70th Birthday*. Aarhus.

———, 2005a. "Neo-Elamite problems" [*Proceedings of the International Conference "The Iron Age in the Iranian World" at Ghent, 17–20 Nov. 2003*], *Iranica Antiqua* 40: 165–177.

———, 2005b. "Cyrus the Great and the Kingdom of Anshan", pp. 7–28 in V. Sarkhosh Curtis & S. Stewart (eds) *Birth of the Persian Empire*. London.

———, 2007. "Foundation houses, fire altars and the *frataraka*: interpreting the iconography of some post-Achaemenid Persian coins", *Iranica Antiqua* 42: 272–300.

———, in press. "The islands of the XIVth satrapy".

Potts D. T. & Roustaei K., eds, 2006. *The Mamasani Archaeological Project Stage One: A Report on the First Two Seasons of the ICAR–University of Sydney Expedition to the Mamasani District, Fars Province, Iran*. Tehran.

Potts D. T., Roustaei K., Weeks L. R. & Petrie C. A., 2006. "The Mamasani district and the archaeology of Southwest Iran", pp. 1–16 in D. T. Potts & K. Roustaei (eds) *The Mamasani Archaeological Project Stage One: A Report on the First Two Seasons of the ICAR–University of Sydney Expedition to the Mamasani District, Fars Province, Iran*. Tehran.

Potts D. T., Askari Chaverdi A., Petrie C. A., Dusting A., Farhadi F., McRae I. K., Shikhi S., Wong E. H., Lashkari A. & Javanmard Zadeh A., 2007. "The Mamasani archaeological project, stage two: Excavations at Qaleh Kali (Tappeh Servan/Jinjun [MS 46])", *Iran* 45: 287–300.

Potts D. T., Askari Chaverdi A., McRae I. K., Alamdari K., Dusting A., Jaffari J., Ellicott T. M., Setoudeh A., Lashkari A., Ameli Rad Sh. & Yazdani A., 2009. "Further excavations at Qaleh Kali (MS 46) by the Joint ICAR–University of Sydney Mamasani Expedition: Results of the 2008 season", *Iranica Antiqua* 44: 207–282.

Preston T., 1595. *A Lamentable Tragedie, Mixed Full of Plesant Mirth, Containing the Life of Cambises King of Percia, from the Beginning of his Kingdom, unto his Death, his Owne Good Deed of Execution, after that Many Wicked Deeds and Tyrannous Murders, Committed by and through him, and Last of All, his Odious Death by Gods Justice Appointed. Done in Such Order as Followeth*. London.

Price W., 1832. *Journal of the British Embassy to Persia; Embellished with Numerous Views Taken in India and Persia: also a Dissertation upon the Antiquities of Persepolis*. 2nd edn. London.

Pritchard J., ed., 1969. *Ancient Near Eastern Texts*. 3rd edn. Princeton.

Quibell J. E., 1908. *Tomb of Yuaa and Thuiu, Catalogue Général des Antiquités du Musée du Caire Nos. 51001–51191*. Cairo.

Quinault P., 1659. *La Mort de Cyrus, Tragédie* [in five acts and in verse]. Paris.

Quintus Curtius Rufus, 1976. *The History of Alexander*. Loeb Classical Library (trans. J. C. Rolfe). Bury St Edmunds.

Rabinowitz I., 1956. "Aramaic inscriptions of the fifth century B.C.E. from a North-Arab shrine in Egypt", *Journal of Near Eastern Studies* 15: 1–9.

Radner K., 2005. *Die Macht des Namens*. Santag, 8. Wiesbaden.

Rahimifar M., 2005. "Clay labels and bullae from Persepolis", *Bastanshenasi* 1/1: 72–77, pls. 16–24.

Ramage A. & Craddock P., 2000. "Prologue", pp. 10–13 in A. Ramage & P. Craddock (eds) *King Croesus' Gold: Excavations at Sardis and the History of Gold Refining*. Archaeological Exploration of Sardis, 11. London.

Rawlinson G., 1885. *The Seven Great Monarchies of the Ancient Eastern World*. New York.

———, 1898. *Memoir of Major-General Sir Henry Creswicke Rawlinson*. London, New York and Bombay.

Razmjou S., 2001. "Des traces de la déesse Spenta Ārmaiti à Persepolis", *Studia Iranica* 30: 7–15.

———, 2002. *Bāzsāzi-ye Yek Banā-ye Nā shenākhteh dar Takht-e Jamshid* [Reconstruction of an unknown building at Persepolis], MA thesis, Azad University, Tehran.

———, 2003. "Unidentified gods in the Achaemenid calendar", *Nāme-ye Irān-e Bāstān* 3/1: 15–35 (in Persian).

Razmjou S., 2004. "The *Lan* ceremony and other ritual ceremonies in the Achaemenid period: the Persepolis Fortification Tablets", *Iran* 42: 103–117.

———, 2005a. "In search of lost Median art" [*Proceedings of the International Conference "The Iron Age in the Iranian World" at Ghent, 17–20 Nov. 2003*] *Iranica Antiqua* 40: 271–314.

———, 2005b. "Religion and burial customs", pp. 150–156 in J. E. Curtis & N. Tallis (eds) *Forgotten Empire: The World of Ancient Persia*. London.

———, 2008. "Ritual practices at Persepolis". PhD thesis, Birkbeck College, University of London.

Reade J. E., 1963. "A glazed brick panel from Nimrud", *Iraq* 25: 38–47.

———, 1967. "Two slabs from Sennacherib's Palace", *Iraq* 29: 42–48.

———, 1976. "Elam and Elamites in Assyrian sculptures", *Archäologische Mitteilungen aus Iran* 9: 97–106.

———, 1986a. "Rassam's excavations at Borsippa and Kutha, 1879–82", *Iraq* 48: 105–116.

———, 1986b. "A hoard of silver currency from Achaemenid Babylonia", *Iran* 24: 79–89, pls I–IV.

———, 1995. "The Khorsabad glazed bricks", pp. 227–251 in A. Caubet (ed.) *Khorsabad, le palais de Sargon II roi d'Assyrie*. Paris.

———, 1998a. "Assyrian illustrations of Arabs", pp. 221–232 in C. S. Phillips, D. T. Potts & S. Searight (eds) *Arabia and its Neighbours: Essays on Prehistorical and Historical Developments, Presented in Honour of Beatrice de Cardi*. Turnhout.

———, 1998b. *Assyrian Sculpture*. London.

———, 2003. "Why did the Medes invade Assyria?", pp. 149–156 in G. Lanfranchi, M. Roaf & R. Rollinger (eds) *Continuity of Empire (?) Assyria, Media, Persia*. Padua.

———, 2005. "Religious ritual in Assyrian sculpture", pp. 7–61 in B. N. Porter (ed.) *Ritual and Politics in Ancient Mesopotamia*. American Oriental Series, 38. New Haven.

Reeder E. D., 1995. *Pandora. Women in Classical Greece*. Baltimore.

———, 1999. "Scythian art", pp. 37–57 in E. D. Reeder (ed.), *Scythian Gold : Treasures from Ancient Ukraine*. New York.

Rehm E., 1992. *Der Schmuck der Achämeniden*. Altertumskunde des Vorderen Orients, 2. Münster.

Reich R., 1992. "The Beth-Zur citadel II—a Persian residency?", *Tel Aviv* 19/1: 113–123.

Reimer P. J., et al. 2004. *Radiocarbon* 46: 1029–1058.

Reiner E. & Roth M. T., eds, 1999. *The Assyrian Dictionary of the University of Chicago*, vol. R. Chicago.

Retsö J., 2003. *The Arabs in Antiquity: Their History from the Assyrians to the Umayyads*. London and New York.

Reuter T., 1999. "Introduction: reading the tenth century", pp. 1–26 in *New Cambridge Mediaeval History* III. Cambridge.

Reuther O., 1926. *Die Innenstadt von Babylon* (*Merkes*). Wissenschaftliche Veröffentlichung der Deutschen Orient-Gesellschaft, 47 (2 vols; reprinted 1968). Leipzig.

Reynolds S., 1994. *Fiefs and Vassals. The Medieval Evidence Reinterpreted*. Oxford.

———, 1997. *Kingdoms and Communities in Western Europe*, 900–1300. Oxford.

Rice C. C., 1916. *Mary Bird in Persia* (with a foreword by the Right Rev. C. H. Stileman). London.

Richter G. M. A., 1920. *The Metropolitan Museum of Art: Catalogue of Engraved Gems of the Classical Style*. New York.

———, 1950. "Greek fifth-century silverware and later imitations", *American Journal of Archaeology* 54: 357–370.

———, 1956. *Catalogue of Engraved Gems: Greek, Etruscan and Roman*. New York.

———, 1968. *Engraved Gems of the Greeks and the Etruscans. A History of Greek Art in Miniature. The Engraved Gems of the Greeks Etruscans and Romans—Part I*. New York.

Riemschneider M., 1966. *Das Reich am Ararat*. Leipzig.

Roaf M., 1974. "The subject peoples on the base of the statue of Darius", *Cahiers de la Délégation Archéologique Française en Iran* 4: 73–160.

———, 1983. *Sculptures and Sculptors at Persepolis*. Iran 21. London.

———, 1990. *Cultural Atlas of Mesopotamia and the Ancient Near East*. Oxford.

———, 1995. "Media and Mesopotamia: history and architecture", pp. 54–66 in J. Curtis (ed.) *Later Mesopotamia and Iran: Tribes and Empires 1600–539 B.C.—Proceedings of a Seminar in Memory of Vladimir G. Lukonin*. London.

———, 2003. "The Median Dark Age", pp. 13–22 in G. Lanfranchi, M. Roaf & R. Rollinger (eds) *Continuity of Empire (?) Assyria, Media, Persia*. Padua.

———, 2004. "Persepolis", *Reallexikon der Assyriologie und Vorderasiatische Archäologie* 10: 393–412.

Robinson E. S. G., 1958. "The beginnings of Achaemenid coinage", *Numismatic Chronicle* 18: 187–193.

Rollinger R., 1993. *Herodots babylonischer Logos: eine kritische Untersuchung der Glaubwürdigkeitsdiskussion.* Innsbrucker Beiträge zur Kulturwissenschaft, Sonderheft, 84. Innsbruck.

———, 1998a. "Überlegungen zu Herodot, Xerxes und dessen angeblicher Zerstörung Babylons", *Altorientalische Forschungen* 25: 339–373.

———, 1998b. "Der Stammbaum des achaimenidischen Königshauses, oder die Frage der Legitimität der Herrschaft des Dareios", *Archäologische Mitteilungen aus Iran und Turan* 30: 155–209.

———, 1999. "Xerxes and Babylon", *NABU* 1999/1 (Mar.): 9–12.

———, 2003. "The western expansion of the Median 'empire': a re-examination", pp. 289–319 in G. Lanfranchi M. Roaf & R. Rollinger (eds) *Continuity of Empire (?) Assyria, Media, Persia.* Padua.

———, 2005a. "The Median 'Empire', the end of Urartu and Cyrus the Great's campaign in 547 B.C. (Nabonidus Chronicle II 16)", accessed 16 Sept., 2005, from Achemenet.com "sous presse" (http://www.achemenet.com/).

———, 2005b. "Das Phantom des Medischen "Grossreichs" und die Behistun-Inschrift", pp. 11–29 in E. Dabrowa (ed.) *Ancient Iran and its Neighbours.* Electrum, 10. Krakow.

———, 2008. "The Median Empire, the end of Urartu, and Cyrus the Great's campaign in 546 BC (Nabonidus Chronicle ii 16)", *Ancient East and West* 7 : 51–65.

Rome, 1956. *Arte Iranica / Iranian Art. Catalogue of the Exhibition of Iranian Art, Rome, Palazzo Brancaccio, Jun.–Aug. 1956.* Rome.

Roos P., 1972. *The Rock-Tombs of Caunus*, vol. 1: *The Architecture.* Studies in Mediterranean Archaeology, 34/1. Göteborg.

———, 1974. *The Rock-Tombs of Caunus*, vol. 2: *The Finds.* Studies in Mediterranean Archaeology, 34/2. Göteborg.

Root M. C., 1979. *The King and Kingship in Achaemenid Art. Essays on the Creation of an Iconography of Empire.* Acta Iranica, 19. Leiden.

———, 1985. "The Parthenon frieze and the Apadana reliefs at Persepolis: reassessing a programmatic relationship", *American Journal of Archaeology* 89: 103–120.

———, 1988. "Evidence from Persepolis for the dating of Persian and archaic Greek coinage", *Numismatic Chronicle* 148: 1–12.

———, 1989. "The Persian archer at Persepolis: Aspects of chronology, style and symbolism", *Revue des études anciennes* 91/1-2: 33–50.

———, 1991. "From the heart: Powerful Persianisms in the art of the Western Empire", pp. 1–29 in H. Sancisi-Weerdenburg & A. Kuhrt (eds) *Achaemenid History VI: Asia Minor and Egypt: Old Cultures in a New Empire.* Leiden.

———, 1996. "The Persepolis Fortification Tablets", pp. 3–27 in M.-F. Boussac & A. Invernizzi (eds) *Archives et Sceaux du Monde Hellénistique.* BCH Supplément 29.

———, 1998. "Pyramidal stamp seals—The Persepolis connection", pp. 257–298 in M. Brosius & A. Kuhrt (eds) *Achaemenid History 11: Studies in Persian History: Essays in Memory of David M. Lewis.* Leiden.

———, 2003a. "Hero and worshipper at Seleucia: Re-inventions of Babylonia on a banded agate cylinder seal of the Achaemenid Empire", pp. 249–283 in T. F. Potts, M. Roaf & D. Stein (eds) *Culture through Objects: Ancient Near Eastern Studies in Honour of P. R. S. Moorey.* Oxford.

———, 2003b. "The lioness of Elam: Politics and fecundity at Persepolis", pp. 9–32 in W. Henkelman & A. Kuhrt (eds) *Persian Perspective. Essays in Memory of Heleen Sancisi-Weerdenburg.* Leiden.

Roscalla F., 1998. *Presenze simboliche dell'ape nella Grecia antica.* Florence.

Ross E. D., 1931. *The Persians.* Oxford.

Rostovtzeff M., 1941. *The Social and Economic History of the Hellenistic World.* 3 vols. Oxford.

Roth M. T., 1987. "Age at marriage and the household: A study of Neo-Babylonian and Neo-Assyrian forms", *Comparative Studies in Society and History* 29: 715–747.

———, 1989/1990. "The material composition of the Neo-Babylonian dowry", *Archiv für Orientforschung* 35/37: 1–55.

———, 1991/1993. "The Neo-Babylonian widow", *Journal of Cuneiform Studies* 43/45: 1–26.

Roustaei K., Alamdari K. & Petrie C. A., 2006. "Landscape and environment of the Mamasani region", pp. 17–30 in D. T. Potts & K. Roustaei (eds) *The Mamasani Archaeological Project Stage One: A Report on the First Two Seasons of the ICAR-University of Sydney Expedition to the Mamasani District, Fars Province, Iran.* Tehran.

Rova E., 2008. "Mirror, distaff, pomegranate, and poppy capsule: On the ambiguity of some attributes of women and goddesses", pp. 557–570 in H. Kühne, R. M. Czichon & F. J. Kreppner (eds) *Proceedings of the 4th International Congress on the Archaeology of the Ancient Near East (ICAANE), Berlin, 29 Mar.–3 Apr., 2004, Volume 1.* 2 vols. Wiesbaden.

Royal Academy, 1931a. *Persian Art. An Illustrated Souvenir of the Exhibition of Persian Art at Burlington House London 1931.* 2nd edn. London.

———, 1931b. *Catalogue of the International Exhibition of Persian Art, 7 Jan.—28 Feb. 1931.* 2nd edn. London.

Rudenko S. I., 1970. *Frozen Tombs of Siberia. The Pazyryk Burials of Iron Age Horsemen* (transl. M. W. Thompson). London.

Russell J. R., 1994. "On the Armeno-Iranian roots of Mithraism", pp. 183–193 in J. R. Hinnells (ed.) *Studies in Mithraism: Papers Associated with the Mithraic Panel Organized on the Occasion of the XVIth Congress of the International Association for the History of Religions, Rome 1990.* Rome.

Rykwert J., 1996. *The Dancing Column: On Order in Architecture.* Cambridge, MA/London.

Sachau E., 1911. *Aramäische Papyrus und Ostraka aus einer jüdischen Militär-Kolonie zu Elephantine: altorientalische Sprachdenkmäler des 5. Jahrhunderts vor Chr.* 2 vols. Leipzig.

Sachs A. J. & Hunger H., 1989. *Astronomical Diaries and Related Texts from Babylonia I: Diaries from 261 B.C. to 165 B.C.* ÖAW, Phil.-hist. Kl., Denkschr. 210. Vienna.

Sackville-West V., 1926. *Passenger to Teheran.* London.

Safar F., 1949. "Soundings at Tell al-Lahm", *Sumer* 5: 154–172.

Sainte-Croix G., 1773. "Observations sur les ruines de Persépolis", (manuscrit inédit (BnF) édité et commenté par S. Montecalvo), *Quaderni di Storia* 59 (2004): 5–57.

———, 1775. *Examen critique des anciens historiens d'Alexandre.* Paris.

———, 1804. *Examen critique des anciens historiens d'Alexandre-le-Grand.* 2nd enlarged edn. Paris.

Sajjadi S. M. S., 2007. "Wall painting from Dahaneh-ye Gholaman (Sistan)", *Ancient Civilizations from Scythia to Siberia* 13/1–2: 129–154.

Saleh M., Sourouzian H. & Liepe J., 1986. *Die Hauptwerke im Ägyptischen Museum Kairo.* Mainz am Rhein.

Salles J.-F., 1990. "Les Achéménides dans le Golfe arabo-persique", pp. 111–130 in S. Sancisi-Weerdenburg & A. Kuhrt (eds) *Achaemenid History IV: Centre and Periphery.* Leiden.

———, 1998. "Antique maritime channels from the Mediterranean to the Indian Ocean", pp. 45–68 in C. Cuillot, D. Lombard & R. Ptak (eds) *From the Mediterranean to the China Sea: Miscellaneous Notes.* Wiesbaden.

Salonen A., 1972. *Die Ziegeleien im Alten Mesopotamien.* Helsinki.

Salvatori G., 1975. "Analysis of the association of types in the protohistoric graveyards of the Swat Valley (Loebanr I, Katelai I, Butkara II)", *East and West* 25: 333–351.

Sami A., 1970. *Persepolis (Takht-e Jamshid).* (sixth edition; translated by The Rev. N. Sharp). Shiraz.

———, 1988. "Was there ever a Median Empire?", pp. 197–212 in A. Kuhrt & H. Sancisi-Weerdenburg (eds) *Achaemenid History III: Method and Theory.* Leiden.

———, 1989. "The personality of Xerxes, King of Kings", pp. 549–561 in L. de Meyer & E. Haerinck (eds) *Archaeologica Iranica et Orientalis. Miscellanea in Honour of L Vanden Berghe.* Ghent [reprinted in E. Bakker, I. de Jong & H. van Wees (eds) *Brill's Companion to Herodotus.* Leiden, 2002, pp. 579–590].

———, 1991. "Introduction. Through travellers' eyes: the Persian monuments as seen by European travellers", pp. 1–35 in H. Sancisi-Weerdenburg & J. W. Drijvers (eds) *Achaemenid History VII: Through Travellers' Eyes.* Leiden.

———, 1994. "The orality of Herodotos' Medikos Logos or: The Median Empire revisited", pp. 39–55 in H. Sancisi-Weerdenburg, A. Kuhrt & M. C. Root (eds) *Achaemenid History VIII: Continuity and Change. Proceedings of the Last Achaemenid History Workshop, Apr. 6–8, 1990—Ann Arbor, Michigan.* Leiden.

———, 1999. "The Persian kings and history", pp. 91–112 in C. S. Kraus (ed.) *The Limit of Historiography: Genre and Narrative in Ancient Historical Texts.* Leiden and Boston.

Sancisi-Weerdenburg H., 1983a. "Exit Atossa. Images of women in Greek historiography on Persia", pp. 22–33 in A. Cameron & A. Kuhrt (eds) *Images of Women in Antiquity.* London.

———, 1983b. "The Zendan and the Ka'aba", pp. 145–151 in H. Koch & D. N. MacKenzie (eds) *Kunst Kultur und Geschichte der Achämenidenzeit und ihr Fortleben.* Archäologische Mitteilungen aus Iran, Ergänzungsbänd 10. Berlin.

———, 1986. "Gifts in the Persian Empire", pp. 129–146 in P. Briant & C. Herrenschmidt (eds) *Le Tribut dans l'Empire perse: actes de la table ronde de Paris, 12–13 décembre 1986.* Paris.

———, 1987a. "Introduction", pp. xi–xiv in H. Sancisi-Weerdenburg (ed.) *Achaemenid History I: Sources, Structures and Syntheses.* Leiden.

———, 1987b. "The fifth oriental monarchy and hellenocentrism: Cyropaedia VIII viii and its influence", pp. 117–131 in H. Sancisi-Weerdenburg &

A. Kuhrt (eds) *Achaemenid History II. The Greek Sources*. Leiden.

———, Kuhrt A. & Root M. C., eds, 1994. *Achaemenid History VIII: Continuity and Change. Proceedings of the Last Achaemenid History Workshop, Apr. 6–8, 1990—Ann Arbor, Michigan*. Leiden.

San-Nicolò M., 1932. "Parerga Babylonica VII: Der §8 des Gesetzbuches Hammurapis in den neubabylonischen Urkunden", *Archiv Orientální* 4: 327–344.

San-Nicolò M. & Petschow H., 1960. *Babylonische Rechtsurkunden aus dem 6. Jahrhundert v. Chr.* Munich.

Santoni M., 1980. "Un site de l'âge du Fer dans la plaine de Kachi, Baluchistan, Pakistan", *Paléorient* 6: 297–302.

Sarraf M. R., 2003. "Archaeological excavations in Tepe Ekbatana (Hamadan) by the Iranian Archaeological Mission between 1983 and 1999", pp. 269–279 in G. Lanfranchi, M. Roaf & R. Rollinger (eds) *Continuity of Empire (?) Assyria, Media, Persia*. Padua.

Sarre F., 1923. *Die Kunst des alten Persien*. Berlin.

Sauer J. A. & Blakely J. A., 1988. "Archaeology along the Spice Route of Yemen", pp. 91–116 in D. T. Potts (ed.) *Araby the Blest: Studies in Arabian Archaeology*. Copenhagen.

Sauvage M., 1998. *La Brique et sa Mise en Œuvre en Mésopotamie: des Origines à l'époque Achéménide*. Paris.

Scerrato U., 1966. "Excavations at Dahan-i Ghulaman (Seistan-Iran): First preliminary report", *East and West* 16: 9–30.

Schachner A. & Bucak E., 2004. "Ceç hitit ya da geç asur? Şanlıurfa arkeoloji müzesi'nde yeni bir ortostat", pp. 659–670 in T. Korkut (ed.) *Anadolu'da Doğdu, Fs Fahri Işık*. Istanbul.

Schaudig H., 2001. *Die Inschriften Nabonids von Babylon und Kyros des Großen*. Alter Orient und Altes Testament [AOAT], 256. Münster.

Scheil V., 1900. *Textes élamites-sémitiques, première série*. Mémoires de la Délégation en Perse, 2. Paris.

———, 1902. *Textes élamites-sémitiques, deuxième série*. Mémoires de la Délégation en Perse, 4. Paris.

Schiffer M. B., 1987. *Formation Processes of the Archaeological Record*. Albuquerque, NM.

Schiltz V., 1994. *Les Scythes et les nomades des steppes, VIIIe siècle av. J.-C.–Ier siècle après J.-C.* Paris.

Schiwek H., 1962. "Der Persische Golf als Schiffahrts- und Seehandelsroute in achämenidischer Zeit und in der Zeit Alexanders des Grossen", *Bonner Jahrbücher* 162: 4–97.

Schlick-Nolte B., 2001. "Glass", pp. 30–33 in *The Oxford Encyclopedia of Ancient Egypt* II. New York.

Schloen J. D., 2001. *The House of the Father as Fact and Symbol: Patrimonialism in Ugarit and the Ancient Near East*. Studies in the Archaeology and History of the Levant, 2. Winona Lake, IN.

Schlumberger D., 1971. "La coiffure du Grand Roi", *Syria* 48: 375–383.

Schmandt-Besserat D. ed., 1978. *Ancient Persia: The Art of an Empire. Catalogue of an Exhibition at the University Museum, The University of Texas at Austin and The Walters Art Gallery, Baltimore*, Austin, TX.

Schmid H., 1981. "Ergebnisse einer Grabung am Kernmassiv der Zikkurrat von Babylon", *Baghdader Mitteilungen* 12: 87–132.

———, 1990. "Rekonstruktionsversuche und Forschungsstand der Zikkurrat von Babylon", pp. 303–342 in R. Koldewey (ed.) *Das wieder erstehende Babylon*. 5th edn, ed. B. Hrouda. Munich.

———, 1995. *Der Tempelturm Etemenanki in Babylon*. Baghdader Forschungen, 17. Mainz am Rhein.

Schmidt E. F., 1939. *The Treasury of Persepolis and Other Discoveries in the Homeland of the Achaemenids*. Oriental Institute Communications [OIC], 21. Chicago.

———, 1953. *Persepolis I: Structures, Reliefs, Inscriptions*. Oriental Institute Publications [OIP], 68. Chicago.

———, 1957. *Persepolis II: Contents of the Treasury and Other Discoveries*. Oriental Institute Publications [OIP], 69. Chicago.

———, 1970. *Persepolis III: The Royal Tombs and Other Monuments*. Oriental Institute Publications [OIP], 70. Chicago.

Schmidt J., 2002. "Das Bit Akitu von Babylon", *Baghdader Mitteilungen* 33: 281–317.

Schmitt R., 1975. "Königtum im alten Iran", *Saeculum* 28/4: 384–395.

———, 1981. *Altpersische Siegel-Inschriften*. Veröffentlichungen der Iranischen Kommission, 10; Sitzungsberichte (Österreichische Akademie der Wissenschaften. Philosophisch-Historische Klasse), 381. Vienna.

———, 1985. "Achaemenid dynasty", *Encyclopaedia Iranica* I: 414–426.

———, 1988. "Achaimenideninschriften in griechischer literarischer Überlieferung", *Acta Iranica* 28: 17–38.

———, 1990. "iii. Darius' inscriptions", *Encyclopaedia Iranica* IV: 299–305.

———, 1999. "Bemerkungen zum Schlussabschnitt von Dareios' Grabinschrift DNb", *Altorientalische Forschungen* 26: 127–139.

Schmitt R., 2000. *The Old Persian Inscriptions of Naqsh-i Rustam and Persepolis*. Corpus Inscriptionum Iranicarum I.I.II. London.

———, 2003. "Die Sprache der Meder—eine grosse Unbekannte", pp. 23–36 in G. Lanfranchi, M. Roaf & R. Rollinger (eds) *Continuity of Empire (?) Assyria, Media, Persia*. Padua.

Schøyen M., 2007. "The Schøyen Collection. MS 2063, the Tower of Babel stele", http://www.schoyencollection.com/babylonianhist.htm#2063, accessed Apr. 2007.

Scurlock J., 2002. "Animals in ancient Mesopotamian religion", pp. 361–387 in B. J. Collins (ed.) *A History of the Animal World in the Ancient Near East*. Leiden.

Secousse D., 1729. "Dissertation sur l'expédition d'Alexandre contre les Perses" (mémoire présenté le 6 avril 1723), *Mémoires de littérature de l'Académie des Inscriptions et Belles-Lettres* 5: 415–430.

Seidl U., 1986. *Die elamischen Felsenreliefs von Kurangun und Naqš-e Rustam*. Iranische Denkmäler 12/2. Berlin.

———, 1989. *Die babylonischen Kudurru-Reliefs. Symbole mesopotamischer Gottheiten*. Orbis Biblicus et Orientalis [OBO], 87. Freiburg.

———, 1999a. "Eine Triumphstele Darius' I. aus Babylon", pp. 297–306 in J. Renger (ed.) *Babylon: Focus mesopotamischer Geschichte, Wiege früher Gelehrsamkeit, Mythos in der Moderne—2. Internationales Colloquium der Deutschen Orient-Gesellschaft 24.–26. März 1998 in Berlin*. Saarbrücken.

———, 1999b. "Ein Monument Dareios' I. aus Babylon", *Zeitschrift für Assyriologie und Vorderasiatische Archäologie* 89: 101–114.

Seipel W., ed., 1999. *Schätze des Orients. Meisterwerke aus dem Miho Museum. Eine Ausstellung des Kunsthistorischen Museums Wien, 22 Juni bis 31 Oktober 1999*. Vienna.

Sekunda N., 1988. "Persian settlement in Hellespontine Phrygia", pp. 175–196 in A. Kuhrt & H. Sancisi-Weerdenburg (eds) *Achaemenid History III: Method and Theory*. Leiden.

———, 1991. "Achaemenid settlement in Caria, Lycia and Greater Phrygia", pp. 83–143 in H. Sancisi-Weerdenburg & A. Kuhrt (eds) *Achaemenid History VI: Asia Minor and Egypt, Old Cultures in a New Empire*. Leiden.

Sekunda N. & Chew S., 1992. *The Persian Army 560–330 BC*. London.

Sellwood D., 1980. *An Introduction to the Coinage of Parthia*. 2nd edn. London.

Settle E., 1671. *Cambyses, King of Persia: A Tragedy. Acted by His Highness the Duke of York's Servants*. London.

Seux M. J., 1980/1983. "Königtum. B. II. und I. Jahrtausend", *Reallexikon der Assyriologie* 6: 140–173.

Sevinç N., Körpe R., Tombul M., Rose C. B., Strahan D., Kiesewetter H. & Wallrodt J., 2001. "A new painted Graeco-Persian sarcophagus from Çan", *Studia Troica* 11: 383–420.

Seyrig H., 1959. "Antiquités syriennes", *Syria* 36: 52–56.

———, 1966. "Divinités de Sidon", *Antiquités Syriennes* 6: 26–30.

Shahbazi A. S., 1972. "The Achaemenid tomb in Buzpar (Gur-i Dukhtar)", *Bastan Chenassi va Honar-e Iran* 9/10: 54–56.

———, 1974. "An Achaemenid symbol, I. A farewell to 'Fravahr' and 'Ahuramazda'", *Archäologische Mitteilungen aus Iran* (N.F.) 7: 135–144.

———, 1975. *The Irano-Lycian Monuments. The Principal Antiquities of Xanthos and its Region as Evidence for Iranian Aspects of Achaemenid Lycia*. Tehran.

———, 1976. "The Persepolis 'Treasury Reliefs' once more", *Archäologischen Mitteilungen aus Iran* (N.F.) 9: 151–156.

———, 1980. "An Achaemenid symbol, II. Farnah '(god given) fortune' symbolized", *Archäologische Mitteilungen aus Iran* (N.F.) 13: 119–147.

———, 1983. "Studies in Sasanian prosopography: I. Narseh's relief at Naqš-i Rustam", *Archäologische Mitteilungen aus Iran* 16: 155–268.

———, 1987. "Astōdān", *Encyclopaedia Iranica* II: 851–853.

———, 1990. "On the $X^w adāy-nāmag$", pp. 208–229 in *Iranica Varia: Papers in Honor of Professor Ehsan Yarshater*. Acta Iranica, 30; Série 3, Textes et mémoires, 16. Leiden.

———, 2002. "Recent speculations on the traditional date of Zoroaster", *Studia Iranica* 31: 7–45.

———, 2004. *The Authoritative Guide of Persepolis*. Tehran.

Shaked S., 1994. *Dualism in Transformation. Varieties of Religion in Sasanian Iran*. London.

———, 2004. *Le satrape de Bactriane et son gouverneur: Documents araméens du IVe s. avant notre ère provenant de Bactriane (Conférences données au Collège de France les 14 et 21 mai 2003)*. Paris.

Sharif M., 1969. "Excavations at Bhir mound, Taxila", *Pakistan Archaeology* 6: 6–99.

Shaw B. D., 1982. "Fear and loathing: The nomad menace and Roman Africa", pp. 29–50 in C. M. Wells (ed.) *L'Afrique Romaine/Roman Africa*. Ottawa.

———, 1983. "Eaters of flesh, drinkers of milk: the ancient Mediterranean ideology of the pastoral nomad", *Ancient Society* 13/14: 5–31.

Shayegan R. 1997. *The Avesta and the Bactria-Margiana Archaeological Complex (BMAC)*, paper presented at

American Oriental Society meeting of Mar. 23–26, 1997, http://www.umich.edu/~aos/abs974.htm

Shea M. O'D., 1983. "The small cuboid incense-burner of the Ancient Near East", *Levant* 15: 76–109.

Shear Jr. T. L., 1982. "The demolished temple at Eleusis", *Hesperia. Supplement* 20: 128–140.

Shefton B. B., 1993. "The white lotus, Rogozen and Colchis: The fate of a motif", pp. 178–209 & corrigenda in J. Chapman & P. Dolukhanov (eds) *Cultural Transformations and Interactions in Eastern Europe*. Avebury.

Sherwin-White S. M. & Kuhrt A., 1993. *From Samarkhand to Sardis: A New Approach to the Seleucid empire*. London and Berkeley, CA.

Simpson St J., 1998a. "Late Achaemenid bowl", *National Art Collections Fund 1997 Review*: 85–86, No. 4439.

Simpson St J., 1998b. "Late Achaemenid silver bowl from Mazanderan", *British Museum Magazine* 32 (autumn/winter): 32.

———, 1998c. "Gilt-silver and clay: A late Sasanian skeuomorphic pitcher from Iran", pp. 335–344 in K. Otavsky (ed.) *Entlang der Seidenstrasse. Frühmittelalterliche Kunst zwischen Persien und China in der Abegg-Stiftung*. Riggisberger Berichte, 6. Riggisburg.

———, 1999. "'The riches of all Persia'", *Minerva* 10/2 (Mar./Apr.): 21–22.

———, 2003. "From Persepolis to Babylon and Nineveh: the rediscovery of the Ancient Near East", pp. 192–201 in K. Sloan (ed.) *Enlightenment. Discovering the World in the Eighteenth Century*. London.

———, 2005. "The royal table", pp. 104–111 in J. Curtis & N. Tallis (eds) *Forgotten Empire. The World of Ancient Persia*. London.

——— & La Niece S., 2006. "Acquisitions: bowl", *British Museum Magazine* 56 (autumn/winter): 59.

———, ed., 2002. *Queen of Sheba: Treasures from Ancient Yemen*. London.

Sinha B. C., 1978. *Serpent Worship in Ancient India*. New Delhi.

Sirocko F., Garbe-Schönberg D. & Devey C., 2000. "Processes controlling trace element geochemistry of Arabian Sea sediments during the last 25,000 years", *Global and Planetary Change* 26: 217–303.

Skjærvø P. O., 1997. "The joy of the cup: a pre-Sasanian Middle Persian inscription on a silver bowl", *Bulletin of the Asia Institute* (N.S.) 11: 93–104.

———, 2005. "The Achaemenids and the *Avesta*", pp. 52–84 in V. Sarkhosh Curtis & S. Stewart (eds) *Birth of the Persian Empire*. London.

Small J. P., 2003. *The Parallel Worlds of Classical Art and Text*. Cambridge.

Smirnov Y. I., 1909. *Oriental Silver*. Leningrad.

Smith II A. M., 2005. "Pathways, roadways, and highways: Networks of communication and exchange in Wadi Araba", *Near Eastern Archaeologist* 68: 180–189.

Smith M., 1963. "II: Isaiah and the Persians", *Journal of the American Oriental Society* 83/4: 415–421.

Smith S., 1924. *Babylonian Historical Texts Relating to the Capture and Downfall of Babylon*. London.

Sotheby's, 1964. *Catalogue of The Ernest Brummer Collection of Egyptian and Near Eastern Antiquities and Works of Art, 16–17 Nov. 1964*. London.

Soudavar A., 2003. *The Aura of Kings: Legitimacy and Divine Sanction in Iranian Kingship*. Costa Mesa, CA.

———, 2006a. "The significance of Av. *cithra*, OPers. *ciça*, MPers *cihr*, and NPers. *cehr*, for the Iranian cosmogony of light", *Iranica Antiqua* 41: 151–185.

———, 2006b. "The Mongol legacy of Persian Farmāns", pp. 407–421 in L. Komaroff (ed.) *Beyond the Legacy of Genghis Khan*. Leiden.

Spanheim E., 1673. *Dissertatio de praesentia et usu numismatum antiquorum*. Rome.

Speck H., 2002. "Alexander at the Persian gates: A study in historiography and topography", *American Journal of Ancient History* 1 (N.S.): 7–234.

Spiegelberg W., 1928. "Drei demotische Schreiben aus der Korrespondenz des Pherendates, des Satrapen Darius I. mit den Chnum-Priestern von Elephantine", *Sitzungsberichte der Preussischen Akademie der Wissenschaften* 30: 604–622.

Spier J., 1992. *Ancient Gems and Finger Rings, Catalogue of the Collections, The J. Paul Getty Museum*. Malibu, CA.

Sprenger A., 1875. *Die alte Geographie Arabiens*. Bern.

Spycket A., 1980. "Women in Persian art", pp. 43–45 in D. Schmandt-Besserat (ed.) *Ancient Persia*. Malibu, CA.

———, 1981. *La statuaire du Proche-Orient ancient*. Handbuch der Orientalistik. 7. Abt., Kunst und Archäologie. 1. Bd., Der Alte Vordere Orient. 2. Abschnitt, Die Denkmäler. B, Vorderasien, Lfg. 2. Leiden.

Stacul G., 1966a. "Preliminary report on the pre-Buddhist necropolises in Swat (W. Pakistan)", *East and West* 16: 37–79.

———, 1966b. "Notes on the discovery of a necropolis near Kherai in the Gorband Valley (Swat, Pakistan)", *East and West* 16: 261–274.

Stacul G., 1967. "Excavations in a rock shelter near Ghaligai (Swat, Pakistan)", *East and West* 17: 185–219.

Stacul G. & Tusa S., 1977. "Report on the excavations at Aligrama (Swat, Pakistan)", *East and West* 27: 151–205.

Stansbury-O'Donnell M., 1999. *Pictorial Narrative in Ancient Greek Art*. Cambridge.

Starr C., 1975. "Greeks and Persians in the fourth century B.C.: A study in cultural contacts before Alexander" (Part One), *Iranica Antiqua* 11: 39–99.

———, 1977. "Greeks and Persians in the fourth century B.C.: A study in cultural contacts before Alexander" (Part Two), *Iranica Antiqua* 12: 49–115.

Stein M. A., 1905. *Report of Archaeological Survey Work in the North-West Frontier Province and Baluchistan, for the Period from Jan. 2nd, 1904 to Mar. 31, 1905.* Peshawar.

———, 1929. *On Alexander's Track to the Indus: Personal Narrative of Explorations on the North-west Frontier of India* (reprinted 2001). London.

———, 1940. *Old Routes of Western Iran*. London.

Steiner R. C., 2001. "The *mbqr* at Qumran, the *episkopos* in the Athenian Empire, and the meaning of *lbqr'* in Ezra 7:14: On the relation of Ezra's mission to the Persian legal project", *Journal of Biblical Literature* 120: 623–646.

Stern E. M., 1999. "Ancient glass in Athenian temple treasures", *Journal of Glass Studies* 41: 19–50.

———, 2001. *Archaeology of the Land of the Bible*, vol. 2. The Anchor Bible Reference Library. New York.

Stewart A., 1997. *Art, Desire and the Body in Ancient Greece*. Cambridge.

Stewart C. E., 1911. *Through Persia in Disguise: with Reminiscences of the Indian Mutiny* (edited from his diaries by Basil Stewart). London and New York.

Stiehl R., 1959. "Chronologie der Frātadāra", pp. 375–379 in F. Altheim (ed.), *Geschichte der Hunnen*, vol. I, Berlin.

Stolper M. W., 1974. *Management and Politics in Later Achaemenid Babylonia: New Texts from the Murašu Archive*. Ann Arbor.

———, 1985. *Entrepreneurs and Empire: the Murašû Archive, the Murašû Firm and Persian Rule in Babylonia*. Istanbul.

Stolper M. W., 1989. "The governor of Babylon and across-the-river in 486 B C ", *Journal of Near Eastern Studies* 48: 283–305.

———, 1992. "The written record: cuneiform texts from Susa", pp. 253–260 in P. O. Harper, J. Aruz & F. Tallon (eds) *The Royal City of Susa: Ancient Near Eastern Treasures in the Louvre*. New York.

———, 1993. *Late Achaemenid, Early Macedonian, and Early Seleucid Records of Deposit and Related Texts*. Supplemento agli Annali, Istituto Universitario Orientale, 77. Naples.

———, 1994. "Aspects of continuity between Achaemenid and Hellenistic Babylonian legal texts", pp. 329–351 in H. Sancisi-Weerdenburg, A. Kuhrt & M. C. Root (eds) *Achaemenid History VIII: Continuity and Change. Proceedings of the Last Achaemenid History Workshop, Apr. 6–8, 1990—Ann Arbor, Michigan.* Leiden.

———, 1997. "Flogging and plucking", *Topoi* Suppl. 1: 347–350.

———, 2001. "Fifth century Nippur: texts of the Murašus and their surroundings", *Journal of Cuneiform Studies* 53: 83–132.

Stone E., 1981. "Texts, architecture and ethnographic analogy: Patterns of residence in Old Babylonian Nippur", *Iraq* 43: 19–33.

———, 1987. *Nippur Neighborhoods*. Studies in Ancient Oriental Civilisation [SAOC], 44. Chicago.

Strassmaier J. N., 1897. *Inschriften von Darius, König von Babylon (521-485 v. Chr.)*. Leipzig.

Streck M., 1916. *Assurbanipal und die letzten assyrischen Könige bis zum Untergange Ninivehs*, Vorderasiatische Bibliothek, 7. Leipzig.

Strelkov A. S., 1937. "The Moscow Artaxerxes cylinder seal", *Bulletin of the American Institute for Iranian Art and Archaeology* 5: 17–21.

Strommenger E. & Hirmer M., 1962. *Fünf Jahrtausende Mesopotamien. Die Kunst von den Anfängen um 5000 v. Chr. bis zu Alexander dem Großen*. Munich.

Stronach D., 1965. "Excavation at Pasargadae: A third preliminary report", *Iran* 3: 9–40.

———, 1966. "The Kuh-i Shahrak fire altar", *Journal of Near Eastern Studies* 25: 217–227.

———, 1971. "A circular symbol on the tomb of Cyrus", *Iran* 9: 155–158.

———, 1972. "Une statue de Darius découverte à Suse—Description and comment", *Journal Asiatique* 260: 235–266.

———, 1978. *Pasargadae. A Report on the Excavations Conducted by the British Institute of Persian Studies from 1961 to 1963.* Oxford.

———, 1989. "Early Achaemenid coinage. Perspectives from the homeland", *Iranica Antiqua* 24: 255–279.

———, 1990. "On the genesis of the old Persian cuneiform script", pp. 195–203 in F. Vallat (ed.) *Contribution à l'histoire de l'Iran: Mélanges Jean Perrot*. Paris.

———, 1997. "Anshan and Parsa: Early Achaemenid history, art and architecture on the Iranian Plateau", pp. 35–53, pls 11–19, IV–X in J. Curtis (ed.)

Mesopotamia and Iran in the Persian Period: Conquest and Imperialism 539-331 B.C.—Proceedings of a Seminar in memory of Vladimir G. Lukonin. London.

———, 2002. "Icons of dominion: Review scenes at Til Barsip and Persepolis", *Iranica Antiqua* 37: 373–402.

———, 2003*a*. "The tomb at Arjan and the history of southwestern Iran in the early sixth century B.C.E.", pp. 249–260 in N. F. Miller & K. Abdi (eds) *Yeki bud, yeki nabud: Essays on the Archaeology of Iran in Honor of William M. Sumner*. Los Angeles.

———, 2003*b*. "Independent Media: archaeological notes from the homeland", pp. 233–248 in G. Lanfranchi, M. Roaf & R. Rollinger (eds) *Continuity of Empire (?) Assyria, Media, Persia*. Padua.

Stronach D. & Roaf M., 2007. *Nush-i Jan I: The Major Buildings of the Median Settlement*. London.

Strong D. E., 1979. *Greek and Roman Gold and Silver Plate* (reprint). London and New York.

Stucky R. A., 1985. "Achämenidische hölzer und elfenbeine aus Ägypten und vorderasien im Louvre", *Antike Kunst* 28: 7–32.

Suhr E. G., 1969. *The Spinning Aphrodite. The Evolution of the Goddess from Earliest Pre-Hellenic Symbolism through Late Classical Times*. New York.

Sulimirski T., 1970. *The Sarmatians*. New York.

Summerer L., 2007. "Picturing Persian victory: The painted battle scene on the Munich Wood", *Ancient Civilization from Scythia to Siberia* (13): 3–30.

Summerer L. & von Kienlin A., 2007. "Kelainai: Afyon'daki Pers Kenti", *ArkeoAtlas*: 74–83.

Summers G., 1993. "Archaeological evidence for the Achaemenid period in Eastern Turkey", *Anatolian Studies* 43: 85–108.

———, 2002. "Preliminary report of the 2002 excavations at Kerkenes Dag", http://www.metu.edu.tr/home/wwwkerk/kerk1/11prelim/2002/english/05exc.html

———, 2003. "Kerkenes: The 2003 season of excavations", http://www.metu.edu.tr/home/wwwkerk/kerk2/11prelim/2003/english/09exclow.html

Sumner W. M., 1986. "Achaemenid settlement in the Persepolis Plain", *American Journal of Archaeology* 90: 3–31.

———, 1994. "Archaeological measures of cultural continuity and the arrival of the Persians in Fars", pp. 97–105 in H. Sancisi-Weerdenburg, A. Kuhrt & M. C. Root (eds) *Achaemenid History VIII: Continuity and Change. Proceedings of the Last Achaemenid History Workshop, Apr. 6–8, 1990—Ann Arbor, Michigan*. Leiden.

Svoboda B. & Concev D., 1956. *Neue Denkmäler antiker Toreutik*. Prague.

Swennen, P., 2004. *D'Indra à Tištrya, Portrait et évolution du cheval sacré dans les mythes indo-iraniens anciens*. Paris.

Sykes E. C., 1898. *Through Persia on a Side-Saddle*. London.

———, 1910. *Persia and its People*. London.

Sykes P. M., 1902. *Ten Thousand Miles in Persia or Eight Years in Iran*. New York.

———, 1915. *A History of Persia*. London.

———, 1922. *Persia*. Oxford.

Tabari, 1983. *Tārīkh-i Tabari* (transl. Arabic to Persian A. Pāyandeh). Tehran.

Tajvidi A. A., 1976 [1355]. *Danestanihaye novin darbaraye honar va bastanshenassiye asr-e hakamanishiye bar bonyad-e kavoshhaye panjsaleye Takht-e Jamshid (New Knowledge on Achaemenid Art and Archaeology based on Five Years' Researches at Persepolis)*. Tehran.

Tallon F., 1997. "Les fouilles de Marcel Dieulafoy à Suse. La résurrection du palais de Darius", pp. 46–55 in N. Chevalier (ed.) *Une Mission en Perse: 1897–1912*. Paris.

Tanabe K. (ed.), 1986. *Sculptures of Palmyra*, I. Memoirs of the Ancient Orient Museum, 1. Tokyo.

Taqizadeh S. H., 1938. *Old Iranian Calendars*. London.

———, 1943–46. "The early Sasanians, some chronological points which possibly call for revision", *Bulletin of the School of Oriental & African Studies* 12: 6–51.

———, 1947. "The era of Zoroaster", *Journal of the Royal Asiatic Society*: 30–40.

Teeter E., 2002. "Animals in Egyptian religion", pp. 335–360 in B. J. Collins (ed.) *A History of the Animal World of the Ancient Near East*. Leiden.

Teeter E. & Wilfong T. G., 2003. *Scarabs, Scaraboids, Seals, and Seal Impressions from Medinet Habu. Based on the Field Notes of Uvo Hölscher and Rudolf Anthes*. Oriental Institute Publications [OIP], 118. Chicago.

Tengberg M. & Lombard P., 2001. "Environnement et économie végétale à Qal'at al-Bahreïn aux périodes Dilmoun et Tylos. Premiers éléments d'archéobotanique", *Paléorient* 27: 167–181.

Ter-Martirossov F., 1996. "Un peuple convoité: l'état arménien et les Achéménides, les Ervandides, les princes hellénistiques et les empereurs romains", pp. 167–249 in J. Santrot (ed.) *Arménie: trésors de l'Arménie ancienne: des origines au IVe siècle*. Nantes.

———, 2001. "The typology of the columnar structures of Armenia in the Achaemenid period", pp. 155–164 in I. Nielsen (ed.) *The Royal Palace Institution in the First Millennium B.C.: Regional Development and Cultural Interchange between East and West*. Monographs of the Danish Institute at Athens, 4. Athens and Aarhus.

Thieme P., 1970. "Die Vedischen Āditya und die Zarathustrischen Ameša Spenta", pp. 397–412 in B. Schlerath (ed.) *Zarathustra*. Darmstadt.

Thomas F., 1993. "Sargon II., der Sohn Tiglat-pileser III", pp. 465–470 in M. Dietrich & O. Loretz (eds) *Mesopotamica—Ugaritica—Biblica. Festschrift für Kurt Bergerhof zur Vollendung seines 70. Lebensjahres am 7. Mai 1992.* Alter Orient und Altes Testament [AOAT], 232. Kevelaer and Neukirchen-Vluyn.

Thompson G., 1965. "Iranian dress in the Achaemenian period: Problems concerning the kandys and other garments", *Iran* 3: 121–126.

Tilia A. B., 1969. "Reconstruction of the parapet on the terrace wall at Persepolis, south and west of Palace H", *East and West* 19: 9–43.

———, 1972. *Studies and Restorations at Persepolis and Other Sites of Fars*. IsMEO Reports and Memoirs, 16. Rome.

———, 1974. "Discovery of an Achaemenian palace near Takht-i Rustam to the north of the terrace of Persepolis", *Iran* 12: 200–204.

———, 1978. *Studies and Restorations at Persepolis and other sites of Fars, Vol. 2*. IsMEO Reports and Memoirs, 18. Rome.

Tomkins C., 1970. *Merchants and Masterpieces. The Story of the Metropolitan Museum of Art*. London and Harlow.

Topbaş A., 1993. "Seyitömer Höyüğü 1991 Yılı Kurtarma Kazısı", pp. 1–30 in *Müze Kurtarma Kazıları Semineri, 26–29 Nisan 1993 Efes, III*. Ankara.

———, 1994. "Seyitömer Höyüğü 1992 Yılı Kurtarma Kazısı", pp. 297–310 in *Müze Kurtarma Kazıları Semineri, 26–29 Nisan 1993 Marmaris, IV*. Ankara.

Tourovets A., 2001. "Nouvelles propositions et problèmes relatifs à l'identification des délégations de l'escalier est de l'Apadana (Persépolis)", *Archäologische Mitteilungen aus Iran und Turan* 33: 219–256.

Triantaffyllidis P., 2000. *Rhodian Glassware 1: The Luxury Hot-formed Transparent Vessels of the Classical and Early Hellenistic Periods*. Athens.

Trowbridge M. L., 1930. *Philological Studies in Ancient Glass*. Urbana, IL.

Tuplin, C. J., 1987. "The administration of the Achaemenid Empire", pp. 109–166 in I. Carradice (ed.) *Coinage and Administration in the Athenian and Persian Empires*. BAR International Series, 343. Oxford.

———, 1989. "Xenophon and the garrisons of the Achaemenid Empire", *Archäologische Mitteilungen aus Iran* 20: 167–245.

———, 1994. "Persians as Medes", pp. 235–256 in H. Sancisi-Weerdenburg, A. Kuhrt & M. C. Root (eds) *Achaemenid History VIII: Continuity and Change. Proceedings of the Last Achaemenid History Workshop, Apr. 6–8, 1990—Ann Arbor, Michigan*. Leiden.

———, 1997. "Xenophon's *Cyropaedia*: education and fiction", pp. 108–133 in A. Sommerstein & C. Atherton (eds) *Education in Greek Fiction*. Bari.

———, 1998. "The seasonal migration of Achaemenid kings. A report on old and new evidence", pp. 63–114 in P. Briant, A. Kuhrt, M. C. Root, H. Sancisi-Weerdenburg & J. Wiesehöfer (eds) *Achaemenid History XI: Studies in Persian History: Essays in Memory of David M. Lewis*. Leiden.

———, 2004a. "The Persian Empire", pp. 154–183 in R. Lane Fox (ed.) *The Long March. Xenophon and the Ten Thousand*. New Haven.

———, 2004b. "Medes in Media, Mesopotamia and Anatolia: Empire, hegemony, domination or illusion?", *Ancient West and East* 3: 223–251.

———, 2005a. "Darius' Accession in (the) Media", pp. 217–244 in P. Bienkowski, C. Mee & E. Slater (eds) *Writing and Ancient Near Eastern Society—Papers in Honour of Alan R. Millard*. New York and London.

———, 2005b. "Fratama", *Arta* 2005.4 (www.achemenet.com).

Tusa S., 1979. "The Swat Valley in the 2nd and 1st Millennium B.C.: A Question of Marginality", *South Asian Archaeology* 4/II: 675–690. Berlin.

Uehlinder C., ed., 2001. *Images as Media. Sources for the Cultural History of the Near East and the Eastern Mediterranean (1st millennium B.C.E.)*. Orbis Biblicus et Orientalis [OBO], 175. Freiburg.

Unger E., 1931. *Babylon, die heilige Stadt nach der Beschreibung der Babylonier*. Leipzig.

Ungnad A., 1908. *Vorderasiatische Schriftdenkmäler der Königlichen Museen zu Berlin*, vol. 6. *Leipzig*.

———, 1911. *Aramäische Papyrus aus Elephantine*. Leipzig.

Usher J., 1865. *A Journey from London to Persepolis*. London.

Ussishkin D., 1993. "Lachish", pp. 897–911 in E. Stern (ed.) *The New Encyclopedia of Archaeological Excavations in the Holy Land, Vol. 1*. Jerusalem.

Vallat F., 2000. "Une inscription élamite sur un rhyton en argent à tête de bélier", *Akkadica* 116: 29–33.

Van Beek G., 1983. "Digging up Tell Jemmeh", *Archaeology* 36/1 (Jan./Feb.): 12–19.

———, 1987. "Arches and vaults in the Ancient Near East", *Scientific American* 257 (Jul.): 78–85.

———, 1993. "Tell Jemmeh", pp. 667–674 in E. Stern (ed.) *The New Encyclopedia of Archaeological Excavations in the Holy Land*, Vol. 2. Jerusalem.

Vanden Berghe L., 1959. *Archéologie de l'Irān ancien*. Documenta et Monumenta Orientis Antiqui, 6. Leiden.

———, 1963. "Les reliefs élamites de Mālamīr", *Iranica Antiqua* 3: 22–39.

———, 1968. *On the Track of the Civilization of Ancient Iran*. Brussels.

———, 1984. *Reliefs Rupestres de l'Irān Ancien*. Brussels.

———, 1986. "Données nouvelles concernant le relief rupestre élamite de Kūrangūn", pp. 157–173 in L. De Meyer, H. Gasche & F. Vallat (eds) *Fragmenta Historiae Elamicae: Mélanges offerts à M. J. Steve*. Paris.

Van den Hoek B. & Shrestha B., 1992. "The sacrifice of serpents: Exchange and non-exchange in the Sarpabali of Indrayani, Kathmandu", *Bulletin de l'École Française d'Extrême-Orient* 79/1: 57–75.

van der Toorn K., 1996. *Family Religion in Babylonia, Syria, and Israel: Continuity and Change in the Forms of Religious Life*. Leiden.

Van Dommelen P., 1998. "Punic persistence: Colonialism and cultural identity in Roman Sardinia", pp. 25–48 in J. Berry & R. Laurence (eds) *Cultural Identity in the Roman Empire*. London.

Van Driel G., 2002. *Elusive Silver—In Search of a Role for a Market in an Agrarian Environment: Aspects of Mesopotamia's Society*. Leiden.

Van Loon M., 1986. "The drooping lotus flower", pp. 245–254 in M. Kelly-Buccellati (ed.) *Insights through Images. Studies in honour of Edith Porada*. Malibu, CA.

van Wees H., 2004. *Greek Warfare: Myths and Realities*. London.

Vargyas P., 2000. "Darius I and the Daric reconsidered", *Iranica Antiqua* 35: 33–46.

Varoli J., 2002. "Scythian gold from Siberia said to predate the Greeks", *New York Times*, 9 Jan. 2002: http://www.nytimes.com/2002/01/09/arts/design/09GOLD.html

Venturi R., 1977. *Complexity and Contradiction in Architecture*. New York.

Verardi G., 2002. *Excavations at Gotihawa and a Territorial Survey in Kapilvastu District of Nepal: A Preliminary Report*. Lumbini International Research Institute Occasional Papers, 2. Lumbini.

Verbrugghe G. & Wickersham J., 1996. *Berossos and Manetho, Introduced and Translated*. Ann Arbor.

Vickers M., 1985. "Early Greek coinage: a reassessment", *Numismatic Chronicle* 145: 1–44.

———, 1991. "Persian, Thracian and Greek gold and silver: questions of metrology", pp. 31–39 in H. Sancisi-Weerdenburg & A. Kuhrt (eds) *Achaemenid History VI: Asia Minor and Egypt: Old Cultures in a New Empire. Proceedings of the 1988 Groningen Achaemenid History Workshop*. Leiden.

———, 1996. "Rock crystal: the key to cut glass and *diatreta* in Persia and Rome", *Journal of Roman Archaeology* 9: 48–65.

Vickers M. & Gill D., 1994. *Artful Crafts. Ancient Greek Silverware and Pottery*. Oxford.

Vittmar G., 1991/92. "Ein altiranischer Titel in demotischer Überlieferung", *Archiv für Orientforschung* 38/39: 159–160.

———, 2003. *Ägypten und die Fremden, Kulturgeschichte der Antiken Welt* 97. Mainz.

Vogel J. P., 1972. *Indian Serpent-lore or The Nagas in Hindu Legend and Art* (reprint). Varanasi and Delhi.

Vogelsang W. J., 1986. "Four short notes on the Bisitun text and monument", *Iranica Antiqua* 21: 131–135.

———, 1988. "A period of acculturation in ancient Gandhara", *South Asian Studies* 4: 103–113.

———, 1990. "The Achaemenids and India", pp. 93–110 in H. Sancisi-Weerdenburg & A. Kuhrt (eds) *Achaemenid History IV: Centre and Periphery*. Leiden.

———, 1992. *The Rise and Organisation of the Achaemenid Empire: The Eastern Iranian Evidence*. Leiden.

———, 1998. "Medes, Scythians and Persians: the rise of Darius in a north–south perspective", *Iranica Antiqua* 33: 195–224.

Voigt M. M. & Young T. C., Jr. 1999. "From Phrygian capital to Achaemenid entrepot: Middle and late Phrygian Gordion", *Iranica Antiqua* 34: 191–242.

Volpilhac-Auger C., 2002. "Montesquieu et l'impérialisme grec: Alexandre ou l'art de la conquête", pp. 49–60 in D. W. Carrithers & P. Coleman (eds) *Montesquieu and the Spirit of Modernity*. Oxford.

von Bolla S., 1941. "Drei Diebstahlsfälle von Tempeleigentum in Uruk", *Archiv Orientální* 12: 113–120.

Von Bothmer D., 1961. *Ancient Art from New York Private Collections. Catalogue of an Exhibition held at the Metropolitan Museum of Art Dec. 17, 1959—Feb. 28, 1960*. New York.

———, 1984. "A Greek and Roman treasury", *The Metropolitan Museum of Art Bulletin* 42/1 (summer): 54–59.

von der Osten H. H., 1931. "The ancient seals from the Near East in the Metropolitan Museum: Old and Middle Persian seals", *The Art Bulletin* 13: 221–241.

———, 1934. *Ancient Oriental Seals in the Collection of Mr. Edward T. Newell*. Oriental Institute Publications [OIP], 22. Chicago.

von Gall H., 1966. "Zu den 'medischen' Felsgräbern in Nordwestiran und Iraqi Kurdistan", *Archäologischer Anzeiger* 19–43.

———, 1972. "Persische und medische Stämme", *Archäologische Mitteilungen aus Iran* 5: 261–283.

———, 1974. "Die Kopfbedeckung des Persichen Ornats bei den Achämeniden", *Archäologische Mitteilungen aus Iran* 7: 145–161, pls 31–36.

———, 1979. "Bemerkungen zum Kyrosgrab in Pasargadae und zu verwandten Denkmälern", *Archaeologische Mitteilungen aus Iran* 12: 271–279.

———, 1988. "Das Felsgrab von Qizqapan", *Bagdader Mitteilungen* 19: 557–582.

———, 1993. "Dā o Doḵtar", *Encyclopaedia Iranica* VI: 529–530.

von Graeve V., 1970. *Der Alexandersarkophag und seine Werkstatt*. Istanbuler Forschungen, 28. Berlin.

von Rad U., Schaaf M., Michels K. H., Schulz H., Berger W. H. & Sirocko F., 1999a. "A 5000-year record of climate change in varved sediments from the oxygen minimum zone off Pakistan, Northeastern Arabian Sea", *Quaternary Research* 51: 39–52.

von Rad U., Schulz H., Reich V., den Dulk M., Berner U., & Sirocko F., 1999b. "Multiple monsoon-controlled breakdown of oxygen-minimum conditions during the past 30,000 years documented in laminated sediments off Pakistan", *Palaeogeography, Palaeoclimatology, Palaeoecology* 152: 129–161.

von Saldern A., 1959. "Glass finds at Gordion", *Journal of Glass Studies* 1: 23–49.

———, 1970. "Other Mesopotamian glass vessels (1500–600 B.C.)", pp. 203–228 in A. L. Oppenheim, R. H. Brill, D. Barag & A. von Saldern, *Glass and Glassmaking in Ancient Mesopotamia*. New York.

———, 1975. "Two Achaemenid glass bowls and a hoard of Hellenistic glass vessels", *Journal of Glass Studies* 17: 37–46.

———, 1995. *Glas. Antike bis Jugendstil. Die Sammlung im Museum für Kunst und Gewerbe Hamburg*. Stuttgart.

von Voigtlander E. N., 1978. *The Bisitun Inscription of Darius the Great. Babylonian Version*. Corpus Inscriptionum Iranicarum. Pt I, vol. II. London.

von Wissmann H., 1982. *Die Geschichte von Saba' II. Das Grossreich der Sabäer bis zu seinem Ende im frühen 4. Jh. v. Chr*. Vienna.

Waerzeggers C., 2003/2004. "The Babylonian revolts against Xerxes and the 'end of archives'", *Archiv für Orientforschung* 50: 150–173.

Wäfler M., 1975. *Nicht-Assyrer neuassyrischer Darstellungen*. Alter Orient und Altes Testament [AOAT], 26. Neukirchen-Vluyn.

Walser G., 1966a. *Die Völkerschaften auf den Reliefs von Persepolis*. Berlin.

———, 1966b. "Archäologische Gesellschaft zu Berlin, Jul. 8, 1965", *Archäologische Anzeiger* 81: 544–549.

———, 1980. *Persepolis. Die Königspfalz des Darius*. Tübingen.

Walters H. B., 1926. *Catalogue of the Engraved Gems and Cameos Greek, Etruscan and Roman in the British Museum*. London.

Wanhill R. J. H., 2003. "Brittle archaeological silver: a fracture mechanisms and mechanics assessment", *Archaeometry* 45/4: 625–636.

Ward W. H., 1910. *The Seal Cylinders of Western Asia*. Washington, DC.

Wasmuth M., 2009. "Reflexion und Repräsentation kultureller Interaktion: Ägypten und die Achämeniden". PhD dissertation. Basel.

Waters M. W., 2004. "Cyrus and the Achaemenids", *Iran* 42: 91–102.

Wedepohl K. H., 2003. *Glass in Antike und Mittelalter*. Stuttgart.

Weeks L. R., Alizadeh K. S., Niakan L., Alamdari K., Khosrowzadeh A. & Zaidi M., 2006. "Excavations at Tol-e Nurabad", pp. 31–88 in D. T. Potts & K. Roustaei (eds) *The Mamasani Archaeological Project Stage One: A Report on the First Two Seasons of the ICAR-University of Sydney Expedition to the Mamasani District, Fars Province, Iran*. Tehran.

Weippert M., 1987. "The relations of the states east of the Jordan with the Mesopotamian powers during the first millennium B.C.", *Studies in the History and Archaeology of Jordan* 3: 97–105. Amman.

Weisberg D. B., 1980. *Texts from the Time of Nebuchadnezzar*. Yale Oriental Series, Babylonian Texts, 17. New Haven.

Weiskopf M., 1989. *The So-Called "Great Satraps' Revolt" 366–36*. Historia: Einzelschriften 63: 1–112.

Weissbach F. H., 1938. "Esagila und Etemenanki nach den keilschriftlichen Quellen", pp. 37–85 in F. Wetzel & F. H. Weissbach (eds) *Das Haupttheiligtum des Marduk in Babylon, Esagila und Etemenanki*. Wissenschaftliche Veröffentlichungen der Deutschen Orient-Gesellschaft, 59. Leipzig.

Weld Blundell H., 1893. "Persepolis", pp. 537–539 in E. Delmar Morgan (ed.) *Transactions of the Ninth International Congress of Orientalists, held in London, 5–12 Sept. 1892*. London.

Wheeler R. E. M., 1962. *Charsada: A Metropolis of the North-West Frontier: Being a Report on the Excavations of 1958*. London.

Whitcomb D. S., 1991. "Pseudo-prehistoric ceramics from southern Iran", pp. 95–112 in K. Schippman, A. Herling & J.-F. Salles (eds) *Golf Archäologie:*

Mesopotamien, Iran, Kuwait, Bahrain, Vereinigte Arabische Emirate und Oman. Göttingen.
White H., 1981. "The value of narrativity in the representation of reality", pp. 1–23 in W. J. T. Mitchell (ed.) *On Narrative*. Chicago.
Whitehouse D., 1972. "Excavations at Siraf: Fifth interim report", *Iran* 10: 63–87.
———, 1974. "Excavations at Siraf: Sixth interim report", *Iran* 12: 1–30.
Whitfield N., 1987. "Motifs and techniques of Celtic filigree: are they original?", pp. 74–84 in M. Ryan (ed.) *Ireland and Insular Art A.D. 500–1200. Proceedings of a Conference at University College, Cork 31 Oct.–3 Nov. 1985*. Dublin.
Who Was Who, 1972, vol. 6: *1961–1970*. London.
Widengren G., 1968. *Les religions de l'Iran*. Paris.
Wiesehöfer J., 1978. *Der Aufstand Gaumātas und die Anfänge Dareios' I*. Habelts Dissertationsdrucke: Reihe Alte Geschichte H. 13. Bonn.
———, 1994. *Die "dunklen Jahrhunderte" der Persis*. Zetemata 90. Munich.
———, 1995. "'Reichsgesetz' oder 'Einzelfallgerechtigkeit'", *ZAR* 1: 36–45.
———, 1996. *Ancient Persia*. London.
———, 1999. "Kyros, der Schah und 2500 Jahre Menschenrechte. Historische Mythenbildung zur Zeit der Pahlavi-Dynastie", pp. 55–68 in S. Conermann (ed.) *Mythen, Geschichte(n), Identitäten: Der Kampf um die Vergangenheit*. Hamburg.
———, 2007. "Fars under Seleucid and Parthian rule", pp. 37–47 in V. S. Curtis & S. Stewart (eds) *The Age of the Parthians*. London and New York.
Wilber D. N., 1969. *Persepolis, The Archaeology of Parsa, Seat of the Persian Kings*. London.
Wilkinson C. K., 1949. "Two ancient silver vessels", *Bulletin of the Metropolitan Museum of Art* 7: 186–198.
Williams A. V., 1990. *The Pahlavi Rivayat Accompanying the Dadestan i Denig*. Historisk-filosofiske Meddelelser, 60, 2 vols. Copenhagen.
Williams D., 2005. "From Phokaia to Persepolis. East Greek, Lydian and Achaemenid jewellery", pp. 105–114 in A. Villing (ed.) *The Greeks in the East*. London.
Williams E. C., 1907. *Across Persia*. London.
Williamson H. G. M., 1985. *Ezra, Nehemiah*. Word Biblical Commentary, 16. Waco.
Winckelman J.-J., 1766. *Histoire de l'art chez les Anciens*, (transl. from the German). Paris.
Winnett F. V., 1937. *A Study of the Lihyanite and Thamudic Inscriptions*. University of Toronto Studies Oriental Series, 3. Toronto.
Winnett F. V. & Reed W. L., 1970. *Ancient Records from North Arabia*. Toronto.
Winter F. T. J., 1912. *Der Alexandersarkophag aus Sidon*. Strassburg.
Winter I., 1976. "Carved ivory furniture panels from Nimrud: a coherent subgroup of the North Syrian style", *Metropolitan Museum Journal* 11: 25–54.
———, 1981. "Royal rhetoric and the development of historical narrative in Neo-Assyrian reliefs", *Studies in Visual Communication* 7/7: 2–38.
———, 1985. "After the battle is over: the 'Stele of the Vultures' and the beginning of historical narrative in the Ancient Near East", pp. 11–32 in H. K. Simpson & M. S. Simpson (eds) *Pictorial Narrative in Antiquity to the Middle Ages (CASVA/Johns Hopkins Symposium in the History of Art)*. Washington, DC.
———, 1986. "The king and the cup. Iconography of the royal presentation scene on Ur III seals", pp. 253–268, pls. 63–66 in M. Kelly-Buccellati (ed.) *Insights through Images. Studies in Honour of Edith Porada*. Malibu, CA.
Woods C. E., 2004. "The sun-god tablet of Nabû-apla-iddina revisited", *Journal of Cuneiform Studies* 56: 23–103.
Woolley C. L., 1962. *Ur Excavations IX: The Neo-Babylonian and Persian Periods*. London.
Wright D., 2001. *The English Amongst the Persians. Imperial Lives in Nineteenth-Century Iran*. rev. edn. London.
Wright F. L., 1994. *Frank Lloyd Wright: Collected Writings, Vol 4*. New York.
Wright G. E., 1955. "Judean Lachish", *The Biblical Archaeologist* 18/1 (Feb.): 9–17.
Wroth W., 1903. *The British Museum Catalogue of the Coins of Parthia*. London.
Wu X., 2005. "Central Asia in the context of the Achaemenid Persian Empire (6th to 4th century B.C.)". PhD thesis, Department of the History of Art, University of Pennsylvania. Philadelphia.
Wübbenhorst H. & Engels G., 1989. *5000 Jahre Gießen von Metallen. Fakten, Daten, Bilder zur Entwicklung der Gießereitechnik*. Düsseldorf.
Wunsch C., 1993. *Die Urkunden des babylonischen Geschäftsmannes Iddin-Marduk: Zum Handel mit Naturalien im 6. Jahrhundert v. Chr*. Cuneiform Monographs 3a, 3b. Groningen.
———, 1995/1996. "Die Frauen der Familie Egibi", *Archiv für Orientforschung* 42/43: 33–63.
———, 2000. "Die Richter des Nabonid", pp. 557–595 in J. Marzahn & H. Neumann (eds) *Assyriologica et Semitica, Festschrift für J. Oelsner*. Alter Orient und Altes Testament [AOAT], 252. Münster.
Wüst W., 1966, *Altpersische Studien, Sprach- und kulturgeschichtliche Beiträge zum Glossar der Achämeniden-Inschriften*. Munich.

Wüstenfeld F., 1874. "Bahrein und Jemama, nach arabischen Geographen beschrieben", *Abhandlungen der königlichen Gesellschaft der Wissenschaften zu Göttingen* 19.

Wynn A., 2003. *Persia in the Great Game. Sir Percy Sykes: Explorer, Consul, Soldier, Spy.* London.

Yağcı E. E., 1995. "Akhaemenid cam kaseleri ve Milas müzesinden yayinlanmamiş iki örnek", *Anadolu Medeniyetleri Müzesi*: 312–326.

Yamauchi E., 1990. *Persia and the Bible.* Grand Rapids, MI.

Yarshater E., 1983. "Iranian national history", pp. 359–477 in E. Yarshater (ed.) *The Cambridge History of Iran*, vol. 3/1: *The Seleucid, Parthian and Sasanian Periods.* Cambridge.

Young R., 2003. *Agriculture and Pastoralism in the Late Bronze and Iron Age, North West Frontier Province, Pakistan.* Bradford Monographs in the Archaeology of Southern Asia, 1; BAR International Series, 1124. Oxford.

Young Jr. T. C., 1966. "Thoughts on the architecture of Hasanlu IV", *Iranica Antiqua* 6: 48–71.

———, 1969. *Excavations at Godin Tepe. First Progress Report.* Toronto.

———, 1988. "The early history of the Medes and the Persians and the Achaemenid Empire to the death of Cambyses", pp. 1–52 in J. Boardman, N. G. L. Hammond, D. M. Lewis & M. Oswald (eds) *Cambridge Ancient History Volume IV: Persia, Greece and the Western Mediterranean c. 525–479 B.C.* 2nd edn. Cambridge.

———, 1992. "Media", pp. 658–659 in *The Anchor Bible Dictionary Volume 4.* New York, London, Toronto, Sydney and Auckland.

———, 1994. "Architectural developments in Iron Age western Iran", *Bulletin of the Canadian Society of Mesopotamian Studies* 27: 25–32.

Young T. C. & Levine L. D., 1974. *Excavations of the Godin Project: Second Progress Report.* Toronto.

Younger J. G., 2005. *Sex in the Ancient World. From A to Z.* London.

Yoyotte J., 1974. "Les inscriptions hiéroglyphiques de la statue de Darius à Suse", *Cahiers de la Délégation Archéologique Française en Iran* 4: 181–183.

Zaehner R. C., 1955. *Zurvan. A Zoroastrian Dilemma.* Oxford.

———, 1956. *The Teachings of the Magi. A Compendium of Zoroastrian Beliefs.* London.

Zaehner R. C., 1961. *The Dawn and Twilight of Zoroastrianism.* New York.

Zahle J., 1975. *Harpyie-monumentet i Xanthos. En lykisk pillegrav.* Copenhagen.

———, 1983. *Arkæologiske studier i lykiske klippegrave og deres relieffer fra ca. 550-300 f.Kr.—Sociale og religiøse aspekter.* Copenhagen.

Zaidi M., McCall B. & Khosrowzadeh A., 2006. "Survey of Dasht-e Rustam Yek and Dasht-e Rustam-Do", pp. 147–168 in D. T. Potts & K. Roustaei (eds) *The Mamasani Archaeological Project Stage One: A Report on the First Two Seasons of the ICAR-University of Sydney Expedition to the Mamasani District, Fars Province, Iran.* Tehran.

Zawadzki S., 1988. *The Fall of Assyria and Median-Babylonian Relations in Light of the Nabopolassar Chronicle* (transl. U. Wolko & P. Lavelle). Poznán and Delft.

———, 2003. "Nebuchadnezzar and Tyre in the light of new texts from the Ebabbar archives in Sippar", Hayim and Miriam Tadmor volume, *Eretz Israel* 27: 276*–281*.

Zazoff P., 1983. *Die antiken Gemmen.* Munich.

Zertal, A., 1990. "The Pahwah of Samaria (Northern Israel) during the Persian period: types of settlement, economy, history and new discoveries", *Transeuphratène* 3: 9-30.

———, 1993. "The Mount Manasseh (Northen Samarian Hills) survey", pp. 1311–12 in E. Stern (ed.) *New Encyclopedia of Archaeological Excavations in the Holy Land* 4. Jerusalem.

Zettler R., 1979. "On the chronological range of Neo-Babylonian and Achaemenid seals", *Journal of Near Eastern Studies* 38: 258–263.

Zick-Nissen J., 1966. "Der Knüpfteppich von Pazyryk und die Frage seiner Datierung", *Archäologischer Anzeiger* 81: 569–581.

Zorn J. R., 1993. "Tell en-Nasbeh: A Re-Evaluation of the Architecture and Stratigraphy of the Early Bronze Age, Iron Age and Later Periods." PhD dissertation. Berkeley, CA.

———, 1994. "Estimating the population size of ancient settlements: methods, problems, solutions, and a case study", *Bulletin of the American Schools of Oriental Research* 295: 31–48.

———, 1997. "Mizpah. Newly discovered stratum reveals Judah"s other capital", *Biblical Archaeology Review* 33/5: 29–38.

Zorn J. R. , Yellin J. and Hayes J., 1994. "The M(W)SH stamp impressions and the Neo-Babylonian period", *Israel Exploration Journal* 44: 161-83.

Zournatzi A., 2000. "The processing of gold and silver tax in the Achaemenid Empire: Herodotus 3.96.2 and the archaeological realities", *Studia Iranica* 29/2: 241–271.

———, 2003. "The Apadana coin hoards, Darius I, and the West", *American Journal of Numismatics* 15: 1–28.

Index

Italic numbers denote reference to illustrations

Ābān Yasht 132, 133
Abdalonymus of Sidon 258
Ablancourt, Nicolas Perrot d' 7
Abradatas 53
Achaemenes 17, 19, 28
Achaemenid bowls 524–5, *527*
Achaemenid dynasty
   in Arabia 445–54
   areas of conflict 463–8, 545–60
   in Central Asia 545–60
   collapse of 379
   continuity/discontinuity
      within 93–4, 95
   and development of
      Zoroastrianism 85, 89, 94,
      103–8, 111, 134
   in Egypt 464–8
   in English drama 33–9
   in Far Eastern part of
      Empire 503–21
   funerary practices of 75–81
   genealogy of 17–19, 93
   goals of 376
   Hellenocentric view of 5, 21–2
   iconography after collapse
      of 379–82, 389–90
   imperial ideology 111–36, 141,
      161, 282, 417, 545
      on coins and seals 323, 324,
         325–6, 327, 332, 333, 334,
         337–56, 366, 367, 376,
         548–54
   in Judah 468–9
   legitimacy of 19
   links with Median Empire 63–9
   in Mesopotamia 481–8
   origins of 315–16
   in Persian Gulf 523–33
   political relations with
      provinces 545–60
   relations with
      subordinates 51–9
   religion of 76, 77, 80–1, 85,
      87–8, 96
   religious tolerance 43, 79–80,
      86, 105
   rise of 63, 445
   royal dress 255–72
   royal titles 492
   royal tombs 77, 80, 91–100
Achaemenid History Workshop 21
Achaemenid robe 255, 260,
   261–3, 264, 265, 271, 272
Ackerman, Phyllis 441
Acts of Christian Martyrs 75
Adad 44, 210
Adad-nirari I 209
Adapa 478
administration 26, 41
   in Arabia 449–50, 452–4
   of Babylonian temples 495–6
   in Bahrain 524
   in Central Asia 545
   courts of law 465–6, 482–8
   local agents 450, 453
   in Mesopotamia 481, 493
   regional diversity of 481, 488
   and rival ethnic groups 467–8
   in Yehud 461
   see also satrapies; taxation;
      tribute
Aelian 475, 477, 478
aerial photography 300–1
Aeschylus 115, 256, 259, 262
Aëtius 421
Afghanistan 504, 519, 520
Afrāsiyāb 130–1
Agathias 80, 525
Agesilaus 53, 312
agriculture 286
Ahriman 81, 526
Ahuramazda 44, 45, 67, 82, 96,
      105, 114, 280
   as Creator 85–9
   Darius as deputy of 125–8
   and *khvarnah* 120, 122–5, 131–3
   primary position of 226
   and winged disc symbol 261
Ai 460
Aizanoi 361
Akhatabu and Abbā, stela of
   538, 539
Akkadian language 54, 55, 56, 96,
      185–6, 316, 353, 483
Akra 506–7, 515, 520
al-Barkeh, Shaykh 532
al-Brukhti 532
al-Hisma depression 447, 452
Alcibiades 81
Alexander III the Great
   at Ephesus 420, 422
   and Babylon 493, 494

Alexander III the
    Great—*Continued*
  on campaign 9
  and collapse of Achaemenid
      Empire 379, 471
  conquest of Swat 505
  and date of Zoroaster 112, 114
  defeat of Persians 12
  destruction of Apadana at
      Susa 410
  in European historiography
      3, 7, 8
  as fanatic or hero 17
  military achievement of 23
  nature of his empire 12, 13
  seizure of Persian Gates
      288, 295
  and tomb of Cyrus the Great 98
  and Tower of Babel 474–5,
      477, 479
  victory at Granicus 532
Alexander IV 475
Alexander, Christopher 201
Alexander, Sir William, Earl of
    Stirling 37–8
Alexander Mosaic, Pompeii 256,
    257–8, *257*, *258*
Alexander Sarcophagus,
    Sidon 142–3, *145*, 156,
    258, *259*
'Ali, Imam 119
Aligrama 505
Alotte de la Füye, M. 382
Alram, Michael 385, 386, 390, 391
Altıntaş 361
Altıntepe 438
Amandry, P. 434
Amarna, North Palace 201
Amarna Period 537
Amasis, Pharaoh 242
amata 57
amber 422
American Numismatic
    Society 383
Amesha Spentas 113, 114, 119
Amisos 424
Ammon/Ammonites 458, 461
Amorges 53
Amorites 458
Amory Jr, Copley 23
Amrit 413
amulets 412–13
Amytis 18, 66

Anahita (deity) 19, 113, 118, 123,
    132–3, 159, 232, 281
  Temple of, Bactria 427
  Temple of, Estakhr 134
Anaïtis 232
Anatolia 66, 217, 315, 316, 449
  conflict in 463–4
  glassware 419–21, 422, 423, 424
  satrapies 463
  seals from 165–6, 168, 170, 215,
      361–7, 557
  silverware 441
Anaximander 81
Anaximenes 81
Andersen, Helmuth 523
Andromache 170
Androsthenes 528
Anglo-Persian Oil Company
    (APOC) 429–31, 432, 433
Angra Mainyu 525
Ankhhapi, stela of *539*, 540
Ansāri, Khājeh 'Abdollāh 113
Anshan 93, 267, 268, 288
Anthemion stele, Daskylion 144,
    148, 150
Antiochus I 388, 391
Antiochus III 385, 492
Antiochus, Crown Prince 475
anušiya 55
anvils 408
Apadana, Persepolis 24, *122*,
    196, 231
  excavation of 221–2, 231
  foundation deposits 128, 221–7
  naming of 231–3
  reliefs 142, 278, 380, 405, 434,
      441, 451, *451*, 538
  staircase 221, 222, 305–6,
      306, 528
Apadana, Susa 208, 410, 415
apadana (word) 231–3
Apam Napāt (deity) 117, 118, 122,
    123, 126–7, 128, 130, 131,
    132, 133, 135, 225, 226
Aperghis, G. G. 294
Apocrypha 37, 39
Apollo of Didyma 479
appliqué ware 511, *516*
appliqués 262–3
Aq-Qoyunlu Empire 134
aquatic deities 132–3
Arabia
  Achaemenid 445, 449–54

  definition of 446
  geography and
      landscape 447–8, 452, 453
  mainland eastern 528–9
  in Neo-Assyrian and Neo-
      Babylonian eras 449
  Persian influence on
      development of 454
Arabian Massif 447, 448
Arachosia 67, 68, 504, 519
Aramaic
  documents 41–9
  language 41, 213, 215, 315
  stelae 535, 537, *539*, 540, 541
archers 496–7
  Assyrian *310*, 311
  on coins and seals 337–56, 372,
      373, *374*, *375*, 376, 380
  crowned 337, 373
  half-figure 339–51, 355
  kneeling 352, 353–5, 356
  organization 497–8
  standing 352–3
architecture
  Babylonian domestic 179–94
  columned halls 195–205
  conflicting views of 23–4, 27
  Median influence 247–52
Arda Viraz Namag 226
Ardashir I 115, 116, 134,
    387, 388
Ardebil-Mughan plain 285, 286
Argishti I 95
Aria 67
Ariaramnes 18, 546
Ariobarzanes 464
Aristagoras 462, 463
Aristes 532
Aristobulus 79, 91, 98, 99
Aristophanes 420, 421, 422
Aristotle 422
Armenia 67, 68, 240, 553
armour 501, 502
Armstrong, J. 189, 190, 192
army, Achaemenid 309–12,
    495–502
  areas of deployment 499–500
  cavalry 498
  chariotry 498–9
  equipment 499, 501–2
  hierarchy 500–1
  infantry 496–8
  weapons 499

Arnold, Arthur 24
aromatics, precious 446–7, 449, 451, 452
Arrian 79–80, 91, 92, 98–9, 256, 271, 475, 494, 505, 530, 532, 533
arrow slots 252
arrowheads, bronze 304
Arsames, satrap of Egypt 18, 19, 41, 42, 43, 44, 45, 47, 48, 464, 466, 467, 552, *553*, 557, 559
arštibara 256–9, *258*
Artabanus 276, 546
Artachate, cylinder seal 553, *555*, 557
Artama 535
Artareme 493
artavan (righteous) 105–6
Artaxerxes I 52, 142, 242, 439, 488, 492, 546
   passing of throne from Xerxes to 276
   personality of 284
   religion under 284
   restoration of Empire under 284
   revolts under 546, 550
   and Treasury reliefs 278, 284
Artaxerxes II 51, 132, 133, 231, 232, 259
Artaxerxes III
   Arabian envoys to 451, 454
   conflict under 550
   tomb of 263, *263*, 451
Artbanu 465
Artemis 232
Artemision, Ephesus 419, 420
Artumazza 497
Artystone, statue of 141
Aryan beliefs 19, 25
Aryan deities 114
ashavans 131
Ashdod 461
Ashkelon 461
Ashmolean Museum 241, 492
Ashur 252
Ashurbanipal 87, 150, 242, 267, 311, 472, 474, 478, 479, 529
Asia
   Central 545–60
   South 503–21

Aššur/Šamaš (deity) 85, 340, 350, 497
Aššur-res-iši 209
Assyrian Empire
   army 310–11, *310*
   art 270
   brick-making 209–10, 212, 217, 411
   campaigns against Arabia 449
   choice of capital 95
   exile of enemies 315, 316
   glass-making 419, 423
   iconography 339–40, 342, 343–4, 352, 355, 374
   overthrow of 63, 67, 68, 460, 472
   reliefs 265, 272
   religion in 113
   weaknesses of 10
astōdān 79
astronomy 526–8
Astyages of Media 18, 64, 65, 66, 68
Aswan *see* Syene
Asyut hoard 372
Ataie, M. T. 304
Athlit 422
Atossa 18
Atradates 65
atravaxsh 106–7, 108
Atta-hamiti-Inshushinak 265–6
Attic vase painting 167, 170, 174, *260*
Aubin, J. 532
audience halls 203
audience scenes 141–51, 154–61, 238, *240*, 243, 277, *382*
Autophradates *see* Vadfradad
Avesta 111
   and Achaemenid inscriptions 114
   and birth date of Zoroaster 112, 116–18
   deities in later 125, 135
   and *khvarnah* 122–3, 130, 131
   writing down of 111, 116, 117, 132, 134, 135–6
Avestan language 112, 135
Avestan tradition 69, 81, 86–7, 89, 105–6, 107–8
axial corridors 201
axiality, negation of 203
Azerbaijan, Iranian 285–6

Ba'al-Aliyan 269
Baba Jan 248
Babelon, Ernest 369, 370, 371–2, 373
Babylon
   Achaemenid palaces in 263
   Achaemenid rule in 491–2, 495
   Assyrian destruction of 474
   Bel-Marduk temple 282, 492
   bricks 209–10, 212, 411
   cylinder seal 19
   Cyrus' capture of 8
   deities 282
   domestic architecture 179–94
   effect of Achaemenid conquest on 481
   Elamite era 472
   excavations at 475
   glassware 422
   iconography 209, 211, 342
   Ishtar Gate and Processional Way 209, 210
   language 41, 222
   looting by 472, 480
   Merkes quarter 188, 189
   revolts against Xerxes 475, 477, 491, 493, 494
   texts 41, 63–4, 222
   wealth of temples 495
Bactria/Bactrians 18, 66, 68, 223, 281, 504, 546, 552, 559
Bactria Margiana Archaeological Complex (BMAC) 113
Bagadad coins 383, 385, 386, 387–9, 391
Bagohi 43, 44, 45
Bahrain 523–8, 533
Bailey, Sir Harold 256
Baker, Heather D. 180
Baker, Valentine 26
Bakun culture 304
Bala Hissar, Charsadda 505, 509, 520
Baluchistan 17, 507–11, 518, 519–20
bandaka 51–2, 54–5
Banks, John 35
Bannu Basin 506–7, 511, 515–18, 519, 520
Bannu Black on Red Ware 506, 507, *508*, 515, 518, 519
banquet tableware 404
banqueting scenes 150–1, 440

Baradkâma 276
Baraklı 372
Bardak-e Siah 317
Bardiya 17, 18, 19, 68, 92, 106, 546
Barnett, R. D. 269–70, 311
Barry, Elizabeth 35
Bastam 286
bathrooms 233
battle scenes, on seals 166, 546–7, *547*, 548–60, *550*, *552*, *553*
Bau-Ēreš 485–7
Bawden, G. 449
Bazira 505
beakers 23, 421, 424, 441
Behistun *see* Bisitun
Bel (deity) 96, 477, 492
Bēl-b Āsir 485
Bel-shimanni 477
bellows 408
Belos, tomb of 477–9
belts, symbolic 52
Benjamin, S.G.W. 24, 26
Benoit, Agnès 416
Berenson, Bernard 23
Berossus 67, 494
Bes 364, 413, *414*
Besenval, R. 511
Beshar Valley 295
Beth-Zur 459, 460
Bethel 460
Beyond the River, satrapy of 459, 468, 469, 491
bezel rings 325, *325*, 331
Bhir mound, Taxila 506, 509, 514–15, 520
Bianchi, Ugo 281
Bianchini, Francesco 371
Bibliothèque Nationale de France 369, 370, 371, 373, 551
bichrome geometric patterns 508–9, *512*, *513*, 515
Bir-kot-ghwandai 505
bird offerings 148, 160
Biruni 115, 116
Bisitun
  iconography 95, 96, 119–20, *124*
  Inscription 55, 56, 67, 68, 88, 93, 106, 114, 119–20, 126, 127, 128, 130, 242, 504, 519, 545, 560
  reliefs 340, 350–1, 366, 380, 548, 553, 555

bit hilani 201
bītu 186, 187
Blenkinsopp, J. 462
Boardman, Sir John 165–6, 215
bodyguards, royal 312
  commander of 276, 277
Boeotians 464
Böhl, Franz 475, 491, 492
Bolaghi gorge and plain xv, 303
Bologna University 303
Bongenaar, A. C. V. M. 502
bonnets 266–7
Book of the Dead 536, 541
booty taking 472, 479–80
Borazjan 317
Borsippa 186, 187, 478, 482, 491, 495, 497
Bossuet J. B. 4, 5, 7
Bosworth, Brian 532
Boucharlat, Rémy 302
bow-fiefs (*bīt qašti*) 496, 497
Bowerstock, G.M. 528
bowls
  Achaemenid bowls 524–5, *527*
  carinated 412
  glass 419–21, 424
  hemispherical 404, 405, *406*
  silver 432–9, *434*, 441
  tulip 290, 291
bows and arrows 499
Boyce, Mary 96, 107, 112, 116, 126, 132, 235–6, 281, 386
BP 430
bracelets 325, 399, 403
  with griffin terminals 397–404, *398*, 407, 408
Bradford University 510
Bradley-Birt, F.B. 23, 26
Breton, J. F. 448
Briant, Pierre 68, 160, 376, 478, 481, 559
bribes 465–7
bricks
  brick-making 209–10, 216–17
  masons' marks 212–16, *214*, *215*, *216*, 217
  origins and parallels 208–9
  polychrome glazed 237, 410
  Susa 207–18, 409–11, *411*, 415–16
brigands 465
Brisson, B. 4
British Museum 299, 432, 506

coins 322, 369, 370, 371, 382, 387
  seals 159, 552, *554*, 557
  silver bowls 429, 434–9, *436*, *437*, *438*, *439*, 441, 472
  Sippar Collections 496
  see also Oxus Treasure
British Museum Friends 434
Bronze Age 76, 507
bronze-work 199
Brosius, Maria 22
Browne, Edward Granville 25, 28
Brummer, Ernest 433
Brummer, Joseph 433, 434, 435
Brummer Galleries, Paris 433
Bryn Mawr College 506
Buddhist texts 526
Buffalo Museum of Science 153–5, 156, 160–1
Bukān bricks 118
Bundahishn 116
Burlington House, London 431
burnt offerings 43–4, 45–6, 282, 457
Bury, R. de 4, 5
Buseirah 449
Butkara 505
Butz, Kilian 528
Buzpar valley 92
Byvanck-Quarles van Ufford, L. 424

Cahill, N. 278–9
Çal dağ 357, 372
calendars 114, 115, 116, 226, 284
Callias, treaty of 284
Callieri, Pierfrancesco 303, 386, 505
Calmeyer, Peter 261, 262
calyx cups 421, 423, 424
Cambises, King of Persia (Preston) 35
Cambridge University 506
Cambyses 465
  death of 95, 221
  decline under 4
  Egyptian campaign 29, 42, 92, 95
  in English drama 35–7, 39
  genealogy 18
  investiture in Babylon 264
  and Jewish temples 43
  kingly ideology 119

military activity under 500
rule in Mesopotamia 481, 486–7, 492
tomb 92
Cambyses, King of Persia: A Tragedy (Settle) 36–7
Cameron, G.G. 491, 492
Çan sarcophagus 367, 558
Canaan/Canaanites 458, 459
Canal Stelae 504
Capisa 504
capital, change of 93, 95
caps 256
caravans 448, 452, 453
Caria/Carians 367, 376, 423, 424, 464, 467–8
   stelae 535, *540*, 541
Carlyle, Thomas 17
Carmania/Carmanians 67, 546
carnelian 167, 325, 402, 403
Carradice, I. 372, 373
Casabonne, O. 377
Cassandane 67, 69
cassia 446
casting *see* hollow casting; lost wax casting
Cataea 531
Caunus 424
cavalry 498, 501
cedars, from Lebanon 498, 499
cemeteries 304, 440, 505
Central Building, Persepolis 380
Centre for Documents, Persepolis 303
ceramics
   Akra and Bannu basin 506, 507, *508, 509*, 515–18
   Bahrain 524–6, *527*
   Baluchistan 508–11, *512, 513*, 518
   columned halls 198–9
   Gandharan 506, 514
   Gilan province 440
   Greek 167, 170, 174, *260*, 549–50
   Mamasani Valleys 289–91, 293
   Parsa-Pasargadae 304
   Phrygian 363
   Yehud 459
   see also tableware
ceremonial 53–4, 58
chalcedony, blue 166, 323, 325
Chaldeans 34, 492, 499, 502
Chalouf stele 533

champlevé work 403, 404
Chardin, J. 4, 5
Charidemus 52, 53
chariot scenes 332–3
chariotry 498–9, 501
Charsadda 505, 509, 510, 515, 518, 520
Chashmeh Sabz pond 133
chiça 124, 128–31
Chichpis *see* Teispes
Chigkamar mound 507
chisels 408
Chitral 506
Chius 421
Choga Zanbil 303
Choresmians 546, 550, 553
Christensen, Arthur 280
Christians, persecution of 75
Christie's 434
Chronicles 458, 459
Cibber, Colley 38–9
Ciçantakhma 67
Cilicia 10, 377, 459, 499
cists 78
Clark, Kenneth 173
clay
   glazed 409, 412
   moulds 408
   tablets 482
   tags 361–7, *363, 364, 365*
clean-shaven figures 238–9, 277
cloaks 256, 259, 266
cloisonné work 400, 401, 403, 404, 408
clubs 501, 502
coffins
   metal 77
   terracotta 76
coins
   Anatolian 216
   Apadana foundation deposits 221, 224–5, 226
   archer 337–56, 372, 373, *374, 375*, 376
      type I 337, 338, *338*, 339–51, 372
      type II 337, 338, 339, 351–5, 356, 373
      type III 337, 372, 377
      type IV 337, 372, 377
   catalogues 370–2
   classification of 372–3, 376
   composition of 376

croeseids 128, *130*, 221, 225, 227, 338
Cypriot 221
darics 321–2, 338, 351, 371, 380
   of Darius I 26
drachms 379, *381*, 385, 386
fakes and forgeries 321, 322
fractions 379, *381*
Frataraka coins of Persis 379–93, *381*
from Abdera 221
from Aegina 221
hoards 321, 338, 372, 382–5
iconography 337–56, *338*, 373–6
identity of kings on 371–2, 373
overstrikes 386–9, 391
Oxus Treasure 321–2
Parthian 385, 391, *392*
as seals 338, 339
of Shāpur and Pāpak 135
sigloi 321–2, 338, *338*, 339, 351, 372, 380
tetradrachms 379, *381*, 382, 383, 385, 386–7, 388
trophy 386, 387, 388, 389, 391
Collins, Treacher 24
colonization 11, 13
colour 236–7, 260–3
column bases 291–2, *293*, 317
columned halls 195–205, 231–3, 252
columns 200–2
Condillac, É.B. de 12
conquerors, devastation caused by 11–12
context of discovery 275–6
continuity
   between Achaemenids and Sasanians 379, 389–90
   between ancient and modern Persia 24, 25
   between Cyrus and Darius 93
corpses, preservation of 97–8
corruption 26
cotton 528
Council Hall, Persepolis 261, 262
Court Style 263–4, 271, 340, 341, 353, 354
courtyard houses 187, 188, 193
courtyards 184, 185, 188, 193
creation
   myth 88
   seven stages of 225, 227

cremation 76, 81
croeseids 128, *130*, 221, 225, 227, 338
Croesus 223, 420
Crown, John 38
crowns 269, 270
crucibles 408
Ctesias xiii, 18, 22, 66, 99, 477, 478, 494
cultural diversity 376
cuneiform documents xiii, 180, 315, 482
Curtius *see* Quintus Curtius
Curzon, George 22, 24, 26, 27, 28, 29, 91, 92, 98, 294
Cyaxares 18, 67–8
cylinder seals 19, 153–5, *154*, 156, 159, 160–1, 325, *325*, 329, 331, 332, 365–7, 552, *554*
cylinders
    archive copies 474
    Cyrus Cylinder 65, 94, 96
    foundation deposits 472–4, 478
    Nebuchadnezzar's fragment 472–4, *472*, 479–80
Cyrus: A Tragedy (Hoole) 35
Cyrus Cylinder 65, 94, 96
Cyrus I 267
Cyrus II the Great 17, 26, 462
    and adoption of Median dress 259
    campaign against Massagetae 546, 559
    conquests of 3, 63, 65, 66
    death of 95
    defeat of Babylon 51, 66, 67, 264, 449
    defeat of Medes 64, 65, 66, 67, 69
    as a deity 270
    dress of 268–72
    and Elamite tradition 94
    in English drama 34–5, 39
    expedition to Central Asia 504
    as founder of empire 283
    Gate R relief, Pasargadae *267*, 268–9, *268*
    genealogy 18, 19, 65, 93, 100
    historiographical status of 10, 65
    and the Jews 66
    kingly ideology 119
    Lydian campaign 10, 66, 223
    marriage 66, 67, 69
    and Orontas 51
    and Persian Gulf 523
    Persian peak under 6, 8
    religion of 94, 96, 118–19
    rise of 63, 65–7
    rule in Mesopotamia 481, 482, 484, 485, 486, 487, 492
    tomb of 25, 80, 91–2, 97, 98–9, 118, 271
    Xenophon's portrayal of 34, 39
Cyrus the Great (Banks) 35
Cyrus the Younger 10, 132, 546
    image on coins 371, 373

Da-u Dukhtar 289, 293
Dabar Kot 511
Dadarshi, satrap 68
daena (world view) 104
daēvas (demons) 86, 87, 119
daggers 499, 501
Dahan-i Ghulaman 518
Dailaman 440
Daivâ Inscription, Persepolis 19, 81, 275, 276, 279–83, *281*, 284
    date of 280
    multiple copies of 282–3, 284
Dalton, O. M. 398
dam construction 303–4, 307
Dandamayev, Mohammad 49, 281
d'Anville, Bourguignon 530, 532
D'Arcy Exploration Company 430–1
darics 321–2, 338, 351, 371, 380
Darius I
    administration of 26, 465, 481, 487–8, 493, 494, 503
    and architectural metaphor 204–5
    Aryan origins 128–31
    bandaka 54–5
    Chalouf stele 533
    co-conspirators 126–8, 133
    conquests of 129–30
    consolidation of empire 559
    construction of Persepolis 221
    cultural tolerance of 283
    discontinuity with Cyrus 93–5, 100, 119
    in English drama 37–8, 39
    extent of empire under 26–7, 222–4
    as fanatic 17
    as founder of dynasty 19, 65
    genealogy 18–19, 93, 100, 128, 133–4, 136, 271
    ghost of 260, *260*
    as a god 115
    image on coins 371
    and Ionian revolt 463
    and Khnum priests 44
    kingly ideology 95, 111, 112, 119–31, 211, 212, 222–4, 227, 337, 503
    military activity under 500
    monotheism 119, 125, 133, 134
    rebellions against 67–8, 92, 340, 504, 546, 559
    and reconstruction of Temple in Jerusalem 114
    rise to power 17, 19, 221, 340, 504
    and royal dress 271
    statements in DPh text 222–4
    Susa palace 207–9, 217, 248
    Susa statue 239, *241*, 413, 528, 529
    tomb 91, *92*, 97, *98*, 99
    and Treasury reliefs 276, 277, 278
    and Zoroastrianism 19, 69, 87, 94, 96, 105, 112, 114, 119, 134, 136, 223
    see also Apadana foundation deposits; Bisitun Inscription; Tachara Palace
Darius II 51, 52
Darius III 52, 530, 532
    Alexander Mosaic 256, *257*
    decadence under 6, 23
    defeat of 12
    despotism 9
    excesses on campaign 6, 8–9
Darius (son of Xerxes) 276, 278
Darius King of Persia: A Tragedy (Crown) 38
Dascyleium *see* Daskylion
Dashtestan 317
Dashli Yar 440
Dasht-e Arjan 295
Dasht-e Nurabad 291
Dasht-e Rostam-e Do 289, 291, 293
Dasht-e Rostam-e Yek 289, 291

Daskylion
  bullae 142, *144*, 156, 161, *238*
  coins 373
  reliefs 233, 379
  ruler of 463
  satrapy 464
  seals 361, 366, 367, 550
  stelae 144, *148*, 150, 151
Datames 390
Davenant, William 36
daxiiunam 118
day and night, realms of 126–8, *128*, 131, 135
dayyĀnu ša šarri see judges of the king
de Blois, François 529
de Jong, Albert 111, 390, 525
de Mably, G. B. 10, 12, 13
de Mecquenem, Roland 207, 410, 415
de Menasce, Jean 280
de Morgan, Jacques 207, 410, 415, 471, 472
de Windt, Harry 23
decadence, Persian 3–9, 13, 22, 23, 26
De Clerq Collection 144, 153, 156, 157, 160
decuries 497
Dedan 449, 450, 460
Deir el-Medineh *537*
deities
  emblems of 118, 119–20
  Mazdaean 225–6
  on seals 156, 159
Délégation scientifique françis en Perse 207
Demetrias, plaque 151
Demetrius II 386
Demetrius (Seleucid general) 452
Democritus of Ephesus 256
demography, Neo-Babylonian 181
dentils 250, *251*, 252
Department of Coal Mines of Turkey 361
"Departure of the Warrior" scenes 168–70
deportations 463–4
descration of tombs 478
desert 445–6, 447, 452–3
despotism 5, 6, 8, 9–10, 13, 26
Deuteronomy, Book of 458, 459
Deve Huyuk 440

dexiai (handshakes) 51, 52
Dieulafoy, Marcel 207, 268, 410, 415
Dilmun 523–8
Dio Cassius 76, 452–3
Diodorus 9, 52, 53, 276, 422, 446, 452, 463–4, 475, 500
Dionysus 386
discontinuity 93–6, 100
Dittman, R. 510
Djedherbes 535–42, *536*
domestic architecture, Babylonian 179–94
domestic images 168–70
doorways, blocking up of 188, 189–90
Doriscus, Battle of 530
Dothan Valley 461
dowries 185, 186
DPh trilingual text 221, 222–4
drachms 379, *381*, 385, 386
Drangiana 67
dress
  of adorants 540
  after fall of Achaemenids 389–90
  female 170
  of nobles 235
  Persian 233–9
  royal 255–72
drills, military 312
Dron service 107
DukKan-i Dāūd 379, 383
Dum-e Mil 289
Dumat al-Ǧandal 529
Dur Khan 509, 510, 515, 518, 520
Dur Sharrukin 95
Durand, E. R. 25
Durrah-i Bust assemblage 511, *516*, *517*, 518, 519
Dusinberre, Elspeth 524
Dussaud, René 529
Dyrbaean 95

Eanna temple, Uruk 479–80, 482, 484, 485, 495–6
Eastern Iran
  Avestan native land 113
  historians' problems over 64
Eastwick, Edward 28
Ebabbara temple, Sippar 478, 482, 484, 495–6, 497–8, 499, 500–1

Ecbatana 25, 64, 231, 232, 387, 439
Edom 446, 447, 449
Egypt
  architecture 201
  art 269, 537
  Artaxerxes' reconquest of 284
  burial customs 422
  conflict in 464–8, 550, 559
  Elephantine rebellion 42–6, 465–7
  foreign residents in 540
  funerary stelae 535–42, *536*
  legal system 488
  Persian conquest of 42
  Persian garrison in 41–2, 49
  Persian rule in 541–2
  satrapy 450, 459, 464
  troops in 499
  vitreous materials 409, 411, 412, 413, 420, 421, 424
Egyptian Museum, Cairo 535
Ekur temple, Nippur 495
El Kargeh 43
Elam 48, 316, 471
  Assyrian defeat of 311
  bricks 210, 211, 217
  hegemony over Babylonia 471, 472
  iconography 211, 343, 355
  religion 44–5, 106–7
  texts 41, 222, 242
  tombs 94
  troops in 499
Elamite Royal Robe 255, 264–8, 270, 271–2
Elamite tablets (Persepolis) 106–7, 108
Elburz mountains 440
Elephantine 41–9, 465–6
  rebellion 42–6
Elfenbein, J. 124, 130
Elizabeth I, Queen 36, 37
embalming 76, 77, 98
empire, overextension and division of 10–13
En-Gedi 459, 460
end of time 88
English drama 33–9
engravers 408
Enlil 495
Enmerkar 478
enthronement scenes 154–61

Ephesus bowl 419–21, *420*, 422, 424
Epyaxa 10
Eretrians 463
erosion 304, 305, 306
erotic art *172*, 173, 174, 331
Erythraean Sea 529, 530, 532
Erythras 532
Esagila temple, Babylon 492, 495
Esarhaddon 474, 479
Esdras, Book of 37
Eshmun'ezer II 461, 468, 469
eširtus 497
Esmā'il I 119, 120, 134
Estakhr *see* Istakhr
Esther, Book of 259, 458
Etemenanki 473–7, *476*, 478, 492
Ethiopia 422
ethnographic commonplaces 24
eunuchs 239, 277
Euphrates River, annual flood 475
Eupolis 55
Euripides 204
excarnation 76, 79, 97
Exhibition of Persian Art, Rome 434
exposure, cult of 75, 76, 79, 80, 97
extended family households 180, 181, 187
Eye of Horus 412–13, *413*
Ezekiel, Book of 270, 458
Ezida temple, Borsippa 495
Ezra, Book of 34, 37, 457, 458, 459, 469, 488

factions, court 17
Fahliyan plain 289
faience 409, 411–12, 415
Fairservis, W. A. 511
Farākh-Kart, lake 132
Farrant, Richard 34
Fars 134, 281, 315
    excavations in western 287, 288–95
Farvardin Yasht 116–18, 123, 133
Fath Ali Shah 26
fatness 171, 173–4
Fergusson, J. 24
Ferrier, R. W. 430
feudo-vassalic relations 54, 57–8
filigree work 401
Firdausi 76
fire, in Mazdaean religion 225–6

fire altars 148, 225, *241*, 251, 252, 391
fire temples 19
fitters' marks 212
fly whisks 142, 154, 156, 159, 161, 239
"Forgotten Empire: the World of Ancient Persia" xiii–xiv, 410
Fort Shalmaneser 212
Fortification Style 341, 352, 353, 354, 355, 450
Fossing, P. 420
foundation deposits 478
Fourth Exhibition of Persian Art, New York 433, 434
Fowler, George 26
fractions 379, *381*
Frangrasyan *see* Afrāsiyāb
Franke-Vogt, U. 511
Frankfort, H. 195–6
frankincense 446, 447, 451
Franks, A. W. 397, 438
Fratadara Temple, Persepolis 301
fratama 55
Frataraka kings of Persis 379, 386
Fravartiš 67
fravashis 115, 123, 131
Frederick the Great 10
free citizens (*mār banê*) 56, 57, 496–7
Freer Gallery of Art, Washington, DC 261
French National Centre for Scientific Research (CNRS) 302, 303
Friends of the Ancient Near East 434
friendship 56
frit 409, 412, 415
Frye, Richard 278, 281
Fukai, S. 421
funerary practices 75–81, 94, 95, 96–9, 113
    Egyptian 536
funerary stelae 150
    Late Egyptian 535–42, *536*
furniture, Macedonian 423

gabled-roofed hut tombs 92, 95
Gabr-i Madar-i Sulaiman 91–2, *93*, 94
Gadatas 53, 118

gadroons 290, *412*
Gallus, Aelius 452–3
Gandhara 503, 504–6, 511, 514–15, 519
Gandharan Grave Culture 505, 506
Ganges, River 515, 521
Garland, Robert 171
garlands 310, 311, 312
Garrison, M. B. 377
Garrison Quarters, Persepolis 279–80, 283, 284
garrisons 452, 461, 465, 466
Gate of All Nations, Persepolis 231, 304–5
Gath 461
Gathas 103, 105, 113, 119
    Zoroaster and 125, 131, 132, 135
Gaumata 17, 19, 55, 57, 92, 106, 126
Gaymay, Sandrine 416
Gaza 461
Gedrosia 520
Gehlken, E. 181
gemstones 165, 166, 167, 168, 170, 171, 422
gender 141–75
geophysical surveys 301, *301*, 302, 303
George V 431
George, Andrew 265
Georgia 240
Gerrha 529
Gershevitch, I. 112, 116
Getty Museum 159
Gezer 459
Ghalekuti 440
Ghaligai 505
Ghirshman, Roman 207, 276–8, 281
Gilan province 439–40
Gillies, John 6, 7–8, 9–10, 12, 13
glass
    colourless 419–25
    hyalos 421–2
    industry 409
    seals 329–30, 524–5, *525*
    vitreous materials 409–16
glaze, silica 412
globular spouted vessels *509*, 515
glyptic art 155, 159, 329, 330, 331, 332, 337, 342, 343, 351, 352, 353, 355, 366, 558, 560

Gnoli, G. 114–15
Gnostic lamentations 113, 135
Gobryas 53, 493
goddesses, on seals 156, 159
Godin Tepe 195, 196, 197, *197*, 198–9, *200*, 202, 203, 204
   architecture 247, 248, 251, 252
gold
   association with sun 226
   in foundation deposits 224–5
   Oxus Treasure 397–408
   sources of 223
goldsmiths 397, 407–8
Golestan Palace, Tehran 385
Gomal plain 506
Gordion 327–8, 424
   seals from 323, 328–34, *329*, *330*, *331*, *332*, *333*, 361
gorgon 364
Grabbe, L. L. 459, 468
Graf, David 528, 529
Granicus plain 367
Granicus, Battle of 532
grave goods 76, 98, 304, 424, 441
graves *see* funerary practices
Graves, Robert 27
Great Prophet 80, 81, 82
Great Satrap's Revolt 464
Great Tomb, Vergina 438
Great Trunk Road 514
Greco-Persian style 376
Greco-Persian wars 21, 22, 23, 27, 28, 309, 549–50, 557, 560
Greece
   Achaemenid Persia measured against 27–8
   alphabet 215
   artwork 166–7, 169, 173, 549–50
   conflict with 309, 559, 560
   glass-making 419–20, 422–5
   mercenaries from 34, 51, 173, 255, 257, 338, 339
   Persian influence on art and culture of 24, 175, 195
   sources from xiii, 21–2, 28, 41, 65, 115–16, 545–6
Grenet, Frantz 386
grey-ware 290
griffins 208, 210, 326, 331, 364, 398
grinding stones 408
grog-tempered ware 511
Grohmann, Adolph 528–9

Grose, D. F. 421, 424–5
guardsmen 310–12
   on roads 461–2
   royal bodyguards 276, 277, 312
Gubaru *see* Gobryas
guest-friendship 54
Gur-i Dokhtar 92
Gurgan province 439, 440
Güterbock, H. G. 312

Hadid 460
Hadish Palace, Persepolis 122, *123*, 233, *234*, *235*, *237*, 241–2
Haerinck, E. 386, 390, 391
Haft Tepe 210
Hagar 529
Haggai 457
hairstyles, female 170–1
Hakemi, Ali 302
half-figure, image of 339–51, 355
Halicarnassus 424
Hamadan *see* Ecbatana
Hamlin, Chauncey J. 154
hammers 408
Hammurapi, stele of 471–2
Hananiah 47, 48–9
hand-over-wrist gesture 150, 171
Handley-Schachler, Morrison 45
Hanne *265*, 266, 268
Harappan civilization 520
Harden, D. B. 420
Harem, Persepolis 231, 243–4, *262*, *263*, 279, 284
Harithat 528, 529
Harmozia 533
Harpagus 18, 64, 462
Harpy tomb, Xanthos 143, *146–7*, 148, 150
Hartmann, Hans 280, 281–2
Hasanlu
   columned buildings 195, 196, *196*, 197, 202
   II 286
   IVB 285
Hastinapura 515
Hathial Ridge 506, 514, 520
Hattusha 201
Hauptburg, Babylon 473, 474
hazarpat (commander of king's bodyguards) 276, 277
Head, Barclay Vincent 369, 370, 371, 372

headdresses
   colour of 236–7
   female 159–60, 161, 236
   in Persepolis reliefs 233–9
Hector of Troy 170
Heeren, Arnold 3, 4
Hejaz 446, 447, 450
Hellespont 309–10, 464
helmets 269
Helwing, Barbara 303
Henning, W. B. 116, 134
Heraclitus of Ephesus 81
Herakles 166, *169*, 170, 366, 387
Herder, Johann Gottfried 8, 11–13
heresy 280–1
Hermitage Museum, St Petersburg 404, 405, 429, 433, 435
hero figures 326, 366, 374, 375, 376, 557–8
Herodotus xiii, 8, 18, 22, 35, 37, 39, 52, 57, 64, 66, 67, 97, 126, 134, 141, 145, 164, 225–6, 239, 247, 259, 282, 309–10, 311, 422, 446, 447, 451, 462, 463, 465, 491, 492, 493, 494, 501, 525, 529–30, 532, 557
Herzfeld, Ernst 134, 141, 221, 231, 233, 243, 244, 261, 262, 270, 279, 280–1, 292, 299, 302, 305, 370, 379, 440, 528
   Persepolis coin hoard 382–5, *384*, 386
Hesychius 256
Heuzey, L. 413
Hibis Temple, El Kargeh 43
hierarchical society 54, 56, 57
hieroglyphics 415, 528
Hieronymus of Cardia 452
Hildebrand, Grant 201
Hill, G. F. 382, 385
Hindush 503, 504, 519–20
Hinz, W. 266, 276, 278
Hippocrates 422
Histiaeus 462, 463
Historia Plantarum (Theophrastus) 528
historiography
   18th-century European 3–13
   battle seals and 554–7, 560
   Eastern Iranian 64

historiography—*Continued*
    new Achaemenid 21–9
    of the study of Persian
        coinage 369–77
Hittites 201, 242, 312, 458, 537
Hofuf 529
Hogarth, D. G. 420
Højlund, Flemming 523
hollow-casting 406, 408
Holofernes 160
homage 51, 57–8
Homera, Babylon 473, 474
honey, corpses covered with 98
hoods 256
Hoole, John 35
Hoover, Oliver D. 387, 388
Hormuz 531
horned parapets 250, *250*
Horomazes 81
horse sacrifices 118
house-tombs 94, 96, 97
households, types of 180–1, 193
houses
    Akkadian terminology 184–5
    division and shared use
        of 185–8, 193
    modifications to 181–4, 187,
        188–93
    Neo-Babylonian and
        Achaemenid 179–94
    rental and ownership 184, 186,
        187, 188
    sale of 186
    title to 185
Huhnur region 288
hunting imagery 555
hupekoos (subordinate) 51, 52,
    53, 54
Hussaini Boi Ziarat Dherai 507
hyalos 421–2
Hyde, Thomas 4
hydraulic culture 448
hyparch 532–3
Hyperbolus 55
hypostyle halls 203
Hyrcanians 66
Hystaspes (father of Darius) 99
Hystaspes (son of Xerxes) 276

Ibn Batutta 528
Ihringen 422
Ikiztepe 435, 439
Immortals 58

Inarus 284
incense-burners 141, 157–8, 159
incrustations 401–2
India
    mathematical astronomy 526
    religious influences 526
Indo-European populations 315
Indo-Scythian period 511
Indra 281
Indus, River 504, 506, 519, 530
infantry 496–8
inlay work 402, 403, 404
Institute of Achaemenid
    Research 299
interment 75–7, 97
International Achaemenid
    Style 419, 423, 424
investiture 52, 388
Ionia/Ionians 66, 280, 351
    glassware 424–5
    philosophy 81
Ionian revolt 340, 463, 479
Iphigenia at Taurus (Euripides) 204
Iran Bâstân Museum 276, 385
Iranian Centre for Archaeological
    Research 288
Iretkherru, stela of *536*
Iron Age
    architecture 198, 201, 202,
        204, 205
    burials 76
    Iranian Azerbaijan 285–6
    Mazanderan 439–40
    Mesopotamia 448
    Pakistan 506, 507–8, 511,
        515, 520
    swords 529, *530*
Išbakatukka 450, *451*, 453
Ishtar Gate, Babylon 209
Ishtar slab, Nineveh 529
Ishtar temple, Uruk 209
Ishtumegu *see* Astyages
Isidore of Charax 76
Isin 189–90, *190*
Isis 540
Iskie/Izki 529
islands of Persian Gulf 529–33
Israel
    enemies of 458–9, 461
    falls to Assyrians 460
    religious development in 85
Issus, Battle of 255, 256, 530
Istakhr 134, 383, 386

Ištar (deity) 495
Italian Organization of
    IsMEO 299
Itti-Nabû-balātu 487
ivory 520

Jacks, Thomas Lavington 429–35,
    430, *431*, *432*
Jacque, Martyrdom of 75
Jameson, J.A. 430–1, *431*
Jamshid 25, 28, 120, 130–1, 132
Jamzadeh, P. 261
Janamejaya 515
Japanese Archaeological
    Mission 440
javelins 310
Jaz Depe I culture 515, 519
Jebusites 458
Jedaniah 466–7
Jenghiz Khan 26
Jericho 459–60, 461
Jerusalem
    citadel 462
    city wall 468
    coins and seal impressions 459
    high priest 44
    Temple of 34, 37, 43, 66, 114,
        457, 469
Jeshua 469
jeweller's stitches 401, 402,
    404, 408
jewellery 397–404
Jews 25
    in Elephantine 42–9, 465–7
    enemies of 458–9
    as mercenaries 43, 44, 48
    offerings of 44, 45
    Passover feast 46–9
    rebuilding of temple 457
    return from captivity 457–8,
        460, 469
    and Zoroastrianism 81
Jinjan *see* Tappeh Servan
Joannès, F. 501
John Hopkins University,
    Baltimore 434
Jones, Janet 424
Judah 460
    enemies of 458–9, 461
    legal system 488
    rebellion in 468, 469
judges of the king 481–8
judiciary 465–6, 482–8

Judith 160
jugs 404, 405–7, *406, 407*
Junge, P. J. 276
Jursa, M. 496–7
Justin 494
Jyotisavedanga 526

Ka'aba-i Zardosht 91, 248, 250, 390
Kachi plain 507, 509, 511, 515, 518, 519
Kaikandrus 531
Kaim, Barbara 303
Kalmākareh grotto silver horde 118
Kalah 479
kantuš (cloak) 256, 271
kapuris (tunic) 256
Karaindash 209
Karlsruhe 399
Kartir 238, *240*
Kassite glyptic 344
Katelai 505
Kaunos 467
Kazerun 294
Kellens, Jean 88, 112, 135
Kent, Ronald 280
Ker Porter engraving *268*, 269
Kerkenes Dağ 196, 197–8
Kerman 281, 519
Khahap, stela of *541*
Kherai 505
Khnum, priests of 43–4, 49, 466–7
Khonsu, coffin of *537*
Khorsabad 212
Khosrow I 111
Khosrow II 132
khrafastras (harmful creatures) 239, 525
Khuzestan 286, 290
khvarnah 120–3, *121, 122, 123,* 127, 136, 271, 391
  origins of the 131–3
  radiance of the 123–5, *126,* 129, 130, 132, 133, 135
  and winged disc symbol 261, 379, 390
kidaris (cap) 256
Kings, Book of 458
Kinneir, John Macdonald 23
kitaris (hood) 256
kitchens 233
Klein, R. 174
Klose, Dietrich 386–7

knighthood 58
Koch, Ebba 203
Koch, Heidemarie 44–5
kohl tubes 141
koinê 211, 217
Konuk, K. 377
Kotwal, Dastur 107
Kouchakji, Fahim 434
Kraay, C. M. 372, 383
Krefter, Friedrich 221, 244
Kreyenbroek, P. G. 115–16
Kritt, Brian 387
Kuhrt, Amélie 22, 282, 475–6, 491
Kūl-i Farah *265*, 266, 268
Kümmel, Hans Martin 486
Kur River Basin 287, 289, 291, 303–4
Kurangun 288, 289, 293
Kurash 267, *547*, 548
Kurdistan 379
Kurdušum 450
Kush 222, 223
Kusheh 532
Kutha 187
Kutir-Nahhunte I 471
Kutir-Nahhunte II 267

Lachish 460
Lahore Fort 515
Lambert, Wilfred G. 483
Lan offerings 44, 45, 106–7, 108
Lane Fox, Robin 173
lapis lazuli 328, 402, 403
Larsa 479
Laslett, P. 180
Late Dilmun palace 523–7, *524, 526,* 533
Late Plain Ware 289, 290
Lateran Baptistry, Rome 205
lathes 405–6
Le Rider, Georges 373
Lecoq, Pierre 114, 126, 281
legal system 465–6, 482–8
Lemaire, A. 460
Lenormant, Charles 371
Lenormant, François 371
Lerner, Judith A. 261–2
Levant 181, 315, 409, 412, 413, 415, 417, 448, 460
Lévy, Isidore 280, 281
levy camps (*madaktu*) 500
Lewis, Sian 170
libation vases 412, 419

Libya, rebellion in 284
Lie-Kings 55, 56, 57
Limyra monument 78
linear houses 184
Linguet, S.-N.-L. 6, 7, 8
lion-bull icons 127–8, *128, 129,* 208, *325,* 326, 343–4, 352, 353
livestock 286
local agents 450, 453
Lod 460
Loebanr 505
Loftus, W. K. 207, 213, 415
Lohra mound 507
Lohra nullah 506
Lombard, Pierre 528
lost wax casting 397, 399–400, *400, 401, 402,* 404, 405, 406, 408
lotus flower emblems 118, 121–2, 123, 124, 263, 424
Louis II de Bourbon, Prince de Condé 7
Louvre, Musée du
  bricks 207–8, 213
  gold objects 402
  seals 144–5, 148–9, *149,* 150, 153, 155, 157, 159, 160
  vitreous materials 409, 415
Lückge, A. 519
Lullubi people 471
Luristan bronzes 431, 432
Luschey, H. 434
Lycia 467–8
  alphabet 215
  tomb architecture 94
Lydia
  alphabet 215
  craftsmen 213, 217
  Cyrus' conquest of 10, 66
  glass 424
  gold 223
  satrapy 464
  see also Sardis
Lydian Treasure 397, 399, 404–5, 439
Lysimachus 391

Macedonia
  funeral customs 423
  glassware 422, 423, 425
  government of 10

Maeandrius 463
Magee, P. 205
magi
　funerary practices 80
　killed by Darius 19
　leadership of Zoroastrian
　　religion 108
　superstition of 9
　tradition of 105
　see also priests
magush 106, 108
Mahabharata 515
Maka province 529
Makran 511, 518, 529
Malandra, W. W. 113
Malcolm, Sir John 22, 24, 25,
　28, 29
Mamasani Archaeological
　Project 289
Mamasani region 288–95
Manaean culture 285
Mandane 18, 65
Manishtushu 471
manpower, army 496–7
mār banê 56, 57, 496–7
Marand plain 285
Marathon, Battle of 8, 9, 27,
　204, 260
Marduk 85, 94, 96, 473, 475, 478,
　491, 492, 494, 495
Margastana 531
Marika 55
Marlowe, Christopher 33
marriage 170
　contracts 186
Marvdasht plain 300, 303, 351
Masistes 546
Massagetae 546
Mas'udi 116
Mathieson, I. J. 541
mausolea 76, 78
Maussolleion 424, 425
Maussolus 424, 464
Mazaios 380
Mazanderan province 429, 434,
　439–41
Mazdayasna 466
Mazdean religion
　and Apadana deposits 225–7
　cosmological aspects 223, 226
　see also Ahuramazda;
　　Zoroastrianism
Mazenes 532, 533

Meda'in Saleh 447
Medes 17, 18, 19, 63, 117
　architecture 203–4, 247–52
　craftsmen 248
　Cyrus' defeat of 64, 65, 66, 67, 69
　deities of 118
　extent of empire 63–4, 67, 68,
　　247–8
　Greek concept of 68
　kingly ideology 117, 118–19,
　　121, 124, 128, 134–5
　Median Rock Tombs 78
　nature of empire 64, 66, 69
　rebel against Darius 67–8
　and rise of Achaemenids 285–6
　royal dress 255–64, 272
　royal family 17
Medina 446
Megabazus 463
Megabernes 53
Mehgarh 507
Memphis 466, 535, 541
mercenaries 49, 502
　Greek 34, 51, 173, 255, 257,
　　338, 339
　Jewish 43, 44, 48
Merodach-baladan II 479
Mesopotamia
　art 270
　artefacts at Susa from 471–2
　astronomy 526
　brick-making 209, 210, 216, 411
　deposits 222, 224
　domestic architecture 179
　glass-making 420, 421
　iconography 119–20, 210,
　　340, 352
　Iron Age empires 448–9
　legal system 482–4, 488
　under Achaemenid rule 481–8
　Ur III texts 288
metal furnaces 302, 408
metalwork
　bronze 199
　gold 397–408
　hoards 440–1
　silver 435–9
Metropolitan Museum of Art 429,
　433, 435
Middle Assyrian period 209,
　342, 353
Middle Elamite period 210, 288,
　290, 291, 293, 411

Miglus, P. 179, 189
Miho Museum 402, 403
Miletus 462, 463, 479
military history 309–12, 495–502
military ritual 312
Mill, James 5
Miller, Margaret 195
Millspaugh, A. C. 24
Ministry of Culture and
　Archaeological
　Organization 299
mints 371, 373, 376
Minû-ana-Bēl-dānu 553, *554*, 557
Miri Qalat 507, 511
Mithra (deity) 19, 82, 113, 114,
　117, 118, 120, 122, 126–7,
　128, 129, 131, 132, 133, 135,
　225, 226, 232, 281
Mithradates 276
Mithradates I 386, 391
Mithropastes 532–3
Mitrobates 463
Mizpeh 459–60
Moabites 458
Mongols 131
monogamy 170
monotheism 25, 113, 119, 125,
　127, 132, 134, 135
monsoon patterns 518–19
Montesquieu 4, 5, 7, 8, 10–11,
　12, 13
Moore, Benjamin Burges 25
Moorey, P.R.S. 159, 435, 440
Mordechai 259
Morier, J. J. 27
Mørkholm, Otto 383, 528–9
Morton, Rosalie 24
Mosah 459
mosques, early
　congregational 203
Mostowfi, Hamdollāh 133–4
mother-of-pearl 402, 403–4
mound sites 291, 361–7, 506–7
mourning colours 236
mud-brick architecture 202, 248,
　251, 291
Mughan plain 285–6
Müller, Walter 529
multiple family households
　180, 187
Munich Coin Cabinet 387
Murashu family 493, 524–5
Murashu Archive, Nippur 553, 559

Muscarella, O. W. 208, 434
Müseler, Wilhelm 387
Mushushu dragons 210
Muweilah 196–7, *198*, 199, 203, 205
Muzeh Melli, Tehran 440
Mycale, Battle of 479
Mycians 529, 530, *530*
Mylasa 424
myrrh 446

Nabataeans 446, 452, 454
Nabonidus 64, 65–6, 67, 96, 449, 450, 474, 483, 484, 486, 497, 523
Nabonidus Chronicle 64, 66, 67, 264
Nabopolassar 474, 478
Nabû (deity) 96, 264, 495
Nabû-balāssu-iqbi 484
Nabû-etel-ilāni 484
Nabû-nāsir 485
Nabûapla-iddina 478
Nadir Shah 26
Nakhthor 464
Napirasu, Queen 150
Napoleon 17
Naqsh-i Rajab *240*
Naqsh-i Rustam 94, 99
   Darius' tomb 91, *92*, 97, *98*, 99
   iconography 53, 128–31, 350–1, 387
   Ka'bah-i Zardusht 91, 248, 250, 390
   tombs 204, 293, 380, 450
Naram-Sîn 471
   stele of 471, 472, 555, 558
Nari River 518
Narseh 132
Naster, P. 340
National Museum of Iran, Tehran 385
National Museums of Scotland Expedition 535
Naumann, R. 201
Nearchus 530, 532, 533
Nebi Samuel 459
Nebuchadnezzar II 209, 212, 243, 483, 497
   cylinder fragment 472–4, *472*, 479–80
   stele of 473, 479
   and Tower of Babel 474, 477
necklaces 325
Negev desert 446, 460
Nehemiah, Book of 37, 458, 459, 462, 468
Nekhau, Pharaoh 242
Nemea 166, *169*, 170
Neo Babylonian Empire 445, 449
   collapse of 449, 481–2
   domestic architecture 179–94
   hold over Levant 460
   legal system 483–4
Neo-Assyrian Empire 277, 352, 448–9
Neo-Elamite period 210, 288, 290, 293
Neo-Elamite style 141, 142, 149–50
Neo-Hittite art 537, 538, 539
Neolithic era 507
Nephthys 540
Neriglissar 483, 484, 486
Netophah 460
New Kingdom 536, 538
New Year festival, Babylon 491, 492–3
Newell, Edward 383, 385
niches, elaborate 250, *251*, 252
Nike 386, 389, 391
Nile Valley 460
Nimchuk, Cindy 128, 340, 351
Nimrud 212, 479
Nineveh 472
   Median sack of 117
   North Palace 150, 310–11, *310*, 501
Ninurta, temple of 473, 474
Nippur 482, 495, 498, 525
   battle seals 550, 553, *554*, *556*
   residential excavations 180
   TA House I 181–4, *182–3*, 186–7, 188
   WC-2 area 188, 189, 190–3, *191*, *192*
Nisa texts 233
nobles, dress 235
Noe, S. P. 370, 372
Nollinger, Marie-Christine 416
nomadic tribes 247–8, 446, 448, 452–3, 546
Nordabschnitt III, Isin 189–90, *190*
North Residential Quarter, Persepolis 302
North West Frontier Province 506, 514, 518
Northern Black Polished Ware 510
Novocherlask 405
nudity, in art 173
Nush-i Jan
   architecture 247, 248–52, *249*
   Central Temple 250, *250*, 251, *251*
   columned halls 195, 196, *196*, 197, 204, 250, 252
   Daivadâna 281
   Fort 252
   Old Western Building 252
Nylander, Carl 23, 24, 213, 214

Oaracta 531, 532–3
oases 448
Oborzos *see* Vahbarz
Odeion of Pericles, Athens 195
offerings 44–5, 106–7, 108, 148, 160, 240
Ogyris 532, 533
Old Elamite period 288
Old Kingdom 539
Old Persian texts/language 41, 86, 88, 89, 222, 232, 242
Old Testament 34, 37, 39, 66, 233, 458
   Zoroastrian influence in 81
Oliver Jr, A. 421
Olivieri, L. M. 505
Olmstead, Albert 22, 276, 281
Oman peninsula 529
omens, astral 526–7
omphaloi 421, 424
One-Hundred-Column-Hall, Persepolis 142, *144*, 154, *156*, 205, 231, 261, 302, 537
Onians, John 204
Ono 460
onyx 402
ophiolatry 526
Organa 531
Oriental Institute of Chicago 383, 385
Oroetes 463
Orontas 51–2, 54
Osirouer 465
ossuaries 76, 77–8, 79
Otanes, silver plaque of 126–8, *127*
Ottoman Empire
   comparison with 5, 9

harems 244
Otys 53
Overlaet, B. 386, 390, 391
Oxus River 397
Oxus Seal 557, 558
Oxus Treasure 159, 233, 235, *238*, 379, 427
   coin hoard 321–2
   cylinder seal with battle scene 548–9, *549*
   gold objects 397–408
   luxury tableware 397, 404–7
   silver objects 439
   votive plaques 389
Ozbaki 248

padam (mouth cover) 239, 242, 390
Pade, king of Qadê 529
Painter, William 34
Pakistan, excavations in 503, 505–21
Pakistan Heritage Society 506
Palace H, Persepolis 390
Palace P, Pasargadae 199, 71
Palace of Pleasure (Painter) 34
Palace of Xerxes *see* Hadish Palace
Panathenaia 24
Panderma 438
Panofski, E. 374
Pantocrator 131
Pāpak *135*
papyri, durability of 482
Pardis, Persepolis 301
Parmenio 294
Parpola, Asko 113
Parr, P. J. 449
Pars, mausolea 78
Pārsā 128, 133–4, 136
Parsa-Pasargadae Research Foundation 299–307
Parsua 315, 316
Parsuwash 267
Parthenon, Athens 204
Parthia/Parthians 66, 68, 546, 552
   and Achaemenid continuity 380, 385
   coins 385, 391, *392*
   funerary practices 76, 80
   religious tolerance 79
   silverware 440
Pasargadae
   archaeological work at xv, *301*,
302, 303
   architecture 248
   as capital 93, 95
   copy of Daivâ Inscription 283, 284
   Darius' inscriptions 17, 18–19
   Gabr-i Madar-i Sulaiman 91–2, *93*, 94
   Gate R reliefs *267*, 268–71, *268*, 272
   iconography 95, 96
   jewellery finds 399
   masons' marks 212, 213, 214, *214*
   Palace P 199, 271
   remains 25
   Zendan-i Sulaiman 91, 92, *94*, 248, 250, *251*, 302, 390
Pasargadae-Marvdasht region 300
Passover 46
pastoral societies 113, 545
Pasu, son of Mannuki 466
Patron the Phocian 255–6
Pausanius 280
Pax Persica 23, 527–8, 533
Pazyryk 153, *158*, 160, 161
pearl emblem 124
"peoples of the lands" 457–9, 461, 463, 468, 469
perfume bottles 419
Periano Ghundai 511
peristyles 201
Perrot, Jean 207
Persepolis
   absence of female depictions at 141, 383
   archaeological work at xv, 221, 231, 299–303, *300*
   architecture 248–52, *249*, *250*, *251*
   audience reliefs 142, *143*, *144*, *382*
   buffer zone *300*, 301
   as ceremonial and ritual centre 244
   colour at 236–7
   columned halls 195, 196, 198
   conflicting views of 23, 24, 27
   copies of Daivâ Inscription at 279–80, 283
   door jamb reliefs 204, 205, 261–2, *551*
   Elamite tablets 106–7, 108
   fortifications around 302
   Frataraka reliefs *380*
   Frataraka rule in 386
   glassware 421, 422
   glazed brick panels 123–4, *126*, *127*
   Herzfeld's coin hoard 383–5, *384*, 386
   iconography 53, 95–6, 120, 123–4, 343–4, 350, 355, 379, 387, 427
   masons' marks 212–13
   palaces 231–44, 250, *250*, 251–2, 271
   preservation and restoration 304–6
   routes to Susa from 286, 288, 292, 294
   royal dress in reliefs 260–3
   seal impressions 235, *239*
   sense of pathos 25–6
   solstice orientation 223, 226
   tombs 293, *382*, 451
   virtual reconstruction xiv
   water system 302–3
   see also Apadana; Council Hall; Hadish Palace; One-Hundred-Column-Hall; Palace H; Palace of Xerxes; seals; Tachara Palace; Treasury
Persepolis Fortification archive xv, 44–5, 148, 155, 232, 241, 287, 295, 337, 338–56, 450, 451, *451*, 462, 519, 528, 529, 545, 548
   see also seals
Persepolis Seal Project 142, 157
Persepolis Treasury Tablets 41, 231, 242, 345, 354, 366, *550*, 551
Persian Gates 289, 294
Persian Gulf 523–33
Persian wars *see* Greco-Persian wars
The Persians (Aeschylus) 256, 260
Persis
   coins of 379–93
   early rulers of 387–8, 391
Peshawar University 510
Peshawar Valley 505–6, 514, 518, 519, 520
Peter the Great 404
Petit, Thierry 51–2, 53, 54, 56,

57, 58
Petra 447, 452
Pharnabazus 53
Pheraulas 53
Pherendates, satrap 44, 49
phialai 419–21, 423, 425
Philip II of Macedonia 438
    authority of 10
Philip Arrhidaeus 475
Philistia/Philistines 461
philoi pistoi 53, 55–6
Philolaus 421
philology 112
philos kai pistos 52, 54
Phoenicia/Phoenicians 460, 461
    art 269–70
    glass-making 420
    stelae 535, 541
Photius 256
Phraortes *see* Fravartiš
Phrygia 323, 327, 332, 333, 532
    glassware 424
    seals and clay tags 361–7
    see also Gordion
pillar tombs 94
Pingree, David 526–7
Pirak 507, 509, 510, *510, 512, 513,* 514, 515, 518
Pirart, E. 135
Pisina 466
pista (pledges) 51, 52
pithoi 363
plastic shaping techniques 397, 400
Plataea, Battle of 8, 27
platforms 252
Plato 4, 37
pliers 408
Plutarch 98, 236, 272
political conflict, Central Asia 545–60
pollution
    by corpses 77, 96
    by harmful creatures 239, 525
Pollux 256, 422
Polyaenus 386
Polybius 4
polychrome traces 236–7, 260–3
Polycrates 463
Pope, A. U. 431, 434
porticoes 201, 202
Postgate, J. N. 180
pottery kilns 304
Potts, Daniel 288, 386, 390

preservation projects 304–6
Preston, Thomas 35–6
priests
    clean-shaven 238, *241*
    dress 235–9
    killing of harmful creatures 239, 525
    see also magi
primary burial 75–7, 79, 80, 81
primary context 275, 279, 283, 284
prisoners of war 499, 552, 553, 557
Processional Way, Babylon 209, 210
Prometheus Vinctus 27
proskynesis 52, 53, 57
prostitutes 175
protection, and kingship 356
proto-Indo-Aryans 113
Ptolemaic Period 538
Ptolemies 13, 391
Ptolemy I 131
Pulvar river 303
punches 408, 435
Punjab, northern 514
Pushkalavati 514
Pushtuns 17
Pydna, seal *155*, 156
Pylora 531
pyramidal stamp seals 323, 325, *325*, 329, 331
Pythagoras 81

Qadê 529
Qalat al-Bahrain 523–7, *525*
Qalaychi 285
Qaleh Kali xv
Qaleh period 291
qānats 4
Qaradaq 285, 286
Qasr 473, 474
Qazvin 528
Qedar, kingdom of 460, 461
Qedarite confederacy 454
Qeshm 531, 532
Qizqapan monument 78–9, 379, *380*, 387
quadriga (four-horsed chariot) 113
Quintus Curtius 7, 37, 38

rab eširti 497
radiocarbon dating 507, 508, 509, 511, 514

Radner, Karen 480
Ramat Rahel 459
Ramhormoz xv
Rana Ghundai 511
Ravenna 422
Rawlinson, George 22, 23, 24, 25, 26, 27, 29
Rawlinson, Henry 27–8
Razmjou, Shahrokh 45, 108, 114, 248
reconciliations 52, 53
reconstructions 415–16
regnal years, tabulations of 115
religious tolerance 43, 79–80, 86, 87, 105, 283
rental, house 184
residence
    and ownership 184
    patterns of 180–1, 185–8
    virilocal 181, 185
restoration projects 304–6, 415–16
Reynolds, S. 57, 58
Reza Shah Pahlavi 91, 383, 385
Rhodes, glassware 422, 423
rhyta 118, 412
    with animal foreparts 417
    inscription 118
    Jacks' silver 432, 434–5
Ribat, seal of 553, *556*, 557
Richter, G. M. A. 435
Richterurkunden documents 483, 484
rikis qabli 499
Rīmūt 486
Rīmūt-Bēl 484
rings
    bezel 325, *325*, 331
    Oxus Treasure 159
    seals 325, *325*
rivets 406–7
road system 461–3
Robinson, E. S. G. 370, 372, 373
rock crystal 153, 328, 402, 419, 422
rock-cut roads 303, *303*, 304
rock-cut tombs 91, 94, 95, 96, 97, 293
Rolfe, John C. 255
Rollin, Charles 4, 5–7, 12
Romans
    coins 390
    trade 446–7

view of Arabia 446, 452–3
roof support
    columns 200, 201–2, 203–4
    mud vaulting struts 251–2
rooms, function of 184–5
Root, Margaret Cool 23, 24, 25, 150, 205, 225, 340, 351, 352, 370, 373, 376–7
Ross, Denison 24
Rostovtzeff, M. 420
rotary tools 408
Roth, M. T. 181
Rothschild, Amschel 434
Roustaei, Kourosh 288
Royal Road 462
Rud-e Fahlian 292
Rumeilah 196–7, 199, *199*, 203

Sachau-Papyrus 6 42, 43, 44, 46–9
sacrifices 45, 107, 118, 148, 241, 282, 283, 525–6
saddlecloth, Pazyryk 153, *158*, 160
Safavid dynasty
    cemeteries 304
    militancy 134
    Shiism under 119
    silks 431, 432
Sagartia/Sagartians 18, 67, 68, 529
Saka/Sakas 222, 223, 399, 547, 550–1, 552, 559
Salamis, Battle of 27, 39
Salles, Jean-François 523, 529
Salt Range 514
šalup 56
Samaria 380, 460–1
Samaryan Delaya 44
Šamaš-iddin 495
Sami, Ali 280, 302
Samos 463
Samsuiluna 479
Samuel, Book of 465
Sancisi-Weerdenburg, Heleen 21, 22, 23, 248, 282
sanctuaries, open-air 148
Sang-e Siah 317
Santoni, M. 509, 510
Saqqara, funerary stelae 535, *536*, *538*, *540*, *541*
Sarangians 529
sarapis (tunic) 256
Sardis 51, 214, 223, 324, 373, 376, 463, 524
    seals from 323–7, *325*, *327*, 333, 334
Sargon II 95, 315, 471, 478, 479
Sari 440–1
Sarmatians 405
Sasanian dynasty 75–6
    archaeological remains 304
    ceramics 511
    coins 391
    continuity with Achaemenids 379
    funerary practices 78, 80, 304
    priests and temples 238, 240
    silverware 440
Šati-dudu 349
satrapies
    Bahrain 524, 525, 526
    capitals 323–4, 331, 334, 449
    estates 57
    government 26, 449–50, 464
    pleasures of court life 167
    rivalry between 463, 464, 468, 469
    satraps' position in society 58
    South Asian 503–4, 514–15, 518, 519–21
    XIVth 529–33
Saudi Arabia 449, 528–9
Saul 85
Sauvage 217
SC Johnson Wax building, Racine, Wisconsin 203
scaraboid seals 165, 168
scarves, tasseled 239
Scheil, Vincent 471
Schiwek, H. 532
Schloen, J. D. 180–1
Schlumberger, D. 373
Schmid, Hansjörg 475–7, 479
Schmidt, Erich F. 99, 231, 243–4, 276, 277, 299, 370, 383, 421, 451
Scott, Sir Walter 28
scriptural religions 104
sculpture
    conflicting views of 23, 24
    women in 141
Scylax of Caryanda 504
Scythians 66
    funerary practices 76
seals
    Achaemenid hegemonic style 326, *328*, 330, 331, *331*, 333
    Anatolian 165, 166, 168, 170, 215, 323–34
    Bahrain 524–5
    battle 166, 546–60, *547*, *549*, *550*, *552*, *553*
    British Museum 159, 552, *554*
    Buffalo cylinder seal 153–5, *154*, 156, 159, 160–1
    clay tags 361–7
    coins as 338, 339
    cylinder 19, 153–5, *154*, 156, 159, 160–1, 325, *325*, 329, 331, 332, 365–7, 552, *554*
    Elamite 267
    from Sardis and Gordion 323–34, *325*, *326*, *327*
    Greco-Persian 165–75, 323, 325, 364
    Herakles 166, *169*, 170
    iconography 165, 167–8, 337, 548–57
    Išbakatukka's 450, *451*, 453
    Louvre 144–5, 148–9, *149*, 150, 153, 155, 157, 159, 160
    Moscow Artaxerxes cylinder 366, 367
    ownership of 155, 156, 170
    personal devices on stamp *216*
    Pydna *155*, 156
    pyramidal stamp 323, 325, *325*, 329, 331
    significance of 323
    stamp 159, 325, 327, 333, 459, 460
    suspension devices 325, *326*
    Zvenigorodsky cylinder 366, 367
Second Exhibition on Persian Art, London 431–2
secondary burial 78, 79
Seidl, U. 96
Seistan 520
Sekunda, N. 54, 57, 58
Seleucid dynasty 13, 452
    continuation of Achaemenid iconography under 379, 380
    Roman conquest 10–11
    support of local dynasts for 385–6
    waning of 386
Seleucus I 383, 385, 386, 387, 388, 389, 391, 475

Sennacherib 95, 474
Sennefer, tomb of *538*
Settle, Elkanah 36–7
settlement patterns
    between Persepolis and
        Susa 287
    Pakistan 518–19
seven, the number 225
sex scenes *172*, 174–5
sexuality, female 170–5, *172*
Seyitgazi 361
Seyitömer Höyük 361–7
Seyrig, Henri 340, 373
Shah Abbas 26
Shah Jahan 203
Shahbazi, Shapur 261, 270, 277
Shahi Tump 507
Shakespeare, William 34
Shalmaneser III 449
Shamash 120, *120*
    temple of (Sippar) 474, 478
Shamash-eriba 477
Shapur 26, *135*
Shara mountains 447
shaving 238
sheet metal production 400, 408
Shekaft-e Salman 150
Sherwin-White, Susan 282,
    475–6, 491
shields 501
Shiism 119, 131
Shilhak-Inshushinak 471
shoes 256, 262
Shush-i Daniel 471
Shushun/Shushin/Shushan/
    Shusha *see* Susa
Shutruk-Nahhunte 471, 480
Shutruk-Nahhunte II 266
Shutruru 266
Siberian Collection 404
Sidon/Sidonians 461, 468, 469
sigloi 321–2, 338, *338*, 339, 351,
    372, 380
Sikavand 379, 383
silica glaze 412
silica paste 410, 411–12, 413
silk 431, 432
silver
    association with moon 226
    composition of
        Achaemenid 438
    in foundation deposits
        224–5

hoards 439, 440–1
Jacks'/British Museum 431–41,
    436, *437*, *438*, *439*, 441
Lydian Treasure 404–5
marks and inscriptions 438–9
silversmiths 435
simple family households
    180–1, 187
Sin (deity) 449
Sind 222, 223, 504, 520
Sippar 471, 474, 478, 482, 484,
    485, 491, 495–6, 497, 498,
    499, 501, 502
Sivand Dam 307
skeuomorphs 508
Skjaervø, P.O. 114, 117–18, 134
skyphos 421, 423
slaves, in Egypt 464
Smerdis *see* Bardiya
Smith, William 35
Smyrna *see* Baraklı
snake deposits, ritual 525–6
snowmelt 518–19
Soapy Red Ware 514, 518
Socrates 422
Sogdiana/Sogdians 222, 547, 550,
    551, 552, 553, 559
solar imagery 120, *120*, 124, 130
soldering 400–1, 402, *404*, 406, 408
solstices 223, 224, 226
Sornay-Setton, Jeanne-Marie 416
Sotheby's 433
sources
    Aramaic 41–9
    Avesta 86–7
    Babylonian 41, 63–4
    for English dramatists 39
    Greek xiii, 21–2, 28, 115–16,
        545–6
South Arabian script 215
South Residential Quarter,
    Persepolis 301, 303
Spanheim, E. 370–1
Sparda 222, 223, 224, 225,
    226, 324
spearbearers 256–9, *258*, 259, *259*,
    263, *263*
spears 167, 168, 205, 277, 278,
    310, *310*, 311, 312, 332,
    365, 367, 372, 416, 499,
    501, 548, 551, 552
Speck, Henry 294
Spell 151, Book of the Dead

536, 541
Spenta-Armaiti 114
sphinxes 120, *121*, 211, *211*, 326
spinning, images of 157, 161
Spitacas 53
Spithridates 53, 54, 58
Sprenger, Alois 528
square houses 184
Sraosha 113
stamp seals 159, 325, 327, 333,
    459, 460
statues and statuettes 413–15,
    414, *415*
Stein, Aurel 289, 295, 505, 511
stereotypes 24
Stevens, Elsie Sheridan 431
Stolper, M.W. 58, 554
Stone, E. 180, 181, 184
stone-masons' marks 212–13, 214
storage jars 304, 363
storehouses, regional 294
Strabo 91, 97, 98, 446, 452, 475,
    494, 532
Straßburger Papyrus 42, 44
Stresiades 422
Stronach, David 94–5, 96, 248,
    268, 269, 270, 271, 280, 293,
    339, 351, 370, 373
subordination rituals 51–4, 57, 58
Sufis 113
Sulaiman Range 506
summer solstice 223
sun and moon
    in Mazdaean religion 226
    motifs 127–8, *129*
sunflower emblems 118, 120,
    121–2, 123, 124
Sunni Islam 119
superstition 9
Susa
    architecture 248
    art 150
    brick motifs and brick
        building 207–17, *214*, *215*,
        216, 237, *239*, 399, 409–11,
        411, 415–16
    early history 471
    Elamite era 267, 268, 471
    French excavations 207, 471
    iconography 96, 120, 124, 208,
        209, 210–12, 217, 379
    jewellery finds 399, 403
    Mesopotamian artefacts at 471–2

Susa—*Continued*
   preserved colour 237, *239*
   reliefs 238–9, 263, 410, 411
   routes to Persepolis 286, 288, 292, 294
   statue of Darius 239, *241*, 413, 528, 529
   vitreous materials 409–11, 412, 413, 415
   war booty found at 479
Susa Foundation Charter 209, 212, 252, 504, 520
Swat Valley 505–6, 514, 519
swords 98, 235, *236*, *238*, 321, 427, 529, *530*
Sydney University 288
Syene 41–2
Syennesis 10
Sykes, Percy 23, 24, 25, 26–7, 29
Syloson 463
Syria 315, 316, 449
   architecture 201
   art 269–70

Tabi, stela of 539, *539*, 541
tableware
   faience 410, 411–12, 415
   gold 397, 404–7
   silver 433–41
Tabriz, Blue Mosque 285
Tachara Palace, Persepolis 231, 233, *236*, 240–2, *243*, 244, 413
Tahhua 553
Taima 41
   temple at 43
Takhmaspâda 276
Takht-i Rustam 92, *94*
Takht-i Jamshid (Persepolis) 25
Tal-e Gach Garan-e Ka Khodada 292–3, 294
Tall-i Takht, Pasargadae xv, 214, *214*, 280, 283
Tamburlaine the Great (Marlowe) 33
Tamukan 317
Tanaoxares *see* Bardiya
Tanefrether 535
Tang-e Bolaghi 303–4, *303*
Tang-i Khas 289, 295
Tappeh Pahnu 292–5
Tappeh Servan 289, 292–5, *292*, *293*
Taqizadeh, S. H. 115, 116
Tardumannu 349

Tarm 528
Tartus 413
Tasrkamuwa *see* Datames
Tatarli paintings 312
Tattenai 469
tauma 56
Tavernier, Jean-Baptiste 4
Tawilan 449–50
taxation 223, 294, 449, 453, 497, 499, 501, 532
Taxila 506, 509, 514, 515, 520
Taxmaspada 68
Tayma 449, 450
Teispes 19, 268, 547, 548
Tekoa 460
Tell al-Lahm 189
Tell al-Rimah 200
Tell Barsip 277
Tell el-Fûl 459
Tell el-Oueili 200
Tell Leilan 200
temple dependents (širkus) 496, 501
temples 148, 242
   archives 496
   Babylonian 495
   contributions to army 496–502
Tempt-Humban-Inshushinak 265, *265*, 272
Ten Thousand 7, 8, 208, 310
Tepe Shiramin 285
Tepe Yahya, Kerman 511, *517*, 519
Ter Kala Dheri 506, 507, 515
Terrace, Persepolis 379, 382–5
tetradrachms 379, *381*, 382, 383, 385, 386–7, 388
Teumman *see* Tempt-Humban-Inshushinak
Thales 81
Thamamaeans 529
Thatagush 503, 504, 507, 518, 519
Thebes 466, *538*
Themistocles 284
Theophrastus 528
Thermopylae, Battle of 38
Third Exhibition on Persian Art, St Petersburg 432–3
Thompson, M. 383
Thrace 463
throne rooms 203
Ti-li-man/Ti-ri-ma-an 528
Tiglath-Pileser I 209
Tiglath-Pileser III 95, 449

Tilia, Ann Britt 261–3, 278, 390
Tilia, Giuseppe 278
Tillya Tepe 508
Tilmun *see* Dilmun
Timargarha 505
Tirutir 266
Tissaphernes 53
Toba Kakar range 518
Tol-e Nurabad 289–91, 294, *288*
Tol-e Spid 288, 289–92, 294, *288*
Toledo Museum of Art 425
tombs 75–9, 91–100
   desecration of 478
   Egyptian 536
   rock-cut 91, 94, 95, 96, 97, 293
Toprak-Kale 95
tourism, damage caused by 306
towel-bearers 154, 160, 161, 238, 240, 277
Tower of Babel 473–4, *476*, 478, 479, 480
   destruction of 474–7, 494
trade
   Gerrha 529
   precious aromatics 446–7, 449, 451, 452
The Tragedy of Darius (Alexander) 37
Trans-Iranian Railway 440
travellers
   Arabian in Persia 450–1, 453
   European 22–3, 28, 445
   in Persian Gulf 526, 533
   reaction to antiquities 25
   safety on roads 461–3
Treasury, Persepolis *240*, 242–3, 276, 472
   as archive 243
   bullae 366, 551
   glass 421
   as museum 243
   Reliefs 275, 276–9, *277*, *278*, *279*, 283, 284
   see also Persepolis Treasury Tablets; seals
tree, image of 353
trial pieces 364
Triantaffyllidis, Pavlos 423
tribal society 17
tribute 49, 86, 211, 221, 283, 447, 449, 450–1, 453, 529
Tripylon Gate, Persepolis 231
Troad 464

trousers (*anaxyrides*) 256, 259, 264, 265, 271
Tübingen University 260
tulip bowls 290, 291
tunics
   Median style 259, 264
   royal 255–6, 260
   spearbearers 257
Tuplin, Christopher 173
turbans 159–60
Turcomans 131, 133
turning spindles 406, 408
Tuspa 95
Tyre 499

Ubaid period 200
Udjahorresnet 48–9
Ulai River, Battle of 265, *265*, 310
Umman-manda 64, 66
Unfinished Gate, Persepolis 303
Untash-Gal 150
Uperi, palace of 523–7, *524*, *526*, 533
upliftedness, quality of 348–51, 355–6
Ur 189, 479, 493, 498
Urartu 117, 201, 250, 252, 285–6, 315
Urmia, Lake 285–6
Uruk 188–9, 200, 209, 479, 482, 484, 485–6, 487, 492, 493, 495–6, 497–8
Usher, John 239
Utians 530
Uttu 157

Vadfradad I 386, 387, 388, 389, 391, 464
Vadfradad II 391
Vadfradad III 391
Vahbarz 386, 387–8
Valerian, Emperor 26
Vallat, F. 118
van der Toorn, Karel 85
van Driel, G. 500
Vanden Berghe, L. 266
Varkana 439
Varuna *see* Apam Napāt
Vedic sacrifices 526
Vendidad 77, 80
Venturi, Robert 202
Venus figurines 171
veraghna 123–4, *127*

Vernacular Style 264
Vickers, Michael 225
Victoria & Albert Museum 398
victory scenes 365–7
victory, trophies of 480
Vidranga 467
Vishtaspa 18, 69, 81, 128, 136, 221
visiting cards 364
vith 56
vitreous materials 409–16
vitreous paste 402, 403
Vitruvius 204
Vivana, satrap 68
von Bothmer, D. 440
von Gall, Hubertus 278
von Wissman, Hermann 529

Wadi Arabah 447
Wadi ed-Daliyeh papyri 461
Wadi Rum 447
Wadi Sirhan 447
Waerzeggers, Caroline 491, 493
waist-hip ratio 174
wall decorations 250–1, *250*
war, booty of 479–80
Warad-Sîn 479
warrior society 58
The Wars of Cyrus (Anon.) 34
Warsaw University 303
water
   in Mazdaean religion 225–6
   as sacred item 232
water canals, underground 4, 301, *301*, 302–3, *302*, 306
water distribution
   Arabia 447–8
   Pakistan 518–19
Waters, M. 95
wax
   corpses covered with 77, 97, 98
   preserving stonework with 305
   see also lost wax casting
way stations 294, 452, 462
weapons 499, 501
   see also bows and arrows; spears; swords
weathering 304
Weippert, M. 450
Weisberg, David B. 485
Weld, Herbert 299
Wheeler, Mortimer 505, 514, 515
Widengren, G. 256
widows 181, 185

Wiesehöfer, Joseph 385–6, 390
Williams Jackson, A.V. 22–3, 25, 27
Williamson, Hugh 457
wills and testaments 185
Wilson, Arnold 430, 431
winged sphere symbol 120, 121–2, 124, 211, 260–1, 332, 339–40, 341, 342, 345, 355, 366, 380
wings, of houses 185
Winthrop, Grenville L. 261
wire production 400, 408
Wištāsp 88
women
   in art 141–51, 153, 167, 383
   on Greco-Persian seals 168–75
   segregation of 185, 244
   sexuality 170–5, *172*
   status of 153–61
   widows 181, 185
Wright, Frank Lloyd 203
Wunsch, Cornelia 483–4, 486, 487

X-ray fluorescence (XRF) 437–8
Xanthos 143, 467
Xenophon xiii, 8
   Agesilaus 53, 312
   Anabasis 51–2, 53, 55, 173, 174, 461–2
   Cyropaedia 3, 4, 18, 34, 39, 53, 56, 66, 256, 259, 441
   Hellenica 53
Xerxes I
   assassination of 23, 276, 283
   depiction of *262*, 263
   in English drama 34, 38–9
   foundation inscription XPf 244
   iconography 122
   image on coins 371
   invasion of Greece 28, 260, 283, 309–10
   moral weakness 22
   motives behind Daivâ Inscription 281, 282
   passing of throne to Artaxerxes I 276
   revised view of 282, 494
   and tomb of Belos 477–9
   and Tower of Babel 475–7, 479, 480
   and Treasury reliefs 278

Xerxes I—*Continued*
   treatment of Babylonia 491–4
   uprisings against 280–2, 283,
      475, 491, 493, 494, 546, 559
   Zoroastrian beliefs 19, 283, 284
   see also Daivâ Inscription;
      Hadish Palace; Harem
Xerxes: A Tragedy (Cibber) 38–9

Yahweh 85, 457
Yaqut 528
Yasna ceremony 107
Yazdgird I 75
Yehud 459–61
Yemen 446
Young, Cuyler 196, 197, 248
Yoyotte, Jean 528, 529

Zagros Mountains 288, 294–5
Zal 28
Zāmyād Yasht 131, 132, 133

Zarathustra 88, 103, 105, 106
Zawadzki, Stefan 499
Zechariah 457
Zendan-i Sulaiman 91, 92, *94*,
   248, 250, *251*, 302, 390
Zephaniah, Book of 458
Zerubbabel 469
ziggurats 94, 473–7, 494
Zincirli, stela from *540*
Ziviyeh *see* Ziwiye
Ziwiye 197, 285
Zoroaster 19, 81, 82, 281
   and Ahuramazda 119
   and Aryan *khvarnah* 131, 132,
      133, 136
   birth date of 68–9, 112–19, 134
   and *Gathas* 125, 131, 132, 135
Zoroastrianism
   calendar 114
   Christian anti-Zoroastrian
      propaganda 75, 80

   Creed 113
   Darius' practice of 19, 69, 114
   deities identified with Greek
      gods 382, 383
   development of 119, 134, 135–6
   and empire 24–5
   funerary practices 75–81
   inclusive nature of 104
   liturgy 107–8
   mythology 88
   oral tradition 104, 116,
      117, 123
   priests 239
   rituals 106–8
   sacrifices 45, 282
   supreme deity 82
   under Achaemenians 103–8, 281
   use of term 81
   see also Ahuramazda; *Avesta*
Zournatzi, Antigoni 225

www.ingramcontent.com/pod-product-compliance
Lightning Source LLC
Chambersburg PA
CBHW082018300426
44117CB00015B/2264